HANDBOOK OF
U.S. LABOR
STATISTICS

Handbook of
U.S. Labor
Statistics

Employment, Earnings, Prices, Productivity, and Other Labor Data

14th Edition
2011

Edited by Mary Meghan Ryan

Bernan Press

Lanham, MD

Published in the United States of America
by Bernan Press, a wholly owned subsidiary of
The Rowman & Littlefield Publishing Group, Inc.
4501 Forbes Boulevard, Suite 200
Lanham, Maryland 20706

Bernan Press
800-865-3457
info@bernan.com
www.bernan.com

ISBN-13: 978-1-59888-479-1
eISBN-13: 978-1-59888-480-7

ISSN: 1526-2553

∞™ The paper used in this publication meets the minimum requirements of
American National Standard for Information Sciences—Permanence of
Paper for Printed Library Materials, ANSI/NISO Z39.48-1992.
Manufactured in the United States of America.

CONTENTS

LIST OF TABLES

Persons with a Disability: Labor Force Characteristics

CHAPTER 2: EMPLOYMENT, HOURS, AND EARNINGS

Employment and Hours

Earnings

Quarterly Census of Employment and Wages

CHAPTER 3: OCCUPATIONAL EMPLOYMENT AND WAGES

CHAPTER 4: LABOR FORCE AND EMPLOYMENT PROJECTIONS BY INDUSTRY AND OCCUPATION

CHAPTER 5: PRODUCTIVITY AND COSTS

CHAPTER 6: COMPENSATION OF EMPLOYEES

CHAPTER 7: RECENT TRENDS IN THE LABOR MARKET

MASS LAYOFFS

JOB OPENINGS, HIRES, AND SEPARATIONS

CHAPTER 8: LABOR-MANAGEMENT RELATIONS

CHAPTER 9: PRICES

PRODUCER PRICE INDEX

CONSUMER PRICE INDEX

EXPORT AND IMPORT PRICE INDEXES

CHAPTER 10: INTERNATIONAL LABOR COMPARISONS

CHAPTER 11: CONSUMER EXPENDITURES

CHAPTER 12: AMERICAN TIME USE SURVEY

CHAPTER 13: INCOME DATA IN THE UNITED STATES (CENSUS BUREAU)

CHAPTER 14: OCCUPATIONAL SAFETY AND HEALTH

LIST OF FIGURES

PREFACE

Bernan Press is pleased to present a compilation of Bureau of Labor Statistics (BLS) data in this 14th edition of its award-winning *Handbook of U.S Labor Statistics: Employment, Earnings, Prices, Productivity, and Other Labor Data*. BLS provides a treasure trove of historical information about all aspects of labor and employment in the United States. The current edition maintains the content of previous editions and updates the text with additional data and new features. The data in this *Handbook* are excellent sources of information for analysts in both government and the private sector.

The *Handbook* addresses many of the issues that are being discussed across the United States, such as high unemployment, the decline in real median household income, the rapidly increasing costs of health care services and prescription drugs, employment projections for the future, and the dramatic aging of the labor force. In addition, this publication provides an abundance of data on topics such as prices, productivity, consumer expenditures, occupational safety and health, international labor comparisons, and much more.

The comprehensive and historical data presented in the *Handbook* allow the user to understand the background of current events and compare today's economy with previous years. Select data in this publication go back to 1913 and several tables have data going back to the 1940s.

FEATURES OF THIS PUBLICATION

- Over 200 tables that present authoritative data on labor market statistics, including employment and unemployment, mass layoffs, prices, productivity, and data from the American Time Use Survey (ATUS).

- Each section is preceded by a figure that calls attention to noteworthy trends in the data.

- In addition to the figures, the introductory material for each chapter also contains highlights of other salient data. For example, the highlights in Chapter 1 showcase the increase in the unemployment and in Chapter 13, the highlights call attention to the decline in real median income in 2009.

- The tables in each section are also preceded by notes and definitions, which contain concise descriptions of the data sources, concepts, definitions, and methodology from which the data are derived.

- The introductory notes also include references to more comprehensive reports. These reports provide additional data and more extensive descriptions of estimation methods, sampling, and reliability measures.

NEW IN THIS EDITION

Several changes have taken place in this edition. Most notably, Chapter 1 "Population, Labor Force, and Employment Status" now includes a section on persons with a disability in the labor force. In addition, Chapter 2 "Employment, Hours, and Earnings" contains tables on average weekly hours, average hourly earnings, and average weekly earnings for all employees as well as for production or nonsupervisory workers. There are also new tables in Chapter 6 "Compensation of Employees" as well as several new figures throughout the book on a variety of topics including retirement benefits, average weekly earnings of all employees, and percent change in producer price indexes for selected commodities.

SOURCES OF ADDITIONAL INFORMATION

BLS data are primarily derived from surveys conducted by the federal government or through federal-state cooperative arrangements. The comparability of data over time can be affected by changes in the surveys, which are essential for keeping pace with the current structure of economic institutions and for taking advantage of improved survey techniques. Revisions of current data are also periodically made as a result of the availability of new information. In addition, some tables in this *Handbook* were dropped due to the data being from a one-time survey that is now outdated or due to the survey being entirely restructured. Introductory notes to each chapter summarize specific factors that may affect the data. In the tables, the ellipsis character ("...") indicates that data are not available.

More extensive methodological information, including further discussion of the sampling and estimation procedures used for each BLS program, is contained in the *BLS Handbook of Methods*. This publication is in the process of being updated, and completed chapters are available on the BLS Web site at <http://www.bls.gov>. Other sources of current data and analytical include the *Monthly Labor Review* and a daily Internet publication, *The Editor's Desk* (TED). All of these publications can be found on the BLS Web site as well. Other relevant publications, including those from the Census Bureau, are noted in the notes and definitions in each chapter.

OTHER PUBLICATIONS BY BERNAN PRESS

The *Handbook of U.S. Labor Statistics Handbook of U.S Labor Statistics: Employment, Earnings, Prices, Productivity, and Other Labor Data* is just one of a number of publications in Bernan Press's award-winning U.S. DataBook Series. Other titles include *The Almanac of American*

Education; *Business Statistics of the United States: Patterns of Economic Change*; *Crime in the United State; States Profiles: The Population and Economy of Each U.S. State; United States Foreign Trade Highlights: Trends in the Global Market*; and *Vital Statistics of the United States: Births, Life Expectancy, Deaths, and Selected Health Data.* In addition, Bernan Press publishes *Employment, Hours, and Earnings: States and Areas* as a special edition of this *Handbook*. Each of these titles provides the public with statistical information from official government sources.

If you have any questions or suggestions as to how we could make future editions even more useful, please contact us by e-mail at info@bernan.com or by letter at Bernan Press, 4051 Forbes Boulevard, Suite 200, Lanham, MD 20706. Please visit our Web site at <http://www.bernan.com>.

Chapter One

POPULATION, LABOR FORCE, AND EMPLOYMENT STATUS

POPULATION, LABOR FORCE, AND EMPLOYMENT STATUS

HIGHLIGHTS

This chapter presents the detailed historical information collected in the Current Population Survey (CPS), a monthly survey of households that gathers data on the employment status of the population. Basic data on labor force, employment, and unemployment are shown for various characteristics of the population, including age, sex, race, Hispanic origin, and marital status.

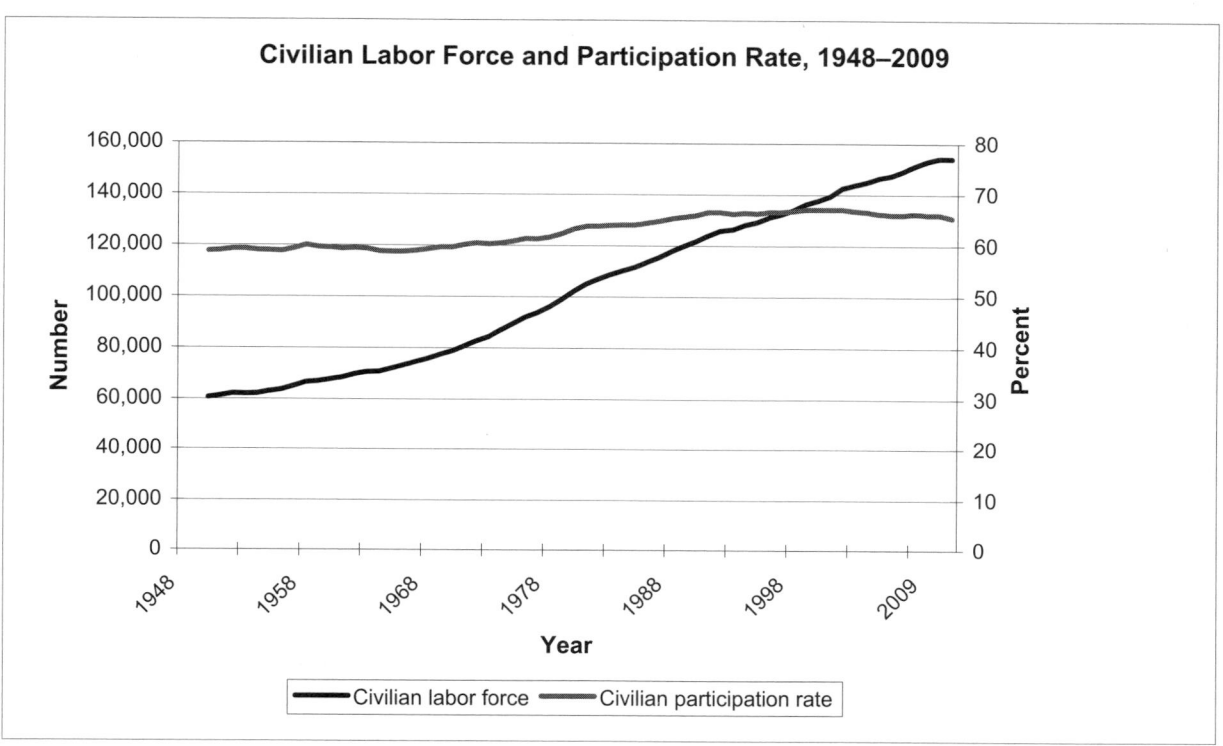

In 2009, the number of people in the labor force declined for the first time since 1951, dropping -0.1 percent from 2008. The civilian labor force participation rate fell to 65.4 percent after remaining steady at 66.0 percent the previous two years. It decreased 1.0 percent for men while it only declined 0.3 percent for women. (See Table 1-1.)

OTHER HIGHLIGHTS

- Employment declined 3.8 percent in 2009 representing the largest single-year decrease since 1954 when it dropped 1.7 percent. Employment declined 3.8 percent in nonagricultural industries and 3.0 percent in agriculture industries. (See Table 1-1.)

- While the civilian labor force participation rate dropped for most age groups in 2009, it increased for those 55 years of age and over. The labor force participation rate for people 55 to 64 years of age increased for the fifth consecutive year while it increased for 11th consecutive year for those 65 years and over. In 2009, the labor force participation rate of those 65 years and over was 17.2 percent—the highest it has been since 1969, when it was 17.3 percent. (See Table 1-8.)

- From 1972 through 1986, the number of Black men exceeded the number of Black women in the labor force. From 1987 through 2009, the number of Black women has exceeded the number of Black men in the labor force. (See Table 1-7.)

NOTES AND DEFINITIONS

CURRENT POPULATION SURVEY OF HOUSEHOLDS

Collection and Coverage

The Current Population Survey (CPS) is a monthly survey that analyzes and publishes statistics on the labor force, employment, and unemployment, classified by a variety of demographic, social, and economic characteristics. This survey is conducted by the Census Bureau for the Bureau of Labor Statistics (BLS). The information is collected from a probability sample of approximately 60,000 households. Respondents are interviewed to obtain information about the employment status of each household member age 16 years and over. Persons under 16 years of age are excluded from the official estimates because child labor laws, compulsory school attendance, and general social custom in the United States severely limit the types and amount of work that these children can do.

The inquiry relates to the household member's employment status during the calendar week, Sunday through Saturday that includes the 12th day of the month. This is known as the "reference week." Actual field interviewing is conducted during the following week (the week that contains the 19th day of the month).

Concepts and Definitions

The concepts and definitions underlying the labor force data have been modified—but not substantially altered—since the inception of the survey in 1940 when it began as a Work Projects Administration program. Current definitions of some of the major concepts used in the CPS are described below.

The civilian noninstitutional population includes persons 16 years of age and over who reside in the 50 states and the District of Columbia who are not inmates of institutions (such as penal and mental facilities and homes for the aged) and who are not on active duty in the armed forces.

An *employed person* is any person who, during the reference week: (1) did any work at all (at least one hour) as a paid employees in their own business, profession, or on their own farm, or who worked 15 hours or more as an unpaid worker in an enterprise operated by a member of the family; and (2) any person who was not working but who had a job or business from which he or she was temporarily absent due to vacation, illness, bad weather, childcare problems, maternity or paternity leave, labor-management disputes, job training, or other family or personal reasons, despite whether the employee was being paid for the time off or was seeking other jobs.

Each employed person is counted only once, even if he or she holds more than one job. For purposes of occupation and industry classification, multiple jobholders are counted as being in the job at which they worked the greatest number of hours during the reference week.

Included in the total are employed citizens of foreign countries who were temporarily in the United States but not living on the premises of an embassy. Excluded are persons whose only activity during the reference week consisted of work around their own house (painting, repairing, or own home housework) or volunteer work for religious, charitable, and similar organizations.

Unemployed persons are all persons who had no employment during the reference week, but who were available for work (except for temporary illness) and had made specific efforts to find employment some time during the four-week period ending with the reference week. Persons who were waiting to be recalled to a job from which they had been laid off need not have been looking for work to be classified as unemployed.

Reasons for unemployment are divided into four major groups: (1) job losers, defined as (a) persons on temporary layoff, who have been given a date to return to work or who expect to return to work within six months; (b) permanent job losers, whose employment ended involuntarily and who began looking for work; and (c) persons who completed a temporary job and began looking for work after the job ended; (2) job leavers, defined as persons who quit or otherwise terminated their employment voluntarily and immediately began looking for work; (3) reentrants, defined as persons who previously worked but were out of the labor force prior to beginning their job search; and (4) new entrants, defined as persons who had never worked but were currently searching for work.

Duration of unemployment represents the length of time (through the current reference week) that persons classified as unemployed had been looking for work. For persons on layoff, duration of unemployment represents the number of full weeks they had been on layoff. Mean duration of unemployment is the arithmetic average computed from single weeks of unemployment; median duration of unemployment is the midpoint of a distribution of weeks of unemployment.

A *spell of unemployment* is a continuous period of unemployment of at least one week's duration and is terminated by either employment or withdrawal from the labor force.

Extent of unemployment refers to the number of workers and proportion of the labor force that were unemployed at some time during the year. The number of weeks unemployed is the total number of weeks accumulated during the entire calendar year.

The *unemployment rate* is the number of unemployed persons as a percentage of the civilian labor force.

The *civilian labor force* comprises all civilians classified as employed or unemployed.

The *participation rate* represents the proportion of the civilian noninstitutional population currently in the labor force.

The *employment-population ratio* represents the proportion of the population that is currently employed.

Persons not in the labor force are all persons in the civilian noninstitutional population who are neither employed nor unemployed. Information is collected about their desire for and availability to take a job at the time of the CPS interview, job search activity during the prior year, and reason for not looking for work during the four-week period ending with the reference week. Persons not in the labor force who want and are available for a job and who have looked for work within the past 12 months (or since the end of their last job, if they had held one within the past 12 months), but who are not currently looking, are designated as *marginally attached to the labor force*. The marginally attached are divided into those not currently looking because they believe their search would be futile—so-called *discouraged workers*—and those not currently looking for other reasons, such as family responsibilities, ill health, or lack of transportation.

Discouraged workers are defined as persons not in the labor force who want and are available for a job and who have looked for work sometime in the past 12 months (or since the end of their last job, if they held one within the past 12 months), but who are not currently looking because they believe that there are no jobs available or there are none for which they would qualify. The reasons for not currently looking for work include a person's belief that no work is available in his or her line of work or area; he or she could not find any work; he or she lacks necessary schooling, training, skills, or experience; employers would think he or she is too young or too old; or he or she would encounter hiring discrimination.

Usual full- or part-time status refers to hours usually worked per week. Full-time workers are those who usually work 35 hours or more (at all jobs). This group includes some individuals who worked less than 35 hours during the reference week for economic or noneconomic reasons. Part-time workers are those who usually work less than 35 hours per week (at all jobs), regardless of the number of hours worked during the reference week. These concepts are used to differentiate a person's normal schedule from his or her specific activity during the reference week. Unemployed persons who are looking for full-time work or who are on layoff from full-time jobs are counted as part of the full-time labor force; unemployed persons who are seeking part-time work or who are on layoff from part-time jobs are counted as part of the part-time labor force.

Year-round, full-time workers are workers who primarily worked at full-time jobs for 50 weeks or more during the preceding calendar year. Part-year workers worked either full- or part-time for 1 to 49 weeks.

At work part-time for economic reasons, sometimes called involuntary part-time, refers to individuals who gave an economic reason for working 1 to 34 hours during the reference week. Economic reasons include slack work or unfavorable business conditions, inability to find full-time work, and seasonal declines in demand. Those who usually work part-time must also indicate that they want and are available to work full-time to be classified as working part-time for economic reasons.

At work part-time for noneconomic reasons refers to persons who usually work part-time and were at work 1 to 34 hours during the reference week for a noneconomic reason. Noneconomic reasons include illness or other medical limitations, childcare problems or other family or personal obligations, school or training, retirement or Social Security limits on earnings, and being in a job where full-time work is less than 35 hours. This also includes workers who gave an economic reason for usually working 1 to 34 hours but said they do not want to work full-time or were unavailable for full-time work.

Absences are defined as instances in which persons who usually work 35 or more hours a week worked less than that during the reference period for reasons of illness or family obligations. Excluded are situations in which work was missed for vacation, holidays, or other reasons. The estimates are based on one-fourth of the sample only.

Earnings are all money income of $1 or more from wages and salaries and all net money income of $1 or more from farm and nonfarm self-employment.

Usual weekly earnings for wage and salary workers include any overtime pay, commissions, or tips usually received (at the main job in the case of multiple jobholders). Earnings reported on a basis other than weekly (such as annual, monthly, or hourly) are converted to weekly. The term "usual" is as perceived by the respondent. If the respondent asks for a definition of usual, interviewers are instructed to define the term as more than half the weeks worked during the past 4 or 5 months.

Minimum wage refers to the prevailing federal minimum wage which was $5.85 per hour from January 2008 to July 23, 2008. Beginning July 24, 2008, the prevailing federal minimum wage increased to $6.55 per hour. On July 24, 2009, the Federal minimum wage increased to $7.25 per hour. Data are for wage and salary workers who were paid hourly rates and refer to a person's earnings at the sole or principal job.

A *multiple jobholder* is an employed person who, during the reference week, had two or more jobs as a wage and salary worker, was self-employed and also held a wage and salary job, or worked as an unpaid family worker and also held a wage and salary job. Self-employed persons with multiple businesses and persons with multiple jobs as unpaid family workers are excluded.

Occupation, industry, and class of worker for members of the employed population are determined by the job held during the reference week. Persons with two or more jobs are classified as being in the job at which they worked the greatest number of hours. The unemployed are classified according to their last job. Beginning with data published in 2003, the systems used to classify occupational and industry data changed. They are currently based on the Standard Occupational Classification (SOC) system and the North American Industry Classification System (NAICS). (See the following section on historical comparability for a discussion of previous classification systems used in the CPS.) The class-of-worker breakdown assigns workers to one of the following categories: private and government wage and salary workers, self-employed workers, and unpaid family workers. Wage and salary workers receive wages, salaries, commissions, tips, or pay in kind from a private employer or from a government unit. Self-employed workers are those who work for profit or fees in their own businesses, professions, trades, or on their own farms. Only the unincorporated self-employed are included in the self-employed category in the class-of-worker typology. Self-employed workers who respond that their businesses are incorporated are included among wage and salary workers, because they are technically paid employees of a corporation. An unpaid family worker is a person working without pay for 15 hours or more per week on a farm or in a business operated by a member of the household to whom he or she is related by birth or marriage.

Educational attainment refers to years of school completed in regular schools, which include graded public, private, and parochial elementary, and high schools, whether day or night school. Colleges, universities, and professional schools are also included.

Tenure refers to length of time a worker has been continuously employed by his or her current employer. These data are collected through a supplement to the CPS. All employed persons were asked how long they had been working continuously for their present employer and, if the length of time was one or two years, a follow-up question was asked about the exact number of months. The follow-up question was included for the first time in the February 1996 supplement to the CPS. CPS supplements that obtained information on tenure in the January of 1983, 1987, and 1991 did not include the follow-up question. Prior to 1983, the question on tenure was asked differently. Data prior to 1983 are thus not strictly comparable to data for subsequent years.

White, Black, and Asian are terms used to describe the race of persons. Persons in these categories are those who selected that race only. Persons in the remaining race categories—American Indian or Alaskan Native, Native Hawaiian or Other Pacific Islander, and persons who selected more than one race category—are included in the esti-

mates of total employment and unemployment but are not shown separately because the number of survey respondents is too small to develop estimates of sufficient quality for monthly publication.

Hispanic origin refers to persons who identified themselves in the enumeration process as being Spanish, Hispanic, or Latino. Persons of Hispanic or Latino origin may be of any race.

Single, never married; married, spouse present; and other marital status are the terms used to define the marital status of individuals at the time of the CPS interview. Married, spouse present, applies to a husband and wife if both were living in the same household, even though one may be temporarily absent on business, vacation, in a hospital, etc. Other marital status applies to persons who are married, spouse absent; widowed; or divorced. Married, spouse absent relates to persons who are separated due to marital problems, as well as husbands and wives living apart because one was employed elsewhere, on duty with the armed forces, or any other reason.

A *household* consists of all persons—related family members and all unrelated persons—who occupy a housing unit and have no other usual address. A house, an apartment, a group of rooms, or a single room is regarded as a housing unit when occupied or intended for occupancy as separate living quarters.

A *householder* is the person (or one of the persons) in whose name the housing unit is owned or rented. The term is not applied to either husbands or wives in married-couple families; it refers only to persons in families maintained by either men or women without a spouse.

A *family* is defined as a group of two or more persons residing together who are related by birth, marriage, or adoption. All such persons are considered as members of one family. Families are classified as either married-couple families or families maintained by women or men without spouses.

Children refer to "own" children of the husband, wife, or person maintaining the family, including sons and daughters, stepchildren, and adopted children. Excluded are other related children, such as grandchildren, nieces, nephews, cousins, and unrelated children.

Persons are referred to as *disabled* if they answer yes to the following questions: 1.) Are you deaf or do you have serious difficulty hearing? 2.) Are you blind or do you serious difficulty seeing even when wearing glasses? 3.) Because of a physical, mental, or emotional condition, do you have serious difficulty concentrating, remembering, or making decisions? 4.) Do you have serious difficulty walking or climbing stairs? 5.) Do you have difficulty dressing or bathing? 6.) Because of a physical, mental, or emotional condition, do you have difficulty doing errands alone such as visiting a doctor's office or shopping? Labor force measures are only tabulated for persons 16 years and over.

Historical Comparability

While the concepts and methods are very similar to those used for the inaugural survey in 1940, a number of changes have been made over the years to improve the accuracy and usefulness of the data. Only recent major changes are described here.

Major changes to the CPS, such as the complete redesign of the questionnaire and the use of computer-assisted interviewing for the entire survey, were introduced in 1994. In addition, there were revisions to some of the labor force concepts and definitions, including the implementation of changes recommended in 1979 by the National Commission on Employment and Unemployment Statistics (NCEUS, also known as the Levitan Commission). Some of the major changes to the survey at this time were:

1) The introduction of a redesigned and automated questionnaire. The CPS questionnaire was totally redesigned in order to obtain more accurate, comprehensive, and relevant information, and to take advantage of state-of-the-art computer interviewing techniques. Computer-assisted interviewing has important benefits, most notably that it facilitates the use of a relatively complex questionnaire that incorporates complicated skip patterns and standardized follow-up questions. Additionally, certain questions are automatically tailored to the individual's situation to make them more understandable.

2) Official labor force measures were defined more precisely. While the labor force status of most people is straightforward, some persons are more difficult to classify correctly, especially if they are engaged in activities that are relatively informal or intermittent. Many of the changes to the questionnaire were made to deal with such cases. This was accomplished by rewording and adding questions to conform more precisely to the official definitions, making the questions easier to understand and answer, minimizing reliance on volunteered responses, revising response categories, and taking advantage of the benefits of an automated interview.

3) The amount of data available was expanded. The questionnaire redesign also made it possible to collect several types of data on topics such as multiple job holding and usual hours regularly for the first time.

4) Several labor definitions were modified. The most important definitional changes concerned discouraged workers. The Levitan Commission had criticized the former definition because it was based on a subjective desire for work and on somewhat arbitrary assumptions about an individual's availability to take a job. As a result of the redesign, two requirements were added: For persons to qualify as discouraged, they must have engaged in some job search within the past year (or since they last worked, if they worked within the past year), and they must be currently available to take a job. (Formerly, availability was inferred from responses to other questions; now, there is a direct ques-

tion.) Also, beginning in January 1994, questions on this subject are asked of the full CPS sample, permitting estimates of the number of discouraged workers to be published monthly (rather than quarterly).

Beginning in January 2003, several other changes were introduced into the CPS. These changes included the following:

1) Population controls that reflected the results of the 2000 census were introduced into the monthly CPS estimation process. The new controls increased the size of the civilian noninstitutional population by about 3.5 million in May 2002. As a result, they also increased the estimated numbers of people unemployed and employed. Because the increases were roughly proportional, however, the overall unemployment rate did not change significantly. Data from January 2000 through December 2002 were revised to reflect these new controls. Over and above these revisions, the U.S. Census Bureau introduced another large upward adjustment to the controls as part of its annual update of population estimates for 2003. These updated population estimates were not available in time to incorporate them into the revised population controls for January 2000 to December 2002. Thus, the data on employment and unemployment levels for January 2003 (and beyond) are not strictly comparable with those for earlier months. The unemployment rate and other ratios, however, were not substantially affected by the 2003 population control revisions.

2) Questions on race and Hispanic origin were modified to comply with the new standards for maintaining, collecting, and presenting federal data on race and ethnicity for federal statistical agencies. The questions were reworded to indicate that individuals could select more than once race category and to convey more clearly that individuals should report their own perception of what race is. These changes had no impact on the overall civilian noninstitutional population and civilian labor force. However, they did reduce the population and labor force levels of Whites, Blacks, and Asians beginning in January 2003.

3) Improvements were introduced to both the second stage and composite weighting procedures. These changes adapted the weighting procedures to the new race/ethnic classification system and enhanced the stability over time for demographic groups. The second-stage weighting procedure substantially reduced the variability of estimates and corrected, to some extent, for CPS underreporting.

Changes in the Occupational and Industrial Classification System

In January 2003, the CPS adopted the 2002 census industry and occupational classification systems, which were derived, respectively, from the 2002 North American Industry Classification System (NAICS) and the 2000 Standard Occupational Classification (SOC) system. The 1990 Census occupational and industry classifications were replaced. The introduction of the new industry and occupational classification systems in 2003 created a complete break in comparability at all levels of industry and occupation aggregation. The composition of detailed occupations and industries changed substantially in the 2002 systems compared with the 1990 systems, as did the structure for aggregating them into major groups. Therefore, any comparisons of data on the different classifications are not possible without major adjustments.

Historical employment series on the 2002 Census classifications are available at broad levels of occupational and industry aggregation back to 1983. However, historical employment series at the detailed occupational and industry levels on the 2002 classifications are available back to 2000 only.

Starting with industry data in 2009, BLS began using the 2007 Census industry classification system, which was derived from the 2007 NAICS series. Several industry titles were revised with no change to the industry definitions. The differences between the 2002 and 2007 classifications are relatively insignificant. BLS did not make any revisions to historical data with the introduction of 2007 NAICS series.

Sources of Additional Information

A complete description of sampling and estimation procedures and further information on the impact of historical changes in the surveys can be found in the updated version of Chapter 1 of the *BLS Handbook of Methods*. This can be found on the BLS Web site at <http://www.bls.gov/opub/hom/>.

Table 1-1. Employment Status of the Civilian Noninstitutional Population, 1947–2009

(Thousands of people, percent.)

Year	Civilian noninstitutional population	Civilian labor force		Employed				Unemployed		Not in labor force
		Total	Participation rate	Total	Percent of population	Agriculture	Nonagricultural industries	Number	Unemploy-ment rate	
1947	101 827	59 350	58.3	57 038	56.0	7 890	49 148	2 311	3.9	42 477
1948	103 068	60 621	58.8	58 343	56.6	7 629	50 714	2 276	3.8	42 447
1949	103 994	61 286	58.9	57 651	55.4	7 658	49 993	3 637	5.9	42 708
1950	104 995	62 208	59.2	58 918	56.1	7 160	51 758	3 288	5.3	42 787
1951	104 621	62 017	59.2	59 961	57.3	6 726	53 235	2 055	3.3	42 604
1952	105 231	62 138	59.0	60 250	57.3	6 500	53 749	1 883	3.0	43 093
1953[1]	107 056	63 015	58.9	61 179	57.1	6 260	54 919	1 834	2.9	44 041
1954	108 321	63 643	58.8	60 109	55.5	6 205	53 904	3 532	5.5	44 678
1955	109 683	65 023	59.3	62 170	56.7	6 450	55 722	2 852	4.4	44 660
1956	110 954	66 552	60.0	63 799	57.5	6 283	57 514	2 750	4.1	44 402
1957	112 265	66 929	59.6	64 071	57.1	5 947	58 123	2 859	4.3	45 336
1958	113 727	67 639	59.5	63 036	55.4	5 586	57 450	4 602	6.8	46 088
1959	115 329	68 369	59.3	64 630	56.0	5 565	59 065	3 740	5.5	46 960
1960[1]	117 245	69 628	59.4	65 778	56.1	5 458	60 318	3 852	5.5	47 617
1961	118 771	70 459	59.3	65 746	55.4	5 200	60 546	4 714	6.7	48 312
1962[1]	120 153	70 614	58.8	66 702	55.5	4 944	61 759	3 911	5.5	49 539
1963	122 416	71 833	58.7	67 762	55.4	4 687	63 076	4 070	5.7	50 583
1964	124 485	73 091	58.7	69 305	55.7	4 523	64 782	3 786	5.2	51 394
1965	126 513	74 455	58.9	71 088	56.2	4 361	66 726	3 366	4.5	52 058
1966	128 058	75 770	59.2	72 895	56.9	3 979	68 915	2 875	3.8	52 288
1967	129 874	77 347	59.6	74 372	57.3	3 844	70 527	2 975	3.8	52 527
1968	132 028	78 737	59.6	75 920	57.5	3 817	72 103	2 817	3.6	53 291
1969	134 335	80 734	60.1	77 902	58.0	3 606	74 296	2 832	3.5	53 602
1970	137 085	82 771	60.4	78 678	57.4	3 463	75 215	4 093	4.9	54 315
1971	140 216	84 382	60.2	79 367	56.6	3 394	75 972	5 016	5.9	55 834
1972[1]	144 126	87 034	60.4	82 153	57.0	3 484	78 669	4 882	5.6	57 091
1973[1]	147 096	89 429	60.8	85 064	57.8	3 470	81 594	4 365	4.9	57 667
1974	150 120	91 949	61.3	86 794	57.8	3 515	83 279	5 156	5.6	58 171
1975	153 153	93 774	61.2	85 846	56.1	3 408	82 438	7 929	8.5	59 377
1976	156 150	96 158	61.6	88 752	56.8	3 331	85 421	7 406	7.7	59 991
1977	159 033	99 008	62.3	92 017	57.9	3 283	88 734	6 991	7.1	60 025
1978[1]	161 910	102 250	63.2	96 048	59.3	3 387	92 661	6 202	6.1	59 659
1979	164 863	104 962	63.7	98 824	59.9	3 347	95 477	6 137	5.8	59 900
1980	167 745	106 940	63.8	99 302	59.2	3 364	95 938	7 637	7.1	60 806
1981	170 130	108 670	63.9	100 397	59.0	3 368	97 030	8 273	7.6	61 460
1982	172 271	110 204	64.0	99 526	57.8	3 401	96 125	10 678	9.7	62 067
1983	174 215	111 550	64.0	100 834	57.9	3 383	97 450	10 717	9.6	62 665
1984	176 383	113 544	64.4	105 005	59.5	3 321	101 685	8 539	7.5	62 839
1985	178 206	115 461	64.8	107 150	60.1	3 179	103 971	8 312	7.2	62 744
1986[1]	180 587	117 834	65.3	109 597	60.7	3 163	106 434	8 237	7.0	62 752
1987	182 753	119 865	65.6	112 440	61.5	3 208	109 232	7 425	6.2	62 888
1988	184 613	121 669	65.9	114 968	62.3	3 169	111 800	6 701	5.5	62 944
1989	186 393	123 869	66.5	117 342	63.0	3 199	114 142	6 528	5.3	62 523
1990[1]	189 164	125 840	66.5	118 793	62.8	3 223	115 570	7 047	5.6	63 324
1991	190 925	126 346	66.2	117 718	61.7	3 269	114 449	8 628	6.8	64 578
1992	192 805	128 105	66.4	118 492	61.5	3 247	115 245	9 613	7.5	64 700
1993	194 838	129 200	66.3	120 259	61.7	3 115	117 144	8 940	6.9	65 638
1994[1]	196 814	131 056	66.6	123 060	62.5	3 409	119 651	7 996	6.1	65 758
1995	198 584	132 304	66.6	124 900	62.9	3 440	121 460	7 404	5.6	66 280
1996	200 591	133 943	66.8	126 708	63.2	3 443	123 264	7 236	5.4	66 647
1997[1]	203 133	136 297	67.1	129 558	63.8	3 399	126 159	6 739	4.9	66 836
1998[1]	205 220	137 673	67.1	131 463	64.1	3 378	128 085	6 210	4.5	67 547
1999[1]	207 753	139 368	67.1	133 488	64.3	3 281	130 207	5 880	4.2	68 385
2000[1]	212 577	142 583	67.1	136 891	64.4	2 464	134 427	5 692	4.0	69 994
2001	215 092	143 734	66.8	136 933	63.7	2 299	134 635	6 801	4.7	71 359
2002	217 570	144 863	66.6	136 485	62.7	2 311	134 174	8 378	5.8	72 707
2003[1]	221 168	146 510	66.2	137 736	62.3	2 275	135 461	8 774	6.0	74 658
2004[1]	223 357	147 401	66.0	139 252	62.3	2 232	137 020	8 149	5.5	75 956
2005	226 082	149 320	66.0	141 730	62.7	2 197	139 532	7 591	5.1	76 762
2006[1]	228 815	151 428	66.2	144 427	63.1	2 206	142 221	7 001	4.6	77 387
2007[1]	231 867	153 124	66.0	146 047	63.0	2 095	143 952	7 078	4.6	78 743
2008[1]	233 788	154 287	66.0	145 362	62.2	2 168	143 194	8 924	5.8	79 501
2009[1]	235 801	154 142	65.4	139 877	59.3	2 103	137 775	14 265	9.3	81 659

[1]Not strictly comparable with data for prior years. See notes and definitions for information on historical comparability.

Table 1-2. Employment Status of the Civilian Noninstitutional Population, by Sex, 1975–2009

(Thousands of people, percent.)

Sex and year	Civilian noninstitutional population	Civilian labor force								Not in labor force
				Employed				Unemployed		
		Total	Participation rate	Total	Percent of population	Agriculture	Non-agricultural industries	Number	Unemployment rate	
Men										
1975	72 291	56 299	77.9	51 857	71.7	2 824	49 032	4 442	7.9	15 993
1976	73 759	57 174	77.5	53 138	72.0	2 744	50 394	4 036	7.1	16 585
1977	75 193	58 396	77.7	54 728	72.8	2 671	52 057	3 667	6.3	16 797
1978[1]	76 576	59 620	77.9	56 479	73.8	2 718	53 761	3 142	5.3	16 956
1979	78 020	60 726	77.8	57 607	73.8	2 686	54 921	3 120	5.1	17 293
1980	79 398	61 453	77.4	57 186	72.0	2 709	54 477	4 267	6.9	17 945
1981	80 511	61 974	77.0	57 397	71.3	2 700	54 697	4 577	7.4	18 537
1982	81 523	62 450	76.6	56 271	69.0	2 736	53 534	6 179	9.9	19 073
1983	82 531	63 047	76.4	56 787	68.8	2 704	54 083	6 260	9.9	19 484
1984	83 605	63 835	76.4	59 091	70.7	2 668	56 423	4 744	7.4	19 771
1985	84 469	64 411	76.3	59 891	70.9	2 535	57 356	4 521	7.0	20 058
1986[1]	85 798	65 422	76.3	60 892	71.0	2 511	58 381	4 530	6.9	20 376
1987	86 899	66 207	76.2	62 107	71.5	2 543	59 564	4 101	6.2	20 692
1988	87 857	66 927	76.2	63 273	72.0	2 493	60 780	3 655	5.5	20 930
1989	88 762	67 840	76.4	64 315	72.5	2 513	61 802	3 525	5.2	20 923
1990[1]	90 377	69 011	76.4	65 104	72.0	2 546	62 559	3 906	5.7	21 367
1991	91 278	69 168	75.8	64 223	70.4	2 589	61 634	4 946	7.2	22 110
1992	92 270	69 964	75.8	64 440	69.8	2 575	61 866	5 523	7.9	22 306
1993	93 332	70 404	75.4	65 349	70.0	2 478	62 871	5 055	7.2	22 927
1994[1]	94 354	70 817	75.1	66 450	70.4	2 554	63 896	4 367	6.2	23 538
1995	95 178	71 360	75.0	67 377	70.8	2 559	64 818	3 983	5.6	23 818
1996	96 206	72 086	74.9	68 207	70.9	2 573	65 634	3 880	5.4	24 119
1997[1]	97 715	73 261	75.0	69 685	71.3	2 552	67 133	3 577	4.9	24 454
1998[1]	98 758	73 959	74.9	70 693	71.6	2 553	68 140	3 266	4.4	24 799
1999[1]	99 722	74 512	74.7	71 446	71.6	2 432	69 014	3 066	4.1	25 210
2000[1]	101 964	76 280	74.8	73 305	71.9	1 861	71 444	2 975	3.9	25 684
2001	103 282	76 886	74.4	73 196	70.9	1 708	71 488	3 690	4.8	26 396
2002	104 585	77 500	74.1	72 903	69.7	1 724	71 179	4 597	5.9	27 085
2003[1]	106 435	78 238	73.5	73 332	68.9	1 695	71 636	4 906	6.3	28 197
2004[1]	107 710	78 980	73.3	74 524	69.2	1 687	72 838	4 456	5.6	28 730
2005[1]	109 151	80 033	73.3	75 973	69.6	1 654	74 319	4 059	5.1	29 119
2006[1]	110 605	81 255	73.5	77 502	70.1	1 663	75 838	3 753	4.6	29 350
2007[1]	112 173	82 136	73.2	78 254	69.8	1 604	76 650	3 882	4.7	30 036
2008[1]	113 113	82 520	73.0	77 486	68.5	1 650	75 836	5 033	6.1	30 593
2009[1]	114 136	82 123	72.0	73 670	64.5	1 607	72 062	8 453	10.3	32 013
Women										
1975	80 860	37 475	46.3	33 989	42.0	584	33 404	3 486	9.3	43 386
1976	82 390	38 983	47.3	35 615	43.2	588	35 027	3 369	8.6	43 406
1977	83 840	40 613	48.4	37 289	44.5	612	36 677	3 324	8.2	43 227
1978[1]	85 334	42 631	50.0	39 569	46.4	669	38 900	3 061	7.2	42 703
1979	86 843	44 235	50.9	41 217	47.5	661	40 556	3 018	6.8	42 608
1980	88 348	45 487	51.5	42 117	47.7	656	41 461	3 370	7.4	42 861
1981	89 618	46 696	52.1	43 000	48.0	667	42 333	3 696	7.9	42 922
1982	90 748	47 755	52.6	43 256	47.7	665	42 591	4 499	9.4	42 993
1983	91 684	48 503	52.9	44 047	48.0	680	43 367	4 457	9.2	43 181
1984	92 778	49 709	53.6	45 915	49.5	653	45 262	3 794	7.6	43 068
1985	93 736	51 050	54.5	47 259	50.4	644	46 615	3 791	7.4	42 686
1986[1]	94 789	52 413	55.3	48 706	51.4	652	48 054	3 707	7.1	42 376
1987	95 853	53 658	56.0	50 334	52.5	666	49 668	3 324	6.2	42 195
1988	96 756	54 742	56.6	51 696	53.4	676	51 020	3 046	5.6	42 014
1989	97 630	56 030	57.4	53 027	54.3	687	52 341	3 003	5.4	41 601
1990[1]	98 787	56 829	57.5	53 689	54.3	678	53 011	3 140	5.5	41 957
1991	99 646	57 178	57.4	53 496	53.7	680	52 815	3 683	6.4	42 468
1992	100 535	58 141	57.8	54 052	53.8	672	53 380	4 090	7.0	42 394
1993	101 506	58 795	57.9	54 910	54.1	637	54 273	3 885	6.6	42 711
1994[1]	102 460	60 239	58.8	56 610	55.3	855	55 755	3 629	6.0	42 221
1995	103 406	60 944	58.9	57 523	55.6	881	56 642	3 421	5.6	42 462
1996	104 385	61 857	59.3	58 501	56.0	871	57 630	3 356	5.4	42 528
1997[1]	105 418	63 036	59.8	59 873	56.8	847	59 026	3 162	5.0	42 382
1998[1]	106 462	63 714	59.8	60 771	57.1	825	59 945	2 944	4.6	42 748
1999[1]	108 031	64 855	60.0	62 042	57.4	849	61 193	2 814	4.3	43 175
2000[1]	110 613	66 303	59.9	63 586	57.5	602	62 983	2 717	4.1	44 310
2001	111 811	66 848	59.8	63 737	57.0	591	63 147	3 111	4.7	44 962
2002	112 985	67 363	59.6	63 582	56.3	587	62 995	3 781	5.6	45 621
2003[1]	114 733	68 272	59.5	64 404	56.1	580	63 824	3 868	5.7	46 461
2004[1]	115 647	68 421	59.2	64 728	56.0	546	64 182	3 694	5.4	47 225
2005[1]	116 931	69 288	59.3	65 757	56.2	544	65 213	3 531	5.1	47 643
2006[1]	118 210	70 173	59.4	66 925	56.6	543	66 382	3 247	4.6	48 037
2007[1]	119 694	70 988	59.3	67 792	56.6	490	67 302	3 196	4.5	48 707
2008[1]	120 675	71 767	59.5	67 876	56.2	518	67 358	3 891	5.4	48 908
2009[1]	121 665	72 019	59.2	66 208	54.4	496	65 712	5 811	8.1	49 646

[1]Not strictly comparable with data for prior years. See notes and definitions for information on historical comparability.

Table 1-3. Employment Status of the Civilian Noninstitutional Population, by Sex, Age, Race, and Hispanic Origin, 1989–2009

(Thousands of people.)

Characteristic	1989	1990	1991	1992	1993	1994	1995	1996	1997	1998	1999
ALL RACES											
Both Sexes											
Civilian noninstitutional population	186 393	189 164	190 925	192 805	194 838	196 814	198 584	200 591	203 133	205 220	207 753
Civilian labor force	123 869	125 840	126 346	128 105	129 200	131 056	132 304	133 943	136 297	137 673	139 368
Employed	117 342	118 793	117 718	118 492	120 259	123 060	124 900	126 708	129 558	131 463	133 488
Agriculture	3 199	3 223	3 269	3 247	3 115	3 409	3 440	3 443	3 399	3 378	3 281
Nonagricultural industries	114 142	115 570	114 449	115 245	117 144	119 651	121 460	123 264	126 159	128 085	130 207
Unemployed	6 528	7 047	8 628	9 613	8 940	7 996	7 404	7 236	6 739	6 210	5 880
Not in labor force	62 523	63 324	64 578	64 700	65 638	65 758	66 280	66 647	66 837	67 547	68 385
Men, 16 Years and Over											
Civilian noninstitutional population	88 762	90 377	91 278	92 270	93 332	94 355	95 178	96 206	97 715	98 758	99 722
Civilian labor force	67 840	69 011	69 168	69 964	70 404	70 817	71 360	72 087	73 261	73 959	74 512
Employed	64 315	65 104	64 223	64 440	65 349	66 450	67 377	68 207	69 685	70 693	71 446
Agriculture	2 513	2 546	2 589	2 575	2 478	2 554	2 559	2 573	2 552	2 553	2 432
Nonagricultural industries	61 802	62 559	61 634	61 866	62 871	63 896	64 818	65 634	67 133	68 140	69 014
Unemployed	3 525	3 906	4 946	5 523	5 055	4 367	3 983	3 880	3 577	3 266	3 066
Not in labor force	20 923	21 367	22 110	22 306	22 927	23 538	23 818	24 119	24 454	24 799	25 210
Men, 20 Years and Over											
Civilian noninstitutional population	81 619	83 030	84 144	85 247	86 256	87 151	87 811	88 606	89 879	90 790	91 555
Civilian labor force	63 704	64 916	65 374	66 213	66 642	66 921	67 324	68 044	69 166	69 715	70 194
Employed	60 837	61 678	61 178	61 496	62 355	63 294	64 085	64 897	66 284	67 135	67 761
Agriculture	2 307	2 329	2 383	2 385	2 293	2 351	2 335	2 356	2 356	2 350	2 244
Nonagricultural industries	58 530	59 349	58 795	59 111	60 063	60 943	61 750	62 541	63 927	64 785	65 517
Unemployed	2 867	3 239	4 195	4 717	4 287	3 627	3 239	3 146	2 882	2 580	2 433
Not in labor force	17 915	18 114	18 770	19 034	19 613	20 230	20 487	20 563	20 713	21 075	21 362
Women, 16 Years and Over											
Civilian noninstitutional population	97 630	98 787	99 646	100 535	101 506	102 460	103 406	104 385	105 418	106 462	108 031
Civilian labor force	56 030	56 829	57 178	58 141	58 795	60 239	60 944	61 857	63 036	63 714	64 855
Employed	53 027	53 689	53 496	54 052	54 910	56 610	57 523	58 501	59 873	60 771	62 042
Agriculture	687	678	680	672	637	855	881	871	847	825	849
Nonagricultural industries	52 341	53 011	52 815	53 380	54 273	55 755	56 642	57 630	59 026	59 945	61 193
Unemployed	3 003	3 140	3 683	4 090	3 885	3 629	3 421	3 356	3 162	2 944	2 814
Not in labor force	41 601	41 957	42 468	42 394	42 711	42 221	42 462	42 528	42 382	42 748	43 175
Women, 20 Years and Over											
Civilian noninstitutional population	90 550	91 614	92 708	93 718	94 647	95 467	96 262	97 050	97 889	98 786	100 158
Civilian labor force	52 212	53 131	53 708	54 796	55 388	56 655	57 215	58 094	59 198	59 702	60 840
Employed	49 745	50 535	50 634	51 328	52 099	53 606	54 396	55 311	56 613	57 278	58 555
Agriculture	642	631	639	625	598	809	830	827	798	768	803
Nonagricultural industries	49 103	49 904	49 995	50 702	51 501	52 796	53 566	54 484	55 815	56 510	57 752
Unemployed	2 467	2 596	3 074	3 469	3 288	3 049	2 819	2 783	2 585	2 424	2 285
Not in labor force	38 339	38 483	39 000	38 922	39 260	38 813	39 047	38 956	38 691	39 084	39 318
Both Sexes, 16 to 19 Years											
Civilian noninstitutional population	14 223	14 520	14 073	13 840	13 935	14 196	14 511	14 934	15 365	15 644	16 040
Civilian labor force	7 954	7 792	7 265	7 096	7 170	7 481	7 765	7 806	7 932	8 256	8 333
Employed	6 759	6 581	5 906	5 669	5 805	6 161	6 419	6 500	6 661	7 051	7 172
Agriculture	250	264	247	237	224	249	275	261	244	261	234
Nonagricultural industries	6 510	6 317	5 659	5 432	5 580	5 912	6 144	6 239	6 417	6 790	6 938
Unemployed	1 194	1 212	1 359	1 427	1 365	1 320	1 346	1 306	1 271	1 205	1 162
Not in labor force	6 270	6 727	6 808	6 745	6 765	6 715	6 746	7 128	7 433	7 388	7 706
WHITE[1]											
Both Sexes											
Civilian noninstitutional population	159 338	160 625	161 759	162 972	164 289	165 555	166 914	168 317	169 993	171 478	173 085
Civilian labor force	106 355	107 447	107 743	108 837	109 700	111 082	111 950	113 108	114 693	115 415	116 509
Employed	101 584	102 261	101 182	101 669	103 045	105 190	106 490	107 808	109 856	110 931	112 235
Agriculture	2 996	2 998	3 026	3 018	2 895	3 162	3 194	3 276	3 208	3 160	3 083
Nonagricultural industries	98 588	99 263	98 157	98 650	100 150	102 027	103 296	104 532	106 648	107 770	109 152
Unemployed	4 770	5 186	6 560	7 169	6 655	5 892	5 459	5 300	4 836	4 484	4 273
Not in labor force	52 983	53 178	54 061	54 135	54 589	54 473	54 965	55 209	55 301	56 064	56 577
Men, 16 Years and Over											
Civilian noninstitutional population	76 468	77 369	77 977	78 651	79 371	80 059	80 733	81 489	82 577	83 352	83 930
Civilian labor force	58 988	59 638	59 656	60 168	60 484	60 727	61 146	61 783	62 639	63 034	63 413
Employed	56 352	56 703	55 797	55 959	56 656	57 452	58 146	58 888	59 998	60 604	61 139
Agriculture	2 345	2 353	2 384	2 378	2 286	2 347	2 347	2 436	2 389	2 376	2 273
Nonagricultural industries	54 007	54 350	53 413	53 580	54 370	55 104	55 800	56 452	57 608	58 228	58 866
Unemployed	2 636	2 935	3 859	4 209	3 828	3 275	2 999	2 896	2 641	2 431	2 274
Not in labor force	17 480	17 731	18 321	18 484	18 887	19 332	19 587	19 706	19 938	20 317	20 517
Men, 20 Years and Over											
Civilian noninstitutional population	70 654	71 457	72 274	73 040	73 721	74 311	74 879	75 454	76 320	76 966	77 432
Civilian labor force	55 441	56 116	56 387	56 976	57 284	57 411	57 719	58 340	59 126	59 421	59 747
Employed	53 292	53 685	53 103	53 357	54 021	54 676	55 254	55 977	56 986	57 500	57 934
Agriculture	2 149	2 148	2 192	2 197	2 114	2 151	2 132	2 224	2 201	2 182	2 094
Nonagricultural industries	51 143	51 537	50 912	51 160	51 907	52 525	53 122	53 753	54 785	55 319	55 839
Unemployed	2 149	2 431	3 284	3 620	3 263	2 735	2 465	2 363	2 140	1 920	1 813
Not in labor force	15 213	15 340	15 887	16 064	16 436	16 900	17 161	17 114	17 194	17 545	17 685

[1]Beginning in 2003, persons who selected this race group only; persons who selected more than one race group are not included. Prior to 2003, persons who reported more than one race group were included in the group they identified as the main race.

Table 1-3. Employment Status of the Civilian Noninstitutional Population, by Sex, Age, Race, and Hispanic Origin, 1989–2009—*Continued*

(Thousands of people.)

Characteristic	2000	2001	2002	2003	2004	2005	2006	2007	2008	2009
ALL RACES										
Both Sexes										
Civilian noninstitutional population	212 577	215 092	217 570	221 168	223 357	226 082	228 815	231 867	233 788	235 801
Civilian labor force	142 583	143 734	144 863	146 510	147 401	149 320	151 428	153 124	154 287	154 142
Employed	136 891	136 933	136 485	137 736	139 252	141 730	144 427	146 047	145 362	139 877
Agriculture	2 464	2 299	2 311	2 275	2 232	2 197	2 206	2 095	2 168	2 103
Nonagricultural industries	134 427	134 635	134 174	135 461	137 020	139 532	142 221	143 952	143 194	137 775
Unemployed	5 692	6 801	8 378	8 774	8 149	7 591	7 001	7 078	8 924	14 265
Not in labor force	69 994	71 359	72 707	74 658	75 956	76 762	77 387	78 743	79 501	81 659
Men, 16 Years and Over										
Civilian noninstitutional population	101 964	103 282	104 585	106 435	107 710	109 151	110 605	112 173	113 113	114 136
Civilian labor force	76 280	76 886	77 500	78 238	78 980	80 033	81 255	82 136	82 520	82 123
Employed	73 305	73 196	72 903	73 332	74 524	75 973	77 502	78 254	77 486	73 670
Agriculture	1 861	1 708	1 724	1 695	1 688	1 654	1 663	1 604	1 650	1 607
Nonagricultural industries	71 444	71 488	71 179	71 636	72 836	74 319	75 838	76 650	75 836	72 062
Unemployed	2 975	3 690	4 597	4 906	4 456	4 059	3 753	3 882	5 033	8 453
Not in labor force	25 684	26 396	27 085	28 197	28 730	29 119	29 350	30 036	30 593	32 013
Men, 20 Years and Over										
Civilian noninstitutional population	93 875	95 181	96 439	98 272	99 476	100 835	102 145	103 555	104 453	105 493
Civilian labor force	72 010	72 816	73 630	74 623	75 364	76 443	77 562	78 596	79 047	78 897
Employed	69 634	69 776	69 734	70 415	71 572	73 050	74 431	75 337	74 750	71 341
Agriculture	1 756	1 613	1 629	1 614	1 596	1 577	1 579	1 514	1 552	1 514
Nonagricultural industries	67 878	68 163	68 104	68 801	69 976	71 473	72 852	73 823	73 198	69 828
Unemployed	2 376	3 040	3 896	4 209	3 791	3 392	3 131	3 259	4 297	7 555
Not in labor force	21 864	22 365	22 809	23 649	24 113	24 392	24 584	24 959	25 406	26 596
Women, 16 Years and Over										
Civilian noninstitutional population	110 613	111 811	112 985	114 733	115 647	116 931	118 210	119 694	120 675	121 665
Civilian labor force	66 303	66 848	67 363	68 272	68 421	69 288	70 173	70 988	71 767	72 019
Employed	63 586	63 737	63 582	64 404	64 728	65 757	66 925	67 792	67 876	66 208
Agriculture	602	591	587	580	547	544	543	490	518	496
Nonagricultural industries	62 983	63 147	62 995	63 824	64 181	65 213	66 382	67 302	67 358	65 712
Unemployed	2 717	3 111	3 781	3 868	3 694	3 531	3 247	3 196	3 891	5 811
Not in labor force	44 310	44 962	45 621	46 461	47 225	47 643	48 037	48 707	48 908	49 646
Women, 20 Years and Over										
Civilian noninstitutional population	102 790	103 983	105 136	106 800	107 658	108 850	109 992	111 330	112 260	113 265
Civilian labor force	62 301	63 016	63 648	64 716	64 923	65 714	66 585	67 516	68 382	68 856
Employed	60 067	60 417	60 420	61 402	61 773	62 702	63 834	64 799	65 039	63 699
Agriculture	567	558	557	550	515	519	520	460	491	471
Nonagricultural industries	59 500	59 860	59 863	60 852	61 258	62 182	63 315	64 339	64 548	63 228
Unemployed	2 235	2 599	3 228	3 314	3 150	3 013	2 751	2 718	3 342	5 157
Not in labor force	40 488	40 967	41 488	42 083	42 735	43 136	43 407	43 814	43 878	44 409
Both Sexes, 16 to 19 Years										
Civilian noninstitutional population	15 912	15 929	15 994	16 096	16 222	16 398	16 678	16 982	17 075	17 043
Civilian labor force	8 271	7 902	7 585	7 170	7 114	7 164	7 281	7 012	6 858	6 390
Employed	7 189	6 740	6 332	5 919	5 907	5 978	6 162	5 911	5 573	4 837
Agriculture	141	128	124	111	121	100	108	121	125	119
Nonagricultural industries	7 049	6 611	6 207	5 808	5 786	5 877	6 054	5 790	5 448	4 719
Unemployed	1 081	1 162	1 253	1 251	1 208	1 186	1 119	1 101	1 285	1 552
Not in labor force	7 642	8 027	8 409	8 926	9 108	9 234	9 397	9 970	10 218	10 654
WHITE[1]										
Both Sexes										
Civilian noninstitutional population	176 220	178 111	179 783	181 292	182 643	184 446	186 264	188 253	189 540	190 902
Civilian labor force	118 545	119 399	120 150	120 546	121 086	122 299	123 834	124 935	125 635	125 644
Employed	114 424	114 430	114 013	114 235	115 239	116 949	118 833	119 792	119 126	114 996
Agriculture	2 320	2 174	2 171	2 148	2 103	2 077	2 063	1 953	2 021	1 968
Nonagricultural industries	112 104	112 256	111 841	112 087	113 136	114 872	116 769	117 839	117 104	113 028
Unemployed	4 121	4 969	6 137	6 311	5 847	5 350	5 002	5 143	6 509	10 648
Not in labor force	57 675	58 713	59 633	60 746	61 558	62 148	62 429	63 319	63 905	65 258
Men, 16 Years and Over										
Civilian noninstitutional population	85 370	86 452	87 361	88 249	89 044	90 027	91 021	92 073	92 725	93 433
Civilian labor force	64 466	64 966	65 308	65 509	65 994	66 694	67 613	68 158	68 351	68 051
Employed	62 289	62 212	61 849	61 866	62 712	63 763	64 883	65 289	64 624	61 630
Agriculture	1 743	1 606	1 611	1 597	1 583	1 562	1 554	1 501	1 539	1 499
Nonagricultural industries	60 546	60 606	60 238	60 269	61 129	62 201	63 330	63 788	63 085	60 131
Unemployed	2 177	2 754	3 459	3 643	3 282	2 931	2 730	2 869	3 727	6 421
Not in labor force	20 905	21 486	22 053	22 740	23 050	23 334	23 408	23 915	24 374	25 382
Men, 20 Years and Over										
Civilian noninstitutional population	78 966	80 029	80 922	81 860	82 615	83 556	84 466	85 420	86 056	86 789
Civilian labor force	60 850	61 519	62 067	62 473	62 944	63 705	64 540	65 214	65 483	65 372
Employed	59 119	59 245	59 124	59 348	60 159	61 255	62 259	62 806	62 304	59 626
Agriculture	1 640	1 512	1 519	1 517	1 495	1 488	1 473	1 417	1 447	1 410
Nonagricultural industries	57 479	57 733	57 605	57 831	58 664	59 767	60 785	61 389	60 857	58 216
Unemployed	1 731	2 275	2 943	3 125	2 785	2 450	2 281	2 408	3 179	5 746
Not in labor force	18 116	18 510	18 855	19 386	19 671	19 851	19 927	20 206	20 573	21 417

[1]Beginning in 2003, persons who selected this race group only; persons who selected more than one race group are not included. Prior to 2003, persons who reported more than one race group were included in the group they identified as the main race.

Table 1-3. Employment Status of the Civilian Noninstitutional Population, by Sex, Age, Race, and Hispanic Origin, 1989–2009—*Continued*

(Thousands of people.)

Characteristic	1989	1990	1991	1992	1993	1994	1995	1996	1997	1998	1999
WHITE[1]											
Women, 16 Years and Over											
Civilian noninstitutional population	82 871	83 256	83 781	84 321	84 918	85 496	86 181	86 828	87 417	88 126	89 156
Civilian labor force	47 367	47 809	48 087	48 669	49 216	50 356	50 804	51 325	52 054	52 380	53 096
Employed	45 232	45 558	45 385	45 710	46 390	47 738	48 344	48 920	49 859	50 327	51 096
Agriculture	651	645	645	641	640	609	815	847	840	819	784	810
Nonagricultural industries	44 581	44 913	44 744	45 070	45 780	46 923	47 497	48 080	49 040	49 543	50 286
Unemployed	2 135	2 251	2 701	2 959	2 827	2 617	2 460	2 404	2 195	2 053	1 999
Not in labor force	35 504	35 447	35 695	35 651	35 702	35 141	35 377	35 503	35 363	35 746	36 060
Women, 20 Years and Over											
Civilian noninstitutional population	77 154	77 539	78 285	78 928	79 490	79 980	80 567	81 041	81 492	82 073	82 953
Civilian labor force	44 105	44 648	45 111	45 839	46 311	47 314	47 686	48 162	48 847	49 029	49 714
Employed	42 346	42 796	42 862	43 327	43 910	45 116	45 643	46 164	47 063	47 342	48 098
Agriculture	608	598	601	594	572	772	799	798	771	729	765
Nonagricultural industries	41 738	42 198	42 261	42 733	43 339	44 344	44 844	45 366	46 292	46 612	47 333
Unemployed	1 758	1 852	2 248	2 512	2 400	2 197	2 042	1 998	1 784	1 688	1 616
Not in labor force	33 050	32 891	33 174	33 089	33 179	32 666	32 881	32 879	32 645	33 044	33 239
Both Sexes, 16 to 19 Years											
Civilian noninstitutional population	11 530	11 630	11 200	11 004	11 078	11 264	11 468	11 822	12 181	12 439	12 700
Civilian labor force	6 809	6 683	6 245	6 022	6 105	6 357	6 545	6 607	6 720	6 965	7 048
Employed	5 946	5 779	5 216	4 985	5 113	5 398	5 593	5 667	5 807	6 089	6 204
Agriculture	239	252	233	228	209	239	262	254	236	250	224
Nonagricultural industries	5 707	5 528	4 984	4 757	4 904	5 158	5 331	5 413	5 571	5 839	5 980
Unemployed	863	903	1 029	1 037	992	960	952	939	912	876	844
Not in labor force	4 721	4 947	4 955	4 982	4 973	4 907	4 923	5 215	5 462	5 475	5 652
BLACK[1]											
Both Sexes											
Civilian noninstitutional population	21 021	21 477	21 799	22 147	22 521	22 879	23 246	23 604	24 003	24 373	24 855
Civilian labor force	13 497	13 740	13 797	14 162	14 225	14 502	14 817	15 134	15 529	15 982	16 365
Employed	11 953	12 175	12 074	12 151	12 382	12 835	13 279	13 542	13 969	14 556	15 056
Agriculture	150	142	160	153	143	136	101	98	117	138	117
Nonagricultural industries	11 803	12 034	11 914	11 997	12 239	12 699	13 178	13 444	13 852	14 417	14 939
Unemployed	1 544	1 565	1 723	2 011	1 844	1 666	1 538	1 592	1 560	1 426	1 309
Not in labor force	7 524	7 737	8 002	7 985	8 296	8 377	8 429	8 470	8 474	8 391	8 490
Men, 16 Years and Over											
Civilian noninstitutional population	9 439	9 573	9 725	9 896	10 083	10 258	10 411	10 575	10 763	10 927	11 143
Civilian labor force	6 701	6 802	6 851	6 997	7 019	7 089	7 183	7 264	7 354	7 542	7 652
Employed	5 928	5 995	5 961	5 930	6 047	6 241	6 422	6 456	6 607	6 871	7 027
Agriculture	127	124	139	138	128	118	93	86	103	118	99
Nonagricultural industries	5 802	5 872	5 822	5 791	5 919	6 122	6 329	6 371	6 504	6 752	6 952
Unemployed	773	806	890	1 067	971	848	762	808	747	671	671
Not in labor force	2 738	2 772	2 874	2 899	3 064	3 169	3 228	3 311	3 409	3 386	3 386
Men, 20 Years and Over											
Civilian noninstitutional population	8 215	8 364	8 479	8 652	8 840	9 171	9 280	9 414	9 575	9 727	9 926
Civilian labor force	6 127	6 221	6 357	6 451	6 568	6 646	6 730	6 806	6 910	7 053	7 182
Employed	5 509	5 602	5 692	5 706	5 681	5 964	6 137	6 167	6 325	6 530	6 702
Agriculture	129	119	117	131	131	115	89	83	101	112	96
Nonagricultural industries	5 381	5 483	5 576	5 575	5 550	5 849	6 048	6 084	6 224	6 418	6 606
Unemployed	617	619	664	745	886	682	593	639	585	524	480
Not in labor force	2 089	2 143	2 122	2 202	801	2 525	2 550	2 608	2 665	2 673	2 743
Women, 16 Years and Over											
Civilian noninstitutional population	11 582	11 904	12 074	12 251	12 438	12 621	12 835	13 029	13 241	13 446	13 711
Civilian labor force	6 796	6 938	6 946	7 166	7 206	7 413	7 634	7 869	8 175	8 441	8 713
Employed	6 025	6 180	6 113	6 221	6 334	6 595	6 857	7 086	7 362	7 685	8 029
Agriculture	24	18	21	15	15	18	8	13	14	20	18
Nonagricultural industries	6 001	6 162	6 092	6 206	6 320	6 577	6 849	7 073	7 348	7 665	8 011
Unemployed	772	758	833	944	872	818	777	784	813	756	684
Not in labor force	4 786	4 965	5 129	5 086	5 231	5 208	5 201	5 159	5 066	5 005	4 999
Women, 20 Years and Over											
Civilian noninstitutional population	10 482	10 760	10 959	11 152	11 332	11 496	11 682	11 833	12 016	12 023	12 451
Civilian labor force	6 352	6 517	6 572	6 778	6 824	7 004	7 175	7 405	7 686	7 912	8 224
Employed	5 727	5 884	5 874	5 978	6 095	6 320	6 556	6 762	7 013	7 290	7 663
Agriculture	23	18	20	15	14	17	7	12	13	19	17
Nonagricultural industries	5 703	5 867	5 853	5 963	6 081	6 303	6 548	6 749	7 000	7 272	7 646
Unemployed	625	633	698	800	729	685	620	643	673	622	561
Not in labor force	4 130	4 243	4 388	4 374	4 508	4 492	4 507	4 428	4 330	4 291	4 226
Both Sexes, 16 to 19 Years											
Civilian noninstitutional population	2 176	2 238	2 187	2 155	2 181	2 211	2 284	2 356	2 412	2 443	2 479
Civilian labor force	925	866	774	816	807	852	911	923	933	1 017	959
Employed	625	598	494	492	494	552	586	613	631	736	691
Agriculture	8	7	8	7	9	1	5	3	3	8	4
Nonagricultural industries	617	591	486	485	485	547	581	611	611	728	687
Unemployed	300	268	280	324	313	300	325	310	310	281	268
Not in labor force	1 251	1 372	1 413	1 339	1 374	1 360	1 372	1 434	1 434	1 427	1 520

[1]Beginning in 2003, persons who selected this race group only; persons who selected more than one race group are not included. Prior to 2003, persons who reported more than one race group were included in the group they identified as the main race.

Table 1-3. Employment Status of the Civilian Noninstitutional Population, by Sex, Age, Race, and Hispanic Origin, 1989–2009—*Continued*

(Thousands of people.)

Characteristic	2000	2001	2002	2003	2004	2005	2006	2007	2008	2009
WHITE[1]										
Women, 16 Years and Over										
Civilian noninstitutional population	90 850	91 660	92 422	93 043	93 599	94 419	95 242	96 180	96 814	97 469
Civilian labor force	54 079	54 433	54 842	55 037	55 092	55 605	56 221	56 777	57 284	57 593
Employed	52 136	52 218	52 164	52 369	52 527	53 186	53 950	54 503	54 501	53 366
Agriculture	578	568	560	551	520	515	510	452	482	469
Nonagricultural industries	51 558	51 650	51 604	51 818	52 007	52 672	53 440	54 050	54 019	52 897
Unemployed	1 944	2 215	2 678	2 668	2 565	2 419	2 271	2 274	2 782	4 227
Not in labor force	36 770	37 227	37 581	38 006	38 508	38 814	39 021	39 403	39 531	39 876
Women, 20 Years and Over										
Civilian noninstitutional population	84 718	85 526	86 266	86 905	87 430	88 200	88 942	89 790	90 400	91 078
Civilian labor force	50 740	51 218	51 717	52 099	52 212	52 643	53 286	53 925	54 508	54 976
Employed	49 145	49 369	49 448	49 823	50 040	50 589	51 359	51 996	52 124	51 231
Agriculture	546	537	532	522	488	492	488	423	457	444
Nonagricultural industries	48 599	48 831	48 916	49 301	49 552	50 097	50 871	51 572	51 667	50 787
Unemployed	1 595	1 849	2 269	2 276	2 172	2 054	1 927	1 930	2 384	3 745
Not in labor force	33 978	34 308	34 548	34 806	35 218	35 557	35 656	35 864	35 892	36 101
Both Sexes, 16 to 19 Years										
Civilian noninstitutional population	12 535	12 556	12 596	12 527	12 599	12 690	12 856	13 043	13 084	13 035
Civilian labor force	6 955	6 661	6 366	5 973	5 929	5 950	6 009	5 795	5 644	5 295
Employed	6 160	5 817	5 441	5 064	5 039	5 105	5 215	4 990	4 697	4 138
Agriculture	135	125	121	109	116	97	102	113	118	114
Nonagricultural industries	6 025	5 692	5 320	4 955	4 923	5 008	5 113	4 877	4 580	4 025
Unemployed	795	845	925	909	890	845	794	805	947	1 157
Not in labor force	5 581	5 894	6 230	6 554	6 669	6 739	6 847	7 248	7 440	7 740
BLACK[1]										
Both Sexes										
Civilian noninstitutional population	24 902	25 138	25 578	25 686	26 065	26 517	27 007	27 485	27 843	28 241
Civilian labor force	16 397	16 421	16 565	16 526	16 638	17 013	17 314	17 496	17 740	17 632
Employed	15 156	15 006	14 872	14 739	14 909	15 313	15 765	16 051	15 953	15 025
Agriculture	77	62	69	63	50	51	60	53	55	66
Nonagricultural industries	15 079	14 944	14 804	14 676	14 859	15 261	15 705	15 998	15 898	14 959
Unemployed	1 241	1 416	1 693	1 787	1 729	1 700	1 549	1 445	1 788	2 606
Not in labor force	8 505	8 717	9 013	9 161	9 428	9 504	9 693	9 989	10 103	10 609
Men, 16 Years and Over										
Civilian noninstitutional population	11 129	11 172	11 391	11 454	11 656	11 882	12 130	12 361	12 516	12 705
Civilian labor force	7 702	7 647	7 794	7 711	7 773	7 998	8 128	8 252	8 347	8 265
Employed	7 082	6 938	6 959	6 820	6 912	7 155	7 354	7 500	7 398	6 817
Agriculture	67	56	63	52	43	43	51	46	49	56
Nonagricultural industries	7 015	6 882	6 896	6 768	6 869	7 111	7 303	7 454	7 350	6 761
Unemployed	620	709	835	891	860	844	774	752	949	1 448
Not in labor force	3 427	3 525	3 597	3 743	3 884	3 884	4 002	4 110	4 169	4 441
Men, 20 Years and Over										
Civilian noninstitutional population	9 952	9 993	10 196	10 278	11 656	10 659	10 864	11 057	11 194	11 379
Civilian labor force	7 240	7 200	7 347	7 346	7 773	7 600	7 720	7 867	7 962	7 914
Employed	6 741	6 627	6 652	6 586	6 912	6 901	7 079	7 245	7 151	6 628
Agriculture	67	55	62	51	274	43	49	45	47	55
Nonagricultural industries	6 675	55	6 591	6 535	6 638	6 858	7 030	7 201	7 104	6 573
Unemployed	499	573	695	760	860	699	640	622	811	1 286
Not in labor force	2 711	2 792	2 848	2 932	3 884	3 060	3 144	3 189	3 232	3 465
Women, 16 Years and Over										
Civilian noninstitutional population	13 772	13 966	14 187	14 232	14 409	14 635	14 877	15 124	15 328	15 536
Civilian labor force	8 695	8 774	8 772	8 815	8 865	9 014	9 186	9 244	9 393	9 367
Employed	8 073	8 068	7 914	7 919	7 997	8 158	8 410	8 551	8 554	8 208
Agriculture	10	6	6	11	7	8	9	7	6	10
Nonagricultural industries	8 064	8 062	7 907	7 908	7 990	8 150	8 402	8 544	8 548	8 198
Unemployed	621	706	858	895	868	856	775	693	839	1 159
Not in labor force	5 078	5 192	5 415	5 418	5 544	5 621	5 691	5 879	5 934	6 169
Women, 20 Years and Over										
Civilian noninstitutional population	12 561	12 758	12 966	13 026	14 409	13 377	13 578	13 788	13 974	14 178
Civilian labor force	8 215	8 323	8 348	8 409	8 865	8 610	8 723	8 828	8 991	8 988
Employed	7 703	7 741	7 610	7 636	7 997	7 876	8 068	8 240	8 260	7 956
Agriculture	9	6	5	10	7	7	7	7	6	10
Nonagricultural industries	7 694	7 735	7 604	7 626	7 701	7 868	8 060	8 233	8 254	7 946
Unemployed	512	582	738	772	868	734	656	588	732	1 032
Not in labor force	4 346	4 434	4 618	4 618	5 544	4 768	4 854	4 960	4 982	5 190
Both Sexes, 16 to 19 Years										
Civilian noninstitutional population	2 389	2 388	2 416	2 382	2 423	2 481	2 565	2 640	2 676	28 241
Civilian labor force	941	898	870	771	762	803	871	801	787	17 632
Employed	711	637	611	516	520	536	618	566	541	15 025
Agriculture	1	1	2	1	0	1	3	1	1	66
Nonagricultural industries	710	637	609	515	520	535	614	564	540	14 959
Unemployed	230	260	260	255	241	267	253	235	246	2 606
Not in labor force	1 448	1 490	1 546	1 611	1 661	1 677	1 694	1 839	1 889	10 609

[1]Beginning in 2003, persons who selected this race group only; persons who selected more than one race group are not included. Prior to 2003, persons who reported more than one race group were included in the group they identified as the main race.

Table 1-3. Employment Status of the Civilian Noninstitutional Population, by Sex, Age, Race, and Hispanic Origin, 1989–2009—*Continued*

(Thousands of people.)

Characteristic	1989	1990	1991	1992	1993	1994	1995	1996	1997	1998	1999
HISPANIC[2]											
Both Sexes											
Civilian noninstitutional population	13 791	15 904	16 425	16 961	17 532	18 117	18 629	19 213	20 321	21 070	21 650
Civilian labor force	9 323	10 720	10 920	11 338	11 610	11 975	12 267	12 774	13 796	14 317	14 665
Employed	8 573	9 845	9 828	10 027	10 361	10 788	11 127	11 642	12 726	13 291	13 720
Agriculture	440	517	512	524	523	560	604	609	660	742	734
Nonagricultural industries	8 133	9 328	9 315	9 503	9 838	10 227	10 524	11 033	12 067	12 549	12 986
Unemployed	750	876	1 092	1 311	1 248	1 187	1 140	1 132	1 069	1 026	945
Not in labor force	4 468	5 184	5 506	5 623	5 922	6 142	6 362	6 439	6 526	6 753	6 985
Men, 16 Years and Over											
Civilian noninstitutional population	6 825	8 041	8 296	8 553	8 824	9 104	9 329	9 604	10 368	10 734	10 713
Civilian labor force	5 595	6 546	6 664	6 900	7 076	7 210	7 376	7 646	8 309	8 571	8 546
Employed	5 172	6 021	5 979	6 093	6 328	6 530	6 725	7 039	7 728	8 018	8 067
Agriculture	393	449	453	468	469	494	527	537	571	651	642
Nonagricultural industries	4 779	5 572	5 526	5 625	5 860	6 036	6 198	6 502	7 157	7 367	7 425
Unemployed	423	524	685	807	747	680	651	607	582	552	480
Not in labor force	1 230	1 495	1 632	1 654	1 749	1 894	1 952	1 957	2 059	2 164	2 167
Men, 20 Years and Over											
Civilian noninstitutional population	6 114	7 126	7 392	7 655	7 930	8 178	8 375	8 611	9 250	9 573	9 523
Civilian labor force	5 195	6 034	6 198	6 432	6 621	6 747	6 898	7 150	7 779	8 005	7 950
Employed	4 853	5 609	5 623	5 757	5 992	6 189	6 367	6 655	7 307	7 570	7 576
Agriculture	366	415	419	437	441	466	501	510	544	621	602
Nonagricultural industries	4 487	5 195	5 204	5 320	5 551	5 722	5 866	6 145	6 763	6 949	6 974
Unemployed	342	425	575	675	629	558	530	495	471	436	374
Not in labor force	919	1 092	1 194	1 223	1 309	1 431	1 477	1 461	1 471	1 568	1 573
Women, 16 Years and Over											
Civilian noninstitutional population	6 965	7 863	8 130	8 408	8 708	9 014	9 300	9 610	9 953	10 335	10 937
Civilian labor force	3 728	4 174	4 256	4 439	4 534	4 765	4 891	5 128	5 486	5 746	6 119
Employed	3 401	3 823	3 848	3 934	4 033	4 258	4 403	4 602	4 999	5 273	5 653
Agriculture	48	68	59	57	55	66	76	72	89	91	92
Nonagricultural industries	3 353	3 755	3 789	3 877	3 978	4 191	4 326	4 531	4 910	5 182	5 561
Unemployed	327	351	407	504	501	508	488	525	488	473	466
Not in labor force	3 237	3 689	3 874	3 969	4 174	4 248	4 409	4 482	4 466	4 589	4 819
Women, 20 Years and Over											
Civilian noninstitutional population	6 278	7 041	7 301	7 569	7 846	8 122	8 382	8 654	8 950	9 292	9 821
Civilian labor force	3 857	3 941	4 110	4 218	4 421	4 520	4 779	5 106	5 304	5 666	6 275
Employed	3 172	3 567	3 603	3 693	3 800	3 989	4 116	4 341	4 705	4 928	5 290
Agriculture	44	62	53	51	49	61	72	69	83	85	88
Nonagricultural industries	3 128	3 505	3 549	3 642	3 751	3 928	4 044	4 272	4 622	4 843	5 202
Unemployed	276	289	339	418	418	431	404	438	401	376	376
Not in labor force	2 830	3 184	3 360	3 459	3 628	3 701	3 863	3 875	3 845	3 988	4 155
Both Sexes, 16 to 19 Years											
Civilian noninstitutional population	1 399	1 737	1 732	1 737	1 756	1 818	1 872	1 948	2 121	2 204	2 307
Civilian labor force	680	829	781	796	771	807	850	845	911	1 007	1 049
Employed	548	668	602	577	570	609	645	646	714	793	854
Agriculture	31	40	41	36	33	32	31	29	33	36	45
Nonagricultural industries	517	628	562	541	537	577	614	617	682	757	809
Unemployed	132	161	179	219	201	198	205	199	197	214	196
Not in labor force	719	907	951	941	985	1 010	1 022	1 103	1 210	1 197	1 257

[2]May be of any race.

Table 1-3. Employment Status of the Civilian Noninstitutional Population, by Sex, Age, Race, and Hispanic Origin, 1989–2009—Continued

(Thousands of people.)

Characteristic	2000	2001	2002	2003	2004	2005	2006	2007	2008	2009
HISPANIC[2]										
Both Sexes										
Civilian noninstitutional population	23 938	24 942	25 963	27 551	28 109	29 133	30 103	31 383	32 141	32 891
Civilian labor force	16 689	17 328	17 943	18 813	19 272	19 824	20 694	21 602	22 024	22 352
Employed	15 735	16 190	16 590	17 372	17 930	18 632	19 613	20 382	20 346	19 647
Agriculture	536	423	448	446	441	423	428	426	441	426
Nonagricultural industries	15 199	15 767	16 141	16 927	17 489	18 209	19 185	19 956	19 904	19 221
Unemployed	954	1 138	1 353	1 441	1 342	1 191	1 081	1 220	1 678	2 706
Not in labor force	7 249	7 614	8 020	8 738	8 837	9 310	9 409	9 781	10 116	10 539
Men, 16 Years and Over										
Civilian noninstitutional population	12 174	12 695	13 221	14 098	14 417	14 962	15 473	16 154	16 524	16 897
Civilian labor force	9 923	10 279	10 609	11 288	11 587	11 985	12 488	13 005	13 255	13 310
Employed	9 428	9 668	9 845	10 479	10 832	11 337	11 887	12 310	12 248	11 640
Agriculture	449	345	361	350	356	350	347	352	364	344
Nonagricultural industries	8 979	9 323	9 484	10 129	10 476	10 987	11 540	11 958	11 884	11 296
Unemployed	494	611	764	809	755	647	601	695	1 007	1 670
Not in labor force	2 252	2 416	2 613	2 810	2 831	2 977	2 985	3 149	3 270	3 588
Men, 20 Years and Over										
Civilian noninstitutional population	10 841	11 386	11 928	12 797	13 082	13 586	14 046	14 649	14 971	15 305
Civilian labor force	9 247	9 595	9 977	10 756	11 020	11 408	11 888	12 403	12 629	12 730
Employed	8 859	9 100	9 341	10 063	10 385	10 872	11 391	11 827	11 769	11 256
Agriculture	423	328	345	336	335	341	337	337	351	332
Nonagricultural industries	8 435	8 773	8 996	9 727	10 050	10 532	11 054	11 490	11 418	10 924
Unemployed	388	495	636	693	635	536	497	576	860	1 474
Not in labor force	1 595	1 791	1 951	2 041	2 061	2 177	2 157	2 246	2 342	2 575
Women, 16 Years and Over										
Civilian noninstitutional population	11 764	12 247	12 742	13 452	13 692	14 172	14 630	15 229	15 616	15 993
Civilian labor force	6 767	7 049	7 334	7 525	7 685	7 839	8 206	8 597	8 769	9 043
Employed	6 307	6 522	6 744	6 894	7 098	7 295	7 725	8 072	8 098	8 007
Agriculture	87	77	87	96	85	73	80	74	77	82
Nonagricultural industries	6 220	6 445	6 657	6 798	7 013	7 222	7 645	7 999	8 021	7 925
Unemployed	460	527	590	631	587	544	480	525	672	1 036
Not in labor force	4 997	5 198	5 408	5 928	6 007	6 333	6 424	6 632	6 847	6 951
Women, 20 Years and Over										
Civilian noninstitutional population	10 574	11 049	11 528	12 211	12 420	12 858	13 262	13 791	14 127	14 463
Civilian labor force	6 557	6 863	7 096	7 096	7 257	7 377	7 735	8 108	8 274	8 560
Employed	5 903	6 121	6 367	6 541	6 752	6 913	7 321	7 662	7 707	59
Agriculture	81	73	84	91	78	70	77	69	75	78
Nonagricultural industries	5 822	6 048	6 283	6 450	6 674	6 843	7 244	7 593	7 632	7 570
Unemployed	371	436	496	555	504	464	414	446	567	911
Not in labor force	4 299	4 492	4 666	5 114	5 163	5 481	5 527	5 682	5 853	5 903
Both Sexes, 16 to 19 Years										
Civilian noninstitutional population	2 523	2 508	2 507	2 543	2 608	2 689	2 796	2 944	3 042	3 123
Civilian labor force	1 168	1 176	1 103	960	995	1 038	1 071	1 091	1 121	1 063
Employed	973	969	882	768	792	847	900	894	870	742
Agriculture	31	22	19	19	25	13	14	20	15	16
Nonagricultural industries	942	947	863	749	767	834	887	874	855	726
Unemployed	194	208	221	192	203	191	170	197	251	321
Not in labor force	1 355	1 331	1 404	1 583	1 612	1 651	1 725	1 853	1 921	2 061

[2]May be of any race.

Table 1-4. Employment Status of the Civilian Noninstitutional Population, by Sex, Race, and Marital Status, 1989–2009

(Thousands of people.)

Race, marital status, and year	Men				Women			
	Civilian noninstitutional population	Civilian labor force			Civilian noninstitutional population	Civilian labor force		
		Total	Employed	Unemployed		Total	Employed	Unemployed
ALL RACES								
Single								
1989	24 831	18 738	16 936	1 801	21 141	14 377	13 175	1 202
1990	25 870	19 357	17 405	1 952	21 901	14 612	13 336	1 276
1991	26 197	19 411	17 011	2 400	22 173	14 681	13 198	1 482
1992	26 436	19 709	17 098	2 611	22 475	14 872	13 263	1 609
1993	26 570	19 706	17 261	2 445	22 713	15 031	13 484	1 547
1994	26 786	19 786	17 604	2 181	23 000	15 333	13 847	1 486
1995	26 918	19 841	17 833	2 007	23 151	15 467	14 053	1 413
1996	27 387	20 071	18 055	2 016	23 623	15 842	14 403	1 439
1997	28 311	20 689	18 783	1 906	24 285	16 492	15 037	1 455
1998	28 693	21 037	19 240	1 798	24 941	17 087	15 755	1 332
1999	29 104	21 351	19 686	1 665	25 576	17 575	16 267	1 308
2000	29 887	22 002	20 339	1 663	25 920	17 849	16 628	1 221
2001	30 646	22 285	20 298	1 988	26 462	18 021	16 635	1 386
2002	31 072	22 289	19 983	2 306	26 999	18 203	16 583	1 621
2003	31 691	22 297	19 841	2 457	27 802	18 397	16 723	1 674
2004	32 422	22 776	20 395	2 381	28 228	18 616	16 995	1 621
2005	33 125	23 214	21 006	2 209	29 046	19 183	17 588	1 595
2006	33 931	23 974	21 907	2 067	29 624	19 474	17 978	1 496
2007	34 650	24 276	22 143	2 132	30 219	19 745	18 322	1 422
2008	35 274	24 643	21 938	2 705	30 980	20 231	18 513	1 717
2009	36 087	24 640	20 628	4 011	31 500	20 224	17 800	2 424
Married, Spouse Present								
1989	53 530	42 036	40 760	1 276	52 885	30 548	29 404	1 145
1990	53 793	42 275	40 829	1 446	52 917	30 901	29 714	1 188
1991	54 158	42 303	40 429	1 875	53 169	31 112	29 698	1 415
1992	54 509	42 491	40 341	2 150	53 501	31 700	30 100	1 600
1993	55 178	42 834	40 935	1 899	53 838	31 980	30 499	1 482
1994	55 560	43 005	41 414	1 592	54 155	32 888	31 536	1 352
1995	56 100	43 472	42 048	1 424	54 716	33 359	32 063	1 296
1996	56 363	43 739	42 417	1 322	54 970	33 618	32 406	1 211
1997	56 396	43 808	42 642	1 167	54 915	33 802	32 755	1 047
1998	56 670	43 957	42 923	1 034	55 331	33 857	32 872	985
1999	57 089	44 244	43 254	990	56 178	34 372	33 450	921
2000	58 167	44 987	44 078	908	57 557	35 146	34 209	937
2001	58 448	45 233	44 007	1 226	57 610	35 236	34 153	1 083
2002	59 102	45 766	44 116	1 650	58 165	35 477	34 153	1 323
2003	60 063	46 404	44 653	1 751	59 069	36 046	34 695	1 352
2004	60 412	46 550	45 084	1 466	59 278	35 845	34 600	1 244
2005	60 545	46 771	45 483	1 287	59 205	35 941	34 773	1 168
2006	60 751	46 842	45 700	1 142	59 576	36 314	35 272	1 042
2007	61 760	47 520	46 314	1 206	60 474	36 881	35 832	1 049
2008	61 794	47 450	45 860	1 590	60 554	37 194	35 869	1 325
2009	61 773	47 114	43 998	3 115	60 675	37 264	35 207	2 057
Divorced, Widowed, or Separated								
1989	10 401	7 066	6 618	448	23 604	11 104	10 448	656
1990	10 714	7 378	6 871	508	23 968	11 315	10 639	676
1991	10 924	7 454	6 783	671	24 304	11 385	10 600	786
1992	11 325	7 763	7 001	762	24 559	11 570	10 689	881
1993	11 584	7 864	7 153	711	24 955	11 784	10 927	856
1994	12 008	8 026	7 432	594	25 304	12 018	11 227	791
1995	12 160	8 048	7 496	551	25 539	12 118	11 407	712
1996	12 456	8 276	7 735	541	25 791	12 397	11 691	706
1997	13 009	8 764	8 260	504	26 218	12 742	12 082	660
1998	13 394	8 965	8 530	435	26 190	12 771	12 143	628
1999	13 528	8 918	8 507	411	26 276	12 909	12 324	585
2000	13 910	9 291	8 888	403	27 135	13 308	12 748	559
2001	14 188	9 367	8 892	476	27 738	13 592	12 949	642
2002	14 411	9 445	8 804	641	27 821	13 683	12 846	837
2003	14 680	9 537	8 838	699	27 862	13 828	12 986	842
2004	14 875	9 654	9 045	608	28 141	13 961	13 133	828
2005	15 481	10 048	9 484	563	28 680	14 163	13 396	768
2006	15 923	10 440	9 895	545	29 010	14 385	13 675	709
2007	15 763	10 341	9 797	544	29 001	14 362	13 638	724
2008	16 044	10 427	9 688	739	29 141	14 342	13 494	849
2009	16 275	10 370	9 043	1 326	29 490	14 531	13 201	1 330

Note: See notes and definitions for information on historical comparability.

Table 1-4. Employment Status of the Civilian Noninstitutional Population, by Sex, Race, and Marital Status, 1989–2009—Continued

(Thousands of people.)

Race, marital status, and year	Men				Women			
	Civilian noninstitutional population	Civilian labor force			Civilian noninstitutional population	Civilian labor force		
		Total	Employed	Unemployed		Total	Employed	Unemployed
WHITE[1]								
Single								
1989	20 076	15 511	14 249	1 263	16 289	11 474	10 741	734
1990	20 746	15 993	14 617	1 376	16 555	11 522	10 729	794
1991	20 899	15 989	14 233	1 756	16 569	11 497	10 557	939
1992	21 025	16 129	14 285	1 844	16 684	11 502	10 526	976
1993	20 974	16 033	14 303	1 730	16 768	11 613	10 633	980
1994	21 071	16 074	14 539	1 535	16 936	11 805	10 885	920
1995	21 132	16 080	14 674	1 406	17 046	11 830	10 967	864
1996	21 454	16 285	14 891	1 394	17 282	11 977	11 099	878
1997	22 236	16 810	15 507	1 303	17 728	12 322	11 443	879
1998	22 513	17 007	15 746	1 261	18 247	12 742	11 945	797
1999	22 788	17 272	16 116	1 157	18 635	13 029	12 206	823
2000	23 266	17 659	16 504	1 154	18 808	13 215	12 449	766
2001	23 979	17 970	16 561	1 409	19 253	13 368	12 491	877
2002	24 289	17 924	16 289	1 635	19 625	13 556	12 550	1 006
2003	24 419	17 755	16 031	1 723	19 924	13 462	12 461	1 001
2004	24 929	18 090	16 435	1 655	20 210	13 597	12 628	969
2005	25 436	18 338	16 833	1 505	20 702	13 906	12 957	949
2006	26 012	18 928	17 500	1 428	21 085	14 109	13 199	909
2007	26 431	19 063	17 580	1 483	21 408	14 255	13 357	897
2008	27 023	19 395	17 474	1 920	22 064	14 648	13 578	1 070
2009	27 559	19 392	16 528	2 864	22 371	14 733	13 193	1 540
Married, Spouse Present								
1989	47 883	37 589	36 545	1 044	47 382	27 030	26 083	947
1990	47 841	37 515	36 338	1 177	47 240	27 271	26 285	986
1991	48 137	37 507	35 923	1 585	47 456	27 479	26 290	1 189
1992	48 416	37 671	35 886	1 785	47 705	27 951	26 623	1 329
1993	48 937	37 953	36 396	1 557	47 944	28 221	26 993	1 228
1994	49 169	38 008	36 719	1 288	48 120	29 017	27 888	1 129
1995	49 597	38 376	37 211	1 165	48 497	29 360	28 290	1 070
1996	49 800	38 616	37 522	1 094	48 684	29 517	28 496	1 020
1997	49 719	38 593	37 636	957	48 542	29 664	28 809	855
1998	49 901	38 629	37 793	836	48 722	29 534	28 727	808
1999	50 091	38 765	37 968	797	49 296	29 806	29 056	749
2000	50 775	39 169	38 451	717	50 194	30 344	29 582	762
2001	50 850	39 246	38 265	981	50 077	30 336	29 472	864
2002	51 284	39 580	38 261	1 319	50 489	30 511	29 463	1 048
2003	51 859	39 908	38 529	1 379	50 957	30 805	29 740	1 065
2004	51 992	39 935	38 774	1 161	50 939	30 544	29 549	996
2005	52 034	40 141	39 130	1 011	50 865	30 599	29 676	922
2006	52 035	40 103	39 207	896	51 200	30 950	30 111	839
2007	52 775	40 559	39 594	965	51 868	31 363	30 533	830
2008	52 708	40 404	39 157	1 247	51 637	31 456	30 367	1 089
2009	52 693	40 142	37 644	2 498	51 786	31 584	29 891	1 694
Divorced, Widowed, or Separated								
1989	8 509	5 887	5 558	329	19 200	8 863	8 409	454
1990	8 782	6 131	5 748	382	19 461	9 016	8 544	471
1991	8 941	6 159	5 641	518	19 757	9 111	8 538	573
1992	9 210	6 368	5 788	580	19 931	9 216	8 561	654
1993	9 459	6 498	5 957	541	20 206	9 382	8 764	618
1994	9 819	6 644	6 193	451	20 439	9 533	8 965	569
1995	10 005	6 689	6 261	428	20 638	9 613	9 087	526
1996	10 234	6 883	6 474	408	20 862	9 831	9 325	506
1997	10 622	7 236	6 855	382	21 147	10 068	9 607	461
1998	10 937	7 398	7 064	334	21 157	10 104	9 656	449
1999	11 050	7 375	7 056	320	21 225	10 261	9 834	427
2000	11 329	7 638	7 333	305	21 847	10 521	10 105	416
2001	11 623	7 750	7 386	364	22 330	10 729	10 255	474
2002	11 789	7 804	7 299	505	22 308	10 775	10 151	624
2003	11 971	7 846	7 305	541	22 162	10 769	10 168	602
2004	12 124	7 969	7 503	466	22 450	10 950	10 350	600
2005	12 558	8 215	7 800	415	22 853	11 101	10 552	548
2006	12 974	8 583	8 176	407	22 957	11 162	10 640	523
2007	12 867	8 536	8 115	421	22 904	11 159	10 613	547
2008	12 995	8 552	7 992	560	23 112	11 180	10 556	624
2009	13 181	8 517	7 459	1 058	23 312	11 275	10 282	993

Note: See notes and definitions for information on historical comparability.

[1]Beginning in 2003, persons who selected this race group only; persons who selected more than one race group are not included. Prior to 2003, persons who reported more than one race group were included in the group they identified as their main race.

Table 1-4. Employment Status of the Civilian Noninstitutional Population, by Sex, Race, and Marital Status, 1989–2009—Continued

(Thousands of people.)

Race, marital status, and year	Men				Women			
	Civilian noninstitutional population	Civilian labor force			Civilian noninstitutional population	Civilian labor force		
		Total	Employed	Unemployed		Total	Employed	Unemployed
ALL OTHER RACES								
Single								
1989	4 755	3 227	2 687	538	4 852	2 903	2 434	468
1990	5 124	3 364	2 788	576	5 346	3 090	2 607	482
1991	5 298	3 422	2 778	644	5 604	3 184	2 641	543
1992	5 411	3 580	2 813	767	5 791	3 370	2 737	633
1993	5 596	3 673	2 958	715	5 945	3 418	2 851	567
1994	5 715	3 712	3 065	646	6 064	3 528	2 962	566
1995	5 786	3 761	3 159	601	6 105	3 637	3 086	549
1996	5 933	3 786	3 164	622	6 341	3 865	3 304	561
1997	6 075	3 879	3 276	603	6 557	4 170	3 594	576
1998	6 180	4 030	3 494	537	6 694	4 345	3 810	535
1999	6 316	4 079	3 570	508	6 941	4 546	4 061	485
2000	6 621	4 343	3 835	509	7 112	4 634	4 179	455
2001	6 667	4 315	3 737	579	7 209	4 653	4 144	509
2002	6 783	4 365	3 694	671	7 374	4 647	4 033	615
2003	7 272	4 542	3 810	734	7 878	4 935	4 262	673
2004	7 493	4 686	3 960	726	8 018	5 019	4 367	652
2005	7 689	4 876	4 173	704	8 344	5 277	4 631	646
2006	7 919	5 046	4 407	639	8 539	5 365	4 779	587
2007	8 219	5 213	4 563	649	8 811	5 490	4 965	525
2008	8 251	5 248	4 464	785	8 916	5 583	4 935	647
2009	8 528	5 248	4 100	1 147	9 129	5 491	4 607	884
Married, Spouse Present								
1989	5 647	4 447	4 215	232	5 503	3 518	3 321	198
1990	5 952	4 760	4 491	269	5 677	3 630	3 429	202
1991	6 021	4 796	4 506	290	5 713	3 633	3 408	226
1992	6 093	4 820	4 455	365	5 796	3 749	3 477	271
1993	6 241	4 881	4 539	342	5 894	3 759	3 506	254
1994	6 391	4 997	4 695	304	6 035	3 871	3 648	223
1995	6 503	5 096	4 837	259	6 219	3 999	3 773	226
1996	6 563	5 123	4 895	228	6 286	4 101	3 910	191
1997	6 677	5 215	5 006	210	6 373	4 138	3 946	192
1998	6 769	5 328	5 130	198	6 609	4 323	4 145	177
1999	6 998	5 479	5 286	193	6 882	4 566	4 394	172
2000	7 392	5 818	5 627	191	7 363	4 802	4 627	175
2001	7 598	5 987	5 742	245	7 533	4 900	4 681	219
2002	7 818	6 186	5 855	331	7 676	4 966	4 690	275
2003	8 204	6 496	6 124	372	8 112	5 241	4 955	287
2004	8 420	6 615	6 310	305	8 339	5 301	5 051	248
2005	8 511	6 630	6 353	276	8 340	5 342	5 097	246
2006	8 716	6 739	6 493	246	8 376	5 364	5 161	203
2007	8 985	6 961	6 720	241	8 606	5 518	5 299	219
2008	9 086	7 046	6 703	343	8 917	5 738	5 502	236
2009	9 080	6 972	6 354	617	8 889	5 680	5 316	363
Divorced, Widowed, or Separated								
1989	1 892	1 179	1 060	119	4 404	2 241	2 039	202
1990	1 932	1 247	1 123	126	4 507	2 299	2 095	205
1991	1 983	1 295	1 142	153	4 547	2 274	2 062	213
1992	2 115	1 395	1 213	182	4 628	2 354	2 128	227
1993	2 125	1 366	1 196	170	4 749	2 402	2 163	238
1994	2 189	1 382	1 239	143	4 865	2 485	2 262	222
1995	2 155	1 359	1 235	123	4 901	2 505	2 320	186
1996	2 222	1 393	1 261	133	4 929	2 566	2 366	200
1997	2 387	1 528	1 405	122	5 071	2 674	2 475	199
1998	2 457	1 567	1 466	101	5 033	2 667	2 487	179
1999	2 478	1 543	1 451	91	5 051	2 648	2 490	158
2000	2 581	1 653	1 555	98	5 288	2 787	2 643	143
2001	2 565	1 617	1 506	112	5 408	2 863	2 694	168
2002	2 622	1 641	1 505	136	5 513	2 908	2 695	213
2003	2 709	1 691	1 533	158	5 700	3 059	2 818	240
2004	2 751	1 685	1 542	142	5 691	3 011	2 783	228
2005	2 923	1 833	1 684	148	5 827	3 062	2 844	220
2006	2 949	1 857	1 719	138	6 053	3 223	3 035	186
2007	2 896	1 805	1 682	123	6 097	3 203	3 025	177
2008	3 049	1 875	1 696	179	6 029	3 162	2 938	225
2009	3 094	1 853	1 584	268	6 178	3 256	2 919	337

Note: See notes and definitions for information on historical comparability.

Table 1-5. Employment Status of the Civilian Noninstitutional Population, by Region, Division, State, and Selected Territory, 2008–2009

(Thousands of people, percent.)

Region, division, and state	2008 Civilian noninstitutional population	2008 Total	2008 Participation rate	2008 Employed	2008 Unemployed	2008 Unemployment rate	2009 Civilian noninstitutional population	2009 Total	2009 Participation rate	2009 Employed	2009 Unemployed	2009 Unemployment rate
UNITED STATES[1]	233 788	154 287	66.0	145 362	8 924	5.8	235 801	154 142	65.4	139 877	14 265	9.3
Northeast	43 280	28 325	65.4	26 809	1 516	5.4	43 565	28 387	65.2	25 995	2 392	8.4
New England	11 363	7 710	67.9	7 297	413	5.4	11 450	7 737	67.6	7 096	641	8.3
Connecticut	2 727	1 870	68.6	1 766	104	5.6	2 748	1 890	68.8	1 734	156	8.2
Maine	1 063	705	66.3	668	38	5.3	1 066	704	66.0	647	57	8.0
Massachusetts	5 185	3 465	66.8	3 282	183	5.3	5 237	3 473	66.3	3 181	293	8.4
New Hampshire	1 050	743	70.8	714	29	3.9	1 056	742	70.3	695	47	6.3
Rhode Island	835	570	68.3	526	43	7.6	837	567	67.7	503	64	11.2
Vermont	504	357	70.8	341	16	4.5	506	360	71.1	335	25	6.9
Middle Atlantic	31 917	20 615	64.6	19 512	1 102	5.3	32 115	20 650	64.3	18 899	1 751	8.5
New Jersey	6 731	4 503	66.9	4 257	246	5.5	6 780	4 537	66.9	4 118	418	9.2
New York	15 293	9 671	63.2	9 157	514	5.3	15 386	9 699	63.0	8 886	813	8.4
Pennsylvania	9 892	6 441	65.1	6 099	342	5.3	9 948	6 414	64.5	5 895	519	8.1
Midwest	51 317	34 922	68.1	32 811	2 111	6.0	51 606	34 723	67.3	31 397	3 327	9.6
East North Central	35 803	23 961	66.9	22 390	1 571	6.6	35 972	23 731	66.0	21 208	2 523	10.6
Illinois	9 822	6 676	68.0	6 248	428	6.4	9 892	6 606	66.8	5 941	665	10.1
Indiana	4 877	3 244	66.5	3 055	189	5.8	4 912	3 185	64.8	2 865	320	10.1
Michigan	7 780	4 976	64.0	4 563	413	8.3	7 782	4 889	62.8	4 224	665	13.6
Ohio	8 939	5 985	67.0	5 592	393	6.6	8 970	5 970	66.6	5 359	611	10.2
Wisconsin	4 386	3 081	70.2	2 933	148	4.8	4 416	3 081	69.8	2 820	262	8.5
West North Central	15 513	10 960	70.7	10 420	540	4.9	15 633	10 992	70.3	10 189	803	7.3
Iowa	2 317	1 678	72.4	1 605	73	4.4	2 330	1 674	71.8	1 574	100	6.0
Kansas	2 112	1 494	70.7	1 428	66	4.4	2 129	1 519	71.3	1 417	102	6.7
Minnesota	4 046	2 938	72.6	2 780	158	5.4	4 081	2 968	72.7	2 732	236	8.0
Missouri	4 577	3 047	66.6	2 861	186	6.1	4 611	3 037	65.9	2 754	283	9.3
Nebraska	1 352	993	73.4	961	33	3.3	1 362	984	72.2	938	45	4.6
North Dakota	498	364	73.1	353	12	3.2	503	365	72.6	349	16	4.3
South Dakota	611	446	73.0	433	14	3.1	617	446	72.3	425	21	4.8
South	85 026	54 880	64.5	51 853	3 027	5.5	86 081	55 063	64.0	50 146	4 917	8.9
South Atlantic	45 059	29 498	65.5	27 814	1 684	5.7	45 574	29 416	64.5	26 634	2 781	9.5
Delaware	678	441	65.0	419	22	4.9	687	435	63.3	400	35	8.1
District of Columbia	480	334	69.6	312	22	6.6	488	332	68.0	298	34	10.2
Florida	14 487	9 206	63.5	8 628	578	6.3	14 602	9 197	63.0	8 232	966	10.5
Georgia	7 197	4 838	67.2	4 536	302	6.2	7 300	4 769	65.3	4 312	457	9.6
Maryland	4 367	3 026	69.3	2 894	133	4.4	4 407	2 987	67.8	2 778	209	7.0
North Carolina	7 019	4 570	65.1	4 287	283	6.2	7 129	4 545	63.8	4 061	484	10.6
South Carolina	3 445	2 143	62.2	1 995	147	6.9	3 497	2 179	62.3	1 924	255	11.7
Virginia	5 936	4 131	69.6	3 968	162	3.9	6 011	4 174	69.4	3 896	278	6.7
West Virginia	1 449	809	55.8	774	34	4.3	1 454	798	54.9	735	63	7.9
East South Central	13 918	8 552	61.4	8 013	539	6.3	14 027	8 505	60.6	7 635	870	10.2
Alabama	3 598	2 156	59.9	2 044	112	5.2	3 627	2 113	58.3	1 900	212	10.1
Kentucky	3 308	2 047	61.9	1 912	135	6.6	3 329	2 080	62.5	1 863	218	10.5
Mississippi	2 189	1 299	59.3	1 210	89	6.8	2 201	1 292	58.7	1 169	123	9.6
Tennessee	4 822	3 050	63.3	2 846	204	6.7	4 870	3 020	62.0	2 703	317	10.5
West South Central	26 049	16 830	64.6	16 026	804	4.8	26 480	17 142	64.7	15 877	1 265	7.4
Arkansas	2 188	1 376	62.9	1 305	72	5.2	2 205	1 370	62.1	1 271	100	7.3
Louisiana	3 360	2 067	61.5	1 975	92	4.5	3 397	2 068	60.9	1 926	141	6.8
Oklahoma	2 748	1 751	63.7	1 687	64	3.7	2 778	1 773	63.8	1 660	114	6.4
Texas	17 753	11 635	65.5	11 059	576	4.9	18 099	11 931	65.9	11 020	911	7.6
West	53 578	35 761	66.7	33 517	2 244	6.3	54 323	35 818	65.9	32 206	3 612	10.1
Mountain	16 353	11 082	67.8	10 511	570	5.1	16 617	11 076	66.7	10 154	922	8.3
Arizona	4 868	3 117	64.0	2 934	183	5.9	4 951	3 143	63.5	2 858	284	9.1
Colorado	3 770	2 728	72.4	2 595	132	4.9	3 840	2 701	70.3	2 493	208	7.7
Idaho	1 132	756	66.8	719	37	4.9	1 147	750	65.4	690	60	8.0
Montana	758	510	67.3	487	23	4.6	765	499	65.2	468	31	6.2
Nevada	1 976	1 347	68.2	1 257	90	6.7	2 001	1 370	68.5	1 209	161	11.8
New Mexico	1 505	961	63.9	918	43	4.5	1 522	956	62.8	887	69	7.2
Utah	1 934	1 368	70.7	1 317	51	3.7	1 973	1 364	69.1	1 275	90	6.6
Wyoming	410	294	71.7	285	9	3.2	417	294	70.5	275	19	6.4
Pacific	37 225	24 680	66.3	23 005	1 674	6.8	37 706	24 741	65.6	22 052	2 689	10.9
Alaska	503	357	71.0	334	23	6.5	515	361	70.1	332	29	8.0
California	27 679	18 252	65.9	16 938	1 313	7.2	28 025	18 250	65.1	16 164	2 086	11.4
Hawaii	985	646	65.6	620	26	4.0	992	638	64.3	595	43	6.8
Oregon	2 970	1 949	65.6	1 823	126	6.5	3 008	1 964	65.3	1 747	217	11.1
Washington	5 087	3 476	68.3	3 290	186	5.4	5 167	3 529	68.3	3 215	314	8.9

Note: Data refer to place of residence. Region and division data are derived from summing the component states. Sub-national data reflect revised population controls and model reestimation.

[1]Due to separate processing and weighing procedures, totals for the United States differ from the results obtained by aggregating data for regions, divisions, or states.

Table 1-6. Civilian Noninstitutional Population, by Age, Race, Sex, and Hispanic Origin, 1948–2009

(Thousands of people.)

Race, Hispanic origin, sex, and year	16 years and over	16 to 19 years			20 years and over						
		Total	16 to 17 years	18 to 19 years	Total	20 to 24 years	25 to 34 years	35 to 44 years	45 to 54 years	55 to 64 years	65 years and over
ALL RACES											
Both Sexes											
1948	103 068	8 449	4 265	4 185	94 618	11 530	22 610	20 097	16 771	12 885	10 720
1949	103 994	8 215	4 139	4 079	95 778	11 312	22 822	20 401	17 002	13 201	11 035
1950	104 995	8 143	4 076	4 068	96 851	11 080	23 013	20 681	17 240	13 469	11 363
1951	104 621	7 865	4 096	3 771	96 755	10 167	22 843	20 863	17 464	13 692	11 724
1952	105 231	7 922	4 234	3 689	97 305	9 389	23 044	21 137	17 716	13 889	12 126
1953	107 056	8 014	4 241	3 773	99 041	8 960	23 266	21 922	17 991	13 830	13 075
1954	108 321	8 224	4 336	3 889	100 095	8 885	23 304	22 135	18 305	14 085	13 375
1955	109 683	8 364	4 440	3 925	101 318	9 036	23 249	22 348	18 643	14 309	13 728
1956	110 954	8 434	4 482	3 953	102 518	9 271	23 072	22 567	19 012	14 516	14 075
1957	112 265	8 612	4 587	4 026	103 653	9 486	22 849	22 786	19 424	14 727	14 376
1958	113 727	8 986	4 872	4 114	104 737	9 733	22 563	23 025	19 832	14 923	14 657
1959	115 329	9 618	5 337	4 282	105 711	9 975	22 201	23 207	20 203	15 134	14 985
1960	117 245	10 187	5 573	4 615	107 056	10 273	21 998	23 437	20 601	15 409	15 336
1961	118 771	10 513	5 462	5 052	108 255	10 583	21 829	23 585	20 893	15 675	15 685
1962	120 153	10 652	5 503	5 150	109 500	10 852	21 503	23 797	20 916	15 874	16 554
1963	122 416	11 370	6 301	5 070	111 045	11 464	21 400	23 948	21 144	16 138	16 945
1964	124 485	12 111	6 974	5 139	112 372	12 017	21 367	23 940	21 452	16 442	17 150
1965	126 513	12 930	6 936	5 995	113 582	12 442	21 417	23 832	21 728	16 727	17 432
1966	128 058	13 592	6 914	6 679	114 463	12 638	21 543	23 579	21 977	17 007	17 715
1967	129 874	13 480	7 003	6 480	116 391	13 421	22 057	23 313	22 256	17 310	18 029
1968	132 028	13 698	7 200	6 499	118 328	13 891	22 912	23 036	22 534	17 614	18 338
1969	134 335	14 095	7 422	6 673	120 238	14 488	23 645	22 709	22 806	17 930	18 657
1970	137 085	14 519	7 643	6 876	122 566	15 323	24 435	22 489	23 059	18 250	19 007
1971	140 216	15 022	7 849	7 173	125 193	16 345	25 337	22 274	23 244	18 581	19 406
1972	144 126	15 510	8 076	7 435	128 614	17 143	26 740	22 358	23 338	19 007	20 023
1973	147 096	15 840	8 227	7 613	131 253	17 692	28 172	22 287	23 431	19 281	20 389
1974	150 120	16 180	8 373	7 809	133 938	17 994	29 439	22 461	23 578	19 517	20 945
1975	153 153	16 418	8 419	7 999	136 733	18 595	30 710	22 526	23 535	19 844	21 525
1976	156 150	16 614	8 442	8 171	139 536	19 109	31 953	22 796	23 409	20 185	22 083
1977	159 033	16 688	8 482	8 206	142 345	19 582	33 117	23 296	23 197	20 557	22 597
1978	161 910	16 695	8 484	8 211	145 216	20 007	34 091	24 099	22 977	20 875	23 166
1979	164 863	16 657	8 389	8 268	148 205	20 353	35 261	24 861	22 752	21 210	23 767
1980	167 745	16 543	8 279	8 264	151 202	20 635	36 558	25 578	22 563	21 520	24 350
1981	170 130	16 214	8 068	8 145	153 916	20 820	37 777	26 291	22 422	21 756	24 850
1982	172 271	15 763	7 714	8 049	156 508	20 845	38 492	27 611	22 264	21 909	25 387
1983	174 215	15 274	7 385	7 889	158 941	20 799	39 147	28 932	22 167	22 003	25 892
1984	176 383	14 735	7 196	7 538	161 648	20 688	39 999	30 251	22 226	22 052	26 433
1985	178 206	14 506	7 232	7 274	163 700	20 097	40 670	31 379	22 418	22 140	26 997
1986	180 587	14 496	7 386	7 110	166 091	19 569	41 731	32 550	22 732	22 011	27 497
1987	182 753	14 606	7 501	7 104	168 147	18 970	42 297	33 755	23 183	21 835	28 108
1988	184 613	14 527	7 284	7 243	170 085	18 434	42 611	34 784	24 004	21 641	28 612
1989	186 393	14 223	6 886	7 338	172 169	18 025	42 845	35 977	24 744	21 406	29 173
1990	189 164	14 520	6 893	7 626	174 644	18 902	42 976	37 719	25 081	20 719	29 247
1991	190 925	14 073	6 901	7 173	176 852	18 963	42 688	39 116	25 709	20 675	29 700
1992	192 805	13 840	6 907	6 933	178 965	18 846	42 278	39 852	27 206	20 604	30 179
1993	194 838	13 935	7 010	6 925	180 903	18 642	41 771	40 733	28 549	20 574	30 634
1994	196 814	14 196	7 245	6 951	182 619	18 353	41 306	41 534	29 778	20 635	31 012
1995	198 584	14 511	7 407	7 104	184 073	17 864	40 798	42 254	30 974	20 735	31 448
1996	200 591	14 934	7 678	7 256	185 656	17 409	40 252	43 086	32 167	20 990	31 751
1997	203 133	15 365	7 861	7 504	187 769	17 442	39 559	43 883	33 391	21 505	31 989
1998	205 220	15 644	7 895	7 749	189 576	17 593	38 778	44 299	34 373	22 296	32 237
1999	207 753	16 040	8 060	7 979	191 713	17 968	37 976	44 635	35 587	23 064	32 484
2000	212 577	15 912	7 978	7 934	196 664	18 311	38 703	44 312	37 642	24 230	33 466
2001	215 092	15 929	8 020	7 909	199 164	18 877	38 505	44 195	38 904	25 011	33 672
2002	217 570	15 994	8 099	7 895	201 576	19 348	38 472	43 894	39 711	26 343	33 808
2003	221 168	16 096	8 561	7 535	205 072	19 801	39 021	43 746	40 522	27 728	34 253
2004	223 357	16 222	8 574	7 648	207 134	20 197	38 939	43 226	41 245	28 919	34 609
2005	226 082	16 398	8 778	7 619	209 685	20 276	39 064	43 005	42 107	30 165	35 068
2006	228 815	16 678	9 089	7 589	212 137	20 265	39 230	42 753	42 901	31 375	35 613
2007	231 867	16 982	9 222	7 760	214 885	20 427	39 751	42 401	43 544	32 533	36 228
2008	233 788	17 075	9 133	7 942	216 713	20 409	39 993	41 699	43 960	33 491	37 161
2009	235 801	17 043	8 944	8 100	218 757	20 524	40 280	40 919	44 365	34 671	37 998

Table 1-6. Civilian Noninstitutional Population, by Age, Race, Sex, and Hispanic Origin, 1948–2009
—Continued

(Thousands of people.)

Race, Hispanic origin, sex, and year	16 years and over	16 to 19 years			20 years and over						
		Total	16 to 17 years	18 to 19 years	Total	20 to 24 years	25 to 34 years	35 to 44 years	45 to 54 years	55 to 64 years	65 years and over
ALL RACES											
Men											
1948	49 996	4 078	2 128	1 951	45 918	5 527	10 767	9 798	8 290	6 441	5 093
1949	50 321	3 946	2 062	1 884	46 378	5 405	10 871	9 926	8 379	6 568	5 226
1950	50 725	3 962	2 043	1 920	46 763	5 270	10 963	10 034	8 472	6 664	5 357
1951	49 727	3 725	2 039	1 687	46 001	4 451	10 709	10 049	8 551	6 737	5 503
1952	49 700	3 767	2 121	1 647	45 932	3 788	10 855	10 164	8 655	6 798	5 670
1953	50 750	3 823	2 122	1 701	46 927	3 482	11 020	10 632	8 878	6 798	6 119
1954	51 395	3 953	2 174	1 780	47 441	3 509	11 067	10 718	9 018	6 885	6 241
1955	52 109	4 022	2 225	1 798	48 086	3 708	11 068	10 804	9 164	6 960	6 380
1956	52 723	4 020	2 238	1 783	48 704	3 970	10 983	10 889	9 322	7 032	6 505
1957	53 315	4 083	2 284	1 800	49 231	4 166	10 889	10 965	9 499	7 109	6 602
1958	54 033	4 293	2 435	1 858	49 740	4 339	10 787	11 076	9 675	7 179	6 683
1959	54 793	4 652	2 681	1 971	50 140	4 488	10 625	11 149	9 832	7 259	6 785
1960	55 662	4 963	2 805	2 159	50 698	4 679	10 514	11 230	10 000	7 373	6 901
1961	56 286	5 112	2 742	2 371	51 173	4 844	10 440	11 286	10 112	7 483	7 006
1962	56 831	5 150	2 764	2 386	51 681	4 925	10 207	11 389	10 162	7 610	7 386
1963	57 921	5 496	3 162	2 334	52 425	5 240	10 165	11 476	10 274	7 740	7 526
1964	58 847	5 866	3 503	2 364	52 981	5 520	10 144	11 466	10 402	7 873	7 574
1965	59 782	6 318	3 488	2 831	53 463	5 701	10 182	11 427	10 512	7 990	7 649
1966	60 262	6 658	3 478	3 180	53 603	5 663	10 224	11 294	10 598	8 099	7 723
1967	60 905	6 537	3 528	3 010	54 367	5 977	10 495	11 161	10 705	8 218	7 809
1968	61 847	6 683	3 634	3 049	55 165	6 127	10 944	11 040	10 819	8 336	7 897
1969	62 898	6 928	3 741	3 187	55 969	6 379	11 309	10 890	10 935	8 464	7 990
1970	64 304	7 145	3 848	3 299	57 157	6 861	11 750	10 810	11 052	8 590	8 093
1971	65 942	7 430	3 954	3 477	58 511	7 511	12 227	10 721	11 129	8 711	8 208
1972	67 835	7 705	4 081	3 624	60 130	8 061	12 911	10 762	11 167	8 895	8 330
1973	69 292	7 855	4 152	3 703	61 436	8 429	13 641	10 746	11 202	8 990	8 426
1974	70 808	8 012	4 231	3 781	62 796	8 600	14 262	10 834	11 315	9 140	8 641
1975	72 291	8 134	4 252	3 882	64 158	8 950	14 899	10 874	11 298	9 286	8 852
1976	73 759	8 244	4 266	3 978	65 515	9 237	15 528	11 010	11 243	9 444	9 053
1977	75 193	8 288	4 290	4 000	66 904	9 477	16 108	11 260	11 144	9 616	9 297
1978	76 576	8 309	4 295	4 014	68 268	9 693	16 598	11 665	11 045	9 758	9 509
1979	78 020	8 310	4 251	4 060	69 709	9 873	17 193	12 046	10 944	9 907	9 746
1980	79 398	8 260	4 195	4 064	71 138	10 023	17 833	12 400	10 861	10 042	9 979
1981	80 511	8 092	4 087	4 005	72 419	10 116	18 427	12 758	10 797	10 151	10 170
1982	81 523	7 879	3 911	3 968	73 644	10 136	18 787	13 410	10 726	10 215	10 371
1983	82 531	7 659	3 750	3 908	74 872	10 140	19 143	14 067	10 689	10 261	10 573
1984	83 605	7 386	3 655	3 731	76 219	10 108	19 596	14 719	10 724	10 285	10 788
1985	84 469	7 275	3 689	3 586	77 195	9 746	19 864	15 265	10 844	10 392	11 084
1986	85 798	7 275	3 768	3 507	78 523	9 498	20 498	15 858	10 986	10 336	11 347
1987	86 899	7 335	3 824	3 510	79 565	9 195	20 781	16 475	11 215	10 267	11 632
1988	87 857	7 304	3 715	3 588	80 553	8 931	20 937	17 008	11 625	10 193	11 859
1989	88 762	7 143	3 524	3 619	81 619	8 743	21 080	17 590	11 981	10 092	12 134
1990	90 377	7 347	3 534	3 813	83 030	9 320	21 117	18 529	12 238	9 778	12 049
1991	91 278	7 134	3 548	3 586	84 144	9 367	20 977	19 213	12 554	9 780	12 254
1992	92 270	7 023	3 542	3 481	85 247	9 326	20 792	19 585	13 271	9 776	12 496
1993	93 332	7 076	3 595	3 481	86 256	9 216	20 569	20 037	13 944	9 773	12 717
1994	94 355	7 203	3 718	3 486	87 151	9 074	20 361	20 443	14 545	9 810	12 918
1995	95 178	7 367	3 794	3 573	87 811	8 835	20 079	20 800	15 111	9 856	13 130
1996	96 206	7 600	3 955	3 645	88 606	8 611	19 775	21 222	15 674	9 997	13 327
1997	97 715	7 836	4 053	3 783	89 879	8 706	19 478	21 669	16 276	10 282	13 469
1998	98 758	7 968	4 059	3 909	90 790	8 804	19 094	21 857	16 773	10 649	13 613
1999	99 722	8 167	4 143	4 024	91 555	8 899	18 565	21 969	17 335	11 008	13 779
2000	101 964	8 089	4 096	3 993	93 875	9 101	19 106	21 683	18 365	11 583	14 037
2001	103 282	8 101	4 102	3 999	95 181	9 368	19 056	21 643	18 987	11 972	14 155
2002	104 585	8 146	4 140	4 006	96 439	9 627	19 037	21 523	19 379	12 641	14 233
2003	106 435	8 163	4 365	3 797	98 272	9 878	19 347	21 463	19 784	13 305	14 496
2004	107 710	8 234	4 318	3 916	99 476	10 125	19 358	21 255	20 160	13 894	14 684
2005	109 151	8 317	4 481	3 836	100 835	10 181	19 446	21 177	20 585	14 502	14 944
2006	110 605	8 459	4 613	3 846	102 145	10 191	19 568	21 082	20 991	15 095	15 219
2007	112 173	8 618	4 658	3 960	103 555	10 291	19 858	20 910	21 313	15 658	15 525
2008	113 113	8 660	4 625	4 035	104 453	10 249	19 999	20 567	21 512	16 123	16 002
2009	114 136	8 643	4 548	4 095	105 493	10 284	20 167	20 199	21 731	16 698	16 414

Table 1-6. Civilian Noninstitutional Population, by Age, Race, Sex, and Hispanic Origin, 1948–2009
—Continued

(Thousands of people.)

Race, Hispanic origin, sex, and year	16 years and over	16 to 19 years			20 years and over						
		Total	16 to 17 years	18 to 19 years	Total	20 to 24 years	25 to 34 years	35 to 44 years	45 to 54 years	55 to 64 years	65 years and over
ALL RACES											
Women											
1948	53 071	4 371	2 137	2 234	48 700	6 003	11 843	10 299	8 481	6 444	5 627
1949	53 670	4 269	2 077	2 195	49 400	5 907	11 951	10 475	8 623	6 633	5 809
1950	54 270	4 181	2 033	2 148	50 088	5 810	12 050	10 647	8 768	6 805	6 006
1951	54 895	4 140	2 057	2 084	50 754	5 716	12 134	10 814	8 913	6 955	6 221
1952	55 529	4 155	2 113	2 042	51 373	5 601	12 189	10 973	9 061	7 091	6 456
1953	56 305	4 191	2 119	2 072	52 114	5 478	12 246	11 290	9 113	7 032	6 956
1954	56 925	4 271	2 162	2 109	52 654	5 376	12 237	11 417	9 287	7 200	7 134
1955	57 574	4 342	2 215	2 127	53 232	5 328	12 181	11 544	9 479	7 349	7 348
1956	58 228	4 414	2 244	2 170	53 814	5 301	12 089	11 678	9 690	7 484	7 570
1957	58 951	4 529	2 303	2 226	54 421	5 320	11 960	11 821	9 925	7 618	7 774
1958	59 690	4 693	2 437	2 256	54 997	5 394	11 776	11 949	10 157	7 744	7 974
1959	60 534	4 966	2 656	2 311	55 570	5 487	11 576	12 058	10 371	7 875	8 200
1960	61 582	5 224	2 768	2 456	56 358	5 594	11 484	12 207	10 601	8 036	8 435
1961	62 484	5 401	2 720	2 681	57 082	5 739	11 389	12 299	10 781	8 192	8 679
1962	63 321	5 502	2 739	2 764	57 819	5 927	11 296	12 408	10 754	8 264	9 168
1963	64 494	5 874	3 139	2 736	58 620	6 224	11 235	12 472	10 870	8 398	9 419
1964	65 637	6 245	3 471	2 775	59 391	6 497	11 223	12 474	11 050	8 569	9 576
1965	66 731	6 612	3 448	3 164	60 119	6 741	11 235	12 405	11 216	8 737	9 783
1966	67 795	6 934	3 436	3 499	60 860	6 975	11 319	12 285	11 379	8 908	9 992
1967	68 968	6 943	3 475	3 470	62 026	7 445	11 562	12 152	11 551	9 092	10 220
1968	70 179	7 015	3 566	3 450	63 164	7 764	11 968	11 996	11 715	9 278	10 441
1969	71 436	7 167	3 681	3 486	64 269	8 109	12 336	11 819	11 871	9 466	10 667
1970	72 782	7 373	3 796	3 578	65 408	8 462	12 684	11 679	12 008	9 659	10 914
1971	74 274	7 591	3 895	3 697	66 682	8 834	13 110	11 553	12 115	9 870	11 198
1972	76 290	7 805	3 994	3 811	68 484	9 082	13 829	11 597	12 171	10 113	11 693
1973	77 804	7 985	4 076	3 909	69 819	9 263	14 531	11 541	12 229	10 290	11 963
1974	79 312	8 168	4 142	4 028	71 144	9 393	15 177	11 627	12 263	10 377	12 304
1975	80 860	8 285	4 168	4 117	72 576	9 645	15 811	11 652	12 237	10 558	12 673
1976	82 390	8 370	4 176	4 194	74 020	9 872	16 425	11 786	12 166	10 742	13 030
1977	83 840	8 400	4 193	4 206	75 441	10 103	17 008	12 036	12 053	10 940	13 300
1978	85 334	8 386	4 189	4 197	76 948	10 315	17 493	12 435	11 932	11 118	13 658
1979	86 843	8 347	4 139	4 208	78 496	10 480	18 070	12 815	11 808	11 303	14 021
1980	88 348	8 283	4 083	4 200	80 065	10 612	18 725	13 177	11 701	11 478	14 372
1981	89 618	8 121	3 981	4 140	81 497	10 705	19 350	13 533	11 625	11 605	14 680
1982	90 748	7 884	3 804	4 081	82 864	10 709	19 705	14 201	11 538	11 694	15 017
1983	91 684	7 616	3 635	3 981	84 069	10 660	20 004	14 865	11 478	11 742	15 319
1984	92 778	7 349	3 542	3 807	85 429	10 580	20 403	15 532	11 501	11 768	15 645
1985	93 736	7 231	3 543	3 688	86 506	10 351	20 805	16 114	11 574	11 748	15 913
1986	94 789	7 221	3 618	3 603	87 567	10 072	21 233	16 692	11 746	11 675	16 150
1987	95 853	7 271	3 677	3 594	88 583	9 776	21 516	17 279	11 968	11 567	16 476
1988	96 756	7 224	3 569	3 655	89 532	9 503	21 674	17 776	12 378	11 448	16 753
1989	97 630	7 080	3 361	3 719	90 550	9 282	21 765	18 387	12 763	11 314	17 039
1990	98 787	7 173	3 359	3 813	91 614	9 582	21 859	19 190	12 843	10 941	17 198
1991	99 646	6 939	3 353	3 586	92 708	9 597	21 711	19 903	13 155	10 895	17 446
1992	100 535	6 818	3 366	3 452	93 718	9 520	21 486	20 267	13 935	10 828	17 682
1993	101 506	6 859	3 415	3 444	94 647	9 426	21 202	20 696	14 605	10 801	17 917
1994	102 460	6 993	3 528	3 465	95 467	9 279	20 945	21 091	15 233	10 825	18 094
1995	103 406	7 144	3 613	3 531	96 262	9 029	20 719	21 454	15 862	10 879	18 318
1996	104 385	7 335	3 723	3 612	97 050	8 798	20 477	21 865	16 493	10 993	18 424
1997	105 418	7 528	3 808	3 721	97 889	8 736	20 081	22 214	17 115	11 224	18 520
1998	106 462	7 676	3 835	3 840	98 786	8 790	19 683	22 442	17 600	11 646	18 625
1999	108 031	7 873	3 917	3 955	100 158	9 069	19 411	22 666	18 251	12 056	18 705
2000	110 613	7 823	3 882	3 941	102 790	9 211	19 597	22 628	19 276	12 647	19 430
2001	111 811	7 828	3 917	3 910	103 983	9 509	19 449	22 552	19 917	13 039	19 517
2002	112 985	7 848	3 959	3 889	105 136	9 721	19 435	22 371	20 332	13 703	19 575
2003	114 733	7 934	4 195	3 738	106 800	9 924	19 674	22 283	20 738	14 423	19 758
2004	115 647	7 989	4 257	3 732	107 658	10 072	19 581	21 970	21 085	15 025	19 925
2005	116 931	8 081	4 297	3 784	108 850	10 095	19 618	21 828	21 521	15 663	20 125
2006	118 210	8 218	4 476	3 742	109 992	10 074	19 662	21 671	21 910	16 280	20 394
2007	119 694	8 364	4 564	3 800	111 330	10 137	19 893	21 491	22 231	16 876	20 703
2008	120 675	8 415	4 508	3 907	112 260	10 160	19 994	21 132	22 448	17 367	21 160
2009	121 665	8 401	4 396	4 004	113 265	10 240	20 113	20 721	22 633	17 973	21 584

Table 1-6. Civilian Noninstitutional Population, by Age, Race, Sex, and Hispanic Origin, 1948–2009 —*Continued*

(Thousands of people.)

Race, Hispanic origin, sex, and year	16 years and over	16 to 19 years			20 years and over						
		Total	16 to 17 years	18 to 19 years	Total	20 to 24 years	25 to 34 years	35 to 44 years	45 to 54 years	55 to 64 years	65 years and over
WHITE											
Both Sexes											
1954	97 705	7 180	3 786	3 394	90 524	7 794	20 818	19 915	16 569	12 993	12 438
1955	98 880	7 292	3 874	3 419	91 586	7 912	20 742	20 110	16 869	13 169	12 785
1956	99 976	7 346	3 908	3 438	92 629	8 106	20 564	20 314	17 198	13 341	13 105
1957	101 119	7 505	4 007	3 498	93 612	8 293	20 342	20 514	17 562	13 518	13 383
1958	102 392	7 843	4 271	3 573	94 547	8 498	20 063	20 734	17 924	13 681	13 645
1959	103 803	8 430	4 707	3 725	95 370	8 697	19 715	20 893	18 257	13 858	13 951
1960	105 282	8 924	4 909	4 016	96 355	8 927	19 470	21 049	18 578	14 070	14 260
1961	106 604	9 211	4 785	4 427	97 390	9 203	19 289	21 169	18 845	14 304	14 581
1962	107 715	9 343	4 818	4 526	98 371	9 484	18 974	21 293	18 872	14 450	15 297
1963	109 705	9 978	5 549	4 430	99 725	10 069	18 867	21 398	19 082	14 681	15 629
1964	111 534	10 616	6 137	4 481	100 916	10 568	18 838	21 375	19 360	14 957	15 816
1965	113 284	11 319	6 049	5 271	101 963	10 935	18 882	21 258	19 604	15 215	16 070
1966	114 566	11 862	5 993	5 870	102 702	11 094	18 989	21 005	19 822	15 469	16 322
1967	116 100	11 682	6 051	5 632	104 417	11 797	19 464	20 745	20 067	15 745	16 602
1968	117 948	11 840	6 225	5 616	106 107	12 184	20 245	20 474	20 310	16 018	16 875
1969	119 913	12 179	6 418	5 761	107 733	12 677	20 892	20 156	20 546	16 305	17 156
1970	122 174	12 521	6 591	5 931	109 652	13 359	21 546	19 929	20 760	16 591	17 469
1971	124 758	12 937	6 750	6 189	111 821	14 208	22 295	19 694	20 907	16 884	17 833
1972	127 906	13 301	6 910	6 392	114 603	14 897	23 555	19 673	20 950	17 250	18 278
1973	130 097	13 533	7 021	6 512	116 563	15 264	24 685	19 532	20 991	17 484	18 607
1974	132 417	13 784	7 114	6 671	118 632	15 502	25 711	19 628	21 061	17 645	19 085
1975	134 790	13 941	7 132	6 808	120 849	15 980	26 746	19 641	20 981	17 918	19 587
1976	137 106	14 055	7 125	6 930	123 050	16 368	27 757	19 827	20 816	18 220	20 064
1977	139 380	14 095	7 150	6 944	125 285	16 728	28 703	20 231	20 575	18 540	20 508
1978	141 612	14 060	7 132	6 928	127 552	17 038	29 453	20 932	20 322	18 799	21 007
1979	143 894	13 994	7 029	6 964	129 900	17 284	30 371	21 579	20 058	19 071	21 538
1980	146 122	13 854	6 912	6 943	132 268	17 484	31 407	22 174	19 837	19 316	22 050
1981	147 908	13 516	6 704	6 813	134 392	17 609	32 367	22 778	19 666	19 485	22 487
1982	149 441	13 076	6 383	6 693	136 366	17 579	32 863	23 910	19 478	19 591	22 945
1983	150 805	12 623	6 089	6 534	138 183	17 492	33 286	25 027	19 349	19 625	23 403
1984	152 347	12 147	5 918	6 228	140 200	17 304	33 889	26 124	19 348	19 629	23 906
1985	153 679	11 900	5 922	5 978	141 780	16 853	34 450	27 100	19 405	19 620	24 352
1986	155 432	11 879	6 036	5 843	143 553	16 353	35 293	28 062	19 587	19 477	24 780
1987	156 958	11 939	6 110	5 829	145 020	15 808	35 667	29 036	19 965	19 242	25 301
1988	158 194	11 838	5 893	5 945	146 357	15 276	35 876	29 818	20 652	18 996	25 739
1989	159 338	11 530	5 506	6 023	147 809	14 879	35 951	30 774	21 287	18 743	26 175
1990	160 625	11 630	5 464	6 166	148 996	15 538	35 661	31 739	21 535	18 204	26 319
1991	161 759	11 200	5 451	5 749	150 558	15 516	35 342	32 854	22 052	18 074	26 721
1992	162 972	11 004	5 478	5 526	151 968	15 354	34 885	33 305	23 364	17 951	27 108
1993	164 289	11 078	5 562	5 516	153 210	15 087	34 365	33 919	24 456	17 892	27 493
1994	165 555	11 264	5 710	5 554	154 291	14 708	33 865	34 582	25 435	17 924	27 776
1995	166 914	11 468	5 822	5 646	155 446	14 313	33 355	35 222	26 418	17 986	28 153
1996	168 317	11 822	6 026	5 796	156 495	13 907	32 852	35 810	27 403	18 136	28 387
1997	169 993	12 181	6 213	5 968	157 812	13 983	32 091	36 325	28 388	18 511	28 514
1998	171 478	12 439	6 264	6 176	159 039	14 138	31 286	36 610	29 132	19 231	28 642
1999	173 085	12 700	6 342	6 358	160 385	14 394	30 516	36 755	30 048	19 855	28 818
2000	176 220	12 535	6 264	6 271	163 685	14 552	30 948	36 261	31 550	20 757	29 617
2001	178 111	12 556	6 291	6 265	165 556	15 001	30 770	36 113	32 475	21 434	29 762
2002	179 783	12 596	6 346	6 250	167 187	15 360	30 676	35 750	33 012	22 540	29 849
2003	181 292	12 527	6 629	5 898	168 765	15 536	30 789	35 352	33 466	23 589	30 033
2004	182 643	12 599	6 561	6 038	170 045	15 817	30 585	34 845	34 005	24 549	30 245
2005	184 446	12 690	6 768	5 921	171 757	15 871	30 592	34 554	34 649	25 534	30 556
2006	186 264	12 856	6 981	5 875	173 408	15 848	30 661	34 217	35 228	26 486	30 968
2007	188 253	13 043	7 026	6 018	175 210	15 945	31 011	33 770	35 665	27 392	31 426
2008	189 540	13 084	6 962	6 122	176 456	15 914	31 234	33 093	35 941	28 109	32 165
2009	190 902	13 035	6 775	6 261	177 867	15 963	31 471	32 378	36 166	29 022	32 867

Table 1-6. Civilian Noninstitutional Population, by Age, Race, Sex, and Hispanic Origin, 1948–2009
—Continued

(Thousands of people.)

Race, Hispanic origin, sex, and year	16 years and over	16 to 19 years			20 years and over						
		Total	16 to 17 years	18 to 19 years	Total	20 to 24 years	25 to 34 years	35 to 44 years	45 to 54 years	55 to 64 years	65 years and over
WHITE											
Men											
1954	46 462	3 455	1 902	1 553	43 007	3 074	9 948	9 688	8 172	6 341	5 787
1955	47 076	3 507	1 945	1 563	43 569	3 241	9 936	9 768	8 303	6 398	5 923
1956	47 602	3 500	1 955	1 546	44 102	3 464	9 851	9 848	8 446	6 455	6 038
1957	48 119	3 556	2 000	1 557	44 563	3 638	9 758	9 917	8 605	6 518	6 127
1958	48 745	3 747	2 140	1 607	44 998	3 783	9 656	10 018	8 765	6 574	6 203
1959	49 408	4 079	2 370	1 710	45 329	3 903	9 499	10 081	8 909	6 639	6 298
1960	50 065	4 349	2 476	1 874	45 716	4 054	9 373	10 131	9 042	6 721	6 395
1961	50 608	4 479	2 407	2 073	46 129	4 204	9 290	10 178	9 148	6 819	6 490
1962	51 054	4 520	2 426	2 094	46 534	4 306	9 080	10 239	9 191	6 917	6 801
1963	52 031	4 827	2 792	2 036	47 204	4 610	9 039	10 309	9 297	7 031	6 919
1964	52 869	5 148	3 090	2 059	47 721	4 862	9 024	10 301	9 417	7 153	6 963
1965	53 681	5 541	3 050	2 492	48 140	5 017	9 056	10 262	9 516	7 261	7 028
1966	54 061	5 820	3 023	2 798	48 241	4 974	9 085	10 136	9 592	7 362	7 092
1967	54 608	5 671	3 058	2 613	48 937	5 257	9 339	10 013	9 688	7 474	7 167
1968	55 434	5 787	3 153	2 635	49 647	5 376	9 752	9 902	9 790	7 585	7 242
1969	56 348	6 005	3 246	2 759	50 343	5 589	10 074	9 760	9 895	7 705	7 320
1970	57 516	6 179	3 329	2 851	51 336	5 988	10 441	9 678	9 999	7 822	7 409
1971	58 900	6 420	3 412	3 008	52 481	6 546	10 841	9 578	10 066	7 933	7 517
1972	60 473	6 627	3 503	3 125	53 845	7 042	11 495	9 568	10 078	8 089	7 573
1973	61 577	6 737	3 555	3 182	54 842	7 312	12 075	9 514	10 099	8 178	7 664
1974	62 791	6 851	3 604	3 247	55 942	7 476	12 599	9 564	10 165	8 288	7 849
1975	63 981	6 929	3 609	3 320	57 052	7 766	13 131	9 578	10 134	8 413	8 031
1976	65 132	6 993	3 609	3 384	58 138	7 987	13 655	9 674	10 063	8 556	8 203
1977	66 301	7 024	3 625	3 399	59 278	8 175	14 139	9 880	9 957	8 708	8 420
1978	67 401	7 022	3 619	3 404	60 378	8 335	14 528	10 236	9 845	8 826	8 608
1979	68 547	7 007	3 568	3 439	61 540	8 470	15 008	10 563	9 730	8 949	8 820
1980	69 634	6 941	3 508	3 433	62 694	8 581	15 529	10 863	9 636	9 059	9 027
1981	70 480	6 764	3 401	3 363	63 715	8 644	16 005	11 171	9 560	9 139	9 195
1982	71 211	6 556	3 249	3 307	64 655	8 621	16 260	11 756	9 463	9 188	9 367
1983	71 922	6 340	3 098	3 242	65 581	8 597	16 499	12 314	9 408	9 208	9 556
1984	72 723	6 113	3 019	3 094	66 610	8 522	16 816	12 853	9 434	9 217	9 768
1985	73 373	5 987	3 026	2 961	67 386	8 246	17 042	13 337	9 488	9 262	10 010
1986	74 390	5 977	3 084	2 894	68 413	8 002	17 564	13 840	9 578	9 201	10 229
1987	75 189	6 015	3 125	2 890	69 175	7 729	17 754	14 338	9 771	9 101	10 481
1988	75 855	5 968	3 015	2 953	69 887	7 473	17 867	14 743	10 114	9 001	10 688
1989	76 468	5 813	2 817	2 996	70 654	7 279	17 908	15 237	10 434	8 900	10 897
1990	77 369	5 913	2 809	3 103	71 457	7 764	17 766	15 770	10 598	8 680	10 879
1991	77 977	5 704	2 805	2 899	72 274	7 748	17 615	16 340	10 856	8 640	11 074
1992	78 651	5 611	2 819	2 792	73 040	7 676	17 403	16 579	11 513	8 602	11 268
1993	79 371	5 650	2 862	2 788	73 721	7 545	17 158	16 900	12 058	8 590	11 470
1994	80 059	5 748	2 938	2 810	74 311	7 357	16 915	17 247	12 545	8 618	11 629
1995	80 733	5 854	2 995	2 859	74 879	7 163	16 653	17 567	13 028	8 653	11 815
1996	81 489	6 035	3 099	2 936	75 454	6 971	16 395	17 868	13 518	8 734	11 968
1997	82 577	6 257	3 209	3 048	76 320	7 087	16 043	18 163	14 030	8 929	12 067
1998	83 352	6 386	3 233	3 153	76 966	7 170	15 644	18 310	14 400	9 286	12 155
1999	83 930	6 498	3 266	3 232	77 432	7 244	15 150	18 340	14 834	9 581	12 283
2000	85 370	6 404	3 224	3 181	78 966	7 329	15 528	18 003	15 578	10 028	12 501
2001	86 452	6 422	3 229	3 194	80 029	7 564	15 486	17 960	16 047	10 369	12 604
2002	87 361	6 439	3 251	3 189	80 922	7 750	15 470	17 792	16 317	10 918	12 676
2003	88 249	6 390	3 378	3 012	81 860	7 856	15 569	17 620	16 555	11 442	12 818
2004	89 044	6 429	3 301	3 129	82 615	8 024	15 486	17 404	16 834	11 922	12 946
2005	90 027	6 471	3 464	3 006	83 556	8 057	15 507	17 286	17 169	12 415	13 123
2006	91 021	6 555	3 551	3 004	84 466	8 052	15 567	17 143	17 467	12 891	13 346
2007	92 073	6 653	3 567	3 086	85 420	8 113	15 762	16 927	17 686	13 341	13 591
2008	92 725	6 669	3 550	3 120	86 056	8 072	15 884	16 599	17 830	13 698	13 972
2009	93 433	6 644	3 469	3 175	86 789	8 076	16 011	16 260	17 956	14 154	14 332

Table 1-6. Civilian Noninstitutional Population, by Age, Race, Sex, and Hispanic Origin, 1948–2009
—Continued

(Thousands of people.)

Race, Hispanic origin, sex, and year	16 years and over	16 to 19 years			20 years and over						
		Total	16 to 17 years	18 to 19 years	Total	20 to 24 years	25 to 34 years	35 to 44 years	45 to 54 years	55 to 64 years	65 years and over
WHITE											
Women											
1954	51 242	3 725	1 884	1 841	47 517	4 720	10 870	10 227	8 397	6 652	6 651
1955	51 802	3 785	1 929	1 856	48 017	4 671	10 806	10 342	8 566	6 771	6 862
1956	52 373	3 846	1 953	1 892	48 527	4 642	10 713	10 466	8 752	6 886	7 067
1957	52 998	3 949	2 007	1 941	49 049	4 655	10 584	10 597	8 957	7 000	7 256
1958	53 645	4 096	2 131	1 966	49 549	4 715	10 407	10 716	9 159	7 107	7 442
1959	54 392	4 351	2 337	2 015	50 041	4 794	10 216	10 812	9 348	7 219	7 653
1960	55 214	4 575	2 433	2 142	50 639	4 873	10 097	10 918	9 536	7 349	7 865
1961	55 993	4 732	2 378	2 354	51 261	4 999	9 999	10 991	9 697	7 485	8 091
1962	56 660	4 823	2 392	2 432	51 837	5 178	9 894	11 054	9 681	7 533	8 496
1963	57 672	5 151	2 757	2 394	52 521	5 459	9 828	11 089	9 785	7 650	8 710
1964	58 663	5 468	3 047	2 422	53 195	5 706	9 814	11 074	9 943	7 804	8 853
1965	59 601	5 778	2 999	2 779	53 823	5 918	9 826	10 996	10 088	7 954	9 042
1966	60 503	6 042	2 970	3 072	54 461	6 120	9 904	10 869	10 230	8 107	9 230
1967	61 491	6 011	2 993	3 019	55 480	6 540	10 125	10 732	10 379	8 271	9 435
1968	62 512	6 053	3 072	2 981	56 460	6 809	10 493	10 572	10 520	8 433	9 633
1969	63 563	6 174	3 172	3 002	57 390	7 089	10 818	10 396	10 651	8 600	9 836
1970	64 656	6 342	3 262	3 080	58 315	7 370	11 105	10 251	10 761	8 769	10 060
1971	65 857	6 518	3 338	3 180	59 340	7 662	11 454	10 117	10 841	8 951	10 315
1972	67 431	6 673	3 407	3 267	60 758	7 855	12 006	10 105	10 872	9 161	10 705
1973	68 517	6 796	3 466	3 331	61 721	7 951	12 610	10 018	10 891	9 306	10 943
1974	69 623	6 933	3 510	3 424	62 690	8 026	13 112	10 064	10 896	9 356	11 236
1975	70 810	7 011	3 523	3 488	63 798	8 214	13 615	10 063	10 847	9 505	11 556
1976	71 974	7 062	3 516	3 546	64 912	8 381	14 102	10 153	10 752	9 664	11 860
1977	73 077	7 071	3 525	3 545	66 007	8 553	14 564	10 351	10 618	9 832	12 088
1978	74 213	7 038	3 513	3 524	67 174	8 704	14 926	10 696	10 476	9 974	12 399
1979	75 347	6 987	3 460	3 527	68 360	8 815	15 363	11 017	10 327	10 122	12 717
1980	76 489	6 914	3 403	3 511	69 575	8 904	15 878	11 313	10 201	10 256	13 022
1981	77 428	6 752	3 303	3 449	70 677	8 965	16 362	11 606	10 106	10 346	13 292
1982	78 230	6 519	3 134	3 385	71 711	8 959	16 603	12 154	10 015	10 402	13 579
1983	78 884	6 282	2 991	3 292	72 601	8 895	16 788	12 714	9 941	10 418	13 847
1984	79 624	6 034	2 899	3 135	73 590	8 782	17 073	13 271	9 914	10 412	14 138
1985	80 306	5 912	2 895	3 017	74 394	8 607	17 409	13 762	9 917	10 358	14 342
1986	81 042	5 902	2 953	2 949	75 140	8 351	17 728	14 223	10 009	10 277	14 551
1987	81 769	5 924	2 985	2 939	75 845	8 079	17 913	14 698	10 194	10 141	14 820
1988	82 340	5 869	2 878	2 991	76 470	7 804	18 009	15 074	10 537	9 994	15 052
1989	82 871	5 716	2 690	3 027	77 154	7 600	18 043	15 537	10 853	9 843	15 278
1990	83 256	5 717	2 654	3 063	77 539	7 774	17 895	15 969	10 937	9 524	15 440
1991	83 781	5 497	2 646	2 850	78 285	7 768	17 726	16 514	11 196	9 435	15 647
1992	84 321	5 393	2 659	2 734	78 928	7 678	17 482	16 727	11 851	9 350	15 841
1993	84 918	5 428	2 700	2 728	79 490	7 542	17 206	17 019	12 398	9 302	16 023
1994	85 496	5 516	2 772	2 744	79 980	7 351	16 950	17 335	12 890	9 306	16 148
1995	86 181	5 614	2 827	2 787	80 567	7 150	16 702	17 654	13 390	9 333	16 337
1996	86 828	5 787	2 927	2 860	81 041	6 936	16 457	17 943	13 884	9 402	16 419
1997	87 417	5 924	3 004	2 920	81 492	6 896	16 047	18 162	14 357	9 582	16 447
1998	88 126	6 053	3 031	3 023	82 073	6 969	15 642	18 300	14 732	9 944	16 486
1999	89 156	6 202	3 076	3 127	82 953	7 150	15 366	18 415	15 214	10 274	16 536
2000	90 850	6 131	3 041	3 090	84 718	7 223	15 420	18 258	15 972	10 729	17 116
2001	91 660	6 134	3 062	3 071	85 526	7 438	15 284	18 153	16 428	11 065	17 158
2002	92 422	6 157	3 096	3 061	86 266	7 611	15 207	17 958	16 695	11 622	17 173
2003	93 043	6 137	3 251	2 886	86 905	7 680	15 220	17 731	16 911	12 147	17 216
2004	93 599	6 169	3 260	2 909	87 430	7 794	15 099	17 441	17 170	12 627	17 299
2005	94 419	6 219	3 304	2 915	88 200	7 814	15 086	17 268	17 480	13 119	17 433
2006	95 242	6 301	3 429	2 871	88 942	7 796	15 094	17 074	17 760	13 596	17 623
2007	96 180	6 390	3 458	2 932	89 790	7 832	15 249	16 843	17 979	14 051	17 835
2008	96 814	6 414	3 412	3 003	90 400	7 842	15 349	16 493	18 111	14 411	18 193
2009	97 469	6 391	3 306	3 086	91 078	7 887	15 460	16 118	18 210	14 868	18 535

Table 1-6. Civilian Noninstitutional Population, by Age, Race, Sex, and Hispanic Origin, 1948–2009
—*Continued*

(Thousands of people.)

Race, Hispanic origin, sex, and year	16 years and over	16 to 19 years			20 years and over						
		Total	16 to 17 years	18 to 19 years	Total	20 to 24 years	25 to 34 years	35 to 44 years	45 to 54 years	55 to 64 years	65 years and over
BLACK											
Both Sexes											
1972	14 526	2 018	1 061	956	12 508	2 027	2 809	2 329	2 139	1 601	1 605
1973	14 917	2 095	1 095	1 000	12 823	2 132	2 957	2 333	2 156	1 616	1 628
1974	15 329	2 137	1 122	1 014	13 192	2 137	3 103	2 382	2 202	1 679	1 689
1975	15 751	2 191	1 146	1 046	13 560	2 228	3 258	2 395	2 211	1 717	1 755
1976	16 196	2 264	1 165	1 098	13 932	2 303	3 412	2 435	2 220	1 736	1 826
1977	16 605	2 273	1 175	1 097	14 332	2 400	3 566	2 493	2 225	1 765	1 883
1978	16 970	2 270	1 169	1 101	14 701	2 483	3 717	2 547	2 226	1 794	1 932
1979	17 397	2 276	1 167	1 109	15 121	2 556	3 899	2 615	2 240	1 831	1 980
1980	17 824	2 289	1 171	1 119	15 535	2 606	4 095	2 687	2 249	1 870	2 030
1981	18 219	2 288	1 161	1 127	15 931	2 642	4 290	2 758	2 260	1 913	2 069
1982	18 584	2 252	1 119	1 134	16 332	2 697	4 438	2 887	2 263	1 935	2 113
1983	18 925	2 225	1 092	1 133	16 700	2 734	4 607	2 999	2 260	1 964	2 135
1984	19 348	2 161	1 056	1 105	17 187	2 783	4 789	3 167	2 288	1 977	2 183
1985	19 664	2 160	1 083	1 077	17 504	2 649	4 873	3 290	2 372	2 060	2 259
1986	19 989	2 137	1 090	1 048	17 852	2 625	5 026	3 410	2 413	2 079	2 298
1987	20 352	2 163	1 123	1 040	18 189	2 578	5 139	3 563	2 460	2 097	2 352
1988	20 692	2 179	1 130	1 049	18 513	2 527	5 234	3 716	2 524	2 110	2 402
1989	21 021	2 176	1 116	1 060	18 846	2 479	5 308	3 900	2 587	2 118	2 454
1990	21 477	2 238	1 101	1 138	19 239	2 554	5 407	4 328	2 618	1 970	2 362
1991	21 799	2 187	1 085	1 102	19 612	2 585	5 419	4 538	2 682	1 985	2 403
1992	22 147	2 155	1 086	1 069	19 992	2 615	5 404	4 722	2 809	1 996	2 446
1993	22 521	2 181	1 113	1 069	20 339	2 600	5 409	4 886	2 941	2 016	2 487
1994	22 879	2 211	1 168	1 044	20 668	2 616	5 362	5 038	3 084	2 045	2 524
1995	23 246	2 284	1 198	1 086	20 962	2 554	5 337	5 178	3 244	2 079	2 571
1996	23 604	2 356	1 238	1 118	21 248	2 519	5 311	5 290	3 408	2 110	2 609
1997	24 003	2 412	1 255	1 158	21 591	2 515	5 279	5 410	3 571	2 164	2 653
1998	24 373	2 443	1 241	1 202	21 930	2 546	5 221	5 510	3 735	2 224	2 695
1999	24 855	2 479	1 250	1 229	22 376	2 615	5 197	5 609	3 919	2 295	2 741
2000	24 902	2 389	1 205	1 183	22 513	2 611	5 089	5 488	4 168	2 407	2 750
2001	25 138	2 388	1 212	1 176	22 750	2 686	5 003	5 467	4 343	2 478	2 775
2002	25 578	2 416	1 235	1 181	23 162	2 779	5 015	5 460	4 513	2 571	2 823
2003	25 686	2 382	1 309	1 074	23 304	2 773	4 978	5 387	4 628	2 692	2 846
2004	26 065	2 423	1 350	1 072	23 643	2 821	5 020	5 335	4 739	2 827	2 899
2005	26 517	2 481	1 341	1 140	24 036	2 835	5 075	5 311	4 869	2 980	2 967
2006	27 007	2 565	1 408	1 157	24 442	2 851	5 133	5 302	4 992	3 137	3 027
2007	27 485	2 640	1 497	1 143	24 845	2 891	5 210	5 271	5 110	3 284	3 080
2008	27 843	2 676	1 459	1 217	25 168	2 914	5 262	5 198	5 183	3 429	3 182
2009	28 241	2 684	1 462	1 221	25 557	2 973	5 349	5 109	5 290	3 596	3 239
BLACK											
Men											
1972	6 538	978	525	453	5 559	921	1 251	1 026	963	720	679
1973	6 704	1 007	539	468	5 697	979	1 327	1 027	962	718	684
1974	6 875	1 027	554	471	5 848	956	1 381	1 055	997	753	707
1975	7 060	1 051	565	486	6 009	1 002	1 452	1 060	997	769	730
1976	7 265	1 099	579	518	6 167	1 036	1 521	1 077	999	774	756
1977	7 431	1 102	586	516	6 329	1 080	1 589	1 102	998	786	774
1978	7 577	1 093	579	514	6 484	1 120	1 657	1 128	995	794	789
1979	7 761	1 100	581	519	6 661	1 151	1 738	1 159	998	809	804
1980	7 944	1 110	583	526	6 834	1 171	1 828	1 191	999	825	822
1981	8 117	1 110	577	534	7 007	1 189	1 914	1 224	1 003	844	835
1982	8 283	1 097	556	542	7 186	1 225	1 983	1 282	1 003	848	846
1983	8 447	1 087	542	545	7 360	1 254	2 068	1 333	1 000	857	847
1984	8 654	1 055	524	531	7 599	1 292	2 164	1 411	1 012	858	861
1985	8 790	1 059	543	517	7 731	1 202	2 180	1 462	1 060	924	902
1986	8 956	1 049	548	503	7 907	1 195	2 264	1 517	1 072	934	924
1987	9 128	1 065	566	499	8 063	1 173	2 320	1 587	1 092	944	947
1988	9 289	1 074	569	505	8 215	1 151	2 367	1 656	1 121	951	970
1989	9 439	1 075	575	501	8 364	1 128	2 403	1 741	1 145	956	989
1990	9 573	1 094	555	540	8 479	1 144	2 412	1 968	1 183	855	917
1991	9 725	1 072	546	526	8 652	1 168	2 417	2 060	1 211	864	933
1992	9 896	1 056	544	512	8 840	1 194	2 409	2 150	1 268	868	951
1993	10 083	1 075	559	516	9 008	1 181	2 425	2 228	1 330	874	969
1994	10 258	1 087	586	501	9 171	1 207	2 399	2 300	1 392	889	985
1995	10 411	1 131	601	530	9 280	1 161	2 388	2 362	1 462	901	1 006
1996	10 575	1 161	623	538	9 414	1 154	2 373	2 413	1 534	914	1 025
1997	10 763	1 188	634	553	9 575	1 153	2 363	2 471	1 607	936	1 045
1998	10 927	1 201	623	578	9 727	1 166	2 335	2 520	1 682	956	1 068
1999	11 143	1 218	628	589	9 926	1 197	2 321	2 566	1 765	986	1 091
2000	11 129	1 178	605	572	9 952	1 195	2 277	2 471	1 889	1 067	1 053
2001	11 172	1 179	606	573	9 993	1 224	2 212	2 440	1 960	1 096	1 060
2002	11 391	1 195	615	580	10 196	1 281	2 223	2 437	2 042	1 137	1 075
2003	11 454	1 176	661	515	10 278	1 291	2 210	2 401	2 094	1 189	1 093
2004	11 656	1 195	680	516	10 461	1 326	2 242	2 382	2 150	1 250	1 111
2005	11 882	1 223	682	541	10 659	1 341	2 277	2 372	2 202	1 319	1 148
2006	12 130	1 266	713	552	10 864	1 355	2 318	2 369	2 261	1 390	1 170
2007	12 361	1 305	742	563	11 057	1 380	2 366	2 352	2 318	1 454	1 186
2008	12 516	1 322	718	604	11 194	1 384	2 398	2 313	2 335	1 519	1 245
2009	12 705	1 326	736	590	11 379	1 410	2 454	2 271	2 392	1 592	1 260

Table 1-6. Civilian Noninstitutional Population, by Age, Race, Sex, and Hispanic Origin, 1948–2009
—Continued

(Thousands of people.)

Race, Hispanic origin, sex, and year	16 years and over	16 to 19 years			20 years and over						
		Total	16 to 17 years	18 to 19 years	Total	20 to 24 years	25 to 34 years	35 to 44 years	45 to 54 years	55 to 64 years	65 years and over
BLACK											
Women											
1972	7 988	1 040	536	503	6 948	1 106	1 558	1 302	1 176	881	925
1973	8 214	1 088	556	532	7 126	1 153	1 631	1 306	1 194	898	944
1974	8 454	1 110	567	542	7 344	1 181	1 723	1 327	1 206	926	981
1975	8 691	1 141	581	560	7 550	1 226	1 806	1 334	1 213	948	1 025
1976	8 931	1 165	585	580	7 765	1 266	1 890	1 357	1 220	962	1 070
1977	9 174	1 171	590	581	8 003	1 320	1 978	1 390	1 228	979	1 108
1978	9 394	1 177	589	588	8 217	1 363	2 061	1 419	1 231	999	1 143
1979	9 636	1 176	586	589	8 460	1 405	2 160	1 455	1 242	1 022	1 176
1980	9 880	1 180	587	593	8 700	1 435	2 267	1 496	1 250	1 045	1 208
1981	10 102	1 178	584	593	8 924	1 453	2 376	1 534	1 257	1 069	1 234
1982	10 300	1 155	563	592	9 146	1 472	2 455	1 605	1 260	1 087	1 267
1983	10 477	1 138	550	588	9 340	1 480	2 539	1 666	1 260	1 107	1 288
1984	10 694	1 106	532	574	9 588	1 491	2 625	1 756	1 276	1 119	1 322
1985	10 873	1 101	540	560	9 773	1 447	2 693	1 828	1 312	1 136	1 357
1986	11 033	1 088	542	545	9 945	1 430	2 762	1 893	1 341	1 145	1 374
1987	11 224	1 098	557	541	10 126	1 405	2 819	1 976	1 368	1 153	1 405
1988	11 402	1 105	561	544	10 298	1 376	2 867	2 060	1 403	1 159	1 432
1989	11 582	1 100	541	559	10 482	1 351	2 905	2 159	1 441	1 162	1 464
1990	11 904	1 144	546	598	10 760	1 410	2 995	2 360	1 435	1 114	1 446
1991	12 074	1 115	539	576	10 959	1 417	3 003	2 478	1 471	1 121	1 470
1992	12 251	1 099	542	557	11 152	1 421	2 995	2 573	1 542	1 127	1 495
1993	12 438	1 106	554	552	11 332	1 419	2 983	2 659	1 611	1 142	1 518
1994	12 621	1 125	582	543	11 496	1 410	2 963	2 738	1 692	1 156	1 538
1995	12 835	1 153	597	556	11 682	1 392	2 948	2 816	1 782	1 178	1 565
1996	13 029	1 195	615	580	11 833	1 364	2 938	2 877	1 874	1 196	1 584
1997	13 241	1 225	620	604	12 016	1 362	2 916	2 939	1 964	1 228	1 608
1998	13 446	1 243	618	624	12 203	1 380	2 886	2 991	2 053	1 268	1 626
1999	13 711	1 261	621	640	12 451	1 418	2 876	3 043	2 153	1 310	1 650
2000	13 772	1 211	600	611	12 561	1 416	2 812	3 017	2 279	1 340	1 697
2001	13 966	1 209	606	603	12 758	1 462	2 790	3 026	2 383	1 382	1 714
2002	14 187	1 221	620	601	12 966	1 498	2 792	3 023	2 471	1 434	1 747
2003	14 232	1 206	648	558	13 026	1 482	2 768	2 986	2 534	1 504	1 753
2004	14 409	1 227	670	557	13 182	1 495	2 778	2 954	2 590	1 577	1 789
2005	14 635	1 258	659	598	13 377	1 494	2 797	2 939	2 666	1 661	1 819
2006	14 877	1 299	694	605	13 578	1 495	2 815	2 933	2 731	1 747	1 857
2007	15 124	1 336	755	581	13 788	1 511	2 844	2 918	2 792	1 830	1 893
2008	15 328	1 354	741	613	13 974	1 530	2 864	2 885	2 848	1 910	1 937
2009	15 536	1 357	726	631	14 178	1 563	2 895	2 839	2 898	2 004	1 979
HISPANIC[1]											
Both Sexes											
1973	6 104	867	. . .	. . .	5 238	. . .	. . .	. . .	. . .	. . .	. . .
1974	6 564	926	. . .	. . .	5 645	. . .	. . .	. . .	. . .	. . .	. . .
1975	6 862	962	. . .	. . .	5 900	. . .	. . .	. . .	. . .	. . .	. . .
1976	6 910	953	494	480	6 075	1 053	1 775	1 261	936	570	479
1977	7 362	1 024	513	508	6 376	1 163	1 869	1 283	989	587	485
1978	7 912	1 076	561	515	6 836	1 265	2 004	1 378	1 033	627	529
1979	8 207	1 095	544	551	7 113	1 296	2 117	1 458	1 015	659	566
1980	9 598	1 281	638	643	8 317	1 564	2 508	1 575	1 190	782	698
1981	10 120	1 301	641	660	8 819	1 650	2 698	1 680	1 231	832	728
1982	10 580	1 307	639	668	9 273	1 724	2 871	1 779	1 264	880	755
1983	11 029	1 304	635	670	9 725	1 790	3 045	1 883	1 298	928	781
1984	11 478	1 300	633	667	10 178	1 839	3 224	1 996	1 336	973	810
1985	11 915	1 298	638	661	10 617	1 864	3 401	2 117	1 377	1 015	843
1986	12 344	1 302	658	644	11 042	1 899	3 510	2 239	1 496	1 023	875
1987	12 867	1 332	651	681	11 536	1 910	3 714	2 464	1 492	1 061	895
1988	13 325	1 354	662	692	11 970	1 948	3 807	2 565	1 571	1 159	920
1989	13 791	1 399	672	727	12 392	1 950	3 953	2 658	1 649	1 182	1 001
1990	15 904	1 737	821	915	14 167	2 428	4 589	3 001	1 817	1 247	1 084
1991	16 425	1 732	819	913	14 693	2 481	4 674	3 243	1 879	1 283	1 134
1992	16 961	1 737	836	901	15 224	2 444	4 806	3 458	1 980	1 321	1 216
1993	17 532	1 756	855	901	15 776	2 487	4 887	3 632	2 094	1 324	1 353
1994	18 117	1 818	902	916	16 300	2 518	5 000	3 756	2 223	1 401	1 401
1995	18 629	1 872	903	969	16 757	2 528	5 050	3 965	2 294	1 483	1 437
1996	19 213	1 948	962	986	17 265	2 524	5 181	4 227	2 275	1 546	1 512
1997	20 321	2 121	1 088	1 033	18 200	2 623	5 405	4 453	2 581	1 580	1 558
1998	21 070	2 204	1 070	1 135	18 865	2 731	5 447	4 636	2 775	1 615	1 662
1999	21 650	2 307	1 113	1 194	19 344	2 700	5 512	4 833	2 868	1 713	1 718
2000	23 938	2 523	1 214	1 309	21 415	3 255	6 466	5 189	3 061	1 736	1 708
2001	24 942	2 508	1 173	1 334	22 435	3 417	6 726	5 346	3 339	1 816	1 792
2002	25 963	2 507	1 216	1 291	23 456	3 508	7 010	5 606	3 494	1 953	1 885
2003	27 551	2 543	1 346	1 197	25 008	3 533	7 506	6 003	3 845	2 093	2 027
2004	28 109	2 608	1 337	1 270	25 502	3 666	7 470	6 055	3 987	2 208	2 115
2005	29 133	2 689	1 415	1 274	26 444	3 647	7 684	6 293	4 217	2 361	2 242
2006	30 103	2 796	1 518	1 277	27 307	3 603	7 856	6 519	4 466	2 516	2 347
2007	31 383	2 944	1 559	1 385	28 440	3 648	8 129	6 785	4 720	2 685	2 473
2008	32 141	3 042	1 620	1 422	29 098	3 620	8 147	6 946	4 937	2 840	2 609
2009	32 891	3 123	1 602	1 522	29 768	3 623	8 099	7 078	5 192	3 017	2 759

[1]May be of any race.
. . . = Not available.

Table 1-6. Civilian Noninstitutional Population, by Age, Race, Sex, and Hispanic Origin, 1948–2009
—Continued

(Thousands of people.)

Race, Hispanic origin, sex, and year	16 years and over	16 to 19 years			20 years and over						
		Total	16 to 17 years	18 to 19 years	Total	20 to 24 years	25 to 34 years	35 to 44 years	45 to 54 years	55 to 64 years	65 years and over
HISPANIC[1]											
Men											
1973	2 891	...	...	...	2 472	...	...	...	...	...	...
1974	3 130	...	...	...	2 680	...	...	...	...	...	...
1975	3 219	...	...	...	2 741	...	...	...	...	...	...
1976	3 241	...	...	...	2 764	...	...	...	...	...	...
1977	3 483	...	...	...	2 982	...	...	...	...	...	...
1978	3 750	...	...	...	3 228	...	...	...	...	...	...
1979	3 917	...	...	...	3 362	...	...	...	...	...	...
1980	4 689	...	...	...	4 036	...	...	...	...	...	...
1981	4 968	...	...	...	4 306	...	...	...	...	...	...
1982	5 203	...	...	...	4 539	...	...	...	...	...	...
1983	5 432	...	...	...	4 771	...	...	...	...	...	...
1984	5 661	...	...	...	5 005	...	...	...	...	...	...
1985	5 885	...	...	...	5 232	...	...	...	...	...	...
1986	6 106	...	...	...	5 451	...	...	...	...	...	...
1987	6 371	...	...	...	5 700	...	...	...	...	...	...
1988	6 604	...	...	...	5 921	...	...	...	...	...	...
1989	6 825	...	...	...	6 114	...	...	...	...	...	...
1990	8 041	...	...	...	7 126	...	...	...	...	...	...
1991	8 296	...	...	...	7 392	...	...	...	...	...	...
1992	8 553	...	...	...	7 655	...	...	...	...	...	...
1993	8 824	...	...	...	7 930	...	...	...	...	...	...
1994	9 104	926	472	454	8 178	1 346	2 627	1 871	1 076	644	614
1995	9 329	954	481	473	8 375	1 337	2 657	1 966	1 127	668	619
1996	9 604	992	485	507	8 611	1 321	2 692	2 144	1 111	712	630
1997	10 368	1 119	585	534	9 250	1 439	2 872	2 275	1 266	747	651
1998	10 734	1 161	586	575	9 573	1 462	2 907	2 377	1 342	771	714
1999	10 713	1 190	571	619	9 523	1 398	2 805	2 407	1 397	767	749
2000	12 174	1 333	640	693	10 841	1 784	3 380	2 626	1 527	799	725
2001	12 695	1 310	619	690	11 386	1 846	3 529	2 765	1 650	848	749
2002	13 221	1 293	615	678	11 928	1 890	3 727	2 875	1 716	902	817
2003	14 098	1 301	674	627	12 797	1 905	4 033	3 098	1 910	989	862
2004	14 417	1 336	664	672	13 082	1 981	4 024	3 147	1 990	1 046	894
2005	14 962	1 376	730	646	13 586	1 956	4 155	3 284	2 114	1 123	953
2006	15 473	1 428	763	664	14 046	1 916	4 266	3 414	2 251	1 204	996
2007	16 154	1 505	790	714	14 649	1 928	4 430	3 563	2 384	1 287	1 058
2008	16 524	1 553	838	716	14 971	1 890	4 438	3 655	2 502	1 365	1 121
2009	16 897	1 593	818	774	15 305	1 875	4 405	3 735	2 647	1 459	1 184
HISPANIC[1]											
Women											
1973	3 213	...	...	...	2 766	...	...	...	...	...	...
1974	3 434	...	...	...	2 959	...	...	...	...	...	...
1975	3 644	...	...	...	3 161	...	...	...	...	...	...
1976	3 669	...	...	...	3 263	...	...	...	...	...	...
1977	3 879	...	...	...	3 377	...	...	...	...	...	...
1978	4 159	...	...	...	3 608	...	...	...	...	...	...
1979	4 291	...	...	...	3 751	...	...	...	...	...	...
1980	4 909	...	...	...	4 281	...	...	...	...	...	...
1981	5 151	...	...	...	4 513	...	...	...	...	...	...
1982	5 377	...	...	...	4 734	...	...	...	...	...	...
1983	5 597	...	...	...	4 954	...	...	...	...	...	...
1984	5 816	...	...	...	5 173	...	...	...	...	...	...
1985	6 029	...	...	...	5 385	...	...	...	...	...	...
1986	6 238	...	...	...	5 591	...	...	...	...	...	...
1987	6 496	...	...	...	5 835	...	...	...	...	...	...
1988	6 721	...	...	...	6 050	...	...	...	...	...	...
1989	6 965	...	...	...	6 278	...	...	...	...	...	...
1990	7 863	...	...	...	7 041	...	...	...	...	...	...
1991	8 130	...	...	...	7 301	...	...	...	...	...	...
1992	8 408	...	...	...	7 569	...	...	...	...	...	...
1993	8 708	...	...	...	7 846	...	...	...	...	...	...
1994	9 014	892	430	462	8 122	1 173	2 373	1 885	1 147	757	787
1995	9 300	918	422	496	8 382	1 191	2 393	1 999	1 167	815	818
1996	9 610	956	477	479	8 654	1 203	2 489	2 082	1 164	834	882
1997	9 953	1 003	503	500	8 950	1 184	2 533	2 178	1 315	833	907
1998	10 335	1 044	483	560	9 292	1 269	2 539	2 259	1 433	844	948
1999	10 937	1 116	542	575	9 821	1 302	2 707	2 425	1 470	947	969
2000	11 764	1 190	574	616	10 574	1 471	3 086	2 564	1 534	937	982
2001	12 247	1 198	554	644	11 049	1 571	3 198	2 581	1 689	968	1 043
2002	12 742	1 214	601	613	11 528	1 617	3 283	2 732	1 777	1 051	1 068
2003	13 452	1 242	672	570	12 211	1 628	3 473	2 905	1 935	1 105	1 166
2004	13 692	1 272	674	598	12 420	1 685	3 447	2 908	1 997	1 162	1 221
2005	14 172	1 313	685	628	12 858	1 692	3 529	3 009	2 103	1 237	1 289
2006	14 630	1 368	755	613	13 262	1 688	3 590	3 105	2 215	1 313	1 351
2007	15 229	1 439	769	670	13 791	1 720	3 698	3 222	2 336	1 398	1 416
2008	15 616	1 489	782	706	14 127	1 730	3 710	3 291	2 435	1 475	1 488
2009	15 993	1 531	783	748	14 463	1 748	3 694	3 343	2 545	1 558	1 576

[1]May be of any race.
. . . = Not available.

Table 1-7. Civilian Labor Force, by Age, Sex, Race, and Hispanic Origin, 1948–2009

(Thousands of people.)

Race, Hispanic origin, sex, and year	16 years and over	16 to 19 years			20 years and over						
		Total	16 to 17 years	18 to 19 years	Total	20 to 24 years	25 to 34 years	35 to 44 years	45 to 54 years	55 to 64 years	65 years and over
ALL RACES											
Both Sexes											
1948	60 621	4 435	1 780	2 654	56 187	7 392	14 258	13 397	10 914	7 329	2 897
1949	61 286	4 288	1 704	2 583	57 000	7 340	14 415	13 711	11 107	7 426	3 010
1950	62 208	4 216	1 659	2 557	57 994	7 307	14 619	13 954	11 444	7 633	3 036
1951	62 017	4 103	1 743	2 360	57 914	6 594	14 668	14 100	11 739	7 796	3 020
1952	62 138	4 064	1 806	2 257	58 075	5 840	14 904	14 383	11 961	7 980	3 005
1953	63 015	4 027	1 727	2 299	58 989	5 481	14 898	15 099	12 249	8 024	3 236
1954	63 643	3 976	1 643	2 300	59 666	5 475	14 983	15 221	12 524	8 269	3 192
1955	65 023	4 092	1 711	2 382	60 931	5 666	15 058	15 400	12 992	8 513	3 305
1956	66 552	4 296	1 878	2 418	62 257	5 940	14 961	15 694	13 407	8 830	3 423
1957	66 929	4 275	1 843	2 433	62 653	6 071	14 826	15 847	13 768	8 853	3 290
1958	67 639	4 260	1 818	2 442	63 377	6 272	14 668	16 028	14 179	9 031	3 199
1959	68 369	4 492	1 971	2 522	63 876	6 413	14 435	16 127	14 518	9 227	3 158
1960	69 628	4 841	2 095	2 747	64 788	6 702	14 382	16 269	14 852	9 385	3 195
1961	70 459	4 936	1 984	2 951	65 524	6 950	14 319	16 402	15 071	9 636	3 146
1962	70 614	4 916	1 919	2 997	65 699	7 082	14 023	16 589	15 096	9 757	3 154
1963	71 833	5 139	2 171	2 966	66 695	7 473	14 050	16 788	15 338	10 006	3 041
1964	73 091	5 388	2 449	2 940	67 702	7 963	14 056	16 771	15 637	10 182	3 090
1965	74 455	5 910	2 486	3 425	68 543	8 259	14 233	16 840	15 756	10 350	3 108
1966	75 770	6 558	2 664	3 893	69 219	8 410	14 458	16 738	15 984	10 575	3 053
1967	77 347	6 521	2 734	3 786	70 825	9 010	15 055	16 703	16 172	10 792	3 097
1968	78 737	6 619	2 817	3 803	72 118	9 305	15 708	16 591	16 397	10 964	3 153
1969	80 734	6 970	3 009	3 959	73 763	9 879	16 336	16 458	16 730	11 135	3 227
1970	82 771	7 249	3 135	4 115	75 521	10 597	17 036	16 437	16 949	11 283	3 222
1971	84 382	7 470	3 192	4 278	76 913	11 331	17 714	16 305	17 024	11 390	3 149
1972	87 034	8 054	3 420	4 636	78 980	12 130	18 960	16 398	16 967	11 412	3 114
1973	89 429	8 507	3 665	4 839	80 924	12 846	20 376	16 492	16 983	11 256	2 974
1974	91 949	8 871	3 810	5 059	83 080	13 314	21 654	16 763	17 131	11 284	2 934
1975	93 775	8 870	3 740	5 131	84 904	13 750	22 864	16 903	17 084	11 346	2 956
1976	96 158	9 056	3 767	5 288	87 103	14 284	24 203	17 317	16 982	11 422	2 895
1977	99 009	9 351	3 919	5 431	89 658	14 825	25 500	17 943	16 878	11 577	2 934
1978	102 251	9 652	4 127	5 526	92 598	15 370	26 703	18 821	16 891	11 744	3 070
1979	104 962	9 638	4 079	5 559	95 325	15 769	27 938	19 685	16 897	11 931	3 104
1980	106 940	9 378	3 883	5 496	97 561	15 922	29 227	20 463	16 910	11 985	3 054
1981	108 670	8 988	3 647	5 340	99 682	16 099	30 392	21 211	16 970	11 969	3 042
1982	110 204	8 526	3 336	5 189	101 679	16 082	31 186	22 431	16 889	12 062	3 030
1983	111 550	8 171	3 073	5 098	103 379	16 052	31 834	23 611	16 851	11 992	3 040
1984	113 544	7 943	3 050	4 894	105 601	16 046	32 723	24 933	17 006	11 961	2 933
1985	115 461	7 901	3 154	4 747	107 560	15 718	33 550	26 073	17 322	11 991	2 907
1986	117 834	7 926	3 287	4 639	109 908	15 441	34 591	27 232	17 739	11 894	3 010
1987	119 865	7 988	3 384	4 604	111 878	14 977	35 233	28 460	18 210	11 877	3 119
1988	121 669	8 031	3 286	4 745	113 638	14 505	35 503	29 435	19 104	11 808	3 284
1989	123 869	7 954	3 125	4 828	115 916	14 180	35 896	30 601	19 916	11 877	3 446
1990	125 840	7 792	2 937	4 856	118 047	14 700	35 929	32 145	20 248	11 575	3 451
1991	126 346	7 265	2 789	4 476	119 082	14 548	35 507	33 312	20 828	11 473	3 413
1992	128 105	7 096	2 769	4 327	121 009	14 521	35 369	33 899	22 160	11 587	3 473
1993	129 200	7 170	2 831	4 338	122 030	14 354	34 780	34 562	23 296	11 599	3 439
1994	131 056	7 481	3 134	4 347	123 576	14 131	34 353	35 226	24 318	11 713	3 834
1995	132 304	7 765	3 225	4 540	124 539	13 688	34 198	35 751	25 223	11 860	3 819
1996	133 943	7 806	3 263	4 543	126 137	13 377	33 833	36 556	26 397	12 146	3 828
1997	136 297	7 932	3 237	4 695	128 365	13 532	33 380	37 326	27 574	12 665	3 887
1998	137 673	8 256	3 335	4 921	129 417	13 638	32 813	37 536	28 368	13 215	3 847
1999	139 368	8 333	3 337	4 996	131 034	13 933	32 143	37 882	29 388	13 682	4 005
2000	142 583	8 271	3 261	5 010	134 312	14 250	32 755	37 567	31 071	14 356	4 312
2001	143 734	7 902	3 088	4 814	135 832	14 557	32 361	37 404	32 025	15 104	4 382
2002	144 863	7 585	2 870	4 715	137 278	14 781	32 196	36 926	32 597	16 309	4 469
2003	146 510	7 170	2 857	4 313	139 340	14 928	32 343	36 695	33 270	17 312	4 792
2004	147 401	7 114	2 747	4 367	140 287	15 154	32 207	36 158	33 758	18 013	4 998
2005	149 320	7 164	2 825	4 339	142 157	15 127	32 341	36 030	34 402	18 979	5 278
2006	151 428	7 281	2 952	4 329	144 147	15 113	32 573	35 848	35 146	19 984	5 484
2007	153 124	7 012	2 771	4 242	146 112	15 205	33 130	35 527	35 697	20 750	5 804
2008	154 287	6 858	2 552	4 306	147 429	15 174	33 332	35 061	36 003	21 615	6 243
2009	154 142	6 390	2 227	4 163	147 752	14 971	33 298	34 239	36 205	22 505	6 534

Table 1-7. Civilian Labor Force, by Age, Sex, Race, and Hispanic Origin, 1948–2009—*Continued*

(Thousands of people.)

Race, Hispanic origin, sex, and year	16 years and over	16 to 19 years			20 years and over						
		Total	16 to 17 years	18 to 19 years	Total	20 to 24 years	25 to 34 years	35 to 44 years	45 to 54 years	55 to 64 years	65 years and over
ALL RACES											
Men											
1948	43 286	2 600	1 109	1 490	40 687	4 673	10 327	9 596	7 943	5 764	2 384
1949	43 498	2 477	1 056	1 420	41 022	4 682	10 418	9 722	8 008	5 748	2 454
1950	43 819	2 504	1 048	1 456	41 316	4 632	10 527	9 793	8 117	5 794	2 453
1951	43 001	2 347	1 081	1 266	40 655	3 935	10 375	9 799	8 205	5 873	2 469
1952	42 869	2 312	1 101	1 210	40 558	3 338	10 585	9 945	8 326	5 949	2 416
1953	43 633	2 320	1 070	1 249	41 315	3 053	10 736	10 437	8 570	5 975	2 543
1954	43 965	2 295	1 023	1 272	41 669	3 051	10 771	10 513	8 702	6 105	2 526
1955	44 475	2 369	1 070	1 299	42 106	3 221	10 806	10 595	8 838	6 122	2 526
1956	45 091	2 433	1 142	1 291	42 658	3 485	10 685	10 663	9 002	6 220	2 602
1957	45 197	2 415	1 127	1 289	42 780	3 629	10 571	10 731	9 153	6 222	2 477
1958	45 521	2 428	1 133	1 295	43 092	3 771	10 475	10 843	9 320	6 304	2 378
1959	45 886	2 596	1 206	1 390	43 289	3 940	10 346	10 899	9 438	6 345	2 322
1960	46 388	2 787	1 290	1 496	43 603	4 123	10 251	10 967	9 574	6 399	2 287
1961	46 653	2 794	1 210	1 583	43 860	4 253	10 176	11 012	9 668	6 530	2 220
1962	46 600	2 770	1 178	1 592	43 831	4 279	9 920	11 115	9 715	6 560	2 241
1963	47 129	2 907	1 321	1 586	44 222	4 514	9 876	11 187	9 836	6 675	2 135
1964	47 679	3 074	1 499	1 575	44 604	4 754	9 876	11 156	9 956	6 741	2 124
1965	48 255	3 397	1 532	1 866	44 857	4 894	9 903	11 120	10 045	6 763	2 132
1966	48 471	3 685	1 609	2 075	44 788	4 820	9 948	10 983	10 100	6 847	2 089
1967	48 987	3 634	1 658	1 976	45 354	5 043	10 207	10 859	10 189	6 937	2 118
1968	49 533	3 681	1 687	1 995	45 852	5 070	10 610	10 725	10 267	7 025	2 154
1969	50 221	3 870	1 770	2 100	46 351	5 282	10 941	10 556	10 344	7 058	2 170
1970	51 228	4 008	1 810	2 199	47 220	5 717	11 327	10 469	10 417	7 126	2 165
1971	52 180	4 172	1 856	2 315	48 009	6 233	11 731	10 347	10 451	7 155	2 090
1972	53 555	4 476	1 955	2 522	49 079	6 766	12 350	10 372	10 412	7 155	2 026
1973	54 624	4 693	2 073	2 618	49 932	7 183	13 056	10 338	10 416	7 028	1 913
1974	55 739	4 861	2 138	2 721	50 879	7 387	13 665	10 401	10 431	7 063	1 932
1975	56 299	4 805	2 065	2 740	51 494	7 565	14 192	10 398	10 401	7 023	1 914
1976	57 174	4 886	2 069	2 817	52 288	7 866	14 784	10 500	10 293	7 020	1 826
1977	58 396	5 048	2 155	2 893	53 348	8 109	15 353	10 771	10 158	7 100	1 857
1978	59 620	5 149	2 227	2 923	54 471	8 327	15 814	11 159	10 083	7 151	1 936
1979	60 726	5 111	2 192	2 919	55 615	8 535	16 387	11 531	10 008	7 212	1 943
1980	61 453	4 999	2 102	2 897	56 455	8 607	16 971	11 836	9 905	7 242	1 893
1981	61 974	4 777	1 957	2 820	57 197	8 648	17 479	12 166	9 868	7 170	1 866
1982	62 450	4 470	1 776	2 694	57 980	8 604	17 793	12 781	9 784	7 174	1 845
1983	63 047	4 303	1 621	2 682	58 744	8 601	18 038	13 398	9 746	7 119	1 842
1984	63 835	4 134	1 591	2 542	59 701	8 594	18 488	14 037	9 776	7 050	1 755
1985	64 411	4 134	1 663	2 471	60 277	8 283	18 808	14 506	9 870	7 060	1 750
1986	65 422	4 102	1 707	2 395	61 320	8 148	19 383	15 029	9 994	6 954	1 811
1987	66 207	4 112	1 745	2 367	62 095	7 837	19 656	15 587	10 176	6 940	1 899
1988	66 927	4 159	1 714	2 445	62 768	7 594	19 742	16 074	10 566	6 831	1 960
1989	67 840	4 136	1 630	2 505	63 704	7 458	19 905	16 622	10 919	6 783	2 017
1990	69 011	4 094	1 537	2 557	64 916	7 866	19 872	17 481	11 103	6 627	1 967
1991	69 168	3 795	1 452	2 343	65 374	7 820	19 641	18 077	11 362	6 550	1 924
1992	69 964	3 751	1 453	2 297	66 213	7 770	19 495	18 347	12 040	6 551	2 010
1993	70 404	3 762	1 497	2 265	66 642	7 671	19 214	18 713	12 562	6 502	1 980
1994	70 817	3 896	1 630	2 266	66 921	7 540	18 854	18 966	12 962	6 423	2 176
1995	71 360	4 036	1 668	2 368	67 324	7 338	18 670	19 189	13 421	6 504	2 201
1996	72 087	4 043	1 665	2 378	68 044	7 104	18 430	19 602	13 967	6 693	2 247
1997	73 261	4 095	1 676	2 419	69 166	7 184	18 110	20 058	14 564	6 952	2 298
1998	73 959	4 244	1 728	2 516	69 715	7 221	17 796	20 242	14 963	7 253	2 240
1999	74 512	4 318	1 732	2 587	70 194	7 291	17 318	20 382	15 394	7 477	2 333
2000	76 280	4 269	1 676	2 594	72 010	7 521	17 844	20 093	16 269	7 795	2 488
2001	76 886	4 070	1 568	2 501	72 816	7 640	17 671	20 018	16 804	8 171	2 511
2002	77 500	3 870	1 431	2 439	73 630	7 769	17 596	19 828	17 143	8 751	2 542
2003	78 238	3 614	1 405	2 209	74 623	7 906	17 767	19 762	17 352	9 144	2 692
2004	78 980	3 616	1 329	2 288	75 364	8 057	17 798	19 539	17 635	9 547	2 787
2005	80 033	3 590	1 368	2 222	76 443	8 054	17 837	19 495	18 053	10 045	2 959
2006	81 255	3 693	1 453	2 240	77 562	8 116	17 944	19 407	18 489	10 509	3 096
2007	82 136	3 541	1 354	2 187	78 596	8 095	18 308	19 299	18 801	10 904	3 188
2008	82 520	3 472	1 238	2 235	79 047	8 065	18 302	18 972	18 928	11 345	3 436
2009	82 123	3 226	1 103	2 123	78 897	7 839	18 211	18 518	19 001	11 730	3 598

Table 1-7. Civilian Labor Force, by Age, Sex, Race, and Hispanic Origin, 1948–2009—Continued

(Thousands of people.)

Race, Hispanic origin, sex, and year	16 years and over	16 to 19 years			20 years and over						
		Total	16 to 17 years	18 to 19 years	Total	20 to 24 years	25 to 34 years	35 to 44 years	45 to 54 years	55 to 64 years	65 years and over
ALL RACES											
Women											
1948	17 335	1 835	671	1 164	15 500	2 719	3 931	3 801	2 971	1 565	513
1949	17 788	1 811	648	1 163	15 978	2 658	3 997	3 989	3 099	1 678	556
1950	18 389	1 712	611	1 101	16 678	2 675	4 092	4 161	3 327	1 839	583
1951	19 016	1 756	662	1 094	17 259	2 659	4 293	4 301	3 534	1 923	551
1952	19 269	1 752	705	1 047	17 517	2 502	4 319	4 438	3 635	2 031	589
1953	19 382	1 707	657	1 050	17 674	2 428	4 162	4 662	3 679	2 049	693
1954	19 678	1 681	620	1 028	17 997	2 424	4 212	4 708	3 822	2 164	666
1955	20 548	1 723	641	1 083	18 825	2 445	4 252	4 805	4 154	2 391	779
1956	21 461	1 863	736	1 127	19 599	2 455	4 276	5 031	4 405	2 610	821
1957	21 732	1 860	716	1 144	19 873	2 442	4 255	5 116	4 615	2 631	813
1958	22 118	1 832	685	1 147	20 285	2 501	4 193	5 185	4 859	2 727	821
1959	22 483	1 896	765	1 132	20 587	2 473	4 089	5 228	5 080	2 882	836
1960	23 240	2 054	805	1 251	21 185	2 579	4 131	5 302	5 278	2 986	908
1961	23 806	2 142	774	1 368	21 664	2 697	4 143	5 390	5 403	3 106	926
1962	24 014	2 146	741	1 405	21 868	2 803	4 103	5 474	5 381	3 197	913
1963	24 704	2 232	850	1 380	22 473	2 959	4 174	5 601	5 502	3 331	906
1964	25 412	2 314	950	1 365	23 098	3 209	4 180	5 615	5 681	3 441	966
1965	26 200	2 513	954	1 559	23 686	3 365	4 330	5 720	5 711	3 587	976
1966	27 299	2 873	1 055	1 818	24 431	3 590	4 510	5 755	5 884	3 728	964
1967	28 360	2 887	1 076	1 810	25 475	3 966	4 848	5 844	5 983	3 855	979
1968	29 204	2 938	1 130	1 808	26 266	4 235	5 098	5 866	6 130	3 939	999
1969	30 513	3 100	1 239	1 859	27 413	4 597	5 395	5 902	6 386	4 077	1 057
1970	31 543	3 241	1 325	1 916	28 301	4 880	5 708	5 968	6 532	4 157	1 056
1971	32 202	3 298	1 336	1 963	28 904	5 098	5 983	5 957	6 573	4 234	1 059
1972	33 479	3 578	1 464	2 114	29 901	5 364	6 610	6 027	6 555	4 257	1 089
1973	34 804	3 814	1 592	2 221	30 991	5 663	7 320	6 154	6 567	4 228	1 061
1974	36 211	4 010	1 672	2 338	32 201	5 926	7 989	6 362	6 699	4 221	1 002
1975	37 475	4 065	1 674	2 391	33 410	6 185	8 673	6 505	6 683	4 323	1 042
1976	38 983	4 170	1 698	2 470	34 814	6 418	9 419	6 817	6 689	4 402	1 069
1977	40 613	4 303	1 765	2 538	36 310	6 717	10 149	7 171	6 720	4 477	1 078
1978	42 631	4 503	1 900	2 603	38 128	7 043	10 888	7 662	6 807	4 593	1 134
1979	44 235	4 527	1 887	2 639	39 708	7 234	11 551	8 154	6 889	4 719	1 161
1980	45 487	4 381	1 781	2 599	41 106	7 315	12 257	8 627	7 004	4 742	1 161
1981	46 696	4 211	1 691	2 520	42 485	7 451	12 912	9 045	7 101	4 799	1 176
1982	47 755	4 056	1 561	2 495	43 699	7 477	13 393	9 651	7 105	4 888	1 185
1983	48 503	3 868	1 452	2 416	44 636	7 451	13 796	10 213	7 105	4 873	1 198
1984	49 709	3 810	1 458	2 351	45 900	7 451	14 234	10 896	7 230	4 911	1 177
1985	51 050	3 767	1 491	2 276	47 283	7 434	14 742	11 567	7 452	4 932	1 156
1986	52 413	3 824	1 580	2 244	48 589	7 293	15 208	12 204	7 746	4 940	1 199
1987	53 658	3 875	1 638	2 237	49 783	7 140	15 577	12 873	8 034	4 937	1 221
1988	54 742	3 872	1 572	2 300	50 870	6 910	15 761	13 361	8 537	4 977	1 324
1989	56 030	3 818	1 495	2 323	52 212	6 721	15 990	13 980	8 997	5 095	1 429
1990	56 829	3 698	1 400	2 298	53 131	6 834	16 058	14 663	9 145	4 948	1 483
1991	57 178	3 470	1 337	2 133	53 708	6 728	15 867	15 235	9 465	4 924	1 489
1992	58 141	3 345	1 316	2 030	54 796	6 750	15 875	15 552	10 120	5 035	1 464
1993	58 795	3 408	1 335	2 073	55 388	6 683	15 566	15 849	10 733	5 097	1 459
1994	60 239	3 585	1 504	2 081	56 655	6 592	15 499	16 259	11 357	5 289	1 658
1995	60 944	3 729	1 557	2 172	57 215	6 349	15 528	16 562	11 801	5 356	1 618
1996	61 857	3 763	1 599	2 164	58 094	6 273	15 403	16 954	12 430	5 452	1 581
1997	63 036	3 837	1 561	2 277	59 198	6 348	15 271	17 268	13 010	5 713	1 590
1998	63 714	4 012	1 607	2 405	59 702	6 418	15 017	17 294	13 405	5 962	1 607
1999	64 855	4 015	1 606	2 410	60 840	6 643	14 826	17 501	13 994	6 204	1 673
2000	66 303	4 002	1 585	2 416	62 301	6 730	14 912	17 473	14 802	6 561	1 823
2001	66 848	3 832	1 520	2 313	63 016	6 917	14 690	17 386	15 221	6 932	1 870
2002	67 363	3 715	1 439	2 277	63 648	7 012	14 600	17 098	15 454	7 559	1 926
2003	68 272	3 556	1 452	2 104	64 716	7 021	14 576	16 933	15 919	8 168	2 099
2004	68 421	3 498	1 418	2 080	64 923	7 097	14 409	16 619	16 123	8 466	2 211
2005	69 288	3 574	1 457	2 117	65 714	7 073	14 503	16 535	16 349	8 934	2 319
2006	70 173	3 588	1 499	2 089	66 585	6 997	14 628	16 441	16 656	9 475	2 388
2007	70 988	3 471	1 417	2 055	67 516	7 110	14 822	16 227	16 896	9 846	2 615
2008	71 767	3 385	1 314	2 071	68 382	7 109	15 030	16 089	17 075	10 270	2 808
2009	72 019	3 163	1 124	2 039	68 856	7 132	15 087	15 720	17 204	10 776	2 937

Table 1-7. Civilian Labor Force, by Age, Sex, Race, and Hispanic Origin, 1948–2009—*Continued*

(Thousands of people.)

Race, Hispanic origin, sex, and year	16 years and over	16 to 19 years			20 years and over						
		Total	16 to 17 years	18 to 19 years	Total	20 to 24 years	25 to 34 years	35 to 44 years	45 to 54 years	55 to 64 years	65 years and over
WHITE											
Both Sexes											
1954	56 816	3 501	1 448	2 054	53 315	4 752	13 226	13 540	11 258	7 591	2 946
1955	58 085	3 598	1 511	2 087	54 487	4 941	13 267	13 729	11 680	7 810	3 062
1956	59 428	3 771	1 656	2 113	55 657	5 194	13 154	14 000	12 061	8 080	3 166
1957	59 754	3 775	1 637	2 135	55 979	5 283	13 044	14 117	12 382	8 091	3 049
1958	60 293	3 757	1 615	2 144	56 536	5 449	12 884	14 257	12 727	8 254	2 964
1959	60 952	4 000	1 775	2 225	56 952	5 544	12 670	14 355	13 048	8 411	2 925
1960	61 915	4 275	1 871	2 405	57 640	5 787	12 594	14 450	13 322	8 522	2 964
1961	62 656	4 362	1 767	2 594	58 294	6 026	12 503	14 557	13 517	8 773	2 917
1962	62 750	4 354	1 709	2 645	58 396	6 164	12 218	14 695	13 551	8 856	2 912
1963	63 830	4 559	1 950	2 608	59 271	6 537	12 229	14 859	13 789	9 067	2 790
1964	64 921	4 784	2 211	2 572	60 137	6 952	12 235	14 852	14 043	9 239	2 817
1965	66 137	5 267	2 221	3 044	60 870	7 189	12 391	14 900	14 162	9 392	2 839
1966	67 276	5 827	2 367	3 460	61 449	7 324	12 591	14 785	14 370	9 583	2 793
1967	68 699	5 749	2 432	3 318	62 950	7 886	13 123	14 765	14 545	9 817	2 821
1968	69 976	5 839	2 519	3 320	64 137	8 109	13 740	14 683	14 756	9 968	2 884
1969	71 778	6 168	2 698	3 470	65 611	8 614	14 289	14 564	15 057	10 132	2 954
1970	73 556	6 442	2 824	3 617	67 113	9 238	14 896	14 525	15 269	10 255	2 930
1971	74 963	6 681	2 894	3 787	68 282	9 889	15 445	14 374	15 343	10 351	2 880
1972	77 275	7 193	3 096	4 098	70 082	10 605	16 584	14 399	15 283	10 402	2 809
1973	79 151	7 579	3 320	4 260	71 572	11 182	17 764	14 440	15 256	10 240	2 687
1974	81 281	7 899	3 441	4 459	73 381	11 600	18 862	14 644	15 375	10 241	2 656
1975	82 831	7 899	3 375	4 525	74 932	12 019	19 897	14 753	15 308	10 287	2 668
1976	84 767	8 088	3 410	4 679	76 678	12 444	20 990	15 088	15 187	10 371	2 599
1977	87 141	8 352	3 562	4 790	78 789	12 892	22 099	15 604	15 053	10 495	2 647
1978	89 634	8 555	3 715	4 839	81 079	13 309	23 067	16 353	15 004	10 602	2 745
1979	91 923	8 548	3 668	4 881	83 375	13 632	24 101	17 123	14 965	10 767	2 787
1980	93 600	8 312	3 485	4 827	85 286	13 769	25 181	17 811	14 956	10 812	2 759
1981	95 052	7 962	3 274	4 688	87 089	13 926	26 208	18 445	14 993	10 764	2 753
1982	96 143	7 518	3 001	4 518	88 625	13 866	26 814	19 491	14 879	10 832	2 742
1983	97 021	7 186	2 765	4 421	89 835	13 816	27 237	20 488	14 798	10 732	2 766
1984	98 492	6 952	2 720	4 232	91 540	13 733	27 958	21 588	14 899	10 701	2 660
1985	99 926	6 841	2 777	4 065	93 085	13 469	28 640	22 591	15 101	10 679	2 605
1986	101 801	6 862	2 895	3 967	94 939	13 176	29 497	23 571	15 379	10 583	2 732
1987	103 290	6 893	2 963	3 931	96 396	12 764	29 956	24 581	15 792	10 497	2 806
1988	104 756	6 940	2 861	4 079	97 815	12 311	30 167	25 358	16 573	10 462	2 943
1989	106 355	6 809	2 685	4 124	99 546	11 940	30 388	26 312	17 278	10 533	3 094
1990	107 447	6 683	2 543	4 140	100 764	12 397	30 174	27 265	17 515	10 290	3 123
1991	107 743	6 245	2 432	3 813	101 498	12 248	29 794	28 213	18 028	10 129	3 086
1992	108 837	6 022	2 388	3 633	102 815	12 187	29 518	28 580	19 200	10 196	3 135
1993	109 700	6 105	2 458	3 647	103 595	11 987	29 027	29 056	20 181	10 215	3 129
1994	111 082	6 357	2 681	3 677	104 725	11 688	28 580	29 626	21 026	10 319	3 486
1995	111 950	6 545	2 749	3 796	105 404	11 266	28 325	30 112	21 804	10 432	3 466
1996	113 108	6 607	2 780	3 826	106 502	11 003	27 901	30 683	22 781	10 648	3 485
1997	114 693	6 720	2 779	3 941	107 973	11 127	27 362	31 171	23 709	11 086	3 517
1998	115 415	6 965	2 860	4 105	108 450	11 244	26 707	31 221	24 282	11 548	3 448
1999	116 509	7 048	2 849	4 199	109 461	11 436	25 978	31 391	25 102	11 960	3 595
2000	118 545	6 955	2 768	4 186	111 590	11 626	26 336	30 968	26 353	12 463	3 846
2001	119 399	6 661	2 626	4 035	112 737	11 883	26 010	30 778	27 062	13 121	3 883
2002	120 150	6 366	2 445	3 921	113 784	12 073	25 908	30 286	27 405	14 148	3 965
2003	120 546	5 973	2 414	3 560	114 572	12 064	25 752	29 788	27 786	14 944	4 238
2004	121 086	5 929	2 309	3 620	115 156	12 192	25 548	29 305	28 181	15 522	4 408
2005	122 299	5 950	2 390	3 560	116 349	12 109	25 548	29 107	28 685	16 275	4 624
2006	123 834	6 009	2 473	3 536	117 825	12 128	25 681	28 849	29 231	17 132	4 805
2007	124 935	5 795	2 326	3 470	119 139	12 176	26 076	28 394	29 627	17 782	5 085
2008	125 635	5 644	2 126	3 518	119 990	12 142	26 210	27 932	29 780	18 464	5 463
2009	125 644	5 295	1 883	3 413	120 349	11 995	26 277	27 263	29 903	19 199	5 711

Table 1-7. Civilian Labor Force, by Age, Sex, Race, and Hispanic Origin, 1948–2009—*Continued*

(Thousands of people.)

Race, Hispanic origin, sex, and year	16 years and over	16 to 19 years			20 years and over						
		Total	16 to 17 years	18 to 19 years	Total	20 to 24 years	25 to 34 years	35 to 44 years	45 to 54 years	55 to 64 years	65 years and over
WHITE											
Men											
1954	39 759	1 989	896	1 095	37 770	2 654	9 695	9 516	7 913	5 653	2 339
1955	40 197	2 056	935	1 121	38 141	2 803	9 721	9 597	8 025	5 654	2 343
1956	40 734	2 114	1 002	1 110	38 620	3 036	9 595	9 661	8 175	5 736	2 417
1957	40 826	2 108	992	1 114	38 718	3 152	9 483	9 719	8 317	5 735	2 307
1958	41 080	2 116	1 001	1 116	38 964	3 278	9 386	9 822	8 465	5 800	2 213
1959	41 397	2 279	1 077	1 202	39 118	3 409	9 261	9 876	8 581	5 833	2 158
1960	41 743	2 433	1 140	1 293	39 310	3 559	9 153	9 919	8 689	5 861	2 129
1961	41 986	2 439	1 067	1 372	39 547	3 681	9 072	9 961	8 776	5 988	2 068
1962	41 931	2 432	1 041	1 391	39 499	3 726	8 846	10 029	8 820	5 995	2 082
1963	42 404	2 563	1 183	1 380	39 841	3 955	8 805	10 079	8 944	6 090	1 967
1964	42 894	2 716	1 345	1 371	40 178	4 166	8 800	10 055	9 053	6 161	1 942
1965	43 400	2 999	1 359	1 639	40 401	4 279	8 824	10 023	9 130	6 188	1 959
1966	43 572	3 253	1 423	1 830	40 319	4 200	8 859	9 892	9 189	6 250	1 928
1967	44 041	3 191	1 464	1 727	40 851	4 416	9 102	9 785	9 260	6 348	1 944
1968	44 553	3 236	1 504	1 732	41 318	4 432	9 477	9 662	9 340	6 427	1 981
1969	45 185	3 413	1 583	1 830	41 772	4 615	9 773	9 509	9 413	6 467	1 996
1970	46 035	3 551	1 629	1 922	42 483	4 988	10 099	9 414	9 487	6 517	1 978
1971	46 904	3 719	1 681	2 039	43 185	5 448	10 444	9 294	9 528	6 550	1 922
1972	48 118	3 980	1 758	2 223	44 138	5 937	11 039	9 278	9 473	6 562	1 846
1973	48 920	4 174	1 875	2 300	44 747	6 274	11 621	9 212	9 445	6 452	1 740
1974	49 843	4 312	1 922	2 391	45 532	6 470	12 135	9 246	9 455	6 464	1 759
1975	50 324	4 290	1 871	2 418	46 034	6 642	12 579	9 231	9 415	6 425	1 742
1976	51 033	4 357	1 869	2 489	46 675	6 890	13 092	9 289	9 310	6 437	1 657
1977	52 033	4 496	1 949	2 548	47 537	7 097	13 575	9 509	9 175	6 492	1 688
1978	52 955	4 565	2 002	2 563	48 390	7 274	13 939	9 858	9 068	6 508	1 744
1979	53 856	4 537	1 974	2 563	49 320	7 421	14 415	10 183	8 968	6 571	1 761
1980	54 473	4 424	1 881	2 543	50 049	7 479	14 893	10 455	8 877	6 618	1 727
1981	54 895	4 224	1 751	2 473	50 671	7 521	15 340	10 740	8 836	6 530	1 704
1982	55 133	3 933	1 602	2 331	51 200	7 438	15 549	11 289	8 727	6 520	1 677
1983	55 480	3 764	1 452	2 312	51 716	7 406	15 707	11 817	8 649	6 446	1 691
1984	56 062	3 609	1 420	2 189	52 453	7 370	16 037	12 348	8 683	6 410	1 606
1985	56 472	3 576	1 467	2 109	52 895	7 122	16 306	12 767	8 730	6 376	1 595
1986	57 217	3 542	1 502	2 040	53 675	6 986	16 769	13 207	8 791	6 260	1 663
1987	57 779	3 547	1 524	2 023	54 232	6 717	16 963	13 674	8 945	6 200	1 733
1988	58 317	3 583	1 487	2 095	54 734	6 468	17 018	14 068	9 285	6 108	1 787
1989	58 988	3 546	1 401	2 146	55 441	6 316	17 077	14 516	9 615	6 082	1 835
1990	59 638	3 522	1 333	2 189	56 116	6 688	16 920	15 026	9 713	5 957	1 811
1991	59 656	3 269	1 266	2 003	56 387	6 619	16 709	15 523	9 926	5 847	1 763
1992	60 168	3 192	1 260	1 932	56 976	6 542	16 512	15 701	10 570	5 821	1 830
1993	60 484	3 200	1 292	1 908	57 284	6 449	16 244	15 971	11 010	5 784	1 825
1994	60 727	3 315	1 403	1 912	57 411	6 294	15 879	16 188	11 327	5 726	1 998
1995	61 146	3 427	1 429	1 998	57 719	6 096	15 669	16 414	11 730	5 809	2 000
1996	61 783	3 444	1 421	2 023	58 340	5 922	15 475	16 728	12 217	5 943	2 054
1997	62 639	3 513	1 440	2 073	59 126	6 029	15 120	17 019	12 710	6 154	2 094
1998	63 034	3 614	1 487	2 127	59 421	6 063	14 770	17 157	13 003	6 415	2 013
1999	63 413	3 666	1 478	2 188	59 747	6 151	14 292	17 201	13 368	6 618	2 117
2000	64 466	3 615	1 422	2 193	60 850	6 244	14 666	16 880	13 977	6 840	2 243
2001	64 966	3 446	1 334	2 112	61 519	6 363	14 536	16 809	14 400	7 169	2 241
2002	65 308	3 241	1 215	2 026	62 067	6 444	14 499	16 583	14 615	7 665	2 261
2003	65 509	3 036	1 193	1 843	62 473	6 479	14 529	16 398	14 708	7 973	2 386
2004	65 994	3 050	1 127	1 923	62 944	6 586	14 429	16 192	14 934	8 326	2 478
2005	66 694	2 988	1 162	1 826	63 705	6 562	14 426	16 080	15 273	8 734	2 631
2006	67 613	3 074	1 222	1 852	64 540	6 597	14 469	15 962	15 606	9 152	2 753
2007	68 158	2 944	1 147	1 798	65 214	6 567	14 715	15 765	15 846	9 500	2 821
2008	68 351	2 868	1 040	1 829	65 483	6 526	14 715	15 436	15 905	9 855	3 046
2009	68 051	2 679	933	1 746	65 372	6 348	14 669	15 066	15 943	10 160	3 186

Table 1-7. Civilian Labor Force, by Age, Sex, Race, and Hispanic Origin, 1948–2009—*Continued*

(Thousands of people.)

Race, Hispanic origin, sex, and year	16 years and over	16 to 19 years			20 years and over						
		Total	16 to 17 years	18 to 19 years	Total	20 to 24 years	25 to 34 years	35 to 44 years	45 to 54 years	55 to 64 years	65 years and over
WHITE											
Women											
1954	17 057	1 512	552	552	15 545	2 098	3 531	4 024	3 345	1 938	607
1955	17 888	1 542	576	576	16 346	2 138	3 546	4 132	3 655	2 156	719
1956	18 694	1 657	654	654	17 037	2 158	3 559	4 339	3 886	2 344	749
1957	18 928	1 667	645	645	17 261	2 131	3 561	4 398	4 065	2 356	742
1958	19 213	1 641	614	614	17 572	2 171	3 498	4 435	4 262	2 454	751
1959	19 555	1 721	698	698	17 834	2 135	3 409	4 479	4 467	2 578	767
1960	20 172	1 842	731	731	18 330	2 228	3 441	4 531	4 633	2 661	835
1961	20 670	1 923	700	700	18 747	2 345	3 431	4 596	4 741	2 785	849
1962	20 819	1 922	668	668	18 897	2 438	3 372	4 666	4 731	2 861	830
1963	21 426	1 996	767	767	19 430	2 582	3 424	4 780	4 845	2 977	823
1964	22 027	2 068	866	866	19 959	2 786	3 435	4 797	4 990	3 078	875
1965	22 737	2 268	862	862	20 469	2 910	3 567	4 877	5 032	3 204	880
1966	23 704	2 574	944	944	21 130	3 124	3 732	4 893	5 181	3 333	865
1967	24 658	2 558	968	968	22 100	3 471	4 021	4 980	5 285	3 469	877
1968	25 423	2 603	1 015	1 015	22 821	3 677	4 263	5 021	5 416	3 541	903
1969	26 593	2 755	1 115	1 115	23 839	3 999	4 516	5 055	5 644	3 665	958
1970	27 521	2 891	1 195	1 195	24 630	4 250	4 797	5 111	5 781	3 738	952
1971	28 060	2 962	1 213	1 213	25 097	4 441	5 001	5 080	5 816	3 801	958
1972	29 157	3 213	1 338	1 338	25 945	4 668	5 544	5 121	5 810	3 839	963
1973	30 231	3 405	1 445	1 445	26 825	4 908	6 143	5 228	5 811	3 788	947
1974	31 437	3 588	1 520	1 520	27 850	5 131	6 727	5 399	5 920	3 777	897
1975	32 508	3 610	1 504	1 504	28 898	5 378	7 318	5 522	5 892	3 862	926
1976	33 735	3 731	1 541	1 541	30 004	5 554	7 898	5 799	5 877	3 935	940
1977	35 108	3 856	1 614	1 614	31 253	5 795	8 523	6 095	5 877	4 003	959
1978	36 679	3 990	1 713	1 713	32 689	6 035	9 128	6 495	5 936	4 094	1 001
1979	38 067	4 011	1 694	1 694	34 056	6 211	9 687	6 940	5 997	4 196	1 024
1980	39 127	3 888	1 605	1 605	35 239	6 290	10 289	7 356	6 079	4 194	1 032
1981	40 157	3 739	1 523	1 523	36 418	6 406	10 868	7 704	6 157	4 235	1 049
1982	41 010	3 585	1 399	1 399	37 425	6 428	11 264	8 202	6 152	4 313	1 065
1983	41 541	3 422	1 314	1 314	38 119	6 410	11 530	8 670	6 149	4 285	1 074
1984	42 431	3 343	1 300	1 300	39 087	6 363	11 922	9 240	6 217	4 292	1 054
1985	43 455	3 265	1 310	1 310	40 190	6 348	12 334	9 824	6 371	4 303	1 010
1986	44 584	3 320	1 393	1 393	41 264	6 191	12 729	10 364	6 588	4 323	1 069
1987	45 510	3 347	1 439	1 439	42 164	6 047	12 993	10 907	6 847	4 297	1 073
1988	46 439	3 358	1 374	1 374	43 081	5 844	13 149	11 291	7 288	4 354	1 156
1989	47 367	3 262	1 284	1 284	44 105	5 625	13 311	11 796	7 663	4 451	1 259
1990	47 809	3 161	1 210	1 210	44 648	5 709	13 254	12 239	7 802	4 333	1 312
1991	48 087	2 976	1 166	1 166	45 111	5 629	13 085	12 689	8 101	4 282	1 324
1992	48 669	2 830	1 128	1 128	45 839	5 645	13 006	12 879	8 630	4 375	1 305
1993	49 216	2 905	1 167	1 167	46 311	5 539	12 783	13 085	9 171	4 430	1 304
1994	50 356	3 042	1 278	1 278	47 314	5 394	12 702	13 439	9 699	4 593	1 487
1995	50 804	3 118	1 320	1 320	47 686	5 170	12 656	13 697	10 074	4 622	1 466
1996	51 325	3 163	1 360	1 360	48 162	5 081	12 426	13 955	10 563	4 706	1 431
1997	52 054	3 207	1 339	1 339	48 847	5 099	12 242	14 153	10 999	4 932	1 422
1998	52 380	3 351	1 373	1 373	49 029	5 180	11 937	14 064	11 279	5 133	1 435
1999	53 096	3 382	1 371	1 371	49 714	5 285	11 685	14 190	11 734	5 342	1 478
2000	54 079	3 339	1 346	1 346	50 740	5 381	11 669	14 088	12 376	5 623	1 602
2001	54 433	3 215	1 292	1 292	51 218	5 519	11 474	13 969	12 662	5 952	1 642
2002	54 842	3 125	1 229	1 229	51 717	5 628	11 409	13 703	12 790	6 482	1 704
2003	55 037	2 937	1 221	1 221	52 099	5 584	11 223	13 390	13 078	6 970	1 852
2004	55 092	2 879	1 182	1 182	52 212	5 606	11 119	13 114	13 247	7 197	1 930
2005	55 605	2 962	1 228	1 228	52 643	5 546	11 123	13 027	13 413	7 542	1 993
2006	56 221	2 935	1 251	1 251	53 286	5 530	11 212	12 886	13 625	7 980	2 052
2007	56 777	2 851	1 179	1 179	53 925	5 609	11 360	12 629	13 781	8 282	2 264
2008	57 284	2 776	1 086	1 086	54 508	5 616	11 495	12 495	13 875	8 609	2 417
2009	57 593	2 616	950	950	54 976	5 647	11 608	12 197	13 960	9 039	2 525

Table 1-7. Civilian Labor Force, by Age, Sex, Race, and Hispanic Origin, 1948–2009—*Continued*

(Thousands of people.)

Race, Hispanic origin, sex, and year	16 years and over	16 to 19 years			20 years and over						
		Total	16 to 17 years	18 to 19 years	Total	20 to 24 years	25 to 34 years	35 to 44 years	45 to 54 years	55 to 64 years	65 years and over
BLACK											
Both Sexes											
1972	8 707	788	293	496	7 919	1 393	2 107	1 735	1 496	909	281
1973	8 976	833	307	525	8 143	1 489	2 242	1 741	1 513	901	258
1974	9 167	851	317	534	8 317	1 492	2 358	1 777	1 517	917	253
1975	9 263	838	312	524	8 426	1 477	2 466	1 775	1 519	929	258
1976	9 561	837	304	532	8 724	1 544	2 646	1 824	1 518	925	268
1977	9 932	861	304	557	9 072	1 641	2 798	1 894	1 530	943	267
1978	10 432	930	341	589	9 501	1 739	2 961	1 975	1 560	978	289
1979	10 678	912	340	572	9 766	1 793	3 094	2 039	1 584	974	281
1980	10 865	891	326	565	9 975	1 802	3 259	2 081	1 596	978	257
1981	11 086	862	308	554	10 224	1 828	3 365	2 164	1 608	1 009	249
1982	11 331	824	268	556	10 507	1 849	3 492	2 303	1 610	1 012	243
1983	11 647	809	248	561	10 838	1 871	3 675	2 406	1 630	1 032	224
1984	12 033	827	268	558	11 206	1 926	3 800	2 565	1 671	1 020	224
1985	12 364	889	311	578	11 476	1 854	3 888	2 681	1 742	1 059	252
1986	12 654	883	322	562	11 770	1 881	4 028	2 793	1 793	1 051	224
1987	12 993	899	336	563	12 094	1 818	4 147	2 942	1 838	1 098	251
1988	13 205	889	344	545	12 316	1 782	4 226	3 069	1 894	1 069	276
1989	13 497	925	353	572	12 573	1 789	4 295	3 227	1 954	1 023	285
1990	13 740	866	306	560	12 874	1 758	4 307	3 566	2 003	977	262
1991	13 797	774	266	508	13 023	1 750	4 254	3 719	2 042	1 001	256
1992	14 162	816	285	532	13 346	1 763	4 309	3 843	2 142	1 029	259
1993	14 225	807	283	524	13 418	1 764	4 232	3 960	2 212	1 013	237
1994	14 502	852	351	501	13 650	1 800	4 199	4 068	2 308	1 007	267
1995	14 817	911	366	545	13 906	1 754	4 267	4 165	2 404	1 046	271
1996	15 134	923	366	556	14 211	1 738	4 305	4 287	2 553	1 073	255
1997	15 529	933	352	580	14 596	1 783	4 329	4 401	2 724	1 093	265
1998	15 982	1 017	370	646	14 966	1 797	4 332	4 531	2 863	1 163	278
1999	16 365	959	352	607	15 406	1 866	4 430	4 653	2 992	1 180	285
2000	16 397	941	356	585	15 456	1 873	4 281	4 515	3 203	1 264	320
2001	16 421	898	332	565	15 524	1 878	4 180	4 483	3 298	1 335	350
2002	16 565	870	297	574	15 695	1 908	4 134	4 458	3 435	1 407	353
2003	16 526	771	289	482	15 755	1 892	4 060	4 465	3 506	1 466	366
2004	16 638	762	272	489	15 876	1 926	4 076	4 380	3 578	1 538	380
2005	17 013	803	279	525	16 209	1 957	4 145	4 370	3 686	1 647	403
2006	17 314	871	318	553	16 443	1 960	4 197	4 348	3 785	1 739	414
2007	17 496	801	300	501	16 695	1 974	4 254	4 357	3 866	1 811	432
2008	17 740	787	270	517	16 953	1 981	4 328	4 316	3 945	1 908	476
2009	17 632	729	231	499	16 902	1 961	4 300	4 175	3 976	1 995	495
BLACK											
Men											
1972	4 816	453	180	272	4 364	761	1 158	935	824	522	165
1973	4 924	460	175	286	4 464	819	1 217	935	842	499	153
1974	5 020	480	189	291	4 540	798	1 279	953	838	519	152
1975	5 016	447	168	279	4 569	790	1 328	948	833	520	150
1976	5 101	454	168	285	4 648	820	1 383	969	824	504	149
1977	5 263	476	178	299	4 787	856	1 441	1 003	818	515	154
1978	5 435	491	186	306	4 943	883	1 504	1 022	829	540	166
1979	5 559	480	179	301	5 079	928	1 577	1 049	844	524	156
1980	5 612	479	181	298	5 134	935	1 659	1 061	830	509	138
1981	5 685	462	169	293	5 223	940	1 702	1 093	829	524	134
1982	5 804	436	137	300	5 368	964	1 769	1 152	824	525	135
1983	5 966	433	134	300	5 533	997	1 840	1 196	845	536	119
1984	6 126	440	141	299	5 686	1 022	1 924	1 270	847	505	118
1985	6 220	471	162	310	5 749	950	1 937	1 313	879	544	125
1986	6 373	458	164	294	5 915	957	2 029	1 359	901	552	116
1987	6 486	463	179	284	6 023	914	2 074	1 406	915	586	130
1988	6 596	469	186	283	6 127	913	2 114	1 459	936	565	139
1989	6 701	480	190	291	6 221	904	2 157	1 544	945	530	141
1990	6 802	445	161	284	6 357	879	2 142	1 733	988	496	119
1991	6 851	400	140	260	6 451	896	2 111	1 806	1 010	507	122
1992	6 997	429	149	280	6 568	900	2 121	1 859	1 037	521	130
1993	7 019	425	154	270	6 594	875	2 118	1 918	1 065	506	112
1994	7 089	443	176	266	6 646	891	2 068	1 975	1 102	484	125
1995	7 183	453	184	269	6 730	866	2 089	1 987	1 148	490	150
1996	7 264	458	182	276	6 806	848	2 077	2 036	1 204	509	132
1997	7 354	444	178	266	6 910	832	2 052	2 096	1 287	508	134
1998	7 542	488	181	307	7 053	837	2 034	2 142	1 343	548	150
1999	7 652	470	180	291	7 182	835	2 069	2 206	1 387	547	138
2000	7 702	462	181	281	7 240	875	1 999	2 105	1 497	612	151
2001	7 647	447	166	281	7 200	853	1 915	2 073	1 537	645	177
2002	7 794	446	149	297	7 347	906	1 909	2 064	1 623	664	181
2003	7 711	365	138	228	7 346	918	1 872	2 058	1 627	685	186
2004	7 773	359	128	231	7 414	927	1 931	2 000	1 654	714	188
2005	7 998	399	139	260	7 600	940	1 948	2 028	1 732	756	196
2006	8 128	409	152	256	7 720	971	1 986	1 999	1 792	777	195
2007	8 252	384	137	247	7 867	981	2 037	2 030	1 822	791	206
2008	8 347	385	124	261	7 962	984	2 047	2 008	1 846	852	225
2009	8 265	350	111	239	7 914	954	2 041	1 932	1 852	904	231

Table 1-7. Civilian Labor Force, by Age, Sex, Race, and Hispanic Origin, 1948–2009—*Continued*

(Thousands of people.)

Race, Hispanic origin, sex, and year	16 years and over	16 to 19 years			20 years and over						
		Total	16 to 17 years	18 to 19 years	Total	20 to 24 years	25 to 34 years	35 to 44 years	45 to 54 years	55 to 64 years	65 years and over
BLACK											
Women											
1972	3 890	335	113	224	3 555	632	949	800	672	387	116
1973	4 052	373	133	240	3 678	670	1 026	806	670	402	105
1974	4 148	371	128	243	3 777	694	1 079	824	679	398	100
1975	4 247	391	144	245	3 857	687	1 138	827	686	409	108
1976	4 460	384	136	247	4 076	723	1 264	855	694	421	119
1977	4 670	385	127	258	4 286	785	1 357	891	712	429	113
1978	4 997	439	155	283	4 558	856	1 456	953	731	439	124
1979	5 119	432	161	271	4 687	865	1 517	990	740	451	124
1980	5 253	412	144	267	4 841	867	1 600	1 020	767	469	119
1981	5 401	400	139	261	5 001	888	1 663	1 071	779	485	115
1982	5 527	387	131	256	5 140	885	1 723	1 151	786	487	108
1983	5 681	375	114	261	5 306	874	1 835	1 210	785	496	105
1984	5 907	387	127	260	5 520	904	1 876	1 294	823	515	106
1985	6 144	417	149	268	5 727	904	1 951	1 368	862	515	127
1986	6 281	425	157	268	5 855	924	1 999	1 434	892	499	107
1987	6 507	435	157	278	6 071	904	2 073	1 537	924	512	121
1988	6 609	419	158	262	6 190	869	2 112	1 610	958	504	137
1989	6 796	445	163	281	6 352	885	2 138	1 683	1 009	493	144
1990	6 938	421	145	276	6 517	879	2 165	1 833	1 015	481	143
1991	6 946	374	126	248	6 572	854	2 143	1 913	1 032	494	135
1992	7 166	387	135	252	6 778	863	2 188	1 985	1 105	508	129
1993	7 206	383	129	254	6 824	889	2 115	2 042	1 147	506	125
1994	7 413	409	174	235	7 004	909	2 131	2 093	1 206	523	142
1995	7 634	458	182	276	7 175	887	2 177	2 178	1 256	556	121
1996	7 869	464	184	280	7 405	890	2 228	2 251	1 349	565	122
1997	8 175	489	175	314	7 686	951	2 277	2 305	1 437	585	131
1998	8 441	528	189	339	7 912	960	2 298	2 390	1 520	615	128
1999	8 713	489	172	316	8 224	1 031	2 360	2 447	1 606	633	147
2000	8 695	479	175	305	8 215	998	2 282	2 409	1 706	652	168
2001	8 774	451	166	284	8 323	1 025	2 265	2 410	1 762	690	173
2002	8 772	424	148	276	8 348	1 002	2 225	2 394	1 812	743	171
2003	8 815	406	151	255	8 409	973	2 188	2 407	1 879	781	180
2004	8 865	403	144	259	8 462	999	2 144	2 380	1 924	824	192
2005	9 014	405	140	265	8 610	1 017	2 197	2 342	1 954	891	207
2006	9 186	462	166	297	8 723	989	2 211	2 349	1 993	963	218
2007	9 244	417	163	254	8 828	993	2 218	2 328	2 044	1 019	227
2008	9 393	402	146	256	8 991	997	2 281	2 308	2 099	1 056	251
2009	9 367	379	119	260	8 988	1 008	2 258	2 243	2 124	1 091	264
HISPANIC[1]											
Both Sexes											
1973	3 673	407	. . .	. . .	. . .	. . .	. . .	. . .	. . .	. . .	. . .
1974	4 012	442	. . .	. . .	. . .	. . .	. . .	. . .	. . .	. . .	. . .
1975	4 171	444	. . .	. . .	. . .	. . .	. . .	. . .	. . .	. . .	. . .
1976	4 205	447	176	285	3 820	729	1 248	875	625	294	48
1977	4 536	493	184	305	4 059	813	1 325	916	656	293	55
1978	4 979	533	221	312	4 446	901	1 446	1 008	701	323	67
1979	5 219	551	207	343	4 668	960	1 532	1 062	704	339	72
1980	6 146	645	241	404	5 502	1 136	1 843	1 163	860	414	85
1981	6 492	603	215	388	5 888	1 231	2 015	1 239	886	430	87
1982	6 734	585	192	393	6 148	1 251	2 163	1 313	891	444	85
1983	7 033	590	189	401	6 442	1 282	2 267	1 380	931	495	86
1984	7 451	618	209	409	6 833	1 325	2 436	1 509	954	524	84
1985	7 698	579	199	379	7 119	1 358	2 571	1 595	985	527	82
1986	8 076	571	203	368	7 505	1 414	2 685	1 713	1 097	511	84
1987	8 541	610	206	404	7 931	1 425	2 890	1 904	1 086	545	81
1988	8 982	671	234	437	8 311	1 486	2 957	1 996	1 147	621	103
1989	9 323	680	224	456	8 643	1 483	3 118	2 092	1 205	625	120
1990	10 720	829	276	554	9 891	1 839	3 590	2 386	1 320	647	110
1991	10 920	781	249	532	10 139	1 835	3 596	2 539	1 376	681	111
1992	11 338	796	263	533	10 542	1 815	3 740	2 735	1 442	687	122
1993	11 610	771	246	525	10 839	1 811	3 800	2 865	1 534	684	145
1994	11 975	807	285	522	11 168	1 863	3 865	2 965	1 626	698	151
1995	12 267	850	291	559	11 417	1 818	3 943	3 113	1 671	720	152
1996	12 774	845	284	561	11 929	1 845	4 054	3 361	1 697	806	166
1997	13 796	911	315	596	12 884	2 004	4 298	3 601	1 945	850	186
1998	14 317	1 007	320	688	13 310	2 077	4 372	3 707	2 090	894	169
1999	14 665	1 049	333	717	13 616	2 052	4 330	3 929	2 178	927	199
2000	16 689	1 168	368	800	15 521	2 546	5 197	4 241	2 387	940	209
2001	17 328	1 176	352	824	16 152	2 616	5 380	4 377	2 583	1 000	195
2002	17 943	1 103	335	769	16 840	2 678	5 645	4 545	2 657	1 091	224
2003	18 813	960	322	638	17 853	2 672	5 960	4 867	2 894	1 201	259
2004	19 272	995	297	698	18 277	2 732	5 931	4 931	3 093	1 284	306
2005	19 824	1 038	331	708	18 785	2 651	6 080	5 110	3 256	1 378	311
2006	20 694	1 071	360	710	19 623	2 681	6 295	5 337	3 452	1 490	369
2007	21 602	1 091	347	744	20 511	2 728	6 559	5 552	3 707	1 569	395
2008	22 024	1 121	353	768	20 903	2 668	6 557	5 698	3 862	1 701	417
2009	22 352	1 063	301	762	21 290	2 647	6 435	5 752	4 116	1 866	472

[1]May be any race.
. . . = Not available.

Table 1-7. Civilian Labor Force, by Age, Sex, Race, and Hispanic Origin, 1948–2009—*Continued*

(Thousands of people.)

Race, Hispanic origin, sex, and year	16 years and over	16 to 19 years			20 years and over						
		Total	16 to 17 years	18 to 19 years	Total	20 to 24 years	25 to 34 years	35 to 44 years	45 to 54 years	55 to 64 years	65 years and over
HISPANIC[1]											
Men											
1973	2 356	...	...	...	2 124	...	...	...	...	...	...
1974	2 556	...	...	...	2 306	...	...	...	...	...	...
1975	2 597	...	...	...	2 343	...	...	...	...	...	...
1976	2 580	260	104	155	2 326	433	771	541	398	189	34
1977	2 817	285	105	179	2 530	485	828	567	416	197	42
1978	3 041	299	129	171	2 742	546	882	620	425	217	52
1979	3 184	315	121	194	2 869	562	941	648	445	216	56
1980	3 818	392	147	245	3 426	697	1 161	713	522	270	62
1981	4 005	359	130	229	3 647	747	1 269	756	535	278	61
1982	4 148	333	111	221	3 815	759	1 361	808	539	290	58
1983	4 362	348	109	239	4 014	789	1 447	852	557	311	58
1984	4 563	345	113	232	4 218	822	1 540	910	570	325	51
1985	4 729	334	116	218	4 395	835	1 629	957	591	331	53
1986	4 948	336	114	222	4 612	888	1 669	1 015	661	323	56
1987	5 163	345	112	233	4 818	865	1 801	1 121	652	325	55
1988	5 409	378	123	255	5 031	897	1 834	1 189	686	355	69
1989	5 595	400	129	271	5 195	909	1 899	1 221	719	375	71
1990	6 546	512	165	346	6 034	1 182	2 230	1 403	775	380	65
1991	6 664	466	141	325	6 198	1 202	2 260	1 487	780	401	67
1992	6 900	468	154	314	6 432	1 141	2 366	1 593	844	414	74
1993	7 076	455	145	310	6 621	1 147	2 417	1 675	900	394	88
1994	7 210	463	163	300	6 747	1 184	2 430	1 713	922	410	89
1995	7 376	479	168	311	6 898	1 153	2 469	1 795	965	417	98
1996	7 646	496	156	340	7 150	1 132	2 510	1 966	967	469	105
1997	8 309	531	177	354	7 779	1 267	2 684	2 091	1 112	511	113
1998	8 571	565	188	377	8 005	1 288	2 733	2 173	1 164	541	106
1999	8 546	596	181	415	7 950	1 231	2 633	2 219	1 205	526	136
2000	9 923	676	204	471	9 247	1 590	3 181	2 451	1 337	555	134
2001	10 279	684	200	484	9 595	1 602	3 294	2 562	1 430	582	125
2002	10 609	632	183	449	9 977	1 627	3 484	2 647	1 478	607	134
2003	11 288	532	164	368	10 756	1 642	3 776	2 877	1 630	680	150
2004	11 587	567	156	410	11 020	1 671	3 765	2 934	1 736	728	186
2005	11 985	577	179	398	11 408	1 645	3 879	3 058	1 855	779	192
2006	12 488	600	189	411	11 888	1 646	4 014	3 203	1 960	838	228
2007	13 005	602	189	412	12 403	1 645	4 170	3 346	2 104	904	233
2008	13 255	626	202	424	12 629	1 594	4 172	3 425	2 216	979	243
2009	13 310	580	160	420	12 730	1 542	4 046	3 472	2 350	1 046	273
HISPANIC[1]											
Women											
1973	1 317	...	...	...	1 142	...	...	...	...	...	...
1974	1 456	...	...	...	1 264	...	...	...	...	...	...
1975	1 574	...	...	...	1 384	...	...	...	...	...	...
1976	1 625	201	71	130	1 454	295	479	334	227	105	13
1977	1 720	204	80	125	1 523	327	497	349	240	96	13
1978	1 938	233	93	142	1 704	354	564	388	275	106	16
1979	2 035	235	86	149	1 800	397	590	413	258	124	15
1980	2 328	252	93	159	2 076	439	682	450	337	144	22
1981	2 486	244	85	159	2 242	484	745	483	351	152	27
1982	2 586	252	81	172	2 333	492	802	504	352	155	28
1983	2 671	242	80	162	2 429	493	820	529	374	184	29
1984	2 888	273	96	177	2 615	503	896	599	384	199	34
1985	2 970	245	84	161	2 725	524	943	639	394	196	29
1986	3 128	236	89	147	2 893	526	1 016	698	436	189	28
1987	3 377	265	94	171	3 112	559	1 090	783	434	220	27
1988	3 573	293	111	182	3 281	589	1 123	806	461	267	34
1989	3 728	280	95	185	3 448	574	1 219	871	486	251	49
1990	4 174	318	110	207	3 857	657	1 360	983	545	268	45
1991	4 256	315	107	207	3 941	633	1 336	1 052	596	279	44
1992	4 439	328	110	219	4 110	674	1 374	1 142	599	273	48
1993	4 534	316	101	215	4 218	664	1 383	1 190	633	290	57
1994	4 765	345	122	222	4 421	679	1 435	1 252	704	288	62
1995	4 891	371	123	249	4 520	666	1 473	1 318	706	303	54
1996	5 128	349	128	221	4 779	713	1 544	1 395	729	338	61
1997	5 486	381	138	242	5 106	737	1 614	1 510	833	338	73
1998	5 746	442	132	310	5 304	789	1 639	1 533	927	353	62
1999	6 119	453	151	302	5 666	821	1 698	1 710	973	401	63
2000	6 767	492	164	328	6 275	956	2 016	1 791	1 051	386	75
2001	7 049	492	152	340	6 557	1 014	2 086	1 815	1 153	418	70
2002	7 334	471	152	320	6 863	1 051	2 161	1 897	1 179	484	90
2003	7 525	428	158	271	7 096	1 030	2 183	1 990	1 264	520	109
2004	7 685	429	141	288	7 257	1 060	2 166	1 998	1 357	556	119
2005	7 839	462	152	310	7 377	1 005	2 201	2 052	1 401	599	119
2006	8 206	471	171	300	7 735	1 035	2 280	2 134	1 492	652	141
2007	8 597	489	158	332	8 108	1 083	2 389	2 205	1 604	665	162
2008	8 769	495	151	344	8 274	1 074	2 384	2 274	1 646	722	174
2009	9 043	483	141	342	8 560	1 105	2 388	2 280	1 767	820	200

[1] May be any race.
... = Not available.

Table 1-8. Civilian Labor Force Participation Rates, by Age, Sex, Race, and Hispanic Origin, 1948–2009

(Percent.)

Race, Hispanic origin, sex, and year	16 years and over	16 to 19 years	20 years and over						
			Total	20 to 24 years	25 to 34 years	35 to 44 years	45 to 54 years	55 to 64 years	65 years and over
ALL RACES									
Both Sexes									
1948	58.8	52.5	59.4	64.1	63.1	66.7	65.1	56.9	27.0
1949	58.9	52.2	59.5	64.9	63.2	67.2	65.3	56.2	27.3
1950	59.2	51.8	59.9	65.9	63.5	67.5	66.4	56.7	26.7
1951	59.2	52.2	59.8	64.8	64.2	67.6	67.2	56.9	25.8
1952	59.0	51.3	59.7	62.2	64.7	68.0	67.5	57.5	24.8
1953	58.9	50.2	59.6	61.2	64.0	68.9	68.1	58.0	24.8
1954	58.8	48.3	59.6	61.6	64.3	68.8	68.4	58.7	23.9
1955	59.3	48.9	60.1	62.7	64.8	68.9	69.7	59.5	24.1
1956	60.0	50.9	60.7	64.1	64.8	69.5	70.5	60.8	24.3
1957	59.6	49.6	60.4	64.0	64.9	69.5	70.9	60.1	22.9
1958	59.5	47.4	60.5	64.4	65.0	69.6	71.5	60.5	21.8
1959	59.3	46.7	60.4	64.3	65.0	69.5	71.9	61.0	21.1
1960	59.4	47.5	60.5	65.2	65.4	69.4	72.2	60.9	20.8
1961	59.3	46.9	60.5	65.7	65.6	69.5	72.1	61.5	20.1
1962	58.8	46.1	60.0	65.3	65.2	69.7	72.2	61.5	19.1
1963	58.7	45.2	60.1	65.1	65.6	70.1	72.5	62.0	17.9
1964	58.7	44.5	60.2	66.3	65.8	70.0	72.9	61.9	18.0
1965	58.9	45.7	60.3	66.4	66.4	70.7	72.5	61.9	17.8
1966	59.2	48.2	60.5	66.5	67.1	71.0	72.7	62.2	17.2
1967	59.6	48.4	60.9	67.1	68.2	71.6	72.7	62.3	17.2
1968	59.6	48.3	60.9	67.0	68.6	72.0	72.8	62.2	17.2
1969	60.1	49.4	61.3	68.2	69.1	72.5	73.4	62.1	17.3
1970	60.4	49.9	61.6	69.2	69.7	73.1	73.5	61.8	17.0
1971	60.2	49.7	61.4	69.3	69.9	73.2	73.2	61.3	16.2
1972	60.4	51.9	61.4	70.8	70.9	73.3	72.7	60.0	15.6
1973	60.8	53.7	61.7	72.6	72.3	74.0	72.5	58.4	14.6
1974	61.3	54.8	62.0	74.0	73.6	74.6	72.7	57.8	14.0
1975	61.2	54.0	62.1	73.9	74.4	75.0	72.6	57.2	13.7
1976	61.6	54.5	62.4	74.7	75.7	76.0	72.5	56.6	13.1
1977	62.3	56.0	63.0	75.7	77.0	77.0	72.8	56.3	13.0
1978	63.2	57.8	63.8	76.8	78.3	78.1	73.5	56.3	13.3
1979	63.7	57.9	64.3	77.5	79.2	79.2	74.3	56.2	13.1
1980	63.8	56.7	64.5	77.2	79.9	80.0	74.9	55.7	12.5
1981	63.9	55.4	64.8	77.3	80.5	80.7	75.7	55.0	12.2
1982	64.0	54.1	65.0	77.1	81.0	81.2	75.9	55.1	11.9
1983	64.0	53.5	65.0	77.2	81.3	81.6	76.0	54.5	11.7
1984	64.4	53.9	65.3	77.6	81.8	82.4	76.5	54.2	11.1
1985	64.8	54.5	65.7	78.2	82.5	83.1	77.3	54.2	10.8
1986	65.3	54.7	66.2	78.9	82.9	83.7	78.0	54.0	10.9
1987	65.6	54.7	66.5	78.9	83.3	84.3	78.6	54.4	11.1
1988	65.9	55.3	66.8	78.7	83.3	84.6	79.6	54.6	11.5
1989	66.5	55.9	67.3	78.7	83.8	85.1	80.5	55.5	11.8
1990	66.5	53.7	67.6	77.8	83.6	85.2	80.7	55.9	11.8
1991	66.2	51.6	67.3	76.7	83.2	85.2	81.0	55.5	11.5
1992	66.4	51.3	67.6	77.0	83.7	85.1	81.5	56.2	11.5
1993	66.3	51.5	67.5	77.0	83.3	84.9	81.6	56.4	11.2
1994	66.6	52.7	67.7	77.0	83.2	84.8	81.7	56.8	12.4
1995	66.6	53.5	67.7	76.6	83.8	84.6	81.4	57.2	12.1
1996	66.8	52.3	67.9	76.8	84.1	84.8	82.1	57.9	12.1
1997	67.1	51.6	68.4	77.6	84.4	85.1	82.6	58.9	12.2
1998	67.1	52.8	68.3	77.5	84.6	84.7	82.5	59.3	11.9
1999	67.1	52.0	68.3	77.5	84.6	84.9	82.6	59.3	12.3
2000	67.1	52.0	68.3	77.8	84.6	84.8	82.5	59.2	12.9
2001	66.8	49.6	68.2	77.1	84.0	84.6	82.3	60.4	13.0
2002	66.6	47.4	68.1	76.4	83.7	84.1	82.1	61.9	13.2
2003	66.2	44.5	67.9	75.4	82.9	83.9	82.1	62.4	14.0
2004	66.0	43.9	67.7	75.0	82.7	83.6	81.8	62.3	14.4
2005	66.0	43.7	67.8	74.6	82.8	83.8	81.7	62.9	15.1
2006	66.2	43.7	67.9	74.6	83.0	83.8	81.9	63.7	15.4
2007	66.0	41.3	68.0	74.4	83.3	83.8	82.0	63.8	16.0
2008	66.0	40.2	68.0	74.4	83.3	84.1	81.9	64.5	16.8
2009	65.4	37.5	67.5	72.9	82.7	83.7	81.6	64.9	17.2

Table 1-8. Civilian Labor Force Participation Rates, by Age, Sex, Race, and Hispanic Origin, 1948–2009
—Continued

(Percent.)

Race, Hispanic origin, sex, and year	16 years and over	16 to 19 years	20 years and over						
			Total	20 to 24 years	25 to 34 years	35 to 44 years	45 to 54 years	55 to 64 years	65 years and over
ALL RACES									
Men									
1948	86.6	63.7	88.6	84.6	95.9	97.9	95.8	89.5	46.8
1949	86.4	62.8	88.5	86.6	95.8	97.9	95.6	87.5	47.0
1950	86.4	63.2	88.4	87.9	96.0	97.6	95.8	86.9	45.8
1951	86.3	63.0	88.2	88.4	96.9	97.5	95.9	87.2	44.9
1952	86.3	61.3	88.3	88.1	97.5	97.8	96.2	87.5	42.6
1953	86.0	60.7	88.0	87.7	97.4	98.2	96.5	87.9	41.6
1954	85.5	58.0	87.8	86.9	97.3	98.1	96.5	88.7	40.5
1955	85.4	58.9	87.6	86.9	97.6	98.1	96.4	87.9	39.6
1956	85.5	60.5	87.6	87.8	97.3	97.9	96.6	88.5	40.0
1957	84.8	59.1	86.9	87.1	97.1	97.9	96.3	87.5	37.5
1958	84.2	56.6	86.6	86.9	97.1	97.9	96.3	87.8	35.6
1959	83.7	55.8	86.3	87.8	97.4	97.8	96.0	87.4	34.2
1960	83.3	56.1	86.0	88.1	97.5	97.7	95.7	86.8	33.1
1961	82.9	54.6	85.7	87.8	97.5	97.6	95.6	87.3	31.7
1962	82.0	53.8	84.8	86.9	97.2	97.6	95.6	86.2	30.3
1963	81.4	52.9	84.4	86.1	97.1	97.5	95.7	86.2	28.4
1964	81.0	52.4	84.2	86.1	97.3	97.3	95.7	85.6	28.0
1965	80.7	53.8	83.9	85.8	97.2	97.3	95.6	84.6	27.9
1966	80.4	55.3	83.6	85.1	97.3	97.2	95.3	84.5	27.1
1967	80.4	55.6	83.4	84.4	97.2	97.3	95.2	84.4	27.1
1968	80.1	55.1	83.1	82.8	96.9	97.1	94.9	84.3	27.3
1969	79.8	55.9	82.8	82.8	96.7	96.9	94.6	83.4	27.2
1970	79.7	56.1	82.6	83.3	96.4	96.9	94.3	83.0	26.8
1971	79.1	56.1	82.1	83.0	95.9	96.5	93.9	82.1	25.5
1972	78.9	58.1	81.6	83.9	95.7	96.4	93.2	80.4	24.3
1973	78.8	59.7	81.3	85.2	95.7	96.2	93.0	78.2	22.7
1974	78.7	60.7	81.0	85.9	95.8	96.0	92.2	77.3	22.4
1975	77.9	59.1	80.3	84.5	95.2	95.6	92.1	75.6	21.6
1976	77.5	59.3	79.8	85.2	95.2	95.4	91.6	74.3	20.2
1977	77.7	60.9	79.7	85.6	95.3	95.7	91.1	73.8	20.0
1978	77.9	62.0	79.8	85.9	95.3	95.7	91.3	73.3	20.4
1979	77.8	61.5	79.8	86.4	95.3	95.7	91.4	72.8	19.9
1980	77.4	60.5	79.4	85.9	95.2	95.5	91.2	72.1	19.0
1981	77.0	59.0	79.0	85.5	94.9	95.4	91.4	70.6	18.4
1982	76.6	56.7	78.7	84.9	94.7	95.3	91.2	70.2	17.8
1983	76.4	56.2	78.5	84.8	94.2	95.2	91.2	69.4	17.4
1984	76.4	56.0	78.3	85.0	94.4	95.4	91.2	68.5	16.3
1985	76.3	56.8	78.1	85.0	94.7	95.0	91.0	67.9	15.8
1986	76.3	56.4	78.1	85.8	94.6	94.8	91.0	67.3	16.0
1987	76.2	56.1	78.0	85.2	94.6	94.6	90.7	67.6	16.3
1988	76.2	56.9	77.9	85.0	94.3	94.5	90.9	67.0	16.5
1989	76.4	57.9	78.1	85.3	94.4	94.5	91.1	67.2	16.6
1990	76.4	55.7	78.2	84.4	94.1	94.3	90.7	67.8	16.3
1991	75.8	53.2	77.7	83.5	93.6	94.1	90.5	67.0	15.7
1992	75.8	53.4	77.7	83.3	93.8	93.7	90.7	67.0	16.1
1993	75.4	53.2	77.3	83.2	93.4	93.4	90.1	66.5	15.6
1994	75.1	54.1	76.8	83.1	92.6	92.8	89.1	65.5	16.8
1995	75.0	54.8	76.7	83.1	93.0	92.3	88.8	66.0	16.8
1996	74.9	53.2	76.8	82.5	93.2	92.4	89.1	67.0	16.9
1997	75.0	52.3	77.0	82.5	93.0	92.6	89.5	67.6	17.1
1998	74.9	53.3	76.8	82.0	93.2	92.6	89.2	68.1	16.5
1999	74.7	52.9	76.7	81.9	93.3	92.8	88.8	67.9	16.9
2000	74.8	52.8	76.7	82.6	93.4	92.7	88.6	67.3	17.7
2001	74.4	50.2	76.5	81.6	92.7	92.5	88.5	68.3	17.7
2002	74.1	47.5	76.3	80.7	92.4	92.1	88.5	69.2	17.9
2003	73.5	44.3	75.9	80.0	91.8	92.1	87.7	68.7	18.6
2004	73.3	43.9	75.8	79.6	91.9	91.9	87.5	68.7	19.0
2005	73.3	43.2	75.8	79.1	91.7	92.1	87.7	69.3	19.8
2006	73.5	43.7	75.9	79.6	91.7	92.1	88.1	69.6	20.3
2007	73.2	41.1	75.9	78.7	92.2	92.3	88.2	69.6	20.5
2008	73.0	40.1	75.7	78.7	91.5	92.2	88.0	70.4	21.5
2009	72.0	37.3	74.8	76.2	90.3	91.7	87.4	70.2	21.9

Table 1-8. Civilian Labor Force Participation Rates, by Age, Sex, Race, and Hispanic Origin, 1948–2009
—Continued

(Percent.)

Race, Hispanic origin, sex, and year	16 years and over	16 to 19 years	20 years and over						
			Total	20 to 24 years	25 to 34 years	35 to 44 years	45 to 54 years	55 to 64 years	65 years and over
ALL RACES									
Women									
1948	32.7	42.0	31.8	45.3	33.2	36.9	35.0	24.3	9.1
1949	33.1	42.4	32.3	45.0	33.4	38.1	35.9	25.3	9.6
1950	33.9	41.0	33.3	46.0	34.0	39.1	37.9	27.0	9.7
1951	34.6	42.4	34.0	46.5	35.4	39.8	39.7	27.6	8.9
1952	34.7	42.2	34.1	44.7	35.4	40.4	40.1	28.7	9.1
1953	34.4	40.7	33.9	44.3	34.0	41.3	40.4	29.1	10.0
1954	34.6	39.4	34.2	45.1	34.4	41.2	41.2	30.0	9.3
1955	35.7	39.7	35.4	45.9	34.9	41.6	43.8	32.5	10.6
1956	36.9	42.2	36.4	46.3	35.4	43.1	45.5	34.9	10.8
1957	36.9	41.1	36.5	45.9	35.6	43.3	46.5	34.5	10.5
1958	37.1	39.0	36.9	46.3	35.6	43.4	47.8	35.2	10.3
1959	37.1	38.2	37.1	45.1	35.3	43.4	49.0	36.6	10.2
1960	37.7	39.3	37.6	46.1	36.0	43.4	49.9	37.2	10.8
1961	38.1	39.7	38.0	47.0	36.4	43.8	50.1	37.9	10.7
1962	37.9	39.0	37.8	47.3	36.3	44.1	50.0	38.7	10.0
1963	38.3	38.0	38.3	47.5	37.2	44.9	50.6	39.7	9.6
1964	38.7	37.0	38.9	49.4	37.2	45.0	51.4	40.2	10.1
1965	39.3	38.0	39.4	49.9	38.5	46.1	50.9	41.1	10.0
1966	40.3	41.4	40.1	51.5	39.8	46.8	51.7	41.8	9.6
1967	41.1	41.6	41.1	53.3	41.9	48.1	51.8	42.4	9.6
1968	41.6	41.9	41.6	54.5	42.6	48.9	52.3	42.4	9.6
1969	42.7	43.2	42.7	56.7	43.7	49.9	53.8	43.1	9.9
1970	43.3	44.0	43.3	57.7	45.0	51.1	54.4	43.0	9.7
1971	43.4	43.4	43.3	57.7	45.6	51.6	54.3	42.9	9.5
1972	43.9	45.8	43.7	59.1	47.8	52.0	53.9	42.1	9.3
1973	44.7	47.8	44.4	61.1	50.4	53.3	53.7	41.1	8.9
1974	45.7	49.1	45.3	63.1	52.6	54.7	54.6	40.7	8.1
1975	46.3	49.1	46.0	64.1	54.9	55.8	54.6	40.9	8.2
1976	47.3	49.8	47.0	65.0	57.3	57.8	55.0	41.0	8.2
1977	48.4	51.2	48.1	66.5	59.7	59.6	55.8	40.9	8.1
1978	50.0	53.7	49.6	68.3	62.2	61.6	57.1	41.3	8.3
1979	50.9	54.2	50.6	69.0	63.9	63.6	58.3	41.7	8.3
1980	51.5	52.9	51.3	68.9	65.5	65.5	59.9	41.3	8.1
1981	52.1	51.8	52.1	69.6	66.7	66.8	61.1	41.4	8.0
1982	52.6	51.4	52.7	69.8	68.0	68.0	61.6	41.8	7.9
1983	52.9	50.8	53.1	69.9	69.0	68.7	61.9	41.5	7.8
1984	53.6	51.8	53.7	70.4	69.8	70.1	62.9	41.7	7.5
1985	54.5	52.1	54.7	71.8	70.9	71.8	64.4	42.0	7.3
1986	55.3	53.0	55.5	72.4	71.6	73.1	65.9	42.3	7.4
1987	56.0	53.3	56.2	73.0	72.4	74.5	67.1	42.7	7.4
1988	56.6	53.6	56.8	72.7	72.7	75.2	69.0	43.5	7.9
1989	57.4	53.9	57.7	72.4	73.5	76.0	70.5	45.0	8.4
1990	57.5	51.6	58.0	71.3	73.5	76.4	71.2	45.2	8.6
1991	57.4	50.0	57.9	70.1	73.1	76.5	72.0	45.2	8.5
1992	57.8	49.1	58.5	70.9	73.9	76.7	72.6	46.5	8.3
1993	57.9	49.7	58.5	70.9	73.4	76.6	73.5	47.2	8.1
1994	58.8	51.3	59.3	71.0	74.0	77.1	74.6	48.9	9.2
1995	58.9	52.2	59.4	70.3	74.9	77.2	74.4	49.2	8.8
1996	59.3	51.3	59.9	71.3	75.2	77.5	75.4	49.6	8.6
1997	59.8	51.0	60.5	72.7	76.0	77.7	76.0	50.9	8.6
1998	59.8	52.3	60.4	73.0	76.3	77.1	76.2	51.2	8.6
1999	60.0	51.0	60.7	73.2	76.4	77.2	76.7	51.5	8.9
2000	59.9	51.2	60.6	73.1	76.1	77.2	76.8	51.9	9.4
2001	59.8	49.0	60.6	72.7	75.5	77.1	76.4	53.2	9.6
2002	59.6	47.3	60.5	72.1	75.1	76.4	76.0	55.2	9.8
2003	59.5	44.8	60.6	70.8	74.1	76.0	76.8	56.6	10.6
2004	59.2	43.8	60.3	70.5	73.6	75.6	76.5	56.3	11.1
2005	59.3	44.2	60.4	70.1	73.9	75.8	76.0	57.0	11.5
2006	59.4	43.7	60.5	69.5	74.4	75.9	76.0	58.2	11.7
2007	59.3	41.5	60.6	70.1	74.5	75.5	76.0	58.3	12.6
2008	59.5	40.2	60.9	70.0	75.2	76.1	76.1	59.1	13.3
2009	59.2	37.7	60.8	69.6	75.0	75.9	76.0	60.0	13.6

Table 1-8. Civilian Labor Force Participation Rates, by Age, Sex, Race, and Hispanic Origin, 1948–2009
—*Continued*

(Percent.)

Race, Hispanic origin, sex, and year	16 years and over	16 to 19 years	20 years and over						
			Total	20 to 24 years	25 to 34 years	35 to 44 years	45 to 54 years	55 to 64 years	65 years and over
WHITE									
Both Sexes									
1954	58.2	48.8	58.9	61.0	63.5	68.0	67.9	58.4	23.7
1955	58.7	49.3	59.5	62.4	64.0	68.3	69.2	59.3	23.9
1956	59.4	51.3	60.1	64.1	64.0	68.9	70.1	60.6	24.2
1957	59.1	50.3	59.8	63.7	64.1	68.8	70.5	59.9	22.8
1958	58.9	47.9	59.8	64.1	64.2	68.8	71.0	60.3	21.7
1959	58.7	47.4	59.7	63.7	64.3	68.7	71.5	60.7	21.0
1960	58.8	47.9	59.8	64.8	64.7	68.6	71.7	60.6	20.8
1961	58.8	47.4	59.9	65.5	64.8	68.8	71.7	61.3	20.0
1962	58.3	46.6	59.4	65.0	64.4	69.0	71.8	61.3	19.0
1963	58.2	45.7	59.4	64.9	64.8	69.4	72.3	61.8	17.9
1964	58.2	45.1	59.6	65.8	64.9	69.5	72.5	61.8	17.8
1965	58.4	46.5	59.7	65.7	65.6	70.1	72.2	61.7	17.7
1966	58.7	49.1	59.8	66.0	66.3	70.4	72.5	61.9	17.1
1967	59.2	49.2	60.3	66.8	67.4	71.2	72.5	62.3	17.0
1968	59.3	49.3	60.4	66.6	67.9	71.7	72.7	62.2	17.1
1969	59.9	50.6	60.9	67.9	68.4	72.3	73.3	62.1	17.2
1970	60.2	51.4	61.2	69.2	69.1	72.9	73.5	61.8	16.8
1971	60.1	51.6	61.1	69.6	69.3	73.0	73.4	61.3	16.1
1972	60.4	54.1	61.2	71.2	70.4	73.2	72.9	60.3	15.4
1973	60.8	56.0	61.4	73.3	72.0	73.9	72.7	58.6	14.4
1974	61.4	57.3	61.9	74.8	73.4	74.6	73.0	58.0	13.9
1975	61.5	56.7	62.0	75.2	74.4	75.1	73.0	57.4	13.6
1976	61.8	57.5	62.3	76.0	75.6	76.1	73.0	56.9	13.0
1977	62.5	59.3	62.9	77.1	77.0	77.1	73.2	56.6	12.9
1978	63.3	60.8	63.6	78.1	78.3	78.1	73.8	56.4	13.1
1979	63.9	61.1	64.2	78.9	79.4	79.3	74.6	56.5	12.9
1980	64.1	60.0	64.5	78.7	80.2	80.3	75.4	56.0	12.5
1981	64.3	58.9	64.8	79.1	81.0	81.0	76.2	55.2	12.2
1982	64.3	57.5	65.0	78.9	81.6	81.5	76.4	55.3	12.0
1983	64.3	56.9	65.0	79.0	81.8	81.9	76.5	54.7	11.8
1984	64.6	57.2	65.3	79.4	82.5	82.6	77.0	54.5	11.1
1985	65.0	57.5	65.7	79.9	83.1	83.4	77.8	54.4	10.7
1986	65.5	57.8	66.1	80.6	83.6	84.0	78.5	54.3	11.0
1987	65.8	57.7	66.5	80.7	84.0	84.7	79.1	54.6	11.1
1988	66.2	58.6	66.8	80.6	84.1	85.0	80.3	55.1	11.4
1989	66.7	59.1	67.3	80.2	84.5	85.5	81.2	56.2	11.8
1990	66.9	57.5	67.6	79.8	84.6	85.9	81.3	56.5	11.9
1991	66.6	55.8	67.4	78.9	84.3	85.9	81.8	56.0	11.6
1992	66.8	54.7	67.7	79.4	84.6	85.8	82.2	56.8	11.6
1993	66.8	55.1	67.6	79.5	84.5	85.7	82.5	57.1	11.4
1994	67.1	56.4	67.9	79.5	84.4	85.7	82.7	57.6	12.5
1995	67.1	57.1	67.8	78.7	84.9	85.5	82.5	58.0	12.3
1996	67.2	55.9	68.1	79.1	84.9	85.7	83.1	58.7	12.3
1997	67.5	55.2	68.4	79.6	85.3	85.8	83.5	59.9	12.3
1998	67.3	56.0	68.2	79.5	85.4	85.3	83.4	60.1	12.0
1999	67.3	55.5	68.2	79.5	85.1	85.4	83.5	60.2	12.5
2000	67.3	55.5	68.2	79.9	85.1	85.4	83.5	60.0	13.0
2001	67.0	53.1	68.1	79.2	84.5	85.2	83.3	61.2	13.0
2002	66.8	50.5	68.1	78.6	84.5	84.7	83.0	62.8	13.3
2003	66.5	47.7	67.9	77.7	83.6	84.3	83.0	63.3	14.1
2004	66.3	47.1	67.7	77.1	83.5	84.1	82.9	63.2	14.6
2005	66.3	46.9	67.7	76.3	83.5	84.2	82.8	63.7	15.1
2006	66.5	46.7	67.9	76.5	83.8	84.3	83.0	64.7	15.5
2007	66.4	44.4	68.0	76.4	84.1	84.1	83.1	64.9	16.2
2008	66.3	43.1	68.0	76.3	83.9	84.4	82.9	65.7	17.0
2009	65.8	40.6	67.7	75.1	83.5	84.2	82.7	66.2	17.4

Table 1-8. Civilian Labor Force Participation Rates, by Age, Sex, Race, and Hispanic Origin, 1948–2009
—Continued

(Percent.)

Race, Hispanic origin, sex, and year	16 years and over	16 to 19 years	20 years and over						
			Total	20 to 24 years	25 to 34 years	35 to 44 years	45 to 54 years	55 to 64 years	65 years and over
WHITE									
Men									
1954	85.6	57.6	87.8	86.3	97.5	98.2	96.8	89.1	40.4
1955	85.4	58.6	87.5	86.5	97.8	98.2	96.7	88.4	39.6
1956	85.6	60.4	87.6	87.6	97.4	98.1	96.8	88.9	40.0
1957	84.8	59.2	86.9	86.6	97.2	98.0	96.7	88.0	37.7
1958	84.3	56.5	86.6	86.7	97.2	98.0	96.6	88.2	35.7
1959	83.8	55.9	86.3	87.3	97.5	98.0	96.3	87.9	34.3
1960	83.4	55.9	86.0	87.8	97.7	97.9	96.1	87.2	33.3
1961	83.0	54.5	85.7	87.6	97.7	97.9	95.9	87.8	31.9
1962	82.1	53.8	84.9	86.5	97.4	97.9	96.0	86.7	30.6
1963	81.5	53.1	84.4	85.8	97.4	97.8	96.2	86.6	28.4
1964	81.1	52.7	84.2	85.7	97.5	97.6	96.1	86.1	27.9
1965	80.8	54.1	83.9	85.3	97.4	97.7	95.9	85.2	27.9
1966	80.6	55.9	83.6	84.4	97.5	97.6	95.8	84.9	27.2
1967	80.6	56.3	83.5	84.0	97.5	97.7	95.6	84.9	27.1
1968	80.4	55.9	83.2	82.4	97.2	97.6	95.4	84.7	27.4
1969	80.2	56.8	83.0	82.6	97.0	97.4	95.1	83.9	27.3
1970	80.0	57.5	82.8	83.3	96.7	97.3	94.9	83.3	26.7
1971	79.6	57.9	82.3	83.2	96.3	97.0	94.7	82.6	25.6
1972	79.6	60.1	82.0	84.3	96.0	97.0	94.0	81.1	24.4
1973	79.4	62.0	81.6	85.8	96.2	96.8	93.5	78.9	22.7
1974	79.4	62.9	81.4	86.6	96.3	96.7	93.0	78.0	22.4
1975	78.7	61.9	80.7	85.5	95.8	96.4	92.9	76.4	21.7
1976	78.4	62.3	80.3	86.3	95.9	96.0	92.5	75.2	20.2
1977	78.5	64.0	80.2	86.8	96.0	96.2	92.1	74.6	20.0
1978	78.6	65.0	80.1	87.3	95.9	96.3	92.1	73.7	20.3
1979	78.6	64.8	80.1	87.6	96.0	96.4	92.2	73.4	20.0
1980	78.2	63.7	79.8	87.2	95.9	96.2	92.1	73.1	19.1
1981	77.9	62.4	79.5	87.0	95.8	96.1	92.4	71.5	18.5
1982	77.4	60.0	79.2	86.3	95.6	96.0	92.2	71.0	17.9
1983	77.1	59.4	78.9	86.1	95.2	96.0	91.9	70.0	17.7
1984	77.1	59.0	78.7	86.5	95.4	96.1	92.0	69.5	16.4
1985	77.0	59.7	78.5	86.4	95.7	95.7	92.0	68.8	15.9
1986	76.9	59.3	78.5	87.3	95.5	95.4	91.8	68.0	16.3
1987	76.8	59.0	78.4	86.9	95.5	95.4	91.6	68.1	16.5
1988	76.9	60.0	78.3	86.6	95.2	95.4	91.8	67.9	16.7
1989	77.1	61.0	78.5	86.8	95.4	95.3	92.2	68.3	16.8
1990	77.1	59.6	78.5	86.2	95.2	95.3	91.7	68.6	16.6
1991	76.5	57.3	78.0	85.4	94.9	95.0	91.4	67.7	15.9
1992	76.5	56.9	78.0	85.2	94.9	94.7	91.8	67.7	16.2
1993	76.2	56.6	77.7	85.5	94.7	94.5	91.3	67.3	15.9
1994	75.9	57.7	77.3	85.5	93.9	93.9	90.3	66.4	17.2
1995	75.7	58.5	77.1	85.1	94.1	93.4	90.0	67.1	16.9
1996	75.8	57.1	77.3	85.0	94.4	93.6	90.4	68.0	17.2
1997	75.9	56.1	77.5	85.1	94.2	93.7	90.6	68.9	17.4
1998	75.6	56.6	77.2	84.6	94.4	93.7	90.3	69.1	16.6
1999	75.6	56.4	77.2	84.9	94.3	93.8	90.1	69.1	17.2
2000	75.5	56.5	77.1	85.2	94.5	93.8	89.7	68.2	17.9
2001	75.1	53.7	76.9	84.1	93.9	93.6	89.7	69.1	17.8
2002	74.8	50.3	76.7	83.2	93.7	93.2	89.6	70.2	17.8
2003	74.2	47.5	76.3	82.5	93.3	93.1	88.8	69.7	18.6
2004	74.1	47.4	76.2	82.1	93.2	93.0	88.7	69.8	19.1
2005	74.1	46.2	76.2	81.4	93.0	93.0	89.0	70.4	20.0
2006	74.3	46.9	76.4	81.9	92.9	93.1	89.3	71.0	20.6
2007	74.0	44.3	76.3	80.9	93.4	93.1	89.6	71.2	20.8
2008	73.7	43.0	76.1	80.8	92.6	93.0	89.2	71.9	21.8
2009	72.8	40.3	75.3	78.6	91.6	92.7	88.8	71.8	22.2

Table 1-8. Civilian Labor Force Participation Rates, by Age, Sex, Race, and Hispanic Origin, 1948–2009
—*Continued*

(Percent.)

Race, Hispanic origin, sex, and year	16 years and over	16 to 19 years	20 years and over						
			Total	20 to 24 years	25 to 34 years	35 to 44 years	45 to 54 years	55 to 64 years	65 years and over
WHITE									
Women									
1954	33.3	40.6	32.7	44.4	32.5	39.3	39.8	29.1	9.1
1955	34.5	40.7	34.0	45.8	32.8	40.0	42.7	31.8	10.5
1956	35.7	43.1	35.1	46.5	33.2	41.5	44.4	34.0	10.6
1957	35.7	42.2	35.2	45.8	33.6	41.5	45.4	33.7	10.2
1958	35.8	40.1	35.5	46.0	33.6	41.4	46.5	34.5	10.1
1959	36.0	39.6	35.6	44.5	33.4	41.4	47.8	35.7	10.0
1960	36.5	40.3	36.2	45.7	34.1	41.5	48.6	36.2	10.6
1961	36.9	40.6	36.6	46.9	34.3	41.8	48.9	37.2	10.5
1962	36.7	39.8	36.5	47.1	34.1	42.2	48.9	38.0	9.8
1963	37.2	38.7	37.0	47.3	34.8	43.1	49.5	38.9	9.4
1964	37.5	37.8	37.5	48.8	35.0	43.3	50.2	39.4	9.9
1965	38.1	39.2	38.0	49.2	36.3	44.4	49.9	40.3	9.7
1966	39.2	42.6	38.8	51.0	37.7	45.0	50.6	41.1	9.4
1967	40.1	42.5	39.8	53.1	39.7	46.4	50.9	41.9	9.3
1968	40.7	43.0	40.4	54.0	40.6	47.5	51.5	42.0	9.4
1969	41.8	44.6	41.5	56.4	41.7	48.6	53.0	42.6	9.7
1970	42.6	45.6	42.2	57.7	43.2	49.9	53.7	42.6	9.5
1971	42.6	45.4	42.3	58.0	43.7	50.2	53.6	42.5	9.3
1972	43.2	48.1	42.7	59.4	46.0	50.7	53.4	41.9	9.0
1973	44.1	50.1	43.5	61.7	48.7	52.2	53.4	40.7	8.7
1974	45.2	51.7	44.4	63.9	51.3	53.6	54.3	40.4	8.0
1975	45.9	51.5	45.3	65.5	53.8	54.9	54.3	40.6	8.0
1976	46.9	52.8	46.2	66.3	56.0	57.1	54.7	40.7	7.9
1977	48.0	54.5	47.3	67.8	58.5	58.9	55.3	40.7	7.9
1978	49.4	56.7	48.7	69.3	61.2	60.7	56.7	41.1	8.1
1979	50.5	57.4	49.8	70.5	63.1	63.0	58.1	41.5	8.1
1980	51.2	56.2	50.6	70.6	64.8	65.0	59.6	40.9	7.9
1981	51.9	55.4	51.5	71.5	66.4	66.4	60.9	40.9	7.9
1982	52.4	55.0	52.2	71.8	67.8	67.5	61.4	41.5	7.8
1983	52.7	54.5	52.5	72.1	68.7	68.2	61.9	41.1	7.8
1984	53.3	55.4	53.1	72.5	69.8	69.6	62.7	41.2	7.5
1985	54.1	55.2	54.0	73.8	70.9	71.4	64.2	41.5	7.0
1986	55.0	56.3	54.9	74.1	71.8	72.9	65.8	42.1	7.3
1987	55.7	56.5	55.6	74.8	72.5	74.2	67.2	42.4	7.2
1988	56.4	57.2	56.3	74.9	73.0	74.9	69.2	43.6	7.7
1989	57.2	57.1	57.2	74.0	73.8	75.9	70.6	45.2	8.2
1990	57.4	55.3	57.6	73.4	74.1	76.6	71.3	45.5	8.5
1991	57.4	54.1	57.6	72.5	73.8	76.8	72.4	45.4	8.5
1992	57.7	52.5	58.1	73.5	74.4	77.0	72.8	46.8	8.2
1993	58.0	53.5	58.3	73.4	74.3	76.9	74.0	47.6	8.1
1994	58.9	55.1	59.2	73.4	74.9	77.5	75.2	49.4	9.2
1995	59.0	55.5	59.2	72.3	75.8	77.6	75.2	49.5	9.0
1996	59.1	54.7	59.4	73.3	75.5	77.8	76.1	50.1	8.7
1997	59.5	54.1	59.9	73.9	76.3	77.9	76.6	51.5	8.6
1998	59.4	55.4	59.7	74.3	76.3	76.9	76.6	51.6	8.7
1999	59.6	54.5	59.9	73.9	76.0	77.1	77.1	52.0	8.9
2000	59.5	54.5	59.9	74.5	75.7	77.2	77.5	52.4	9.4
2001	59.4	52.4	59.9	74.2	75.1	77.0	77.1	53.8	9.6
2002	59.3	50.8	60.0	74.0	75.0	76.3	76.6	55.8	9.9
2003	59.2	47.9	59.9	72.7	73.7	75.5	77.3	57.4	10.8
2004	58.9	46.7	59.7	71.9	73.6	75.2	77.1	57.0	11.2
2005	58.9	47.6	59.7	71.0	73.7	75.4	76.7	57.5	11.4
2006	59.0	46.6	59.9	70.9	74.3	75.5	76.7	58.7	11.6
2007	59.0	44.6	60.1	71.6	74.5	75.0	76.6	58.9	12.7
2008	59.2	43.3	60.3	71.6	74.9	75.8	76.6	59.7	13.3
2009	59.1	40.9	60.4	71.6	75.1	75.7	76.7	60.8	13.6

Table 1-8. Civilian Labor Force Participation Rates, by Age, Sex, Race, and Hispanic Origin, 1948–2009
—Continued

(Percent.)

Race, Hispanic origin, sex, and year	16 years and over	16 to 19 years	20 years and over						
			Total	20 to 24 years	25 to 34 years	35 to 44 years	45 to 54 years	55 to 64 years	65 years and over
BLACK									
Both Sexes									
1972	59.9	39.1	63.3	68.6	74.9	74.4	70.0	56.9	17.5
1973	60.2	39.8	63.4	69.7	75.7	74.5	70.3	55.9	16.0
1974	59.8	39.8	63.0	69.8	75.8	74.6	69.1	54.7	15.1
1975	58.8	38.2	62.0	66.1	75.6	74.1	69.0	54.3	14.9
1976	59.0	37.0	62.5	66.8	77.4	74.9	68.6	53.4	14.9
1977	59.8	37.9	63.2	68.2	78.3	75.9	69.0	53.7	14.5
1978	61.5	41.0	64.5	69.9	79.6	77.4	70.4	54.8	15.3
1979	61.4	40.1	64.5	70.0	79.2	77.9	71.1	53.5	14.5
1980	61.0	38.9	64.1	69.0	79.5	77.4	71.4	52.6	13.0
1981	60.8	37.7	64.2	69.2	78.5	78.4	71.2	52.8	12.0
1982	61.0	36.6	64.3	68.6	78.7	79.8	71.1	52.3	11.5
1983	61.5	36.4	64.9	68.4	79.8	80.2	72.1	52.5	10.5
1984	62.2	38.3	65.2	69.2	79.3	81.0	73.0	51.6	10.3
1985	62.9	41.2	65.6	70.0	79.8	81.5	73.4	51.4	11.2
1986	63.3	41.3	65.9	71.7	80.1	81.9	74.3	50.6	9.7
1987	63.8	41.6	66.5	70.5	80.7	82.6	74.7	52.4	10.7
1988	63.8	40.8	66.5	70.5	80.8	82.6	75.0	50.6	11.5
1989	64.2	42.5	66.7	72.2	80.9	82.7	75.5	48.3	11.6
1990	64.0	38.7	66.9	68.8	79.7	82.4	76.5	49.6	11.1
1991	63.3	35.4	66.4	67.7	78.5	82.0	76.2	50.4	10.7
1992	63.9	37.9	66.8	67.4	79.7	81.4	76.2	51.6	10.6
1993	63.2	37.0	66.0	67.8	78.3	81.0	75.2	50.2	9.5
1994	63.4	38.5	66.0	68.8	78.3	80.8	74.8	49.3	10.6
1995	63.7	39.9	66.3	68.7	80.0	80.4	74.1	50.3	10.5
1996	64.1	39.2	66.9	69.0	81.1	81.0	74.9	50.9	9.8
1997	64.7	38.7	67.6	70.9	82.0	81.4	76.3	50.5	10.0
1998	65.6	41.6	68.2	70.6	83.0	82.2	76.7	52.3	10.3
1999	65.8	38.7	68.9	71.4	85.2	83.0	76.4	51.4	10.4
2000	65.8	39.4	68.7	71.8	84.1	82.3	76.9	52.5	11.6
2001	65.3	37.6	68.2	69.9	83.6	82.0	75.9	53.9	12.6
2002	64.8	36.0	67.8	68.6	82.4	81.6	76.1	54.7	12.5
2003	64.3	32.4	67.6	68.2	81.6	82.9	75.8	54.4	12.9
2004	63.8	31.4	67.2	68.3	81.2	82.1	75.5	54.4	13.1
2005	64.2	32.4	67.4	69.0	81.7	82.3	75.7	55.3	13.6
2006	64.1	34.0	67.3	68.8	81.8	82.0	75.8	55.4	13.7
2007	63.7	30.3	67.2	68.3	81.7	82.7	75.7	55.1	14.0
2008	63.7	29.4	67.4	68.0	82.2	83.0	76.1	55.6	15.0
2009	62.4	27.2	66.1	66.0	80.4	81.7	75.2	55.5	15.3
BLACK									
Men									
1972	73.6	46.3	78.5	82.7	92.7	91.1	85.4	72.5	24.2
1973	73.4	45.7	78.4	83.7	91.8	91.0	87.4	69.5	22.3
1974	72.9	46.7	77.6	83.6	92.8	90.4	84.0	68.9	21.6
1975	70.9	42.6	76.0	78.7	91.6	89.4	83.5	67.7	20.7
1976	70.0	41.3	75.4	79.0	90.9	89.9	82.4	65.1	19.8
1977	70.6	43.2	75.6	79.2	90.7	91.0	82.0	65.5	20.0
1978	71.5	44.9	76.2	78.8	90.9	90.5	83.2	67.9	21.1
1979	71.3	43.6	76.3	80.7	90.8	90.4	84.5	64.8	19.5
1980	70.3	43.2	75.1	79.9	90.9	89.1	83.0	61.9	16.9
1981	70.0	41.6	74.5	79.2	88.9	89.3	82.7	62.1	16.0
1982	70.1	39.8	74.7	78.7	89.2	89.8	82.2	61.9	15.9
1983	70.6	39.9	75.2	79.4	89.0	89.7	84.5	62.6	14.0
1984	70.8	41.7	74.8	79.1	88.9	90.0	83.7	58.9	13.7
1985	70.8	44.6	74.4	79.0	88.8	89.8	83.0	58.9	13.9
1986	71.2	43.7	74.8	80.1	89.6	89.6	84.1	59.1	12.6
1987	71.1	43.6	74.7	77.8	89.4	88.6	83.7	62.1	13.7
1988	71.0	43.8	74.6	79.3	89.3	88.2	83.5	59.4	14.3
1989	71.0	44.6	74.4	80.2	89.7	88.7	82.5	55.5	14.3
1990	71.0	40.7	75.0	76.8	88.8	88.1	83.5	58.0	13.0
1991	70.4	37.3	74.6	76.7	87.3	87.7	83.4	58.7	13.0
1992	70.7	40.6	74.3	75.4	88.0	86.5	81.8	60.0	13.7
1993	69.6	39.5	73.2	74.1	87.3	86.1	80.0	57.9	11.6
1994	69.1	40.8	72.5	73.9	86.2	85.9	79.1	54.5	12.7
1995	69.0	40.1	72.5	74.6	87.5	84.1	78.5	54.4	14.9
1996	68.7	39.5	72.3	73.4	87.5	84.4	78.5	55.6	12.9
1997	68.3	37.4	72.2	72.1	86.8	84.8	80.1	54.3	12.9
1998	69.0	40.7	72.5	71.8	87.1	85.0	79.9	57.3	14.0
1999	68.7	38.6	72.4	69.8	89.2	86.0	78.5	55.5	12.7
2000	69.2	39.2	72.8	73.3	87.8	85.2	79.2	57.4	14.4
2001	68.4	37.9	72.1	69.7	86.6	84.9	78.4	58.9	16.7
2002	68.4	37.3	72.1	70.7	85.9	84.7	79.5	58.4	16.9
2003	67.3	31.1	71.5	71.1	84.7	85.7	77.7	57.6	17.0
2004	66.7	30.0	70.9	69.9	86.1	84.0	76.9	57.1	17.0
2005	67.3	32.6	71.3	70.1	85.5	85.5	78.6	57.3	17.1
2006	67.0	32.3	71.1	71.6	85.7	84.4	79.2	55.9	16.7
2007	66.8	29.4	71.2	71.1	86.1	86.3	78.6	54.4	17.3
2008	66.7	29.1	71.1	71.1	85.3	86.8	79.1	56.1	18.1
2009	65.0	26.4	69.6	67.6	83.2	85.1	77.4	56.8	18.3

Table 1-8. Civilian Labor Force Participation Rates, by Age, Sex, Race, and Hispanic Origin, 1948–2009
—*Continued*

(Percent.)

Race, Hispanic origin, sex, and year	16 years and over	16 to 19 years	20 years and over						
			Total	20 to 24 years	25 to 34 years	35 to 44 years	45 to 54 years	55 to 64 years	65 years and over
BLACK									
Women									
1972	48.7	32.2	51.2	57.0	60.8	61.4	57.2	44.0	12.6
1973	49.3	34.2	51.6	58.0	62.7	61.7	56.1	44.7	11.4
1974	49.0	33.4	51.4	58.8	62.4	62.2	56.4	42.8	10.4
1975	48.8	34.2	51.1	55.9	62.8	62.0	56.6	43.1	10.7
1976	49.8	32.9	52.5	56.9	66.7	63.0	56.8	43.7	11.3
1977	50.8	32.9	53.6	59.3	68.5	64.1	57.9	43.7	10.5
1978	53.1	37.3	55.5	62.7	70.6	67.2	59.4	43.8	11.1
1979	53.1	36.8	55.4	61.5	70.1	68.0	59.6	44.0	10.9
1980	53.1	34.9	55.6	60.2	70.5	68.1	61.4	44.8	10.2
1981	53.5	34.0	56.0	61.1	70.0	69.8	62.0	45.4	9.3
1982	53.7	33.5	56.2	60.1	70.2	71.7	62.4	44.8	8.5
1983	54.2	33.0	56.8	59.1	72.3	72.6	62.3	44.8	8.2
1984	55.2	35.0	57.6	60.7	71.5	73.7	64.5	46.1	8.0
1985	56.5	37.9	58.6	62.5	72.4	74.8	65.7	45.3	9.4
1986	56.9	39.1	58.9	64.6	72.4	75.8	66.5	43.6	7.8
1987	58.0	39.6	60.0	64.4	73.5	77.8	67.5	44.4	8.6
1988	58.0	37.9	60.1	63.2	73.7	78.1	68.3	43.4	9.6
1989	58.7	40.4	60.6	65.5	73.6	78.0	70.0	42.4	9.8
1990	58.3	36.8	60.6	62.4	72.3	77.7	70.7	43.2	9.9
1991	57.5	33.5	60.0	60.3	71.4	77.2	70.2	44.1	9.2
1992	58.5	35.2	60.8	60.8	73.1	77.1	71.7	45.1	8.6
1993	57.9	34.6	60.2	62.6	70.9	76.8	71.2	44.4	8.3
1994	58.7	36.3	60.9	64.5	71.9	76.4	71.3	45.3	9.2
1995	59.5	39.8	61.4	63.7	73.9	77.3	70.5	47.2	7.7
1996	60.4	38.9	62.6	65.2	75.9	78.2	72.0	47.2	7.7
1997	61.7	39.9	64.0	69.9	78.1	78.4	73.2	47.6	8.2
1998	62.8	42.5	64.8	69.6	79.6	79.9	74.0	48.5	7.9
1999	63.5	38.8	66.1	72.7	82.1	80.4	74.6	48.4	8.9
2000	63.1	39.6	65.4	70.5	81.1	79.9	74.9	48.6	9.9
2001	62.8	37.3	65.2	70.1	81.2	79.6	73.9	49.9	10.1
2002	61.8	34.7	64.4	66.9	79.7	79.2	73.3	51.8	9.8
2003	61.9	33.7	64.6	65.7	79.1	80.6	74.2	51.9	10.3
2004	61.5	32.8	64.2	66.8	77.2	80.6	74.3	52.3	10.7
2005	61.6	32.2	64.4	68.1	78.5	79.7	73.3	53.7	11.4
2006	61.7	35.6	64.2	66.2	78.6	80.1	73.0	55.1	11.8
2007	61.1	31.2	64.0	65.7	78.0	79.8	73.2	55.7	12.0
2008	61.3	29.7	64.3	65.2	79.6	80.0	73.7	55.3	13.0
2009	60.3	27.9	63.4	64.5	78.0	79.0	73.3	54.4	13.3
HISPANIC[1]									
Both Sexes									
1973	60.2	46.9	. . .	. . .	. . .	. . .	. . .	. . .	. . .
1974	61.1	47.7	. . .	. . .	. . .	. . .	. . .	. . .	. . .
1975	60.8	46.2	. . .	. . .	. . .	. . .	. . .	. . .	. . .
1976	60.8	46.9	62.9	. . .	. . .	. . .	. . .	. . .	. . .
1977	61.6	48.2	63.7	. . .	. . .	. . .	. . .	. . .	. . .
1978	62.9	49.6	65.0	. . .	. . .	. . .	. . .	. . .	. . .
1979	63.6	50.3	65.6	. . .	. . .	. . .	. . .	. . .	. . .
1980	64.0	50.3	66.2	. . .	. . .	. . .	. . .	. . .	. . .
1981	64.1	46.4	66.8	. . .	. . .	. . .	. . .	. . .	. . .
1982	63.6	44.8	66.3	. . .	. . .	. . .	. . .	. . .	. . .
1983	63.8	45.3	66.2	. . .	. . .	. . .	. . .	. . .	. . .
1984	64.9	47.5	67.1	. . .	. . .	. . .	. . .	. . .	. . .
1985	64.6	44.6	67.1	. . .	. . .	. . .	. . .	. . .	. . .
1986	65.4	43.9	68.0	. . .	. . .	. . .	. . .	. . .	. . .
1987	66.4	45.8	68.8	. . .	. . .	. . .	. . .	. . .	. . .
1988	67.4	49.6	69.4	. . .	. . .	. . .	. . .	. . .	. . .
1989	67.6	48.6	69.7	. . .	. . .	. . .	. . .	. . .	. . .
1990	67.4	47.8	69.8	. . .	. . .	. . .	. . .	. . .	. . .
1991	66.5	45.1	69.0	. . .	. . .	. . .	. . .	. . .	. . .
1992	66.8	45.8	69.2	. . .	. . .	. . .	. . .	. . .	. . .
1993	66.2	43.9	68.7	. . .	. . .	. . .	. . .	. . .	. . .
1994	66.1	44.4	68.5	74.0	77.3	78.9	73.1	49.8	10.7
1995	65.8	45.4	68.1	71.9	78.1	78.5	72.8	48.6	10.5
1996	66.5	43.4	69.1	73.1	78.2	79.5	74.6	52.2	11.0
1997	67.9	43.0	70.8	76.4	79.5	80.9	75.4	53.8	11.9
1998	67.9	45.7	70.6	76.1	80.3	80.0	75.3	55.4	10.1
1999	67.7	45.5	70.4	76.0	78.6	81.3	75.9	54.1	11.6
2000	69.7	46.3	72.5	78.2	80.4	81.7	78.0	54.2	12.3
2001	69.5	46.9	72.0	76.6	80.0	81.9	77.4	55.1	10.9
2002	69.1	44.0	71.8	76.3	80.5	81.1	76.1	55.8	11.9
2003	68.3	37.7	71.4	75.6	79.4	81.1	75.3	57.4	12.8
2004	68.6	38.2	71.7	74.5	79.4	81.4	77.6	58.1	14.5
2005	68.0	38.6	71.0	72.7	79.1	81.2	77.2	58.4	13.9
2006	68.7	38.3	71.9	74.4	80.1	81.9	77.3	59.2	15.7
2007	68.8	37.1	72.1	74.8	80.7	81.8	78.6	58.5	16.0
2008	68.5	36.9	71.8	73.7	80.5	82.0	78.2	59.9	16.0
2009	68.0	34.0	71.5	73.1	79.5	81.3	79.3	61.9	17.1

[1]May be of any race.
. . . = Not available.

Table 1-8. Civilian Labor Force Participation Rates, by Age, Sex, Race, and Hispanic Origin, 1948–2009
—*Continued*

(Percent.)

Race, Hispanic origin, sex, and year	16 years and over	16 to 19 years	20 years and over						
			Total	20 to 24 years	25 to 34 years	35 to 44 years	45 to 54 years	55 to 64 years	65 years and over
HISPANIC[1]									
Men									
1973	81.5	. . .	85.9	. . .	. . .	. . .	. . .	. . .	. . .
1974	81.7	. . .	86.0	. . .	. . .	. . .	. . .	. . .	. . .
1975	80.7	. . .	85.5	. . .	. . .	. . .	. . .	. . .	. . .
1976	79.6	. . .	84.2	. . .	. . .	. . .	. . .	. . .	. . .
1977	80.9	. . .	84.8	. . .	. . .	. . .	. . .	. . .	. . .
1978	81.1	. . .	84.9	. . .	. . .	. . .	. . .	. . .	. . .
1979	81.3	. . .	85.3	. . .	. . .	. . .	. . .	. . .	. . .
1980	81.4	. . .	84.9	. . .	. . .	. . .	. . .	. . .	. . .
1981	80.6	. . .	84.7	. . .	. . .	. . .	. . .	. . .	. . .
1982	79.7	. . .	84.0	. . .	. . .	. . .	. . .	. . .	. . .
1983	80.3	. . .	84.1	. . .	. . .	. . .	. . .	. . .	. . .
1984	80.6	. . .	84.3	. . .	. . .	. . .	. . .	. . .	. . .
1985	80.3	. . .	84.0	. . .	. . .	. . .	. . .	. . .	. . .
1986	81.0	. . .	84.6	. . .	. . .	. . .	. . .	. . .	. . .
1987	81.0	. . .	84.5	. . .	. . .	. . .	. . .	. . .	. . .
1988	81.9	. . .	85.0	. . .	. . .	. . .	. . .	. . .	. . .
1989	82.0	. . .	85.0	. . .	. . .	. . .	. . .	. . .	. . .
1990	81.4	. . .	84.7	. . .	. . .	. . .	. . .	. . .	. . .
1991	80.3	. . .	83.8	. . .	. . .	. . .	. . .	. . .	. . .
1992	80.7	. . .	84.0	. . .	. . .	. . .	. . .	. . .	. . .
1993	80.2	. . .	83.5	. . .	. . .	. . .	. . .	. . .	. . .
1994	79.2	50.0	82.5	88.0	92.5	91.5	85.7	63.6	14.4
1995	79.1	50.2	82.4	86.2	92.9	91.3	85.6	62.4	15.8
1996	79.6	50.0	83.0	85.7	93.2	91.7	87.0	65.9	16.7
1997	80.1	47.4	84.1	88.1	93.5	91.9	87.8	68.4	17.3
1998	79.8	48.7	83.6	88.1	94.0	91.4	86.7	70.2	14.9
1999	79.8	50.1	83.5	88.1	93.9	92.2	86.2	68.6	18.2
2000	81.5	50.7	85.3	89.1	94.1	93.3	87.6	69.4	18.5
2001	81.0	52.2	84.3	86.8	93.4	92.7	86.7	68.6	16.8
2002	80.2	48.8	83.6	86.1	93.5	92.1	86.1	67.3	16.3
2003	80.1	40.9	84.1	86.2	93.6	92.9	85.4	68.8	17.4
2004	80.4	42.4	84.2	84.4	93.6	93.2	87.2	69.6	20.8
2005	80.1	41.9	84.0	84.1	93.3	93.1	87.7	69.3	20.1
2006	80.7	42.0	84.6	85.9	94.1	93.8	87.1	69.6	22.9
2007	80.5	40.0	84.7	85.3	94.1	93.9	88.3	70.3	22.0
2008	80.2	40.3	84.4	84.3	94.0	93.7	88.6	71.7	21.7
2009	78.8	36.4	83.2	82.3	91.9	93.0	88.8	71.7	23.0
HISPANIC[1]									
Women									
1973	41.0	. . .	41.3	. . .	. . .	. . .	. . .	. . .	. . .
1974	42.4	. . .	42.7	. . .	. . .	. . .	. . .	. . .	. . .
1975	43.2	. . .	43.8	. . .	. . .	. . .	. . .	. . .	. . .
1976	44.3	. . .	44.6	. . .	. . .	. . .	. . .	. . .	. . .
1977	44.3	. . .	45.1	. . .	. . .	. . .	. . .	. . .	. . .
1978	46.6	. . .	47.2	. . .	. . .	. . .	. . .	. . .	. . .
1979	47.4	. . .	48.0	. . .	. . .	. . .	. . .	. . .	. . .
1980	47.4	. . .	48.5	. . .	. . .	. . .	. . .	. . .	. . .
1981	48.3	. . .	49.7	. . .	. . .	. . .	. . .	. . .	. . .
1982	48.1	. . .	49.3	. . .	. . .	. . .	. . .	. . .	. . .
1983	47.7	. . .	49.0	. . .	. . .	. . .	. . .	. . .	. . .
1984	49.6	. . .	50.5	. . .	. . .	. . .	. . .	. . .	. . .
1985	49.3	. . .	50.6	. . .	. . .	. . .	. . .	. . .	. . .
1986	50.1	. . .	51.7	. . .	. . .	. . .	. . .	. . .	. . .
1987	52.0	. . .	53.3	. . .	. . .	. . .	. . .	. . .	. . .
1988	53.2	. . .	54.2	. . .	. . .	. . .	. . .	. . .	. . .
1989	53.5	. . .	54.9	. . .	. . .	. . .	. . .	. . .	. . .
1990	53.1	. . .	54.8	. . .	. . .	. . .	. . .	. . .	. . .
1991	52.4	. . .	54.0	. . .	. . .	. . .	. . .	. . .	. . .
1992	52.8	. . .	54.3	. . .	. . .	. . .	. . .	. . .	. . .
1993	52.1	. . .	53.8	. . .	. . .	. . .	. . .	. . .	. . .
1994	52.9	38.7	54.4	57.9	60.5	66.4	61.4	38.1	7.9
1995	52.6	40.4	53.9	55.9	61.6	65.9	60.5	37.2	6.6
1996	53.4	36.5	55.2	59.2	62.0	67.0	62.7	40.5	6.9
1997	55.1	38.0	57.0	62.3	63.7	69.3	63.3	40.6	8.1
1998	55.6	42.4	57.1	62.2	64.5	67.9	64.7	41.9	6.6
1999	55.9	40.6	57.7	63.0	62.7	70.5	66.2	42.4	6.5
2000	57.5	41.4	59.3	65.0	65.3	69.9	68.5	41.2	7.7
2001	57.6	41.1	59.3	64.6	65.2	70.3	68.3	43.2	6.7
2002	57.6	38.8	59.5	65.0	65.8	69.5	66.3	46.1	8.5
2003	55.9	34.5	58.1	63.3	62.9	68.5	65.3	47.1	9.4
2004	56.1	33.7	58.4	62.9	62.9	68.7	67.9	47.8	9.8
2005	55.3	35.2	57.4	59.4	62.4	68.2	66.6	48.4	9.3
2006	56.1	34.4	58.3	61.3	63.5	68.7	67.4	49.7	10.4
2007	56.5	34.0	58.8	62.9	64.6	68.4	68.7	47.6	11.4
2008	56.2	33.3	58.6	62.1	64.3	69.1	67.6	48.9	11.7
2009	56.5	31.6	59.2	63.2	64.7	68.2	69.4	52.6	12.7

[1]May be of any race.
. . . = Not available.

Table 1-9. Employed and Unemployed Full- and Part-Time Workers, by Age, Sex, and Race, 1999–2009

(Thousands of people.)

Race, sex, age, and year	Employed[1]								Unemployed	
	Full-time workers				Part-time workers				Looking for full-time work	Looking for part-time work
	Total	At work		Not at work	Total	At work[2]		Not at work		
		35 hours or more	1 to 34 hours for economic or noneconomic reasons			For economic reasons	For noneconomic reasons			
ALL RACES										
Both Sexes, 16 Years and Over										
1999	110 302	96 276	10 079	3 947	23 186	2 216	19 509	1 461	4 669	1 211
2000	113 846	100 533	9 125	4 188	23 044	2 003	19 548	1 493	4 538	1 154
2001	113 573	99 047	10 464	4 061	23 361	2 297	19 494	1 570	5 546	1 254
2002	112 700	99 042	9 746	3 912	23 785	2 755	19 549	1 481	7 063	1 314
2003	113 324	99 539	9 841	3 944	24 412	3 184	19 702	1 525	7 361	1 413
2004	114 518	100 496	10 053	3 969	24 734	3 113	20 109	1 513	6 762	1 388
2005	117 016	103 044	9 983	3 990	24 714	2 963	20 229	1 522	6 175	1 415
2006	119 688	105 328	10 223	4 137	24 739	2 774	20 356	1 609	5 675	1 326
2007	121 091	106 990	9 976	4 125	24 956	2 851	20 511	1 594	5 789	1 289
2008	120 030	105 575	10 426	4 030	25 332	3 814	20 009	1 509	7 446	1 478
2009	112 634	95 911	12 853	3 870	27 244	6 353	19 327	1 563	12 523	1 741
Both Sexes, 20 Years and Over										
1999	107 917	94 270	9 754	3 893	18 399	1 939	15 187	1 273	4 094	624
2000	111 353	98 439	8 787	4 127	18 348	1 747	15 297	1 304	3 978	632
2001	111 323	97 161	10 156	4 006	18 870	2 013	15 486	1 371	4 956	682
2002	110 679	97 342	9 474	3 862	19 475	2 448	15 704	1 322	6 395	730
2003	111 578	98 087	9 587	3 904	20 239	2 875	16 001	1 363	6 705	818
2004	112 747	99 034	9 789	3 924	20 598	2 817	16 436	1 345	6 178	764
2005	115 206	101 534	9 729	3 942	20 546	2 698	16 489	1 359	5 619	786
2006	117 844	103 779	9 974	4 090	20 421	2 510	16 478	1 433	5 117	765
2007	119 317	105 499	9 738	4 080	20 819	2 587	16 819	1 413	5 234	742
2008	118 404	104 212	10 204	3 989	21 385	3 492	16 543	1 350	6 790	849
2009	111 414	94 928	12 647	3 839	23 626	5 934	16 286	1 406	11 651	1 061
Men, 16 Years and Over										
1999	63 930	57 034	4 971	1 924	7 516	946	6 178	392	2 548	518
2000	65 930	59 345	4 555	2 030	7 375	856	6 105	414	2 486	488
2001	65 623	58 386	5 241	1 996	7 573	1 021	6 129	424	3 144	546
2002	65 205	58 318	4 971	1 916	7 697	1 246	6 050	401	4 029	568
2003	65 379	58 428	5 023	1 927	7 953	1 473	6 056	423	4 291	615
2004	66 444	59 363	5 148	1 933	8 080	1 405	6 258	417	3 843	613
2005	67 858	60 825	5 096	1 937	8 115	1 316	6 370	429	3 444	616
2006	69 307	62 087	5 237	1 984	8 194	1 232	6 510	452	3 192	561
2007	70 035	62 965	5 095	1 975	8 220	1 319	6 424	477	3 326	556
2008	68 853	61 436	5 443	1 974	8 634	1 842	6 349	442	4 396	637
2009	63 951	55 317	6 772	1 862	9 719	3 035	6 170	514	7 696	757
Men, 20 Years and Over										
1999	62 514	55 827	4 790	1 897	5 247	809	4 127	311	2 222	211
2000	64 464	58 095	4 370	2 000	5 170	733	4 109	328	2 162	214
2001	64 311	57 273	5 072	1 966	5 465	881	4 253	331	2 801	239
2002	64 006	57 302	4 815	1 889	5 728	1 093	4 299	336	3 642	254
2003	64 364	57 580	4 879	1 905	6 051	1 314	4 388	348	3 906	302
2004	65 377	58 471	5 000	1 906	6 196	1 251	4 600	345	3 511	281
2005	66 803	59 934	4 955	1 914	6 247	1 182	4 705	360	3 118	274
2006	68 193	61 140	5 095	1 958	6 238	1 100	4 762	376	2 861	270
2007	68 968	62 057	4 959	1 952	6 369	1 190	4 782	397	2 990	268
2008	67 895	60 625	5 315	1 955	6 855	1 675	4 802	378	3 994	303
2009	63 242	54 738	6 659	1 845	8 099	2 827	4 828	445	7 151	404
Women, 16 Years and Over										
1999	46 372	39 242	5 108	2 022	15 670	1 270	13 330	1 069	2 121	693
2000	47 916	41 188	4 570	2 158	15 670	1 147	13 443	1 080	2 052	666
2001	47 950	40 661	5 223	2 065	15 788	1 276	13 365	1 146	2 402	709
2002	47 494	40 723	4 775	1 996	16 088	1 509	13 498	1 080	3 034	747
2003	47 946	41 111	4 818	2 017	16 459	1 711	13 646	1 102	3 070	798
2004	48 073	41 133	4 905	2 036	16 654	1 708	13 851	1 096	2 919	775
2005	49 158	42 219	4 887	2 052	16 598	1 647	13 859	1 092	2 732	799
2006	50 380	43 241	4 986	2 153	16 545	1 542	13 846	1 157	2 483	764
2007	51 056	44 025	4 881	2 150	16 736	1 532	14 087	1 117	2 463	732
2008	51 178	44 139	4 983	2 056	16 698	1 972	13 660	1 067	3 050	841
2009	48 683	40 594	6 080	2 009	17 525	3 318	13 157	1 050	4 827	984

Note: Beginning in January 2004, data reflect revised population controls used in the household survey. See notes and definitions for information on historical comparability.

[1] Employed persons are classified as full- or part-time workers based on their usual weekly hours at all jobs, regardless of the number of hours they were at work during the reference week. Persons absent from work are also classified according to their usual status.
[2] Includes some persons at work 35 hours or more classified by their reason for working part time.

Table 1-9. Employed and Unemployed Full- and Part-Time Workers, by Age, Sex, and Race, 1999–2009 —Continued

(Thousands of people.)

Race, sex, age, and year	Employed[1]								Unemployed	
	Full-time workers				Part-time workers					
		At work				At work[2]				
	Total	35 hours or more	1 to 34 hours for economic or noneconomic reasons	Not at work	Total	For economic reasons	For noneconomic reasons	Not at work	Looking for full-time work	Looking for part-time work
ALL RACES										
Women, 20 Years and Over										
1999	45 403	38 443	4 964	1 996	13 152	1 131	11 059	962	1 872	413
2000	46 889	40 344	4 417	2 128	13 178	1 013	11 188	976	1 816	419
2001	47 012	39 889	5 083	2 040	13 405	1 132	11 233	1 040	2 155	444
2002	46 673	40 040	4 660	1 973	13 747	1 355	11 406	986	2 752	476
2003	47 215	40 507	4 708	2 000	14 188	1 560	11 613	1 015	2 799	515
2004	47 371	40 563	4 790	2 017	14 402	1 567	11 836	1 000	2 667	483
2005	48 403	41 600	4 774	2 028	14 299	1 516	11 784	999	2 501	512
2006	49 651	42 639	4 880	2 132	14 183	1 410	11 716	1 057	2 256	495
2007	50 349	43 442	4 779	2 128	14 450	1 397	12 037	1 016	2 244	474
2008	50 509	43 587	4 888	2 034	14 530	1 817	11 740	973	2 796	546
2009	48 171	40 190	5 988	1 994	15 527	3 107	11 459	961	4 500	657
WHITE[3]										
Men, 16 Years and Over										
1999	54 756	48 834	4 274	1 647	6 383	730	5 314	339	1 883	391
2000	56 068	50 434	3 896	1 738	6 221	656	5 213	351	1 798	379
2001	55 830	49 625	4 504	1 701	6 381	793	5 225	364	2 323	431
2002	55 369	49 459	4 267	1 644	6 480	980	5 150	350	3 017	443
2003	55 216	49 323	4 266	1 628	6 650	1 146	5 148	357	3 164	479
2004	55 926	49 891	4 396	1 638	6 786	1 092	5 331	363	2 805	477
2005	56 955	50 965	4 334	1 656	6 808	1 014	5 424	370	2 459	471
2006	58 063	51 894	4 484	1 685	6 820	947	5 481	393	2 299	432
2007	58 494	52 460	4 359	1 676	6 795	1 022	5 368	406	2 444	425
2008	57 432	51 104	4 653	1 675	7 192	1 433	5 379	379	3 235	492
2009	53 506	46 153	5 770	1 583	8 124	2 438	5 240	446	5 819	602
Men, 20 Years and Over										
1999	53 513	47 764	4 124	1 626	4 420	618	3 534	268	1 651	162
2000	54 778	49 335	3 733	1 710	4 341	558	3 505	278	1 566	165
2001	54 666	48 636	4 354	1 676	4 579	677	3 616	285	2 080	195
2002	54 333	48 581	4 133	1 619	4 790	857	3 640	293	2 743	200
2003	54 339	48 585	4 145	1 609	5 010	1 016	3 703	291	2 893	231
2004	55 005	49 124	4 267	1 614	5 154	961	3 895	299	2 567	217
2005	56 050	50 203	4 213	1 634	5 205	905	3 990	310	2 242	209
2006	57 108	51 081	4 365	1 662	5 150	840	3 987	324	2 074	208
2007	57 591	51 691	4 243	1 656	5 216	915	3 967	334	2 204	204
2008	56 623	50 421	4 542	1 660	5 681	1 302	4 055	324	2 944	235
2009	52 899	45 654	5 676	1 569	6 728	2 269	4 075	384	5 421	325
Women, 16 Years and Over										
1999	37 417	31 577	4 157	1 684	13 679	947	11 768	964	1 469	530
2000	38 438	32 942	3 729	1 767	13 698	867	11 870	961	1 422	521
2001	38 445	32 491	4 252	1 702	13 773	971	11 787	1 015	1 664	551
2002	38 152	32 623	3 896	1 633	14 011	1 152	11 903	956	2 084	595
2003	38 249	32 659	3 939	1 652	14 120	1 304	11 860	956	2 038	629
2004	38 240	32 555	4 018	1 667	14 287	1 280	12 038	969	1 968	597
2005	38 973	33 325	3 976	1 672	14 213	1 207	12 043	963	1 807	612
2006	39 813	33 980	4 082	1 751	14 137	1 157	11 967	1 013	1 670	601
2007	40 238	34 486	4 014	1 738	14 265	1 143	12 148	973	1 694	579
2008	40 292	34 569	4 076	1 647	14 209	1 518	11 761	931	2 119	664
2009	38 456	31 885	4 946	1 626	14 910	2 579	11 418	913	3 442	785
Women, 20 Years and Over										
1999	36 602	30 905	4 036	1 662	11 496	839	9 789	867	1 297	319
2000	37 585	32 242	3 600	1 743	11 560	754	9 935	872	1 256	339
2001	37 658	31 839	4 139	1 680	11 711	853	9 933	924	1 492	357
2002	37 467	32 049	3 803	1 615	11 981	1 029	10 079	873	1 888	381
2003	37 640	32 158	3 845	1 637	12 183	1 180	10 124	879	1 866	411
2004	37 663	32 085	3 927	1 652	12 377	1 166	10 326	885	1 795	377
2005	38 354	32 820	3 882	1 652	12 235	1 108	10 248	879	1 653	401
2006	39 232	33 500	3 998	1 733	12 128	1 050	10 151	927	1 524	402
2007	39 670	34 015	3 932	1 722	12 326	1 037	10 402	887	1 547	383
2008	39 765	34 128	4 005	1 632	12 359	1 392	10 116	851	1 949	435
2009	38 033	31 547	4 872	1 614	13 198	2 411	9 952	835	3 216	529

Note: Beginning in January 2004, data reflect revised population controls used in the household survey. See notes and definitions for information on historical comparability.

[1]Employed persons are classified as full- or part-time workers based on their usual weekly hours at all jobs, regardless of the number of hours they were at work during the reference week. Persons absent from work are also classified according to their usual status.
[2]Includes some persons at work 35 hours or more classified by their reason for working part time.
[3]Beginning in 2003, persons who selected this race group only; persons who selected more than one race group are not included. Prior to 2003, persons who reported more than one race group were included in the group they identified as their main race.

Table 1-9. Employed and Unemployed Full- and Part-Time Workers, by Age, Sex, and Race, 1999–2009
—Continued

(Thousands of people.)

Race, sex, age, and year	Employed[1]								Unemployed	
	Full-time workers				Part-time workers					
		At work				At work[2]				
	Total	35 hours or more	1 to 34 hours for economic or noneconomic reasons	Not at work	Total	For economic reasons	For noneconomic reasons	Not at work	Looking for full-time work	Looking for part-time work
BLACK[3]										
Men, 16 Years and Over										
1999	6 263	5 574	494	196	764	163	568	33	528	97
2000	6 350	5 704	445	202	732	144	548	41	542	78
2001	6 178	5 509	468	200	761	165	557	39	626	83
2002	6 194	5 541	480	173	765	188	546	30	749	86
2003	6 055	5 414	453	188	765	221	505	39	804	87
2004	6 177	5 538	460	179	736	205	499	32	763	98
2005	6 381	5 745	463	174	773	207	533	33	742	102
2006	6 529	5 907	446	176	825	201	590	34	681	93
2007	6 673	6 068	429	176	826	195	589	42	660	92
2008	6 548	5 935	440	173	850	276	542	32	849	100
2009	5 871	5 166	556	150	946	379	530	36	1 348	100
Men, 20 Years and Over										
1999	6 140	5 477	471	192	561	142	392	27	446	35
2000	6 222	5 594	429	199	520	125	363	32	468	31
2001	6 069	5 417	455	197	558	145	382	31	542	31
2002	6 073	5 437	465	171	579	166	387	26	660	35
2003	5 980	5 355	439	185	607	201	372	34	717	43
2004	6 089	5 463	449	177	592	189	376	27	689	44
2005	6 287	5 662	452	174	614	189	397	28	655	44
2006	6 424	5 816	433	175	655	185	441	30	596	44
2007	6 574	5 983	417	174	671	181	452	37	580	43
2008	6 461	5 860	430	171	690	252	409	29	764	46
2009	5 811	5 119	544	148	817	355	428	34	1 238	49
Women, 16 Years and Over										
1999	6 641	5 651	734	256	1 388	257	1 059	72	554	130
2000	6 780	5 862	632	287	1 293	211	1 005	77	515	106
2001	6 761	5 777	715	270	1 307	223	998	85	584	122
2002	6 588	5 685	640	263	1 326	259	991	76	744	114
2003	6 552	5 709	595	247	1 367	274	1 017	76	774	121
2004	6 597	5 740	611	246	1 399	306	1 022	71	744	124
2005	6 750	5 871	619	260	1 407	320	1 018	70	723	133
2006	7 001	6 131	605	265	1 410	274	1 054	82	655	120
2007	7 119	6 272	584	263	1 432	273	1 085	75	589	104
2008	7 105	6 238	596	272	1 449	302	1 070	77	717	122
2009	6 666	5 696	718	252	1 542	480	984	78	1 027	132
Women, 20 Years and Over										
1999	6 519	5 549	717	252	1 145	230	850	65	486	75
2000	6 651	5 753	615	283	1 052	197	788	67	456	56
2001	6 647	5 684	695	268	1 094	203	816	75	521	61
2002	6 492	5 605	626	261	1 117	234	816	68	671	67
2003	6 468	5 639	583	246	1 168	257	842	69	698	75
2004	6 512	5 674	595	243	1 195	287	844	64	679	76
2005	6 653	5 789	606	258	1 222	298	861	63	660	74
2006	6 893	6 042	588	263	1 175	255	848	72	588	67
2007	7 024	6 194	570	260	1 216	254	897	65	527	61
2008	7 006	6 160	580	267	1 254	283	902	68	654	78
2009	6 600	5 644	705	250	1 356	449	837	71	951	82

Note: Beginning in January 2004, data reflect revised population controls used in the household survey. See notes and definitions for information on historical comparability.

[1]Employed persons are classified as full- or part-time workers based on their usual weekly hours at all jobs, regardless of the number of hours they were at work during the reference week. Persons absent from work are also classified according to their usual status.
[2]Includes some persons at work 35 hours or more classified by their reason for working part time.
[3]Beginning in 2003, persons who selected this race group only; persons who selected more than one race group are not included. Prior to 2003, persons who reported more than one race group were included in the group they identified as their main race.

Table 1-10. Persons Not in the Labor Force, by Age, Sex, and Desire and Availability for Work, 2004–2009

(Thousands of people.)

Category	Total		16 to 24 years		25 to 54 years		55 years and over		Men		Women	
	2004	2005	2004	2005	2004	2005	2004	2005	2004	2005	2004	2005
TOTAL, NOT IN THE LABOR FORCE	75 956	76 762	14 151	14 383	21 288	21 403	40 517	40 976	28 730	29 119	47 225	47 643
Do Not Want a Job Now[1]	71 103	71 777	12 422	12 585	19 136	19 238	39 545	39 954	26 565	26 926	44 538	44 851
Want a Job[1]	4 852	4 985	1 729	1 798	2 152	2 165	971	1 022	2 165	2 193	2 687	2 792
Did not search for work in the previous year	2 715	2 841	886	963	1 145	1 163	684	715	1 126	1 173	1 590	1 668
Searched for work in the previous year[2]	2 137	2 144	843	836	1 006	1 002	288	307	1 040	1 020	1 097	1 124
Not available to work now	563	599	279	285	242	260	42	54	230	231	333	368
Available to work now	1 574	1 545	565	551	764	742	245	252	809	789	765	756
Reason not currently looking:												
Discouragement over job prospects[3]	466	436	142	141	240	217	84	78	288	260	178	176
Reasons other than discouragement	1 108	1 109	423	410	524	525	161	175	521	529	587	580
Family responsibilities	157	159	28	32	104	105	24	22	38	36	119	123
In school or training	244	217	199	179	43	35	2	2	131	118	112	99
Ill health or disability	123	119	18	16	71	69	35	34	56	64	67	55
Other[4]	584	614	178	182	306	316	100	116	296	311	2	302

Category	Total		16 to 24 years		25 to 54 years		55 years and over		Men		Women	
	2006	2007	2006	2007	2006	2007	2006	2007	2006	2007	2006	2007
TOTAL, NOT IN THE LABOR FORCE	77 387	78 743	14 549	15 192	21 318	21 343	41 520	42 207	30 036	30 036	48 037	48 707
Do Not Want a Job Now[1]	72 602	74 040	12 867	13 510	19 221	19 256	40 514	41 275	27 914	27 914	45 354	46 126
Want a Job[1]	4 786	4 703	1 682	1 683	2 097	2 088	1 006	933	2 122	2 122	2 684	2 581
Did not search for work in the previous year	2 758	2 748	883	931	1 155	1 148	720	668	1 173	1 173	1 612	1 575
Searched for work in the previous year[2]	2 028	1 955	800	751	942	939	286	264	950	950	1 071	1 005
Not available to work now	580	560	282	272	252	234	46	53	223	223	354	336
Available to work now	1 448	1 395	518	479	690	705	240	211	726	726	717	669
Reason not currently looking:												
Discouragement over job prospects[3]	381	369	118	110	195	199	68	61	226	226	152	143
Reasons other than discouragement	1 067	1 026	399	370	495	506	172	150	500	500	565	526
Family responsibilities	152	160	31	31	97	109	24	21	37	37	117	123
In school or training	207	180	177	149	28	27	2	3	102	102	96	78
Ill health or disability	130	114	18	11	76	66	36	37	57	57	68	58
Other[4]	578	572	174	178	294	304	110	90	305	305	285	267

Category	Total		16 to 24 years		25 to 54 years		55 years and over		Men		Women	
	2008	2009	2008	2009	2008	2009	2008	2009	2008	2009	2008	2009
TOTAL, NOT IN THE LABOR FORCE	79 501	81 659	15 452	16 207	21 255	21 823	42 794	43 629	30 593	32 013	48 908	49 646
Do Not Want a Job Now[1]	74 519	75 765	13 719	14 263	19 087	19 199	41 712	42 303	28 365	29 234	46 154	46 531
Want a Job[1]	4 983	5 894	1 733	1 944	2 168	2 624	1 082	1 325	2 228	2 779	2 755	3 115
Did not search for work in the previous year	2 826	3 075	913	960	1 145	1 241	768	874	1 187	1 344	1 639	1 731
Searched for work in the previous year[2]	2 157	2 818	819	983	1 023	1 383	314	452	1 041	1 435	1 115	1 384
Not available to work now	543	592	252	275	244	256	48	61	214	251	329	341
Available to work now	1 614	2 226	568	708	780	1 127	266	391	827	1 184	787	1 043
Reason not currently looking:												
Discouragement over job prospects[3]	462	778	145	200	226	427	90	151	282	485	180	293
Reasons other than discouragement	1 152	1 449	422	509	554	699	176	240	545	699	607	749
Family responsibilities	171	209	35	38	111	131	25	41	45	50	126	159
In school or training	218	306	173	234	42	65	3	7	108	163	109	144
Ill health or disability	124	136	16	19	68	68	40	49	55	70	69	66
Other[4]	640	798	199	219	332	435	108	144	337	417	303	381

[1]Includes some persons who were not asked if they wanted a job.
[2]Persons who had a job during the prior 12 months must have searched since the end of that job.
[3]Includes believes no work available, could not find work, lacks necessary schooling or training, employer thinks too young or old, and other types of discrimination.
[4]Includes those who did not actively look for work in the prior four weeks for reasons such as childcare and transportation problems, as well as a small number for whom reason for nonparticipation was not ascertained.

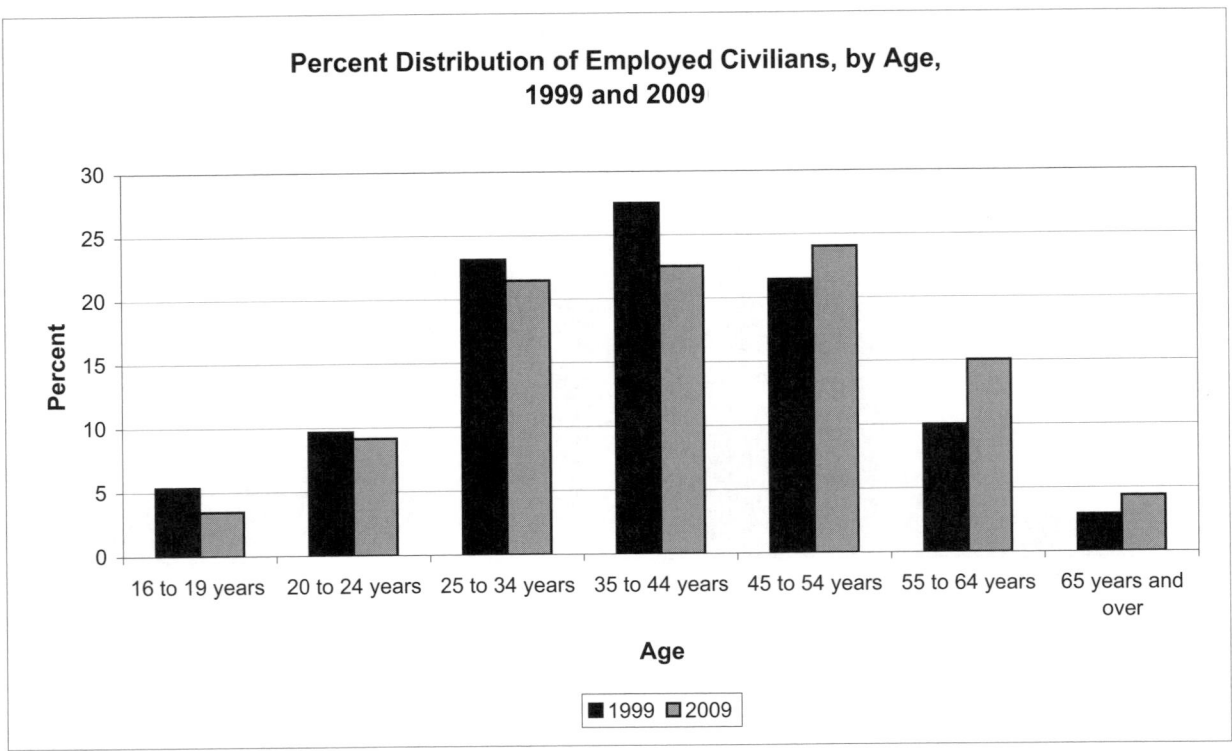

Percent Distribution of Employed Civilians, by Age, 1999 and 2009

The change in the distribution of employed civilians by age reflects, in part, the aging of the baby-boom population. From 1999 to 2009, the proportion of employed persons age 45 years and over increased significantly, while the proportion of employed persons age 16 to 44 years declined. In 1999, workers 45 years of age and over only made up 34.3 percent of employed civilians, however in 2009, they compiled 43.4 percent of employed civilians. (See Table 1-11.)

OTHER HIGHLIGHTS

- The percent of employed civilians that are women has gradually increased the past few years. Women made up 46.4 percent of employed civilians in 2007 and 46.7 percent in 2008. In 2009, 47.3 percent of employed civilians were women. The number of women significantly outnumbered men in the following occupations: healthcare support, personal care and services, office and administrative, and education, training, and library. (See Table 1-13.)

- Employment declined for every level of educational attainment in 2009 for persons 25 years of age and over. Those with less than a high school diploma experienced the greatest decline at 6.3 percent followed by those with some college but no degree (4.9 percent). People with an Associate's degree experienced the smallest decline at 0.6 percent. (See Table 1-16.)

- In May 1970, only 15.7 percent of multiple jobholders were women. By May 2010, 51.0 percent were women. (See Table 1-17.)

Table 1-11. Employed Civilians, by Age, Sex, Race, and Hispanic Origin, 1948–2009

(Thousands of people.)

Race, Hispanic origin, sex, and year	16 years and over	16 to 19 years			20 years and over						
		Total	16 to 17 years	18 to 19 years	Total	20 to 24 years	25 to 34 years	35 to 44 years	45 to 54 years	55 to 64 years	65 years and over
ALL RACES											
Both Sexes											
1948	58 343	4 026	1 600	2 426	54 318	6 937	13 801	13 050	10 624	7 103	2 804
1949	57 651	3 712	1 466	2 246	53 940	6 660	13 639	13 108	10 636	7 042	2 864
1950	58 918	3 703	1 433	2 270	55 218	6 746	13 917	13 424	10 966	7 265	2 899
1951	59 961	3 767	1 575	2 192	56 196	6 321	14 233	13 746	11 421	7 558	2 917
1952	60 250	3 719	1 626	2 092	56 536	5 572	14 515	14 058	11 687	7 785	2 919
1953	61 179	3 720	1 577	2 142	57 460	5 225	14 519	14 774	11 969	7 806	3 166
1954	60 109	3 475	1 422	2 053	56 634	4 971	14 190	14 541	11 976	7 895	3 060
1955	62 170	3 642	1 500	2 143	58 528	5 270	14 481	14 879	12 556	8 158	3 185
1956	63 799	3 818	1 647	2 171	59 983	5 545	14 407	15 218	12 978	8 519	3 314
1957	64 071	3 778	1 613	2 167	60 291	5 641	14 253	15 348	13 320	8 553	3 179
1958	63 036	3 582	1 519	2 063	59 454	5 571	13 675	15 157	13 448	8 559	3 045
1959	64 630	3 838	1 670	2 168	60 791	5 870	13 709	15 454	13 915	8 822	3 023
1960	65 778	4 129	1 770	2 360	61 648	6 119	13 630	15 598	14 238	8 989	3 073
1961	65 746	4 108	1 621	2 486	61 638	6 227	13 429	15 552	14 320	9 120	2 987
1962	66 702	4 195	1 607	2 588	62 508	6 446	13 311	15 901	14 491	9 346	3 013
1963	67 762	4 255	1 751	2 504	63 508	6 815	13 318	16 114	14 749	9 596	2 915
1964	69 305	4 516	2 013	2 503	64 789	7 303	13 449	16 166	15 094	9 804	2 973
1965	71 088	5 036	2 075	2 962	66 052	7 702	13 704	16 294	15 320	10 028	3 005
1966	72 895	5 721	2 269	3 452	67 178	7 964	14 017	16 312	15 615	10 310	2 961
1967	74 372	5 682	2 334	3 348	68 690	8 499	14 575	16 281	15 789	10 536	3 011
1968	75 920	5 781	2 403	3 377	70 141	8 762	15 265	16 220	16 083	10 745	3 065
1969	77 902	6 117	2 573	3 543	71 785	9 319	15 883	16 100	16 410	10 919	3 155
1970	78 678	6 144	2 598	3 546	72 534	9 731	16 318	15 922	16 473	10 974	3 118
1971	79 367	6 208	2 596	3 613	73 158	10 201	16 781	15 675	16 451	11 009	3 040
1972	82 153	6 746	2 787	3 959	75 407	10 999	18 082	15 822	16 457	11 044	3 003
1973	85 064	7 271	3 032	4 239	77 793	11 839	19 509	16 041	16 553	10 966	2 886
1974	86 794	7 448	3 111	4 338	79 347	12 101	20 610	16 203	16 633	10 964	2 835
1975	85 846	7 104	2 941	4 162	78 744	11 885	21 087	15 953	16 190	10 827	2 801
1976	88 752	7 336	2 972	4 363	81 416	12 570	22 493	16 468	16 224	10 912	2 747
1977	92 017	7 688	3 138	4 550	84 329	13 196	23 850	17 157	16 212	11 126	2 787
1978	96 048	8 070	3 330	4 739	87 979	13 887	25 281	18 128	16 338	11 400	2 946
1979	98 824	8 083	3 340	4 743	90 741	14 327	26 492	18 981	16 357	11 585	2 999
1980	99 303	7 710	3 106	4 605	91 593	14 087	27 204	19 523	16 234	11 586	2 960
1981	100 397	7 225	2 866	4 359	93 172	14 122	28 180	20 145	16 255	11 525	2 945
1982	99 526	6 549	2 505	4 044	92 978	13 690	28 149	20 879	15 923	11 414	2 923
1983	100 834	6 342	2 320	4 022	94 491	13 722	28 756	21 960	15 812	11 315	2 927
1984	105 005	6 444	2 404	4 040	98 562	14 207	30 348	23 598	16 178	11 395	2 835
1985	107 150	6 434	2 492	3 941	100 716	13 980	31 208	24 732	16 509	11 474	2 813
1986	109 597	6 472	2 622	3 850	103 125	13 790	32 201	25 861	16 949	11 405	2 919
1987	112 440	6 640	2 736	3 905	105 800	13 524	33 105	27 179	17 487	11 465	3 041
1988	114 968	6 805	2 713	4 092	108 164	13 244	33 574	28 269	18 447	11 433	3 197
1989	117 342	6 759	2 588	4 172	110 582	12 962	34 045	29 443	19 279	11 499	3 355
1990	118 793	6 581	2 410	4 171	112 213	13 401	33 935	30 817	19 525	11 189	3 346
1991	117 718	5 906	2 202	3 704	111 812	12 975	33 061	31 593	19 882	11 001	3 300
1992	118 492	5 669	2 128	3 540	112 824	12 872	32 667	31 923	21 022	10 998	3 341
1993	120 259	5 805	2 226	3 579	114 455	12 840	32 385	32 666	22 175	11 058	3 331
1994	123 060	6 161	2 510	3 651	116 899	12 758	32 286	33 599	23 348	11 228	3 681
1995	124 900	6 419	2 573	3 846	118 481	12 443	32 356	34 202	24 378	11 435	3 666
1996	126 708	6 500	2 646	3 853	120 208	12 138	32 077	35 051	25 514	11 739	3 690
1997	129 558	6 661	2 648	4 012	122 897	12 380	31 809	35 908	26 744	12 296	3 761
1998	131 463	7 051	2 762	4 289	124 413	12 557	31 394	36 278	27 587	12 872	3 725
1999	133 488	7 172	2 793	4 379	126 316	12 891	30 865	36 728	28 635	13 315	3 882
2000	136 891	7 189	2 759	4 431	129 701	13 229	31 549	36 433	30 310	14 002	4 179
2001	136 933	6 740	2 558	4 182	130 194	13 348	30 863	36 049	31 036	14 645	4 253
2002	136 485	6 332	2 330	4 002	130 154	13 351	30 306	35 235	31 281	15 674	4 306
2003	137 736	5 919	2 312	3 607	131 817	13 433	30 383	34 881	31 914	16 598	4 608
2004	139 252	5 907	2 193	3 714	133 345	13 723	30 423	34 580	32 469	17 331	4 819
2005	141 730	5 978	2 284	3 694	135 752	13 792	30 680	34 630	33 207	18 349	5 094
2006	144 427	6 162	2 444	3 719	138 265	13 878	31 051	34 569	34 052	19 389	5 325
2007	146 047	5 911	2 286	3 625	140 136	13 964	31 586	34 302	34 563	20 108	5 614
2008	145 362	5 573	1 989	3 584	139 790	13 629	31 383	33 457	34 529	20 812	5 979
2009	139 877	4 837	1 651	3 187	135 040	12 764	30 014	31 517	33 613	21 019	6 114

Table 1-11. Employed Civilians, by Age, Sex, Race, and Hispanic Origin, 1948–2009—*Continued*

(Thousands of people.)

Race, Hispanic origin, sex, and year	16 years and over	16 to 19 years			20 years and over						
		Total	16 to 17 years	18 to 19 years	Total	20 to 24 years	25 to 34 years	35 to 44 years	45 to 54 years	55 to 64 years	65 years and over
ALL RACES											
Men											
1948	41 725	2 344	996	1 348	39 382	4 349	10 038	9 363	7 742	5 587	2 303
1949	40 925	2 124	911	1 213	38 803	4 197	9 879	9 308	7 661	5 438	2 329
1950	41 578	2 186	909	1 277	39 394	4 255	10 060	9 445	7 790	5 508	2 336
1951	41 780	2 156	979	1 177	39 626	3 780	10 134	9 607	8 012	5 711	2 382
1952	41 682	2 107	985	1 121	39 578	3 183	10 352	9 753	8 144	5 804	2 343
1953	42 430	2 136	976	1 159	40 296	2 901	10 500	10 229	8 374	5 808	2 483
1954	41 619	1 985	881	1 104	39 634	2 724	10 254	10 082	8 330	5 830	2 414
1955	42 621	2 095	936	1 159	40 526	2 973	10 453	10 267	8 553	5 857	2 424
1956	43 379	2 164	1 008	1 156	41 216	3 245	10 337	10 385	8 732	6 004	2 512
1957	43 357	2 115	987	1 130	41 239	3 346	10 222	10 427	8 851	6 002	2 394
1958	42 423	2 012	948	1 064	40 411	3 293	9 790	10 291	8 828	5 955	2 254
1959	43 466	2 198	1 015	1 183	41 267	3 597	9 862	10 492	9 048	6 058	2 210
1960	43 904	2 361	1 090	1 271	41 543	3 754	9 759	10 552	9 182	6 105	2 191
1961	43 656	2 315	989	1 325	41 342	3 795	9 591	10 505	9 195	6 155	2 098
1962	44 177	2 362	990	1 372	41 815	3 898	9 475	10 711	9 333	6 260	2 138
1963	44 657	2 406	1 073	1 334	42 251	4 118	9 431	10 801	9 478	6 385	2 038
1964	45 474	2 587	1 242	1 345	42 886	4 370	9 531	10 832	9 637	6 478	2 039
1965	46 340	2 918	1 285	1 634	43 422	4 583	9 611	10 837	9 792	6 542	2 057
1966	46 919	3 253	1 389	1 863	43 668	4 599	9 709	10 764	9 904	6 668	2 024
1967	47 479	3 186	1 417	1 769	44 294	4 809	9 988	10 674	9 990	6 774	2 058
1968	48 114	3 255	1 453	1 802	44 859	4 812	10 405	10 554	10 102	6 893	2 093
1969	48 818	3 430	1 526	1 904	45 388	5 012	10 736	10 401	10 187	6 931	2 122
1970	48 990	3 409	1 504	1 905	45 581	5 237	10 936	10 216	10 170	6 928	2 094
1971	49 390	3 478	1 510	1 968	45 912	5 593	11 218	10 028	10 139	6 916	2 019
1972	50 896	3 765	1 598	2 167	47 130	6 138	11 884	10 088	10 139	6 929	1 953
1973	52 349	4 039	1 721	2 318	48 310	6 655	12 617	10 126	10 197	6 857	1 856
1974	53 024	4 103	1 744	2 359	48 922	6 739	13 119	10 135	10 181	6 880	1 869
1975	51 857	3 839	1 621	2 219	48 018	6 484	13 205	9 891	9 902	6 722	1 811
1976	53 138	3 947	1 626	2 321	49 190	6 915	13 869	10 069	9 881	6 724	1 732
1977	54 728	4 174	1 733	2 441	50 555	7 232	14 483	10 399	9 832	6 848	1 761
1978	56 479	4 336	1 800	2 535	52 143	7 559	15 124	10 845	9 806	6 954	1 855
1979	57 607	4 300	1 799	2 501	53 308	7 791	15 688	11 202	9 735	7 015	1 876
1980	57 186	4 085	1 672	2 412	53 101	7 532	15 832	11 355	9 548	6 999	1 835
1981	57 397	3 815	1 526	2 289	53 582	7 504	16 266	11 613	9 478	6 909	1 812
1982	56 271	3 379	1 307	2 072	52 891	7 197	16 002	11 902	9 234	6 781	1 776
1983	56 787	3 300	1 213	2 087	53 487	7 232	16 216	12 450	9 133	6 686	1 770
1984	59 091	3 322	1 244	2 078	55 769	7 571	17 166	13 309	9 326	6 694	1 703
1985	59 891	3 328	1 300	2 029	56 562	7 339	17 564	13 800	9 411	6 753	1 695
1986	60 892	3 323	1 352	1 971	57 569	7 250	18 092	14 266	9 554	6 654	1 753
1987	62 107	3 381	1 393	1 988	58 726	7 058	18 487	14 898	9 750	6 682	1 850
1988	63 273	3 492	1 403	2 089	59 781	6 918	18 702	15 457	10 201	6 591	1 911
1989	64 315	3 477	1 327	2 150	60 837	6 799	18 952	16 002	10 569	6 548	1 968
1990	65 104	3 427	1 254	2 173	61 678	7 151	18 779	16 771	10 690	6 378	1 909
1991	64 223	3 044	1 135	1 909	61 178	6 909	18 265	17 086	10 813	6 245	1 860
1992	64 440	2 944	1 096	1 848	61 496	6 819	17 966	17 230	11 365	6 173	1 943
1993	65 349	2 994	1 155	1 839	62 355	6 805	17 877	17 665	11 927	6 166	1 916
1994	66 450	3 156	1 288	1 868	63 294	6 771	17 741	18 111	12 439	6 142	2 089
1995	67 377	3 292	1 316	1 977	64 085	6 665	17 709	18 374	12 958	6 272	2 108
1996	68 207	3 310	1 318	1 992	64 897	6 429	17 527	18 816	13 483	6 470	2 172
1997	69 685	3 401	1 355	2 045	66 284	6 548	17 338	19 327	14 107	6 735	2 229
1998	70 693	3 558	1 398	2 161	67 135	6 638	17 097	19 634	14 544	7 052	2 171
1999	71 446	3 685	1 437	2 249	67 761	6 729	16 694	19 811	14 991	7 274	2 263
2000	73 305	3 671	1 394	2 276	69 634	6 974	17 241	19 537	15 871	7 606	2 406
2001	73 196	3 420	1 268	2 151	69 776	6 952	16 915	19 305	16 268	7 900	2 437
2002	72 903	3 169	1 130	2 040	69 734	6 978	16 573	18 932	16 419	8 378	2 455
2003	73 332	2 917	1 115	1 802	70 415	7 065	16 670	18 774	16 588	8 733	2 585
2004	74 524	2 952	1 037	1 915	71 572	7 246	16 818	18 700	16 951	9 174	2 683
2005	75 973	2 923	1 067	1 855	73 050	7 279	16 993	18 780	17 429	9 714	2 857
2006	77 502	3 071	1 182	1 888	74 431	7 412	17 134	18 765	17 920	10 192	3 008
2007	78 254	2 917	1 091	1 827	75 337	7 374	17 452	18 666	18 210	10 556	3 080
2008	77 486	2 736	926	1 810	74 750	7 145	17 183	18 097	18 124	10 919	3 282
2009	73 670	2 328	786	1 543	71 341	6 510	16 223	16 918	17 443	10 890	3 357

Table 1-11. Employed Civilians, by Age, Sex, Race, and Hispanic Origin, 1948–2009—*Continued*

(Thousands of people.)

Race, Hispanic origin, sex, and year	16 years and over	16 to 19 years			20 years and over						
		Total	16 to 17 years	18 to 19 years	Total	20 to 24 years	25 to 34 years	35 to 44 years	45 to 54 years	55 to 64 years	65 years and over
ALL RACES											
Women											
1948	16 617	1 682	604	1 078	14 936	2 588	3 763	3 687	2 882	1 516	501
1949	16 723	1 588	555	1 033	15 137	2 463	3 760	3 800	2 975	1 604	535
1950	17 340	1 517	524	993	15 824	2 491	3 857	3 979	3 176	1 757	563
1951	18 181	1 611	596	1 015	16 570	2 541	4 099	4 139	3 409	1 847	535
1952	18 568	1 612	641	971	16 958	2 389	4 163	4 305	3 543	1 981	576
1953	18 749	1 584	601	983	17 164	2 324	4 019	4 545	3 595	1 998	683
1954	18 490	1 490	541	949	17 000	2 247	3 936	4 459	3 646	2 065	646
1955	19 551	1 547	564	984	18 002	2 297	4 028	4 612	4 003	2 301	761
1956	20 419	1 654	639	1 015	18 767	2 300	4 070	4 833	4 246	2 515	802
1957	20 714	1 663	626	1 037	19 052	2 295	4 031	4 921	4 469	2 551	785
1958	20 613	1 570	571	999	19 043	2 278	3 885	4 866	4 620	2 604	791
1959	21 164	1 640	655	985	19 524	2 273	3 847	4 962	4 867	2 764	813
1960	21 874	1 768	680	1 089	20 105	2 365	3 871	5 046	5 056	2 884	882
1961	22 090	1 793	632	1 161	20 296	2 432	3 838	5 047	5 125	2 965	889
1962	22 525	1 833	617	1 216	20 693	2 548	3 836	5 190	5 158	3 086	875
1963	23 105	1 849	678	1 170	21 257	2 697	3 887	5 313	5 271	3 211	877
1964	23 831	1 929	771	1 158	21 903	2 933	3 918	5 334	5 457	3 326	934
1965	24 748	2 118	790	1 328	22 630	3 119	4 093	5 457	5 528	3 486	948
1966	25 976	2 468	880	1 589	23 510	3 365	4 308	5 548	5 711	3 642	937
1967	26 893	2 496	917	1 579	24 397	3 690	4 587	5 607	5 799	3 762	953
1968	27 807	2 526	950	1 575	25 281	3 950	4 860	5 666	5 981	3 852	972
1969	29 084	2 687	1 047	1 639	26 397	4 307	5 147	5 699	6 223	3 988	1 033
1970	29 688	2 735	1 094	1 641	26 952	4 494	5 382	5 706	6 303	4 046	1 023
1971	29 976	2 730	1 086	1 645	27 246	4 609	5 563	5 647	6 313	4 093	1 021
1972	31 257	2 980	1 188	1 792	28 276	4 861	6 197	5 734	6 318	4 115	1 051
1973	32 715	3 231	1 310	1 920	29 484	5 184	6 893	5 915	6 356	4 109	1 029
1974	33 769	3 345	1 367	1 978	30 424	5 363	7 492	6 068	6 451	4 084	966
1975	33 989	3 263	1 320	1 943	30 726	5 401	7 882	6 061	6 288	4 105	989
1976	35 615	3 389	1 346	2 043	32 226	5 655	8 624	6 400	6 343	4 188	1 017
1977	37 289	3 514	1 403	2 110	33 775	5 965	9 367	6 758	6 380	4 279	1 027
1978	39 569	3 734	1 530	2 204	35 836	6 328	10 157	7 282	6 532	4 446	1 091
1979	41 217	3 783	1 541	2 242	37 434	6 538	10 802	7 779	6 622	4 569	1 124
1980	42 117	3 625	1 433	2 192	38 492	6 555	11 370	8 168	6 686	4 587	1 125
1981	43 000	3 411	1 340	2 070	39 590	6 618	11 914	8 532	6 777	4 616	1 133
1982	43 256	3 170	1 198	1 972	40 086	6 492	12 147	8 977	6 689	4 634	1 147
1983	44 047	3 043	1 107	1 935	41 004	6 490	12 540	9 510	6 678	4 629	1 157
1984	45 915	3 122	1 161	1 962	42 793	6 636	13 182	10 289	6 852	4 700	1 133
1985	47 259	3 105	1 193	1 913	44 154	6 640	13 644	10 933	7 097	4 721	1 118
1986	48 706	3 149	1 270	1 879	45 556	6 540	14 109	11 595	7 395	4 751	1 165
1987	50 334	3 260	1 343	1 917	47 074	6 466	14 617	12 281	7 737	4 783	1 191
1988	51 696	3 313	1 310	2 003	48 383	6 326	14 872	12 811	8 246	4 841	1 286
1989	53 027	3 282	1 261	2 021	49 745	6 163	15 093	13 440	8 711	4 950	1 388
1990	53 689	3 154	1 156	1 998	50 535	6 250	15 155	14 046	8 835	4 811	1 437
1991	53 496	2 862	1 067	1 794	50 634	6 066	14 796	14 507	9 069	4 756	1 440
1992	54 052	2 724	1 032	1 692	51 328	6 053	14 701	14 693	9 657	4 825	1 398
1993	54 910	2 811	1 071	1 740	52 099	6 035	14 508	15 002	10 248	4 892	1 414
1994	56 610	3 005	1 222	1 783	53 606	5 987	14 545	15 488	10 908	5 085	1 592
1995	57 523	3 127	1 258	1 869	54 396	5 779	14 647	15 828	11 421	5 163	1 558
1996	58 501	3 190	1 328	1 862	55 311	5 709	14 549	16 235	12 031	5 269	1 518
1997	59 873	3 260	1 293	1 967	56 613	5 831	14 471	16 581	12 637	5 561	1 532
1998	60 771	3 493	1 364	2 128	57 278	5 919	14 298	16 644	13 043	5 820	1 554
1999	62 042	3 487	1 357	2 130	58 555	6 163	14 171	16 917	13 644	6 041	1 619
2000	63 586	3 519	1 364	2 154	60 067	6 255	14 308	16 897	14 438	6 396	1 773
2001	63 737	3 320	1 289	2 031	60 417	6 396	13 948	16 744	14 768	6 745	1 815
2002	63 582	3 162	1 200	1 962	60 420	6 374	13 733	16 303	14 863	7 296	1 851
2003	64 404	3 002	1 197	1 805	61 402	6 367	13 714	16 106	15 326	7 866	2 023
2004	64 728	2 955	1 156	1 799	61 773	6 477	13 605	15 880	15 518	8 157	2 135
2005	65 757	3 055	1 217	1 838	62 702	6 513	13 687	15 850	15 779	8 635	2 238
2006	66 925	3 091	1 261	1 830	63 834	6 467	13 917	15 804	16 132	9 198	2 316
2007	67 792	2 994	1 195	1 798	64 799	6 590	14 133	15 636	16 353	9 553	2 534
2008	67 876	2 837	1 063	1 774	65 039	6 484	14 200	15 360	16 406	9 893	2 697
2009	66 208	2 509	865	1 644	63 699	6 254	13 791	14 599	16 170	10 128	2 757

Table 1-11. Employed Civilians, by Age, Sex, Race, and Hispanic Origin, 1948–2009—*Continued*

(Thousands of people.)

Race, Hispanic origin, sex, and year	16 years and over	16 to 19 years			20 years and over						
		Total	16 to 17 years	18 to 19 years	Total	20 to 24 years	25 to 34 years	35 to 44 years	45 to 54 years	55 to 64 years	65 years and over
WHITE											
Both Sexes											
1954	53 957	3 078	1 257	1 822	50 879	4 358	12 616	13 000	10 811	7 262	2 831
1955	55 833	3 225	1 330	1 896	52 608	4 637	12 855	13 327	11 322	7 510	2 957
1956	57 269	3 389	1 465	1 922	53 880	4 897	12 748	13 637	11 706	7 822	3 068
1957	57 465	3 374	1 442	1 931	54 091	4 952	12 619	13 716	12 009	7 829	2 951
1958	56 613	3 216	1 370	1 847	53 397	4 908	12 128	13 571	12 113	7 849	2 828
1959	58 006	3 475	1 520	1 955	54 531	5 138	12 144	13 830	12 552	8 063	2 805
1960	58 850	3 700	1 598	2 103	55 150	5 331	12 021	13 930	12 820	8 192	2 855
1961	58 913	3 693	1 472	2 220	55 220	5 460	11 835	13 905	12 906	8 335	2 778
1962	59 698	3 774	1 447	2 327	55 924	5 676	11 703	14 173	13 066	8 511	2 795
1963	60 622	3 851	1 600	2 250	56 771	6 036	11 689	14 341	13 304	8 718	2 683
1964	61 922	4 076	1 846	2 230	57 846	6 444	11 794	14 380	13 596	8 916	2 717
1965	63 446	4 562	1 892	2 670	58 884	6 752	11 992	14 473	13 804	9 116	2 748
1966	65 021	5 176	2 052	3 124	59 845	6 986	12 268	14 449	14 072	9 356	2 713
1967	66 361	5 114	2 121	2 993	61 247	7 493	12 763	14 429	14 224	9 596	2 746
1968	67 750	5 195	2 193	3 002	62 555	7 687	13 410	14 386	14 487	9 781	2 804
1969	69 518	5 508	2 347	3 161	64 010	8 182	13 935	14 270	14 788	9 947	2 888
1970	70 217	5 571	2 386	3 185	64 645	8 559	14 326	14 092	14 854	9 979	2 835
1971	70 878	5 670	2 404	3 266	65 208	9 000	14 713	13 858	14 843	10 014	2 780
1972	73 370	6 173	2 581	3 592	67 197	9 718	15 904	13 940	14 845	10 077	2 714
1973	75 708	6 623	2 806	3 816	69 086	10 424	17 099	14 083	14 886	9 983	2 610
1974	77 184	6 796	2 881	3 916	70 388	10 676	18 040	14 196	14 948	9 958	2 568
1975	76 411	6 487	2 721	3 770	69 924	10 546	18 485	13 979	14 555	9 827	2 533
1976	78 853	6 724	2 762	3 962	72 129	11 119	19 662	14 407	14 549	9 923	2 470
1977	81 700	7 068	2 926	4 142	74 632	11 696	20 844	14 984	14 483	10 107	2 518
1978	84 936	7 367	3 085	4 282	77 569	12 251	22 008	15 809	14 550	10 311	2 642
1979	87 259	7 356	3 079	4 278	79 904	12 594	23 033	16 578	14 522	10 477	2 699
1980	87 715	7 021	2 861	4 161	80 694	12 405	23 653	17 071	14 405	10 475	2 684
1981	88 709	6 588	2 645	3 943	82 121	12 477	24 551	17 617	14 414	10 386	2 676
1982	87 903	5 984	2 317	3 667	81 918	12 097	24 531	18 268	14 083	10 283	2 656
1983	88 893	5 799	2 156	3 643	83 094	12 138	24 955	19 194	13 961	10 169	2 678
1984	92 120	5 836	2 209	3 627	86 284	12 451	26 235	20 552	14 239	10 227	2 580
1985	93 736	5 768	2 270	3 498	87 968	12 235	26 945	21 552	14 459	10 247	2 530
1986	95 660	5 792	2 386	3 406	89 869	12 027	27 746	22 515	14 750	10 176	2 654
1987	97 789	5 898	2 468	3 431	91 890	11 748	28 429	23 596	15 216	10 164	2 738
1988	99 812	6 030	2 424	3 606	93 782	11 438	28 796	24 468	16 054	10 153	2 874
1989	101 584	5 946	2 278	3 668	95 638	11 084	29 091	25 442	16 775	10 223	3 024
1990	102 261	5 779	2 141	3 638	96 481	11 498	28 773	26 282	16 933	9 960	3 035
1991	101 182	5 216	1 971	3 246	95 966	11 116	27 989	26 883	17 269	9 719	2 990
1992	101 669	4 985	1 904	3 081	96 684	11 031	27 552	27 097	18 285	9 701	3 019
1993	103 045	5 113	1 990	3 123	97 932	10 931	27 274	27 645	19 273	9 772	3 037
1994	105 190	5 398	2 210	3 188	99 792	10 736	27 101	28 442	20 247	9 912	3 354
1995	106 490	5 593	2 273	3 320	100 897	10 400	27 014	28 951	21 127	10 070	3 335
1996	107 808	5 667	2 325	3 343	102 141	10 149	26 678	29 566	22 071	10 313	3 364
1997	109 856	5 807	2 341	3 466	104 049	10 362	26 294	30 137	23 061	10 785	3 411
1998	110 931	6 089	2 436	3 653	104 842	10 512	25 729	30 320	23 662	11 272	3 347
1999	112 235	6 204	2 435	3 769	106 032	10 716	25 113	30 548	24 507	11 657	3 491
2000	114 424	6 160	2 383	3 777	108 264	10 944	25 500	30 151	25 762	12 169	3 738
2001	114 430	5 817	2 224	3 593	108 613	11 054	24 948	29 793	26 301	12 743	3 774
2002	114 013	5 441	2 037	3 404	108 572	11 096	24 568	29 049	26 401	13 630	3 828
2003	114 235	5 064	1 999	3 065	109 171	11 052	24 399	28 501	26 762	14 375	4 083
2004	115 239	5 039	1 895	3 145	110 199	11 233	24 337	28 176	27 228	14 965	4 260
2005	116 949	5 105	1 999	3 106	111 844	11 231	24 443	28 102	27 801	15 788	4 480
2006	118 833	5 215	2 099	3 117	113 618	11 296	24 652	27 929	28 419	16 652	4 670
2007	119 792	4 990	1 965	3 026	114 802	11 325	25 024	27 492	28 779	17 262	4 921
2008	119 126	4 697	1 703	2 994	114 428	11 055	24 875	26 736	28 686	17 829	5 247
2009	114 996	4 138	1 443	2 696	110 858	10 438	23 957	25 237	27 891	17 978	5 357

Table 1-11. Employed Civilians, by Age, Sex, Race, and Hispanic Origin, 1948–2009—*Continued*

(Thousands of people.)

Race, Hispanic origin, sex, and year	16 years and over	16 to 19 years			20 years and over						
		Total	16 to 17 years	18 to 19 years	Total	20 to 24 years	25 to 34 years	35 to 44 years	45 to 54 years	55 to 64 years	65 years and over
WHITE											
Men											
1954	37 846	1 723	771	953	36 123	2 394	9 287	9 175	7 614	5 412	2 241
1955	38 719	1 824	821	1 004	36 895	2 607	9 461	9 351	7 792	5 431	2 254
1956	39 368	1 893	890	1 002	37 475	2 850	9 330	9 449	7 950	5 559	2 336
1957	39 349	1 865	874	990	37 484	2 930	9 226	9 480	8 067	5 542	2 234
1958	38 591	1 783	852	932	36 808	2 896	8 861	9 386	8 061	5 501	2 103
1959	39 494	1 961	915	1 046	37 533	3 153	8 911	9 560	8 261	5 588	2 060
1960	39 755	2 092	973	1 119	37 663	3 264	8 777	9 589	8 372	5 618	2 043
1961	39 588	2 055	891	1 164	37 533	3 311	8 630	9 566	8 394	5 670	1 961
1962	40 016	2 098	883	1 215	37 918	3 426	8 514	9 718	8 512	5 749	1 998
1963	40 428	2 156	972	1 184	38 272	3 646	8 463	9 782	8 650	5 844	1 887
1964	41 115	2 316	1 128	1 188	38 799	3 856	8 538	9 800	8 787	5 945	1 872
1965	41 844	2 612	1 159	1 453	39 232	4 025	8 598	9 795	8 924	5 998	1 892
1966	42 331	2 913	1 245	1 668	39 418	4 028	8 674	9 719	9 029	6 096	1 871
1967	42 833	2 849	1 278	1 571	39 985	4 231	8 931	9 632	9 093	6 208	1 892
1968	43 411	2 908	1 319	1 589	40 503	4 226	9 315	9 522	9 198	6 208	1 892
1969	44 048	3 070	1 385	1 685	40 978	4 401	9 608	9 379	9 279	6 359	1 953
1970	44 178	3 066	1 374	1 692	41 112	4 601	9 784	9 202	9 271	6 340	1 914
1971	44 595	3 157	1 393	1 764	41 438	4 935	10 026	9 026	9 256	6 339	1 856
1972	45 944	3 416	1 470	1 947	42 528	5 431	10 664	9 047	9 236	6 363	1 786
1973	47 085	3 660	1 590	2 071	43 424	5 863	11 268	9 046	9 257	6 299	1 786
1974	47 674	3 728	1 611	2 117	43 946	5 965	11 701	9 027	9 242	6 304	1 706
1975	46 697	3 505	1 502	2 002	43 192	5 770	11 783	8 818	9 005	6 160	1 656
1976	47 775	3 604	1 501	2 103	44 171	6 140	12 362	8 944	8 968	6 176	1 579
1977	49 150	3 824	1 607	2 217	45 326	6 437	12 893	9 212	8 898	6 279	1 605
1978	50 544	3 950	1 664	2 286	46 594	6 717	13 413	9 608	8 840	6 339	1 677
1979	51 452	3 904	1 654	2 250	47 546	6 868	13 888	9 930	8 748	6 406	1 707
1980	51 127	3 708	1 534	2 174	47 419	6 652	14 009	10 077	8 586	6 412	1 684
1981	51 315	3 469	1 402	2 066	47 846	6 652	14 398	10 307	8 518	6 309	1 662
1982	50 287	3 079	1 214	1 865	47 209	6 372	14 164	10 593	8 267	6 188	1 624
1983	50 621	3 003	1 124	1 879	47 618	6 386	14 297	11 062	8 152	6 084	1 637
1984	52 462	3 001	1 140	1 861	49 461	6 647	15 045	11 776	8 320	6 108	1 564
1985	53 046	2 985	1 185	1 800	50 061	6 428	15 374	12 214	8 374	6 118	1 552
1986	53 785	2 966	1 225	1 741	50 818	6 340	15 790	12 620	8 442	6 012	1 612
1987	54 647	2 999	1 252	1 747	51 649	6 150	16 084	13 138	8 596	5 991	1 690
1988	55 550	3 084	1 248	1 836	52 466	5 987	16 241	13 590	8 992	5 909	1 748
1989	56 352	3 060	1 171	1 889	53 292	5 839	16 383	14 046	9 335	5 891	1 797
1990	56 703	3 018	1 119	1 899	53 685	6 179	16 124	14 496	9 383	5 744	1 760
1991	55 797	2 694	1 017	1 677	53 103	5 942	15 644	14 743	9 488	5 578	1 707
1992	55 959	2 602	990	1 612	53 357	5 855	15 357	14 842	10 027	5 503	1 707
1993	56 656	2 634	1 031	1 603	54 021	5 830	15 230	15 178	10 497	5 514	1 772
1994	57 452	2 776	1 144	1 632	54 676	5 738	15 052	15 562	10 910	5 490	1 925
1995	58 146	2 892	1 169	1 723	55 254	5 613	14 958	15 793	11 359	5 609	1 921
1996	58 888	2 911	1 161	1 750	55 977	5 444	14 820	16 136	11 834	5 755	1 987
1997	59 998	3 011	1 206	1 806	56 986	5 590	14 567	16 470	12 352	5 972	2 037
1998	60 604	3 103	1 233	1 870	57 500	5 659	14 259	16 715	12 661	6 251	1 955
1999	61 139	3 205	1 254	1 951	57 934	5 753	13 851	16 781	13 046	6 447	2 056
2000	62 289	3 169	1 205	1 965	59 119	5 876	14 238	16 477	13 675	6 678	2 175
2001	62 212	2 967	1 102	1 865	59 245	5 870	13 989	16 280	13 987	6 941	2 178
2002	61 849	2 725	987	1 738	59 124	5 882	13 727	15 910	14 060	7 360	2 184
2003	61 866	2 518	972	1 546	59 348	5 890	13 731	15 675	14 117	7 640	2 295
2004	62 712	2 553	903	1 650	60 159	6 026	13 735	15 572	14 418	8 018	2 390
2005	63 763	2 508	942	1 566	61 255	6 041	13 840	15 544	14 810	8 471	2 550
2006	64 883	2 625	1 020	1 605	62 259	6 114	13 903	15 480	15 189	8 893	2 680
2007	65 289	2 483	951	1 531	62 806	6 066	14 112	15 287	15 399	9 215	2 727
2008	64 624	2 320	808	1 512	62 304	5 858	13 931	14 775	15 300	9 518	2 922
2009	61 630	2 004	692	1 312	59 626	5 379	13 230	13 858	14 710	9 465	2 984

Table 1-11. Employed Civilians, by Age, Sex, Race, and Hispanic Origin, 1948–2009—*Continued*

(Thousands of people.)

Race, Hispanic origin, sex, and year	16 years and over	16 to 19 years			20 years and over						
		Total	16 to 17 years	18 to 19 years	Total	20 to 24 years	25 to 34 years	35 to 44 years	45 to 54 years	55 to 64 years	65 years and over
WHITE											
Women											
1954	16 111	1 355	486	869	14 756	1 964	3 329	3 825	3 197	1 850	590
1955	17 114	1 401	509	892	15 713	2 030	3 394	3 976	3 530	2 079	703
1956	17 901	1 496	575	920	16 405	2 047	3 418	4 188	3 756	2 263	732
1957	18 116	1 509	568	941	16 607	2 022	3 393	4 236	3 942	2 287	717
1958	18 022	1 433	518	915	16 589	2 012	3 267	4 185	4 052	2 348	725
1959	18 512	1 514	605	909	16 998	1 985	3 233	4 270	4 291	2 475	745
1960	19 095	1 608	625	984	17 487	2 067	3 244	4 341	4 448	2 574	812
1961	19 325	1 638	581	1 056	17 687	2 149	3 205	4 339	4 512	2 665	817
1962	19 682	1 676	564	1 112	18 006	2 250	3 189	4 455	4 554	2 762	797
1963	20 194	1 695	628	1 066	18 499	2 390	3 226	4 559	4 654	2 874	796
1964	20 807	1 760	718	1 042	19 047	2 588	3 256	4 580	4 809	2 971	845
1965	21 602	1 950	733	1 217	19 652	2 727	3 394	4 678	4 880	3 118	856
1966	22 690	2 263	807	1 456	20 427	2 958	3 594	4 730	5 043	3 260	842
1967	23 528	2 265	843	1 422	21 263	3 262	3 832	4 797	5 131	3 388	854
1968	24 339	2 287	874	1 413	22 052	3 461	4 095	4 864	5 289	3 465	878
1969	25 470	2 438	962	1 476	23 032	3 781	4 327	4 891	5 509	3 588	935
1970	26 039	2 505	1 012	1 493	23 534	3 959	4 542	4 890	5 582	3 640	921
1971	26 283	2 513	1 011	1 502	23 770	4 065	4 687	4 831	5 588	3 675	924
1972	27 426	2 755	1 111	1 645	24 669	4 286	5 240	4 893	5 608	3 714	928
1973	28 623	2 962	1 217	1 746	25 661	4 562	5 831	5 036	5 628	3 684	920
1974	29 511	3 069	1 269	1 799	26 442	4 711	6 340	5 169	5 706	3 654	862
1975	29 714	2 983	1 215	1 767	26 731	4 775	6 701	5 161	5 550	3 667	877
1976	31 078	3 120	1 260	1 860	27 958	4 978	7 300	5 462	5 580	3 746	891
1977	32 550	3 244	1 319	1 923	29 306	5 259	7 950	5 772	5 585	3 829	912
1978	34 392	3 416	1 420	1 996	30 975	5 535	8 595	6 201	5 710	3 972	964
1979	35 807	3 451	1 423	2 027	32 357	5 726	9 145	6 648	5 773	4 071	993
1980	36 587	3 314	1 327	1 986	33 275	5 753	9 644	6 994	5 818	4 064	1 001
1981	37 394	3 119	1 242	1 877	34 275	5 826	10 153	7 311	5 896	4 077	1 013
1982	37 615	2 905	1 103	1 802	34 710	5 724	10 367	7 675	5 816	4 095	1 032
1983	38 272	2 796	1 032	1 764	35 476	5 751	10 659	8 132	5 809	4 084	1 041
1984	39 659	2 835	1 069	1 766	36 823	5 804	11 190	8 776	5 920	4 118	1 015
1985	40 690	2 783	1 085	1 698	37 907	5 807	11 571	9 338	6 084	4 128	978
1986	41 876	2 825	1 160	1 665	39 050	5 687	11 956	9 895	6 307	4 164	1 042
1987	43 142	2 900	1 216	1 684	40 242	5 598	12 345	10 459	6 620	4 172	1 047
1988	44 262	2 946	1 176	1 770	41 316	5 450	12 555	10 878	7 062	4 244	1 126
1989	45 232	2 886	1 107	1 779	42 346	5 245	12 708	11 395	7 440	4 332	1 227
1990	45 558	2 762	1 023	1 739	42 796	5 319	12 649	11 785	7 551	4 217	1 275
1991	45 385	2 523	954	1 569	42 862	5 174	12 344	12 139	7 781	4 141	1 283
1992	45 710	2 383	915	1 468	43 327	5 176	12 195	12 254	8 258	4 198	1 246
1993	46 390	2 479	959	1 520	43 910	5 101	12 044	12 467	8 776	4 258	1 265
1994	47 738	2 622	1 066	1 556	45 116	4 997	12 049	12 880	9 338	4 423	1 429
1995	48 344	2 701	1 104	1 597	45 643	4 787	12 056	13 157	9 768	4 461	1 415
1996	48 920	2 756	1 164	1 592	46 164	4 705	11 858	13 430	10 237	4 558	1 376
1997	49 859	2 796	1 136	1 660	47 063	4 773	11 727	13 667	10 709	4 813	1 374
1998	50 327	2 986	1 203	1 783	47 342	4 853	11 470	13 604	11 001	5 021	1 392
1999	51 096	2 999	1 181	1 817	48 098	4 963	11 262	13 767	11 461	5 211	1 435
2000	52 136	2 991	1 178	1 813	49 145	5 068	11 262	13 674	12 087	5 490	1 564
2001	52 218	2 850	1 122	1 727	49 369	5 184	10 959	13 513	12 314	5 802	1 597
2002	52 164	2 716	1 050	1 665	49 448	5 214	10 842	13 138	12 341	6 269	1 644
2003	52 369	2 546	1 027	1 519	49 823	5 161	10 668	12 826	12 645	6 735	1 788
2004	52 527	2 486	991	1 495	50 040	5 207	10 602	12 604	12 810	6 947	1 870
2005	53 186	2 597	1 057	1 540	50 589	5 190	10 603	12 558	12 991	7 317	1 930
2006	53 950	2 590	1 079	1 512	51 359	5 182	10 750	12 449	13 230	7 758	1 991
2007	54 503	2 507	1 013	1 494	51 996	5 259	10 912	12 205	13 380	8 047	2 193
2008	54 501	2 377	895	1 482	52 124	5 197	10 943	11 961	13 386	8 312	2 325
2009	53 366	2 134	751	1 383	51 231	5 060	10 727	11 379	13 181	8 513	2 373

Table 1-11. Employed Civilians, by Age, Sex, Race, and Hispanic Origin, 1948–2009—*Continued*

(Thousands of people.)

Race, Hispanic origin, sex, and year	16 years and over	16 to 19 years			20 years and over						
		Total	16 to 17 years	18 to 19 years	Total	20 to 24 years	25 to 34 years	35 to 44 years	45 to 54 years	55 to 64 years	65 years and over
BLACK											
Both Sexes											
1972	7 802	509	180	329	7 292	1 166	1 924	1 629	1 434	872	269
1973	8 128	570	194	378	7 559	1 258	2 062	1 659	1 460	872	249
1974	8 203	554	190	364	7 649	1 231	2 157	1 682	1 452	884	243
1975	7 894	507	183	325	7 386	1 115	2 145	1 617	1 393	874	241
1976	8 227	508	170	338	7 719	1 193	2 309	1 679	1 416	870	252
1977	8 540	508	169	339	8 031	1 244	2 443	1 754	1 448	892	251
1978	9 102	571	191	380	8 531	1 359	2 641	1 848	1 479	932	273
1979	9 359	579	204	376	8 780	1 424	2 759	1 902	1 502	927	266
1980	9 313	547	192	356	8 765	1 376	2 827	1 910	1 487	925	239
1981	9 355	505	170	335	8 849	1 346	2 872	1 957	1 489	954	231
1982	9 189	428	138	290	8 761	1 283	2 830	2 025	1 469	928	225
1983	9 375	416	123	294	8 959	1 280	2 976	2 107	1 456	937	204
1984	10 119	474	146	328	9 645	1 423	3 223	2 311	1 533	945	209
1985	10 501	532	175	356	9 969	1 399	3 325	2 427	1 598	985	235
1986	10 814	536	183	353	10 278	1 429	3 464	2 524	1 666	982	214
1987	11 309	587	203	385	10 722	1 421	3 614	2 695	1 714	1 036	241
1988	11 658	601	223	378	11 057	1 433	3 725	2 839	1 783	1 018	261
1989	11 953	625	237	388	11 328	1 467	3 801	2 981	1 844	970	265
1990	12 175	598	194	404	11 577	1 409	3 803	3 287	1 897	933	248
1991	12 074	494	161	334	11 580	1 373	3 714	3 401	1 892	957	243
1992	12 151	492	157	335	11 659	1 343	3 699	3 441	1 964	965	246
1993	12 382	494	171	323	11 888	1 377	3 700	3 584	2 059	941	226
1994	12 835	552	224	328	12 284	1 449	3 732	3 722	2 178	953	251
1995	13 279	586	223	363	12 693	1 443	3 844	3 861	2 288	1 004	253
1996	13 542	613	233	380	12 929	1 411	3 851	3 974	2 426	1 025	241
1997	13 969	631	229	401	13 339	1 456	3 903	4 094	2 588	1 048	249
1998	14 556	736	246	490	13 820	1 496	3 967	4 238	2 739	1 118	262
1999	15 056	691	243	448	14 365	1 594	4 091	4 404	2 872	1 134	271
2000	15 156	711	260	451	14 444	1 593	3 993	4 261	3 073	1 226	300
2001	15 006	637	230	408	14 368	1 571	3 840	4 200	3 139	1 283	335
2002	14 872	611	193	417	14 262	1 543	3 726	4 109	3 220	1 332	332
2003	14 739	516	196	320	14 222	1 516	3 618	4 080	3 289	1 373	346
2004	14 909	520	169	351	14 389	1 572	3 635	4 039	3 332	1 452	359
2005	15 313	536	164	372	14 776	1 599	3 722	4 060	3 464	1 555	375
2006	15 765	618	215	402	15 147	1 643	3 809	4 072	3 570	1 659	394
2007	16 051	566	202	364	15 485	1 674	3 888	4 120	3 658	1 732	413
2008	15 953	541	172	369	15 411	1 625	3 870	4 015	3 670	1 791	440
2009	15 025	442	131	310	14 584	1 474	3 582	3 686	3 562	1 827	453
BLACK											
Men											
1972	4 368	309	114	195	4 058	648	1 074	890	793	499	156
1973	4 527	330	112	220	4 197	711	1 142	898	816	483	148
1974	4 527	322	114	209	4 204	668	1 176	912	803	500	145
1975	4 275	276	98	179	3 998	595	1 159	865	755	487	137
1976	4 404	283	100	184	4 120	635	1 217	897	763	472	137
1977	4 565	291	105	186	4 273	659	1 271	940	777	484	143
1978	4 796	312	106	206	4 483	697	1 357	969	788	516	155
1979	4 923	316	111	205	4 606	754	1 425	983	801	498	147
1980	4 798	299	109	191	4 498	713	1 438	975	770	478	126
1981	4 794	273	95	178	4 520	693	1 457	991	764	492	123
1982	4 637	223	65	158	4 414	660	1 414	997	750	471	122
1983	4 753	222	64	158	4 531	684	1 483	1 034	749	477	105
1984	5 124	252	79	173	4 871	750	1 635	1 138	780	460	108
1985	5 270	278	92	186	4 992	726	1 669	1 187	795	501	114
1986	5 428	278	96	182	5 150	732	1 756	1 211	831	507	112
1987	5 661	304	109	195	5 357	728	1 821	1 283	853	547	124
1988	5 824	316	122	193	5 509	736	1 881	1 348	878	536	131
1989	5 928	327	124	202	5 602	742	1 931	1 415	886	498	131
1990	5 995	303	99	204	5 692	702	1 895	1 586	926	469	114
1991	5 961	255	85	170	5 706	695	1 859	1 634	923	481	114
1992	5 930	249	78	170	5 681	679	1 819	1 650	930	478	124
1993	6 047	254	88	166	5 793	674	1 858	1 717	978	461	106
1994	6 241	276	107	169	5 964	718	1 850	1 795	1 030	455	115
1995	6 422	285	111	174	6 137	714	1 895	1 836	1 085	468	138
1996	6 456	289	109	180	6 167	685	1 867	1 878	1 129	482	126
1997	6 607	282	108	174	6 325	668	1 874	1 955	1 215	487	127
1998	6 871	341	120	221	6 530	686	1 886	2 008	1 284	524	142
1999	7 027	325	120	205	6 702	700	1 926	2 092	1 327	525	131
2000	7 082	341	129	211	6 741	730	1 865	1 984	1 425	596	142
2001	6 938	311	115	196	6 627	703	1 757	1 931	1 452	614	170
2002	6 959	306	95	212	6 652	725	1 729	1 899	1 503	624	172
2003	6 820	234	89	145	6 586	726	1 660	1 868	1 518	638	176
2004	6 912	231	76	155	6 681	739	1 720	1 840	1 534	668	180
2005	7 155	254	76	178	6 901	748	1 759	1 886	1 616	711	182
2006	7 354	275	99	175	7 079	804	1 797	1 882	1 680	734	184
2007	7 500	254	82	172	7 245	816	1 851	1 916	1 717	750	195
2008	7 398	247	70	177	7 151	794	1 805	1 854	1 703	792	204
2009	6 817	189	56	133	6 628	689	1 635	1 662	1 622	813	206

Table 1-11. Employed Civilians, by Age, Sex, Race, and Hispanic Origin, 1948–2009—*Continued*

(Thousands of people.)

Race, Hispanic origin, sex, and year	16 years and over	16 to 19 years			20 years and over						
		Total	16 to 17 years	18 to 19 years	Total	20 to 24 years	25 to 34 years	35 to 44 years	45 to 54 years	55 to 64 years	65 years and over
BLACK											
Women											
1972	3 433	200	65	134	3 233	519	850	739	641	373	113
1973	3 601	239	81	158	3 362	546	920	761	644	389	101
1974	3 677	232	77	155	3 445	562	981	770	649	383	98
1975	3 618	231	85	146	3 388	520	985	752	638	387	104
1976	3 823	224	70	154	3 599	558	1 092	782	653	398	115
1977	3 975	217	64	153	3 758	585	1 172	814	671	408	109
1978	4 307	260	85	175	4 047	662	1 283	879	691	416	118
1979	4 436	263	92	171	4 174	670	1 333	919	702	428	119
1980	4 515	248	82	165	4 267	663	1 389	936	717	448	113
1981	4 561	232	75	157	4 329	653	1 415	966	725	462	108
1982	4 552	205	73	132	4 347	623	1 416	1 028	719	457	103
1983	4 622	194	59	136	4 428	596	1 493	1 073	707	460	99
1984	4 995	222	67	155	4 773	673	1 588	1 173	753	485	101
1985	5 231	254	83	171	4 977	673	1 656	1 240	804	484	121
1986	5 386	259	87	171	5 128	696	1 708	1 313	835	475	102
1987	5 648	283	93	190	5 365	693	1 793	1 412	860	489	117
1988	5 834	285	101	184	5 548	697	1 844	1 491	905	482	129
1989	6 025	298	113	185	5 727	725	1 870	1 566	959	472	134
1990	6 180	296	96	200	5 884	707	1 907	1 701	971	464	135
1991	6 113	239	76	164	5 874	677	1 855	1 768	969	476	129
1992	6 221	243	79	164	5 978	664	1 880	1 791	1 034	487	123
1993	6 334	239	82	157	6 095	703	1 842	1 867	1 081	480	121
1994	6 595	275	117	158	6 320	731	1 882	1 926	1 147	497	136
1995	6 857	301	112	189	6 556	729	1 949	2 025	1 202	536	114
1996	7 086	324	124	200	6 762	726	1 984	2 096	1 297	543	115
1997	7 362	349	122	227	7 013	789	2 029	2 139	1 373	561	122
1998	7 685	395	126	268	7 290	810	2 081	2 230	1 455	594	120
1999	8 029	366	123	243	7 663	893	2 165	2 312	1 545	609	139
2000	8 073	370	131	240	7 703	862	2 128	2 277	1 647	630	158
2001	8 068	327	115	212	7 741	868	2 084	2 269	1 686	668	165
2002	7 914	304	99	205	7 610	819	1 997	2 209	1 717	708	160
2003	7 919	283	107	175	7 636	790	1 959	2 211	1 770	735	171
2004	7 997	289	93	196	7 707	833	1 914	2 199	1 798	784	179
2005	8 158	282	88	194	7 876	852	1 964	2 175	1 848	844	193
2006	8 410	343	116	227	8 068	839	2 012	2 191	1 890	925	210
2007	8 551	311	120	191	8 240	858	2 037	2 205	1 941	982	218
2008	8 554	294	102	192	8 260	831	2 065	2 161	1 967	1 000	236
2009	8 208	252	75	178	7 956	784	1 947	2 024	1 939	1 014	246
HISPANIC¹											
Both Sexes											
1973	3 396	325	...	...	...	...	...	...	...	...	...
1974	3 687	355	...	...	...	...	...	...	...	...	...
1975	3 663	322	...	...	...	...	...	...	...	...	...
1976	3 720	341	124	230	3 436	614	1 135	803	573	269	42
1977	4 079	381	135	245	3 715	715	1 212	860	608	269	50
1978	4 527	423	159	264	4 104	803	1 330	942	661	307	62
1979	4 785	445	152	292	4 340	860	1 430	996	666	319	69
1980	5 527	500	174	325	5 028	998	1 675	1 074	811	389	80
1981	5 813	459	155	304	5 354	1 060	1 837	1 147	829	399	82
1982	5 805	410	119	291	5 394	1 030	1 896	1 173	816	399	80
1983	6 072	423	125	297	5 649	1 068	1 997	1 224	837	441	81
1984	6 651	468	148	320	6 182	1 160	2 201	1 385	883	474	79
1985	6 888	438	144	294	6 449	1 187	2 316	1 473	913	486	75
1986	7 219	430	146	284	6 789	1 231	2 427	1 570	1 011	474	76
1987	7 790	474	149	325	7 316	1 273	2 668	1 775	1 010	512	76
1988	8 250	523	171	353	7 727	1 341	2 749	1 876	1 078	585	97
1989	8 573	548	165	383	8 025	1 325	2 900	1 968	1 129	589	114
1990	9 845	668	208	460	9 177	1 672	3 327	2 229	1 235	611	103
1991	9 828	602	169	433	9 225	1 622	3 264	2 333	1 266	637	103
1992	10 027	577	169	408	9 450	1 575	3 350	2 468	1 316	628	112
1993	10 361	570	160	410	9 792	1 574	3 446	2 605	1 402	630	135
1994	10 788	609	195	415	10 178	1 643	3 517	2 737	1 495	647	139
1995	11 127	645	194	450	10 483	1 609	3 618	2 889	1 565	666	135
1996	11 642	646	199	447	10 996	1 628	3 758	3 115	1 595	748	152
1997	12 726	714	228	487	12 012	1 798	4 029	3 371	1 846	794	173
1998	13 291	793	230	563	12 498	1 883	4 113	3 504	1 994	846	158
1999	13 720	854	254	600	12 866	1 881	4 097	3 738	2 074	886	190
2000	15 735	973	285	688	14 762	2 356	4 950	4 052	2 308	898	197
2001	16 190	969	268	701	15 221	2 404	5 065	4 149	2 472	944	187
2002	16 590	882	254	628	15 708	2 413	5 272	4 273	2 511	1 029	209
2003	17 372	768	242	525	16 604	2 399	5 541	4 573	2 711	1 132	249
2004	17 930	792	211	581	17 138	2 477	5 560	4 671	2 932	1 210	288
2005	18 632	847	253	595	17 785	2 423	5 756	4 879	3 114	1 317	296
2006	19 613	900	287	614	18 712	2 487	6 001	5 106	3 324	1 441	354
2007	20 382	894	269	625	19 488	2 516	6 237	5 314	3 547	1 499	376
2008	20 346	870	248	622	19 476	2 361	6 119	5 371	3 620	1 619	385
2009	19 647	742	192	550	18 905	2 218	5 704	5 168	3 700	1 680	435

¹May be of any race.
... = Not available.

Table 1-11. Employed Civilians, by Age, Sex, Race, and Hispanic Origin, 1948–2009—*Continued*

(Thousands of people.)

Race, Hispanic origin, sex, and year	16 years and over	16 to 19 years			20 years and over						
		Total	16 to 17 years	18 to 19 years	Total	20 to 24 years	25 to 34 years	35 to 44 years	45 to 54 years	55 to 64 years	65 years and over
HISPANIC[1]											
Men											
1973	2 198	...	...	...	2 010	...	...	...	...	...	...
1974	2 369	...	...	...	2 165	...	...	...	...	...	...
1975	2 301	...	...	...	2 117	...	...	...	...	...	...
1976	2 303	199	74	125	2 109	364	708	504	369	173	...
1977	2 564	225	78	147	2 335	427	763	540	394	184	...
1978	2 808	241	93	147	2 568	494	824	590	405	207	...
1979	2 962	260	93	168	2 701	511	891	615	427	205	...
1980	3 448	306	109	198	3 142	611	1 065	662	491	254	...
1981	3 597	272	90	182	3 325	642	1 157	707	504	259	...
1982	3 583	229	66	162	3 354	621	1 192	729	498	261	...
1983	3 771	248	71	177	3 523	655	1 280	760	499	275	...
1984	4 083	258	78	180	3 825	718	1 398	841	530	292	...
1985	4 245	251	82	169	3 994	727	1 473	888	550	308	...
1986	4 428	254	82	172	4 174	773	1 510	929	614	297	...
1987	4 713	268	81	188	4 444	777	1 664	1 044	606	303	...
1988	4 972	292	87	205	4 680	815	1 706	1 120	645	331	...
1989	5 172	319	94	225	4 853	821	1 787	1 152	676	350	...
1990	6 021	412	126	286	5 609	1 083	2 076	1 312	722	355	...
1991	5 979	356	94	263	5 623	1 063	2 050	1 360	719	369	...
1992	6 093	336	97	238	5 757	985	2 127	1 437	768	372	...
1993	6 328	337	95	242	5 992	1 003	2 200	1 527	822	360	...
1994	6 530	341	109	233	6 189	1 056	2 227	1 600	847	379	79
1995	6 725	358	110	248	6 367	1 030	2 284	1 675	908	384	85
1996	7 039	384	107	277	6 655	1 015	2 345	1 842	918	438	96
1997	7 728	420	130	290	7 307	1 142	2 547	1 978	1 059	477	105
1998	8 018	449	133	315	7 570	1 173	2 592	2 077	1 115	512	101
1999	8 067	491	139	352	7 576	1 135	2 524	2 135	1 151	502	130
2000	9 428	570	159	411	8 859	1 486	3 063	2 358	1 295	532	126
2001	9 668	568	149	419	9 100	1 473	3 142	2 446	1 375	545	119
2002	9 845	504	141	363	9 341	1 476	3 271	2 503	1 396	569	125
2003	10 479	415	121	294	10 063	1 485	3 537	2 724	1 533	639	144
2004	10 832	446	108	338	10 385	1 514	3 557	2 801	1 654	687	174
2005	11 337	465	137	328	10 872	1 511	3 711	2 939	1 781	748	183
2006	11 887	496	146	350	11 391	1 535	3 845	3 088	1 894	809	220
2007	12 310	483	145	338	11 827	1 524	3 982	3 220	2 012	869	220
2008	12 248	479	140	340	11 769	1 406	3 897	3 233	2 080	929	224
2009	11 640	383	94	289	11 256	1 287	3 576	3 108	2 104	930	251
HISPANIC[1]											
Women											
1973	1 198	...	...	...	1 060	...	...	...	...	...	...
1974	1 319	...	...	...	1 166	...	...	...	...	...	...
1975	1 362	...	...	...	1 224	...	...	...	...	...	...
1976	1 417	155	50	106	1 288	249	427	300	204	96	...
1977	1 516	155	57	98	1 370	288	449	320	214	86	...
1978	1 719	182	65	117	1 537	308	506	352	256	99	...
1979	1 824	185	60	125	1 638	349	539	381	241	115	...
1980	2 079	193	65	128	1 886	387	610	412	320	136	...
1981	2 216	187	65	122	2 029	418	680	440	326	139	...
1982	2 222	181	52	129	2 040	409	704	444	318	139	...
1983	2 301	175	54	120	2 127	413	717	464	338	166	...
1984	2 568	211	71	140	2 357	442	804	544	354	181	...
1985	2 642	187	62	125	2 456	460	843	585	362	178	...
1986	2 791	176	64	112	2 615	458	917	641	397	177	...
1987	3 077	206	69	137	2 872	496	1 004	732	405	209	...
1988	3 278	231	84	147	3 047	526	1 042	756	434	254	...
1989	3 401	229	71	158	3 172	504	1 114	816	453	239	...
1990	3 823	256	82	174	3 567	588	1 251	917	513	256	...
1991	3 848	246	76	170	3 603	559	1 214	972	548	268	...
1992	3 934	242	72	170	3 693	591	1 223	1 031	548	256	...
1993	4 033	233	65	168	3 800	571	1 246	1 077	581	269	...
1994	4 258	268	86	182	3 989	587	1 290	1 137	648	268	59
1995	4 403	287	85	202	4 116	579	1 334	1 213	657	282	50
1996	4 602	261	92	169	4 341	612	1 412	1 273	677	310	56
1997	4 999	294	98	196	4 705	656	1 482	1 393	787	318	69
1998	5 273	345	97	247	4 928	710	1 521	1 428	879	334	57
1999	5 653	363	115	248	5 290	746	1 574	1 603	923	384	60
2000	6 307	404	127	277	5 903	870	1 887	1 695	1 013	366	72
2001	6 522	401	119	282	6 121	931	1 923	1 703	1 097	398	67
2002	6 744	378	113	265	6 367	937	2 001	1 770	1 114	460	84
2003	6 894	353	121	231	6 541	914	2 004	1 849	1 178	493	105
2004	7 098	346	103	243	6 752	964	2 003	1 870	1 279	523	114
2005	7 295	382	116	266	6 913	912	2 045	1 940	1 333	569	113
2006	7 725	404	140	264	7 321	951	2 155	2 018	1 430	632	135
2007	8 072	410	124	287	7 662	991	2 255	2 094	1 535	631	155
2008	8 098	391	108	282	7 707	955	2 222	2 138	1 541	690	161
2009	8 007	358	98	261	7 649	931	2 128	2 060	1 596	751	183

[1]May be of any race.
. . . = Not available.

Table 1-12. Civilian Employment-Population Ratios, by Sex, Age, Race, and Hispanic Origin, 1948–2009

(Percent.)

Race, Hispanic origin, and year	Both sexes			Men			Women		
	16 years and over	16 to 19 years	20 years and over	16 years and over	16 to 19 years	20 years and over	16 years and over	16 to 19 years	20 years and over
ALL RACES									
1948	56.6	47.7	57.4	83.5	57.5	85.8	31.3	38.5	30.7
1949	55.4	45.2	56.3	81.3	53.8	83.7	31.2	37.2	30.6
1950	56.1	45.5	57.0	82.0	55.2	84.2	32.0	36.3	31.6
1951	57.3	47.9	58.1	84.0	57.9	86.1	33.1	38.9	32.6
1952	57.3	46.9	58.1	83.9	55.9	86.2	33.4	38.8	33.0
1953	57.1	46.4	58.0	83.6	55.9	85.9	33.3	37.8	32.9
1954	55.5	42.3	56.6	81.0	50.2	83.5	32.5	34.9	32.3
1955	56.7	43.5	57.8	81.8	52.1	84.3	34.0	35.6	33.8
1956	57.5	45.3	58.5	82.3	53.8	84.6	35.1	37.5	34.9
1957	57.1	43.9	58.2	81.3	51.8	83.8	35.1	36.7	35.0
1958	55.4	39.9	56.8	78.5	46.9	81.2	34.5	33.5	34.6
1959	56.0	39.9	57.5	79.3	47.2	82.3	35.0	33.0	35.1
1960	56.1	40.5	57.6	78.9	47.6	81.9	35.5	33.8	35.7
1961	55.4	39.1	56.9	77.6	45.3	80.8	35.4	33.2	35.6
1962	55.5	39.4	57.1	77.7	45.9	80.9	35.6	33.3	35.8
1963	55.4	37.4	57.2	77.1	43.8	80.6	35.8	31.5	36.3
1964	55.7	37.3	57.7	77.3	44.1	80.9	36.3	30.9	36.9
1965	56.2	38.9	58.2	77.5	46.2	81.2	37.1	32.0	37.6
1966	56.9	42.1	58.7	77.9	48.9	81.5	38.3	35.6	38.6
1967	57.3	42.2	59.0	78.0	48.7	81.5	39.0	35.9	39.3
1968	57.5	42.2	59.3	77.8	48.7	81.3	39.6	36.0	40.0
1969	58.0	43.4	59.7	77.6	49.5	81.1	40.7	37.5	41.1
1970	57.4	42.3	59.2	76.2	47.7	79.7	40.8	37.1	41.2
1971	56.6	41.3	58.4	74.9	46.8	78.5	40.4	36.0	40.9
1972	57.0	43.5	58.6	75.0	48.9	78.4	41.0	38.2	41.3
1973	57.8	45.9	59.3	75.5	51.4	78.6	42.0	40.5	42.2
1974	57.8	46.0	59.2	74.9	51.2	77.9	42.6	41.0	42.8
1975	56.1	43.3	57.6	71.7	47.2	74.8	42.0	39.4	42.3
1976	56.8	44.2	58.3	72.0	47.9	75.1	43.2	40.5	43.5
1977	57.9	46.1	59.2	72.8	50.4	75.6	44.5	41.8	44.8
1978	59.3	48.3	60.6	73.8	52.2	76.4	46.4	44.5	46.6
1979	59.9	48.5	61.2	73.8	51.7	76.5	47.5	45.3	47.7
1980	59.2	46.6	60.6	72.0	49.5	74.6	47.7	43.8	48.1
1981	59.0	44.6	60.5	71.3	47.1	74.0	48.0	42.0	48.6
1982	57.8	41.5	59.4	69.0	42.9	71.8	47.7	40.2	48.4
1983	57.9	41.5	59.5	68.8	43.1	71.4	48.0	40.0	48.8
1984	59.5	43.7	61.0	70.7	45.0	73.2	49.5	42.5	50.1
1985	60.1	44.4	61.5	70.9	45.7	73.3	50.4	42.9	51.0
1986	60.7	44.6	62.1	71.0	45.7	73.3	51.4	43.6	52.0
1987	61.5	45.5	62.9	71.5	46.1	73.8	52.5	44.8	53.1
1988	62.3	46.8	63.6	72.0	47.8	74.2	53.4	45.9	54.0
1989	63.0	47.5	64.2	72.5	48.7	74.5	54.3	46.4	54.9
1990	62.8	45.3	64.3	72.0	46.6	74.3	54.3	44.0	55.2
1991	61.7	42.0	63.2	70.4	42.7	72.7	53.7	41.2	54.6
1992	61.5	41.0	63.0	69.8	41.9	72.1	53.8	40.0	54.8
1993	61.7	41.7	63.3	70.0	42.3	72.3	54.1	41.0	55.0
1994	62.5	43.4	64.0	70.4	43.8	72.6	55.3	43.0	56.2
1995	62.9	44.2	64.4	70.8	44.7	73.0	55.6	43.8	56.5
1996	63.2	43.5	64.7	70.9	43.6	73.2	56.0	43.5	57.0
1997	63.8	43.4	65.5	71.3	43.4	73.7	56.8	43.3	57.8
1998	64.1	45.1	65.6	71.6	44.7	73.9	57.1	45.5	58.0
1999	64.3	44.7	65.9	71.6	45.1	74.0	57.4	44.3	58.5
2000	64.4	45.2	66.0	71.9	45.4	74.2	57.5	45.0	58.4
2001	63.7	42.3	65.4	70.9	42.2	73.3	57.0	42.4	58.1
2002	62.7	39.6	64.6	69.7	38.9	72.3	56.3	40.3	57.5
2003	62.3	36.8	64.3	68.9	35.7	71.7	56.1	37.8	57.5
2004	62.3	36.4	64.4	69.2	35.9	71.9	56.0	37.0	57.4
2005	62.7	36.5	64.7	69.6	35.1	72.4	56.2	37.8	57.6
2006	63.1	36.9	65.2	70.1	36.3	72.9	56.6	37.6	58.0
2007	63.0	34.8	65.2	69.8	33.9	72.8	56.6	35.8	58.2
2008	62.2	32.6	64.5	68.5	31.6	71.6	56.2	33.7	57.9
2009	59.3	28.4	61.7	64.5	26.9	67.6	54.4	29.9	56.2

Table 1-12. Civilian Employment-Population Ratios, by Sex, Age, Race, and Hispanic Origin, 1948–2009
—*Continued*

(Percent.)

Race, Hispanic origin, and year	Both sexes			Men			Women		
	16 years and over	16 to 19 years	20 years and over	16 years and over	16 to 19 years	20 years and over	16 years and over	16 to 19 years	20 years and over
WHITE[1]									
1954	55.2	42.9	56.2	81.5	49.9	84.0	31.4	36.4	31.1
1955	56.5	44.2	57.4	82.2	52.0	84.7	33.0	37.0	32.7
1956	57.3	46.1	58.2	82.7	54.1	85.0	34.2	38.9	33.8
1957	56.8	45.0	57.8	81.8	52.4	84.1	34.2	38.2	33.9
1958	55.3	41.0	56.5	79.2	47.6	81.8	33.6	35.0	33.5
1959	55.9	41.2	57.2	79.9	48.1	82.8	34.0	34.8	34.0
1960	55.9	41.5	57.2	79.4	48.1	82.4	34.6	35.1	34.5
1961	55.3	40.1	56.7	78.2	45.9	81.4	34.5	34.6	34.5
1962	55.4	40.4	56.9	78.4	46.4	81.5	34.7	34.8	34.7
1963	55.3	38.6	56.9	77.7	44.7	81.1	35.0	32.9	35.2
1964	55.5	38.4	57.3	77.8	45.0	81.3	35.5	32.2	35.8
1965	56.0	40.3	57.8	77.9	47.1	81.5	36.2	33.7	36.5
1966	56.8	43.6	58.3	78.3	50.1	81.7	37.5	37.5	37.5
1967	57.2	43.8	58.7	78.4	50.2	81.7	38.3	37.7	38.3
1968	57.4	43.9	59.0	78.3	50.3	81.6	38.9	37.8	39.1
1969	58.0	45.2	59.4	78.2	51.1	81.4	40.1	39.5	40.1
1970	57.5	44.5	59.0	76.8	49.6	80.1	40.3	39.5	40.4
1971	56.8	43.8	58.3	75.7	49.2	79.0	39.9	38.6	40.1
1972	57.4	46.4	58.6	76.0	51.5	79.0	40.7	41.3	40.6
1973	58.2	48.9	59.3	76.5	54.3	79.2	41.8	43.6	41.6
1974	58.3	49.3	59.3	75.9	54.4	78.6	42.4	44.3	42.2
1975	56.7	46.5	57.9	73.0	50.6	75.7	42.0	42.5	41.9
1976	57.5	47.8	58.6	73.4	51.5	76.0	43.2	44.2	43.1
1977	58.6	50.1	59.6	74.1	54.4	76.5	44.5	45.9	44.4
1978	60.0	52.4	60.8	75.0	56.3	77.2	46.3	48.5	46.1
1979	60.6	52.6	61.5	75.1	55.7	77.3	47.5	49.4	47.3
1980	60.0	50.7	61.0	73.4	53.4	75.6	47.8	47.9	47.8
1981	60.0	48.7	61.1	72.8	51.3	75.1	48.3	46.2	48.5
1982	58.8	45.8	60.1	70.6	47.0	73.0	48.1	44.6	48.4
1983	58.9	45.9	60.1	70.4	47.4	72.6	48.5	44.5	48.9
1984	60.5	48.0	61.5	72.1	49.1	74.3	49.8	47.0	50.0
1985	61.0	48.5	62.0	72.3	49.9	74.3	50.7	47.1	51.0
1986	61.5	48.8	62.6	72.3	49.6	74.3	51.7	47.9	52.0
1987	62.3	49.4	63.4	72.7	49.9	74.7	52.8	49.0	53.1
1988	63.1	50.9	64.1	73.2	51.7	75.1	53.8	50.2	54.0
1989	63.8	51.6	64.7	73.7	52.6	75.4	54.6	50.5	54.9
1990	63.7	49.7	64.8	73.3	51.0	75.1	54.7	48.3	55.2
1991	62.6	46.6	63.7	71.6	47.2	73.5	54.2	45.9	54.8
1992	62.4	45.3	63.6	71.1	46.4	73.1	54.2	44.2	54.9
1993	62.7	46.2	63.9	71.4	46.6	73.3	54.6	45.7	55.2
1994	63.5	47.9	64.7	71.8	48.3	73.6	55.8	47.5	56.4
1995	63.8	48.8	64.9	72.0	49.4	73.8	56.1	48.1	56.7
1996	64.1	47.9	65.3	72.3	48.2	74.2	56.3	47.6	57.0
1997	64.6	47.7	65.9	72.7	48.1	74.7	57.0	47.2	57.8
1998	64.7	48.9	65.9	72.7	48.6	74.7	57.1	49.3	57.7
1999	64.8	48.8	66.1	72.8	49.3	74.8	57.3	48.3	58.0
2000	64.9	49.1	66.1	73.0	49.5	74.9	57.4	48.8	58.0
2001	64.2	46.3	65.6	72.0	46.2	74.0	57.0	46.5	57.7
2002	63.4	43.2	64.9	70.8	42.3	73.1	56.4	44.1	57.3
2003	63.0	40.4	64.7	70.1	39.4	72.5	56.3	41.5	57.3
2004	63.1	40.0	64.8	70.4	39.7	72.8	56.1	40.3	57.2
2005	63.4	40.2	65.1	70.8	38.8	73.3	56.3	41.8	57.4
2006	63.8	40.6	65.5	71.3	40.0	73.7	56.6	41.1	57.7
2007	63.6	38.3	65.5	70.9	37.3	73.5	56.7	39.2	57.9
2008	62.8	35.9	64.8	69.7	34.8	72.4	56.3	37.1	57.7
2009	60.2	31.7	62.3	66.0	30.2	68.7	54.8	33.4	56.3

[1]Beginning in 2003, persons who selected this race group only; persons who selected more than one race group are not included. Prior to 2003, persons who reported more than one race group were included in the group they identified as their main race.

Table 1-12. Civilian Employment-Population Ratios, by Sex, Age, Race, and Hispanic Origin, 1948–2009
—Continued

(Percent.)

Race, Hispanic origin, and year	Both sexes			Men			Women		
	16 years and over	16 to 19 years	20 years and over	16 years and over	16 to 19 years	20 years and over	16 years and over	16 to 19 years	20 years and over
BLACK[1]									
1972	53.7	25.2	58.3	66.8	31.6	73.0	43.0	19.2	46.5
1973	54.5	27.2	58.9	67.5	32.8	73.7	43.8	22.0	47.2
1974	53.5	25.9	58.0	65.8	31.4	71.9	43.5	20.9	46.9
1975	50.1	23.1	54.5	60.6	26.3	66.5	41.6	20.2	44.9
1976	50.8	22.4	55.4	60.6	25.8	66.8	42.8	19.2	46.4
1977	51.4	22.3	56.0	61.4	26.4	67.5	43.3	18.5	47.0
1978	53.6	25.2	58.0	63.3	28.5	69.1	45.8	22.1	49.3
1979	53.8	25.4	58.1	63.4	28.7	69.1	46.0	22.4	49.3
1980	52.3	23.9	56.4	60.4	27.0	65.8	45.7	21.0	49.1
1981	51.3	22.1	55.5	59.1	24.6	64.5	45.1	19.7	48.5
1982	49.4	19.0	53.6	56.0	20.3	61.4	44.2	17.7	47.5
1983	49.5	18.7	53.6	56.3	20.4	61.6	44.1	17.0	47.4
1984	52.3	21.9	56.1	59.2	23.9	64.1	46.7	20.1	49.8
1985	53.4	24.6	57.0	60.0	26.3	64.6	48.1	23.1	50.9
1986	54.1	25.1	57.6	60.6	26.5	65.1	48.8	23.8	51.6
1987	55.6	27.1	58.9	62.0	28.5	66.4	50.3	25.8	53.0
1988	56.3	27.6	59.7	62.7	29.4	67.1	51.2	25.8	53.9
1989	56.9	28.7	60.1	62.8	30.4	67.0	52.0	27.1	54.6
1990	56.7	26.7	60.2	62.6	27.7	67.1	51.9	25.8	54.7
1991	55.4	22.6	59.0	61.3	23.8	65.9	50.6	21.5	53.6
1992	54.9	22.8	58.3	59.9	23.6	64.3	50.8	22.1	53.6
1993	55.0	22.6	58.4	60.0	23.6	64.3	50.9	21.6	53.8
1994	56.1	24.9	59.4	60.8	25.4	65.0	52.3	24.5	55.0
1995	57.1	25.7	60.5	61.7	25.2	66.1	53.4	26.1	56.1
1996	57.4	26.0	60.8	61.1	24.9	65.5	54.4	27.1	57.1
1997	58.2	26.1	61.8	61.4	23.7	66.1	55.6	28.5	58.4
1998	59.7	30.1	63.0	62.9	28.4	67.1	57.2	31.8	59.7
1999	60.6	27.9	64.2	63.1	26.7	67.5	58.6	29.0	61.5
2000	60.9	29.8	64.2	63.6	28.9	67.7	58.6	30.6	61.3
2001	59.7	26.7	63.2	62.1	26.4	66.3	57.8	27.0	60.7
2002	58.1	25.3	61.6	61.1	25.6	65.2	55.8	24.9	58.7
2003	57.4	21.7	61.0	59.5	19.9	64.1	55.6	23.4	58.6
2004	57.2	21.5	60.9	59.3	19.3	63.9	55.5	23.6	58.5
2005	57.7	21.6	61.5	60.2	20.8	64.7	55.7	22.4	58.9
2006	58.4	24.1	62.0	60.6	21.7	65.2	56.5	26.4	59.4
2007	58.4	21.4	62.3	60.7	19.5	65.5	56.5	23.3	59.8
2008	57.3	20.2	61.2	59.1	18.7	63.9	55.8	21.7	59.1
2009	53.2	16.5	57.1	53.7	14.3	58.2	52.8	18.6	56.1
HISPANIC[2]									
1973	55.6	...	...	...	...	...	...	...	...
1974	56.2	...	...	...	...	...	...	...	...
1975	53.4	...	...	...	...	...	...	...	...
1976	53.8	...	56.6	...	...	...	...	...	...
1977	55.4	...	58.3	...	...	...	...	...	...
1978	57.2	...	60.0	...	...	...	...	...	...
1979	58.3	...	61.0	...	...	...	...	...	...
1980	57.6	...	60.5	...	...	...	...	...	...
1981	57.4	...	60.7	...	...	...	...	...	...
1982	54.9	...	58.2	...	...	...	...	...	...
1983	55.1	...	58.1	...	...	...	...	...	...
1984	57.9	...	60.7	...	...	...	...	...	...
1985	57.8	...	60.7	...	...	...	...	...	...
1986	58.5	...	61.5	...	...	...	...	...	...
1987	60.5	...	63.4	...	...	...	...	...	...
1988	61.9	...	64.6	...	...	...	...	...	...
1989	62.2	...	64.8	...	...	...	...	...	...
1990	61.9	...	64.8	...	...	...	...	...	...
1991	59.8	...	62.8	...	...	...	...	...	...
1992	59.1	...	62.1	...	...	...	...	...	...
1993	59.1	...	62.1	...	...	...	...	...	...
1994	59.5	33.5	62.4	71.7	36.8	...	47.2	30.1	...
1995	59.7	34.4	62.6	72.1	37.5	...	47.3	31.3	...
1996	60.6	33.1	63.7	73.3	38.8	...	47.9	27.3	...
1997	62.6	33.7	66.0	74.5	37.6	...	50.2	29.3	...
1998	63.1	36.0	66.2	74.7	38.6	...	51.0	33.0	...
1999	63.4	37.0	66.5	75.3	41.2	...	51.7	32.5	...
2000	65.7	38.6	68.9	77.4	42.8	81.7	53.6	33.9	55.8
2001	64.9	38.6	67.8	76.2	43.3	79.9	53.3	33.5	55.4
2002	63.9	35.2	67.0	74.5	39.0	78.3	52.9	31.1	55.2
2003	63.1	30.2	66.4	74.3	31.9	78.6	51.2	28.4	53.6
2004	63.8	30.4	67.2	75.1	33.4	79.4	51.8	27.2	54.4
2005	64.0	31.5	67.3	75.8	33.8	80.0	51.5	29.1	53.8
2006	65.2	32.2	68.5	76.8	34.8	81.1	52.8	29.5	55.2
2007	64.9	30.4	68.5	76.2	32.1	80.7	53.0	28.5	55.6
2008	63.3	28.6	66.9	74.1	30.9	78.6	51.9	26.2	54.6
2009	59.7	23.7	63.5	68.9	24.1	73.5	50.1	23.4	52.9

[1]Beginning in 2003, persons who selected this race group only; persons who selected more than one race group are not included. Prior to 2003, persons who reported more than one race group were included in the group they identified as their main race.
[2]May be of any race.
. . . = Not available.

Table 1-13. Employed Civilians, by Sex, Race, Hispanic Origin, and Occupation, 2007–2009

(Thousands of people.)

Year and occupation	Total	Men	Women	White[1]	Black[1]	Hispanic[2]
2007						
All Occupations	146 047	78 254	67 792	119 792	16 051	20 382
Management, professional, and related occupations	51 788	25 593	26 195	43 235	4 343	3 621
Management, business, and financial operations	21 577	12 375	9 203	18 511	1 626	1 580
Computer and mathematical occupations	3 441	2 560	881	2 523	247	179
Architecture and engineering occupations	2 932	2 511	421	2 449	154	189
Life, physical and social science occupations	1 382	792	591	1 094	80	64
Community and social service occupations	2 265	890	1 375	1 720	416	216
Legal occupations	1 668	809	858	1 481	111	100
Education, training, and library occupations	8 485	2 267	6 218	7 215	814	646
Arts, design, entertainment, sports, and media occupations	2 789	1 476	1 313	2 453	159	241
Healthcare practitioner and technical occupations	7 248	1 913	5 335	5 788	736	407
Healthcare support occupations	3 138	338	2 800	2 182	753	441
Protective service occupations	3 071	2 380	691	2 347	581	307
Food preparation and serving related occupations	7 699	3 354	4 345	6 121	888	1 633
Building and grounds cleaning and maintenance occupations	5 469	3 280	2 189	4 325	833	1 875
Personal care and service occupations	4 760	986	3 774	3 612	678	648
Sales and related occupations	16 698	8 424	8 275	13 888	1 658	1 891
Office and administrative support occupations	19 513	4 840	14 673	15 772	2 543	2 415
Farming, fishing, and forestry occupations	960	759	201	859	47	388
Construction and extraction occupations	9 535	9 276	258	8 504	636	2 851
Installation, maintenance, and repair occupations	5 245	5 043	202	4 517	436	725
Production occupations	9 395	6 563	2 832	7 566	1 184	1 921
Transportation and material moving occupations	8 776	7 420	1 355	6 863	1 471	1 667
2008						
All Occupations	145 362	77 486	67 876	119 126	15 953	20 346
Management, professional, and related occupations	52 761	25 948	26 813	44 090	4 374	3 723
Management, business, and financial operations	22 059	12 647	9 412	18 938	1 599	1 652
Computer and mathematical occupations	3 676	2 765	911	2 730	267	188
Architecture and engineering occupations	2 931	2 536	395	2 446	148	196
Life, physical and social science occupations	1 307	704	603	1 030	93	62
Community and social service occupations	2 293	909	1 383	1 741	436	205
Legal occupations	1 671	803	867	1 481	116	110
Education, training, and library occupations	8 605	2 234	6 371	7 337	792	641
Arts, design, entertainment, sports, and media occupations	2 820	1 471	1 349	2 466	172	234
Healthcare practitioner and technical occupations	7 399	1 878	5 521	5 920	751	434
Healthcare support occupations	3 212	359	2 853	2 156	827	436
Protective service occupations	3 047	2 352	695	2 330	582	332
Food preparation and serving related occupations	7 824	3 443	4 381	6 199	946	1 645
Building and grounds cleaning and maintenance occupations	5 445	3 254	2 192	4 295	818	1 821
Personal care and service occupations	4 923	1 064	3 859	3 701	722	699
Sales and related occupations	35 544	13 067	22 477	29 160	4 075	4 361
Office and administrative support occupations	19 249	4 845	14 404	15 563	2 499	2 459
Farming, fishing, and forestry occupations	988	780	208	878	45	389
Construction and extraction occupations	8 667	8 448	219	7 747	545	2 564
Installation, maintenance, and repair occupations	5 152	4 953	199	4 451	437	749
Production occupations	8 973	6 313	2 661	7 210	1 093	1 892
Transportation and material moving occupations	8 827	7 507	1 319	6 909	1 487	1 736
2009						
All Occupations	139 877	73 670	66 208	114 996	15 025	19 647
Management, professional, and related occupations	52 219	25 385	26 833	43 649	4 388	3 817
Management, business, and financial operations	21 529	12 330	9 199	18 582	1 516	1 642
Computer and mathematical occupations	3 481	2 618	863	2 633	233	189
Architecture and engineering occupations	2 740	2 363	377	2 276	151	196
Life, physical and social science occupations	1 328	707	621	1 052	80	1 328
Community and social service occupations	2 341	868	1 474	1 764	463	2 341
Legal occupations	1 710	859	851	1 510	110	85
Education, training, and library occupations	8 627	2 221	6 407	7 343	797	671
Arts, design, entertainment, sports, and media occupations	2 724	1 453	1 271	2 387	183	239
Healthcare practitioner and technical occupations	7 738	1 968	5 770	6 101	855	488
Healthcare support occupations	3 309	350	2 959	2 258	836	456
Protective service occupations	3 164	2 457	707	2 411	594	389
Food preparation and serving related occupations	7 733	3 422	4 310	6 184	884	1 672
Building and grounds cleaning and maintenance occupations	5 349	3 186	2 163	4 304	737	1 823
Personal care and service occupations	5 043	1 106	3 937	3 804	733	721
Sales and related occupations	33 787	12 498	21 289	27 777	3 793	1 864
Office and administrative support occupations	18 146	4 618	13 527	14 715	2 298	2 313
Farming, fishing, and forestry occupations	926	736	190	834	46	377
Construction and extraction occupations	7 439	7 248	191	6 682	447	2 123
Installation, maintenance, and repair occupations	4 957	4 751	206	4 286	418	726
Production occupations	15 951	12 530	3 421	12 808	2 149	1 675
Transportation and material moving occupations	8 297	7 028	1 269	6 587	1 270	1 689

[1]Beginning in 2003, persons who selected this race group only; persons who selected more than one race group are not included. Prior to 2003, persons who reported more than one race group were included in the group they identified as the main race.
[2]May be of any race.

Table 1-14. Employed Civilians, by Selected Occupation and Industry, 2007–2009

(Thousands of people.)

Year and industry	Total employed	Agriculture, forestry, fishing, and hunting	Mining	Construction	Manufacturing Total	Durable goods	Nondurable goods	Wholesale trade
2007								
All Occupations	146 047	2 095	736	11 856	16 302	10 363	5 938	4 367
Management, professional, and related occupations	51 788	1 013	171	1 931	4 654	3 169	1 485	704
Management, business, and financial operations	21 577	971	110	1 717	2 616	1 672	944	534
Computer and mathematical occupations	3 441	3	4	21	431	358	73	62
Architecture and engineering occupations	2 932	4	34	147	1 062	902	159	34
Life, physical and social science occupations	1 382	30	17	10	247	51	196	14
Community and social service occupations	2 265	1	X	0	3	3	1	X
Legal occupations	1 668	1	2	5	23	15	8	6
Education, training, and library occupations	8 485	1	X	5	25	16	9	6
Arts, design, entertainment, sports, and media occupations	2 789	1	1	24	210	132	78	35
Healthcare practitioner and technical occupations	7 248	2	2	2	36	19	17	13
Healthcare support occupations	3 138	0	X	0	11	5	5	2
Protective service occupations	3 071	26	1	15	38	24	14	6
Food preparation and serving related occupations	7 699	2	0	3	35	7	29	9
Building and grounds cleaning and maintenance occupations	5 469	22	4	48	129	74	55	22
Personal care and service occupations	4 760	29	X	3	8	3	5	3
Sales and related occupations	16 698	8	10	125	621	343	278	1 583
Office and administrative support occupations	19 513	77	59	621	1 521	931	590	19 513
Farming, fishing, and forestry occupations	960	785	1	6	65	11	54	47
Construction and extraction occupations	9 535	15	257	8 077	354	292	62	23
Installation, maintenance, and repair occupations	5 245	25	69	567	794	506	288	192
Production occupations	18 171	93	164	460	8 071	4 997	3 074	980
Transportation and material moving occupations	8 776	73	115	297	1 260	679	582	825
2008								
All Occupations	145 362	2 168	819	10 974	15 904	10 273	5 631	4 052
Management, professional, and related occupations	52 761	1 041	199	2 018	4 688	3 243	1 445	693
Management, business, and financial operations	22 059	996	117	1 804	2 523	1 639	884	553
Computer and mathematical occupations	3 676	4	8	18	513	425	88	56
Architecture and engineering occupations	2 931	4	45	159	1 107	955	152	24
Life, physical and social science occupations	1 307	24	20	7	242	47	194	12
Community and social service occupations	2 293	X	X	1	3	3	X	1
Legal occupations	1 671	1	4	2	24	13	11	7
Education, training, and library occupations	8 605	4	1	1	27	14	13	3
Arts, design, entertainment, sports, and media occupations	2 820	7	4	24	212	127	85	29
Healthcare practitioner and technical occupations	7 399	2	0	2	37	19	17	9
Healthcare support occupations	3 212	0	X	0	5	3	2	3
Protective service occupations	3 047	25	5	14	32	20	11	7
Food preparation and serving related occupations	7 824	2	1	2	38	11	27	14
Building and grounds cleaning and maintenance occupations	5 445	29	4	46	144	74	70	25
Personal care and service occupations	4 923	36	X	4	12	6	7	2
Sales and related occupations	16 295	11	11	81	625	334	291	1 468
Office and administrative support occupations	19 249	82	57	610	1 507	924	583	697
Farming, fishing, and forestry occupations	988	836	2	3	48	7	41	41
Construction and extraction occupations	8 667	6	285	7 241	322	254	68	38
Installation, maintenance, and repair occupations	5 152	19	74	527	798	538	260	151
Production occupations	8 973	14	63	169	6 434	4 158	2 275	123
Transportation and material moving occupations	8 827	66	120	260	1 250	700	551	788
2009								
All Occupations	139 877	2 103	707	9 702	14 202	8 927	5 275	3 808
Management, professional, and related occupations	52 219	1 008	187	1 987	4 406	3 044	1 362	677
Management, business, and financial operations	21 529	977	108	1 746	2 433	1 604	829	528
Computer and mathematical occupations	3 481	3	11	21	455	368	87	149
Architecture and engineering occupations	2 740	3	38	171	1 017	866	151	33
Life, physical and social science occupations	1 328	20	23	8	216	42	174	11
Community and social service occupations	2 341	0	X	3	1	0	1	1
Legal occupations	1 710	0	4	6	24	16	8	5
Education, training, and library occupations	8 627	1	1	1	23	14	8	8
Arts, design, entertainment, sports, and media occupations	2 724	2	1	28	194	117	77	23
Healthcare practitioner and technical occupations	7 738	2	2	2	42	17	26	8
Healthcare support occupations	3 309	1	X	1	8	4	4	2
Protective service occupations	3 164	17	7	12	31	21	10	4
Food preparation and serving related occupations	7 733	6	2	5	47	11	36	9
Building and grounds cleaning and maintenance occupations	5 349	24	4	46	156	78	79	36
Personal care and service occupations	5 043	46	X	3	9	3	6	1
Sales and related occupations	15 641	15	7	101	643	358	285	1 424
Office and administrative support occupations	18 146	76	58	560	1 337	831	506	616
Farming, fishing, and forestry occupations	926	779	2	5	43	5	38	40
Construction and extraction occupations	7 439	8	236	6 114	299	230	69	30
Installation, maintenance, and repair occupations	4 957	25	64	499	760	495	265	131
Production occupations	15 951	98	142	368	6 463	3 847	2 616	838
Transportation and material moving occupations	8 297	77	93	240	1 108	556	552	701

X = Not applicable.

Table 1-14. Employed Civilians, by Selected Occupation and Industry, 2007–2009—*Continued*

(Thousands of people.)

Year and industry	Retail trade	Transportation and warehousing	Utilities	Information	Finance and insurance	Real estate and rental and leasing	Professional and technical services
2007							
All Occupations	16 570	6 457	1 193	3 566	7 306	3 182	9 208
Management, professional, and related occupations	1 734	666	386	1 847	3 623	971	7 151
Management, business, and financial operations	916	550	195	714	3 017	893	2 597
Computer and mathematical occupations	142	45	42	315	379	29	4 554
Architecture and engineering occupations	17	31	100	133	14	6	1 004
Life, physical and social science occupations	18	5	22	12	23	3	341
Community and social service occupations	2	1	X	0	15	5	7
Legal occupations	21	3	6	12	90	17	1 089
Education, training, and library occupations	19	16	9	123	18	6	33
Arts, design, entertainment, sports, and media occupations	174	12	9	536	34	8	680
Healthcare practitioner and technical occupations	424	3	3	2	33	5	180
Healthcare support occupations	42	3	0	1	5	6	52
Protective service occupations	71	55	11	6	30	19	23
Food preparation and serving related occupations	327	18	1	33	4	22	5
Building and grounds cleaning and maintenance occupations	160	52	14	16	23	205	31
Personal care and service occupations	50	195	1	37	3	20	24
Sales and related occupations	9 269	112	18	413	1 259	1 229	262
Office and administrative support occupations	77	59	621	1 521	931	590	1 620
Farming, fishing, and forestry occupations	13	6	1	X	0	0	2
Construction and extraction occupations	114	61	123	15	11	58	52
Installation, maintenance, and repair occupations	646	336	165	415	31	154	97
Production occupations	1 688	3 312	268	147	29	130	152
Transportation and material moving occupations	1 177	3 214	56	65	12	105	36
2008							
All Occupations	16 533	6 501	1 225	3 481	7 279	2 949	9 362
Management, professional, and related occupations	1 746	726	380	1 815	3 679	878	7 367
Management, business, and financial operations	913	591	194	711	3 076	806	2 718
Computer and mathematical occupations	128	60	42	297	403	28	2 718
Architecture and engineering occupations	24	44	98	107	13	6	1 371
Life, physical and social science occupations	12	6	19	12	18	2	317
Community and social service occupations	4	1	X	X	18	5	7
Legal occupations	8	3	6	9	65	14	1 133
Education, training, and library occupations	24	12	5	109	24	3	39
Arts, design, entertainment, sports, and media occupations	209	8	10	565	29	8	641
Healthcare practitioner and technical occupations	425	2	6	4	33	5	156
Healthcare support occupations	46	3	X	2	3	5	51
Protective service occupations	60	40	11	4	30	15	30
Food preparation and serving related occupations	336	14	0	29	5	21	4
Building and grounds cleaning and maintenance occupations	153	53	20	21	22	215	30
Personal care and service occupations	51	183	1	36	6	19	22
Sales and related occupations	9 127	116	18	377	1 278	1 150	257
Office and administrative support occupations	2 481	1 610	217	657	2 198	329	1 321
Farming, fishing, and forestry occupations	13	4	X	0	1	0	0
Construction and extraction occupations	100	63	127	14	6	50	41
Installation, maintenance, and repair occupations	663	362	187	384	24	141	82
Production occupations	481	101	210	77	15	30	156
Transportation and material moving occupations	1 277	3 225	54	65	12	97	31
2009							
All Occupations	15 877	6 012	1 233	3 239	6 826	2 796	9 159
Management, professional, and related occupations	1 677	690	388	1 659	3 473	888	7 197
Management, business, and financial operations	860	562	186	639	2 914	819	2 615
Computer and mathematical occupations	817	128	202	1 020	559	69	4 583
Architecture and engineering occupations	24	49	122	87	8	5	884
Life, physical and social science occupations	13	4	21	17	21	3	335
Community and social service occupations	2	0	0	1	19	5	10
Legal occupations	11	6	6	7	66	18	1 175
Education, training, and library occupations	23	12	5	109	24	3	10
Arts, design, entertainment, sports, and media occupations	181	4	7	540	24	9	629
Healthcare practitioner and technical occupations	444	2	5	2	28	7	189
Healthcare support occupations	30	2	X	1	3	6	41
Protective service occupations	66	31	7	11	36	25	24
Food preparation and serving related occupations	299	5	1	26	4	24	6
Building and grounds cleaning and maintenance occupations	149	54	18	19	22	183	23
Personal care and service occupations	46	171	0	32	6	24	33
Sales and related occupations	8 762	98	24	405	1 188	1 011	234
Office and administrative support occupations	2 417	1 478	200	604	2 037	330	1 291
Farming, fishing, and forestry occupations	13	7	1	X	0	X	1
Construction and extraction occupations	89	73	120	18	9	52	49
Installation, maintenance, and repair occupations	628	320	229	326	22	130	94
Production occupations	1 699	3 084	244	138	27	123	165
Transportation and material moving occupations	1 211	2 997	51	64	7	99	47

X = Not applicable.

Table 1-14. Employed Civilians, by Selected Occupation and Industry, 2007–2009—*Continued*

(Thousands of people.)

Year and industry	Management, administrative, and waste services	Educational services	Health care and social assistance	Arts, entertainment, and recreation	Accommodation and food services	Other services (except public administration)	Public administration
2007							
All Occupations	6 412	12 828	17 834	2 833	9 582	6 972	6 746
Management, professional, and related occupations	1 200	9 727	9 411	947	1 425	1 488	2 738
Management, business, and financial operations	820	1 131	1 488	232	1 348	586	1 144
Computer and mathematical occupations	381	8 597	7 923	715	78	902	1 594
Architecture and engineering occupations	59	36	26	5	6	17	196
Life, physical and social science occupations	24	188	218	11	1	17	182
Community and social service occupations	9	297	914	6	2	647	354
Legal occupations	33	8	29	1	1	16	304
Education, training, and library occupations	14	7 396	615	71	16	36	77
Arts, design, entertainment, sports, and media occupations	36	209	48	591	28	104	49
Healthcare practitioner and technical occupations	113	273	5 922	11	8	27	189
Healthcare support occupations	72	26	2 735	16	8	117	42
Protective service occupations	515	108	69	127	39	15	1 899
Food preparation and serving related occupations	14	452	378	266	6 053	49	29
Building and grounds cleaning and maintenance occupations	2 250	554	486	269	476	569	135
Personal care and service occupations	33	206	1 613	658	92	1 711	74
Sales and related occupations	354	67	66	175	683	410	34
Office and administrative support occupations	1 404	1 219	2 683	389	1 100	1 099	1 383
Farming, fishing, and forestry occupations	9	2	2	2	0	4	14
Construction and extraction occupations	83	80	45	18	13	32	103
Installation, maintenance, and repair occupations	171	132	95	63	52	1 074	168
Production occupations	660	320	318	78	323	814	163
Transportation and material moving occupations	444	274	154	57	214	313	84
2008							
All Occupations	6 178	13 169	18 233	2 972	9 795	7 005	6 763
Management, professional, and related occupations	1 114	9 895	9 655	1 017	1 511	1 539	2 799
Management, business, and financial operations	795	1 164	1 540	305	1 439	641	1 174
Computer and mathematical occupations	67	195	163	15	14	33	260
Architecture and engineering occupations	X	X	0	X	X	X	0
Life, physical and social science occupations	24	184	202	12	2	12	181
Community and social service occupations	9	309	897	4	5	645	384
Legal occupations	34	14	25	2	1	18	300
Education, training, and library occupations	15	7 531	608	64	15	51	68
Arts, design, entertainment, sports, and media occupations	35	190	69	600	20	96	63
Healthcare practitioner and technical occupations	93	273	6 130	5	7	30	182
Healthcare support occupations	78	35	2 791	20	12	118	39
Protective service occupations	526	110	60	142	46	21	1 868
Food preparation and serving related occupations	19	452	382	252	6 168	48	37
Building and grounds cleaning and maintenance occupations	2 151	599	485	274	467	581	128
Personal care and service occupations	26	239	1 678	689	101	1 741	75
Sales and related occupations	307	75	64	184	711	401	36
Office and administrative support occupations	988	1 189	2 664	226	415	657	1 343
Farming, fishing, and forestry occupations	5	5	1	3	1	3	22
Construction and extraction occupations	103	63	38	14	18	38	99
Installation, maintenance, and repair occupations	185	137	101	59	52	1 053	154
Production occupations	678	369	314	92	292	805	164
Transportation and material moving occupations	463	314	137	72	189	310	96
2009							
All Occupations	5 849	13 188	18 632	3 018	9 717	6 935	6 875
Management, professional, and related occupations	1 125	10 011	9 980	994	1 464	1 558	2 850
Management, business, and financial operations	796	1 203	1 547	276	1 387	689	1 244
Computer and mathematical occupations	329	8 808	8 433	718	77	869	1 606
Architecture and engineering occupations	32	42	24	11	7	10	175
Life, physical and social science occupations	17	203	191	10	2	11	202
Community and social service occupations	12	339	960	7	2	618	362
Legal occupations	33	11	37	3	0	14	285
Education, training, and library occupations	12	339	960	7	2	618	362
Arts, design, entertainment, sports, and media occupations	48	195	56	602	24	93	64
Healthcare practitioner and technical occupations	93	287	6 402	4	6	23	189
Healthcare support occupations	62	37	2 912	18	5	131	48
Protective service occupations	517	124	77	186	42	22	1 925
Food preparation and serving related occupations	21	419	376	278	6 121	52	32
Building and grounds cleaning and maintenance occupations	2 067	603	474	274	500	562	135
Personal care and service occupations	24	234	1 755	721	104	1 756	79
Sales and related occupations	285	65	81	143	721	403	30
Office and administrative support occupations	861	1 124	2 568	234	403	621	1 331
Farming, fishing, and forestry occupations	8	2	1	4	1	1	18
Construction and extraction occupations	91	49	38	19	12	29	106
Installation, maintenance, and repair occupations	195	139	101	71	49	1 023	151
Production occupations	593	381	268	76	297	777	170
Transportation and material moving occupations	415	340	131	61	211	349	94

X = Not applicable.

Table 1-15. Employed Civilians in Agriculture and Nonagricultural Industries, by Class of Worker and Sex, 1989–2009

(Thousands of people.)

Sex and year	Total employed	Agriculture				Nonagricultural industries						
		Total	Wage and salary workers	Self-employed workers	Unpaid family workers	Total employed	Wage and salary workers				Self-employed workers	Unpaid family workers
							Total	Government	Private household	Other industries except private households		
Both Sexes												
1989	117 341	3 199	1 665	1 403	131	114 142	105 259	17 469	1 101	86 689	8 605	279
1990	118 793	3 223	1 740	1 378	105	115 570	106 598	17 769	1 027	87 802	8 719	253
1991	117 718	3 269	1 729	1 423	118	114 449	105 373	17 934	1 010	86 429	8 851	226
1992	118 492	3 247	1 750	1 385	112	115 245	106 437	18 136	1 135	87 166	8 575	233
1993	120 259	3 115	1 689	1 320	106	117 144	107 966	18 579	1 126	88 261	8 959	218
1994	123 060	3 409	1 715	1 645	49	119 651	110 517	18 293	966	91 258	9 003	131
1995	124 900	3 440	1 814	1 580	45	121 460	112 448	18 362	963	93 123	8 902	110
1996	126 707	3 443	1 869	1 518	56	123 264	114 171	18 217	928	95 026	8 971	122
1997	129 558	3 399	1 890	1 457	51	126 159	116 983	18 131	915	97 937	9 056	120
1998	131 463	3 378	2 000	1 341	38	128 085	119 019	18 383	962	99 674	8 962	103
1999	133 488	3 281	1 944	1 297	40	130 207	121 323	18 903	933	101 487	8 790	95
2000	136 891	2 464	1 421	1 010	33	134 427	125 114	19 248	718	105 148	9 205	108
2001	136 933	2 299	1 283	988	28	134 635	125 407	19 335	694	105 378	9 121	107
2002	136 485	2 311	1 282	1 003	26	134 174	125 156	19 636	757	104 764	8 923	95
2003	137 736	2 275	1 299	951	25	135 461	126 015	19 634	764	105 616	9 344	101
2004	139 252	2 232	1 242	964	27	137 020	127 463	19 983	779	106 701	9 467	90
2005	141 730	2 197	1 212	955	30	139 532	129 931	20 357	812	108 761	9 509	93
2006	144 427	2 206	1 287	901	18	142 221	132 449	20 337	803	111 309	9 685	87
2007	146 047	2 095	1 220	856	19	143 952	134 283	21 003	813	112 467	9 557	112
2008	145 362	2 168	1 279	860	28	143 194	133 882	21 258	805	111 819	9 219	93
2009	139 877	2 103	1 242	836	25	137 775	128 713	21 178	783	106 752	8 995	66
Men												
1989	64 315	2 513	1 302	1 167	44	61 802	56 202	8 116	156	47 930	5 562	38
1990	65 105	2 546	1 355	1 151	39	62 559	56 913	8 245	149	48 519	5 597	48
1991	64 223	2 589	1 359	1 185	45	61 634	55 899	8 300	143	47 456	5 700	35
1992	64 441	2 575	1 371	1 164	40	61 866	56 212	8 348	156	47 708	5 613	41
1993	65 349	2 478	1 323	1 117	39	62 871	56 926	8 435	146	48 345	5 894	50
1994	66 450	2 554	1 330	1 197	27	63 896	58 300	8 327	99	49 874	5 560	37
1995	67 377	2 559	1 395	1 138	26	64 818	59 332	8 267	96	50 969	5 461	25
1996	68 207	2 573	1 418	1 124	31	65 634	60 133	8 110	99	51 924	5 465	36
1997	69 685	2 552	1 439	1 084	29	67 133	61 595	8 015	81	53 499	5 506	31
1998	70 693	2 553	1 526	1 005	23	68 140	62 630	8 178	86	54 366	5 480	29
1999	71 446	2 432	1 450	962	20	69 014	63 624	8 278	74	55 272	5 366	25
2000	73 305	1 861	1 116	725	20	71 444	65 838	8 309	71	57 458	5 573	33
2001	73 196	1 708	990	703	15	71 488	65 930	8 342	63	57 524	5 527	31
2002	72 903	1 724	979	731	14	71 179	65 726	8 437	76	57 212	5 425	29
2003	73 332	1 695	991	694	11	71 636	65 871	8 368	59	57 444	5 736	30
2004	74 525	1 687	970	702	15	72 838	66 951	8 616	60	58 275	5 860	27
2005	75 973	1 654	949	688	17	74 319	68 345	8 760	67	59 518	5 944	30
2006	77 502	1 663	989	664	10	75 838	69 811	8 696	60	61 055	6 004	23
2007	78 254	1 604	973	623	8	76 650	70 697	9 022	76	61 599	5 920	32
2008	77 486	1 650	997	637	16	75 836	70 072	9 089	70	60 912	5 736	29
2009	73 670	1 607	977	613	17	72 062	66 517	9 013	74	57 430	5 527	19
Women												
1989	53 028	687	363	236	87	52 341	49 057	9 353	945	38 759	3 043	240
1990	53 689	678	385	227	66	53 011	49 685	9 524	879	39 282	3 122	205
1991	53 495	680	369	237	73	52 815	49 474	9 635	867	38 972	3 150	191
1992	54 052	672	379	221	73	53 380	50 225	9 788	979	39 458	2 963	192
1993	54 910	637	367	204	67	54 273	51 040	10 144	980	39 916	3 065	168
1994	56 610	855	384	448	23	55 755	52 217	9 965	867	41 385	3 443	95
1995	57 523	881	419	442	20	56 642	53 115	10 095	867	42 153	3 440	86
1996	58 501	871	452	394	25	57 630	54 037	10 107	830	43 100	3 506	87
1997	59 873	847	451	373	23	59 026	55 388	10 116	834	44 438	3 550	89
1998	60 770	825	474	336	15	59 945	56 389	10 205	876	45 308	3 482	74
1999	62 042	849	494	335	20	61 193	57 699	10 625	859	46 215	3 424	70
2000	63 586	602	305	285	12	62 983	59 277	10 939	647	47 690	3 631	76
2001	63 737	591	293	284	13	63 147	59 477	10 993	630	47 853	3 594	75
2002	63 582	587	303	272	12	62 995	59 431	11 199	680	47 552	3 499	66
2003	64 404	580	309	257	14	63 824	60 144	11 267	705	48 172	3 609	72
2004	64 728	546	271	262	12	64 182	60 512	11 367	719	48 426	3 607	63
2005	65 757	544	263	267	13	65 213	61 586	11 598	745	49 243	3 565	63
2006	66 925	543	298	237	8	66 382	62 638	11 641	742	50 254	3 681	64
2007	67 792	490	247	233	11	67 302	63 586	11 981	737	50 868	3 637	80
2008	67 876	518	282	224	12	67 358	63 810	12 169	735	50 907	3 483	65
2009	66 208	496	265	223	8	65 712	62 197	12 165	709	49 322	3 468	47

Note: See notes and definitions for information on historical comparabilty.

Table 1-16. Number of Employed Persons Age 25 Years and Over, by Educational Attainment, Sex, Race, and Hispanic Origin, 1999–2009

(Thousands of people.)

Race, Hispanic origin, sex, and year	Total	Less than a high school diploma	High school graduate, no college	Some college, no degree	Associate's degree	College graduate or higher	
						Total	Bachelor's degree only
All Races							
1999	113 425	11 294	36 017	21 129	10 079	34 905	22 973
2000	116 473	11 692	36 452	21 601	10 707	36 020	23 706
2001	116 846	11 669	36 078	21 459	11 127	36 514	23 907
2002	116 802	11 535	35 779	20 928	11 166	37 395	24 570
2003	118 385	11 537	35 857	21 107	11 313	38 570	25 188
2004	119 622	11 408	35 944	21 284	11 693	39 293	25 484
2005	121 960	11 712	36 398	21 380	12 245	40 225	26 027
2006	124 386	11 892	36 702	21 630	12 514	41 649	26 960
2007	126 172	11 521	36 857	22 076	12 535	43 182	28 055
2008	126 161	11 073	36 097	22 092	12 948	43 951	28 460
2009	122 277	10 371	34 487	21 016	12 872	43 531	27 964
Men							
1999	61 032	6 921	19 125	10 941	4 838	19 208	12 343
2000	62 661	7 199	19 388	11 260	5 013	19 800	12 742
2001	62 824	7 188	19 274	11 076	5 226	20 060	12 872
2002	62 756	7 220	19 154	10 811	5 221	20 350	13 076
2003	63 349	7 290	19 200	10 858	5 231	20 770	13 354
2004	64 326	7 276	19 535	10 896	5 426	21 192	13 575
2005	65 772	7 487	20 127	10 993	5 739	21 427	13 687
2006	67 019	7 614	20 345	11 110	5 835	22 114	14 138
2007	67 963	7 450	20 434	11 382	5 862	22 835	14 680
2008	67 605	7 108	20 093	11 356	6 021	23 027	14 845
2009	64 831	6 569	19 085	10 772	5 864	22 541	14 368
Women							
1999	52 392	4 372	16 893	10 189	5 242	15 697	10 630
2000	53 812	4 493	17 064	10 341	5 694	16 220	10 964
2001	54 021	4 480	16 804	10 383	5 901	16 453	11 035
2002	54 046	4 315	16 624	10 117	5 945	17 045	11 493
2003	55 035	4 248	16 657	10 249	6 081	17 800	11 834
2004	55 296	4 132	16 409	10 387	6 267	18 101	11 908
2005	56 188	4 226	16 271	10 388	6 506	18 798	12 340
2006	57 367	4 278	16 357	10 520	6 678	19 535	12 822
2007	58 209	4 071	16 423	10 695	6 674	20 346	13 375
2008	58 555	3 965	16 004	10 737	6 926	20 924	13 614
2009	57 445	3 802	15 402	10 244	7 008	20 990	13 597
White[1]							
1999	95 316	9 235	30 211	17 388	8 556	29 925	19 668
2000	97 320	9 544	30 438	17 770	9 075	30 493	20 078
2001	97 560	9 550	30 126	17 671	9 393	30 821	20 136
2002	97 476	9 394	29 836	17 209	9 440	31 597	20 670
2003	98 120	9 437	29 645	17 227	9 476	32 335	21 103
2004	98 967	9 335	29 571	17 445	9 817	32 799	21 299
2005	100 613	9 579	29 911	17 515	10 256	33 352	21 550
2006	102 322	9 720	30 188	17 632	10 424	34 357	22 272
2007	103 477	9 446	30 140	17 936	10 419	35 535	23 138
2008	103 373	9 036	29 495	17 873	10 742	36 228	23 511
2009	100 419	8 497	28 372	16 983	10 714	35 854	23 109
Black[1]							
1999	12 771	1 488	4 631	2 924	1 108	2 621	1 814
2000	12 852	1 499	4 571	2 910	1 160	2 713	1 866
2001	12 797	1 492	4 492	2 871	1 216	2 727	1 921
2002	12 719	1 498	4 453	2 843	1 210	2 715	1 955
2003	12 706	1 376	4 465	2 780	1 199	2 887	2 056
2004	12 817	1 326	4 606	2 717	1 195	2 973	2 097
2005	13 177	1 369	4 742	2 720	1 288	3 057	2 106
2006	13 504	1 389	4 697	2 816	1 338	3 263	2 243
2007	13 811	1 293	4 783	2 912	1 389	3 435	2 362
2008	13 786	1 234	4 719	2 972	1 439	3 423	2 354
2009	13 110	1 096	4 375	2 855	1 422	3 363	2 253
Hispanic[2]							
1999	10 985	3 926	3 213	1 696	660	1 491	1 034
2000	12 406	4 468	3 658	1 828	756	1 696	1 198
2001	12 817	4 601	3 796	1 916	781	1 723	1 223
2002	13 294	4 744	3 921	1 900	823	1 906	1 370
2003	14 205	5 073	4 169	2 037	889	2 039	1 468
2004	14 661	5 135	4 330	2 137	931	2 127	1 538
2005	15 362	5 367	4 535	2 230	997	2 232	1 595
2006	16 225	5 620	4 801	2 282	1 095	2 428	1 698
2007	16 973	5 677	5 110	2 382	1 160	2 644	1 898
2008	17 115	5 426	5 232	2 484	1 236	2 736	1 930
2009	16 687	5 233	5 069	2 414	1 242	2 729	1 933

[1]Beginning in 2003, persons who selected this race group only; persons who selected more than one race group are not included. Prior to 2003, persons who reported more than one race group were included in the group they identified as their main race.
[2]May be of any race.

Table 1-16. Number of Employed Persons Age 25 Years and Over, by Educational Attainment, Sex, Race, and Hispanic Origin, 1999–2009—*Continued*

(Thousands of people.)

Race, Hispanic origin, sex, and year	Total	Less than a high school diploma	High school graduate, no college	Some college, no degree	Associate's degree	College graduate or higher — Total	Bachelor's degree only
White Men[1]							
1999	52 180	5 883	16 193	9 182	4 160	16 763	10 806
2000	53 243	6 085	16 373	9 435	4 320	17 030	11 029
2001	53 375	6 080	16 292	9 344	4 501	17 158	11 060
2002	53 242	6 072	16 148	9 102	4 497	17 423	11 217
2003	53 458	6 192	16 068	9 042	4 431	17 725	11 461
2004	54 133	6 188	16 297	9 125	4 613	17 910	11 555
2005	55 214	6 368	16 750	9 225	4 851	18 021	11 551
2006	56 145	6 448	17 018	9 244	4 952	18 483	11 881
2007	56 740	6 364	17 039	9 409	4 964	18 964	12 260
2008	56 446	6 066	16 741	9 397	5 070	19 171	12 482
2009	54 248	5 583	15 966	8 937	4 948	18 813	12 112
White Women[1]							
1999	43 135	3 352	14 018	8 207	4 396	13 162	8 862
2000	44 077	3 459	14 065	8 335	4 755	13 463	9 049
2001	44 184	3 469	13 834	8 327	4 891	13 663	9 075
2002	44 234	3 322	13 688	8 107	4 944	14 173	9 453
2003	44 662	3 245	13 576	8 185	5 045	14 610	9 643
2004	44 834	3 146	13 275	8 320	5 203	14 888	9 744
2005	45 399	3 211	13 162	8 290	5 405	15 331	9 999
2006	46 177	3 272	13 171	8 388	5 473	15 874	10 391
2007	46 737	3 082	13 102	8 527	5 455	16 571	10 878
2008	46 928	2 970	12 753	8 477	5 672	17 056	11 029
2009	46 172	2 913	12 406	8 046	5 766	17 040	10 997
Black Men[1]							
1999	6 001	741	2 339	1 313	469	1 140	789
2000	6 011	755	2 253	1 326	466	1 210	828
2001	5 924	762	2 232	1 258	486	1 186	834
2002	5 928	785	2 212	1 264	482	1 185	855
2003	5 860	693	2 190	1 256	492	1 230	890
2004	5 942	676	2 287	1 172	503	1 305	931
2005	6 153	697	2 417	1 171	558	1 310	938
2006	6 276	720	2 338	1 249	535	1 433	1 002
2007	6 429	653	2 340	1 320	570	1 547	1 076
2008	6 357	616	2 358	1 296	579	1 508	1 036
2009	5 939	551	2 199	1 225	544	1 419	958
Black Women[1]							
1999	6 770	746	2 292	1 612	639	1 481	1 025
2000	6 841	743	2 318	1 583	694	1 503	1 038
2001	6 873	730	2 260	1 612	729	1 541	1 087
2002	6 791	713	2 241	1 579	729	1 530	1 101
2003	6 846	683	2 275	1 524	707	1 657	1 166
2004	6 874	650	2 319	1 545	691	1 668	1 166
2005	7 024	672	2 325	1 549	730	1 748	1 169
2006	7 228	669	2 359	1 567	803	1 830	1 241
2007	7 382	641	2 443	1 592	819	1 888	1 286
2008	7 429	617	2 361	1 676	859	1 915	1 318
2009	7 171	544	2 176	1 631	877	1 943	1 295
Hispanic Men[2]							
1999	6 441	2 554	1 839	917	334	797	540
2000	7 373	2 937	2 128	995	397	916	634
2001	7 628	3 041	2 174	1 082	386	945	669
2002	7 865	3 141	2 244	1 029	415	1 035	732
2003	8 578	3 424	2 461	1 105	451	1 137	806
2004	8 872	3 508	2 583	1 158	468	1 155	837
2005	9 361	3 639	2 775	1 251	503	1 193	847
2006	9 856	3 823	2 932	1 260	547	1 293	891
2007	10 303	3 947	3 100	1 285	567	1 403	1 000
2008	10 363	3 714	3 231	1 371	607	1 439	1 008
2009	9 969	3 508	3 114	1 321	595	1 431	992
Hispanic Women[2]							
1999	4 544	1 372	1 373	778	327	694	494
2000	5 033	1 531	1 529	833	359	780	564
2001	5 190	1 560	1 622	834	395	778	553
2002	5 429	1 604	1 676	871	408	871	638
2003	5 627	1 649	1 708	932	438	901	661
2004	5 789	1 628	1 746	980	463	972	701
2005	6 000	1 728	1 759	979	495	1 039	748
2006	6 370	1 797	1 868	1 021	548	1 135	807
2007	6 670	1 730	2 010	1 097	593	1 241	898
2008	6 752	1 712	2 001	1 113	629	1 297	922
2009	6 718	1 724	1 955	1 093	647	1 298	941

[1]Beginning in 2003, persons who selected this race group only; persons who selected more than one race group are not included. Prior to 2003, persons who reported more than one race group were included in the group they identified as their main race.
[2]May be of any race.

Table 1-17. Multiple Jobholders and Multiple Jobholding Rates, by Selected Characteristics, May of Selected Years, 1970–2010

(Thousands of people, percent, not seasonally adjusted.)

| Year | Total employed | Multiple jobholders | | | | Multiple jobholding rate[1] | | | | | | |
		Total	Men	Women Number	Women Percent of all multiple jobholders	Total	Men	Women	White	Black[2]	Asian	Hispanic[3]
1970	78 358	4 048	3 412	636	15.7	5.2	7.0	2.2	5.3	4.4	...	...
1971	78 708	4 035	3 270	765	19.0	5.1	6.7	2.6	5.3	3.8	...	...
1972	81 224	3 770	3 035	735	19.5	4.6	6.0	2.4	4.8	3.7	...	...
1973	83 758	4 262	3 393	869	20.4	5.1	6.6	2.7	5.1	4.7	...	...
1974	85 786	3 889	3 022	867	22.3	4.5	5.8	2.6	4.6	3.8	...	...
1975	84 146	3 918	2 962	956	24.4	4.7	5.8	2.9	4.8	3.7	...	...
1976	87 278	3 948	3 037	911	23.1	4.5	5.8	2.6	4.7	2.8	...	...
1977	90 482	4 558	3 317	1 241	27.2	5.0	6.2	3.4	5.3	2.6	...	...
1978	93 904	4 493	3 212	1 281	28.5	4.8	5.8	3.3	5.0	3.1	...	...
1979	96 327	4 724	3 317	1 407	29.8	4.9	5.9	3.5	5.1	3.0	...	...
1980	96 809	4 759	3 210	1 549	32.5	4.9	5.8	3.8	5.1	3.2	...	...
1985	106 878	5 730	3 537	2 192	38.3	5.4	5.9	4.7	5.7	3.2	...	...
1989	117 084	7 225	4 115	3 109	43.0	6.2	6.4	5.9	6.5	4.3	...	...
1991	116 626	7 183	4 054	3 129	43.6	6.2	6.4	5.9	6.4	4.9	...	...
1994	122 946	7 316	3 973	3 343	45.7	6.0	6.0	5.9	6.1	4.9	...	3.8
1995	124 554	7 952	4 225	3 727	46.9	6.4	6.3	6.5	6.6	5.2	...	3.6
1996	126 391	7 846	4 352	3 494	44.5	6.2	6.4	6.0	6.4	5.1	...	4.0
1997	129 565	8 197	4 398	3 800	46.4	6.3	6.3	6.4	6.5	5.7	...	4.1
1998	131 476	8 126	4 438	3 688	45.4	6.2	6.3	6.1	6.3	5.5	...	4.4
1999	133 411	7 895	4 117	3 778	47.9	5.9	5.8	6.1	6.0	5.5	...	3.6
2000	136 685	7 751	4 084	3 667	47.3	5.7	5.6	5.8	5.9	4.9	3.4	3.2
2001	137 121	7 540	3 914	3 626	48.1	5.5	5.3	5.7	5.6	5.3	3.7	3.4
2002	136 559	7 247	3 736	3 511	48.4	5.3	5.1	5.5	5.5	4.7	4.0	3.8
2003	137 567	7 338	3 841	3 498	47.7	5.3	5.3	5.4	5.5	4.3	4.2	3.4
2004	138 867	7 258	3 653	3 605	49.7	5.2	4.9	5.6	5.3	5.1	3.7	3.4
2005	141 591	7 348	3 741	3 607	49.1	5.2	4.9	5.5	5.4	4.4	3.5	2.8
2006	144 041	7 641	3 863	3 778	49.4	5.3	5.0	5.7	5.3	5.4	3.7	3.1
2007	145 864	7 693	3 835	3 858	50.1	5.3	4.9	5.7	5.5	4.4	3.7	3.0
2008	145 927	7 653	3 842	3 812	49.8	5.2	4.9	5.6	5.4	4.9	3.8	2.9
2009	140 363	7 265	3 540	3 725	51.3	5.2	4.8	5.6	5.3	4.8	3.9	3.0
2010	139 497	7 261	3 559	3 702	51.0	5.2	4.8	5.6	5.4	4.6	3.1	3.1

Note: Data prior to 1985 reflect 1970 census–based population controls; years 1985–1991 reflect 1980 census–based controls; years 1994–1999 reflect 1990 census–based controls adjusted for the estimated undercount; and data for years 2000–2002 have been revised to incorporate population controls from the 2000 census. Prior to 1994, data on multiple jobholders were collected only through special periodic supplements to the Current Population Survey (CPS) in May of various years; these supplemental surveys were not conducted in 1981–1984, 1986–1988, 1990, or 1992–1993. Beginning in 1994, data reflect the introduction of a major redesign of the CPS, including the the collection of monthly data on multiple jobholders.

[1]Multiple jobholders as a percent of all employed persons in specified group.
[2]Data for years prior to 1977 refer to the Black-and-Other population group.
[3]May be of any race.
. . . = Not available.

Table 1-18. Multiple Jobholders, by Sex, Age, Marital Status, Race, Hispanic Origin, and Job Status, 2006–2009

(Thousands of people, percent.)

Characteristic	Both sexes				Men				Women			
	Number		Rate[1]		Number		Rate[1]		Number		Rate[1]	
	2006	2007	2006	2007	2006	2007	2006	2007	2006	2007	2006	2007
Age												
Total, 16 years and over[2]	7 576	7 655	5.2	5.2	3 822	3 833	4.9	4.9	3 753	3 822	5.6	5.6
16 to 19 years	270	249	4.4	4.2	103	96	3.4	3.3	167	153	5.4	5.1
20 to 24 years	774	738	5.6	5.3	341	309	4.6	4.2	432	429	6.7	6.5
25 to 34 years	1 577	1 662	5.1	5.3	850	876	5.0	5.0	727	786	5.2	5.6
35 to 44 years	1 856	1 844	5.4	5.4	969	948	5.2	5.1	887	896	5.6	5.7
45 to 54 years	1 934	1 926	5.7	5.6	940	959	5.2	5.3	994	967	6.2	5.9
55 to 64 years	988	1 022	5.1	5.1	517	522	5.1	4.9	471	501	5.1	5.2
65 years and over	176	214	3.3	3.8	101	123	3.4	4.0	75	91	3.2	3.6
Marital Status												
Single	2 131	2 101	5.3	5.2	962	952	4.4	4.3	1 169	1 149	6.5	6.3
Married, spouse present	4 136	4 215	5.1	5.1	2 420	2 435	5.3	5.3	1 716	1 780	4.9	5.0
Widowed, divorced, or separated	1 308	1 339	5.6	5.7	440	446	4.4	4.6	868	893	6.3	6.5
Race and Hispanic Origin												
White[3]	6 321	6 467	5.3	5.4	3 199	3 250	4.9	5.0	3 122	3 217	5.8	5.9
Black[3]	818	753	5.2	4.7	404	375	5.5	5.0	415	379	4.9	4.4
Hispanic[4]	598	638	3.0	3.1	337	353	2.8	2.9	261	284	3.4	3.5
Full- or Part-Time Status												
Primary job full time, secondary job part time	3 981	4 174	. . .	. . .	3 822	2 320	. . .	. . .	3 753	1 854	. . .	. . .
Primary and secondary jobs, both part time	1 676	1 764	. . .	. . .	508	531	. . .	. . .	1 168	1 233	. . .	. . .
Primary and secondary jobs, both full time	310	288	. . .	. . .	208	193	. . .	. . .	102	95	. . .	. . .
Hours vary on primary or secondary job	1 564	1 383	. . .	. . .	849	765	. . .	. . .	715	618	. . .	. . .

Characteristic	Both sexes				Men				Women			
	Number		Rate[1]		Number		Rate[1]		Number		Rate[1]	
	2008	2009	2008	2009	2008	2009	2008	2009	2008	2009	2008	2009
Age												
Total, 16 years and over[2]	7 620	7 271	5.2	5.2	3 837	3 530	5.0	4.8	3 783	3 741	5.6	5.6
16 to 19 years	225	186	4.0	3.8	94	71	3.4	3.1	131	115	4.6	4.6
20 to 24 years	752	710	5.5	5.6	329	307	4.6	4.7	423	403	6.5	6.4
25 to 34 years	1 555	1 546	5.0	5.1	846	795	4.9	4.9	710	750	5.0	5.4
35 to 44 years	1 841	1 675	5.5	5.3	941	822	5.2	4.9	900	853	5.9	5.8
45 to 54 years	1 958	1 903	5.7	5.7	959	907	5.3	5.2	999	996	6.1	6.2
55 to 64 years	1 067	1 039	5.1	4.9	539	507	4.9	4.7	528	532	5.3	5.2
65 years and over	223	212	3.7	3.5	129	120	3.9	3.6	94	92	3.5	3.3
Marital Status												
Single	2 089	1 989	5.2	5.2	989	890	4.5	4.3	1 100	1 099	5.9	6.2
Married, spouse present	4 166	3 993	5.1	5.0	2 386	2 212	5.2	5.0	1 780	1 781	5.0	5.1
Widowed, divorced, or separated	1 365	1 289	5.9	5.8	462	429	4.8	4.7	903	861	6.7	6.5
Race and Hispanic Origin												
White[3]	6 405	6 166	5.4	5.4	1 923	3 016	5.0	4.9	3 151	3 150	5.8	5.9
Black[3]	756	714	4.7	4.8	240	319	5.0	4.7	385	395	4.5	4.8
Hispanic[4]	671	643	3.3	3.3	235	354	3.1	3.0	294	289	3.6	3.6
Full- or Part-Time Status												
Primary job full time, secondary job part time	4 165	3 868	. . .	. . .	2 289	2 042	. . .	. . .	1 876	1 825	. . .	. . .
Primary and secondary jobs, both part time	1 791	1 821	. . .	. . .	588	599	. . .	. . .	1 203	1 222	. . .	. . .
Primary and secondary jobs, both full time	284	249	. . .	. . .	192	157	. . .	. . .	92	92	. . .	. . .
Hours vary on primary or secondary job	1 338	1 287	. . .	. . .	747	704	. . .	. . .	591	583	. . .	. . .

Note: Estimates for the above race groups (White or Black) do not sum to totals because data are not presented for all races. Beginning in January 2003, data reflect the revised population controls used in the household survey.

[1]Multiple jobholders as a percent of all employed persons in specified group.
[2]Includes a small number of persons who work part time at their primary job and full time at their secondary job(s), not shown separately.
[3]Beginning in 2003, persons who selected this race group only; persons who selected more than one race group are not included. Prior to 2003, persons who reported more than one race group were included in the group they identified as their main race.
[4]May be of any race.
. . . = Not available.

Table 1-19. Multiple Jobholders, by Sex and Industry of Principal Secondary Job, Annual Averages, 2007–2009

(Thousands of people.)

Year and industry of secondary job	Both sexes	Men	Women
2007			
All Nonagricultural Industries, Wage and Salary Workers	5 315	2 440	2 875
Mining	2	2	0
Construction	268	210	58
Manufacturing	177	106	71
Durable goods	93	65	28
Nondurable goods	84	41	43
Wholesale and retail trade	1 127	446	681
Wholesale trade	75	49	26
Retail trade	1 051	396	655
Transportation and utilities	210	157	53
Transportation and warehousing	194	146	48
Utilities	16	11	5
Information	175	118	57
Financial activities	400	227	173
Professional and business services	861	493	368
Education and health services	1 516	506	1 009
Leisure and hospitality	1 142	558	585
Other services	560	241	319
Other services, except private households	478	239	239
Other services, private households	82	2	80
Public administration	199	134	65
2008			
All Nonagricultural Industries, Wage and Salary Workers	5 322	2 480	2 842
Mining	6	5	1
Construction	242	202	40
Manufacturing	173	108	65
Durable goods	101	72	29
Nondurable goods	72	36	36
Wholesale and retail trade	1 142	461	681
Wholesale trade	78	46	31
Retail trade	1 065	415	650
Transportation and utilities	188	145	43
Transportation and warehousing	171	133	39
Utilities	17	13	4
Information	135	89	46
Financial activities	354	215	139
Professional and business services	863	521	342
Education and health services	1 527	544	983
Leisure and hospitality	1 146	519	626
Other services	622	287	335
Other services, except private households	535	279	256
Other services, private households	87	8	79
Public administration	190	123	67
2009			
All Nonagricultural Industries, Wage and Salary Workers	5 245	2 325	2 920
Mining	2	2	0
Construction	206	165	40
Manufacturing	159	98	60
Durable goods	96	63	33
Nondurable goods	63	35	28
Wholesale and retail trade	1 060	435	626
Wholesale trade	77	47	30
Retail trade	984	388	596
Transportation and utilities	173	124	50
Transportation and warehousing	151	107	44
Utilities	22	17	5
Information	148	97	51
Financial activities	340	208	132
Professional and business services	784	446	338
Education and health services	1 635	510	1 125
Leisure and hospitality	1 173	549	623
Other services	582	266	316
Other services, except private households	498	259	239
Other services, private households	84	7	77
Public administration	186	119	67

Table 1-20. Employment and Unemployment in Families, by Race and Hispanic Origin, Annual Averages, 2000–2009

(Thousands of people, percent.)

Characteristic	2000	2001	2002	2003	2004	2005	2006	2007	2008	2009
ALL RACES										
Total Families	71 680	73 306	74 169	75 301	75 872	76 443	77 017	77 894	77 943	78 361
With employed member(s)	59 626	60 707	61 121	61 761	62 424	62 933	63 492	64 330	64 058	63 010
As percent of total families	83.2	82.8	82.4	82.0	82.3	82.3	82.4	82.6	82.2	80.4
Some usually work full time[1]	55 683	56 519	56 742	57 229	57 813	58 276	58 918	59 616	59 116	57 037
With no employed member	12 054	12 600	13 048	13 540	13 447	13 509	13 525	13 564	13 884	15 351
As percent of total families	16.8	17.2	17.6	18.0	17.7	17.7	17.6	17.4	17.8	19.6
With unemployed member(s)	4 110	4 847	5 809	6 079	5 593	5 318	4 913	4 914	6 104	9 381
As percent of total families	5.7	6.6	7.8	8.1	7.4	7.0	6.4	6.3	7.8	12.0
Some member(s) employed	2 973	3 494	4 126	4 285	3 915	3 717	3 419	3 497	4 319	6 438
As percent of families with unemployed member(s)	72.3	72.1	71.0	70.5	70.0	69.9	69.6	71.2	70.8	68.6
Some usually work full time[1]	2 675	3 122	3 668	3 790	3 494	3 310	3 049	3 096	3 830	5 460
As percent of families with unemployed member(s)	65.1	64.4	63.1	62.3	62.5	62.2	62.1	63.0	62.7	58.2
WHITE[2]										
Total Families	59 918	60 921	61 494	61 995	62 250	62 567	62 977	63 667	63 490	63 774
With employed member(s)	49 877	50 505	50 785	51 002	51 350	51 645	52 054	52 669	52 273	51 494
As percent of total families	83.2	83.0	82.6	82.3	82.5	82.5	82.7	82.7	82.3	80.7
Some usually work full time[1]	46 639	47 060	47 193	47 356	47 620	47 883	48 395	48 879	48 271	46 629
With no employed member	10 042	10 416	10 709	10 993	10 900	10 922	10 923	10 997	11 217	12 280
As percent of total families	16.8	17.0	17.4	17.7	17.5	17.5	17.3	17.3	17.7	19.3
With unemployed member(s)	3 010	3 553	4 275	4 411	4 078	3 801	3 556	3 587	4 506	7 089
As percent of total families	5.0	5.8	7.0	7.1	6.6	6.1	5.6	5.6	7.1	11.1
Some member(s) employed	2 276	2 661	3 164	3 245	3 000	2 782	2 582	2 653	3 332	5 072
As percent of families with unemployed member(s)	75.6	74.9	74.0	73.6	73.6	73.2	72.6	73.9	74.0	71.5
Some usually work full time[1]	2 052	2 379	2 808	2 873	2 677	2 477	2 306	2 350	2 955	4 294
As percent of families with unemployed member(s)	68.2	67.0	65.7	65.1	65.7	65.2	64.8	65.5	65.6	60.6
BLACK[2]										
Total Families	8 600	8 674	8 845	8 869	8 860	8 952	9 058	9 184	9 297	9 318
With employed member(s)	6 964	6 933	6 987	6 906	6 920	6 986	7 078	7 249	7 290	7 022
As percent of total families	81.0	80.0	79.0	77.9	78.1	78.0	78.1	78.9	78.4	75.4
Some usually work full time[1]	6 401	6 373	6 390	6 270	6 292	6 353	6 437	6 608	6 622	6 265
With no employed member	1 636	1 742	1 858	1 963	1 940	1 966	1 980	1 935	2 006	2 296
As percent of total families	19.0	20.1	21.0	22.1	21.9	22.0	21.9	21.1	21.6	24.6
With unemployed member(s)	881	990	1 162	1 213	1 127	1 140	1 036	990	1 188	1 624
As percent of total families	10.2	11.4	13.1	13.7	12.7	12.7	11.4	10.8	12.8	17.4
Some member(s) employed	535	596	689	695	625	657	596	591	686	886
As percent of families with unemployed member(s)	60.8	60.2	59.3	57.3	55.5	57.7	57.6	59.7	57.8	54.5
Some usually work full time[1]	476	533	611	612	556	583	526	519	605	748
As percent of families with unemployed member(s)	54.1	53.8	52.6	50.5	49.3	51.1	50.8	52.4	50.9	46.0
HISPANIC[3]										
Total Families	7 581	8 140	8 650	9 185	9 305	9 603	9 905	10 332	10 500	10 489
With employed member(s)	6 633	7 100	7 485	7 907	8 071	8 312	8 641	9 048	9 135	8 852
As percent of total families	87.5	87.2	86.5	86.1	86.7	86.6	87.2	87.6	87.0	84.4
Some usually work full time[1]	6 255	6 692	6 989	7 383	7 566	7 786	8 129	8 492	8 466	7 923
With no employed member	947	1 040	1 165	1 277	1 235	1 291	1 264	1 285	1 365	1 637
As percent of total families	12.5	12.8	13.5	13.9	13.3	13.4	12.8	12.4	13.0	15.6
With unemployed member(s)	679	809	965	1 020	950	860	793	876	1 159	1 770
As percent of total families	9.0	9.9	11.2	11.1	10.2	9.0	8.0	8.5	11.0	16.9
Some member(s) employed	493	592	686	715	664	606	544	619	846	1 228
As percent of families with unemployed member(s)	72.7	73.2	71.1	70.1	69.9	70.5	68.6	70.6	73.0	69.3
Some usually work full time[1]	446	537	615	640	594	544	491	554	743	1 021
As percent of families with unemployed member(s)	65.8	66.4	63.7	62.7	62.5	63.2	61.9	63.2	64.1	57.7

Note: The race or ethnicity of the family is determined by the race of the householder. Estimates for the above race groups (White or Black) do not sum to totals because data are not presented for all races. Detail may not sum to total due to rounding. Data for 2003 reflect the revised population controls used in the Current Population Survey (CPS). Estimates for 2000 are not strictly comparable with data for later years due to population controls reflecting Census 2000 results.

[1] Usually work 35 hours or more a week at all jobs.
[2] Beginning in 2003, families where the householder selected this race group only; families where the householder selected more than one race group are excluded. Prior to 2003, families where the householder selected more than one race group were included in the group that the householder identified as the main race.
[3] May be of any race.

Table 1-21. Families, by Presence and Relationship of Employed Members and Family Type, Annual Averages, 2000–2009

(Thousands of people, percent.)

Characteristic	Number of families									
	2000	2001	2002	2003	2004	2005	2006	2007	2008	2009
MARRIED-COUPLE FAMILIES										
Total	54 704	55 749	56 280	57 074	57 188	57 167	57 509	58 145	58 125	58 124
Member(s) employed, total	45 967	46 680	46 976	47 535	47 767	47 895	48 196	48 676	48 541	47 876
Husband only	10 500	10 833	11 174	11 403	11 712	11 562	11 399	11 509	11 351	11 371
Wife only	2 946	3 257	3 613	3 863	3 843	3 715	3 754	3 858	4 036	4 909
Husband and wife	29 128	29 241	28 873	29 077	28 991	29 330	29 799	30 055	29 854	28 211
Other employment combinations	3 394	3 350	3 317	3 193	3 222	3 288	3 244	3 254	3 300	3 384
No member(s) employed	8 737	9 068	9 303	9 539	9 420	9 272	9 313	9 469	9 585	10 248
FAMILIES MAINTAINED BY WOMEN[1]										
Total	12 775	13 037	13 215	13 450	13 614	14 035	14 208	14 423	14 383	14 610
Member(s) employed, total	10 026	10 131	10 169	10 187	10 358	10 609	10 796	11 087	10 929	10 642
Householder only	5 581	5 667	5 944	5 987	6 021	6 052	6 103	6 307	6 250	6 135
Householder and other member(s)	2 806	2 778	2 559	2 539	2 701	2 830	2 955	2 994	2 870	2 642
Other member(s), not householder	1 639	1 686	1 666	1 660	1 636	1 727	1 738	1 785	1 809	1 866
No member(s) employed	2 749	2 906	3 047	3 263	3 255	3 426	3 412	3 336	3 454	3 968
FAMILIES MAINTAINED BY MEN[1]										
Total	4 200	4 521	4 674	4 777	5 071	5 242	5 300	5 327	5 435	5 627
Member(s) employed, total	3 632	3 895	3 976	4 039	4 299	4 430	4 500	4 568	4 589	4 492
Householder only	1 761	1 875	1 939	1 954	2 060	2 093	2 089	2 170	2 178	2 104
Householder and other member(s)	1 358	1 450	1 440	1 427	1 557	1 639	1 715	1 696	1 659	1 557
Other member(s), not householder	514	570	598	658	682	698	696	701	752	831
No member(s) employed	567	625	698	739	772	812	800	759	845	1 135

Characteristic	Percent distribution									
	2000	2001	2002	2003	2004	2005	2006	2007	2008	2009
MARRIED-COUPLE FAMILIES										
Total	100.0	100.0	100.0	100.0	100.0	100.0	100.0	100.0	100.0	100.0
Member(s) employed, total	84.0	83.7	83.5	83.3	83.5	83.8	83.8	83.7	83.5	82.4
Husband only	19.2	19.4	19.9	20.0	20.5	20.2	19.8	19.8	19.5	19.6
Wife only	5.4	5.8	6.4	6.8	6.7	6.5	6.5	6.6	6.9	8.4
Husband and wife	53.2	52.5	51.3	50.9	50.7	51.3	51.8	51.7	51.4	48.5
Other employment combinations	6.2	6.0	5.9	5.6	5.6	5.8	5.6	5.6	5.7	5.8
No member(s) employed	16.0	16.3	16.5	16.7	16.5	16.2	16.2	16.3	16.5	17.6
FAMILIES MAINTAINED BY WOMEN[1]										
Total	100.0	100.0	100.0	100.0	100.0	100.0	100.0	100.0	100.0	100.0
Member(s) employed, total	78.5	77.7	77.0	75.7	76.1	75.6	76.0	76.9	76.0	72.8
Householder only	43.7	43.5	45.0	44.5	44.2	43.1	43.0	43.7	43.5	42.0
Householder and other member(s)	22.0	21.3	19.4	18.9	19.8	20.2	20.8	20.8	20.0	18.1
Other member(s), not householder	12.8	12.9	12.6	12.3	12.0	12.3	12.2	12.4	12.6	12.8
No member(s) employed	21.5	22.3	23.1	24.3	23.9	24.4	24.0	23.1	24.0	27.2
FAMILIES MAINTAINED BY MEN[1]										
Total	100.0	100.0	100.0	100.0	100.0	100.0	100.0	100.0	100.0	100.0
Member(s) employed, total	86.5	86.2	85.1	84.6	84.8	84.5	84.9	85.7	84.4	79.8
Householder only	41.9	41.5	41.5	40.9	40.6	39.9	39.4	40.7	40.1	37.4
Householder and other member(s)	32.3	32.1	30.8	29.9	30.7	31.3	32.4	31.8	30.5	27.7
Other member(s), not householder	12.2	12.6	12.8	13.8	13.5	13.3	13.1	13.2	13.8	14.8
No member(s) employed	13.5	13.8	14.9	15.5	15.2	15.5	15.1	14.3	15.6	20.2

Note: Detail may not sum to total due to rounding. Estimates for 2000 are not strictly comparable with data for later years due to population controls reflecting Census 2000 results.

[1]No spouse present.

Table 1-22. Unemployment in Families, by Presence and Relationship of Employed Members and Family Type, Annual Averages, 2000–2009

(Thousands of people, percent.)

Characteristic	Number									
	2000	2001	2002	2003	2004	2005	2006	2007	2008	2009
MARRIED-COUPLE FAMILIES										
With Unemployed Member(s), Total	2 584	3 081	3 772	3 857	3 521	3 243	2 968	2 978	3 796	6 056
No member employed	411	531	676	713	615	580	526	512	663	1 218
Some member(s) employed	2 174	2 550	3 096	3 144	2 906	2 664	2 442	2 467	3 133	4 838
Husband unemployed	836	1 160	1 523	1 600	1 333	1 190	1 061	1 110	1 439	2 808
Wife employed	531	736	993	1 023	850	753	679	725	927	1 799
Wife unemployed	789	918	1 117	1 129	1 041	1 004	898	902	1 114	1 630
Husband employed	694	809	969	991	913	873	772	783	975	1 397
Other family member unemployed	959	1 003	1 133	1 129	1 147	1 049	1 010	966	1 243	1 618
FAMILIES MAINTAINED BY WOMEN[1]										
With Unemployed Member(s), Total	1 194	1 324	1 504	1 612	1 521	1 539	1 429	1 416	1 666	2 309
No member employed	587	643	787	842	829	797	753	701	849	1 244
Some member(s) employed	607	681	717	770	692	743	675	714	817	1 065
Householder unemployed	522	593	737	791	758	746	688	650	796	1 141
Other member(s) employed	102	129	147	162	146	161	132	144	181	225
Other member(s) unemployed	672	731	767	821	764	793	740	766	870	1 168
FAMILIES MAINTAINED BY MEN[1]										
With Unemployed Member(s), Total	331	442	533	610	551	536	516	520	642	1 016
No member employed	139	178	220	239	234	225	215	205	274	482
Some member(s) employed	192	264	313	371	316	310	301	316	368	535
Householder unemployed	173	234	303	340	296	301	284	294	385	626
Other member(s) employed	67	96	129	158	117	122	118	137	164	239
Other member(s) unemployed	158	208	230	270	255	235	232	226	257	391

Characteristic	Percent distribution									
	2000	2001	2002	2003	2004	2005	2006	2007	2008	2009
MARRIED-COUPLE FAMILIES										
With Unemployed Member(s), Total	100.0	100.0	100.0	100.0	100.0	100.0	100.0	100.0	100.0	100.0
No member employed	15.9	17.2	17.9	18.5	17.5	17.9	17.7	17.2	17.5	20.1
Some member(s) employed	84.0	82.8	82.1	81.5	82.5	82.1	82.3	82.8	82.5	79.9
Husband unemployed	32.0	37.7	40.4	41.5	37.9	36.7	35.7	37.3	37.9	46.4
Wife employed	20.5	23.9	26.3	26.5	24.2	23.2	22.9	24.3	24.4	29.7
Wife unemployed	31.0	29.8	29.6	29.3	29.6	31.0	30.3	30.3	29.3	26.9
Husband employed	26.8	26.3	25.7	25.7	25.9	26.9	26.0	26.3	25.7	23.1
Other family member unemployed	37.0	32.6	30.0	29.3	32.6	32.4	34.0	32.4	32.7	26.7
FAMILIES MAINTAINED BY WOMEN[1]										
With Unemployed Member(s), Total	100.0	100.0	100.0	100.0	100.0	100.0	100.0	100.0	100.0	100.0
No member employed	49.1	48.6	52.3	52.3	54.5	51.8	52.7	49.5	50.9	53.9
Some member(s) employed	50.9	51.4	47.7	47.8	45.5	48.2	47.3	50.5	49.1	46.1
Householder unemployed	43.7	44.8	49.0	49.1	49.8	48.5	48.2	45.9	47.8	49.4
Other member(s) employed	8.5	9.7	9.8	10.0	9.6	10.5	9.3	10.2	10.9	9.7
Other member(s) unemployed	56.3	55.2	51.0	50.9	50.2	51.5	51.8	54.1	52.2	50.6
FAMILIES MAINTAINED BY MEN[1]										
With Unemployed Member(s), Total	100.0	100.0	100.0	100.0	100.0	100.0	100.0	100.0	100.0	100.0
No member employed	42.0	40.3	41.3	39.2	42.5	42.1	41.7	39.3	42.7	47.4
Some member(s) employed	58.0	59.7	58.7	60.8	57.5	57.9	58.3	60.7	57.3	52.6
Householder unemployed	52.2	52.9	56.8	55.7	53.7	56.1	55.0	56.6	60.0	61.6
Other member(s) employed	20.4	21.7	24.2	25.9	21.3	22.8	22.8	26.3	25.6	23.5
Other member(s) unemployed	47.8	47.1	43.2	44.3	46.3	43.9	45.0	43.4	40.0	38.4

Note: Detail may not sum to total due to rounding. Estimates for 2000 are not strictly comparable with data for later years due to population controls reflecting Census 2000 results.

[1]No spouse present.

Table 1-23. Employment Status of the Population, by Sex, Marital Status, and Presence and Age of Own Children Under 18 Years, Annual Averages, 2000–2009

(Thousands of people, percent.)

Characteristic	2000 Both sexes	2000 Men	2000 Women	2001 Both sexes	2001 Men	2001 Women	2002 Both sexes	2002 Men	2002 Women	2003 Both sexes	2003 Men	2003 Women	2004 Both sexes	2004 Men	2004 Women
With Own Children Under 18 Years, Total															
Civilian noninstitutional population	63 267	27 673	35 595	64 100	28 076	36 024	64 399	28 137	36 263	64 932	28 402	36 530	64 758	28 272	36 486
Civilian labor force	51 944	26 202	25 742	52 489	26 551	25 938	52 566	26 529	26 036	52 727	26 739	25 988	52 288	26 607	25 681
Participation rate	82.1	94.7	72.3	81.9	94.6	72.0	81.6	94.3	71.8	81.2	94.1	71.1	80.7	94.1	70.4
Employed	50 259	25 622	24 637	50 455	25 750	24 704	50 022	25 474	24 549	50 103	25 638	24 466	49 957	25 696	24 261
Employment-population ratio	79.4	92.6	69.2	78.7	91.7	68.6	77.7	90.5	67.7	77.2	90.3	67.0	77.1	90.9	66.5
Full-time workers[1]	43 365	24 922	18 443	43 424	24 964	18 460	42 884	24 644	18 240	42 880	24 762	18 118	42 758	24 794	17 964
Part-time workers[2]	6 894	699	6 195	7 031	787	6 244	7 138	829	6 308	7 223	876	6 347	7 200	902	6 298
Unemployed	1 685	581	1 104	2 034	801	1 233	2 543	1 056	1 488	2 624	1 101	1 523	2 331	911	1 420
Unemployment rate	3.2	2.2	4.3	3.9	3.0	4.8	4.8	4.0	5.7	5.0	4.1	5.9	4.5	3.4	5.5
Married, Spouse Present															
Civilian noninstitutional population	51 415	25 540	25 874	51 981	25 796	26 185	51 947	25 781	26 166	52 476	26 049	26 427	52 109	25 852	26 258
Civilian labor force	42 361	24 290	18 072	42 712	24 512	18 201	42 492	24 425	18 067	42 776	24 638	18 138	42 247	24 449	17 798
Participation rate	82.4	95.1	69.8	82.2	95.0	69.5	81.8	94.7	69.0	81.5	94.6	68.6	81.1	94.6	67.8
Employed	41 357	23 816	17 541	41 431	23 849	17 581	40 867	23 533	17 334	41 128	23 712	17 416	40 847	23 703	17 144
Employment-population ratio	80.4	93.2	67.8	79.7	92.5	67.1	78.7	91.3	66.2	78.4	91.0	65.9	78.4	91.7	65.3
Full-time workers[1]	35 793	23 212	12 581	35 772	23 169	12 603	35 180	22 825	12 356	35 315	22 954	12 360	35 141	22 935	12 206
Part-time workers[2]	5 564	604	4 960	5 659	680	4 979	5 687	708	4 979	5 813	757	5 056	5 706	768	4 938
Unemployed	1 004	474	531	1 282	662	619	1 625	893	733	1 648	926	722	1 400	747	653
Unemployment rate	2.4	2.0	2.9	3.0	2.7	3.4	3.8	3.7	4.1	3.9	3.8	4.0	3.3	3.1	3.7
Other Marital Status[3]															
Civilian noninstitutional population	11 853	2 132	9 720	12 119	2 280	9 839	12 452	2 355	10 096	12 455	2 354	10 102	12 649	2 420	10 229
Civilian labor force	9 583	1 913	7 670	9 777	2 039	7 737	10 073	2 103	7 970	9 950	2 100	7 850	10 042	2 158	7 883
Participation rate	80.8	89.7	78.9	80.7	89.4	78.6	80.9	89.3	78.9	79.9	89.2	77.7	79.4	89.2	77.1
Employed	8 902	1 806	7 096	9 024	1 902	7 123	9 155	1 941	7 215	8 975	1 926	7 050	9 110	1 993	7 117
Employment-population ratio	75.1	84.7	73.0	74.5	83.4	72.4	73.5	82.4	71.5	72.1	81.8	69.8	72.0	82.4	69.6
Full-time workers[1]	7 572	1 710	5 862	7 652	1 795	5 857	7 704	1 820	5 885	7 566	1 807	5 759	7 617	1 859	5 757
Part-time workers[2]	1 330	96	1 234	1 372	107	1 265	1 451	122	1 329	1 411	118	1 291	1 494	134	1 360
Unemployed	681	107	574	752	138	614	918	163	755	976	175	800	931	165	766
Unemployment rate	7.1	5.6	7.5	7.7	6.8	7.9	9.1	7.8	9.5	9.8	8.3	10.2	9.3	7.6	9.7
With Own Children 6 to 17 Years, None Younger															
Civilian noninstitutional population	34 737	15 165	19 572	35 523	15 486	20 038	35 829	15 580	20 250	35 943	15 653	20 290	35 874	15 597	20 277
Civilian labor force	29 576	14 178	15 398	30 182	14 489	15 693	30 371	14 541	15 830	30 362	14 572	15 790	30 182	14 516	15 666
Participation rate	85.1	93.5	78.7	85.0	93.6	78.3	84.8	93.3	78.2	84.5	93.1	77.8	84.1	93.1	77.3
Employed	28 744	13 877	14 868	29 174	14 096	15 078	29 122	14 023	15 099	29 040	14 008	15 032	29 013	14 056	14 957
Employment-population ratio	82.7	91.5	76.0	82.1	91.0	75.2	81.3	90.0	74.6	80.8	89.5	74.1	80.9	90.1	73.8
Full-time workers[1]	25 042	13 513	11 529	25 382	13 689	11 693	25 225	13 586	11 638	25 116	13 558	11 557	25 069	13 597	11 473
Part-time workers[2]	3 703	364	3 339	3 792	407	3 385	3 898	437	3 461	3 925	450	3 475	3 944	459	3 485
Unemployed	832	302	530	1 008	393	615	1 249	518	731	1 322	564	758	1 170	460	709
Unemployment rate	2.8	2.1	3.4	3.3	2.7	3.9	4.1	3.6	4.6	4.4	3.9	4.8	3.9	3.2	4.5
With Own Children Under 6 Years															
Civilian noninstitutional population	28 530	12 508	16 022	28 577	12 590	15 986	28 570	12 557	16 013	28 988	12 749	16 240	28 884	12 675	16 210
Civilian labor force	22 368	12 024	10 344	22 307	12 062	10 245	22 194	11 988	10 206	22 365	12 167	10 198	22 106	12 091	10 014
Participation rate	78.4	96.1	64.6	78.1	95.8	64.1	77.7	95.5	63.7	77.2	95.4	62.8	76.5	95.4	61.8
Employed	21 515	11 745	9 770	21 280	11 654	9 626	20 900	11 450	9 450	21 063	11 630	9 433	20 944	11 640	9 304
Employment-population ratio	75.4	93.9	61.0	74.5	92.6	60.2	73.2	91.2	59.0	72.7	91.2	58.1	72.5	91.8	57.4
Full-time workers[1]	18 323	11 410	6 914	18 041	11 274	6 767	17 660	11 058	6 602	17 764	11 203	6 561	17 689	11 197	6 491
Part-time workers[2]	3 191	335	2 856	3 239	380	2 859	3 240	392	2 848	3 299	426	2 872	3 256	443	2 813
Unemployed	853	279	574	1 026	408	619	1 294	538	757	1 302	538	765	1 162	451	710
Unemployment rate	3.8	2.3	5.6	4.6	3.4	6.0	5.8	4.5	7.4	5.8	4.4	7.5	5.3	3.7	7.1
With No Own Children Under 18 Years															
Civilian noninstitutional population	145199	71 825	73 374	149643	73 857	75 786	151715	74 993	76 722	154714	76 510	78 204	156900	77 739	79 160
Civilian labor force	88 014	48 140	39 874	90 171	49 249	40 922	90 971	49 644	41 327	92 319	50 036	42 284	93 511	50 771	42 740
Participation rate	60.6	67.0	54.3	60.3	66.7	54.0	60.0	66.2	53.9	59.7	65.4	54.1	59.6	65.3	54.0
Employed	84 058	45 781	38 278	85 421	46 371	39 050	85 187	46 154	39 034	86 233	46 294	39 939	87 748	47 282	40 467
Employment-population ratio	57.9	63.7	52.2	57.1	62.8	51.5	56.1	61.5	50.9	55.7	60.5	51.1	55.9	60.8	51.1
Full-time workers[1]	68 046	39 136	28 910	69 074	39 596	29 478	68 574	39 319	29 254	69 073	39 245	29 827	70 244	40 134	30 110
Part-time workers[2]	16 012	6 645	9 367	16 347	6 776	9 572	16 614	6 834	9 779	17 160	7 049	10 111	17 505	7 148	10 357
Unemployed	3 956	2 359	1 596	4 750	2 878	1 872	5 784	3 491	2 293	6 087	3 741	2 345	5 763	3 489	2 274
Unemployment rate	4.5	4.9	4.0	5.3	5.8	4.6	6.4	7.0	5.5	6.6	7.5	5.5	6.2	6.9	5.3

Note: Own children include sons, daughters, stepchildren, and adopted children. Not included are nieces, nephews, grandchildren, and other related and unrelated children. Detail may not sum to total due to rounding. Estimates for 2000 are not strictly comparable with data for later years due to population controls reflecting Census 2000 results.

[1] Usually work 35 hours or more a week at all jobs.
[2] Usually work less than 35 hours a week at all jobs.
[3] Includes never-married, divorced, separated, and widowed persons.

Table 1-23. Employment Status of the Population, by Sex, Marital Status, and Presence and Age of Own Children Under 18 Years, Annual Averages, 2000–2009—*Continued*

(Thousands of people, percent.)

Characteristic	2005			2006			2007			2008			2009		
	Both sexes	Men	Women	Both sexes	Men	Women	Both sexes	Men	Women	Both sexes	Men	Women	Both sexes	Men	Women
With Own Children Under 18 Years, Total															
Civilian noninstitutional population	64 482	28 065	36 417	65 941	29 449	36 492	66 801	29 684	37 117	65 655	29 142	36 513	64 854	28 778	36 076
Civilian labor force	52 056	26 399	25 657	53 590	27 730	25 861	54 370	28 002	26 368	53 506	27 422	26 085	52 748	26 985	25 763
Participation rate	81.0	94.0	71.0	81.0	94.0	71.0	81.0	94.0	71.0	82.0	94.0	71.0	81.0	94.0	71.0
Employed	49 882	25 587	24 294	51 561	26 948	24 614	52 373	27 216	25 157	51 017	26 380	24 637	48 621	24 989	23 632
Employment-population ratio	77.0	91.0	67.0	78.0	92.0	67.0	78.0	92.0	68.0	78.0	91.0	68.0	75.0	87.0	66.0
Full-time workers[1]	42 852	24 713	18 139	44 634	26 033	18 601	45 336	26 282	19 053	43 967	25 338	18 629	41 003	23 583	17 419
Part-time workers[2]	7 029	875	6 155	6 927	914	6 013	7 037	933	6 104	7 050	1 042	6 008	7 618	1 406	6 212
Unemployed	2 174	811	1 363	2 029	782	1 247	1 998	786	1 211	2 490	1 041	1 448	4 128	1 996	2 132
Unemployment rate	4.2	3.1	5.3	3.8	2.8	4.8	3.7	2.8	4.6	4.7	3.8	5.6	7.8	7.4	8.3
Married, Spouse Present															
Civilian noninstitutional population	51 519	25 578	25 942	52 930	26 908	26 022	53 432	27 205	26 227	52 433	26 647	25 786	51 634	26 249	25 385
Civilian labor force	41 905	24 215	17 690	43 336	25 494	17 842	43 824	25 784	18 041	43 137	25 205	17 933	42 424	24 763	17 661
Participation rate	81.0	95.0	68.0	82.0	95.0	69.0	82.0	95.0	69.0	82.0	95.0	70.0	82.0	94.0	70.0
Employed	40 614	23 556	17 058	42 134	24 854	17 280	42 625	25 134	17 492	41 611	24 353	17 258	39 732	23 100	16 632
Employment-population ratio	79.0	92.0	66.0	80.0	92.0	66.0	80.0	92.0	67.0	79.0	91.0	67.0	77.0	88.0	66.0
Full-time workers[1]	35 086	22 808	12 278	36 649	24 074	12 575	37 120	24 332	12 788	36 128	23 444	12 685	33 846	21 871	11 975
Part-time workers[2]	5 528	748	4 780	5 485	780	4 705	5 505	802	4 704	5 482	909	4 573	5 886	1 229	4 657
Unemployed	1 291	659	632	1 202	640	562	1 199	650	549	1 527	852	675	2 692	1 663	1 029
Unemployment rate	3.1	2.7	3.6	2.8	2.5	3.1	2.7	2.5	3.0	3.5	3.4	3.8	6.3	6.7	5.8
Other Marital Status[3]															
Civilian noninstitutional population	12 963	2 487	10 475	13 010	2 541	10 470	13 369	2 479	10 890	13 222	2 495	10 727	13 221	2 529	10 691
Civilian labor force	10 151	2 184	7 967	10 255	2 236	8 019	10 546	2 219	8 328	10 369	2 217	8 152	10 325	2 223	8 102
Participation rate	78.0	88.0	76.0	79.0	88.0	77.0	79.0	90.0	77.0	78.0	89.0	76.0	78.0	88.0	76.0
Employed	9 268	2 032	7 236	9 427	2 094	7 333	9 747	2 082	7 665	9 406	2 027	7 379	8 889	1 889	7 000
Employment-population ratio	72.0	82.0	69.0	73.0	82.0	70.0	73.0	84.0	70.0	71.0	81.0	69.0	67.0	75.0	66.0
Full-time workers[1]	7 766	1 905	5 861	7 985	1 960	6 026	8 216	1 950	6 266	7 838	1 894	5 944	7 157	1 712	5 445
Part-time workers[2]	1 502	127	1 375	1 442	134	1 308	1 531	132	1 400	1 568	133	1 435	1 732	177	1 555
Unemployed	883	152	731	827	142	686	799	137	662	963	190	773	1 436	334	1 103
Unemployment rate	8.7	7.0	9.2	8.1	6.3	8.5	7.6	6.2	8.0	9.3	8.6	9.5	13.9	15.0	13.6
With Own Children 6 to 17 Years, None Younger															
Civilian noninstitutional population	35 937	15 590	20 348	36 530	16 212	20 318	36 983	16 384	20 599	36 581	16 256	20 325	35 885	15 982	19 903
Civilian labor force	30 068	14 496	15 572	30 675	15 091	15 585	31 179	15 269	15 910	30 846	15 128	15 718	30 200	14 821	15 379
Participation rate	84.0	93.0	77.0	84.0	93.0	77.0	84.0	93.0	77.0	84.0	93.0	77.0	84.0	93.0	77.0
Employed	28 953	14 066	14 887	29 643	14 690	14 952	30 176	14 866	15 310	29 590	14 588	15 003	28 059	13 775	14 284
Employment-population ratio	81.0	90.0	73.0	81.0	91.0	74.0	82.0	91.0	74.0	81.0	90.0	74.0	78.0	86.0	72.0
Full-time workers[1]	25 074	13 606	11 468	25 835	14 206	11 629	26 288	14 378	11 910	25 733	14 054	11 679	23 864	13 067	10 798
Part-time workers[2]	3 880	460	3 419	3 808	485	3 323	3 888	488	3 400	3 858	534	3 324	4 194	708	3 486
Unemployed	1 115	430	684	1 032	400	632	1 003	403	600	1 255	541	715	2 141	1 046	1 095
Unemployment rate	3.7	3.0	4.4	3.4	2.7	4.1	3.2	2.6	3.8	4.1	3.6	4.5	7.1	7.1	7.1
With Own Children Under 6 Years															
Civilian noninstitutional population	28 545	12 475	16 070	29 411	13 237	16 174	29 818	13 299	16 518	29 074	12 886	16 188	28 969	12 796	16 173
Civilian labor force	21 988	11 903	10 085	22 915	12 639	10 276	23 192	12 733	10 458	22 661	12 293	10 367	22 549	12 164	10 384
Participation rate	77.0	95.0	63.0	78.0	96.0	64.0	78.0	96.0	63.0	78.0	95.0	64.0	78.0	95.0	64.0
Employed	20 928	11 521	9 407	21 919	12 257	9 661	22 197	12 350	9 847	21 426	11 792	9 634	20 562	11 214	9 348
Employment-population ratio	73.0	92.0	59.0	75.0	93.0	60.0	74.0	93.0	60.0	74.0	92.0	60.0	71.0	88.0	58.0
Full-time workers[1]	17 778	11 107	6 671	18 800	11 828	6 972	19 048	11 904	7 143	18 234	11 284	6 950	17 138	10 517	6 622
Part-time workers[2]	3 150	414	2 736	3 119	430	2 689	3 149	446	2 704	3 193	508	2 684	3 424	697	2 726
Unemployed	1 060	381	678	997	382	615	995	383	611	1 234	501	733	1 987	950	1 036
Unemployment rate	4.8	3.2	6.7	4.3	3.0	6.0	4.3	3.0	5.8	5.4	4.1	7.1	8.8	7.8	10.0
With No Own Children Under 18 Years															
Civilian noninstitutional population	159751	79 237	80 514	162874	81 156	81 718	165066	82 489	82 577	168133	83 971	84 162	170947	85 358	85 589
Civilian labor force	95 545	51 914	43 631	97 837	53 525	44 312	98 754	54 134	44 620	100780	55 098	45 682	101394	55 138	46 256
Participation rate	60.0	66.0	54.0	60.0	66.0	54.0	60.0	66.0	54.0	60.0	66.0	54.0	59.0	65.0	54.0
Employed	90 171	48 709	41 462	92 866	50 554	42 312	93 674	51 039	42 635	94 346	51 106	43 239	91 257	48 681	42 576
Employment-population ratio	56.0	62.0	52.0	57.0	62.0	52.0	57.0	62.0	52.0	56.0	61.0	51.0	53.0	57.0	50.0
Full-time workers[1]	72 515	41 496	31 019	75 054	43 274	31 780	75 755	43 752	32 003	76 064	43 515	32 549	71 631	40 368	31 263
Part-time workers[2]	17 657	7 213	10 444	17 812	7 280	10 532	17 919	7 286	10 632	18 282	7 592	10 690	19 626	8 313	11 313
Unemployed	5 374	3 205	2 169	4 971	2 971	2 000	5 080	3 095	1 984	6 435	3 992	2 443	10 137	6 457	3 680
Unemployment rate	5.6	6.2	5.0	5.1	5.6	4.5	5.1	5.7	4.4	6.4	7.2	5.3	10.0	11.7	8.0

Note: Own children include sons, daughters, stepchildren, and adopted children. Not included are nieces, nephews, grandchildren, and other related and unrelated children. Detail may not sum to total due to rounding. Estimates for 2000 are not strictly comparable with data for later years due to population controls reflecting Census 2000 results.

[1] Usually work 35 hours or more a week at all jobs.
[2] Usually work less than 35 hours a week at all jobs.
[3] Includes never-married, divorced, separated, and widowed persons.

Table 1-24. Employment Status of Mothers with Own Children Under 3 Years of Age, by Age of Youngest Child and Marital Status, Annual Averages, 2000–2009

(Thousands of people, percent.)

Year and characteristic	Civilian noninsti-tutional population	Civilian labor force		Employed				Unemployed	
		Total	Percent of population	Total	Percent of population	Full-time workers[1]	Part-time workers[2]	Number	Percent of labor force
2000									
Total Mothers with Own Children Under 3 Years	9 356	5 653	60.4	5 311	56.8	3 614	1 697	342	6.0
2 years	2 803	1 807	64.5	1 712	61.1	1 193	519	95	5.3
1 year	3 300	2 069	62.7	1 939	58.8	1 310	629	130	6.3
Under 1 year	3 253	1 777	54.6	1 660	51.0	1 112	548	117	6.6
Married, Spouse Present with Own Children Under 3 Years	7 056	4 090	58.0	3 940	55.8	2 613	1 327	150	3.7
2 years	2 096	1 276	60.9	1 233	58.9	823	411	42	3.3
1 year	2 499	1 503	60.1	1 448	57.9	953	495	55	3.6
Under 1 year	2 461	1 312	53.3	1 259	51.1	837	421	53	4.1
Other Marital Status with Own Children Under 3 Years[3]	2 300	1 563	67.9	1 371	59.6	1 002	370	191	12.2
2 years	707	531	75.1	478	67.6	370	108	53	9.9
1 year	801	566	70.7	491	61.3	357	134	75	13.2
Under 1 year	792	465	58.8	402	50.7	275	127	64	13.7
2001									
Total Mothers with Own Children Under 3 Years	9 352	5 613	60.0	5 227	55.9	3 591	1 636	387	6.9
2 years	2 844	1 868	65.7	1 751	61.6	1 218	533	117	6.3
1 year	3 405	2 050	60.2	1 911	56.1	1 308	603	140	6.8
Under 1 year	3 103	1 695	54.6	1 565	50.4	1 065	500	130	7.7
Married, Spouse Present with Own Children Under 3 Years	7 079	4 058	57.3	3 884	54.9	2 601	1 282	175	4.3
2 years	2 120	1 310	61.8	1 258	59.3	839	419	53	4.0
1 year	2 589	1 479	57.1	1 416	54.7	940	475	63	4.3
Under 1 year	2 370	1 269	53.5	1 210	51.1	822	388	59	4.6
Other Marital Status with Own Children Under 3 Years[3]	2 269	1 555	68.5	1 343	59.2	989	352	212	13.6
2 years	723	558	77.2	493	68.2	379	114	65	11.6
1 year	814	571	70.1	495	60.8	367	127	76	13.3
Under 1 year	732	426	58.2	355	48.5	243	111	71	16.7
2002									
Total Mothers with Own Children Under 3 Years	9 350	5 632	60.2	5 181	55.4	3 513	1 667	451	8.0
2 years	2 949	1 895	64.3	1 758	59.6	1 234	524	137	7.2
1 year	3 310	2 003	60.5	1 852	56.0	1 241	610	151	7.5
Under 1 year	3 091	1 734	56.1	1 571	50.8	1 038	533	163	9.4
Married, Spouse Present with Own Children Under 3 Years	7 073	4 071	57.6	3 869	54.7	2 572	1 297	203	5.0
2 years	2 201	1 333	60.6	1 274	57.9	870	404	59	4.4
1 year	2 509	1 446	57.6	1 379	55.0	902	477	67	4.6
Under 1 year	2 363	1 292	54.7	1 216	51.5	800	416	77	6.0
Other Marital Status with Own Children Under 3 Years[3]	2 278	1 562	68.6	1 313	57.6	941	372	248	15.9
2 years	748	562	75.1	484	64.7	364	120	77	13.7
1 year	802	557	69.5	473	59.0	340	134	84	15.1
Under 1 year	728	443	60.9	356	48.9	237	118	87	19.6
2003									
Total Mothers with Own Children Under 3 Years	9 450	5 563	58.9	5 115	54.1	3 430	1 685	446	8.0
2 years	2 987	1 896	63.5	1 752	58.7	1 205	547	143	7.5
1 year	3 353	1 997	59.6	1 842	54.9	1 223	619	154	7.7
Under 1 year	3 110	1 670	53.7	1 521	48.9	1 002	519	149	8.9
Married, Spouse Present with Own Children Under 3 Years	7 165	4 068	56.8	3 872	54.0	2 529	1 342	197	4.8
2 years	2 243	1 350	60.2	1 281	57.1	853	428	69	5.1
1 year	2 541	1 458	57.4	1 395	54.9	906	488	64	4.4
Under 1 year	2 381	1 260	52.9	1 196	50.2	770	426	64	5.1
Other Marital Status with Own Children Under 3 Years[3]	2 287	1 495	65.4	1 244	54.4	902	341	250	16.7
2 years	744	546	73.4	471	63.3	352	118	75	13.7
1 year	813	539	66.3	448	55.1	317	131	91	16.9
Under 1 year	730	410	56.2	325	44.5	233	92	84	20.5
2004									
Total Mothers with Own Children Under 3 Years	9 345	5 377	57.5	4 964	53.1	3 360	1 604	414	7.7
2 years	2 813	1 746	62.1	1 630	57.9	1 152	477	116	6.6
1 year	3 273	1 906	58.2	1 759	53.7	1 172	587	147	7.7
Under 1 year	3 259	1 725	52.9	1 575	48.3	1 035	540	151	8.7
Married, Spouse Present with Own Children Under 3 Years	7 071	3 910	55.3	3 740	52.9	2 513	1 227	170	4.4
2 years	2 111	1 246	59.0	1 200	56.8	839	361	46	3.7
1 year	2 519	1 401	55.6	1 337	53.1	877	459	65	4.6
Under 1 year	2 441	1 262	51.7	1 203	49.3	797	406	59	4.7
Other Marital Status with Own Children Under 3 Years[3]	2 274	1 467	64.5	1 224	53.8	847	377	243	16.6
2 years	702	499	71.1	430	61.2	314	116	70	13.9
1 year	754	505	66.9	422	56.0	295	127	82	16.3
Under 1 year	818	463	56.6	372	45.4	238	134	91	19.7

Note: Own children include sons, daughters, stepchildren, and adopted children. Not included are nieces, nephews, grandchildren, and other related and unrelated children. Detail may not sum to total due to rounding. Updated population controls are introduced annually with the release of January data.

[1] Usually work 35 hours or more a week at all jobs.
[2] Usually work less than 35 hours a week at all jobs.
[3] Includes never-married, divorced, separated, and widowed persons.

Table 1-24. Employment Status of Mothers with Own Children Under 3 Years of Age, by Age of Youngest Child and Marital Status, Annual Averages, 2000–2009—Continued

(Thousands of people, percent.)

Year and characteristic	Civilian noninsti- tutional population	Civilian labor force						Unemployed	
		Total	Percent of population	Employed				Number	Percent of labor force
				Total	Percent of population	Full-time workers[1]	Part-time workers[2]		
2005									
Total Mothers with Own Children Under 3 Years	9 365	5 470	58.4	5 077	54.2	3 501	1 576	393	7.2
2 years	2 845	1 773	62.3	1 654	58.1	1 162	492	119	6.7
1 year	3 287	1 958	59.6	1 823	55.5	1 247	576	135	6.9
Under 1 year	3 233	1 740	53.8	1 600	49.5	1 092	508	140	8.0
Married, Spouse Present with Own Children Under 3 Years	6 951	3 939	56.7	3 776	54.3	2 588	1 188	164	4.2
2 years	2 118	1 268	59.9	1 214	57.3	840	374	55	4.3
1 year	2 435	1 389	57.0	1 337	54.9	901	436	52	3.7
Under 1 year	2 398	1 282	53.5	1 225	51.1	847	378	58	4.5
Other Marital Status with Own Children Under 3 Years[3]	2 414	1 531	63.4	1 301	53.9	913	388	230	15.0
2 years	726	504	69.5	440	60.6	322	118	64	12.7
1 year	852	569	66.8	486	57.0	346	139	83	14.6
Under 1 year	836	457	54.7	375	44.9	245	130	82	18.0
2006									
Total Mothers with Own Children Under 3 Years	9 431	5 675	60.2	5 315	56.4	3 751	1 564	360	6.3
2 years	2 864	1 847	64.5	1 746	61.0	1 280	466	101	5.5
1 year	3 318	2 006	60.5	1 883	56.7	1 305	577	123	6.1
Under 1 year	3 248	1 822	56.1	1 686	51.9	1 166	520	136	7.4
Married, Spouse Present with Own Children Under 3 Years	6 998	4 076	58.2	3 933	56.2	2 756	1 177	143	3.5
2 years	2 114	1 305	61.7	1 265	59.8	910	354	40	3.1
1 year	2 494	1 456	58.4	1 404	56.3	962	442	52	3.6
Under 1 year	2 390	1 315	55.0	1 264	52.9	883	381	51	3.9
Other Marital Status with Own Children Under 3 Years[3]	2 433	1 600	65.7	1 382	56.8	996	386	217	13.6
2 years	750	543	72.3	481	64.2	369	112	61	11.3
1 year	824	550	66.7	479	58.1	344	135	71	13.0
Under 1 year	859	507	59.0	422	49.2	283	139	85	16.7
2007									
Total Mothers with Own Children Under 3 Years	9 659	5 721	59.2	5 354	55.4	3 783	1 571	367	6.4
2 years	2 812	1 808	64.3	1 694	60.2	1 225	469	114	6.3
1 year	3 501	2 068	59.1	1 938	55.4	1 350	589	130	6.3
Under 1 year	3 346	1 845	55.1	1 721	51.4	1 208	513	123	6.7
Married, Spouse Present with Own Children Under 3 Years	7 018	4 027	57.4	3 888	55.4	2 730	1 157	140	3.5
2 years	2 076	1 281	61.7	1 230	59.2	881	349	51	4.0
1 year	2 536	1 433	56.5	1 388	54.7	954	434	46	3.2
Under 1 year	2 406	1 313	54.6	1 270	52.8	896	374	43	3.3
Other Marital Status with Own Children Under 3 Years[3]	2 641	1 694	64.1	1 466	55.5	1 052	414	227	13.4
2 years	736	528	71.6	464	63.1	344	120	63	12.0
1 year	965	635	65.8	551	57.1	396	155	84	13.2
Under 1 year	940	531	56.5	451	48.0	312	139	80	15.1
2008									
Total Mothers with Own Children Under 3 Years	9 595	5 792	60.4	5 354	55.8	3 782	1 573	438	7.6
2 years	2 934	1 852	63.1	1 734	59.1	1 264	470	118	6.4
1 year	3 342	2 069	61.9	1 905	57.0	1 337	568	164	7.9
Under 1 year	3 319	1 871	56.4	1 715	51.7	1 180	535	156	8.4
Married, Spouse Present with Own Children Under 3 Years	6 868	4 035	58.7	3 848	56.0	2 717	1 132	186	4.6
2 years	2 088	1 255	60.1	1 206	57.8	871	335	49	3.9
1 year	2 414	1 450	60.1	1 380	57.2	970	410	70	4.8
Under 1 year	2 366	1 330	56.2	1 263	53.4	875	388	67	5.0
Other Marital Status with Own Children Under 3 Years[3]	2 727	1 758	64.4	1 506	55.2	1 065	441	252	14.3
2 years	847	597	70.5	528	62.4	393	135	69	11.5
1 year	928	619	66.7	525	56.6	367	159	94	15.1
Under 1 year	953	542	56.8	452	47.5	305	147	89	16.5
2009									
Total Mothers with Own Children Under 3 Years	9 476	5 787	61.1	5 191	54.8	3 626	1 565	595	10.3
2 years	2 848	1 855	65.1	1 693	59.4	1 195	498	162	8.7
1 year	3 398	2 104	61.9	1 880	55.3	1 314	566	224	10.6
Under 1 year	3 231	1 828	56.6	1 619	50.1	1 117	502	209	11.4
Married, Spouse Present with Own Children Under 3 Years	6 784	4 047	59.7	3 780	55.7	2 657	1 123	267	6.6
2 years	2 053	1 288	62.7	1 208	58.8	858	350	80	6.2
1 year	2 425	1 465	60.4	1 369	56.4	963	406	96	6.6
Under 1 year	2 306	1 293	56.1	1 204	52.2	836	368	90	7.0
Other Marital Status with Own Children Under 3 Years[3]	2 693	1 740	64.6	1 411	52.4	969	442	328	18.9
2 years	795	567	71.3	485	61.0	337	148	82	14.4
1 year	973	639	65.6	511	52.5	351	160	127	20.0
Under 1 year	925	534	57.8	415	44.9	281	134	119	22.3

Note: Own children include sons, daughters, stepchildren, and adopted children. Not included are nieces, nephews, grandchildren, and other related and unrelated children. Detail may not sum to total due to rounding. Updated population controls are introduced annually with the release of January data.

[1]Usually work 35 hours or more a week at all jobs.
[2]Usually work less than 35 hours a week at all jobs.
[3]Includes never-married, divorced, separated, and widowed persons.

UNEMPLOYMENT

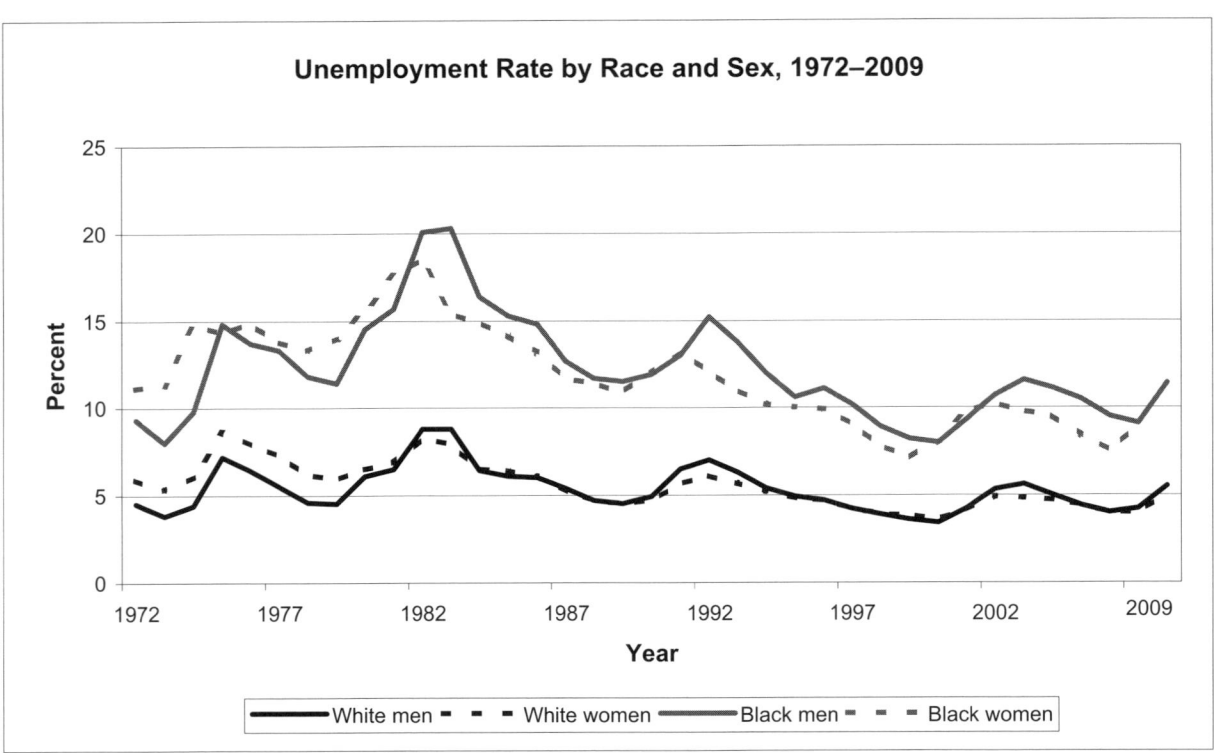

The unemployment rate rose significantly in 2009 to 9.3 percent. It was substantially higher for men (10.3 percent) than for women (8.1 percent). All racial and ethnic groups experienced an increase in unemployment in 2009. Blacks continued to have the highest unemployment rate at 14.8 percent, followed by Hispanics (12.1 percent) and Whites (8.5 percent). From 2008 to 2009, the unemployment rate increased by 4.7 percent for Blacks, 4.5 percent for Hispanics, and 3.3 percent for Whites. (See Table 1-27.)

OTHER HIGHLIGHTS

- Although unemployment rates increased for every age group, the disparity in unemployment rates among age groups continued to be substantial as younger workers experienced much higher levels of unemployment. In 2009, the unemployment rate for those age 16 to 19 years was 24.3 percent, compared to 6.6 percent for those age 55 to 64 years. (See Table 1-27.)

- Among the major industries, construction had the highest unemployment rate at 19.0 percent, followed by agriculture and private wage salary workers at 14.3 percent. Government workers had the lowest unemployment rate at 3.6 percent. (See Table 1-29.)

- In 2009, Michigan had the highest unemployment rate among all the state at 13.6 percent followed by Nevada at 11.8 percent and South Carolina at 11.7 percent. North Dakota had the lowest unemployment rate at 4.3 percent. (See Table 1-5.)

Table 1-25. Unemployment Rate, by Selected Characteristics, 1948–2009

(Unemployment as a percent of civilian labor force.)

Year	All civilian workers	Both sexes, 16 to 19 years	Men, 20 years and over	Women, 20 years and over	White[1]	Black[1]	Asian[1]	Hispanic[2]	Men Single, never married	Men Married, spouse present	Men Widowed, divorced, or separated	Women Single, never married	Women Married, spouse present	Women Widowed, divorced, or separated
1948	3.8	9.2	3.2	3.6	...	...	...	...	...	...	...	...	...	...
1949	5.9	13.4	5.4	5.3	...	...	...	...	...	...	...	...	...	...
1950	5.3	12.2	4.7	5.1	...	...	...	...	...	...	...	...	...	...
1951	3.3	8.2	2.5	4.0	...	...	...	...	...	...	...	...	...	...
1952	3.0	8.5	2.4	3.2	...	...	...	...	...	...	...	...	...	...
1953	2.9	7.6	2.5	2.9	...	...	...	...	...	...	...	...	...	...
1954	5.5	12.6	4.9	5.5	5.0	...	...	...	...	...	...	...	...	...
1955	4.4	11.0	3.8	4.4	3.9	...	...	...	8.6	2.6	7.1	5.0	3.7	5.0
1956	4.1	11.1	3.4	4.2	3.6	...	...	...	7.7	2.3	6.2	5.3	3.6	5.0
1957	4.3	11.6	3.6	4.1	3.8	...	...	...	9.2	2.8	6.8	5.6	4.3	4.7
1958	6.8	15.9	6.2	6.1	6.1	...	...	...	13.3	5.1	11.2	7.4	6.5	6.7
1959	5.5	14.6	4.7	5.2	4.8	...	...	...	11.6	3.6	8.6	7.1	5.2	6.2
1960	5.5	14.7	4.7	5.1	5.0	...	...	...	11.7	3.7	8.4	7.5	5.2	5.9
1961	6.7	16.8	5.7	6.3	6.0	...	...	...	13.1	4.6	10.3	8.7	6.4	7.4
1962	5.5	14.7	4.6	5.4	4.9	...	...	...	11.2	3.6	9.9	7.9	5.4	6.4
1963	5.7	17.2	4.5	5.4	5.0	...	...	...	12.4	3.4	9.6	8.9	5.4	6.7
1964	5.2	16.2	3.9	5.2	4.6	...	...	...	11.5	2.8	8.9	8.7	5.1	6.4
1965	4.5	14.8	3.2	4.5	4.1	...	...	...	10.1	2.4	7.2	8.2	4.5	5.4
1966	3.8	12.8	2.5	3.8	3.4	...	...	...	8.6	1.9	5.5	7.9	3.7	4.7
1967	3.8	12.9	2.3	4.2	3.4	...	...	...	8.3	1.8	4.9	7.5	4.5	4.6
1968	3.6	12.7	2.2	3.8	3.2	...	...	...	8.0	1.6	4.2	7.6	3.9	4.2
1969	3.5	12.2	2.1	3.7	3.1	...	...	...	8.0	1.5	4.0	7.3	3.9	4.0
1970	4.9	15.3	3.5	4.8	4.5	...	...	...	11.2	2.6	6.4	9.0	4.9	5.2
1971	5.9	16.9	4.4	5.7	5.4	...	...	...	13.2	3.2	7.4	10.5	5.7	6.3
1972	5.6	16.2	4.0	5.4	5.1	10.4	...	...	12.4	2.8	7.0	10.1	5.4	6.1
1973	4.9	14.5	3.3	4.9	4.3	9.4	...	7.5	10.4	2.3	5.4	9.4	4.7	5.8
1974	5.6	16.0	3.8	5.5	5.0	10.5	...	8.1	11.8	2.7	6.2	10.5	5.3	6.3
1975	8.5	19.9	6.8	8.0	7.8	14.8	...	12.2	16.1	5.1	11.0	13.0	7.9	8.9
1976	7.7	19.0	5.9	7.4	7.0	14.0	...	11.5	14.9	4.2	9.8	12.1	7.1	8.7
1977	7.1	17.8	5.2	7.0	6.2	14.0	...	10.1	13.5	3.6	8.2	12.1	6.5	7.9
1978	6.1	16.4	4.3	6.0	5.2	12.8	...	9.1	11.7	2.8	6.6	10.9	5.5	6.9
1979	5.8	16.1	4.2	5.7	5.1	12.3	...	8.3	11.1	2.8	6.5	10.4	5.1	6.7
1980	7.1	17.8	5.9	6.4	6.3	14.3	...	10.1	13.6	4.2	8.6	10.9	5.8	7.2
1981	7.6	19.6	6.3	6.8	6.7	15.6	...	10.4	14.6	4.3	9.1	11.9	6.0	8.1
1982	9.7	23.2	8.8	8.3	8.6	18.9	...	13.8	17.7	6.5	12.4	13.6	7.4	9.5
1983	9.6	22.4	8.9	8.1	8.4	19.5	...	13.7	17.3	6.5	13.0	13.1	7.0	9.9
1984	7.5	18.9	6.6	6.8	6.5	15.9	...	10.7	13.5	4.6	9.4	11.1	5.7	8.4
1985	7.2	18.6	6.2	6.6	6.2	15.1	...	10.5	12.7	4.3	9.2	10.7	5.6	8.3
1986	7.0	18.3	6.1	6.2	6.0	14.5	...	10.6	12.2	4.4	8.8	10.7	5.2	7.7
1987	6.2	16.9	5.4	5.4	5.3	13.0	...	8.8	11.1	3.9	7.6	9.5	4.3	7.0
1988	5.5	15.3	4.8	4.9	4.7	11.7	...	8.2	9.9	3.3	7.0	8.6	3.9	6.3
1989	5.3	15.0	4.5	4.7	4.5	11.4	...	8.0	9.6	3.0	6.3	8.4	3.7	5.9
1990	5.6	15.5	5.0	4.9	4.8	11.4	...	8.2	10.1	3.4	6.9	8.7	3.8	6.0
1991	6.8	18.7	6.4	5.7	6.1	12.5	...	10.0	12.4	4.4	9.0	10.1	4.5	6.9
1992	7.5	20.1	7.1	6.3	6.6	14.2	...	11.6	13.2	5.1	9.8	10.8	5.0	7.6
1993	6.9	19.0	6.4	5.9	6.1	13.0	...	10.8	12.4	4.4	9.0	10.3	4.6	7.3
1994	6.1	17.6	5.4	5.4	5.3	11.5	...	9.9	11.0	3.7	7.4	9.7	4.1	6.6
1995	5.6	17.3	4.8	4.9	4.9	10.4	...	9.3	10.1	3.3	6.9	9.1	3.9	5.9
1996	5.4	16.7	4.6	4.8	4.7	10.5	...	8.9	10.0	3.0	6.5	9.1	3.6	5.7
1997	4.9	16.0	4.2	4.4	4.2	10.0	...	7.7	9.2	2.7	5.8	8.8	3.1	5.2
1998	4.5	14.6	3.7	4.1	3.9	8.9	...	7.2	8.5	2.4	4.8	7.8	2.9	4.9
1999	4.2	13.9	3.5	3.8	3.7	8.0	...	6.4	7.8	2.2	4.6	7.4	2.7	4.5
2000	4.0	13.1	3.3	3.6	3.5	7.6	3.6	5.7	7.6	2.0	4.3	6.8	2.7	4.2
2001	4.7	14.7	4.2	4.1	4.2	8.6	4.5	6.6	8.9	2.7	5.1	7.7	3.1	4.7
2002	5.8	16.5	5.3	5.1	5.1	10.2	5.9	7.5	10.3	3.6	6.8	8.9	3.7	6.1
2003	6.0	17.5	5.6	5.1	5.2	10.8	6.0	7.7	11.0	3.8	7.3	9.1	3.7	6.1
2004	5.5	17.0	5.0	4.9	4.8	10.4	4.4	7.0	10.5	3.1	6.3	8.7	3.5	5.9
2005	5.1	16.6	4.4	4.6	4.4	10.0	4.0	6.0	9.5	2.8	5.6	8.3	3.3	5.4
2006	4.6	15.4	4.0	4.1	4.0	8.9	3.0	5.2	8.6	2.4	5.2	7.7	2.9	4.9
2007	4.6	15.7	4.1	4.0	4.1	8.3	3.2	5.6	8.8	2.5	5.3	7.2	2.8	5.0
2008	5.8	18.7	5.4	4.9	5.2	10.1	4.0	7.6	11.0	3.4	7.1	8.5	3.6	5.9
2009	9.3	24.3	9.6	7.5	8.5	14.8	7.3	12.1	16.3	6.6	12.8	12.0	5.5	9.2

Note: See notes and definitions for information on historical comparability.

[1] Beginning in 2003, persons who selected this race group only; persons who selected more than one race group are not included. Prior to 2003, persons who reported more than one race group were included in the group they identified as their main race.
[2] May be of any race.
... = Not available.

Table 1-26. Unemployed Persons, by Age, Sex, Race, and Hispanic Origin, 1948–2009

(Thousands of people.)

Race, Hispanic origin, sex, and year	16 years and over	16 to 19 years			20 years and over						
		Total	16 to 17 years	18 to 19 years	Total	20 to 24 years	25 to 34 years	35 to 44 years	45 to 54 years	55 to 64 years	65 years and over
ALL RACES											
Both Sexes											
1948	2 276	409	180	228	1 869	455	457	347	290	226	93
1949	3 637	576	238	337	3 060	680	776	603	471	384	146
1950	3 288	513	226	287	2 776	561	702	530	478	368	137
1951	2 055	336	168	168	1 718	273	435	354	318	238	103
1952	1 883	345	180	165	1 539	268	389	325	274	195	86
1953	1 834	307	150	157	1 529	256	379	325	280	218	70
1954	3 532	501	221	247	3 032	504	793	680	548	374	132
1955	2 852	450	211	239	2 403	396	577	521	436	355	120
1956	2 750	478	231	247	2 274	395	554	476	429	311	109
1957	2 859	497	230	266	2 362	430	573	499	448	300	111
1958	4 602	678	299	379	3 923	701	993	871	731	472	154
1959	3 740	654	301	354	3 085	543	726	673	603	405	135
1960	3 852	712	325	387	3 140	583	752	671	614	396	122
1961	4 714	828	363	465	3 886	723	890	850	751	516	159
1962	3 911	721	312	409	3 191	636	712	688	605	411	141
1963	4 070	884	420	462	3 187	658	732	674	589	410	126
1964	3 786	872	436	437	2 913	660	607	605	543	378	117
1965	3 366	874	411	463	2 491	557	529	546	436	322	103
1966	2 875	837	395	441	2 041	446	441	426	369	265	92
1967	2 975	839	400	438	2 140	511	480	422	383	256	86
1968	2 817	838	414	426	1 978	543	443	371	314	219	88
1969	2 832	853	436	416	1 978	560	453	358	320	216	72
1970	4 093	1 106	537	569	2 987	866	718	515	476	309	104
1971	5 016	1 262	596	665	3 755	1 130	933	630	573	381	109
1972	4 882	1 308	633	676	3 573	1 132	878	576	510	368	111
1973	4 365	1 235	634	600	3 130	1 008	866	451	430	290	88
1974	5 156	1 422	699	722	3 733	1 212	1 044	559	498	321	99
1975	7 929	1 767	799	968	6 161	1 865	1 776	951	893	520	155
1976	7 406	1 719	796	924	5 687	1 714	1 710	849	758	510	147
1977	6 991	1 663	781	881	5 330	1 629	1 650	785	666	450	147
1978	6 202	1 583	796	787	4 620	1 483	1 422	694	552	345	123
1979	6 137	1 555	739	816	4 583	1 442	1 446	705	540	346	104
1980	7 637	1 669	778	890	5 969	1 835	2 024	940	676	399	94
1981	8 273	1 763	781	981	6 510	1 976	2 211	1 065	715	444	98
1982	10 678	1 977	831	1 145	8 701	2 392	3 037	1 552	966	647	107
1983	10 717	1 829	753	1 076	8 888	2 330	3 078	1 650	1 039	677	114
1984	8 539	1 499	646	854	7 039	1 838	2 374	1 335	828	566	97
1985	8 312	1 468	662	806	6 844	1 738	2 341	1 340	813	518	93
1986	8 237	1 454	665	789	6 783	1 651	2 390	1 371	790	489	91
1987	7 425	1 347	648	700	6 077	1 453	2 129	1 281	723	412	78
1988	6 701	1 226	573	653	5 475	1 261	1 929	1 166	657	375	87
1989	6 528	1 194	537	657	5 333	1 218	1 851	1 159	637	379	91
1990	7 047	1 212	527	685	5 835	1 299	1 995	1 328	723	386	105
1991	8 628	1 359	587	772	7 269	1 573	2 447	1 719	946	473	113
1992	9 613	1 427	641	787	8 186	1 649	2 702	1 976	1 138	589	132
1993	8 940	1 365	606	759	7 575	1 514	2 395	1 896	1 121	541	108
1994	7 996	1 320	624	696	6 676	1 373	2 067	1 627	971	485	153
1995	7 404	1 346	652	695	6 058	1 244	1 841	1 549	844	425	153
1996	7 236	1 306	617	689	5 929	1 239	1 757	1 505	883	406	139
1997	6 739	1 271	589	683	5 467	1 152	1 571	1 418	830	369	127
1998	6 210	1 205	573	632	5 005	1 081	1 419	1 258	782	343	122
1999	5 880	1 162	544	618	4 718	1 042	1 278	1 154	753	367	124
2000	5 692	1 081	502	579	4 611	1 022	1 207	1 133	762	355	132
2001	6 801	1 162	531	632	5 638	1 209	1 498	1 355	989	458	129
2002	8 378	1 253	540	714	7 124	1 430	1 890	1 691	1 315	635	163
2003	8 774	1 251	545	706	7 523	1 495	1 960	1 815	1 356	713	183
2004	8 149	1 208	554	653	6 942	1 431	1 784	1 578	1 288	682	179
2005	7 591	1 186	541	645	6 405	1 335	1 661	1 400	1 195	630	184
2006	7 001	1 119	509	610	5 882	1 234	1 521	1 279	1 094	595	159
2007	7 078	1 101	485	616	5 976	1 241	1 544	1 225	1 135	642	190
2008	8 924	1 285	563	722	7 639	1 545	1 949	1 604	1 473	803	264
2009	14 265	1 552	576	976	12 712	2 207	3 284	2 722	2 592	1 487	421

Table 1-26. Unemployed Persons, by Age, Sex, Race, and Hispanic Origin, 1948–2009—*Continued*

(Thousands of people.)

Race, Hispanic origin, sex, and year	16 years and over	16 to 19 years			20 years and over						
		Total	16 to 17 years	18 to 19 years	Total	20 to 24 years	25 to 34 years	35 to 44 years	45 to 54 years	55 to 64 years	65 years and over
ALL RACES											
Men											
1948	1 559	256	113	142	1 305	324	289	233	201	177	81
1949	2 572	353	145	207	2 219	485	539	414	347	310	125
1950	2 239	318	139	179	1 922	377	467	348	327	286	117
1951	1 221	191	102	89	1 029	155	241	192	193	162	87
1952	1 185	205	116	89	980	155	233	192	182	145	73
1953	1 202	184	94	90	1 019	152	236	208	196	167	60
1954	2 344	310	142	168	2 035	327	517	431	372	275	112
1955	1 854	274	134	140	1 580	248	353	328	285	265	102
1956	1 711	269	134	135	1 442	240	348	278	270	216	90
1957	1 841	300	140	159	1 541	283	349	304	302	220	83
1958	3 098	416	185	231	2 681	478	685	552	492	349	124
1959	2 420	398	191	207	2 022	343	484	407	390	287	112
1960	2 486	426	200	225	2 060	369	492	415	392	294	96
1961	2 997	479	221	258	2 518	458	585	507	473	375	122
1962	2 423	408	188	220	2 016	381	445	404	382	300	103
1963	2 472	501	248	252	1 971	396	445	386	358	290	97
1964	2 205	487	257	230	1 718	384	345	324	319	263	85
1965	1 914	479	247	232	1 435	311	292	283	253	221	75
1966	1 551	432	220	212	1 120	221	239	219	196	179	65
1967	1 508	448	241	207	1 060	235	219	185	199	163	60
1968	1 419	426	234	193	993	258	205	171	165	132	61
1969	1 403	440	244	196	963	270	205	155	157	127	48
1970	2 238	599	306	294	1 638	479	391	253	247	198	71
1971	2 789	693	346	347	2 097	640	513	320	313	239	71
1972	2 659	711	357	355	1 948	628	466	284	272	227	73
1973	2 275	653	352	300	1 624	528	439	211	219	171	57
1974	2 714	757	394	362	1 957	649	546	266	250	183	63
1975	4 442	966	445	521	3 476	1 081	986	507	499	302	103
1976	4 036	939	443	496	3 098	951	914	431	411	296	94
1977	3 667	874	421	453	2 794	877	869	373	326	252	97
1978	3 142	813	426	388	2 328	768	691	314	277	198	81
1979	3 120	811	393	418	2 308	744	699	329	272	196	67
1980	4 267	913	429	485	3 353	1 076	1 137	482	357	243	58
1981	4 577	962	431	531	3 615	1 144	1 213	552	390	261	55
1982	6 179	1 090	469	621	5 089	1 407	1 791	879	550	393	69
1983	6 260	1 003	408	595	5 257	1 369	1 822	947	613	433	73
1984	4 744	812	348	464	3 932	1 023	1 322	728	450	356	53
1985	4 521	806	363	443	3 715	944	1 244	706	459	307	55
1986	4 530	779	355	424	3 751	899	1 291	763	440	301	58
1987	4 101	732	353	379	3 369	779	1 169	689	426	258	49
1988	3 655	667	311	356	2 987	676	1 040	617	366	240	49
1989	3 525	658	303	355	2 867	660	953	619	351	234	49
1990	3 906	667	283	384	3 239	715	1 092	711	413	249	59
1991	4 946	751	317	433	4 195	911	1 375	990	550	305	64
1992	5 523	806	357	449	4 717	951	1 529	1 118	675	378	67
1993	5 055	768	342	426	4 287	865	1 338	1 049	636	336	64
1994	4 367	740	342	398	3 627	768	1 113	855	522	281	88
1995	3 983	744	352	391	3 239	673	961	815	464	233	94
1996	3 880	733	347	387	3 146	675	903	786	484	223	76
1997	3 577	694	321	373	2 882	636	772	732	457	217	69
1998	3 266	686	330	355	2 580	583	699	609	420	201	69
1999	3 066	633	295	338	2 433	562	624	571	403	203	70
2000	2 975	599	281	317	2 376	547	602	557	398	189	83
2001	3 690	650	300	350	3 040	688	756	714	536	272	74
2002	4 597	700	301	399	3 896	792	1 023	897	725	373	87
2003	4 906	697	291	407	4 209	841	1 097	988	764	412	107
2004	4 456	664	292	372	3 791	811	980	839	684	373	104
2005	4 059	667	300	367	3 392	775	844	715	624	331	102
2006	3 753	622	271	352	3 131	705	810	642	569	318	88
2007	3 882	623	263	360	3 259	721	856	634	591	349	108
2008	5 033	736	312	425	4 297	920	1 119	875	804	425	153
2009	8 453	898	317	581	7 555	1 329	1 988	1 600	1 558	840	241

Table 1-26. Unemployed Persons, by Age, Sex, Race, and Hispanic Origin, 1948–2009—*Continued*

(Thousands of people.)

Race, Hispanic origin, sex, and year	16 years and over	16 to 19 years			20 years and over						
		Total	16 to 17 years	18 to 19 years	Total	20 to 24 years	25 to 34 years	35 to 44 years	45 to 54 years	55 to 64 years	65 years and over
ALL RACES											
Women											
1948	717	153	67	86	564	131	168	114	89	49	12
1949	1 065	223	93	130	841	195	237	189	124	74	21
1950	1 049	195	87	108	854	184	235	182	151	82	20
1951	834	145	66	79	689	118	194	162	125	76	16
1952	698	140	64	76	559	113	156	133	92	50	13
1953	632	123	56	67	510	104	143	117	84	51	10
1954	1 188	191	79	79	997	177	276	249	176	99	20
1955	998	176	77	99	823	148	224	193	151	90	18
1956	1 039	209	97	112	832	155	206	198	159	95	19
1957	1 018	197	90	107	821	147	224	195	146	80	28
1958	1 504	262	114	148	1 242	223	308	319	239	123	30
1959	1 320	256	110	147	1 063	200	242	266	213	118	23
1960	1 366	286	125	162	1 080	214	260	256	222	102	26
1961	1 717	349	142	207	1 368	265	305	343	278	141	37
1962	1 488	313	124	189	1 175	255	267	284	223	111	38
1963	1 598	383	172	210	1 216	262	287	288	231	120	29
1964	1 581	385	179	207	1 195	276	262	281	224	115	32
1965	1 452	395	164	231	1 056	246	237	263	183	101	28
1966	1 324	405	175	229	921	225	202	207	173	86	27
1967	1 468	391	159	231	1 078	277	261	237	184	93	26
1968	1 397	412	180	233	985	285	238	200	149	87	27
1969	1 429	413	192	220	1 015	290	248	203	163	89	24
1970	1 855	506	231	275	1 349	387	327	262	229	111	33
1971	2 227	568	250	318	1 658	489	420	310	260	142	38
1972	2 222	598	276	322	1 625	503	413	293	237	141	38
1973	2 089	583	282	301	1 507	480	427	240	212	119	31
1974	2 441	665	305	360	1 777	564	497	294	248	137	36
1975	3 486	802	355	447	2 684	783	791	444	395	219	52
1976	3 369	780	352	429	2 588	763	795	417	346	214	53
1977	3 324	789	361	428	2 535	752	782	412	340	198	50
1978	3 061	769	370	399	2 292	714	731	381	275	148	43
1979	3 018	743	346	396	2 276	697	748	375	268	150	38
1980	3 370	755	349	407	2 615	760	886	459	318	155	36
1981	3 696	800	350	450	2 895	833	998	513	325	184	43
1982	4 499	886	362	524	3 613	985	1 246	673	416	254	38
1983	4 457	825	344	481	3 632	961	1 255	703	427	244	41
1984	3 794	687	298	390	3 107	815	1 052	607	378	211	45
1985	3 791	661	298	363	3 129	794	1 098	634	355	211	39
1986	3 707	675	310	365	3 032	752	1 099	609	350	189	33
1987	3 324	616	295	321	2 709	674	960	592	298	155	30
1988	3 046	558	262	297	2 487	585	889	550	291	136	38
1989	3 003	536	234	302	2 467	558	897	540	286	144	41
1990	3 140	544	243	301	2 596	584	902	617	310	137	46
1991	3 683	608	270	338	3 074	662	1 071	728	396	168	49
1992	4 090	621	283	338	3 469	698	1 173	858	463	210	66
1993	3 885	597	264	333	3 288	648	1 058	847	485	205	45
1994	3 629	580	282	298	3 049	605	954	772	449	204	66
1995	3 421	602	299	303	2 819	571	880	735	381	193	60
1996	3 356	573	270	303	2 783	564	854	720	399	183	63
1997	3 162	577	268	310	2 585	516	800	686	373	152	58
1998	2 944	519	242	277	2 424	498	720	650	362	141	53
1999	2 814	529	249	280	2 285	480	654	584	350	163	54
2000	2 717	483	221	262	2 235	475	604	577	364	165	50
2001	3 111	512	230	282	2 599	521	742	641	453	187	55
2002	3 781	553	238	315	3 228	638	866	795	591	263	76
2003	3 868	554	255	299	3 314	654	863	827	592	302	76
2004	3 694	543	262	281	3 150	619	804	739	605	309	75
2005	3 531	519	240	278	3 013	560	817	685	571	299	82
2006	3 247	496	238	258	2 751	530	711	637	524	277	71
2007	3 196	478	222	256	2 718	520	688	591	544	293	81
2008	3 891	549	251	297	3 342	625	830	730	669	377	111
2009	5 811	654	259	395	5 157	878	1 296	1 121	1 034	647	180

Table 1-26. Unemployed Persons, by Age, Sex, Race, and Hispanic Origin, 1948–2009—*Continued*

(Thousands of people.)

Race, Hispanic origin, sex, and year	16 years and over	16 to 19 years			20 years and over						
		Total	16 to 17 years	18 to 19 years	Total	20 to 24 years	25 to 34 years	35 to 44 years	45 to 54 years	55 to 64 years	65 years and over
WHITE											
Both Sexes											
1954	2 859	423	191	232	2 436	394	610	540	447	329	115
1955	2 252	373	181	191	1 879	304	412	402	358	300	105
1956	2 159	382	191	191	1 777	297	406	363	355	258	98
1957	2 289	401	195	204	1 888	331	425	401	373	262	98
1958	3 680	541	245	297	3 139	541	756	686	614	405	136
1959	2 946	525	255	270	2 421	406	526	525	496	348	120
1960	3 065	575	273	302	2 490	456	573	520	502	330	109
1961	3 743	669	295	374	3 074	566	668	652	611	438	139
1962	3 052	580	262	318	2 472	488	515	522	485	345	117
1963	3 208	708	350	358	2 500	501	540	518	485	349	107
1964	2 999	708	365	342	2 291	508	441	472	447	323	100
1965	2 691	705	329	374	1 986	437	399	427	358	276	91
1966	2 255	651	315	336	1 604	338	323	336	298	227	80
1967	2 338	635	311	325	1 703	393	360	336	321	221	75
1968	2 226	644	326	318	1 582	422	330	297	269	187	80
1969	2 260	660	351	309	1 601	432	354	294	269	185	66
1970	3 339	871	438	432	2 468	679	570	433	415	275	95
1971	4 085	1 011	491	521	3 074	887	732	517	500	338	100
1972	3 906	1 021	515	506	2 885	887	679	459	439	324	95
1973	3 442	955	513	443	2 486	758	664	358	371	257	77
1974	4 097	1 104	561	544	2 993	925	821	448	427	283	88
1975	6 421	1 413	657	755	5 007	1 474	1 413	774	753	460	136
1976	5 914	1 364	649	715	4 550	1 326	1 329	682	637	448	128
1977	5 441	1 284	636	648	4 157	1 195	1 255	621	569	388	129
1978	4 698	1 189	631	558	3 509	1 059	1 059	543	453	290	104
1979	4 664	1 193	589	603	3 472	1 038	1 068	545	443	290	87
1980	5 884	1 291	625	666	4 593	1 364	1 528	740	550	335	74
1981	6 343	1 374	629	745	4 968	1 449	1 658	827	578	379	77
1982	8 241	1 534	683	851	6 707	1 770	2 283	1 223	796	549	86
1983	8 128	1 387	609	778	6 741	1 678	2 282	1 294	837	563	88
1984	6 372	1 116	510	605	5 256	1 282	1 723	1 036	660	475	81
1985	6 191	1 074	507	567	5 117	1 235	1 695	1 039	642	432	75
1986	6 140	1 070	509	561	5 070	1 149	1 751	1 056	629	407	78
1987	5 501	995	495	500	4 506	1 017	1 527	984	576	333	68
1988	4 944	910	437	473	4 033	874	1 371	890	520	309	69
1989	4 770	863	407	456	3 908	856	1 297	871	503	311	70
1990	5 186	903	401	502	4 283	899	1 401	983	582	330	88
1991	6 560	1 029	461	568	5 532	1 132	1 805	1 330	759	410	96
1992	7 169	1 037	484	553	6 132	1 156	1 967	1 483	915	495	116
1993	6 655	992	468	523	5 663	1 057	1 754	1 411	907	442	92
1994	5 892	960	471	489	4 933	952	1 479	1 184	779	407	132
1995	5 459	952	476	476	4 507	866	1 311	1 161	676	362	131
1996	5 300	939	456	484	4 361	854	1 223	1 117	709	336	122
1997	4 836	912	438	475	3 924	765	1 068	1 035	648	302	106
1998	4 484	876	424	451	3 608	731	978	901	620	276	101
1999	4 273	844	414	430	3 429	720	865	843	595	303	104
2000	4 121	795	386	409	3 326	682	835	817	591	294	107
2001	4 969	845	402	443	4 124	829	1 062	985	761	378	109
2002	6 137	925	407	518	5 212	977	1 340	1 237	1 004	518	137
2003	6 311	909	414	495	5 401	1 012	1 354	1 287	1 025	569	155
2004	5 847	890	414	476	4 957	959	1 211	1 130	953	557	148
2005	5 350	845	391	454	4 505	878	1 106	1 006	884	488	144
2006	5 002	794	375	419	4 208	832	1 029	920	813	480	135
2007	5 143	805	361	444	4 338	851	1 052	902	848	520	164
2008	6 509	947	422	524	5 562	1 087	1 336	1 196	1 094	634	216
2009	10 648	1 157	440	717	9 491	1 556	2 320	2 026	2 012	1 221	355

Table 1-26. Unemployed Persons, by Age, Sex, Race, and Hispanic Origin, 1948–2009—*Continued*

(Thousands of people.)

Race, Hispanic origin, sex, and year	16 years and over	16 to 19 years			20 years and over						
		Total	16 to 17 years	18 to 19 years	Total	20 to 24 years	25 to 34 years	35 to 44 years	45 to 54 years	55 to 64 years	65 years and over
WHITE											
Men											
1954	1 913	266	125	142	1 647	260	408	341	299	241	98
1955	1 478	232	114	117	1 246	196	260	246	233	223	89
1956	1 366	221	112	108	1 145	186	265	212	225	177	81
1957	1 477	243	118	124	1 234	222	257	239	250	193	73
1958	2 489	333	149	184	2 156	382	525	436	404	299	110
1959	1 903	318	162	156	1 585	256	350	316	320	245	98
1960	1 988	341	167	174	1 647	295	376	330	317	243	86
1961	2 398	384	176	208	2 014	370	442	395	382	318	107
1962	1 915	334	158	176	1 581	300	332	311	308	246	84
1963	1 976	407	211	196	1 569	309	342	297	294	246	80
1964	1 779	400	217	183	1 379	310	262	255	266	216	70
1965	1 556	387	200	186	1 169	254	226	228	206	190	67
1966	1 241	340	178	162	901	172	185	173	160	154	57
1967	1 208	342	186	156	866	185	171	153	167	140	52
1968	1 142	328	185	143	814	206	162	140	142	111	55
1969	1 137	343	198	145	794	214	165	130	134	108	43
1970	1 857	485	255	230	1 372	388	316	212	216	177	64
1971	2 309	562	288	275	1 747	513	418	268	272	211	66
1972	2 173	564	288	276	1 610	506	375	231	237	199	60
1973	1 836	513	284	229	1 323	411	353	166	188	153	51
1974	2 169	584	311	274	1 585	505	434	218	213	161	53
1975	3 627	785	369	416	2 841	871	796	412	411	265	86
1976	3 258	754	368	385	2 504	750	730	346	341	259	78
1977	2 883	672	342	330	2 211	660	682	297	276	213	82
1978	2 411	615	338	277	1 797	558	525	250	227	169	68
1979	2 405	633	319	313	1 773	553	526	253	220	165	56
1980	3 345	716	347	369	2 629	827	884	378	291	206	44
1981	3 580	755	349	406	2 825	869	943	433	317	221	42
1982	4 846	854	387	467	3 991	1 066	1 385	696	460	331	53
1983	4 859	761	328	433	4 098	1 019	1 410	755	497	362	54
1984	3 600	608	280	328	2 992	722	991	572	363	302	42
1985	3 426	592	282	310	2 834	694	931	553	356	257	43
1986	3 433	576	276	299	2 857	645	978	586	349	248	51
1987	3 132	548	272	276	2 584	568	879	536	350	209	43
1988	2 766	499	239	260	2 268	480	777	477	293	200	40
1989	2 636	487	230	257	2 149	476	694	470	280	191	38
1990	2 935	504	214	290	2 431	510	796	530	330	214	51
1991	3 859	575	249	327	3 284	677	1 064	780	438	269	55
1992	4 209	590	270	319	3 620	686	1 155	858	543	318	58
1993	3 828	565	261	305	3 263	619	1 015	793	512	270	53
1994	3 275	540	259	280	2 735	555	827	626	417	236	74
1995	2 999	535	260	275	2 465	483	711	621	371	200	79
1996	2 896	532	260	273	2 363	478	655	592	383	188	67
1997	2 641	502	234	268	2 140	439	553	549	358	182	58
1998	2 431	510	254	257	1 920	405	512	441	342	164	58
1999	2 274	461	223	237	1 813	398	441	419	322	172	61
2000	2 177	446	217	229	1 731	368	428	403	302	162	68
2001	2 754	479	232	247	2 275	494	547	529	413	229	64
2002	3 459	516	228	288	2 943	562	772	672	554	305	77
2003	3 643	518	221	298	3 125	589	798	723	591	333	91
2004	3 282	497	224	274	2 785	560	694	620	516	307	88
2005	2 931	480	220	260	2 450	522	586	536	463	263	81
2006	2 730	449	202	247	2 281	483	567	482	417	259	73
2007	2 869	461	195	266	2 408	501	604	478	447	285	93
2008	3 727	548	231	317	3 179	668	784	662	604	337	124
2009	6 421	675	241	434	5 746	969	1 439	1 208	1 233	695	202

Table 1-26. Unemployed Persons, by Age, Sex, Race, and Hispanic Origin, 1948–2009—*Continued*

(Thousands of people.)

Race, Hispanic origin, sex, and year	16 years and over	16 to 19 years			20 years and over						
		Total	16 to 17 years	18 to 19 years	Total	20 to 24 years	25 to 34 years	35 to 44 years	45 to 54 years	55 to 64 years	65 years and over
WHITE											
Women											
1954	946	157	66	90	789	134	202	199	148	88	17
1955	774	141	67	74	633	108	152	156	125	77	16
1956	793	161	79	83	632	111	141	151	130	81	17
1957	812	158	77	80	654	109	168	162	123	69	25
1958	1 191	208	96	113	983	159	231	250	210	106	26
1959	1 043	207	93	114	836	150	176	209	176	103	22
1960	1 077	234	106	128	843	161	197	190	185	87	23
1961	1 345	285	119	166	1 060	196	226	257	229	120	32
1962	1 137	246	104	142	891	188	183	211	177	99	33
1963	1 232	301	139	162	931	192	198	221	191	103	27
1964	1 220	308	148	159	912	198	179	217	181	107	30
1965	1 135	318	129	188	817	183	173	199	152	86	24
1966	1 014	311	137	174	703	166	138	163	138	73	23
1967	1 130	293	125	169	837	209	189	183	154	81	23
1968	1 084	316	141	175	768	216	168	157	127	76	25
1969	1 123	317	153	164	806	218	189	164	135	77	23
1970	1 482	386	183	202	1 096	291	254	221	199	98	31
1971	1 777	449	203	246	1 328	376	314	249	228	126	34
1972	1 733	457	227	230	1 275	381	304	227	202	125	35
1973	1 606	442	228	214	1 164	347	311	192	183	104	26
1974	1 927	519	250	270	1 408	420	387	230	214	122	35
1975	2 794	628	288	340	2 166	602	617	362	342	195	49
1976	2 656	611	280	330	2 045	577	598	336	296	188	49
1977	2 558	612	294	318	1 946	536	573	323	293	175	47
1978	2 287	574	292	281	1 713	500	533	294	226	122	37
1979	2 260	560	270	290	1 699	485	542	293	223	125	32
1980	2 540	576	278	298	1 964	537	645	362	259	129	31
1981	2 762	620	281	339	2 143	580	715	394	261	158	36
1982	3 395	680	296	384	2 715	704	898	527	337	217	33
1983	3 270	626	282	345	2 643	659	872	539	340	201	33
1984	2 772	508	231	277	2 264	559	731	464	297	173	39
1985	2 765	482	225	257	2 283	541	763	486	286	175	32
1986	2 708	495	233	262	2 213	504	773	470	281	159	27
1987	2 369	447	223	224	1 922	449	648	448	227	124	25
1988	2 177	412	198	214	1 766	393	594	413	227	110	30
1989	2 135	376	177	199	1 758	380	603	401	223	120	32
1990	2 251	399	187	212	1 852	389	605	453	251	116	37
1991	2 701	453	212	241	2 248	455	741	550	320	141	41
1992	2 959	447	214	233	2 512	469	811	625	372	177	58
1993	2 827	426	208	219	2 400	438	739	618	395	172	39
1994	2 617	420	211	208	2 197	397	652	558	361	170	58
1995	2 460	418	216	201	2 042	384	600	540	306	162	52
1996	2 404	407	196	211	1 998	376	568	525	326	148	55
1997	2 195	411	204	207	1 784	326	515	486	290	119	49
1998	2 053	365	171	195	1 688	327	467	460	279	112	43
1999	1 999	383	190	193	1 616	322	423	423	273	131	43
2000	1 944	349	168	180	1 595	314	407	414	289	133	39
2001	2 215	366	170	196	1 849	335	515	456	348	150	45
2002	2 678	409	179	230	2 269	415	567	565	449	213	60
2003	2 668	391	194	197	2 276	423	555	564	434	235	64
2004	2 565	393	191	202	2 172	399	516	510	437	250	60
2005	2 419	365	172	193	2 054	356	520	469	421	225	63
2006	2 271	345	173	172	1 927	349	462	437	395	222	62
2007	2 274	344	166	178	1 930	350	448	425	401	235	71
2008	2 782	399	191	207	2 384	419	552	534	489	298	92
2009	4 227	482	199	283	3 745	587	881	818	780	526	153

Table 1-26. Unemployed Persons, by Age, Sex, Race, and Hispanic Origin, 1948–2009—*Continued*

(Thousands of people.)

Race, Hispanic origin, sex, and year	16 years and over	16 to 19 years			20 years and over						
		Total	16 to 17 years	18 to 19 years	Total	20 to 24 years	25 to 34 years	35 to 44 years	45 to 54 years	55 to 64 years	65 years and over
BLACK											
Both Sexes											
1972	906	279	113	167	627	226	183	106	62	37	12
1973	846	262	114	148	584	231	181	82	53	29	9
1974	965	297	127	170	666	261	201	95	65	33	10
1975	1 369	330	130	200	1 040	362	321	157	126	54	17
1976	1 334	330	134	195	1 005	350	338	145	101	54	16
1977	1 393	354	135	218	1 040	397	355	140	81	51	16
1978	1 330	360	150	210	972	379	320	127	82	47	17
1979	1 319	333	137	197	986	369	335	137	82	48	15
1980	1 553	343	134	210	1 209	426	433	171	109	53	18
1981	1 731	357	138	219	1 374	483	493	207	119	55	17
1982	2 142	396	130	266	1 747	565	662	278	141	84	17
1983	2 272	392	125	267	1 879	591	700	299	174	95	21
1984	1 914	353	122	230	1 561	504	577	253	138	75	15
1985	1 864	357	135	221	1 507	455	562	254	143	74	18
1986	1 840	347	138	209	1 493	453	564	269	127	69	10
1987	1 684	312	134	178	1 373	397	533	247	124	62	10
1988	1 547	288	121	167	1 259	349	502	230	111	51	15
1989	1 544	300	116	184	1 245	322	494	246	109	53	20
1990	1 565	268	112	156	1 297	349	505	278	106	44	14
1991	1 723	280	105	175	1 443	378	539	318	151	44	13
1992	2 011	324	127	197	1 687	421	610	402	178	64	13
1993	1 844	313	112	201	1 530	387	532	376	153	72	11
1994	1 666	300	127	173	1 366	351	468	346	130	55	16
1995	1 538	325	143	182	1 213	311	423	303	116	42	18
1996	1 592	310	133	177	1 282	327	454	313	127	48	13
1997	1 560	302	123	179	1 258	327	426	307	136	45	16
1998	1 426	281	124	156	1 146	301	366	294	125	45	16
1999	1 309	268	109	159	1 041	273	339	249	121	46	14
2000	1 241	230	96	134	1 011	281	289	254	131	38	20
2001	1 416	260	102	158	1 155	307	340	283	159	52	15
2002	1 693	260	103	156	1 433	365	407	349	215	76	21
2003	1 787	255	93	162	1 532	375	442	385	217	93	20
2004	1 729	241	103	138	1 487	353	441	341	245	86	21
2005	1 700	267	115	152	1 433	358	423	310	222	92	28
2006	1 549	253	102	151	1 296	318	388	276	214	81	19
2007	1 445	235	98	138	1 210	300	367	237	208	79	19
2008	1 788	246	98	148	1 542	355	458	301	275	117	36
2009	2 606	288	99	189	2 319	488	717	489	415	168	42
BLACK											
Men											
1972	448	143	66	77	305	113	84	45	31	23	9
1973	395	128	62	66	267	108	75	37	27	16	5
1974	494	159	75	82	336	129	103	41	35	19	8
1975	741	170	71	100	571	195	169	83	78	33	13
1976	698	170	69	103	528	185	166	73	60	32	13
1977	698	187	73	114	512	197	170	63	40	31	12
1978	641	180	80	101	462	185	148	53	40	24	11
1979	636	164	68	97	473	174	152	66	44	27	10
1980	815	179	72	108	636	222	222	88	60	32	12
1981	891	188	73	115	703	248	245	102	65	32	10
1982	1 167	213	72	141	954	304	355	154	74	54	12
1983	1 213	211	70	142	1 002	313	358	162	96	59	14
1984	1 003	188	62	126	815	272	289	132	67	45	9
1985	951	193	69	124	757	224	268	127	85	43	11
1986	946	180	68	112	765	225	273	148	70	44	5
1987	826	160	70	90	666	186	253	122	61	39	6
1988	771	154	64	90	617	177	233	111	58	30	8
1989	773	153	65	88	619	162	226	129	59	33	10
1990	806	142	62	80	664	177	247	146	62	27	6
1991	890	145	54	91	745	201	252	172	87	25	7
1992	1 067	180	71	109	886	221	301	208	107	42	6
1993	971	170	66	104	801	201	260	201	87	46	7
1994	848	167	69	97	682	173	218	180	72	29	10
1995	762	168	73	95	593	153	195	150	63	21	11
1996	808	169	73	96	639	163	210	158	75	26	7
1997	747	162	70	92	585	165	178	141	72	22	7
1998	671	147	61	86	524	151	148	133	60	24	8
1999	626	145	60	85	480	135	143	114	60	22	7
2000	620	121	52	70	499	145	134	121	72	17	9
2001	709	136	51	85	573	150	159	142	84	31	7
2002	835	140	54	85	695	181	180	165	120	40	9
2003	891	132	49	83	760	192	212	189	109	47	10
2004	860	128	52	75	733	188	211	160	120	46	8
2005	844	145	63	82	699	192	189	143	116	45	14
2006	774	134	53	81	640	167	189	118	112	43	11
2007	752	130	55	75	622	166	186	114	106	41	10
2008	949	138	54	84	811	190	242	154	143	61	21
2009	1 448	161	55	106	1 286	264	406	270	230	91	24

Table 1-26. Unemployed Persons, by Age, Sex, Race, and Hispanic Origin, 1948–2009—*Continued*

(Thousands of people.)

Race, Hispanic origin, sex, and year	16 years and over	16 to 19 years			20 years and over						
		Total	16 to 17 years	18 to 19 years	Total	20 to 24 years	25 to 34 years	35 to 44 years	45 to 54 years	55 to 64 years	65 years and over
BLACK											
Women											
1972	458	136	47	90	322	113	99	61	31	14	3
1973	451	134	51	82	317	123	105	45	26	13	4
1974	470	139	51	87	331	132	98	55	30	14	2
1975	629	160	60	100	469	167	153	75	48	22	4
1976	637	160	66	93	477	165	172	73	41	23	3
1977	695	167	63	104	528	200	185	77	41	21	4
1978	690	179	70	110	510	194	173	74	41	23	6
1979	683	169	69	100	513	195	183	71	38	21	5
1980	738	164	62	102	574	204	211	83	49	21	6
1981	840	169	65	104	671	235	248	105	54	23	7
1982	975	182	58	124	793	261	307	123	67	29	5
1983	1 059	181	56	125	878	278	342	137	77	36	7
1984	911	165	60	104	747	231	288	121	71	30	5
1985	913	164	66	98	750	231	295	127	58	31	7
1986	894	167	70	97	728	228	291	121	57	25	5
1987	858	152	64	88	706	211	280	125	63	23	4
1988	776	134	57	78	642	172	269	118	53	22	7
1989	772	147	51	96	625	160	267	118	50	21	9
1990	758	126	49	76	633	172	258	132	44	17	8
1991	833	135	51	84	698	177	288	145	64	19	6
1992	944	144	56	88	800	200	308	194	71	22	6
1993	872	143	46	97	729	186	272	175	66	26	5
1994	818	133	57	76	685	178	249	166	59	26	6
1995	777	157	. . .	87	620	158	228	153	53	20	7
1996	784	141	60	80	643	164	244	155	52	21	7
1997	813	140	53	87	673	163	248	166	64	24	9
1998	756	134	63	71	622	150	218	160	65	21	8
1999	684	123	49	74	561	138	196	135	61	25	7
2000	621	109	44	65	512	136	154	132	59	22	10
2001	706	124	52	72	582	157	181	141	75	21	8
2002	858	120	49	71	738	183	228	185	95	35	12
2003	895	123	44	79	772	183	230	195	109	46	10
2004	868	114	51	63	755	166	230	180	126	40	13
2005	856	123	52	70	734	166	233	168	106	47	14
2006	775	120	50	70	656	150	199	158	102	38	8
2007	693	106	43	63	588	135	181	123	103	38	9
2008	839	108	44	64	732	166	216	147	132	56	15
2009	1 159	127	44	82	1 032	223	311	219	185	77	17
HISPANIC[1]											
Both Sexes											
1973	277	80	. . .	. . .	. . .	. . .	. . .	. . .	. . .	. . .	. . .
1974	325	88	. . .	. . .	. . .	. . .	. . .	. . .	. . .	. . .	. . .
1975	508	123	. . .	. . .	. . .	. . .	. . .	. . .	. . .	. . .	. . .
1976	485	106	51	55	385	116	113	72	53	26	6
1977	456	113	50	60	344	98	114	56	48	24	5
1978	452	110	63	47	342	98	116	65	41	16	5
1979	434	106	54	51	329	100	102	65	37	20	4
1980	620	145	66	79	474	138	168	90	49	24	5
1981	678	144	60	84	533	171	178	92	57	31	5
1982	929	175	73	102	754	221	267	140	75	45	6
1983	961	167	64	104	793	214	270	156	93	54	6
1984	800	149	60	88	651	164	235	124	71	51	5
1985	811	141	55	85	670	171	256	123	73	41	7
1986	857	141	57	84	716	183	258	143	85	38	9
1987	751	136	57	79	615	152	222	128	75	33	5
1988	732	148	63	84	585	145	209	120	69	36	6
1989	750	132	59	73	618	158	218	124	76	36	6
1990	876	161	68	94	714	167	263	156	85	36	7
1991	1 092	179	79	99	913	214	332	206	110	44	8
1992	1 311	219	94	124	1 093	240	390	267	126	59	10
1993	1 248	201	86	115	1 047	237	354	261	132	54	10
1994	1 187	198	90	108	989	220	348	227	132	51	12
1995	1 140	205	96	109	934	209	325	224	106	54	16
1996	1 132	199	85	114	933	217	296	246	101	59	14
1997	1 069	197	87	110	872	206	269	229	99	56	13
1998	1 026	214	89	125	812	194	260	203	96	48	11
1999	945	196	79	117	750	171	233	190	104	42	10
2000	954	194	83	112	759	190	247	189	79	42	12
2001	1 138	208	84	123	931	212	315	228	111	56	9
2002	1 353	221	81	140	1 132	265	373	271	146	62	15
2003	1 441	192	79	113	1 249	273	419	294	183	69	10
2004	1 342	203	86	117	1 139	255	371	261	161	74	18
2005	1 191	191	78	113	1 000	227	324	231	142	61	15
2006	1 081	170	74	97	911	194	294	231	128	49	14
2007	1 220	197	78	119	1 023	213	322	238	161	70	19
2008	1 678	251	105	146	1 427	307	437	328	242	81	32
2009	2 706	321	109	212	2 385	429	731	584	416	186	38

[1]May be of any race.
. . . = Not available.

Table 1-26. Unemployed Persons, by Age, Sex, Race, and Hispanic Origin, 1948–2009—Continued

(Thousands of people.)

Race, Hispanic origin, sex, and year	16 years and over	16 to 19 years			20 years and over						
		Total	16 to 17 years	18 to 19 years	Total	20 to 24 years	25 to 34 years	35 to 44 years	45 to 54 years	55 to 64 years	65 years and over
HISPANIC[1]											
Men											
1973	158	...	...	...	114	...	...	...	...	...	...
1974	187	...	...	...	139	...	...	...	...	...	...
1975	296	...	...	...	225	...	63	504	29	16	...
1976	278	60	30	31	217	69	65	540	22	15	...
1977	253	60	27	33	195	57	59	590	20	10	...
1978	234	59	35	24	175	51	50	615	19	11	...
1979	223	55	29	27	168	52	50		19	11	...
1980	370	86	39	47	284	85	96	662	31	16	...
1981	408	87	40	47	321	105	113	707	31	19	...
1982	565	104	45	59	461	138	169	729	40	29	...
1983	591	100	38	62	491	134	168	760	57	36	...
1984	480	87	36	51	393	103	142	841	41	33	...
1985	483	82	34	49	401	108	156	888	40	23	...
1986	520	82	33	50	438	115	159	929	46	26	...
1987	451	77	32	45	374	88	137	1 044	46	22	...
1988	437	86	36	50	351	83	128	1 120	42	24	...
1989	423	81	36	45	342	88	113	1 152	43	25	...
1990	524	100	40	60	425	99	154	1 312	53	25	...
1991	685	110	47	62	575	139	210	1 360	62	33	...
1992	807	132	56	75	675	156	239	1 437	75	42	...
1993	747	118	50	68	629	144	217	1 527	79	33	...
1994	680	121	54	67	558	128	203	1 600	75	30	9
1995	651	121	59	63	530	123	185	1 675	57	33	13
1996	607	112	49	63	495	117	165	1 842	49	31	9
1997	582	110	47	63	471	125	137	1 978	54	35	8
1998	552	117	54	62	436	115	142	2 077	49	29	5
1999	480	106	42	63	374	96	109	2 135	54	24	7
2000	494	106	46	60	388	105	118	2 358	42	23	8
2001	611	117	52	65	495	129	152	2 446	55	36	6
2002	764	127	42	86	636	151	213	2 503	82	38	8
2003	809	116	42	74	693	157	239	2 724	98	41	5
2004	755	120	48	72	635	158	207	2 801	82	41	13
2005	647	112	42	70	536	134	168	2 939	74	31	9
2006	601	104	43	61	497	110	169	3 088	66	29	8
2007	695	119	44	74	576	121	189	3 220	92	35	13
2008	1 007	147	63	84	860	188	275	3 233	136	50	19
2009	1 670	196	66	131	1 474	255	470	3 108	246	117	21
HISPANIC[1]											
Women											
1973	119	...	...	...	83	...	...	...	...	...	...
1974	137	...	...	...	98	...	...	...	...	...	...
1975	212	...	...	...	160	...	...	...	...	...	...
1976	207	45	22	24	166	47	52	33	22	10	...
1977	204	50	23	27	153	40	49	28	25	11	...
1978	219	51	28	23	168	46	58	36	20	8	...
1979	211	50	26	24	160	48	52	32	18	10	...
1980	249	59	28	31	190	53	72	39	18	8	...
1981	269	57	20	37	212	65	65	43	25	13	...
1982	364	71	28	43	293	83	98	60	35	16	...
1983	369	68	26	42	302	80	102	65	36	18	...
1984	320	62	25	37	258	61	93	55	30	17	...
1985	327	58	22	37	269	63	100	54	32	18	...
1986	337	59	25	35	278	68	99	57	39	12	...
1987	300	59	25	34	241	64	85	51	29	11	...
1988	296	62	27	34	234	63	81	50	27	12	...
1989	327	51	23	28	276	70	105	55	33	11	...
1990	351	62	28	34	289	68	109	65	32	11	...
1991	407	69	32	37	339	74	122	80	48	12	...
1992	504	87	38	49	418	84	151	111	51	17	...
1993	501	83	36	47	418	93	136	113	53	21	...
1994	508	77	36	40	431	92	145	115	57	21	2
1995	488	84	38	46	404	86	140	104	50	21	3
1996	525	88	36	52	438	100	131	122	52	27	5
1997	488	87	40	46	401	81	132	117	46	21	4
1998	473	98	35	63	376	80	118	106	48	19	5
1999	466	90	36	54	376	75	124	107	50	17	3
2000	460	88	37	51	371	86	129	96	38	19	4
2001	527	91	33	58	436	83	163	112	56	20	3
2002	590	94	39	54	496	113	160	127	65	24	7
2003	631	76	37	39	555	116	180	141	86	28	5
2004	587	83	38	45	504	97	164	128	78	32	5
2005	544	80	36	43	464	93	156	112	68	30	6
2006	480	67	31	36	414	84	125	116	62	20	6
2007	525	79	34	45	446	92	134	111	69	35	6
2008	672	104	42	62	567	119	162	136	105	32	13
2009	1 036	125	44	81	911	174	260	220	170	70	17

[1]May be of any race.
. . . = Not available.

Table 1-27. Unemployment Rates of Civilian Workers, by Age, Sex, Race, and Hispanic Origin, 1948–2009

(Percent of labor force.)

Race, Hispanic origin, sex, and year	16 years and over	16 to 19 years			20 years and over						
		Total	16 to 17 years	18 to 19 years	Total	20 to 24 years	25 to 34 years	35 to 44 years	45 to 54 years	55 to 64 years	65 years and over
ALL RACES											
Both Sexes											
1948	3.8	9.2	10.1	8.6	3.3	6.2	3.2	2.6	2.7	3.1	3.2
1949	5.9	13.4	14.0	13.0	5.4	9.3	5.4	4.4	4.2	5.1	4.9
1950	5.3	12.2	13.6	11.2	4.8	7.7	4.8	3.8	4.2	4.7	4.5
1951	3.3	8.2	9.6	7.1	3.0	4.1	3.0	2.5	2.7	3.2	3.4
1952	3.0	8.5	10.0	7.3	2.7	4.6	2.6	2.3	2.3	2.6	2.9
1953	2.9	7.6	8.7	6.8	2.6	4.7	2.5	2.2	2.3	2.6	2.2
1954	5.5	12.6	13.5	10.7	5.1	9.2	5.3	4.5	4.4	4.4	4.1
1955	4.4	11.0	12.3	10.0	3.9	7.0	3.8	3.4	3.4	4.0	3.6
1956	4.1	11.1	12.3	10.2	3.7	6.6	3.7	3.0	3.2	3.4	3.2
1957	4.3	11.6	12.5	10.9	3.8	7.1	3.9	3.1	3.3	3.4	3.4
1958	6.8	15.9	16.4	15.5	6.2	11.2	6.8	5.4	5.2	5.1	4.8
1959	5.5	14.6	15.3	14.0	4.8	8.5	5.0	4.2	4.2	4.4	4.3
1960	5.5	14.7	15.5	14.1	4.8	8.7	5.2	4.1	4.1	4.1	3.8
1961	6.7	16.8	18.3	15.8	5.9	10.4	6.2	5.2	5.0	5.3	5.1
1962	5.5	14.7	16.3	13.6	4.9	9.0	5.1	4.1	4.0	4.3	4.5
1963	5.7	17.2	19.3	15.6	4.8	8.8	5.2	4.0	3.8	4.1	4.1
1964	5.2	16.2	17.8	14.9	4.3	8.3	4.3	3.6	3.5	3.7	3.8
1965	4.5	14.8	16.5	13.5	3.6	6.7	3.7	3.2	2.8	3.2	3.3
1966	3.8	12.8	14.8	11.3	2.9	5.3	3.1	2.5	2.3	2.6	3.0
1967	3.8	12.9	14.6	11.6	3.0	5.7	3.2	2.5	2.4	2.5	2.8
1968	3.6	12.7	14.7	11.2	2.7	5.8	2.8	2.2	1.9	2.2	2.8
1969	3.5	12.2	14.5	10.5	2.7	5.7	2.8	2.2	1.9	2.0	2.2
1970	4.9	15.3	17.1	13.8	4.0	8.2	4.2	3.1	2.8	2.8	3.2
1971	5.9	16.9	18.7	15.5	4.9	10.0	5.3	3.9	3.4	3.4	3.5
1972	5.6	16.2	18.5	14.6	4.5	9.3	4.6	3.5	3.0	3.3	3.6
1973	4.9	14.5	17.3	12.4	3.9	7.8	4.2	2.7	2.5	2.7	3.0
1974	5.6	16.0	18.3	14.3	4.5	9.1	4.8	3.3	2.9	3.0	3.4
1975	8.5	19.9	21.4	18.9	7.3	13.6	7.8	5.6	5.2	4.7	5.2
1976	7.7	19.0	21.1	17.5	6.5	12.0	7.1	4.9	4.5	4.6	5.1
1977	7.1	17.8	19.9	16.2	5.9	11.0	6.5	4.4	3.9	4.1	5.0
1978	6.1	16.4	19.3	14.2	5.0	9.6	5.3	3.7	3.3	3.2	4.0
1979	5.8	16.1	18.1	14.7	4.8	9.1	5.2	3.6	3.2	3.0	3.4
1980	7.1	17.8	20.0	16.2	6.1	11.5	6.9	4.6	4.0	3.3	3.1
1981	7.6	19.6	21.4	18.4	6.5	12.3	7.3	5.0	4.2	3.6	3.2
1982	9.7	23.2	24.9	22.1	8.6	14.9	9.7	6.9	5.7	5.0	3.5
1983	9.6	22.4	24.5	21.1	8.6	14.5	9.7	7.0	6.2	5.3	3.7
1984	7.5	18.9	21.2	17.4	6.7	11.5	7.3	5.4	4.9	4.5	3.3
1985	7.2	18.6	21.0	17.0	6.4	11.1	7.0	5.1	4.7	4.1	3.2
1986	7.0	18.3	20.2	17.0	6.2	10.7	6.9	5.0	4.5	3.9	3.0
1987	6.2	16.9	19.1	15.2	5.4	9.7	6.0	4.5	4.0	3.3	2.5
1988	5.5	15.3	17.4	13.8	4.8	8.7	5.4	4.0	3.4	3.1	2.7
1989	5.3	15.0	17.2	13.6	4.6	8.6	5.2	3.8	3.2	3.1	2.6
1990	5.6	15.5	17.9	14.1	4.9	8.8	5.6	4.1	3.6	3.3	3.0
1991	6.8	18.7	21.0	17.2	6.1	10.8	6.9	5.2	4.5	3.9	3.3
1992	7.5	20.1	23.1	18.2	6.8	11.4	7.6	5.8	5.1	4.8	3.8
1993	6.9	19.0	21.4	17.5	6.2	10.5	6.9	5.5	4.8	4.3	3.2
1994	6.1	17.6	19.9	16.0	5.4	9.7	6.0	4.6	4.0	4.1	4.0
1995	5.6	17.3	20.2	15.3	4.9	9.1	5.4	4.3	3.3	3.7	4.0
1996	5.4	16.7	18.9	15.2	4.7	9.3	5.2	4.1	3.3	3.4	3.6
1997	4.9	16.0	18.2	14.5	4.3	8.5	4.7	3.8	3.0	3.0	3.3
1998	4.5	14.6	17.2	12.8	3.9	7.9	4.3	3.4	2.8	2.7	3.2
1999	4.2	13.9	16.3	12.4	3.6	7.5	4.0	3.0	2.6	2.8	3.1
2000	4.0	13.1	15.4	11.6	3.4	7.2	3.7	3.0	2.5	2.6	3.1
2001	4.7	14.7	17.2	13.1	4.2	8.3	4.6	3.6	3.1	3.0	2.9
2002	5.8	16.5	18.8	15.1	5.2	9.7	5.9	4.6	4.0	3.8	3.6
2003	6.0	17.5	19.1	16.4	5.4	10.0	6.1	4.9	4.1	4.1	3.8
2004	5.5	17.0	20.2	15.0	4.9	9.4	5.5	4.4	3.8	3.7	3.6
2005	5.1	16.6	19.1	14.9	4.5	8.8	5.1	3.9	3.5	3.4	3.5
2006	4.6	15.4	17.2	14.1	4.1	8.2	4.7	3.6	3.1	3.0	2.9
2007	4.6	15.7	17.5	14.5	4.1	8.2	4.7	3.4	3.2	3.1	3.3
2008	5.8	18.7	22.1	16.8	5.2	10.2	5.8	4.6	4.1	3.8	4.2
2009	9.3	24.3	25.9	23.4	8.6	14.7	9.9	7.9	7.2	6.6	6.4

Table 1-27. Unemployment Rates of Civilian Workers, by Age, Sex, Race, and Hispanic Origin, 1948–2009 —Continued

(Percent of labor force.)

Race, Hispanic origin, sex, and year	16 years and over	16 to 19 years			20 years and over						
		Total	16 to 17 years	18 to 19 years	Total	20 to 24 years	25 to 34 years	35 to 44 years	45 to 54 years	55 to 64 years	65 years and over
ALL RACES											
Men											
1948	3.6	9.8	10.2	9.5	3.2	6.9	2.8	2.4	2.5	3.1	3.4
1949	5.9	14.3	13.7	14.6	5.4	10.4	5.2	4.3	4.3	5.4	5.1
1950	5.1	12.7	13.3	12.3	4.7	8.1	4.4	3.6	4.0	4.9	4.8
1951	2.8	8.1	9.4	7.0	2.5	3.9	2.3	2.0	2.4	2.8	3.5
1952	2.8	8.9	10.5	7.4	2.4	4.6	2.2	1.9	2.2	2.4	3.0
1953	2.8	7.9	8.8	7.2	2.5	5.0	2.2	2.0	2.3	2.8	2.4
1954	5.3	13.5	13.9	13.2	4.9	10.7	4.8	4.1	4.3	4.5	4.4
1955	4.2	11.6	12.5	10.8	3.8	7.7	3.3	3.1	3.2	4.3	4.0
1956	3.8	11.1	11.7	10.5	3.4	6.9	3.3	2.6	3.0	3.5	3.5
1957	4.1	12.4	12.4	12.3	3.6	7.8	3.3	2.8	3.3	3.5	3.4
1958	6.8	17.1	16.3	17.8	6.2	12.7	6.5	5.1	5.3	5.5	5.2
1959	5.2	15.3	15.8	14.9	4.7	8.7	4.7	3.7	4.1	4.5	4.8
1960	5.4	15.3	15.5	15.0	4.7	8.9	4.8	3.8	4.1	4.6	4.2
1961	6.4	17.1	18.3	16.3	5.7	10.8	5.7	4.6	4.9	5.7	5.5
1962	5.2	14.7	16.0	13.8	4.6	8.9	4.5	3.6	3.9	4.6	4.6
1963	5.2	17.2	18.8	15.9	4.5	8.8	4.5	3.5	3.6	4.3	4.5
1964	4.6	15.8	17.1	14.6	3.9	8.1	3.5	2.9	3.2	3.9	4.0
1965	4.0	14.1	16.1	12.4	3.2	6.4	2.9	2.5	2.5	3.3	3.5
1966	3.2	11.7	13.7	10.2	2.5	4.6	2.4	2.0	1.9	2.6	3.1
1967	3.1	12.3	14.5	10.5	2.3	4.7	2.1	1.7	2.0	2.3	2.8
1968	2.9	11.6	13.9	9.7	2.2	5.1	1.9	1.6	1.6	1.9	2.8
1969	2.8	11.4	13.8	9.3	2.1	5.1	1.9	1.5	1.5	1.8	2.2
1970	4.4	15.0	16.9	13.4	3.5	8.4	3.5	2.4	2.4	2.8	3.3
1971	5.3	16.6	18.7	15.0	4.4	10.3	4.4	3.1	3.0	3.3	3.4
1972	5.0	15.9	18.3	14.1	4.0	9.3	3.8	2.7	2.6	3.2	3.6
1973	4.2	13.9	17.0	11.4	3.3	7.3	3.4	2.0	2.1	2.4	3.0
1974	4.9	15.6	18.4	13.3	3.8	8.8	4.0	2.6	2.4	2.6	3.3
1975	7.9	20.1	21.6	19.0	6.8	14.3	6.9	4.9	4.8	4.3	5.4
1976	7.1	19.2	21.4	17.6	5.9	12.1	6.2	4.1	4.0	4.2	5.1
1977	6.3	17.3	19.5	15.6	5.2	10.8	5.7	3.5	3.2	3.6	5.2
1978	5.3	15.8	19.1	13.3	4.3	9.2	4.4	2.8	2.7	2.8	4.2
1979	5.1	15.9	17.9	14.3	4.2	8.7	4.3	2.9	2.7	2.7	3.4
1980	6.9	18.3	20.4	16.7	5.9	12.5	6.7	4.1	3.6	3.4	3.1
1981	7.4	20.1	22.0	18.8	6.3	13.2	6.9	4.5	4.0	3.6	2.9
1982	9.9	24.4	26.4	23.1	8.8	16.4	10.1	6.9	5.6	5.5	3.7
1983	9.9	23.3	25.2	22.2	8.9	15.9	10.1	7.1	6.3	6.1	3.9
1984	7.4	19.6	21.9	18.3	6.6	11.9	7.2	5.2	4.6	5.0	3.0
1985	7.0	19.5	21.9	17.9	6.2	11.4	6.6	4.9	4.6	4.3	3.1
1986	6.9	19.0	20.8	17.7	6.1	11.0	6.7	5.1	4.4	4.3	3.2
1987	6.2	17.8	20.2	16.0	5.4	9.9	5.9	4.4	4.2	3.7	2.6
1988	5.5	16.0	18.2	14.6	4.8	8.9	5.3	3.8	3.5	3.5	2.5
1989	5.2	15.9	18.6	14.2	4.5	8.8	4.8	3.7	3.2	3.5	2.4
1990	5.7	16.3	18.4	15.0	5.0	9.1	5.5	4.1	3.7	3.8	3.0
1991	7.2	19.8	21.8	18.5	6.4	11.6	7.0	5.5	4.8	4.6	3.3
1992	7.9	21.5	24.6	19.5	7.1	12.2	7.8	6.1	5.6	5.8	3.3
1993	7.2	20.4	22.9	18.8	6.4	11.3	7.0	5.6	5.1	5.2	3.2
1994	6.2	19.0	21.0	17.6	5.4	10.2	5.9	4.5	4.0	4.4	4.0
1995	5.6	18.4	21.1	16.5	4.8	9.2	5.1	4.2	3.5	3.6	4.3
1996	5.4	18.1	20.8	16.3	4.6	9.5	4.9	4.0	3.5	3.3	3.4
1997	4.9	16.9	19.1	15.4	4.2	8.9	4.3	3.6	3.1	3.1	3.0
1998	4.4	16.2	19.1	14.1	3.7	8.1	3.9	3.0	2.8	2.8	3.1
1999	4.1	14.7	17.0	13.1	3.5	7.7	3.6	2.8	2.6	2.7	3.0
2000	3.9	14.0	16.8	12.2	3.3	7.3	3.4	2.8	2.4	2.4	3.3
2001	4.8	16.0	19.1	14.0	4.2	9.0	4.3	3.6	3.2	3.3	3.0
2002	5.9	18.1	21.1	16.4	5.3	10.2	5.8	4.5	4.2	4.3	3.4
2003	6.3	19.3	20.7	18.4	5.6	10.6	6.2	5.0	4.4	4.5	4.0
2004	5.6	18.4	22.0	16.3	5.0	10.1	5.5	4.3	3.9	3.9	3.7
2005	5.1	18.6	22.0	16.5	4.4	9.6	4.7	3.7	3.5	3.3	3.4
2006	4.6	16.9	18.6	15.7	4.0	8.7	4.5	3.3	3.1	3.0	2.8
2007	4.7	17.6	19.4	16.5	4.1	8.9	4.7	3.3	3.1	3.2	3.4
2008	6.1	21.2	25.2	19.0	5.4	11.4	6.1	4.6	4.2	3.8	4.5
2009	10.3	27.8	28.7	27.4	9.6	17.0	10.9	8.6	8.2	7.2	6.7

Table 1-27. Unemployment Rates of Civilian Workers, by Age, Sex, Race, and Hispanic Origin, 1948–2009
—Continued

(Percent of labor force.)

Race, Hispanic origin, sex, and year	16 years and over	16 to 19 years			20 years and over						
		Total	16 to 17 years	18 to 19 years	Total	20 to 24 years	25 to 34 years	35 to 44 years	45 to 54 years	55 to 64 years	65 years and over
ALL RACES											
Women											
1948	4.1	8.3	10.0	7.4	3.6	4.8	4.3	3.0	3.0	3.1	2.3
1949	6.0	12.3	14.4	11.2	5.3	7.3	5.9	4.7	4.0	4.4	3.8
1950	5.7	11.4	14.2	9.8	5.1	6.9	5.7	4.4	4.5	4.5	3.4
1951	4.4	8.3	10.0	7.2	4.0	4.4	4.5	3.8	3.5	4.0	2.9
1952	3.6	8.0	9.1	7.3	3.2	4.5	3.6	3.0	2.5	2.5	2.2
1953	3.3	7.2	8.5	6.4	2.9	4.3	3.4	2.5	2.3	2.5	1.4
1954	6.0	11.4	12.7	7.7	5.5	7.3	6.6	5.3	4.6	4.6	3.0
1955	4.9	10.2	12.0	9.1	4.4	6.1	5.3	4.0	3.6	3.8	2.3
1956	4.8	11.2	13.2	9.9	4.2	6.3	4.8	3.9	3.6	3.6	2.3
1957	4.7	10.6	12.6	9.4	4.1	6.0	5.3	3.8	3.2	3.0	3.4
1958	6.8	14.3	16.6	12.9	6.1	8.9	7.3	6.2	4.9	4.5	3.7
1959	5.9	13.5	14.4	13.0	5.2	8.1	5.9	5.1	4.2	4.1	2.8
1960	5.9	13.9	15.5	12.9	5.1	8.3	6.3	4.8	4.2	3.4	2.9
1961	7.2	16.3	18.3	15.1	6.3	9.8	7.4	6.4	5.1	4.5	4.0
1962	6.2	14.6	16.7	13.5	5.4	9.1	6.5	5.2	4.1	3.5	4.2
1963	6.5	17.2	20.2	15.2	5.4	8.9	6.9	5.1	4.2	3.6	3.2
1964	6.2	16.6	18.8	15.2	5.2	8.6	6.3	5.0	3.9	3.3	3.3
1965	5.5	15.7	17.2	14.8	4.5	7.3	5.5	4.6	3.2	2.8	2.9
1966	4.8	14.1	16.6	12.6	3.8	6.3	4.5	3.6	2.9	2.3	2.8
1967	5.2	13.5	14.8	12.8	4.2	7.0	5.4	4.1	3.1	2.4	2.7
1968	4.8	14.0	15.9	12.9	3.8	6.7	4.7	3.4	2.4	2.2	2.7
1969	4.7	13.3	15.5	11.8	3.7	6.3	4.6	3.4	2.6	2.2	2.3
1970	5.9	15.6	17.4	14.4	4.8	7.9	5.7	4.4	3.5	2.7	3.1
1971	6.9	17.2	18.7	16.2	5.7	9.6	7.0	5.2	4.0	3.3	3.6
1972	6.6	16.7	18.8	15.2	5.4	9.4	6.2	4.9	3.6	3.3	3.5
1973	6.0	15.3	17.7	13.5	4.9	8.5	5.8	3.9	3.2	2.8	2.9
1974	6.7	16.6	18.2	15.4	5.5	9.5	6.2	4.6	3.7	3.2	3.6
1975	9.3	19.7	21.2	18.7	8.0	12.7	9.1	6.8	5.9	5.1	5.0
1976	8.6	18.7	20.8	17.4	7.4	11.9	8.4	6.1	5.2	4.9	5.0
1977	8.2	18.3	20.5	16.9	7.0	11.2	7.7	5.7	5.1	4.4	4.7
1978	7.2	17.1	19.5	15.3	6.0	10.1	6.7	5.0	4.0	3.2	3.8
1979	6.8	16.4	18.3	15.0	5.7	9.6	6.5	4.6	3.9	3.2	3.3
1980	7.4	17.2	19.6	15.6	6.4	10.4	7.2	5.3	4.5	3.3	3.1
1981	7.9	19.0	20.7	17.9	6.8	11.2	7.7	5.7	4.6	3.8	3.6
1982	9.4	21.9	23.2	21.0	8.3	13.2	9.3	7.0	5.9	5.2	3.2
1983	9.2	21.3	23.7	19.9	8.1	12.9	9.1	6.9	6.0	5.0	3.4
1984	7.6	18.0	20.4	16.6	6.8	10.9	7.4	5.6	5.2	4.3	3.8
1985	7.4	17.6	20.0	16.0	6.6	10.7	7.4	5.5	4.8	4.3	3.3
1986	7.1	17.6	19.6	16.3	6.2	10.3	7.2	5.0	4.5	3.8	2.8
1987	6.2	15.9	18.0	14.3	5.4	9.4	6.2	4.6	3.7	3.1	2.4
1988	5.6	14.4	16.6	12.9	4.9	8.5	5.6	4.1	3.4	2.7	2.9
1989	5.4	14.0	15.7	13.0	4.7	8.3	5.6	3.9	3.2	2.8	2.9
1990	5.5	14.7	17.4	13.1	4.9	8.5	5.6	4.2	3.4	2.8	3.1
1991	6.4	17.5	20.2	15.9	5.7	9.8	6.8	4.8	4.2	3.4	3.3
1992	7.0	18.6	21.5	16.6	6.3	10.3	7.4	5.5	4.6	4.2	4.5
1993	6.6	17.5	19.8	16.1	5.9	9.7	6.8	5.3	4.5	4.0	3.1
1994	6.0	16.2	18.7	14.3	5.4	9.2	6.2	4.7	4.0	3.9	4.0
1995	5.6	16.1	19.2	14.0	4.9	9.0	5.7	4.4	3.2	3.6	3.7
1996	5.4	15.2	16.9	14.0	4.8	9.0	5.5	4.2	3.2	3.4	4.0
1997	5.0	15.0	17.2	13.6	4.4	8.1	5.2	4.0	2.9	2.7	3.6
1998	4.6	12.9	15.1	11.5	4.1	7.8	4.8	3.8	2.7	2.4	3.3
1999	4.3	13.2	15.5	11.6	3.8	7.2	4.4	3.3	2.5	2.6	3.2
2000	4.1	12.1	13.9	10.8	3.6	7.1	4.1	3.3	2.5	2.5	2.7
2001	4.7	13.4	15.2	12.2	4.1	7.5	5.1	3.7	3.0	2.7	2.9
2002	5.6	14.9	16.6	13.8	5.1	9.1	5.9	4.6	3.8	3.5	3.9
2003	5.7	15.6	17.5	14.2	5.1	9.3	5.9	4.9	3.7	3.7	3.6
2004	5.4	15.5	18.5	13.5	4.9	8.7	5.6	4.4	3.7	3.6	3.4
2005	5.1	14.5	16.5	13.1	4.6	7.9	5.6	4.1	3.5	3.3	3.5
2006	4.6	13.8	15.9	12.4	4.1	7.6	4.9	3.9	3.1	2.9	3.0
2007	4.5	13.8	15.7	12.5	4.0	7.3	4.6	3.6	3.2	3.0	3.1
2008	5.4	16.2	19.1	14.3	4.9	8.8	5.5	4.5	3.9	3.7	3.9
2009	8.1	20.7	23.1	19.4	7.5	12.3	8.6	7.1	6.0	6.0	6.1

Table 1-27. Unemployment Rates of Civilian Workers, by Age, Sex, Race, and Hispanic Origin, 1948–2009
—*Continued*

(Percent of labor force.)

Race, Hispanic origin, sex, and year	16 years and over	16 to 19 years			20 years and over						
		Total	16 to 17 years	18 to 19 years	Total	20 to 24 years	25 to 34 years	35 to 44 years	45 to 54 years	55 to 64 years	65 years and over
WHITE											
Both Sexes											
1954	5.0	12.1	13.2	11.3	4.6	8.3	4.6	4.0	4.0	4.3	3.9
1955	3.9	10.4	12.0	9.2	3.4	6.2	3.1	2.9	3.1	3.8	3.4
1956	3.6	10.1	11.5	9.0	3.2	5.7	3.1	2.6	2.9	3.2	3.1
1957	3.8	10.6	11.9	9.6	3.4	6.3	3.3	2.8	3.0	3.2	3.2
1958	6.1	14.4	15.2	13.9	5.6	9.9	5.9	4.8	4.8	4.9	4.6
1959	4.8	13.1	14.4	12.1	4.3	7.3	4.2	3.7	3.8	4.1	4.1
1960	5.0	13.5	14.6	12.6	4.3	7.9	4.5	3.6	3.8	3.9	3.7
1961	6.0	15.3	16.7	14.4	5.3	9.4	5.3	4.5	4.5	5.0	4.8
1962	4.9	13.3	15.3	12.0	4.2	7.9	4.2	3.6	3.6	3.9	4.0
1963	5.0	15.5	17.9	13.7	4.2	7.7	4.4	3.5	3.5	3.8	3.8
1964	4.6	14.8	16.5	13.3	3.8	7.3	3.6	3.2	3.2	3.5	3.5
1965	4.1	13.4	14.8	12.3	3.3	6.1	3.2	2.9	2.5	2.9	3.2
1966	3.4	11.2	13.3	9.7	2.6	4.6	2.6	2.3	2.1	2.4	2.9
1967	3.4	11.0	12.8	9.8	2.7	5.0	2.7	2.3	2.2	2.3	2.7
1968	3.2	11.0	12.9	9.6	2.5	5.2	2.4	2.0	1.8	1.9	2.8
1969	3.1	10.7	13.0	8.9	2.4	5.0	2.5	2.0	1.8	1.8	2.2
1970	4.5	13.5	15.5	11.9	3.7	7.3	3.8	3.0	2.7	2.7	3.2
1971	5.4	15.1	17.0	13.8	4.5	9.0	4.7	3.6	3.3	3.3	3.5
1972	5.1	14.2	16.6	12.3	4.1	8.4	4.1	3.2	2.9	3.1	3.4
1973	4.3	12.6	15.4	10.4	3.5	6.8	3.7	2.5	2.4	2.5	2.9
1974	5.0	14.0	16.3	12.2	4.1	8.0	4.4	3.1	2.8	2.8	3.3
1975	7.8	17.9	19.5	16.7	6.7	12.3	7.1	5.2	4.9	4.5	5.1
1976	7.0	16.9	19.0	15.3	5.9	10.7	6.3	4.5	4.2	4.3	4.9
1977	6.2	15.4	17.9	13.5	5.3	9.3	5.7	4.0	3.8	3.7	4.9
1978	5.2	13.9	17.0	11.5	4.3	8.0	4.6	3.3	3.0	2.7	3.8
1979	5.1	14.0	16.1	12.4	4.2	7.6	4.4	3.2	3.0	2.7	3.1
1980	6.3	15.5	17.9	13.8	5.4	9.9	6.1	4.2	3.7	3.1	2.7
1981	6.7	17.3	19.2	15.9	5.7	10.4	6.3	4.5	3.9	3.5	2.8
1982	8.6	20.4	22.8	18.8	7.6	12.8	8.5	6.3	5.4	5.1	3.1
1983	8.4	19.3	22.0	17.6	7.5	12.1	8.4	6.3	5.7	5.2	3.2
1984	6.5	16.0	18.8	14.3	5.7	9.3	6.2	4.8	4.4	4.4	3.0
1985	6.2	15.7	18.3	13.9	5.5	9.2	5.9	4.6	4.3	4.0	2.9
1986	6.0	15.6	17.6	14.1	5.3	8.7	5.9	4.5	4.1	3.8	2.9
1987	5.3	14.4	16.7	12.7	4.7	8.0	5.1	4.0	3.7	3.2	2.4
1988	4.7	13.1	15.3	11.6	4.1	7.1	4.5	3.5	3.1	3.0	2.4
1989	4.5	12.7	15.2	11.1	3.9	7.2	4.3	3.3	2.9	3.0	2.3
1990	4.8	13.5	15.8	12.1	4.3	7.3	4.6	3.6	3.3	3.2	2.8
1991	6.1	16.5	19.0	14.9	5.5	9.2	6.1	4.7	4.2	4.0	3.1
1992	6.6	17.2	20.3	15.2	6.0	9.5	6.7	5.2	4.8	4.9	3.7
1993	6.1	16.2	19.0	14.4	5.5	8.8	6.0	4.9	4.5	4.3	3.0
1994	5.3	15.1	17.6	13.3	4.7	8.1	5.2	4.0	3.7	3.9	3.8
1995	4.9	14.5	17.3	12.5	4.3	7.7	4.6	3.9	3.1	3.5	3.8
1996	4.7	14.2	16.4	12.6	4.1	7.8	4.4	3.6	3.1	3.2	3.5
1997	4.2	13.6	15.8	12.0	3.6	6.9	3.9	3.3	2.7	2.7	3.0
1998	3.9	12.6	14.8	11.0	3.3	6.5	3.7	2.9	2.6	2.4	2.9
1999	3.7	12.0	14.5	10.2	3.1	6.3	3.3	2.7	2.4	2.5	2.9
2000	3.5	11.4	13.9	9.8	3.0	5.9	3.2	2.6	2.2	2.4	2.8
2001	4.2	12.7	15.3	11.0	3.7	7.0	4.1	3.2	2.8	2.9	2.8
2002	5.1	14.5	16.7	13.2	4.6	8.1	5.2	4.1	3.7	3.7	3.5
2003	5.2	15.2	17.2	13.9	4.7	8.4	5.3	4.3	3.7	3.8	3.7
2004	4.8	15.0	17.9	13.1	4.3	7.9	4.7	3.9	3.4	3.6	3.3
2005	4.4	14.2	16.4	12.7	3.9	7.2	4.3	3.5	3.1	3.0	3.1
2006	4.0	13.2	15.1	11.9	3.6	6.9	4.0	3.2	2.8	2.8	2.8
2007	4.1	13.9	15.5	12.8	3.6	7.0	4.0	3.2	2.9	2.9	3.2
2008	5.2	16.8	19.9	14.9	4.6	9.0	5.1	4.3	3.7	3.4	4.0
2009	8.5	21.8	23.4	21.0	7.9	13.0	8.8	7.4	6.7	6.4	6.2

Table 1-27. Unemployment Rates of Civilian Workers, by Age, Sex, Race, and Hispanic Origin, 1948–2009
—Continued

(Percent of labor force.)

Race, Hispanic origin, sex, and year	16 years and over	16 to 19 years			20 years and over						
		Total	16 to 17 years	18 to 19 years	Total	20 to 24 years	25 to 34 years	35 to 44 years	45 to 54 years	55 to 64 years	65 years and over
WHITE											
Men											
1954	4.8	13.4	14.0	13.0	4.4	9.8	4.2	3.6	3.8	4.3	4.2
1955	3.7	11.3	12.2	10.4	3.3	7.0	2.7	2.6	2.9	3.9	3.8
1956	3.4	10.5	11.2	9.7	3.0	6.1	2.8	2.2	2.8	3.1	3.4
1957	3.6	11.5	11.9	11.1	3.2	7.0	2.7	2.5	3.0	3.4	3.2
1958	6.1	15.7	14.9	16.5	5.5	11.7	5.6	4.4	4.8	5.2	5.0
1959	4.6	14.0	15.0	13.0	4.1	7.5	3.8	3.2	3.7	4.2	4.5
1960	4.8	14.0	14.6	13.5	4.2	8.3	4.1	3.3	3.6	4.1	4.0
1961	5.7	15.7	16.5	15.2	5.1	10.1	4.9	4.0	4.4	5.3	5.2
1962	4.6	13.7	15.2	12.7	4.0	8.1	3.8	3.1	3.5	4.1	4.0
1963	4.7	15.9	17.8	14.2	3.9	7.8	3.9	2.9	3.3	4.0	4.1
1964	4.1	14.7	16.1	13.3	3.4	7.4	3.0	2.5	2.9	3.5	3.6
1965	3.6	12.9	14.7	11.3	2.9	5.9	2.6	2.3	2.3	3.1	3.4
1966	2.8	10.5	12.5	8.9	2.2	4.1	2.1	1.7	1.7	2.5	3.0
1967	2.7	10.7	12.7	9.0	2.1	4.2	1.9	1.6	1.8	2.2	2.7
1968	2.6	10.1	12.3	8.3	2.0	4.6	1.7	1.4	1.5	1.7	2.8
1969	2.5	10.0	12.5	7.9	1.9	4.6	1.7	1.4	1.4	1.7	2.2
1970	4.0	13.7	15.7	12.0	3.2	7.8	3.1	2.3	2.3	2.7	3.2
1971	4.9	15.1	17.1	13.5	4.0	9.4	4.0	2.9	2.9	3.2	3.4
1972	4.5	14.2	16.4	12.4	3.6	8.5	3.4	2.5	2.5	3.0	3.3
1973	3.8	12.3	15.2	10.0	3.0	6.6	3.0	1.8	2.0	2.4	2.9
1974	4.4	13.5	16.2	11.5	3.5	7.8	3.6	2.4	2.2	2.5	3.0
1975	7.2	18.3	19.7	17.2	6.2	13.1	6.3	4.5	4.4	4.1	5.0
1976	6.4	17.3	19.7	15.5	5.4	10.9	5.6	3.7	3.7	4.0	4.7
1977	5.5	15.0	17.6	13.0	4.7	9.3	5.0	3.1	3.0	3.3	4.9
1978	4.6	13.5	16.9	10.8	3.7	7.7	3.8	2.5	2.5	2.6	3.9
1979	4.5	13.9	16.1	12.2	3.6	7.5	3.7	2.5	2.5	2.5	3.2
1980	6.1	16.2	18.5	14.5	5.3	11.1	5.9	3.6	3.3	3.1	2.5
1981	6.5	17.9	19.9	16.4	5.6	11.6	6.1	4.0	3.6	3.4	2.4
1982	8.8	21.7	24.2	20.0	7.8	14.3	8.9	6.2	5.3	5.1	3.2
1983	8.8	20.2	22.6	18.7	7.9	13.8	9.0	6.4	5.7	5.6	3.2
1984	6.4	16.8	19.7	15.0	5.7	9.8	6.2	4.6	4.2	4.7	2.6
1985	6.1	16.5	19.2	14.7	5.4	9.7	5.7	4.3	4.1	4.0	2.7
1986	6.0	16.3	18.4	14.7	5.3	9.2	5.8	4.4	4.0	4.0	3.0
1987	5.4	15.5	17.9	13.7	4.8	8.4	5.2	3.9	3.9	3.4	2.5
1988	4.7	13.9	16.1	12.4	4.1	7.4	4.6	3.4	3.2	3.3	2.2
1989	4.5	13.7	16.4	12.0	3.9	7.5	4.1	3.2	2.9	3.1	2.1
1990	4.9	14.3	16.1	13.2	4.3	7.6	4.7	3.5	3.4	3.6	2.8
1991	6.5	17.6	19.7	16.3	5.8	10.2	6.4	5.0	4.4	4.6	3.1
1992	7.0	18.5	21.5	16.5	6.4	10.5	7.0	5.5	5.1	5.5	3.2
1993	6.3	17.7	20.2	16.0	5.7	9.6	6.2	5.0	4.7	4.7	2.9
1994	5.4	16.3	18.5	14.7	4.8	8.8	5.2	3.9	3.7	4.1	3.7
1995	4.9	15.6	18.2	13.8	4.3	7.9	4.5	3.8	3.2	3.4	4.0
1996	4.7	15.5	18.3	13.5	4.1	8.1	4.2	3.5	3.1	3.2	3.2
1997	4.2	14.3	16.3	12.9	3.6	7.3	3.7	3.2	2.8	3.0	2.7
1998	3.9	14.1	17.1	12.1	3.2	6.7	3.5	2.6	2.6	2.6	2.9
1999	3.6	12.6	15.1	10.8	3.0	6.5	3.1	2.4	2.4	2.6	2.9
2000	3.4	12.3	15.3	10.4	2.8	5.9	2.9	2.4	2.2	2.4	3.0
2001	4.2	13.9	17.4	11.7	3.7	7.8	3.8	3.1	2.9	3.2	2.8
2002	5.3	15.9	18.8	14.2	4.7	8.7	5.3	4.1	3.8	4.0	3.4
2003	5.6	17.1	18.5	16.1	5.0	9.1	5.5	4.4	4.0	4.2	3.8
2004	5.0	16.3	19.8	14.2	4.4	8.5	4.8	3.8	3.5	3.7	3.5
2005	4.4	16.1	18.9	14.3	3.8	7.9	4.1	3.3	3.0	3.0	3.1
2006	4.0	14.6	16.5	13.4	3.5	7.3	3.9	3.0	2.7	2.8	2.7
2007	4.2	15.7	17.0	14.8	3.7	7.6	4.1	3.0	2.8	3.0	3.3
2008	5.5	19.1	22.2	17.3	4.9	10.2	5.3	4.3	3.8	3.4	4.1
2009	9.4	25.2	25.9	24.8	8.8	15.3	9.8	8.0	7.7	6.8	6.3

Table 1-27. Unemployment Rates of Civilian Workers, by Age, Sex, Race, and Hispanic Origin, 1948–2009
—Continued

(Percent of labor force.)

Race, Hispanic origin, sex, and year	16 years and over	16 to 19 years			20 years and over						
		Total	16 to 17 years	18 to 19 years	Total	20 to 24 years	25 to 34 years	35 to 44 years	45 to 54 years	55 to 64 years	65 years and over
WHITE											
Women											
1954	5.5	10.4	12.0	9.4	5.1	6.4	5.7	4.9	4.4	4.5	2.8
1955	4.3	9.1	11.6	7.7	3.9	5.1	4.3	3.8	3.4	3.6	2.2
1956	4.2	9.7	12.1	8.3	3.7	5.1	4.0	3.5	3.3	3.5	2.3
1957	4.3	9.5	11.9	7.8	3.8	5.1	4.7	3.7	3.0	2.9	3.4
1958	6.2	12.7	15.6	11.0	5.6	7.3	6.6	5.6	4.9	4.3	3.5
1959	5.3	12.0	13.3	11.1	4.7	7.0	5.2	4.7	3.9	4.0	2.9
1960	5.3	12.7	14.5	11.5	4.6	7.2	5.7	4.2	4.0	3.3	2.8
1961	6.5	14.8	17.0	13.6	5.7	8.4	6.6	5.6	4.8	4.3	3.8
1962	5.5	12.8	15.6	11.3	4.7	7.7	5.4	4.5	3.7	3.5	4.0
1963	5.8	15.1	18.1	13.2	4.8	7.4	5.8	4.6	3.9	3.5	3.3
1964	5.5	14.9	17.1	13.2	4.6	7.1	5.2	4.5	3.6	3.5	3.4
1965	5.0	14.0	15.0	13.4	4.0	6.3	4.9	4.1	3.0	2.7	2.7
1966	4.3	12.1	14.5	10.7	3.3	5.3	3.7	3.3	2.7	2.2	2.7
1967	4.6	11.5	12.9	10.6	3.8	6.0	4.7	3.7	2.9	2.3	2.6
1968	4.3	12.1	13.9	11.0	3.4	5.9	3.9	3.1	2.3	2.1	2.8
1969	4.2	11.5	13.7	10.0	3.4	5.5	4.2	3.2	2.4	2.1	2.4
1970	5.4	13.4	15.3	11.9	4.4	6.9	5.3	4.3	3.4	2.6	3.3
1971	6.3	15.1	16.7	14.1	5.3	8.5	6.3	4.9	3.9	3.3	3.6
1972	5.9	14.2	17.0	12.3	4.9	8.2	5.5	4.4	3.5	3.3	3.7
1973	5.3	13.0	15.8	10.9	4.3	7.1	5.1	3.7	3.2	2.7	2.8
1974	6.1	14.5	16.4	13.0	5.1	8.2	5.8	4.3	3.6	3.2	3.9
1975	8.6	17.4	19.2	16.1	7.5	11.2	8.4	6.5	5.8	5.0	5.3
1976	7.9	16.4	18.2	15.1	6.8	10.4	7.6	5.8	5.0	4.8	5.3
1977	7.3	15.9	18.2	14.2	6.2	9.3	6.7	5.3	5.0	4.4	4.9
1978	6.2	14.4	17.1	12.4	5.2	8.3	5.8	4.5	3.8	3.0	3.7
1979	5.9	14.0	15.9	12.5	5.0	7.8	5.6	4.2	3.7	3.0	3.1
1980	6.5	14.8	17.3	13.1	5.6	8.5	6.3	4.9	4.3	3.1	3.0
1981	6.9	16.6	18.4	15.3	5.9	9.1	6.6	5.1	4.2	3.7	3.4
1982	8.3	19.0	21.2	17.6	7.3	10.9	8.0	6.4	5.5	5.0	3.1
1983	7.9	18.3	21.4	16.4	6.9	10.3	7.6	6.2	5.5	4.7	3.1
1984	6.5	15.2	17.8	13.6	5.8	8.8	6.1	5.0	4.8	4.0	3.7
1985	6.4	14.8	17.2	13.1	5.7	8.5	6.2	4.9	4.5	4.1	3.1
1986	6.1	14.9	16.7	13.6	5.4	8.1	6.1	4.5	4.3	3.7	2.6
1987	5.2	13.4	15.5	11.7	4.6	7.4	5.0	4.1	3.3	2.9	2.4
1988	4.7	12.3	14.4	10.8	4.1	6.7	4.5	3.7	3.1	2.5	2.6
1989	4.5	11.5	13.8	10.1	4.0	6.8	4.5	3.4	2.9	2.7	2.5
1990	4.7	12.6	15.5	10.9	4.1	6.8	4.6	3.7	3.2	2.7	2.8
1991	5.6	15.2	18.2	13.3	5.0	8.1	5.7	4.3	4.0	3.3	3.1
1992	6.1	15.8	18.9	13.7	5.5	8.3	6.2	4.9	4.3	4.0	4.5
1993	5.7	14.7	17.8	12.6	5.2	7.9	5.8	4.7	4.3	3.9	3.0
1994	5.2	13.8	16.6	11.8	4.6	7.4	5.1	4.2	3.7	3.7	3.9
1995	4.8	13.4	16.4	11.2	4.3	7.4	4.7	3.9	3.0	3.5	3.5
1996	4.7	12.9	14.4	11.7	4.1	7.4	4.6	3.8	3.1	3.1	3.8
1997	4.2	12.8	15.2	11.1	3.7	6.4	4.2	3.4	2.6	2.4	3.4
1998	3.9	10.9	12.4	9.8	3.4	6.3	3.9	3.3	2.5	2.2	3.0
1999	3.8	11.3	13.9	9.6	3.3	6.1	3.6	3.0	2.3	2.5	2.9
2000	3.6	10.4	12.5	9.0	3.1	5.8	3.5	2.9	2.3	2.4	2.4
2001	4.1	11.4	13.1	10.2	3.6	6.1	4.5	3.3	2.7	2.5	2.7
2002	4.9	13.1	14.6	12.1	4.4	7.4	5.0	4.1	3.5	3.3	3.5
2003	4.8	13.3	15.9	11.5	4.4	7.6	4.9	4.2	3.3	3.4	3.5
2004	4.7	13.6	16.1	11.9	4.2	7.1	4.6	3.9	3.3	3.5	3.1
2005	4.4	12.3	14.0	11.1	3.9	6.4	4.7	3.6	3.1	3.0	3.2
2006	4.0	11.7	13.8	10.2	3.6	6.3	4.1	3.4	2.9	2.8	3.0
2007	4.0	12.1	14.1	10.6	3.6	6.2	3.9	3.4	2.9	2.8	3.1
2008	4.9	14.4	17.6	12.3	4.4	7.5	4.8	4.3	3.5	3.5	3.8
2009	7.3	18.4	20.9	17.0	6.8	10.4	7.6	6.7	5.6	5.8	6.0

Table 1-27. Unemployment Rates of Civilian Workers, by Age, Sex, Race, and Hispanic Origin, 1948–2009
—*Continued*

(Percent of labor force.)

Race, Hispanic origin, sex, and year	16 years and over	16 to 19 years			20 years and over						
		Total	16 to 17 years	18 to 19 years	Total	20 to 24 years	25 to 34 years	35 to 44 years	45 to 54 years	55 to 64 years	65 years and over
BLACK											
Both Sexes											
1972	10.4	35.4	38.7	33.6	7.9	16.3	8.7	6.1	4.2	4.1	4.3
1973	9.4	31.5	37.0	28.1	7.2	15.5	8.1	4.7	3.5	3.2	3.5
1974	10.5	35.0	40.0	31.8	8.0	17.5	8.5	5.4	4.3	3.6	3.9
1975	14.8	39.5	41.6	38.1	12.3	24.5	13.0	8.9	8.3	5.9	6.6
1976	14.0	39.3	44.2	36.7	11.5	22.7	12.8	8.0	6.7	5.9	5.9
1977	14.0	41.1	44.5	39.2	11.5	24.2	12.7	7.4	5.3	5.5	5.9
1978	12.8	38.7	43.9	35.7	10.2	21.8	10.8	6.4	5.2	4.8	5.8
1979	12.3	36.5	40.2	34.4	10.1	20.6	10.8	6.7	5.2	4.9	5.3
1980	14.3	38.5	41.1	37.1	12.1	23.6	13.3	8.2	6.8	5.4	6.9
1981	15.6	41.4	44.8	39.5	13.4	26.4	14.7	9.5	7.4	5.5	7.0
1982	18.9	48.0	48.6	47.8	16.6	30.6	19.0	12.1	8.7	8.3	7.1
1983	19.5	48.5	50.5	47.6	17.3	31.6	19.0	12.4	10.7	9.2	9.2
1984	15.9	42.7	45.7	41.2	13.9	26.1	15.2	9.9	8.2	7.4	6.5
1985	15.1	40.2	43.6	38.3	13.1	24.5	14.5	9.5	8.2	7.0	7.0
1986	14.5	39.3	43.0	37.2	12.7	24.1	14.0	9.6	7.1	6.6	4.5
1987	13.0	34.7	39.7	31.6	11.3	21.8	12.8	8.4	6.8	5.6	3.9
1988	11.7	32.4	35.1	30.7	10.2	19.6	11.9	7.5	5.9	4.8	5.5
1989	11.4	32.4	32.9	32.2	9.9	18.0	11.5	7.6	5.6	5.2	6.9
1990	11.4	30.9	36.5	27.8	10.1	19.9	11.7	7.8	5.3	4.6	5.3
1991	12.5	36.1	39.5	34.4	11.1	21.6	12.7	8.5	7.4	4.4	5.2
1992	14.2	39.7	44.7	37.1	12.6	23.8	14.2	10.5	8.3	6.2	4.9
1993	13.0	38.8	39.7	38.4	11.4	21.9	12.6	9.5	6.9	7.1	4.7
1994	11.5	35.2	36.1	34.6	10.0	19.5	11.1	8.5	5.6	5.4	6.2
1995	10.4	35.7	39.1	33.4	8.7	17.7	9.9	7.3	4.8	4.0	6.7
1996	10.5	33.6	36.3	31.7	9.0	18.8	10.5	7.3	5.0	4.4	5.3
1997	10.0	32.4	35.0	30.8	8.6	18.3	9.9	7.0	5.0	4.2	6.1
1998	8.9	27.6	33.6	24.2	7.7	16.8	8.4	6.5	4.4	3.9	5.6
1999	8.0	27.9	31.0	26.2	6.8	14.6	7.6	5.3	4.0	3.9	5.0
2000	7.6	24.5	26.9	22.9	6.5	15.0	6.7	5.6	4.1	3.0	6.1
2001	8.6	29.0	30.8	27.9	7.4	16.3	8.1	6.3	4.8	3.9	4.3
2002	10.2	29.8	34.9	27.2	9.1	19.1	9.9	7.8	6.3	5.4	5.9
2003	10.8	33.0	32.2	33.5	9.7	19.8	10.9	8.6	6.2	6.3	5.4
2004	10.4	31.7	37.8	28.3	9.4	18.4	10.8	7.8	6.9	5.6	5.5
2005	10.0	33.3	41.2	29.0	8.8	18.3	10.2	7.1	6.0	5.6	6.9
2006	8.9	29.1	32.2	27.3	7.9	16.2	9.3	6.3	5.7	4.6	4.7
2007	8.3	29.4	32.6	27.4	7.2	15.2	8.6	5.4	5.4	4.3	4.5
2008	10.1	31.2	36.3	28.5	9.1	17.9	10.6	7.0	7.0	6.1	7.5
2009	14.8	39.5	43.1	37.8	13.7	24.9	16.7	11.7	10.4	8.4	8.5
BLACK											
Men											
1972	9.3	31.7	36.7	28.4	7.0	14.9	7.2	4.8	3.8	4.4	5.4
1973	8.0	27.8	35.7	23.0	6.0	13.2	6.2	3.9	3.2	3.2	3.3
1974	9.8	33.1	39.9	28.3	7.4	16.2	8.1	4.3	4.2	3.6	5.3
1975	14.8	38.1	41.9	35.9	12.5	24.7	12.7	8.7	9.3	6.3	8.7
1976	13.7	37.5	40.8	36.0	11.4	22.6	12.0	7.5	7.3	6.3	8.7
1977	13.3	39.2	41.0	38.2	10.7	23.0	11.8	6.2	4.9	6.0	7.8
1978	11.8	36.7	43.0	32.9	9.3	21.0	9.8	5.1	4.9	4.4	6.6
1979	11.4	34.2	37.9	32.2	9.3	18.7	9.6	6.3	5.2	5.1	6.4
1980	14.5	37.5	39.7	36.2	12.4	23.7	13.4	8.2	7.2	6.2	8.7
1981	15.7	40.7	43.2	39.2	13.5	26.4	14.4	9.3	7.8	6.1	7.5
1982	20.1	48.9	52.7	47.1	17.8	31.5	20.1	13.4	9.0	10.3	9.3
1983	20.3	48.8	52.2	47.3	18.1	31.4	19.4	13.5	11.4	11.0	11.8
1984	16.4	42.7	44.0	42.2	14.3	26.6	15.0	10.4	7.9	8.9	7.9
1985	15.3	41.0	42.9	40.0	13.2	23.5	13.8	9.6	9.7	7.9	8.9
1986	14.8	39.3	41.4	38.2	12.9	23.5	13.5	10.9	7.8	8.0	4.3
1987	12.7	34.4	39.0	31.6	11.1	20.3	12.2	8.7	6.7	6.6	4.3
1988	11.7	32.7	34.4	31.7	10.1	19.4	11.0	7.6	6.2	5.2	5.6
1989	11.5	31.9	34.4	30.3	10.0	17.9	10.5	8.4	6.2	6.2	7.4
1990	11.9	31.9	38.8	28.0	10.4	20.1	11.5	8.4	6.3	5.4	4.6
1991	13.0	36.3	39.0	34.8	11.5	22.4	11.9	9.5	8.6	5.0	6.1
1992	15.2	42.0	47.5	39.1	13.5	24.6	14.2	11.2	10.3	8.1	4.9
1993	13.8	40.1	42.7	38.6	12.1	23.0	12.3	10.5	8.1	9.0	5.8
1994	12.0	37.6	39.3	36.5	10.3	19.4	10.6	9.1	6.5	6.0	8.2
1995	10.6	37.1	39.7	35.4	8.8	17.6	9.3	7.6	5.5	4.4	7.6
1996	11.1	36.9	39.9	34.9	9.4	19.2	10.1	7.8	6.3	5.2	5.0
1997	10.2	36.5	39.5	34.4	8.5	19.8	8.7	6.7	5.6	4.2	5.5
1998	8.9	30.1	33.9	27.9	7.4	18.0	7.3	6.2	4.4	4.5	5.2
1999	8.2	30.9	33.3	29.4	6.7	16.2	6.9	5.2	4.3	3.9	5.0
2000	8.0	26.2	28.5	24.7	6.9	16.6	6.7	5.8	4.8	2.7	6.3
2001	9.3	30.4	30.5	30.4	8.0	17.6	8.3	6.9	5.5	4.8	4.0
2002	10.7	31.3	36.6	28.7	9.5	20.0	9.4	8.0	7.4	6.1	5.0
2003	11.6	36.0	35.6	36.3	10.3	20.9	11.3	9.2	6.7	6.8	5.6
2004	11.1	35.6	40.8	32.7	9.9	20.3	10.9	8.0	7.2	6.4	4.2
2005	10.5	36.3	45.1	31.5	9.2	20.5	9.7	7.0	6.7	5.9	7.1
2006	9.5	32.7	34.8	31.5	8.3	17.2	9.5	5.9	6.3	5.5	5.8
2007	9.1	33.8	40.1	30.2	7.9	16.9	9.1	5.6	5.8	5.2	5.0
2008	11.4	35.9	43.9	32.0	10.2	19.3	11.8	7.7	7.7	7.1	9.5
2009	17.5	46.0	49.3	44.5	16.3	27.7	19.9	14.0	12.4	10.1	10.6

Table 1-27. Unemployment Rates of Civilian Workers, by Age, Sex, Race, and Hispanic Origin, 1948–2009
—Continued

(Percent of labor force.)

Race, Hispanic origin, sex, and year	16 years and over	16 to 19 years			20 years and over						
		Total	16 to 17 years	18 to 19 years	Total	20 to 24 years	25 to 34 years	35 to 44 years	45 to 54 years	55 to 64 years	65 years and over
BLACK											
Women											
1972	11.8	40.5	42.0	40.1	9.0	17.9	10.5	7.6	4.6	3.7	2.6
1973	11.1	36.1	38.6	34.2	8.6	18.4	10.3	5.6	3.9	3.3	3.7
1974	11.3	37.4	40.2	36.0	8.8	19.0	9.0	6.6	4.4	3.6	1.9
1975	14.8	41.0	41.2	40.6	12.2	24.3	13.4	9.0	7.0	5.3	3.6
1976	14.3	41.6	48.4	37.6	11.7	22.8	13.6	8.5	5.9	5.4	2.4
1977	14.9	43.4	49.5	40.4	12.3	25.5	13.6	8.7	5.8	4.8	3.4
1978	13.8	40.8	45.0	38.7	11.2	22.7	11.9	7.8	5.6	5.2	4.7
1979	13.3	39.1	42.7	36.9	10.9	22.6	12.1	7.2	5.2	4.7	3.9
1980	14.0	39.8	42.9	38.2	11.9	23.5	13.2	8.2	6.4	4.5	4.9
1981	15.6	42.2	46.5	39.8	13.4	26.4	14.9	9.8	6.9	4.7	6.0
1982	17.6	47.1	44.2	48.6	15.4	29.6	17.8	10.7	8.5	6.1	4.5
1983	18.6	48.2	48.6	48.0	16.5	31.8	18.6	11.4	9.9	7.3	6.3
1984	15.4	42.6	47.5	40.2	13.5	25.6	15.4	9.4	8.6	5.9	4.9
1985	14.9	39.2	44.3	36.4	13.1	25.6	15.1	9.3	6.8	6.0	5.2
1986	14.2	39.2	44.6	36.1	12.4	24.7	14.6	8.5	6.4	5.0	4.9
1987	13.2	34.9	40.5	31.7	11.6	23.3	13.5	8.1	6.9	4.5	3.4
1988	11.7	32.0	35.9	29.6	10.4	19.8	12.7	7.4	5.6	4.3	5.4
1989	11.4	33.0	31.1	34.0	9.8	18.1	12.5	7.0	5.0	4.2	6.4
1990	10.9	29.9	34.1	27.6	9.7	19.6	11.9	7.2	4.3	3.6	5.9
1991	12.0	36.0	40.1	33.9	10.6	20.7	13.4	7.6	6.2	3.8	4.4
1992	13.2	37.2	41.7	34.8	11.8	23.1	14.1	9.8	6.4	5.1	3.6
1993	12.1	37.4	36.1	38.1	10.7	20.9	12.9	8.6	5.8	5.1	3.6
1994	11.0	32.6	32.9	32.5	9.8	19.6	11.7	8.0	4.9	4.9	4.4
1995	10.2	34.3	38.5	31.5	8.6	17.8	10.5	7.0	4.2	3.6	. . .
1996	10.0	30.3	32.8	28.6	8.7	18.4	11.0	6.9	3.8	3.8	5.6
1997	9.9	28.7	30.3	27.8	8.8	17.1	10.9	7.2	4.4	4.1	6.6
1998	9.0	25.3	33.2	20.9	7.9	15.7	9.5	6.7	4.3	3.4	6.1
1999	7.8	25.1	28.5	23.3	6.8	13.4	8.3	5.5	3.8	3.9	5.0
2000	7.1	22.8	25.3	21.3	6.2	13.6	6.8	5.5	3.4	3.3	6.0
2001	8.1	27.5	31.2	25.4	7.0	15.3	8.0	5.8	4.3	3.1	4.6
2002	9.8	28.3	33.2	25.6	8.8	18.3	10.2	7.7	5.3	4.7	6.9
2003	10.2	30.3	29.1	31.1	9.2	18.8	10.5	8.1	5.8	5.9	5.3
2004	9.8	28.2	35.2	24.3	8.9	16.6	10.7	7.6	6.5	4.8	6.8
2005	9.5	30.3	37.3	26.6	8.5	16.3	10.6	7.2	5.4	5.3	6.6
2006	8.4	25.9	29.9	23.6	7.5	15.2	9.0	6.7	5.1	3.9	3.7
2007	7.5	25.3	26.4	24.7	6.7	13.6	8.1	5.3	5.0	3.7	4.0
2008	8.9	26.8	29.9	25.0	8.1	16.6	9.5	6.4	6.3	5.3	5.8
2009	12.4	33.4	37.2	31.7	11.5	22.2	13.8	9.7	8.7	7.1	6.6
HISPANIC[1]											
Both Sexes											
1973	7.5	19.7	23.4	17.3	6.0	8.5	5.7	5.6	4.7	5.5	3.9
1974	8.1	19.8	23.5	17.2	6.6	9.8	6.3	5.9	4.6	6.1	6.3
1975	12.2	27.7	30.0	26.5	10.3	16.7	9.9	8.6	8.1	7.7	9.9
1976	11.5	23.8	29.2	19.2	10.1	15.9	9.1	8.2	8.4	8.8	12.6
1977	10.1	22.9	27.0	19.6	8.5	12.0	8.6	6.1	7.3	8.2	9.2
1978	9.1	20.7	28.3	15.1	7.7	10.9	8.0	6.5	5.8	5.0	7.5
1979	8.3	19.2	26.0	14.9	7.0	10.4	6.7	6.2	5.2	6.0	5.7
1980	10.1	22.5	27.6	19.5	8.6	12.1	9.1	7.7	5.7	5.9	6.0
1981	10.4	23.9	28.0	21.7	9.1	13.9	8.8	7.4	6.4	7.3	5.4
1982	13.8	29.9	38.1	25.9	12.3	17.7	12.3	10.7	8.4	10.1	6.5
1983	13.7	28.4	33.8	25.8	12.3	16.7	11.9	11.3	10.0	10.9	5.8
1984	10.7	24.1	28.9	21.6	9.5	12.4	9.7	8.2	7.5	9.7	6.1
1985	10.5	24.3	27.8	22.5	9.4	12.6	9.9	7.7	7.4	7.8	8.1
1986	10.6	24.7	28.1	22.9	9.5	12.9	9.6	8.4	7.8	7.3	10.1
1987	8.8	22.3	27.7	19.5	7.8	10.6	7.7	6.7	6.9	6.0	6.5
1988	8.2	22.0	27.1	19.3	7.0	9.8	7.1	6.0	6.0	5.8	5.6
1989	8.0	19.4	26.4	16.0	7.2	10.7	7.0	5.9	6.3	5.8	5.3
1990	8.2	19.5	24.5	16.9	7.2	9.1	7.3	6.6	6.4	5.6	6.0
1991	10.0	22.9	31.9	18.7	9.0	11.6	9.2	8.1	8.0	6.5	7.0
1992	11.6	27.5	35.7	23.4	10.4	13.2	10.4	9.8	8.8	8.6	8.1
1993	10.8	26.1	35.1	21.8	9.7	13.1	9.3	9.1	8.6	8.0	6.6
1994	9.9	24.5	31.7	20.6	8.9	11.8	9.0	7.7	8.1	7.3	7.9
1995	9.3	24.1	33.1	19.5	8.2	11.5	8.2	7.2	6.4	7.5	10.6
1996	8.9	23.6	30.0	20.3	7.8	11.8	7.3	7.3	6.0	7.3	8.2
1997	7.7	21.6	27.7	18.4	6.8	10.3	6.3	6.4	5.1	6.5	6.8
1998	7.2	21.3	28.0	18.1	6.1	9.4	5.9	5.5	4.6	5.3	6.4
1999	6.4	18.6	23.7	16.3	5.5	8.3	5.4	4.8	4.8	4.5	5.0
2000	5.7	16.6	22.5	13.9	4.9	7.5	4.8	4.5	3.3	4.5	5.7
2001	6.6	17.7	24.0	15.0	5.8	8.1	5.9	5.2	4.3	5.6	4.5
2002	7.5	20.1	24.2	18.2	6.7	9.9	6.6	6.0	5.5	5.7	6.8
2003	7.7	20.0	24.6	17.7	7.0	10.2	7.0	6.0	6.3	5.7	3.9
2004	7.0	20.4	29.0	16.8	6.2	9.3	6.3	5.3	5.2	5.8	6.0
2005	6.0	18.4	23.6	16.0	5.3	8.6	5.3	4.5	4.4	4.4	4.9
2006	5.2	15.9	20.4	13.6	4.6	7.2	4.7	4.3	3.7	3.3	3.9
2007	5.6	18.1	22.5	16.0	5.0	7.8	4.9	4.3	4.3	4.5	4.9
2008	7.6	22.4	29.8	19.0	6.8	11.5	6.7	5.8	6.3	4.8	7.8
2009	12.1	30.2	36.3	27.8	11.2	16.2	11.4	10.2	10.1	10.0	8.0

[1] May be of any race.
. . . = Not available.

Table 1-27. Unemployment Rates of Civilian Workers, by Age, Sex, Race, and Hispanic Origin, 1948–2009
—Continued

(Percent of labor force.)

Race, Hispanic origin, sex, and year	16 years and over	16 to 19 years			20 years and over						
		Total	16 to 17 years	18 to 19 years	Total	20 to 24 years	25 to 34 years	35 to 44 years	45 to 54 years	55 to 64 years	65 years and over
HISPANIC[1]											
Men											
1973	6.7	19.0	20.9	17.7	5.4	8.2	5.0	4.2	4.5	5.4	. . .
1974	7.3	19.0	22.0	17.1	6.0	9.9	5.5	5.0	4.3	5.4	. . .
1975	11.4	27.6	29.3	26.5	9.6	16.3	9.6	7.9	7.0	6.8	. . .
1976	10.8	23.3	28.7	19.7	9.4	16.0	8.1	7.0	7.4	8.7	. . .
1977	9.0	20.9	25.9	18.2	7.7	11.7	7.9	4.9	5.4	7.4	. . .
1978	7.7	19.7	27.5	13.9	6.4	9.4	6.6	4.8	4.8	4.4	. . .
1979	7.0	17.5	23.5	13.8	5.8	9.2	5.3	5.1	4.4	5.0	. . .
1980	9.7	21.9	26.2	19.3	8.3	12.2	8.3	7.1	6.0	5.9	. . .
1981	10.2	24.3	30.9	20.3	8.8	14.1	8.9	6.5	5.9	6.7	. . .
1982	13.6	31.3	40.2	26.8	12.1	18.2	12.4	9.9	7.5	10.0	. . .
1983	13.6	28.7	34.7	25.9	12.2	17.0	11.6	10.8	10.3	11.7	. . .
1984	10.5	25.2	31.5	22.2	9.3	12.5	9.2	7.6	7.2	10.2	. . .
1985	10.2	24.7	29.1	22.4	9.1	12.9	9.6	7.2	6.8	7.0	. . .
1986	10.5	24.5	28.5	22.4	9.5	13.0	9.5	8.5	7.0	8.0	. . .
1987	8.7	22.2	28.2	19.3	7.8	10.2	7.6	6.9	7.1	6.7	. . .
1988	8.1	22.7	29.5	19.5	7.0	9.2	7.6	6.9	7.1	6.7	. . .
1989	7.6	20.2	27.6	16.8	6.6	9.7	5.9	5.7	6.0	6.6	. . .
1990	8.0	19.5	24.0	17.4	7.0	8.4	6.9	6.5	6.8	6.5	. . .
1991	10.3	23.5	33.6	19.2	9.3	11.6	9.3	8.5	7.9	8.1	. . .
1992	11.7	28.2	36.6	24.0	10.5	13.7	10.1	9.8	8.9	10.2	. . .
1993	10.6	25.9	34.5	21.9	9.5	12.6	9.0	8.8	8.9	10.2	. . .
1994	9.4	26.3	33.3	22.5	8.3	10.8	8.4	6.6	8.1	7.4	10.5
1995	8.8	25.3	34.8	20.2	7.7	10.6	7.5	6.7	5.9	7.9	12.9
1996	7.9	22.5	31.5	18.4	6.9	10.3	6.6	6.3	5.1	6.7	8.3
1997	7.0	20.8	26.5	17.9	6.1	9.8	5.1	5.4	4.8	6.8	7.2
1998	6.4	20.6	29.0	16.4	5.4	8.9	5.2	4.5	4.2	5.3	5.0
1999	5.6	17.8	23.4	15.3	4.7	7.8	4.1	3.8	4.5	4.6	5.0
2000	5.0	15.7	22.3	12.8	4.2	6.6	3.7	3.8	3.1	4.1	6.2
2001	5.9	17.1	25.8	13.4	5.2	8.1	4.6	4.5	3.8	6.3	4.8
2002	7.2	20.2	22.9	19.1	6.4	9.3	6.1	5.4	5.5	6.2	6.3
2003	7.2	21.9	25.9	20.1	6.4	9.6	6.3	5.3	6.0	6.0	3.6
2004	6.5	21.2	30.7	17.6	5.8	9.4	5.5	4.5	4.7	5.7	6.9
2005	5.4	19.3	23.4	17.5	4.7	8.2	4.3	3.9	4.0	4.0	4.8
2006	4.8	17.3	22.6	14.8	4.2	6.7	4.2	3.6	3.4	3.5	3.7
2007	5.3	19.7	23.4	18.0	4.6	7.4	4.5	3.8	4.4	3.9	5.5
2008	7.6	23.4	30.9	19.9	6.8	11.8	6.6	5.6	6.2	5.1	7.8
2009	12.5	33.8	41.1	31.1	11.6	16.6	11.6	10.5	10.5	11.2	7.8
HISPANIC[1]											
Women											
1973	9.0	20.7	26.8	16.7	7.3	9.0	6.9	8.3	5.1	5.6	. . .
1974	9.4	20.8	25.3	17.4	7.7	9.7	7.7	7.5	5.3	7.5	. . .
1975	13.5	27.9	31.0	26.4	11.5	17.2	10.5	9.9	10.0	9.3	. . .
1976	12.7	22.2	30.3	18.7	11.4	15.8	10.8	10.0	9.8	9.0	. . .
1977	11.9	24.4	28.5	21.9	10.1	12.1	9.8	8.2	10.6	11.0	. . .
1978	11.3	21.8	29.9	16.6	9.8	13.0	10.3	9.2	7.4	7.2	. . .
1979	10.3	21.2	30.0	15.8	8.9	12.1	8.9	7.7	7.1	7.9	. . .
1980	10.7	23.4	29.7	19.8	9.2	12.0	10.6	8.6	5.3	5.8	. . .
1981	10.8	23.4	23.5	23.4	9.5	13.5	8.7	8.9	7.2	8.4	. . .
1982	14.1	28.2	35.1	25.0	12.5	16.8	12.2	11.9	9.9	10.4	. . .
1983	13.8	28.0	32.5	25.7	12.4	16.2	12.5	12.2	9.7	9.6	. . .
1984	11.1	22.8	26.1	21.0	9.9	12.2	10.3	9.1	7.9	8.8	. . .
1985	11.0	23.8	26.2	22.6	9.9	12.1	10.6	8.5	8.1	9.2	. . .
1986	10.8	25.1	27.6	23.6	9.6	12.9	9.8	8.2	8.9	6.2	. . .
1987	8.9	22.4	27.1	19.9	7.7	11.4	7.8	6.5	6.7	5.0	. . .
1988	8.3	21.0	24.5	18.9	7.1	10.7	7.2	6.2	5.9	4.6	. . .
1989	8.8	18.2	24.7	14.9	8.0	12.2	8.6	6.3	6.7	4.5	. . .
1990	8.4	19.4	25.4	16.2	7.5	10.4	8.0	6.7	6.0	4.3	. . .
1991	9.6	21.9	29.6	17.9	8.6	11.7	9.1	7.6	8.1	4.1	. . .
1992	11.4	26.4	34.5	22.4	10.2	12.4	11.0	9.7	8.5	6.2	. . .
1993	11.0	26.3	36.0	21.7	9.9	14.0	9.9	9.5	8.3	7.2	. . .
1994	10.7	22.2	29.7	18.1	9.8	13.5	10.1	9.2	8.0	7.1	3.6
1995	10.0	22.6	30.7	18.7	8.9	13.0	9.5	7.9	7.0	6.8	6.4
1996	10.2	25.1	28.2	23.3	9.2	14.1	8.5	8.7	7.2	8.1	8.0
1997	8.9	22.7	29.2	19.1	7.9	11.0	8.2	7.7	5.5	6.1	6.0
1998	8.2	22.1	26.4	20.2	7.1	10.1	7.2	6.9	5.1	5.4	8.8
1999	7.6	19.8	24.0	17.7	6.6	9.1	7.3	6.3	5.1	4.3	4.8
2000	6.8	18.0	22.7	15.6	5.9	9.0	6.4	5.4	3.6	5.0	4.8
2001	7.5	18.5	21.6	17.1	6.6	8.2	6.2	4.8	4.8	4.8	4.0
2002	8.0	19.9	25.8	17.0	7.2	10.8	7.4	6.7	5.5	5.0	7.5
2003	8.4	17.7	23.2	14.4	7.8	11.3	8.2	7.1	6.8	5.3	4.4
2004	7.6	19.3	27.0	15.5	7.0	9.1	7.6	6.4	5.8	5.8	4.6
2005	6.9	17.2	23.8	14.0	6.3	9.2	7.1	5.5	4.8	5.0	5.1
2006	5.9	14.1	18.1	11.9	5.3	8.1	5.5	5.5	4.2	3.1	4.2
2007	6.1	16.1	21.3	13.6	5.5	8.5	5.6	5.1	4.3	5.2	4.0
2008	7.7	21.1	28.1	18.0	6.9	11.1	6.8	6.0	6.4	4.4	7.7
2009	11.5	25.8	30.8	23.8	10.6	15.7	10.9	9.7	9.6	8.5	8.3

[1]May be of any race.
. . . = Not available.

Table 1-28. Unemployed Persons and Unemployment Rates, by Selected Occupation, 2000–2009

(Thousands of people, percent of civilian labor force.)

Occupation	2000	2001	2002	2003	2004	2005	2006	2007	2008	2009
Total Unemployed Persons, 16 Years and Over[1]	5 692	6 801	8 378	8 774	8 149	7 591	7 001	7 078	8 924	14 265
Management, professional, and related	827	1 102	1 482	1 556	1 346	1 172	1 065	1 090	1 463	2 531
Management, business, and financial operations	320	455	622	627	544	464	427	429	619	1 105
Professional and related	507	647	859	929	801	708	638	662	844	1 427
Services	1 132	1 311	1 544	1 681	1 617	1 587	1 485	1 521	1 769	2 605
Sales and office	1 446	1 652	2 110	2 070	1 937	1 820	1 667	1 638	2 006	3 143
Sales and related	673	779	998	995	912	874	812	835	980	1 501
Office and administrative support	773	873	1 112	1 076	1 025	946	856	804	1 026	1 642
Natural resources, construction, and maintenance	758	943	1 155	1 244	1 140	1 069	1 007	1 052	1 421	2 464
Farming, fishing, and forestry	133	163	142	136	132	103	101	89	112	179
Construction and extraction	507	626	788	814	786	751	699	781	1 067	1 825
Installation, maintenance, and repair	119	154	225	295	222	214	207	182	243	459
Production, transportation, and material moving	1 081	1 318	1 530	1 555	1 393	1 245	1 127	1 128	1 474	2 453
Production	575	759	848	807	714	677	544	564	746	1 322
Transportation and material moving	505	559	682	748	679	568	583	564	727	1 131
Total Unemployment Rate, 16 Years and Over[1]	4.0	4.7	5.8	6.0	5.5	5.1	4.6	4.6	5.8	9.3
Management, professional, and related	1.8	2.3	3.0	3.1	2.7	2.3	2.1	2.1	2.7	4.6
Management, business, and financial operations	1.6	2.2	3.0	3.1	2.6	2.2	2.0	1.9	2.7	4.9
Professional and related	1.9	2.3	3.0	3.2	2.8	2.4	2.1	2.1	2.7	4.4
Services	5.2	5.8	6.6	7.1	6.6	6.4	5.9	5.9	6.7	9.6
Sales and office	3.8	4.4	5.6	5.5	5.2	4.8	4.4	4.3	5.3	8.5
Sales and related	4.1	4.7	5.9	5.9	5.4	5.0	4.7	4.8	5.7	8.8
Office and administrative support	3.6	4.2	5.4	5.2	5.0	4.6	4.2	4.0	5.1	8.3
Natural resources, construction, and maintenance	5.3	6.4	7.8	8.1	7.3	6.5	6.0	6.3	8.8	15.6
Farming, fishing, and forestry	10.2	13.4	12.0	11.4	11.8	9.6	9.5	8.5	10.2	16.2
Construction and extraction	6.2	7.3	9.1	9.1	8.4	7.6	6.8	7.6	11.0	19.7
Installation, maintenance, and repair	2.4	3.2	4.6	5.5	4.2	3.9	3.7	3.4	4.5	8.5
Production, transportation, and material moving	5.1	6.4	7.6	7.9	7.2	6.5	5.8	5.8	7.6	13.3
Production	4.8	6.6	7.8	7.7	7.0	6.7	5.5	5.7	7.7	14.7
Transportation and material moving	5.6	6.2	7.4	8.2	7.4	6.2	6.2	6.0	7.6	12.0

[1]Includes persons with no work experience and persons whose last job was in the armed forces.

Table 1-29. Unemployed Persons and Unemployment Rates, by Class of Worker and Industry, 2000–2009

(Thousands of people, percent.)

Class of worker and industry	2000	2001	2002	2003	2004	2005	2006	2007	2008	2009
Total Unemployed Persons, 16 Years and Over	5 692	6 801	8 378	8 774	8 149	7 591	7 001	7 078	8 924	14 265
Nonagricultural private wage and salary workers	4 483	5 540	6 926	7 131	6 484	5 989	5 523	5 559	7 118	11 654
Mining	21	23	33	37	21	20	22	25	25	90
Construction	513	609	800	810	769	712	671	757	1 030	1 770
Manufacturing	691	992	1 205	1 166	966	812	699	706	945	1 890
Durable goods	400	630	789	762	590	485	410	436	597	1 279
Nondurable goods	290	362	416	404	375	326	289	270	348	611
Wholesale trade and retail trade	837	945	1 202	1 237	1 197	1 137	1 039	975	1 205	1 844
Transportation and utilities	193	236	274	283	236	232	229	233	312	525
Information	124	190	253	246	189	163	126	120	167	294
Financial activities	208	252	320	319	332	272	264	289	380	598
Professional and business services	573	768	1 009	1 042	861	792	746	740	921	1 522
Education and health services	383	463	570	640	617	627	568	575	698	1 100
Leisure and hospitality	720	833	961	1 006	972	921	865	896	1 102	1 543
Other services	219	229	301	347	324	301	293	241	332	477
Agriculture and related private wage and salary workers	134	153	139	140	129	104	95	78	123	200
Government workers	422	430	512	568	548	534	473	505	534	799
Self-employed and unpaid family workers	219	218	265	294	303	298	293	309	383	577
Total Unemployment Rate, 16 Years and Over[1]	4.0	4.7	5.8	6.0	5.5	5.1	4.6	4.6	5.8	9.3
Nonagricultural private wage and salary workers	4.1	5.0	6.2	6.3	5.7	5.2	4.7	4.7	5.9	9.8
Mining	4.4	4.2	6.3	6.7	3.9	3.1	3.2	3.4	3.1	11.6
Construction	6.2	7.1	9.2	9.3	8.4	7.4	6.7	7.4	10.6	19.0
Manufacturing	3.5	5.2	6.7	6.6	5.7	4.9	4.2	4.3	5.8	12.1
Durable goods	3.2	5.2	6.9	6.9	5.5	4.6	3.9	4.2	5.6	12.9
Nondurable goods	4.0	5.2	6.2	6.1	5.9	5.3	4.8	4.5	6.0	10.6
Wholesale trade and retail trade	4.3	4.9	6.1	6.0	5.8	5.4	4.9	4.7	5.9	9.0
Transportation and utilities	3.4	4.3	4.9	5.3	4.4	4.1	4.0	3.9	5.1	8.9
Information	3.2	4.9	6.9	6.8	5.7	5.0	3.7	3.6	5.0	9.2
Financial activities	2.4	2.9	3.5	3.5	3.6	2.9	2.7	3.0	3.9	6.4
Professional and business services	4.8	6.1	7.9	8.2	6.8	6.2	5.6	5.3	6.5	10.8
Education and health services	2.5	2.8	3.4	3.6	3.4	3.4	3.0	3.0	3.5	5.3
Leisure and hospitality	6.6	7.5	8.4	8.7	8.3	7.8	7.3	7.4	8.6	11.7
Other services	3.9	4.0	5.1	5.7	5.3	4.8	4.7	3.9	5.3	7.5
Agriculture and related private wage and salary workers	9.0	11.2	10.1	10.2	9.9	8.3	7.2	6.3	9.2	14.3
Government workers	2.1	2.2	2.5	2.8	2.7	2.6	2.3	2.3	2.4	3.6
Self-employed and unpaid family workers	2.1	2.1	2.6	2.7	2.8	2.7	2.7	2.8	3.6	5.5

Note: See notes and definitions for information on historical comparability.

[1]Includes persons with no work experience and persons whose last job was in the armed forces.

Table 1-30. Unemployed Persons, by Duration of Unemployment, 1948–2009

(Thousands of people, number of weeks.)

Year	Total unemployed	Less than 5 weeks		5 to 14 weeks		15 weeks and over		15 to 26 weeks		27 weeks and over		Average duration, in weeks	Median duration, in weeks
		Number	Percent	Number	Percent	Number	Percent	Number	Percent	Number	Percent		
1948	2 276	1 300	57.1	669	29.4	309	13.6	193	8.5	116	5.1	8.6	. . .
1949	3 637	1 756	48.3	1 194	32.8	684	18.8	428	11.8	256	7.0	10.0	. . .
1950	3 288	1 450	44.1	1 055	32.1	782	23.8	425	12.9	357	10.9	12.1	. . .
1951	2 055	1 177	57.3	574	27.9	303	14.7	166	8.1	137	6.7	9.7	. . .
1952	1 883	1 135	60.3	516	27.4	232	12.3	148	7.9	84	4.5	8.4	. . .
1953	1 834	1 142	62.3	482	26.3	210	11.5	132	7.2	78	4.3	8.0	. . .
1954	3 532	1 605	45.4	1 116	31.6	812	23.0	495	14.0	317	9.0	11.8	. . .
1955	2 852	1 335	46.8	815	28.6	702	24.6	366	12.8	336	11.8	13.0	. . .
1956	2 750	1 412	51.3	805	29.3	533	19.4	301	10.9	232	8.4	11.3	. . .
1957	2 859	1 408	49.2	891	31.2	560	19.6	321	11.2	239	8.4	10.5	. . .
1958	4 602	1 753	38.1	1 396	30.3	1 452	31.6	785	17.1	667	14.5	13.9	. . .
1959	3 740	1 585	42.4	1 114	29.8	1 040	27.8	469	12.5	571	15.3	14.4	. . .
1960	3 852	1 719	44.6	1 176	30.5	957	24.8	503	13.1	454	11.8	12.8	. . .
1961	4 714	1 806	38.3	1 376	29.2	1 532	32.5	728	15.4	804	17.1	15.6	. . .
1962	3 911	1 663	42.5	1 134	29.0	1 119	28.6	534	13.7	585	15.0	14.7	. . .
1963	4 070	1 751	43.0	1 231	30.2	1 088	26.7	535	13.1	553	13.6	14.0	. . .
1964	3 786	1 697	44.8	1 117	29.5	973	25.7	491	13.0	482	12.7	13.3	. . .
1965	3 366	1 628	48.4	983	29.2	755	22.4	404	12.0	351	10.4	11.8	. . .
1966	2 875	1 573	54.7	779	27.1	526	18.3	287	10.0	239	8.3	10.4	. . .
1967	2 975	1 634	54.9	893	30.0	448	15.1	271	9.1	177	5.9	8.7	2.3
1968	2 817	1 594	56.6	810	28.8	412	14.6	256	9.1	156	5.5	8.4	4.5
1969	2 832	1 629	57.5	827	29.2	375	13.2	242	8.5	133	4.7	7.8	4.4
1970	4 093	2 139	52.3	1 290	31.5	663	16.2	428	10.4	235	5.8	8.6	4.9
1971	5 016	2 245	44.8	1 585	31.6	1 187	23.7	668	13.3	519	10.4	11.3	6.3
1972	4 882	2 242	45.9	1 472	30.2	1 167	23.9	601	12.3	566	11.6	12.0	6.2
1973	4 365	2 224	51.0	1 314	30.1	826	18.9	483	11.1	343	7.9	10.0	5.2
1974	5 156	2 604	50.5	1 597	31.0	955	18.5	574	11.1	381	7.4	9.8	5.2
1975	7 929	2 940	37.1	2 484	31.3	2 505	31.6	1 303	16.4	1 203	15.2	14.2	8.4
1976	7 406	2 844	38.4	2 196	29.6	2 366	32.0	1 018	13.8	1 348	18.2	15.8	8.2
1977	6 991	2 919	41.8	2 132	30.5	1 942	27.8	913	13.1	1 028	14.7	14.3	7.0
1978	6 202	2 865	46.2	1 923	31.0	1 414	22.8	766	12.3	648	10.5	11.9	5.9
1979	6 137	2 950	48.1	1 946	31.7	1 241	20.2	706	11.5	535	8.7	10.8	5.4
1980	7 637	3 295	43.2	2 470	32.3	1 871	24.5	1 052	13.8	820	10.7	11.9	6.5
1981	8 273	3 449	41.7	2 539	30.7	2 285	27.6	1 122	13.6	1 162	14.0	13.7	6.9
1982	10 678	3 883	36.4	3 311	31.0	3 485	32.6	1 708	16.0	1 776	16.6	15.6	8.7
1983	10 717	3 570	33.3	2 937	27.4	4 210	39.3	1 652	15.4	2 559	23.9	20.0	10.1
1984	8 539	3 350	39.2	2 451	28.7	2 737	32.1	1 104	12.9	1 634	19.1	18.2	7.9
1985	8 312	3 498	42.1	2 509	30.2	2 305	27.7	1 025	12.3	1 280	15.4	15.6	6.8
1986	8 237	3 448	41.9	2 557	31.0	2 232	27.1	1 045	12.7	1 187	14.4	15.0	6.9
1987	7 425	3 246	43.7	2 196	29.6	1 983	26.7	943	12.7	1 040	14.0	14.5	6.5
1988	6 701	3 084	46.0	2 007	30.0	1 610	24.0	801	12.0	809	12.1	13.5	5.9
1989	6 528	3 174	48.6	1 978	30.3	1 375	21.1	730	11.2	646	9.9	11.9	4.8
1990	7 047	3 265	46.3	2 257	32.0	1 525	21.6	822	11.7	703	10.0	12.0	5.3
1991	8 628	3 480	40.3	2 791	32.4	2 357	27.3	1 246	14.4	1 111	12.9	13.7	6.8
1992	9 613	3 376	35.1	2 830	29.4	3 408	35.4	1 453	15.1	1 954	20.3	17.7	8.7
1993	8 940	3 262	36.5	2 584	28.9	3 094	34.6	1 297	14.5	1 798	20.1	18.0	8.3
1994	7 996	2 728	34.1	2 408	30.1	2 860	35.8	1 237	15.5	1 623	20.3	18.8	9.2
1995	7 404	2 700	36.5	2 342	31.6	2 363	31.9	1 085	14.6	1 278	17.3	16.6	8.3
1996	7 236	2 633	36.4	2 287	31.6	2 316	32.0	1 053	14.6	1 262	17.4	16.7	8.3
1997	6 739	2 538	37.7	2 138	31.7	2 062	30.6	995	14.8	1 067	15.8	15.8	8.0
1998	6 210	2 622	42.2	1 950	31.4	1 637	26.4	763	12.3	875	14.1	14.5	6.7
1999	5 880	2 568	43.7	1 832	31.2	1 480	25.2	755	12.8	725	12.3	13.4	6.4
2000	5 692	2 558	44.9	1 815	31.9	1 318	23.2	669	11.8	649	11.4	12.6	5.9
2001	6 801	2 853	42.0	2 196	32.3	1 752	25.8	951	14.0	801	11.8	13.1	6.8
2002	8 378	2 893	34.5	2 580	30.8	2 904	34.7	1 369	16.3	1 535	18.3	16.6	9.1
2003	8 774	2 785	31.7	2 612	29.8	3 378	38.5	1 442	16.4	1 936	22.1	19.2	10.1
2004	8 149	2 696	33.1	2 382	29.2	3 072	37.7	1 293	15.9	1 779	21.8	19.6	9.8
2005	7 591	2 667	35.1	2 304	30.4	2 619	34.5	1 130	14.9	1 490	19.6	18.4	8.9
2006	7 001	2 614	37.3	2 121	30.3	2 266	32.4	1 031	14.7	1 235	17.6	16.8	8.3
2007	7 078	2 542	35.9	2 232	31.5	2 303	32.5	1 061	15.0	1 243	17.6	16.8	8.5
2008	8 924	2 932	32.8	2 804	31.4	3 188	35.7	1 427	16.0	1 761	19.7	17.9	9.4
2009	14 265	3 165	22.2	3 828	26.8	7 272	51.0	2 775	19.5	4 496	31.5	24.4	15.1

. . . = Not available.

Table 1-31. Long-Term Unemployment, by Industry and Selected Occupation, 2000–2009

(Thousands of people.)

Length of unemployment, industry, and occupation	2000	2001	2002	2003	2004	2005	2006	2007	2008	2009
UNEMPLOYED 15 WEEKS AND OVER										
Total	1 318	1 752	2 904	3 378	3 072	2 619	2 266	2 303	3 188	7 272
Wage and Salary Workers, by Industry										
Agriculture and related	32	44	39	44	38	29	30	28	42	96
Mining [1]	7	7	11	17	8	8	5	6	7	44
Construction	107	130	236	262	248	216	177	215	339	907
Manufacturing	184	303	528	575	467	326	257	259	385	1 059
Durable goods	99	183	348	389	293	199	140	162	246	702
Nondurable goods	86	120	180	186	174	127	116	97	139	357
Wholesale and retail trade	186	241	423	472	455	415	337	334	440	962
Transportation and utilities	57	71	124	132	114	91	87	95	142	290
Information	33	52	119	128	87	76	55	49	66	170
Financial activities	58	75	131	144	139	91	103	100	168	357
Professional and business services	143	217	377	440	345	299	266	247	346	810
Education and health services	124	149	232	300	304	271	263	253	320	691
Leisure and hospitality	146	196	279	328	321	277	259	274	356	755
Other services	54	58	95	132	126	117	97	80	132	245
Public administration	41	36	51	59	72	62	34	51	55	107
Experienced Workers, by Occupation										
Management, professional, and related	213	313	603	692	571	436	373	368	569	1 331
Services	246	323	447	564	565	511	464	482	595	1 243
Sales and office	331	419	759	810	750	641	561	560	741	1 675
Natural resources, construction, and maintenance	161	212	346	424	386	341	294	299	463	1 224
Production, transportation, and material moving	273	360	575	654	561	461	380	384	570	1 302
UNEMPLOYED 27 WEEKS AND OVER										
Total	649	801	1 535	1 936	1 779	1 490	1 235	1 243	1 761	4 496
Wage and Salary Workers, by Industry										
Agriculture and related	13	16	18	21	18	16	13	14	17	51
Mining [1]	4	3	5	10	6	4	3	3	4	23
Construction	44	60	111	132	133	108	92	107	168	530
Manufacturing	100	132	291	366	302	195	140	152	230	657
Durable goods	50	75	191	255	196	124	75	93	150	428
Nondurable goods	50	57	100	111	106	71	64	58	80	229
Wholesale and retail trade	80	114	226	261	261	230	183	171	237	607
Transportation and utilities	27	33	67	74	63	50	42	58	77	180
Information	18	21	62	80	58	41	30	29	38	115
Financial activities	32	34	131	88	79	56	56	50	97	232
Professional and business services	67	90	377	262	193	172	144	130	184	510
Education and health services	63	71	232	167	168	156	144	132	182	432
Leisure and hospitality	69	90	279	166	169	148	135	142	196	445
Other services	26	31	95	71	76	74	51	43	73	161
Public administration	23	18	51	33	44	38	21	29	29	66
Experienced Workers, by Occupation										
Management, professional, and related	101	135	340	429	356	269	206	207	569	840
Services	128	156	225	295	307	284	249	251	595	750
Sales and office	151	185	397	459	419	354	299	285	741	1 067
Natural resources, construction, and maintenance	74	96	164	229	221	186	158	157	463	724
Production, transportation, and material moving	140	162	313	388	336	261	206	219	570	814

Note: Beginning in January 2004, data reflect revised population controls used in the household survey. See notes and definitions for information on historical comparability.

[1] For 2009, mining includes quarrying, and oil and gas extraction.

Table 1-32. Unemployed Persons and Unemployment Rates, by Reason for Unemployment, Sex, and Age, 1975–2009

(Thousands of people, percent.)

Sex, age, and year	Number of unemployed					Unemployed as a percent of the total civilian labor force			
	Total	Job losers and persons who completed temporary jobs	Job leavers	Entrants		Job losers and persons who completed temporary jobs	Job leavers	Entrants	
				Reentrants	New entrants			Reentrants	New entrants
Both Sexes, 16 Years and Over									
1975	7 929	4 386	827	1 892	823	4.7	0.9	2.0	0.9
1976	7 406	3 679	903	1 928	895	3.8	0.9	2.0	0.9
1977	6 991	3 166	909	1 963	953	3.2	0.9	2.0	1.0
1978	6 202	2 585	874	1 857	885	2.5	0.9	1.8	0.9
1979	6 137	2 635	880	1 806	817	2.5	0.8	1.7	0.8
1980	7 637	3 947	891	1 927	872	3.7	0.8	1.8	0.8
1981	8 273	4 267	923	2 102	981	3.9	0.8	1.9	0.9
1982	10 678	6 268	840	2 384	1 185	5.7	0.8	2.2	1.1
1983	10 717	6 258	830	2 412	1 216	5.6	0.7	2.2	1.1
1984	8 539	4 421	823	2 184	1 110	3.9	0.7	1.9	1.0
1985	8 312	4 139	877	2 256	1 039	3.6	0.8	2.0	0.9
1986	8 237	4 033	1 015	2 160	1 029	3.4	0.9	1.8	0.9
1987	7 425	3 566	965	1 974	920	3.0	0.8	1.6	0.8
1988	6 701	3 092	983	1 809	816	2.5	0.8	1.5	0.7
1989	6 528	2 983	1 024	1 843	677	2.4	0.8	1.5	0.5
1990	7 047	3 387	1 041	1 930	688	2.7	0.8	1.5	0.5
1991	8 628	4 694	1 004	2 139	792	3.7	0.8	1.7	0.6
1992	9 613	5 389	1 002	2 285	937	4.2	0.8	1.8	0.7
1993	8 940	4 848	976	2 198	919	3.8	0.8	1.7	0.7
1994	7 996	3 815	791	2 786	604	2.9	0.6	2.1	0.5
1995	7 404	3 476	824	2 525	579	2.6	0.6	1.9	0.4
1996	7 236	3 370	774	2 512	580	2.5	0.6	1.9	0.4
1997	6 739	3 037	795	2 338	569	2.2	0.6	1.7	0.4
1998	6 210	2 822	734	2 132	520	2.1	0.5	1.5	0.4
1999	5 880	2 622	783	2 005	469	1.9	0.6	1.4	0.3
2000	5 692	2 517	780	1 961	434	1.8	0.5	1.4	0.3
2001	6 801	3 476	835	2 031	459	2.4	0.6	1.6	0.3
2002	8 378	4 607	866	2 368	536	3.2	0.6	1.7	0.4
2003	8 774	4 838	818	2 477	641	3.3	0.6	1.6	0.4
2004	8 149	4 197	858	2 408	686	2.8	0.6	1.6	0.5
2005	7 591	3 667	872	2 386	666	2.5	0.6	1.6	0.4
2006	7 001	3 321	827	2 237	616	2.2	0.5	1.5	0.4
2007	7 078	3 515	793	2 142	627	2.3	0.5	1.4	0.4
2008	8 924	4 789	896	2 472	766	3.1	0.6	1.6	0.5
2009	14 265	9 160	882	3 187	1 035	5.9	0.6	2.1	0.7
Both Sexes, 16 to 19 Years									
1975	1 767	450	155	529	634	5.1	1.7	6.0	7.1
1976	1 719	387	153	496	683	4.3	1.7	5.5	7.5
1977	1 663	318	156	477	711	3.4	1.7	5.1	7.6
1978	1 583	300	167	455	660	3.1	1.7	4.7	6.8
1979	1 555	319	184	452	599	3.3	1.9	4.7	6.2
1980	1 669	388	156	481	643	4.1	1.7	5.1	6.9
1981	1 763	385	162	487	728	4.3	1.8	5.4	8.1
1982	1 977	460	134	509	874	5.4	1.6	6.0	10.2
1983	1 829	370	110	482	867	4.6	1.3	5.9	10.6
1984	1 499	271	114	370	745	3.4	1.4	4.7	9.4
1985	1 468	275	113	390	689	3.5	1.4	4.9	8.7
1986	1 454	240	145	374	695	3.0	1.8	4.7	8.8
1987	1 347	210	146	375	617	2.7	1.8	4.7	7.7
1988	1 226	207	159	310	550	2.6	2.0	3.9	6.8
1989	1 194	198	200	345	452	2.5	2.5	4.3	5.7
1990	1 212	233	181	338	460	3.0	2.3	4.3	5.9
1991	1 359	289	180	365	524	4.0	2.5	5.0	7.2
1992	1 427	259	149	377	643	3.6	2.1	5.3	9.1
1993	1 365	233	151	353	628	3.3	2.1	4.9	8.8
1994	1 320	185	84	634	416	2.5	1.1	8.5	5.6
1995	1 346	214	102	615	415	2.8	1.3	7.9	5.3
1996	1 306	182	91	625	409	2.3	1.2	8.0	5.2
1997	1 271	174	104	606	388	2.2	1.3	7.6	4.9
1998	1 205	181	86	577	361	2.2	1.0	7.0	4.4
1999	1 162	173	114	547	328	2.1	1.4	6.6	3.9
2000	1 081	157	109	516	299	1.9	1.3	6.2	3.6
2001	1 162	185	98	568	311	2.3	1.2	7.2	3.9
2002	1 253	197	91	597	368	2.6	1.2	7.9	4.9
2003	1 251	188	85	554	424	2.6	1.2	7.7	5.9
2004	1 208	165	76	510	456	2.3	1.1	7.2	6.4
2005	1 186	155	76	489	466	2.2	1.1	6.8	6.5
2006	1 119	145	78	461	435	2.0	1.1	6.3	6.0
2007	1 101	176	71	435	419	2.5	1.0	6.2	6.0
2008	1 285	203	80	490	511	3.0	1.2	7.1	7.5
2009	1 552	271	56	548	677	4.2	0.9	8.6	10.6

Note: See notes and definitions for information on historical comparability.

Table 1-32. Unemployed Persons and Unemployment Rates, by Reason for Unemployment, Sex, and Age, 1975–2009—*Continued*

(Thousands of people, percent.)

Sex, age, and year	Number of unemployed					Unemployed as a percent of the total civilian labor force			
	Total	Job losers and persons who completed temporary jobs	Job leavers	Entrants		Job losers and persons who completed temporary jobs	Job leavers	Entrants	
				Reentrants	New entrants			Reentrants	New entrants
Men, 20 Years and Over									
1975	3 476	2 598	298	506	76	5.0	0.6	1.0	0.1
1976	3 098	2 167	323	521	86	4.1	0.6	1.0	0.2
1977	2 794	1 816	335	540	103	3.4	0.6	1.0	0.2
1978	2 328	1 433	337	471	86	2.6	0.6	0.9	0.2
1979	2 308	1 464	325	446	73	2.6	0.6	0.8	0.1
1980	3 353	2 389	359	516	90	4.2	0.6	0.9	0.2
1981	3 615	2 565	356	592	102	4.5	0.6	1.0	0.2
1982	5 089	3 965	327	678	119	6.8	0.6	1.2	0.2
1983	5 257	4 088	336	695	138	6.9	0.6	1.2	0.2
1984	3 932	2 800	324	663	146	4.7	0.5	1.1	0.2
1985	3 715	2 568	352	671	124	4.3	0.6	1.1	0.2
1986	3 751	2 568	444	611	128	4.1	0.7	1.0	0.2
1987	3 369	2 289	413	558	108	3.7	0.7	0.9	0.2
1988	2 987	1 939	416	534	98	3.1	0.7	0.9	0.2
1989	2 867	1 843	394	541	88	2.9	0.6	0.8	0.1
1990	3 239	2 100	431	626	82	3.2	0.7	1.0	0.1
1991	4 195	2 982	411	698	105	4.6	0.6	1.1	0.2
1992	4 717	3 420	421	765	111	5.2	0.6	1.2	0.2
1993	4 287	2 996	429	747	114	4.5	0.6	1.1	0.2
1994	3 627	2 296	367	898	65	3.4	0.5	1.3	0.1
1995	3 239	2 051	356	775	57	3.0	0.5	1.2	0.1
1996	3 146	2 043	322	731	51	3.0	0.5	1.1	0.1
1997	2 882	1 795	358	675	55	2.6	0.5	1.0	0.1
1998	2 580	1 588	318	611	63	2.3	0.5	0.9	0.1
1999	2 433	1 459	336	592	46	2.1	0.5	0.8	0.1
2000	2 376	1 416	328	577	55	2.0	0.5	0.8	0.1
2001	3 040	1 999	372	612	56	2.7	0.5	0.8	0.1
2002	3 896	2 702	386	743	65	3.7	0.5	1.0	0.1
2003	4 209	2 899	376	846	88	3.9	0.5	1.1	0.1
2004	3 791	2 503	398	791	99	3.3	0.5	1.0	0.1
2005	4 059	2 188	445	1 067	359	2.7	0.5	1.0	0.1
2006	3 131	1 927	368	757	78	2.5	0.5	1.0	0.1
2007	3 259	2 064	371	723	101	2.6	0.5	0.9	0.1
2008	4 297	2 918	410	969	856	3.7	0.5	1.1	0.1
2009	7 555	5 796	407	1 190	162	7.3	0.5	1.5	0.2
Women, 20 Years and Over									
1975	2 684	1 339	375	858	114	4.0	1.1	2.6	0.3
1976	2 588	1 124	427	912	126	3.2	1.2	2.6	0.4
1977	2 535	1 031	419	945	140	2.8	1.2	2.6	0.4
1978	2 292	852	371	930	138	2.2	1.0	2.4	0.4
1979	2 276	851	370	908	145	2.1	0.9	2.3	0.4
1980	2 615	1 170	376	930	139	2.8	0.9	2.3	0.3
1981	2 895	1 317	404	1 023	151	3.1	1.0	2.4	0.4
1982	3 613	1 844	379	1 197	192	4.2	0.9	2.7	0.4
1983	3 632	1 801	384	1 235	212	4.0	0.9	2.8	0.5
1984	3 107	1 350	386	1 151	220	2.9	0.8	2.5	0.5
1985	3 129	1 296	412	1 195	227	2.7	0.9	2.5	0.5
1986	3 032	1 225	426	1 175	206	2.5	0.9	2.4	0.4
1987	2 709	1 067	406	1 041	194	2.2	0.8	2.1	0.4
1988	2 487	946	408	965	168	1.9	0.8	1.9	0.3
1989	2 467	942	430	958	137	1.8	0.8	1.8	0.3
1990	2 596	1 054	429	966	146	2.0	0.8	1.8	0.3
1991	3 074	1 423	413	1 075	163	2.6	0.8	2.0	0.3
1992	3 469	1 710	433	1 142	183	3.1	0.8	2.1	0.3
1993	3 288	1 619	395	1 098	176	2.9	0.7	2.0	0.3
1994	3 049	1 334	339	1 253	122	2.4	0.6	2.2	0.2
1995	2 819	1 211	366	1 135	107	2.1	0.6	2.0	0.2
1996	2 783	1 145	361	1 156	120	2.0	0.6	2.0	0.2
1997	2 585	1 069	333	1 057	126	1.8	0.6	1.8	0.2
1998	2 424	1 053	330	944	97	1.8	0.6	1.6	0.2
1999	2 285	990	333	866	96	1.6	0.5	1.4	0.2
2000	2 235	943	343	868	80	1.5	0.6	1.4	0.1
2001	2 599	1 291	365	850	92	2.0	0.6	1.3	0.1
2002	3 228	1 708	389	1 028	102	2.7	0.6	1.6	0.2
2003	3 314	1 751	357	1 076	130	2.7	0.6	1.7	0.2
2004	3 150	1 529	384	1 107	131	2.4	0.6	1.7	0.2
2005	3 013	1 417	391	1 103	101	2.2	0.6	1.7	0.2
2006	2 751	1 249	380	1 019	103	1.9	0.6	1.5	0.2
2007	2 718	1 276	351	984	107	1.9	0.5	1.7	0.4
2008	3 342	1 668	406	1 126	143	2.4	0.6	1.6	0.2
2009	5 157	3 093	419	1 449	196	4.5	0.6	2.1	0.3

Note: See notes and definitions for information on historical comparability.

Table 1-33. Percent of the Population with Work Experience During the Year, by Age and Sex, 1987–2009

(Percent.)

Sex and year	Total	16 to 17 years	18 to 19 years	20 to 24 years	25 to 34 years	35 to 44 years	45 to 54 years	55 to 59 years	60 to 64 years	65 to 69 years	70 years and over
Both Sexes											
1987	69.7	51.8	76.6	85.5	85.7	86.1	81.6	69.4	51.3	26.2	10.2
1988	70.2	50.6	75.5	85.7	86.0	86.8	82.2	70.5	52.2	27.9	10.3
1989	70.5	51.9	75.4	84.9	86.6	86.9	82.8	70.4	52.5	28.4	10.0
1990	70.2	48.6	74.2	84.1	86.2	87.0	82.8	70.9	53.4	28.3	10.2
1991	69.5	43.4	70.8	83.4	85.9	86.6	83.0	70.3	52.9	27.2	9.8
1992	69.1	43.8	69.9	82.7	85.2	85.9	82.8	70.8	53.5	25.5	9.8
1993	69.2	42.1	70.4	82.0	85.0	85.3	82.8	71.6	51.6	27.5	10.7
1994	69.6	44.1	71.5	82.5	85.5	85.6	83.8	72.2	52.8	27.5	10.0
1995	69.6	44.4	71.2	82.0	85.6	85.9	83.4	72.2	53.3	28.0	10.2
1996	69.9	43.3	70.5	83.1	86.1	85.7	84.3	73.3	54.3	27.8	10.4
1997	70.1	43.6	70.5	83.0	87.1	85.9	84.4	73.8	53.8	28.5	10.0
1998	70.1	42.1	69.9	82.9	86.7	86.3	84.2	73.7	54.5	29.2	10.6
1999	70.7	43.7	71.2	82.7	87.3	86.9	85.0	72.3	55.8	30.5	11.6
2000	70.5	42.2	69.6	82.6	87.1	87.0	84.6	72.9	55.1	30.8	11.4
2001	69.4	37.7	66.7	80.8	86.1	85.8	83.7	73.5	56.7	30.6	10.5
2002	68.5	34.5	62.8	78.5	84.4	85.0	83.7	74.7	56.8	33.1	10.4
2003	67.8	32.0	61.7	77.5	83.7	84.0	82.9	73.9	56.5	33.2	11.4
2004	67.7	32.6	59.8	76.9	83.3	84.2	82.6	73.9	57.0	32.7	12.2
2005	67.8	31.1	60.1	77.3	83.7	84.1	82.8	74.4	58.2	32.0	12.1
2006	67.9	30.9	58.3	76.9	84.4	84.3	82.8	74.5	58.2	33.6	12.6
2007	67.8	28.5	57.3	76.6	84.2	84.4	82.4	75.6	59.7	35.2	13.0
2008	67.1	24.6	55.3	76.0	84.1	83.9	81.8	74.6	60.3	34.9	13.5
2009	65.0	21.9	48.7	71.0	81.6	82.0	80.5	73.8	59.3	35.3	12.8
Men											
1987	78.9	52.4	77.4	90.4	94.3	94.1	91.9	83.3	63.2	34.2	15.4
1988	79.1	51.8	78.9	90.7	94.3	94.6	91.6	82.1	63.1	35.6	15.6
1989	79.4	53.2	77.7	89.9	94.7	94.7	91.9	82.0	64.2	35.4	15.1
1990	78.9	50.3	76.7	88.7	94.4	94.7	91.3	82.0	65.8	35.8	14.0
1991	77.9	45.4	72.2	87.9	93.5	93.6	91.3	81.5	63.6	35.0	14.4
1992	77.4	46.6	73.7	87.1	93.3	92.8	89.9	80.9	63.2	32.4	14.3
1993	76.8	43.9	71.4	86.6	92.5	92.0	89.3	79.8	59.1	34.3	15.3
1994	77.2	44.4	74.7	87.2	92.9	92.0	90.0	81.3	61.4	33.9	14.8
1995	77.0	43.7	73.6	86.4	92.6	92.2	89.7	81.5	62.1	34.5	14.9
1996	77.2	44.1	71.8	86.7	93.4	92.1	90.4	81.8	62.5	33.6	15.2
1997	77.1	43.4	70.3	86.6	94.1	92.3	90.7	81.4	62.9	33.8	13.9
1998	76.9	40.4	71.6	86.4	93.5	92.7	90.1	81.7	63.5	35.5	14.7
1999	77.3	44.7	72.3	85.5	93.9	93.2	89.9	79.2	65.1	37.4	16.5
2000	77.1	42.1	70.2	85.1	93.4	93.6	89.8	80.6	64.4	38.4	16.0
2001	76.3	37.4	67.7	84.8	93.2	92.2	89.1	80.4	64.3	37.8	14.5
2002	75.2	34.7	62.8	82.1	91.6	91.8	88.9	80.7	64.3	39.3	14.6
2003	74.3	32.8	61.7	80.2	90.8	90.9	87.7	80.9	63.1	37.3	15.8
2004	74.2	32.1	58.9	80.2	91.0	91.1	87.9	80.1	64.5	37.1	16.7
2005	74.6	31.1	60.7	80.8	91.3	91.6	88.2	80.1	64.3	37.6	17.0
2006	74.5	30.9	57.9	80.1	91.9	91.8	88.0	80.6	64.1	38.3	17.3
2007	74.3	28.5	59.0	80.5	90.5	91.5	88.2	80.3	66.2	39.3	17.9
2008	73.2	24.4	55.1	78.7	90.7	91.1	86.4	79.3	66.0	40.3	17.9
2009	70.8	22.2	48.0	73.3	87.7	89.1	85.0	78.3	64.8	39.8	17.2
Women											
1987	61.3	51.1	75.8	81.0	77.3	78.5	71.9	56.7	41.0	19.6	6.8
1988	62.1	49.3	72.2	81.0	78.1	79.4	73.5	60.0	42.5	21.4	6.8
1989	62.3	50.6	73.1	80.2	78.6	79.3	74.2	59.9	42.4	22.5	6.7
1990	62.2	46.8	71.7	79.6	78.0	79.6	74.9	60.4	42.5	22.1	7.7
1991	61.8	41.4	69.4	79.0	78.3	79.9	75.3	59.9	43.6	20.6	6.7
1992	61.5	40.9	66.1	78.4	77.2	79.1	76.1	61.5	44.4	20.0	6.7
1993	62.1	40.3	69.4	77.5	77.6	78.7	76.5	63.9	44.7	22.1	7.7
1994	62.5	43.7	68.4	77.8	78.1	79.4	78.0	63.9	45.0	22.2	6.8
1995	62.8	45.2	68.7	77.7	78.8	79.8	77.6	63.2	45.6	22.4	7.1
1996	63.2	42.5	69.2	79.5	78.9	79.5	78.4	65.4	46.9	23.0	7.1
1997	63.6	43.9	70.7	79.5	80.1	79.6	78.4	66.7	45.6	24.0	7.3
1998	63.7	44.1	68.2	79.4	80.1	80.0	78.6	66.3	46.2	23.8	7.8
1999	64.5	42.6	70.1	79.9	80.9	80.7	80.3	66.2	47.3	24.4	8.2
2000	64.3	42.3	69.0	80.2	80.9	80.5	79.5	65.7	47.0	23.9	8.2
2001	63.1	38.1	65.7	76.9	79.2	79.5	78.6	67.1	49.8	24.2	7.9
2002	62.3	34.3	62.8	74.9	77.2	78.4	78.7	69.1	50.0	27.8	7.4
2003	61.7	31.2	61.6	74.6	76.6	77.2	78.4	67.3	50.7	29.6	8.3
2004	61.5	33.1	60.7	73.7	75.6	77.4	77.5	68.2	50.3	28.7	9.0
2005	61.4	31.2	59.6	73.7	76.1	76.8	77.6	68.9	52.7	27.1	8.7
2006	61.6	30.9	58.7	73.7	76.9	76.9	77.9	68.8	53.0	29.5	9.3
2007	61.6	28.5	55.6	72.6	77.8	77.4	76.9	71.2	53.7	31.5	9.5
2008	61.3	24.8	55.4	73.2	77.3	76.7	77.3	70.1	55.0	30.1	10.3
2009	59.6	21.6	49.5	68.6	75.4	75.0	76.1	69.5	54.4	31.1	9.7

Note: See notes and definitions for information on historical comparability.

Table 1-34. Persons with Work Experience During the Year, by Industry and Class of Worker of Job Held the Longest, 2002–2009

(Thousands of people.)

Industry and class of worker	2002	2003	2004	2005	2006	2007	2008	2009
TOTAL	151 546	151 553	153 024	155 127	157 352	158 468	158 317	154 772
Agriculture	2 490	2 521	2 492	2 344	2 332	2 407	2 382	2 581
Wage and salary workers	1 583	1 605	1 549	1 501	1 495	1 525	1 522	1 733
Self-employed workers	875	894	918	829	812	846	824	813
Unpaid family workers	33	22	25	14	25	36	37	35
Nonagricultural Industries	149 055	149 032	150 532	152 783	155 021	156 061	155 934	152 191
Wage and salary workers	139 909	139 747	140 885	143 002	145 152	146 485	146 521	142 946
Mining	594	576	630	696	758	746	840	778
Construction	9 488	9 423	10 076	10 423	10 989	10 547	10 234	9 443
Manufacturing	17 660	17 349	17 196	17 243	17 112	16 641	16 332	14 956
Durable goods	11 013	10 622	10 814	10 930	10 995	10 687	10 477	9 342
Nondurable goods	6 647	6 727	6 382	6 313	6 116	5 954	5 855	5 613
Wholesale and retail trade	21 615	21 650	22 091	22 479	21 822	21 837	21 838	21 210
Wholesale trade	4 402	4 691	4 470	4 517	4 395	4 017	4 016	3 849
Retail trade	17 213	16 959	17 621	17 962	17 427	17 820	17 822	17 361
Transportation and utilities	7 039	6 934	7 040	7 248	7 413	8 023	7 675	7 309
Transportation and warehousing	5 745	5 736	5 827	6 095	6 197	6 750	6 365	6 025
Utilities	1 294	1 198	1 213	1 153	1 216	1 273	1 310	1 284
Information	3 989	3 755	3 359	3 495	3 710	3 687	3 455	3 375
Financial activities	9 591	9 822	9 956	9 748	10 101	10 013	9 671	9 409
Finance and insurance	6 986	7 135	7 192	7 011	7 190	7 347	6 994	6 792
Real estate and rental and leasing	2 605	2 687	2 764	2 737	2 912	2 666	2 677	2 617
Professional and business services	13 883	13 485	13 277	13 537	14 412	14 659	14 868	14 633
Professional, scientific, and technical services	7 989	7 855	7 793	7 768	8 294	8 676	8 742	8 475
Management, administration, and waste management services	5 894	5 629	5 484	5 769	6 118	5 982	6 127	6 159
Education and health services	29 343	29 571	29 814	30 552	31 314	31 921	32 828	33 465
Education services	12 765	13 026	13 169	13 282	13 659	13 989	14 396	14 457
Health care and social assistance services	16 578	16 544	16 645	17 270	17 655	17 932	18 432	19 008
Leisure and hospitality	13 260	13 110	13 345	13 405	13 455	13 959	14 242	13 917
Arts, entertainment, and recreation	2 852	2 789	2 888	2 877	2 797	3 124	3 047	3 284
Accommodation and food services	10 408	10 321	10 457	10 528	10 658	10 835	11 195	10 633
Other services and private household	6 416	6 529	6 473	6 490	6 341	6 603	6 590	6 233
Private households	873	897	907	866	912	888	912	757
Public administration	6 290	6 734	6 897	6 917	7 076	7 095	7 121	7 332
Self-employed workers	9 023	9 169	9 520	9 658	9 733	9 451	9 332	9 121
Unpaid family workers	124	116	128	123	135	126	82	124

Note: See notes and definitions for information on historical comparability.

Table 1-35. Number of Persons with Work Experience During the Year, by Extent of Employment and Sex, 1987–2009

(Thousands of people.)

Sex and year	Total	Full-time workers				Part-time workers			
		Total	50 to 52 weeks	27 to 49 weeks	1 to 26 weeks	Total	50 to 52 weeks	27 to 49 weeks	1 to 26 weeks
Both Sexes									
1987	128 315	100 288	77 015	13 361	9 912	28 027	10 973	6 594	10 460
1988	130 451	102 131	79 627	12 875	9 629	28 320	11 384	6 624	10 312
1989	132 817	104 876	81 117	14 271	9 488	27 941	11 275	6 987	9 679
1990	133 535	105 323	80 932	14 758	9 633	28 212	11 507	7 012	9 693
1991	133 410	104 472	80 385	14 491	9 596	28 938	11 946	7 003	9 989
1992	133 912	104 813	81 523	13 587	9 703	29 099	12 326	6 841	9 932
1993	136 354	106 299	83 384	13 054	9 861	30 055	12 818	6 777	10 460
1994	138 468	108 141	85 764	13 051	9 326	30 327	12 936	6 956	10 435
1995	139 724	110 063	88 173	12 970	8 920	29 661	12 725	6 831	10 105
1996	142 201	112 313	90 252	12 997	9 064	29 888	13 382	6 643	9 863
1997	143 968	113 879	92 631	12 508	8 740	30 089	13 810	6 565	9 714
1998	145 566	116 412	95 772	12 156	8 484	29 155	13 538	6 480	9 137
1999	148 295	119 096	97 941	12 294	8 861	29 199	13 680	6 317	9 202
2000	149 361	120 591	100 349	12 071	8 171	28 770	13 865	6 161	8 744
2001	151 042	121 921	100 357	13 172	8 392	29 121	14 038	6 139	8 944
2002	151 546	121 726	100 659	12 544	8 523	29 819	14 635	6 184	9 000
2003	151 553	121 158	100 700	11 972	8 486	30 395	15 333	6 027	9 035
2004	153 024	122 404	102 427	11 862	8 115	30 621	15 552	6 077	8 992
2005	155 127	124 683	104 876	11 816	7 991	30 444	15 374	6 161	8 909
2006	157 352	127 340	107 734	11 736	7 870	30 012	15 131	6 223	8 657
2007	158 468	128 332	108 617	11 901	7 814	30 136	15 477	6 194	8 466
2008	158 317	125 937	104 023	13 421	8 493	32 380	16 562	6 630	9 188
2009	154 772	121 355	99 306	12 350	9 698	33 418	17 417	6 674	9 327
Men									
1987	69 144	59 736	47 040	7 503	5 193	9 408	3 260	2 191	3 957
1988	70 021	60 504	48 299	7 329	4 876	9 517	3 468	2 199	3 850
1989	71 640	62 108	49 693	7 642	4 773	9 532	3 619	2 254	3 659
1990	71 953	62 319	49 175	8 188	4 956	9 634	3 650	2 322	3 662
1991	71 700	61 636	47 895	8 324	5 417	10 064	3 820	2 342	3 902
1992	72 007	61 722	48 300	7 965	5 457	10 285	3 864	2 354	4 067
1993	72 872	62 513	49 832	7 317	5 364	10 359	4 005	2 144	4 210
1994	73 958	63 634	51 582	7 094	4 958	10 324	3 948	2 358	4 018
1995	74 381	64 145	52 671	6 973	4 501	10 236	4 034	2 257	3 945
1996	75 760	65 356	53 795	6 891	4 670	10 404	4 321	2 136	3 947
1997	76 408	66 089	54 918	6 638	4 533	10 319	4 246	2 274	3 799
1998	76 918	67 250	56 953	6 208	4 089	9 669	4 197	2 090	3 382
1999	78 145	68 347	57 520	6 401	4 426	9 797	4 297	2 062	3 438
2000	78 804	68 925	58 756	6 094	4 075	9 879	4 485	1 957	3 437
2001	79 971	70 074	58 715	7 087	4 272	9 897	4 306	1 989	3 602
2002	80 282	70 132	58 765	6 804	4 563	10 151	4 519	2 042	3 590
2003	80 317	69 766	58 778	6 479	4 509	10 551	5 042	1 872	3 637
2004	81 261	70 780	60 096	6 428	4 256	10 482	4 987	1 992	3 503
2005	82 735	72 056	61 510	6 299	4 247	10 679	5 153	2 074	3 452
2006	83 767	73 578	63 058	6 373	4 147	10 189	4 747	2 046	3 396
2007	84 292	73 734	62 994	6 583	4 157	10 558	4 933	2 165	3 460
2008	83 889	72 204	59 869	7 645	4 690	11 685	5 425	2 457	3 803
2009	81 835	69 178	56 058	7 339	5 780	12 658	5 911	2 526	4 221
Women									
1987	59 171	40 552	29 975	5 858	4 719	18 619	7 713	4 403	6 503
1988	60 430	41 627	31 328	5 546	4 753	18 803	7 916	4 425	6 462
1989	61 178	42 768	31 424	6 629	4 715	18 410	7 656	4 733	6 021
1990	61 582	43 004	31 757	6 570	4 677	18 578	7 857	4 690	6 031
1991	61 712	42 837	32 491	6 167	4 179	18 875	8 126	4 662	6 087
1992	61 904	43 090	33 223	5 621	4 246	18 814	8 462	4 487	5 865
1993	63 481	43 785	33 552	5 736	4 497	19 696	8 813	4 633	6 250
1994	64 511	44 508	34 182	5 957	4 369	20 003	8 988	4 598	6 417
1995	65 342	45 917	35 502	5 997	4 418	19 425	8 691	4 574	6 160
1996	66 439	46 955	36 457	6 105	4 393	19 484	9 061	4 507	5 916
1997	67 559	47 790	37 713	5 870	4 207	19 769	9 564	4 291	5 914
1998	68 648	49 162	38 819	5 948	4 395	19 486	9 341	4 390	5 755
1999	70 150	50 748	40 421	5 892	4 435	19 402	9 383	4 255	5 764
2000	70 556	51 665	41 593	5 977	4 095	18 891	9 380	4 204	5 307
2001	71 071	51 848	41 642	6 085	4 120	19 223	9 731	4 150	5 342
2002	71 263	51 593	41 893	5 741	3 959	19 671	10 117	4 143	5 411
2003	71 236	51 391	41 921	5 493	3 977	19 844	10 291	4 155	5 398
2004	71 763	51 624	42 331	5 434	3 859	20 139	10 565	4 085	5 489
2005	72 392	52 627	43 366	5 517	3 744	19 765	10 222	4 087	5 456
2006	73 585	53 762	44 676	5 364	3 723	19 823	10 384	4 178	5 261
2007	74 176	54 598	45 622	5 318	3 657	19 579	10 543	4 029	5 006
2008	74 428	53 733	44 154	5 776	3 803	20 695	11 137	4 172	5 385
2009	72 937	52 177	43 248	5 012	3 918	20 760	11 506	4 147	5 107

Note: See notes and definitions for information on historical comparability.

Table 1-36. Percent Distribution of the Population with Work Experience During the Year, by Extent of Employment and Sex, 1987–2009

(Percent of total people with work experience.)

Sex and year	Total	Full-time workers				Part-time workers			
		Total	50 to 52 weeks	27 to 49 weeks	1 to 26 weeks	Total	50 to 52 weeks	27 to 49 weeks	1 to 26 weeks
Both Sexes									
1987	100.0	78.1	60.0	10.4	7.7	21.9	8.6	5.1	8.2
1988	100.0	78.3	61.0	9.9	7.4	21.7	8.7	5.1	7.9
1989	100.0	78.9	61.1	10.7	7.1	21.1	8.5	5.3	7.3
1990	100.0	78.9	60.6	11.1	7.2	21.2	8.6	5.3	7.3
1991	100.0	78.4	60.3	10.9	7.2	21.7	9.0	5.2	7.5
1992	100.0	78.2	60.9	10.1	7.2	21.7	9.2	5.1	7.4
1993	100.0	78.0	61.2	9.6	7.2	22.1	9.4	5.0	7.7
1994	100.0	78.0	61.9	9.4	6.7	21.8	9.3	5.0	7.5
1995	100.0	78.8	63.1	9.3	6.4	21.2	9.1	4.9	7.2
1996	100.0	79.0	63.5	9.1	6.4	21.0	9.4	4.7	6.9
1997	100.0	79.1	64.3	8.7	6.1	20.9	9.6	4.6	6.7
1998	100.0	80.0	65.8	8.4	5.8	20.1	9.3	4.5	6.3
1999	100.0	80.3	66.0	8.3	6.0	19.7	9.2	4.3	6.2
2000	100.0	80.8	67.2	8.1	5.5	19.3	9.3	4.1	5.9
2001	100.0	80.7	66.4	8.7	5.6	19.3	9.3	4.1	5.9
2002	100.0	80.3	66.4	8.3	5.6	19.7	9.7	4.1	5.9
2003	100.0	79.9	66.4	7.9	5.6	20.1	10.1	4.0	6.0
2004	100.0	80.0	66.9	7.8	5.3	20.1	10.2	4.0	5.9
2005	100.0	80.4	67.6	7.6	5.2	19.6	9.9	4.0	5.7
2006	100.0	80.9	68.5	7.5	5.0	19.1	9.6	4.0	5.5
2007	100.0	81.0	68.5	7.5	4.9	19.0	9.8	3.9	5.3
2008	100.0	79.5	65.7	8.5	5.4	20.5	10.5	4.2	5.8
2009	100.0	78.4	64.2	8.0	6.3	21.6	11.3	4.3	6.0
Men									
1987	100.0	86.4	68.0	10.9	7.5	13.6	4.7	3.2	5.7
1988	100.0	86.5	69.0	10.5	7.0	13.6	5.0	3.1	5.5
1989	100.0	86.8	69.4	10.7	6.7	13.3	5.1	3.1	5.1
1990	100.0	86.6	68.3	11.4	6.9	13.4	5.1	3.2	5.1
1991	100.0	86.0	66.8	11.6	7.6	14.0	5.3	3.3	5.4
1992	100.0	85.8	67.1	11.1	7.6	14.3	5.4	3.3	5.6
1993	100.0	85.8	68.4	10.0	7.4	14.2	5.5	2.9	5.8
1994	100.0	86.0	69.7	9.6	6.7	13.9	5.3	3.2	5.4
1995	100.0	86.3	70.8	9.4	6.1	13.7	5.4	3.0	5.3
1996	100.0	86.3	71.0	9.1	6.2	13.7	5.7	2.8	5.2
1997	100.0	86.5	71.9	8.7	5.9	13.6	5.6	3.0	5.0
1998	100.0	87.4	74.0	8.1	5.3	12.6	5.5	2.7	4.4
1999	100.0	87.5	73.6	8.2	5.7	12.5	5.5	2.6	4.4
2000	100.0	87.5	74.6	7.7	5.2	12.6	5.7	2.5	4.4
2001	100.0	87.6	73.4	8.9	5.3	12.4	5.4	2.5	4.5
2002	100.0	87.4	73.2	8.5	5.7	12.6	5.6	2.5	4.5
2003	100.0	86.9	73.2	8.1	5.6	13.1	6.3	2.3	4.5
2004	100.0	87.1	74.0	7.9	5.2	12.9	6.1	2.5	4.3
2005	100.0	87.0	74.3	7.6	5.1	12.9	6.2	2.5	4.2
2006	100.0	87.8	75.3	7.6	5.0	12.2	5.7	2.4	4.1
2007	100.0	87.5	74.7	7.8	4.9	12.5	5.9	2.6	4.1
2008	100.0	86.1	71.4	9.1	5.6	13.9	6.5	2.9	4.5
2009	100.0	84.5	68.5	9.0	7.1	15.5	7.2	3.1	5.2
Women									
1987	100.0	68.6	50.7	9.9	8.0	31.4	13.0	7.4	11.0
1988	100.0	68.9	51.8	9.2	7.9	31.1	13.1	7.3	10.7
1989	100.0	69.9	51.4	10.8	7.7	30.0	12.5	7.7	9.8
1990	100.0	69.9	51.6	10.7	7.6	30.2	12.8	7.6	9.8
1991	100.0	69.4	52.6	10.0	6.8	30.7	13.2	7.6	9.9
1992	100.0	69.7	53.7	9.1	6.9	30.4	13.7	7.2	9.5
1993	100.0	69.0	52.9	9.0	7.1	31.0	13.9	7.3	9.8
1994	100.0	69.0	53.0	9.2	6.8	30.9	13.9	7.1	9.9
1995	100.0	70.3	54.3	9.2	6.8	29.7	13.3	7.0	9.4
1996	100.0	70.7	54.9	9.2	6.6	29.3	13.6	6.8	8.9
1997	100.0	70.7	55.8	8.7	6.2	29.4	14.2	6.4	8.8
1998	100.0	71.6	56.5	8.7	6.4	28.4	13.6	6.4	8.4
1999	100.0	72.3	57.6	8.4	6.3	27.7	13.4	6.1	8.2
2000	100.0	73.2	58.9	8.5	5.8	26.8	13.3	6.0	7.5
2001	100.0	73.0	58.6	8.6	5.8	27.0	13.7	5.8	7.5
2002	100.0	72.5	58.8	8.1	5.6	27.6	14.2	5.8	7.6
2003	100.0	72.1	58.8	7.7	5.6	27.8	14.4	5.8	7.6
2004	100.0	72.0	59.0	7.6	5.4	28.0	14.7	5.7	7.6
2005	100.0	72.7	59.9	7.6	5.2	27.2	14.1	5.6	7.5
2006	100.0	73.1	60.7	7.3	5.1	26.9	14.1	5.7	7.1
2007	100.0	73.6	61.5	7.2	4.9	26.4	14.2	5.4	6.7
2008	100.0	72.2	59.3	7.8	5.1	27.8	15.0	5.6	7.2
2009	100.0	71.5	59.3	6.9	5.4	28.5	15.8	5.7	7.0

Note: See notes and definitions for information on historical comparability.

Table 1-37. Extent of Unemployment During the Year, by Sex, 1987–2009

(Thousands of people, percent.)

Sex and extent of unemployment	1987	1988	1989	1990	1991	1992	1993	1994	1995	1996	1997
BOTH SEXES											
Total Who Worked or Looked for Work	130 353	132 185	134 394	135 408	135 826	136 654	139 786	141 325	142 413	144 528	146 096
Percent with unemployment	14.1	12.9	12.9	14.6	15.7	15.7	14.7	13.4	12.7	11.6	10.7
Total with Unemployment	18 399	17 096	17 273	19 809	21 276	21 455	20 527	18 966	18 067	16 789	15 637
Did not work but looked for work	2 037	1 735	1 577	1 874	2 415	2 742	3 432	2 857	2 690	2 329	2 129
Worked during the year	16 362	15 362	15 697	17 936	18 861	18 714	17 094	16 109	15 377	14 460	13 508
Year-round workers with 1 or 2 weeks of unemployment	792	830	833	1 056	966	871	688	746	715	589	611
Part-year workers with unemployment	15 570	14 532	14 864	16 880	17 895	17 843	16 406	15 363	14 662	13 871	12 897
1 to 4 weeks	3 363	3 256	3 489	3 645	3 224	2 944	2 626	2 788	2 812	2 550	2 582
5 to 10 weeks	3 191	3 148	3 359	3 669	3 655	3 496	2 898	2 983	2 725	2 671	2 601
11 to 14 weeks	2 258	2 128	2 235	2 501	2 587	2 574	2 300	2 265	2 147	2 020	1 822
15 to 26 weeks	3 904	3 479	3 600	4 316	4 927	4 877	4 549	4 158	4 013	3 662	3 378
27 weeks or more	2 854	2 521	2 181	2 749	3 502	3 952	4 033	3 169	2 965	2 968	2 514
With 2 or more spells of unemployment	5 149	5 136	5 073	5 811	5 864	5 734	5 338	4 783	4 468	4 237	4 044
2 spells	2 442	2 460	2 460	2 855	2 738	2 698	2 572	2 207	1 963	1 982	1 853
3 or more spells	2 707	2 676	2 613	2 956	3 126	3 036	2 766	2 576	2 505	2 255	2 191
MEN											
Total Who Worked or Looked for Work	69 995	70 738	72 362	72 844	72 909	73 387	74 516	75 244	75 698	76 786	77 385
Percent with unemployment	15.0	13.7	13.5	15.5	17.3	17.5	15.7	14.1	13.2	11.9	11.1
Total with Unemployment	10 504	9 696	9 792	11 307	12 642	12 844	11 723	10 582	9 996	9 157	8 604
Did not work but looked for work	852	717	723	891	1 210	1 379	1 641	1 286	1 317	1 026	978
Worked during the year	9 653	8 978	9 071	10 415	11 432	11 466	10 082	9 296	8 679	8 130	7 626
Year-round workers with 1 or 2 weeks of unemployment	536	585	568	711	612	567	449	527	462	395	382
Part-year workers with unemployment	9 117	8 393	8 503	9 704	10 820	10 899	9 633	8 769	8 217	7 735	7 244
1 to 4 weeks	1 561	1 633	1 742	1 819	1 591	1 563	1 343	1 365	1 398	1 272	1 275
5 to 10 weeks	1 824	1 808	1 890	2 041	2 111	2 039	1 647	1 666	1 434	1 478	1 474
11 to 14 weeks	1 415	1 279	1 365	1 462	1 659	1 615	1 354	1 370	1 253	1 258	1 068
15 to 26 weeks	2 514	2 124	2 188	2 645	3 206	3 165	2 862	2 449	2 439	2 076	1 949
27 weeks or more	1 803	1 549	1 318	1 737	2 253	2 517	2 427	1 919	1 693	1 651	1 478
With 2 or more spells of unemployment	3 300	3 366	3 178	3 689	3 886	3 889	3 451	2 940	2 793	2 554	2 437
2 spells	1 488	1 560	1 517	1 676	1 742	1 781	1 580	1 266	1 110	1 109	1 078
3 or more spells	1 812	1 806	1 661	2 013	2 144	2 108	1 871	1 674	1 683	1 445	1 359
WOMEN											
Total Who Worked or Looked for Work	60 357	61 447	62 032	62 564	62 917	63 267	65 270	66 081	66 716	67 742	68 710
Percent with unemployment	13.1	12.0	12.1	13.6	13.7	13.6	13.5	12.7	12.1	11.3	10.2
Total with Unemployment	7 895	7 400	7 481	8 502	8 634	8 611	8 804	8 383	8 070	7 632	7 033
Did not work but looked for work	1 185	1 017	854	982	1 205	1 363	1 791	1 570	1 373	1 303	1 151
Worked during the year	6 710	6 382	6 628	7 520	7 427	7 247	7 014	6 813	6 696	6 330	5 882
Year-round workers with 1 or 2 weeks of unemployment	255	244	265	344	354	304	239	219	253	194	229
Part-year workers with unemployment	6 455	6 138	6 363	7 176	7 073	6 943	6 775	6 594	6 443	6 136	5 653
1 to 4 weeks	1 802	1 623	1 747	1 827	1 633	1 380	1 284	1 422	1 413	1 279	1 307
5 to 10 weeks	1 368	1 340	1 469	1 627	1 544	1 457	1 252	1 317	1 291	1 192	1 127
11 to 14 weeks	844	849	870	1 038	927	959	946	896	893	762	754
15 to 26 weeks	1 391	1 354	1 413	1 671	1 720	1 712	1 687	1 708	1 574	1 586	1 429
27 weeks or more	1 050	972	864	1 013	1 249	1 435	1 606	1 251	1 272	1 317	1 036
With 2 or more spells of unemployment	1 849	1 769	1 895	2 122	1 979	1 844	1 887	1 843	1 675	1 682	1 607
2 spells	954	899	943	1 179	997	916	992	941	853	872	775
3 or more spells	895	870	952	943	982	928	895	902	822	810	832

Table 1-37. Extent of Unemployment During the Year, by Sex, 1987–2009—*Continued*

(Thousands of people, percent.)

Sex and extent of unemployment	1998	1999	2000	2001	2002	2003	2004	2005	2006	2007	2008	2009
BOTH SEXES												
Total Who Worked or Looked for Work	147 295	149 798	150 786	153 056	154 205	154 315	155 576	157 549	159 259	160 565	161 506	160 624
Percent with unemployment	9.5	8.7	8.1	10.4	10.9	10.7	9.7	9.2	9.1	9.4	13.1	16.3
Total with Unemployment	14 044	13 068	12 269	15 843	16 824	16 462	15 074	14 558	14 447	15 130	21 231	26 151
Did not work but looked for work	1 729	1 503	1 425	2 014	2 660	2 762	2 551	2 422	1 907	2 097	3 189	5 851
Worked during the year	12 316	11 566	10 845	13 829	14 164	13 699	12 522	12 136	12 540	13 033	18 042	20 300
Year-round workers with 1 or 2 weeks of unemployment	630	562	573	602	584	534	465	431	450	500	763	693
Part-year workers with unemployment	11 686	11 004	10 272	13 227	13 580	13 165	12 057	11 705	12 090	12 533	17 279	19 607
1 to 4 weeks	2 323	2 361	2 233	2 368	2 002	1 839	1 985	1 941	2 601	2 593	2 794	2 528
5 to 10 weeks	2 495	2 218	2 014	2 557	2 373	2 264	2 100	2 170	2 107	2 090	2 944	2 562
11 to 14 weeks	1 701	1 594	1 505	2 038	1 970	1 749	1 773	1 698	1 615	1 888	2 438	2 414
15 to 26 weeks	3 019	2 803	2 641	3 683	3 848	3 778	3 448	3 349	3 176	3 373	4 859	5 698
27 weeks or more	2 148	2 028	1 879	2 582	3 387	3 535	2 751	2 547	2 592	2 589	4 244	6 405
With 2 or more spells of unemployment	3 628	3 225	3 079	3 421	3 226	3 093	2 896	3 095	3 076	3 108	3 991	4 152
2 spells	1 650	1 449	1 397	1 643	1 556	1 585	1 344	1 477	1 564	1 427	1 987	1 918
3 or more spells	1 978	1 776	1 682	1 779	1 670	1 508	1 552	1 618	1 513	1 681	2 004	2 234
MEN												
Total Who Worked or Looked for Work	77 704	78 905	79 546	80 975	81 651	81 804	82 478	83 951	84 736	85 368	85 563	85 161
Percent with unemployment	9.4	9.0	8.6	11.0	11.8	11.4	10.0	9.7	9.6	10.2	14.4	18.6
Total with Unemployment	7 284	7 091	6 806	8 928	9 621	9 339	8 256	8 116	8 115	8 698	12 331	15 877
Did not work but looked for work	787	760	742	1 004	1 369	1 487	1 217	1 216	969	1 076	1 674	3 325
Worked during the year	6 497	6 332	6 064	7 924	8 252	7 854	7 039	6 899	7 146	7 622	10 656	12 552
Year-round workers with 1 or 2 weeks of unemployment	386	373	379	421	365	359	289	296	295	365	484	458
Part-year workers with unemployment	6 111	5 959	5 685	7 502	7 887	7 495	6 750	6 603	6 850	7 257	10 172	12 093
1 to 4 weeks	1 085	1 166	1 070	1 247	1 075	958	1 028	1 052	1 283	1 367	1 523	1 466
5 to 10 weeks	1 363	1 168	1 135	1 446	1 342	1 314	1 170	1 209	1 267	1 214	1 701	1 594
11 to 14 weeks	980	937	880	1 207	1 186	1 039	1 021	1 024	961	1 163	1 467	1 558
15 to 26 weeks	1 585	1 655	1 595	2 191	2 282	2 178	2 065	1 923	1 868	2 058	3 035	3 564
27 weeks or more	1 098	1 033	1 005	1 412	2 002	2 006	1 466	1 395	1 472	1 455	2 445	3 911
With 2 or more spells of unemployment	2 014	1 845	1 809	2 100	1 920	1 882	1 828	1 975	1 936	1 992	2 623	2 865
2 spells	880	787	804	1 002	914	946	808	940	945	847	1 234	1 299
3 or more spells	1 134	1 058	1 005	1 099	1 006	936	1 020	1 035	991	1 145	1 389	1 566
WOMEN												
Total Who Worked or Looked for Work	69 591	70 893	71 240	72 081	72 554	72 511	73 097	73 598	74 523	75 197	75 943	75 463
Percent with unemployment	9.7	8.4	7.7	9.6	9.9	9.8	9.3	8.8	8.5	8.6	11.7	13.6
Total with Unemployment	6 760	5 976	5 463	6 915	7 203	7 123	6 818	6 442	6 332	6 432	8 900	10 274
Did not work but looked for work	942	743	683	1 010	1 291	1 275	1 334	1 206	938	1 021	1 514	2 526
Worked during the year	5 816	5 234	4 779	5 905	5 913	5 848	5 484	5 236	5 394	5 411	7 385	7 748
Year-round workers with 1 or 2 weeks of unemployment	243	189	193	180	220	176	177	136	154	135	279	235
Part-year workers with unemployment	5 573	5 045	4 586	5 725	5 693	5 672	5 307	5 100	5 240	5 276	7 106	7 513
1 to 4 weeks	1 237	1 194	1 164	1 121	927	882	957	888	1 317	1 226	1 270	1 061
5 to 10 weeks	1 131	1 050	878	1 111	1 031	950	929	961	840	876	1 243	968
11 to 14 weeks	721	657	625	831	784	710	752	674	655	725	971	857
15 to 26 weeks	1 434	1 148	1 045	1 492	1 566	1 600	1 384	1 426	1 307	1 316	1 823	2 134
27 weeks or more	1 050	996	874	1 170	1 385	1 530	1 285	1 151	1 120	1 134	1 800	2 494
With 2 or more spells of unemployment	1 614	1 379	1 270	1 321	1 306	1 211	1 069	1 120	1 140	1 116	1 368	1 287
2 spells	770	662	593	641	642	639	537	537	619	580	753	619
3 or more spells	844	717	677	680	664	572	532	583	521	536	616	668

Table 1-38. Percent Distribution of Persons with Unemployment During the Year, by Sex and Extent of Unemployment, 1987–2009

(Percent.)

Sex and extent of unemployment	1987	1988	1989	1990	1991	1992	1993	1994	1995	1996	1997
BOTH SEXES											
Total with Unemployment Who Worked During the Year	100.0	99.9	99.9	100.0	99.9	100.1	100.1	100.0	100.0	100.1	100.0
Year-round workers with 1 or 2 weeks of unemployment	4.8	5.4	5.3	5.9	5.1	4.7	4.0	4.6	4.6	4.1	4.5
Part-year workers with unemployment	95.2	94.5	94.6	94.1	94.8	95.4	96.1	95.4	95.4	96.0	95.5
1 to 4 weeks	20.6	21.2	22.2	20.3	17.1	15.7	15.4	17.3	18.3	17.6	19.1
5 to 10 weeks	19.5	20.5	21.4	20.5	19.4	18.7	17.0	18.5	17.7	18.5	19.3
11 to 14 weeks	13.8	13.8	14.2	13.9	13.7	13.8	13.5	14.1	14.0	14.0	13.5
15 to 26 weeks	23.9	22.6	22.9	24.1	26.1	26.1	26.6	25.8	26.1	25.3	25.0
27 weeks or more	17.4	16.4	13.9	15.3	18.5	21.1	23.6	19.7	19.3	20.6	18.6
With 2 or more spells of unemployment	31.4	33.4	32.3	32.4	31.1	30.6	31.2	29.7	29.1	29.3	29.9
2 spells	14.9	16.0	15.7	15.9	14.5	14.4	15.0	13.7	12.8	13.7	13.7
3 or more spells	16.5	17.4	16.6	16.5	16.6	16.2	16.2	16.0	16.3	15.6	16.2
MEN											
Total with Unemployment Who Worked During the Year	100.1	99.9	100.0	100.0	100.0	99.9	99.9	100.0	100.0	100.0	100.1
Year-round workers with 1 or 2 weeks of unemployment	5.6	6.5	6.3	6.8	5.4	4.9	4.4	5.7	5.3	4.9	5.0
Part-year workers with unemployment	94.5	93.4	93.7	93.2	94.6	95.0	95.5	94.3	94.7	95.1	95.1
1 to 4 weeks	16.2	18.2	19.2	17.5	13.9	13.6	13.3	14.7	16.1	15.6	16.7
5 to 10 weeks	18.9	20.1	20.8	19.6	18.5	17.8	16.3	17.9	16.5	18.2	19.3
11 to 14 weeks	14.7	14.2	15.1	14.0	14.5	14.1	13.4	14.7	14.4	15.5	14.0
15 to 26 weeks	26.0	23.7	24.1	25.4	28.0	27.6	28.4	26.4	28.1	25.5	25.6
27 weeks or more	18.7	17.2	14.5	16.7	19.7	21.9	24.1	20.6	19.5	20.3	19.4
With 2 or more spells of unemployment	34.2	37.5	35.0	35.4	34.0	33.9	34.3	31.6	32.2	31.4	31.9
2 spells	15.4	17.4	16.7	16.1	15.2	15.5	15.7	13.6	12.8	13.6	14.1
3 or more spells	18.8	20.1	18.3	19.3	18.8	18.4	18.6	18.0	19.4	17.8	17.8
WOMEN											
Total With Unemployment Who Worked During the Year	100.1	99.9	100.0	99.9	100.1	99.9	100.0	99.9	100.0	100.0	100.0
Year-round workers with 1 or 2 weeks of unemployment	3.8	3.8	4.0	4.6	4.8	4.2	3.4	3.2	3.8	3.1	3.9
Part-year workers with unemployment	96.3	96.1	96.0	95.3	95.3	95.7	96.6	96.7	96.2	96.9	96.1
1 to 4 weeks	26.9	25.4	26.4	24.3	22.0	19.0	18.3	20.9	21.1	20.2	22.2
5 to 10 weeks	20.4	21.0	22.2	21.6	20.8	20.1	17.8	19.3	19.3	18.8	19.2
11 to 14 weeks	12.6	13.3	13.1	13.8	12.5	13.2	13.5	13.1	13.3	12.0	12.8
15 to 26 weeks	20.7	21.2	21.3	22.2	23.2	23.6	24.1	25.1	23.5	25.1	24.3
27 weeks or more	15.7	15.2	13.0	13.4	16.8	19.8	22.9	18.3	19.0	20.8	17.6
With 2 or more spells of unemployment	27.5	27.7	28.6	28.2	26.6	25.4	26.9	27.0	25.0	26.6	27.3
2 spells	14.2	14.1	14.2	15.7	13.4	12.6	14.1	13.8	12.7	13.8	13.2
3 or more spells	13.3	13.6	14.4	12.5	13.2	12.8	12.8	13.2	12.3	12.8	14.1

Table 1-38. Percent Distribution of Persons with Unemployment During the Year, by Sex and Extent of Unemployment, 1987–2009—*Continued*

(Percent.)

Sex and extent of unemployment	1998	1999	2000	2001	2002	2003	2004	2005	2006	2007	2008	2009
BOTH SEXES												
Total with Unemployment Who Worked During the Year	100.1	100.0	100.1	100.0	100.0	100.0	100.0	100.0	100.0	100.0	100.0	100.0
Year-round workers with 1 or 2 weeks of unemployment	5.1	4.9	5.3	4.4	4.1	3.9	3.7	3.6	3.6	3.8	4.2	3.4
Part-year workers with unemployment	95.0	95.1	94.8	95.6	95.9	96.1	96.3	96.4	96.4	96.1	95.8	96.5
1 to 4 weeks	18.9	20.4	20.6	17.1	14.1	13.4	15.9	16.0	20.7	19.9	15.5	12.5
5 to 10 weeks	20.3	19.2	18.6	18.5	16.8	16.5	16.8	17.9	16.8	16.0	16.3	12.6
11 to 14 weeks	13.8	13.8	13.9	14.7	13.9	12.8	14.2	14.0	12.9	14.5	13.5	11.9
15 to 26 weeks	24.5	24.2	24.4	26.6	27.2	27.6	27.5	27.6	25.3	25.9	26.9	28.1
27 weeks or more	17.5	17.5	17.3	18.7	23.9	25.8	22.0	20.9	20.7	19.8	23.5	31.5
With 2 or more spells of unemployment	29.5	27.9	28.4	24.8	22.8	22.6	23.1	25.5	24.5	23.8	22.1	20.5
2 spells	13.4	12.5	12.9	11.9	11.0	11.6	10.7	12.2	12.5	10.9	11.0	9.4
3 or more spells	16.1	15.4	15.5	12.9	11.8	11.0	12.4	13.3	12.1	12.9	11.1	11.0
MEN												
Total with Unemployment Who Worked During the Year	100.0	99.9	99.9	100.0	100.0	100.0	100.0	100.0	100.0	100.0	100.0	100.0
Year-round workers with 1 or 2 weeks of unemployment	5.9	5.9	6.3	5.3	4.4	4.6	4.1	4.3	4.1	4.8	4.5	3.7
Part-year workers with unemployment	94.1	94.0	93.6	94.7	95.6	95.4	95.9	95.7	95.9	95.2	95.5	96.4
1 to 4 weeks	16.7	18.4	17.6	15.7	13.0	12.2	14.6	15.3	18.0	17.9	14.3	11.7
5 to 10 weeks	21.0	18.4	18.7	18.2	16.3	16.7	16.6	17.5	17.7	15.9	16.0	12.7
11 to 14 weeks	15.1	14.8	14.5	15.2	14.4	13.2	14.5	14.8	13.4	15.3	13.8	12.4
15 to 26 weeks	24.4	26.1	26.3	27.6	27.7	27.7	29.3	27.9	26.1	27.0	28.5	28.4
27 weeks or more	16.9	16.3	16.5	17.8	24.3	25.5	20.8	20.2	20.6	19.1	22.9	31.2
With 2 or more spells of unemployment	31.0	29.1	29.9	26.5	23.3	24.0	26.0	28.6	27.1	26.1	24.6	22.8
2 spells	13.5	12.4	13.3	12.6	11.1	12.1	11.5	13.6	13.2	11.1	11.6	10.3
3 or more spells	17.5	16.7	16.6	13.9	12.2	11.9	14.5	15.0	13.9	15.0	13.0	12.5
WOMEN												
Total With Unemployment Who Worked During the Year	100.0	100.0	100.0	100.0	100.0	100.0	100.0	100.0	100.0	100.0	100.0	100.0
Year-round workers with 1 or 2 weeks of unemployment	4.2	3.6	4.0	3.1	3.7	3.0	3.2	2.6	2.9	2.5	3.8	3.0
Part-year workers with unemployment	95.8	96.4	96.0	96.9	96.3	97.0	96.8	97.4	97.1	97.4	96.2	96.9
1 to 4 weeks	21.3	22.8	24.3	19.0	15.7	15.1	17.4	17.0	24.4	22.6	17.2	13.7
5 to 10 weeks	19.4	20.1	18.4	18.8	17.4	16.2	16.9	18.4	15.6	16.2	16.8	12.5
11 to 14 weeks	12.4	12.6	13.1	14.1	13.3	12.1	13.7	12.9	12.1	13.4	13.1	11.1
15 to 26 weeks	24.7	21.9	21.9	25.3	26.5	27.4	25.2	27.2	24.2	24.3	24.7	27.5
27 weeks or more	18.0	19.0	18.3	19.8	23.4	26.2	23.5	22.0	20.8	20.9	24.4	32.1
With 2 or more spells of unemployment	27.7	26.3	26.6	22.4	22.1	20.7	19.5	21.4	21.1	20.6	18.5	16.6
2 spells	13.2	12.6	12.4	10.9	10.9	10.9	9.8	10.3	11.5	10.7	10.2	8.0
3 or more spells	14.5	13.7	14.2	11.5	11.2	9.8	9.7	11.1	9.7	9.9	8.3	8.6

Table 1-39. Number and Median Annual Earnings of Year-Round, Full-Time Wage and Salary Workers, by Age, Sex, and Race, 1987–2009

(Thousands of people, dollars.)

Sex, age, and race	1987	1988	1989	1990	1991	1992	1993	1994	1995	1996	1997
NUMBER											
Both Sexes, 16 Years and Over	71 069	73 598	74 898	74 728	74 449	75 517	77 427	79 875	83 407	85 611	86 905
16 to 24 years	7 563	7 400	7 471	6 978	6 571	6 224	6 685	6 684	6 892	6 809	7 063
25 to 44 years	42 211	44 036	45 082	45 086	44 811	45 022	45 951	47 150	48 695	49 225	49 513
25 to 34 years	22 884	23 727	23 721	23 201	22 541	22 469	22 637	23 193	23 310	23 071	23 186
35 to 44 years	19 327	20 309	21 361	21 885	22 270	22 553	23 314	23 957	25 385	26 154	26 327
45 to 54 years	12 764	13 506	13 848	14 070	14 718	15 652	16 424	17 366	18 436	19 714	20 109
55 to 64 years	7 406	7 529	7 321	7 458	7 219	7 590	7 208	7 500	8 122	8 455	8 901
65 years and over	1 125	1 127	1 177	1 137	1 130	1 029	1 159	1 174	1 263	1 408	1 318
Men, 16 Years and Over	42 490	43 785	45 107	44 574	43 523	43 894	45 494	47 255	49 334	50 407	50 772
16 to 24 years	4 145	4 165	4 223	3 982	3 596	3 457	3 853	3 918	4 094	3 942	4 021
25 to 44 years	25 293	26 246	27 321	27 069	26 353	26 335	27 161	28 000	28 940	29 282	29 453
25 to 34 years	13 659	14 163	14 439	13 941	13 303	13 146	13 400	13 749	13 844	13 817	13 735
35 to 44 years	11 634	12 083	12 882	13 128	13 050	13 189	13 761	14 251	15 096	15 465	15 718
45 to 54 years	7 726	8 086	8 276	8 168	8 479	8 908	9 522	10 120	10 589	11 372	11 388
55 to 64 years	4 654	4 616	4 562	4 650	4 403	4 588	4 238	4 460	4 884	4 908	5 133
65 years and over	672	672	725	705	694	606	719	757	827	903	775
Women, 16 Years and Over	28 579	29 812	29 791	30 155	30 925	31 622	31 933	32 619	34 073	35 203	36 133
16 to 24 years	3 418	3 235	3 249	2 995	2 976	2 767	2 832	2 767	2 798	2 867	3 041
25 to 44 years	16 918	17 790	17 760	18 017	18 458	18 688	18 790	19 150	19 755	19 942	20 060
25 to 34 years	9 225	9 564	9 282	9 260	9 238	9 323	9 237	9 444	9 467	9 254	9 451
35 to 44 years	7 693	8 226	8 478	8 757	9 220	9 365	9 553	9 706	10 288	10 688	10 609
45 to 54 years	5 037	5 420	5 572	5 902	6 239	6 744	6 902	7 246	7 847	8 343	8 721
55 to 64 years	2 752	2 913	2 758	2 808	2 816	3 002	2 970	3 040	3 238	3 547	3 767
65 years and over	453	455	451	433	436	423	439	417	436	505	543
White, 16 Years and Over	61 546	63 357	64 246	64 128	63 926	64 706	65 656	67 370	70 430	72 068	72 650
Men	37 461	38 449	39 430	38 915	38 018	38 267	39 347	40 589	42 608	43 554	43 429
Women	24 085	24 908	24 815	25 213	25 908	26 439	26 309	26 782	27 822	28 514	29 221
Black, 16 Years and Over	7 440	7 907	8 140	8 027	7 941	7 995	8 478	9 074	9 446	9 706	10 248
Men	3 838	3 976	4 219	4 162	4 001	4 011	4 259	4 598	4 686	4 682	5 026
Women	3 602	3 931	3 920	3 865	3 940	3 984	4 219	4 476	4 759	5 024	5 222
MEDIAN ANNUAL EARNINGS											
Both Sexes, 16 Years and Over	21 000	22 000	23 000	24 000	25 000	25 871	26 000	26 620	27 000	28 000	30 000
16 to 24 years	13 000	13 500	14 000	14 400	14 100	15 000	15 000	15 000	15 500	15 600	16 000
25 to 34 years	20 000	21 000	22 000	22 000	23 000	24 000	24 000	24 480	25 000	25 300	27 000
35 to 44 years	25 000	26 000	27 000	27 970	28 000	29 483	30 000	30 000	30 000	31 000	32 000
45 to 54 years	25 000	26 000	27 000	28 000	29 000	30 000	30 500	32 343	32 000	33 000	35 000
55 to 64 years	23 000	24 000	26 000	26 000	27 000	27 430	28 000	30 000	30 000	30 000	32 000
65 years and over	18 000	19 500	23 000	23 841	22 000	24 000	24 000	24 377	29 600	26 496	28 200
Men, 16 Years and Over	25 900	26 570	27 300	28 000	29 120	30 000	30 000	30 000	31 000	32 000	34 000
16 to 24 years	14 000	14 200	15 000	15 000	15 000	15 000	15 000	15 000	16 000	17 000	17 000
25 to 34 years	23 000	24 000	24 000	25 000	25 000	26 000	25 000	26 000	27 000	28 000	29 852
35 to 44 years	30 000	31 000	32 000	32 000	33 000	34 000	35 000	35 000	35 000	36 000	37 000
45 to 54 years	31 200	32 000	34 000	35 000	36 000	37 000	38 000	40 000	40 000	40 000	41 000
55 to 64 years	29 181	30 000	32 000	31 875	33 000	33 000	34 000	36 000	36 000	36 000	39 000
65 years and over	24 000	25 000	30 000	29 000	28 000	30 000	28 000	30 000	36 000	33 000	36 400
Women, 16 Years and Over	17 000	18 000	18 574	20 000	20 000	21 500	22 000	22 150	23 000	24 000	25 000
16 to 24 years	12 000	13 000	13 167	13 392	13 800	14 000	14 872	14 560	15 000	15 000	15 000
25 to 34 years	17 000	18 000	19 000	19 500	20 000	21 000	21 000	22 000	22 000	23 000	24 000
35 to 44 years	19 000	20 000	20 200	22 000	22 510	23 397	24 000	25 000	25 000	25 000	26 000
45 to 54 years	18 148	19 000	20 000	21 000	22 000	24 000	24 000	25 000	25 000	26 000	27 040
55 to 64 years	17 000	17 000	18 000	19 000	20 000	22 000	21 500	22 000	22 500	24 000	24 800
65 years and over	16 000	15 600	17 566	18 586	17 000	18 500	20 000	19 000	23 290	20 800	24 000
White, 16 Years and Over	22 000	23 000	24 000	25 000	25 000	26 200	27 000	28 000	28 000	29 000	30 000
Men	26 500	27 489	28 500	29 000	30 000	31 000	30 700	32 000	32 000	33 000	35 000
Women	17 000	18 000	19 000	20 000	20 500	22 000	22 000	23 000	23 000	24 000	25 000
Black, 16 Years and Over	17 000	18 000	19 000	19 350	20 000	21 000	20 800	21 000	22 000	23 784	24 000
Men	18 850	20 000	20 000	20 800	22 000	22 312	23 000	23 500	24 500	26 000	26 000
Women	15 500	16 200	17 115	18 000	18 500	20 000	19 843	20 000	20 000	21 000	22 000

Table 1-39. Number and Median Annual Earnings of Year-Round, Full-Time Wage and Salary Workers, by Age, Sex, and Race, 1987–2009—*Continued*

(Thousands of people, dollars.)

Sex, age, and race	1998	1999	2000	2001	2002	2003	2004	2005	2006	2007	2008	2009
NUMBER												
Both Sexes, 16 Years and Over	89 748	91 722	94 359	94 531	94 526	94 731	96 098	98 632	101 353	102 441	98 493	94 012
16 to 24 years	7 618	7 631	8 384	7 989	7 903	7 631	7 702	7 956	8 113	8 064	7 242	6 302
25 to 44 years	50 264	50 532	51 159	49 939	49 120	48 343	48 421	49 149	50 056	49 725	47 364	44 579
25 to 34 years	23 048	22 952	23 044	22 744	22 657	22 512	22 405	22 808	23 613	23 646	22 786	21 572
35 to 44 years	27 216	27 580	28 115	27 195	26 463	25 831	26 016	26 341	26 443	26 080	24 578	23 007
45 to 54 years	21 274	22 375	23 307	23 855	23 999	24 507	25 074	25 661	26 338	26 566	25 722	24 877
55 to 64 years	9 273	9 594	9 870	10 948	11 584	12 207	12 812	13 605	14 340	15 248	15 286	15 274
65 years and over	1 318	1 590	1 639	1 800	1 921	2 042	2 090	2 262	2 507	2 837	2 879	2 980
Men, 16 Years and Over	52 509	53 132	54 477	54 630	54 420	54 575	55 610	57 020	58 533	58 673	55 973	52 362
16 to 24 years	4 479	4 347	4 602	4 605	4 570	4 421	4 493	4 663	4 812	4 719	4 112	3 494
25 to 44 years	29 763	29 738	30 080	29 271	28 855	28 499	28 763	29 151	29 589	29 004	27 546	25 324
25 to 34 years	13 612	13 471	13 497	13 386	13 400	13 288	13 430	13 629	13 933	13 706	13 208	12 085
35 to 44 years	16 151	16 267	16 583	15 885	15 455	15 211	15 333	15 522	15 655	15 298	14 337	13 239
45 to 54 years	12 030	12 546	13 045	13 363	13 330	13 616	13 975	14 382	14 758	14 810	14 199	13 521
55 to 64 years	5 438	5 498	5 693	6 253	6 502	6 872	7 165	7 489	7 905	8 449	8 397	8 289
65 years and over	801	1 003	1 057	1 138	1 163	1 165	1 213	1 334	1 469	1 692	1 720	1 733
Women, 16 Years and Over	37 239	38 591	39 887	39 901	40 106	40 156	40 488	41 613	42 820	43 768	42 520	41 650
16 to 24 years	3 140	3 285	3 782	3 384	3 333	3 210	3 209	3 293	3 301	3 345	3 130	2 808
25 to 44 years	20 503	20 794	21 081	20 668	20 264	19 844	19 656	19 997	20 467	20 721	19 819	19 255
25 to 34 years	9 437	9 481	9 548	9 358	9 257	9 224	8 974	9 179	9 679	9 940	9 578	9 487
35 to 44 years	11 066	11 313	11 533	11 310	11 007	10 620	10 682	10 818	10 788	10 782	10 240	9 768
45 to 54 years	9 244	9 829	10 263	10 493	10 669	10 891	11 099	11 279	11 580	11 757	11 524	11 356
55 to 64 years	3 836	4 096	4 178	4 695	5 082	5 335	5 647	6 116	6 434	6 799	6 889	6 984
65 years and over	517	586	583	662	758	877	877	927	1 038	1 146	1 158	1 247
White, 16 Years and Over	75 046	76 203	77 790	78 306	77 632	77 545	78 236	80 546	82 411	83 139	79 980	76 470
Men	44 901	45 211	46 105	46 373	45 823	45 816	46 317	47 790	48 897	48 825	46 608	43 622
Women	30 145	30 992	31 685	31 933	31 809	31 729	31 919	32 756	33 513	34 314	33 372	32 848
Black, 16 Years and Over	10 532	11 145	11 899	11 001	10 966	10 979	11 301	11 417	11 988	11 987	11 424	10 716
Men	5 202	5 411	5 636	5 281	5 150	5 196	5 470	5 402	5 679	5 689	5 377	4 952
Women	5 329	5 734	6 264	5 720	5 816	5 783	5 832	6 015	6 309	6 299	6 046	5 764
MEDIAN ANNUAL EARNINGS												
Both Sexes, 16 Years and Over	30 000	31 000	32 000	34 000	35 000	35 000	35 672	36 400	38 000	40 000	40 000	41 000
16 to 24 years	18 000	18 000	19 000	20 000	20 000	20 000	20 000	20 000	21 000	22 421	24 000	23 532
25 to 34 years	28 500	30 000	30 000	31 000	31 800	32 000	33 000	33 000	35 000	35 000	36 500	38 000
35 to 44 years	33 000	34 992	35 000	36 000	37 000	39 000	40 000	40 000	41 000	43 000	45 000	45 000
45 to 54 years	35 000	36 000	38 000	39 500	40 000	40 000	40 000	42 000	44 000	45 000	45 000	46 000
55 to 64 years	34 000	35 000	35 000	36 400	39 145	40 000	40 000	40 000	45 000	45 000	46 000	48 000
65 years and over	26 000	30 000	32 000	32 000	33 000	32 000	35 000	35 000	35 001	40 000	42 000	42 000
Men, 16 Years and Over	35 000	36 000	37 600	38 500	40 000	40 000	40 000	40 051	42 000	45 000	46 000	48 000
16 to 24 years	18 720	19 000	20 000	20 000	20 000	20 800	20 800	20 800	22 000	23 000	25 000	25 000
25 to 34 years	30 000	32 000	33 500	34 000	34 740	35 000	35 000	35 000	36 000	38 000	40 000	40 000
35 to 44 years	38 000	40 000	40 000	42 000	43 000	43 900	45 000	45 000	48 000	50 000	50 000	50 000
45 to 54 years	42 000	44 616	45 000	45 000	47 000	48 000	48 000	50 000	50 000	50 000	52 000	53 004
55 to 64 years	40 000	40 853	44 000	45 000	47 000	50 000	50 000	50 000	50 000	52 000	54 000	55 000
65 years and over	35 000	36 000	35 999	35 000	37 861	42 000	40 000	41 000	44 000	44 000	50 000	49 000
Women, 16 Years and Over	25 000	26 000	27 500	29 000	30 000	30 000	30 001	32 000	33 000	35 000	35 000	36 000
16 to 24 years	17 000	17 000	18 000	19 000	19 000	20 000	20 000	20 000	20 000	22 000	22 000	22 000
25 to 34 years	25 000	26 000	27 000	28 080	29 500	30 000	30 000	30 000	31 000	33 000	34 000	35 000
35 to 44 years	27 200	28 000	29 000	30 000	30 400	32 000	32 800	35 000	35 000	36 000	38 000	38 000
45 to 54 years	28 132	30 000	30 000	32 000	32 000	33 466	34 771	35 000	36 000	37 163	38 000	40 000
55 to 64 years	25 775	27 000	28 000	30 000	31 410	32 000	33 000	33 000	35 000	37 100	39 000	40 000
65 years and over	22 000	20 800	24 000	25 000	28 000	26 000	27 000	28 768	27 878	31 000	34 193	36 000
White, 16 Years and Over	31 000	32 000	34 000	35 000	35 000	36 000	37 000	38 000	40 000	40 000	41 600	42 000
Men	36 000	37 200	39 000	40 000	40 000	40 000	42 000	42 000	44 707	45 000	48 000	49 000
Women	26 000	27 000	28 000	30 000	30 000	31 000	31 800	32 000	34 000	35 000	35 500	36 002
Black, 16 Years and Over	25 000	25 760	26 000	28 500	29 000	30 000	30 000	30 000	31 000	33 000	34 000	35 000
Men	27 000	30 000	30 000	30 000	30 000	32 000	30 000	33 000	34 000	35 000	37 500	38 000
Women	23 000	24 000	25 000	26 000	26 000	27 000	28 000	29 141	30 000	30 000	30 002	32 000

Table 1-40. Number and Median Annual Earnings of Year-Round, Full-Time Wage and Salary Workers, by Sex and Occupation of Job Held the Longest, 2002–2009

(Thousands of people, dollars.)

Sex and occupation	2002	2003	2004	2005	2006	2007	2008	2009
Both Sexes, Number of Workers								
Management, business, and financial operations	15 707	15 552	15 575	16 299	16 806	17 115	17 259	16 491
Management	11 350	11 102	11 125	11 685	11 866	12 191	12 256	11 733
Business and financial operations	4 357	4 450	4 451	4 613	4 941	4 924	5 003	4 758
Professional and related	19 149	19 607	19 592	20 093	21 268	21 939	21 748	21 831
Computer and mathematical	2 644	2 598	2 680	2 779	2 888	3 180	3 089	3 100
Architecture and engineering	2 257	2 273	2 349	2 361	2 491	2 467	2 360	2 133
Life, physical, and social sciences	1 094	1 010	999	1 096	1 142	1 026	1 044	1 054
Community and social services	1 694	1 698	1 632	1 728	1 835	1 791	1 754	1 827
Legal	1 006	1 149	1 087	1 093	1 168	1 159	1 228	1 230
Education, training, and library	4 606	4 918	4 742	4 894	5 195	5 482	5 478	5 500
Arts, design, entertainment, sports, and media	1 453	1 374	1 416	1 362	1 633	1 554	1 415	1 404
Health care practitioner and technical	4 395	4 586	4 688	4 780	4 916	5 278	5 380	5 583
Services	12 011	11 990	12 457	13 117	13 236	13 553	13 034	12 944
Health care support	1 767	1 703	1 781	2 027	2 081	2 027	2 019	2 135
Protective services	2 042	2 385	2 406	2 429	2 506	2 511	2 472	2 593
Food preparation and serving related	3 592	3 223	3 383	3 586	3 646	3 769	3 504	3 307
Building and grounds cleaning and maintenance	2 843	2 942	3 116	3 285	3 120	3 198	3 027	2 870
Personal care and services	1 767	1 735	1 771	1 790	1 883	2 048	2 012	2 038
Sales and office	23 791	23 766	23 619	24 010	24 467	24 472	23 058	22 320
Sales and related	9 929	9 804	9 951	10 251	10 497	10 301	9 763	9 275
Office and administrative support	13 862	13 962	13 668	13 758	13 970	14 171	13 294	13 045
Natural resources, construction, and maintenance	9 823	9 709	10 574	10 864	11 295	10 745	10 002	8 599
Farming, fishing, and forestry	573	562	629	556	585	607	581	555
Construction and extraction	5 256	5 070	5 711	6 145	6 484	5 885	5 158	4 172
Installation, maintenance, and repair	3 994	4 077	4 234	4 163	4 226	4 252	4 264	3 872
Production, transportation, and material moving	13 386	13 391	13 648	13 586	13 704	13 907	12 649	11 062
Production	7 736	7 670	7 787	7 623	7 762	7 589	6 652	5 834
Transportation and material moving	5 650	5 721	5 861	5 963	5 942	6 318	5 997	5 228
Armed forces	658	717	632	664	576	709	744	765
Both Sexes, Median Annual Earnings								
Management, business, and financial operations	50 000	52 000	55 000	57 000	60 000	60 000	60 800	60 000
Management	55 000	58 000	60 000	60 000	62 500	65 000	65 000	65 000
Business and financial operations	44 000	45 000	45 000	49 000	50 000	50 000	52 000	55 000
Professional and related	46 000	46 000	48 000	50 000	50 000	51 000	54 000	55 000
Computer and mathematical	60 000	60 000	62 000	62 400	68 000	70 000	70 000	72 000
Architecture and engineering	59 400	62 000	60 000	65 000	69 000	70 000	70 000	70 000
Life, physical, and social sciences	50 000	50 000	50 000	53 500	57 000	60 000	57 532	60 000
Community and social services	34 000	34 349	36 000	36 000	36 780	39 000	40 000	40 000
Legal	61 860	75 000	70 000	72 000	70 000	70 000	75 000	80 000
Education, training, and library	38 000	39 000	40 000	40 000	40 282	44 984	45 000	46 000
Arts, design, entertainment, sports, and media	43 500	40 000	40 000	42 000	45 000	44 297	47 000	49 000
Health care practitioner and technical	46 000	48 000	50 000	50 000	52 000	52 800	55 000	55 000
Services	22 000	22 000	22 000	23 000	24 000	25 000	25 000	26 000
Health care support	22 100	22 000	22 000	22 000	23 000	24 500	26 000	26 000
Protective services	38 000	42 000	42 000	42 000	45 000	45 000	45 000	46 000
Food preparation and serving related	18 000	18 000	18 000	19 656	19 000	20 000	20 800	20 000
Building and grounds cleaning and maintenance	20 000	20 000	20 000	21 000	23 000	23 000	24 000	24 024
Personal care and services	21 840	20 678	22 537	23 000	23 000	25 000	25 000	25 000
Sales and office	30 000	30 000	30 000	31 200	32 002	34 000	35 000	35 000
Sales and related	35 000	35 000	35 000	35 000	37 000	38 000	38 500	38 000
Office and administrative support	28 000	29 000	30 000	30 000	30 000	32 000	32 500	34 000
Natural resources, construction, and maintenance	33 000	34 000	35 000	35 000	35 000	36 000	40 000	40 000
Farming, fishing, and forestry	20 000	20 000	20 000	21 000	20 000	24 000	24 000	24 000
Construction and extraction	31 200	32 000	33 000	32 000	35 000	35 000	39 000	40 000
Installation, maintenance, and repair	36 000	38 000	38 300	40 000	40 000	40 000	42 000	44 192
Production, transportation, and material moving	28 704	30 000	30 000	30 200	30 000	33 000	34 000	34 000
Production	28 000	30 000	30 000	30 000	30 000	33 000	34 000	32 006
Transportation and material moving	29 000	30 000	30 000	30 800	30 000	33 800	34 000	35 000
Armed forces	36 000	36 000	40 000	39 000	40 000	42 000	45 000	47 000

Table 1-40. Number and Median Annual Earnings of Year-Round, Full-Time Wage and Salary Workers, by Sex and Occupation of Job Held the Longest, 2002–2009—*Continued*

(Thousands of people, dollars.)

Sex and occupation	2002	2003	2004	2005	2006	2007	2008	2009
Men, Number of Workers								
Management, business, and financial operations	9 178	8 961	8 849	9 496	9 519	9 784	9 836	9 418
Management	7 145	6 991	6 911	7 477	7 361	7 619	7 714	7 300
Business and financial operations	2 033	1 970	1 938	2 019	2 157	2 165	2 122	2 117
Professional and related	9 299	9 535	9 497	9 561	10 387	10 274	10 074	10 036
Computer and mathematical	1 953	1 913	1 972	2 060	2 159	2 378	2 348	2 227
Architecture and engineering	1 984	2 004	2 049	2 041	2 174	2 172	2 068	1 859
Life, physical, and social sciences	667	668	626	668	748	611	581	575
Community and social services	726	730	705	713	756	744	675	707
Legal	490	610	537	490	546	515	595	645
Education, training, and library	1 407	1 476	1 386	1 421	1 587	1 651	1 535	1 650
Arts, design, entertainment, sports, and media	847	811	848	789	953	790	782	829
Health care practitioner and technical	1 225	1 323	1 374	1 378	1 464	1 413	1 490	1 544
Services	5 988	6 204	6 314	6 658	6 715	6 871	6 389	6 379
Health care support	181	178	208	240	252	261	204	247
Protective services	1 689	1 967	1 906	1 919	1 998	2 000	1 930	2 026
Food preparation and serving related	1 836	1 638	1 716	1 873	1 991	1 985	1 816	1 744
Building and grounds cleaning and maintenance	1 788	1 914	2 002	2 153	1 939	2 048	1 911	1 832
Personal care and services	494	508	482	473	535	576	527	530
Sales and office	9 453	9 398	9 380	9 464	9 747	9 694	9 128	8 680
Sales and related	5 933	5 891	5 892	5 896	6 125	6 019	5 690	5 231
Office and administrative support	3 520	3 507	3 488	3 568	3 622	3 675	3 438	3 449
Natural resources, construction, and maintenance	9 434	9 348	10 178	10 503	10 904	10 343	9 627	8 225
Farming, fishing, and forestry	463	470	536	469	482	516	489	425
Construction and extraction	5 156	4 972	5 576	6 026	6 344	5 753	5 056	4 068
Installation, maintenance, and repair	3 815	3 905	4 065	4 008	4 078	4 074	4 081	3 732
Production, transportation, and material moving	10 472	10 492	10 812	10 747	10 733	11 047	10 226	8 921
Production	5 517	5 513	5 637	5 503	5 525	5 461	4 983	4 370
Transportation and material moving	4 955	4 979	5 176	5 244	5 208	5 585	5 242	4 552
Armed forces	600	636	580	591	528	660	696	703
Men, Median Annual Earnings								
Management, business, and financial operations	60 000	60 200	65 000	69 000	68 000	70 000	72 000	72 000
Management	65 000	65 000	70 000	70 000	70 000	75 000	75 000	75 000
Business and financial operations	52 000	51 000	55 000	60 000	60 000	60 000	65 000	65 000
Professional and related	55 000	58 000	58 000	60 000	61 000	62 000	67 000	65 000
Computer and mathematical	60 000	65 000	65 000	65 000	70 000	70 000	74 000	75 000
Architecture and engineering	60 000	64 558	61 785	66 921	70 000	72 000	74 000	72 000
Life, physical, and social sciences	52 000	50 801	55 000	62 000	61 000	65 000	65 000	65 000
Community and social services	35 000	35 000	38 000	40 000	39 000	40 000	44 085	45 000
Legal	100 000	100 000	101 000	108 000	100 000	104 146	130 000	120 000
Education, training, and library	45 600	48 000	47 000	50 000	50 000	50 000	54 000	52 000
Arts, design, entertainment, sports, and media	46 000	45 000	45 000	50 000	50 000	50 000	52 000	50 000
Health care practitioner and technical	72 000	65 500	70 000	70 000	72 000	75 000	75 000	74 000
Services	25 000	26 000	25 000	26 000	29 000	29 000	30 000	30 000
Health care support	24 000	22 537	20 400	22 880	25 000	25 000	28 000	30 000
Protective services	40 000	44 000	44 000	45 000	46 886	49 000	49 000	49 500
Food preparation and serving related	20 000	18 720	18 720	20 000	20 000	21 000	21 500	21 000
Building and grounds cleaning and maintenance	24 500	22 156	24 000	24 000	25 000	25 000	27 012	26 000
Personal care and services	30 000	28 559	26 000	30 000	30 000	30 000	30 500	30 000
Sales and office	38 000	39 000	40 000	40 000	40 000	42 000	40 000	42 002
Sales and related	41 600	41 000	44 000	42 000	45 000	45 000	48 000	48 002
Office and administrative support	32 000	32 000	34 000	34 000	35 000	36 000	35 000	37 400
Natural resources, construction, and maintenance	33 592	34 283	35 000	35 000	35 674	36 000	40 000	40 000
Farming, fishing, and forestry	22 000	22 000	22 000	22 500	20 000	24 000	24 000	25 000
Construction and extraction	31 304	32 000	33 000	32 000	35 000	35 000	40 000	40 000
Installation, maintenance, and repair	36 000	38 000	38 870	40 000	40 000	40 000	42 685	45 000
Production, transportation, and material moving	30 000	32 000	33 000	34 000	33 358	35 000	35 360	35 198
Production	30 360	32 000	34 000	35 000	35 000	36 000	36 000	36 000
Transportation and material moving	30 000	30 000	32 000	32 760	32 000	35 000	35 000	35 000
Armed forces	36 000	36 000	40 000	40 000	40 000	42 000	45 000	47 000

Table 1-40. Number and Median Annual Earnings of Year-Round, Full-Time Wage and Salary Workers, by Sex and Occupation of Job Held the Longest, 2002–2009—*Continued*

(Thousands of people, dollars.)

Sex and occupation	2002	2003	2004	2005	2006	2007	2008	2009
Women, Number of Workers								
Management, business, and financial operations	6 529	6 591	6 726	6 803	7 287	7 332	7 423	7 073
Management	4 205	4 111	4 214	4 209	4 504	4 573	4 542	4 432
Business and financial operations	2 324	2 479	2 512	2 594	2 783	2 759	2 881	2 641
Professional and related	9 851	10 071	10 095	10 532	10 881	11 664	11 675	11 795
Computer and mathematical	691	685	708	718	729	802	741	873
Architecture and engineering	273	269	300	320	317	295	293	274
Life, physical, and social sciences	428	342	373	428	394	415	462	479
Community and social services	968	968	927	1 015	1 079	1 047	1 079	1 119
Legal	516	539	550	603	622	645	633	585
Education, training, and library	3 199	3 441	3 356	3 473	3 608	3 831	3 944	3 850
Arts, design, entertainment, sports, and media	606	563	568	573	681	764	633	575
Health care practitioner and technical	3 170	3 263	3 314	3 403	3 452	3 865	3 890	4 039
Services	6 026	5 786	6 144	6 459	6 522	6 682	6 645	6 565
Health care support	1 586	1 525	1 573	1 787	1 829	1 766	1 815	1 888
Protective services	354	419	500	510	509	511	541	567
Food preparation and serving related	1 757	1 585	1 668	1 713	1 655	1 784	1 688	1 563
Building and grounds cleaning and maintenance	1 055	1 029	1 115	1 132	1 181	1 150	1 116	1 038
Personal care and services	1 274	1 228	1 289	1 317	1 349	1 471	1 485	1 508
Sales and office	14 338	14 368	14 239	14 546	14 720	14 778	13 930	13 640
Sales and related	3 996	3 913	4 060	4 355	4 372	4 282	4 073	4 044
Office and administrative support	10 342	10 455	10 180	10 191	10 348	10 496	9 856	9 596
Natural resources, construction, and maintenance	391	361	396	360	391	402	376	374
Farming, fishing, and forestry	111	92	93	87	104	92	91	130
Construction and extraction	100	97	135	119	140	132	101	104
Installation, maintenance, and repair	180	172	169	155	148	178	183	140
Production, transportation, and material moving	2 914	2 899	2 835	2 839	2 971	2 861	2 423	2 141
Production	2 219	2 157	2 150	2 120	2 237	2 128	1 668	1 464
Transportation and material moving	695	742	685	719	734	733	755	676
Armed forces	58	81	52	73	48	49	49	62
Women, Median Annual Earnings								
Management, business, and financial operations	41 000	43 000	43 000	46 000	50 000	50 000	50 000	50 000
Management	44 000	47 000	46 000	50 000	52 000	52 000	55 000	52 999
Business and financial operations	38 500	40 000	40 000	41 000	46 000	45 000	48 000	48 000
Professional and related	40 000	40 000	40 000	42 000	43 000	45 000	46 000	48 002
Computer and mathematical	51 627	52 000	57 000	57 000	60 000	60 000	62 000	65 000
Architecture and engineering	50 000	48 000	47 500	55 000	52 000	55 000	50 000	61 000
Life, physical, and social sciences	44 000	45 000	45 995	50 000	48 000	48 000	49 000	54 651
Community and social services	33 000	33 000	35 000	35 000	36 000	37 000	37 700	39 000
Legal	45 000	45 000	46 000	47 500	50 000	47 500	52 001	60 000
Education, training, and library	35 000	35 000	37 000	38 000	38 632	41 000	42 000	43 000
Arts, design, entertainment, sports, and media	40 000	35 000	36 000	35 000	38 000	40 000	40 000	45 000
Health care practitioner and technical	41 000	43 000	45 000	46 000	48 000	50 000	50 000	52 000
Services	20 000	20 000	20 000	20 000	20 500	22 000	23 516	24 000
Health care support	22 000	22 000	22 000	21 000	23 000	24 500	26 000	25 000
Protective services	30 900	32 000	32 000	34 344	37 896	35 000	35 000	38 000
Food preparation and serving related	16 160	17 000	16 000	18 000	18 000	19 000	20 000	19 000
Building and grounds cleaning and maintenance	16 491	16 000	16 866	18 000	19 000	19 500	20 000	20 000
Personal care and services	20 000	20 000	21 000	20 800	20 000	24 000	24 000	24 700
Sales and office	26 989	28 000	28 000	29 000	30 000	30 000	30 600	31 400
Sales and related	25 000	26 000	26 000	26 000	26 000	28 000	29 000	30 000
Office and administrative support	27 000	28 000	28 000	29 800	30 000	30 002	32 000	32 100
Natural resources, construction, and maintenance	26 000	28 000	30 000	30 200	27 000	37 025	30 000	30 000
Farming, fishing, and forestry	17 000	16 000	15 700	18 000	18 808	24 117	24 685	21 000
Construction and extraction	26 000	29 500	40 000	31 200	24 980	40 000	34 500	31 000
Installation, maintenance, and repair	34 000	37 000	33 000	36 000	40 000	42 000	33 913	38 139
Production, transportation, and material moving	22 000	22 100	23 000	23 000	23 000	25 000	25 000	25 000
Production	21 632	22 000	23 000	23 400	23 000	25 000	25 000	25 000
Transportation and material moving	22 000	22 710	23 000	21 000	24 000	27 000	24 000	25 000
Armed forces	40 000	32 000	35 100	32 652	32 000	41 000	32 000	43 600

Table 1-41. Wage and Salary Workers Paid Hourly Rates with Earnings at or Below the Prevailing Federal Minimum Wage, by Selected Characteristics, 2008–2009

(Thousands of people, percent.)

Characteristic	Workers paid hourly rates				
	Total	Below prevailing federal minimum wage	At prevailing federal minimum wage	Total at or below prevailing federal minimum wage	
				Number	Percent of hourly-paid workers
2008					
Age and Sex					
Both sexes, 16 years and over	75 305	1 940	286	2 226	3.0
16 to 24 years	15 680	961	161	1 122	7.2
25 years and over	59 626	979	125	1 104	1.9
Men, 16 years and over	37 334	638	90	728	2.0
16 to 24 years	7 978	326	58	384	4.8
25 years and over	29 356	313	32	345	1.2
Women, 16 years and over	37 972	1 302	196	1 497	3.9
16 to 24 years	7 701	635	103	738	9.6
25 years and over	30 270	666	93	759	2.5
Race, Sex, and Hispanic Origin					
White, 16 years and over	60 464	1 568	215	1 783	2.9
Men	30 533	495	65	560	1.8
Women	29 931	1 073	151	1 223	4.1
Black, 16 years and over	9 866	259	49	308	3.1
Men	4 408	105	17	123	2.8
Women	5 457	154	32	186	3.4
Asian, 16 years and over	2 844	58	11	69	2.4
Men	1 301	24	3	27	2.1
Women	1 543	34	8	41	2.7
Hispanic,[1] 16 years and over	13 070	285	39	324	2.5
Men	7 756	117	15	132	1.7
Women	5 313	168	23	191	3.6
Full- and Part-Time Status[2] and Sex					
Full-time workers	56 837	778	95	873	1.5
Men	31 363	313	27	341	1.1
Women	25 474	464	68	532	2.1
Part-time workers	18 334	1 162	191	1 353	7.4
Men	5 903	325	63	388	6.6
Women	12 431	837	128	965	7.8
2009					
Age and Sex					
Both sexes, 16 years and over	72 611	2 592	980	3 572	4.9
16 to 24 years	14 389	1 229	508	1 737	12.1
25 years and over	58 222	1 363	472	1 835	3.2
Men, 16 years and over	35 185	990	368	1 358	3.9
16 to 24 years	7 045	460	214	674	9.6
25 years and over	28 140	530	154	684	2.4
Women, 16 years and over	37 426	1 603	612	2 215	5.9
16 to 24 years	7 344	769	295	1 064	14.5
25 years and over	30 082	833	318	1 151	3.8
Race, Sex, and Hispanic Origin					
White, 16 years and over	58 633	2 094	763	2 857	4.9
Men	28 873	774	300	1 074	3.7
Women	29 760	1 320	463	1 783	6.0
Black, 16 years and over	9 269	327	168	495	5.3
Men	4 038	142	50	192	4.8
Women	5 231	185	117	303	5.8
Asian, 16 years and over	2 718	96	21	117	4.3
Men	1 258	41	6	47	3.8
Women	1 460	55	15	70	4.8
Hispanic,[1] 16 years and over	12 740	439	183	622	4.9
Men	7 291	210	80	291	4.0
Women	5 449	229	102	331	6.1
Full- and Part-Time Status[2] and Sex					
Full-time workers	52 454	952	320	1 273	2.4
Men	28 388	442	137	579	2.0
Women	24 066	511	183	694	2.9
Part-time workers	20 027	1 625	656	2 281	11.4
Men	6 721	540	229	768	11.4
Women	13 307	1 085	428	1 513	11.4

Note: In 2008, the minimum wage was $5.85 per hour until July 23, 2008. Beginning July 24, 2008, the prevailing federal minimum wage increased to $6.55 per hour. It remained $6.55 until July 23, 2009. Beginning July 24, 2009, the prevailing federal minimum wage increased to $7.25 per hour. Data are for wage and salary workers, excluding the incorporated self-employed. The data refer to a person's earnings on the sole or principal job, and pertain only to workers who are paid hourly rates. Salaried workers and other nonhourly workers are not included. The presence of workers with hourly earnings below the minimum wage does not necessarily indicate violation of the Fair Labor Standards Act, as there are exceptions to the minimum wage provisions of the law. In addition, some survey respondents reported hourly earnings below the minimum wage even though they earned the minimum wage or higher. Updated population controls are introduced annually with the release of January data.

[1] May be of any race.
[2] The distinction between full- and part-time workers is based on the hours usually worked. These data will not sum to totals because full- or part-time status on the principal job is not identifiable for a small number of multiple jobholders.
. . . = Not available.

Table 1-42. Absences from Work of Employed Full-Time Wage and Salary Workers, by Age and Sex, 2007–2009

(Thousands of people, percent.)

Year, sex, and age	Total employed	Absence rate[1]			Lost worktime rate[2]		
		Total	Illness or injury	Other reasons	Total	Illness or injury	Other reasons
2007							
Both Sexes, 16 Years and Over	107 164	3.2	2.2	1.0	1.7	1.2	0.5
16 to 19 years	1 674	2.8	1.9	1.0	1.5	0.9	0.6
20 to 24 years	9 527	2.9	1.9	1.0	1.5	0.9	0.6
25 years and over	95 964	3.2	2.2	1.0	1.7	1.2	0.5
25 to 54 years	79 438	3.1	2.1	1.0	1.7	1.1	0.6
55 years and over	16 526	3.5	2.8	0.7	2.0	1.7	0.3
Men, 16 Years and Over	60 262	2.3	1.7	0.6	1.2	1.0	0.3
16 to 19 years	1 011	1.8	1.4	0.4	0.8	0.6	0.2
20 to 24 years	5 435	2.1	1.7	0.5	1.0	0.8	0.2
25 years and over	53 817	2.3	1.7	0.6	1.3	1.0	0.3
25 to 54 years	44 895	2.2	1.6	0.6	1.2	0.9	0.3
55 years and over	8 922	3.0	2.4	0.5	1.7	1.5	0.2
Women, 16 Years and Over	46 902	4.3	2.7	1.5	2.4	1.5	0.9
16 to 19 years	663	4.4	2.6	1.9	2.7	1.4	1.3
20 to 24 years	4 092	4.0	2.2	1.8	2.2	1.0	1.2
25 years and over	42 147	4.3	2.8	1.5	2.4	1.5	0.9
25 to 54 years	34 544	4.3	2.7	1.6	2.4	1.4	1.0
55 years and over	7 603	4.2	3.3	0.9	2.4	1.9	0.5
2008							
Both Sexes, 16 Years and Over	102 307	3.1	2.2	0.9	1.7	1.2	0.5
16 to 19 years	1 345	2.4	1.5	0.9	1.3	0.7	0.5
20 to 24 years	8 528	2.9	2.0	0.9	1.4	0.9	0.6
25 years and over	92 433	3.2	2.2	0.9	1.7	1.2	0.5
25 to 54 years	75 837	3.1	2.1	1.0	1.7	1.1	0.6
55 years and over	16 597	3.6	2.9	0.7	2.0	1.7	0.3
Men, 16 Years and Over	57 019	2.3	1.8	0.5	1.2	1.0	0.3
16 to 19 years	799	1.5	1.0	0.5	0.6	0.5	0.2
20 to 24 years	4 797	2.0	1.5	0.4	0.9	0.7	0.2
25 years and over	51 424	2.3	1.8	0.5	1.3	1.0	0.3
25 to 54 years	42 477	2.2	1.7	0.5	1.2	0.9	0.3
55 years and over	8 946	3.0	2.5	0.5	1.8	1.5	0.3
Women, 16 Years and Over	45 288	4.1	2.7	1.4	2.3	1.4	0.9
16 to 19 years	546	3.6	2.2	1.4	2.2	1.1	1.1
20 to 24 years	3 732	4.0	2.5	1.5	2.2	1.1	1.0
25 years and over	41 010	4.2	2.8	1.4	2.3	1.4	0.8
25 to 54 years	33 359	4.2	2.6	1.5	2.3	1.3	0.9
55 years and over	7 650	4.2	3.4	0.8	2.3	1.9	0.4
2009							
Both Sexes, 16 Years and Over	99 838	3.3	2.3	1.0	1.7	1.2	0.5
16 to 19 years	1 135	4.0	2.8	1.2	1.3	0.8	0.4
20 to 24 years	7 804	3.2	2.2	1.0	1.4	0.9	0.5
25 years and over	90 898	3.3	2.3	1.0	1.7	1.2	0.5
25 to 54 years	73 626	3.2	2.2	1.0	1.7	1.1	0.6
55 years and over	17 272	3.5	2.9	0.7	1.9	1.6	0.3
Men, 16 Years and Over	55 047	2.4	1.8	0.6	1.2	1.0	0.2
16 to 19 years	662	2.8	2.1	0.7	0.9	0.8	0.1
20 to 24 years	4 305	2.2	1.7	0.6	0.8	0.6	0.2
25 years and over	50 080	2.4	1.9	0.5	1.3	1.0	0.2
25 to 54 years	40 870	2.3	1.7	0.5	1.2	0.9	0.3
55 years and over	9 210	3.0	2.4	0.5	1.7	1.5	0.2
Women, 16 Years and Over	44 791	4.4	2.9	1.5	2.3	1.4	0.9
16 to 19 years	473	5.7	3.9	1.8	1.8	0.9	0.9
20 to 24 years	3 499	4.4	2.9	1.5	2.0	1.1	0.9
25 years and over	40 818	4.4	2.9	1.5	2.3	1.5	0.9
25 to 54 years	32 756	4.4	2.8	1.6	2.4	1.4	1.0
55 years and over	8 062	4.2	3.4	0.8	2.2	1.9	0.4

Note: Data for 2009 reflect a modification in the estimation of the absence universe and are not strictly comparable with absence measures for prior years.

[1] Absences are defined as instances when persons who usually work 35 or more hours a week worked less than 35 hours during the reference week for reasons including own illness, injury, or medical problems; childcare problems; other family or personal obligations; civic or military duty; and maternity or paternity leave. Excluded are situations in which work was missed due to vacation or personal days, holidays, labor disputes, and other reasons. For multiple jobholders, absence data refer only to work missed at their main jobs. The absence rate is the ratio of workers with absences to total full-time wage and salary employment. The estimates of full-time wage and salary employment shown in this table do not match those in other tables because the estimates in this table are based on the full Current Population Survey (CPS) sample. Those in the other tables are based on a quarter of the sample only.
[2] Hours absent as a percentage of hours usually worked.

Table 1-43. Median Years of Tenure with Current Employer for Employed Wage and Salary Workers, by Age and Sex, Selected Years, February 1996–January 2010

(Number of years.)

Sex and age	February 1996	February 1998	February 2000	January 2002	January 2004	January 2006	January 2008	January 2010
Both Sexes								
16 years and over	3.8	3.6	3.5	3.7	4.0	4.0	4.1	4.4
16 to 17 years	0.7	0.6	0.6	0.7	0.7	0.6	0.7	0.7
18 to 19 years	0.7	0.7	0.7	0.8	0.8	0.7	0.8	1.0
20 to 24 years	1.2	1.1	1.1	1.2	1.3	1.3	1.3	1.5
25 years and over	5.0	4.7	4.7	4.7	4.9	4.9	5.1	5.2
25 to 34 years	2.8	2.7	2.6	2.7	2.9	2.9	2.7	3.1
35 to 44 years	5.3	5.0	4.8	4.6	4.9	4.9	4.9	5.1
45 to 54 years	8.3	8.1	8.2	7.6	7.7	7.3	7.6	7.8
55 to 64 years	10.2	10.1	10.0	9.9	9.6	9.3	9.9	10.0
65 years and over	8.4	7.8	9.4	8.6	9.0	8.8	10.2	9.9
Men								
16 years and over	4.0	3.8	3.8	3.9	4.1	4.1	4.2	4.6
16 to 17 years	0.6	0.6	0.6	0.8	0.7	0.7	0.7	0.7
18 to 19 years	0.7	0.7	0.7	0.8	0.8	0.7	0.8	1.0
20 to 24 years	1.2	1.2	1.2	1.4	1.3	1.4	1.4	1.6
25 years and over	5.3	4.9	4.9	4.9	5.1	5.0	5.2	5.3
25 to 34 years	3.0	2.8	2.7	2.8	3.0	2.9	2.8	3.2
35 to 44 years	6.1	5.5	5.3	5.0	5.2	5.1	5.2	5.3
45 to 54 years	10.1	9.4	9.5	9.1	9.6	8.1	8.2	8.5
55 to 64 years	10.5	11.2	10.2	10.2	9.8	9.5	10.1	10.4
65 years and over	8.3	7.1	9.0	8.1	8.2	8.3	10.4	9.7
Women								
16 years and over	3.5	3.4	3.3	3.4	3.8	3.9	3.9	4.2
16 to 17 years	0.7	0.6	0.6	0.7	0.6	0.6	0.6	0.7
18 to 19 years	0.7	0.7	0.7	0.8	0.8	0.7	0.8	1.0
20 to 24 years	1.2	1.1	1.0	1.1	1.3	1.2	1.3	1.5
25 years and over	4.7	4.4	4.4	4.4	4.7	4.8	4.9	5.1
25 to 34 years	2.7	2.5	2.5	2.5	2.8	2.8	2.6	3.0
35 to 44 years	4.8	4.5	4.3	4.2	4.5	4.6	4.7	4.9
45 to 54 years	7.0	7.2	7.3	6.5	6.4	6.7	7.0	7.1
55 to 64 years	10.0	9.6	9.9	9.6	9.2	9.2	9.8	9.7
65 years and over	8.4	8.7	9.7	9.4	9.6	9.5	9.9	10.1

Table 1-44. Median Years of Tenure with Current Employer for Employed Wage and Salary Workers, by Industry, Selected Years, February 2000–January 2010

(Number of years.)

Industry	February 2000	January 2002	January 2004	January 2006	January 2008	January 2010
TOTAL, 16 YEARS AND OVER	3.5	3.7	4.0	4.0	4.1	4.4
Private Sector	3.2	3.3	3.5	3.6	3.6	4.0
Agriculture and related industries	3.7	4.2	3.7	3.8	4.3	4.8
Nonagricultural industries	3.2	3.3	3.5	3.6	3.6	4.0
Mining	4.8	4.5	5.2	3.8	4.1	4.8
Construction	2.7	3.0	3.0	3.0	3.5	4.2
Manufacturing	4.9	5.4	5.8	5.5	5.9	6.1
Durable goods manufacturing	4.8	5.5	6.0	5.6	6.1	6.6
Nonmetallic mineral product	5.5	5.3	4.8	5.0	4.8	7.7
Primary metals and fabricated metal product	5.0	6.3	6.4	6.2	5.2	7.2
Machinery manufacturing	5.3	6.8	6.4	6.6	6.0	8.3
Computers and electronic product	3.9	4.7	5.2	5.9	6.7	5.9
Electrical equipment and appliances	5.0	5.5	9.8	6.2	6.2	8.3
Transportation equipment	6.4	7.0	7.7	7.2	7.8	4.7
Wood product	3.7	4.3	5.0	4.7	6.2	5.0
Furniture and fixtures	4.4	4.7	4.7	4.2	5.2	5.4
Miscellaneous manufacturing	3.7	4.5	4.6	3.9	4.7	5.5
Nondurable goods manufacturing	5.0	5.3	5.5	5.4	5.4	4.7
Food manufacturing	4.6	5.0	4.9	5.2	4.3	8.1
Beverage and tobacco product	5.5	4.6	8.0	5.4	6.9	4.7
Textiles, apparel, and leather	4.7	5.0	5.0	4.4	4.6	6.8
Paper and printing	5.1	6.2	6.9	6.3	5.5	5.1
Petroleum and coal product	9.5	9.8	11.4	5.0	4.3	7.3
Chemicals	6.0	5.7	5.3	6.1	7.6	7.4
Plastics and rubber product	4.6	5.3	5.7	5.0	5.3	3.6
Wholesale and retail trade	2.7	2.8	3.1	3.1	3.2	5.2
Wholesale trade	3.9	3.9	4.3	4.6	5.0	3.3
Retail trade	2.5	2.6	2.8	2.8	2.9	5.3
Transportation and utilities	4.7	4.9	5.3	4.9	5.1	5.0
Transportation and warehousing	4.0	4.3	4.7	4.3	4.6	9.1
Utilities	11.5	13.4	13.3	10.4	10.1	5.0
Information[1]	3.4	3.3	4.3	4.8	4.7	5.6
Publishing, except Internet	4.2	4.8	4.7	5.3	4.7	3.8
Motion picture and sound recording industries	1.6	2.3	2.2	1.9	1.9	4.3
Broadcasting, except Internet	3.6	3.1	4.0	4.6	3.4	6.6
Telecommunications	4.3	3.4	4.6	5.3	6.9	4.6
Financial activities	3.5	3.6	3.9	4.0	4.5	4.8
Finance and insurance	3.6	3.9	4.1	4.1	4.7	4.5
Finance	3.3	3.6	4.0	3.9	4.4	5.5
Insurance	4.4	4.5	4.4	4.7	5.2	3.9
Real estate and rental and leasing	3.1	3.0	3.3	3.4	3.7	4.1
Real estate	3.1	3.2	3.5	3.5	3.9	3.3
Rental and leasing services	3.0	2.2	2.9	3.1	3.0	3.4
Professional and business services	2.4	2.7	3.2	3.2	3.1	4.0
Professional and technical services	2.6	3.1	3.6	3.8	3.3	2.9
Management, administrative, and waste services[1]	2.0	2.1	2.6	2.5	2.5	2.8
Administrative and support services	1.8	1.9	2.4	2.4	2.4	2.9
Waste management and remediation services	3.6	4.3	3.4	4.1	4.1	4.1
Education and health services	3.4	3.5	3.6	4.0	4.1	4.4
Education services	3.2	3.6	3.8	4.0	4.3	4.1
Health care and social assistance	3.5	3.5	3.6	4.1	4.1	5.3
Hospitals	5.1	4.9	4.7	5.2	5.4	3.6
Health services, except hospitals	3.2	3.1	3.3	3.6	3.6	3.1
Social assistance	2.4	2.5	2.8	3.1	3.0	2.5
Leisure and hospitality	1.7	1.8	2.0	1.9	2.1	3.3
Arts, entertainment, and recreation	2.6	2.3	2.8	3.1	2.8	2.3
Accommodation and food services	1.5	1.6	1.9	1.6	1.9	3.3
Accommodation	2.8	2.7	3.1	2.5	3.1	2.2
Food services and drinking places	1.4	1.4	1.6	1.4	1.6	4.0
Other services	3.1	3.3	3.3	3.2	3.3	4.1
Other services, except private households	3.2	3.3	3.5	3.3	3.4	4.0
Repair and maintenance	3.0	3.0	3.2	2.9	3.0	3.5
Personal and laundry services	2.7	2.8	3.4	2.8	3.2	4.5
Membership associations and organizations	4.0	4.1	3.9	4.2	4.4	3.4
Other services, private households	3.0	2.7	2.3	2.8	2.8	
Public Sector	7.1	6.7	6.9	6.9	7.2	7.2
Federal government	11.5	11.3	10.4	9.9	9.9	7.9
State government	5.5	5.4	6.4	6.3	6.5	6.4
Local government	6.7	6.2	6.4	6.6	7.1	7.5

Note: Data beginning in 2000 reflect the introduction of Census 2000 population controls. Data for 2004 forward reflect updated population controls introduced annually with the release of January data.

[1]Includes other industries not shown separately.

Table 1-45. Employment Status of the Population, by Sex and Marital Status, March 1990–March 2010

(Thousands of people, percent.)

Marital status and year	Men						Women					
	Population	Labor force		Employed			Population	Labor force		Employed		
		Total			Unemployed			Total			Unemployed	
		Number	Percent of population	Employed	Number	Percent of labor force		Number	Percent of population	Employed	Number	Percent of labor force
Single												
1990	25 757	18 829	73.1	16 893	1 936	10.3	21 088	14 003	66.4	12 856	1 147	8.2
1991	26 220	19 014	72.5	16 418	2 596	13.7	21 688	14 125	65.1	12 887	1 238	8.8
1992	26 529	19 229	72.5	16 401	2 828	14.7	21 738	14 072	64.7	12 793	1 279	9.1
1993	26 951	19 625	72.8	16 858	2 767	14.1	21 848	14 091	64.5	12 711	1 380	9.8
1994	28 350	20 365	71.8	17 826	2 539	12.5	22 885	14 903	65.1	13 419	1 484	10.0
1995	28 318	20 449	72.2	18 286	2 163	10.6	22 853	14 974	65.5	13 673	1 301	8.7
1996	28 695	20 561	71.7	18 097	2 464	12.0	23 632	15 417	65.2	14 084	1 333	8.6
1997	29 294	20 942	71.5	18 683	2 259	10.8	24 215	16 178	66.8	14 747	1 431	8.8
1998	29 558	21 255	71.9	19 124	2 131	10.0	24 808	16 885	68.1	15 626	1 259	7.5
1999	29 883	21 329	71.4	19 465	1 864	8.7	25 674	17 486	68.1	16 185	1 301	7.4
2000	30 232	21 641	71.6	19 823	1 818	8.4	25 863	17 749	68.6	16 446	1 303	7.3
2001	30 968	22 232	71.8	20 239	1 993	9.0	26 180	17 900	68.4	16 631	1 269	7.1
2002	32 220	22 761	70.6	20 066	2 695	11.8	26 942	18 079	67.1	16 499	1 580	8.7
2003	32 852	22 821	69.5	20 194	2 627	11.5	27 527	17 901	65.0	16 219	1 682	9.4
2004	33 786	23 212	68.7	20 434	2 778	12.0	28 033	18 089	64.5	16 506	1 583	8.8
2005	34 069	23 335	68.5	20 831	2 504	10.7	28 508	18 554	65.1	16 902	1 652	8.9
2006	34 906	24 369	69.8	21 961	2 408	9.9	29 357	18 989	64.7	17 444	1 545	8.1
2007	35 359	24 506	69.3	22 224	2 281	9.3	29 695	19 218	64.7	17 935	1 284	6.7
2008	36 522	25 229	69.1	22 695	2 534	10.0	30 772	19 889	64.6	18 369	1 520	7.6
2009	36 907	24 930	67.5	20 645	4 284	17.2	31 038	19 785	63.7	17 714	2 071	10.5
2010	38 110	25 663	67.3	21 038	4 626	18.0	32 085	19 973	62.3	17 517	2 457	12.3
Married, Spouse Present												
1990	52 464	41 020	78.2	39 562	1 458	3.6	53 207	30 967	58.2	29 870	1 097	3.5
1991	52 460	40 883	77.9	38 843	2 040	5.0	53 176	31 103	58.5	29 668	1 435	4.6
1992	52 780	40 930	77.5	38 650	2 280	5.6	53 464	31 686	59.3	30 130	1 556	4.9
1993	53 488	41 255	77.1	39 069	2 186	5.3	54 146	32 158	59.4	30 757	1 401	4.4
1994	53 436	40 993	76.7	39 085	1 908	4.7	54 198	32 863	60.6	31 397	1 466	4.5
1995	54 166	41 806	77.2	40 262	1 544	3.7	54 902	33 563	61.1	32 267	1 296	3.9
1996	53 996	41 837	77.5	40 356	1 481	3.5	54 640	33 382	61.1	32 258	1 124	3.4
1997	53 981	41 967	77.7	40 628	1 339	3.2	54 611	33 907	62.1	32 836	1 071	3.2
1998	54 685	42 288	77.3	41 039	1 249	3.0	55 241	34 136	61.8	33 028	1 108	3.2
1999	55 256	42 557	77.0	41 476	1 081	2.5	55 801	34 349	61.6	33 403	946	2.8
2000	55 897	43 254	77.4	42 261	993	2.3	56 432	34 959	61.9	33 998	961	2.7
2001	56 152	43 463	77.4	42 245	1 218	2.8	56 740	35 234	62.1	34 273	961	2.7
2002	57 325	44 271	77.2	42 508	1 763	4.0	57 883	35 624	61.5	34 295	1 329	3.7
2003	57 940	44 700	77.1	42 797	1 903	4.3	58 545	36 185	61.8	34 806	1 379	3.8
2004	58 395	44 860	76.8	43 247	1 613	3.6	59 008	35 918	60.9	34 582	1 336	3.7
2005	58 854	45 263	76.9	43 763	1 500	3.3	59 449	35 809	60.2	34 738	1 071	3.0
2006	58 850	45 082	76.6	43 877	1 205	2.7	59 476	36 192	60.9	35 185	1 007	2.8
2007	60 126	46 129	76.7	44 813	1 317	2.9	60 656	37 335	61.6	36 370	965	2.6
2008	59 455	45 451	76.4	43 958	1 493	3.3	60 108	37 074	61.7	35 919	1 155	3.1
2009	60 132	45 741	76.1	42 667	3 074	6.7	60 818	37 536	61.7	35 540	1 996	5.3
2010	59 694	45 110	75.6	41 762	3 348	7.4	60 339	37 201	61.7	34 964	2 237	6.0
Widowed, Divorced, or Separated												
1990	11 152	7 513	67.4	6 959	554	7.4	23 857	11 168	46.8	10 530	638	5.7
1991	11 588	7 804	67.3	6 985	819	10.5	24 105	11 145	46.2	10 386	759	6.8
1992	11 927	8 049	67.5	7 140	909	11.3	24 582	11 486	46.7	10 610	876	7.6
1993	11 861	7 956	67.1	7 055	901	11.3	24 661	11 308	45.9	10 528	780	6.9
1994	12 239	8 156	66.6	7 382	774	9.5	25 098	11 879	47.3	10 995	884	7.4
1995	12 410	8 315	67.0	7 632	683	8.2	25 373	12 001	47.3	11 308	693	5.8
1996	13 176	8 697	66.0	7 976	721	8.3	25 786	12 430	48.2	11 742	688	5.5
1997	14 113	9 420	66.7	8 715	705	7.5	26 301	12 814	48.7	12 071	743	5.8
1998	14 166	9 482	66.9	8 954	528	5.6	26 092	12 880	49.4	12 235	645	5.0
1999	14 225	9 449	66.4	8 971	478	5.1	26 199	12 951	49.4	12 307	644	5.0
2000	14 289	9 623	67.3	9 152	471	4.9	26 354	13 228	50.2	12 657	571	4.3
2001	14 392	9 421	65.5	8 927	494	5.2	26 747	13 454	50.3	12 887	567	4.2
2002	14 617	9 650	66.0	8 931	719	7.5	27 802	13 716	49.3	12 855	861	6.3
2003	15 180	9 855	64.9	9 020	835	8.5	28 240	14 154	50.1	13 240	914	6.5
2004	15 059	9 789	65.0	9 059	730	7.5	28 228	14 194	50.3	13 324	870	6.1
2005	15 779	10 256	65.0	9 569	687	6.7	28 576	14 233	49.8	13 472	761	5.3
2006	16 405	10 815	65.9	10 141	674	6.2	28 981	14 220	49.1	13 539	681	4.8
2007	16 247	10 799	66.5	10 150	650	6.0	28 950	14 320	49.5	13 620	700	4.9
2008	16 718	10 896	65.2	10 083	812	7.5	29 419	14 553	49.5	13 765	787	5.4
2009	16 719	10 687	63.9	9 224	1 463	13.7	29 471	14 449	49.0	13 169	1 281	8.9
2010	17 016	10 863	63.8	9 188	1 675	15.4	29 915	14 707	49.2	13 285	1 422	9.7

Note: See notes and definitions for information on historical comparability.

Table 1-45. Employment Status of the Population, by Sex and Marital Status, March 1990–March 2010
—Continued

(Thousands of people, percent.)

Marital status and year	Men						Women					
	Population	Labor force					Population	Labor force				
		Total		Employed	Unemployed			Total		Employed	Unemployed	
		Number	Percent of population		Number	Percent of labor force		Number	Percent of population		Number	Percent of labor force
Widowed												
1990	2 331	519	22.3	490	29	5.6	11 477	2 243	19.5	2 149	94	4.2
1991	2 385	486	20.4	448	38	7.8	11 288	2 150	19.0	2 044	106	4.9
1992	2 529	566	22.4	501	65	11.5	11 325	2 131	18.8	2 029	102	4.8
1993	2 468	596	24.1	535	61	10.2	11 214	1 961	17.5	1 856	105	5.4
1994	2 220	474	21.4	440	34	7.2	11 073	1 945	17.6	1 825	120	6.2
1995	2 282	496	21.7	469	27	5.4	11 080	1 941	17.5	1 844	97	5.0
1996	2 476	487	19.7	466	21	4.3	11 070	1 916	17.3	1 820	96	5.0
1997	2 686	559	20.8	529	30	5.4	11 058	2 018	18.2	1 926	92	4.6
1998	2 567	563	21.9	551	12	2.1	11 027	2 157	19.6	2 071	86	4.0
1999	2 540	562	22.1	532	30	5.3	10 943	2 039	18.6	1 942	97	4.8
2000	2 601	583	22.4	547	36	6.2	11 061	2 011	18.2	1 911	100	5.0
2001	2 638	568	21.5	546	22	3.9	11 182	2 137	19.1	2 045	92	4.3
2002	2 635	629	23.9	581	48	7.6	11 411	2 001	17.5	1 887	114	5.7
2003	2 694	628	23.3	588	40	6.4	11 295	2 087	18.5	1 991	96	4.6
2004	2 651	581	21.9	558	23	4.0	11 159	2 157	19.3	2 048	109	5.1
2005	2 729	618	22.6	590	28	4.5	11 125	2 111	19.0	2 005	106	5.0
2006	2 626	610	23.2	563	47	7.7	11 305	2 164	19.1	2 094	70	3.2
2007	2 697	631	23.4	588	43	6.8	11 220	2 058	18.3	1 971	87	4.2
2008	2 911	656	22.5	611	44	6.8	11 399	2 218	19.5	2 101	117	5.3
2009	2 813	632	22.5	543	90	14.2	11 446	2 174	19.0	2 032	143	6.6
2010	2 969	776	26.1	684	92	11.8	11 379	2 214	19.5	2 036	178	8.0
Divorced												
1990	6 256	5 004	80.0	4 639	365	7.3	8 845	6 678	75.5	6 333	345	5.2
1991	6 586	5 262	79.9	4 722	540	10.3	9 152	6 779	74.1	6 365	414	6.1
1992	6 743	5 418	80.3	4 823	595	11.0	9 569	7 076	73.9	6 578	498	7.0
1993	6 770	5 330	78.7	4 736	594	11.1	9 879	7 183	72.7	6 736	447	6.2
1994	7 222	5 548	76.8	5 028	520	9.4	10 113	7 473	73.9	6 962	511	6.8
1995	7 343	5 739	78.2	5 266	473	8.2	10 262	7 559	73.7	7 206	353	4.7
1996	7 734	5 954	77.0	5 468	486	8.2	10 508	7 829	74.5	7 468	361	4.6
1997	8 191	6 298	76.9	5 851	447	7.1	11 102	8 092	72.9	7 666	426	5.3
1998	8 307	6 378	76.8	6 045	333	5.2	11 065	8 038	72.6	7 687	351	4.4
1999	8 529	6 481	76.0	6 151	330	5.1	11 130	8 171	73.4	7 841	330	4.0
2000	8 532	6 583	77.2	6 279	304	4.6	11 061	8 505	76.9	8 217	288	3.4
2001	8 580	6 403	74.6	6 074	329	5.1	11 719	8 662	73.9	8 335	327	3.8
2002	8 643	6 519	75.4	6 053	466	7.1	12 227	8 902	72.8	8 416	486	5.5
2003	8 938	6 621	74.1	6 052	569	8.6	12 653	9 191	72.6	8 673	518	5.6
2004	8 942	6 622	74.1	6 104	518	7.8	12 817	9 246	72.1	8 706	540	5.8
2005	9 196	6 754	73.4	6 281	473	7.0	12 950	9 253	71.5	8 836	417	4.5
2006	9 646	7 065	73.2	6 631	434	6.1	13 107	9 188	70.1	8 799	389	4.2
2007	9 608	7 110	74.0	6 679	431	6.1	13 214	9 334	70.6	8 896	439	4.7
2008	9 767	7 106	72.8	6 607	499	7.0	13 551	9 387	69.3	8 938	449	4.8
2009	9 938	7 052	71.0	6 064	988	14.0	13 301	9 176	69.0	8 402	774	8.4
2010	9 944	7 018	70.6	5 888	1 131	16.1	13 758	9 394	68.3	8 510	885	9.4
Separated												
1990	2 565	1 990	77.6	1 830	160	8.0	3 535	2 247	63.6	2 048	199	8.9
1991	2 616	2 057	78.6	1 816	241	11.7	3 665	2 216	60.5	1 977	239	10.8
1992	2 655	2 065	77.8	1 816	249	12.1	3 688	2 279	61.8	2 003	276	12.1
1993	2 623	2 030	77.4	1 784	246	12.1	3 568	2 165	60.7	1 937	228	10.5
1994	2 797	2 134	76.3	1 914	220	10.3	3 911	2 461	62.9	2 208	253	10.3
1995	2 784	2 081	74.7	1 898	183	8.8	4 031	2 501	62.0	2 258	243	9.7
1996	2 966	2 255	76.0	2 041	214	9.5	4 209	2 684	63.8	2 453	231	8.6
1997	3 236	2 563	79.2	2 335	228	8.9	4 141	2 705	65.3	2 480	225	8.3
1998	3 293	2 542	77.2	2 358	184	7.2	4 000	2 683	67.1	2 476	207	7.7
1999	3 156	2 405	76.2	2 287	118	4.9	4 126	2 740	66.4	2 523	217	7.9
2000	3 157	2 456	77.8	2 326	130	5.3	4 012	2 711	67.6	2 528	183	6.8
2001	3 174	2 450	77.2	2 307	143	5.8	3 846	2 654	69.0	2 507	147	5.5
2002	3 339	2 502	74.9	2 297	205	8.2	4 164	2 812	67.5	2 551	261	9.3
2003	3 548	2 606	73.4	2 380	226	8.7	4 293	2 877	67.0	2 576	301	10.5
2004	3 466	2 586	74.6	2 397	189	7.3	4 251	2 791	65.7	2 569	222	8.0
2005	3 855	2 884	74.8	2 698	186	6.4	4 501	2 870	63.8	2 632	238	8.3
2006	4 132	3 141	76.0	2 947	194	6.2	4 569	2 869	62.8	2 647	222	7.7
2007	3 943	3 058	77.6	2 883	176	5.7	4 516	2 927	64.8	2 753	174	6.0
2008	4 040	3 134	77.6	2 865	269	8.6	4 469	2 947	65.9	2 726	221	7.5
2009	3 968	3 002	75.7	2 617	386	12.8	4 725	3 099	65.6	2 734	364	11.8
2010	4 103	3 069	74.8	2 616	452	14.7	4 778	3 099	64.8	2 739	359	11.6

Note: See notes and definitions for information on historical comparability.

Table 1-46. Employment Status of All Women and Single Women, by Presence and Age of Children, March 1990–March 2010

(Thousands of women, percent.)

Presence and age of children and year	All women							Single women						
	Civilian labor force	Civilian labor force as percent of population	Employed			Unemployed		Civilian labor force	Civilian labor force as percent of population	Employed			Unemployed	
			Number	Percent full time	Percent part time	Number	Percent of labor force			Number	Percent full time	Percent part time	Number	Percent of labor force
Women with No Children Under 18 Years														
1990	33 942	52.3	32 391	74.4	25.6	1 551	4.6	12 478	68.1	11 611	65.9	34.1	866	6.9
1991	34 047	52.0	32 167	74.0	26.0	1 880	5.5	12 472	67.0	11 529	66.2	33.8	943	7.6
1992	34 487	52.3	32 481	74.3	25.7	2 006	5.8	12 355	66.9	11 374	66.6	33.4	982	7.9
1993	34 495	52.1	32 476	74.6	25.4	2 020	5.9	12 223	66.4	11 201	66.1	33.9	1 022	8.4
1994	35 454	53.1	33 343	72.7	27.3	2 110	6.0	12 737	66.8	11 674	64.5	35.5	1 063	8.3
1995	35 843	52.9	34 054	72.9	27.1	1 789	5.0	12 870	67.1	11 919	64.5	35.5	951	7.4
1996	36 509	53.0	34 698	73.3	26.7	1 811	5.0	13 172	66.1	12 255	64.6	35.4	918	7.0
1997	37 295	53.6	35 572	73.7	26.3	1 723	4.6	13 405	66.5	12 442	64.0	36.0	964	7.2
1998	38 253	54.1	36 680	74.1	25.9	1 573	4.1	13 888	67.2	13 082	64.8	35.2	806	5.8
1999	39 316	54.3	37 589	74.6	25.4	1 727	4.4	14 435	67.1	13 491	65.6	34.4	944	6.5
2000	40 142	54.8	38 408	75.4	24.6	1 733	4.3	14 677	67.6	13 713	66.6	33.4	964	6.6
2001	40 836	54.9	39 219	75.7	24.3	1 617	4.0	14 877	67.4	13 993	67.3	32.7	884	5.9
2002	41 278	54.0	39 038	75.1	24.9	2 241	5.4	14 855	65.6	13 682	65.9	34.1	1 173	7.9
2003	42 039	54.1	39 667	74.8	25.2	2 372	5.6	14 678	63.5	13 430	65.1	34.9	1 249	8.5
2004	42 289	53.8	40 000	74.6	25.4	2 289	5.4	14 828	63.0	13 670	65.5	34.5	1 157	7.8
2005	42 039	54.1	39 667	74.8	25.2	2 372	5.6	14 678	63.5	13 430	65.1	34.9	1 249	8.5
2006	43 392	53.6	41 440	75.3	24.7	1 952	4.5	15 673	63.4	14 547	66.5	33.5	1 125	7.2
2007	44 039	53.9	42 279	75.3	24.7	1 760	4.0	15 704	63.4	14 801	66.4	33.6	903	5.7
2008	45 585	54.3	43 417	75.7	24.3	2 168	4.8	16 378	63.4	15 261	67.4	32.6	1 116	6.8
2009	45 649	53.8	42 343	73.3	26.7	3 306	7.2	16 112	62.1	14 607	64.9	35.1	1 506	9.3
2010	46 098	53.5	42 256	73.5	26.5	3 842	8.3	16 331	60.7	14 533	65.6	34.4	1 798	11.0
Women with Children Under 18 Years														
1990	22 196	66.7	20 865	73.0	27.0	1 331	6.0	1 525	55.2	1 244	79.1	20.9	280	18.4
1991	22 327	66.6	20 774	73.0	27.0	1 552	7.0	1 654	53.6	1 358	76.4	23.6	296	17.9
1992	22 756	67.2	21 052	73.8	26.2	1 704	7.5	1 716	52.5	1 420	75.9	24.1	297	17.3
1993	23 063	66.9	21 521	73.9	26.1	1 541	6.7	1 869	54.4	1 510	74.8	25.2	359	19.2
1994	24 191	68.4	22 467	70.8	29.2	1 724	7.1	2 166	56.9	1 745	73.9	26.1	421	19.4
1995	24 695	69.7	23 195	71.7	28.3	1 500	6.1	2 104	57.5	1 754	73.6	26.4	350	16.6
1996	24 720	70.2	23 386	72.6	27.4	1 334	5.4	2 245	60.5	1 829	73.5	26.5	416	18.5
1997	25 604	72.1	24 082	74.1	25.9	1 522	5.9	2 772	68.1	2 305	76.6	23.4	467	16.8
1998	25 647	72.3	24 209	74.0	26.0	1 438	5.6	2 997	72.5	2 544	75.6	24.4	453	15.1
1999	25 469	72.1	24 305	74.1	25.9	1 165	4.6	3 051	73.4	2 694	75.8	24.2	357	11.7
2000	25 795	72.9	24 693	74.6	25.4	1 102	4.3	3 073	73.9	2 734	79.7	20.3	339	11.0
2001	25 751	73.1	24 572	75.6	24.4	1 179	4.6	3 022	73.8	2 638	81.8	18.2	385	12.7
2002	26 140	72.2	24 612	74.8	25.2	1 529	5.8	3 224	75.3	2 818	79.1	20.9	406	12.6
2003	26 202	71.7	24 598	74.3	25.7	1 603	6.1	3 222	73.1	2 789	79.5	20.5	433	13.4
2004	25 913	70.7	24 413	74.2	25.8	1 501	5.8	3 262	72.6	2 836	76.8	23.2	426	13.1
2005	26 202	71.7	24 598	74.3	25.7	1 603	6.1	3 222	73.1	2 789	79.5	20.5	433	13.4
2006	26 009	70.6	24 728	75.6	24.4	1 281	4.9	3 317	71.5	2 896	77.8	22.2	420	12.7
2007	26 834	71.3	25 646	75.2	24.8	1 188	4.4	3 514	71.4	3 133	76.4	23.6	381	10.8
2008	25 930	71.2	24 637	75.7	24.3	1 294	5.0	3 511	71.0	3 108	78.0	22.0	403	11.5
2009	26 122	71.6	24 079	74.6	25.4	2 043	7.8	3 673	72.0	3 108	75.8	24.2	566	18.2
2010	25 783	71.3	23 510	73.7	26.3	2 273	8.8	3 642	70.1	2 984	71.9	28.1	659	18.1
Women with Children Under 6 Years														
1990	9 397	58.2	8 732	69.6	30.4	664	7.1	929	48.7	736	75.0	25.0	194	20.9
1991	9 636	58.4	8 758	69.5	30.5	878	9.1	1 050	48.8	819	72.2	27.8	231	22.0
1992	9 573	58.0	8 662	70.2	29.8	911	9.5	1 029	45.8	829	73.2	26.8	200	19.4
1993	9 621	57.9	8 764	70.1	29.9	857	8.9	1 125	47.4	869	70.0	30.0	257	22.8
1994	10 328	60.3	9 394	67.1	32.9	935	9.1	1 379	52.2	1 062	70.0	30.0	317	23.0
1995	10 395	62.3	9 587	67.5	32.5	809	7.8	1 328	53.0	1 069	68.6	31.4	259	19.5
1996	10 293	62.3	9 592	68.4	31.6	701	6.8	1 378	55.1	1 099	67.3	32.7	279	20.2
1997	10 610	65.0	9 800	70.5	29.5	810	7.6	1 755	65.1	1 424	71.6	28.4	330	18.8
1998	10 619	65.2	9 839	69.8	30.2	780	7.3	1 755	67.3	1 448	71.7	28.3	307	17.5
1999	10 322	64.4	9 674	69.0	31.0	648	6.3	1 811	68.1	1 565	71.0	29.0	246	13.6
2000	10 316	65.3	9 763	70.5	29.5	553	5.4	1 835	70.5	1 603	75.3	24.7	232	12.6
2001	10 200	64.9	9 618	71.2	28.8	582	5.7	1 783	69.7	1 542	79.1	20.9	242	13.6
2002	10 193	64.1	9 441	70.4	29.6	752	7.4	1 819	71.0	1 568	74.5	25.5	251	13.8
2003	10 209	62.9	9 433	70.0	30.0	776	7.6	1 893	70.2	1 614	75.2	24.8	279	14.7
2004	10 131	62.2	9 407	69.4	30.6	724	7.1	1 885	68.4	1 605	70.1	29.9	279	14.8
2005	10 209	62.9	9 433	70.0	30.0	776	7.6	1 893	70.2	1 614	75.2	24.8	279	14.7
2006	10 430	63.0	9 779	72.0	28.0	651	6.2	1 934	68.6	1 659	72.8	27.2	276	14.3
2007	10 894	63.5	10 305	71.9	28.1	589	5.4	2 066	67.4	1 827	72.7	27.3	239	11.6
2008	10 452	63.6	9 794	72.1	27.9	657	6.3	1 982	66.0	1 705	72.2	27.8	277	14.0
2009	10 497	63.6	9 517	71.8	28.2	980	9.3	2 137	67.8	1 754	70.3	29.7	383	17.9
2010	10 536	64.2	9 452	70.9	29.1	1 085	10.3	2 076	65.6	1 643	67.0	33.0	433	20.9

Note: See notes and definitions for information on historical comparability.

Table 1-47. Employment Status of Ever-Married Women and Married Women, Spouse Present, by Presence and Age of Children, March 1990–March 2010

(Thousands of women, percent.)

Presence and age of children and year	Ever-married women[1]						Married women, spouse present					
	Civilian labor force	Civilian labor force as percent of population	Employed		Unemployed		Civilian labor force	Civilian labor force as percent of population	Employed		Unemployed	
			Number	Percent full time	Percent part time	Number	Percent of labor force			Number	Percent full time	Percent part time	Number	Percent of labor force

Presence and age of children and year	CLF	CLF % pop	Emp Number	Emp % FT	Emp % PT	Unemp Number	Unemp %	CLF	CLF % pop	Emp Number	Emp % FT	Emp % PT	Unemp Number	Unemp %
Women with No Children Under 18														
1990	21 464	46.1	20 779	79.1	20.9	685	3.2	14 467	51.1	14 068	77.3	22.7	399	2.8
1991	21 575	46.1	20 637	78.4	21.6	937	4.3	14 529	51.2	13 976	77.6	22.4	552	3.8
1992	22 132	46.6	21 108	78.5	21.5	1 024	4.6	14 851	51.9	14 247	77.8	22.2	604	4.1
1993	22 273	46.6	21 275	79.0	21.0	998	4.5	15 211	52.4	14 630	77.6	22.4	581	3.8
1994	22 716	47.6	21 669	77.1	22.9	1 047	4.6	15 234	53.2	14 641	75.6	24.4	593	3.9
1995	22 973	47.3	22 134	77.4	22.6	839	3.7	15 594	53.2	15 072	76.3	23.7	522	3.3
1996	23 337	47.7	22 444	78.1	21.9	893	3.8	15 628	53.4	15 123	76.8	23.2	506	3.2
1997	23 890	48.3	23 130	78.9	21.1	760	3.2	15 750	54.2	15 315	77.7	22.3	435	2.8
1998	24 366	48.7	23 598	79.3	20.7	767	3.1	16 007	54.1	15 581	78.3	21.7	426	2.7
1999	24 881	48.9	24 098	79.7	20.3	783	3.1	16 484	54.4	16 061	78.2	21.8	423	2.6
2000	25 465	49.4	24 695	80.3	19.7	769	3.0	16 786	54.7	16 357	79.1	20.9	429	2.6
2001	25 959	49.6	25 226	80.4	19.6	733	2.8	16 909	54.8	16 528	78.7	21.3	381	2.3
2002	26 423	49.1	25 356	80.0	20.0	1 068	4.0	17 353	54.8	16 780	78.4	21.6	573	3.3
2003	27 361	50.1	26 238	79.7	20.3	1 123	4.1	17 901	55.7	17 273	78.6	21.4	628	3.5
2004	27 461	49.8	26 329	79.3	20.7	1 131	4.1	17 965	55.0	17 367	78.6	21.4	598	3.3
2005	27 361	50.1	26 238	79.7	20.3	1 123	4.1	17 901	55.7	17 273	78.6	21.4	628	3.5
2006	27 719	49.3	26 893	80.1	19.9	827	3.0	18 124	54.8	17 691	79.3	20.7	434	2.4
2007	28 335	49.8	27 477	80.1	19.9	858	3.0	18 766	55.4	18 326	79.6	20.4	441	2.3
2008	29 207	50.3	28 156	80.2	19.8	1 052	3.6	19 188	55.9	18 650	79.8	20.2	539	2.8
2009	29 536	50.2	27 737	77.8	22.2	1 800	6.1	19 541	55.8	18 521	77.3	22.7	1 019	5.2
2010	29 767	50.2	27 723	77.7	22.3	2 044	6.9	19 579	55.8	18 454	77.3	22.7	1 125	5.7
Women with Children Under 18 Years														
1990	20 671	67.8	19 621	72.6	27.4	1 051	5.1	16 500	66.3	15 803	69.8	30.2	698	4.2
1991	20 673	67.9	19 416	72.8	27.2	1 257	6.1	16 575	66.8	15 692	70.1	29.9	883	5.3
1992	21 040	68.8	19 633	73.6	26.4	1 407	6.7	16 835	67.8	15 884	71.3	28.7	952	5.7
1993	21 194	68.3	20 011	73.9	26.1	1 183	5.6	16 947	67.5	16 127	71.4	28.6	820	4.8
1994	22 025	69.8	20 722	70.5	29.5	1 303	5.9	17 628	69.0	16 755	68.0	32.0	873	5.0
1995	22 591	71.1	21 441	71.5	28.5	1 150	5.1	17 969	70.2	17 195	68.8	31.2	774	4.3
1996	22 475	71.4	21 556	72.5	27.5	919	4.1	17 754	70.0	17 136	69.6	30.4	618	3.5
1997	22 831	72.6	21 777	73.9	26.1	1 054	4.6	18 157	71.1	17 521	71.6	28.4	636	3.5
1998	22 650	72.3	21 665	73.8	26.2	985	4.3	18 129	70.6	17 447	71.5	28.5	682	3.8
1999	22 419	71.9	21 611	73.9	26.1	808	3.6	17 865	70.1	17 342	71.5	28.5	523	2.9
2000	22 722	72.7	21 960	74.0	26.0	763	3.4	18 174	70.6	17 641	71.7	28.3	533	2.9
2001	22 729	73.0	21 934	74.9	25.1	795	3.5	18 325	70.8	17 745	72.6	27.4	580	3.2
2002	22 917	71.8	21 794	74.3	25.7	1 122	4.9	18 271	69.6	17 515	71.7	28.3	756	4.1
2003	22 979	71.5	21 809	73.7	26.3	1 170	5.1	18 284	69.2	17 533	71.0	29.0	751	4.1
2004	22 651	70.5	21 576	73.8	26.2	1 075	4.7	17 953	68.2	17 215	71.3	28.7	738	4.1
2005	22 979	71.5	21 809	73.7	26.3	1 170	5.1	18 284	69.2	17 533	71.0	29.0	751	4.1
2006	22 692	70.5	21 831	75.3	24.7	861	3.8	18 067	68.4	17 494	73.0	27.0	574	3.2
2007	23 320	71.3	22 513	75.0	25.0	807	3.5	18 569	69.3	18 045	72.6	27.4	524	2.8
2008	22 419	71.2	21 529	75.4	24.6	890	4.0	17 886	69.4	17 269	73.6	26.4	616	3.4
2009	22 449	71.5	20 972	74.5	25.5	1 477	6.6	17 995	69.8	17 018	73.1	26.9	977	5.4
2010	22 141	71.5	20 526	74.0	26.0	1 615	7.3	17 622	69.7	16 510	72.6	27.4	1 112	6.3
Women with Children Under 6 Years														
1990	8 467	59.5	7 996	69.1	30.9	471	5.6	7 247	58.9	6 901	67.4	32.6	346	4.8
1991	8 585	59.9	7 938	69.2	30.8	647	7.5	7 434	59.9	6 933	67.5	32.5	501	6.7
1992	8 544	60.0	7 832	69.9	30.1	711	8.3	7 333	59.9	6 819	68.5	31.5	514	7.0
1993	8 496	59.6	7 895	70.2	29.8	600	7.1	7 289	59.6	6 840	68.8	31.2	450	6.2
1994	8 949	61.8	8 332	66.7	33.3	617	6.9	7 723	61.7	7 291	65.4	34.6	432	5.6
1995	9 067	63.9	8 517	67.4	32.6	550	6.1	7 759	63.5	7 349	66.1	33.9	409	5.3
1996	8 915	63.6	8 493	68.6	31.4	422	4.7	7 590	62.7	7 297	66.5	33.5	293	3.9
1997	8 856	64.9	8 376	70.3	29.7	480	5.4	7 582	63.6	7 252	69.1	30.9	330	4.4
1998	8 864	64.8	8 391	69.5	30.5	473	5.3	7 655	63.7	7 309	68.1	31.9	346	4.5
1999	8 511	63.7	8 109	68.6	31.4	402	4.7	7 246	61.8	6 979	67.1	32.9	267	3.7
2000	8 481	64.3	8 159	69.5	30.5	321	3.8	7 341	62.8	7 087	68.1	31.9	254	3.5
2001	8 417	64.0	8 077	69.7	30.3	340	4.0	7 319	62.5	7 062	68.5	31.5	257	3.5
2002	8 373	62.8	7 873	69.6	30.4	501	6.0	7 166	60.8	6 804	67.7	32.3	363	5.1
2003	8 315	61.4	7 818	68.9	31.1	497	6.0	7 175	59.8	6 826	67.1	32.9	349	4.9
2004	8 246	61.0	7 801	69.3	30.7	445	5.4	7 107	59.3	6 774	68.1	31.9	332	4.7
2005	8 315	61.4	7 818	68.9	31.1	497	6.0	7 175	59.8	6 826	67.1	32.9	349	4.9
2006	8 496	61.9	8 121	71.8	28.2	375	4.4	7 366	60.3	7 092	70.6	29.4	274	3.7
2007	8 829	62.7	8 479	71.7	28.3	350	4.0	7 664	61.5	7 407	70.8	29.2	257	3.4
2008	8 470	63.0	8 089	72.1	27.9	381	4.5	7 285	61.6	6 999	70.9	29.1	285	3.9
2009	8 360	62.6	7 763	72.1	27.9	597	7.1	7 231	61.6	6 805	71.4	28.6	426	5.9
2010	8 460	63.8	7 809	71.7	28.3	651	7.7	7 227	62.5	6 741	71.5	28.5	486	6.7

[1]Ever-married women are women who are, or have ever been, married.

Table 1-48. Employment Status of Women Who Maintain Families, by Marital Status and Presence and Age of Children, March 1990–March 2010

(Thousands of women, percent.)

Marital status, age of children, and year	Civilian noninstitutional population	Civilian labor force					Not in the labor force
		Number	Percent of the population	Employed	Unemployed		
					Number	Percent of the labor force	
Total, Women Who Maintain Families							
1990	11 309	7 088	62.7	6 471	617	8.7	4 221
1991	11 765	7 329	62.3	6 657	672	9.2	4 436
1992	12 214	7 517	61.5	6 798	719	9.6	4 697
1993	12 489	7 777	62.3	7 093	684	8.8	4 712
1994	12 963	8 214	63.4	7 413	801	9.8	4 750
1995	12 762	8 192	64.2	7 527	665	8.1	4 570
1996	12 993	8 460	65.1	7 832	628	7.4	4 532
1997	13 258	8 998	67.9	8 192	806	9.0	4 260
1998	13 102	8 976	68.5	8 309	667	7.4	4 127
1999	13 191	9 213	69.8	8 596	617	6.7	3 978
2000	13 145	9 226	70.2	8 592	634	6.9	3 918
2001	12 930	9 034	69.9	8 453	581	6.4	3 897
2002	13 489	9 523	70.6	8 755	768	8.1	3 966
2003	14 000	9 759	69.7	8 898	861	8.8	4 241
2004	14 165	9 869	69.7	9 054	815	8.3	4 297
2005	14 391	9 941	69.1	9 140	801	8.1	4 450
2006	14 485	9 966	68.8	9 227	739	7.4	4 520
2007	14 833	10 172	68.6	9 510	661	6.5	4 662
2008	14 820	10 166	68.6	9 447	719	7.1	4 654
2009	14 813	10 140	68.5	9 034	1 106	10.9	4 673
2010	15 214	10 206	67.1	9 027	1 179	11.6	5 008
Women with No Children Under 18 Years							
1990	4 290	2 227	51.9	2 132	95	4.3	2 062
1991	4 447	2 364	53.2	2 231	133	5.6	2 083
1992	4 651	2 427	52.2	2 307	120	4.9	2 223
1993	4 708	2 466	52.4	2 339	127	5.2	2 242
1994	4 758	2 609	54.8	2 489	120	4.6	2 149
1995	4 610	2 471	53.6	2 394	77	3.1	2 139
1996	4 847	2 552	52.7	2 462	90	3.5	2 295
1997	4 909	2 663	54.2	2 571	92	3.4	2 246
1998	4 952	2 649	53.5	2 578	71	2.7	2 303
1999	4 942	2 667	54.0	2 556	111	4.2	2 275
2000	5 097	2 707	53.1	2 546	161	6.0	2 390
2001	5 185	2 772	53.5	2 668	104	3.8	2 413
2002	5 119	2 764	54.0	2 628	136	4.9	2 355
2003	5 457	2 934	53.8	2 728	206	7.0	2 522
2004	5 551	3 052	55.0	2 855	197	6.4	2 499
2005	5 692	3 095	54.4	2 961	134	4.3	2 597
2006	5 693	3 088	54.2	2 945	143	4.6	2 604
2007	5 823	3 124	53.7	2 990	134	4.3	2 699
2008	6 022	3 352	55.7	3 167	185	5.5	2 670
2009	6 068	3 332	54.9	3 075	258	7.7	2 735
2010	6 414	3 417	53.3	3 131	286	8.4	2 997
Women with Children Under 18 Years							
1990	7 018	4 860	69.3	4 338	522	10.7	2 159
1991	7 318	4 965	67.8	4 426	539	10.9	2 353
1992	7 564	5 090	67.3	4 491	599	11.8	2 473
1993	7 781	5 311	68.3	4 755	556	10.5	2 470
1994	8 205	5 604	68.3	4 924	680	12.1	2 601
1995	8 152	5 720	70.2	5 132	588	10.3	2 431
1996	8 146	5 908	72.5	5 370	538	9.1	2 237
1997	8 348	6 335	75.9	5 621	714	11.3	2 014
1998	8 151	6 327	77.6	5 731	596	9.4	1 823
1999	8 248	6 546	79.4	6 040	506	7.7	1 702
2000	8 048	6 520	81.0	6 046	474	7.3	1 528
2001	7 746	6 261	80.8	5 785	476	7.6	1 484
2002	8 370	6 759	80.8	6 127	632	9.4	1 611
2003	8 543	6 825	79.9	6 170	655	9.6	1 718
2004	8 614	6 817	79.1	6 199	618	9.1	1 798
2005	8 699	6 846	78.7	6 179	667	9.7	1 853
2006	8 793	6 878	78.2	6 282	596	8.7	1 915
2007	9 010	7 047	78.2	6 520	527	7.5	1 963
2008	8 798	6 814	77.4	6 280	535	7.8	1 984
2009	8 745	6 807	77.8	5 959	848	12.5	1 938
2010	8 800	6 789	77.1	5 896	893	13.2	2 011
Single Women with No Children Under 18 Years							
1990	642	450	70.1	425	25	5.6	192
1991	682	469	68.8	441	28	6.0	214
1992	745	505	67.8	475	30	5.9	241
1993	752	531	70.6	494	37	7.0	221
1994	704	490	69.6	451	39	8.0	213
1995	779	534	68.5	508	26	4.9	245
1996	895	588	65.7	572	16	2.7	308
1997	860	585	68.0	563	22	3.8	275
1998	893	637	71.3	613	24	3.8	256
1999	969	674	69.6	638	36	5.3	295

Note: See notes and definitions for information on historical comparability.

Table 1-48. Employment Status of Women Who Maintain Families, by Marital Status and Presence and Age of Children, March 1990–March 2010—*Continued*

(Thousands of women, percent.)

Marital status, age of children, and year	Civilian noninstitutional population	Civilian labor force			Unemployed		Not in the labor force
		Number	Percent of the population	Employed	Number	Percent of the labor force	
Single Women with No Children Under 18 Years—*Continued*							
2000	1 004	720	71.7	642	78	10.8	284
2001	1 096	787	71.8	756	31	3.9	309
2002	1 154	796	69.0	747	49	6.2	358
2003	1 254	814	64.9	713	101	12.4	440
2004	1 381	977	70.7	887	90	9.2	404
2005	1 388	926	66.7	855	71	7.7	463
2006	1 370	933	68.1	861	72	7.7	437
2007	1 413	986	69.8	930	57	5.7	427
2008	1 515	1 057	69.8	989	68	6.5	458
2009	1 531	1 069	69.8	967	102	9.6	462
2010	1 718	1 166	67.9	1 041	125	10.7	552
Single Women with Children Under 18 Years							
1990	1 953	1 095	56.1	874	221	20.2	858
1991	2 208	1 187	53.8	985	202	17.0	1 021
1992	2 376	1 256	52.9	1 067	189	15.0	1 120
1993	2 445	1 414	57.8	1 161	253	17.9	1 031
1994	2 790	1 625	58.2	1 328	297	18.3	1 165
1995	2 613	1 510	57.8	1 261	249	16.5	1 102
1996	2 639	1 633	61.9	1 346	287	17.6	1 006
1997	3 012	2 087	69.3	1 749	338	16.2	925
1998	3 083	2 280	74.0	1 960	320	14.0	803
1999	3 163	2 415	76.4	2 146	269	11.1	748
2000	3 167	2 413	76.2	2 151	262	10.9	754
2001	3 097	2 351	75.9	2 055	296	12.6	745
2002	3 315	2 566	77.4	2 241	325	12.7	749
2003	3 421	2 584	75.5	2 272	312	12.1	837
2004	3 414	2 568	75.2	2 233	335	13.0	846
2005	3 591	2 708	75.4	2 325	383	14.1	882
2006	3 671	2 710	73.8	2 370	340	12.6	961
2007	3 748	2 782	74.2	2 491	291	10.4	966
2008	3 721	2 743	73.7	2 448	295	10.8	978
2009	3 872	2 877	74.3	2 448	429	14.9	995
2010	3 948	2 868	72.6	2 379	488	17.0	1 081
Widowed, Divorced, or Separated Women with No Children Under 18 Years							
1990	3 648	1 778	48.7	1 708	70	3.9	1 870
1991	3 765	1 896	50.4	1 791	105	5.5	1 869
1992	3 905	1 923	49.2	1 832	91	4.7	1 982
1993	3 956	1 935	48.9	1 845	90	4.6	2 021
1994	4 054	2 118	52.2	2 037	81	3.8	1 936
1995	3 831	1 938	50.6	1 887	51	2.6	1 894
1996	3 952	1 964	49.7	1 890	74	3.8	1 988
1997	4 049	2 077	51.3	2 008	69	3.3	1 971
1998	4 058	2 011	49.6	1 965	46	2.3	2 047
1999	3 974	1 993	50.2	1 918	75	3.8	1 980
2000	4 093	1 987	48.5	1 904	83	4.2	2 106
2001	4 088	1 985	48.6	1 912	73	3.7	2 104
2002	3 964	1 968	49.6	1 882	86	4.4	1 997
2003	4 203	2 121	50.5	2 016	105	5.0	2 082
2004	4 170	2 075	49.8	1 968	107	5.2	2 095
2005	4 304	2 170	50.4	2 106	64	3.0	2 135
2006	4 323	2 156	49.9	2 084	72	3.3	2 168
2007	4 410	2 138	48.5	2 061	77	3.6	2 272
2008	4 507	2 295	50.9	2 178	117	5.1	2 213
2009	4 536	2 263	49.9	2 108	155	6.9	2 273
2010	4 696	2 251	47.9	2 090	161	7.1	2 445
Widowed, Divorced, or Separated Women with Children Under 18 Years							
1990	5 065	3 765	74.3	3 464	301	8.0	1 301
1991	5 109	3 778	73.9	3 441	337	8.9	1 331
1992	5 187	3 834	73.9	3 424	410	10.7	1 353
1993	5 336	3 897	73.0	3 594	303	7.8	1 439
1994	5 415	3 979	73.5	3 596	383	9.6	1 436
1995	5 539	4 210	76.0	3 871	339	8.0	1 329
1996	5 507	4 275	77.6	4 024	251	5.9	1 231
1997	5 337	4 248	79.6	3 872	376	8.8	1 089
1998	5 068	4 047	79.9	3 771	276	6.8	1 020
1999	5 086	4 131	81.2	3 894	237	5.7	955
2000	4 881	4 107	84.1	3 895	212	5.2	774
2001	4 649	3 910	84.1	3 730	180	4.6	739
2002	5 056	4 193	82.9	3 886	307	7.3	862
2003	5 122	4 241	82.8	3 898	343	8.1	881
2004	5 201	4 249	81.7	3 966	283	6.7	952
2005	5 108	4 137	81.0	3 854	283	6.8	971
2006	5 121	4 167	81.4	3 912	255	6.1	955
2007	5 262	4 266	81.1	4 029	237	5.6	997
2008	5 077	4 071	80.2	3 832	239	5.9	1 006
2009	4 873	3 930	80.7	3 511	420	10.7	943
2010	4 852	3 922	80.8	3 517	405	10.3	931

Note: See notes and definitions for information on historical comparability.

Table 1-49. Number and Age of Children in Families, by Type of Family and Labor Force Status of Mother, March 1990–March 2010

(Thousands of children.)

Age of children and year	Total children	Mother in labor force	Mother not in labor force	Married-couple families			Families maintained by women			Families maintained by men
				Total	Mother in labor force	Mother not in labor force	Total	Mother in labor force	Mother not in labor force	
Children Under 18 Years										
1990	59 596	36 712	21 110	45 898	29 077	16 820	11 925	7 635	4 290	1 774
1991	60 330	36 968	21 526	45 912	29 056	16 856	12 582	7 912	4 670	1 836
1992	61 262	38 081	21 176	45 966	29 882	16 084	13 291	8 199	5 093	2 005
1993	62 020	38 542	21 444	46 499	30 054	16 445	13 487	8 488	4 999	2 034
1994	63 407	40 186	21 188	47 247	31 279	15 968	14 127	8 907	5 220	2 033
1995	63 989	41 365	20 421	47 675	32 190	15 486	14 111	9 176	4 935	2 202
1996	64 506	41 573	20 449	47 484	31 764	15 720	14 538	9 809	4 729	2 484
1997	64 710	42 747	19 223	47 529	32 263	15 265	14 441	10 483	3 958	2 740
1998	65 043	43 156	19 069	47 909	32 533	15 376	14 317	10 623	3 694	2 818
1999	65 191	43 419	19 074	47 945	32 193	15 752	14 547	11 226	3 322	2 699
2000	65 601	44 188	18 674	48 902	33 149	15 753	13 960	11 039	2 921	2 739
2001	65 777	44 051	18 864	49 352	33 436	15 916	13 563	10 615	2 948	2 862
2002	65 978	43 821	19 243	48 836	32 673	16 163	14 228	11 149	3 079	2 914
2003	66 521	43 769	19 782	49 004	32 411	16 593	14 547	11 359	3 189	2 970
2004	66 386	43 144	20 229	48 656	31 892	16 764	14 717	11 252	3 465	3 014
2005	66 526	43 239	20 179	48 688	31 886	16 802	14 729	11 352	3 377	3 108
2006	66 883	43 278	20 440	48 853	31 946	16 908	14 865	11 332	3 532	3 165
2007	67 228	44 116	20 073	48 927	32 496	16 431	15 263	11 620	3 643	3 038
2008	67 153	43 798	19 966	48 303	32 110	16 193	15 461	11 688	3 773	3 388
2009	66 913	43 509	20 074	48 384	32 065	16 315	15 204	11 444	3 759	3 326
2010	66 811	43 335	19 913	47 730	31 686	16 044	15 518	11 649	3 869	3 563
Children 6 to 17 Years										
1990	39 095	25 805	12 079	29 726	20 067	9 659	8 157	5 737	2 420	1 211
1991	39 470	25 806	12 392	29 598	19 907	9 691	8 599	5 899	2 701	1 272
1992	40 064	26 666	12 067	29 673	20 586	9 087	9 060	6 079	2 980	1 331
1993	40 622	27 046	12 291	30 233	20 796	9 437	9 104	6 249	2 854	1 285
1994	41 795	28 179	12 287	30 895	21 663	9 233	9 570	6 516	3 054	1 329
1995	42 423	28 931	12 000	31 298	22 239	9 059	9 633	6 692	2 941	1 492
1996	42 964	29 381	11 897	31 231	22 092	9 139	10 047	7 289	2 758	1 685
1997	43 488	30 308	11 400	31 509	22 602	8 906	10 199	7 705	2 493	1 781
1998	43 771	30 579	11 367	31 707	22 706	9 001	10 238	7 873	2 365	1 826
1999	44 110	30 885	11 370	31 975	22 706	9 269	10 281	8 179	2 101	1 855
2000	44 562	31 531	11 198	32 732	23 393	9 339	9 997	8 138	1 859	1 833
2001	44 458	31 411	11 153	32 957	23 599	9 358	9 608	7 813	1 795	1 894
2002	44 865	31 437	11 510	32 799	23 296	9 504	10 148	8 142	2 006	1 918
2003	45 273	31 559	11 635	32 782	23 160	9 622	10 412	8 399	2 013	2 080
2004	45 066	31 040	11 968	32 506	22 736	9 769	10 502	8 304	2 199	2 058
2005	45 027	30 930	11 995	32 412	22 565	9 847	10 514	8 366	2 148	2 102
2006	45 039	30 591	12 250	32 311	22 315	9 996	10 530	8 276	2 254	2 198
2007	45 155	31 252	11 855	32 417	22 788	9 629	10 690	8 464	2 226	2 048
2008	44 909	30 853	11 874	31 990	22 413	9 577	10 737	8 440	2 297	2 182
2009	44 595	30 600	11 811	31 966	22 425	9 537	10 449	8 175	2 274	2 180
2010	44 456	30 209	11 922	31 468	21 957	9 510	10 663	8 251	2 412	2 325
Children Under 6 Years										
1990	20 502	10 907	9 031	16 171	9 010	7 161	3 767	1 897	1 870	563
1991	20 860	11 162	9 134	16 313	9 148	7 165	3 983	2 013	1 969	563
1992	21 198	11 415	9 109	16 293	9 296	6 997	4 232	2 119	2 112	674
1993	21 398	11 496	9 153	16 266	9 258	7 008	4 383	2 239	2 145	749
1994	21 612	12 007	8 901	16 352	9 617	6 735	4 556	2 391	2 166	704
1995	21 566	12 435	8 421	16 377	9 951	6 427	4 478	2 484	1 995	710
1996	21 542	12 192	8 552	16 253	9 672	6 581	4 491	2 520	1 971	799
1997	21 222	12 439	7 823	16 020	9 661	6 359	4 243	2 778	1 464	959
1998	21 272	12 577	7 703	16 201	9 827	6 375	4 079	2 751	1 328	992
1999	21 081	12 533	7 704	15 971	9 487	6 484	4 267	3 046	1 220	844
2000	21 039	12 657	7 476	16 170	9 757	6 413	3 963	2 901	1 062	906
2001	21 318	12 640	7 711	16 395	9 837	6 558	3 956	2 802	1 153	968
2002	21 113	12 384	7 733	16 037	9 377	6 660	4 080	3 007	1 073	996
2003	21 248	12 210	8 147	16 222	9 251	6 971	4 136	2 960	1 176	890
2004	21 321	12 104	8 261	16 151	9 156	6 995	4 214	2 948	1 266	956
2005	21 498	12 308	8 184	16 276	9 321	6 955	4 216	2 987	1 229	1 006
2006	21 844	12 687	8 190	16 542	9 631	6 911	4 335	3 057	1 278	968
2007	22 073	12 864	8 218	16 509	9 708	6 802	4 572	3 156	1 416	991
2008	22 244	12 946	8 092	16 313	9 697	6 616	4 724	3 248	1 476	1 207
2009	22 318	12 909	8 263	16 418	9 640	6 778	4 755	3 270	1 485	1 146
2010	22 355	13 127	7 991	16 262	9 729	6 533	4 855	3 398	1 457	1 237

Note: See notes and definitions for information on historical comparability.

Table 1-50. Number of Families and Median Family Income, by Type of Family and Earner Status of Members, 1990–2009

(Thousands of families, dollars.)

Number and type of families and median family income	1990	1991	1992	1993	1994	1995	1996	1997	1998	1999
NUMBER OF FAMILIES										
Married-Couple Families, Total	52 241	52 549	53 254	53 248	53 929	53 621	53 654	54 362	54 829	55 352
No earners	6 765	7 101	7 250	7 281	7 225	7 276	7 145	7 286	7 257	7 160
One earner	11 630	11 553	12 053	11 806	11 715	11 708	11 493	11 700	12 246	12 290
Husband	9 110	8 907	9 182	8 715	8 673	8 792	8 611	8 770	9 173	9 062
Wife	1 816	1 987	2 145	2 405	2 364	2 251	2 207	2 298	2 411	2 585
Other family member	703	659	726	686	678	666	674	632	662	643
Two earners	25 896	26 037	26 344	26 742	27 263	27 180	27 260	27 712	27 593	28 010
Husband and wife	23 697	23 880	24 255	24 543	25 123	25 274	25 274	25 731	25 696	26 134
Husband and other family member	1 711	1 633	1 447	1 582	1 565	1 393	1 483	1 406	1 306	1 325
Husband not an earner	487	524	642	617	574	513	502	575	590	552
Three earners or more	7 950	7 858	7 606	7 419	7 727	7 456	7 756	7 664	7 733	7 892
Husband and wife	7 029	7 052	6 882	6 723	6 987	6 770	7 126	7 023	7 102	7 220
Husband, not wife	756	595	550	535	543	531	479	478	456	528
Husband not an earner	165	211	175	162	196	155	150	163	176	144
Families Maintained by Women, Total	11 771	12 214	12 504	12 982	12 771	13 007	13 277	13 115	13 206	13 164
No earners	2 623	2 925	2 968	3 100	2 848	2 664	2 574	2 332	2 143	1 883
One earner	5 672	5 926	6 184	6 407	6 506	6 815	7 027	7 091	7 351	7 441
Householder	4 585	4 812	5 042	5 278	5 415	5 590	5 817	5 841	6 167	6 127
Other family member	1 087	1 114	1 142	1 129	1 091	1 225	1 211	1 251	1 183	1 314
Two earners or more	3 476	3 363	3 352	3 476	3 417	3 527	3 675	3 692	3 712	3 840
Householder and other family member(s)	3 146	3 058	2 998	3 139	3 126	3 225	3 431	3 398	3 399	3 508
Householder not an earner	330	305	354	337	291	302	245	294	313	332
Families Maintained by Men, Total	2 948	3 079	3 094	2 992	3 287	3 557	3 924	3 982	4 041	4 086
No earners	296	310	345	329	383	357	359	344	381	376
One earner	1 396	1 541	1 544	1 593	1 705	1 800	1 972	2 104	2 027	2 044
Householder	1 133	1 289	1 305	1 352	1 428	1 548	1 667	1 791	1 725	1 721
Other family member	263	253	239	241	277	253	305	313	302	323
Two earners or more	1 257	1 228	1 204	1 070	1 198	1 400	1 593	1 534	1 634	1 666
Householder and other family member(s)	1 180	1 157	1 117	1 002	1 128	1 302	1 469	1 427	1 532	1 522
Householder not an earner	76	71	88	67	71	98	124	107	102	143
MEDIAN FAMILY INCOME										
Married-Couple Families, Total	39 802	40 746	42 000	43 000	44 893	47 000	49 614	51 475	54 043	56 792
No earners	19 221	20 415	20 023	19 983	20 604	21 888	22 622	23 782	24 525	25 262
One earner	31 020	31 671	32 500	32 084	33 393	35 100	36 468	39 140	40 519	41 261
Husband	32 422	33 208	34 714	34 401	35 000	36 052	38 150	40 300	42 000	44 200
Wife	25 228	26 500	27 343	27 502	28 661	32 098	30 301	34 050	35 625	35 546
Other family member	33 262	33 042	33 622	30 254	32 578	37 784	39 644	40 317	42 414	41 120
Two earners	44 000	45 359	47 737	49 650	51 190	53 500	56 000	58 020	61 300	64 007
Husband and wife	44 031	45 516	48 050	49 980	51 500	53 626	56 392	58 564	61 900	64 950
Husband and other family member	42 602	45 000	45 694	48 862	48 517	52 530	49 610	53 854	57 680	53 541
Husband not an earner	39 494	40 495	40 124	38 800	42 800	47 121	46 990	47 979	50 955	52 466
Three earners or more	59 336	61 120	61 640	63 535	66 172	68 996	70 400	75 593	78 973	81 940
Husband and wife	55 846	61 448	62 674	64 099	66 674	69 371	71 148	76 105	79 907	83 000
Husband, not wife	59 675	60 592	57 015	60 712	63 633	60 360	61 824	68 890	71 001	69 561
Husband not an earner	49 107	44 874	47 551	54 805	54 655	61 196	55 495	62 684	63 205	69 275
Families Maintained by Women, Total	16 351	16 054	16 431	16 800	17 600	19 306	19 416	20 470	21 875	23 100
No earners	5 880	6 060	5 964	6 492	6 805	7 440	7 092	7 476	7 737	8 010
One earner	15 987	16 284	16 468	16 745	17 226	18 824	18 500	19 000	20 000	20 092
Householder	15 001	15 542	15 905	15 700	16 603	17 890	18 000	18 000	18 800	19 000
Other family member	20 173	20 220	19 709	20 800	21 300	23 166	21 000	22 870	25 981	26 800
Two earners or more	30 500	31 508	32 705	33 300	33 820	35 000	36 400	39 275	40 000	41 144
Householder and other family member(s)	30 367	31 550	33 280	33 165	33 357	34 674	36 400	39 000	39 713	40 855
Householder not an earner	32 800	29 477	30 460	35 394	37 531	39 444	38 249	47 471	43 725	48 004
Families Maintained by Men, Total	28 493	28 000	27 400	25 856	27 486	30 000	31 500	32 984	35 000	37 000
No earners	11 386	11 196	9 416	10 900	11 293	12 240	12 030	14 252	15 468	13 752
One earner	25 000	23 715	23 020	22 300	24 011	25 337	26 100	26 897	29 125	31 038
Householder	24 150	23 309	23 000	22 079	24 000	25 069	25 874	27 000	29 125	30 483
Other family member	27 620	25 720	24 359	26 916	26 253	27 291	28 584	25 486	28 241	34 756
Two earners or more	40 000	37 700	39 000	38 000	41 439	43 100	44 275	49 900	51 288	51 040
Householder and other family member(s)	40 256	37 550	39 300	38 363	41 534	43 000	43 065	50 000	50 954	50 960
Householder not an earner	34 064	40 000	36 445	33 700	37 386	55 133	47 001	44 786	68 257	57 407

Note: See notes and definitions for information on historical comparability.

Table 1-50. Number of Families and Median Family Income, by Type of Family and Earner Status of Members, 1990–2009—*Continued*

(Thousands of families, dollars.)

Number and type of families and median family income	2000	2001	2002	2003	2004	2005	2006	2007	2008	2009
NUMBER OF FAMILIES										
Married-Couple Families, Total	55 650	56 798	57 362	57 767	58 180	58 225	59 050	58 490	59 181	58 521
No earners	7 297	7 662	7 803	8 043	7 998	8 017	8 091	7 914	8 083	8 467
One earner	12 450	12 852	13 503	14 061	14 385	14 301	14 562	14 272	14 625	15 046
Husband	9 319	9 573	10 121	10 478	10 853	10 611	10 706	10 396	10 567	10 570
Wife	2 545	2 689	2 821	3 027	2 993	3 097	3 264	3 267	3 437	3 854
Other family member	586	590	560	557	539	593	591	608	620	621
Two earners	28 329	28 779	28 891	28 693	28 806	28 802	29 216	29 256	29 466	28 371
Husband and wife	26 447	26 829	26 966	26 860	26 758	26 833	27 241	27 264	27 531	26 298
Husband and other family member	1 277	1 424	1 391	1 322	1 462	1 376	1 358	1 393	1 308	1 363
Husband not an earner	605	526	534	511	586	594	616	599	627	710
Three earners or more	7 575	7 504	7 165	6 970	6 991	7 104	7 181	7 048	7 008	6 638
Husband and wife	6 917	6 859	6 565	6 349	6 459	6 535	6 620	6 452	6 393	6 024
Husband, not wife	537	530	455	467	381	445	397	452	432	425
Husband not an earner	120	115	145	154	152	124	165	144	182	189
Families Maintained by Women, Total	12 950	13 517	14 033	14 196	14 404	14 505	14 852	14 846	14 842	15 236
No earners	1 786	2 076	2 228	2 451	2 610	2 616	2 627	2 502	2 678	3 076
One earner	7 462	7 693	8 153	8 012	8 074	8 052	8 303	8 418	8 381	8 475
Householder	6 132	6 436	6 832	6 725	6 788	6 724	6 904	7 020	6 978	6 941
Other family member	1 331	1 257	1 321	1 286	1 285	1 329	1 398	1 398	1 404	1 533
Two earners or more	3 702	3 748	3 652	3 733	3 720	3 836	3 923	3 925	3 783	3 685
Householder and other family member(s)	3 376	3 442	3 290	3 364	3 399	3 468	3 547	3 572	3 467	3 281
Householder not an earner	325	306	362	369	321	368	376	353	316	405
Families Maintained by Men, Total	4 316	4 499	4 747	4 778	4 953	5 193	5 119	5 181	5 301	5 630
No earners	380	461	466	530	492	537	555	532	611	539
One earner	2 223	2 319	2 434	2 466	2 573	2 661	2 584	2 703	2 636	2 801
Householder	1 879	1 911	2 026	2 053	2 152	2 196	2 155	2 297	2 199	2 261
Other family member	344	408	408	413	421	464	429	406	437	539
Two earners or more	1 713	1 719	1 847	1 782	1 888	1 995	1 979	1 947	2 054	2 030
Householder and other family member(s)	1 585	1 629	1 709	1 625	1 736	1 848	1 828	1 812	1 889	1 822
Householder not an earner	128	90	138	157	152	147	152	134	165	208
MEDIAN FAMILY INCOME										
Married-Couple Families, Total	59 200	60 100	61 000	62 388	63 627	65 586	69 300	72 802	72 805	71 464
No earners	25 356	25 900	25 954	26 312	26 798	28 376	30 000	30 134	31 164	32 093
One earner	44 424	44 400	45 000	46 546	47 749	50 000	50 400	52 686	53 865	53 087
Husband	47 010	47 500	48 004	48 948	50 000	52 000	53 360	55 350	56 000	53 333
Wife	36 458	36 140	39 072	41 180	41 000	43 505	45 000	47 000	47 015	55 333
Other family member	45 492	44 270	40 927	45 936	46 324	50 263	49 352	48 922	55 114	47 550
Two earners	67 500	69 543	71 282	73 309	75 100	76 960	81 500	85 012	85 500	55 166
Husband and wife	68 132	70 000	72 150	74 500	76 000	77 539	82 762	86 000	86 842	86 361
Husband and other family member	56 503	65 240	62 848	60 100	66 120	67 350	68 828	71 573	68 755	87 939
Husband not an earner	53 430	58 725	54 840	58 000	63 050	65 622	63 657	68 032	66 445	73 720
Three earners or more	83 990	86 090	88 632	93 000	94 212	98 000	103 803	106 747	105 618	70 017
Husband and wife	84 634	87 000	89 962	94 353	95 524	99 800	104 045	107 630	106 493	107 000
Husband, not wife	79 050	76 230	82 180	77 316	87 000	79 417	91 965	101 771	99 731	108 703
Husband not an earner	68 050	80 661	68 400	91 771	73 137	84 638	97 510	92 428	93 961	85 574
										95 251
Families Maintained by Women, Total	25 000	25 064	26 000	26 000	26 400	27 000	28 218	30 000	29 698	29 025
No earners	8 988	8 160	8 808	8 344	8 400	8 228	8 657	8 873	9 404	10 037
One earner	22 306	23 008	24 597	24 752	25 040	25 308	26 393	27 795	28 060	29 000
Householder	21 400	22 001	23 760	23 832	24 801	24 505	25 381	26 644	27 000	27 928
Other family member	27 524	28 476	29 524	28 857	29 700	31 700	31 462	31 950	34 814	34 421
Two earners or more	43 035	45 244	46 580	47 576	48 549	50 000	52 400	55 749	54 369	54 500
Householder and other family member(s)	43 000	44 842	46 000	46 701	47 974	48 989	51 479	55 010	54 306	54 448
Householder not an earner	45 600	51 000	51 248	57 267	56 799	64 805	61 699	64 094	54 978	56 203
Families Maintained by Men, Total	37 040	36 000	37 440	37 914	40 000	40 293	41 130	44 001	43 050	41 000
No earners	14 946	12 840	15 200	15 408	14 167	13 950	15 462	12 921	15 557	15 653
One earner	30 160	30 800	30 139	32 097	35 000	35 001	35 100	37 716	36 806	35 116
Householder	30 816	30 500	30 014	31 355	35 000	35 075	35 011	37 720	37 569	35 117
Other family member	29 118	31 052	32 000	35 525	35 438	35 000	37 840	37 522	34 404	35 086
Two earners or more	55 010	55 024	55 000	57 840	57 600	60 024	61 000	63 600	64 077	64 747
Householder and other family member(s)	55 400	54 850	55 220	57 400	57 058	60 000	61 000	64 000	63 416	64 743
Householder not an earner	51 945	61 824	49 852	64 658	65 400	70 879	62 000	60 498	69 794	65 618

Note: See notes and definitions for information on historical comparability.

Table 1-51. Employment Status of the Foreign-Born and Native-Born Populations, by Selected Characteristics, 2008–2009

(Thousands of people, percent.)

Year and characteristic	Civilian noninstitutional population	Civilian labor force				
		Total	Participation rate	Employed	Unemployed	
					Number	Rate
2008						
TOTAL						
Both sexes, 16 years and over	233 788	154 287	66.0	145 362	8 924	5.8
Men	113 113	82 520	73.0	77 486	5 033	6.1
Women	120 675	71 767	59.5	67 876	3 891	5.4
FOREIGN BORN						
Both sexes, 16 years and over	35 317	24 063	68.1	22 660	1 403	5.8
Men	17 688	14 400	81.4	13 578	822	5.7
Women	17 629	9 663	54.8	9 082	581	6.0
Age						
16 to 24 years	3 845	2 211	57.5	1 979	232	10.5
25 to 34 years	7 992	6 236	78.0	5 866	371	5.9
35 to 44 years	8 327	6 814	81.8	6 473	341	5.0
45 to 54 years	6 602	5 380	81.5	5 083	297	5.5
55 to 64 years	4 126	2 700	65.4	2 580	120	4.5
65 years and over	4 424	721	16.3	679	42	5.9
Race and Hispanic Origin						
White, non-Hispanic	7 517	4 531	60.3	4 305	226	5.0
Black, non-Hispanic	2 743	2 007	73.2	1 863	144	7.2
Asian, non-Hispanic	7 894	5 382	68.2	5 185	197	3.7
Hispanic[1]	16 816	11 889	70.7	11 067	822	6.9
Educational Attainment						
Total, 25 years and over	31 472	21 852	69.4	20 681	1 171	5.4
Less than a high school diploma	9 420	5 759	61.1	5 316	443	7.7
High school graduate, no college[2]	8 098	5 514	68.1	5 201	312	5.7
Some college or associate's degree	4 951	3 648	73.7	3 457	190	5.2
Bachelor's degree or higher[3]	9 003	6 931	77.0	6 705	226	3.3
NATIVE BORN						
Both sexes, 16 years and over	198 471	130 224	65.6	122 703	7 521	5.8
Men	95 424	68 119	71.4	63 908	4 211	6.2
Women	103 047	62 104	60.3	58 795	3 310	5.3
Age						
16 to 24 years	33 639	19 821	58.9	17 223	2 599	13.1
25 to 34 years	32 001	27 096	84.7	25 517	1 579	5.8
35 to 44 years	33 372	28 247	84.6	26 984	1 264	4.5
45 to 54 years	37 357	30 623	82.0	29 446	1 177	3.8
55 to 64 years	29 364	18 915	64.4	18 232	682	3.6
65 years and over	32 737	5 522	16.9	5 300	222	4.0
Race and Hispanic Origin						
White, non-Hispanic	152 157	100 679	66.2	95 909	4 770	4.7
Black, non-Hispanic	24 157	15 101	62.5	13 524	1 577	10.4
Asian, non-Hispanic	2 669	1 674	62.7	1 600	74	4.4
Hispanic[1]	15 325	10 135	66.1	9 279	856	8.4
Educational Attainment						
Total, 25 years and over	164 832	110 403	67.0	105 480	4 923	4.5
Less than a high school diploma	16 702	6 406	38.4	5 757	649	10.1
High school graduates, no college[2]	53 017	32 749	61.8	30 896	1 854	5.7
Some college or associate's degree	46 153	33 070	71.7	31 582	1 488	4.5
Bachelor's degree or higher[3]	48 959	38 177	78.0	37 245	932	2.4

Note: Due to the introduction of revised population controls in January 2009, estimated levels for 2009 are not strictly comparable with those for 2008.

[1]May be of any race.
[2]Includes persons with a high school diploma or equivalent.
[3]Includes persons with bachelor's, master's, professional, and doctoral degrees.

Table 1-51. Employment Status of the Foreign-Born and Native-Born Populations, by Selected Characteristics, 2008–2009—*Continued*

(Thousands of people, percent.)

Year and characteristic	Civilian noninstitutional population	Civilian labor force			Unemployed	
		Total	Participation rate	Employed	Number	Rate
2009						
TOTAL						
Both sexes, 16 years and over	235 801	154 142	65.4	139 877	14 265	9.3
Men	114 136	82 123	72.0	73 670	8 453	10.3
Women	121 665	72 019	59.2	66 208	5 811	8.1
FOREIGN BORN						
Both sexes, 16 years and over	35 216	23 926	67.9	21 608	2 317	9.7
Men	17 628	14 190	80.5	12 765	1 426	10.0
Women	17 588	9 735	55.4	8 844	891	9.2
Age						
16 to 24 years	3 542	1 986	56.1	1 681	304	15.3
25 to 34 years	7 637	5 907	77.3	5 330	577	9.8
35 to 44 years	8 379	6 847	81.7	6 210	637	9.3
45 to 54 years	6 819	5 588	81.9	5 096	491	8.8
55 to 64 years	4 321	2 838	65.7	2 590	249	8.8
65 years and over	4 517	760	16.8	701	59	7.8
Race and Hispanic Origin						
White, non-Hispanic	7 249	4 334	59.8	4 002	332	7.7
Black, non-Hispanic	2 812	2 037	72.4	1 807	231	11.3
Asian, non-Hispanic	7 876	5 332	67.7	4 967	365	6.8
Hispanic[1]	16 933	11 982	70.8	10 612	1 370	11.4
Educational Attainment						
Total, 25 years and over	31 674	21 940	69.3	19 927	2 013	9.2
Less than a high school diploma	9 542	5 862	61.4	5 122	740	12.6
High school graduates, no college[2]	7 992	5 371	67.2	4 875	496	9.2
Some college or associate degree	5 070	3 735	73.7	3 406	328	8.8
Bachelor's degree and higher[3]	9 070	6 972	76.9	6 524	448	6.4
NATIVE BORN						
Both sexes, 16 years and over	200 585	130 216	64.9	118 269	11 947	9.2
Men	96 508	67 933	70.4	60 905	7 028	10.3
Women	104 077	62 284	59.8	57 364	4 920	7.9
Age						
16 to 24 years	34 025	19 375	56.9	15 920	3 455	17.8
25 to 34 years	32 643	27 392	83.9	24 684	2 707	9.9
35 to 44 years	32 540	27 391	84.2	25 307	2 085	7.6
45 to 54 years	37 546	30 617	81.5	28 517	2 101	6.9
55 to 64 years	30 349	19 667	64.8	18 429	1 238	6.3
65 years and over	33 481	5 774	17.2	5 413	362	6.3
Race and Hispanic Origin						
White, non-Hispanic	153 104	100 525	65.7	92 681	7 844	7.8
Black, non-Hispanic	24 466	14 971	61.2	12 700	2 271	15.2
Asian, non-Hispanic	2 756	1 681	61.0	1 542	138	8.2
Hispanic[1]	15 958	10 370	65.0	9 034	1 336	12.9
Educational Attainment						
Total, 25 years and over	166 560	110 842	66.5	102 349	8 492	7.7
Less than a high school diploma	16 587	6 284	37.9	5 249	1 035	16.5
High school graduates, no college[2]	53 477	32 815	61.4	29 612	3 203	9.8
Some college or associate degree	46 657	33 080	70.9	30 482	2 599	7.9
Bachelor's degree or higher[3]	49 839	38 662	77.6	37 007	1 655	4.3

Note: Due to the introduction of revised population controls in January 2009, estimated levels for 2009 are not strictly comparable with those for 2008.

[1]May be of any race.
[2]Includes persons with a high school diploma or equivalent.
[3]Includes persons with bachelor's, master's, professional, and doctoral degrees.

Table 1-52. Employment Status of the Foreign-Born and Native-Born Populations Age 16 Years and Over, by Sex and Presence and Age of Youngest Child, Annual Averages, 2008–2009

(Thousands of people, percent.)

Characteristic	2008			2009		
	Both sexes	Men	Women	Both sexes	Men	Women
FOREIGN BORN						
With Own Children Under 18 Years						
Civilian noninstitutional population	13 864	6 618	7 245	13 723	6 585	7 138
Civilian labor force	10 626	6 228	4 399	10 577	6 209	4 368
Participation rate	76.6	94.1	60.7	77.1	94.3	61.2
Employed	10 047	5 929	4 118	9 573	5 645	3 928
Employment-population ratio	72.5	89.6	56.8	69.8	85.7	55.0
Unemployed	580	299	281	1 003	563	440
Unemployment rate	5.5	4.8	6.4	9.5	9.1	10.1
With Own Children 6 to 17 Years, None Younger						
Civilian noninstitutional population	7 173	3 359	3 814	7 180	3 395	3 785
Civilian labor force	5 791	3 123	2 668	5 834	3 176	2 658
Participation rate	80.7	93.0	69.9	81.2	93.5	70.2
Employed	5 505	2 985	2 520	5 292	2 876	2 416
Employment-population ratio	76.7	88.9	66.1	73.7	84.7	63.8
Unemployed	286	138	148	542	299	242
Unemployment rate	4.9	4.4	5.5	9.3	9.4	9.1
With Own Children Under 6 Years						
Civilian noninstitutional population	6 691	3 259	3 431	6 543	3 190	3 353
Civilian labor force	4 835	3 104	1 731	4 743	3 033	1 710
Participation rate	72.3	95.2	50.4	72.5	95.1	51.0
Employed	4 542	2 944	1 598	4 281	2 769	1 512
Employment-population ratio	67.9	90.3	46.6	65.4	86.8	45.1
Unemployed	294	161	133	461	264	198
Unemployment rate	6.1	5.2	7.7	9.7	8.7	11.6
With Own Children Under 3 Years						
Civilian noninstitutional population	3 923	1 927	1 996	3 758	1 852	1 907
Civilian labor force	2 727	1 837	890	2 632	1 758	874
Participation rate	69.5	95.3	44.6	70.0	95.0	45.8
Employed	2 558	1 745	813	2 379	1 612	767
Employment-population ratio	65.2	90.6	40.7	63.3	87.0	40.2
Unemployed	169	92	78	253	146	107
Unemployment rate	6.2	5.0	8.7	9.6	8.3	12.2
With No Own Children Under 18 Years						
Civilian noninstitutional population	21 453	11 070	10 383	21 493	11 043	10 450
Civilian labor force	13 436	8 173	5 264	13 349	7 982	5 367
Participation rate	62.6	73.8	50.7	62.1	72.3	51.4
Employed	12 613	7 650	4 964	12 035	7 119	4 916
Employment-population ratio	58.8	69.1	47.8	56.0	64.5	47.0
Unemployed	823	523	300	1 314	862	452
Unemployment rate	6.1	6.4	5.7	9.8	10.8	8.4

Note: Due to the introduction of revised population controls in January 2009, estimated levels for 2009 are not strictly comparable with those for 2008.

Table 1-52. Employment Status of the Foreign-Born and Native-Born Populations Age 16 Years and Over, by Sex and Presence and Age of Youngest Child, Annual Averages, 2008–2009—*Continued*

(Thousands of people, percent.)

Characteristic	2008			2009		
	Both sexes	Men	Women	Both sexes	Men	Women
NATIVE BORN						
With Own Children Under 18 Years						
Civilian noninstitutional population	51 642	22 467	29 175	50 974	22 132	28 841
Civilian labor force	42 762	21 144	21 617	42 050	20 720	21 330
Participation rate	82.8	94.1	74.1	82.5	93.6	74.0
Employed	40 859	20 403	20 455	38 934	19 291	19 642
Employment-population ratio	79.1	90.8	70.1	76.4	87.2	68.1
Unemployed	1 903	741	1 162	3 116	1 429	1 687
Unemployment rate	4.5	3.5	5.4	7.4	6.9	7.9
With Own Children 6 to 17 Years, None Younger						
Civilian noninstitutional population	29 259	12 841	16 418	28 548	12 527	16 021
Civilian labor force	24 936	11 955	12 981	24 244	11 589	12 655
Participation rate	85.2	93.1	79.1	84.9	92.5	79.0
Employed	23 974	11 555	12 419	22 653	10 847	11 806
Employment-population ratio	81.9	90.0	75.6	79.4	86.6	73.7
Unemployed	963	400	562	1 591	743	848
Unemployment rate	3.9	3.3	4.3	6.6	6.4	6.7
With Own Children Under 6 Years						
Civilian noninstitutional population	22 384	9 627	12 757	22 426	9 606	12 820
Civilian labor force	17 825	9 189	8 636	17 806	9 131	8 675
Participation rate	79.6	95.5	67.7	79.4	95.1	67.7
Employed	16 885	8 849	8 036	16 281	8 445	7 836
Employment-population ratio	75.4	91.9	63.0	72.6	87.9	61.1
Unemployed	940	340	600	1 525	686	839
Unemployment rate	5.3	3.7	6.9	8.6	7.5	9.7
With Own Children Under 3 Years						
Civilian noninstitutional population	13 358	5 758	7 600	13 293	5 723	7 570
Civilian labor force	10 419	5 517	4 902	10 350	5 438	4 913
Participation rate	78.0	95.8	64.5	77.9	95.0	64.9
Employed	9 841	5 299	4 542	9 442	5 018	4 424
Employment-population ratio	73.7	92.0	59.8	71.0	87.7	58.4
Unemployed	578	218	360	908	420	488
Unemployment rate	5.5	3.9	7.4	8.8	7.7	9.9
With No Own Children Under 18 Years						
Civilian noninstitutional population	146 829	72 957	73 872	149 611	74 375	75 236
Civilian labor force	87 462	46 975	40 487	88 167	47 213	40 954
Participation rate	59.6	64.4	54.8	58.9	63.5	54.4
Employed	81 844	43 505	38 339	79 335	41 614	37 722
Employment-population ratio	55.7	59.6	51.9	53.0	56.0	50.1
Unemployed	5 618	3 470	2 148	8 831	5 599	3 232
Unemployment rate	6.4	7.4	5.3	10.0	11.9	7.9

Note: Due to the introduction of revised population controls in January 2009, estimated levels for 2009 are not strictly comparable with those for 2008.

Table 1-53. Employment Status of the Foreign-Born and Native-Born Populations Age 25 Years and Over, by Educational Attainment, Race, and Hispanic Origin, Annual Averages, 2008–2009

(Thousands of people, percent.)

Characteristic	2008				2009			
	Less than a high school diploma	High school graduate, no college[1]	Some college or associate's degree	Bachelor's degree or higher[2]	Less than a high school diploma	High school graduate, no college[1]	Some college or associate's degree	Bachelor's degree or higher[2]
FOREIGN BORN								
White, Non-Hispanic								
Civilian noninstitutional population	891	1 884	1 360	2 744	832	1 729	1 370	2 763
Civilian labor force	276	990	885	2 024	266	899	865	2 004
Participation rate	30.9	52.5	65.1	73.7	32.0	52.0	63.1	72.5
Employed	253	939	838	1 952	238	823	804	1 877
Employment-population ratio	28.4	49.9	61.6	71.2	28.6	47.6	58.6	67.9
Unemployed	22	50	48	71	28	77	61	127
Unemployment rate	8.1	5.1	5.4	3.5	10.7	8.5	7.1	6.4
Black, Non-Hispanic								
Civilian noninstitutional population	334	758	629	677	347	748	661	719
Civilian labor force	192	561	501	582	194	544	525	615
Participation rate	57.4	74.0	79.7	86.0	56.0	72.7	79.5	85.5
Employed	176	516	466	559	164	482	474	563
Employment-population ratio	52.9	68.1	74.0	82.5	47.2	64.4	71.7	78.3
Unemployed	15	45	36	24	30	62	52	52
Unemployment rate	7.9	8.0	7.1	4.1	15.7	11.4	9.8	8.5
Asian, Non-Hispanic								
Civilian noninstitutional population	864	1 453	1 033	3 880	936	1 425	1 032	3 881
Civilian labor force	402	951	758	2 979	419	878	759	3 016
Participation rate	46.6	65.5	73.4	76.8	44.8	61.6	73.6	77.7
Employed	375	913	725	2 898	386	814	696	2 841
Employment-population ratio	43.4	62.8	70.2	74.7	41.3	57.2	67.5	73.2
Unemployed	27	39	33	81	33	64	64	175
Unemployment rate	6.8	4.1	4.4	2.7	7.9	7.3	8.4	5.8
Hispanic[3]								
Civilian noninstitutional population	7 292	3 940	1 852	1 579	7 376	4 020	1 929	1 596
Civilian labor force	4 871	2 967	1 439	1 245	4 959	3 002	1 526	1 247
Participation rate	66.8	75.3	77.7	78.9	67.2	74.7	79.1	78.1
Employed	4 495	2 790	1 368	1 198	4 314	2 712	1 378	1 158
Employment-population ratio	61.6	70.8	73.9	75.9	58.5	67.5	71.5	72.5
Unemployed	376	177	71	47	644	289	147	89
Unemployment rate	7.7	6.0	5.0	3.7	13.0	9.6	9.7	7.1
NATIVE BORN								
White, Non-Hispanic								
Civilian noninstitutional population	10 723	41 180	35 972	41 982	10 507	41 552	36 165	42 586
Civilian labor force	3 975	24 863	25 386	32 458	3 860	24 975	25 328	32 751
Participation rate	37.1	60.4	70.6	77.3	36.7	60.1	70.0	76.9
Employed	3 644	23 659	24 397	31 727	3 295	22 797	23 543	31 445
Employment-population ratio	34.0	57.5	67.8	75.6	31.4	54.9	65.1	73.8
Unemployed	331	1 204	990	731	565	2 178	1 785	1 306
Unemployment rate	8.3	4.8	3.9	2.3	14.6	8.7	7.0	4.0
Black, Non-Hispanic								
Civilian noninstitutional population	3 128	6 923	5 533	3 582	3 112	6 897	5 738	3 659
Civilian labor force	1 167	4 467	4 125	2 881	1 099	4 392	4 158	2 923
Participation rate	37.3	64.5	74.6	80.4	35.3	63.7	72.5	79.9
Employed	979	4 046	3 815	2 769	851	3 760	3 673	2 717
Employment-population ratio	31.3	58.4	69.0	77.3	27.4	54.5	64.0	74.3
Unemployed	187	420	310	113	248	631	486	206
Unemployment rate	16.0	9.4	7.5	3.9	22.6	14.4	11.7	7.0
Asian, Non-Hispanic								
Civilian noninstitutional population	147	360	442	929	126	360	465	962
Civilian labor force	57	210	308	737	51	201	315	779
Participation rate	38.9	58.2	69.6	79.3	40.2	55.7	67.8	81.0
Employed	55	200	301	715	47	186	291	743
Employment-population ratio	37.7	55.4	68.2	76.9	37.3	51.5	62.5	77.2
Unemployed	2	10	6	23	4	15	25	36
Unemployment rate	2.9	4.9	2.1	3.1	7.4	7.6	7.8	4.7
Hispanic[3]								
Civilian noninstitutional population	2 264	3 587	3 131	1 835	2 388	3 716	3 174	1 947
Civilian labor force	1 040	2 609	2 476	1 588	1 105	2 656	2 501	1 648
Participation rate	45.9	72.8	79.1	86.5	46.3	71.5	78.8	84.7
Employed	931	2 442	2 353	1 537	918	2 357	2 278	1 571
Employment-population ratio	41.1	68.1	75.2	83.8	38.5	63.4	71.8	80.7
Unemployed	109	167	123	50	186	299	223	77
Unemployment rate	10.4	6.4	5.0	3.2	16.9	11.3	8.9	4.7

Note: Due to the introduction of revised population controls in January 2009, estimated levels for 2009 are not strictly comparable with those for 2008. Data for race/ethnicity groups do not sum to total because data are not presented for all races.

[1] Includes persons with a high school diploma or equivalent.
[2] Includes persons with bachelor's, master's, professional, and doctoral degrees.
[3] May be of any race.

Table 1-54. Employed Foreign-Born and Native-Born Persons Age 16 Years and Over, by Occupation and Sex, 2008–2009 Annual Averages

(Thousands of people, percent.)

Occupation	2008					
	Foreign born			Native born		
	Both sexes	Male	Female	Both sexes	Male	Female
TOTAL EMPLOYED	22 660	13 578	9 082	122 703	63 908	58 795
Percent Employed	100.0	100.0	100.0	100.0	100.0	100.0
Management, professional, and related	28.2	25.9	31.5	37.8	35.1	40.7
Management, business, and financial operations	10.8	10.6	11.0	16.0	17.5	14.3
Management	7.7	8.3	6.8	11.5	13.8	9.0
Business and financial operations	3.1	2.3	4.2	4.5	3.8	5.3
Professional and related	17.4	15.3	20.5	21.8	17.6	26.4
Computer and mathematical	3.6	4.7	2.1	2.3	3.3	1.2
Architecture and engineering	2.0	2.9	0.8	2.0	3.4	0.6
Life, physical, and social sciences	1.2	1.2	1.2	0.9	0.9	0.8
Community and social services	0.9	0.7	1.1	1.7	1.3	2.2
Legal	0.4	0.3	0.7	1.3	1.2	1.4
Education, training, and library	3.3	1.8	5.4	6.4	3.1	10.0
Arts, design, entertainment, sports, and media	1.4	1.2	1.6	2.0	2.0	2.0
Health care practitioner and technical	4.6	2.6	7.8	5.2	2.4	8.2
Services	23.2	17.7	31.3	15.6	12.6	18.9
Health care support	2.5	0.5	5.4	2.2	0.5	4.0
Protective services	0.9	1.1	0.6	2.3	3.4	1.1
Food preparation and serving related	7.5	7.3	7.7	5.0	3.8	6.3
Building and grounds cleaning and maintenance	8.2	7.2	9.7	2.9	3.6	2.2
Personal care and services	4.1	1.5	7.9	3.3	1.3	5.3
Sales and office	17.2	12.4	24.3	25.8	17.8	34.5
Sales and related	8.9	7.8	10.6	11.6	11.2	12.1
Office and administrative support	8.3	4.6	13.8	14.2	6.6	22.4
Natural resources, construction, and maintenance	15.1	24.2	1.5	9.3	17.0	0.8
Farming, fishing, and forestry	1.7	2.2	0.9	0.5	0.7	0.2
Construction and extraction	10.4	17.2	0.4	5.1	9.6	0.3
Installation, maintenance, and repair	3.0	4.8	0.2	3.6	6.7	0.3
Production, transportation, and material moving	16.4	19.7	11.3	11.5	17.4	5.0
Production	9.3	9.9	8.4	5.6	7.8	3.2
Transportation and material moving	7.1	9.9	2.9	5.9	9.6	1.8

Occupation	2009					
	Foreign born			Native born		
	Both sexes	Male	Female	Both sexes	Male	Female
TOTAL EMPLOYED	21 608	12 765	8 844	118 269	60 905	57 364
Percent Employed	100.0	100.0	100.0	100.0	100.0	100.0
Management, professional, and related	28.9	26.5	32.5	38.9	36.1	41.8
Management, business, and financial operations	10.7	10.7	10.7	16.3	18.0	14.4
Management	7.6	8.6	6.3	11.7	14.1	9.1
Business and financial operations	3.0	2.1	4.3	4.6	3.9	5.3
Professional and related	18.2	15.8	21.8	22.6	18.1	27.4
Computer and mathematical	3.3	4.2	2.1	2.3	3.4	1.2
Architecture and engineering	2.1	3.1	0.7	1.9	3.2	0.5
Life, physical, and social sciences	1.2	1.2	1.3	0.9	0.9	0.9
Community and social services	1.0	0.7	1.4	1.8	1.3	2.4
Legal	0.5	0.4	0.6	1.4	1.3	1.4
Education, training, and library	3.5	2.1	5.5	6.7	3.2	10.3
Arts, design, entertainment, sports, and media	1.3	1.3	1.5	2.1	2.1	2.0
Health care practitioner and technical	5.3	2.8	8.7	5.6	2.6	8.7
Services	24.7	19.0	32.8	16.3	13.3	19.5
Health care support	2.6	0.6	5.6	2.3	0.4	4.3
Protective services	1.0	1.3	0.6	2.5	3.8	1.1
Food preparation and serving related	8.0	8.0	8.0	5.1	3.9	6.3
Building and grounds cleaning and maintenance	8.5	7.4	10.2	3.0	3.7	2.2
Personal care and services	4.5	1.7	8.5	3.4	1.5	5.6
Sales and office	17.0	12.8	23.1	25.5	17.8	33.5
Sales and related	8.9	8.1	10.0	11.6	11.2	12.0
Office and administrative support	8.2	4.7	13.1	13.9	6.6	21.6
Natural resources, construction, and maintenance	13.5	21.9	1.4	8.8	16.3	0.8
Farming, fishing, and forestry	1.6	2.2	0.8	0.5	0.7	0.2
Construction and extraction	8.8	14.8	0.3	4.7	8.8	0.3
Installation, maintenance, and repair	3.0	4.9	0.3	3.6	6.8	0.3
Production, transportation, and material moving	15.8	19.8	10.1	10.6	16.4	4.4
Production	8.5	9.2	7.5	4.9	7.1	2.6
Transportation and material moving	7.4	10.6	2.7	5.7	9.3	1.8

Note: Due to the introduction of revised population controls in January 2009, estimated levels for 2009 are not strictly comparable with those for 2008.

Table 1-55.   Median Usual Weekly Earnings of Full-Time Wage and Salary Workers for the Foreign-Born and Native-Born Populations, by Selected Characteristics, 2008–2009 Annual Averages

(Thousands of people, dollars, percent.)

Year and characteristic	Foreign born		Native born		Earnings of foreign born as a percent of earnings of native born[1]
	Number	Median weekly earnings	Number	Median weekly earnings	
2008					
Both Sexes, 16 Years and Over	17 328	595	89 320	744	79.9
Men	10 848	613	48 591	842	72.9
Women	6 480	557	40 729	651	85.5
Age					
16 to 24 years	1 337	402	9 284	451	89.1
25 to 34 years	4 786	572	20 857	689	83.0
35 to 44 years	5 118	635	21 290	842	75.4
45 to 54 years	3 846	663	22 794	848	78.2
55 to 64 years	1 849	661	12 914	849	77.9
65 years and over	392	568	2 181	659	86.2
Race and Hispanic Origin					
White, non-Hispanic	2 984	846	68 334	788	107.3
Black, non-Hispanic	1 472	601	10 905	588	102.2
Asian, non-Hispanic	3 988	864	1 184	865	99.8
Hispanic[2]	8 686	483	7 122	621	77.8
Educational Attainment					
Total, 25 years and over	15 992	614	80 036	788	78.0
Less than a high school diploma	4 213	417	3 908	493	84.6
High school graduate, no college[3]	3 920	523	23 472	633	82.7
Some college	2 582	651	23 944	729	89.3
Bachelor's degree or higher[4]	5 277	1 092	28 713	1 119	97.6
2009					
Both Sexes, 16 Years and Over	15 965	602	83 855	761	79.1
Men	9 867	620	45 241	864	71.7
Women	6 099	567	38 614	670	84.6
Age					
16 to 24 years	1 085	400	7 873	452	88.5
25 to 34 years	4 185	555	19 675	704	78.8
35 to 44 years	4 709	647	19 659	856	75.5
45 to 54 years	3 718	679	21 605	866	78.4
55 to 64 years	1 886	672	12 842	865	77.7
65 years and over	383	574	2 201	703	81.6
Race and Hispanic Origin					
White, non-Hispanic	2 693	863	64 497	808	106.7
Black, non-Hispanic	1 397	613	9 956	601	102.1
Asian, non-Hispanic	3 726	877	1 101	908	96.6
Hispanic[2]	7 964	479	6 660	632	75.8
Educational Attainment					
Total, 25 years and over	14 881	621	75 982	805	77.1
Less than a high school diploma	3 817	415	3 472	498	83.3
High school graduates, no college[3]	3 611	530	21 766	644	82.3
Some college	2 460	641	22 657	733	87.4
Bachelor's degree and higher[4]	4 993	1 129	28 088	1 138	99.2

Note: Due to the introduction of revised population controls in January 2009, estimated levels for 2009 are not strictly comparable with those for 2008. Data for race/ethnicity groups do not sum to total because data are not presented for all races.

[1]These figures are computed using unrounded medians and may differ slightly from percentages computed using the rounded medians displayed in this table.
[2]May be of any race.
[3]Includes persons with a high school diploma or equivalent.
[4]Includes persons with bachelor's, master's, professional, and doctoral degrees.

Table 1-56. Percent Distribution of the Civilian Labor Force Age 25 to 64 Years, by Educational Attainment, Sex, and Race, March 1990–March 2010

(Thousands of people, percent.)

Sex, race, and year	Civilian labor force	Percent distribution				
		Total	Less than a high school diploma	4 years of high school only	1 to 3 years of college	4 or more years of college
Both Sexes						
1990	99 175	100.0	13.4	39.5	20.7	26.4
1991	100 480	100.0	13.0	39.4	21.1	26.5
1992	102 387	100.0	12.2	36.2	25.2	26.4
1993	103 504	100.0	11.5	35.2	26.3	27.0
1994	104 868	100.0	11.0	34.0	27.7	27.3
1995	106 519	100.0	10.8	33.1	27.8	28.3
1996	108 037	100.0	10.9	32.9	27.7	28.5
1997	110 514	100.0	10.9	33.0	27.4	28.6
1998	111 857	100.0	10.7	32.8	27.4	29.1
1999	112 542	100.0	10.3	32.3	27.4	30.0
2000	114 052	100.0	9.8	31.8	27.9	30.4
2001	115 073	100.0	9.8	31.4	28.1	30.7
2002	117 738	100.0	10.1	30.6	27.7	31.6
2003	119 261	100.0	10.1	30.1	27.8	31.9
2004	119 392	100.0	9.7	30.1	27.8	32.4
2005	120 461	100.0	9.8	30.1	27.8	32.3
2006	122 541	100.0	9.8	29.6	28.0	32.6
2007	124 581	100.0	9.8	29.3	27.3	33.6
2008	125 493	100.0	9.0	28.8	27.9	34.4
2009	125 655	100.0	9.0	28.7	27.9	34.3
2010	126 363	100.0	8.8	29.1	27.5	34.5
Men						
1990	54 476	100.0	15.1	37.2	19.7	28.0
1991	55 165	100.0	14.7	37.5	20.2	27.6
1992	55 917	100.0	13.9	34.7	23.8	27.5
1993	56 544	100.0	13.2	33.9	24.7	28.1
1994	56 633	100.0	12.7	32.9	25.8	28.6
1995	57 454	100.0	12.2	32.3	25.7	29.7
1996	58 121	100.0	12.7	32.2	26.0	29.1
1997	59 268	100.0	12.8	32.2	25.8	29.2
1998	59 905	100.0	12.3	32.3	25.8	29.6
1999	60 030	100.0	11.7	32.0	25.8	30.5
2000	60 510	100.0	11.1	31.8	26.1	30.9
2001	61 091	100.0	11.0	31.6	26.3	31.1
2002	62 794	100.0	11.8	30.6	25.9	31.7
2003	63 466	100.0	12.0	30.1	25.8	32.1
2004	63 699	100.0	11.5	30.5	25.8	32.2
2005	64 562	100.0	11.6	31.4	25.4	31.6
2006	65 708	100.0	11.8	30.7	25.7	31.8
2007	66 742	100.0	11.7	30.6	25.1	32.7
2008	66 957	100.0	11.0	30.3	25.8	33.0
2009	66 843	100.0	10.8	30.4	26.0	32.8
2010	67 261	100.0	10.6	31.2	25.3	32.9
Women						
1990	44 699	100.0	11.3	42.4	21.9	24.5
1991	45 315	100.0	10.9	41.6	22.2	25.2
1992	46 469	100.0	10.2	37.9	26.9	25.0
1993	46 961	100.0	9.3	36.7	28.2	25.8
1994	48 235	100.0	9.1	35.3	29.8	25.8
1995	49 065	100.0	9.1	34.1	30.2	26.6
1996	49 916	100.0	8.8	33.7	29.7	27.8
1997	51 246	100.0	8.7	34.0	29.3	28.0
1998	51 953	100.0	8.8	33.3	29.3	28.6
1999	52 512	100.0	8.7	32.7	29.2	29.5
2000	53 541	100.0	8.4	31.8	30.0	29.8
2001	53 982	100.0	8.5	31.1	30.1	30.2
2002	54 944	100.0	8.2	30.6	29.7	31.5
2003	55 795	100.0	8.0	30.1	30.1	31.8
2004	55 693	100.0	7.7	29.6	30.2	32.5
2005	55 899	100.0	7.8	28.6	30.5	33.1
2006	56 833	100.0	7.6	28.2	30.6	33.6
2007	57 839	100.0	7.5	27.9	29.9	34.6
2008	58 536	100.0	6.7	27.0	30.4	35.9
2009	58 811	100.0	7.0	26.9	30.2	35.9
2010	59 102	100.0	6.8	26.8	30.1	36.3

Table 1-56. Percent Distribution of the Civilian Labor Force Age 25 to 64 Years, by Educational Attainment, Sex, and Race, March 1990–March 2010—*Continued*

(Thousands of people, percent.)

Sex, race, and year	Civilian labor force	Percent distribution				
		Total	Less than a high school diploma	4 years of high school only	1 to 3 years of college	4 or more years of college
White[1]						
1990	85 238	100.0	12.6	39.6	20.6	27.1
1991	86 344	100.0	12.2	39.3	21.1	27.4
1992	87 656	100.0	11.3	36.1	25.5	27.1
1993	88 457	100.0	10.7	35.0	26.4	27.9
1994	89 009	100.0	10.5	33.7	27.7	28.1
1995	90 192	100.0	10.0	32.8	27.8	29.3
1996	91 506	100.0	10.4	32.8	27.5	29.3
1997	93 179	100.0	10.4	32.8	27.3	29.5
1998	93 527	100.0	10.2	32.7	27.4	29.8
1999	94 216	100.0	9.8	32.2	27.2	30.8
2000	95 073	100.0	9.5	31.8	27.7	31.0
2001	95 562	100.0	9.5	31.0	28.0	31.4
2002	97 699	100.0	9.8	30.6	27.6	32.0
2003	98 241	100.0	9.9	30.0	27.7	32.4
2004	98 030	100.0	9.5	29.8	27.8	32.9
2005	98 581	100.0	9.7	29.8	27.8	32.7
2006	100 205	100.0	9.7	29.3	28.1	32.9
2007	101 548	100.0	9.7	29.1	27.3	33.9
2008	102 077	100.0	8.9	28.7	27.8	34.6
2009	102 261	100.0	9.1	28.6	27.7	34.6
2010	102 634	100.0	8.8	29.0	27.4	34.8
Black[1]						
1990	10 537	100.0	19.9	42.5	22.1	15.5
1991	10 650	100.0	19.5	42.9	22.1	15.4
1992	10 936	100.0	19.2	40.3	24.9	15.6
1993	11 051	100.0	16.8	39.5	27.6	16.1
1994	11 368	100.0	14.5	39.3	29.2	17.0
1995	11 695	100.0	14.1	38.6	29.6	17.7
1996	11 891	100.0	14.2	37.2	31.2	17.4
1997	12 253	100.0	14.3	37.8	31.3	16.6
1998	12 893	100.0	14.3	37.3	30.1	18.2
1999	12 945	100.0	13.0	37.2	30.4	19.5
2000	13 383	100.0	11.8	36.1	31.5	20.7
2001	13 617	100.0	12.0	37.1	31.1	19.8
2002	13 319	100.0	12.4	34.5	32.0	21.0
2003	13 315	100.0	11.3	35.6	31.5	21.6
2004	13 372	100.0	11.0	36.6	30.5	21.9
2005	13 635	100.0	11.2	37.3	29.9	21.6
2006	13 855	100.0	10.9	35.6	30.4	23.0
2007	14 186	100.0	10.1	35.4	31.4	23.1
2008	14 356	100.0	9.5	34.3	32.1	24.1
2009	14 325	100.0	8.5	35.1	33.0	23.5
2010	14 483	100.0	8.9	34.5	32.4	24.2

[1]Beginning in 2003, persons who selected this race group only; persons who selected more than one race group are not included. Prior to 2003, persons who reported more than one race group were included in the group they identified as their main race.

Table 1-57. Labor Force Participation Rates of Persons Age 25 to 64 Years, by Educational Attainment, Sex, and Race, March 1990–March 2010

(Civilian labor force as a percent of the civilian noninstitutional population.)

Sex, race, and year	Participation rates				
	Total	Less than a high school diploma	4 years of high school only	1 to 3 years of college	4 or more years of college
Both Sexes					
1990	78.6	60.7	78.2	83.3	88.4
1991	78.6	60.7	78.1	83.2	88.4
1992	79.0	60.3	78.3	83.5	88.4
1993	78.9	59.6	77.7	82.9	88.3
1994	78.9	58.3	77.8	83.2	88.2
1995	79.3	59.8	77.3	83.2	88.7
1996	79.4	60.2	77.9	83.7	87.8
1997	80.1	61.7	78.5	83.7	88.5
1998	80.2	63.0	78.4	83.5	88.0
1999	80.0	62.7	78.1	83.0	87.6
2000	80.3	62.7	78.4	83.2	87.8
2001	80.2	63.5	78.4	83.0	87.0
2002	79.7	63.5	77.7	82.1	86.7
2003	79.4	64.1	76.9	81.9	86.2
2004	78.8	63.2	76.1	81.2	85.9
2005	78.5	62.9	75.7	81.1	85.7
2006	78.7	63.2	75.9	81.0	85.9
2007	79.0	63.7	76.3	81.1	85.9
2008	79.0	62.5	76.0	80.9	86.1
2009	78.6	62.3	75.7	80.3	85.9
2010	78.7	62.7	76.2	79.7	85.7
Men					
1990	88.8	75.1	89.9	91.5	94.5
1991	88.6	75.1	89.3	92.0	94.2
1992	88.6	75.1	89.0	91.8	93.7
1993	88.1	74.9	88.1	90.6	93.7
1994	87.0	71.5	86.8	90.3	93.2
1995	87.4	72.0	86.9	90.1	93.8
1996	87.5	74.3	86.9	90.0	92.9
1997	87.7	75.2	86.4	90.6	93.5
1998	87.8	75.3	86.7	90.0	93.4
1999	87.5	74.4	86.6	89.4	93.0
2000	87.5	74.9	86.2	88.9	93.3
2001	87.4	75.4	85.8	89.1	92.9
2002	87.0	75.5	85.3	88.8	92.4
2003	86.4	76.1	84.3	87.5	92.2
2004	85.9	75.2	83.8	87.0	91.9
2005	86.0	75.7	83.7	87.5	91.7
2006	86.0	76.3	83.4	87.8	91.7
2007	86.2	75.7	83.9	87.2	92.4
2008	85.8	74.8	83.6	86.5	91.9
2009	85.1	73.7	82.3	86.0	91.9
2010	85.3	74.5	83.2	85.3	91.5
Women					
1990	68.9	46.2	68.7	75.9	81.1
1991	69.1	46.2	68.6	75.2	81.8
1992	70.0	45.6	69.1	76.2	82.2
1993	70.0	44.2	68.8	76.1	82.2
1994	71.1	44.7	70.0	77.0	82.5
1995	71.5	47.2	68.9	77.3	82.8
1996	71.8	45.7	69.8	78.1	82.3
1997	72.8	47.1	71.4	77.6	83.2
1998	73.0	49.8	70.9	77.8	82.3
1999	72.8	50.5	70.4	77.4	81.9
2000	73.5	50.4	71.2	78.3	82.0
2001	73.4	51.7	71.3	77.7	80.9
2002	72.7	50.4	70.4	76.4	81.0
2003	72.6	50.5	69.8	77.1	80.1
2004	72.0	49.7	68.6	76.2	80.0
2005	71.4	48.7	67.4	75.8	79.8
2006	71.7	48.3	68.2	75.3	80.4
2007	72.1	49.6	68.4	76.0	79.7
2008	72.5	47.9	68.2	76.1	80.9
2009	72.4	49.0	68.7	75.4	80.5
2010	72.3	48.9	68.6	75.0	80.4

Table 1-57. Labor Force Participation Rates of Persons Age 25 to 64 Years, by Educational Attainment, Sex, and Race, March 1990–March 2010—*Continued*

(Civilian labor force as a percent of the civilian noninstitutional population.)

Sex, race, and year	Participation rates				
	Total	Less than a high school diploma	4 years of high school only	1 to 3 years of college	4 or more years of college
White[1]					
1990	79.2	62.5	78.4	83.3	88.3
1991	79.4	62.5	78.3	83.1	88.6
1992	79.8	61.5	78.7	83.8	88.7
1993	79.7	61.1	78.2	83.1	88.8
1994	79.8	60.3	78.3	83.5	88.5
1995	80.1	61.6	77.9	83.4	88.8
1996	80.4	62.5	78.6	83.9	88.2
1997	81.0	63.8	79.2	83.9	89.0
1998	80.6	63.8	78.6	83.5	88.3
1999	80.6	64.2	78.5	83.3	87.9
2000	80.8	64.2	78.7	83.1	87.9
2001	80.7	64.5	78.7	83.1	87.2
2002	80.3	65.0	78.2	82.4	87.0
2003	80.1	65.7	77.5	82.3	86.5
2004	79.5	64.6	76.7	81.6	86.2
2005	79.2	63.8	76.4	81.5	86.1
2006	79.5	65.1	76.5	81.4	86.2
2007	79.6	65.1	77.2	81.4	86.1
2008	79.6	63.8	76.8	81.2	86.3
2009	79.4	64.7	76.4	80.7	86.2
2010	79.5	64.5	77.1	80.4	86.0
Black[1]					
1990	74.6	54.5	78.2	84.2	92.0
1991	73.9	53.9	77.1	84.1	90.2
1992	74.4	55.4	76.9	83.4	89.1
1993	73.8	53.4	74.7	83.0	89.6
1994	73.5	49.4	75.2	82.4	89.5
1995	74.2	51.0	74.5	82.8	90.9
1996	73.7	50.1	74.3	83.0	87.9
1997	74.9	52.9	75.0	83.8	89.0
1998	77.7	59.3	77.0	85.0	88.8
1999	76.5	55.1	76.5	82.9	88.6
2000	77.9	55.5	77.0	84.2	90.3
2001	78.1	58.7	76.8	83.0	90.5
2002	76.4	56.6	75.0	81.7	88.9
2003	75.8	55.4	73.9	81.2	88.2
2004	75.0	55.2	73.4	79.0	87.9
2005	75.2	58.2	72.6	79.5	87.2
2006	75.0	54.0	73.3	79.6	87.7
2007	75.6	55.3	72.5	80.7	88.0
2008	75.6	54.3	72.8	80.0	87.5
2009	74.4	50.0	72.6	78.7	86.2
2010	74.2	52.2	71.7	77.5	87.0

[1]Beginning in 2003, persons who selected this race group only; persons who selected more than one race group are not included. Prior to 2003, persons who reported more than one race group were included in the group they identified as their main race.

Table 1-58. Unemployment Rates of Persons Age 25 to 64 Years, by Educational Attainment and Sex, March 1990–March 2010

(Unemployment as a percent of the civilian labor force.)

Sex, race, and year	Unemployment rates				
	Total	Less than a high school diploma	4 years of high school only	1 to 3 years of college	4 or more years of college
Both Sexes					
1990	4.5	9.6	4.9	3.7	1.9
1991	6.1	12.3	6.7	5.0	2.9
1992	6.7	13.5	7.7	5.9	2.9
1993	6.4	13.0	7.3	5.5	3.2
1994	5.8	12.6	6.7	5.0	2.9
1995	4.8	10.0	5.2	4.5	2.5
1996	4.8	10.9	5.5	4.1	2.2
1997	4.4	10.4	5.1	3.8	2.0
1998	4.0	8.5	4.8	3.6	1.8
1999	3.5	7.7	4.0	3.1	1.9
2000	3.3	7.9	3.8	3.0	1.5
2001	3.5	8.1	4.2	2.9	2.0
2002	5.0	10.2	6.1	4.5	2.8
2003	5.3	9.9	6.4	5.2	3.0
2004	5.1	10.5	5.9	4.9	2.9
2005	4.4	9.0	5.5	4.1	2.3
2006	4.1	8.3	4.7	3.9	2.3
2007	3.9	8.5	4.7	3.7	1.8
2008	4.4	10.1	5.8	4.2	2.1
2009	8.1	15.8	10.4	8.0	4.3
2010	9.1	16.8	12.1	8.8	4.7
Men					
1990	4.8	9.6	5.3	3.9	2.1
1991	6.8	13.4	7.7	5.2	3.2
1992	7.5	14.8	8.8	6.4	3.2
1993	7.3	14.1	8.7	6.3	3.4
1994	6.2	12.8	7.2	5.3	2.9
1995	5.1	10.9	5.7	4.4	2.6
1996	5.3	11.0	6.4	4.5	2.3
1997	4.7	9.9	5.6	4.0	2.1
1998	4.1	8.0	5.1	3.7	1.7
1999	3.5	7.0	4.1	3.2	1.9
2000	3.3	7.1	3.9	3.1	1.6
2001	3.7	7.5	4.6	3.2	1.9
2002	5.5	9.9	6.7	4.9	3.0
2003	5.8	9.5	6.9	6.0	3.2
2004	5.4	9.4	6.6	5.4	3.0
2005	4.7	7.9	6.0	4.3	2.5
2006	4.3	7.6	5.0	4.2	2.4
2007	4.3	8.4	5.5	3.9	1.9
2008	4.9	10.9	6.3	4.2	2.0
2009	9.5	16.5	12.4	9.3	4.7
2010	10.5	17.8	13.8	10.2	5.1
Women					
1990	4.2	9.5	4.6	3.5	1.7
1991	5.2	10.7	5.5	4.8	2.5
1992	5.7	11.4	6.5	5.3	2.5
1993	5.2	11.2	5.8	4.6	2.9
1994	5.4	12.4	6.2	4.7	2.9
1995	4.4	8.6	4.6	4.5	2.4
1996	4.1	10.7	4.4	3.8	2.1
1997	4.1	11.3	4.5	3.6	2.0
1998	3.9	9.3	4.4	3.5	1.9
1999	3.5	8.8	3.9	3.0	1.9
2000	3.2	9.1	3.6	2.9	1.4
2001	3.3	8.9	3.8	2.6	2.0
2002	4.6	10.6	5.4	4.1	2.6
2003	4.8	10.6	5.9	4.4	2.8
2004	4.7	12.2	5.2	4.3	2.9
2005	4.2	10.9	4.8	4.0	2.2
2006	3.8	9.4	4.4	3.7	2.1
2007	3.4	8.5	3.8	3.6	1.8
2008	4.0	8.5	5.1	4.2	2.1
2009	6.6	14.5	7.9	6.7	4.0
2010	7.5	15.0	9.8	7.5	4.3

Table 1-58. Unemployment Rates of Persons Age 25 to 64 Years, by Educational Attainment and Sex, March 1990–March 2010—*Continued*

(Unemployment as a percent of the civilian labor force.)

Sex, race, and year	Unemployment rates				
	Total	Less than a high school diploma	4 years of high school only	1 to 3 years of college	4 or more years of college
White[1]					
1990	4.0	8.3	4.4	3.3	1.8
1991	5.6	11.6	6.2	4.6	2.7
1992	6.0	12.9	6.8	5.3	2.7
1993	5.8	12.4	6.5	5.0	3.1
1994	5.2	11.7	5.8	4.5	2.6
1995	4.3	9.2	4.6	4.2	2.3
1996	4.2	10.2	4.6	3.7	2.1
1997	3.9	9.4	4.6	3.4	1.8
1998	3.5	7.5	4.2	3.2	1.7
1999	3.1	7.0	3.4	2.8	1.7
2000	3.0	7.5	3.3	2.7	1.4
2001	3.1	7.2	3.6	2.7	1.8
2002	4.6	9.1	5.5	4.1	2.6
2003	4.7	9.0	5.7	4.5	2.7
2004	4.6	9.6	5.4	4.4	2.8
2005	3.9	7.7	4.9	3.6	2.2
2006	3.5	7.1	4.0	3.5	2.1
2007	3.5	7.8	4.2	3.3	1.7
2008	4.0	9.2	5.1	3.7	1.9
2009	7.6	15.2	9.9	7.4	4.0
2010	8.4	16.3	11.3	8.1	4.3
Black[1]					
1990	8.6	15.9	8.6	6.5	1.9
1991	10.1	15.9	10.3	8.0	5.2
1992	12.4	17.2	14.1	10.7	4.8
1993	10.9	17.3	12.4	8.7	4.1
1994	10.6	17.4	12.2	8.3	4.9
1995	7.7	13.7	8.4	6.3	4.1
1996	8.9	15.3	10.8	6.9	3.3
1997	8.1	16.6	8.2	6.1	4.4
1998	7.3	13.4	8.4	6.4	2.1
1999	6.3	12.0	6.7	5.2	3.3
2000	5.4	10.4	6.3	4.3	2.5
2001	6.5	14.0	7.7	4.3	3.3
2002	8.1	15.4	9.7	6.0	4.1
2003	9.0	14.7	9.9	8.9	4.7
2004	8.4	15.8	9.3	7.9	3.7
2005	8.3	17.9	8.6	7.5	3.6
2006	7.8	16.4	9.0	6.5	3.6
2007	6.5	14.0	7.7	5.7	2.5
2008	7.6	16.7	9.3	6.5	3.3
2009	12.1	22.0	14.0	11.2	7.2
2010	14.1	22.4	17.5	12.9	7.9

[1]Beginning in 2003, persons who selected this race group only; persons who selected more than one race group are not included. Prior to 2003, persons who reported more than one race group were included in the group they identified as their main race.

Table 1-59. Workers Age 25 to 64 Years, by Educational Attainment, Occupation of Longest Job Held, and Sex, 2008–2009

(Thousands of people with work experience during the year.)

Year, sex, and occupation	Total	Less than a high school diploma	4 years of high school only	1 to 3 years of college	4 or more years of college
2008					
Both Sexes	128 339	11 478	36 732	36 103	44 027
Management, business, and financial operations	20 566	406	3 516	5 037	11 608
Management	14 645	360	2 768	3 595	7 923
Business and financial operations	5 921	45	748	1 442	3 685
Professional and related	28 527	167	2 117	6 279	19 965
Computer and mathematical	3 494	14	240	828	2 412
Architecture and engineering	2 574	4	228	643	1 699
Life, physical, and social sciences	1 242	1	67	138	1 036
Community and social services	2 065	27	178	351	1 509
Legal	1 545	3	86	218	1 238
Education, training, and library	8 201	41	547	1 112	6 501
Arts, design, entertainment, sports, and media	2 404	49	293	552	1 510
Health care practitioner and technical	7 001	27	477	2 437	4 060
Services	19 346	3 536	7 368	5 877	2 565
Health care support	2 762	267	970	1 220	305
Protective services	2 594	90	707	1 089	708
Food preparation and serving related	5 056	1 143	2 129	1 227	557
Building and grounds cleaning and maintenance	4 886	1 496	2 118	958	313
Personal care and services	4 048	539	1 444	1 382	682
Sales and office	29 191	1 375	9 606	10 798	7 412
Sales and related	12 864	768	3 764	4 103	4 230
Office and administrative support	16 326	607	5 842	6 695	3 183
Natural resources, construction, and maintenance	13 756	2 878	6 121	3 773	984
Farming, fishing, and forestry	891	446	286	100	58
Construction and extraction	8 094	1 962	3 754	1 850	528
Installation, maintenance, and repair	4 771	470	2 081	1 822	398
Production, transportation, and material moving	16 323	3 112	7 869	4 066	1 276
Production	8 206	1 618	3 853	2 092	642
Transportation and material moving	8 117	1 494	4 016	1 974	633
Armed forces	631	4	136	274	217
Men	68 130	7 341	20 570	17 879	22 340
Management, business, and financial operations	11 549	286	1 937	2 646	6 680
Management	9 098	271	1 757	2 179	4 891
Business and financial operations	2 452	15	179	468	1 790
Professional and related	11 866	75	741	2 259	8 792
Computer and mathematical	2 593	13	172	607	1 801
Architecture and engineering	2 240	2	177	575	1 485
Life, physical, and social sciences	634	1	34	80	519
Community and social services	709	17	56	115	521
Legal	753	3	15	23	712
Education, training, and library	2 008	3	46	166	1 793
Arts, design, entertainment, sports, and media	1 240	30	178	306	727
Health care practitioner and technical	1 690	6	64	387	1 233
Services	7 910	1 455	2 902	2 365	1 188
Health care support	258	20	80	100	58
Protective services	1 961	59	517	863	522
Food preparation and serving related	2 139	511	864	522	242
Building and grounds cleaning and maintenance	2 784	802	1 171	620	191
Personal care and services	768	63	270	259	176
Sales and office	10 468	539	2 884	3 479	3 566
Sales and related	6 756	303	1 674	2 104	2 675
Office and administrative support	3 712	237	1 210	1 375	890
Natural resources, construction, and maintenance	13 166	2 735	5 910	3 612	909
Farming, fishing, and forestry	680	341	233	64	41
Construction and extraction	7 901	1 942	3 666	1 790	502
Installation, maintenance, and repair	4 585	452	2 011	1 757	365
Production, transportation, and material moving	12 591	2 248	6 071	3 265	1 008
Production	5 803	1 043	2 715	1 610	435
Transportation and material moving	6 788	1 204	3 356	1 655	573
Armed forces	579	3	126	253	197
Women	60 209	4 137	16 162	18 224	21 687
Management, business, and financial operations	9 017	120	1 579	2 391	4 927
Management	5 548	90	1 011	1 416	3 032
Business and financial operations	3 469	30	569	975	1 896
Professional and related	16 660	92	1 376	4 020	11 173
Computer and mathematical	902	1	68	221	611
Architecture and engineering	334	2	51	68	214
Life, physical, and social sciences	608	. . .	33	58	517
Community and social services	1 356	10	122	236	988
Legal	792	. . .	71	194	526
Education, training, and library	6 193	38	501	946	4 708
Arts, design, entertainment, sports, and media	1 164	19	115	247	783
Health care practitioner and technical	5 311	21	414	2 050	2 826
Services	11 435	2 081	4 465	3 512	1 377
Health care support	2 504	247	890	1 119	247
Protective services	632	31	189	226	186
Food preparation and serving related	2 918	633	1 264	706	315
Building and grounds cleaning and maintenance	2 102	694	947	338	123
Personal care and services	3 279	476	1 174	1 123	507
Sales and office	18 723	836	6 722	7 319	3 846
Sales and related	6 108	465	2 090	1 999	1 554
Office and administrative support	12 614	370	4 632	5 320	2 292
Natural resources, construction, and maintenance	591	142	212	161	75
Farming, fishing, and forestry	211	104	54	36	17
Construction and extraction	193	20	88	60	26
Installation, maintenance, and repair	186	18	70	65	32
Production, transportation, and material moving	3 731	865	1 798	801	267
Production	2 402	575	1 138	482	207
Transportation and material moving	1 329	290	660	319	61
Armed forces	52	1	10	21	20

. . . = Not available.

Table 1-59. Workers Age 25 to 64 Years, by Educational Attainment, Occupation of Longest Job Held, and Sex, 2008–2009—*Continued*

(Thousands of people with work experience during the year.)

Year, sex, and occupation	Total	Less than a high school diploma	4 years of high school only	1 to 3 years of college	4 or more years of college
2009					
Both Sexes	126 188	10 799	36 267	35 059	44 064
Management, business, and financial operations	19 958	420	3 371	4 832	11 335
Management	14 294	368	2 697	3 519	7 711
Business and financial operations	5 664	52	674	1 313	3 624
Professional and related	28 756	147	2 304	6 412	19 893
Computer and mathematical	3 465	13	269	920	2 263
Architecture and engineering	2 425	. . .	220	582	1 623
Life, physical, and social sciences	1 261	4	99	130	1 028
Community and social services	2 156	20	170	399	1 566
Legal	1 530	6	76	230	1 218
Education, training, and library	8 235	35	615	1 074	6 510
Arts, design, entertainment, sports, and media	2 487	46	309	577	1 555
Health care practitioner and technical	7 197	23	545	2 500	4 128
Services	19 912	3 435	7 580	6 097	2 800
Health care support	2 941	280	1 047	1 274	340
Protective services	2 838	88	796	1 197	757
Food preparation and serving related	5 026	1 099	2 026	1 277	624
Building and grounds cleaning and maintenance	4 946	1 495	2 182	904	365
Personal care and services	4 161	473	1 528	1 445	714
Sales and office	28 602	1 320	9 438	10 268	7 576
Sales and related	12 528	726	3 771	3 768	4 263
Office and administrative support	16 074	594	5 668	6 500	3 313
Natural resources, construction, and maintenance	13 406	2 710	6 154	3 518	1 025
Farming, fishing, and forestry	930	433	304	128	64
Construction and extraction	7 854	1 810	3 745	1 767	532
Installation, maintenance, and repair	4 622	466	2 104	1 623	429
Production, transportation, and material moving	14 866	2 760	7 269	3 626	1 211
Production	7 502	1 496	3 553	1 830	623
Transportation and material moving	7 364	1 264	3 716	1 796	588
Armed forces	689	6	151	306	225
Men	66 826	6 847	20 605	17 084	22 290
Management, business, and financial operations	11 359	306	1 892	2 580	6 581
Management	8 870	283	1 678	2 103	4 807
Business and financial operations	2 489	24	214	476	1 774
Professional and related	11 980	65	865	2 281	8 769
Computer and mathematical	2 462	9	171	650	1 633
Architecture and engineering	2 108	. . .	194	503	1 412
Life, physical, and social sciences	628	3	59	65	501
Community and social services	746	9	63	133	541
Legal	735	. . .	17	27	691
Education, training, and library	2 128	8	79	165	1 876
Arts, design, entertainment, sports, and media	1 367	32	189	342	804
Health care practitioner and technical	1 805	4	94	396	1 312
Services	8 351	1 403	3 124	2 483	1 341
Health care support	300	27	83	122	68
Protective services	2 186	58	593	961	574
Food preparation and serving related	2 246	496	906	539	305
Building and grounds cleaning and maintenance	2 794	739	1 260	576	219
Personal care and services	825	83	281	286	175
Sales and office	10 284	528	2 940	3 291	3 525
Sales and related	6 419	315	1 648	1 907	2 549
Office and administrative support	3 865	213	1 292	1 384	975
Natural resources, construction, and maintenance	12 731	2 542	5 919	3 334	936
Farming, fishing, and forestry	661	298	249	72	42
Construction and extraction	7 633	1 785	3 638	1 707	504
Installation, maintenance, and repair	4 436	459	2 032	1 556	390
Production, transportation, and material moving	11 512	1 999	5 720	2 843	950
Production	5 370	968	2 613	1 353	437
Transportation and material moving	6 141	1 031	3 107	1 490	513
Armed forces	610	5	144	272	188
Women	59 362	3 952	15 662	17 975	21 774
Management, business, and financial operations	8 598	114	1 479	2 252	4 753
Management	5 424	85	1 019	1 416	2 904
Business and financial operations	3 175	29	459	837	1 850
Professional and related	16 776	82	1 439	4 132	11 124
Computer and mathematical	1 003	3	99	270	631
Architecture and engineering	317	. . .	26	80	211
Life, physical, and social sciences	633	2	40	64	527
Community and social services	1 410	11	108	266	1 026
Legal	795	6	60	203	527
Education, training, and library	6 107	27	536	909	4 634
Arts, design, entertainment, sports, and media	1 120	14	120	235	751
Health care practitioner and technical	5 391	19	451	2 105	2 816
Services	11 561	2 033	4 456	3 614	1 459
Health care support	2 641	253	964	1 152	272
Protective services	652	30	203	237	183
Food preparation and serving related	2 780	603	1 120	738	319
Building and grounds cleaning and maintenance	2 153	756	923	329	145
Personal care and services	3 336	391	1 247	1 159	539
Sales and office	18 319	793	6 498	6 977	4 051
Sales and related	6 109	412	2 122	1 861	1 714
Office and administrative support	12 210	381	4 376	5 116	2 337
Natural resources, construction, and maintenance	675	168	234	184	88
Farming, fishing, and forestry	268	135	55	56	22
Construction and extraction	221	25	108	60	27
Installation, maintenance, and repair	186	8	71	68	39
Production, transportation, and material moving	3 354	761	1 549	782	261
Production	2 132	528	940	477	186
Transportation and material moving	1 222	232	609	306	75
Armed forces	79	2	6	34	37

. . . = Not available.

Table 1-60. Percent Distribution of Workers Age 25 to 64 Years, by Educational Attainment, Occupation of Longest Job Held, and Sex, 2008–2009

(Percent of total workers in occupation.)

Year, sex, and occupation	Total	Less than a high school diploma	4 years of high school only	1 to 3 years of college	4 or more years of college
2008					
Both Sexes	100.0	8.9	28.6	28.1	34.3
Management, business, and financial operations	100.0	2.0	17.1	24.5	56.4
Management	100.0	2.5	18.9	24.5	54.1
Business and financial operations	100.0	0.8	12.6	24.4	62.2
Professional and related	100.0	0.6	7.4	22.0	70.0
Computer and mathematical	100.0	0.4	6.9	23.7	69.0
Architecture and engineering	100.0	0.1	8.9	25.0	66.0
Life, physical, and social sciences	100.0	0.1	5.4	11.1	83.4
Community and social services	100.0	1.3	8.6	17.0	73.1
Legal	100.0	0.2	5.6	14.1	80.1
Education, training, and library	100.0	0.5	6.7	13.6	79.3
Arts, design, entertainment, sports, and media	100.0	2.0	12.2	23.0	62.8
Health care practitioner and technical	100.0	0.4	6.8	34.8	58.0
Services	100.0	18.3	38.1	30.4	13.3
Health care support	100.0	9.7	35.1	44.2	11.0
Protective services	100.0	3.5	27.2	42.0	27.3
Food preparation and serving related	100.0	22.6	42.1	24.3	11.0
Building and grounds cleaning and maintenance	100.0	30.6	43.3	19.6	6.4
Personal care and services	100.0	13.3	35.7	34.1	16.9
Sales and office	100.0	4.7	32.9	37.0	25.4
Sales and related	100.0	6.0	29.3	31.9	32.9
Office and administrative support	100.0	3.7	35.8	41.0	19.5
Natural resources, construction, and maintenance	100.0	20.9	44.5	27.4	7.2
Farming, fishing, and forestry	100.0	50.0	32.1	11.3	6.6
Construction and extraction	100.0	24.2	46.4	22.9	6.5
Installation, maintenance, and repair	100.0	9.9	43.6	38.2	8.3
Production, transportation, and material moving	100.0	19.1	48.2	24.9	7.8
Production	100.0	19.7	47.0	25.5	7.8
Transportation and material moving	100.0	18.4	49.5	24.3	7.8
Armed forces	100.0	0.7	21.5	43.5	34.4
Men	100.0	10.8	30.2	26.2	32.8
Management, business, and financial operations	100.0	2.5	16.8	22.9	57.8
Management	100.0	3.0	19.3	24.0	53.8
Business and financial operations	100.0	0.6	7.3	19.1	73.0
Professional and related	100.0	0.6	6.2	19.0	74.1
Computer and mathematical	100.0	0.5	6.6	23.4	69.4
Architecture and engineering	100.0	0.1	7.9	25.7	66.3
Life, physical, and social sciences	100.0	0.1	5.4	12.6	81.9
Community and social services	100.0	2.3	7.9	16.3	73.5
Legal	100.0	0.5	1.9	3.1	94.5
Education, training, and library	100.0	0.1	2.3	8.3	89.3
Arts, design, entertainment, sports, and media	100.0	2.4	14.3	24.7	58.6
Health care practitioner and technical	100.0	0.4	3.8	22.9	73.0
Services	100.0	18.4	36.7	29.9	15.0
Health care support	100.0	7.7	31.0	38.8	22.5
Protective services	100.0	3.0	26.4	44.0	26.6
Food preparation and serving related	100.0	23.9	40.4	24.4	11.3
Building and grounds cleaning and maintenance	100.0	28.8	42.0	22.3	6.8
Personal care and services	100.0	8.3	35.1	33.7	22.9
Sales and office	100.0	5.2	27.5	33.2	34.1
Sales and related	100.0	4.5	24.8	31.1	39.6
Office and administrative support	100.0	6.4	32.6	37.0	24.0
Natural resources, construction, and maintenance	100.0	20.8	44.9	27.4	6.9
Farming, fishing, and forestry	100.0	50.2	34.2	9.5	6.1
Construction and extraction	100.0	24.6	46.4	22.7	6.4
Installation, maintenance, and repair	100.0	9.9	43.9	38.3	8.0
Production, transportation, and material moving	100.0	17.9	48.2	25.9	8.0
Production	100.0	18.0	46.8	27.7	7.5
Transportation and material moving	100.0	17.7	49.4	24.4	8.4
Armed forces	100.0	0.5	21.8	43.8	34.0
Women	100.0	6.9	26.8	30.3	36.0
Management, business, and financial operations	100.0	1.3	17.5	26.5	54.6
Management	100.0	1.6	18.2	25.5	54.7
Business and financial operations	100.0	0.9	16.4	28.1	54.6
Professional and related	100.0	0.6	8.3	24.1	67.1
Computer and mathematical	100.0	0.1	7.5	24.6	67.8
Architecture and engineering	100.0	0.5	15.2	20.4	63.9
Life, physical, and social sciences	100.0	0.0	5.5	9.5	85.0
Community and social services	100.0	0.8	9.0	17.4	72.8
Legal	100.0	0.0	9.0	24.6	66.4
Education, training, and library	100.0	0.6	8.1	15.3	76.0
Arts, design, entertainment, sports, and media	100.0	1.7	9.9	21.2	67.3
Health care practitioner and technical	100.0	0.4	7.8	38.6	53.2
Services	100.0	18.2	39.0	30.7	12.0
Health care support	100.0	9.9	35.6	44.7	9.9
Protective services	100.0	4.9	29.9	35.8	29.4
Food preparation and serving related	100.0	21.7	43.3	24.2	10.8
Building and grounds cleaning and maintenance	100.0	33.0	45.1	16.1	5.8
Personal care and services	100.0	14.5	35.8	34.2	15.4
Sales and office	100.0	4.5	35.9	39.1	20.5
Sales and related	100.0	7.6	34.2	32.7	25.4
Office and administrative support	100.0	2.9	36.7	42.2	18.2
Natural resources, construction, and maintenance	100.0	24.1	35.8	27.3	12.8
Farming, fishing, and forestry	100.0	49.4	25.4	17.1	8.1
Construction and extraction	100.0	10.2	45.5	30.9	13.4
Installation, maintenance, and repair	100.0	9.9	37.6	35.1	17.3
Production, transportation, and material moving	100.0	23.2	48.2	21.5	7.2
Production	100.0	23.9	47.4	20.1	8.6
Transportation and material moving	100.0	21.8	49.7	24.0	4.6
Armed forces	100.0	2.6	18.6	40.2	38.6

Table 1-60. Percent Distribution of Workers Age 25 to 64 Years, by Educational Attainment, Occupation of Longest Job Held, and Sex, 2008–2009—Continued

(Percent of total workers in occupation.)

Year, sex, and occupation	Total	Less than a high school diploma	4 years of high school only	1 to 3 years of college	4 or more years of college
2009					
Both Sexes	100.0	8.6	28.7	27.8	34.9
Management, business, and financial operations	100.0	2.1	16.9	24.2	56.8
Management	100.0	2.6	18.9	24.6	53.9
Business and financial operations	100.0	0.9	11.9	23.2	64.0
Professional and related	100.0	0.5	8.0	22.3	69.2
Computer and mathematical	100.0	0.4	7.8	26.6	65.3
Architecture and engineering	100.0	0.0	9.1	24.0	66.9
Life, physical, and social sciences	100.0	0.4	7.8	10.3	81.5
Community and social services	100.0	0.9	7.9	18.5	72.7
Legal	100.0	0.4	5.0	15.0	79.6
Education, training, and library	100.0	0.4	7.5	13.0	79.1
Arts, design, entertainment, sports, and media	100.0	1.9	12.4	23.2	62.5
Health care practitioner and technical	100.0	0.3	7.6	34.7	57.4
Services	100.0	17.3	38.1	30.6	14.1
Health care support	100.0	9.5	35.6	43.3	11.6
Protective services	100.0	3.1	28.0	42.2	26.7
Food preparation and serving related	100.0	21.9	40.3	25.4	12.4
Building and grounds cleaning and maintenance	100.0	30.2	44.1	18.3	7.4
Personal care and services	100.0	11.4	36.7	34.7	17.2
Sales and office	100.0	4.6	33.0	35.9	26.5
Sales and related	100.0	5.8	30.1	30.1	34.0
Office and administrative support	100.0	3.7	35.3	40.4	20.6
Natural resources, construction, and maintenance	100.0	20.2	45.9	26.2	7.6
Farming, fishing, and forestry	100.0	46.6	32.7	13.7	6.9
Construction and extraction	100.0	23.0	47.7	22.5	6.8
Installation, maintenance, and repair	100.0	10.1	45.5	35.1	9.3
Production, transportation, and material moving	100.0	18.6	48.9	24.4	8.1
Production	100.0	19.9	47.4	24.4	8.3
Transportation and material moving	100.0	17.2	50.5	24.4	8.0
Armed forces	100.0	0.9	21.9	44.4	32.7
Men	100.0	10.2	30.8	25.6	33.4
Management, business, and financial operations	100.0	2.7	16.7	22.7	57.9
Management	100.0	3.2	18.9	23.7	54.2
Business and financial operations	100.0	1.0	8.6	19.1	71.3
Professional and related	100.0	0.5	7.2	19.0	73.2
Computer and mathematical	100.0	0.4	6.9	26.4	66.3
Architecture and engineering	100.0	0.0	9.2	23.8	67.0
Life, physical, and social sciences	100.0	0.4	9.4	10.4	79.8
Community and social services	100.0	1.2	8.4	17.9	72.5
Legal	100.0	0.0	2.3	3.7	94.0
Education, training, and library	100.0	0.4	3.7	7.7	88.2
Arts, design, entertainment, sports, and media	100.0	2.4	13.8	25.0	58.8
Health care practitioner and technical	100.0	0.2	5.2	21.9	72.7
Services	100.0	16.8	37.4	29.7	16.1
Health care support	100.0	9.1	27.6	40.7	22.6
Protective services	100.0	2.7	27.1	43.9	26.3
Food preparation and serving related	100.0	22.1	40.4	24.0	13.6
Building and grounds cleaning and maintenance	100.0	26.5	45.1	20.6	7.9
Personal care and services	100.0	10.0	34.1	34.7	21.2
Sales and office	100.0	5.1	28.6	32.0	34.3
Sales and related	100.0	4.9	25.7	29.7	39.7
Office and administrative support	100.0	5.5	33.4	35.8	25.2
Natural resources, construction, and maintenance	100.0	20.0	46.5	26.2	7.4
Farming, fishing, and forestry	100.0	45.1	37.7	10.8	6.4
Construction and extraction	100.0	23.4	47.7	22.4	6.6
Installation, maintenance, and repair	100.0	10.3	45.8	35.1	8.8
Production, transportation, and material moving	100.0	17.4	49.7	24.7	8.2
Production	100.0	18.0	48.7	25.2	8.1
Transportation and material moving	100.0	16.8	50.6	24.3	8.4
Armed forces	100.0	0.8	23.7	44.7	30.9
Women	100.0	6.7	26.4	30.3	36.7
Management, business, and financial operations	100.0	1.3	17.2	26.2	55.3
Management	100.0	1.6	18.8	26.1	53.5
Business and financial operations	100.0	0.9	14.5	26.4	58.3
Professional and related	100.0	0.5	8.6	24.6	66.3
Computer and mathematical	100.0	0.3	9.8	26.9	62.9
Architecture and engineering	100.0	0.0	8.2	25.1	66.7
Life, physical, and social sciences	100.0	0.3	6.3	10.1	83.3
Community and social services	100.0	0.8	7.6	18.9	72.7
Legal	100.0	0.7	7.5	25.5	66.2
Education, training, and library	100.0	0.4	8.8	14.9	75.9
Arts, design, entertainment, sports, and media	100.0	1.3	10.7	21.0	67.1
Health care practitioner and technical	100.0	0.3	8.4	39.0	52.2
Services	100.0	17.6	38.5	31.3	12.6
Health care support	100.0	9.6	36.5	43.6	10.3
Protective services	100.0	4.6	31.1	36.3	28.0
Food preparation and serving related	100.0	21.7	40.3	26.5	11.5
Building and grounds cleaning and maintenance	100.0	35.1	42.9	15.3	6.8
Personal care and services	100.0	11.7	37.4	34.7	16.2
Sales and office	100.0	4.3	35.5	38.1	22.1
Sales and related	100.0	6.7	34.7	30.5	28.1
Office and administrative support	100.0	3.1	35.8	. . .	19.1
Natural resources, construction, and maintenance	100.0	24.9	34.8	27.3	13.1
Farming, fishing, and forestry	100.0	50.3	20.6	20.9	8.1
Construction and extraction	100.0	11.4	48.9	27.2	12.4
Installation, maintenance, and repair	100.0	4.1	38.4	36.4	21.1
Production, transportation, and material moving	100.0	22.7	46.2	23.3	7.8
Production	100.0	24.8	44.1	22.4	8.7
Transportation and material moving	100.0	19.0	49.8	25.0	6.1
Armed forces	100.0	2.2	8.2	42.6	46.9

. . . = Not available.

Table 1-61. Median Annual Earnings of Year-Round, Full-Time Wage and Salary Workers Age 25 to 64 Years, by Educational Attainment and Sex, 1999–2009

(Thousands of workers, dollars.)

Year and sex	Total	Less than a high school diploma	4 years of high school only	1 to 3 years of college	4 or more years of college
1999					
Both Sexes					
Number of workers	82 501	7 208	25 792	23 380	26 120
Median annual earnings	33 000	20 000	27 000	33 000	48 000
Men					
Number of workers	47 781	4 693	14 806	12 824	15 459
Median annual earnings	38 500	22 000	32 000	39 000	55 600
Women					
Number of workers	34 720	2 516	10 986	10 556	10 662
Median annual earnings	27 040	15 000	22 000	27 280	40 000
2000					
Both Sexes					
Number of workers	84 337	7 354	26 144	24 064	26 775
Median annual earnings	35 000	20 000	28 600	34 000	50 000
Men					
Number of workers	48 816	4 738	15 057	13 242	15 780
Median annual earnings	40 000	22 500	33 000	40 000	60 000
Women					
Number of workers	35 521	2 616	11 087	10 822	10 995
Median annual earnings	29 000	16 000	24 000	28 000	40 000
2001					
Both Sexes					
Number of workers	84 743	7 623	25 522	23 719	27 879
Median annual earnings	35 000	20 800	29 000	35 000	50 000
Men					
Number of workers	48 887	5 049	14 655	12 968	16 215
Median annual earnings	40 000	24 000	33 800	40 000	60 000
Women					
Number of workers	35 856	2 574	10 867	10 751	11 664
Median annual earnings	30 000	17 000	24 000	30 000	42 000
2002					
Both Sexes					
Number of workers	84 702	7 578	25 078	23 604	28 443
Median annual earnings	36 000	21 000	30 000	35 100	52 000
Men					
Number of workers	48 687	5 102	14 306	12 677	16 602
Median annual earnings	41 000	23 400	34 000	41 500	61 000
Women					
Number of workers	36 015	2 476	10 772	10 927	11 841
Median annual earnings	30 000	18 000	25 000	30 000	43 500
2003					
Both Sexes					
Number of workers	85 058	7 245	25 352	23 702	28 759
Median annual earnings	37 752	21 000	30 000	36 000	53 000
Men					
Number of workers	48 988	4 879	14 657	12 766	16 686
Median annual earnings	42 000	24 000	35 000	42 000	62 000
Women					
Number of workers	36 070	2 366	10 695	10 936	12 073
Median annual earnings	32 000	18 000	25 111	31 000	45 000
2004					
Both Sexes					
Number of workers	86 306	7 648	25 786	23 897	28 976
Median annual earnings	38 000	21 840	30 000	37 000	55 000
Men					
Number of workers	49 904	5 178	15 263	12 822	16 642
Median annual earnings	42 900	24 000	35 000	43 000	65 000
Women					
Number of workers	36 402	2 470	10 523	11 074	12 334
Median annual earnings	32 000	18 000	25 280	31 200	45 000

Table 1-61. Median Annual Earnings of Year-Round, Full-Time Wage and Salary Workers Age 25 to 64 Years, by Educational Attainment and Sex, 1999–2009—*Continued*

(Thousands of workers, dollars.)

Year and sex	Total	Less than a high school diploma	4 years of high school only	1 to 3 years of college	4 or more years of college
2005					
Both Sexes					
Number of workers	88 415	7 758	26 023	24 623	30 012
Median annual earnings	39 768	22 880	31 000	38 000	55 000
Men					
Number of workers	51 022	5 376	15 451	13 199	16 996
Median annual earnings	44 000	25 000	35 360	45 000	65 000
Women					
Number of workers	37 393	2 381	10 571	11 424	13 016
Median annual earnings	33 644	18 200	26 000	32 000	46 700
2006					
Both Sexes					
Number of workers	90 733	7 951	26 233	24 737	31 812
Median annual earnings	40 000	23 000	32 000	39 482	57 588
Men					
Number of workers	52 252	5 485	15 525	13 204	18 038
Median annual earnings	45 000	25 000	36 665	45 000	68 000
Women					
Number of workers	38 481	2 466	10 708	11 533	13 774
Median annual earnings	35 000	19 000	26 800	33 000	49 000
2007					
Both Sexes					
Number of workers	91 540	7 123	25 925	25 574	32 918
Median annual earnings	41 000	24 000	33 000	40 000	60 000
Men					
Number of workers	52 262	4 902	15 390	13 655	18 316
Median annual earnings	47 000	25 000	38 000	45 188	70 000
Women					
Number of workers	39 277	2 221	10 535	11 919	14 603
Median annual earnings	35 000	19 200	27 120	35 000	50 000
2008					
Both Sexes					
Number of workers	88 373	6 600	24 531	24 887	32 355
Median annual earnings	42 000	24 000	34 000	40 000	60 000
Men					
Number of workers	50 141	4 503	14 480	13 283	17 876
Median annual earnings	49 564	27 000	39 040	47 000	72 000
Women					
Number of workers	38 231	2 097	10 051	11 604	14 479
Median annual earnings	36 000	19 567	28 000	35 000	50 000
2009					
Both Sexes					
Number of workers	84 730	5 847	23 277	23 515	32 091
Median annual earnings	43 000	24 000	34 320	40 000	60 000
Men					
Number of workers	47 135	3 809	13 620	12 283	17 424
Median annual earnings	50 000	26 000	40 000	49 000	71 000
Women					
Number of workers	37 595	2 037	9 657	11 233	14 667
Median annual earnings	38 000	20 000	29 000	35 000	52 000

Table 1-62. Employment Status of the Civilian Noninstitutional Population by Disability Status and Selected Characteristics, 2009 Annual Averages

(Thousands of people, percent.)

Characteristic	Civilian noninstitutional population	Civilian labor force						Not in labor force
		Total	Participation rate	Employed		Unemployed		
				Total	Percent	Total	Rate	
TOTAL								
Total, 16 Years and Over	235 801	154 142	65.4	139 877	59.3	14 265	9.3	81 659
Men	114 136	82 123	72.0	73 670	64.5	8 453	10.3	32 013
Women	121 665	72 019	59.2	66 208	54.4	5 811	8.1	49 646
PERSONS WITH A DISABILITY	26 981	6 050	22.4	5 174	19.2	876	14.5	20 931
Total, 16 Years and Over	12 184	3 221	26.4	2 735	22.4	486	15.1	8 963
Men	14 797	2 829	19.1	2 439	16.5	390	13.8	11 968
16 to 64 years	14 845	5 220	35.2	4 406	29.7	814	15.6	9 625
16 to 19 years	597	173	28.9	107	17.9	66	38.2	424
20 to 24 years	792	376	47.5	279	35.2	97	25.9	416
25 to 34 years	1 646	758	46.1	606	36.8	153	20.1	887
35 to 44 years	2 230	931	41.8	782	35.1	149	16.0	1 298
45 to 54 years	4 182	1 476	35.3	1 278	30.6	198	13.4	2 706
55 to 64 years	5 398	1 505	27.9	1 354	25.1	152	10.1	3 893
65 years and over	12 136	830	6.8	768	6.3	61	7.4	11 306
Race and Hispanic Origin								
White	22 039	5 066	23.0	4 391	19.9	675	13.3	16 972
Black or African American	3 493	633	18.1	493	14.1	140	22.1	2 861
Asian	621	117	18.9	104	16.7	14	11.6	504
Hispanic[1]	2 478	562	22.7	455	18.4	107	19.0	1 915
Educational Attainment								
Total, 25 years and over	25 591	5 501	21.5	4 788	18.7	712	12.9	20 091
Less than a high school diploma	6 558	705	10.8	574	8.7	132	18.7	5 852
High school graduates, no college[2]	9 160	1 773	19.4	1 535	16.8	238	13.4	7 387
Some college or associate degree	6 174	1 782	28.9	1 542	25.0	240	13.5	4 393
Bachelor's degree and higher[3]	3 700	1 241	33.5	1 138	30.8	103	8.3	2 459

[1] May be of any race.
[2] Includes persons with a high school diploma or equivalent.
[3] Includes persons with bachelor's, master's, professional, and doctoral degrees.

Table 1-63. Employed Full- and Part-Time Workers by Disability Status and Age, 2009 Annual Averages

(Thousands of people.)

Disability status and age	Employed			At work part-time for economic reasons[1]
	Total	Usually work full-time	Usually work part-time	
TOTAL				
Total, 16 Years and Over	139 877	112 634	27 244	8 913
16 to 64 years	133 764	109 155	24 609	8 671
65 years and over	6 114	3 479	2 635	241
Persons With a Disability				
16 years and over	5 174	3 502	1 672	425
16 to 64 years	4 406	3 134	1 271	394
65 years and over	768	368	401	31
Persons Without a Disability				
16 years and over	134 703	109 132	25 572	8 488
16 to 64 years	129 358	106 021	23 337	8 278
65 years and over	5 345	3 111	2 234	210

Note: Full time refers to persons who usually work 35 hours or more per week; part time refers to persons who usually work less than 35 hours per week.

[1] Refers to persons who, whether they usually work full or part time, worked 1 to 34 hours during the reference week for an economic reason such as slack work or unfavorable business conditions, inability to find full-time work, or seasonal declines in demand.

Table 1-64. Employed Persons by Disability Status, Occupation, and Sex, 2009 Annual Averages

(Number in thousands, percent.)

Occupation	Persons with a disability			Persons with no disability		
	Total	Men	Women	Total	Men	Women
TOTAL EMPLOYED	5 174	2 735	2 439	134 703	70 935	63 769
Occupation as a Percent of Total Employed						
Management, professional, and related	30.5	28.5	32.7	37.6	34.7	40.8
Management, business, and financial operations	13.3	15.0	11.5	15.5	16.8	14.0
Management	9.8	12.3	7.1	11.1	13.2	8.8
Business and financial operations	3.5	2.7	4.4	4.4	3.6	5.2
Professional and related	17.1	13.5	21.2	22.1	17.9	26.8
Computer and mathematical	1.6	2.4	0.8	2.5	3.6	1.3
Architecture and engineering	1.3	2.2	0.4	2.0	3.2	0.6
Life, physical, and social science	0.6	0.6	0.6	1.0	1.0	1.0
Community and social services	1.9	1.4	2.5	1.7	1.2	2.2
Legal	0.9	0.9	0.9	1.2	1.2	1.3
Education, training, and library	5.3	2.7	8.2	6.2	3.0	9.7
Arts, design, entertainment, sports, and media	1.6	1.6	1.5	2.0	2.0	1.9
Healthcare practitioner and technical	3.8	1.7	6.3	5.6	2.7	8.8
Service	20.3	16.8	24.3	17.5	14.2	21.1
Healthcare support	2.6	0.7	4.9	2.4	0.5	4.5
Protective service	2	3	1	2	3	1
Food preparation and serving related	5.5	4.3	6.8	5.5	4.7	6.5
Building and grounds cleaning and maintenance	5.8	7.0	4.6	3.7	4.2	3.2
Personal care and service	4.4	1.8	7.3	3.6	1.5	5.9
Sales and office	25.5	17.4	34.6	24.1	16.9	32.1
Sales and related	11.3	10.4	12.3	11.2	10.7	11.7
Office and administrative support	14.2	7.0	22.3	12.9	6.2	20.4
Natural resources, construction, and maintenance	9.2	16.6	0.9	9.5	17.3	0.9
Farming, fishing, and forestry	0.7	1.2	0.3	0.7	1.0	0.3
Construction and extraction	4.9	8.8	0.5	5.3	9.9	0.3
Installation, maintenance, and repair	3.6	6.7	0.2	3.5	6.4	0.3
Production, transportation, and material moving	14.4	20.6	7.4	11.3	16.9	5.1
Production	7.6	10.1	4.7	5.4	7.4	3.2
Transportation and material moving	6.9	10.6	2.7	5.9	9.5	1.9

Table 1-65. Persons Not in the Labor Force by Disability Status, Age, and Sex, 2009 Annual Averages

(Thousands of people, percent distribution.)

Category	Total, 16 years and over	16 to 64 years			Total, 65 years and over
		Total	Men	Women	
Persons With a Disability					
Total not in the labor force	20 931	9 625	4 489	5 136	11 306
Persons who currently want a job	620	459	220	239	161
Marginally attached to the labor force[1]	193	166	87	79	27
Discouraged workers[2]	60	50	29	20	10
Other persons marginally attached to the labor force[3]	133	116	58	58	17
Persons Without a Disability					
Total not in the labor force	60 728	40 570	14 707	25 863	20 158
Persons who currently want a job	5 273	4 821	2 270	2 550	453
Marginally attached to the labor force[1]	2 034	1 927	1 027	900	107
Discouraged workers[2]	718	673	426	247	45
Other persons marginally attached to the labor force[3]	1 315	1 254	601	653	62

[1]Data refer to persons who want a job, have searched for work during the prior 12 months, and were available to take a job during the reference week, but had not looked for work in the past 4 weeks.
[2]Includes those who did not actively look for work in the prior 4 weeks for reasons such as thinks no work available, could not find work, lacks schooling or training, employer thinks too young or old, and other types of discrimination.
[3]Includes those who did not actively look for work in the prior 4 weeks for such reasons as school or family responsibilities, ill health, and transportation problems, as well as a number for whom reason for nonparticipation was not determined.

Chapter Two

EMPLOYMENT, HOURS, AND EARNINGS

EMPLOYMENT AND HOURS

HIGHLIGHTS

The employment, hours, and earnings data in this section are presented by industry and state and are derived from the Current Employment Statistics (CES) survey, which covers approximately 440,000 individual worksites and 140,000 business and government agencies. The employment numbers differ from those presented in the household survey in Chapter 1 because of dissimilarities in methodology, concepts, definitions, and coverage. As the CES survey data are obtained from payroll records, they are consistent for industry classifications.

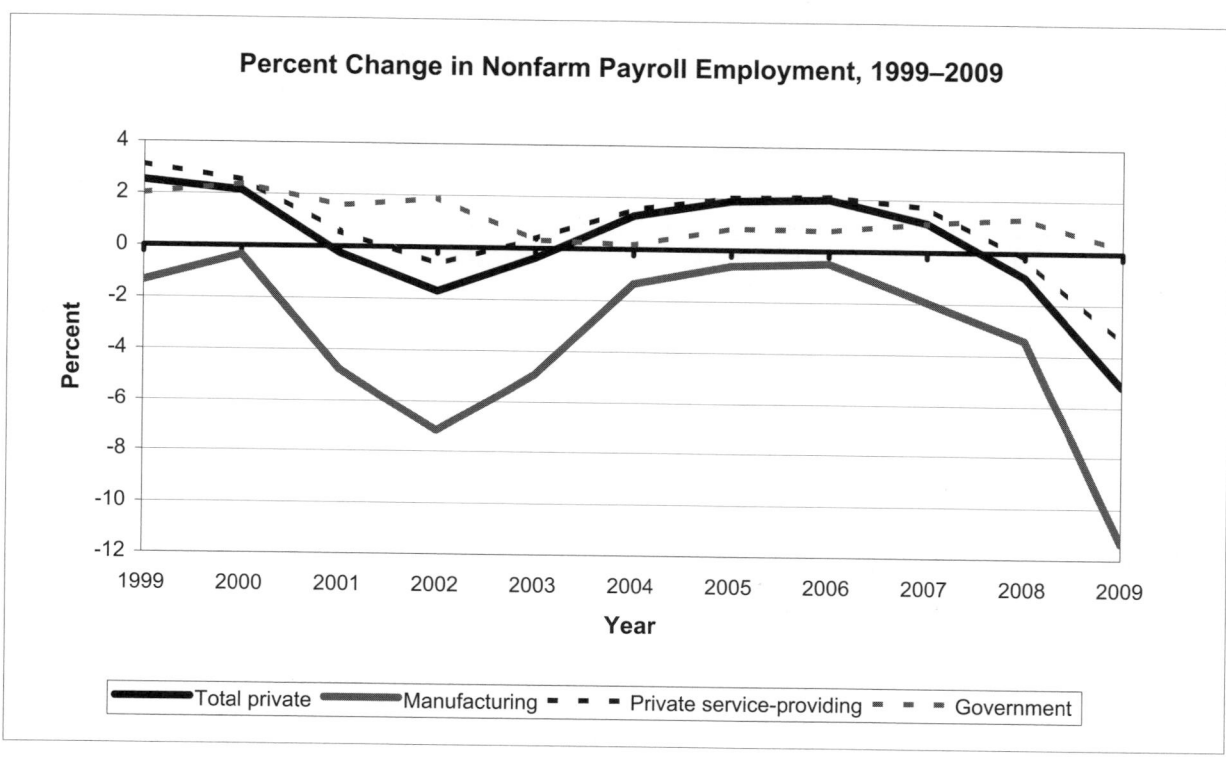

Percent Change in Nonfarm Payroll Employment, 1999–2009

In 2009, total employment declined 4.3 percent after only declining 0.6 percent in 2008. In contrast, employment increased each year from 2004 to 2007. Employment in the private service-providing sector declined 3.4 percent while employment in government actually increased 0.2 percent in 2009. (See Table 2-1.)

OTHER HIGHLIGHTS

- The goods-producing industries experienced substantial job losses in 2009 as employment declined 12.7 percent. Construction employment declined to its lowest level since 1997 while manufacturing employment declined to its lowest level since 1940. (See Table 2-1.)

- Most super sectors experienced a decline in employment in 2009. Employment increased in the following super sectors: education and health services (1.9 percent), utilities (0.4 percent), and government (0.2 percent). (See Table 2-1.)

- The number of men on nonfarm payrolls declined by 5.8 percent from 2008 to 2009 while the number of women on nonfarm payrolls only declined 2.8 percent. (See Tables 2-1 and 2-2)

- Average weekly hours of all employees on private nonfarm payrolls has gradually declined from 34.6 in 2007 to 33.9 in 2009. Mining and logging and utilities were the only major super sectors where average weekly hours topped 40 hours. (See Table 2-6.)

NOTES AND DEFINITIONS

EMPLOYMENT, HOURS, AND EARNINGS

Collection and Coverage

The Bureau of Labor Statistics (BLS) works with State Employment Security Agencies (SESAs) to conduct the Current Employment Statistics (CES), or establishment, survey. This survey collects monthly data on employment, hours, and earnings from a sample of nonfarm establishments (including government). The CES sample includes about 140,000 businesses and government agencies and covers approximately 440,000 individual worksites. Over 1,900 published monthly employment series are available for all employees and production and nonsupervisory employees. In addition, around 3,700 series, which cover approximately 750 industries average weekly earnings, average hourly earnings, average weekly hours, and, in manufacturing, average weekly overtime hours, are available. From these data, a large number of employment, hours, and earnings series are prepared and published.

Establishments reporting on the schedule (form BLS 790) are classified into industries based on their principal product or activity. Data defined on the 790 form are submitted each month by the respondent and edited by the state agency. Data submitted on the schedule are used in developing statewide and major metropolitan area estimates. The state also transmits sample data and state-developed geographic estimates to Washington. All states' samples are combined to form a collective sample for developing national industry estimates. Statewide samples range from nearly 30,000 sample units in California to about 1,000 units in smaller states. It should be noted that state estimation procedures are designed to produce accurate data for each individual state. BLS independently develops the national employment series and does not force state estimates to sum to national totals nor vice versa.

Data are collected by telephone, touch-tone self response, computer-assisted interviews, fax technology, voice recognition, and mail. The use of electronic media has resulted in more rapid response times and higher response rates.

Industry Classification

The CES survey completed a conversion from its original quota sample design to a probability-based sample survey design, and switched from the Standard Industrial Classification (SIC) system to the North American Industry Classification System (NAICS) in 2003. The industry-coding update included reconstruction of historical estimates in order to preserve time series for data users. The foundation of industrial classification with NAICS has changed how establishments are classified into industries and how businesses, as they exist today, are recognized. With the

release of January 2008 data on February 1, 2008, the CES National Nonfarm Payroll series was updated to the 2007 North American Industry Classification System (NAICS) from the 2002 NAICS basis. This resulted in relatively minor changes.

Industry Employment

Employment data refer to persons on establishment payrolls who received pay for any part of the pay period containing the 12th day of the month. The data exclude proprietors, the self-employed, unpaid volunteer or family workers, farm workers, and domestic workers. Salaried officers of corporations are included. Government employment covers only civilian employees; military personnel are excluded. Employees of the Central Intelligence Agency, the National Security Agency, the National Imagery and Mapping Agency, and the Defense Intelligence Agency are also excluded.

Persons on establishment payrolls who were on paid sick leave (for cases in which pay is received directly from the firm), paid holiday, or vacation leave, or who work during part of the pay period despite being unemployed or on strike during the rest of the period were counted as employed. Not counted as employed were persons on layoff, on leave without pay, on strike for the entire period, or who had been hired but had not yet reported during to their new jobs.

Beginning with the June 2003 publication of May 2003 data, the CES national federal government employment series has been estimated from a sample of federal establishments and benchmarked annually to counts from unemployment insurance tax records. It reflects employee counts as of the pay period containing the 12th day of the month, which is consistent with other CES industry series. Previously, the national series was an end-of-month count produced by the Office of Personnel Management.

The exclusion of farm employment, self-employment, and domestic service employment accounts from the payroll survey accounts for the differences in employment figures between the household and payroll surveys. The payroll survey also excludes workers on leave without pay. (These workers are counted as employed in the household survey.) Persons who worked in more than one establishment during the reporting period are counted each time their names appear on payrolls; these persons are only counted once in the household survey.

Concepts and Definitions

Production and related workers. This category includes working supervisors and all nonsupervisory workers (including group leaders and trainees) engaged in fabricating, processing, assembling, inspecting, receiving, storing, handling, packing, warehousing, shipping, trucking, hauling, maintenance, repair, janitorial, guard services, product development, auxiliary production for plant's own use (such as a power plant), record-keeping, and other services closely associated with production operations.

Construction workers. This group includes the following employees in the construction division: working supervisors, qualified craft workers, mechanics, apprentices, helpers, and laborers engaged in new work, alterations, demolition, repair, maintenance, and the like, whether working at the site of construction or at jobs in shops or yards at jobs (such as precutting and pre-assembling) ordinarily performed by members of the construction trades.

Nonsupervisory workers. This category consists of employees such as office and clerical workers, repairers, salespersons, operators, drivers, physicians, lawyers, accountants, nurses, social workers, research aides, teachers, drafters, photographers, beauticians, musicians, restaurant workers, custodial workers, attendants, line installers and repairers, laborers, janitors, guards, and other employees at similar occupational levels whose services are closely associated with those of the employees listed. It excludes persons in executive, managerial, and supervisory positions.

Payroll. This refers to payments made to full- and part-time production, construction, or nonsupervisory workers who received pay for any part of the pay period containing the 12th day of the month. The payroll is reported before deductions of any kind, such as those for old age and unemployment insurance, group insurance, withholding tax, bonds, or union dues. Also included is pay for overtime, holidays, and vacation, as well as for sick leave paid directly by the firm. Bonuses (unless earned and paid regularly each pay period), other pay not earned in the pay period reported (such as retroactive pay), tips, and the value of free rent, fuel, meals, or other payment-in-kind are excluded. Employee benefits (such as health and other types of insurance and contributions to retirement, as paid by the employer) are also excluded.

Total hours. During the pay period, total hours include all hours worked (including overtime hours), hours paid for standby or reporting time, and equivalent hours for which employees received pay directly from the employer for sick leave, holidays, vacations, and other leave. Overtime and other premium pay hours are not converted to straight-time equivalent hours. The concept of total hours differs from those of scheduled hours and hours worked. The average weekly hours derived from paid total hours reflect the effects of such factors as unpaid absenteeism, labor turnover, part-time work, and work stoppages, as well as fluctuations in work schedules.

Average weekly hours. The workweek information relates to the average hours for which pay was received and is different from standard or scheduled hours. Such factors as unpaid absenteeism, labor turnover, part-time work, and

work stoppages cause average weekly hours to be lower than scheduled hours of work for an establishment. Group averages further reflect changes in the workweeks of component industries.

Overtime hours. These are hours worked by production or related workers for which overtime premiums were paid because the hours were in excess of the number of hours of either the straight-time workday or the total workweek. Weekend and holiday hours are included only if overtime premiums were paid. Hours for which only shift differential, hazard, incentive, or other similar types of premiums were paid are excluded.

Average overtime hours. Overtime hours represent the portion of average weekly hours that exceeded regular hours and for which overtime premiums were paid. If an employee worked during a paid holiday at regular rates, receiving as total compensation his or her holiday pay plus straight-time pay for hours worked that day, no overtime hours would be reported.

Since overtime hours are premium hours by definition, weekly hours and overtime hours do not necessarily move in the same direction from month to month. Factors such as work stoppages, absenteeism, and labor turnover may not have the same influence on overtime hours as on average hours. Diverse trends at the industry group level may also be caused by a marked change in hours for a component industry in which little or no overtime was worked in both the previous and current months.

Industry hours and earnings. Average hours and earnings data are derived from reports of payrolls and hours for production and related workers in manufacturing and natural resources and mining, construction workers in construction, and nonsupervisory employees in private service-providing industries.

Indexes of aggregate weekly hours and payrolls. The indexes of aggregate weekly hours are calculated by dividing the current month's aggregate by the average of the 12 monthly figures for 2002. For basic industries, the hours aggregates are the product of average weekly hours and production worker or nonsupervisory worker employment. At all higher levels of industry aggregation, hours aggregates are the sum of the component aggregates.

The indexes of aggregate weekly payrolls are calculated by dividing the current month's aggregate by the average of the 12 monthly figures for 2002. For basic industries, the payroll aggregates are the product of average hourly earnings and aggregate weekly hours. At all higher levels of industry aggregation, payroll aggregates are the sum of the component aggregates.

Average hourly earnings. Average hourly earnings are on a "gross" basis. They reflect not only changes in basic hourly and incentive wage rates, but also such variable factors as premium pay for overtime and late-shift work and changes in output of workers paid on an incentive plan. They also reflect shifts in the number of employees between relatively high-paid and low-paid work and changes in workers' earnings in individual establishments. Averages for groups and divisions further reflect changes in average hourly earnings for individual industries.

Averages of hourly earnings differ from wage rates. Earnings are the actual return to the worker for a stated period; rates are the amount stipulated for a given unit of work or time. The earnings series do not measure the level of total labor costs on the part of the employer because the following items are excluded: irregular bonuses, retroactive items, payroll taxes paid by employers, and earnings for those employees not covered under the definitions of production workers, construction workers, or nonsupervisory employees.

Average hourly earnings, excluding overtime-premium pay, are computed by dividing the total production worker payroll for the industry group by the sum of total production worker hours and one-half of total overtime hours. No adjustments are made for other premium payment provisions, such as holiday pay, late-shift premiums, and overtime rates other than time and one-half.

Average weekly earnings. These estimates are derived by multiplying average weekly hours estimates by average hourly earnings estimates. Therefore, weekly earnings are affected not only by changes in average hourly earnings but also by changes in the length of the workweek. Monthly variations in factors, such as the proportion of part-time workers, work stoppages, labor turnover during the survey period, and absenteeism for which employees are not paid may cause the average workweek to fluctuate.

Long-term trends of average weekly earnings can be affected by structural changes in the makeup of the workforce. For example, persistent long-term increases in the proportion of part-time workers in retail trade and many of the services industries have reduced average workweeks in

these industries and have affected the average weekly earnings series.

These earnings are in constant dollars and are calculated from the earnings averages for the current month using a deflator derived from the Consumer Price Index for Urban Wage Earnings and Clerical Workers (CPI-W). The reference year for these series is 1982.

Seasonally adjusted. This removes the change in employment that is due to normal seasonal hiring or layoffs, thus leaving an over-the-month change that reflects only employment changes due to trend and irregular movements. Seasonally adjusted estimates of employment and other series are generated using the X-12 ARIMA program developed by the United States Census Bureau.

Benchmarks

Employment estimates are adjusted annually to a complete count of jobs—called benchmarks—which are primarily derived from tax reports submitted by employers covered by state unemployment laws (which cover most establishments). A comprehensive account of employment is derived in March. In this re-anchoring of sample-based employment estimates to full population counts, the original sample-based estimates are replaced with the benchmark data from the previous year. The benchmark information is used to adjust monthly estimates between the new benchmark and the preceding benchmark, thereby preserving the continuity of the series and establishing the level of employment for the new benchmark month.

Sources of Additional Information

For further information on sampling and estimation methods for national data, visit the Employment, Hours, and Earnings homepage on the BLS Web site at <http://www.bls.gov/ces>. For more information on state and area data, please visit the BLS Web site at <http://www.bls.gov/sae>.

Table 2-1. Employees on Nonfarm Payrolls, by Super Sector and Selected Component Groups, NAICS Basis, 2000–2009

(Thousands of people.)

Industry	2000	2001	2002	2003	2004	2005	2006	2007	2008	2009
TOTAL	131 785	131 826	130 341	129 999	131 435	133 703	136 086	137 598	136 790	130 920
Total Private	110 995	110 708	108 828	108 416	109 814	111 899	114 113	115 380	114 281	108 371
Goods-Producing	24 649	23 873	22 557	21 816	21 882	22 190	22 531	22 233	21 334	18 620
Mining and Logging	599	606	583	572	591	628	684	724	767	700
Mining	520	533	512	503	523	562	620	664	710	650
Logging	79	74	70	69	68	65	64	60	57	50
Construction	6 787	6 826	6 716	6 735	6 976	7 336	7 691	7 630	7 162	6 037
Construction of buildings	1 633	1 589	1 575	1 576	1 630	1 712	1 805	1 774	1 642	1 366
Heavy and civil engineering	937	953	931	903	907	951	985	1 005	965	847
Specialty trade contractors	4 217	4 284	4 210	4 256	4 439	4 673	4 901	4 850	4 556	3 824
Manufacturing	17 263	16 441	15 259	14 510	14 315	14 226	14 155	13 879	13 406	11 883
Durable goods	10 877	10 336	9 485	8 964	8 925	8 956	8 981	8 808	8 463	7 309
Wood product	613	574	555	538	550	559	559	515	456	361
Nonmetallic mineral product	554	545	516	494	506	505	510	501	465	398
Primary metals	622	571	509	477	467	466	464	456	442	365
Fabricated metal product	1 753	1 676	1 549	1 479	1 497	1 522	1 553	1 563	1 528	1 318
Machinery	1 457	1 371	1 232	1 152	1 145	1 166	1 183	1 187	1 188	1 029
Computer and electronic product	1 820	1 749	1 507	1 355	1 323	1 316	1 308	1 273	1 244	1 136
Electrical equipment and appliances	591	557	497	460	445	434	433	429	424	377
Transportation equipment	2 057	1 939	1 830	1 775	1 767	1 772	1 769	1 712	1 608	1 353
Furniture and related product	683	645	607	576	576	568	560	531	480	386
Miscellaneous manufacturing	728	710	683	658	651	647	644	642	629	587
Nondurable goods	6 386	6 105	5 774	5 546	5 390	5 271	5 174	5 071	4 943	4 574
Food manufacturing	1 553	1 551	1 526	1 518	1 494	1 478	1 479	1 484	1 481	1 459
Beverage and tobacco product	207	209	207	200	195	192	194	198	198	188
Textile mills	378	333	291	261	237	218	195	170	151	126
Textile product mills	230	217	204	188	183	176	167	158	147	127
Apparel	484	415	350	304	278	251	232	215	199	170
Paper and paper product	605	578	547	516	496	484	471	458	445	407
Printing and related support activities	807	768	707	681	663	646	634	622	594	524
Petroleum and coal product	123	121	118	114	112	112	113	115	117	115
Chemicals	980	959	928	906	887	872	866	861	847	803
Plastics and rubber product	951	896	847	814	805	802	786	757	729	627
Private Service-Providing	86 346	86 834	86 271	86 600	87 932	89 709	91 582	93 147	92 947	89 751
Trade, Transportation, and Utilities	26 225	25 983	25 497	25 287	25 533	25 959	26 276	26 630	26 293	24 949
Wholesale Trade	5 933	5 773	5 652	5 608	5 663	5 764	5 905	6 015	5 943	5 625
Durable goods	3 251	3 130	3 008	2 941	2 951	2 999	3 075	3 122	3 052	2 827
Nondurable goods	2 065	2 031	2 015	2 005	2 010	2 022	2 041	2 062	2 048	1 980
Electronic markets, agents, and brokers	618	611	629	662	702	743	789	832	843	818
Retail Trade	15 280	15 239	15 025	14 917	15 058	15 280	15 353	15 520	15 283	14 528
Motor vehicle and parts dealers	1 847	1 855	1 879	1 883	1 902	1 919	1 910	1 908	1 831	1 640
Furniture and home furnishing stores	544	541	539	547	563	576	587	575	531	450
Electronic and appliance stores	564	555	525	512	516	536	541	549	541	487
Building material and garden supply stores	1 142	1 152	1 177	1 185	1 227	1 276	1 324	1 309	1 248	1 163
Food and beverage stores	2 993	2 951	2 882	2 838	2 822	2 818	2 821	2 844	2 862	2 829
Health and personal care stores	928	952	939	938	941	954	961	993	1 003	984
Gasoline stations	936	925	896	882	876	871	864	862	842	827
Clothing and clothing accessories stores	1 322	1 321	1 313	1 305	1 364	1 415	1 451	1 500	1 468	1 369
Sporting goods, hobby, and music stores	686	679	661	647	641	647	646	656	651	616
General merchandise stores	2 820	2 842	2 812	2 822	2 863	2 934	2 935	3 021	3 026	2 956
Miscellaneous store retailers	1 007	993	960	931	914	900	881	865	843	785
Nonstore retailers	492	474	444	427	429	435	433	438	438	422
Transportation and Warehousing	4 410	4 372	4 224	4 185	4 249	4 361	4 470	4 541	4 508	4 235
Air transportation	614	615	564	528	515	501	487	492	491	460
Rail transportation	232	227	218	218	226	228	228	234	231	219
Water transportation	56	54	53	55	56	61	63	66	67	64
Truck transportation	1 406	1 387	1 339	1 326	1 352	1 398	1 436	1 439	1 389	1 266
Transit and ground passenger transportation	372	375	381	382	385	389	399	412	423	419
Pipeline transportation	46	45	42	40	38	38	39	39	42	42
Scenic and sightseeing transportation	28	29	26	27	27	29	28	29	28	28
Support activities for transportation	537	539	525	520	535	552	571	584	592	549
Couriers and messengers	605	587	561	562	557	571	582	581	573	547
Warehousing and storage	514	514	517	528	558	595	638	665	672	642
Utilities	601	599	596	577	564	554	549	553	559	561
Information	3 630	3 629	3 395	3 188	3 118	3 061	3 038	3 032	2 984	2 807
Publishing industries, except Internet	1 035	1 021	964	925	909	904	902	901	880	796
Motion picture and sound recording industry	383	377	388	376	385	378	376	381	371	350
Broadcasting, except Internet	344	345	334	324	325	328	328	325	319	301
Internet publishing and broadcasting and web search portals	111	100	76	67	66	67	69	73	81	83
Telecommunications	1 397	1 424	1 281	1 167	1 115	1 071	1 048	1 031	1 019	975
Other information services	157	147	124	116	117	118	121	126	134	135

Table 2-1. Employees on Nonfarm Payrolls, by Super Sector and Selected Component Groups, NAICS Basis, 2000–2009—*Continued*

(Thousands of people.)

Industry	2000	2001	2002	2003	2004	2005	2006	2007	2008	2009
Financial Activities	7 687	7 808	7 847	7 977	8 031	8 153	8 328	8 301	8 145	7 758
Finance and insurance	5 677	5 769	5 814	5 919	5 945	6 019	6 156	6 132	6 015	5 763
Monetary authorities, central bank	23	23	23	23	22	21	21	22	22	21
Credit intermediation	2 548	2 598	2 686	2 792	2 817	2 869	2 925	2 866	2 733	2 597
Securities, commodity contracts, and investments	805	831	789	758	766	786	818	849	864	810
Insurance carriers and related activities	2 221	2 234	2 233	2 266	2 259	2 259	2 304	2 307	2 305	2 247
Funds, trusts, and other financial vehicles	81	84	82	80	82	84	88	89	91	88
Real estate and rental and leasing	2 011	2 038	2 033	2 058	2 086	2 134	2 173	2 169	2 130	1 995
Real estate	1 316	1 343	1 357	1 387	1 419	1 461	1 499	1 500	1 485	1 417
Rental and leasing services	667	666	649	643	641	646	646	640	617	552
Lessors of nonfinancial intangible assets	28	29	28	27	26	27	28	28	28	26
Professional and Business Services	16 666	16 476	15 976	15 987	16 394	16 954	17 566	17 942	17 735	16 580
Professional and technical services	6 702	6 871	6 649	6 603	6 747	7 025	7 357	7 660	7 799	7 509
Management of companies and enterprises	1 796	1 779	1 705	1 687	1 724	1 759	1 811	1 866	1 905	1 856
Administrative and waste services	8 168	7 826	7 622	7 697	7 923	8 170	8 398	8 416	8 032	7 215
Administrative and support services	7 855	7 509	7 304	7 375	7 594	7 833	8 050	8 061	7 675	6 864
Waste management and remediation services	313	317	318	322	329	338	348	355	357	351
Education and Health Services	15 109	15 645	16 199	16 588	16 953	17 372	17 826	18 322	18 838	19 191
Education services	2 390	2 511	2 643	2 695	2 763	2 836	2 901	2 941	3 040	3 090
Health care and social assistance	12 718	13 134	13 556	13 893	14 190	14 536	14 925	15 380	15 798	16 101
Ambulatory health care services	4 320	4 462	4 633	4 786	4 952	5 114	5 286	5 474	5 647	5 777
Hospitals	3 954	4 051	4 160	4 245	4 285	4 345	4 423	4 515	4 627	4 677
Nursing and residential health facilities	2 583	2 676	2 743	2 786	2 818	2 855	2 893	2 958	3 016	3 081
Social assistance	1 860	1 946	2 020	2 075	2 135	2 222	2 324	2 433	2 508	2 565
Leisure and Hospitality	11 862	12 036	11 986	12 173	12 493	12 816	13 110	13 427	13 436	13 102
Arts, entertainment, and recreation	1 788	1 824	1 783	1 813	1 850	1 892	1 929	1 969	1 970	1 915
Performing arts and spectator sports	382	382	364	372	368	376	399	405	406	397
Museums, historical sites	110	115	114	115	118	121	124	130	132	130
Amusements, gambling, and recreation	1 296	1 327	1 305	1 327	1 364	1 395	1 406	1 434	1 433	1 387
Accommodation and food services	10 074	10 211	10 203	10 360	10 643	10 923	11 181	11 457	11 466	11 188
Accommodation	1 884	1 852	1 779	1 775	1 790	1 819	1 832	1 867	1 869	1 760
Food services and drinking places	8 189	8 359	8 425	8 584	8 854	9 104	9 349	9 590	9 598	9 428
Other Services	5 168	5 258	5 372	5 401	5 409	5 395	5 438	5 494	5 515	5 364
Repair and maintenance	1 242	1 257	1 247	1 234	1 229	1 236	1 249	1 253	1 227	1 154
Personal and laundry services	1 243	1 255	1 257	1 264	1 273	1 277	1 288	1 310	1 323	1 282
Membership associations and organizations	2 683	2 746	2 868	2 904	2 908	2 882	2 901	2 931	2 966	2 928
Government	20 790	21 118	21 513	21 583	21 621	21 804	21 974	22 218	22 509	22 549
Federal	2 865	2 764	2 766	2 761	2 730	2 732	2 732	2 734	2 762	2 828
Federal, excluding U.S. Postal Service	1 985	1 891	1 924	1 952	1 948	1 957	1 963	1 965	2 014	2 124
State	4 786	4 905	5 029	5 002	4 982	5 032	5 075	5 122	5 177	5 180
State, excluding education	2 756	2 792	2 786	2 748	2 744	2 772	2 782	2 804	2 823	2 809
Local	13 139	13 449	13 718	13 820	13 909	14 041	14 167	14 362	14 571	14 542
Local, excluding education	5 845	5 970	6 063	6 110	6 144	6 185	6 254	6 376	6 487	6 480

Table 2-2. Women Employees on Nonfarm Payrolls, by Super Sector and Selected Component Groups, NAICS Basis, 2000–2009

(Thousands of people.)

Industry	2000	2001	2002	2003	2004	2005	2006	2007	2008	2009
TOTAL NONFARM	63 223	63 684	63 360	63 237	63 739	64 718	65 525	66 805	67 084	65 234
Total Private	51 452	51 669	51 033	50 901	51 404	52 329	53 307	54 227	54 175	52 339
Goods-Producing	6 297	5 961	5 486	5 192	5 117	5 104	5 082	5 041	4 866	4 303
Mining and logging	92	90	85	80	80	79	82	93	101	99
Construction	846	832	827	822	841	890	944	947	916	804
Manufacturing	5 359	5 039	4 574	4 290	4 197	4 135	4 057	4 001	3 848	3 400
Private Service-Providing	45 155	45 708	45 547	45 709	46 287	47 225	48 224	49 186	49 310	48 037
Trade, transportation, and utilities	10 859	10 768	10 466	10 321	10 364	10 535	10 627	10 849	10 782	10 244
Wholesale trade	1 827	1 770	1 718	1 700	1 714	1 738	1 796	1 831	1 820	1 717
Retail trade	7 680	7 635	7 449	7 339	7 387	7 524	7 587	7 758	7 713	7 361
Transportation and warehousing	1 202	1 212	1 149	1 134	1 117	1 130	1 098	1 110	1 098	1 024
Utilities	151	151	150	147	146	143	146	150	151	142
Information	1 697	1 684	1 554	1 428	1 366	1 333	1 306	1 285	1 260	1 172
Financial activities	4 638	4 726	4 755	4 830	4 831	4 896	5 031	4 959	4 813	4 600
Professional and business services	7 680	7 591	7 314	7 248	7 360	7 574	7 779	8 007	7 946	7 472
Education and health services	11 586	12 037	12 474	12 786	13 073	13 408	13 764	14 178	14 574	14 851
Leisure and hospitality	6 082	6 224	6 215	6 319	6 516	6 708	6 903	7 054	7 056	6 877
Other services	2 614	2 677	2 769	2 779	2 776	2 772	2 814	2 854	2 880	2 821
Government	11 771	12 015	12 327	12 337	12 335	12 389	12 218	12 578	12 908	12 895
Federal	1 231	1 148	1 155	1 173	1 168	1 177	1 194	1 202	1 224	1 255
State	2 464	2 534	2 621	2 599	2 562	2 575	2 630	2 651	2 684	2 634
Local	8 076	8 333	8 551	8 565	8 606	8 637	8 395	8 725	9 000	9 006

Table 2-3. Production Workers on Private Nonfarm Payrolls, by Super Sector, NAICS Basis, 2000–2009

(Thousands of people.)

Industry	2000	2001	2002	2003	2004	2005	2006	2007	2008	2009
TOTAL PRIVATE	90 336	89 983	88 393	87 658	88 937	91 135	93 451	94 903	94 270	89 271
Goods-Producing	18 169	17 466	16 400	15 732	15 821	16 145	16 559	16 405	15 724	13 447
Mining and logging	446	457	436	420	440	473	519	547	574	514
Construction	5 295	5 332	5 196	5 123	5 309	5 611	5 903	5 883	5 521	4 583
Manufacturing	12 428	11 677	10 768	10 189	10 072	10 060	10 137	9 975	9 629	8 350
Private Service-Providing	72 167	72 517	71 993	71 926	73 116	74 990	76 893	78 498	78 546	75 823
Trade, transportation, and utilities	21 965	21 709	21 337	21 078	21 319	21 830	22 166	22 546	22 337	21 149
Wholesale trade	4 686	4 555	4 474	4 396	4 444	4 584	4 724	4 851	4 822	4 536
Retail trade	13 734	13 425	13 295	13 225	13 438	13 677	13 736	13 954	13 302	12 819
Transportation and warehousing	3 753	3 718	3 611	3 563	3 637	3 774	3 889	3 935	3 931	3 687
Utilities	485	483	478	464	450	443	443	444	450	451
Information	2 502	2 531	2 398	2 347	2 371	2 386	2 399	2 403	2 388	2 243
Financial activities	5 737	5 810	5 872	5 967	5 989	6 090	6 281	6 326	6 269	5 999
Professional and business services	13 790	13 588	13 049	12 911	13 287	13 854	14 446	14 784	14 585	13 525
Education and health services	13 362	13 846	14 311	14 532	14 771	15 129	15 539	15 999	16 488	16 839
Leisure and hospitality	10 516	10 662	10 576	10 666	10 955	11 263	11 568	11 861	11 873	11 583
Other services	4 296	4 373	4 449	4 426	4 425	4 438	4 494	4 578	4 606	4 486

Table 2-4. Production Workers on Manufacturing Payrolls, by Industry, NAICS Basis, 2000–2009

(Thousands of people.)

Industry	2000	2001	2002	2003	2004	2005	2006	2007	2008	2009
Total Manufacturing	12 428	11 677	10 768	10 189	10 072	10 060	10 137	9 975	9 629	8 350
Durable Goods	7 659	7 164	6 530	6 152	6 140	6 220	6 355	6 250	5 975	5 008
Wood products	506	468	449	433	444	453	450	406	356	278
Nometallic mineral products	440	427	399	375	388	387	391	384	363	305
Primary metals	490	447	396	370	364	363	363	358	348	275
Fabricated metal products	1 326	1 254	1 147	1 093	1 109	1 129	1 162	1 171	1 143	965
Machinery	961	891	787	732	730	749	770	774	772	641
Computer and electronic products	949	876	744	673	656	700	756	744	730	654
Electrical equipment and appliances	433	402	352	320	307	300	303	305	305	268
Transportation equipment	1 498	1 399	1 310	1 269	1 265	1 277	1 304	1 275	1 177	952
Furniture and related products	546	511	477	446	446	437	434	410	365	286
Miscellaneous manufacturing	510	490	469	442	432	424	423	425	416	384
Nondurable Goods	4 769	4 513	4 238	4 037	3 932	3 841	3 782	3 725	3 653	3 341
Food manufacturing	1 228	1 221	1 202	1 193	1 178	1 170	1 172	1 184	1 184	1 163
Beverage and tobacco products	117	116	120	106	107	112	115	118	112	112
Textile mills	315	276	242	217	194	174	158	137	122	100
Textile products mills	183	174	162	148	147	143	135	123	115	99
Apparel	404	341	286	242	219	193	182	173	163	134
Leather and allied products	55	47	40	35	33	31	29	27	28	24
Paper and paper products	468	446	421	393	374	365	357	351	344	313
Printing and related support	576	544	493	471	460	447	447	443	425	371
Petroleum and coal products	83	81	78	74	77	75	72	73	77	70
Chemicals	980	959	928	906	887	872	866	861	847	803
Plastics and rubber products	951	896	847	814	805	802	786	757	729	627

Table 2-5. Total Employees on Manufacturing Payrolls, by Industry, NAICS Basis, 2000–2009

(Thousands of people.)

Industry	2000	2001	2002	2003	2004	2005	2006	2007	2008	2009
Total Manufacturing	17 263	16 441	15 259	14 510	14 315	14 226	14 155	13 879	13 406	11 883
Durable Goods	10 877	10 336	9 485	8 964	8 925	8 956	8 981	8 808	8 463	7 309
Wood products	613	574	555	538	550	559	559	515	456	361
Nometallic mineral products	554	545	516	494	506	505	510	501	465	398
Primary metals	622	571	509	477	467	466	464	456	442	365
Fabricated metal products	1 753	1 676	1 549	1 479	1 497	1 522	1 553	1 563	1 528	1 318
Machinery	1 457	1 371	1 232	1 152	1 145	1 166	1 183	1 187	1 188	1 029
Computer and electronic products	1 820	1 749	1 507	1 355	1 323	1 316	1 308	1 273	1 244	1 136
Electrical equipment and appliances	591	557	497	460	445	434	433	429	424	377
Transportation equipment	2 057	1 939	1 830	1 775	1 767	1 772	1 769	1 712	1 608	1 353
Furniture and related products	683	645	607	576	576	568	560	531	480	386
Miscellaneous manufacturing	728	710	683	658	651	647	644	642	629	587
Nondurable Goods	6 386	6 105	5 774	5 546	5 390	5 271	5 174	5 071	4 943	4 574
Food manufacturing	1 553	1 551	1 526	1 518	1 494	1 478	1 479	1 484	1 481	1 459
Beverage and tobacco products	207	209	207	200	195	192	194	198	198	188
Textile mills	378	333	291	261	237	218	195	170	151	126
Textile products mills	230	217	204	188	183	176	167	158	147	127
Apparel	484	415	350	304	278	251	232	215	199	170
Leather and allied products	69	58	50	45	42	40	37	34	33	29
Paper and paper products	605	578	547	516	496	484	471	458	445	407
Printing and related support	807	768	707	681	663	646	634	622	594	524
Petroleum and coal products	123	121	118	114	112	112	113	115	117	115
Chemicals	980	959	928	906	887	872	866	861	847	803
Plastics and rubber products	951	896	847	814	805	802	786	757	729	627

Table 2-6. Average Weekly Hours of All Employees on Private Nonfarm Payrolls by NAICS Super Sector, 2006–2009

(Hours per week, seasonally adjusted.)

Year and month	Total private	Mining and logging	Construction	Manufacturing	Trade, transportation, and utilities				Information	Financial activities	Professional and business services	Education and health services	Leisure and hospitality	Other services
					Total	Wholesale trade	Retail trade	Utilities						
2007	34.6	44.0	38.0	40.0	34.6	38.1	31.7	41.8	36.1	36.6	35.4	33.5	26.1	32.9
2008	34.5	43.7	37.8	39.8	34.4	38.4	31.4	42.0	36.5	36.5	35.2	33.7	26.1	32.9
2009	33.9	42.1	37.2	39.0	34.1	37.9	31.3	40.9	36.5	36.6	35.0	33.0	25.9	31.6
2006														
January	...	...	...	...	...	...	...	...	...	...	...	...	...	...
February	...	...	...	...	...	...	...	...	...	...	...	...	...	...
March	34.5	42.7	37.7	40.0	34.0	37.8	31.1	40.9	36.3	36.7	35.2	33.4	26.2	33.3
April	34.5	42.9	37.5	40.1	34.1	37.6	31.3	41.3	36.5	36.7	35.2	33.5	26.2	33.3
May	34.5	42.8	37.8	40.1	34.1	37.5	31.4	41.2	36.5	36.7	35.1	33.5	26.3	33.2
June	34.7	42.9	37.9	40.0	34.3	37.8	31.6	41.4	36.5	36.8	35.5	33.5	26.3	33.4
July	34.5	43.2	37.6	40.0	34.3	37.8	31.5	41.9	36.5	36.6	35.3	33.4	26.1	33.2
August	34.4	42.6	37.6	39.8	34.2	37.7	31.5	41.6	36.5	36.5	35.1	33.3	26.1	33.0
September	34.5	42.6	37.8	39.8	34.3	37.8	31.5	41.4	36.3	36.7	35.5	33.4	26.1	33.0
October	34.5	42.3	38.3	39.8	34.4	37.7	31.7	41.8	36.2	36.6	35.1	33.3	26.1	32.9
November	34.5	41.8	37.9	39.7	34.4	37.8	31.7	41.5	36.1	36.6	35.4	33.3	26.1	32.9
December	34.8	42.7	38.8	39.9	34.8	37.9	32.3	41.5	36.0	36.7	35.7	33.4	26.5	32.8
2007														
January	34.5	42.5	37.9	40.0	34.3	37.4	31.7	41.1	36.0	36.5	35.2	33.2	26.3	32.6
February	34.5	43.0	37.4	39.9	34.2	37.7	31.4	41.4	36.1	36.5	35.7	33.2	26.2	32.7
March	34.6	43.3	38.1	40.1	34.5	38.2	31.7	41.6	36.1	36.5	35.5	33.5	26.2	33.0
April	34.7	44.7	37.9	40.2	34.6	38.2	31.8	41.8	36.0	36.5	35.5	33.7	26.2	33.1
May	34.7	44.3	38.3	40.1	34.5	38.1	31.7	42.0	35.9	36.4	35.4	33.7	26.2	33.0
June	34.7	44.2	38.1	40.0	34.8	38.2	32.0	42.0	36.0	36.7	35.5	33.6	26.2	33.1
July	34.6	44.3	37.8	40.1	34.6	38.3	31.8	41.9	36.1	36.5	35.4	33.6	26.0	32.9
August	34.5	43.7	37.5	39.9	34.5	38.2	31.7	42.0	36.1	36.5	35.4	33.5	25.9	32.7
September	34.6	44.7	38.3	40.0	34.5	38.1	31.6	42.4	36.0	36.5	35.5	33.5	25.9	32.7
October	34.5	44.2	38.4	39.7	34.5	38.1	31.7	41.5	36.1	36.5	35.3	33.5	25.9	32.7
November	34.6	43.8	38.3	39.9	34.5	38.2	31.7	41.6	36.2	36.5	35.4	33.5	26.1	32.7
December	34.7	44.1	38.5	40.2	34.7	38.3	31.9	42.0	36.4	36.6	35.5	33.5	26.2	32.6
2008														
January	34.5	43.7	38.2	40.1	34.5	38.1	31.6	42.4	36.5	36.4	35.2	33.4	26.1	32.5
February	34.5	43.8	38.0	40.1	34.4	38.2	31.5	41.9	36.5	36.5	35.4	33.5	26.1	32.7
March	34.7	44.9	38.3	40.4	34.6	38.4	31.6	42.7	36.6	36.5	35.3	33.8	26.2	33.1
April	34.6	43.2	38.1	40.1	34.6	38.4	31.6	42.2	36.7	36.5	35.3	33.9	26.1	33.2
May	34.6	43.7	37.8	40.0	34.5	38.4	31.5	42.0	36.5	36.7	35.2	33.9	26.1	33.0
June	34.6	43.8	38.0	40.1	34.6	38.5	31.6	42.5	36.4	36.6	35.2	33.8	26.0	32.9
July	34.5	43.4	37.6	39.7	34.5	38.7	31.5	41.8	36.5	36.5	35.2	33.8	25.8	32.8
August	34.4	43.3	37.5	39.7	34.5	38.7	31.4	41.5	36.6	36.6	35.3	33.7	25.7	32.9
September	34.4	43.0	37.7	39.5	34.4	38.5	31.3	41.9	36.7	36.5	35.3	33.6	25.7	32.9
October	34.4	43.9	37.8	39.5	34.4	38.4	31.3	41.6	36.8	36.5	35.3	33.6	25.8	32.7
November	34.3	44.3	37.5	39.5	34.3	38.3	31.3	41.8	36.7	36.5	35.2	33.6	25.8	32.6
December	34.2	43.1	37.4	39.1	34.3	38.3	31.2	41.4	36.5	36.5	35.2	33.5	25.7	32.6
2009														
January	34.2	43.5	37.5	39.0	34.3	38.2	31.3	41.5	36.5	36.6	35.1	33.4	25.7	32.5
February	34.1	42.9	37.5	39.1	34.3	38.2	31.3	41.9	36.4	36.5	35.1	33.3	25.7	32.3
March	34.0	42.4	37.3	38.7	34.3	38.0	31.4	41.1	36.3	36.5	35.1	33.3	25.7	31.9
April	33.9	42.2	37.4	38.7	34.2	37.9	31.3	40.8	36.4	36.5	35.0	33.1	25.6	31.7
May	33.9	41.8	37.4	38.7	34.2	37.9	31.3	40.8	36.5	36.5	35.0	33.0	25.6	31.6
June	33.8	41.7	37.2	38.7	34.1	37.8	31.2	40.5	36.4	36.4	35.0	32.9	25.5	31.5
July	33.8	41.8	37.4	38.8	34.1	37.8	31.3	40.7	36.4	36.5	34.9	32.9	25.5	31.5
August	33.8	42.5	37.2	39.1	34.1	37.8	31.3	40.9	36.5	36.5	34.9	32.9	25.6	31.5
September	33.8	41.8	37.0	39.0	34.1	37.7	31.4	40.6	36.6	36.6	34.9	32.8	25.5	31.4
October	33.7	41.6	36.7	39.1	34.1	37.7	31.3	40.9	36.6	36.6	34.9	32.7	25.4	31.3
November	33.9	42.2	37.2	39.6	34.0	37.7	31.2	41.0	36.5	36.7	35.1	32.7	25.5	31.3
December	33.8	42.1	36.9	39.6	34.0	37.6	31.2	40.5	36.5	36.7	35.1	32.7	25.6	31.3

. . . = Not available.

Table 2-7. Average Weekly Hours of Production Workers on Private Nonfarm Payrolls, by Super Sector, NAICS Basis, 2000–2009

(Hours.)

Industry	2000	2001	2002	2003	2004	2005	2006	2007	2008	2009
TOTAL PRIVATE	34.3	34.0	33.9	33.7	33.7	33.8	33.9	33.9	33.6	33.1
Goods-Producing	40.7	39.9	39.9	39.8	40.0	40.1	40.5	40.6	40.2	39.2
Mining and logging	44.4	44.6	43.2	43.6	44.5	45.6	45.6	45.9	45.1	43.3
Construction	39.2	38.7	38.4	38.4	38.3	38.6	39.0	39.0	38.5	37.6
Manufacturing	41.3	40.3	40.5	40.4	40.8	40.7	41.1	41.2	40.8	39.8
Private Service-Providing	32.7	32.5	32.5	32.3	32.3	32.4	32.5	32.4	32.3	32.1
Trade, transportation, and utilities	33.8	33.5	33.6	33.6	33.5	33.4	33.4	33.3	33.2	32.9
Wholesale trade	38.8	38.4	38.0	37.9	37.8	37.7	38.0	38.2	38.2	37.6
Retail trade	30.7	30.7	30.9	30.9	30.7	30.6	30.5	30.2	30.0	29.9
Transportation and warehousing	37.4	36.7	36.8	36.8	37.2	37.0	36.9	37.0	36.4	36.0
Utilities	42.0	41.4	40.9	41.1	40.9	41.1	41.4	42.4	42.7	42.1
Information	36.8	36.9	36.5	36.2	36.3	36.5	36.6	36.5	36.7	36.6
Financial activities	35.9	35.8	35.6	35.5	35.5	35.9	35.7	35.9	35.8	36.1
Professional and business services	34.5	34.2	34.2	34.1	34.2	34.2	34.6	34.8	34.8	34.7
Education and health services	32.2	32.3	32.4	32.3	32.4	32.6	32.5	32.6	32.5	32.3
Leisure and hospitality	26.1	25.8	25.8	25.6	25.7	25.7	25.7	25.5	25.2	24.8
Other services	32.5	32.3	32.0	31.4	31.0	30.9	30.9	30.9	30.8	30.5

Table 2-8. Employees on Total Nonfarm Payrolls, by State and Selected Territory, 1969–2009

(Thousands of people.)

State	1969	1970	1971	1972	1973	1974	1975	1976	1977	1978	1979	1980	1981	1982	1983
UNITED STATES	70 512	71 006	71 335	73 798	76 912	78 389	77 069	79 502	82 593	86 826	89 932	90 528	91 289	89 677	90 280
Alabama	1 000	1 010	1 022	1 072	1 136	1 170	1 155	1 207	1 269	1 336	1 362	1 356	1 348	1 312	1 329
Alaska	87	93	98	104	110	128	162	172	163	164	167	169	186	200	214
Arizona	517	547	581	646	714	746	729	759	809	895	980	1 014	1 041	1 030	1 078
Arkansas	534	536	551	582	614	641	624	660	696	733	750	742	740	720	741
California	6 932	6 946	6 917	7 210	7 622	7 834	7 847	8 154	8 600	9 200	9 665	9 849	9 985	9 810	9 918
Colorado	721	750	787	869	936	960	964	1 003	1 058	1 150	1 218	1 251	1 295	1 317	1 327
Connecticut	1 194	1 198	1 164	1 190	1 239	1 264	1 223	1 240	1 282	1 346	1 398	1 427	1 438	1 428	1 444
Delaware	212	217	225	232	239	233	230	237	239	248	257	259	259	259	266
District of Columbia	575	567	567	572	574	580	576	576	579	596	612	616	611	598	597
Florida	2 070	2 152	2 276	2 513	2 779	2 864	2 746	2 784	2 933	3 181	3 381	3 576	3 736	3 762	3 905
Georgia	1 532	1 558	1 603	1 695	1 802	1 828	1 756	1 839	1 926	2 050	2 128	2 159	2 199	2 202	2 280
Hawaii	276	294	302	313	328	336	343	349	359	377	394	404	405	399	406
Idaho	201	208	217	236	252	267	273	291	307	331	338	330	328	312	318
Illinois	4 376	4 346	4 296	4 315	4 467	4 546	4 419	4 565	4 656	4 789	4 880	4 850	4 732	4 593	4 531
Indiana	1 880	1 849	1 841	1 922	2 028	2 031	1 942	2 024	2 114	2 206	2 236	2 130	2 114	2 028	2 030
Iowa	873	877	883	912	961	999	999	1 037	1 079	1 119	1 132	1 110	1 089	1 042	1 040
Kansas	686	679	678	718	763	790	801	835	871	912	947	945	950	921	922
Kentucky	896	910	932	988	1 039	1 066	1 058	1 103	1 148	1 210	1 245	1 210	1 196	1 161	1 152
Louisiana	1 033	1 034	1 056	1 129	1 176	1 221	1 250	1 314	1 365	1 464	1 517	1 579	1 630	1 607	1 565
Maine	330	332	332	344	355	362	357	375	388	406	416	418	419	416	425
Maryland	1 272	1 349	1 372	1 415	1 472	1 494	1 479	1 498	1 546	1 626	1 691	1 712	1 716	1 676	1 724
Massachusetts	2 249	2 244	2 211	2 252	2 333	2 354	2 273	2 324	2 416	2 526	2 604	2 654	2 672	2 642	2 696
Michigan	3 081	2 999	2 995	3 119	3 284	3 278	3 137	3 283	3 442	3 609	3 637	3 443	3 364	3 193	3 223
Minnesota	1 300	1 315	1 310	1 357	1 436	1 481	1 474	1 521	1 597	1 689	1 767	1 770	1 761	1 707	1 718
Mississippi	573	584	602	649	693	711	692	728	766	814	838	829	819	791	793
Missouri	1 672	1 668	1 661	1 700	1 771	1 789	1 741	1 798	1 862	1 953	2 011	1 970	1 956	1 922	1 937
Montana	196	199	205	215	224	234	238	251	265	280	284	280	282	274	276
Nebraska	474	484	491	517	541	562	558	572	594	610	631	628	623	610	611
Nevada	194	203	210	224	245	256	263	280	308	350	384	400	411	401	403
New Hampshire	259	258	260	278	298	300	293	313	337	360	378	385	395	394	410
New Jersey	2 570	2 606	2 608	2 672	2 760	2 783	2 700	2 754	2 837	2 962	3 027	3 060	3 099	3 093	3 165
New Mexico	288	293	306	328	346	360	370	390	415	444	461	465	476	474	480
New York	7 182	7 156	7 011	7 038	7 132	7 077	6 830	6 790	6 858	7 044	7 179	7 207	7 287	7 255	7 313
North Carolina	1 747	1 783	1 814	1 912	2 018	2 048	1 980	2 083	2 171	2 278	2 373	2 380	2 392	2 347	2 419
North Dakota	158	164	167	176	184	194	204	215	221	234	244	245	249	250	251
Ohio	3 887	3 881	3 840	3 938	4 113	4 169	4 016	4 095	4 230	4 395	4 485	4 367	4 318	4 124	4 092
Oklahoma	748	762	774	812	852	887	900	931	972	1 036	1 088	1 138	1 201	1 217	1 171
Oregon	709	711	729	775	816	838	837	878	937	1 009	1 056	1 044	1 019	961	967
Pennsylvania	4 375	4 352	4 291	4 400	4 506	4 515	4 436	4 513	4 565	4 716	4 806	4 753	4 729	4 580	4 524
Rhode Island	346	344	343	358	366	367	349	367	382	396	400	398	401	390	396
South Carolina	820	842	863	920	984	1 016	983	1 038	1 082	1 138	1 176	1 189	1 196	1 162	1 189
South Dakota	173	175	179	190	199	207	209	219	227	237	241	238	236	230	235
Tennessee	1 310	1 328	1 357	1 450	1 531	1 558	1 506	1 575	1 648	1 737	1 777	1 747	1 755	1 703	1 719
Texas	1 310	1 328	1 357	1 450	1 531	1 558	1 506	1 575	1 648	1 737	1 777	1 747	1 755	1 703	1 719
Utah	348	357	369	393	415	434	440	463	489	525	548	551	558	561	567
Vermont	146	148	148	154	161	163	162	168	178	191	198	200	204	203	206
Virginia	1 436	1 519	1 567	1 656	1 753	1 805	1 779	1 848	1 930	2 034	2 115	2 157	2 161	2 146	2 207
Washington	1 120	1 079	1 064	1 100	1 152	1 199	1 226	1 283	1 367	1 485	1 581	1 608	1 612	1 569	1 586
West Virginia	1 120	1 079	1 064	1 100	1 152	1 199	1 226	1 283	1 367	1 485	1 581	1 608	1 612	1 569	1 586
Wisconsin	1 525	1 530	1 525	1 581	1 660	1 703	1 677	1 726	1 799	1 887	1 960	1 938	1 923	1 867	1 867
Wyoming	107	108	111	117	126	136	146	157	171	187	201	210	224	218	202
Puerto Rico	. . .	. . .	. . .	. . .	. . .	. . .	. . .	. . .	. . .	. . .	. . .	693	680	642	646
Virgin Islands	. . .	. . .	. . .	. . .	. . .	. . .	33	31	32	34	36	37	38	36	36

. . . = Not available.

Table 2-8. Employees on Total Nonfarm Payrolls, by State and Selected Territory, 1969–2009—*Continued*

(Thousands of people.)

State	1984	1985	1986	1987	1988	1989	1990	1991	1992	1993	1994	1995	1996
UNITED STATES	94 530	97 511	99 474	102 088	105 345	108 014	109 487	108 375	108 726	110 844	114 291	117 298	119 708
Alabama	1 388	1 427	1 463	1 508	1 559	1 601	1 636	1 642	1 674	1 717	1 758	1 804	1 829
Alaska	226	231	221	210	214	227	238	243	247	253	259	262	264
Arizona	1 182	1 279	1 338	1 386	1 419	1 454	1 483	1 491	1 517	1 584	1 692	1 793	1 892
Arkansas	780	797	814	837	865	893	924	937	963	994	1 034	1 070	1 087
California	10 390	10 770	11 086	11 473	11 912	12 238	12 500	12 359	12 154	12 045	12 160	12 422	12 743
Colorado	1 402	1 419	1 408	1 413	1 436	1 482	1 521	1 545	1 597	1 671	1 756	1 835	1 901
Connecticut	1 517	1 558	1 598	1 638	1 667	1 666	1 620	1 557	1 526	1 531	1 544	1 562	1 582
Delaware	280	293	303	321	334	344	347	342	341	349	356	366	376
District of Columbia	614	629	640	656	674	681	686	677	674	670	659	643	623
Florida	4 204	4 410	4 599	4 848	5 067	5 261	5 376	5 283	5 348	5 560	5 788	5 985	6 172
Georgia	2 449	2 570	2 672	2 782	2 876	2 941	2 992	2 938	2 987	3 109	3 266	3 402	3 527
Hawaii	413	426	439	460	478	506	528	539	543	539	536	533	531
Idaho	330	336	328	333	349	366	385	398	414	433	459	475	489
Illinois	4 672	4 755	4 791	4 928	5 098	5 214	5 288	5 233	5 235	5 330	5 463	5 593	5 685
Indiana	2 122	2 169	2 222	2 305	2 396	2 479	2 522	2 507	2 554	2 627	2 713	2 786	2 814
Iowa	1 075	1 074	1 074	1 109	1 156	1 200	1 226	1 238	1 252	1 278	1 320	1 358	1 383
Kansas	961	968	985	1 005	1 035	1 064	1 092	1 097	1 116	1 135	1 167	1 200	1 228
Kentucky	1 214	1 250	1 274	1 328	1 382	1 433	1 470	1 475	1 508	1 548	1 597	1 643	1 672
Louisiana	1 602	1 591	1 518	1 484	1 512	1 538	1 588	1 611	1 625	1 656	1 720	1 770	1 808
Maine	446	458	477	501	527	542	535	514	512	519	532	538	542
Maryland	1 814	1 888	1 952	2 028	2 102	2 155	2 173	2 102	2 084	2 104	2 148	2 184	2 213
Massachusetts	2 856	2 931	2 992	3 071	3 138	3 118	2 988	2 824	2 798	2 843	2 907	2 980	3 039
Michigan	3 381	3 562	3 657	3 736	3 819	3 922	3 946	3 884	3 919	3 999	4 141	4 268	4 352
Minnesota	1 820	1 866	1 892	1 962	2 028	2 087	2 136	2 146	2 194	2 252	2 320	2 388	2 442
Mississippi	821	839	848	864	896	919	936	938	960	1 002	1 056	1 074	1 089
Missouri	2 033	2 095	2 143	2 198	2 259	2 315	2 345	2 309	2 334	2 395	2 470	2 521	2 567
Montana	281	279	275	274	283	291	297	304	317	326	340	352	362
Nebraska	635	650	652	667	688	708	731	740	752	769	798	819	837
Nevada	426	446	468	500	538	581	621	629	639	672	738	786	843
New Hampshire	442	466	490	513	529	529	508	482	487	502	523	540	554
New Jersey	3 329	3 414	3 488	3 576	3 651	3 690	3 635	3 499	3 458	3 493	3 553	3 600	3 639
New Mexico	503	520	526	529	548	562	580	585	602	626	657	682	694
New York	7 570	7 751	7 908	8 059	8 187	8 247	8 214	7 888	7 732	7 762	7 833	7 894	7 941
North Carolina	2 565	2 651	2 744	2 863	2 987	3 074	3 122	3 076	3 140	3 243	3 351	3 451	3 536
North Dakota	252	252	250	252	257	260	266	271	277	285	295	302	309
Ohio	4 260	4 373	4 472	4 583	4 701	4 818	4 882	4 819	4 848	4 918	5 076	5 221	5 296
Oklahoma	1 180	1 165	1 124	1 108	1 132	1 164	1 189	1 204	1 215	1 240	1 273	1 309	1 347
Oregon	1 007	1 030	1 058	1 100	1 153	1 206	1 256	1 254	1 276	1 318	1 372	1 428	1 485
Pennsylvania	4 655	4 730	4 791	4 915	5 042	5 138	5 170	5 084	5 076	5 123	5 192	5 253	5 306
Rhode Island	416	429	443	452	459	462	454	424	424	430	434	439	441
South Carolina	1 262	1 296	1 338	1 392	1 449	1 500	1 540	1 510	1 525	1 568	1 605	1 644	1 673
South Dakota	247	249	252	257	266	276	288	296	308	318	331	342	347
Tennessee	1 812	1 868	1 930	2 012	2 092	2 167	2 193	2 184	2 245	2 328	2 423	2 499	2 533
Texas	1 812	1 868	1 930	2 012	2 092	2 167	2 193	2 184	2 245	2 328	2 423	2 499	2 533
Utah	601	624	634	640	660	691	724	745	769	810	860	908	954
Vermont	215	225	234	246	256	262	258	249	251	257	264	270	275
Virginia	2 333	2 455	2 558	2 680	2 772	2 862	2 894	2 829	2 848	2 919	3 004	3 070	3 136
Washington	1 660	1 710	1 770	1 852	1 941	2 047	2 143	2 177	2 222	2 253	2 304	2 347	2 416
West Virginia	1 660	1 710	1 770	1 852	1 941	2 047	2 143	2 177	2 222	2 253	2 304	2 347	2 416
Wisconsin	1 949	1 983	2 024	2 090	2 168	2 236	2 292	2 302	2 358	2 413	2 491	2 559	2 601
Wyoming	204	207	196	183	189	193	198	203	206	210	217	219	221
Puerto Rico	684	692	728	764	818	837	846	838	858	872	898	930	973
Virgin Islands	37	37	38	40	42	42	43	44	45	48	44	42	41

Table 2-8. Employees on Total Nonfarm Payrolls, by State and Selected Territory, 1969–2009—*Continued*

(Thousands of people.)

State	1997	1998	1999	2000	2001	2002	2003	2004	2005	2006	2007	2008	2009
UNITED STATES	122 776	125 930	128 993	131 785	131 826	130 341	129 999	131 435	133 703	136 086	137 598	136 790	130 920
Alabama	1 866	1 898	1 920	1 931	1 909	1 883	1 876	1 902	1 945	1 980	2 006	1 992	1 886
Alaska	269	275	278	284	289	295	299	304	310	315	318	322	321
Arizona	1 985	2 075	2 163	2 243	2 265	2 265	2 296	2 381	2 509	2 634	2 674	2 616	2 426
Arkansas	1 105	1 122	1 142	1 159	1 154	1 146	1 145	1 158	1 178	1 199	1 204	1 202	1 165
California	13 130	13 596	13 992	14 488	14 602	14 458	14 393	14 533	14 801	15 060	15 174	14 981	14 079
Colorado	1 980	2 058	2 133	2 214	2 227	2 184	2 153	2 180	2 226	2 279	2 331	2 350	2 244
Connecticut	1 608	1 643	1 669	1 693	1 681	1 665	1 644	1 650	1 662	1 681	1 698	1 699	1 627
Delaware	388	400	413	420	420	415	416	425	433	438	438	436	416
District of Columbia	618	614	627	650	654	664	666	674	682	688	694	704	703
Florida	6 403	6 625	6 816	7 070	7 160	7 169	7 250	7 499	7 800	8 002	8 018	7 736	7 260
Georgia	3 614	3 741	3 855	3 949	3 943	3 870	3 845	3 898	4 001	4 089	4 146	4 102	3 877
Hawaii	532	531	535	551	555	557	568	583	602	617	625	619	592
Idaho	506	521	539	560	568	568	572	588	611	638	655	649	610
Illinois	5 771	5 899	5 958	6 045	5 995	5 884	5 811	5 816	5 862	5 933	5 980	5 950	5 658
Indiana	2 858	2 917	2 970	3 000	2 933	2 901	2 895	2 929	2 955	2 974	2 986	2 957	2 787
Iowa	1 407	1 443	1 469	1 478	1 466	1 447	1 440	1 457	1 480	1 504	1 519	1 524	1 478
Kansas	1 270	1 314	1 328	1 346	1 349	1 336	1 313	1 325	1 333	1 354	1 380	1 391	1 345
Kentucky	1 711	1 753	1 795	1 827	1 805	1 789	1 783	1 799	1 824	1 847	1 867	1 852	1 770
Louisiana	1 848	1 887	1 894	1 918	1 915	1 896	1 906	1 918	1 892	1 853	1 916	1 938	1 899
Maine	554	569	586	604	608	606	607	612	612	615	618	617	595
Maryland	2 269	2 326	2 392	2 455	2 472	2 480	2 487	2 518	2 556	2 589	2 608	2 600	2 521
Massachusetts	3 114	3 184	3 243	3 329	3 339	3 259	3 198	3 195	3 212	3 246	3 280	3 290	3 173
Michigan	4 439	4 513	4 585	4 676	4 564	4 487	4 416	4 399	4 389	4 326	4 267	4 162	3 876
Minnesota	2 500	2 564	2 622	2 685	2 690	2 664	2 660	2 681	2 723	2 758	2 771	2 763	2 650
Mississippi	1 107	1 134	1 153	1 154	1 130	1 124	1 115	1 124	1 130	1 141	1 153	1 148	1 097
Missouri	2 639	2 684	2 727	2 749	2 730	2 699	2 680	2 694	2 735	2 774	2 795	2 789	2 688
Montana	367	376	384	391	392	396	401	411	421	432	445	446	429
Nebraska	856	878	894	911	917	908	910	918	930	942	957	965	944
Nevada	891	926	983	1 027	1 051	1 052	1 088	1 153	1 223	1 280	1 292	1 264	1 148
New Hampshire	570	589	606	622	627	618	618	627	636	642	646	646	624
New Jersey	3 724	3 801	3 901	3 994	3 997	3 984	3 979	3 999	4 039	4 071	4 079	4 048	3 892
New Mexico	708	720	730	745	757	766	776	790	809	832	844	847	812
New York	8 069	8 239	8 458	8 638	8 595	8 462	8 410	8 465	8 537	8 618	8 734	8 793	8 556
North Carolina	3 653	3 758	3 849	3 915	3 894	3 836	3 788	3 836	3 915	4 041	4 145	4 135	3 916
North Dakota	314	319	324	328	330	330	333	338	345	352	358	367	366
Ohio	5 392	5 482	5 564	5 625	5 543	5 445	5 398	5 408	5 427	5 436	5 428	5 362	5 074
Oklahoma	1 387	1 432	1 453	1 480	1 494	1 474	1 445	1 461	1 500	1 540	1 568	1 593	1 539
Oregon	1 537	1 562	1 586	1 618	1 606	1 585	1 574	1 607	1 654	1 704	1 731	1 718	1 612
Pennsylvania	5 406	5 495	5 586	5 691	5 682	5 641	5 611	5 644	5 702	5 756	5 798	5 799	5 608
Rhode Island	450	458	466	477	478	479	484	488	491	493	493	482	459
South Carolina	1 718	1 783	1 830	1 859	1 823	1 804	1 807	1 833	1 866	1 907	1 944	1 926	1 821
South Dakota	353	360	370	378	379	378	378	384	390	399	406	411	404
Tennessee	2 584	2 638	2 685	2 729	2 688	2 664	2 663	2 706	2 743	2 783	2 797	2 775	2 619
Texas	2 584	2 638	2 685	2 729	2 688	2 664	2 663	2 706	2 743	2 783	2 797	2 775	2 619
Utah	994	1 023	1 048	1 075	1 081	1 073	1 074	1 104	1 148	1 204	1 253	1 252	1 192
Vermont	279	285	292	299	302	299	299	303	306	308	308	307	297
Virginia	3 232	3 320	3 412	3 516	3 517	3 494	3 498	3 584	3 664	3 726	3 761	3 763	3 637
Washington	2 515	2 595	2 649	2 711	2 697	2 654	2 658	2 701	2 777	2 859	2 934	2 959	2 826
West Virginia	2 515	2 595	2 649	2 711	2 697	2 654	2 658	2 701	2 777	2 859	2 934	2 959	2 826
Wisconsin	2 656	2 718	2 784	2 834	2 814	2 782	2 775	2 807	2 842	2 866	2 884	2 878	2 748
Wyoming	224	228	233	239	245	248	250	255	264	277	289	298	286
Puerto Rico	989	997	1 011	1 025	1 009	1 005	1 022	1 046	1 048	1 041	1 028	1 010	963
Virgin Islands	42	42	41	42	44	43	42	43	44	46	46	46	44

Table 2-9. Employees on Total Private Payrolls, by State and Selected Territory, 1995–2009

(Thousands of people.)

State	1995	1996	1997	1998	1999	2000	2001	2002	2003	2004	2005	2006	2007	2008	2009
UNITED STATES	97 865	100 169	103 113	106 021	108 686	110 995	110 708	108 828	108 416	109 814	111 899	114 113	115 380	114 281	108 371
Alabama	1 460	1 486	1 520	1 551	1 569	1 580	1 557	1 529	1 517	1 542	1 582	1 609	1 629	1 608	1 502
Alaska	189	190	196	201	204	209	210	214	218	223	229	234	236	239	237
Arizona	1 483	1 574	1 656	1 733	1 809	1 876	1 887	1 875	1 903	1 982	2 106	2 226	2 253	2 184	2 004
Arkansas	892	907	921	937	954	968	960	951	947	958	974	991	994	989	949
California	10 315	10 630	10 989	11 430	11 752	12 170	12 220	12 011	11 967	12 135	12 381	12 608	12 679	12 462	11 582
Colorado	1 531	1 592	1 665	1 735	1 804	1 877	1 883	1 829	1 797	1 821	1 863	1 912	1 957	1 966	1 853
Connecticut	1 341	1 360	1 382	1 416	1 434	1 451	1 437	1 416	1 398	1 407	1 418	1 435	1 449	1 446	1 379
Delaware	316	324	335	346	358	364	363	358	358	367	373	377	377	374	354
District of Columbia	. . .	382	385	388	405	426	428	432	435	443	448	455	463	469	461
Florida	5 067	5 244	5 461	5 671	5 850	6 068	6 136	6 129	6 197	6 433	6 719	6 903	6 896	6 609	6 142
Georgia	2 832	2 958	3 037	3 155	3 265	3 352	3 334	3 246	3 214	3 264	3 355	3 430	3 473	3 412	3 187
Hawaii	421	420	420	419	422	437	440	439	448	463	482	496	503	494	466
Idaho	380	392	406	419	434	451	458	456	459	474	496	522	538	530	490
Illinois	4 794	4 875	4 963	5 082	5 133	5 205	5 145	5 023	4 958	4 971	5 016	5 087	5 131	5 094	4 800
Indiana	2 399	2 428	2 471	2 523	2 572	2 595	2 523	2 484	2 473	2 503	2 529	2 548	2 555	2 516	2 347
Iowa	1 128	1 150	1 172	1 207	1 229	1 235	1 220	1 203	1 196	1 213	1 235	1 257	1 269	1 272	1 224
Kansas	963	995	1 034	1 074	1 089	1 101	1 101	1 085	1 063	1 074	1 082	1 099	1 122	1 131	1 082
Kentucky	1 356	1 383	1 420	1 458	1 494	1 519	1 493	1 474	1 471	1 489	1 510	1 528	1 543	1 529	1 445
Louisiana	1 412	1 446	1 484	1 520	1 524	1 544	1 542	1 521	1 526	1 535	1 518	1 505	1 560	1 573	1 531
Maine	445	450	461	474	490	504	506	503	503	507	507	510	514	513	492
Maryland	1 761	1 790	1 846	1 892	1 948	2 005	2 015	2 016	2 024	2 055	2 090	2 118	2 130	2 112	2 028
Massachusetts	2 576	2 630	2 700	2 762	2 814	2 894	2 899	2 823	2 772	2 774	2 787	2 816	2 848	2 853	2 736
Michigan	3 628	3 709	3 791	3 858	3 917	3 995	3 878	3 800	3 730	3 719	3 715	3 661	3 612	3 512	3 230
Minnesota	2 001	2 054	2 111	2 174	2 226	2 277	2 280	2 250	2 248	2 269	2 308	2 342	2 357	2 344	2 234
Mississippi	860	872	888	910	926	920	892	884	874	882	889	902	909	900	846
Missouri	2 131	2 167	2 226	2 270	2 306	2 323	2 302	2 268	2 248	2 265	2 306	2 340	2 355	2 343	2 234
Montana	274	283	288	294	301	307	308	311	315	325	335	347	358	358	340
Nebraska	668	686	704	727	742	756	760	749	751	758	769	779	795	801	776
Nevada	689	742	784	814	866	905	925	921	954	1 014	1 079	1 129	1 136	1 101	990
New Hampshire	464	476	491	509	524	538	541	530	528	537	545	550	553	551	527
New Jersey	3 027	3 068	3 154	3 230	3 324	3 406	3 394	3 370	3 357	3 366	3 398	3 424	3 431	3 401	3 243
New Mexico	516	523	532	542	549	562	572	575	580	592	607	634	649	649	613
New York	6 478	6 541	6 663	6 816	7 014	7 171	7 127	6 970	6 922	6 981	7 048	7 133	7 233	7 277	7 032
North Carolina	2 908	2 982	3 084	3 172	3 252	3 300	3 265	3 202	3 154	3 191	3 259	3 368	3 457	3 429	3 200
North Dakota	231	238	244	249	253	255	257	256	257	263	270	277	283	291	289
Ohio	4 472	4 544	4 635	4 719	4 791	4 840	4 749	4 645	4 595	4 607	4 627	4 636	4 631	4 566	4 283
Oklahoma	1 040	1 076	1 110	1 154	1 170	1 193	1 197	1 173	1 150	1 160	1 187	1 219	1 243	1 264	1 200
Oregon	1 178	1 228	1 277	1 296	1 314	1 339	1 324	1 300	1 294	1 324	1 369	1 417	1 442	1 420	1 312
Pennsylvania	4 541	4 594	4 692	4 783	4 870	4 966	4 954	4 902	4 866	4 900	4 957	5 010	5 053	5 050	4 853
Rhode Island	378	379	387	395	402	412	413	413	418	423	426	428	428	418	397
South Carolina	1 350	1 378	1 419	1 474	1 515	1 536	1 500	1 479	1 481	1 508	1 539	1 576	1 608	1 580	1 472
South Dakota	272	278	284	291	300	307	305	303	304	309	315	323	331	335	326
Tennessee	2 126	2 152	2 204	2 253	2 295	2 330	2 285	2 254	2 252	2 291	2 330	2 366	2 376	2 347	2 191
Texas	6 583	6 805	7 130	7 439	7 625	7 870	7 928	7 790	7 724	7 841	8 056	8 359	8 660	8 828	8 491
Utah	744	788	821	846	869	890	891	878	878	905	946	999	1 046	1 041	978
Vermont	225	230	234	239	244	249	252	248	247	251	252	254	254	253	242
Virginia	2 472	2 540	2 635	2 718	2 801	2 892	2 888	2 859	2 860	2 933	3 002	3 052	3 078	3 068	2 940
Washington	1 902	1 965	2 057	2 129	2 174	2 228	2 192	2 138	2 137	2 177	2 250	2 329	2 400	2 413	2 276
West Virginia	551	560	569	578	585	593	594	590	585	594	603	611	613	615	594
Wisconsin	2 180	2 217	2 269	2 325	2 385	2 428	2 400	2 368	2 362	2 395	2 427	2 451	2 468	2 456	2 323
Wyoming	162	163	166	170	174	178	184	185	186	191	199	212	222	229	215
Puerto Rico	. . .	. . .	. . .	. . .	. . .	. . .	726	710	721	738	743	741	730	710	669
Virgin Islands	28	27	28	28	27	28	32	30	29	31	32	33	33	33	31

. . . = Not available.

Table 2-10. Employees on Manufacturing Payrolls, by State and Selected Territory, NAICS Basis, 1995–2009

(Thousands of people.)

State	1995	1996	1997	1998	1999	2000	2001	2002	2003	2004	2005	2006	2007	2008	2009
UNITED STATES	17 241	17 237	17 419	17 560	17 322	17 263	16 441	15 259	14 510	14 315	14 226	14 155	13 879	13 406	11 883
Alabama	370	362	364	365	358	351	326	307	294	292	299	303	296	284	248
Alaska	15	14	14	13	12	12	12	11	12	12	13	13	13	13	13
Arizona	191	199	205	211	207	210	202	184	175	177	182	186	182	173	153
Arkansas	246	241	241	242	241	240	227	214	206	204	202	200	191	184	164
California	1 719	1 777	1 826	1 856	1 829	1 856	1 781	1 634	1 545	1 523	1 505	1 490	1 464	1 425	1 281
Colorado	179	181	187	191	187	189	180	164	154	152	150	149	147	144	130
Connecticut	249	245	245	248	240	236	227	211	200	197	195	194	191	187	172
Delaware	43	41	43	44	44	42	39	37	36	35	33	34	33	32	28
District of Columbia	5	5	4	4	4	4	3	3	3	2	2	2	2	2	1
Florida	479	485	486	482	478	477	455	428	410	411	416	416	399	371	323
Georgia	547	552	555	553	550	538	505	471	452	448	450	448	431	409	357
Hawaii	16	16	16	16	16	16	16	15	15	15	15	15	15	15	14
Idaho	63	66	68	69	69	70	69	66	62	62	64	66	66	63	55
Illinois	894	899	902	906	882	871	815	754	714	697	688	683	675	657	578
Indiana	653	647	652	658	666	665	615	588	573	572	571	565	550	521	440
Iowa	237	235	239	251	253	251	240	227	220	223	229	231	230	227	204
Kansas	180	186	198	206	204	201	195	184	175	177	180	183	186	187	168
Kentucky	299	298	302	307	309	310	292	275	265	264	262	261	256	245	213
Louisiana	182	183	185	185	181	177	172	161	156	153	152	153	157	153	142
Maine	83	81	81	81	81	80	75	68	64	63	61	60	59	59	53
Maryland	175	172	173	173	172	172	166	155	145	141	139	135	132	128	119
Massachusetts	412	411	412	413	400	403	389	349	324	313	305	300	295	286	259
Michigan	874	867	874	890	899	897	822	762	718	699	679	650	619	574	462
Minnesota	375	381	391	397	395	397	379	356	343	343	347	346	342	336	300
Mississippi	241	231	228	234	233	223	201	188	179	180	178	176	170	160	141
Missouri	377	376	377	378	373	365	345	325	315	311	309	307	300	289	256
Montana	21	22	22	22	23	23	21	20	19	19	20	20	21	20	17
Nebraska	110	111	112	114	113	114	111	106	102	101	101	102	101	101	94
Nevada	36	38	40	41	41	43	44	43	44	46	48	50	50	48	40
New Hampshire	97	99	102	104	101	103	97	85	80	80	80	78	78	76	68
New Jersey	449	437	435	429	422	422	401	368	350	338	330	324	311	299	267
New Mexico	43	43	43	43	41	42	41	38	37	36	36	38	37	35	30
New York	809	795	796	790	771	749	707	651	612	596	579	566	552	532	477
North Carolina	828	809	800	796	777	758	704	644	599	577	565	553	539	516	448
North Dakota	20	21	22	23	23	24	24	24	24	25	26	26	26	26	24
Ohio	1 037	1 030	1 027	1 030	1 028	1 021	953	885	843	822	812	796	771	739	629
Oklahoma	161	162	168	175	177	177	170	152	143	142	145	149	151	150	130
Oregon	211	218	227	229	224	225	216	202	195	200	204	207	204	195	167
Pennsylvania	881	867	871	874	864	864	822	760	712	691	679	670	659	644	574
Rhode Island	80	77	76	75	72	71	68	62	59	57	55	53	51	48	42
South Carolina	347	339	339	341	336	336	314	290	276	268	261	253	250	242	214
South Dakota	44	44	44	44	44	44	41	38	38	39	40	42	42	43	38
Tennessee	524	507	503	504	500	493	454	429	413	412	409	399	380	361	310
Texas	994	1 016	1 044	1 077	1 063	1 067	1 026	948	899	890	897	924	934	924	840
Utah	117	122	126	127	126	126	122	114	112	115	118	123	128	126	113
Vermont	41	43	44	45	45	46	46	41	38	37	37	36	36	35	31
Virginia	373	371	374	376	367	364	341	320	305	299	296	288	278	265	239
Washington	311	325	350	361	343	332	316	285	267	264	273	286	293	291	266
West Virginia	78	78	77	78	77	76	72	69	65	63	62	61	59	57	51
Wisconsin	567	568	579	593	595	594	560	528	504	503	505	506	501	493	436
Wyoming	10	10	10	10	10	10	10	10	9	9	10	10	10	10	9
Puerto Rico	. . .	. . .	. . .	. . .	. . .	. . .	132	121	118	118	115	110	107	101	92
Virgin Islands	2	2	2	2	2	2	2	2	2	2	2	2	2	2	2

. . . = Not available.

Table 2-11. Employees on Government Payrolls, by State and Selected Territory, NAICS Basis, 1995–2009

(Thousands of people.)

State	1995	1996	1997	1998	1999	2000	2001	2002	2003	2004	2005	2006	2007	2008	2009
UNITED STATES	19 432	19 539	19 664	19 909	20 307	20 790	21 118	21 513	21 583	21 621	21 804	21 974	22 218	22 509	22 549
Alabama	343	343	346	347	351	352	352	355	358	359	363	370	377	384	383
Alaska	73	73	73	74	74	74	79	81	82	81	81	81	82	83	84
Arizona	310	318	328	341	354	367	378	390	394	399	403	409	421	432	423
Arkansas	177	180	183	185	187	191	194	195	199	200	204	208	211	214	217
California	2 107	2 113	2 141	2 166	2 239	2 318	2 382	2 447	2 426	2 398	2 420	2 452	2 495	2 519	2 497
Colorado	304	309	316	322	328	337	344	355	356	359	363	367	375	384	391
Connecticut	221	223	226	228	235	242	244	249	246	243	244	246	249	253	248
Delaware	51	52	53	54	55	57	57	57	57	57	58	59	61	62	62
District of Columbia	255	240	233	226	222	224	226	232	231	231	234	233	231	235	242
Florida	918	928	942	955	966	1 002	1 023	1 039	1 053	1 066	1 081	1 099	1 123	1 127	1 118
Georgia	570	570	577	586	590	597	610	624	631	635	647	660	673	691	690
Hawaii	111	111	112	112	113	115	115	118	119	120	120	121	122	125	126
Idaho	96	97	100	103	105	109	110	112	113	114	115	116	117	119	120
Illinois	799	809	808	816	826	840	850	861	853	845	846	846	849	856	857
Indiana	387	386	387	394	398	405	410	417	423	426	426	426	431	441	440
Iowa	230	233	235	236	239	243	245	244	245	245	245	247	250	253	255
Kansas	237	234	236	240	240	245	248	251	250	251	251	255	258	260	262
Kentucky	287	289	291	295	301	308	312	315	313	310	314	318	323	323	324
Louisiana	358	362	364	367	370	373	374	375	379	382	374	348	356	365	368
Maine	93	93	93	95	97	100	102	103	104	105	105	104	104	104	103
Maryland	423	423	423	433	444	450	457	465	462	463	466	471	478	488	493
Massachusetts	404	409	414	422	428	435	440	436	426	422	425	429	433	437	437
Michigan	641	644	647	656	667	681	685	687	685	680	674	665	656	650	647
Minnesota	387	389	389	391	397	408	409	414	413	412	415	416	415	419	417
Mississippi	215	217	219	223	227	234	238	240	241	242	241	239	244	248	250
Missouri	390	401	413	414	421	426	429	431	432	429	429	434	440	446	454
Montana	78	79	80	81	82	84	84	85	86	87	86	86	87	88	89
Nebraska	151	151	152	151	151	154	157	159	160	160	161	162	162	164	169
Nevada	97	101	107	112	117	122	127	131	135	139	144	150	157	162	158
New Hampshire	76	78	79	80	82	84	86	88	90	90	91	92	93	95	97
New Jersey	573	571	570	572	578	589	603	614	622	633	642	647	648	647	649
New Mexico	166	171	177	178	180	183	186	191	195	198	201	198	195	198	199
New York	1 416	1 400	1 406	1 424	1 445	1 467	1 467	1 492	1 487	1 484	1 489	1 485	1 501	1 516	1 524
North Carolina	544	554	569	587	597	615	629	634	634	645	656	672	688	706	716
North Dakota	71	70	70	70	71	73	73	74	75	75	75	76	76	76	78
Ohio	749	752	758	763	772	785	794	800	803	802	800	800	797	796	790
Oklahoma	270	271	276	278	283	288	296	301	296	302	312	321	325	329	338
Oregon	250	257	260	266	272	279	282	286	280	282	285	286	290	298	300
Pennsylvania	712	713	715	712	716	725	728	739	746	744	745	746	745	749	756
Rhode Island	61	61	63	63	63	64	65	66	66	66	65	65	64	64	62
South Carolina	294	295	299	309	315	323	323	326	326	325	328	331	337	346	349
South Dakota	70	69	69	69	70	71	73	74	75	75	75	75	76	76	78
Tennessee	373	382	380	386	390	399	403	410	411	413	415	413	421	428	428
Texas	1 446	1 458	1 483	1 504	1 535	1 562	1 586	1 626	1 646	1 656	1 684	1 707	1 735	1 779	1 820
Utah	164	167	172	177	180	185	190	195	197	199	202	205	207	212	214
Vermont	45	45	46	46	48	49	50	51	52	52	53	54	54	54	55
Virginia	598	596	597	602	611	625	629	635	638	651	662	675	683	694	697
Washington	444	451	458	466	474	483	505	516	521	524	527	530	534	546	549
West Virginia	136	139	139	141	141	143	141	143	143	143	144	145	145	147	150
Wisconsin	379	384	387	393	399	406	414	415	413	412	415	415	416	422	425
Wyoming	58	58	58	58	59	61	62	63	64	65	65	65	67	69	72
Puerto Rico	. . .	. . .	. . .	. . .	. . .	. . .	282	295	301	307	305	300	297	299	295
Virgin Islands	14	14	14	14	13	13	12	13	13	12	12	13	13	13	13

. . . = Not available.

EARNINGS

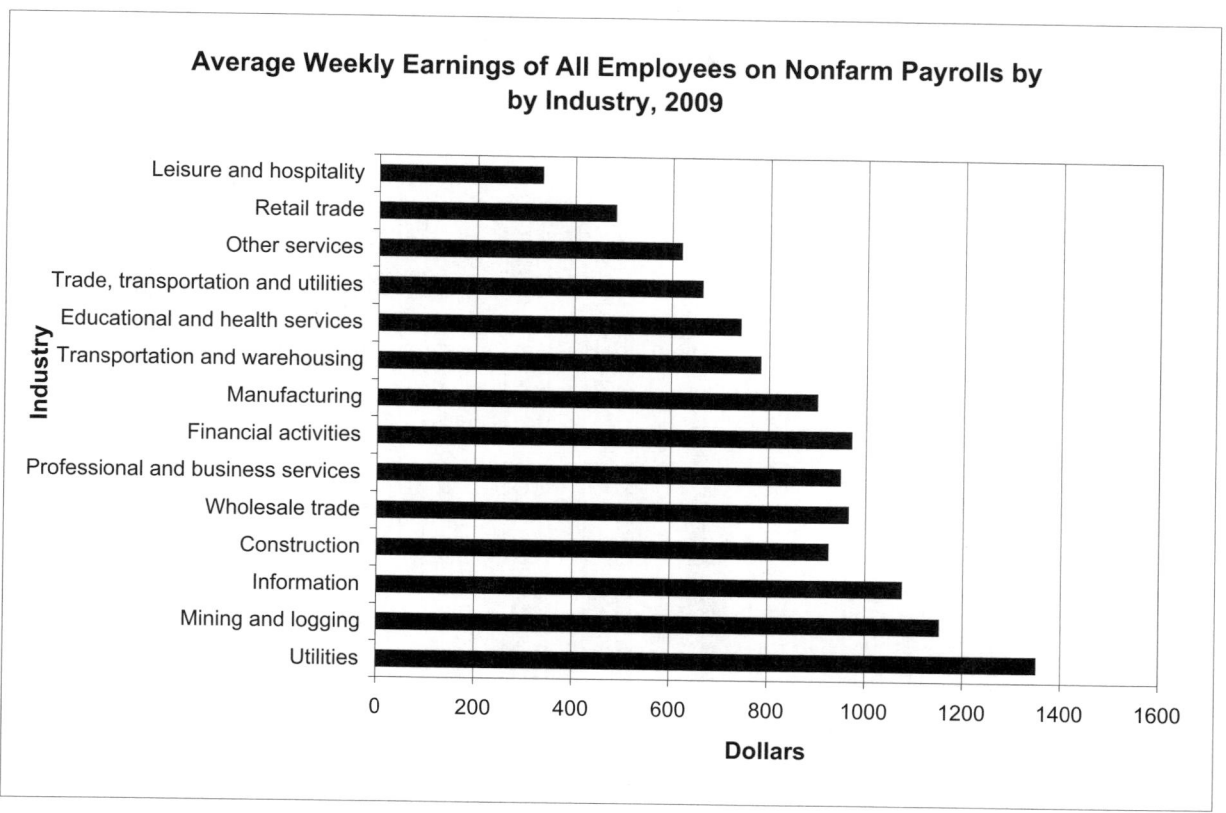

Average weekly earnings of all employees on nonfarm payrolls rose from $744.80 in 2008 to $753.02 in 2009, an increase of 1.1 percent. When adjusted for inflation, average weekly earnings increased 1.5 percent. Average weekly earnings ranged from $331.47 in leisure and hospitality to $1,348.43 in utilities. (See Table 2-14.)

OTHER HIGHLIGHTS

- In 2009, average weekly earnings for all employees also varied significantly by state. Earnings were highest in the District of Columbia ($1,138.73) followed by Connecticut ($918.06) and Washington ($905.75). Average weekly earnings were the lowest in South Dakota ($597.40). (See Table 2-17.)

- Average weekly earnings were $617.11 for all production workers on nonfarm private payrolls in 2009, an increase of 1.5 percent from 2008. Earnings ranged from $275.80 in leisure and hospitality to $1,243.76 in utilites. (See Table 2-15.)

- Average hourly earnings for all employees on private nonfarm payrolls rose 2.7 percent in 2009 after increasing by 3.1 percent from 2007 to 2008. Meanwhile, average hourly earnings rose 3.0 percent for production workers in 2009 following and increase of 3.7 percent from 2007 to 2008. (See Tables 2-12 and 2-13.)

Table 2-12. Average Hourly Earnings of All Employees on Total Private Payrolls by NAICS Super Sector, 2006–2009

(Dollars.)

| Year and month | Total private | Mining and logging | Construc-tion | Manufac-turing | Trade, transportation, and utilities | | | | | Informa-tion | Financial activities | Profes-sional and business services | Education and health services | Leisure and hospitality | Other services |
					Total	Total	Wholesale trade	Retail trade	Utilities						
2007	20.97	24.91	23.02	21.50	18.58	18.58	23.96	15.13	30.27	28.09	25.62	24.68	21.35	12.39	17.62
2008	21.62	26.20	23.96	22.16	18.93	18.93	24.37	15.21	32.22	28.66	26.16	25.82	22.12	12.77	18.17
2009	22.21	27.30	24.84	23.03	19.34	19.34	25.42	15.40	32.94	29.38	26.48	27.02	22.41	12.96	19.52
2006															
January	...	...	...	...	...	...	...	...	...	...	...	...	...	...	...
February	...	...	...	...	...	...	...	...	...	...	...	...	...	...	...
March	20.08	22.91	21.84	20.74	18.24	18.24	22.83	15.26	29.30	26.69	23.92	23.40	20.28	11.54	17.20
April	20.37	23.64	22.02	20.98	18.52	18.52	23.33	15.44	29.70	27.22	24.85	23.87	20.37	11.59	17.33
May	20.08	23.21	21.93	20.69	18.22	18.22	22.90	15.19	29.20	26.98	24.28	23.24	20.29	11.65	17.25
June	20.05	23.47	22.05	20.70	18.25	18.25	22.91	15.22	28.90	26.90	24.21	23.14	20.34	11.55	17.14
July	20.29	23.77	22.19	20.91	18.46	18.46	23.52	15.27	28.90	27.18	24.90	23.68	20.49	11.54	17.13
August	20.14	23.39	22.20	20.80	18.19	18.19	23.14	15.07	28.90	27.05	24.69	23.31	20.46	11.58	17.13
September	20.36	23.63	22.43	20.95	18.37	18.37	23.50	15.19	29.20	27.45	24.71	23.64	20.55	11.78	17.32
October	20.52	24.32	22.55	21.10	18.39	18.39	23.55	15.16	29.60	27.54	25.14	23.97	20.56	11.93	17.36
November	20.45	24.85	22.51	21.10	18.19	18.19	23.52	14.94	29.50	27.31	25.12	23.81	20.61	12.01	17.35
December	20.61	24.81	22.75	21.42	18.22	18.22	23.88	14.89	29.40	27.48	25.11	24.22	20.70	12.17	17.49
2007															
January	20.70	24.93	22.65	21.32	18.44	18.44	23.74	15.11	29.40	27.91	25.03	24.42	20.70	12.21	17.51
February	20.79	25.18	22.71	21.34	18.54	18.54	23.75	15.16	29.50	27.93	25.30	24.56	20.73	12.30	17.50
March	20.82	25.00	22.72	21.33	18.46	18.46	23.63	15.12	29.90	27.88	25.28	24.45	21.28	12.24	17.48
April	21.05	25.18	22.80	21.56	18.75	18.75	24.13	15.30	30.50	28.34	25.77	24.84	21.32	12.30	17.66
May	20.83	24.71	22.88	21.40	18.46	18.46	23.73	15.10	30.20	28.07	25.50	24.46	21.23	12.35	17.50
June	20.82	24.88	22.85	21.42	18.53	18.53	23.84	15.13	29.90	27.80	25.47	24.45	21.30	12.27	17.51
July	20.99	24.88	23.00	21.55	18.64	18.64	24.08	15.15	30.40	28.08	25.78	24.85	21.43	12.29	17.59
August	20.85	24.60	23.04	21.45	18.47	18.47	23.87	15.02	30.10	27.94	25.59	24.44	21.40	12.28	17.59
September	21.18	24.65	23.26	21.61	18.80	18.80	24.25	15.29	30.60	28.34	26.01	24.91	21.61	12.46	17.78
October	21.07	24.78	23.21	21.48	18.66	18.66	24.03	15.16	30.80	28.29	25.70	24.65	21.60	12.53	17.70
November	21.13	24.82	23.33	21.66	18.57	18.57	24.13	15.01	30.70	28.12	25.83	24.80	21.69	12.62	17.72
December	21.37	25.34	23.67	21.92	18.62	18.62	24.32	14.97	31.40	28.32	26.14	25.33	21.81	12.90	17.90
2008															
January	21.35	25.73	23.48	21.83	18.76	18.76	24.21	15.10	31.50	28.33	25.85	25.33	21.80	12.77	17.83
February	21.43	25.16	23.57	21.88	18.87	18.87	24.23	15.20	32.20	28.31	26.04	25.48	21.81	12.85	17.89
March	21.58	26.57	23.60	22.02	18.90	18.90	24.37	15.20	31.90	28.85	26.24	25.72	22.02	12.80	18.18
April	21.49	25.29	23.60	21.99	18.92	18.92	24.22	15.28	31.60	28.58	26.12	25.46	22.01	12.78	18.14
May	21.46	25.13	23.73	22.02	18.88	18.88	24.11	15.27	31.80	28.48	26.13	25.47	21.96	12.77	18.11
June	21.53	25.60	23.69	22.11	18.99	18.99	24.28	15.27	32.60	28.66	26.22	25.72	21.98	12.65	18.18
July	21.49	26.40	23.87	22.08	18.93	18.93	24.31	15.19	32.00	28.68	26.06	25.59	22.12	12.57	18.12
August	21.54	26.65	24.12	22.06	18.92	18.92	24.42	15.20	32.30	28.72	26.11	25.66	22.14	12.62	18.14
September	21.74	26.38	24.27	22.20	19.05	19.05	24.39	15.36	32.60	28.87	26.22	25.89	22.33	12.80	18.28
October	21.78	26.36	24.34	22.35	18.95	18.95	24.35	15.20	32.50	28.82	26.23	26.05	22.30	12.81	18.28
November	22.03	27.39	24.46	22.62	19.07	19.07	24.77	15.22	32.90	28.90	26.45	26.73	22.43	12.89	18.44
December	22.02	27.51	24.80	22.76	18.91	18.91	24.78	15.04	33.00	28.72	26.24	26.74	22.56	13.02	18.48
2009															
January	22.11	27.49	24.68	22.87	19.20	19.20	24.98	15.30	32.80	28.75	26.13	26.89	22.48	12.99	18.60
February	22.29	27.67	24.65	23.04	19.38	19.38	25.29	15.41	33.10	29.24	26.46	27.37	22.52	13.01	18.64
March	22.25	27.85	24.80	23.06	19.35	19.35	25.17	15.40	33.20	29.09	26.39	27.32	22.19	12.94	19.72
April	22.16	27.56	24.74	23.09	19.31	19.31	25.18	15.39	32.90	28.85	26.26	27.02	22.29	12.91	19.63
May	22.07	27.42	24.67	22.99	19.26	19.26	25.11	15.40	33.00	29.18	26.36	26.84	22.21	12.85	19.61
June	21.99	27.15	24.64	22.93	19.19	19.19	25.03	15.33	32.80	29.07	26.26	26.73	22.26	12.77	19.50
July	22.03	27.04	24.73	22.98	19.24	19.24	25.23	15.37	32.70	29.50	26.29	26.83	22.35	12.72	19.48
August	22.19	27.26	24.86	22.97	19.51	19.51	25.76	15.54	32.80	29.84	26.66	26.97	22.35	12.79	19.62
September	22.23	26.95	24.93	23.06	19.47	19.47	25.64	15.61	32.80	29.60	26.45	26.97	22.45	13.00	19.77
October	22.29	27.07	25.11	22.99	19.41	19.41	25.67	15.40	33.00	29.83	26.67	26.87	22.56	13.09	19.78
November	22.47	26.89	25.10	23.17	19.49	19.49	25.97	15.42	33.20	30.01	27.02	27.25	22.58	13.22	19.94
December	22.41	27.16	25.26	23.22	19.31	19.31	25.98	15.23	33.10	29.64	26.78	27.17	22.68	13.31	20.00

. . . = Not available.

Table 2-13. Average Hourly Earnings of Production Workers on Private Nonfarm Payrolls, by Super Sector, NAICS Basis, 2000–2009

(Dollars.)

Industry	2000	2001	2002	2003	2004	2005	2006	2007	2008	2009
TOTAL PRIVATE	14.02	14.54	14.97	15.37	15.69	16.13	16.76	17.43	18.08	18.62
Goods-Producing	15.27	15.78	16.33	16.80	17.19	17.60	18.02	18.67	19.33	19.90
Natural resources and mining	16.55	17.00	17.19	17.56	18.07	18.72	19.90	20.97	22.50	23.29
Construction	17.48	18.00	18.52	18.95	19.23	19.46	20.02	20.95	21.87	22.67
Manufacturing	14.32	14.76	15.29	15.74	16.14	16.56	16.81	17.26	17.75	18.23
Private Service-Providing	13.62	14.18	14.59	14.99	15.29	15.74	16.42	17.11	17.77	18.35
Trade, transportation, and utilities	13.31	13.70	14.02	14.34	14.58	14.92	15.39	15.78	16.16	16.50
Wholesale trade	16.28	16.77	16.98	17.36	17.65	18.16	18.91	19.59	20.13	20.85
Retail trade	10.86	11.29	11.67	11.90	12.08	12.36	12.57	12.75	12.87	13.02
Transportation and warehousing	15.05	15.33	15.76	16.25	16.52	16.70	17.28	17.72	18.41	18.80
Utilities	22.75	23.58	23.96	24.77	25.61	26.68	27.40	27.88	28.83	29.56
Information	19.07	19.80	20.20	21.01	21.40	22.06	23.23	23.96	24.78	25.45
Financial activities	14.98	15.59	16.17	17.14	17.52	17.95	18.80	19.64	20.28	20.83
Professional and business services	15.52	16.33	16.81	17.21	17.48	18.08	19.13	20.15	21.18	22.35
Education and health services	13.95	14.64	15.21	15.64	16.15	16.71	17.38	18.11	18.87	19.49
Leisure and hospitality	8.32	8.57	8.81	9.00	9.15	9.38	9.75	10.41	10.84	11.11
Other services	12.73	13.27	13.72	13.84	13.98	14.34	14.77	15.42	16.09	16.59

Table 2-14. Average Weekly Earnings of All Employees on Nonfarm Payrolls, by Industry, in Current and 1982–1984 Dollars, NAICS Basis, 2007–2009

(Dollars.)

Industry	2007	2008	2009
TOTAL PRIVATE			
Current dollars	725.22	744.80	753.02
1982–1984 dollars	349.77	345.93	351.00
Goods-Producing			
Current dollars	873.51	899.62	915.88
1982–1984 dollars	421.29	417.84	426.91
Mining and logging			
Current dollars	1 094.85	1 144.59	1 150.38
1982–1984 dollars	528.04	531.62	536.22
Construction			
Current dollars	875.28	905.68	923.11
1982–1984 dollars	422.14	420.65	430.28
Manufacturing			
Current dollars	861.22	882.19	898.19
1982–1984 dollars	415.36	409.74	418.66
Private Service-Providing			
Current dollars	689.95	709.65	718.86
1982–1984 dollars	332.76	329.61	335.08
Trade, transportation, and utilities			
Current dollars	641.97	651.96	660.41
1982–1984 dollars	309.62	302.81	307.83
Wholesale trade			
Current dollars	913.00	936.17	963.49
1982–1984 dollars	440.34	434.82	449.10
Retail trade			
Current dollars	479.91	477.87	481.24
1982–1984 dollars	231.46	221.95	224.32
Transportation and warehousing			
Current dollars	758.26	780.55	780.37
1982–1984 dollars	365.70	362.54	363.75
Utilities			
Current dollars	1 264.45	1 352.50	1 348.43
1982–1984 dollars	609.84	628.18	628.53
Information			
Current dollars	1 014.38	1 047.50	1 073.14
1982–1984 dollars	489.23	486.52	500.21
Financial activities			
Current dollars	936.56	954.82	968.64
1982–1984 dollars	451.70	443.48	451.50
Professional and business services			
Current dollars	874.68	909.23	946.84
1982–1984 dollars	421.85	422.30	441.34
Education and health services			
Current dollars	715.84	745.03	739.19
1982–1984 dollars	345.25	346.04	344.55
Leisure and hospitality			
Current dollars	323.54	330.32	331.47
1982–1984 dollars	156.04	153.42	154.50
Other services			
Current dollars	578.84	597.13	617.72
1982–1984 dollars	279.17	277.34	287.93

Table 2-15. Average Weekly Earnings of Production Workers on Nonfarm Payrolls, by Industry, in Current and 1982–1984 Dollars, NAICS Basis, 2000–2009

(Dollars.)

Industry	2000	2001	2002	2003	2004	2005	2006	2007	2008	2009
TOTAL PRIVATE										
Current dollars	481.01	493.79	506.75	518.06	529.09	544.33	567.87	590.04	607.95	617.11
1982 dollars	284.79	284.61	288.09	288.13	286.77	284.99	288.11	290.99	288.06	294.38
Goods-Producing										
Current dollars	621.86	630.01	651.61	669.13	688.13	705.31	730.16	757.34	776.66	779.83
1982 dollars	368.18	363.12	370.44	372.15	372.97	369.27	370.45	373.50	367.99	372.00
Mining and logging										
Current dollars	734.92	757.92	741.97	765.94	803.82	853.71	907.95	962.64	1 014.69	1 007.85
1982 dollars	435.12	436.84	421.81	426.00	435.67	446.97	460.65	474.75	480.77	480.78
Construction										
Current dollars	685.78	695.89	711.82	726.83	735.55	750.22	781.21	816.66	842.61	852.45
1982 dollars	406.03	401.09	404.67	404.24	398.67	392.79	396.35	402.76	399.24	406.65
Manufacturing										
Current dollars	590.77	595.19	618.75	635.99	658.49	673.30	691.02	711.56	724.46	725.87
1982 dollars	349.78	343.05	351.76	353.72	356.91	352.51	350.59	350.92	343.26	346.26
Private Service-Providing										
Current dollars	445.74	461.08	473.80	484.68	494.22	509.58	532.78	554.89	574.35	588.07
1982 dollars	263.91	265.75	269.36	269.57	267.87	266.80	270.31	273.66	272.14	280.53
Trade, transportation, and utilities										
Current dollars	449.88	459.53	471.27	481.14	488.42	498.43	514.34	526.07	536.06	542.36
1982 dollars	266.36	264.86	267.92	267.60	264.73	260.96	260.95	259.45	253.99	258.72
Wholesale trade										
Current dollars	631.40	643.45	644.38	657.29	667.09	685.00	718.63	748.94	769.62	784.75
1982 dollars	373.83	370.86	366.33	365.57	361.57	358.64	364.60	369.36	364.66	374.35
Retail trade										
Current dollars	333.38	346.16	360.81	367.15	371.13	377.58	383.02	385.11	386.21	388.72
1982 dollars	197.38	199.52	205.12	204.20	201.15	197.69	194.33	189.93	182.99	185.43
Transportation and warehousing										
Current dollars	562.31	562.70	579.88	598.41	614.96	618.58	636.97	654.95	670.37	677.44
1982 dollars	266.36	264.86	267.92	267.60	264.73	260.96	260.95	259.45	253.99	258.72
Utilities										
Current dollars	955.66	977.18	979.09	1 017.27	1 048.44	1 095.90	1 135.34	1 182.65	1 230.69	1 243.76
1982 dollars	565.81	563.22	556.62	565.78	568.26	573.77	576.02	583.26	583.12	593.31
Information										
Current dollars	700.86	730.88	737.77	760.45	777.25	805.08	850.42	874.65	908.99	931.93
1982 dollars	414.96	421.26	419.43	422.94	421.27	421.51	431.47	431.36	430.69	444.56
Financial activities										
Current dollars	537.37	557.92	575.54	609.08	622.87	644.99	672.21	705.13	727.07	751.21
1982 dollars	318.16	321.57	327.20	338.75	337.60	337.69	341.05	347.75	344.50	358.35
Professional and business services										
Current dollars	535.07	557.84	574.66	587.02	597.56	618.87	662.27	700.82	737.70	775.81
1982 dollars	316.80	321.52	326.70	326.48	323.88	324.02	336.01	345.63	349.53	370.09
Education and health services										
Current dollars	449.29	473.39	492.74	505.69	523.78	544.59	564.94	590.09	613.73	628.56
1982 dollars	266.01	272.85	280.13	281.25	283.89	285.13	286.63	291.02	290.79	299.84
Leisure and hospitality										
Current dollars	217.20	220.73	227.17	230.42	234.86	241.36	250.34	265.52	273.39	275.80
1982 dollars	128.60	127.22	129.15	128.15	127.30	126.37	127.01	130.95	129.54	131.57
Other services										
Current dollars	413.41	428.64	439.76	434.41	433.04	443.37	456.50	477.06	495.57	506.28
1982 dollars	244.77	247.05	250.01	241.61	234.71	232.13	231.61	235.27	234.81	241.51

Table 2-16. Average Hourly Earnings of All Employees on Total Private Payrolls, by State, NAICS Basis, 2007–2009

(Dollars.)

State	2007	2008	2009
UNITED STATES	20.97	21.62	22.21
Alabama	19.37	19.56	19.68
Alaska	24.70	25.01	24.80
Arizona	19.84	20.69	22.03
Arkansas	16.27	17.21	17.97
California	24.69	24.70	25.48
Colorado	23.13	23.80	23.78
Connecticut	26.59	27.71	27.82
Delaware	21.98	22.73	22.38
District of Columbia	. . .	32.37	31.37
Florida	20.58	21.00	21.61
Georgia	20.43	20.77	21.08
Hawaii	20.68	20.80	21.11
Idaho	16.51	17.53	19.26
Illinois	22.94	22.67	23.05
Indiana	19.94	20.30	20.56
Iowa	18.01	18.35	20.01
Kansas	19.64	20.13	20.18
Kentucky	17.73	18.07	18.82
Louisiana	18.73	19.22	19.46
Maine	18.74	18.96	19.16
Maryland	24.04	24.56	25.42
Massachusetts	26.07	26.38	26.85
Michigan	21.55	21.62	21.90
Minnesota	23.13	23.23	23.41
Mississippi	16.46	16.89	17.87
Missouri	19.78	20.57	20.94
Montana	17.80	18.43	19.86
Nebraska	19.92	19.79	20.19
Nevada	19.64	19.75	19.56
New Hampshire	22.06	22.66	22.70
New Jersey	24.84	25.32	25.92
New Mexico	18.57	18.73	18.92
New York	25.26	25.48	25.70
North Carolina	19.25	19.90	20.57
North Dakota	18.34	18.75	19.21
Ohio	20.22	20.11	19.95
Oklahoma	17.33	17.43	18.08
Oregon	20.61	20.93	21.33
Pennsylvania	20.07	20.43	20.74
Rhode Island	22.17	22.50	22.52
South Carolina	18.76	18.80	19.17
South Dakota	16.47	16.53	17.94
Tennessee	19.01	19.40	19.52
Texas	21.07	21.30	21.40
Utah	21.41	21.10	22.48
Vermont	20.42	21.35	22.41
Virginia	22.46	22.31	22.58
Washington	24.19	25.23	26.33
West Virginia	17.04	17.70	18.09
Wisconsin	20.45	20.67	21.12
Wyoming	20.03	20.83	21.07

. . . = Not available.

Table 2-17. Average Weekly Earnings of All Employees on Total Nonfarm Payrolls, by State, NAICS Basis, 2007–2009

(Dollars.)

State	2007	2008	2009
UNITED STATES	725.22	744.80	753.02
Alabama	708.94	704.16	686.83
Alaska	876.85	882.85	868.00
Arizona	698.37	720.01	766.64
Arkansas	569.45	605.79	621.76
California	851.81	844.74	861.22
Colorado	807.24	828.24	815.65
Connecticut	912.04	942.14	918.06
Delaware	753.91	768.27	731.83
District of Columbia	. . .	1 158.85	1 138.73
Florida	728.53	739.20	756.35
Georgia	727.31	733.18	729.37
Hawaii	674.17	678.08	686.08
Idaho	566.29	594.27	647.14
Illinois	789.14	777.58	792.92
Indiana	707.87	710.50	711.38
Iowa	615.94	620.23	668.33
Kansas	615.94	620.23	668.33
Kentucky	652.46	654.13	666.23
Louisiana	670.53	701.53	702.51
Maine	640.91	650.33	638.03
Maryland	836.59	852.23	876.99
Massachusetts	873.35	889.01	902.16
Michigan	752.10	739.40	729.27
Minnesota	781.79	778.21	763.17
Mississippi	587.62	601.28	632.60
Missouri	680.43	709.67	709.87
Montana	633.68	595.29	619.63
Nebraska	667.32	666.92	680.40
Nevada	732.57	730.75	700.25
New Hampshire	734.60	743.25	742.29
New Jersey	844.56	850.75	870.91
New Mexico	642.52	663.04	664.09
New York	861.37	868.87	868.66
North Carolina	669.90	682.57	695.27
North Dakota	605.22	607.50	614.72
Ohio	685.46	681.73	658.35
Oklahoma	606.55	618.77	634.61
Oregon	704.86	707.43	708.16
Pennsylvania	678.37	688.49	686.49
Rhode Island	742.70	767.25	763.43
South Carolina	675.36	669.28	665.20
South Dakota	543.51	543.84	597.40
Tennessee	671.05	682.88	687.10
Texas	769.06	773.19	755.42
Utah	747.21	730.06	804.78
Vermont	696.32	734.44	764.18
Virginia	790.59	780.85	781.27
Washington	853.91	872.96	905.75
West Virginia	599.81	623.04	622.30
Wisconsin	672.81	682.11	680.06
Wyoming	725.09	764.46	750.09

. . . = Not available.

NOTES AND DEFINITIONS

QUARTERLY CENSUS OF EMPLOYMENT AND WAGES

The Quarterly Census of Employment and Wages (QCEW), often referred to as the ES-202 program, is a cooperative endeavor of the Bureau of Labor Statistics (BLS) and the State Employment Security Agencies (SESAs). Using quarterly data submitted by the agencies, BLS summarizes the employment and wage data for workers covered by state unemployment insurance laws and civilian workers covered by the Unemployment Compensation for Federal Employees (UCFE) program.

Since the introduction of 2001 data, the QCEW data have been coded according to the North American Classification System, either NAICS 2002, which was used for the data up through 2006, or NAICS 2007 which will be used for data for the period from 2007 forward. NAICS is the statistical classification standard underlying all establishment-based federal economic statistics classified by industry. Before 2001, QCEW data were coded according to the Standard Industrial Classification (SIC) system. Due to the differences in the classification systems, data coded according to NAICS are often not directly comparable to SIC coded data.

Most industry definitions remained the same under NAICS 2007 as they were under NAICS 2002. However, there were a few industries with substantial changes. As QCEW data coded to the NAICS 2007 system become available, users will need to exercise caution in making comparisons that span the transition.

The QCEW data series is the most complete universe of employment and wage information by industry, county, and state. It includes 98% of all wage and salary civilian employment. These data serve as the basic source of benchmark information for employment by industry in the Current Employment Statistics (CES) survey, which is described in the first section of notes in this chapter. Therefore, the entire employment series is not presented here. The wage series is presented because the CES only provides earnings only for production and nonsupervisory employees. The QCEW is more comprehensive. BLS aggregates the data by industry and ownership; these aggregations are available at the national, state, county, and metropolitan statistical area (MSA) levels.

Collection and Coverage

Employment data under the QCEW program represent the number of covered workers who worked during, or received pay for, the pay period including the 12th of the month. Excluded are members of the armed forces, the self-employed, proprietors, domestic workers, unpaid family workers, and railroad workers covered by the railroad unemployment insurance system. Wages represent total compensation paid during the calendar quarter, regardless of when services were performed. Included in wages are pay for vacation and other paid leave, bonuses, stock options, tips, the cash value of meals and lodging, and in some states, contributions to deferred compensation plans (such as 401(k) plans). The QCEW program does provide partial information on agricultural industries and employees in private households.

Data from the QCEW program serve as an important input to many BLS programs. The QCEW data are used as the benchmark source for employment by the Current Employment Statistics program and the Occupational employment statistics program. The UI administrative records collected under the QCEW program serve as a sampling frame for BLS establishment surveys.

In addition, data from the QCEW program serve as an input to other federal and state programs. The Bureau of Economic Analysis (BEA) of the Department of Commerce uses QCEW data as the base for developing the wage and salary component of personal income. The Employment and Training Administration (ETA) of the Department of Labor and the SESAs use QCEW data to administer the employment security program. The QCEW data accurately reflect the extent of coverage of the state UI laws and are used to measure UI revenues; national, state and local area employment; and total and UI taxable wage trends.

Sources of Additional Information

Additional information is available on the BLS Web site at <http://www.bls.gov/cew>.

Table 2-18. Employment and Average Annual Pay for Covered Workers,[1] by Industry, NAICS Basis, 2004–2009

(Number, dollars.)

Industry	2004		2005		2006	
	Employment	Average annual pay	Employment	Average annual pay	Employment	Average annual pay
Total Private	108 490 066	39 134	110 611 016	40 505	112 718 858	42 414
Agriculture, forestry, fishing, and hunting	1 155 106	22 337	1 163 629	23 117	1 160 179	24 132
Mining and logging	519 931	66 632	560 416	72 226	616 598	78 224
Construction	6 916 398	40 521	7 269 317	42 100	7 602 148	44 496
Manufacturing	14 257 380	47 861	14 190 394	49 287	14 110 663	51 427
Wholesale trade	5 642 537	53 310	5 752 802	55 262	5 885 194	58 046
Retail trade	15 060 686	24 415	15 256 340	24 930	15 370 040	25 567
Transportation and warehousing	4 009 165	38 834	4 098 553	39 515	4 204 514	40 848
Utilities	563 931	72 403	550 593	75 208	546 521	78 341
Information	3 099 633	60 722	3 056 431	62 853	3 040 577	65 962
Financial activities	7 890 786	61 487	8 037 850	64 398	8 162 063	68 901
Professional and business services	16 294 776	47 401	16 869 852	49 574	17 469 679	51 974
Education and health services	16 084 963	36 548	16 479 482	37 654	16 916 228	39 115
Leisure and hospitality	12 467 597	16 624	12 739 466	17 068	13 024 615	17 781
Other services	4 287 999	25 152	4 324 015	25 883	4 364 889	26 923
Total Government	20 788 110	40 500	20 960 607	41 585	21 114 976	43 180
Federal	2 739 596	57 782	2 733 675	59 864	2 728 974	62 274
State	4 484 997	41 118	4 527 514	42 249	4 565 908	43 875
Local	13 563 517	36 805	13 699 418	37 718	13 820 093	39 179

Industry	2007		2008		2009	
	Employment	Average annual pay	Employment	Average annual pay	Employment	Average annual pay
Total Private	114 012 221	44 362	113 188 643	45 371	106 947 104	45 155
Agriculture, forestry, fishing, and hunting	1 166 333	25 191	1 169 029	25 986	1 142 192	26 031
Mining and logging	660 276	82 019	713 398	87 160	641 366	85 526
Construction	7 562 732	46 784	7 124 886	49 013	5 948 837	49 322
Manufacturing	13 833 022	53 489	13 382 697	54 400	11 810 371	54 873
Wholesale trade	5 987 206	60 719	5 954 915	61 843	5 561 787	61 595
Retail trade	15 509 017	26 124	15 307 933	26 179	14 544 111	26 162
Transportation and warehousing	4 292 445	42 615	4 271 969	42 962	3 985 037	42 823
Utilities	549 539	82 275	557 983	84 153	560 713	84 877
Information	3 029 789	69 140	2 989 161	70 787	2 807 721	71 191
Financial activities	8 145 981	73 980	7 968 376	74 133	7 589 821	70 045
Professional and business services	17 859 796	55 139	17 705 280	57 476	16 488 835	58 344
Education and health services	17 433 162	40 528	17 954 103	41 984	18 321 635	43 042
Leisure and hospitality	13 327 559	18 495	13 395 477	18 946	13 001 028	18 899
Other services	4 438 439	27 970	4 484 907	28 773	4 369 780	28 814
Total Government	21 353 885	44 968	21 617 017	46 568	21 660 738	47 552
Federal	2 726 300	64 871	2 762 055	66 293	2 826 713	67 756
State	4 611 395	45 903	4 642 650	47 980	4 639 715	48 742
Local	14 016 190	40 790	14 212 311	42 274	14 194 311	43 140

[1]Includes workers covered by unemployment insurance (UI) and Unemployment Compensation for Federal Employees (UCFE) programs.

Table 2-19. Employment and Average Annual Pay for Covered Workers,[1] by State and Selected Territory, 2004–2009

(Number, dollars.)

State	2004		2005		2006	
	Employment	Average annual pay	Employment	Average annual pay	Employment	Average annual pay
UNITED STATES	129 278 176	39 354	131 571 623	40 677	133 833 834	42 535
Alabama	1 851 769	33 414	1 894 616	34 598	1 928 281	36 204
Alaska	296 292	39 062	302 330	40 216	307 637	41 750
Arizona	2 354 660	36 646	2 489 462	38 154	2 614 344	40 019
Arkansas	1 129 018	30 245	1 147 615	31 266	1 167 925	32 389
California	14 953 022	44 641	15 234 188	46 211	15 503 144	48 345
Colorado	2 142 352	40 276	2 189 516	41 601	2 242 012	43 506
Connecticut	1 631 240	51 007	1 644 274	52 954	1 672 109	54 814
Delaware	411 298	42 487	417 692	44 622	422 187	46 285
District of Columbia	659 542	63 887	667 512	66 696	671 143	70 151
Florida	7 463 255	35 186	7 747 729	36 800	7 952 023	38 485
Georgia	3 840 663	37 866	3 932 315	39 096	4 024 699	40 370
Hawaii	585 131	35 198	603 668	36 353	618 178	37 799
Idaho	591 355	29 871	614 548	30 777	643 671	32 580
Illinois	5 700 643	42 277	5 748 355	43 744	5 821 022	45 650
Indiana	2 848 873	34 694	2 873 795	35 431	2 892 419	36 553
Iowa	1 422 454	32 097	1 446 568	33 070	1 470 742	34 320
Kansas	1 296 618	32 738	1 305 440	33 864	1 327 677	35 696
Kentucky	1 729 015	33 165	1 757 997	33 965	1 779 202	35 201
Louisiana	1 865 164	31 880	1 841 046	33 566	1 807 563	36 604
Maine	597 238	31 906	594 481	32 701	598 525	33 794
Maryland	2 459 362	42 579	2 497 487	44 368	2 530 011	46 162
Massachusetts	3 138 738	48 916	3 159 934	50 095	3 194 914	52 435
Michigan	4 301 743	40 373	4 297 017	41 214	4 235 650	42 157
Minnesota	2 600 360	40 398	2 640 326	40 800	2 670 222	42 185
Mississippi	1 105 915	28 535	1 111 269	29 763	1 122 474	31 194
Missouri	2 627 401	34 845	2 664 447	35 951	2 699 860	37 143
Montana	403 432	27 830	413 460	29 150	426 182	30 596
Nebraska	882 263	31 507	892 397	32 422	902 383	33 814
Nevada	1 145 762	37 106	1 215 783	38 763	1 271 634	40 070
New Hampshire	613 310	39 176	620 893	40 551	627 371	42 447
New Jersey	3 873 787	48 064	3 917 397	49 471	3 951 210	51 645
New Mexico	760 449	31 411	778 233	32 605	807 063	34 567
New York	8 271 927	49 941	8 348 739	51 937	8 429 519	55 479
North Carolina	3 777 872	34 791	3 856 748	35 912	3 965 479	37 439
North Dakota	321 108	28 987	328 097	29 956	335 718	31 316
Ohio	5 292 088	36 441	5 308 808	37 333	5 314 572	38 568
Oklahoma	1 427 618	30 743	1 465 969	31 721	1 507 196	34 022
Oregon	1 595 003	35 630	1 652 773	36 588	1 699 932	38 077
Pennsylvania	5 496 599	38 555	5 552 301	39 661	5 607 139	41 349
Rhode Island	475 628	37 651	477 420	38 751	480 570	40 454
South Carolina	1 789 447	31 839	1 819 217	32 927	1 855 842	34 281
South Dakota	369 632	28 281	375 707	29 149	383 876	30 291
Tennessee	2 644 749	34 549	2 685 491	35 879	2 728 694	37 564
Texas	9 323 537	38 511	9 583 457	40 150	9 922 313	42 458
Utah	1 071 855	32 171	1 115 375	33 328	1 170 587	35 130
Vermont	298 454	33 274	300 919	34 197	303 205	35 542
Virginia	3 495 767	40 534	3 578 558	42 287	3 636 417	44 051
Washington	2 694 933	39 361	2 766 451	40 721	2 850 073	42 897
West Virginia	686 936	30 382	695 382	31 347	705 189	32 728
Wisconsin	2 714 847	34 743	2 744 006	35 471	2 767 141	36 821
Wyoming	248 051	31 210	254 418	33 251	266 894	36 662
Puerto Rico	1 043 949	22 259	1 048 004	22 859	1 036 802	23 707
Virgin Islands	30 669	43 156	32 023	44 464	32 632	45 114

[1]Includes workers covered by the unemployment insurance (UI) and Unemployment Compensation for Federal Employees (UCFE) programs.

Table 2-19. Employment and Average Annual Pay for Covered Workers,[1] by State and Selected Territory, 2004–2009—Continued

(Number, dollars.)

State	2007 Employment	2007 Average annual pay	2008 Employment	2008 Average annual pay	2009 Employment	2009 Average annual pay
UNITED STATES	135 366 106	44 458	134 805 659	45 563	128 607 842	45 559
Alabama	1 952 091	37 492	1 936 489	38 734	1 829 487	39 422
Alaska	310 810	43 972	315 285	45 805	313 802	47 103
Arizona	2 647 691	41 551	2 583 215	42 518	2 396 362	42 832
Arkansas	1 173 852	34 118	1 172 208	34 919	1 134 488	35 692
California	15 640 575	50 538	15 494 915	51 487	14 629 953	51 566
Colorado	2 292 630	45 396	2 310 865	46 614	2 201 427	46 861
Connecticut	1 686 043	58 029	1 687 902	58 395	1 615 356	57 771
Delaware	423 412	47 308	423 083	47 569	402 343	47 770
District of Columbia	678 119	73 450	685 069	76 518	681 875	77 483
Florida	7 945 162	39 746	7 666 374	40 568	7 182 815	40 970
Georgia	4 077 184	42 178	4 031 467	42 585	3 796 429	42 902
Hawaii	625 862	39 466	619 703	40 675	592 171	41 328
Idaho	660 683	33 544	653 108	33 897	613 814	34 124
Illinois	5 869 157	47 685	5 841 692	48 719	5 551 930	48 358
Indiana	2 905 725	37 528	2 872 442	38 403	2 705 331	38 270
Iowa	1 485 627	35 738	1 490 575	36 964	1 445 627	37 158
Kansas	1 356 966	37 044	1 366 878	38 178	1 317 029	38 154
Kentucky	1 801 907	36 480	1 791 017	37 434	1 710 677	37 996
Louisiana	1 868 986	38 229	1 890 007	40 381	1 849 303	40 579
Maine	602 321	35 129	602 074	36 317	581 796	36 617
Maryland	2 547 351	48 241	2 537 752	49 535	2 461 109	50 579
Massachusetts	3 234 357	55 244	3 245 983	56 746	3 135 497	56 267
Michigan	4 179 122	43 357	4 070 914	44 245	3 775 435	43 645
Minnesota	2 687 482	44 375	2 679 527	45 826	2 569 651	45 319
Mississippi	1 135 336	32 291	1 131 096	33 508	1 081 138	33 847
Missouri	2 719 380	38 603	2 715 183	40 361	2 607 595	40 022
Montana	436 656	32 224	437 591	33 305	421 566	33 762
Nebraska	916 580	35 238	922 929	36 243	901 470	36 644
Nevada	1 284 502	42 149	1 252 987	42 984	1 138 036	42 743
New Hampshire	630 204	43 863	628 763	44 912	605 004	44 932
New Jersey	3 961 341	53 853	3 934 789	55 280	3 771 296	55 168
New Mexico	821 484	36 379	825 736	37 910	791 509	38 529
New York	8 554 012	59 439	8 608 351	60 288	8 343 862	57 739
North Carolina	4 062 955	38 909	4 043 486	39 740	3 823 299	39 844
North Dakota	341 705	33 086	350 440	35 075	349 560	35 970
Ohio	5 306 812	39 917	5 235 972	40 784	4 943 970	40 900
Oklahoma	1 534 802	35 491	1 550 489	37 284	1 497 855	37 238
Oregon	1 727 886	39 569	1 713 764	40 500	1 607 915	40 757
Pennsylvania	5 652 547	43 239	5 658 771	44 381	5 468 176	44 829
Rhode Island	480 132	41 646	469 701	43 029	448 842	43 439
South Carolina	1 891 255	35 393	1 876 081	36 252	1 765 739	36 759
South Dakota	392 060	31 655	397 108	32 822	389 360	33 352
Tennessee	2 745 099	39 082	2 721 990	39 996	2 565 288	40 242
Texas	10 231 906	44 695	10 452 907	45 939	10 149 694	45 692
Utah	1 219 207	37 054	1 221 052	37 980	1 157 704	38 614
Vermont	303 448	36 956	302 627	38 328	292 406	38 778
Virginia	3 672 958	45 995	3 665 654	47 241	3 545 623	48 239
Washington	2 925 908	45 021	2 950 773	46 569	2 836 283	47 470
West Virginia	706 172	34 106	709 657	35 987	691 998	36 897
Wisconsin	2 780 924	38 050	2 772 889	39 119	2 644 190	39 131
Wyoming	277 721	39 254	286 333	41 487	274 758	40 709
Puerto Rico	1 016 362	24 741	1 001 120	25 554	954 555	26 359
Virgin Islands	33 097	45 922	32 661	45 796	30 691	43 799

[1]Includes workers covered by the unemployment insurance (UI) and Unemployment Compensation for Federal Employees (UCFE) programs.

BUSINESS EMPLOYMENT DYNAMICS

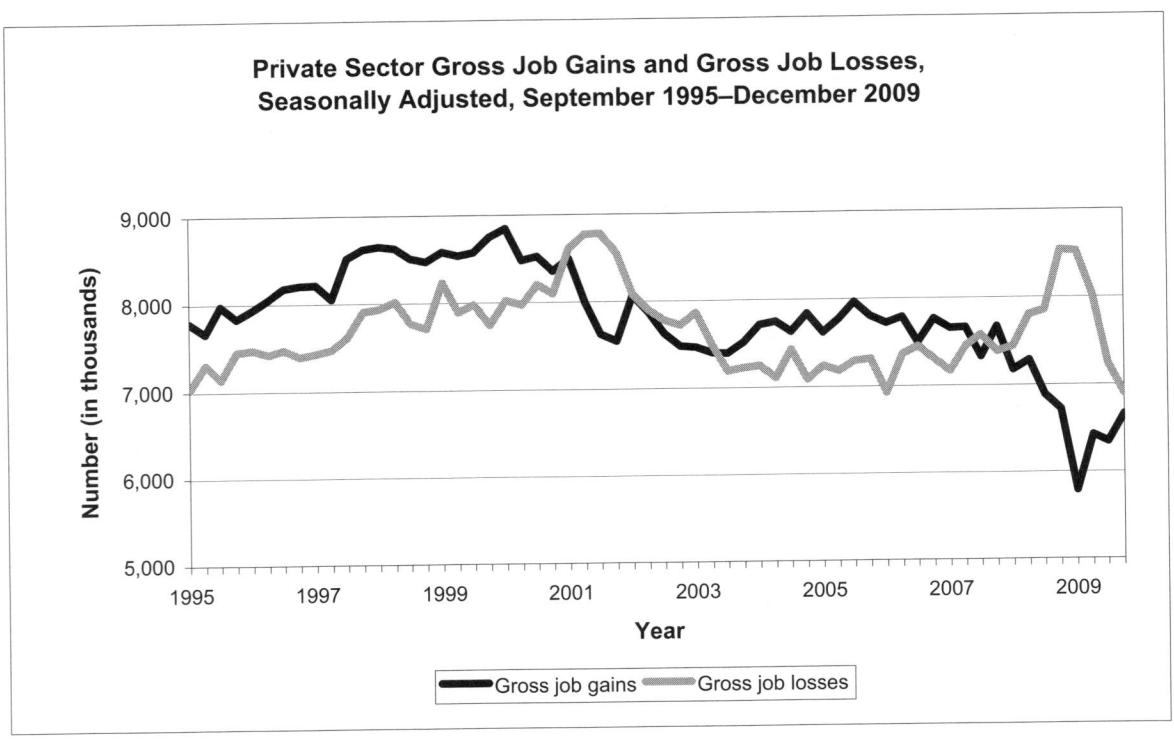

Private Sector Gross Job Gains and Gross Job Losses, Seasonally Adjusted, September 1995–December 2009

The change in the number of jobs is the net result of the gross increase in the number of jobs from expanding and opening establishments and the gross decrease in jobs from contracting and closing establishments. The net loss of 228,000 jobs in the fourth quarter of 2009 resulted from 6.662 million gross job gains and 6.890 million gross job losses. There has been a net loss in each quarter of 2008 and 2009. In comparison, from 2004 to 2007, there was only a net loss in one quarter. (See Table 2-20.)

OTHER HIGHLIGHTS

- Educational and health services was the only sector that experienced more job gains than job losses in the first quarter of 2010. In the fourth quarter of 2009, job gains exceeded the number of job losses in educational and health services and professional and business services. (See Table 2-22.)

- In the first quarter of 2010, gross job losses exceeded gross job gains in the goods-producing industries by 193,000. The net employment change was -137,000 in construction and -55,000 in manufacturing. (See Table 2-22.)

- In service-providing industries, gross job losses exceeded gross losses 118,000 in the first quarter of 2010. Financial activities experienced the worst net employment change at -43,000. (See Table 2-22.)

- In the first quarter of 2010 quarter, gross job losses exceeded gross job losses in 35 states. In California, gross job losses exceeded gross job gains by 57,060, however, in Texas, gross job gains exceeded gross job losses by 33,494. (See Table 2-23.)

NOTES AND DEFINITIONS

BUSINESS EMPLOYMENT DYNAMICS (BED)

The Business Employment Dynamics (BED) data are a set of statistics generated from the federal-state cooperative program known as the Quarterly Census of Employment and Wages (QCEW), or the ES-202 program. These quarterly data series consist of gross job gains and gross job losses statistics from 1992 forward.

The Bureau of Labor Statistics (BLS) compiles the BED data from existing quarterly state unemployment insurance (UI) records. Most employers in the United States are required to file quarterly reports on the employment and wages of workers covered by UI laws and to pay quarterly UI taxes. The quarterly UI reports are sent by the State Workforce Agencies (SWAs) to BLS. These reports form the basis of the BLS establishment universe-sampling frame.

In the BED program, the quarterly UI records are linked across quarters to provide a longitudinal history for each establishment. The linkage process allows the tracking of net employment changes at the establishment level, which in turn allows estimations of jobs gained at opening and expanding establishments and of jobs lost at closing and contracting establishments. BLS publishes three different establishment-based employment measures for every given quarter. Each of these measures—the Current Employment Statistics (CES) survey, the QCEW program, and the BED data each make use of the quarterly UI employment reports. However, each measure has somewhat different types of universal coverage, estimation procedures, and publication products. (See the notes and corresponding tables for CES and QCEW in earlier sections of this chapter.)

Concepts and Definitions

The BED data measure the net change in employment at the establishment level. These changes can come about in four different ways. A net increase in employment can come from either opening establishments or expanding establishments. A net decrease in employment can come from either closing establishments or contracting establishments.

Gross job gains include the sum of all jobs added at either opening or expanding establishments.

Gross job losses include the sum of all jobs lost in either closing or contracting establishments. The net change in employment is the difference between gross job gains and gross job losses.

Openings consist of establishments with positive third-month employment for the first time in the current quarter, with no links to the prior quarter, or with positive third-month employment in the current quarter, following zero employment in the previous quarter.

Expansions include establishments with positive employment in the third month in both the previous and current quarters, with a net increase in employment over this period.

Closings consist of establishments with positive third-month employment in the previous quarter, with no employment or zero employment reported in the current quarter.

Contractions include establishments with positive employment in the third month in both the previous and current quarters, with a net decrease in employment over this period.

Sources of Additional Information

For additional information, see BLS news release 10-1602, "Business Employment Dynamics: First Quarter 2010." An extensive article on the BED data appeared in the April 2004 edition of the *Monthly Labor Review*. These resources can be found on the BLS Web site at <http://www.bls.gov>.

Table 2-20. Private Sector Gross Job Gains and Job Losses, Seasonally Adjusted, March 1995–December 2009

(Thousands of jobs.)

Year and month	Net change[1]	Gross job gains			Gross job losses		
		Total	Expanding establishments	Opening establishments	Total	Contracting establishments	Closing establishments
1995							
March	758	7 787	6 124	1 663	7 029	5 652	1 377
June	358	7 666	6 006	1 660	7 308	5 840	1 468
September	845	7 983	6 341	1 642	7 138	5 645	1 493
December	378	7 830	6 140	1 690	7 452	5 929	1 523
1996							
March	457	7 933	6 179	1 754	7 476	5 967	1 509
June	631	8 051	6 282	1 769	7 420	5 903	1 517
September	704	8 177	6 373	1 804	7 473	5 942	1 531
December	816	8 206	6 396	1 810	7 390	5 875	1 515
1997							
March	784	8 214	6 407	1 807	7 430	5 886	1 544
June	584	8 055	6 330	1 725	7 471	5 931	1 540
September	901	8 515	6 718	1 797	7 614	5 927	1 687
December	708	8 617	6 697	1 920	7 909	6 024	1 885
1998							
March	711	8 648	6 599	2 049	7 937	6 077	1 860
June	610	8 629	6 552	2 077	8 019	6 224	1 795
September	742	8 508	6 607	1 901	7 766	6 093	1 673
December	768	8 475	6 737	1 738	7 707	6 025	1 682
1999							
March	353	8 585	6 626	1 959	8 232	6 395	1 837
June	644	8 539	6 661	1 878	7 895	6 210	1 685
September	588	8 571	6 734	1 837	7 983	6 250	1 733
December	1 005	8 749	6 956	1 793	7 744	6 076	1 668
2000							
March	827	8 849	6 960	1 889	8 022	6 342	1 680
June	503	8 479	6 794	1 685	7 976	6 373	1 603
September	324	8 525	6 756	1 769	8 201	6 479	1 722
December	251	8 351	6 673	1 678	8 100	6 444	1 656
2001							
March	-119	8 491	6 728	1 763	8 610	6 717	1 893
June	-780	7 991	6 302	1 689	8 771	7 036	1 735
September	-1 148	7 630	5 945	1 685	8 778	6 990	1 788
December	-1 009	7 547	5 912	1 635	8 556	6 870	1 686
2002							
March	-10	8 071	6 298	1 773	8 081	6 434	1 647
June	-30	7 868	6 145	1 723	7 898	6 274	1 624
September	-151	7 630	6 039	1 591	7 781	6 248	1 533
December	-241	7 483	5 938	1 545	7 724	6 185	1 539
2003							
March	-393	7 467	5 928	1 539	7 860	6 307	1 553
June	-90	7 398	5 929	1 469	7 488	6 030	1 458
September	204	7 392	5 923	1 469	7 188	5 828	1 360
December	297	7 521	6 005	1 516	7 224	5 800	1 424
2004							
March	470	7 715	6 204	1 511	7 245	5 795	1 450
June	644	7 754	6 235	1 519	7 110	5 639	1 471
September	206	7 633	6 060	1 573	7 427	5 888	1 539
December	757	7 844	6 243	1 601	7 087	5 663	1 424
2005							
March	384	7 620	6 131	1 489	7 236	5 801	1 435
June	593	7 774	6 231	1 543	7 181	5 776	1 405
September	677	7 965	6 387	1 578	7 288	5 844	1 444
December	494	7 807	6 252	1 555	7 313	5 948	1 365
2006							
March	806	7 726	6 293	1 433	6 920	5 635	1 285
June	424	7 789	6 273	1 516	7 365	5 998	1 367
September	45	7 495	6 057	1 438	7 450	6 098	1 352
December	462	7 765	6 241	1 524	7 303	5 954	1 349
2007							
March	491	7 657	6 243	1 414	7 166	5 870	1 296
June	207	7 661	6 250	1 411	7 454	6 056	1 398
September	-249	7 328	5 855	1 473	7 577	6 223	1 354
December	286	7 670	6 197	1 473	7 384	6 028	1 356
2008							
March	-275	7 172	5 778	1 394	7 447	6 083	1 364
June	-520	7 285	5 878	1 407	7 805	6 332	1 473
September	-966	6 888	5 521	1 367	7 854	6 469	1 385
December	-1 814	6 720	5 357	1 363	8 534	7 041	1 493
2009							
March	-2 741	5 783	4 611	1 172	8 524	7 109	1 415
June	-1 604	6 421	5 117	1 304	8 025	6 644	1 381
September	-900	6 341	5 124	1 217	7 241	5 883	1 358
December	-228	6 662	5 326	1 336	6 890	5 598	1 292

[1]Net change is the difference between total gross job gains and total gross job losses.

Table 2-21. Private Sector Gross Job Gains and Job Losses, as a Percent of Employment,[1] Seasonally Adjusted, March 1995–March 2010

(Percent.)

Year and month	Net change[2]	Gross job gains			Gross job losses		
		Total	Expanding establishments	Opening establishments	Total	Contracting establishments	Closing establishments
1995							
March	0.8	8.1	6.4	1.7	7.3	5.9	1.4
June	0.3	7.9	6.2	1.7	7.6	6.1	1.5
September	0.9	8.2	6.5	1.7	7.3	5.8	1.5
December	0.3	8.0	6.3	1.7	7.7	6.1	1.6
1996							
March	0.5	8.1	6.3	1.8	7.6	6.1	1.5
June	0.7	8.2	6.4	1.8	7.5	6.0	1.5
September	0.7	8.2	6.4	1.8	7.5	6.0	1.5
December	0.8	8.2	6.4	1.8	7.4	5.9	1.5
1997							
March	0.9	8.2	6.4	1.8	7.3	5.8	1.5
June	0.6	7.9	6.2	1.7	7.3	5.8	1.5
September	1.0	8.4	6.6	1.8	7.4	5.8	1.6
December	0.8	8.4	6.5	1.9	7.6	5.8	1.8
1998							
March	0.7	8.4	6.4	2.0	7.7	5.9	1.8
June	0.6	8.3	6.3	2.0	7.7	6.0	1.7
September	0.7	8.1	6.3	1.8	7.4	5.8	1.6
December	0.7	8.0	6.4	1.6	7.3	5.7	1.6
1999							
March	0.3	8.0	6.2	1.8	7.7	6.0	1.7
June	0.6	8.0	6.2	1.8	7.4	5.8	1.6
September	0.6	8.0	6.3	1.7	7.4	5.8	1.6
December	1.0	8.1	6.4	1.7	7.1	5.6	1.5
2000							
March	0.8	8.1	6.4	1.7	7.3	5.8	1.5
June	0.4	7.7	6.2	1.5	7.3	5.8	1.5
September	0.2	7.7	6.1	1.6	7.5	5.9	1.6
December	0.2	7.5	6.0	1.5	7.3	5.8	1.5
2001							
March	-0.1	7.7	6.1	1.6	7.8	6.1	1.7
June	-0.8	7.2	5.7	1.5	8.0	6.4	1.6
September	-1.1	6.9	5.4	1.5	8.0	6.4	1.6
December	-1.0	7.0	5.5	1.5	8.0	6.4	1.6
2002							
March	0.0	7.5	5.9	1.6	7.5	6.0	1.5
June	0.0	7.3	5.7	1.6	7.3	5.8	1.5
September	-0.1	7.1	5.6	1.5	7.2	5.8	1.4
December	-0.3	6.9	5.5	1.4	7.2	5.8	1.4
2003							
March	-0.5	6.9	5.5	1.4	7.4	5.9	1.5
June	0.0	7.0	5.6	1.4	7.0	5.6	1.4
September	0.1	6.9	5.5	1.4	6.8	5.5	1.3
December	0.3	7.0	5.6	1.4	6.7	5.4	1.3
2004							
March	0.5	7.2	5.8	1.4	6.7	5.4	1.3
June	0.6	7.2	5.8	1.4	6.6	5.2	1.4
September	0.3	7.1	5.6	1.5	6.8	5.4	1.4
December	0.7	7.2	5.7	1.5	6.5	5.2	1.3
2005							
March	0.4	7.0	5.6	1.4	6.6	5.3	1.3
June	0.6	7.1	5.7	1.4	6.5	5.2	1.3
September	0.6	7.2	5.8	1.4	6.6	5.3	1.3
December	0.4	7.0	5.6	1.4	6.6	5.4	1.2
2006							
March	0.8	6.9	5.6	1.3	6.1	5.0	1.1
June	0.4	6.9	5.6	1.3	6.5	5.3	1.2
September	0.1	6.7	5.4	1.3	6.6	5.4	1.2
December	0.3	6.8	5.5	1.3	6.5	5.3	1.2
2007							
March	0.4	6.7	5.5	1.2	6.3	5.2	1.1
June	0.2	6.7	5.5	1.2	6.5	5.3	1.2
September	-0.3	6.4	5.1	1.3	6.7	5.5	1.2
December	0.2	6.7	5.4	1.3	6.5	5.3	1.2
2008							
March	-0.2	6.3	5.1	1.2	6.5	5.3	1.2
June	-0.5	6.4	5.2	1.2	6.9	5.6	1.3
September	-0.8	6.1	4.9	1.2	6.9	5.7	1.2
December	-1.6	6.0	4.8	1.2	7.6	6.3	1.3
2009							
March	-2.5	5.3	4.2	1.1	7.8	6.5	1.3
June	-1.5	6.0	4.8	1.2	7.5	6.2	1.3
September	-1.0	5.9	4.8	1.1	6.9	5.6	1.3
December	-0.1	6.4	5.1	1.3	6.5	5.3	1.2
2010							
March	-0.3	5.8	4.7	1.1	6.1	5.0	1.1

[1]The rates measure gross job gains and job losses as a percentage of the average of the previous and current employment.
[2]Net change is the difference between total gross job gains and total gross job losses.

Table 2-22. Three-Month Private Sector Job Gains and Losses, by Industry, Seasonally Adjusted, March 2009–March 2010

(Thousands of jobs.)

Industry	Gross job gains and job losses (3 months ended)					Gross job gains and losses as a percent of employment (3 months ended)				
	March 2009	June 2009	September 2009	December 2009	March 2010	March 2009	June 2009	September 2009	December 2009	March 2010
TOTAL PRIVATE[1]										
Gross job gains	5 783	6 421	6 341	6 662	6 110	5.3	6.0	5.9	6.4	5.8
Gross job losses	8 524	8 025	7 241	6 890	6 421	7.8	7.5	6.9	6.5	6.1
Net employment change	-2 741	-1 604	-900	-228	-311	-2.5	-1.5	-1.0	-0.1	-0.3
Goods-Producing										
Gross job gains	1 090	1 273	1 343	1 313	1 266	5.2	6.4	7.0	6.9	6.7
Gross job losses	2 309	2 147	1 675	1 590	1 459	11.0	10.8	8.7	8.4	7.8
Net employment change	-1 219	-874	-332	-277	-193	-5.8	-4.4	-1.7	-1.5	-1.1
Natural Resources and Mining										
Gross job gains	231	285	256	285	270	12.4	15.9	14.5	16.3	15.4
Gross job losses	346	304	287	292	271	18.6	16.9	16.3	16.7	15.4
Net employment change	-115	-19	-31	-7	-1	-6.2	-1.0	-1.8	-0.4	0.0
Construction										
Gross job gains	566	620	614	615	591	8.7	10.2	10.5	10.9	10.7
Gross job losses	1 001	946	814	773	728	15.4	15.5	13.9	13.6	13.1
Net employment change	-435	-326	-200	-158	-137	-6.7	-5.3	-3.4	-2.7	-2.4
Manufacturing										
Gross job gains	293	368	473	413	405	2.4	3.0	4.0	3.6	3.5
Gross job losses	962	897	574	525	460	7.6	7.5	4.9	4.5	4.0
Net employment change	-669	-529	-101	-112	-55	-5.2	-4.5	-0.9	-0.9	-0.5
Service-Providing[1]										
Gross job gains	4 693	5 148	4 998	5 349	4 844	5.3	5.9	5.8	6.2	5.6
Gross job losses	6 215	5 878	5 566	5 300	4 962	7.1	6.7	6.4	6.2	5.8
Net employment change	-1 522	-730	-568	49	-118	-1.8	-0.8	-0.6	0.0	-0.2
Wholesale Trade										
Gross job gains	224	240	235	259	248	3.9	4.3	4.3	4.7	4.6
Gross job losses	384	355	306	283	274	6.7	6.3	5.5	5.1	5.0
Net employment change	-160	-115	-71	-24	-26	-2.8	-2.0	-1.2	-0.4	-0.4
Retail Trade										
Gross job gains	757	871	832	816	784	5.1	5.9	5.7	5.7	5.4
Gross job losses	1 030	931	940	936	805	6.9	6.4	6.5	6.5	5.6
Net employment change	-273	-60	-108	-120	-21	-1.8	-0.5	-0.8	-0.8	-0.2
Transportation and Warehousing										
Gross job gains	176	186	188	220	183	4.2	4.6	4.7	5.5	4.7
Gross job losses	312	289	238	222	223	7.5	7.1	6.0	5.7	5.6
Net employment change	-136	-103	-50	-2	-40	-3.3	-2.5	-1.3	-0.2	-0.9
Utilities										
Gross job gains	12	12	12	11	9	2.2	2.2	2.2	2.0	1.6
Gross job losses	10	15	12	14	9	1.8	2.7	2.2	2.5	1.6
Net employment change	2	-3	0	-3	0	0.4	-0.5	0.0	-0.5	0.0
Information										
Gross job gains	114	111	113	123	106	3.9	3.9	4.0	4.4	3.8
Gross job losses	174	158	161	144	130	6.0	5.6	5.8	5.2	4.7
Net employment change	-60	-47	-48	-21	-24	-2.1	-1.7	-1.8	-0.8	-0.9
Financial Activities										
Gross job gains	337	341	327	356	326	4.3	4.5	4.4	4.8	4.3
Gross job losses	458	446	420	400	369	5.9	5.8	5.6	5.4	5.0
Net employment change	-121	-105	-93	-44	-43	-1.6	-1.3	-1.2	-0.6	-0.7
Professional and Business Services										
Gross job gains	989	1 144	1 152	1 368	1 125	5.8	6.9	7.1	8.3	6.8
Gross job losses	1 549	1 474	1 302	1 184	1 130	9.1	8.9	8.0	7.2	6.8
Net employment change	-560	-330	-150	184	-5	-3.3	-2.0	-0.9	1.1	0.0
Education and Health Services										
Gross job gains	752	773	769	825	730	4.1	4.2	4.1	4.5	3.9
Gross job losses	725	712	727	677	690	4.0	3.9	4.0	3.7	3.7
Net employment change	27	61	42	148	40	0.1	0.3	0.1	0.8	0.2
Leisure and Hospitality										
Gross job gains	1 028	1 122	1 047	1 032	1 000	7.8	8.6	8.0	7.9	7.7
Gross job losses	1 234	1 179	1 135	1 141	1 037	9.3	9.0	8.8	8.8	8.0
Net employment change	-206	-57	-88	-109	-37	-1.5	-0.4	-0.8	-0.9	-0.3
Other Services										
Gross job gains	252	267	250	262	247	6.6	7.1	6.7	7.0	6.7
Gross job losses	310	292	293	272	263	8.1	7.7	7.8	7.3	7.1
Net employment change	-58	-25	-43	-10	-16	-1.5	-0.6	-1.1	-0.3	-0.4

[1]Includes unclassified sector, not shown separately.

Table 2-23. Private Sector Gross Job Gains and Losses, by State and Selected Territory, Seasonally Adjusted, March 2009–March 2010

(Number.)

State	Gross job gains (3 months ended)					Gross job losses (3 months ended)				
	March 2009	June 2009	September 2009	December 2009	March 2010	March 2009	June 2009	September 2009	December 2009	March 2010
UNITED STATES	5 783 000	6 421 000	6 341 000	6 662 000	6 110 000	8 524 000	8 025 000	7 241 000	6 890 000	6 421 000
Alabama	74 930	84 427	86 122	86 379	82 695	117 183	107 020	103 661	92 544	83 327
Alaska	23 204	25 541	22 773	24 288	25 078	25 481	25 071	24 951	25 288	23 147
Arizona	113 031	115 874	127 354	131 273	116 334	176 039	166 696	143 497	140 298	123 728
Arkansas	53 264	51 935	55 002	57 989	52 233	67 476	68 745	62 142	54 247	49 809
California	690 931	779 930	760 570	845 478	759 025	1 062 484	982 275	942 350	831 793	816 085
Colorado	109 610	120 243	117 376	122 327	117 669	161 005	152 052	138 028	132 705	124 210
Connecticut	62 583	71 988	70 301	70 946	66 227	92 159	87 054	80 384	77 470	81 300
Delaware	18 489	21 917	18 960	20 397	19 505	27 952	24 535	23 740	24 289	20 984
District of Columbia	26 365	24 915	23 127	26 592	23 480	27 652	27 823	26 867	24 332	21 514
Florida	358 171	391 465	404 628	440 522	362 571	508 029	493 113	484 765	448 286	370 546
Georgia	192 577	205 284	190 528	204 380	197 155	265 768	259 305	229 914	215 423	195 344
Hawaii	22 180	23 451	24 230	24 368	23 639	30 141	30 432	27 797	25 953	25 062
Idaho	35 379	38 283	39 554	38 431	35 560	54 869	48 675	38 929	40 220	38 578
Illinois	212 065	246 810	236 220	255 104	229 254	332 172	324 057	285 983	275 576	243 415
Indiana	115 299	129 098	143 632	134 249	129 707	186 633	177 927	142 079	135 204	125 181
Iowa	64 063	68 686	66 045	68 771	63 734	86 988	81 401	72 674	74 300	65 573
Kansas	54 342	58 666	57 332	62 377	55 897	78 133	80 690	67 642	67 646	61 303
Kentucky	74 310	81 454	84 435	89 347	77 786	110 419	103 021	90 271	86 416	83 376
Louisiana	95 342	92 714	98 620	100 019	95 060	116 203	122 894	112 255	103 173	94 395
Maine	30 418	37 139	36 365	35 430	30 442	42 403	39 573	36 687	37 779	34 497
Maryland	115 732	127 520	117 084	119 515	124 598	148 730	138 482	137 169	132 550	125 093
Massachusetts	122 170	154 078	147 604	145 704	145 413	180 949	169 339	160 301	160 961	143 996
Michigan	165 441	206 933	232 306	210 533	183 635	285 447	304 525	222 019	228 170	191 162
Minnesota	113 299	132 666	126 020	123 644	120 648	165 987	156 444	139 662	132 265	131 091
Mississippi	48 953	48 855	51 467	51 744	50 450	66 147	65 129	58 923	52 347	49 877
Missouri	122 348	123 254	124 865	122 278	123 242	163 212	157 408	143 070	132 033	129 143
Montana	24 485	27 363	25 345	27 841	25 855	36 272	29 118	27 383	29 098	27 670
Nebraska	38 671	39 998	39 640	40 153	39 893	50 261	47 980	42 323	46 789	40 899
Nevada	54 428	55 091	58 646	68 915	51 824	91 602	81 824	74 075	66 626	65 187
New Hampshire	30 515	35 768	33 238	33 650	34 318	41 235	40 800	36 849	36 107	35 737
New Jersey	168 478	212 882	187 286	196 657	176 313	234 802	229 390	217 472	210 510	193 790
New Mexico	36 766	39 134	39 429	37 662	37 821	52 545	50 040	42 791	42 496	37 739
New York	363 051	432 347	402 733	420 489	373 307	500 717	495 342	440 840	428 924	390 777
North Carolina	175 000	190 464	189 566	196 885	182 350	262 778	247 884	213 945	213 043	188 187
North Dakota	16 786	19 353	19 688	19 816	19 787	21 853	19 393	18 154	19 189	18 824
Ohio	204 363	233 452	236 910	234 522	219 390	319 756	319 866	262 345	255 910	228 984
Oklahoma	69 578	67 104	67 384	68 999	66 668	100 417	95 963	84 628	76 133	66 249
Oregon	78 635	87 457	87 415	89 357	87 342	126 159	107 811	94 954	96 934	87 279
Pennsylvania	224 409	256 071	255 221	267 074	249 634	315 422	306 124	286 693	274 524	248 312
Rhode Island	21 303	24 992	22 109	23 191	22 628	29 590	26 660	26 578	24 865	21 893
South Carolina	79 504	86 102	84 871	85 984	87 466	122 020	110 584	96 487	92 731	82 707
South Dakota	17 753	20 773	19 792	19 762	19 139	24 052	24 006	21 277	21 189	21 608
Tennessee	100 656	118 348	116 655	121 455	108 572	162 691	157 260	136 883	119 337	111 023
Texas	436 995	439 009	441 368	476 502	467 608	609 113	592 395	512 968	484 059	434 114
Utah	56 719	62 938	63 095	65 512	63 614	84 784	81 966	71 601	67 768	63 688
Vermont	15 185	17 600	16 606	19 496	15 542	21 607	20 181	17 421	18 017	17 756
Virginia	150 177	168 871	160 078	166 982	151 244	202 453	198 841	183 506	168 916	162 007
Washington	151 632	156 533	158 859	151 742	153 771	203 909	187 414	171 447	181 151	155 633
West Virginia	33 605	33 270	33 315	37 101	33 246	43 437	44 133	37 630	34 836	34 478
Wisconsin	110 692	125 603	122 694	130 553	125 693	173 335	158 994	141 594	138 015	129 422
Wyoming	18 202	16 081	17 008	16 108	17 159	26 468	25 196	18 099	18 573	18 274
Puerto Rico	37 391	37 741	41 636	45 647	38 617	56 275	51 493	44 872	41 169	44 755
Virgin Islands	1 673	1 711	1 931	2 361	2 632	2 633	2 610	2 190	1 899	1 897

Table 2-24. Private Sector Gross Job Gains and Losses as a Percent of Total Employment, by State and Selected Territory, Seasonally Adjusted, March 2009–March 2010

(Percent.)

State	Gross job gains (3 months ended)					Gross job losses (3 months ended)				
	March 2009	June 2009	September 2009	December 2009	March 2010	March 2009	June 2009	September 2009	December 2009	March 2010
UNITED STATES	5.3	6.0	5.9	6.4	5.8	7.8	7.5	6.9	6.5	6.1
Alabama	4.9	5.7	6.0	6.0	5.8	7.7	7.3	7.1	6.4	5.8
Alaska	9.8	10.9	9.7	10.3	10.6	10.7	10.6	10.7	10.8	9.8
Arizona	5.4	5.7	6.4	6.7	5.9	8.5	8.3	7.2	7.1	6.3
Arkansas	5.6	5.6	6.0	6.3	5.7	7.1	7.3	6.7	5.9	5.4
California	5.6	6.5	6.4	7.2	6.5	8.7	8.2	8.0	7.1	7.0
Colorado	5.9	6.5	6.5	6.8	6.5	8.5	8.3	7.6	7.3	6.9
Connecticut	4.5	5.3	5.2	5.3	4.9	6.6	6.4	5.9	5.7	6.0
Delaware	5.3	6.3	5.5	6.0	5.8	7.9	7.2	7.0	7.2	6.3
District of Columbia	5.9	5.6	5.3	6.0	5.3	6.2	6.2	6.2	5.5	4.9
Florida	5.7	6.4	6.7	7.3	6.1	8.1	8.0	7.9	7.4	6.2
Georgia	6.0	6.5	6.2	6.6	6.4	8.3	8.3	7.4	7.0	6.4
Hawaii	4.6	5.0	5.2	5.2	5.1	6.3	6.5	5.9	5.5	5.4
Idaho	6.8	7.7	8.0	7.8	7.2	10.7	9.8	7.8	8.1	7.8
Illinois	4.4	5.1	5.0	5.5	4.9	6.8	6.8	6.1	5.9	5.3
Indiana	4.9	5.6	6.3	5.8	5.7	7.9	7.7	6.2	5.9	5.5
Iowa	5.2	5.7	5.5	5.8	5.4	7.1	6.8	6.1	6.2	5.5
Kansas	5.0	5.5	5.5	6.0	5.4	7.1	7.5	6.4	6.5	5.8
Kentucky	5.1	5.8	6.0	6.4	5.6	7.7	7.2	6.5	6.2	5.9
Louisiana	6.2	6.2	6.7	6.7	6.4	7.6	8.2	7.5	7.0	6.4
Maine	6.2	7.8	7.6	7.4	6.4	8.7	8.2	7.6	8.0	7.3
Maryland	5.7	6.4	5.9	6.1	6.4	7.4	7.0	6.9	6.8	6.4
Massachusetts	4.4	5.7	5.5	5.5	5.4	6.6	6.3	6.0	6.0	5.4
Michigan	5.0	6.5	7.4	6.7	5.9	8.7	9.5	7.1	7.2	6.1
Minnesota	5.1	6.0	5.8	5.7	5.6	7.4	7.1	6.4	6.1	6.1
Mississippi	5.7	5.8	6.2	6.3	6.1	7.7	7.8	7.1	6.4	6.0
Missouri	5.5	5.6	5.8	5.7	5.8	7.4	7.2	6.6	6.2	6.0
Montana	7.1	8.0	7.5	8.3	7.7	10.5	8.5	8.1	8.6	8.2
Nebraska	5.1	5.4	5.4	5.5	5.4	6.7	6.4	5.7	6.3	5.6
Nevada	5.3	5.5	6.0	7.2	5.4	8.9	8.3	7.6	6.9	6.7
New Hampshire	5.8	6.9	6.5	6.6	6.7	7.8	7.9	7.1	7.0	7.0
New Jersey	5.2	6.7	5.9	6.2	5.6	7.2	7.2	6.8	6.7	6.2
New Mexico	5.9	6.5	6.6	6.3	6.4	8.5	8.2	7.2	7.1	6.4
New York	5.1	6.3	5.9	6.1	5.5	7.1	7.2	6.4	6.3	5.7
North Carolina	5.4	6.1	6.1	6.4	5.9	8.2	7.8	6.9	6.9	6.1
North Dakota	5.8	6.9	6.9	7.0	7.0	7.6	6.8	6.4	6.7	6.5
Ohio	4.7	5.5	5.7	5.6	5.3	7.4	7.6	6.2	6.2	5.5
Oklahoma	5.7	5.6	5.8	6.0	5.8	8.2	8.1	7.3	6.6	5.8
Oregon	5.8	6.6	6.7	6.8	6.7	9.2	8.1	7.2	7.4	6.6
Pennsylvania	4.6	5.3	5.4	5.7	5.3	6.5	6.4	6.0	5.9	5.3
Rhode Island	5.4	6.4	5.7	6.1	5.9	7.5	6.8	6.9	6.5	5.6
South Carolina	5.4	6.0	6.0	6.1	6.3	8.3	7.7	6.9	6.6	5.9
South Dakota	5.5	6.6	6.2	6.3	6.1	7.4	7.6	6.7	6.7	6.8
Tennessee	4.5	5.5	5.5	5.7	5.1	7.3	7.2	6.4	5.6	5.2
Texas	5.1	5.3	5.3	5.8	5.7	7.2	7.1	6.2	5.8	5.3
Utah	5.8	6.5	6.6	6.9	6.8	8.6	8.5	7.6	7.2	6.8
Vermont	6.2	7.4	6.9	8.2	6.5	8.8	8.4	7.3	7.5	7.4
Virginia	5.1	5.9	5.6	5.9	5.4	7.0	6.9	6.5	5.9	5.8
Washington	6.5	6.9	7.1	6.7	6.9	8.8	8.2	7.6	8.1	7.0
West Virginia	5.9	6.0	6.1	6.8	6.0	7.7	7.9	6.8	6.4	6.3
Wisconsin	4.8	5.6	5.4	5.9	5.6	7.5	7.0	6.3	6.2	5.8
Wyoming	8.3	7.6	8.3	7.8	8.4	12.0	11.9	8.8	9.0	8.9
Puerto Rico	5.3	5.5	6.2	6.7	5.7	8.1	7.5	6.7	6.1	6.7
Virgin Islands	5.2	5.6	6.4	7.8	8.5	8.3	8.5	7.2	6.3	6.1

Chapter Three

OCCUPATIONAL EMPLOYMENT AND WAGES

OCCUPATIONAL EMPLOYMENT AND WAGES

HIGHLIGHTS

This chapter presents employment and wage statistics from the Bureau of Labor Statistics Occupational Employment Statistics (OES) program.

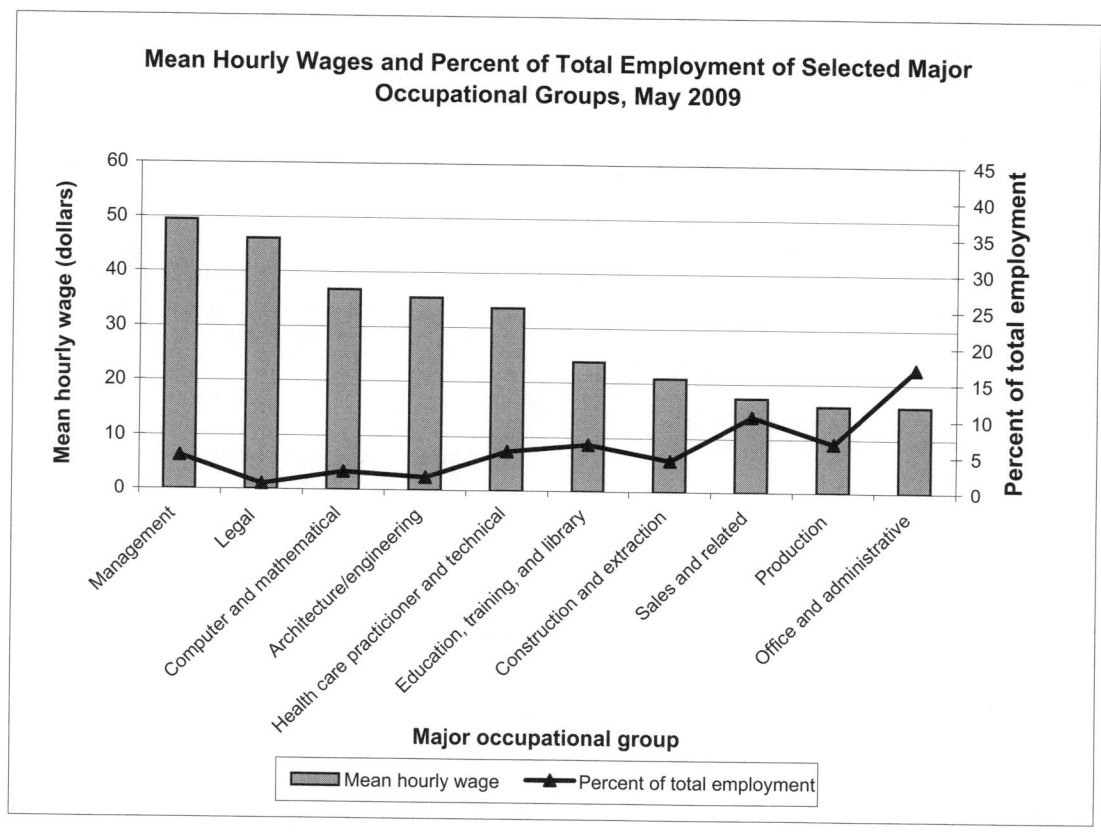

Mean Hourly Wages and Percent of Total Employment of Selected Major Occupational Groups, May 2009

The mean hourly wage for all occupations was $20.90 while the mean annual wage was $43,460 in May 2009. Office and administration support occupations continued to employ the largest percentage of workers in any major group (17.1 percent). The mean hourly wage for office and administration support occupations ($15.86) ranked 16th (from highest to lowest) among the 22 major occupational groups compared. Management workers continued to have the highest mean hourly wage at $49.47. (See Table 3-1.)

OTHER HIGHLIGHTS

- In addition to management occupations, the following occupational groups all had a mean hourly wage above $35.00 in 2009: legal ($46.07), computer and mathematical ($36.68) and architecture and engineering ($35.38). (See Table 3-1.)

- Food preparation workers, the third largest occupational group with 8.6 percent of workers, continued to be the lowest paying occupational group in May 2009 with a mean hourly wage of only $10.04. Food preparation workers were the only workers with a mean hourly wage below $11.50. (See Table 3-1.)

- Sales was the only major occupational group that had a lower mean annual wage in 2009 than in 2008. Mean annual wages rose the highest in the legal profession and protective services at 3.8 percent. (See Table 3-1.)

- The mean average wages of those in managerial positions ranged from $37,530 for education administrators of preschool and child care centers to $167,280 for chief executives. (See Table 3-3.)

NOTES AND DEFINITIONS

Collection and Coverage

The Occupational Employment Statistics (OES) survey is a federal-state cooperative program conducted by the Bureau of Labor Statistics (BLS) and the State Workforce Agencies (SWAs). The OES program collects data on wage and salary workers in nonfarm establishments in order to produce employment and wage estimates for about 801 detailed occupations. Data from self-employed persons are not collected and are not included in the estimates. BLS funds the survey and provides procedural and technical support, while the SWAs collect the necessary data.

OES estimated are created from a sample of 1.2 million establishments. In March and November of each year, forms are mailed to two semiannual panels of around 200,000 establishments. May 2009 estimates are based on responses from six semiannual panels collected over a 3-year period: May 2009, November 2008, May 2008, November 2007, May 2007, and November 2006.

Scope of the Survey

Prior to 1996, the OES program collected only occupational employment data for selected industries in each year of the three-year survey cycle, and produced only industry-specific estimates of occupational employment. The 1996 survey round was the first year that the OES program began collecting occupational employment and wage data in every state. In addition, the program's three-year survey cycle was modified to collect data from all covered industries each year. In 1997, the OES program began producing estimates of cross-industry as well as industry-specific occupational employment and wages.

In 1999, the OES survey began using the Standard Occupational Classification (SOC) system. The SOC system is the first occupational classification system for federal agencies required by the Office of Management and Budget (OMB). The SOC system consists of 821 detailed occupations grouped into 449 broad occupations, 96 minor occupational groups, and 23 major occupational groups. The OES survey uses 22 of the 23 major occupational groups from the SOC to categorize workers into 801 detailed occupations. Military-specific occupations, which are not covered by the OES survey, are not included.

In 2002, the OES survey switched from the Standard Industrial Classification System (SIC) to the North American Industry Classification System (NAICS). In 2008, the OES survey switched to the 2007 NAICS from the 2002 NAICS. The most significant revisions were in the infor-mation sector, particularly within the telecommunications area. More information about NAICS can be found on the BLS Web site at <http://www.bls.gov/bls/naics.htm>.

Concepts and Definitions

Employment is the estimate of total wage and salary employment in an occupation across the industries in which it was reported. The OES survey defines employment as the number of workers who can be classified as full-time or part-time employees, including workers on paid vacations or other types of leave; workers on unpaid short-term absences; employees who are salaried officers, executives, or staff members of incorporated firms; employees temporarily assigned to other units; and employees for whom the reporting unit is their permanent duty station regardless of whether that unit prepares their paycheck. Self-employed owners, partners in unincorporated firms, household workers, and unpaid family workers are excluded.

Occupations are classified based on work performed and required skills. Employees are assigned to an occupation based on the work they perform and not on their education or training. For example, an employee trained as an engineer but working as a drafter is reported as a drafter. Employees who perform the duties of two or more occupations are reported as being in either the occupation that requires the highest level of skill or the occupation in which the most time is spent (if there is no measurable difference in skill requirements).

Wages are money that is paid or received for work or services performed in a specified period. Base rate, cost-of-living allowances, guaranteed pay, hazardous-duty pay, incentive pay (including commissions and production bonuses), tips, and on-call pay are included. Excluded are back pay, jury duty pay, overtime pay, severance pay, shift differentials, nonproduction bonuses, employer cost of supplementary benefits, and tuition reimbursements.

Mean wage refers to an average wage; an occupational mean wage estimate is calculated by summing the wages of all the employees in a given occupation and then dividing the total wages by the number of employees.

An *establishment* is defined as an economic unit that processes goods or provides services, such as a factory, store, or mine. The establishment is generally at a single physical location and is primarily engaged in one type of economic activity.

An *industry* is a group of establishments that produce similar products or provide similar services. For example, all establishments that manufacture automobiles are in the same industry. A given industry, or even a particular establishment in that industry, might have employees in dozens of occupations. The North American Industry Classification System (NAICS) groups similar establishments into industries.

Additional Information

For additional data including area data, see BLS news release USDL 10-0646, "Occupational Employment and Wages, May 2009," and special reports on the BLS Web site at <http://www.bls.gov/OES/>.

Table 3-1. Employment and Wages, by Major Occupational Group, May 2006–May 2009

(Number, percent, dollars.)

Occupation	May 2006				May 2007			
	Employment		Mean hourly wage	Mean annual wage[1]	Employment		Mean hourly wage	Mean annual wage[1]
	Number	Percent			Number	Percent		
All Occupations	132 604 980	100.0	18.84	39 190	134 354 250	100.0	19.56	40 690
Management	5 892 900	4.4	44.20	91 930	6 003 930	4.5	46.22	96 150
Business and financial operations	5 826 140	4.4	28.85	60 000	6 015 500	4.5	30.01	62 410
Computer and mathematical sciences	3 076 200	2.3	33.29	69 240	3 191 360	2.4	34.71	72 190
Architecture and engineering	2 430 250	1.8	31.82	66 190	2 486 020	1.9	33.11	68 880
Life, physical, and social sciences	1 231 070	0.9	28.68	59 660	1 255 670	0.9	29.82	62 020
Community and social services	1 749 210	1.3	18.75	39 000	1 793 040	1.3	19.49	40 540
Legal	976 740	0.7	41.04	85 360	998 590	0.7	42.53	88 450
Education, training, and library	8 206 440	6.2	21.79	45 320	8 316 360	6.2	22.41	46 610
Arts, design, entertainment, sports, and media	1 727 380	1.3	22.17	46 110	1 761 270	1.3	23.27	48 410
Health care practitioner and technical	6 713 780	5.1	29.82	62 030	6 877 680	5.1	31.26	65 020
Health care support	3 483 270	2.6	11.83	24 610	3 625 240	2.7	12.31	25 600
Protective services	3 024 840	2.3	17.81	37 040	3 087 650	2.3	18.63	38 750
Food preparation and serving related	11 029 280	8.3	8.86	18 430	11 273 850	8.4	9.35	19 440
Building and grounds cleaning and maintenance	4 396 250	3.3	10.86	22 580	4 403 900	3.3	11.33	23 560
Personal care and services	3 249 760	2.5	11.02	22 920	3 339 510	2.5	11.53	23 980
Sales and related	14 114 860	10.6	16.52	34 350	14 332 020	10.7	11.41	35 240
Office and administrative support	23 077 190	17.4	14.60	30 370	23 270 810	17.3	15.00	31 200
Farming, fishing, and forestry	450 040	0.3	10.49	21 810	448 000	0.3	10.89	22 640
Construction and extraction	6 680 710	5.0	18.89	39 290	6 708 200	5.0	19.53	40 620
Installation, maintenance, and repair	5 352 420	4.0	18.78	39 060	5 390 090	4.0	19.20	39 930
Production	10 268 510	7.7	14.65	30 480	10 146 560	7.6	15.05	31 310
Transportation and material moving	9 647 730	7.3	14.16	29 460	9 629 030	7.2	14.75	30 680

Occupation	May 2008				May 2009			
	Employment		Mean hourly wage	Mean annual wage[1]	Employment		Mean hourly wage	Mean annual wage[1]
	Number	Percent			Number	Percent		
All Occupations	135 185 230	100.0	20.32	42 270	130 647 610	100.0	20.90	43 460
Management	6 152 650	4.6	48.23	100 310	6 116 380	4.7	49.47	102 900
Business and financial operations	6 135 520	4.5	31.12	64 720	6 063 670	4.6	31.68	65 900
Computer and mathematical sciences	3 308 260	2.4	35.82	74 500	3 303 690	2.5	36.68	76 290
Architecture and engineering	2 521 630	1.9	34.34	71 430	2 412 730	1.8	35.38	73 590
Life, physical, and social sciences	1 296 840	1.0	30.90	64 280	1 308 380	1.0	31.57	65 660
Community and social services	1 861 750	1.4	20.09	41 790	1 891 320	1.4	20.55	42 750
Legal	1 003 270	0.7	44.36	92 270	999 020	0.8	46.07	95 820
Education, training, and library	8 451 250	6.3	23.30	48 460	8 488 740	6.5	23.81	49 530
Arts, design, entertainment, sports, and media	1 804 940	1.3	24.36	50 670	1 745 670	1.3	24.87	51 720
Health care practitioner and technical	7 076 800	5.2	32.64	67 890	7 200 950	5.5	33.51	69 690
Health care support	3 779 280	2.8	12.66	26 340	3 886 690	3.0	12.84	26 710
Protective services	3 128 960	2.3	19.33	40 200	3 172 420	2.4	20.07	41 740
Food preparation and serving related	11 438 550	8.5	9.72	20 220	11 218 260	8.6	10.04	20 880
Building and grounds cleaning and maintenance	4 429 870	3.3	11.72	24 370	4 269 480	3.3	12.00	24 970
Personal care and services	3 437 520	2.5	11.59	24 120	3 461 910	2.6	11.87	24 680
Sales and related	14 336 430	10.6	17.35	36 080	13 715 050	10.5	17.32	36 020
Office and administrative support	23 231 750	17.2	15.49	32 220	22 336 450	17.1	15.86	32 990
Farming, fishing, and forestry	438 490	0.3	11.32	23 560	419 200	0.3	11.53	23 990
Construction and extraction	6 548 760	4.8	20.36	42 350	5 751 630	4.4	20.84	43 350
Installation, maintenance, and repair	5 374 850	4.0	19.82	41 230	5 114 150	3.9	20.30	42 210
Production	9 919 120	7.3	15.54	32 320	8 927 130	6.8	16.01	33 290
Transportation and material moving	9 508 750	7.0	15.12	31 450	8 844 700	6.8	15.47	32 180

[1]The annual wage has been calculated by multiplying the hourly mean wage by a "year-round, full-time" hours figure of 2,080 hours; for occupations with no published hourly mean wage, the annual wage has been directly calculated from the reported survey data.

Table 3-2. Distribution of Employment, by Wage Range and Occupational Group, May 2008–May 2009

(Percent distribution.)

Occupation	Total	Wage range, May 2008								
		Under $9.50	$9.50 to $11.99	$12.00 to $15.24	$15.25 to $19.24	$19.25 to $24.49	$24.50 to $30.99	$31.00 to $39.24	$39.25 to $49.74	$49.75 and over
Management	100.0	1.1	0.7	2.1	4.5	8.1	12.2	16.1	17.5	37.7
Business and financial operations	100.0	1.3	1.8	5.5	11.9	18.3	20.9	18.4	12.0	9.9
Computer and mathematical sciences	100.0	0.5	1.3	3.5	7.0	12.0	17.2	21.4	20.1	17.1
Architecture and engineering	100.0	0.5	1.5	4.2	7.9	13.4	19.4	20.5	17.8	14.8
Life, physical, and social sciences	100.0	1.5	2.9	7.3	12.4	17.1	18.3	16.5	12.2	11.8
Community and social services	100.0	6.0	9.8	17.7	20.9	19.4	14.4	7.7	3.0	0.9
Legal	100.0	0.9	1.8	5.5	9.9	12.9	13.4	12.1	10.7	32.7
Education, training, and library	100.0	9.7	8.1	10.2	14.4	19.7	16.9	11.5	5.6	3.9
Arts, design, entertainment, sports, and media	100.0	10.5	8.9	12.7	15.3	16.1	13.6	10.0	6.2	6.7
Health care practitioner and technical	100.0	1.8	4.0	7.7	11.3	16.7	20.0	16.2	9.3	13.1
Health care support	100.0	23.2	29.2	25.7	14.1	5.5	1.8	0.5	0.1	-
Protective services	100.0	14.5	14.6	15.5	14.0	14.2	12.9	8.8	4.1	1.3
Food preparation and serving related	100.0	63.8	18.1	10.3	4.8	2.0	0.7	0.2	0.1	-
Building and grounds cleaning and maintenance	100.0	38.5	25.2	18.4	10.3	5.2	1.7	0.5	0.1	-
Personal care and services	100.0	46.1	22.7	14.3	7.9	4.8	2.6	1.2	0.3	0.1
Sales and related	100.0	35.9	15.9	11.9	9.8	8.2	6.2	4.6	3.2	4.2
Office and administrative support	100.0	15.0	17.9	23.9	20.1	13.5	7.0	1.9	0.5	0.1
Farming, fishing, and forestry	100.0	53.3	18.4	12.1	7.9	5.0	2.2	0.8	0.2	-
Construction and extraction	100.0	5.6	10.6	18.9	19.6	17.7	13.7	9.1	3.8	1.1
Installation, maintenance, and repair	100.0	6.5	9.8	16.6	20.3	20.5	16.3	7.4	2.1	0.5
Production	100.0	17.2	19.2	22.0	18.5	12.1	7.2	2.8	0.8	0.2
Transportation and material moving	100.0	24.3	18.3	19.7	16.1	11.3	6.3	2.3	0.8	0.9

Occupation	Total	Wage range, May 2009								
		Under $9.50	$9.50 to $11.99	$12.00 to $15.24	$15.25 to $19.24	$19.25 to $24.49	$24.50 to $30.99	$31.00 to $39.24	$39.25 to $49.74	$49.75 and over
Management	100.0	1.5	1.5	3.5	6.2	10.3	14.1	16.9	16.4	29.6
Business and financial operations	100.0	2.5	4.0	9.6	15.3	20.0	19.4	14.7	8.2	6.4
Computer and mathematical sciences	100.0	1.2	2.6	5.6	9.3	14.7	19.1	21.0	16.1	10.4
Architecture and engineering	100.0	1.2	3.0	6.3	10.3	16.7	20.0	19.2	14.1	9.2
Life, physical, and social sciences	100.0	3.1	5.7	10.5	15.0	17.6	17.2	13.9	9.3	7.6
Community and social services	100.0	12.4	14.8	20.5	18.8	16.6	10.2	4.8	1.4	0.4
Legal	100.0	2.3	4.0	8.1	11.1	12.9	12.2	11.1	10.1	28.3
Education, training, and library	100.0	15.5	9.3	12.5	16.6	18.7	13.5	8.1	3.4	2.5
Arts, design, entertainment, sports, and media	100.0	17.0	11.1	14.3	14.9	14.4	11.4	7.9	4.3	4.8
Health care practitioner and technical	100.0	4.6	6.4	9.9	13.5	18.7	17.9	12.1	6.7	10.1
Health care support	100.0	45.9	25.9	17.0	7.3	2.8	0.8	0.2	0.1	-
Protective services	100.0	24.3	14.3	14.5	13.2	13.9	10.5	6.1	2.5	0.7
Food preparation and serving related	100.0	78.0	11.7	6.1	2.6	1.1	0.4	0.1	-	-
Building and grounds cleaning and maintenance	100.0	57.4	19.7	12.8	6.1	3.0	0.8	0.2	-	-
Personal care and services	100.0	64.2	15.6	9.2	5.3	3.3	1.6	0.7	0.2	-
Sales and related	100.0	50.0	12.0	9.9	7.9	6.5	4.9	3.5	2.3	2.9
Office and administrative support	100.0	27.5	21.7	21.5	14.8	10.1	3.1	1.0	0.2	0.1
Farming, fishing, and forestry	100.0	68.7	12.4	8.7	5.4	3.0	1.3	0.4	0.1	-
Construction and extraction	100.0	12.5	16.0	19.8	17.2	15.3	10.9	6.0	1.9	0.4
Installation, maintenance, and repair	100.0	13.2	13.9	19.1	19.4	18.2	11.1	4.0	0.9	0.2
Production	100.0	30.1	20.6	19.8	13.9	9.1	4.6	1.5	0.4	0.1
Transportation and material moving	100.0	37.4	18.9	17.1	12.4	8.2	3.6	1.2	0.5	0.6

- = Quantity represents or rounds to zero.

Table 3-3. Employment and Wages, by Occupation, May 2008 and May 2009

(Number of people, dollars.)

Occupation	May 2008				May 2009			
	Employ-ment	Median hourly wage	Mean hourly wage	Mean annual wage[1]	Employ-ment	Median hourly wage	Mean hourly wage	Mean annual wage[1]
ALL OCCUPATIONS	135 185 230	15.57	20.32	42 270	130 647 610	15.95	20.90	43 460
Management								
Chief executives	301 930	76.23	77.13	160 440	297 640	77.27	80.43	167 280
General and operations managers	1 697 690	44.02	51.91	107 970	1 689 680	44.55	53.15	110 550
Legislators	64 650	([2])	([2])	37 980	65 750	([2])	([2])	37 530
Advertising and promotions managers	36 100	38.57	45.54	94 720	35 760	39.60	46.96	97 670
Marketing managers	166 790	52.20	56.81	118 160	169 330	52.90	57.73	120 070
Sales managers	333 910	46.76	53.07	110 390	328 980	46.53	53.64	111 570
Public relations managers	51 730	43.00	48.66	101 220	53 270	43.12	48.97	101 850
Administrative services managers	246 930	35.35	38.22	79 500	243 580	36.31	39.20	81 530
Computer and information systems managers	276 820	53.95	57.07	118 710	287 210	54.67	58.00	120 640
Financial managers	500 590	47.76	53.19	110 640	495 180	48.65	54.68	113 730
Compensation and benefits managers	38 810	41.59	44.91	93 410	35 630	42.33	45.78	95 230
Training and development managers	29 350	42.16	45.11	93 830	29 320	42.35	45.37	94 360
Human resources managers, all other	60 980	46.22	49.96	103 920	62 990	46.42	50.73	105 510
Industrial production managers	154 030	40.04	43.85	91 200	147 250	40.90	45.03	93 650
Purchasing managers	67 150	42.86	45.34	94 300	65 080	43.96	46.59	96 910
Transportation, storage, and distribution managers	96 300	37.98	40.64	84 520	92 380	38.22	41.09	85 470
Farm, ranch, and other agricultural managers	3 410	27.03	30.00	62 400	3 250	28.58	31.13	64 760
Farmers and ranchers	490	16.13	23.62	49 140	520	15.55	20.53	42 710
Construction managers	220 550	38.39	43.16	89 770	204 760	39.58	44.85	93 290
Education administrators, preschool and child care center/program	49 630	19.20	22.29	46 370	51 140	19.74	23.16	48 170
Education administrators, elementary and secondary school	219 100	([2])	([2])	86 060	219 280	([2])	([2])	87 390
Education administrators, postsecondary	97 410	38.79	44.67	92 920	105 900	39.81	45.84	95 340
Education administrators, all other	28 090	34.44	37.13	77 220	28 710	35.54	38.53	80 140
Engineering managers	182 300	55.42	57.97	120 580	178 110	56.25	59.04	122 810
Food service managers	196 080	22.27	24.19	50 320	190 250	22.70	24.71	51 400
Funeral directors	25 680	25.10	28.27	58 810	25 820	26.14	29.04	60 390
Gaming managers	3 790	32.83	35.33	73 480	3 390	32.40	35.59	74 030
Lodging managers	32 460	22.02	25.26	52 550	31 660	22.26	25.72	53 500
Medical and health services managers	258 130	38.58	42.67	88 750	271 710	39.35	43.74	90 970
Natural sciences managers	43 060	54.23	59.20	123 140	44 180	55.08	61.06	127 000
Postmasters and mail superintendents	26 410	28.52	28.44	59 150	24 890	28.26	28.65	59 600
Property, real estate, and community association managers	159 700	22.18	27.05	56 250	150 850	23.30	28.20	58 660
Social and community service managers	117 150	26.92	29.12	60 570	113 760	27.21	29.44	61 240
Managers, all other	365 460	43.38	46.10	95 890	369 170	44.52	47.64	99 100
Business and Financial Operations								
Agents and business managers of artists, performers, and athletes	12 110	30.26	39.21	81 550	11 700	29.76	42.04	87 430
Purchasing agents and buyers, farm products	13 010	23.88	28.25	58 760	11 690	25.56	30.02	62 450
Wholesale and retail buyers, except farm products	132 420	23.42	26.70	55 540	116 900	23.39	26.68	55 480
Purchasing agents, except wholesale, retail, and farm products	286 990	25.93	27.70	57 630	281 910	26.35	28.15	58 550
Claims adjusters, examiners, and investigators	277 230	26.81	27.67	57 550	273 930	27.46	28.26	58 780
Insurance appraisers, auto damage	11 280	25.69	25.95	53 980	10 960	26.63	27.01	56 180
Compliance officers, except agriculture, construction, health and safety, and transportation	242 270	23.50	25.85	53 760	247 900	23.92	26.49	55 100
Cost estimators	218 400	27.17	29.00	60 320	197 330	27.55	29.42	61 190
Emergency management specialists	12 260	24.26	25.70	53 460	13 060	25.28	27.36	56 900
Employment, recruitment, and placement specialists	205 800	21.86	25.90	53 870	198 190	22.21	26.21	54 530
Compensation, benefits, and job analysis specialists	116 250	25.89	27.43	57 060	111 890	26.74	28.13	58 520
Training and development specialists	206 890	24.73	26.36	54 830	205 020	25.06	26.59	55 310
Human resources, training, and labor relations specialists, all other	217 440	26.79	28.00	58 230	219 240	27.14	28.40	59 070
Logisticians	98 590	31.96	32.98	68 600	100 420	32.67	33.85	70 400
Management analysts	535 850	35.37	39.87	82 920	552 770	36.18	40.70	84 650
Meeting and convention planners	47 960	21.28	22.84	47 500	51 530	21.53	23.11	48 060
Business operations specialists, all other	1 030 320	28.81	31.25	64 990	1 036 450	29.14	31.71	65 960
Accountants and auditors	1 133 580	28.57	31.65	65 840	1 106 980	29.01	32.42	67 430
Appraisers and assessors of real estate	66 260	22.77	25.68	53 410	64 770	23.00	25.73	53 520
Budget analysts	62 630	31.41	32.76	68 140	60 970	32.05	33.29	69 240
Credit analysts	74 400	26.56	31.05	64 580	67 950	27.63	32.32	67 230
Financial analysts	236 720	35.17	40.76	84 780	235 240	35.42	40.98	85 240
Personal financial advisors	146 690	33.20	44.69	92 970	149 460	32.79	45.28	94 180
Insurance underwriters	98 690	27.31	30.09	62 600	98 430	27.80	30.45	63 330
Financial examiners	26 020	34.10	37.59	78 180	26 050	34.49	38.01	79 070
Loan counselors	29 430	18.02	20.18	41 970	30 360	17.94	19.68	40 930
Loan officers	321 850	26.30	30.55	63 540	298 200	26.38	30.39	63 210
Tax examiners, collectors, and revenue agents	66 030	23.12	25.53	53 090	69 500	23.34	25.87	53 800
Tax preparers	63 030	14.14	17.08	35 520	61 130	14.45	17.34	36 060
Financial specialists, all other	145 110	27.48	30.71	63 880	153 720	28.05	31.16	64 810

[1] Annual wages have been calculated by multiplying the hourly mean wage by a "year-round, full-time" hours figure of 2,080 hours; for occupations with no published hourly mean wage, the annual wage has been directly calculated from the reported survey data.

[2] Wages for some occupations that do not generally entail year-round, full-time employment are reported as either hourly wages or annual salaries (depending on how employees are typically paid).

Table 3-3. Employment and Wages, by Occupation, May 2008 and May 2009—*Continued*

(Number of people, dollars.)

Occupation	May 2008				May 2009			
	Employ-ment	Median hourly wage	Mean hourly wage	Mean annual wage[1]	Employ-ment	Median hourly wage	Mean hourly wage	Mean annual wage[1]
Computer and Mathematical Science								
Computer and information scientists, research	26 610	47.10	48.51	100 900	26 130	48.83	50.66	105 370
Computer programmers	394 230	33.47	35.32	73 470	367 880	34.10	35.91	74 690
Computer software engineers, applications	494 160	41.07	42.26	87 900	495 500	42.06	43.35	90 170
Computer software engineers, systems software	381 830	44.44	45.44	94 520	385 200	44.94	46.45	96 620
Computer support specialists	545 520	20.89	22.29	46 370	540 560	21.30	22.77	47 360
Computer systems analysts	489 890	36.30	37.90	78 830	512 720	37.06	38.67	80 430
Database administrators	115 770	33.53	35.05	72 900	108 080	34.40	35.72	74 290
Network and computer systems administrators	327 850	31.88	33.45	69 570	338 890	32.55	34.10	70 930
Network systems and data communications analysts	230 410	34.18	35.50	73 830	226 080	35.22	36.81	76 560
Computer specialists, all other	191 780	36.13	36.54	76 000	195 890	37.02	37.50	78 010
Actuaries	18 220	40.77	46.14	95 980	17 940	41.93	46.85	97 450
Mathematicians	2 770	45.75	45.65	94 960	2 770	44.99	45.16	93 920
Operations research analysts	60 860	33.17	35.68	74 220	60 960	33.69	36.23	75 370
Statisticians	20 680	34.91	35.96	74 790	21 370	35.01	36.16	75 220
Mathematical technicians	1 100	18.46	20.24	42 100	1 090	19.83	21.27	44 230
Mathematical scientists, all other	6 600	26.44	31.55	65 630	2 610	23.18	29.74	61 850
Architecture and Engineering								
Architects, except landscape and naval	110 990	33.81	36.90	76 750	101 630	34.95	37.93	78 880
Landscape architects	21 130	28.35	30.77	64 000	18 940	29.12	31.69	65 910
Cartographers and photogrammetrists	11 690	24.60	27.87	57 980	11 750	25.50	28.53	59 340
Surveyors	55 780	25.47	26.91	55 980	50 360	26.05	27.61	57 420
Aerospace engineers	67 800	44.48	45.18	93 980	70 570	45.57	46.29	96 270
Agricultural engineers	2 640	33.04	35.02	72 850	2 620	33.44	35.89	74 640
Biomedical engineers	15 220	37.21	39.00	81 120	14 760	37.92	39.69	82 550
Chemical engineers	30 970	40.71	42.67	88 760	29 000	42.44	44.07	91 670
Civil engineers	261 360	35.87	37.77	78 560	259 320	36.82	39.03	81 180
Computer hardware engineers	73 370	46.83	48.16	100 180	65 410	47.51	48.75	101 410
Electrical engineers	154 670	39.50	41.04	85 350	151 660	39.96	41.47	86 250
Electronics engineers, except computer	139 930	41.52	42.63	88 670	135 990	42.94	44.01	91 540
Environmental engineers	52 590	35.59	37.49	77 970	50 610	37.04	38.82	80 750
Health and safety engineers, except mining safety engineers and inspectors	25 190	34.85	35.50	73 830	24 070	35.62	36.45	75 810
Industrial engineers	214 580	35.49	36.41	75 740	209 300	36.11	37.06	77 090
Marine engineers and naval architects	6 480	35.64	37.46	77 920	5 270	35.74	38.10	79 240
Materials engineers	24 160	39.34	40.48	84 200	22 510	39.99	41.18	85 660
Mechanical engineers	233 610	36.02	37.59	78 200	232 660	37.03	38.74	80 580
Mining and geological engineers, including mining safety engineers	6 900	36.52	38.42	79 910	6 310	38.19	39.46	82 080
Nuclear engineers	16 640	46.68	47.96	99 750	16 710	46.59	48.25	100 350
Petroleum engineers	20 880	51.93	57.28	119 140	25 540	52.36	57.67	119 960
Engineers, all other	169 240	42.58	42.83	89 080	159 680	43.06	43.56	90 600
Architectural and civil drafters	114 910	21.39	22.30	46 390	105 320	21.92	22.94	47 710
Electrical and electronics drafters	32 710	24.67	25.85	53 770	30 590	25.04	26.34	54 800
Mechanical drafters	77 070	22.42	23.36	48 600	71 890	22.98	23.94	49 790
Drafters, all other	20 720	21.60	22.73	47 290	18 290	21.79	23.18	48 210
Aerospace engineering and operations technicians	8 540	26.46	27.06	56 280	7 940	27.39	28.76	59 820
Civil engineering technicians	88 140	21.29	21.98	45 730	82 690	22.10	22.80	47 420
Electrical and electronic engineering technicians	162 330	25.60	25.96	53 990	154 050	26.36	26.64	55 410
Electro-mechanical technicians	16 290	22.27	23.13	48 110	15 640	23.08	23.98	49 880
Environmental engineering technicians	20 740	19.76	21.36	44 440	20 630	20.36	21.99	45 730
Industrial engineering technicians	72 820	22.69	24.07	50 070	65 460	22.48	23.57	49 030
Mechanical engineering technicians	45 770	23.14	24.06	50 040	43 580	23.54	24.38	50 700
Engineering technicians, except drafters, all other	73 870	27.33	27.19	56 560	69 070	27.66	28.04	58 330
Surveying and mapping technicians	71 920	16.88	18.03	37 500	62 940	17.88	18.98	39 470
Life, Physical, and Social Sciences								
Animal scientists	2 760	26.94	29.64	61 640	2 190	27.38	31.02	64 510
Food scientists and technologists	10 510	28.61	31.06	64 610	10 790	28.67	30.95	64 370
Soil and plant scientists	10 790	28.07	30.82	64 110	11 830	28.45	31.34	65 180
Biochemists and biophysicists	22 230	39.83	42.53	88 450	22 860	39.61	42.57	88 550
Microbiologists	15 750	30.94	33.73	70 150	16 260	32.01	34.61	71 980
Zoologists and wildlife biologists	17 780	26.58	28.28	58 820	17 460	27.16	29.17	60 670
Biological scientists, all other	28 290	31.29	32.71	68 030	29 630	31.98	33.38	69 430
Conservation scientists	15 830	28.23	28.93	60 170	16 810	28.92	29.41	61 180
Foresters	10 160	25.84	26.46	55 040	10 230	25.89	26.55	55 220
Epidemiologists	4 370	29.50	31.01	64 500	4 610	29.66	31.22	64 950
Medical scientists, except epidemiologists	99 750	34.90	39.36	81 870	101 760	35.86	40.75	84 760
Life scientists, all other	12 030	29.55	33.18	69 020	12 320	30.76	34.90	72 590
Astronomers	1 280	48.70	47.95	99 730	1 240	50.35	49.40	102 740
Physicists	14 810	49.47	51.17	106 440	13 630	51.15	53.49	111 250
Atmospheric and space scientists	8 860	39.08	39.46	82 080	8 320	40.73	40.94	85 160
Chemists	83 080	31.84	34.17	71 070	79 910	32.80	34.97	72 740
Materials scientists	9 650	38.57	39.23	81 600	8 880	38.61	39.59	82 350
Environmental scientists and specialists, including health	80 120	28.72	31.39	65 280	83 530	29.33	32.38	67 360
Geoscientists, except hydrologists and geographers	31 260	38.06	42.93	89 300	31 860	39.05	44.57	92 710
Hydrologists	7 590	34.35	35.36	73 540	7 150	35.42	36.91	76 760

[1] Annual wages have been calculated by multiplying the hourly mean wage by a "year-round, full-time" hours figure of 2,080 hours; for occupations with no published hourly mean wage, the annual wage has been directly calculated from the reported survey data.

Table 3-3. Employment and Wages, by Occupation, May 2008 and May 2009—*Continued*

(Number of people, dollars.)

Occupation	May 2008				May 2009			
	Employ-ment	Median hourly wage	Mean hourly wage	Mean annual wage[1]	Employ-ment	Median hourly wage	Mean hourly wage	Mean annual wage[1]
Life, Physical, and Social Sciences—*Continued*								
Physical scientists, all other	22 900	43.99	44.16	91 850	25 310	45.17	45.62	94 880
Economists	12 600	40.19	43.67	90 830	13 160	41.79	46.31	96 320
Market research analysts	230 070	29.36	32.37	67 340	226 410	29.61	32.45	67 500
Survey researchers	21 100	17.42	20.22	42 060	20 300	17.01	20.35	42 330
Clinical, counseling, and school psychologists	97 880	30.84	33.74	70 190	98 330	31.75	34.77	72 310
Industrial-organizational psychologists	1 460	37.03	41.57	86 460	1 710	40.03	49.31	102 570
Psychologists, all other	9 870	41.41	43.49	90 460	10 260	41.60	40.49	84 220
Sociologists	4 390	32.96	36.28	75 460	4 430	33.47	36.63	76 190
Urban and regional planners	37 120	28.75	30.00	62 400	38 950	29.72	31.10	64 680
Anthropologists and archeologists	5 230	25.92	27.55	57 300	5 570	25.70	27.52	57 230
Geographers	1 120	32.02	32.13	66 830	1 170	34.36	34.33	71 420
Historians	3 700	26.22	27.49	57 180	3 620	24.54	27.09	56 350
Political scientists	3 530	50.06	47.75	99 320	3 970	50.04	48.58	101 050
Social scientists and related workers, all other	28 680	33.04	34.49	71 730	29 250	33.59	35.31	73 450
Agricultural and food science technicians	18 930	16.34	17.53	36 470	18 490	16.54	17.72	36 850
Biological technicians	72 200	18.46	19.67	40 900	74 560	18.61	19.78	41 140
Chemical technicians	65 830	20.25	21.02	43 710	64 420	20.23	21.11	43 900
Geological and petroleum technicians	14 570	25.65	27.44	57 080	14 460	25.60	28.08	58 400
Nuclear technicians	6 360	32.64	32.17	66 910	6 290	32.37	32.07	66 700
Social science research assistants	18 120	17.14	18.23	37 920	21 720	18.03	19.39	40 340
Environmental science and protection technicians, including health	33 370	19.34	20.76	43 180	30 870	19.61	20.92	43 520
Forensic science technicians	11 990	23.97	25.46	52 960	12 870	24.75	26.47	55 070
Forest and conservation technicians	30 850	15.39	16.98	35 320	31 440	15.80	17.49	36 370
Life, physical, and social science technicians, all other	58 070	19.25	20.63	42 910	59 530	20.24	21.57	44 870
Community and Social Science								
Substance abuse and behavioral disorder counselors	79 180	17.80	19.07	39 670	78 470	18.13	19.43	40 420
Educational, vocational, and school counselors	243 100	24.54	25.74	53 540	251 050	25.27	26.46	55 030
Marriage and family therapists	24 520	21.44	22.56	46 930	26 450	22.56	23.57	49 020
Mental health counselors	104 650	17.70	19.36	40 270	106 920	18.28	20.05	41 710
Rehabilitation counselors	112 700	14.87	16.64	34 600	112 690	15.01	16.69	34 710
Counselors, all other	29 980	19.20	20.31	42 240	30 900	19.86	21.35	44 400
Child, family, and school social workers	274 140	19.01	20.73	43 120	277 670	19.21	20.93	43 540
Medical and public health social workers	131 730	21.95	22.87	47 560	133 510	22.26	23.24	48 340
Mental health and substance abuse social workers	131 010	17.89	19.05	39 630	127 140	18.37	19.88	41 350
Social workers, all other	68 230	22.22	23.16	48 180	73 250	23.76	24.26	50 470
Health educators	62 120	21.16	23.36	48 590	63 320	21.32	23.59	49 060
Probation officers and correctional treatment specialists	97 130	22.07	23.81	49 520	92 910	22.37	24.28	50 500
Social and human service assistants	332 880	13.12	14.03	29 170	344 050	13.44	14.37	29 880
Community and social service specialists, all other	107 910	18.11	19.21	39 950	109 120	18.07	19.48	40 530
Clergy	42 040	20.06	21.85	45 440	42 670	20.65	22.58	46 960
Directors, religious activities and education	14 790	17.35	19.36	40 260	15 060	17.40	19.60	40 770
Religious workers, all other	5 640	13.30	15.56	32 360	6 140	14.14	15.94	33 160
Legal								
Lawyers	553 690	53.17	59.98	124 750	556 790	54.44	62.03	129 020
Administrative law judges, adjudicators, and hearing officers	13 370	36.99	38.88	80 870	13 140	40.35	42.13	87 620
Arbitrators, mediators, and conciliators	9 570	24.36	28.68	59 650	8 110	25.37	30.41	63 250
Judges, magistrate judges, and magistrates	25 470	52.99	48.29	100 450	26 350	54.24	49.99	103 990
Paralegals and legal assistants	253 040	22.18	23.46	48 790	246 810	22.58	24.08	50 080
Court reporters	17 930	23.90	24.98	51 960	18 780	22.98	25.22	52 460
Law clerks	31 500	17.85	19.51	40 580	32 630	18.46	20.17	41 960
Title examiners, abstractors, and searchers	59 390	18.41	20.24	42 090	56 820	18.64	20.65	42 960
Legal support workers, all other	39 310	24.16	27.24	56 660	39 590	25.03	28.19	58 630
Education, Training, and Library								
Business teachers, postsecondary	69 690	([2])	([2])	77 340	73 790	([2])	([2])	83 840
Computer science teachers, postsecondary	32 520	([2])	([2])	74 050	32 240	([2])	([2])	75 860
Mathematical science teachers, postsecondary	45 710	([2])	([2])	68 130	48 100	([2])	([2])	70 550
Architecture teachers, postsecondary	6 430	([2])	([2])	75 450	7 090	([2])	([2])	77 830
Engineering teachers, postsecondary	32 070	([2])	([2])	90 070	34 270	([2])	([2])	92 970
Agricultural sciences teachers, postsecondary	10 000	([2])	([2])	77 770	10 230	([2])	([2])	80 790
Biological science teachers, postsecondary	51 930	([2])	([2])	83 270	54 810	([2])	([2])	87 220
Forestry and conservation science teachers, postsecondary	2 450	([2])	([2])	67 400	2 380	([2])	([2])	72 290
Atmospheric, earth, marine, and space sciences teachers, postsecondary	9 650	([2])	([2])	81 470	9 900	([2])	([2])	83 320
Chemistry teachers, postsecondary	19 950	([2])	([2])	76 310	20 370	([2])	([2])	77 350
Environmental science teachers, postsecondary	4 870	([2])	([2])	74 610	4 820	([2])	([2])	73 700
Physics teachers, postsecondary	12 350	([2])	([2])	81 880	12 870	([2])	([2])	83 320
Anthropology and archeology teachers, postsecondary	5 500	([2])	([2])	73 410	5 880	([2])	([2])	75 530
Area, ethnic, and cultural studies teachers, postsecondary	7 570	([2])	([2])	70 560	8 070	([2])	([2])	75 130
Economics teachers, postsecondary	12 540	([2])	([2])	88 330	12 860	([2])	([2])	89 320

[1]Annual wages have been calculated by multiplying the hourly mean wage by a "year-round, full-time" hours figure of 2,080 hours; for occupations with no published hourly mean wage, the annual wage has been directly calculated from the reported survey data.
[2]Wages for some occupations that do not generally entail year-round, full-time employment are reported as either hourly wages or annual salaries (depending on how employees are typically paid).

Table 3-3. Employment and Wages, by Occupation, May 2008 and May 2009—*Continued*

(Number of people, dollars.)

Occupation	May 2008				May 2009			
	Employment	Median hourly wage	Mean hourly wage	Mean annual wage[1]	Employment	Median hourly wage	Mean hourly wage	Mean annual wage[1]
Education, Training, and Library—*Continued*								
Geography teachers, postsecondary	4 030	([2])	([2])	67 480	3 930	([2])	([2])	69 840
Political science teachers, postsecondary	14 340	([2])	([2])	75 960	15 180	([2])	([2])	76 990
Psychology teachers, postsecondary	31 420	([2])	([2])	69 560	33 450	([2])	([2])	72 140
Sociology teachers, postsecondary	16 440	([2])	([2])	68 900	16 380	([2])	([2])	71 970
Social sciences teachers, postsecondary, all other	5 720	([2])	([2])	74 720	5 830	([2])	([2])	77 040
Health specialties teachers, postsecondary	125 100	([2])	([2])	102 000	133 070	([2])	([2])	103 340
Nursing instructors and teachers, postsecondary	46 890	([2])	([2])	62 660	49 140	([2])	([2])	65 240
Education teachers, postsecondary	55 880	([2])	([2])	60 080	56 880	([2])	([2])	62 160
Library science teachers, postsecondary	3 960	([2])	([2])	61 630	3 940	([2])	([2])	64 270
Criminal justice and law enforcement teachers, postsecondary	11 630	([2])	([2])	59 830	12 610	([2])	([2])	62 750
Law teachers, postsecondary	12 490	([2])	([2])	101 170	12 690	([2])	([2])	109 150
Social work teachers, postsecondary	7 930	([2])	([2])	64 680	8 290	([2])	([2])	67 410
Art, drama, and music teachers, postsecondary	76 810	([2])	([2])	65 030	80 790	([2])	([2])	68 230
Communications teachers, postsecondary	24 360	([2])	([2])	63 330	25 090	([2])	([2])	65 190
English language and literature teachers, postsecondary	62 230	([2])	([2])	63 610	65 490	([2])	([2])	65 860
Foreign language and literature teachers, postsecondary	26 400	([2])	([2])	65 280	27 020	([2])	([2])	63 300
History teachers, postsecondary	21 020	([2])	([2])	68 360	21 810	([2])	([2])	69 280
Philosophy and religion teachers, postsecondary	18 370	([2])	([2])	65 140	19 630	([2])	([2])	67 610
Graduate teaching assistants	124 380	([2])	([2])	31 710	122 120	([2])	([2])	32 770
Home economics teachers, postsecondary	4 820	([2])	([2])	70 420	4 800	([2])	([2])	68 210
Recreation and fitness studies teachers, postsecondary	17 410	([2])	([2])	60 700	16 850	([2])	([2])	60 580
Vocational education teachers, postsecondary	112 940	22.76	24.46	50 870	114 420	23.05	25.01	52 030
Postsecondary teachers, all other	242 780	([2])	([2])	71 320	205 760	([2])	([2])	74 330
Preschool teachers, except special education	392 170	11.48	12.80	26 610	389 660	11.80	13.20	27 450
Kindergarten teachers, except special education	174 530	([2])	([2])	49 770	181 810	([2])	([2])	50 380
Elementary school teachers, except special education	1 544 270	([2])	([2])	52 240	1 544 300	([2])	([2])	53 150
Middle school teachers, except special and vocational education	661 820	([2])	([2])	52 570	665 420	([2])	([2])	53 550
Vocational education teachers, middle school	15 720	([2])	([2])	50 150	14 060	([2])	([2])	51 520
Secondary school teachers, except special and vocational education	1 090 490	([2])	([2])	54 390	1 091 710	([2])	([2])	55 150
Vocational education teachers, secondary school	99 800	([2])	([2])	53 700	92 980	([2])	([2])	54 420
Special education teachers, preschool, kindergarten, and elementary school	226 250	([2])	([2])	52 970	228 580	([2])	([2])	53 770
Special education teachers, middle school	100 650	([2])	([2])	53 540	102 490	([2])	([2])	54 750
Special education teachers, secondary school	147 210	([2])	([2])	55 050	146 240	([2])	([2])	56 420
Adult literacy, remedial education, and GED teachers and instructors	73 050	22.26	23.95	49 830	68 430	22.08	24.23	50 390
Self-enrichment education teachers	163 190	17.17	19.68	40 920	162 330	17.52	19.88	41 360
Teachers and instructors, all other	574 540	([2])	([2])	40 770	599 500	([2])	([2])	41 110
Archivists	5 330	21.64	23.18	48 220	4 900	22.34	23.85	49 600
Curators	10 820	22.70	24.78	51 540	10 410	23.04	25.16	52 330
Museum technicians and conservators	10 200	17.63	19.59	40 750	10 170	17.85	19.87	41 330
Librarians	151 170	25.26	26.30	54 700	150 520	25.82	26.76	55 670
Library technicians	113 510	13.86	14.49	30 130	111 390	14.22	14.93	31 060
Audio-visual collections specialists	6 160	20.86	21.90	45 540	6 800	21.10	22.35	46 490
Farm and home management advisors	10 760	19.97	21.46	44 630	9 830	21.24	22.29	46 370
Instructional coordinators	122 180	27.35	28.74	59 780	124 480	28.26	29.46	61 270
Teacher assistants	1 266 900	([2])	([2])	23 560	1 275 410	([2])	([2])	24 280
Education, training, and library workers, all other	99 900	17.07	19.50	40 560	104 500	17.45	20.13	41 880
Arts, Design, Entertainment, Sports, and Media								
Art directors	33 670	37.01	42.55	88 510	31 660	37.78	44.00	91 520
Craft artists	5 440	13.98	15.66	32 570	5 380	13.92	15.90	33 070
Fine artists, including painters, sculptors, and illustrators	9 380	20.51	23.22	48 300	8 900	21.23	24.34	50 630
Multi-media artists and animators	31 500	27.08	29.99	62 380	28 800	28.01	30.20	62 810
Artists and related workers, all other	8 470	24.81	26.51	55 140	8 100	25.54	27.63	57 470
Commercial and industrial designers	32 940	27.57	29.60	61 580	29 170	27.92	29.52	61 400
Fashion designers	16 920	29.41	34.33	71 400	15 780	30.90	35.78	74 410
Floral designers	57 500	11.17	11.78	24 510	51 470	11.31	11.99	24 940
Graphic designers	209 290	20.39	22.48	46 750	200 870	20.76	22.99	47 820
Interior designers	53 290	21.61	24.53	51 020	46 010	22.20	24.99	51 990
Merchandise displayers and window trimmers	63 320	12.47	13.73	28 560	61 280	12.49	13.69	28 480
Set and exhibit designers	7 940	21.47	23.40	48 660	7 940	21.83	24.33	50 600
Designers, all other	11 160	21.07	24.10	50 130	10 510	21.16	24.24	50 420
Actors	44 360	16.59	29.05	([2])	39 880	16.20	28.79	([2])
Producers and directors	78 060	30.98	39.92	83 030	79 780	32.08	41.77	86 870
Athletes and sports competitors	13 960	([2])	([2])	79 460	13 620	([2])	([2])	80 950
Coaches and scouts	175 720	([2])	([2])	35 580	179 830	([2])	([2])	35 740
Umpires, referees, and other sports officials	12 970	([2])	([2])	28 330	14 860	([2])	([2])	28 490
Dancers	11 370	12.22	15.06	([2])	10 700	13.74	16.37	([2])
Choreographers	13 860	18.52	20.13	41 870	14 700	18.20	20.25	42 130

[1]Annual wages have been calculated by multiplying the hourly mean wage by a "year-round, full-time" hours figure of 2,080 hours; for occupations with no published hourly mean wage, the annual wage has been directly calculated from the reported survey data.

[2]Wages for some occupations that do not generally entail year-round, full-time employment are reported as either hourly wages or annual salaries (depending on how employees are typically paid).

Table 3-3. Employment and Wages, by Occupation, May 2008 and May 2009—Continued

(Number of people, dollars.)

Occupation	May 2008				May 2009			
	Employ-ment	Median hourly wage	Mean hourly wage	Mean annual wage[1]	Employ-ment	Median hourly wage	Mean hourly wage	Mean annual wage[1]
Arts, Design, Entertainment, Sports, and Media—*Continued*								
Music directors and composers	9 120	19.84	26.36	54 840	14 330	21.68	25.68	53 410
Musicians and singers	47 030	21.24	28.28	([2])	47 260	22.36	29.10	([2])
Entertainers and performers, sports and related workers, all other	36 190	14.62	17.91	([2])	23 500	14.78	18.41	([2])
Radio and television announcers	37 290	12.95	19.43	40 410	35 130	13.23	19.99	41 590
Public address system and other announcers	8 280	13.18	18.04	37 530	7 280	13.08	17.37	36 130
Broadcast news analysts	6 310	24.65	34.00	70 730	5 820	24.23	32.69	67 990
Reporters and correspondents	50 690	16.75	21.17	44 030	46 130	16.52	20.80	43 270
Public relations specialists	240 610	24.65	28.34	58 960	242 670	24.98	28.55	59 370
Editors	110 010	24.04	27.49	57 180	105 040	24.42	28.10	58 440
Technical writers	47 460	29.62	30.87	64 210	46 270	30.16	31.55	65 610
Writers and authors	44 170	25.51	31.04	64 560	43 390	25.91	31.04	64 560
Interpreters and translators	36 610	18.68	20.74	43 130	40 000	19.65	21.97	45 700
Media and communication workers, all other	24 470	19.99	22.97	47 770	25 460	20.52	24.37	50 680
Audio and video equipment technicians	45 200	18.30	19.86	41 310	46 070	18.80	20.41	42 450
Broadcast technicians	33 550	15.82	18.30	38 070	31 220	15.85	18.43	38 330
Radio operators	820	17.85	18.52	38 520	870	20.69	20.86	43 400
Sound engineering technicians	16 600	22.83	25.53	53 110	15 560	22.29	25.93	53 940
Photographers	61 670	14.15	17.14	35 640	57 760	14.31	17.48	36 370
Camera operators, television, video, and motion picture	19 270	20.03	22.94	47 710	17 540	20.64	23.84	49 590
Film and video editors	18 720	24.31	30.05	62 500	17 550	24.42	30.62	63 680
Media and communication equipment workers, all other	19 770	25.45	26.98	56 120	17 610	27.64	28.79	59 880
Health Care Practitioner and Technical								
Chiropractors	27 050	31.97	39.11	81 340	26 310	32.53	38.65	80 390
Dentists, general	85 910	68.69	74.17	154 270	86 270	68.31	75.41	156 850
Oral and maxillofacial surgeons	4 760	([3])	91.55	190 420	5 390	([3])	101.30	210 710
Orthodontists	5 500	([3])	93.72	194 930	5 410	([3])	99.13	206 190
Prosthodontists	370	([3])	81.64	169 810	660	53.42	60.29	125 400
Dentists, all other specialists	4 770	66.33	68.30	142 070	5 010	73.70	73.83	153 570
Dietitians and nutritionists	53 630	24.32	24.75	51 470	53 220	25.07	25.59	53 230
Optometrists	25 970	46.31	50.58	105 200	26 480	46.22	51.42	106 960
Pharmacists	266 410	51.16	50.13	104 260	267 860	52.49	51.27	106 630
Anesthesiologists	34 230	([3])	94.99	197 570	37 450	([3])	101.80	211 750
Family and general practitioners	106 210	([3])	77.64	161 490	99 000	77.18	81.03	168 550
Internists, general	46 980	([3])	84.97	176 740	48 270	([3])	88.46	183 990
Obstetricians and gynecologists	19 750	([3])	92.68	192 780	20 380	([3])	98.31	204 470
Pediatricians, general	29 170	70.21	73.74	153 370	29 460	73.19	77.60	161 410
Psychiatrists	22 140	74.13	74.06	154 050	22 210	77.04	78.68	163 660
Surgeons	47 070	([3])	99.41	206 770	44 560	([3])	105.66	219 770
Physicians and surgeons, all other	262 850	([3])	79.33	165 000	274 160	([3])	83.59	173 860
Physician assistants	71 950	39.05	39.24	81 610	76 900	40.58	40.78	84 830
Podiatrists	9 670	54.60	60.46	125 760	9 720	55.89	63.33	131 730
Registered nurses	2 542 760	30.03	31.31	65 130	2 583 770	30.65	31.99	66 530
Audiologists	12 480	29.82	31.49	65 500	12 590	30.40	32.14	66 850
Occupational therapists	94 800	32.10	32.65	67 920	97 840	33.48	33.98	70 680
Physical therapists	167 300	35.00	35.77	74 410	174 490	35.81	36.64	76 220
Radiation therapists	14 850	35.05	36.28	75 450	15 570	35.66	37.18	77 340
Recreational therapists	22 510	18.45	19.20	39 930	21 960	18.96	19.84	41 270
Respiratory therapists	103 870	25.10	25.55	53 150	107 270	25.64	26.06	54 200
Speech-language pathologists	107 340	30.25	31.80	66 130	111 640	31.29	32.86	68 350
Therapists, all other	12 960	24.37	26.32	54 750	13 440	24.70	26.16	54 400
Veterinarians	53 110	38.01	43.10	89 450	54 130	38.71	43.32	90 110
Health diagnosing and treating practitioners, all other	34 890	31.67	37.76	78 540	32 960	31.36	37.32	77 630
Medical and clinical laboratory technologists	166 510	25.72	25.99	54 050	166 860	26.51	26.74	55 620
Medical and clinical laboratory technicians	149 670	17.01	17.86	37 150	152 420	17.32	18.20	37 860
Dental hygienists	173 090	32.00	32.19	66 950	173 900	32.38	32.63	67 860
Cardiovascular technologists and technicians	48 040	22.60	23.38	48 640	48 070	23.22	23.91	49 730
Diagnostic medical sonographers	48 920	29.80	30.12	62 660	51 630	30.30	30.60	63 640
Nuclear medicine technologists	21 200	32.05	32.44	67 480	21 670	32.65	32.91	68 450
Radiologic technologists and technicians	208 570	25.10	25.59	53 230	213 560	25.59	26.05	54 180
Emergency medical technicians and paramedics	207 610	14.10	15.38	31 980	217 920	14.42	15.88	33 020
Dietetic technicians	24 620	12.54	13.26	27 580	24 510	12.98	13.72	28 530
Pharmacy technicians	324 110	13.32	13.70	28 500	331 890	13.49	13.92	28 940
Psychiatric technicians	54 800	14.06	15.48	32 190	70 730	13.53	14.77	30 730
Respiratory therapy technicians	16 210	20.40	21.00	43 670	15 100	21.49	21.96	45 680
Surgical technologists	89 600	18.62	19.27	40 070	91 250	18.94	19.57	40 710
Veterinary technologists and technicians	78 920	13.89	14.35	29 850	79 200	14.08	14.70	30 580
Licensed practical and licensed vocational nurses	730 500	18.77	19.28	40 110	728 670	19.14	19.66	40 900

[1]Annual wages have been calculated by multiplying the hourly mean wage by a "year-round, full-time" hours figure of 2,080 hours; for occupations with no published hourly mean wage, the annual wage has been directly calculated from the reported survey data.
[2]Wages for some occupations that do not generally entail year-round, full-time employment are reported as either hourly wages or annual salaries (depending on how employees are typically paid).
[3]Median hourly wage is equal to or greater than $80.00 per hour.

Table 3-3. Employment and Wages, by Occupation, May 2008 and May 2009—Continued

(Number of people, dollars.)

Occupation	May 2008				May 2009			
	Employ-ment	Median hourly wage	Mean hourly wage	Mean annual wage[1]	Employ-ment	Median hourly wage	Mean hourly wage	Mean annual wage[1]
Health Care Practitioner and Technical—*Continued*								
Medical records and health information technicians	168 650	14.71	15.85	32 960	170 580	15.04	16.29	33 880
Opticians, dispensing	59 470	15.77	16.85	35 060	60 840	15.74	16.73	34 790
Orthotists and prosthetists	5 490	30.09	31.76	66 060	5 470	29.84	32.02	66 600
Health technologists and technicians, all other	74 990	18.25	19.89	41 380	78 600	18.51	20.28	42 180
Occupational health and safety specialists	53 250	29.93	30.31	63 030	51 850	30.40	30.87	64 200
Occupational health and safety technicians	10 540	21.81	22.79	47 410	10 070	21.56	22.73	47 280
Athletic trainers	15 070	(^{2})	(^{2})	41 620	15 260	(^{2})	(^{2})	44 020
Healthcare practitioners and technical workers, all other	55 750	20.98	24.28	50 510	56 520	21.47	25.05	52 110
Health Care Support								
Home health aides	892 410	9.84	10.31	21 440	955 220	9.85	10.39	21 620
Nursing aides, orderlies, and attendants	1 422 720	11.46	11.84	24 620	1 438 010	11.56	12.01	24 980
Psychiatric aides	59 050	12.77	13.10	27 260	62 610	12.33	13.19	27 430
Occupational therapist assistants	25 610	23.19	23.29	48 440	26 680	24.16	24.44	50 830
Occupational therapist aides	7 410	12.96	14.22	29 580	8 040	12.37	13.89	28 890
Physical therapist assistants	61 820	22.18	22.26	46 300	63 750	23.22	23.36	48 590
Physical therapist aides	44 410	11.42	11.91	24 770	44 160	11.49	12.01	24 990
Massage therapists	51 250	16.78	19.16	39 850	55 920	16.94	19.13	39 780
Dental assistants	293 090	15.57	15.95	33 170	294 020	15.98	16.35	34 000
Medical assistants	475 950	13.60	13.97	29 060	495 970	13.77	14.16	29 450
Medical equipment preparers	44 340	13.66	14.08	29 290	47 070	13.93	14.32	29 780
Medical transcriptionists	86 200	15.41	15.84	32 960	82 810	15.68	16.03	33 350
Pharmacy aides	53 190	9.66	10.34	21 500	52 230	10.00	10.74	22 330
Veterinary assistants and laboratory animal caretakers	71 950	10.20	10.96	22 790	71 350	10.43	11.25	23 400
Healthcare support workers, all other	189 890	14.11	14.74	30 650	188 850	14.39	15.07	31 340
Protective Services								
First-line supervisors/managers of correctional officers	40 840	27.58	28.07	58 380	45 540	27.74	28.76	59 810
First-line supervisors/managers of police and detectives	92 840	36.29	36.93	76 820	99 900	36.78	37.78	78 580
First-line supervisors/managers of fire fighting and prevention workers	53 300	32.42	34.07	70 860	57 750	32.81	34.46	71 680
First-line supervisors/managers, protective service workers, all other	49 310	20.95	22.93	47 700	49 360	21.38	23.39	48 640
Fire fighters	298 900	21.28	21.97	45 700	305 500	21.66	22.72	47 270
Fire inspectors and investigators	12 920	25.50	26.37	54 840	12 180	25.83	27.07	56 310
Forest fire inspectors and prevention specialists	1 580	15.09	17.50	36 400	1 540	15.83	18.36	38 180
Bailiffs	19 290	18.18	18.79	39 090	17 140	18.25	19.35	40 240
Correctional officers and jailers	428 040	18.45	19.88	41 340	455 350	18.78	20.49	42 610
Detectives and criminal investigators	104 480	29.29	30.69	63 840	110 380	29.86	31.66	65 860
Fish and game wardens	7 720	23.53	26.94	56 030	7 530	23.46	26.42	54 950
Parking enforcement workers	9 530	15.57	16.36	34 020	9 670	16.74	17.00	35 360
Police and sheriff's patrol officers	633 710	24.72	25.39	52 810	641 590	25.58	26.53	55 180
Transit and railroad police	3 830	22.44	23.34	48 540	3 930	24.49	25.17	52 350
Animal control workers	15 480	14.57	15.38	31 990	15 320	15.17	16.14	33 560
Private detectives and investigators	35 820	20.08	22.35	46 480	31 250	20.25	22.66	47 130
Gaming surveillance officers and gaming investigators	9 100	13.87	15.17	31 550	7 670	14.53	15.60	32 460
Security guards	1 046 760	11.28	12.42	25 840	1 028 830	11.45	12.70	26 430
Crossing guards	68 530	10.96	11.68	24 290	68 470	11.24	12.23	25 430
Lifeguards, ski patrol, and other recreational protective service workers	111 560	8.87	9.58	19 930	115 640	8.99	9.85	20 490
Protective service workers, all other	85 440	14.00	15.66	32 580	87 880	14.14	15.70	32 650
Food Preparation and Serving Related								
Chefs and head cooks	98 040	18.64	20.39	42 410	94 300	19.27	21.27	44 240
First-line supervisors/managers of food preparation and serving workers	805 360	13.93	14.81	30 810	791 750	14.17	15.12	31 460
Cooks, fast food	559 160	8.12	8.47	17 620	539 520	8.52	8.76	18 230
Cooks, institution and cafeteria	370 920	10.68	11.19	23 260	383 540	10.88	11.48	23 870
Cooks, private household	960	11.57	14.91	31 020	770	11.87	13.33	27 720
Cooks, restaurant	899 620	10.57	10.94	22 750	898 820	10.66	11.11	23 110
Cooks, short order	168 770	9.26	9.73	20 230	166 140	9.38	9.94	20 670
Cooks, all other	17 340	11.09	11.91	24 770	19 210	10.99	11.89	24 730
Food preparation workers	880 480	8.96	9.54	19 850	849 400	9.15	9.82	20 420
Bartenders	503 420	8.54	9.84	20 460	492 480	8.82	10.08	20 970
Combined food preparation and serving workers, including fast food	2 708 840	7.90	8.36	17 400	2 695 740	8.28	8.71	18 120
Counter attendants, cafeteria, food concession, and coffee shop	527 530	8.42	8.90	18 520	490 980	8.74	9.13	18 990
Waiters and waitresses	2 371 750	8.01	9.41	19 580	2 302 070	8.50	9.80	20 380
Food servers, nonrestaurant	188 390	9.32	10.19	21 190	194 950	9.42	10.39	21 620
Dining room and cafeteria attendants and bartender helpers	416 410	8.05	8.72	18 140	402 020	8.51	9.09	18 900
Dishwashers	521 150	8.19	8.54	17 750	512 990	8.54	8.81	18 330
Hosts and hostesses, restaurant, lounge, and coffee shop	349 990	8.42	8.93	18 570	334 310	8.71	9.23	19 190
Food preparation and serving related workers, all other	50 420	9.39	10.32	21 460	49 260	9.54	10.61	22 060

[1]Annual wages have been calculated by multiplying the hourly mean wage by a "year-round, full-time" hours figure of 2,080 hours; for occupations with no published hourly mean wage, the annual wage has been directly calculated from the reported survey data.
[2]Wages for some occupations that do not generally entail year-round, full-time employment are reported as either hourly wages or annual salaries (depending on how employees are typically paid).

Table 3-3. Employment and Wages, by Occupation, May 2008 and May 2009—*Continued*

(Number of people, dollars.)

Occupation	May 2008				May 2009			
	Employ-ment	Median hourly wage	Mean hourly wage	Mean annual wage[1]	Employ-ment	Median hourly wage	Mean hourly wage	Mean annual wage[1]
Building and Grounds Cleaning and Maintenance								
First-line supervisors/managers of housekeeping and janitorial workers	183 560	16.34	17.46	36 310	177 730	16.73	17.88	37 180
First-line supervisors/managers of landscaping, lawn service, and groundskeeping workers	108 940	19.19	20.67	42 990	103 540	19.69	21.19	44 080
Janitors and cleaners, except maids and housekeeping cleaners	2 145 320	10.31	11.30	23 500	2 090 400	10.56	11.60	24 120
Maids and housekeeping cleaners	917 120	9.13	9.76	20 290	887 890	9.26	10.02	20 840
Building cleaning workers, all other	13 580	13.09	13.78	28 660	12 290	13.16	13.55	28 190
Pest control workers	63 180	14.37	14.92	31 040	63 500	14.62	15.43	32 100
Landscaping and groundskeeping workers	921 900	11.13	11.95	24 860	859 960	11.29	12.18	25 340
Pesticide handlers, sprayers, and applicators, vegetation	25 060	14.31	15.01	31 210	23 530	14.39	15.11	31 420
Tree trimmers and pruners	35 420	14.41	15.12	31 450	37 830	14.57	15.43	32 090
Grounds maintenance workers, all other	15 790	10.76	13.07	27 180	12 840	11.49	13.65	28 400
Personal Care Services								
Gaming supervisors	26 110	21.87	22.40	46 600	24 760	23.05	23.52	48 920
Slot key persons	15 390	12.24	13.68	28 460	14 310	12.45	13.73	28 560
First-line supervisors/managers of personal service workers	129 070	16.78	18.38	38 230	129 890	16.99	18.53	38 540
Animal trainers	10 030	13.11	14.99	31 190	10 080	12.95	14.94	31 080
Nonfarm animal caretakers	126 740	9.31	10.36	21 550	132 860	9.40	10.50	21 830
Gaming dealers	91 130	7.84	9.56	19 890	86 900	8.19	9.76	20 290
Gaming and sports book writers and runners	16 140	9.46	10.96	22 800	14 790	9.78	11.28	23 460
Gaming service workers, all other	13 910	11.58	12.16	25 290	12 050	11.47	12.20	25 380
Motion picture projectionists	10 200	9.46	10.91	22 700	10 310	9.82	11.03	22 950
Ushers, lobby attendants, and ticket takers	106 570	8.35	9.18	19 100	104 360	8.68	9.43	19 610
Amusement and recreation attendants	258 820	8.40	9.10	18 930	257 350	8.71	9.35	19 450
Costume attendants	5 120	12.62	15.46	32 150	5 150	12.60	15.47	32 180
Locker room, coatroom, and dressing room attendants	18 170	9.48	10.33	21 490	18 470	9.49	10.41	21 640
Entertainment attendants and related workers, all other	43 930	9.39	10.06	20 920	45 080	9.21	10.10	21 020
Embalmers	8 090	18.32	18.90	39 320	8 190	19.53	19.80	41 180
Funeral attendants	33 060	10.63	11.19	23 270	31 900	10.83	11.48	23 880
Barbers	10 330	11.56	12.79	26 610	10 550	11.61	13.29	27 650
Hairdressers, hairstylists, and cosmetologists	355 990	11.13	12.82	26 660	349 210	11.21	13.02	27 070
Makeup artists, theatrical and performance	1 930	12.63	18.76	39 020	1 930	15.12	21.64	45 010
Manicurists and pedicurists	51 590	9.46	10.60	22 040	53 020	9.48	10.65	22 150
Shampooers	15 570	8.32	8.80	18 300	16 170	8.61	9.08	18 890
Skin care specialists	26 300	13.81	15.40	32 040	28 210	13.74	15.38	31 990
Baggage porters and bellhops	49 770	9.49	11.14	23 170	49 380	9.65	11.34	23 580
Concierges	20 380	13.07	13.52	28 120	20 470	13.11	13.83	28 760
Tour guides and escorts	31 760	11.19	12.09	25 150	31 630	11.42	12.50	25 990
Travel guides	4 510	14.60	16.18	33 660	4 270	15.05	16.01	33 300
Flight attendants	99 480	(2)	(2)	39 840	95 810	(2)	(2)	43 350
Transportation attendants, except flight attendants and baggage porters	21 870	9.98	10.76	22 370	22 450	9.90	11.17	23 230
Child care workers	581 670	9.12	9.79	20 350	595 650	9.25	10.07	20 940
Personal and home care aides	614 190	9.22	9.47	19 690	630 740	9.46	9.75	20 280
Fitness trainers and aerobics instructors	229 030	14.04	16.50	34 310	228 170	14.74	16.99	35 340
Recreation workers	282 680	10.56	11.81	24 570	286 230	10.71	12.04	25 040
Residential advisors	52 240	11.26	12.17	25 320	57 280	11.61	12.54	26 070
Personal care and service workers, all other	75 780	9.59	10.88	22 630	74 310	9.69	10.99	22 860
Sales and Related								
First-line supervisors/managers of retail sales workers	1 186 270	16.97	19.19	39 910	1 163 040	16.78	18.81	39 130
First-line supervisors/managers of non-retail sales workers	275 390	32.74	38.40	79 870	261 200	32.44	38.27	79 610
Cashiers	3 545 610	8.49	9.08	18 880	3 439 380	8.57	9.15	19 030
Gaming change persons and booth cashiers	22 280	10.57	11.00	22 890	19 480	10.62	11.11	23 110
Counter and rental clerks	448 480	10.05	11.74	24 430	416 950	10.24	11.87	24 680
Parts salespersons	226 530	13.71	14.83	30 850	208 350	13.52	14.65	30 460
Retail salespersons	4 426 280	9.86	12.04	25 050	4 209 500	9.74	11.84	24 630
Advertising sales agents	161 550	20.90	25.56	53 170	152 420	20.85	25.57	53 190
Insurance sales agents	327 780	21.84	29.06	60 440	325 710	21.87	29.48	61 330
Securities, commodities, and financial services sales agents	271 900	33.02	44.26	92 050	271 670	32.18	43.94	91 390
Travel agents	86 420	14.70	15.61	32 470	76 990	14.80	15.60	32 450
Sales representatives, services, all other	569 130	23.77	28.38	59 030	543 560	23.76	28.49	59 250
Sales representatives, wholesale and manufacturing, technical and scientific products	415 120	33.75	38.11	79 260	406 140	34.30	39.12	81 370
Sales representatives, wholesale and manufacturing, except technical and scientific products	1 493 760	24.68	29.55	61 470	1 409 780	24.48	29.52	61 400
Demonstrators and product promoters	83 540	11.18	13.05	27 150	80 910	10.82	12.81	26 640
Models	1 660	13.18	14.50	30 160	1 510	13.14	17.51	36 420
Real estate brokers	51 390	27.64	37.13	77 240	48 380	26.80	37.68	78 360
Real estate sales agents	164 080	19.30	26.16	54 410	151 550	19.28	25.53	53 100
Sales engineers	78 030	39.95	43.16	89 770	71 640	40.00	43.53	90 540
Telemarketers	345 220	10.56	11.91	24 770	307 730	10.49	11.90	24 760
Door-to-door sales workers, news and street vendors, and related workers	9 520	10.09	13.27	27 600	8 460	10.24	12.65	26 320
Sales and related workers, all other	146 480	16.99	20.10	41 810	140 680	16.91	20.12	41 840

[1]Annual wages have been calculated by multiplying the hourly mean wage by a "year-round, full-time" hours figure of 2,080 hours; for occupations with no published hourly mean wage, the annual wage has been directly calculated from the reported survey data.
[2]Wages for some occupations that do not generally entail year-round, full-time employment are reported as either hourly wages or annual salaries (depending on how employees are typically paid).

Table 3-3. Employment and Wages, by Occupation, May 2008 and May 2009—*Continued*

(Number of people, dollars.)

Occupation	May 2008				May 2009			
	Employ-ment	Median hourly wage	Mean hourly wage	Mean annual wage[1]	Employ-ment	Median hourly wage	Mean hourly wage	Mean annual wage[1]
Office and Administrative Support								
First-line supervisors/managers of office and administrative support workers	1 404 330	22.02	23.42	48 700	1 381 060	22.55	24.04	49 990
Switchboard operators, including answering service	153 860	11.65	12.14	25 250	146 980	11.93	12.50	26 000
Telephone operators	22 820	15.23	16.25	33 800	21 960	14.70	15.58	32 410
Communications equipment operators, all other	3 500	16.85	17.79	37 000	2 810	18.12	18.68	38 850
Bill and account collectors	408 760	14.73	15.47	32 180	403 100	14.87	15.65	32 560
Billing and posting clerks and machine operators	512 120	14.88	15.44	32 120	493 780	15.25	15.82	32 900
Bookkeeping, accounting, and auditing clerks	1 855 010	15.63	16.25	33 800	1 757 870	16.08	16.71	34 750
Gaming cage workers	17 060	11.97	12.48	25 970	16 070	12.08	12.68	26 360
Payroll and timekeeping clerks	203 210	16.74	17.07	35 500	190 810	17.31	17.60	36 600
Procurement clerks	79 610	16.72	16.96	35 280	78 150	17.36	17.51	36 430
Tellers	600 380	11.35	11.66	24 250	576 580	11.53	11.91	24 780
Brokerage clerks	68 430	18.61	19.89	41 370	62 470	19.32	20.55	42 750
Correspondence clerks	13 450	14.73	15.04	31 280	10 370	15.35	15.86	32 990
Court, municipal, and license clerks	115 070	15.96	16.88	35 120	120 690	16.12	17.10	35 570
Credit authorizers, checkers, and clerks	65 020	14.61	15.37	31 980	57 220	15.36	16.20	33 700
Customer service representatives	2 233 270	14.36	15.28	31 790	2 195 860	14.56	15.58	32 410
Eligibility interviewers, government programs	112 510	18.90	19.16	39 850	110 850	19.32	19.56	40 680
File clerks	204 760	11.44	12.16	25 290	188 510	11.89	12.66	26 320
Hotel, motel, and resort desk clerks	230 230	9.37	9.92	20 630	224 360	9.53	10.16	21 130
Interviewers, except eligibility and loan	224 690	13.53	13.96	29 040	215 930	13.78	14.32	29 780
Library assistants, clerical	114 740	10.88	11.68	24 290	115 310	11.05	11.92	24 790
Loan interviewers and clerks	212 340	15.61	16.29	33 890	195 310	16.03	16.67	34 670
New accounts clerks	87 300	14.53	14.90	30 990	81 650	14.73	15.14	31 490
Order clerks	248 030	13.46	14.08	29 300	227 190	13.71	14.37	29 890
Human resources assistants, except payroll and timekeeping	164 340	17.19	17.70	36 810	161 920	17.62	18.19	37 840
Receptionists and information clerks	1 097 610	11.80	12.21	25 400	1 052 120	12.05	12.50	26 010
Reservation and transportation ticket agents and travel clerks	163 880	14.94	15.41	32 060	142 500	15.03	15.58	32 400
All other information and record clerks	215 780	16.15	16.78	34 910	212 090	17.09	17.45	36 300
Cargo and freight agents	85 950	17.92	18.67	38 830	82 440	17.77	18.72	38 940
Couriers and messengers	96 110	11.22	12.07	25 100	93 460	11.43	12.36	25 710
Police, fire, and ambulance dispatchers	96 360	16.19	16.99	35 340	98 090	16.73	17.53	36 470
Dispatchers, except police, fire, and ambulance	193 210	16.28	17.58	36 560	185 100	16.58	17.94	37 310
Meter readers, utilities	44 730	15.84	16.77	34 890	42 330	16.58	17.50	36 400
Postal service clerks	78 250	24.54	24.11	50 150	73 690	25.26	24.84	51 670
Postal service mail carriers	354 570	23.94	22.58	46 970	339 030	25.10	23.53	48 940
Postal service mail sorters, processors, and processing machine operators	185 770	24.05	21.87	45 490	162 940	25.25	23.20	48 260
Production, planning, and expediting clerks	281 660	19.46	20.26	42 150	274 140	19.98	20.80	43 260
Shipping, receiving, and traffic clerks	760 950	13.30	14.03	29 180	715 130	13.58	14.35	29 840
Stock clerks and order fillers	1 873 390	10.00	11.13	23 140	1 864 410	10.08	11.28	23 460
Weighers, measurers, checkers, and samplers, recordkeeping	72 720	12.95	13.70	28 500	69 890	13.13	13.88	28 860
Executive secretaries and administrative assistants	1 491 520	19.24	20.35	42 340	1 361 170	20.03	21.16	44 010
Legal secretaries	257 810	19.16	20.02	41 640	244 380	19.75	20.65	42 940
Medical secretaries	454 500	14.27	14.81	30 800	469 740	14.51	15.12	31 450
Secretaries, except legal, medical, and executive	1 872 070	13.96	14.42	29 990	1 797 670	14.41	14.93	31 060
Computer operators	107 450	17.11	17.82	37 070	94 730	17.36	18.05	37 540
Data entry keyers	272 810	12.56	13.04	27 110	243 550	13.05	13.46	28 000
Word processors and typists	128 010	15.09	15.73	32 710	109 470	15.67	16.21	33 720
Desktop publishers	26 210	17.59	18.62	38 740	22 810	17.53	18.73	38 960
Insurance claims and policy processing clerks	237 800	15.91	16.75	34 830	235 480	16.36	17.18	35 740
Mail clerks and mail machine operators, except postal service	137 350	12.07	12.70	26 420	131 750	12.36	13.05	27 150
Office clerks, general	2 906 600	12.17	12.90	26 830	2 815 240	12.57	13.32	27 700
Office machine operators, except computer	79 470	12.40	13.13	27 310	70 230	12.79	13.49	28 060
Proofreaders and copy markers	15 300	14.66	15.50	32 240	14 050	14.76	15.63	32 500
Statistical assistants	16 900	16.76	17.32	36 020	15 900	17.27	18.03	37 500
Office and administrative support workers, all other	272 190	14.10	15.15	31 510	266 090	14.29	15.37	31 960
Farming, Fishing, and Forestry								
First-line supervisors/managers of farming, fishing, and forestry workers	20 800	19.11	20.55	42 740	20 200	19.47	21.02	43 720
Farm labor contractors	1 110	16.10	17.62	36 640	1 000	14.62	17.37	36 130
Agricultural inspectors	14 340	19.80	19.87	41 330	14 030	19.95	20.12	41 860
Animal breeders	2 080	13.02	15.90	33 070	1 700	14.27	16.93	35 210
Graders and sorters, agricultural products	37 500	9.06	9.85	20 490	40 160	9.14	9.93	20 640
Agricultural equipment operators	22 110	10.92	11.77	24 490	22 420	11.28	12.12	25 220
Farmworkers and laborers, crop, nursery, and greenhouse	242 390	8.64	9.27	19 280	233 650	8.91	9.51	19 780
Farmworkers, farm and ranch animals	38 110	10.13	11.02	22 920	35 000	10.42	11.37	23 640
Agricultural workers, all other	7 680	12.00	13.13	27 310	7 420	12.31	13.48	28 040
Fishers and related fishing workers	1 110	13.44	13.68	28 460	670	11.34	12.79	26 600
Forest and conservation workers	8 280	10.98	12.55	26 110	5 840	12.30	14.14	29 410
Fallers	7 120	14.66	16.43	34 180	6 480	15.49	17.10	35 570
Logging equipment operators	27 010	15.18	15.76	32 780	23 630	15.31	15.80	32 870
Log graders and scalers	3 610	15.64	16.51	34 330	2 940	16.20	17.09	35 550
Logging workers, all other	5 180	15.96	15.82	32 900	4 010	16.56	16.43	34 180

[1]Annual wages have been calculated by multiplying the hourly mean wage by a "year-round, full-time" hours figure of 2,080 hours; for occupations with no published hourly mean wage, the annual wage has been directly calculated from the reported survey data.

Table 3-3. Employment and Wages, by Occupation, May 2008 and May 2009—*Continued*

(Number of people, dollars.)

Occupation	May 2008				May 2009			
	Employ-ment	Median hourly wage	Mean hourly wage	Mean annual wage[1]	Employ-ment	Median hourly wage	Mean hourly wage	Mean annual wage[1]
Construction and Extraction								
First-line supervisors/managers of construction trades and extraction workers	577 390	27.95	29.46	61 280	531 840	28.04	29.68	61 730
Boilermakers	20 400	25.13	25.53	53 100	22 400	26.97	27.25	56 680
Brickmasons and blockmasons	106 270	21.94	22.95	47 740	87 780	22.47	23.68	49 250
Stonemasons	18 910	18.17	19.68	40 930	14 080	17.68	19.24	40 030
Carpenters	899 920	18.72	20.64	42 940	743 760	18.98	20.98	43 640
Carpet installers	34 390	17.80	19.87	41 330	29 080	17.90	19.98	41 560
Floor layers, except carpet, wood, and hard tiles	14 250	17.50	19.03	39 580	11 870	17.34	18.84	39 190
Floor sanders and finishers	8 220	15.41	16.93	35 220	7 000	15.76	16.89	35 140
Tile and marble setters	51 210	18.85	20.13	41 870	41 140	18.83	20.41	42 450
Cement masons and concrete finishers	201 730	16.87	18.75	39 000	165 700	17.04	18.95	39 410
Terrazzo workers and finishers	5 550	17.25	18.90	39 300	4 290	18.38	19.89	41 360
Construction laborers	1 020 290	13.71	15.51	32 250	856 440	14.01	15.96	33 190
Paving, surfacing, and tamping equipment operators	61 230	16.00	17.54	36 490	54 850	16.36	18.10	37 660
Pile-driver operators	4 790	23.01	24.83	51 640	4 240	22.24	24.72	51 410
Operating engineers and other construction equipment operators	398 910	18.88	20.97	43 630	368 200	19.12	21.24	44 180
Drywall and ceiling tile installers	128 740	18.12	19.68	40 940	102 880	17.88	19.75	41 080
Tapers	31 850	21.03	22.07	45 900	24 050	21.37	22.54	46 880
Electricians	633 010	22.32	23.98	49 890	579 150	22.68	24.45	50 850
Glaziers	51 730	17.11	18.74	38 990	46 400	17.11	19.05	39 630
Insulation workers, floor, ceiling, and wall	28 390	15.34	16.79	34 920	26 500	15.65	17.35	36 090
Insulation workers, mechanical	30 150	17.95	19.99	41 570	29 620	17.81	19.86	41 310
Painters, construction and maintenance	250 310	15.85	17.56	36 510	214 240	16.21	17.94	37 320
Paperhangers	4 610	16.76	19.00	39 520	5 140	18.00	20.34	42 310
Pipelayers	54 440	15.72	17.45	36 300	49 190	16.12	17.81	37 040
Plumbers, pipefitters, and steamfitters	437 540	21.94	23.65	49 200	400 970	22.27	23.97	49 870
Plasterers and stucco masons	43 290	18.01	19.27	40 070	34 280	18.16	19.84	41 260
Reinforcing iron and rebar workers	28 620	19.18	21.34	44 380	24 200	18.97	21.42	44 560
Roofers	120 200	16.17	18.00	37 430	108 180	16.33	17.98	37 390
Sheet metal workers	163 480	19.37	21.30	44 310	146 690	19.54	21.58	44 890
Structural iron and steel workers	68 670	20.68	22.68	47 170	65 130	21.40	23.30	48 470
Helpers—brickmasons, blockmasons, stonemasons, and tile and marble setters	53 300	13.19	14.24	29 610	40 770	13.29	14.34	29 830
Helpers—carpenters	81 260	12.21	12.69	26 390	62 020	12.43	12.87	26 770
Helpers—electricians	104 050	12.69	13.20	27 450	90 930	12.86	13.40	27 870
Helpers—painters, paperhangers, plasterers, and stucco masons	19 900	11.23	11.70	24 330	15 740	11.21	11.68	24 300
Helpers—pipelayers, plumbers, pipefitters, and steamfitters	79 870	12.73	13.10	27 260	68 270	12.91	13.24	27 530
Helpers—roofers	18 730	11.47	11.85	24 660	15 440	11.35	11.71	24 360
Helpers, construction trades, all other	27 210	12.01	13.04	27 130	21 390	12.17	13.28	27 630
Construction and building inspectors	96 000	24.12	25.08	52 160	90 730	24.77	25.75	53 550
Elevator installers and repairers	25 070	33.35	32.57	67 750	23 450	33.20	32.67	67 950
Fence erectors	25 710	13.49	14.49	30 130	21 840	13.47	14.49	30 140
Hazardous materials removal workers	42 500	17.94	19.37	40 290	41 100	17.92	19.36	40 270
Highway maintenance workers	136 420	16.35	16.84	35 040	139 490	16.47	16.98	35 310
Rail-track laying and maintenance equipment operators	15 020	21.26	21.57	44 870	14 880	21.94	22.11	46 000
Septic tank servicers and sewer pipe cleaners	24 730	16.19	17.09	35 550	24 690	16.03	17.05	35 470
Segmental pavers	1 170	13.17	13.68	28 450	1 040	13.33	13.81	28 730
Construction and related workers, all other	55 820	15.65	16.91	35 170	47 630	16.34	17.55	36 490
Derrick operators, oil and gas	23 590	20.15	20.18	41 980	21 080	20.66	20.96	43 590
Rotary drill operators, oil and gas	27 020	23.94	26.14	54 370	25 500	25.49	28.63	59 560
Service unit operators, oil, gas, and mining	36 850	18.07	19.86	41 320	36 450	18.49	20.52	42 690
Earth drillers, except oil and gas	20 220	18.39	19.88	41 360	17 850	18.82	20.22	42 070
Explosives workers, ordnance handling experts, and blasters	6 060	20.18	21.39	44 490	6 280	20.41	21.65	45 030
Continuous mining machine operators	10 920	22.09	21.91	45 570	11 230	22.56	22.44	46 680
Mine cutting and channeling machine operators	9 190	19.94	19.96	41 510	7 940	20.68	20.73	43 120
Mining machine operators, all other	4 650	20.62	20.79	43 240	4 830	20.88	20.93	43 540
Rock splitters, quarry	4 210	13.41	14.50	30 160	3 430	13.96	14.64	30 440
Roof bolters, mining	4 950	21.74	21.97	45 690	5 470	22.80	22.96	47 750
Roustabouts, oil and gas	62 540	14.72	15.70	32 660	61 320	15.31	16.44	34 190
Helpers—extraction workers	25 550	15.74	16.36	34 030	24 210	16.62	17.73	36 870
Extraction workers, all other	7 800	18.49	19.89	41 370	7 340	19.17	19.81	41 210
Installation, Maintenance, and Repair								
First-line supervisors/managers of mechanics, installers, and repairers	443 840	27.55	28.44	59 160	427 560	28.18	29.15	60 630
Computer, automated teller, and office machine repairers	122 400	18.18	18.95	39 420	111 600	18.09	18.95	39 420
Radio mechanics	5 440	19.36	20.45	42 530	5 690	19.74	20.31	42 250
Telecommunications equipment installers and repairers, except line installers	195 170	26.73	25.31	52 650	189 850	26.71	25.48	52 990
Avionics technicians	18 360	23.71	23.73	49 360	17 960	24.31	24.20	50 330
Electric motor, power tool, and related repairers	23 400	16.96	17.84	37 110	20 660	17.44	18.40	38 280
Electrical and electronics installers and repairers, transportation equipment	15 860	21.37	21.60	44 940	13 900	22.03	22.38	46 550
Electrical and electronics repairers, commercial and industrial equipment	77 270	23.29	23.68	49 260	72 520	24.39	24.62	51 210
Electrical and electronics repairers, powerhouse, substation, and relay	23 180	29.34	29.18	60 700	22 870	29.94	29.66	61 700
Electronic equipment installers and repairers, motor vehicles	19 980	13.29	14.31	29 770	17 090	13.49	14.36	29 880
Electronic home entertainment equipment installers and repairers	38 680	15.42	16.26	33 830	34 200	15.54	16.36	34 030
Security and fire alarm systems installers	62 720	17.63	18.57	38 630	63 690	18.13	19.15	39 830
Aircraft mechanics and service technicians	116 310	24.71	24.83	51 650	112 130	25.39	25.47	52 970
Automotive body and related repairers	147 200	17.81	19.21	39 950	133 290	18.26	19.72	41 020
Automotive glass installers and repairers	18 330	15.44	15.95	33 180	15 920	15.91	16.34	33 980

[1]Annual wages have been calculated by multiplying the hourly mean wage by a "year-round, full-time" hours figure of 2,080 hours; for occupations with no published hourly mean wage, the annual wage has been directly calculated from the reported survey data.

Table 3-3. Employment and Wages, by Occupation, May 2008 and May 2009—*Continued*

(Number of people, dollars.)

Occupation	May 2008				May 2009			
	Employ-ment	Median hourly wage	Mean hourly wage	Mean annual wage[1]	Employ-ment	Median hourly wage	Mean hourly wage	Mean annual wage[1]
Installation, Maintenance, and Repair—*Continued*								
Automotive service technicians and mechanics	649 460	16.88	18.05	37 540	606 990	17.03	18.21	37 880
Bus and truck mechanics and diesel engine specialists	248 620	18.94	19.57	40 710	232 810	19.35	20.00	41 590
Farm equipment mechanics	30 240	15.32	15.79	32 850	30 250	15.85	16.32	33 950
Mobile heavy equipment mechanics, except engines	125 930	20.59	21.30	44 300	120 450	21.21	21.94	45 630
Rail car repairers	20 780	21.48	21.59	44 920	20 910	22.33	22.32	46 430
Motorboat mechanics	19 640	16.60	17.35	36 080	18 180	17.03	17.85	37 120
Motorcycle mechanics	16 850	15.08	16.10	33 490	16 070	15.30	16.29	33 870
Outdoor power equipment and other small engine mechanics	26 440	13.91	14.41	29 970	26 010	14.08	14.61	30 400
Bicycle repairers	9 690	11.15	11.61	24 140	9 290	11.28	11.65	24 240
Recreational vehicle service technicians	13 400	15.14	16.05	33 380	10 860	15.45	16.50	34 320
Tire repairers and changers	98 520	10.80	11.46	23 830	92 440	11.11	11.83	24 610
Mechanical door repairers	17 530	16.11	17.00	35 360	15 330	16.64	17.44	36 270
Control and valve installers and repairers, except mechanical door	43 900	22.62	22.72	47 260	42 180	22.71	23.01	47 860
Heating, air conditioning, and refrigeration mechanics and installers	261 610	19.08	20.31	42 240	244 410	19.76	21.00	43 670
Home appliance repairers	37 300	16.30	17.16	35 690	34 670	16.44	17.11	35 590
Industrial machinery mechanics	280 620	20.99	21.77	45 280	276 230	21.38	22.19	46 160
Maintenance and repair workers, general	1 305 170	16.21	17.13	35 630	1 268 930	16.65	17.56	36 520
Maintenance workers, machinery	73 650	17.69	18.56	38 610	66 390	18.16	19.03	39 570
Millwrights	46 250	22.87	24.05	50 030	41 640	23.14	24.09	50 110
Refractory materials repairers, except brickmasons	2 450	19.78	20.07	41 750	2 080	19.97	20.82	43 310
Electrical power-line installers and repairers	111 580	26.49	26.11	54 300	108 980	27.24	26.86	55 860
Telecommunications line installers and repairers	168 050	23.12	22.75	47 330	162 400	23.61	23.23	48 310
Camera and photographic equipment repairers	3 820	16.49	18.27	37 990	3 290	17.03	18.85	39 210
Medical equipment repairers	34 260	19.96	21.17	44 030	34 550	20.34	21.61	44 950
Musical instrument repairers and tuners	5 310	15.90	17.28	35 950	5 580	15.77	17.47	36 330
Watch repairers	2 770	16.66	18.08	37 600	2 350	18.12	19.62	40 810
Precision instrument and equipment repairers, all other	12 990	23.54	24.23	50 400	13 240	24.11	24.41	50 770
Coin, vending, and amusement machine servicers and repairers	41 280	14.39	14.89	30 970	38 470	14.64	15.27	31 760
Commercial divers	2 370	22.28	26.42	54 940	3 030	25.26	27.91	58 060
Fabric menders, except garment	960	13.69	13.42	27 920	840	13.50	13.28	27 630
Locksmiths and safe repairers	18 500	16.57	17.26	35 900	16 910	17.20	18.05	37 550
Manufactured building and mobile home installers	8 290	13.58	14.17	29 460	6 780	13.81	14.34	29 820
Riggers	13 490	19.77	20.49	42 620	13 310	20.37	21.15	43 990
Signal and track switch repairers	6 570	23.89	23.59	49 060	6 450	24.78	24.29	50 520
Helpers—installation, maintenance, and repair workers	149 350	11.46	12.34	25 670	135 880	11.61	12.62	26 260
Installation, maintenance, and repair workers, all other	139 100	16.46	17.89	37 220	127 060	17.08	18.49	38 450
Production								
First-line supervisors/managers of production and operating workers	658 500	24.25	25.72	53 500	605 560	25.03	26.51	55 150
Aircraft structure, surfaces, rigging, and systems assemblers	43 330	21.22	20.96	43 600	39 870	21.86	21.44	44 600
Coil winders, tapers, and finishers	22 160	13.33	13.81	28 720	18 730	13.48	14.05	29 210
Electrical and electronic equipment assemblers	215 230	13.22	14.14	29 410	193 570	13.77	14.76	30 690
Electromechanical equipment assemblers	62 310	14.11	14.67	30 520	56 460	14.75	15.24	31 700
Engine and other machine assemblers	39 270	15.70	16.78	34 900	34 080	16.58	17.86	37 150
Structural metal fabricators and fitters	111 620	15.58	16.28	33 860	96 870	16.29	16.87	35 080
Fiberglass laminators and fabricators	30 890	13.48	13.79	28 680	22 360	13.65	14.07	29 270
Team assemblers	1 131 060	12.32	13.28	27 630	997 390	12.89	13.87	28 840
Timing device assemblers, adjusters, and calibrators	2 700	13.73	14.76	30 710	2 260	13.50	14.41	29 970
Assemblers and fabricators, all other	318 060	13.37	15.79	32 840	267 780	13.39	15.52	32 280
Bakers	141 130	11.20	12.03	25 020	140 510	11.36	12.19	25 350
Butchers and meat cutters	128 210	13.60	14.28	29 700	125 510	13.87	14.55	30 270
Meat, poultry, and fish cutters and trimmers	166 150	10.49	10.77	22 400	168 700	10.64	11.01	22 900
Slaughterers and meat packers	97 000	11.07	11.19	23 270	97 530	11.30	11.42	23 740
Food and tobacco roasting, baking, and drying machine operators and tenders	17 870	12.81	13.76	28 610	16 260	13.11	13.88	28 870
Food batchmakers	99 170	11.62	12.64	26 290	100 190	11.68	12.85	26 730
Food cooking machine operators and tenders	39 300	11.00	11.59	24 110	37 060	11.11	11.84	24 630
Computer-controlled machine tool operators, metal and plastic	143 030	16.03	16.60	34 520	129 780	16.57	17.10	35 570
Numerical tool and process control programmers	16 990	21.30	22.29	46 360	15 480	22.12	23.19	48 230
Extruding and drawing machine setters, operators, and tenders, metal and plastic	92 160	14.31	14.92	31 030	81 610	14.94	15.54	32 320
Forging machine setters, operators, and tenders, metal and plastic	28 800	14.90	15.56	32 370	24 590	15.62	16.20	33 700
Rolling machine setters, operators, and tenders, metal and plastic	34 970	16.40	17.02	35 410	32 880	17.03	17.63	36 670
Cutting, punching, and press machine setters, operators, and tenders, metal and plastic	242 970	13.54	14.15	29 420	209 730	14.02	14.65	30 480
Drilling and boring machine tool setters, operators, and tenders, metal and plastic	33 550	14.83	15.64	32 520	28 140	15.13	15.84	32 940
Grinding, lapping, polishing, and buffing machine tool setters, operators, and tenders, metal and plastic	91 990	14.16	15.01	31 230	81 740	14.56	15.43	32 090
Lathe and turning machine tool setters, operators, and tenders, metal and plastic	56 500	15.84	16.38	34 070	51 260	16.29	16.83	35 000
Milling and planing machine setters, operators, and tenders, metal and plastic	26 220	16.00	16.56	34 450	23 770	16.69	17.40	36 190
Machinists	419 070	17.41	18.03	37 490	380 720	18.10	18.72	38 940
Metal-refining furnace operators and tenders	19 280	17.47	17.94	37 310	16 960	18.22	18.67	38 830
Pourers and casters, metal	15 320	15.66	16.11	33 510	13 090	16.24	16.71	34 760
Model makers, metal and plastic	8 990	19.55	21.49	44 700	7 710	19.82	21.44	44 590
Patternmakers, metal and plastic	6 220	17.75	18.98	39 490	5 220	17.54	18.62	38 730
Foundry mold and coremakers	15 240	14.13	14.61	30 390	13 550	14.41	14.93	31 050

[1]Annual wages have been calculated by multiplying the hourly mean wage by a "year-round, full-time" hours figure of 2,080 hours; for occupations with no published hourly mean wage, the annual wage has been directly calculated from the reported survey data.

Table 3-3. Employment and Wages, by Occupation, May 2008 and May 2009—*Continued*

(Number of people, dollars.)

Occupation	May 2008				May 2009			
	Employ-ment	Median hourly wage	Mean hourly wage	Mean annual wage[1]	Employ-ment	Median hourly wage	Mean hourly wage	Mean annual wage[1]
Installation, Maintenance, and Repair—*Continued*								
Molding, coremaking, and casting machine setters, operators, and tenders, metal and plastic	145 760	13.17	14.07	29 270	126 840	13.40	14.30	29 750
Multiple machine tool setters, operators, and tenders, metal and plastic	87 800	14.87	15.76	32 780	76 130	15.01	15.80	32 860
Tool and die makers	85 610	22.32	23.17	48 180	73 640	22.55	23.43	48 730
Welders, cutters, solderers, and brazers	392 520	16.13	17.01	35 370	357 740	16.71	17.61	36 630
Welding, soldering, and brazing machine setters, operators, and tenders	51 840	15.20	16.20	33 700	41 580	15.74	16.43	34 170
Heat treating equipment setters, operators, and tenders, metal and plastic	23 630	15.40	15.93	33 140	20 420	15.70	16.24	33 790
Lay-out workers, metal and plastic	8 340	16.79	17.87	37 170	9 020	17.77	18.38	38 240
Plating and coating machine setters, operators, and tenders, metal and plastic	40 300	13.65	14.46	30 090	34 310	13.75	14.57	30 300
Tool grinders, filers, and sharpeners	16 410	15.37	16.29	33 880	13 740	16.00	16.88	35 110
Metal workers and plastic workers, all other	43 690	15.61	17.10	35 570	35 190	15.46	16.78	34 910
Bindery workers	60 560	13.17	13.99	29 100	53 870	13.55	14.40	29 960
Bookbinders	6 150	14.92	16.33	33 970	6 430	14.72	16.26	33 830
Job printers	42 640	16.21	16.98	35 330	39 180	16.56	17.24	35 860
Prepress technicians and workers	61 170	16.84	17.52	36 440	53 710	17.21	17.96	37 360
Printing machine operators	193 510	15.46	16.42	34 150	174 720	15.85	16.84	35 030
Laundry and dry-cleaning workers	221 230	9.14	9.72	20 230	211 490	9.28	10.00	20 790
Pressers, textile, garment, and related materials	67 500	9.15	9.55	19 860	60 440	9.31	9.78	20 330
Sewing machine operators	190 440	9.55	10.43	21 690	165 680	9.74	10.70	22 250
Shoe and leather workers and repairers	8 170	11.00	11.60	24 130	7 190	11.16	11.83	24 610
Shoe machine operators and tenders	4 910	12.06	12.22	25 420	3 990	12.69	12.80	26 620
Sewers, hand	7 050	10.58	11.14	23 170	6 020	11.07	11.71	24 350
Tailors, dressmakers, and custom sewers	31 700	12.01	12.94	26 920	26 450	12.81	13.60	28 300
Textile bleaching and dyeing machine operators and tenders	16 180	11.38	11.77	24 480	12 980	11.22	11.82	24 580
Textile cutting machine setters, operators, and tenders	20 170	10.88	11.45	23 810	17 890	11.35	11.95	24 850
Textile knitting and weaving machine setters, operators, and tenders	30 250	12.21	12.33	25 650	24 530	12.33	12.46	25 910
Textile winding, twisting, and drawing out machine setters, operators, and tenders	36 540	11.53	11.83	24 600	30 530	12.10	12.40	25 780
Extruding and forming machine setters, operators, and tenders, synthetic and glass fibers	14 440	14.98	15.29	31 800	13 680	15.12	15.48	32 190
Fabric and apparel patternmakers	7 500	18.15	20.28	42 190	6 640	18.75	20.64	42 940
Upholsterers	39 090	13.94	14.69	30 560	33 810	14.42	15.21	31 640
Textile, apparel, and furnishings workers, all other	17 430	11.85	13.20	27 450	14 220	12.24	13.95	29 010
Cabinetmakers and bench carpenters	120 960	13.93	14.72	30 620	99 870	14.22	14.95	31 100
Furniture finishers	21 630	12.93	13.66	28 410	18 760	13.26	14.00	29 120
Model makers, wood	1 740	15.06	17.16	35 690	1 900	14.72	16.33	33 970
Patternmakers, wood	1 930	16.35	18.61	38 720	1 540	15.48	18.53	38 540
Sawing machine setters, operators, and tenders, wood	51 830	12.41	13.01	27 070	41 750	12.51	13.12	27 290
Woodworking machine setters, operators, and tenders, except sawing	88 510	11.89	12.44	25 880	72 560	12.25	12.81	26 630
Woodworkers, all other	11 260	11.57	12.78	26 570	9 980	11.43	13.03	27 090
Nuclear power reactor operators	4 970	35.25	35.34	73 510	4 840	34.93	35.66	74 180
Power distributors and dispatchers	9 820	31.68	31.76	66 070	10 000	32.21	32.17	66 910
Power plant operators	34 700	28.11	28.05	58 340	36 860	29.04	28.97	60 270
Stationary engineers and boiler operators	39 000	23.94	24.36	50 660	37 270	24.70	25.02	52 040
Water and liquid waste treatment plant and system operators	110 300	18.48	19.21	39 950	109 090	19.16	19.99	41 580
Chemical plant and system operators	44 600	25.23	25.07	52 150	45 750	26.09	25.97	54 010
Gas plant operators	14 500	26.81	26.61	55 350	14 040	27.02	26.86	55 860
Petroleum pump system operators, refinery operators, and gaugers	45 710	26.45	26.42	54 950	46 230	27.37	27.40	56 990
Plant and system operators, all other	12 370	23.37	23.36	48 590	11 050	23.92	23.97	49 860
Chemical equipment operators and tenders	52 890	21.76	21.92	45 580	48 360	21.70	21.68	45 100
Separating, filtering, clarifying, precipitating, and still machine setters, operators, and tenders	41 200	17.64	18.27	38 010	37 490	18.04	18.49	38 450
Crushing, grinding, and polishing machine setters, operators, and tenders	41 270	14.38	15.08	31 360	38 360	15.14	15.80	32 860
Grinding and polishing workers, hand	40 290	12.36	13.03	27 100	32 350	12.78	13.40	27 870
Mixing and blending machine setters, operators, and tenders	140 120	15.04	15.70	32 650	129 250	15.43	16.09	33 460
Cutters and trimmers, hand	24 700	11.38	12.28	25 540	20 180	11.64	12.59	26 190
Cutting and slicing machine setters, operators, and tenders	76 500	13.85	14.44	30 020	70 700	14.23	14.77	30 720
Extruding, forming, pressing, and compacting machine setters, operators, and tenders	85 130	13.92	14.63	30 430	72 770	14.36	15.08	31 370
Furnace, kiln, oven, drier, and kettle operators and tenders	22 950	15.31	15.84	32 950	19 900	16.00	16.54	34 410
Inspectors, testers, sorters, samplers, and weighers	467 010	15.02	16.29	33 890	430 450	15.54	16.75	34 840
Jewelers and precious stone and metal workers	24 780	15.84	17.00	35 360	23 410	16.38	17.60	36 620
Dental laboratory technicians	42 640	16.43	17.78	36 990	40 480	16.74	18.12	37 690
Medical appliance technicians	12 930	16.57	18.58	38 640	13 760	16.83	18.55	38 590
Ophthalmic laboratory technicians	32 930	13.08	14.01	29 130	30 580	13.57	14.37	29 880
Packaging and filling machine operators and tenders	357 480	11.73	12.76	26 550	338 920	12.08	13.13	27 320
Coating, painting, and spraying machine setters, operators, and tenders	103 310	13.66	14.27	29 680	89 430	14.06	14.69	30 550
Painters, transportation equipment	50 310	17.86	19.37	40 300	46 810	18.38	19.82	41 220
Painting, coating, and decorating workers	31 200	11.57	12.54	26 090	28 460	11.44	12.47	25 940
Photographic process workers	21 040	12.51	14.14	29 410	18 390	12.73	14.28	29 710
Photographic processing machine operators	49 550	9.79	10.93	22 740	46 680	9.69	10.74	22 330
Semiconductor processors	32 230	15.49	16.43	34 170	25 750	15.18	15.92	33 110
Cementing and gluing machine operators and tenders	19 640	13.23	13.96	29 030	16 190	13.89	14.46	30 080
Cleaning, washing, and metal pickling equipment operators and tenders	18 870	11.53	12.57	26 140	19 550	11.86	12.88	26 800
Cooling and freezing equipment operators and tenders	9 940	12.05	13.11	27 260	9 160	12.75	13.96	29 040
Etchers and engravers	10 760	13.22	14.14	29 400	8 920	13.35	14.27	29 690

[1] Annual wages have been calculated by multiplying the hourly mean wage by a "year-round, full-time" hours figure of 2,080 hours; for occupations with no published hourly mean wage, the annual wage has been directly calculated from the reported survey data.

Table 3-3. Employment and Wages, by Occupation, May 2008 and May 2009—*Continued*

(Number of people, dollars.)

Occupation	May 2008				May 2009			
	Employ-ment	Median hourly wage	Mean hourly wage	Mean annual wage[1]	Employ-ment	Median hourly wage	Mean hourly wage	Mean annual wage[1]
Installation, Maintenance, and Repair—*Continued*								
Molders, shapers, and casters, except metal and plastic	41 900	13.40	13.98	29 090	35 430	13.69	14.33	29 800
Paper goods machine setters, operators, and tenders	104 170	15.91	16.35	34 010	94 210	16.40	16.85	35 040
Tire builders	21 740	19.35	18.31	38 080	17 820	18.95	18.19	37 830
Helpers—production workers	499 870	10.48	11.21	23 320	433 370	10.75	11.54	24 000
Production workers, all other	280 160	12.86	14.57	30 310	239 550	13.33	14.97	31 130
Aircraft cargo handling supervisors	4 950	19.23	22.43	46 660	5 370	20.43	23.46	48 790
First-line supervisors/managers of helpers, laborers, and material movers, hand	186 230	20.18	21.33	44 380	174 540	20.65	21.76	45 250
First-line supervisors/managers of transportation and material-moving machine and vehicle operators	218 480	24.67	25.94	53 960	205 780	25.12	26.32	54 750
Airline pilots, copilots, and flight engineers	77 090	(2)	(2)	119 750	74 420	(2)	(2)	117 060
Commercial pilots	31 250	(2)	(2)	75 500	29 180	(2)	(2)	73 060
Air traffic controllers	24 260	53.78	51.97	108 090	24 420	52.81	51.44	106 990
Airfield operations specialists	8 050	19.88	20.46	42 550	7 670	20.10	20.79	43 250
Ambulance drivers and attendants, except emergency medical technicians	21 790	10.77	11.25	23 400	19 570	10.66	11.13	23 140
Bus drivers, transit and intercity	184 160	16.32	17.16	35 700	177 510	16.43	17.30	35 990
Bus drivers, school	460 100	12.79	13.01	27 060	459 480	13.17	13.49	28 050
Driver/sales workers	372 720	10.70	12.52	26 050	363 050	10.93	12.83	26 690
Truck drivers, heavy and tractor-trailer	1 672 580	17.92	18.62	38 720	1 550 930	18.14	18.87	39 260
Truck drivers, light or delivery services	908 960	13.27	14.55	30 260	834 780	13.62	14.96	31 120
Taxi drivers and chauffeurs	170 520	10.36	11.32	23 540	167 740	10.56	11.51	23 930
Motor vehicle operators, all other	78 610	11.97	14.26	29 650	73 410	12.56	14.95	31 100
Locomotive engineers	42 760	23.29	25.71	53 470	43 560	23.01	25.77	53 590
Locomotive firers	970	23.17	25.46	52 950	960	22.63	24.71	51 400
Rail yard engineers, dinkey operators, and hostlers	5 480	15.68	16.76	34 850	5 360	16.02	17.35	36 090
Railroad brake, signal, and switch operators	24 610	22.94	23.75	49 400	24 270	23.09	23.85	49 600
Railroad conductors and yardmasters	39 580	25.40	26.02	54 120	41 540	25.93	26.39	54 900
Subway and streetcar operators	7 430	25.59	23.72	49 330	6 050	27.11	25.38	52 800
Rail transportation workers, all other	4 660	21.12	21.25	44 200	4 310	20.92	21.14	43 960
Sailors and marine oilers	32 420	16.53	17.25	35 880	31 950	17.22	17.94	37 310
Captains, mates, and pilots of water vessels	30 600	29.79	32.56	67 730	30 450	30.88	34.01	70 740
Motorboat operators	3 380	15.34	17.54	36 480	3 070	15.97	18.46	38 390
Ship engineers	11 190	29.18	31.80	66 140	10 850	30.59	33.38	69 420
Bridge and lock tenders	4 490	19.54	19.20	39 930	4 290	20.38	20.02	41 630
Parking lot attendants	136 470	9.04	9.67	20 120	129 990	9.23	9.90	20 600
Service station attendants	84 480	9.11	9.78	20 340	79 480	9.27	10.01	20 820
Traffic technicians	7 030	19.00	20.10	41 810	6 570	19.87	20.90	43 470
Transportation inspectors	24 940	26.56	28.46	59 200	24 250	27.06	29.38	61 110
Transportation workers, all other	43 330	15.87	17.11	35 590	39 870	15.39	16.94	35 240
Conveyor operators and tenders	41 920	13.95	14.46	30 090	38 730	13.92	14.59	30 350
Crane and tower operators	44 490	20.13	21.84	45 430	40 770	21.22	22.93	47 700
Dredge operators	1 910	16.70	18.77	39 040	1 990	16.63	18.43	38 330
Excavating and loading machine and dragline operators	65 160	16.93	18.36	38 180	57 990	17.28	18.53	38 540
Loading machine operators, underground mining	3 670	20.54	21.26	44 230	3 570	21.36	21.14	43 970
Hoist and winch operators	2 810	17.50	19.87	41 340	2 990	17.89	20.01	41 620
Industrial truck and tractor operators	620 450	13.98	14.78	30 750	568 270	14.21	15.02	31 240
Cleaners of vehicles and equipment	330 850	9.35	10.43	21 700	298 500	9.47	10.63	22 110
Laborers and freight, stock, and material movers, hand	2 335 510	10.89	11.87	24 690	2 135 790	11.11	12.16	25 290
Machine feeders and offbearers	144 820	12.29	12.92	26 880	129 180	12.64	13.19	27 430
Packers and packagers, hand	777 630	9.16	10.15	21 100	706 240	9.36	10.47	21 780
Gas compressor and gas pumping station operators	4 050	21.45	21.35	44 410	4 160	23.49	23.01	47 860
Pump operators, except wellhead pumpers	9 280	18.81	19.72	41 020	10 310	18.97	19.95	41 490
Wellhead pumpers	17 050	18.20	18.96	39 430	15 360	18.48	19.33	40 210
Refuse and recyclable material collectors	129 080	14.93	15.76	32 790	128 940	15.42	16.23	33 760
Shuttle car operators	3 050	20.29	20.53	42 700	3 520	21.91	22.31	46 400
Tank car, truck, and ship loaders	12 330	18.14	19.00	39 510	11 560	18.76	19.49	40 530
Material moving workers, all other	41 140	15.68	16.68	34 700	32 180	15.39	16.45	34 220

[1]Annual wages have been calculated by multiplying the hourly mean wage by a "year-round, full-time" hours figure of 2,080 hours; for occupations with no published hourly mean wage, the annual wage has been directly calculated from the reported survey data.
[2]Wages for some occupations that do not generally entail year-round, full-time employment are reported as either hourly wages or annual salaries (depending on how employees are typically paid).

Chapter Four

LABOR FORCE AND EMPLOYMENT PROJECTIONS BY INDUSTRY AND OCCUPATION

LABOR FORCE AND EMPLOYMENT PROJECTIONS BY INDUSTRY AND OCCUPATION

HIGHLIGHTS

Every two years, the Bureau of Labor Statistics (BLS) develops decade-long projections for industry output, employment, and occupations. This chapter presents the employment outlook for the 2008–2018 period. The projections are based on a set of explicit assumptions and an application of a model of economic relationships.

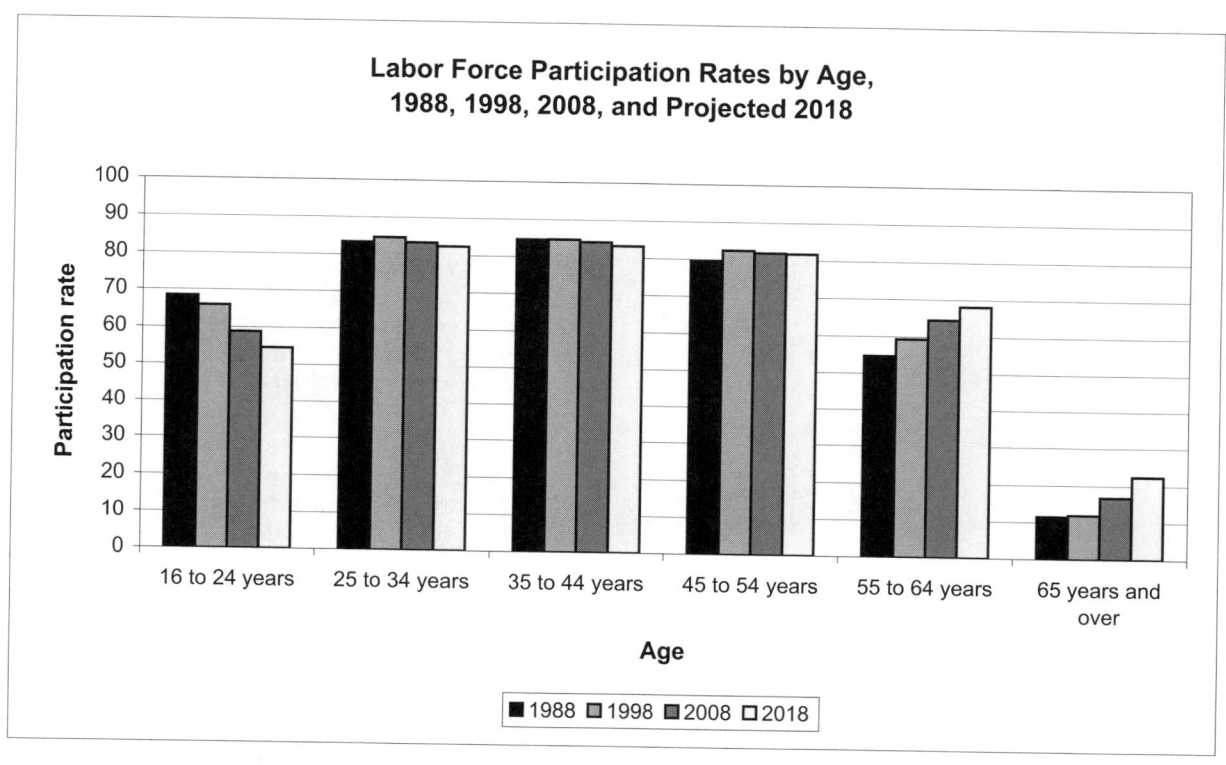

The civilan labor force is projected to grow by 8.2 percent from 2008 to 2018, a much slower rate than the 12.1 percent increase from 1998 to 2008 or the 13.2 percent increase from 1988 to 1998. The aging of baby boomers has lead to a significant projected increase in the labor force of older workers. The labor force of those age 55 years and over is expected to grow by 43.0 percent and 81.4 percent for those in the 65- to 74-year age group. (See Table 4-1.)

OTHER HIGHLIGHTS

- The labor force in 2018 is expected to more diverse. From 2008 to 2018, the number of Hispanics in the labor force is projected to increase by 33.1 percent, followed by the number of Asians at 29.8 percent and the number of Blacks at 14.1 percent. Meanwhile, the number of non-Hispanic Whites in the labor force is only projected to increase by 1.5 percent. (Hispanics may be of any race.) (See Table 4-1.)

- While the number of women in the labor force is projected to increase from 2008 to 2018, the number is increasing at declining rate. From 1988 to 1998, the number of women in the labor force increased 16.4 percent and from 1998 to 2008, the number increased 12.6 percent. It is projected that the number of women will increase by only 9.0 percent from 2008 to 2018. (See Table 4-1.)

- The number of 16- to 24-year-olds as well as the number of 35- to 54-year-olds in the labor force is expected to decline from 2008 to 2018. (See Table 4-1.)

NOTES AND DEFINITIONS

The Bureau of Labor Statistics (BLS) develops long-term projections of likely employment patterns in the U.S. economy. Since the early 1970s, projections have been prepared on a 2-year cycle. The projections cover the future size and composition of the labor force, aggregate economic growth, detailed estimates of industry production, and industry and occupational employment. The resulting data serve a variety of users who need information about expected patterns of economic growth and the effects these patterns are expected to have on employment. For example, information about future employment opportunities by occupation is used by counselors, educators, and others helping people choose a career and by officials who plan education and training programs.

The labor force projections are a function of two components—projections of the population and projections of labor force participation rates. Population projections are provided by the Census Bureau for detailed age, sex, race, and ethnicity groupings. BLS extrapolates participation rates for these same categories by applying well-specified smoothing and time series techniques to historical time series for the detailed participation rates.

Concepts and Definitions

Employment. In the employment projections survey, employment is defined as a count of jobs, not a count of individual workers.

Employment change. The numerical change in employment measures the projected number of job gains or losses.

Employment change, percent. The percent change in employment measures the projected rate of change of employment in an occupation. A rapidly growing occupation usually indicates favorable prospects for employment. However, even modest employment growth in a large occupation can result in many more job openings due to growth than can rapid employment growth in a small occupation.

Job openings due to growth and replacement needs. Estimates of the projected number of net entrants into an occupation. For occupations that require training, the data may be used to assess the minimum number of workers who will need to be trained. The number of openings due to growth is the positive employment change from 2008 to 2018. If employment declines, then there are no job openings due to growth. The number of openings due to replacement needs is the net number of workers leaving an occupation who will need to be replaced. Replacement needs are calculated from monthly CPS data for 1999 to 2008.

Median annual wages quartile. This measure indicates where the median annual wages of an occupation rank in comparison to the wages for all workers across the Nation. Occupations in which the median wage is higher than that earned by 75 percent of all workers are classified as having "very high" (VH) earnings. Occupations in which the median wage is above the national median for all workers are classified as having "high" (H) earnings. Occupations with a median wage below the national median are classified as having "low" (L) earnings, and occupations in which the median wage falls into the lowest 25 percent of national wages are classified as occupations with "very low" (VL) earnings.

Short-term on-the-job training. Skills needed for a worker to become fully qualified can be acquired during a short demonstration of job duties or during one month or less of on-the-job experience or instruction. Examples include retail salespersons and restaurant servers.

Moderate-term on-the-job training. Skills needed for a worker to become fully qualified can be acquired during 1 to 12 months of combined on-the-job experience and informal training. Examples include heavy and tractor-trailer truckdrivers and medical secretaries.

Long-term on-the-job training. More than 12 months of on-the-job training or, alternatively, combined work experience and formal classroom instruction are needed for workers to develop the skills to become fully qualified. This category includes formal or informal apprenticeships that may last up to 5 years. Long-term on-the-job training also includes intensive occupation-specific, employer-sponsored programs that workers must complete. Such programs include those offered by fire and police academies and schools for air traffic controllers and flight attendants. In other occupations—nuclear power reactor operators, for example—trainees take formal courses, often provided at the jobsite, to prepare for the required licensing exams. Individuals undergoing training usually are considered to be employed in the occupation. Also included in this category is the development of some natural ability—such as that possessed by musicians, athletes, actors, and other entertainers—that must be cultivated over several years, frequently in a nonwork setting.

Sources of Additional Information

A complete presentation of the projections, including analysis of results and additional tables and a comprehensive description of the methodology, can be found in the November 2009 edition of the *Monthly Labor Review* which is available on the BLS Web site at <http://www.bls.gov/opub/mlr/2009/11/home.htm>. In addition, more information on employment projections can be found on the BLS Web site at <http://www.bls.gov/emp/>.

Table 4-1. Civilian Labor Force, by Age, Sex, Race, and Hispanic Origin, 1988, 1998, 2008, and Projected 2018

(Numbers in thousands, percent.)

Age, sex, race, and Hispanic origin	Labor force				Change			Percent change		
	1988	1998	2008	2018	1988–1998	1998–2008	2008–2018	1988–1998	1998–2008	2008–2018
Both Sexes, 16 Years and Over	121 669	137 673	154 287	166 911	16 004	16 614	12 624	13.2	12.1	8.2
16 to 24 years	22 536	21 894	22 032	21 131	-642	138	-901	-2.8	0.6	-4.1
16 to 19 years	8 031	8 256	6 858	5 868	225	-1 398	-990	2.8	-16.9	-14.4
20 to 24 years	14 505	13 638	15 174	15 263	-867	1 536	89	-6.0	11.3	0.6
25 to 54 years	84 041	98 718	104 396	105 944	14 677	5 678	1 548	17.5	5.8	1.5
25 to 34 years	35 503	32 813	33 332	36 814	-2 690	519	3 482	-7.6	1.6	10.4
35 to 44 years	29 435	37 536	35 061	34 787	8 101	-2 475	-274	27.5	-6.6	-0.8
45 to 54 years	19 104	28 368	36 003	34 343	9 264	7 635	-1 660	48.5	26.9	-4.6
55 years and over	15 092	17 062	27 858	39 836	1 970	10 796	11 978	13.1	63.3	43.0
55 to 64 years	11 808	13 215	21 615	28 754	1 407	8 400	7 139	11.9	63.6	33.0
65 to 74 years	2 814	3 179	4 985	9 045	365	1 806	4 060	13.0	56.8	81.4
75 years and over	471	668	1 258	2 037	197	590	779	41.8	88.3	61.9
Men, 16 Years and Over	66 927	73 959	82 520	88 682	7 032	8 561	6 162	10.5	11.6	7.5
16 to 24 years	11 752	11 464	11 538	10 987	-288	74	-551	-2.5	0.6	-4.8
16 to 19 years	4 159	4 244	3 472	2 923	85	-772	-549	2.0	-18.2	-15.8
20 to 24 years	7 594	7 221	8 065	8 064	-373	844	-1	-4.9	11.7	0.0
25 to 54 years	46 382	53 002	56 202	57 309	6 620	3 200	1 107	14.3	6.0	2.0
25 to 34 years	19 742	17 796	18 302	20 173	-1 946	506	1 871	-9.9	2.8	10.2
35 to 44 years	16 074	20 242	18 972	19 109	4 168	-1 270	137	25.9	-6.3	0.7
45 to 54 years	10 566	14 963	18 928	18 027	4 397	3 965	-901	41.6	26.5	-4.8
55 years and over	8 793	9 493	14 780	20 386	700	5 287	5 606	8.0	55.7	37.9
55 to 64 years	6 831	7 253	11 345	14 479	422	4 092	3 134	6.2	56.4	27.6
65 to 74 years	1 657	1 826	2 724	4 753	169	898	2 029	10.2	49.2	74.5
75 years and over	304	413	711	1 154	109	298	443	35.9	72.2	62.3
Women, 16 Years and Over	54 742	63 714	71 767	78 229	8 972	8 053	6 462	16.4	12.6	9.0
16 to 24 years	10 783	10 430	10 494	10 144	-353	64	-350	-3.3	0.6	-3.3
16 to 19 years	3 872	4 012	3 385	2 946	140	-627	-439	3.6	-15.6	-13.0
20 to 24 years	6 910	6 418	7 109	7 198	-492	691	89	-7.1	10.8	1.3
25 to 54 years	37 659	45 716	48 195	48 635	8 057	2 479	440	21.4	5.4	0.9
25 to 34 years	15 761	15 017	15 030	16 641	-744	13	1 611	-4.7	0.1	10.7
35 to 44 years	13 361	17 294	16 089	15 678	3 933	-1 205	-411	29.4	-7.0	-2.6
45 to 54 years	8 537	13 405	17 075	16 316	4 868	3 670	-759	57.0	27.4	-4.4
55 years and over	6 301	7 569	13 078	19 449	1 268	5 509	6 371	20.1	72.8	48.7
55 to 64 years	4 977	5 962	10 270	14 275	985	4 308	4 005	19.8	72.3	39.0
65 to 74 years	1 157	1 352	2 261	4 291	195	909	2 030	16.9	67.2	89.8
75 years and over	167	255	547	883	88	292	336	52.7	114.5	61.4
White, 16 Years and Over	104 756	115 415	125 635	132 490	10 659	10 220	6 855	10.2	8.9	5.5
Men	58 317	63 034	68 351	71 731	4 717	5 317	3 380	8.1	8.4	4.9
Women	46 439	52 380	57 284	60 759	5 941	4 904	3 475	12.8	9.4	6.1
Black, 16 Years and Over	13 205	15 982	17 740	20 244	2 777	1 758	2 504	21.0	11.0	14.1
Men	6 596	7 542	8 347	9 579	946	805	1 232	14.3	10.7	14.8
Women	6 609	8 441	9 393	10 665	1 832	952	1 272	27.7	11.3	13.5
Asian, 16 Years and Over	3 718	6 278	7 202	9 345	2 560	924	2 143	68.9	14.7	29.8
Men	2 017	3 383	3 852	4 895	1 366	469	1 043	67.7	13.9	27.1
Women	1 701	2 895	3 350	4 450	1 194	455	1 100	70.2	15.7	32.8
All Other Groups,[1] 16 Years and Over	. . .	. . .	3 710	4 832	. . .	. . .	1 122	. . .	. . .	30.2
Men	. . .	. . .	1 970	2 477	. . .	. . .	507	. . .	. . .	25.7
Women	. . .	. . .	1 740	2 355	. . .	. . .	615	. . .	. . .	35.3
Hispanic,[2] 16 Years and Over	8 982	14 317	22 024	29 304	5 335	7 707	7 280	59.4	53.8	33.1
Men	5 409	8 571	13 255	17 051	3 162	4 684	3 796	58.5	54.6	28.6
Women	3 573	5 746	8 769	12 253	2 173	3 023	3 484	60.8	52.6	39.7
Non-Hispanic, 16 Years and Over	112 687	123 356	132 263	137 607	10 669	8 907	5 344	9.5	7.2	4.0
Men	61 518	65 388	69 265	71 631	3 870	3 877	2 366	6.3	5.9	3.4
Women	51 169	57 968	62 998	65 976	6 799	5 030	2 978	13.3	8.7	4.7
White Non-Hispanic, 16 Years and Over	96 141	101 767	105 210	106 834	5 626	3 443	1 624	5.9	3.4	1.5
Men	53 122	54 833	55 971	57 075	1 711	1 138	1 104	3.2	2.1	2.0
Women	43 018	46 935	49 238	49 759	3 917	2 303	521	9.1	4.9	1.1

[1] The "All other groups" category includes respondents who reported the racial categories of "American Indian and Alaska Native" or "Native Hawaiian and Other Pacific Islander," as well as those who reported two or more races. This category was not defined prior to 2003.
[2] May be of any race.
. . . = Not available.

Table 4-1. Civilian Labor Force, by Age, Sex, Race, and Hispanic Origin, 1988, 1998, 2008, and Projected 2018—*Continued*

(Numbers in thousands, percent.)

Age, sex, race, and Hispanic origin	Percent distribution				Annual growth rate (percent)		
	1988	1998	2008	2018	1988–1998	1998–2008	2008–2018
Both Sexes, 16 Years and Over	100.0	100.0	100.0	100.0	1.2	1.1	0.8
16 to 24 years	18.5	15.9	14.3	12.7	-0.3	0.1	-0.4
16 to 19 years	6.6	6.0	4.4	3.5	0.3	-1.8	-1.5
20 to 24 years	11.9	9.9	9.8	9.1	-0.6	1.1	0.1
25 to 54 years	69.1	71.7	67.7	63.5	1.6	0.6	0.1
25 to 34 years	29.2	23.8	21.6	22.1	-0.8	0.2	1.0
35 to 44 years	24.2	27.3	22.7	20.8	2.5	-0.7	-0.1
45 to 54 years	15.7	20.6	23.3	20.6	4.0	2.4	-0.5
55 years and over	12.4	12.4	18.1	23.9	1.2	5.0	3.6
55 to 64 years	9.7	9.6	14.0	17.2	1.1	5.0	2.9
65 to 74 years	2.3	2.3	3.2	5.4	1.2	4.6	6.1
75 years and over	0.4	0.5	0.8	1.2	3.6	6.5	4.9
Men, 16 Years and Over	55.0	53.7	53.5	53.1	1.0	1.1	0.7
16 to 24 years	9.7	8.3	7.5	6.6	-0.2	0.1	-0.5
16 to 19 years	3.4	3.1	2.3	1.8	0.2	0.0	-1.7
20 to 24 years	6.2	5.2	5.2	4.8	-0.5	1.1	0.0
25 to 54 years	38.1	38.5	36.4	34.3	1.3	0.6	0.2
25 to 34 years	16.2	12.9	11.9	12.1	-1.0	0.3	1.0
35 to 44 years	13.2	14.7	12.3	11.4	2.3	-0.6	0.1
45 to 54 years	8.7	10.9	12.3	10.8	3.5	2.4	-0.5
55 years and over	7.2	6.9	9.6	12.2	0.8	4.5	3.3
55 to 64 years	5.6	5.3	7.4	8.7	0.6	4.6	2.5
65 to 74 years	1.4	1.3	1.8	2.8	1.0	4.1	5.7
75 years and over	0.2	0.3	0.5	0.7	3.1	5.6	5.0
Women, 16 Years and Over	45.0	46.3	46.5	46.9	1.5	1.2	0.9
16 to 24 years	8.9	7.6	6.8	6.1	-0.3	0.1	-0.3
16 to 19 years	3.2	2.9	2.2	1.8	0.4	-1.7	-1.4
20 to 24 years	5.7	4.7	4.6	4.3	-0.7	1.0	0.1
25 to 54 years	31.0	33.2	31.2	29.1	2.0	0.5	0.1
25 to 34 years	13.0	10.9	9.7	10.0	-0.5	0.0	1.0
35 to 44 years	11.0	12.6	10.4	9.4	2.6	-0.7	-0.3
45 to 54 years	7.0	9.7	11.1	9.8	4.6	2.4	-0.5
55 years and over	5.2	5.5	8.5	11.7	1.9	5.6	4.0
55 to 64 years	4.1	4.3	6.7	8.6	1.8	5.6	3.3
65 to 74 years	1.0	1.0	1.5	2.6	1.6	5.3	6.6
75 years and over	0.1	0.2	0.4	0.5	4.3	7.9	4.9
White, 16 Years and Over	86.1	83.8	81.4	79.4	1.0	0.9	0.5
Men	47.9	45.8	44.3	43.0	0.8	0.8	0.5
Women	38.2	38.0	37.1	36.4	1.2	0.9	0.6
Black, 16 Years and Over	10.9	11.6	11.5	12.1	1.9	1.0	1.3
Men	5.4	5.5	5.4	5.7	1.3	1.0	1.4
Women	5.4	6.1	6.1	6.4	2.5	1.1	1.3
Asian, 16 Years and Over	3.1	4.6	4.7	5.6	5.4	1.4	2.6
Men	1.7	2.5	2.5	2.9	5.3	1.3	2.4
Women	1.4	2.1	2.2	2.7	5.5	1.5	2.9
All Other Groups,[1] 16 Years and Over	...	...	2.4	2.9	...	...	2.7
Men	...	...	1.3	1.5	...	...	2.3
Women	...	...	1.1	1.4	...	...	3.1
Hispanic,[2] 16 Years and Over	7.4	10.4	14.3	17.6	4.8	4.4	2.9
Men	4.4	6.2	8.6	10.2	4.7	4.5	2.6
Women	2.9	4.2	5.7	7.3	4.9	4.3	3.4
Non-Hispanic, 16 Years and Over	92.6	89.6	85.7	82.4	0.9	0.7	0.4
Men	50.6	47.5	44.9	42.9	0.6	0.6	0.3
Women	42.1	42.1	40.8	39.5	1.3	0.8	0.5
White Non-Hispanic, 16 Years and Over	79.0	73.9	68.2	64.0	0.6	0.3	0.2
Men	43.7	39.8	36.3	34.2	0.3	0.2	0.2
Women	35.4	34.1	31.9	29.8	0.9	0.5	0.1

[1]The "All other groups" category includes respondents who reported the racial categories of "American Indian and Alaska Native" or "Native Hawaiian and Other Pacific Islander," as well as those who reported two or more races. This category was not defined prior to 2003.
[2]May be of any race.
. . . = Not available.

PROJECTED EMPLOYMENT

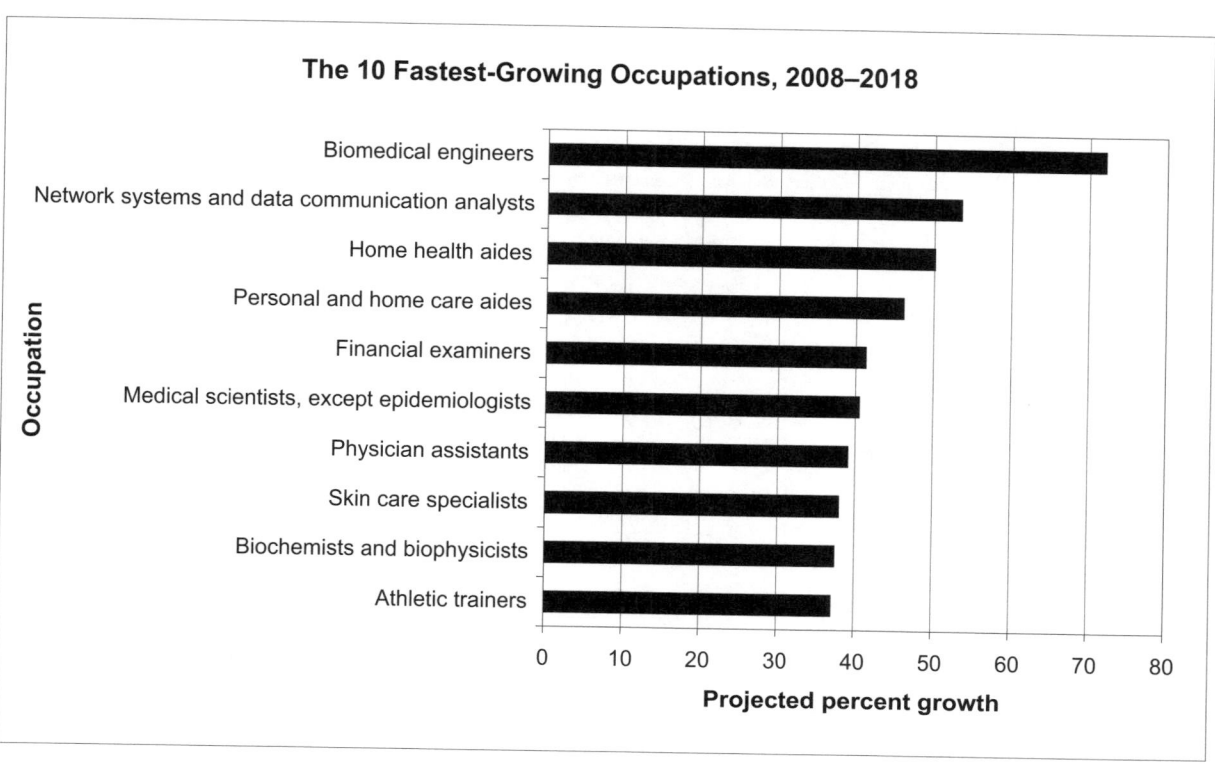

The 10 Fastest-Growing Occupations, 2008–2018

Although biomedical engineering was the fastest-growing occupation, employment is only projected to be at 28,000 in 2018. In contrast, network systems and data communications analysts—the second fastest-growing occupation—is projected to provide 448,000 jobs in 2018. (See Table 4-2.)

OTHER HIGHLIGHTS

- Of the ten occupations with the fastest job growth, seven require a bachelor's degree or more, two require short-term on-the-job training, and one requires a postsecondary vocational award. (See Table 4-2.)

- Many of the largest declines in employment can be found in the manufacturing sector. Employment in semiconductor and other electronic component manufacturing is projected to decline by 146,000, while employment in motor vehicle parts manufacturing is projected to decline by 101,000 between 2008 and 2018. (See Table 4-4.)

- The occupations projected to add the most jobs from 2008 to 2018 are registered nurses (582,000), home health aides (461,000), and customer service representatives (400,000). Seventeen of the thirty fastest-growing occupations are related to health care or medical research. (See Table 4-7.)

Table 4-2. Fastest-Growing Occupations, 2008–2018

(Numbers in thousands, percent.)

Occupation	Occupational group	Employment		Change		Most significant source of postsecondary education or training[1]
		2008	2018	Number	Percent	
Biomedical engineers	Professional and related	16	28	12	72.0	Bachelor's degree
Network systems and data communications analysts	Professional and related	292	448	156	53.4	Bachelor's degree
Home health aides	Service	922	1 383	461	50.0	Short-term on-the-job training
Personal and home care aides	Service	817	1 193	376	46.0	Short-term on-the-job training
Financial examiners	Management, business, and financial	27	38	11	41.2	Bachelor's degree
Medical scientists, except epidemiologists	Professional and related	109	154	44	40.4	Doctoral degree
Physician assistants	Professional and related	75	104	29	39.0	Master's degree
Skin care specialists	Service	39	54	15	37.9	Postsecondary vocational award
Biochemists and biophysicists	Professional and related	23	32	9	37.4	Doctoral degree
Athletic trainers	Professional and related	16	22	6	37.0	Bachelor's degree
Physical therapist aides	Service	46	63	17	36.3	Short-term on-the-job training
Dental hygienists	Professional and related	174	237	63	36.1	Associate's degree
Veterinary technologists and technicians	Professional and related	80	108	29	35.8	Associate's degree
Dental assistants	Service	295	401	106	35.8	Moderate-term on-the-job training
Computer software engineers, applications	Professional and related	515	690	175	34.0	Bachelor's degree
Medical assistants	Service	484	648	164	33.9	Moderate-term on-the-job-training
Physical therapist assistants	Service	64	85	21	33.3	Associate's degree
Veterinarians	Professional and related	60	79	20	33.0	First professional degree
Self-enrichment education teachers	Professional and related	254	335	81	32.1	Work experience
Compliance officers, except agriculture, construction, health and safety, and transportation	Management, business, and financial	260	341	81	31.1	Long-term on-the-job training
Occupational therapist aides	Service	8	10	2	30.7	Short-term on-the-job training
Environmental engineers	Professional and related	54	71	17	30.6	Bachelor's degree
Pharmacy technicians	Professional and related	326	426	100	30.6	Moderate-term on-the-job training
Computer software engineers, systems software	Professional and related	395	515	120	30.4	Bachelor's degree
Survey researchers	Professional and related	23	31	7	30.4	Bachelor's degree
Physical therapists	Professional and related	186	242	56	30.3	Master's degree
Personal financial advisors	Management, business, and financial	208	271	63	30.1	Bachelor's degree
Environmental engineering technicians	Professional and related	21	28	6	30.1	Associate's degree
Occupational therapist assistants	Service	27	35	8	29.8	Associate's degree
Fitness trainers and aerobics instructors	Service	261	338	77	29.4	Post-secondary vocational award

[1]An occupation is placed into 1 of 11 categories that best describes the education or training needed by most workers to become fully qualified in that occupation.

Table 4-3. Occupations with the Largest Job Growth, 2008–2018

(Numbers in thousands, percent.)

Occupation	Occupational group	Employment		Change		Most significant source of postsecondary education or training[1]
		2008	2018	Number	Percent	
Registered nurses	Professional and related	2 619	3 200	582	22.2	Associate's degree
Home health aides	Service	922	1 383	461	50.0	Short-term on-the-job training
Customer service representatives	Office and administrative support	2 252	2 652	400	17.7	Moderate-term on-the-job training
Combined food preparation and serving workers, including fast food	Service	2 702	3 096	394	14.6	Short-term on-the-job training
Personal and home care aides	Service	817	1 193	376	46.0	Short-term on-the-job training
Retail salespersons	Sales and related	4 489	4 864	375	8.4	Short-term on-the-job training
Office clerks, general	Office and administrative support	3 024	3 383	359	11.9	Short-term on-the-job training
Accountants and auditors	Management, business, and financial	1 291	1 570	279	21.7	Bachelor's degree
Nursing aides, orderlies, and attendants	Service	1 470	1 746	276	18.8	Postsecondary vocational award
Postsecondary teachers	Professional and related	1 699	1 956	257	15.1	Doctoral degree
Construction laborers	Construction and extraction	1 249	1 505	256	20.5	Moderate-term on-the-job training
Elementary school teachers, except special education	Professional and related	1 550	1 794	244	15.8	Bachelor's degree
Truck drivers, heavy and tractor-trailer	Transportation and material moving	1 798	2 031	233	13.0	Short-term on-the-job training
Landscaping and groundskeeping workers	Service	1 206	1 423	217	18.0	Short-term on-the-job training
Bookkeeping, accounting, and auditing clerks	Office and administrative support	2 064	2 276	212	10.3	Moderate-term on-the-job training
Executive secretaries and administrative assistants	Office and administrative support	1 594	1 799	204	12.8	Work experience
Management analysts	Management, business, and financial	747	925	178	23.9	Bachelor's or higher degree
Computer software engineers, applications	Professional and related	515	690	175	34.0	Bachelor's degree
Receptionists and information clerks	Office and administrative support	1 139	1 312	173	15.2	Short term on-the-job training
Carpenters	Construction and extraction	1 285	1 450	165	12.9	Long-term on-the-job training
Medical assistants	Service	484	648	164	33.9	Moderate-term on-the-job training
First-line supervisors/managers of office and, administrative support workers	Office and administrative support	1 457	1 618	160	11.0	Work experience
Network systems and data communications analysts	Professional and related	292	448	156	53.4	Bachelor's degree
Licensed practical and licensed vocational nurses	Professional and related	754	909	156	20.7	Post secondary vocational award
Security guards	Service	1 077	1 229	153	14.2	Short-term on-the-job-training
Waiters and waitresses	Service	2 382	2 533	152	6.4	Short-term on-the-job training
Maintenance and repair workers, general	Installation, maintenance, and repair occupations	1 361	1 509	148	10.9	Moderate-term on-the-job training
Physicians and surgeons	Professional and related	661	806	144	21.8	First professional degree
Child care workers	Service	1 302	1 444	142	10.9	Short-term on-the-job training
Teacher assistants	Professional and related	1 313	1 448	135	10.3	Short-term on-the-job training

[1]An occupation is placed into 1 of 11 categories that best describes the education or training needed by most workers to become fully qualified in that occupation.

Table 4-4. Industries with the Largest Wage and Salary Employment Growth and Declines, 2008–2018

(Number in thousands, percent.)

Industry	Sector	Employment		Change	
		2008	2018	Number	Percent
Largest Growth					
Management, scientific, and technical consulting services	Professional and business services	1 009	1 844	835	82.8
Offices of physicians	Health care and social assistance	2 266	3 038	772	34.1
Computer systems design and related services	Professional and business services	1 450	2 107	656	45.3
Other general merchandise stores	Retail trade	1 490	2 097	607	40.7
Employment services	Professional and business services	3 144	3 744	600	19.1
Local government, excluding education and hospitals	Government	5 819	6 306	487	8.4
Home health care services	Health care and social assistance	958	1 399	441	46.1
Services for the elderly and persons with disabilities	Health care and social assistance	585	1 016	431	73.8
Nursing care facilities	Health care and social assistance	1 614	2 007	394	24.4
Full-service restaurants	Accommodation and food services	4 598	4 942	343	7.5
Largest Declines					
Department stores	Retail trade	1 557	1 398	-159	-10.2
Semiconductor and other electronic component manufacturing	Manufacturting	432	287	-146	-33.7
Motor vehicle parts manufacturing	Manufacturting	544	443	-101	-18.6
Postal service	Government	748	650	-98	-13.0
Printing and related support activities	Manufacturing	594	499	-95	-16.0
Cut and sew apparel manufacturing	Manufacturing	155	67	-89	-57.0
Newspaper publishers	Information	326	245	-81	-24.8
Support activities for mining	Mining	328	252	-76	-23.2
Gasoline stations	Retail trade	843	769	-75	-8.9
Wired telecommunications carriers	Information	666	593	-73	-11.0

Table 4-5. Employment and Total Job Openings, by Education Cluster, 2008–2018

(Numbers in thousands, percent, dollars.)

Education cluster	Employment				Change in employment, 2008–2018		Total job openings due to growth and net replacements[1]		May 2008 median annual wages[2]
	Number		Percent distribution		Number	Percent	Number	Percent distribution	
	2008	2018	2008	2018					
TOTAL, ALL OCCUPATIONS	150 932	166 206	100.0	100.0	15 274	10.1	50 929	100.0	32 390
First professional degree	2 001	2 354	1.3	1.4	353	17.6	746	1.5	122 550
Doctoral degree	2 085	2 430	1.4	1.5	345	16.6	743	1.5	61 200
Master's degree	2 531	2 995	1.7	1.8	464	18.3	1 008	2.0	55 170
Bachelor's or higher degree, plus work experience	6 519	7 068	4.3	4.3	550	8.4	2 106	4.1	89 720
Bachelor's degree	18 584	21 669	12.3	13.0	3 085	16.6	7 072	13.9	57 770
Associate's degree	6 129	7 297	4.1	4.4	1 168	19.1	2 372	4.7	54 320
Postsecondary vocational award	8 787	9 952	5.8	6.0	1 164	13.2	2 927	5.7	32 380
Work experience in a related occupation	14 517	15 697	9.6	9.4	1 180	8.1	4 196	8.2	45 650
Long-term on-the-job training	10 815	11 621	7.2	7.0	806	7.5	3 081	6.1	39 630
Moderate-term on-the-job training	24 569	26 531	16.3	16.0	1 963	8.0	7 059	13.9	30 640
Short-term on-the-job training	54 396	58 593	36.0	35.3	4 197	7.7	19 619	38.5	21 320

[1]Total job openings are given by the sum of net employment increases and net replacements. If employment change is negative, job openings due to growth are zero and total job openings equal net replacements.
[2] Data for wage and salary workers are derived from the Occupational Employment Statistics Survey.

Table 4-6. Employment and Output, by Industry, 1998, 2008, and Projected 2018

(Number, percent, dollars.)

Industry	Employment							Output				
	Number of jobs (thousands)			Change		Average annual rate of change (percent)		Billions of chained (2000) dollars			Average annual rate of change (percent)	
	1998	2008	2018	1998–2018	2008–2018	1998–2008	2008–2018	1998	2008	2018	1998–2008	2008–2018
TOTAL[1,2]	140 564	150 932	166 206	10 368	15 274	0.7	1.0	17 050	21 028	27 703	2.0	2.8
Nonagriculture Wage and Salary Workers	126 625	137 815	152 444	11 190	14 629	0.9	1.0	16 785	20 735	27 371	2.1	2.8
Mining	565	717	613	152	-104	2.4	-1.6	205	232	227	1.2	-0.2
Oil and gas extraction	141	162	136	21	-26	1.4	-1.7	131	126	122	-0.5	-0.3
Mining (except oil and gas)	243	228	226	-15	-2	-0.7	-0.1	49	46	56	-0.7	2.0
Coal mining	85	81	84	-5	3.0	-0.6	0.4	20	20	24	0.5	1.5
Metal ore mining	46	40	36	-6	-4	-1.5	-1.1	11	8	8	-3.5	0.6
Nonmetallic mineral mining and quarrying	12	107	106	-4	-1	-0.4	-0.1	19	18	23	-0.7	2.8
Mining support activities	181	328	252	147	-76	6.1	-2.6	25	56	54	8.4	-0.3
Utilities	613	560	501	-54	-59	-0.9	-1.1	299	319	349	0.7	0.9
Electric power generation, transmission, and distribution	444	405	346	-39	-59	-0.9	-1.6	206	247	282	1.8	1.3
Natural gas distribution	129	107	101	-22	-6	-1.8	-0.6	85	68	67	-2.3	-0.1
Water, sewage, and other systems	41	48	54	7	6	1.6	1.2	7	8	10	1.2	1.6
Construction	6 149	7 215	8 552	1 066	1 337	1.6	1.7	852	861	1 141	0.1	2.9
Manufacturing	17 560	13 431	12 225	-4 128	-1 206	-2.6	-0.9	4 061	3 985	4 923	-0.2	2.1
Food	1 555	1 485	1 483	-70	-2	-0.5	0.0	417	434	533	0.4	2.1
Animal food	55	51	49	-4	-2	-0.8	-0.4	24	21	32	-1.4	4.2
Grain and oilseed milling	68	63	61	-5	-1	-0.8	-0.2	44	34	52	-2.4	4.2
Sugar and confectionery product	98	71	64	-28	-7	-3.2	-1.1	25	25	29	0.0	1.7
Fruit and vegetable preserving and specialty food	203	174	155	-29	-19	-1.5	-1.1	50	56	66	1.1	1.7
Dairy product	131	129	126	-2	-3	-0.2	-0.2	59	59	64	0.1	0.8
Animal slaughtering and processing	499	512	539	13	27	0.3	0.5	110	126	145	1.3	1.4
Seafood product preparation and packaging	47	41	45	-7	4	-1.5	1.0	8	10	12	2.4	2.0
Bakery and tortilla	306	281	275	-25	-6	-0.8	-0.2	46	45	57	-0.2	2.4
Other food	148	164	169	16	5	1.1	0.3	52	62	79	1.9	2.4
Beverage and tobacco product	209	199	181	-10	-18	-0.5	-0.9	168	144	140	-1.5	-0.3
Beverage	171	177	164	6	-13	0.4	-0.8	72	81	98	1.1	2.0
Tobacco	38	22	17	-16	-5	-5.3	-2.7	96	65	50	-3.9	-2.6
Textile mills	425	151	79	-273	-72	-9.8	-6.3	56	31	29	-5.8	-0.4
Fiber, yarn, and thread mills	87	37	21	-50	-17	-8.1	-5.7	12	8	8	-4.2	0.5
Fabric mills	221	65	35	-156	-30	-11.5	-6.1	29	15	14	-6.5	-0.2
Textile fabric finishing/fabric coating mills	116	48	24	-68	-25	-8.4	-7.0	15	8	7	-5.8	-1.5
Textile product mills	235	148	91	-87	-56	-4.5	-4.7	31	23	24	-3.0	0.6
Textile furnishings mills	127	75	42	-51	-34	-5.1	-5.7	21	16	18	-2.4	1.1
Other textile product mills	108	72	49	-36	-23	-4.0	-3.7	10	6	6	-4.4	-0.8
Apparel	622	198	88	-423	-110	-10.8	-7.8	67	31	22	-7.3	-3.6
Apparel knitting mills	87	26	13	-60	-14	-11.3	-7.1	9	5	3	-6.0	-3.0
Cut and sew apparel	498	155	67	-343	-89	-11.0	-8.1	54	25	16	-7.5	-4.1
Apparel accessories and other apparel	37	17	9	-20	-8	-7.5	-6.0	5	2	2	-8.0	0.2
Leather and allied product	83	34	23	-49	-11	-8.6	-3.7	23	12	11	-6.7	-0.4
Leather and hide tanning and finishing	43	18	13	-25	-5	-8.5	-3.1	8	4	4	-6.9	-0.4
Footwear	40	16	10	-24	-6	-8.8	-4.5	16	8	8	-6.6	-0.4
Wood product	609	460	424	-150	-35	-2.8	-0.8	92	91	95	-0.2	0.4
Sawmills and wood preservation	135	104	85	-31	-19	-2.6	-2.0	28	30	31	0.6	0.5
Veneer, plywood, and engineered wood product	113	91	100	-22	9	-2.1	0.9	20	21	22	0.4	0.3
Other wood product	362	265	240	-97	-26	-3.1	-1.0	44	40	42	-1.0	0.5
Paper	625	446	338	-179	-108	-3.3	-2.7	165	142	128	-1.5	-1.0
Pulp, paper, and paperboard mills	208	126	82	-82	-44	-4.9	-4.2	78	67	62	-1.5	-0.7
Converted paper product	417	320	256	-97	-64	-2.6	-2.2	88	75	66	-1.6	-1.2
Printing and related support activities	828	594	499	-234	-95	-3.3	-1.7	107	92	80	-1.5	-1.4
Petroleum and coal product	135	117	91	-17	-26	-1.4	-2.5	226	224	279	-0.1	2.2
Chemical	993	850	793	-143	-57	-1.5	-0.7	430	464	613	0.8	2.8
Basic chemical	213	152	100	-61	-52	-3.3	-4.1	112	104	136	-0.7	2.7
Resin, synthetic rubber, and artificial and synthetic fiber and filament	140	105	95	-35	-10	-2.8	-1.0	70	66	85	-0.5	2.5
Pesticide, fertilizer, and other agricultural chemical	50	36	35	-14	-1	-3.2	-0.3	24	17	19	-3.5	1.6
Pharmaceutical and medicine	247	290	307	43	18	1.6	0.6	108	141	195	2.6	3.3
Paint, coating, and adhesive	78	63	65	-15	3	-2.1	0.4	27	26	30	-0.2	1.4
Soap, cleaning compound, and toilet preparation	131	108	101	-22	-7	-1.9	-0.7	55	75	98	3.1	2.8
Other chemical product and preparation	135	95	89	-39	-6	-3.4	-0.7	35	40	49	1.3	1.9
Plastics and rubber product	941	734	678	-207	-56	-2.5	-0.8	165	160	227	-0.3	3.5
Plastics product	728	589	555	-139	-34	-2.1	-0.6	130	138	193	0.6	3.4
Rubber product	214	145	123	-68	-23	-3.8	-1.7	34	22	33	-4.3	4.2
Nonmetallic mineral product	535	468	480	-67	12	-1.3	0.3	95	85	104	-1.1	2.0
Clay product and refractory	82	52	54	-30	2	-4.4	0.3	9	8	9	-1.9	1.9
Glass and glass product	142	97	84	-45	-13	-3.8	-1.4	23	22	30	-0.4	3.0
Cement and concrete product	217	223	248	6	24	0.3	1.0	40	36	45	-1.3	2.3
Lime and gypsum product	94	96	95	2	-1	0.2	-0.1	22	21	22	-0.7	0.7
Primary metal	642	443	400	-198	-44	-3.6	-1.0	162	152	144	-0.6	-0.6
Iron and steel mills ferroalloy	144	99	80	-45	-19	-3.7	-2.1	52	45	47	-1.5	0.4
Steel product from purchased steel	73	60	59	-12	-1	-1.9	-0.2	19	15	16	-2.6	0.6
Alumina and aluminum production and processing	100	68	65	-32	-3	-3.8	-0.5	33	42	40	2.5	-0.5
Nonferrous (except aluminum) production and processing	102	67	63	-35	-5	-4.1	-0.7	29	24	16	-1.9	-4.1
Foundries	223	149	133	-74	-16	-4.0	-1.1	30	30	28	0.3	-0.9

[1]Employment data for wage and salary workers are from the BLS Current Employment Statistics (CES) Survey, which counts jobs, whereas data for self-employed, unpaid family workers, and agriculture, forestry, fishing, and hunting workers are from the Current Population Survey (CPS, or household, survey), which counts workers.
[2]Output subcategories do not necessarily add to higher categories as a by-product of chain weighting.

Table 4-6. Employment and Output, by Industry, 1998, 2008, and Projected 2018—*Continued*

(Number, percent, dollars.)

Industry	Employment							Output				
	Number of jobs (thousands)			Change		Average annual rate of change (percent)		Billions of chained (2000) dollars			Average annual rate of change (percent)	
	1998	2008	2018	1998–2018	2008–2018	1998–2008	2008–2018	1998	2008	2018	1998–2008	2008–2018
Manufacturing—*Continued*												
Fabricated metal product	1 740	1 528	1 399	-211	-129	-1.3	-0.9	255	251	286	-0.2	1.3
Forging and stamping	146	108	85	-38	-23	-3.0	-2.4	26	24	25	-0.6	0.3
Cutlery and handtool	80	49	36	-31	-13	-4.7	-3.1	11	11	11	-0.4	0.3
Architectural and structural metals	396	409	429	14	20	0.3	0.5	57	59	75	0.3	2.4
Boiler, tank, and shipping container	109	96	89	-13	-7	-1.2	-0.7	24	21	24	-1.3	1.3
Hardware	54	29	24	-24	-5	-5.8	-2.0	11	10	10	-0.8	0.0
Spring and wire product	83	52	42	-31	-10	-4.6	-2.0	9	7	9	-2.0	2.2
Machine shops; turned product; and screw, nut, and bolt	371	360	320	-11	-41	-0.3	-1.2	45	47	56	0.4	1.7
Coating, engraving, heat treating, and allied activities	173	144	125	-29	-19	-1.8	-1.4	20	23	25	1.4	1.0
Other fabricated metal product	330	282	250	-48	-32	-1.6	-1.2	52	49	53	-0.6	0.7
Machinery	1 514	1 186	1 095	-329	-90	-2.4	-0.8	276	280	334	0.2	1.8
Agriculture, construction, and mining machinery	241	242	250	1	8	0.0	0.3	57	57	77	0.0	3.0
Industrial machinery	171	121	93	-50	-28	-3.4	-2.6	32	34	32	0.7	-0.5
Ventilation, heating, air-conditioning, and commercial refrigeration	186	150	113	-36	-37	-2.1	-2.8	32	35	38	0.8	0.9
Metalworking machinery	289	192	190	-97	-2	-4.0	-0.1	32	28	33	-1.1	1.4
Engine, turbine, and power transmission equipment	114	104	97	-10	-7	-0.9	-0.7	32	38	54	1.7	3.4
Other general purpose machinery	365	273	249	-92	-24	-2.9	-0.9	64	64	74	0.0	1.4
Computer and electronic product	1 831	1 248	1 007	-583	-241	-3.8	-2.1	407	515	946	2.4	6.3
Computer and peripheral equipment	322	183	125	-139	-58	-5.5	-3.8	88	201	967	8.6	17.0
Communications equipment	237	129	120	-108	-9	-5.9	-0.7	81	75	109	-0.8	3.8
Audio and video equipment	53	27	15	-26	-12	-6.6	-6.0	8	5	11	-4.7	8.4
Semiconductor and other electronic component	650	432	287	-217	-146	-4.0	-4.0	127	173	309	3.2	5.9
Navigational, measuring, electromedical, and control instruments	509	442	434	-68	-7	-1.4	-0.2	94	92	128	-0.1	3.3
Manufacturing and reproducing magnetic and optical media	59	35	26	-24	-9	-5.1	-2.9	11	10	13	-0.1	1.8
Electrical equipment, appliance, and component	592	425	368	-167	-57	-3.3	-1.4	114	100	113	-1.4	1.3
Electric lighting equipment	85	57	46	-28	-11	-3.9	-2.2	13	13	15	-0.3	1.9
Household appliance	108	72	55	-36	-17	-4.0	-2.7	21	24	30	1.0	2.5
Electrical equipment	215	159	129	-56	-29	-3.0	-2.0	36	28	30	-2.4	0.6
Other electrical equipment and component	184	137	138	-47	1	-2.9	0.0	44	36	39	-2.1	0.8
Transportation equipment	2 078	1 607	1 437	-472	-169	-2.5	-1.1	638	583	744	-0.9	2.5
Motor vehicle	284	191	160	-93	-31	-3.9	-1.8	239	237	322	-0.1	3.1
Motor vehicle body and trailer	170	142	131	-28	-11	-1.8	-0.8	32	28	36	-1.2	2.7
Motor vehicle parts	818	544	443	-274	-101	-4.0	-2.0	179	169	190	-0.6	1.2
Aerospace product and parts	579	504	502	-75	-2	-1.4	0.0	154	115	148	-2.8	2.5
Railroad rolling stock	35	28	18	-7	-11	-2.0	-4.7	9	5	7	-6.2	3.9
Ship and boat building	154	157	140	3	-17	0.2	-1.1	18	16	24	-0.8	3.9
Other transportation equipment	40	41	44	1	3	0.2	0.8	10	13	22	2.8	5.7
Furniture and related product	644	481	512	-163	31	-2.9	0.6	70	63	95	-1.1	4.2
Household and institutional furniture and kitchen cabinet	418	306	339	-112	33	-3.1	1.0	40	36	57	-1.2	4.8
Office furniture (including fixtures)	173	131	130	-42	-1	-2.7	-0.1	23	21	30	-0.9	3.4
Other furniture related product	53	44	42	-9	-2	-1.8	-0.3	7	6	8	-1.4	2.7
Miscellaneous	727	631	759	-96	128	-1.4	1.9	105	134	222	2.4	5.2
Medical equipment and supplies	301	310	360	8	50	0.3	1.5	49	72	133	3.9	6.3
Other miscellaneous	426	321	399	-105	78	-2.8	2.2	56	61	89	0.9	3.8
Wholesale Trade	5 795	5 964	6 220	169	256	0.3	0.4	780	1 064	1 777	3.2	5.3
Retail Trade	14 610	15 356	16 010	747	654	0.5	0.4	872	1 232	1 864	3.5	4.2
Transportation and Warehousing	4 168	4 505	4 950	337	446	0.8	0.9	595	678	906	1.3	2.9
Air transportation	563	493	529	-70	37	-1.3	0.7	121	102	152	-1.7	4.1
Rail transportation	225	230	240	5	11	0.2	0.5	44	50	59	1.5	1.6
Water transportation	51	65	67	15.0	2	2.6	0.3	28	21	32	-2.9	4.2
Truck transportation	1 354	1 391	1 534	37	143	0.3	1.0	199	275	375	3.3	3.1
Transit and ground passenger transportation	363	418	471	55	53	1.4	1.2	32	38	47	1.9	2.1
Pipeline transportation	48	42	38	-6	-4	-1.3	-0.9	20	17	17	-1.8	-0.1
Scenic and sightseeing transportation	522	618	726	96	108	1.7	1.6	116	137	173	1.7	2.3
Support activities for transportation	881	748	650	-133	-98	-1.6	-1.4	62	57	62	-0.8	0.9
Couriers and messengers	568	576	588	8	12	0.1	0.2	59	72	95	2.1	2.7
Warehousing and storage	474	673	756	199	83	3.6	1.2	36	43	55	1.9	2.5
Information	3 218	2 997	3 115	-222	118	-0.7	0.4	769	1 106	1 865	3.7	5.4
Publishing industries, except Internet	982	883	842	-100	-41	-1.1	-0.5	224	308	468	3.2	4.3
Newspaper, periodical, book, and directory publishers	767	619	499	-149	-120	-2.1	-2.1	136	127	120	-0.7	-0.6
Software publishers	215	264	343	49	79	2.1	2.7	88	195	530	8.2	10.5
Motion picture, video, and sound recording industries	369	382	428	12	46	0.3	1.1	74	87	116	1.7	2.9
Broadcasting, except Internet	321	316	340	-5	24	-0.2	0.7	63	85	104	2.9	2.1
Telecommunications	1 167	1 022	932	-146	-90	-1.3	-0.9	351	480	822	3.2	5.5
Data processing, hosting, related services, and other information services	378	395	574	17	179	0.4	3.8	58	142	345	9.3	9.3
Finance and Insurance	5 529	6 015	6 337	487	322	0.8	0.5	58	142	345	9.3	9.3
Monetary authorities, credit intermediation, and related activities	2 554	2 758	2 896	205	137	0.8	0.5	560	847	1 217	4.2	3.7
Securities, commodity contracts, and other financial investments and related activities	692	858	959	166	101	2.2	1.1	199	436	883	8.1	7.3
Insurance carriers	1 443	1 402	1 338	-41	-64	-0.3	-0.5	309	362	421	1.6	1.5
Agencies, brokerages, and other insurance-related activities	766	907	1 038	141	131	1.7	1.4	112	124	161	1.0	2.7
Funds, trusts, and other financial vehicles	73	90	106	17	16	2.1	1.6	71	88	99	2.1	1.2
Real estate	1 278	1 481	1 677	203	196	1.5	1.3	690	859	1 065	2.2	2.2
Automotive equipment rental and leasing	189	195	215	6	20	0.3	1.0	37	40	53	0.8	3.0
Consumer goods rental and general rental centers	344	298	308	-46	10	-1.4	0.3	22	24	30	0.8	2.3
Commercial and industrial machinery and equipment rental and leasing	98	128	128	30	0	2.7	0.0	36	45	52	2.3	1.3
Lessors of nonfinancial intangible assets (except copyrighted works)	25	28	38	3	10	1.1	3.0	92	146	235	4.8	4.9

Table 4-6. Employment and Output, by Industry, 1998, 2008, and Projected 2018—*Continued*

(Number, percent, dollars.)

Industry	Employment — Number of jobs (thousands)			Change		Average annual rate of change (percent)		Output — Billions of chained (2000) dollars			Average annual rate of change (percent)	
	1998	2008	2018	1998–2018	2008–2018	1998–2008	2008–2018	1998	2008	2018	1998–2008	2008–2018
Professional, Scientific, and Technical Services	5 992	7 830	10 486	1 838	2 657	2.7	3.0	877	1 279	1 752	3.8	3.2
Legal services	1 021	1 164	1 417	143	253	1.3	2.0	183	202	249	1.0	2.1
Accounting, tax preparation, bookkeeping, and payroll services	802	950	1 149	148	199	1.7	1.9	90	108	118	1.9	0.9
Architectural, engineering, and related services	1 115	1 445	1 770	330	325	2.6	2.0	148	229	269	4.5	1.6
Specialized design services	120	143	209	23	66	1.8	3.8	21	26	35	2.2	3.0
Computer systems design and related services	975	1 450	2 107	475	656	4.1	3.8	143	207	302	3.8	3.8
Management, scientific, and technical consulting services	590	1 009	1 844	419	835	5.5	6.2	96	172	287	6.0	5.3
Scientific research and development services	486	622	779	136	157	2.5	2.3	66	159	289	9.2	6.1
Advertising and related services	453	462	499	9	37	0.2	0.8	68	96	131	3.4	3.2
Other professional, scientific, and technical services	430	585	713	155	128	3.1	2.0	64	87	107	3.2	2.1
Management of companies and enterprises	1 756	1 895	1 997	139	102	0.8	0.5	379	634	964	5.3	4.3
Administrative and support and waste management and remediation services	7 398	8 054	9 485	656	1 431	0.9	1.6	422	593	837	3.5	3.5
Administrative and support services	7 099	7 694	9 034	595	1 340	0.8	1.6	370	526	731	3.6	3.3
Office administrative services	265	403	483	139	80	4.3	1.8	23	50	68	8.2	3.1
Facilities support services	89	133	174	44	41	4.1	2.7	12	17	18	3.4	0.6
Employment services	3 246	3 144	3 744	-101	600	-0.3	1.8	130	174	238	2.9	3.2
Business support services	772	823	948	51	125	0.6	1.4	43	57	68	2.9	1.8
Travel arrangement and reservation services	304	228	225	-77	-3	-2.9	-0.1	26	28	37	0.7	2.7
Investigation and and security services	659	807	960	148	153	2.0	1.8	28	40	54	3.6	3.0
Services to buildings and dwellings	1 460	1 847	2 183	387	336	2.4	1.7	77	121	198	4.6	5.0
Other support services	304	308	317	5	9	0.2	0.3	31	39	51	2.3	2.7
Waste management and remediation services	299	360	451	61	91	1.9	2.3	52	67	105	2.6	4.6
Education services	2 233	3 037	3 842	804	806	3.1	2.4	123	156	184	2.4	1.7
Elementary and secondary schools	651	855	1 090	204	235	2.8	2.5	26	30	37	1.5	2.2
Junior colleges, colleges, universities, and professional schools	1 234	1 603	1 857	369	255	2.6	1.5	68	92	102	3.0	1.0
Other education services	348	579	895	231	316	5.2	4.5	29	34	44	1.7	2.7
Health care and social assistance	12 214	15 819	19 816	3 605	3 997	2.6	2.3	924	1 302	1 861	3.5	3.6
Ambulatory health care services	4 161	5 661	7 676	1 500	2 015	3.1	3.1	426	636	973	4.1	4.3
Offices of health practitioners	2 815	3 713	4 979	898	1 265	2.8	3.0	312	468	714	4.2	4.3
Home health care services	660	958	1 399	299	441	3.8	3.9	33	53	79	4.8	4.1
Outpatient, laboratory, and other ambulatory services	687	990	1 298	303	308	3.7	2.8	82	116	180	3.5	4.5
Hospitals, private	3 892	4 641	5 192	749	551	1.8	1.1	306	426	580	3.4	3.2
Nursing and residential care facilities	2 487	3 008	3 645	521	637	1.9	1.9	111	131	160	1.6	2.0
Nursing care facilities	. . .	. . .	. . .	. . .	. . .	. . .	. . .	. . .	. . .	. . .	. . .	. . .
Residential care facilities	. . .	. . .	. . .	. . .	. . .	. . .	. . .	. . .	. . .	. . .	. . .	. . .
Social assistance	1 673	2 509	3 303	836	794	4.1	2.8	81	111	157	3.2	3.5
Individual and family services	597	1 109	1 639	511	530	6.4	4.0	32	46	69	3.7	4.1
Community, and vocational rehabilitation services	460	541	672	81	131	1.6	2.2	18	24	40	3.2	5.2
Child day care services	615	859	992	244	133	3.4	1.4	31	41	49	2.7	1.9
Arts, entertainment, and recreation	1 645	1 970	2 274	324	304	1.8	1.4	134	173	209	2.6	1.9
Performing arts, speccator sports, and related industries	350	406	468	56	62	1.5	1.4	70	78	89	1.2	1.3
Performing arts companies	128	118	127	-10	9	-0.8	0.7	13	10	11	-3.2	1.2
Spectator sports	110	129	146	19	17	1.6	1.3	22	27	33	2.0	2.1
Promoters of events, and agents and managers	77	109	131	32	21	3.5	1.8	15	21	21	3.4	0.0
Independent artists, writers, and performers	35	50	65	15	14	3.7	2.5	20	21	25	0.8	1.6
Museums, historical sites, and similar institutions	97	132	161	34	29	3.1	2.0	5	7	8	2.5	1.2
Amusement, gambling, and recreation industries	1 198	1 431	1 645	233	214	1.8	1.4	59	88	113	4.1	2.5
Accommodation and food services	9 586	11 489	12 327	1 903	838	1.8	0.7	473	575	675	2.0	1.6
Accommodation	1 774	1 857	1 957	84	99	0.5	0.5	129	145	176	1.1	2.0
Food services and drinking places	7 813	9 632	10 371	1 819	739	2.1	0.7	344	430	499	2.3	1.5
Other services	5 750	6 333	7 142	583	809	1.0	1.2	401	463	539	1.4	1.5
Repair and maintenance	1 189	1 228	1 291	39	63	0.3	0.5	141	157	180	1.1	1.4
Automotive repair and maintenance	828	858	912	30	54	0.4	0.6	88	99	105	1.2	0.6
Electronic and precision equipment repair and maintenance	113	104	111	-9	6	-0.8	0.6	20	21	23	0.6	1.0
Commercial and industrial machinery and equipment (except automotive and electronic) repair and maintenance	163	192	200	28	8	1.6	0.4	17	23	41	3.2	6.0
Personal and household goods repair and maintenance	85	74	68	-11	-6	-1.3	-0.8	17	14	14	-1.5	-0.4
Personal and laundry services	1 206	1 327	1 589	121	262	1.0	1.8	105	124	153	1.6	2.2
Personal care services	469	622	819	153	198	2.9	2.8	33	40	54	1.8	3.0
Death care services	134	136	145	3	9	0.2	0.6	13	11	9	-2.0	-1.1
Dry-cleaning and laundry services	383	335	348	-48	13	-1.3	0.4	22	22	22	-0.2	0.3
Other personal services	220	234	276	14	42	0.6	1.7	37	52	70	3.3	3.0
Religious, grantmaking, civic, professional, and similar organizations	2 581	2 973	3 353	392	379	1.4	1.2	140	168	189	1.9	1.2
Religious organizations	1 460	1 684	1 882	224	198	1.4	1.1	47	51	57	0.9	1.1
Grantmaking and giving services and social advocacy organizations	265	351	387	87	36	2.9	1.0	29	44	47	4.4	0.5
Civic, social, professional, and similar organizations	857	938	1 083	81	145	0.9	1.5	64	73	86	1.3	1.6
Private households	774	805	910	31	105	0.4	1.2	15	14	17	-0.4	2.0
Federal Government	2 772	2 764	2 859	-8	95	0.0	0.3	573	760	868	2.9	1.3
Postal Service	881	748	650	-133	-98	-1.6	-1.4	62	57	62	-0.8	0.9
Federal electric utilities	30	24	19	-6	-5	-2.1	-2.3	10	11	12	1.3	0.7
Federal enterprises except Postal Service and electric utilities	86	64	45	-22	-19	-3.0	-3.4	8	11	13	3.5	1.4
Federal government except enterprises	1 776	1 929	2 145	153	216	0.8	1.1	495	681	785	3.2	1.4
Federal defense government	550	496	547	-54	51.0	-1.0	1.0	323	463	548	3.7	1.7
Federal non-defense government except enterprises	1 226	1 433	1 598	207	165	1.6	1.1	172	225	246	2.7	0.9

. . . = Not available.

Table 4-6. Employment and Output, by Industry, 1998, 2008, and Projected 2018—*Continued*

(Number, percent, dollars.)

Industry	Employment							Output				
	Number of jobs (thousands)			Change		Average annual rate of change (percent)		Billions of chained (2000) dollars			Average annual rate of change (percent)	
	1998	2008	2018	1998–2018	2008–2018	1998–2008	2008–2018	1998	2008	2018	1998–2008	2008–2018
State and Local Government	17 137	19 735	21 327	2 598	1 592	1.4	0.8	1 254	1 504	1 728	1.8	1.4
Local government passenger transit	214	269	343	55	74	2.3	2.5	8	9	11	1.1	2.1
Local government enterprises except passenger transit	1 078	1 326	1 499	249	173	2.1	1.2	140	176	211	2.3	1.8
Local government hospitals	630	663	669	32	6	0.5	0.1	23	27	29	1.9	0.6
Local government educational services	6 921	8 076	8 728	1 155	653	1.6	0.8	271	305	323	1.2	0.6
Local government excluding enterprises, educational services, and hospitals	3 682	4 224	4 464	542	240	1.4	0.6	164	185	189	1.2	0.2
State government enterprises	504	534	578	30	45	0.6	0.8	21	25	30	2.1	1.8
State government hospitals-compensation	346	363	377	17	14	0.5	0.4	19	20	21	0.1	0.9
State government	1 922	2 359	2 584	437	225	2.1	0.9	75	87	89	1.4	0.2
State government, other compensation	1 840	1 922	2 084	81	162	0.4	0.8	97	101	103	0.4	0.2
State and local government capital services	...	...	...	...	...	...	...	77	109	139	3.5	2.4
General state and local government except compensation and capital services	...	...	...	...	...	...	...	360	462	590	2.5	2.5
Owner-Occupied Dwellings	...	...	...	...	...	...	...	699	899	1 093	2.6	2.0
Agriculture, Forestry, Fishing, and Hunting	2 528	2 098	2 020	-430	-78.0	-1.8	-0.4	265	293	319	1.0	0.9
Crop production	1 085	951	881	-135	-70	-1.3	-0.8	110	131	141	1.8	0.7
Animal production	1 120	861	824	-259	-37	-2.6	-0.4	104	115	128	1.0	1.1
Forestry	17	17	18	0	1	-0.2	0.7	7	6	8	-1.7	3.2
Logging	123	82	100	-41	18	-4.0	2.0	24	23	23	-0.7	0.1
Fishing, hunting and trapping	58	47	47	-11	0	-2.0	0.0	6	7	6	1.1	-1.1
Support activities for agriculture and forestry	126	141	150	16	9	1.2	0.6	13	8	11	-4.0	2.9
Nonagriculture Self-Employed and Unpaid Family Worker[3]	9 342	9 313	9 943	-30	631	0.0	0.7	...	...	...	...	...
Secondary Wage and Salary Jobs in Agriculture and Private Household Industries[4]	173	182	192	9	10	0.5	0.5	...	...	...	...	...
Secondary Jobs as a Self-Employed or Unpaid Family Worker[5]	1 897	1 524	1 607	-372	83	-2.2	0.5	...	...	...	...	...

[3]Comparable estimate of output growth is not available.
[4]Workers who hold a secondary wage and salary job in agricultural production, forestry, fishing, and private household industries.
[5]Wage and salary workers who hold a secondary job as a self-employed or unpaid family worker.
. . . = Not available.

Table 4-7. Employment, by Occupation, 2008 and Projected 2018

(Numbers in thousands, percent.)

Occupation	Employment				Change, 2008–2018		Total job openings due to growth and net replacements, 2008–2018[1]
	Number		Percent distribution		Number	Percent	
	2008	2018	2008	2018			
ALL OCCUPATIONS	150 932	166 206	100.0	100.0	15 274	10.1	50 929
Management, Business, and Financial	15 747	17 411	10.4	10.5	1 664	10.6	5 035
Management	8 912	9 367	5.9	5.6	454	5.1	2 460
Top executives	2 201	2 194	1.5	1.3	-7	-0.3	634
Chief executives	400	395	0.3	0.2	-6	-1.4	113
General and operations managers	1 733	1 731	1.1	1.0	-2	-0.1	502
Legislators	68	68	0.0	0.0	1	0.7	20
Advertising, marketing, promotions, public relations, and sales managers	624	704	0.4	0.4	80	12.9	217
Advertising and promotions managers	45	44	0.0	0.0	-1	-1.7	11
Marketing and sales managers	522	596	0.3	0.4	74	14.1	186
Marketing managers	176	198	0.1	0.1	22	12.5	60
Sales managers	347	399	0.2	0.2	52	14.9	127
Public relations managers	57	64	0.0	0.0	7	12.9	21
Operations specialties managers	1 552	1 672	1.0	1.0	120	7.7	467
Administrative services managers	259	292	0.2	0.2	32	12.5	87
Computer and information systems managers	293	343	0.2	0.2	50	16.9	97
Financial managers	539	581	0.4	0.3	41	7.6	138
Human resources managers	134	147	0.1	0.1	13	9.6	41
Compensation and benefits managers	41	44	0.0	0.0	3	8.5	12
Training and development managers	30	34	0.0	0.0	4	11.9	10
Human resources managers, all other	63	69	0.0	0.0	6	9.2	19
Industrial production managers	156	144	0.1	0.1	-12	-7.6	55
Purchasing managers	70	71	0.0	0.0	1	1.5	21
Transportation, storage, and distribution managers	100	94	0.1	0.1	-5	-5.3	27
Other management occupations	4 536	4 797	3.0	2.9	261	5.8	1 141
Agricultural managers	1 234	1 169	0.8	0.7	-65	-5.2	125
Farm, ranch, and other agricultural managers	248	263	0.2	0.2	15	5.9	65
Farmers and ranchers	986	907	0.7	0.5	-79	-8.0	60
Construction managers	551	646	0.4	0.4	95	17.2	138
Education administrators	445	483	0.3	0.3	37	8.3	170
Education administrators, preschool and childcare center/program	59	66	0.0	0.0	7	11.8	25
Education administrators, elementary and secondary school	231	250	0.2	0.2	20	8.6	89
Education administrators, postsecondary	125	127	0.1	0.1	3	2.3	40
Education administrators, all other	31	39	0.0	0.0	8	23.9	17
Engineering managers	184	195	0.1	0.1	11	6.2	49
Food service managers	339	357	0.2	0.2	18	5.3	84
Funeral directors	30	34	0.0	0.0	4	11.9	10
Gaming managers	6	7	0.0	0.0	1	11.8	20
Lodging managers	60	63	0.0	0.0	3	4.7	16
Medical and health services managers	284	329	0.2	0.2	45	16.0	99
Natural sciences managers	45	52	0.0	0.0	7	15.5	2
Postmasters and mail superintendents	26	22	0.0	0.0	-4	-15.1	5
Property, real estate, and community association managers	304	330	0.2	0.2	26	8.4	78
Social and community service managers	131	149	0.1	0.1	18	13.8	48
Managers, all other	898	964	0.6	0.6	66	7.3	298
Business and Financial Operations	6 834	8 044	4.5	4.8	1 210	17.7	2 575
Business operations specialists	4 043	4 762	2.7	2.9	720	17.8	1 609
Agents and business managers of artists, performers, and athletes	23	28	0.0	0.0	5	22.4	10
Buyers and purchasing agents	457	495	0.3	0.3	37	8.2	159
Purchasing agents and buyers, farm products	14	14	0.0	0.0	0	-1.1	3
Wholesale and retail buyers, except farm products	148	144	0.1	0.1	-3	-2.2	37
Purchasing agents, except wholesale, retail, and farm products	295	336	0.2	0.2	41	13.9	119
Claims adjusters, appraisers, examiners, and investigators	306	327	0.2	0.2	21	6.8	99
Claims adjusters, examiners, and investigators	295	316	0.2	0.2	21	7.1	96
Insurance appraisers, auto damage	12	12	0.0	0.0	0	0.5	3
Compliance officers, except agriculture, construction, health and safety, and transportation	260	341	0.2	0.2	81	31.0	109
Cost estimators	218	273	0.1	0.2	55	25.3	104
Emergency management specialists	13	16	0.0	0.0	3	21.7	6
Human resources, training, and labor relations specialists	771	956	0.5	0.6	185	23.9	386
Employment, recruitment, and placement specialists	208	266	0.1	0.2	58	27.9	112
Compensation, benefits, and job analysis specialists	122	151	0.1	0.1	29	23.6	61
Training and development specialists	217	267	0.1	0.2	51	23.3	107
Human resources, training, and labor relations specialists, all other	225	272	0.1	0.2	47	21.0	106
Logisticians	100	120	0.1	0.1	20	19.5	42
Management analysts	747	925	0.5	0.6	178	23.9	307
Meeting and convention planners	57	65	0.0	0.0	9	15.6	21
Business operation specialists, all other	1 091	1 217	0.7	0.7	126	11.5	368
Financial specialists	2 792	3 282	1.8	2.0	491	17.6	966
Accountants and auditors	1 291	1 570	0.9	0.9	279	21.6	498
Appraisers and assessors of real estate	92	97	0.1	0.1	4	4.6	21
Budget analysts	67	77	0.0	0.0	10	15.1	22
Credit analysts	73	84	0.0	0.1	11	15.0	24
Financial analysts and advisers	562	670	0.4	0.4	108	19.2	210
Financial analysts	251	300	0.2	0.2	50	19.8	95
Personal financial advisers	208	271	0.1	0.2	63	30.1	85
Insurance underwriters	103	99	0.1	0.1	-4	-4.1	30
Financial examiners	27	38	0.0	0.0	11	41.2	16
Loan counselors and officers	360	399	0.2	0.2	38	10.6	78
Loan counselors	32	38	0.0	0.0	5	16.3	9
Loan officers	328	361	0.2	0.2	33	10.1	69
Tax examiners, collectors, preparers, and revenue agents	169	181	0.1	0.1	12	7.3	54
Tax examiners, collectors, and revenue agents	73	82	0.0	0.0	10	13.0	35
Tax preparers	96	99	0.1	0.1	3	2.9	19
Financial specialists, all other	151	166	0.1	0.1	16	10.5	43

Note: Data may not sum to totals or 100 percent due to rounding.

[1]Total job openings represent the sum of employment increases and net replacements. If employment change is negative, job openings due to growth are zero and total job openings equal net replacements.

Table 4-7. Employment, by Occupation, 2008 and Projected 2018—*Continued*

(Numbers in thousands, percent.)

Occupation	Employment				Change, 2008–2018		Total job openings due to growth and net replacements, 2008–2018[1]
	Number		Percent distribution		Number	Percent	
	2008	2018	2008	2018			
Computer and Mathematical Sciences	3 540	4 326	2.3	2.6	786	22.2	1 441
Computer specialists	3 424	4 187	2.3	2.5	763	22.3	1 384
Computer and information scientists, research	29	36	0.0	0.0	7	24.2	13
Computer programmers	427	414	0.3	0.2	-12	-2.9	80
Computer software engineers	910	1 205	0.6	0.7	295	32.5	372
Computer software engineers, applications	515	690	0.3	0.4	175	34.0	218
Computer software engineers, systems software	395	515	0.3	0.3	120	30.4	153
Computer support specialists	566	644	0.4	0.4	78	13.8	235
Computer systems analysts	532	640	0.4	0.4	108	20.3	223
Database administrators	120	145	0.1	0.1	24	20.3	44
Network and computer systems administrators	340	418	0.2	0.3	79	23.2	136
Network systems and data communications analysts	292	448	0.2	0.3	156	53.4	208
Computer specialists, all other	209	237	0.1	0.1	28	13.1	73
Mathematical science occupations	116	139	0.1	0.1	23	19.8	57
Actuaries	20	24	0.0	0.0	4	21.4	10
Mathematicians	3	4	0.0	0.0	1	22.5	2
Operations research analysts	63	77	0.0	0.0	14	22.0	32
Statisticians	23	26	0.0	0.0	3	13.1	10
Miscellaneous mathematical science occupations	8	9	0.0	0.0	1	16.2	4
Mathematical technicians	1	1	0.0	0.0	0	8.5	1
Mathematical scientists, all other	7	8	0.0	0.0	1	17.6	3
Architecture and engineering	2 636	2 907	1.7	1.7	271	10.3	838
Architects, surveyors, and cartographers	238	278	0.2	0.2	40	16.8	86
Architects, except naval	168	196	0.1	0.1	28	16.8	57
Architects, except landscape and naval	141	164	0.1	0.1	23	16.2	47
Landscape architects	27	32	0.0	0.0	5	19.7	10
Surveyors, cartographers, and photogrammetrists	70	82	0.0	0.0	12	17.0	30
Cartographers and photogrammetrists	12	16	0.0	0.0	3	26.8	6
Surveyors	58	66	0.0	0.0	9	14.9	23
Engineers	1 572	1 750	1.0	1.1	178	11.3	531
Aerospace engineers	72	79	0.0	0.0	7	10.4	22
Agricultural engineers	3	3	0.0	0.0	0	12.1	1
Biomedical engineers	16	28	0.0	0.0	12	72.0	15
Chemical engineers	32	31	0.0	0.0	-1	-2.0	8
Civil engineers	278	346	0.2	0.2	68	24.3	115
Computer hardware engineers	75	78	0.0	0.0	3	3.8	24
Electrical and electronics engineers	302	305	0.2	0.2	3	1.0	72
Electrical engineers	158	161	0.1	0.1	3	1.7	39
Electronics engineers, except computer	144	144	0.1	0.1	0	0.3	33
Environmental engineers	54	71	0.0	0.0	17	30.6	28
Industrial engineers, including health and safety	240	274	0.2	0.2	33	13.8	95
Health and safety engineers, except mining safety engineers and inspectors	26	28	0.0	0.0	3	10.3	9
Industrial engineers	215	245	0.1	0.1	31	14.2	85
Marine engineers and naval architects	9	9	0.0	0.0	1	5.8	2
Materials engineers	24	27	0.0	0.0	2	9.3	8
Mechanical engineers	239	253	0.2	0.2	14	6.0	76
Mining and geological engineers, including mining safety engineers	7	8	0.0	0.0	1	15.3	3
Nuclear engineers	17	19	0.0	0.0	2	10.9	5
Petroleum engineers	22	26	0.0	0.0	4	18.4	9
Engineers, all other	183	195	0.1	0.1	12	6.7	50
Drafters, engineering, and mapping technicians	826	878	0.5	0.5	52	6.3	220
Drafters	252	263	0.2	0.2	11	4.2	66
Architectural and civil drafters	118	129	0.1	0.1	11	9.1	36
Electrical and electronics drafters	34	34	0.0	0.0	0	0.8	8
Mechanical drafters	79	78	0.1	0.0	-1	-1.1	17
Drafters, all other	21	22	0.0	0.0	1	2.3	5
Engineering technicians, except drafters	497	523	0.3	0.3	26	5.2	125
Aerospace engineering and operations technicians	9	9	0.0	0.0	0	2.3	2
Civil engineering technicians	92	107	0.1	0.1	16	16.9	33
Electrical and electronic engineering technicians	164	160	0.1	0.1	-4	-2.2	31
Electromechanical technicians	16	16	0.0	0.0	-1	-4.9	3
Environmental engineering technicians	21	28	0.0	0.0	6	30.1	10
Industrial engineering technicians	73	77	0.0	0.0	5	6.6	19
Mechanical engineering technicians	46	46	0.0	0.0	-1	-1.5	9
Engineering technicians, except drafters, all other	77	81	0.1	0.0	4	5.2	19
Surveying and mapping technicians	77	93	0.1	0.1	16	20.4	29
Life, Physical, and Social Sciences	1 461	1 738	1.0	1.0	277	19.0	715
Life scientists	279	354	0.2	0.2	75	26.7	144
Agricultural and food scientists	31	36	0.0	0.0	5	15.6	16
Animal scientists	4	4	0.0	0.0	1	13.1	2
Food scientists and technologists	13	16	0.0	0.0	2	16.3	7
Soil and plant scientists	14	16	0.0	0.0	2	15.5	7
Biological scientists	91	111	0.1	0.1	19	21.0	49
Biochemists and biophysicists	23	32	0.0	0.0	9	37.4	16
Microbiologists	17	19	0.0	0.0	2	12.2	8
Zoologists and wildlife biologists	20	22	0.0	0.0	3	12.8	9
Biological scientists, all other	32	38	0.0	0.0	6	18.8	16
Conservation scientists and foresters	30	33	0.0	0.0	4	12.0	7
Conservation scientists	18	21	0.0	0.0	2	11.9	4
Foresters	12	13	0.0	0.0	1	12.1	3
Medical scientists	114	159	0.1	0.1	45	39.3	68
Epidemiologists	5	6	0.0	0.0	1	15.1	2
Medical scientists, except epidemiologists	109	154	0.1	0.1	44	40.4	66
Life scientists, all other	13	15	0.0	0.0	2	16.3	5

Note: Data may not sum to totals or 100 percent due to rounding.

[1]Total job openings represent the sum of employment increases and net replacements. If employment change is negative, job openings due to growth are zero and total job openings equal net replacements.

Table 4-7. Employment, by Occupation, 2008 and Projected 2018—*Continued*

(Numbers in thousands, percent.)

Occupation	Employment				Change, 2008–2018		Total job openings due to growth and net replacements, 2008–2018[1]
	Number		Percent distribution		Number	Percent	
	2008	2018	2008	2018			
Life, Physical, and Social Sciences—*Continued*							
Physical scientists	276	317	0.2	0.2	42	15.1	123
Astronomers and physicists	17	20	0.0	0.0	3	15.9	8
Astronomers	2	2	0.0	0.0	0	16.0	1
Physicists	16	18	0.0	0.0	3	15.9	7
Atmospheric and space scientists	9	11	0.0	0.0	1	14.7	3
Chemists and materials scientists	94	97	0.1	0.1	3	3.5	34
Chemists	84	86	0.1	0.1	2	2.5	30
Materials scientists	10	11	0.0	0.0	1	11.9	4
Environmental scientists and geoscientists	128	159	0.1	0.1	31	24.5	68
Environmental scientists and specialists, including health	86	110	0.1	0.1	24	27.9	48
Geoscientists, except hydrologists and geologists	34	39	0.0	0.0	6	17.5	15
Hydrologists	8	10	0.0	0.0	2	18.3	4
Physical scientists, all other	27	30	0.0	0.0	3	11.1	10
Social scientists and related	549	666	0.4	0.4	117	21.3	275
Economists	15	16	0.0	0.0	1	5.8	5
Market and survey researchers	273	351	0.2	0.2	77	28.3	151
Market research analysts	250	320	0.2	0.2	70	28.1	137
Survey researchers	23	31	0.0	0.0	7	30.4	13
Psychologists	170	190	0.1	0.1	20	11.6	68
Clinical, counseling, and school psychologists	152	169	0.1	0.1	17	11.1	60
Industrial-organizational psychologists	2	3	0.0	0.0	1	26.3	1
Psychologists, all other	16	18	0.0	0.0	2	14.4	7
Sociologists	5	6	0.0	0.0	1	21.9	2
Urban and regional planners	38	46	0.0	0.0	7	19.0	15
Miscellaneous social scientists and related workers	48	59	0.0	0.0	11	22.0	35
Anthropologists and archeologists	6	7	0.0	0.0	2	28.1	5
Geographers	1	2	0.0	0.0	0	26.2	1
Historians	4	5	0.0	0.0	1	11.5	3
Political scientists	40	5	0.0	0.0	1	19.5	3
Social scientists and related workers, all other	33	40	0.0	0.0	7	22.4	24
Life, physical, and social science technicians	357	401	0.2	0.2	44	12.4	173
Agricultural and food science technicians	22	24	0.0	0.0	2	8.8	10
Biological technicians	80	94	0.1	0.1	14	17.6	42
Chemical technicians	66	66	0.0	0.0	-1	-0.8	13
Geological and petroleum technicians	15	15	0.0	0.0	0	1.5	6
Nuclear technicians	6	7	0.0	0.0	1	9.2	3
Social science research assistants	21	25	0.0	0.0	4	17.8	13
Other life, physical, and social science technicians	147	171	0.1	0.1	24	16.5	87
Environmental science and protection technicians, including health	35	45	0.0	0.0	10	28.9	25
Forensic science technicians	13	15	0.0	0.0	3	19.6	8
Forest and conservation technicians	34	37	0.0	0.0	3	8.6	18
Life, physical, and social science technicians, all other	65	73	0.0	0.0	9	13.3	36
Community and Social Services	2 724	3 172	1.8	1.9	448	16.5	1 033
Counselors, social workers, and other community and social service specialists	1 945	2 295	1.3	1.4	350	18.0	780
Counselors	666	782	0.4	0.5	117	17.5	251
Substance abuse and behavioral disorder counselors	86	104	0.1	0.1	18	21.0	36
Educational, vocational, and school counselors	276	314	0.2	0.2	39	14.0	94
Marriage and family therapists	27	31	0.0	0.0	4	14.5	10
Mental health counselors	113	140	0.1	0.1	27	24.0	50
Rehabilitation counselors	130	154	0.1	0.1	25	18.9	51
Counselors, all other	33	38	0.0	0.0	4	13.1	11
Social workers	642	745	0.4	0.4	103	16.1	265
Child, family, and school social workers	293	329	0.2	0.2	36	12.3	110
Medical and public health social workers	139	170	0.1	0.1	31	22.4	66
Mental health and substance abuse social workers	137	164	0.1	0.1	27	19.5	61
Social workers, all other	73	83	0.0	0.0	9	12.8	28
Miscellaneous community and social service specialists	637	767	0.4	0.5	130	20.3	265
Health educators	66	78	0.0	0.0	12	18.1	26
Probation officers and correctional treatment specialists	103	123	0.1	0.1	20	19.3	42
Social and human service assistants	352	432	0.2	0.3	79	22.6	154
Community and social service specialists, all other	116	134	0.1	0.1	18	15.7	43
Religious workers	779	878	0.5	0.5	99	12.7	252
Clergy	670	755	0.4	0.5	85	12.7	218
Directors, religious activities and education	80	91	0.1	0.1	10	12.6	26
Religious workers, all other	28	32	0.0	0.0	4	12.5	8
Legal	1 251	1 439	0.8	0.9	188	15.1	397
Lawyers, judges, and related workers	810	911	0.5	0.5	100	12.4	253
Lawyers	759	858	0.5	0.5	99	13.0	240
Judges, magistrates, and other judicial workers	51	53	0.0	0.0	2	3.6	12
Administrative law judges, adjudicators, and hearing officers	14	16	0.0	0.0	1	8.0	4
Arbitrators, mediators, and conciliators	10	11	0.0	0.0	1	13.9	3
Judges, magistrate judges, and magistrates	27	26	0.0	0.0	-1	-2.6	5
Legal support workers	441	529	0.3	0.3	88	20.0	145
Paralegals and legal assistants	264	338	0.2	0.2	74	28.1	104
Miscellaneous legal support workers	177	191	0.1	0.1	14	7.9	41
Court reporters	22	25	0.0	0.0	4	18.3	7
Law clerks	38	43	0.0	0.0	5	13.9	11
Title examiners, abstractors, and searchers	70	69	0.0	0.0	-1	-0.7	10
Legal support workers, all other	48	53	0.0	0.0	5	11.0	12

Note: Data may not sum to totals or 100 percent due to rounding.

[1]Total job openings represent the sum of employment increases and net replacements. If employment change is negative, job openings due to growth are zero and total job openings equal net replacements.

Table 4-7. Employment, by Occupation, 2008 and Projected 2018—*Continued*

(Numbers in thousands, percent.)

Occupation	Employment				Change, 2008–2018		Total job openings due to growth and net replacements, 2008–2018[1]
	Number		Percent distribution		Number	Percent	
	2008	2018	2008	2018			
Education, Training, and Library	9 210	10 534	6.1	6.3	1 324	14.4	3 332
Postsecondary teachers	1 699	1 956	1.1	1.2	257	15.1	553
Primary, secondary, and special education teachers	4 522	5 169	3.0	3.1	647	14.3	1 748
Preschool and kindergarten teachers	637	750	0.4	0.5	114	17.8	241
Preschool teachers, except special education	457	544	0.3	0.3	87	19.0	178
Kindergarten teachers, except special education	180	207	0.1	0.1	27	15.0	63
Elementary and middle school teachers	2 225	2 571	1.5	1.5	346	15.5	852
Elementary school teachers, except special education	1 550	1 794	1.0	1.1	244	15.8	597
Middle school teachers, except special and vocational education	660	761	0.4	0.5	101	15.3	251
Vocational education teachers, middle school	16	16	0.0	0.0	1	3.2	4
Secondary school teachers	1 187	1 293	0.8	0.8	106	8.9	451
Secondary school teachers, except special and vocational education	1 088	1 184	0.7	0.7	96	8.9	412
Vocational education teachers, secondary school	99	109	0.1	0.1	10	9.6	39
Special education teachers	473	555	0.3	0.3	82	17.3	205
Special education teachers, preschool, kindergarten, and elementary school	226	270	0.1	0.2	44	19.6	103
Special education teachers, middle school	100	118	0.1	0.1	18	18.1	44
Special education teachers, secondary school	147	166	0.1	0.1	20	13.3	58
Other teachers and instructors	1 099	1 306	0.7	0.8	206	18.8	375
Adult literacy, remedial education, and GED teachers and instructors	96	110	0.1	0.1	15	15.1	29
Self-enrichment education teachers	254	335	0.2	0.2	81	32.0	120
Teachers and instructors, all other	750	860	0.5	0.5	110	14.7	226
Archivists, curators, and librarians	310	339	0.2	0.2	29	9.4	134
Archivists, curators, and museum technicians	29	35	0.0	0.0	6	20.4	15
Archivists	6	7	0.0	0.0	0	6.5	2
Curators	12	14	0.0	0.0	3	23.0	6
Museum technicians and conservators	11	14	0.0	0.0	3	25.6	6
Librarians	160	172	0.1	0.1	13	7.8	55
Library technicians	121	131	0.1	0.1	11	8.8	65
Other education, training, and library	1 580	1 765	1.0	1.1	185	11.7	521
Audio-visual collections specialists	7	8	0.0	0.0	1	10.3	2
Farm and home management advisers	13	13	0.0	0.0	0	1.2	3
Instructional coordinators	134	165	0.1	0.1	31	23.2	61
Teacher assistants	1 313	1 448	0.9	0.9	135	10.3	413
Education, training, and library workers, all other	113	131	0.1	0.1	18	15.8	43
Arts, Design, Entertainment, Sports, and Media	2 741	3 073	1.8	1.8	333	12.1	1 030
Art and design	834	922	0.6	0.6	88	10.6	328
Artists and related workers	222	248	0.1	0.1	26	11.6	76
Art directors	84	94	0.1	0.1	10	11.7	29
Craft artists	14	15	0.0	0.0	1	7.2	4
Fine artists, including painters, sculptors, and illustrators	24	26	0.0	0.0	2	9.0	7
Multimedia artists and animators	79	90	0.1	0.1	11	14.2	29
Artists and related workers, all other	22	23	0.0	0.0	2	7.9	7
Designers	612	674	0.4	0.4	62	10.2	252
Commercial and industrial designers	44	48	0.0	0.0	4	9.0	18
Fashion designers	23	23	0.0	0.0	0	0.8	7
Floral designers	76	74	0.1	0.0	-2	-2.5	23
Graphic designers	286	323	0.2	0.2	37	12.9	125
Interior designers	72	86	0.0	0.1	14	19.4	36
Merchandise displayers and window trimmers	85	91	0.1	0.1	6	7.1	32
Set and exhibit designers	11	13	0.0	0.0	2	16.6	5
Designers, all other	15	17	0.0	0.0	2	9.6	6
Entertainers and performers, sports and related	741	845	0.5	0.5	105	14.1	274
Actors, producers, and directors	155	172	0.1	0.1	17	10.9	61
Actors	57	64	0.0	0.0	7	12.8	21
Producers and directors	99	108	0.1	0.1	10	9.8	40
Athletes, coaches, umpires, and related workers	258	318	0.2	0.2	60	23.1	109
Athletes and sports competitors	17	18	0.0	0.0	2	11.8	5
Coaches and scouts	226	282	0.1	0.2	56	24.8	99
Umpires, referees, and other sports officials	16	18	0.0	0.0	2	10.4	5
Dancers and choreographers	29	31	0.0	0.0	2	6.0	15
Dancers	13	14	0.0	0.0	1	6.8	7
Choreographers	16	17	0.0	0.0	1	5.3	8
Musicians, singers, and related workers	240	260	0.2	0.2	20	8.2	68
Music directors and composers	54	59	0.0	0.0	5	10.0	16
Musicians and singers	186	201	0.1	0.1	14	7.6	52
Entertainers and performers, sports and related, all other	58	65	0.0	0.0	7	11.8	21
Media and communication	827	933	0.5	0.6	105	12.7	311
Announcers	67	65	0.0	0.0	-2	-3.5	20
Radio and television announcers	55	52	0.0	0.0	-3	-6.1	16
Public address system and other announcers	12	13	0.0	0.0	1	8.2	5
News analysts, reporters, and correspondents	69	65	0.0	0.0	-4	-6.3	19
Broadcast news analysts	8	8	0.0	0.0	0	4.1	2
Reporters and correspondents	62	57	0.0	0.0	-5	-7.6	17
Public relations specialists	275	341	0.2	0.2	66	24.0	131
Writers and editors	330	361	0.2	0.2	31	9.4	105
Editors	130	129	0.1	0.1	0	-0.3	34
Technical writers	49	58	0.0	0.0	9	18.2	17
Writers and authors	152	174	0.1	0.1	23	14.8	54
Miscellaneous media and communication workers	85	100	0.1	0.1	15	17.4	35
Interpreters and translators	51	62	0.0	0.0	11	22.2	23
Media and communication workers, all other	34	38	0.0	0.0	4	10.4	12

Note: Data may not sum to totals or 100 percent due to rounding.

[1]Total job openings represent the sum of employment increases and net replacements. If employment change is negative, job openings due to growth are zero and total job openings equal net replacements.

Table 4-7. Employment, by Occupation, 2008 and Projected 2018—*Continued*

(Numbers in thousands, percent.)

Occupation	Employment				Change, 2008–2018		Total job openings due to growth and net replacements, 2008–2018[1]
	Number		Percent distribution		Number	Percent	
	2008	2018	2008	2018			
Arts, Design, Entertainment, Sports, and Media—*Continued*							
Media and communication equipment occupations	339	374	0.2	0.2	35	10.2	117
Broadcast and sound engineering technicians and radio operators	115	124	0.1	0.1	9	7.8	44
Audio and video equipment technicians	55	62	0.0	0.0	7	12.6	24
Broadcast technicians	39	39	0.0	0.0	1	1.8	12
Radio operators	1	1	0.0	0.0	0	9.0	0
Sound engineering technicians	20	21	0.0	0.0	1	6.3	7
Photographers	152	170	0.1	0.1	18	11.5	48
Television, video, and motion picture camera operators and editors	52	57	0.0	0.0	5	10.5	18
Camera operators, television, video, and motion picture	26	29	0.0	0.0	2	9.2	9
Film and video editors	26	29	0.0	0.0	3	11.9	9
Media and communication equipment workers, all other	21	23	0.0	0.0	3	12.5	8
Health Care Practitioner and Technical	7 491	9 091	5.0	5.5	1 600	21.4	3 139
Health diagnosing and treating practitioners	4 630	5 646	3.1	3.4	1 015	21.9	1 866
Chiropractors	49	59	0.0	0.0	10	19.5	18
Dentists	142	164	0.1	0.1	22	15.6	62
Dentists, general	120	139	0.1	0.1	18	15.3	52
Oral and maxillofacial surgeons	7	8	0.0	0.0	1	15.3	3
Orthodontists	8	9	0.0	0.0	2	19.8	4
Prosthodontists	1	1	0.0	0.0	0	27.7	0
Dentists, all other specialists	7	8	0.0	0.0	1	14.7	3
Dietitians and nutritionists	60	66	0.0	0.0	6	9.2	26
Optometrists	35	43	0.0	0.0	9	24.4	20
Pharmacists	270	316	0.2	0.2	46	17.0	106
Physicians and surgeons	661	806	0.4	0.5	144	21.8	261
Physician assistants	75	104	0.0	0.1	29	39.0	43
Podiatrists	12	13	0.0	0.0	1	9.0	3
Registered nurses	2 619	3 200	1.7	1.9	582	22.2	1 039
Therapists	599	740	0.4	0.4	142	23.7	244
Audiologists	13	16	0.0	0.0	3	25.0	6
Occupational therapists	105	131	0.1	0.1	27	25.6	46
Physical therapists	186	242	0.1	0.1	56	30.3	79
Radiation therapists	15	19	0.0	0.0	4	27.1	7
Recreational therapists	23	27	0.0	0.0	3	14.6	12
Respiratory therapists	106	128	0.1	0.1	22	20.9	41
Speech-language pathologists	119	141	0.1	0.1	22	18.5	44
Therapists, all other	32	36	0.0	0.0	4	11.5	10
Veterinarians	60	79	0.0	0.0	20	33.0	30
Health diagnosing and treating practitioners, all other	49	55	0.0	0.0	6	13.0	15
Health technologists and technicians	2 719	3 280	1.8	2.0	561	20.6	1 202
Clinical laboratory technologists and technicians	328	374	0.2	0.2	46	13.9	108
Medical and clinical laboratory technologists	172	193	0.1	0.1	21	11.9	53
Medical and clinical laboratory technicians	156	181	0.1	0.1	25	16.1	55
Dental hygienists	174	237	0.1	0.1	63	36.1	98
Diagnostic related technologists and technicians	336	398	0.2	0.2	62	18.3	110
Cardiovascular technologists and technicians	50	61	0.0	0.0	12	24.1	19
Diagnostic medical sonographers	50	60	0.0	0.0	9	18.3	17
Nuclear medicine technologists	22	25	0.0	0.0	4	16.3	7
Radiologic technologists and technicians	215	252	0.1	0.2	37	17.2	68
Emergency medical technicians and paramedics	211	230	0.1	0.1	19	9.0	62
Health diagnosing and treating practitioner support technicians	596	753	0.4	0.5	157	26.4	308
Dietetic technicians	25	29	0.0	0.0	4	13.9	10
Pharmacy technicians	326	426	0.2	0.3	100	30.6	182
Psychiatric technicians	57	60	0.0	0.0	2	4.2	17
Respiratory therapy technicians	17	16	0.0	0.0	0	-1.1	4
Surgical technologists	92	115	0.1	0.1	23	25.3	46
Veterinary technologists and technicians	80	108	0.1	0.1	29	35.8	49
Licensed practical and licensed vocational nurses	754	909	0.5	0.5	156	20.6	391
Medical records and health information technicians	173	208	0.1	0.1	35	20.3	70
Opticians, dispensing	60	68	0.0	0.0	8	13.4	20
Miscellaneous health technologists and technicians	88	104	0.1	0.1	16	18.5	34
Orthotists and prosthetists	6	7	0.0	0.0	1	15.5	2
Health care technologists and technicians, all other	82	97	0.1	0.1	15	18.7	32
Other health care practitioner and technical	142	165	0.1	0.1	23	16.4	71
Occupational health and safety specialists and technicians	67	75	0.0	0.0	8	11.7	30
Occupational health and safety specialists	56	62	0.0	0.0	6	11.2	25
Occupational health and safety technicians	11	13	0.0	0.0	2	14.4	5
Miscellaneous health care practitioner and technical	75	91	0.0	0.1	15	20.5	41
Athletic trainers	16	22	0.0	0.0	6	36.9	12
Health care practitioner and technical workers, all other	59	68	0.0	0.0	9	15.9	29
Health Care Support	3 982	5 130	2.6	3.1	1 147	28.8	1 595
Nursing, psychiatric, and home health aides	2 454	3 194	1.6	1.9	741	30.2	985
Home health aides	922	1 383	0.6	0.8	461	50.0	553
Nursing aides, orderlies, and attendants	1 470	1 746	1.0	1.1	276	18.8	422
Psychiatric aides	63	66	0.0	0.0	4	5.8	10
Occupational and physical therapist assistants and aides	144	193	0.1	0.1	48	33.5	69
Occupational therapist assistants and aides	34	45	0.0	0.0	10	30.0	15
Occupational therapist assistants	27	35	0.0	0.0	8	29.8	12
Occupational therapist aides	8	10	0.0	0.0	2	30.7	4
Physical therapist assistants and aides	110	148	0.1	0.1	38	34.5	54
Physical therapist assistants	64	85	0.0	0.1	21	33.3	31
Physical therapist aides	46	63	0.0	0.0	17	36.3	23

Note: Data may not sum to totals or 100 percent due to rounding.

[1]Total job openings represent the sum of employment increases and net replacements. If employment change is negative, job openings due to growth are zero and total job openings equal net replacements.

Table 4-7. Employment, by Occupation, 2008 and Projected 2018—*Continued*

(Numbers in thousands, percent.)

Occupation	Employment				Change, 2008–2018		Total job openings due to growth and net replacements, 2008–2018[1]
	Number		Percent distribution		Number	Percent	
	2008	2018	2008	2018			
Health Care Support—*Continued*							
Other health care support	1 384	1 743	0.9	1.0	358	25.9	541
Massage therapists	122	146	0.1	0.1	23	18.9	40
Miscellaneous health care support	1 262	1 597	0.8	1.0	335	26.6	502
Dental assistants	295	401	0.2	0.2	106	35.8	161
Medical assistants	484	648	0.3	0.4	164	33.9	218
Medical equipment preparers	47	53	0.0	0.0	6	12.8	11
Medical transcriptionists	105	117	0.1	0.1	12	11.1	24
Pharmacy aides	55	52	0.0	0.0	-4	-6.3	6
Veterinary assistants and laboratory animal caretakers	75	92	0.0	0.1	17	22.8	26
Health care support workers, all other	201	235	0.1	0.1	34	17.1	57
Protective Services	3 270	3 670	2.2	2.2	400	12.2	1 304
First-line supervisors/managers of protective service workers	252	274	0.2	0.2	23	9.0	129
First-line supervisors/managers of law enforcement workers	141	152	0.1	0.1	12	8.2	70
First-line supervisors/managers of correctional officers	44	47	0.0	0.0	4	8.5	19
First-line supervisors/managers of police and detectives	97	105	0.1	0.1	8	8.1	51
First-line supervisors/managers of fire fighting and prevention workers	55	60	0.0	0.0	5	8.2	33
First-line supervisors/managers of protective service workers, all other	56	62	0.0	0.0	7	12.0	27
Fire fighting and prevention workers	327	386	0.2	0.2	59	18.1	159
Firefighters	310	368	0.2	0.2	58	18.5	153
Fire inspectors	17	18	0.0	0.0	2	9.2	6
Fire inspectors and investigators	15	16	0.0	0.0	1	9.3	5
Forest fire inspectors and prevention specialists	2	2	0.0	0.0	0	8.4	1
Law enforcement workers	1 271	1 393	0.8	0.8	122	9.6	426
Bailiffs, correctional officers, and jailers	475	519	0.3	0.3	45	9.4	150
Bailiffs	20	22	0.0	0.0	2	8.4	6
Correctional officers and jailers	455	498	0.3	0.3	43	9.4	144
Detectives and criminal investigators	112	131	0.1	0.1	19	16.6	42
Fish and game wardens	8	9	0.0	0.0	1	8.3	3
Parking enforcement workers	10	10	0.0	0.0	0	-0.1	2
Police officers	666	723	0.4	0.4	58	8.6	229
Police and sheriff's patrol officers	662	719	0.4	0.4	57	8.7	228
Transit and railroad police	4	5	0.0	0.0	0	5.3	1
Other protective services	1 420	1 617	0.9	1.0	197	13.9	590
Animal control workers	16	18	0.0	0.0	2	9.0	6
Private detectives and investigators	46	56	0.0	0.0	10	22.0	19
Security guards and gaming surveillance officers	1 086	1 240	0.7	0.7	154	14.1	377
Gaming surveillance officers and gaming investigators	9	10	0.0	0.0	1	11.7	3
Security guards	1 077	1 229	0.7	0.7	153	14.2	374
Miscellaneous protective services	273	305	0.2	0.2	32	11.7	188
Crossing guards	70	77	0.0	0.0	7	9.4	26
Lifeguards, ski patrol, and other recreational protective service workers	115	128	0.1	0.1	13	11.2	91
Protective service workers, all other	88	100	0.1	0.1	12	14.0	72
Food Preparation and Serving Related	11 552	12 560	7.7	7.6	1 008	8.7	5 101
Supervisors of food preparation and serving workers	942	997	0.6	0.6	55	5.9	145
Chefs and head cooks	108	109	0.1	0.1	0	0.2	11
First-line supervisors/managers of food preparation and serving workers	833	889	0.6	0.5	55	6.6	134
Cooks and food preparation workers	2 958	3 150	2.0	1.9	192	6.5	1 040
Cooks	2 066	2 220	1.4	1.3	154	7.4	682
Cooks, fast food	566	608	0.4	0.4	42	7.5	187
Cooks, institution and cafeteria	392	430	0.3	0.3	38	9.7	138
Cooks, private household	5	5	0.0	0.0	0	4.3	2
Cooks, restaurant	914	984	0.6	0.6	70	7.7	304
Cooks, short order	171	172	0.1	0.1	0	0.0	44
Cooks, all other	18	21	0.0	0.0	3	16.3	8
Food preparation workers	892	930	0.6	0.6	38	4.2	357
Food and beverage serving workers	6 307	6 962	4.2	4.2	655	10.4	3 142
Bartenders	509	550	0.3	0.3	41	8.0	222
Fast food and counter workers	3 227	3 670	2.1	2.2	443	13.7	1 402
Combined food preparation and serving workers, including fast food	2 702	3 096	1.8	1.9	394	14.6	967
Counter attendants, cafeteria, food concession, and coffee shop	525	574	0.3	0.3	49	9.3	435
Waiters and waitresses	2 382	2 533	1.6	1.5	152	6.4	1 466
Food servers, nonrestaurant	190	209	0.1	0.1	19	10.2	52
Other food preparation and serving related workers	1 345	1 451	0.9	0.9	106	7.9	774
Dining room and cafeteria attendants and bartender helpers	421	444	0.3	0.3	23	5.5	206
Dishwashers	523	583	0.3	0.4	60	11.6	276
Hosts and hostesses, restaurant, lounge, and coffee shop	351	373	0.2	0.2	23	6.5	267
Food preparation and serving related workers, all other	51	50	0.0	0.0	-1	-1.7	26
Building and Grounds Cleaning and Maintenance	5 727	6 211	3.8	3.7	484	8.4	1 434
Supervisors of building and grounds cleaning and maintenance workers	469	514	0.3	0.3	45	9.6	95
First-line supervisors/managers of housekeeping and janitorial workers	251	264	0.2	0.2	13	5.1	39
First-line supervisors/managers of landscaping, lawn service, and groundskeeping workers	218	250	0.1	0.2	32	14.9	56
Building cleaning and pest control workers	3 956	4 157	2.6	2.5	202	5.1	946
Building cleaning workers	3 888	4 079	2.6	2.5	192	4.9	912
Janitors and cleaners, except maids and housekeeping workers	2 375	2 479	1.6	1.5	104	4.4	553
Maids and housekeeping cleaners	1 498	1 584	1.0	1.0	86	5.7	354
Building cleaning workers, all other	15	16	0.0	0.0	2	12.1	5
Pest control workers	68	78	0.0	0.0	10	15.3	34
Grounds maintenance	1 303	1 540	0.9	0.9	237	18.2	394
Landscaping and groundskeeping	1 206	1 423	0.8	0.9	217	18.0	362
Pesticide handlers, sprayers, and applicators, vegetation	31	36	0.0	0.0	5	17.7	9
Tree trimmers and pruners	45	57	0.0	0.0	12	26.3	17
Grounds maintenance workers, all other	21	24	0.0	0.0	3	11.8	5

Note: Data may not sum to totals or 100 percent due to rounding.

[1]Total job openings represent the sum of employment increases and net replacements. If employment change is negative, job openings due to growth are zero and total job openings equal net replacements.

Table 4-7. Employment, by Occupation, 2008 and Projected 2018—*Continued*

(Numbers in thousands, percent.)

Occupation	Employment				Change, 2008–2018		Total job openings due to growth and net replacements, 2008–2018[1]
	Number		Percent distribution		Number	Percent	
	2008	2018	2008	2018			
Personal Care and Services	5 044	6 075	3.3	3.7	1 031	20.4	2 284
Supervisors of personal care and service workers	278	317	0.2	0.2	38	13.7	111
First-line supervisors/managers of gaming workers	65	71	0.0	0.0	6	8.4	20
Gaming supervisors	41	46	0.0	0.0	5	11.8	14
Slot key persons	24	25	0.0	0.0	1	2.8	6
First-line supervisors/managers of personal service workers	213	246	0.1	0.1	33	15.4	91
Animal care and service workers	220	266	0.1	0.2	46	20.6	93
Animal trainers	47	57	0.0	0.0	10	20.4	19
Nonfarm animal caretakers	173	209	0.1	0.1	36	20.7	74
Entertainment attendants and related workers	569	652	0.4	0.4	83	14.6	378
Gaming services workers	121	142	0.1	0.1	21	17.4	73
Gaming dealers	91	108	0.1	0.1	17	19.0	56
Gaming and sports book writers and runners	16	18	0.0	0.0	2	13.2	9
Gaming service workers, all other	14	16	0.0	0.0	2	11.7	8
Motion picture projectionists	11	11	0.0	0.0	0	0.6	5
Ushers, lobby attendants, and ticket takers	106	121	0.1	0.1	15	13.7	82
Miscellaneous entertainment attendants and related workers	331	378	0.2	0.2	47	14.3	219
Amusement and recreation attendants	263	298	0.2	0.2	35	13.3	171
Costume attendants	5	6	0.0	0.0	1	13.8	3
Locker room, coatroom, and dressing room attendants	19	21	0.0	0.0	2	13.2	12
Funeral service	43	53	0.0	0.0	10	22.1	30
Embalmers	9	9	0.0	0.0	0	5.2	5
Funeral attendants	35	44	0.0	0.0	9	26.2	26
Personal appearance	825	991	0.5	0.6	166	20.1	287
Barbers and cosmetologists	684	817	0.5	0.5	133	19.5	234
Barbers	54	60	0.0	0.0	6	11.6	14
Hairdressers, hairstylists, and cosmetologists	631	758	0.4	0.5	127	20.1	220
Miscellaneous personal appearance	141	173	0.1	0.1	33	23.3	53
Makeup artists, theatrical and performance	3	3	0.0	0.0	1	16.9	1
Manicurists and pedicurists	76	90	0.1	0.1	14	18.8	25
Shampooers	23	26	0.0	0.0	3	14.6	7
Skin care specialists	39	54	0.0	0.0	15	37.9	20
Transportation, tourism, and lodging attendants	236	261	0.2	0.2	25	10.5	89
Baggage porters, bellhops, and concierges	71	81	0.0	0.0	9	13.0	28
Baggage porters and bellhops	51	57	0.0	0.0	6	12.7	20
Concierges	21	24	0.0	0.0	3	13.7	8
Tour and travel guides	44	49	0.0	0.0	5	10.4	23
Tour guides and escorts	38	43	0.0	0.0	5	11.7	21
Travel guides	6	6	0.0	0.0	0	1.7	2
Transportation attendants	120	131	0.1	0.1	11	9.1	38
Flight attendants	99	107	0.1	0.1	8	8.1	30
Transportation attendants, except flight attendants and baggage porters	22	25	0.0	0.0	3	13.3	8
Other personal care and services	2 873	3 537	1.9	2.1	664	23.1	1 297
Childcare workers	1 302	1 444	0.9	0.9	142	10.9	523
Personal and home care aides	817	1 193	0.5	0.7	376	46.0	478
Recreation and fitness workers	589	714	0.4	0.4	125	21.2	231
Fitness trainers and aerobics instructors	261	338	0.2	0.2	77	29.4	124
Recreation workers	328	376	0.2	0.2	48	14.7	107
Residential advisers	57	62	0.0	0.0	5	9.1	25
Personal care and service workers, all other	109	124	0.1	0.1	16	14.3	40
Sales and Related	15 903	16 883	10.5	10.2	980	6.2	5 713
Supervisors of sales workers	2 192	2 305	1.5	1.4	113	5.1	580
First-line supervisors/managers of retail sales workers	1 686	1 774	1.1	1.1	88	5.2	450
First-line supervisors/managers of non-retail sales workers	507	531	0.3	0.3	24	4.8	130
Retail sales	8 737	9 251	5.8	5.6	514	5.9	3 573
Cashiers	3 572	3 696	2.4	2.2	123	3.4	1 730
Cashiers, except gaming	3 550	3 676	2.4	2.2	126	3.5	1 720
Gaming change persons and booth cashiers	22	20	0.0	0.0	-2	-10.4	10
Counter and rental clerks and parts salespersons	676	692	0.4	0.4	16	2.4	216
Counter and rental clerks	448	462	0.3	0.3	14	3.1	134
Parts salespersons	228	230	0.2	0.1	2	1.0	83
Retail salespersons	4 489	4 864	3.0	2.9	375	8.3	1 627
Sales representatives, services	1 614	1 788	1.1	1.1	174	10.8	561
Advertising sales agents	167	179	0.1	0.1	12	7.2	45
Insurance sales agents	435	486	0.3	0.3	52	11.9	153
Securities, commodities, and financial services sales agents	317	347	0.2	0.2	30	9.3	127
Travel agents	105	104	0.1	0.1	-1	-1.1	8
Sales representatives, services, all other	590	672	0.4	0.4	82	13.9	228
Sales representatives, wholesale and manufacturing	1 973	2 116	1.3	1.3	143	7.3	600
Sales representatives, wholesale and manufacturing, technical and scientific products	433	475	0.3	0.3	42	9.7	142
Sales representatives, wholesale and manufacturing, except technical and scientific products	1 540	1 641	1.0	1.0	101	6.6	458
Other sales and related workers	1 386	1 423	0.9	0.9	37	2.6	400
Models, demonstrators, and product promoters	105	113	0.1	0.1	8	7.3	38
Demonstrators and product promoters	103	110	0.1	0.1	7	7.1	37
Models	2	3	0.0	0.0	0	16.0	1
Real estate brokers and sales agents	518	592	0.3	0.4	74	14.4	159
Real estate brokers	123	134	0.1	0.1	11	8.6	31
Real estate sales agents	394	458	0.3	0.3	64	16.2	128
Sales engineers	78	85	0.1	0.1	7	8.8	35
Telemarketers	342	304	0.2	0.2	-38	-11.1	86

Note: Data may not sum to totals or 100 percent due to rounding.

[1]Total job openings represent the sum of employment increases and net replacements. If employment change is negative, job openings due to growth are zero and total job openings equal net replacements.

Table 4-7. Employment, by Occupation, 2008 and Projected 2018—*Continued*

(Numbers in thousands, percent.)

Occupation	Employment				Change, 2008–2018		Total job openings due to growth and net replacements, 2008–2018[1]
	Number		Percent distribution		Number	Percent	
	2008	2018	2008	2018			
Sales and Related—*Continued*							
Miscellaneous sales and related	344	329	0.2	0.2	-15	-4.2	82
Door-to-door sales workers, news and street vendors, and related workers	182	155	0.1	0.1	-27	-14.8	33
Sales and related workers, all other	162	175	0.1	0.1	12	7.6	49
Office and Administrative Support	24 101	25 943	16.0	15.6	1 842	7.6	7 255
Supervisors of office and administrative support workers	1 457	1 618	1.0	1.0	160	11.0	489
First-line supervisors/managers of office and administrative support workers	1 457	1 618	1.0	1.0	160	11.0	489
Communications equipment operators	182	163	0.1	0.1	-18	-10.0	37
Switchboard operators, including answering service	155	138	0.1	0.1	-17	-10.9	32
Telephone operators	23	22	0.0	0.0	-1	-3.6	4
Communications equipment operators, all other	4	3	0.0	0.0	0	-12.2	1
Financial clerks	3 911	4 313	2.6	2.6	402	10.3	1 152
Bill and account collectors	411	491	0.3	0.3	80	19.3	157
Billing and posting clerks and machine operators	529	610	0.4	0.4	81	15.3	168
Bookkeeping, accounting, and auditing clerks	2 064	2 276	1.4	1.4	212	10.3	460
Gaming cage workers	17	15	0.0	0.0	-2	-10.4	3
Payroll and timekeeping clerks	209	198	0.1	0.1	-11	-5.2	50
Procurement clerks	82	86	0.1	0.1	5	5.8	30
Tellers	601	638	0.4	0.4	38	6.2	284
Information and record clerks	5 685	6 230	3.8	3.7	546	9.6	2 352
Brokerage clerks	68	66	0.0	0.0	-2	-2.6	19
Correspondence clerks	14	12	0.0	0.0	-2	-13.8	4
Court, municipal, and license clerks	122	132	0.1	0.1	10	8.2	45
Credit authorizers, checkers, and clerks	64	66	0.0	0.0	2	2.8	20
Customer service representatives	2 252	2 652	1.5	1.6	400	17.7	1 108
Eligibility interviewers, government programs	120	131	0.1	0.1	11	9.2	39
File clerks	212	163	0.1	0.1	-50	-23.4	52
Hotel, motel, and resort desk clerks	230	262	0.2	0.2	32	13.7	110
Interviewers, except eligibility and loan	233	270	0.2	0.2	36	15.6	92
Library assistants, clerical	122	136	0.1	0.1	14	11.1	64
Loan interviewers and clerks	210	219	0.1	0.1	9	4.3	61
New accounts clerks	87	87	0.1	0.1	0	0.1	25
Order clerks	246	182	0.2	0.1	-64	-26.1	70
Human resources assistants, except payroll and timekeeping	170	160	0.1	0.1	-10	-5.7	48
Receptionists and information clerks	1 139	1 312	0.8	0.8	173	15.2	480
Reservation and transportation ticket agents and travel clerks	168	182	0.1	0.1	14	8.1	52
Information and record clerks, all other	227	200	0.2	0.1	-27	-11.8	64
Material recording, scheduling, dispatching, and distributing occupations	4 113	4 145	2.7	2.5	32	0.8	1 147
Cargo and freight agents	86	107	0.1	0.1	21	23.9	40
Couriers and messengers	122	122	0.1	0.1	0	-0.3	28
Dispatchers	296	308	0.2	0.2	13	4.3	79
Police, fire, and ambulance dispatchers	100	118	0.1	0.1	18	17.8	38
Dispatchers, except police, fire, and ambulance	196	191	0.1	0.1	-5	-2.6	40
Meter readers, utilities	45	36	0.0	0.0	-9	-20.0	13
Postal service workers	599	527	0.4	0.3	-72	-12.0	140
Postal service clerks	751	62	0.1	0.0	-14	-18.0	16
Postal service mail carriers	343	339	0.2	0.2	-4	-1.1	107
Postal service mail sorters, processors, and processing machine operators	180	125	0.1	0.1	-55	-30.3	17
Production, planning, and expediting clerks	284	288	0.2	0.2	4	1.5	74
Shipping, receiving, and traffic clerks	751	701	0.5	0.4	-49	-6.6	186
Stock clerks and order fillers	1 859	1 993	1.2	1.2	134	7.2	563
Weighers, measurers, checkers, and samplers, recordkeeping	72	62	0.0	0.0	-9	-13.1	25
Secretaries and administrative assistants	4 348	4 820	2.9	2.9	472	10.8	1 057
Executive secretaries and administrative assistants	1 594	1 799	1.1	1.1	204	12.8	419
Legal secretaries	263	311	0.2	0.2	48	18.4	84
Medical secretaries	471	597	0.3	0.4	126	26.6	189
Secretaries, except legal, medical, and executive	2 020	2 113	1.3	1.3	93	4.6	366
Other office and administrative support	4 405	4 654	2.9	2.8	249	5.7	1 021
Computer operators	110	90	0.1	0.1	-21	-18.6	12
Data entry and information processing	426	401	0.3	0.2	-26	-6.0	70
Data entry keyers	284	267	0.2	0.2	-17	-6.1	59
Word processors and typists	142	134	0.1	0.1	-8	-5.7	11
Desktop publishers	26	20	0.0	0.0	-6	-22.5	4
Insurance claims and policy processing clerks	254	254	0.2	0.2	1	0.3	34
Mail clerks and mail machine operators, except postal service	141	125	0.1	0.1	-17	-11.8	26
Office clerks, general	3 024	3 383	2.0	2.0	359	11.9	771
Office machine operators, except computer	80	74	0.1	0.0	-6	-7.6	27
Proofreaders and copy markers	18	17	0.0	0.0	-1	-6.1	3
Statistical assistants	18	19	0.0	0.0	1	5.1	4
Office and administrative support workers, all other	307	271	0.2	0.2	-36	-11.6	70
Farming, Fishing, and Forestry	1 035	1 026	0.7	0.6	-9	-0.9	291
Supervisors of farming, fishing, and forestry workers	49	52	0.0	0.0	4	7.8	16
Agricultural workers	872	857	0.6	0.5	-15	-1.7	239
Agricultural inspectors	17	19	0.0	0.0	2	12.8	6
Animal breeders	15	16	0.0	0.0	1	5.8	5
Graders and sorters, agricultural products	33	34	0.0	0.0	0	0.2	7
Miscellaneous agricultural	807	789	0.5	0.5	-18	-2.3	222
Fishing and hunting	36	33	0.0	0.0	-3	-7.6	9
Fishers and related fishing	36	33	0.0	0.0	-3	-7.7	9
Forest, conservation, and logging	79	84	0.1	0.1	5	6.3	27
Forest and conservation	13	14	0.0	0.0	1	8.5	5
Logging	66	70	0.0	0.0	4	5.9	22
Fallers	11	11	0.0	0.0	0	-2.9	3
Logging equipment operators	42	45	0.0	0.0	3	7.7	14
Log graders and scalers	6	5	0.0	0.0	0	-1.8	2
Logging workers, all other	8	9	0.0	0.0	1	13.5	3

Note: Data may not sum to totals or 100 percent due to rounding.

[1]Total job openings represent the sum of employment increases and net replacements. If employment change is negative, job openings due to growth are zero and total job openings equal net replacements.

Table 4-7. Employment, by Occupation, 2008 and Projected 2018—*Continued*

(Numbers in thousands, percent.)

Occupation	Employment				Change, 2008–2018		Total job openings due to growth and net replacements, 2008–2018[1]
	Number		Percent distribution		Number	Percent	
	2008	2018	2008	2018			
Construction and Extraction	7 810	8 829	5.2	5.3	1 019	13.0	2 396
Supervisors of construction and extraction workers	698	805	0.5	0.5	107	15.4	242
First-line supervisors/managers of construction and extraction workers	698	805	0.5	0.5	107	15.4	242
Construction trades and related	6 018	6 826	4.0	4.1	808	13.4	1 777
Boilermakers	20	24	0.0	0.0	4	18.8	8
Brickmasons, blockmasons, and stonemasons	160	179	0.1	0.1	19	11.5	59
Brickmasons and blockmasons	136	152	0.1	0.1	16	11.5	50
Stonemasons	24	27	0.0	0.0	3	11.6	9
Carpenters	1 285	1 450	0.9	0.9	165	12.9	325
Carpet, floor, and tile installers and finishers	161	172	0.1	0.1	11	7.1	54
Carpet installers	51	51	0.0	0.0	-1	-1.1	13
Floor layers, except carpet, wood, and hard tiles	21	21	0.0	0.0	0	-1.0	6
Floor sanders and finishers	12	14	0.0	0.0	1	11.3	5
Tile and marble setters	76	87	0.1	0.1	11	14.3	31
Cement masons, concrete finishers, and terrazzo workers	207	233	0.1	0.1	27	12.9	79
Cement masons and concrete finishers	201	227	0.1	0.1	26	12.9	76
Terrazzo workers and finishers	6	6	0.0	0.0	1	12.7	2
Construction laborers	1 249	1 505	0.8	0.9	256	20.5	339
Construction equipment operators	469	526	0.3	0.3	56	12.0	136
Paving, surfacing, and tamping equipment operators	60	67	0.0	0.0	7	11.5	17
Pile-driver operators	5	5	0.0	0.0	1	13.1	1
Operating engineers and other construction equipment operators	405	453	0.3	0.3	49	12.0	118
Drywall installers, ceiling tile installers, and tapers	189	214	0.1	0.1	25	13.4	46
Drywall and ceiling tile installers	151	172	0.1	0.1	21	13.5	37
Tapers	37	42	0.0	0.0	5	13.0	9
Electricians	695	778	0.5	0.5	83	11.9	251
Glaziers	54	58	0.0	0.0	4	7.7	24
Insulation workers	57	67	0.0	0.0	10	17.4	29
Insulation workers, floor, ceiling, and wall	28	32	0.0	0.0	4	15.2	13
Insulation workers, mechanical	30	36	0.0	0.0	6	19.4	16
Painters and paperhangers	450	480	0.3	0.3	30	6.6	107
Painters, construction and maintenance	443	474	0.3	0.3	31	7.0	107
Paperhangers	7	6	0.0	0.0	-1	-14.5	0
Pipelayers, plumbers, pipefitters, and steamfitters	556	642	0.4	0.4	86	15.5	198
Pipelayers	61	72	0.0	0.0	11	17.2	23
Plumbers, pipefitters, and steamfitters	495	571	0.3	0.3	76	15.3	176
Plasterers and stucco masons	49	52	0.0	0.0	3	6.6	11
Reinforcing iron and rebar workers	28	31	0.0	0.0	4	12.6	8
Roofers	149	155	0.1	0.1	6	3.8	30
Sheet metal workers	171	182	0.1	0.1	11	6.5	52
Structural iron and steel workers	70	79	0.0	0.0	9	12.4	20
Helpers—construction trades	382	456	0.3	0.3	75	19.5	156
Helpers—brickmasons, blockmasons, stonemasons, and tile and marble setters	51	59	0.0	0.0	8	16.4	19
Helpers—carpenters	80	99	0.1	0.1	19	23.3	35
Helpers—electricians	106	132	0.1	0.1	26	24.7	48
Helpers—painters, paperhangers, plasterers, and stucco masons	19	19	0.0	0.0	-1	-3.4	4
Helpers—pipelayers, plumbers, pipefitters, and steamfitters	80	101	0.1	0.1	21	25.7	37
Helpers—roofers	19	17	0.0	0.0	-2	-9.4	4
Helpers—construction trades, all other	27	30	0.0	0.0	3	12.3	9
Other construction and related	456	514	0.3	0.3	59	12.9	174
Construction and building inspectors	106	124	0.1	0.1	18	16.8	40
Elevator installers and repairers	25	27	0.0	0.0	2	9.2	9
Fence erectors	34	38	0.0	0.0	5	13.6	8
Hazardous materials removal	43	49	0.0	0.0	6	14.8	18
Highway maintenance	146	158	0.1	0.1	12	8.5	52
Rail-track laying and maintenance equipment operators	16	18	0.0	0.0	2	14.8	7
Septic tank servicers and sewer pipe cleaners	26	32	0.0	0.0	6	23.8	13
Miscellaneous construction and related	61	68	0.0	0.0	7	11.0	27
Segmental pavers	1	1	0.0	0.0	0	7.1	1
Construction and related workers, all other	60	66	0.0	0.0	7	11.1	27
Extraction workers	257	227	0.2	0.1	-30	-11.7	47
Derrick, rotary drill, and service unit operators, oil, gas, and mining	93	75	0.1	0.0	-18	-19.0	16
Derrick operators, oil and gas	25	19	0.0	0.0	-6	-23.0	4
Rotary drill operators, oil and gas	29	23	0.0	0.0	-6	-21.5	5
Service unit operators, oil, gas, and mining	39	33	0.0	0.0	-6	-14.7	7
Earth drillers, except oil and gas	23	25	0.0	0.0	2	7.1	6
Explosives workers, ordnance handling experts, and blasters	6	7	0.0	0.0	0	4.0	1
Mining machine operators	25	25	0.0	0.0	0	-0.8	5
Continuous mining machine operators	11	11	0.0	0.0	-1	-5.5	2
Mine cutting and channeling machine operators	9	10	0.0	0.0	0	4.4	2
Mining machine operators, all other	5	5	0.0	0.0	0	-0.4	1
Rock splitters, quarry	4	4	0.0	0.0	0	-1.7	1
Roof bolters, mining	5	5	0.0	0.0	0	-5.7	1
Roustabouts, oil and gas	66	57	0.0	0.0	-8	-12.5	11
Helpers—extraction workers	26	21	0.0	0.0	-5	-19.2	5
Extraction workers, all other	8	8	0.0	0.0	-1	-7.3	1
Installation, Maintenance, and Repair	5 798	6 238	3.8	3.8	440	7.6	1 586
Supervisors of installation, maintenance, and repair workers	449	468	0.3	0.3	19	4.3	137
First-line supervisors/managers of mechanics, installers, and repairers	449	468	0.3	0.3	19	4.3	137
Electrical and electronic equipment mechanics, installers, and repairers	659	683	0.4	0.4	24	3.7	150
Computer, automated teller, and office machine repairers	153	146	0.1	0.1	-7	-4.4	26
Radio and telecommunications equipment installers and reporters	209	208	0.1	0.1	-1	-0.3	37
Radio mechanics	6	6	0.0	0.0	0	-4.0	1
Telecommunications equipment installers and repairers, except line installers	203	203	0.1	0.1	-1	-0.2	36
Miscellaneous electrical and electronic equipment mechanics, installers, and repairers	297	329	0.2	0.2	32	10.6	87
Avionics technicians	19	21	0.0	0.0	2	10.6	5

Note: Data may not sum to totals or 100 percent due to rounding.

[1] Total job openings represent the sum of employment increases and net replacements. If employment change is negative, job openings due to growth are zero and total job openings equal net replacements.

Table 4-7. Employment, by Occupation, 2008 and Projected 2018—*Continued*

(Numbers in thousands, percent.)

Occupation	Employment				Change, 2008–2018		Total job openings due to growth and net replacements, 2008–2018[1]
	Number		Percent distribution		Number	Percent	
	2008	2018	2008	2018			
Installation, Maintenance, and Repair—*Continued*							
Electric motor, power tool, and related repairers	24	25	0.0	0.0	1	5.1	9
Electrical and electronics installers and repairers, transportation equipment	16	17	0.0	0.0	1	4.1	3
Electrical and electronics repairers, commercial and industrial equipment	78	81	0.1	0.0	3	3.8	16
Electrical and electronics repairers, powerhouse, substation, and relay	23	26	0.0	0.0	3	11.5	7
Electronic equipment installers and repairers, motor vehicles	20	20	0.0	0.0	0	0.1	3
Electronic home entertainment equipment installers and repairers	51	57	0.0	0.0	6	10.8	14
Security and fire alarm systems installers	66	83	0.0	0.0	16	24.8	28
Vehicle and mobile equipment mechanics, installers, and repairers	1 722	1 806	1.1	1.1	84	4.9	438
Aircraft mechanics and service technicians	122	129	0.1	0.1	8	6.4	31
Automotive technicians and repairers	950	987	0.6	0.6	37	3.9	230
Automotive body and related repairers	166	167	0.1	0.1	1	0.5	44
Automotive glass installers and repairers	20	20	0.0	0.0	0	1.8	4
Automotive service technicians and mechanics	764	800	0.5	0.5	36	4.7	182
Bus and truck mechanics and diesel engine specialists	263	278	0.2	0.2	15	5.7	75
Heavy vehicle and mobile equipment service technicians and mechanics	191	206	0.1	0.1	16	8.1	52
Farm equipment mechanics	31	33	0.0	0.0	2	6.9	8
Mobile heavy equipment mechanics, except engines	136	148	0.1	0.1	12	8.7	38
Rail car repairers	23	25	0.0	0.0	2	6.5	6
Small engine mechanics	70	75	0.0	0.0	5	6.8	19
Motorboat mechanics	22	23	0.0	0.0	1	5.6	6
Motorcycle mechanics	19	21	0.0	0.0	2	8.8	6
Outdoor power equipment and other small engine mechanics	29	31	0.0	0.0	2	6.4	8
Miscellaneous vehicle and mobile equipment mechanics, installers, and repairers	127	131	0.1	0.1	4	2.9	30
Bicycle repairers	10	12	0.0	0.0	2	19.3	4
Recreational vehicle service technicians	14	15	0.0	0.0	1	6.6	4
Tire repairers and changers	103	104	0.1	0.1	1	0.9	22
Other installation, maintenance, and repair occupations	2 969	3 282	2.0	2.0	313	10.6	863
Control and valve installers and repairers	62	63	0.0	0.0	1	2.1	11
Mechanical door repairers	17	19	0.0	0.0	2	10.9	5
Control and valve installers and repairers, except mechanical door	45	44	0.0	0.0	-1	-1.3	7
Heating, air-conditioning, and refrigeration mechanics and installers	308	395	0.2	0.2	87	28.1	136
Home appliance repairers	50	51	0.0	0.0	1	2.2	9
Industrial machinery installation, repair, and maintenance	1 772	1 945	1.2	1.2	173	9.7	445
Industrial machinery mechanics	288	309	0.2	0.2	21	7.3	62
Maintenance and repair workers, general	1 361	1 509	0.9	0.9	148	10.9	358
Maintenance workers, machinery	75	79	0.0	0.0	3	4.6	15
Millwrights	45	46	0.0	0.0	1	1.4	10
Refractory materials repairers, except brickmasons	3	2	0.0	0.0	0	-6.4	0
Line installers and repairers	285	292	0.2	0.2	7	2.3	73
Electrical power line installers and repairers	114	119	0.1	0.1	5	4.5	46
Telecommunications line installers and repairers	171	173	0.1	0.1	2	0.9	28
Precision instrument and equipment repairers	71	82	0.0	0.0	11	14.7	32
Camera and photographic equipment repairers	5	4	0.0	0.0	-1	-15.4	1
Medical equipment repairers	41	53	0.0	0.0	11	27.2	23
Musical instrument repairers and tuners	6	6	0.0	0.0	0	0.1	2
Watch repairers	3	3	0.0	0.0	0	-13.8	1
Precision instrument and equipment repairers, all other	16	16	0.0	0.0	0	2.5	5
Miscellaneous installation, maintenance, and repair	421	455	0.3	0.3	34	8.2	156
Coin, vending, and amusement machine servicers and repairers	44	47	0.0	0.0	3	7.0	18
Commercial divers	2	3	0.0	0.0	0	5.8	1
Fabric menders, except garment	1	1	0.0	0.0	0	-29.8	0
Locksmiths and safe repairers	22	25	0.0	0.0	3	12.0	6
Manufactured building and mobile home installers	10	11	0.0	0.0	1	5.2	1
Riggers	14	14	0.0	0.0	0	0.3	2
Signal and track switch repairers	7	7	0.0	0.0	0	1.2	1
Helpers—installation, maintenance, and repair	151	164	0.1	0.1	13	8.3	85
Installation, maintenance, and repair workers, all other	170	186	0.1	0.1	16	9.2	42
Production	10 083	9 734	6.7	5.9	-349	-3.5	2 156
Supervisors of production workers	681	646	0.5	0.4	-36	-5.2	92
First-line supervisors/managers of production and operating workers	681	646	0.5	0.4	-36	-5.2	92
Assemblers and fabricators	1 951	1 913	1.3	1.2	-38	-1.9	426
Aircraft structure, surfaces, rigging, and systems assemblers	44	48	0.0	0.0	4	9.4	13
Electrical, electronics, and electromechanical assemblers	298	254	0.2	0.2	-43	-14.5	46
Coil winders, tapers, and finishers	22	17	0.0	0.0	-6	-25.2	3
Electrical and electronic equipment assemblers	213	182	0.1	0.1	-31	-14.7	33
Electromechanical equipment assemblers	62	56	0.0	0.0	-6	-10.3	10
Engine and other machine assemblers	40	37	0.0	0.0	-3	-8.0	8
Structural metal fabricators and fitters	114	114	0.1	0.1	0	-0.4	24
Miscellaneous assemblers and fabricators	1 455	1 460	1.0	0.9	5	0.3	334
Fiberglass laminators and fabricators	30	29	0.0	0.0	-1	-4.6	7
Team assemblers	1 112	1 113	0.7	0.7	0	0.0	251
Timing device assemblers, adjusters, and calibrators	3	3	0.0	0.0	0	-4.4	1
Assemblers and fabricators, all other	310	316	0.2	0.2	6	1.9	76
Food processing	707	734	0.5	0.4	27	3.9	234
Bakers	152	152	0.1	0.1	0	0.2	39
Butchers and other meat, poultry, and fish processing	397	414	0.3	0.2	17	4.2	144
Butchers and meat cutters	129	131	0.1	0.1	2	1.5	43
Meat, poultry, and fish cutters and trimmers	170	180	0.1	0.1	11	6.4	65
Slaughterers and meat packers	98	103	0.1	0.1	4	4.2	36
Miscellaneous food processing	158	168	0.1	0.1	10	6.5	51
Food and tobacco roasting, baking, and drying machine operators and tenders	18	18	0.0	0.0	0	0.3	5
Food batchmakers	101	109	0.1	0.1	9	8.7	33
Food cooking machine operators and tenders	39	41	0.0	0.0	2	3.8	13
Metal workers and plastic	2 159	1 999	1.4	1.2	-159	-7.4	443
Computer control programmers and operators	158	165	0.1	0.1	7	4.2	40
Computer-controlled machine tool operators, metal and plastic	141	150	0.1	0.1	9	6.6	37

Note: Data may not sum to totals or 100 percent due to rounding.

[1]Total job openings represent the sum of employment increases and net replacements. If employment change is negative, job openings due to growth are zero and total job openings equal net replacements.

Table 4-7. Employment, by Occupation, 2008 and Projected 2018—*Continued*

(Numbers in thousands, percent.)

Occupation	Employment				Change, 2008–2018		Total job openings due to growth and net replacements, 2008–2018[1]
	Number		Percent distribution		Number	Percent	
	2008	2018	2008	2018			
Production—*Continued*							
Numerical tool and process control programmers	17	14	0.0	0.0	-3	-15.4	3
Forming machine setters, operators, and tenders, metal and plastic	153	138	0.1	0.1	-16	-10.1	30
Extruding and drawing machine setters, operators, and tenders, metal and plastic	91	86	0.1	0.1	-5	-5.2	18
Forging machine setters, operators, and tenders, metal and plastic	28	23	0.0	0.0	-6	-19.5	6
Rolling machine setters, operators, and tenders, metal and plastic	34	29	0.0	0.0	-5	-15.5	7
Machine tool cutting setters, operators, and tenders, metal and plastic	444	368	0.3	0.2	-76	-17.1	77
Cutting, punching, and press machine setters, operators, and tenders, metal and plastic	237	204	0.2	0.1	-33	-14.1	47
Drilling and boring machine tool setters, operators, and tenders, metal and plastic	33	24	0.0	0.0	-9	-26.9	3
Grinding, lapping, polishing, and buffing machine, tool setters, operators, and tenders, metal and plastic	93	78	0.1	0.0	-15	-15.9	14
Lathe and turning machine tool setters, operators, and tenders, metal and plastic	56	41	0.0	0.0	-15	-26.7	9
Milling and planing machine setters, operators, and tenders, metal and plastic	26	22	0.0	0.0	-4	-15.8	5
Machinists	422	402	0.3	0.2	-19	-4.6	56
Metal furnace and kiln operators and tenders	34	31	0.0	0.0	-3	-9.1	7
Metal-refining furnace operators and tenders	19	17	0.0	0.0	-2	-8.6	4
Pourers and casters, metal	15	14	0.0	0.0	-2	-9.6	3
Model makers and patternmakers, metal and plastic	17	16	0.0	0.0	-1	-5.8	1
Model makers, metal and plastic	10	10	0.0	0.0	-1	-5.9	1
Patternmakers, metal and plastic	7	7	0.0	0.0	0	-5.7	0
Molders and molding machine setters, operators, and tenders, metal and plastic	159	151	0.1	0.1	-8	-5.1	33
Foundry mold and coremakers	15	13	0.0	0.0	-2	-12.0	3
Molding, coremaking, and casting machine setters, operators and tenders, metal and plastic	144	137	0.1	0.1	-6	-4.4	30
Multiple machine tool setters, operators, and tenders, metal and plastic	86	73	0.1	0.0	-13	-14.7	17
Tool and die makers	84	78	0.1	0.0	-7	-8.0	5
Welding, soldering, and brazing	466	456	0.3	0.3	-11	-2.3	143
Welders, cutters, solderers, and brazers	412	406	0.3	0.2	-7	-1.6	126
Welding, soldering, and brazing machine setters, operators, and tenders	54	50	0.0	0.0	-4	-7.0	17
Miscellaneous metalworkers and plastic	135	122	0.1	0.1	-13	-9.7	35
Heat treating equipment setters, operators, and tenders, matal and plastic	23	21	0.0	0.0	-3	-10.6	11
Lay out workers, metal and plastic	8	7	0.0	0.0	-1	-11.6	2
Plating and coating machine setters, operators, and tenders, metal and plastic	40	35	0.0	0.0	-5	-12.4	11
Tool grinders, filers, and sharpeners	19	17	0.0	0.0	-1	-7.5	6
Metal workers and plastic workers, all other	45	42	0.0	0.0	-3	-7.4	6
Printing occupations	369	331	0.2	0.2	-38	-10.3	60
Bookbinders and bindery workers	67	54	0.0	0.0	-13	-19.3	10
Bindery workers	60	48	0.0	0.0	-12	-20.1	9
Bookbinders	6	5	0.0	0.0	-1	-12.1	1
Printers	303	278	0.2	0.2	-25	-8.3	50
Job printers	46	42	0.0	0.0	-4	-7.6	2
Prepress technicians and workers	61	50	0.0	0.0	-11	-17.7	8
Printing machine operators	196	185	0.1	0.1	-11	-5.5	41
Textile, apparel, and furnishings occupations	788	668	0.5	0.4	-120	-15.2	96
Laundry and dry-cleaning	235	242	0.2	0.1	7	2.8	48
Pressers, textile, garment, and related materials	67	61	0.0	0.0	-6	-8.2	3
Sewing machine operators	212	141	0.1	0.1	-72	-33.7	12
Shoe and leather	14	11	0.0	0.0	-3	-21.3	2
Shoe and leather workers and repairers	9	8	0.0	0.0	-1	-14.3	1
Shoe machine operators and tenders	5	3	0.0	0.0	-2	-34.8	1
Tailors, dressmakers, and sewers	67	65	0.0	0.0	-2	-3.1	7
Sewers, hand	12	11	0.0	0.0	-1	-8.2	1
Tailors, dressmakers, and custom sewers	55	54	0.0	0.0	-1	-2.0	6
Textile machine setters, operators, and tenders	100	61	0.1	0.0	-39	-39.0	13
Textile bleaching and dyeing machine operators and tenders	16	9	0.0	0.0	-7	-44.8	2
Textile cutting machine setters, operators, and tenders	19	13	0.0	0.0	-6	-31.0	3
Textile knitting and weaving machine setters, operators, and tenders	29	18	0.0	0.0	-12	-39.3	2
Textile winding, twisting, and drawing out machine setters, operators, and tenders	35	21	0.0	0.0	-14	-40.7	6
Miscellaneous textile, apparel, and furnishings workers	93	87	0.1	0.1	-6	-6.1	12
Extruding and forming machine setters, operators, and tenders, synthetic or glass fibers	14	9	0.0	0.0	-5	-33.9	2
Fabric and apparel patternmakers	8	6	0.0	0.0	-2	-27.2	1
Upholsterers	53	56	0.0	0.0	4	6.8	7
Textile, apparel, and furnishings workers, all other	18	16	0.0	0.0	-2	-12.7	3
Woodworkers	323	344	0.2	0.2	21	6.4	89
Cabinetmakers and bench carpenters	132	144	0.1	0.1	12	9.1	42
Furniture finishers	27	28	0.0	0.0	1	4.5	7
Model makers and patternmakers, wood	4	4	0.0	0.0	0	-0.6	1
Model makers, wood	2	2	0.0	0.0	0	2.4	0
Patternmakers, wood	2	2	0.0	0.0	0	-3.2	0
Woodworking machine setters, operators, and tenders	138	145	0.1	0.1	7	4.9	34
Sawing machine setters, operators, and tenders, wood	53	53	0.0	0.0	1	1.4	10
Woodworking machine setters, operators, and tenders, except sawing	86	92	0.1	0.1	6	7.0	24
Woodworkers, all other	23	24	0.0	0.0	1	3.3	6
Plant and system operators	325	332	0.2	0.2	7	2.2	102
Power plant operators, distributors, and dispatchers	50	51	0.0	0.0	0	0.4	18
Nuclear power reactor operators	5	6	0.0	0.0	1	18.9	3
Power distributors and dispatchers	10	10	0.0	0.0	0	-2.2	4
Power plant operators	35	35	0.0	0.0	-1	-1.6	12
Stationary engineers and boiler operators	42	44	0.0	0.0	2	5.2	9
Water and liquid waste treatment plant and system operators	113	136	0.1	0.1	23	19.8	47
Miscellaneous plant and system operators	120	102	0.1	0.1	-18	-14.7	28
Chemical plant and system operators	45	36	0.0	0.0	-9	-20.6	10
Gas plant operators	15	14	0.0	0.0	-1	-4.2	3
Petroleum pump system operators, refinery operators, and gaugers	47	40	0.0	0.0	-7	-15.2	11
Plant and system operators, all other	13	12	0.0	0.0	-1	-4.7	3

Note: Data may not sum to totals or 100 percent due to rounding.

[1]Total job openings represent the sum of employment increases and net replacements. If employment change is negative, job openings due to growth are zero and total job openings equal net replacements.

Table 4-7. Employment, by Occupation, 2008 and Projected 2018—*Continued*

(Numbers in thousands, percent.)

Occupation	Employment				Change, 2008–2018		Total job openings due to growth and net replacements, 2008–2018[1]
	Number		Percent distribution		Number	Percent	
	2008	2018	2008	2018			
Production—*Continued*							
Other production	2 781	2 767	1.8	1.7	-14	-0.5	614
Chemical processing machine setters, operators, and tenders	94	92	0.1	0.1	-2	-2.2	12
Chemical equipment operators and tenders	53	47	0.0	0.0	-6	-12.1	4
Separating, filtering, clarifying, precipitating, and still machine setters, operators, and tenders	41	45	0.0	0.0	4	10.6	8
Crushing, grinding, polishing, mixing, and blending	223	247	0.1	0.1	24	11.0	63
Crushing, grinding, and polishing machine setters, operators, and tenders	41	41	0.0	0.0	-1	-1.4	7
Grinding and polishing workers, hand	40	43	0.0	0.0	3	7.6	10
Mixing and blending machine setters, operators, and tenders	142	164	0.1	0.1	22	15.5	46
Cutting	99	93	0.1	0.1	-7	-6.8	21
Cutters and trimmers, hand	24	21	0.0	0.0	-3	-13.1	5
Cutting and slicing machine setters, operators, and tenders	75	72	0.0	0.0	-4	-4.8	16
Extruding, forming, pressing, and compacting machine setters, operators, and tenders	83	96	0.1	0.1	13	15.0	30
Furnace, kiln, oven, drier, and kettle operators and tenders	25	23	0.0	0.0	-2	-7.0	3
Inspectors, testers, sorters, samplers, and weighers	465	448	0.3	0.3	-17	-3.6	78
Jewelers and precious stone and metal	52	55	0.0	0.0	3	5.3	14
Medical, dental, and ophthalmic laboratory technicians	95	108	0.1	0.1	13	13.8	32
Dental laboratory technicians	46	52	0.0	0.0	6	13.9	15
Medical appliance technicians	14	15	0.0	0.0	2	10.9	4
Ophthalmic laboratory technicians	35	40	0.0	0.0	5	14.7	12
Packaging and filling machine operators and tenders	349	347	0.2	0.2	-2	-0.7	59
Painting workers	193	200	0.1	0.1	7	3.8	58
Coating, painting, and spraying machine setters, operators, and tenders	108	111	0.1	0.1	4	3.3	32
Painters, transportation equipment	52	53	0.0	0.0	0	0.8	14
Painting, coating, and decorating workers	33	36	0.0	0.0	3	10.2	12
Photographic process workers and processing machine operators	73	61	0.0	0.0	-12	-16.1	19
Photographic process workers	22	22	0.0	0.0	1	3.1	6
Photographic processing machine operators	51	39	0.0	0.0	-13	-24.3	13
Semiconductor processors	32	22	0.0	0.0	-10	-31.5	7
Miscellaneous production	999	976	0.7	0.6	-22	-2.2	221
Cementing and gluing machine operators and tenders	20	18	0.0	0.0	-2	-11.4	5
Cleaning, washing, and metal pickling equipment operators, and tenders	18	17	0.0	0.0	-1	-3.5	4
Cooling and freezing equipment operators and tenders	10	10	0.0	0.0	0	-0.4	2
Etchers and engravers	12	12	0.0	0.0	0	0.0	1
Molders, shapers, and casters, except metal and plastic	48	50	0.0	0.0	1	2.8	25
Paper goods machine setters, operators, and tenders	103	81	0.1	0.0	-22	-21.5	22
Tire builders	21	18	0.0	0.0	-4	-17.6	7
Helpers—production	484	484	0.3	0.3	0	-0.1	85
Production workers, all other	282	288	0.2	0.2	6	2.0	71
Transportation and Material Moving	9 826	10 217	6.5	6.1	391	4.0	2 857
Supervisors of transportation and material moving workers	406	405	0.3	0.2	-1	-0.3	77
Aircraft cargo handling supervisors	5	5	0.0	0.0	0	7.2	1
First-line supervisors/managers of helpers, laborers, and material movers, hand	184	190	0.1	0.1	7	3.6	39
First-line supervisors/managers of transportation and material moving machine and vehicle operators	218	210	0.1	0.1	-8	-3.7	38
Air transportation	150	169	0.1	0.1	18	12.1	69
Aircraft pilots and flight engineers	116	130	0.1	0.1	14	11.8	53
Airline pilots, copilots, and flight engineers	77	83	0.1	0.1	6	8.4	33
Commercial pilots	39	47	0.0	0.0	7	18.5	21
Air traffic controllers and airfield operations specialists	34	39	0.0	0.0	5	13.0	16
Air traffic controllers	26	30	0.0	0.0	3	13.0	12
Airfield operations specialists	8	9	0.0	0.0	1	13.0	4
Motor vehicle operators	4 171	4 552	2.8	2.7	381	9.1	1 124
Ambulance drivers and attendants, except emergency medical technicians	22	25	0.0	0.0	2	10.3	6
Bus drivers	648	691	0.4	0.4	44	6.8	157
Bus drivers, transit and intercity	194	210	0.1	0.1	16	8.2	50
Bus drivers, school	454	482	0.3	0.3	28	6.2	107
Driver/sales workers and truck drivers	3 189	3 481	2.1	2.1	292	9.2	863
Driver/sales workers	406	424	0.3	0.3	18	4.4	90
Truck drivers, heavy and tractor trailer	1 798	2 031	1.2	1.2	233	12.9	555
Truck drivers, light or delivery services	985	1 026	0.7	0.6	41	4.2	218
Taxi drivers and chauffeurs	232	268	0.2	0.2	36	15.5	77
Motor vehicle operators, all other	80	86	0.1	0.1	7	8.4	21
Rail transportation	131	142	0.1	0.1	12	9.2	55
Locomotive engineers and operators	51	56	0.0	0.0	5	9.9	22
Railroad brake, signal, and switch operators	26	28	0.0	0.0	2	9.4	11
Railroad conductors and yardmasters	41	44	0.0	0.0	3	6.9	17
Subway and streetcar operators	8	9	0.0	0.0	1	18.8	4
Rail transportation workers, all other	5	5	0.0	0.0	0	4.2	2
Water transportation	81	93	0.1	0.1	12	14.8	46
Sailors and marine oilers	33	37	0.0	0.0	4	11.7	18
Ship and boat captains and operators	37	43	0.0	0.0	6	16.3	21
Captains, mates, and pilots of water vessels	33	39	0.0	0.0	6	17.3	20
Motorboat operators	4	4	0.0	0.0	0	8.1	2
Ship engineers	12	14	0.0	0.0	2	18.6	7
Other transportation	303	319	0.2	0.2	16	5.2	128
Bridge and lock tenders	5	5	0.0	0.0	0	8.4	2
Parking lot attendants	136	142	0.1	0.1	6	4.2	55
Service station attendants	83	82	0.1	0.0	-2	-2.2	35
Traffic technicians	7	8	0.0	0.0	1	10.3	3
Transportation inspectors	27	32	0.0	0.0	5	18.3	11
Transportation workers, all other	44	50	0.0	0.0	6	12.7	22

Note: Data may not sum to totals or 100 percent due to rounding.

[1]Total job openings represent the sum of employment increases and net replacements. If employment change is negative, job openings due to growth are zero and total job openings equal net replacements.

Table 4-7. Employment, by Occupation, 2008 and Projected 2018—*Continued*

(Numbers in thousands, percent.)

Occupation	Employment				Change, 2008–2018		Total job openings due to growth and net replacements, 2008–2018[1]
	Number		Percent distribution		Number	Percent	
	2008	2018	2008	2018			
Transportation and Material Moving—*Continued*							
Material moving	4 584	4 537	3.0	2.7	-47	-1.0	1 357
Conveyor operators and tenders	41	37	0.0	0.0	-4	-9.3	12
Crane and tower operators	44	41	0.0	0.0	-3	-6.7	10
Dredge, excavating, and loading machine operators	82	89	0.1	0.1	6	7.7	31
Dredge operators	2	2	0.0	0.0	0	7.0	1
Excavating and loading machine and dragline operators	76	82	0.1	0.0	7	8.6	29
Loading machine operators, underground mining	4	4	0.0	0.0	0	-7.4	1
Hoist and winch operators	3	3	0.0	0.0	0	-8.0	1
Industrial truck and tractor operators	610	627	0.4	0.4	17	2.7	199
Laborers and material movers, hand	3 566	3 485	2.4	2.1	-80	-2.3	1 016
Cleaners of vehicles and equipment	349	353	0.2	0.2	4	1.0	128
Laborers and freight, stock, and material movers hand	2 317	2 299	1.5	1.4	-19	-0.8	746
Machine feeders and offbearers	141	110	0.1	0.1	-31	-22.2	16
Packers and packagers, hand	759	725	0.5	0.4	-34	-4.5	126
Pumping station operators	33	25	0.0	0.0	-8	-24.7	10
Gas compressor and gas pumping station operators	4	3	0.0	0.0	-1	-20.6	1
Laborers and freight, stock, and material movers, hand	10	8	0.0	0.0	-2	-19.6	3
Wellhead pumpers	19	13	0.0	0.0	-5	-28.4	5
Refuse and recyclable material collectors	149	177	0.1	0.1	28	18.6	71
Shuttle car operators	3	3	0.0	0.0	0	-4.0	1
Tank car, truck, and ship loaders	12	11	0.0	0.0	-1	-7.4	4
Material moving workers, all other	41	40	0.0	0.0	-1	-2.4	5

Note: Data may not sum to totals or 100 percent due to rounding.

[1]Total job openings represent the sum of employment increases and net replacements. If employment change is negative, job openings due to growth are zero and total job openings equal net replacements.

Chapter Five

PRODUCTIVITY AND COSTS

PRODUCTIVITY AND COSTS

HIGHLIGHTS

This chapter covers two kinds of productivity measures produced by the Bureau of Labor Statistics (BLS): output per hour (or labor productivity) and multifactor productivity. Multifactor productivity is designed to combine the joint influence of technological change, efficiency improvements, returns to scale, and other factors on economic growth. Industry data are based on the North American Industry Classification System (NAICS).

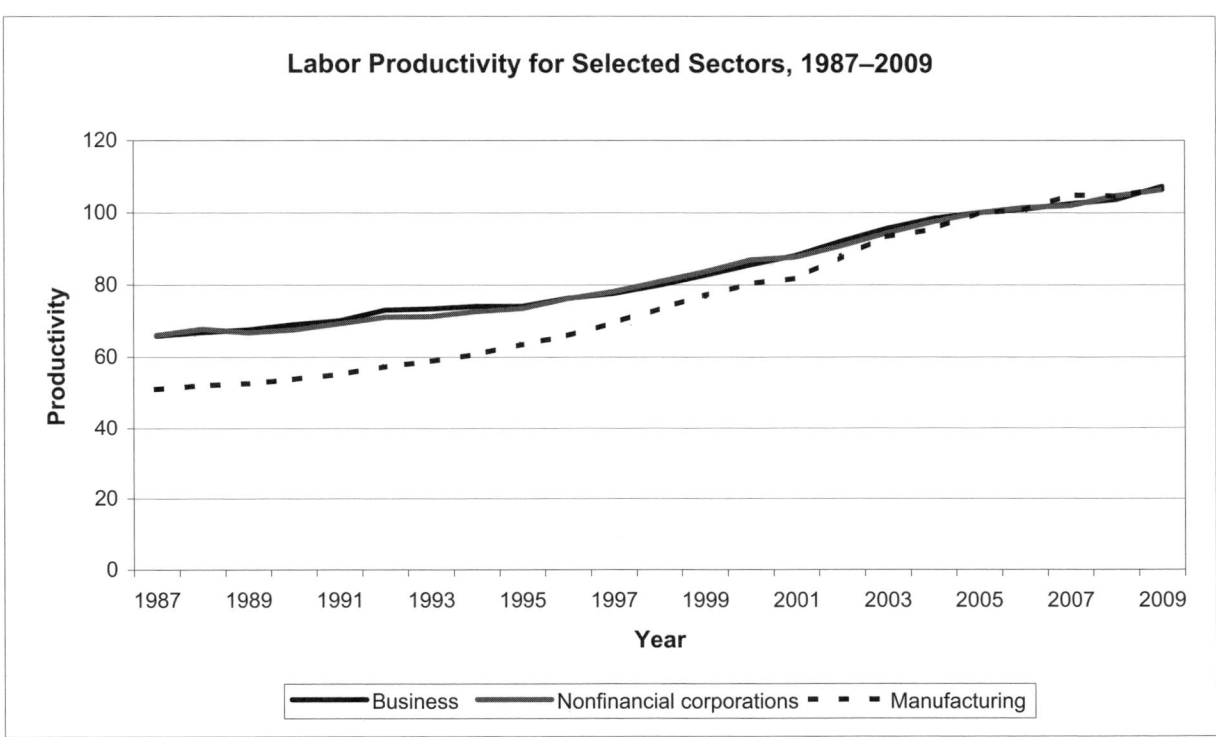

The levels of the output indexes for business, nonfinancial corporations, and manufacturing are not directly comparable because of different sources of the data. However, trends can be examined in output per hour or labor productivity. In 2009, labor productivity grew 3.6 percent in the business sector which is the fastest that it has grown since 2003. Productivity in manufacturing and nonfinancial corporations also grew but at much slower rates (2.0 percent and 2.6 percent respectively. (See Table 5-1.)

OTHER HIGHLIGHTS

- From 2008 to 2009, the number of hours in business declined 6.9 percent—the largest decline ever in one year since data has been collected. The next largest decline came in 1958 when hours declined by 4.5 percent. (See Table 5-1.)

- Labor productivity increased in retail trade and food services in 2008–2009 after decreasing in 2007–2008; however, it continued to decline in wholesale trade. From 1987 to 2009, the average annual percentage change in labor productivity was positive for all three industries. (See Table 5-3.)

- Within retail trade, output per hour increased in 29 industries. Florists (16.0 percent), other motor vehicle dealers (14.1 percent), and specialty food stores (13.9 percent) experienced the largest increases while vending machine operators (-9.2 percent) showed the biggest decline. (See Table 5-3.)

NOTES AND DEFINITIONS

PRODUCTIVITY AND COSTS

The Bureau of Labor Statistics (BLS) publishes three sets of productivity measures for the major sectors and subsectors of the U.S. economy, each using a distinct methodology. One measure includes labor productivity for the major sectors of business, nonfarm business, and nonfinancial corporations and for the subsectors of total, durable, and nondurable manufacturing. The second set includes multifactor productivity for major sectors; and the third measures multifactor productivity for total industries. Each set of measures involves a comparison of output and input measures.

Indexes of labor productivity show changes in the ratio of output to hours of labor input. These measures are used in economic analysis, public and private policymaking, and forecasting and analysis of prices, wages, and technological change.

Concepts and Definitions

Business sector output is constructed by excluding the following outputs from gross domestic product (GDP): general government, nonprofit institutions, paid employees of private households, and the rental value of owner-occupied dwellings. Corresponding exclusions are also made in labor inputs. These activities are excluded because theoretical or practical difficulties make it impossible to use them as a basis for the computation of meaningful productivity measures.

Hourly compensation costs are defined as the sum of wage and salary accruals and supplements to wages and salaries. Wage and salary accruals consist of the monetary remuneration of employees, including the compensation of corporate officers; commissions, tips, and bonuses; voluntary employee contributions to certain deferred compensation plans, such as 401(k) plans; employee gains from exercising nonqualified stock options; and receipts in kind that represent income. Supplements to wages and salaries consist of employer contributions for social insurance and employer payments (including payments in kind) to private pension and profit-sharing plans, group health and life insurance plans, privately administered workers' compensation plans. For employees (wage and salary workers), hourly compensation is measured relative to hours at work and includes payments made by employers for time not at work, such as vacation, holiday, and sick pay. Because compensation costs for the business and nonfarm business sectors would otherwise be severely understated, an estimate of the hourly compensation of proprietors of unincorporated businesses is made by assuming that their hourly compensation is equal to that of employees in the same sector.

Hours at work include paid time working, traveling between job sites, coffee breaks, and machine downtime.

Hours at work, however, exclude hours for which employees are paid but not at work.

The *nonfarm business sector* is a subset of the domestic economy and excludes the economic activities of the following: general government, private households, nonprofit organizations serving individuals, and farms.

Nonfinancial corporations are a subset of the domestic economy and excludes the economic activities of the following: general government, private households, nonprofit organizations serving individuals, and those corporations classified as offices of bank holding companies, offices of other holding companies, or offices in the finance and insurance sector.

Nonlabor payments include profits, consumption of fixed capital, taxes on production and imports less subsidies, net interest and miscellaneous payments, business current transfer payments, rental income of persons, and the current surplus of government enterprises.

Output is measured as an annual-weighted index of the changes in the various products or services (in real terms) provided for sale outside the industry. Real industry output is usually derived by deflating nominal sales or values of production using BLS price indexes, but for some industries it is measured by physical quantities of output. Industry output measures are constructed primarily using data from the economic censuses and annual surveys of the U.S. Census Bureau, U.S. Department of Commerce, together with information on price changes primarily from BLS. Output measures for some mining and utilities industries are based on physical quantity data from the Energy Information Administration, U.S. Department of Energy, while output measures for some transportation industries are based on physical quantity data from the Bureau of Transportation Statistics, U.S. Department of Transportation. Other data sources for some industries include the U.S. Geological Survey, U.S. Department of the Interior; the U.S. Postal Service; the Federal Deposit Insurance Corporation; and the Postal Rate Commission.

Productivity measures describe the relationship between industry output and the labor time involved in its production. They show the changes from period to period in the amount of goods and services produced per hour. Although the labor productivity measures relate output to hours of employees or all persons in an industry, they do not measure the specific contribution of labor or any other factor of production. Rather, they reflect the joint effects of many influences, including changes in technology; capital investment; utilization of capacity, energy, and materials; the use of purchased services inputs, including contract employment services; the organization of production; managerial skill; and the characteristics and effort of the workforce.

Unit labor costs show the growth in compensation relative to that of real output. These costs are calculated by dividing total labor compensation by real output. Changes in unit labor costs can be approximated by subtracting the change in productivity from the change in hourly compensation.

Multifactor Productivity Concepts and Definitions

Multifactor productivity indexes for private business and private nonfarm business are derived by dividing an output index by an index of labor input and capital services. The output indexes are computed as chained superlative indexes of components of real output. BLS adjusts output measures from the Bureau of Economic Analysis (BEA) to remove the output of government enterprises.

Capital services measures the services derived from the stock of physical assets and software. The assets included are computers, software, communications and other information processing equipment, other fixed business equipment, structures, inventories, rental residences, and land. Investments, depreciation, capital income, and rental prices are estimated for each of these eight aggregates. Rental prices reflect the nominal rates of return and rates of economic depreciation and revaluation for the specific asset. Rental prices are adjusted for the effects of taxes. Data on investments in physical assets are obtained from BEA. Capital input measures constructed for the preliminary MFP measures are based on less detail than those for full MFP measure.

Combined inputs involve combining labor and capital inputs using a Tornqvist index. Growth rates of labor and capital input are combined with weights that represent each component's share of total costs. Total costs are defined as the value of output (Gross Product Originating) less a portion of taxes on production and imports. Most taxes on production and imports, such as excise taxes, are excluded from costs; however, property and motor vehicle taxes remain in total costs. The index uses changing weights: The share in each year is averaged with the preceding year's share.

Labor input is total hours worked multiplied by a labor composition index. Hours paid of employees are largely obtained from BLS's Current Employment Survey (CES). These hours of employees are then converted to an at-work basis by using information from the Employment Cost Index (ECI) of the National Compensation Survey (NCS) and the Hours at Work Survey. Hours at work for non-production and supervisory workers are derived using data from the CPS, the CES, and the NCS. The hours at work of proprietors, unpaid family workers, and farm employees are derived from the Current Population Survey.

Multifactor productivity measures describe the relationship between output in real terms and the inputs involved in its production. They do not measure the specific contributions of labor, capital, or any other factor of production. Rather, multifactor productivity is designed to measure the joint influences of output, capital, and labor on economic growth of technological change, efficiency improvements, returns to scale, reallocation of resources due to shifts in factor inputs across industries, and other factors. The multifactor productivity indexes for private business and private nonfarm business are derived by dividing an output index by an index of labor input and capital services. The output indexes are computed as chained superlative indexes (Fisher Ideal indexes) of components of real output. BLS adjusts BEA output measures to remove the output of government enterprises.

Sources of Additional Information

Productivity concepts and methodology are described in Chapters 10 and 11 of the *BLS Handbook of Methods*. More information on productivity can be found in BLS news releases on the BLS Web site at <http://www.bls.gov/lpc/>.

Table 5-1. Indexes of Productivity and Related Data, 1947–2009

(2005 = 100.)

Year	Business											
	Output per hour	Output	Hours	Hourly compensation	Real hourly compensation	Unit labor costs	Unit nonlabor payments	Implicit price deflator	Employment	Output per person	Compensation in current dollars	Nonlabor payments in current dollars
1947	23.5	12.6	53.6	4.3	34.3	18.2	14.1	16.6	46.3	27.2	2.3	1.8
1948	24.6	13.3	54.0	4.7	34.4	18.9	15.6	17.6	46.9	28.4	2.5	2.1
1949	25.2	13.2	52.3	4.7	35.3	18.7	15.5	17.4	45.8	28.8	2.5	2.0
1950	27.3	14.5	53.0	5.1	37.3	18.5	16.3	17.6	46.3	31.3	2.7	2.4
1951	28.1	15.4	54.7	5.5	37.9	19.7	17.9	19.0	47.5	32.4	3.0	2.8
1952	28.9	15.9	54.9	5.9	39.5	20.3	17.6	19.2	47.7	33.3	3.2	2.8
1953	30.0	16.6	55.5	6.3	41.7	20.9	17.1	19.4	48.4	34.4	3.5	2.8
1954	30.6	16.4	53.7	6.5	42.7	21.1	17.0	19.5	47.2	34.8	3.5	2.8
1955	31.9	17.8	55.7	6.6	44.0	20.7	18.2	19.7	48.6	36.6	3.7	3.2
1956	31.9	18.1	56.5	7.1	46.2	22.1	17.7	20.4	49.6	36.4	4.0	3.2
1957	33.0	18.4	55.7	7.5	47.6	22.8	18.3	21.0	49.5	37.1	4.2	3.4
1958	33.9	18.0	53.2	7.8	48.3	23.1	18.7	21.4	47.6	37.9	4.2	3.4
1959	35.2	19.5	55.4	8.2	50.0	23.2	19.0	21.5	49.1	39.8	4.5	3.7
1960	35.8	19.9	55.5	8.5	51.2	23.8	18.8	21.8	49.3	40.3	4.7	3.7
1961	37.1	20.3	54.7	8.8	52.6	23.8	19.1	21.9	48.8	41.5	4.8	3.9
1962	38.8	21.6	55.7	9.2	54.4	23.8	19.7	22.2	49.4	43.7	5.1	4.2
1963	40.3	22.6	56.1	9.6	55.6	23.7	20.1	22.3	49.7	45.4	5.4	4.5
1964	41.6	24.0	57.7	9.9	57.0	23.8	20.6	22.5	50.6	47.4	5.7	4.9
1965	43.1	25.7	59.6	10.3	58.2	23.9	21.4	22.9	52.1	49.3	6.1	5.5
1966	44.9	27.4	61.2	11.0	60.3	24.5	21.9	23.5	53.6	51.2	6.7	6.0
1967	45.8	28.0	61.0	11.6	61.9	25.3	22.3	24.1	54.4	51.5	7.1	6.2
1968	47.4	29.4	61.9	12.5	64.2	26.5	22.9	25.1	55.4	53.0	7.8	6.7
1969	47.7	30.3	63.5	13.4	65.1	28.2	23.2	26.2	57.2	52.9	8.5	7.0
1970	48.6	30.3	62.2	14.4	66.3	29.7	23.7	27.3	57.0	53.1	9.0	7.2
1971	50.6	31.4	62.1	15.4	67.5	30.3	25.7	28.5	57.1	55.0	9.5	8.1
1972	52.2	33.4	64.0	16.3	69.6	31.3	26.9	29.5	58.8	56.9	10.5	9.0
1973	53.8	35.8	66.5	17.7	71.0	32.9	28.3	31.1	61.3	58.3	11.8	10.1
1974	52.9	35.2	66.6	19.4	70.1	36.7	30.1	34.1	62.3	56.6	12.9	10.6
1975	54.8	34.9	63.7	21.4	70.8	39.0	34.9	37.4	60.4	57.8	13.6	12.2
1976	56.6	37.2	65.8	23.2	72.7	41.1	36.7	39.4	62.3	59.8	15.3	13.7
1977	57.5	39.3	68.3	25.1	73.7	43.6	38.8	41.7	65.0	60.5	17.1	15.3
1978	58.1	41.8	71.8	27.3	74.9	46.9	41.3	44.7	68.5	60.9	19.6	17.2
1979	58.1	43.2	74.3	29.9	74.9	51.4	44.0	48.5	71.2	60.6	22.2	19.0
1980	58.0	42.7	73.6	33.1	74.6	57.0	46.4	52.8	71.4	59.8	24.3	19.8
1981	59.2	43.9	74.1	36.2	74.5	61.2	52.4	57.7	72.1	60.8	26.8	23.0
1982	58.7	42.5	72.5	38.8	75.4	66.1	53.2	61.0	70.9	60.0	28.1	22.6
1983	60.8	44.8	73.7	40.4	75.3	66.5	57.9	63.1	71.5	62.7	29.8	25.9
1984	62.4	48.7	78.0	42.1	75.4	67.5	61.0	64.9	75.2	64.8	32.9	29.7
1985	63.8	51.0	79.9	44.1	76.3	69.1	62.4	66.4	77.0	66.2	35.2	31.8
1986	65.7	52.9	80.5	46.4	78.8	70.6	62.9	67.5	78.3	67.5	37.3	33.3
1987	65.9	54.6	82.9	48.0	79.0	72.9	63.4	69.2	80.4	67.9	39.8	34.6
1988	66.9	57.0	85.2	50.5	80.1	75.6	64.9	71.3	82.9	68.7	43.0	37.0
1989	67.6	59.1	87.4	51.9	78.9	76.8	69.6	74.0	84.7	69.8	45.4	41.1
1990	69.0	60.0	86.9	55.2	80.0	80.0	71.4	76.6	85.2	70.4	48.0	42.8
1991	70.1	59.5	84.9	58.0	81.1	82.8	73.3	79.1	83.9	70.9	49.3	43.6
1992	73.0	61.8	84.7	61.1	83.3	83.7	75.8	80.6	83.4	74.1	51.7	46.9
1993	73.4	63.8	86.9	62.5	83.1	85.2	77.7	82.2	85.2	74.9	54.3	49.5
1994	74.0	66.9	90.4	63.4	82.6	85.7	80.5	83.6	88.1	76.0	57.3	53.8
1995	74.1	68.8	92.9	64.7	82.3	87.4	81.6	85.1	90.5	76.0	60.1	56.2
1996	76.2	71.9	94.4	66.9	82.9	87.8	84.4	86.5	92.5	77.8	63.2	60.7
1997	77.6	75.7	97.5	69.1	83.8	89.1	85.9	87.8	95.0	79.6	67.4	65.0
1998	79.9	79.4	99.4	73.3	87.7	91.8	83.3	88.4	97.0	81.9	72.9	66.2
1999	82.7	83.9	101.4	76.6	89.8	92.7	83.7	89.1	98.5	85.1	77.7	70.3
2000	85.6	87.7	102.4	82.3	93.3	96.1	82.6	90.8	100.2	87.5	84.3	72.4
2001	88.1	88.4	100.3	86.1	95.0	97.7	84.2	92.4	99.4	88.9	86.4	74.4
2002	92.1	90.1	97.8	88.8	96.3	96.4	88.0	93.1	97.2	92.7	86.9	79.3
2003	95.6	92.9	97.2	93.0	98.7	97.3	90.0	94.4	97.0	95.8	90.4	83.6
2004	98.4	96.7	98.3	96.2	99.5	97.8	95.4	96.9	98.2	98.5	94.6	92.3
2005	100.0	100.0	100.0	100.0	100.0	100.0	100.0	100.0	100.0	100.0	100.0	100.0
2006	100.9	103.1	102.1	103.8	100.5	102.8	103.1	102.9	101.8	101.2	106.0	106.2
2007	102.5	105.2	102.6	108.1	101.8	105.4	106.0	105.7	102.6	102.5	110.9	111.4
2008	103.6	104.2	100.5	111.5	101.1	107.6	107.5	107.6	101.1	103.0	112.1	112.0
2009	107.3	100.4	93.6	113.6	103.4	105.9	111.6	108.1	95.5	105.1	106.3	112.0

Table 5-1. Indexes of Productivity and Related Data, 1947–2009—*Continued*

(2005 = 100.)

Year	Nonfarm business											
	Output per hour	Output	Hours	Hourly compensation	Real hourly compensation	Unit labor costs	Unit nonlabor payments	Implicit price deflator	Employment	Output per person	Compensation in current dollars	Nonlabor payments in current dollars
1947	27.2	12.4	45.5	4.6	36.7	16.9	13.3	15.5	38.9	31.8	2.1	1.6
1948	28.0	12.9	46.3	5.0	36.9	17.9	14.5	16.5	39.7	32.6	2.3	1.9
1949	28.9	12.9	44.5	5.1	38.5	17.8	14.9	16.7	38.6	33.3	2.3	1.9
1950	30.8	14.2	45.9	5.4	40.2	17.7	15.6	16.8	39.5	35.8	2.5	2.2
1951	31.7	15.2	48.1	5.9	40.5	18.7	16.8	17.9	41.3	36.8	2.8	2.6
1952	32.2	15.7	48.6	6.2	42.0	19.4	16.7	18.3	41.8	37.4	3.0	2.6
1953	33.0	16.4	49.8	6.6	44.0	20.0	16.6	18.7	43.1	38.1	3.3	2.7
1954	33.6	16.2	48.1	6.8	45.0	20.2	16.6	18.8	41.9	38.6	3.3	2.7
1955	35.0	17.5	50.1	7.1	46.9	20.1	17.7	19.2	43.2	40.6	3.5	3.1
1956	34.8	17.8	51.3	7.5	49.0	21.5	17.2	19.8	44.4	40.2	3.8	3.1
1957	35.7	18.2	51.0	7.9	50.2	22.2	17.8	20.5	44.6	40.7	4.0	3.2
1958	36.4	17.8	48.9	8.2	50.7	22.6	18.0	20.8	43.1	41.4	4.0	3.2
1959	37.9	19.4	51.1	8.6	52.3	22.6	18.6	21.0	44.6	43.4	4.4	3.6
1960	38.3	19.7	51.4	8.9	53.7	23.3	18.1	21.3	45.1	43.7	4.6	3.6
1961	39.5	20.1	50.9	9.2	54.9	23.3	18.5	21.4	44.8	44.9	4.7	3.7
1962	41.3	21.5	52.0	9.6	56.5	23.2	19.2	21.6	45.6	47.1	5.0	4.1
1963	42.7	22.5	52.6	9.9	57.7	23.2	19.6	21.8	46.1	48.7	5.2	4.4
1964	44.0	24.0	54.5	10.2	58.7	23.3	20.3	22.1	47.2	50.8	5.6	4.9
1965	45.3	25.7	56.6	10.6	59.7	23.3	20.9	22.4	48.9	52.5	6.0	5.4
1966	46.9	27.5	58.6	11.2	61.5	23.8	21.4	22.9	50.8	54.1	6.6	5.9
1967	47.8	28.0	58.6	11.8	63.1	24.8	21.8	23.6	51.7	54.1	6.9	6.1
1968	49.4	29.4	59.6	12.8	65.3	25.8	22.5	24.5	52.9	55.7	7.6	6.6
1969	49.5	30.3	61.3	13.6	66.2	27.6	22.7	25.6	54.8	55.4	8.4	6.9
1970	50.2	30.3	60.4	14.6	67.1	29.1	23.2	26.8	54.8	55.3	8.8	7.0
1971	52.2	31.5	60.2	15.5	68.3	29.8	25.1	27.9	55.0	57.2	9.4	7.9
1972	54.0	33.6	62.2	16.6	70.5	30.7	25.9	28.8	56.6	59.2	10.3	8.7
1973	55.7	36.0	64.7	17.9	71.8	32.2	26.2	29.8	59.2	60.9	11.6	9.4
1974	54.8	35.5	64.8	19.7	71.0	35.9	28.3	32.9	60.1	59.0	12.7	10.1
1975	56.3	34.9	62.0	21.6	71.6	38.4	33.4	36.4	58.4	59.8	13.4	11.6
1976	58.1	37.4	64.2	23.5	73.4	40.3	35.5	38.4	60.4	61.9	15.1	13.3
1977	59.1	39.4	66.8	25.4	74.5	42.9	37.7	40.9	63.1	62.5	16.9	14.9
1978	59.8	42.0	70.3	27.6	75.8	46.1	39.7	43.6	66.6	63.1	19.4	16.7
1979	59.6	43.4	72.8	30.2	75.7	50.7	42.2	47.3	69.5	62.4	22.0	18.3
1980	59.4	42.9	72.2	33.4	75.4	56.2	45.2	51.9	69.7	61.5	24.1	19.4
1981	60.3	43.8	72.7	36.7	75.5	60.8	50.7	56.8	70.5	62.2	26.6	22.2
1982	59.6	42.4	71.1	39.3	76.3	65.8	51.9	60.4	69.3	61.1	27.9	22.0
1983	62.2	45.1	72.5	40.9	76.2	65.7	57.0	62.3	70.0	64.4	29.6	25.7
1984	63.5	48.8	76.9	42.6	76.2	67.0	59.5	64.1	73.8	66.2	32.7	29.0
1985	64.5	50.9	78.9	44.5	76.9	68.9	61.3	65.9	75.9	67.1	35.1	31.2
1986	66.5	52.9	79.5	46.8	79.5	70.4	61.9	67.0	77.2	68.5	37.2	32.8
1987	66.7	54.7	81.9	48.5	79.7	72.7	62.4	68.6	79.4	68.9	39.7	34.1
1988	67.8	57.2	84.3	50.9	80.8	75.1	64.0	70.7	81.9	69.8	42.9	36.6
1989	68.3	59.2	86.6	52.2	79.4	76.4	68.4	73.3	83.8	70.7	45.2	40.5
1990	69.6	60.0	86.3	55.5	80.3	79.7	70.3	76.0	84.4	71.1	47.9	42.2
1991	70.7	59.5	84.2	58.4	81.6	82.6	72.5	78.6	83.0	71.7	49.1	43.1
1992	73.5	61.7	84.0	61.5	83.9	83.7	74.8	80.2	82.5	74.8	51.7	46.2
1993	73.9	63.9	86.4	62.7	83.5	84.9	77.0	81.8	84.5	75.6	54.2	49.2
1994	74.7	66.9	89.6	63.9	83.2	85.6	79.8	83.3	87.2	76.7	57.2	53.3
1995	75.0	69.0	92.0	65.2	82.9	87.0	81.3	84.8	89.7	76.9	60.0	56.1
1996	76.9	72.0	93.7	67.3	83.4	87.6	83.4	85.9	91.8	78.4	63.1	60.1
1997	78.1	75.7	96.9	69.4	84.2	88.9	85.3	87.5	94.4	80.2	67.3	64.6
1998	80.4	79.6	99.0	73.6	88.0	91.6	83.0	88.2	96.5	82.5	72.9	66.0
1999	83.0	84.0	101.2	76.8	89.9	92.4	83.8	89.0	98.2	85.5	77.7	70.4
2000	85.9	87.7	102.2	82.5	93.5	96.1	82.7	90.8	100.0	87.8	84.3	72.5
2001	88.4	88.5	100.2	86.2	95.0	97.5	84.3	92.3	99.3	89.1	86.3	74.6
2002	92.4	90.2	97.7	88.9	96.5	96.2	88.4	93.1	97.0	93.0	86.8	79.7
2003	95.7	92.9	97.1	93.1	98.8	97.2	89.9	94.3	96.9	95.9	90.4	83.5
2004	98.4	96.8	98.3	96.2	99.4	97.8	94.8	96.6	98.2	98.5	94.6	91.7
2005	100.0	100.0	100.0	100.0	100.0	100.0	100.0	100.0	100.0	100.0	100.0	100.0
2006	100.9	103.1	102.2	103.8	100.5	102.8	103.3	103.0	101.9	101.2	106.0	106.5
2007	102.5	105.3	102.7	107.9	101.6	105.3	105.8	105.5	102.7	102.6	110.9	111.4
2008	103.6	104.2	100.6	111.5	101.1	107.6	107.0	107.4	101.1	103.0	112.1	111.5
2009	107.2	100.3	93.5	113.5	103.3	105.9	111.9	108.3	95.5	105.0	106.2	112.3

Table 5-1. Indexes of Productivity and Related Data, 1947–2008—*Continued*

(2005 = 100.)

Year	Nonfinancial corporations												
	Output per hour	Output	Hours	Hourly compensation	Real hourly compensation	Unit labor costs	Unit nonlabor costs	Unit profits	Implicit price deflator	Employment	Output per person	Compensation in current dollars	Nonlabor payments in current dollars
1947	...	...	...	...	...	...	...	...	...	...	...	...	...
1948	...	...	...	...	...	...	...	...	...	...	...	...	...
1949	...	...	...	...	...	...	...	...	...	...	...	...	...
1950	...	...	...	...	...	...	...	...	...	...	...	...	...
1951	...	...	...	...	...	...	...	...	...	...	...	...	...
1952	...	...	...	...	...	...	...	...	...	...	...	...	...
1953	...	...	...	...	...	...	...	...	...	...	...	...	...
1954	...	...	...	...	...	...	...	...	...	...	...	...	...
1955	...	...	...	...	...	...	...	...	...	...	...	...	...
1956	...	...	...	...	...	...	...	...	...	...	...	...	...
1957	...	...	...	...	...	...	...	...	...	...	...	3.9	3.5
1958	36.7	14.8	40.4	9.7	59.5	26.3	21.2	28.6	25.4	35.9	41.3	4.3	4.1
1959	38.5	16.5	42.9	10.0	61.3	26.0	20.4	33.3	25.6	37.6	43.9		
1960	39.2	17.1	43.5	10.4	62.7	26.6	20.8	30.7	25.7	38.4	44.4	4.5	4.1
1961	40.4	17.4	43.1	10.8	64.1	26.6	21.2	30.7	25.8	38.1	45.7	4.6	4.3
1962	42.2	18.9	44.8	11.2	65.9	26.5	20.9	33.2	26.0	39.4	48.0	5.0	4.8
1963	43.7	20.1	45.9	11.5	67.0	26.3	20.8	35.1	26.1	40.2	49.9	5.3	5.1
1964	44.4	21.5	48.3	11.7	67.4	26.4	20.7	36.4	26.3	41.7	51.5	5.7	5.6
1965	45.5	23.3	51.1	12.1	68.3	26.5	20.6	39.1	26.7	43.9	53.0	6.2	6.3
1966	46.4	24.9	53.8	12.8	70.1	27.5	20.6	38.9	27.3	46.4	53.7	6.9	6.7
1967	47.1	25.6	54.4	13.5	71.8	28.6	21.9	36.4	27.9	47.7	53.7	7.3	6.9
1968	48.8	27.3	55.9	14.5	74.1	29.7	23.3	36.3	29.0	49.4	55.2	8.1	7.6
1969	48.9	28.4	58.0	15.5	75.1	31.6	25.1	32.9	30.2	51.6	55.0	9.0	7.9
1970	49.2	28.1	57.2	16.6	76.0	33.6	28.3	26.8	31.5	51.7	54.4	9.5	7.8
1971	51.3	29.3	57.1	17.6	77.4	34.3	29.6	30.3	32.6	51.9	56.5	10.0	8.8
1972	52.4	31.6	60.2	18.5	79.0	35.4	29.6	32.9	33.7	54.5	57.9	11.2	9.7
1973	52.9	33.5	63.3	20.0	80.1	37.7	31.2	33.3	35.6	57.5	58.3	12.6	10.7
1974	51.9	33.0	63.5	21.9	78.9	42.1	35.8	29.5	39.0	58.6	56.3	13.9	11.1
1975	53.9	32.5	60.3	24.0	79.4	44.6	40.7	38.2	42.8	56.4	57.6	14.5	12.9
1976	55.7	35.1	63.1	26.0	81.2	46.6	40.5	43.2	44.7	58.9	59.7	16.4	14.5
1977	57.2	37.7	66.0	28.0	82.3	49.0	42.0	47.1	47.1	61.9	61.0	18.5	16.5
1978	57.9	40.2	69.4	30.6	84.1	52.9	44.1	48.9	50.2	65.4	61.5	21.3	18.4
1979	57.4	41.4	72.2	33.4	83.7	58.2	48.0	45.9	54.1	68.6	60.4	24.1	19.6
1980	57.2	41.0	71.7	36.7	82.9	64.2	56.2	41.2	59.4	68.9	59.5	26.3	20.9
1981	58.6	42.6	72.7	40.0	82.5	68.3	64.1	49.0	64.8	70.0	60.9	29.1	25.1
1982	58.8	41.6	70.8	42.7	82.9	72.6	71.1	45.3	68.7	68.5	60.8	30.2	25.9
1983	60.7	43.6	71.8	44.2	82.4	72.9	71.3	55.0	70.2	68.8	63.3	31.8	28.6
1984	62.1	47.4	76.4	46.1	82.5	74.2	70.5	66.0	72.3	72.8	65.1	35.2	32.7
1985	63.4	49.5	78.1	48.2	83.3	76.0	72.4	63.2	73.5	74.9	66.1	37.6	34.3
1986	64.7	50.7	78.4	50.5	85.9	78.1	75.8	54.2	74.5	76.0	66.8	39.6	34.7
1987	66.0	53.4	80.8	52.2	85.8	79.1	75.1	61.0	75.8	78.1	68.4	42.2	37.5
1988	67.7	56.5	83.4	54.4	86.3	80.3	76.0	67.5	77.7	80.7	70.0	45.4	41.3
1989	66.8	57.4	86.0	55.8	84.8	83.5	80.9	61.9	80.1	82.7	69.4	47.9	42.7
1990	67.5	58.3	86.3	58.4	84.6	86.6	84.5	59.5	82.6	84.1	69.3	50.4	44.3
1991	69.2	58.0	83.8	61.4	85.8	88.7	88.9	58.6	84.9	82.3	70.4	51.4	45.5
1992	71.0	59.8	84.2	64.3	87.7	90.6	86.7	62.1	86.0	82.4	72.6	54.1	46.8
1993	71.2	61.3	86.2	65.5	87.1	92.0	86.0	71.0	87.9	84.0	73.0	56.4	49.6
1994	72.7	65.3	89.9	66.7	86.8	91.8	86.4	83.2	89.4	87.1	75.0	59.9	55.7
1995	73.4	68.4	93.1	67.8	86.3	92.4	86.7	86.3	90.2	90.2	75.8	63.2	59.2
1996	76.2	72.2	94.8	69.8	86.5	91.7	86.2	93.4	90.6	92.5	78.0	66.2	64.0
1997	78.1	76.9	98.4	72.0	87.3	92.1	86.1	95.6	91.1	95.4	80.6	70.8	68.7
1998	80.8	81.3	100.5	76.3	91.2	94.3	86.5	83.9	91.1	97.7	83.2	76.7	69.6
1999	83.7	86.0	102.8	79.6	93.3	95.2	88.6	77.7	91.4	99.8	86.2	81.9	73.0
2000	87.0	90.6	104.1	85.5	97.0	98.4	91.7	64.7	92.5	101.8	89.0	89.1	74.7
2001	87.7	88.9	101.4	88.3	97.4	100.7	97.3	52.2	93.7	100.5	88.4	89.5	72.8
2002	90.9	89.3	98.3	90.7	98.4	99.8	97.9	60.0	94.3	97.7	91.4	89.1	75.8
2003	94.4	91.5	96.9	94.7	100.6	100.4	97.7	66.6	95.4	96.8	94.5	91.8	79.6
2004	97.5	95.8	98.2	96.9	100.2	99.4	96.5	88.6	97.3	98.0	97.8	95.2	89.9
2005	100.0	100.0	100.0	100.0	100.0	100.0	100.0	100.0	100.0	100.0	100.0	100.0	100.0
2006	101.4	103.7	102.3	102.8	99.6	101.4	103.1	111.7	103.1	102.0	101.7	105.2	110.0
2007	102.0	105.1	103.1	106.4	100.2	104.3	108.8	99.7	104.8	103.0	102.1	109.7	111.1
2008	104.7	106.1	101.3	110.1	99.8	105.1	112.9	85.5	104.5	101.6	104.4	111.5	109.8

. . . = Not available.

Table 5-1. Indexes of Productivity and Related Data, 1947–2009—*Continued*

(2005 = 100.)

Year	Manufacturing											
	Output per hour	Output	Hours	Hourly compen- sation	Real hourly compen- sation	Unit labor costs	Unit nonlabor payments	Implicit price deflator	Employment	Output per person	Compen- sation in current dollars	Nonlabor payments in current dollars
1947	. . .	. . .	. . .	. . .	. . .	. . .	. . .	. . .	. . .	. . .	. . .	. . .
1948	. . .	. . .	. . .	. . .	. . .	. . .	. . .	. . .	. . .	. . .	. . .	. . .
1949	. . .	. . .	. . .	. . .	. . .	. . .	. . .	. . .	. . .	. . .	. . .	. . .
1950	. . .	. . .	. . .	. . .	. . .	. . .	. . .	. . .	. . .	. . .	. . .	. . .
1951	. . .	. . .	. . .	. . .	. . .	. . .	. . .	. . .	. . .	. . .	. . .	. . .
1952	. . .	. . .	. . .	. . .	. . .	. . .	. . .	. . .	. . .	. . .	. . .	. . .
1953	. . .	. . .	. . .	. . .	. . .	. . .	. . .	. . .	. . .	. . .	. . .	. . .
1954	. . .	. . .	. . .	. . .	. . .	. . .	. . .	. . .	. . .	. . .	. . .	. . .
1955	. . .	. . .	. . .	. . .	. . .	. . .	. . .	. . .	. . .	. . .	. . .	. . .
1956	. . .	. . .	. . .	. . .	. . .	. . .	. . .	. . .	. . .	. . .	. . .	. . .
1957	. . .	. . .	. . .	. . .	. . .	. . .	. . .	. . .	. . .	. . .	. . .	. . .
1958	. . .	. . .	. . .	. . .	. . .	. . .	. . .	. . .	. . .	. . .	. . .	. . .
1959	. . .	. . .	. . .	. . .	. . .	. . .	. . .	. . .	. . .	. . .	. . .	. . .
1960	. . .	. . .	. . .	. . .	. . .	. . .	. . .	. . .	. . .	. . .	. . .	. . .
1961	. . .	. . .	. . .	. . .	. . .	. . .	. . .	. . .	. . .	. . .	. . .	. . .
1962	. . .	. . .	. . .	. . .	. . .	. . .	. . .	. . .	. . .	. . .	. . .	. . .
1963	. . .	. . .	. . .	. . .	. . .	. . .	. . .	. . .	. . .	. . .	. . .	. . .
1964	. . .	. . .	. . .	. . .	. . .	. . .	. . .	. . .	. . .	. . .	. . .	. . .
1965	. . .	. . .	. . .	. . .	. . .	. . .	. . .	. . .	. . .	. . .	. . .	. . .
1966	. . .	. . .	. . .	. . .	. . .	. . .	. . .	. . .	. . .	. . .	. . .	. . .
1967	. . .	. . .	. . .	. . .	. . .	. . .	. . .	. . .	. . .	. . .	. . .	. . .
1968	. . .	. . .	. . .	. . .	. . .	. . .	. . .	. . .	. . .	. . .	. . .	. . .
1969	. . .	. . .	. . .	. . .	. . .	. . .	. . .	. . .	. . .	. . .	. . .	. . .
1970	. . .	. . .	. . .	. . .	. . .	. . .	. . .	. . .	. . .	. . .	. . .	. . .
1971	. . .	. . .	. . .	. . .	. . .	. . .	. . .	. . .	. . .	. . .	. . .	. . .
1972	. . .	. . .	. . .	. . .	. . .	. . .	. . .	. . .	. . .	. . .	. . .	. . .
1973	. . .	. . .	. . .	. . .	. . .	. . .	. . .	. . .	. . .	. . .	. . .	. . .
1974	. . .	. . .	. . .	. . .	. . .	. . .	. . .	. . .	. . .	. . .	. . .	. . .
1975	. . .	. . .	. . .	. . .	. . .	. . .	. . .	. . .	. . .	. . .	. . .	. . .
1976	. . .	. . .	. . .	. . .	. . .	. . .	. . .	. . .	. . .	. . .	. . .	. . .
1977	. . .	. . .	. . .	. . .	. . .	. . .	. . .	. . .	. . .	. . .	. . .	. . .
1978	. . .	. . .	. . .	. . .	. . .	. . .	. . .	. . .	. . .	. . .	. . .	. . .
1979	. . .	. . .	. . .	. . .	. . .	. . .	. . .	. . .	. . .	. . .	. . .	. . .
1980	. . .	. . .	. . .	. . .	. . .	. . .	. . .	. . .	. . .	. . .	. . .	. . .
1981	. . .	. . .	. . .	. . .	. . .	. . .	. . .	. . .	. . .	. . .	. . .	. . .
1982	. . .	. . .	. . .	. . .	. . .	. . .	. . .	. . .	. . .	. . .	. . .	. . .
1983	. . .	. . .	. . .	. . .	. . .	. . .	. . .	. . .	. . .	. . .	. . .	. . .
1984	. . .	. . .	. . .	. . .	. . .	. . .	. . .	. . .	. . .	. . .	. . .	. . .
1985	. . .	. . .	. . .	. . .	. . .	. . .	. . .	. . .	. . .	. . .	. . .	. . .
1986	. . .	. . .	. . .	. . .	. . .	. . .	. . .	. . .	. . .	. . .	. . .	. . .
1987	51.0	62.9	123.2	49.4	81.2	96.8	71.5	78.4	123.2	51.0	60.8	45.0
1988	52.1	66.1	126.9	51.2	81.1	98.1	74.2	80.7	125.4	52.7	64.9	49.0
1989	52.7	67.2	127.7	52.7	80.1	100.1	78.3	84.2	126.1	53.3	67.3	52.6
1990	53.8	67.0	124.5	55.2	80.0	102.7	81.2	87.0	124.2	53.9	68.8	54.4
1991	55.2	65.8	119.3	58.5	81.8	106.0	80.7	87.6	119.9	54.9	69.8	53.1
1992	57.3	68.0	118.7	61.3	83.5	107.0	81.8	88.7	117.9	57.7	72.7	55.6
1993	58.8	70.7	120.3	62.7	83.4	106.7	82.7	89.2	118.0	59.9	75.3	58.4
1994	60.8	74.8	123.1	64.2	83.7	105.6	84.1	90.0	119.5	62.6	79.0	63.0
1995	63.6	78.8	123.9	65.2	83.0	102.6	87.3	91.5	121.2	65.0	80.8	68.7
1996	65.9	81.4	123.6	66.4	82.2	100.7	88.8	92.0	121.0	67.3	82.0	72.3
1997	69.5	87.4	125.9	68.0	82.4	97.8	88.5	91.1	122.1	71.6	85.6	77.4
1998	73.3	92.1	125.5	72.2	86.3	98.5	84.2	88.1	123.1	74.8	90.6	77.5
1999	76.9	95.9	124.7	75.4	88.3	97.9	84.5	88.2	121.2	79.2	94.0	81.1
2000	80.4	98.9	123.1	81.2	92.0	101.0	85.5	89.8	120.9	81.8	99.9	84.6
2001	81.9	94.2	115.0	84.3	92.9	102.9	83.9	89.1	115.3	81.7	96.9	79.1
2002	87.8	93.9	106.9	88.9	96.5	101.2	83.4	88.2	107.0	87.8	95.0	78.3
2003	93.4	94.9	101.7	96.0	101.9	102.8	84.9	89.8	101.9	93.1	97.6	80.6
2004	95.5	96.6	101.1	96.8	100.0	101.4	91.3	94.1	100.5	96.1	97.9	88.2
2005	100.0	100.0	100.0	100.0	100.0	100.0	100.0	100.0	100.0	100.0	100.0	100.0
2006	100.8	101.5	100.8	102.0	98.8	101.2	104.4	103.6	99.4	102.1	102.8	106.0
2007	105.0	104.0	99.0	105.3	99.2	100.3	107.6	105.6	97.7	106.4	104.3	111.9
2008	104.7	99.4	95.0	109.5	99.3	104.6	116.0	112.9	94.2	105.5	104.1	115.4
2009	106.8	88.7	83.0	115.2	104.9	107.9	. . .	. . .	83.9	105.7	95.7	. . .

. . . = Not available.

Table 5-2. Average Annual Percent Change in Output Per Hour and Related Series, Selected Industries, 1987–2008 and 2007–2008

(Number, percent.)

Industry	NAICS code	2008 employment (thousands)	Average annual percent change, 1987–2008			Annual percent change, 2007–2008		
			Output per hour	Output	Hours	Output per hour	Output	Hours
Mining								
Mining	21	725	-0.4	-0.2	0.2	-3.0	0.9	4.0
Oil and gas extraction	211	161	0.5	-0.8	-1.3	-9.0	1.5	11.6
Mining, except oil and gas	212	230	2.0	0.8	-1.1	-0.7	-1.4	-0.7
Coal mining	2121	82	2.4	0.1	-2.3	-5.7	2.2	8.4
Metal ore mining	2122	40	1.9	2.2	0.4	-3.4	6.9	10.6
Nonmetallic mineral mining and quarrying	2123	108	1.0	0.6	-0.4	0.1	-10.7	-10.8
Support activities for mining	213	334	3.1	5.6	2.4	23.8	29.3	4.4
Utilities								
Power generation and supply	2211	404	2.4	1.1	-1.3	-4.1	-1.6	2.6
Natural gas distribution	2212	107	2.8	1.3	-1.5	0.8	1.0	0.2
Transportation and Warehousing								
Air transportation	481	427	2.9	3.1	0.2	-1.4	-3.1	-1.8
Line-haul railroads	482111	184	4.2	2.2	-1.9	-1.0	-1.0	0.1
General freight trucking	4841	1 196	1.3	2.5	1.1	0.2	-3.1	-3.3
General freight trucking, local	48411	315	3.1	4.0	0.8	-0.1	-5.8	-5.7
General freight trucking, long-distance	48412	881	1.3	2.8	1.5	-0.1	-2.4	-2.3
Used household and office goods moving	48421	95	-0.6	-0.2	0.4	6.5	-5.7	-11.4
Postal service	491	747	0.9	0.7	-0.2	-1.4	-4.9	-3.5
Couriers and messengers	492	612	-0.2	2.2	2.4	4.9	-6.2	-10.5
Warehousing and storage	493	681	2.7	6.1	3.4	0.3	4.1	3.8
General warehousing and storage	49311	574	5.0	8.5	3.3	0.2	4.6	4.4
Refrigerated warehousing and storage	49312	49	-0.3	3.0	3.2	3.0	0.6	-2.3
Information								
Publishing	511	912	3.8	4.1	0.3	1.7	-1.3	-2.9
Newspaper, book, and directory publishers	5111	648	0.0	-1.0	-1.0	-2.0	-6.1	-4.1
Software publishers	5112	265	14.4	21.9	6.5	4.3	4.2	-0.1
Motion picture and video exhibition	51213	133	1.2	1.9	0.7	-3.3	-2.2	1.1
Broadcasting, except Internet	515	328	1.6	2.7	1.1	2.4	0.3	-2.0
Radio and television broadcasting	5151	241	0.4	0.6	0.1	0.0	-1.0	-1.0
Cable and other subscription programming	5152	88	3.6	8.3	4.5	6.3	1.8	-4.2
Wired telecommunications carriers	5171	683	4.4	3.8	-0.5	3.2	2.9	-0.3
Wireless telecommunications carriers	5172	203	9.5	22.4	11.9	18.8	12.8	-5.1
Finance and Insurance								
Commercial banking	52211	1 358	3.5	3.5	0.0	0.2	0.7	0.5
Real Estate and Rental and Leasing								
Passenger car rental	532111	124	1.8	2.9	1.1	4.9	-4.0	-8.4
Truck, trailer, and RV rental and leasing	53212	60	3.7	2.9	-0.8	-4.7	-5.5	-0.8
Video tape and disc rental	53223	109	4.2	4.4	0.2	-6.9	-10.3	-3.7
Professional and Technical Services								
Tax preparation services	541213	152	0.7	3.3	2.6	-3.3	1.2	4.7
Architectural services	54131	234	1.5	3.9	2.3	4.6	1.2	-3.2
Engineering services	54133	969	1.8	4.0	2.2	9.4	9.6	0.1
Advertising agencies	54181	195	2.0	2.4	0.4	4.6	3.0	-1.5
Photography studios, portrait	541921	80	0.1	2.3	2.2	3.3	0.2	-3.1
Administrative and Waste Services								
Employment placement agencies	561311	260	7.6	8.9	1.2	16.7	4.8	-10.2
Travel agencies	56151	119	6.2	5.1	-1.0	1.4	-1.2	-2.6
Janitorial services	56172	1 225	2.2	4.2	2.0	2.5	2.9	0.3
Healthcare and Social Assistance								
Medical and diagnostic laboratories	6215	227	4.3	7.4	3.0	11.8	8.9	-2.5
Medical laboratories	621511	152	3.6	6.1	2.4	9.4	7.1	-2.1
Diagnostic imaging centers	621512	75	5.0	9.4	4.2	15.5	11.4	-3.5
Arts, Entertainment, and Recreation								
Amusement and theme parks	71311	138	0.1	3.0	2.9	0.7	-1.0	-1.7
Bowling centers	71395	76	0.4	-1.5	-1.9	1.6	-4.2	-5.7
Accommodation and Food Services								
Accommodation and food services	72	11 742	0.9	2.4	1.5	-0.9	-1.6	-0.7
Accommodation	721	1 900	1.7	2.9	1.2	-0.8	-2.2	-1.4
Traveler accommodation	7211	1 825	1.7	2.9	1.2	-1.0	-2.3	-1.3
Food services and drinking places	722	9 842	0.6	2.3	1.6	-0.8	-1.4	-0.6
Full-service restaurants	7221	4 617	0.6	2.3	1.7	-1.8	-3.2	-1.4
Limited-service eating places	7222	4 178	0.6	2.5	1.8	0.3	0.5	0.2
Special food services	7223	686	1.7	2.9	1.1	-0.8	-0.9	0.0
Drinking places (alcoholic beverages)	7224	362	-0.4	-0.6	-0.1	-2.0	-2.3	-0.4

Table 5-2. Average Annual Percent Change in Output Per Hour and Related Series, Selected Industries, 1987–2008 and 2007–2008—*Continued*

(Number, percent.)

Industry	NAICS code	2008 employment (thousands)	Average annual percent change, 1987–2008			Annual percent change, 2007–2008		
			Output per hour	Output	Hours	Output per hour	Output	Hours
Other Services								
Automotive repair and maintenance	8111	1 115	1.0	1.6	0.6	-0.5	-5.1	-4.6
Reupholstery and furniture repair	81142	25	-0.2	-2.0	-1.8	-3.5	-6.2	-2.8
Hair, nail, and skin care services	81211	917	2.3	3.1	0.8	2.3	0.2	-2.1
Funeral homes and funeral services	81221	108	-0.5	-0.2	0.4	-5.1	-0.8	4.5
Drycleaning and laundry services	8123	370	0.9	0.6	-0.3	0.6	-0.7	-1.3
Coin-operated laundries and drycleaners	812310	49	1.9	0.7	-1.2	-4.4	-2.5	2.0
Drycleaning and laundry services	812320	183	0.6	-0.6	-1.2	2.0	-2.3	-4.2
Linen and uniform supply	81233	137	0.3	1.7	1.3	0.0	1.3	1.3
Photofinishing	81292	24	0.7	-4.8	-5.4	7.0	-2.2	-8.6
Manufacturing								
Food	311	1 511	1.1	1.4	0.3	-0.4	-0.6	-0.1
Animal food	3111	53	2.7	2.0	-0.7	-6.0	-0.6	5.8
Grain and oilseed milling	3112	62	2.1	1.3	-0.8	-3.7	1.4	5.3
Sugar and confectionery products	3113	74	0.8	-0.1	-0.9	-7.7	-8.2	-0.6
Fruit and vegetable preserving and specialty	3114	173	1.6	1.3	-0.3	-2.3	-2.5	-0.1
Dairy products	3115	132	1.6	1.0	-0.6	7.9	2.3	-5.2
Animal slaughtering and processing	3116	514	0.9	2.3	1.4	2.5	1.6	-0.9
Seafood product preparation and packaging	3117	39	0.9	0.1	-0.8	-12.8	-13.6	-1.0
Bakeries and tortilla manufacturing	3118	300	0.4	0.3	-0.2	-7.5	-5.1	2.6
Other food products	3119	164	0.5	2.0	1.6	1.4	-0.1	-1.5
Beverages and tobacco products	312	200	0.6	-0.3	-0.9	-2.5	-6.9	-4.5
Beverages	3121	179	1.9	1.5	-0.4	0.1	-5.3	-5.4
Tobacco and tobacco products	3122	22	0.5	-3.1	-3.6	-13.0	-10.6	2.7
Textile mills	313	161	3.5	-2.6	-5.9	-1.6	-15.6	-14.2
Fiber, yarn, and thread mills	3131	37	4.2	-1.5	-5.4	1.3	-13.4	-14.5
Fabric mills	3132	72	4.8	-2.6	-7.1	5.3	-13.5	-17.8
Textile and fabric finishing mills	3133	52	0.6	-3.6	-4.2	-14.7	-22.2	-8.8
Textile product mills	314	163	0.8	-1.1	-1.9	-3.2	-8.6	-5.7
Textile furnishings mills	3141	82	0.7	-1.5	-2.2	-2.6	-12.6	-10.2
Other textile product mills	3149	81	1.4	-0.2	-1.5	-0.5	-1.1	-0.6
Apparel	315	221	-1.3	-8.1	-6.9	-1.8	-13.7	-12.1
Apparel knitting mills	3151	32	-0.6	-6.8	-6.2	-3.4	-15.0	-12.0
Cut and sew apparel	3152	172	-1.4	-8.5	-7.2	-1.6	-13.2	-11.9
Accessories and other apparel	3159	17	-2.6	-6.9	-4.4	0.0	-14.6	-14.6
Leather and allied products	316	36	2.2	-4.5	-6.6	3.6	-5.7	-9.0
Leather and hide tanning and finishing	3161	5	0.7	-4.8	-5.4	-2.7	-12.3	-9.9
Footwear	3162	17	2.5	-5.6	-7.9	18.1	11.6	-5.5
Other leather products	3169	15	1.5	-3.5	-4.9	-4.8	-16.5	-12.2
Wood products	321	486	1.3	0.1	-1.3	-2.0	-14.3	-12.5
Sawmills and wood preservation	3211	106	2.5	0.1	-2.3	3.5	-9.4	-12.5
Plywood and engineered wood products	3212	90	0.7	-0.1	-0.8	-4.0	-18.3	-14.9
Other wood products	3219	290	1.1	0.1	-1.0	-3.4	-14.6	-11.6
Paper and paper products	322	446	2.0	0.2	-1.7	-0.6	-4.3	-3.7
Pulp, paper, and paperboard mills	3221	127	3.0	-0.2	-3.1	0.5	-4.1	-4.6
Converted paper products	3222	319	1.5	0.5	-1.0	-1.2	-4.5	-3.4
Printing and related support activities	323	623	1.5	0.1	-1.3	1.4	-6.0	-7.3
Petroleum and coal products	324	118	2.6	1.2	-1.3	-3.0	0.6	3.7
Chemicals	325	855	1.8	1.0	-0.7	-6.7	-9.6	-3.1
Basic chemicals	3251	153	2.7	0.5	-2.1	-15.1	-12.3	3.4
Resin, rubber, and artificial fibers	3252	104	2.2	0.5	-1.6	-8.5	-13.2	-5.2
Agricultural chemicals	3253	37	2.6	0.5	-2.1	-1.1	-8.6	-7.6
Pharmaceuticals and medicines	3254	292	0.7	3.0	2.4	-1.3	-4.2	-2.9
Paints, coatings, and adhesives	3255	62	1.0	-0.3	-1.4	-4.0	-9.1	-5.3
Soaps, cleaning compounds, and toiletries	3256	112	3.0	2.3	-0.7	-5.6	-9.6	-4.3
Other chemical products and preparations	3259	96	2.4	0.0	-2.3	0.8	-6.0	-6.7
Plastics and rubber products	326	734	2.0	1.7	-0.3	-5.3	-9.2	-4.2
Plastics products	3261	589	1.9	2.0	0.1	-4.8	-8.8	-4.2
Rubber products	3262	145	2.1	0.4	-1.7	-7.5	-11.4	-4.2
Nonmetallic mineral products	327	481	1.2	0.7	-0.5	-4.5	-11.9	-7.7
Clay products and refractories	3271	57	1.3	-1.1	-2.4	-1.4	-9.4	-8.1
Glass and glass products	3272	104	2.0	0.5	-1.5	-4.0	-3.5	0.5
Cement and concrete products	3273	223	0.4	1.1	0.6	-7.1	-17.6	-11.3
Lime and gypsum products	3274	18	1.0	0.0	-1.0	-1.7	-7.2	-5.6
Other nonmetallic mineral products	3279	79	1.7	1.5	-0.2	1.2	-6.1	-7.2
Primary metals	331	443	2.6	0.5	-2.1	4.9	0.0	-4.7
Iron and steel mills and ferroalloy production	3311	100	5.2	2.5	-2.6	8.5	6.7	-1.7
Steel products from purchased steel	3312	62	-0.9	-1.6	-0.7	-4.6	-7.9	-3.5
Alumina and aluminum production	3313	66	2.5	-0.1	-2.5	-1.6	-9.4	-8.0

Table 5-2. Average Annual Percent Change in Output Per Hour and Related Series, Selected Industries, 1987–2008 and 2007–2008—Continued

(Number, percent.)

Industry	NAICS code	2008 employment (thousands)	Average annual percent change, 1987–2008			Annual percent change, 2007–2008		
			Output per hour	Output	Hours	Output per hour	Output	Hours
Manufacturing—Continued								
Other nonferrous metal production	3314	67	1.5	-0.9	-2.3	4.6	2.1	-2.4
Foundries	3315	148	2.0	0.1	-1.9	-7.1	-13.4	-6.8
Fabricated metal products	332	1 550	1.6	1.5	-0.2	1.4	-3.2	-4.6
Forging and stamping	3321	107	2.9	1.8	-1.0	0.1	-3.6	-3.7
Cutlery and hand tools	3322	49	1.4	-0.9	-2.3	-3.3	-11.8	-8.8
Architectural and structural metals	3323	412	1.1	1.8	0.7	-0.9	-4.5	-3.7
Boilers, tanks, and shipping containers	3324	98	0.8	0.3	-0.5	-2.1	-2.4	-0.3
Hardware	3325	30	1.3	-2.6	-3.8	7.7	-13.8	-19.9
Spring and wire products	3326	53	2.8	0.7	-2.0	4.3	-6.6	-10.4
Machine shops and threaded products	3327	370	2.5	3.3	0.8	3.7	-0.9	-4.4
Coating, engraving, and heat treating metals	3328	145	3.0	3.4	0.3	1.2	-0.1	-1.3
Other fabricated metal products	3329	286	1.7	0.9	-0.8	4.0	-2.0	-5.8
Machinery	333	1 201	2.5	1.9	-0.6	-1.4	-2.0	-0.6
Agriculture, construction, and mining machinery	3331	244	3.0	3.6	0.6	2.2	4.0	1.7
Industrial machinery	3332	124	2.5	1.6	-0.9	-9.7	-13.6	-4.4
Commercial and service industry machinery	3333	105	1.6	-0.2	-1.7	6.3	-0.4	-6.2
HVAC and commercial refrigeration equipment	3334	151	2.1	1.7	-0.4	-0.5	-2.9	-2.4
Metalworking machinery	3335	195	2.1	0.6	-1.5	0.1	0.5	0.4
Turbine and power transmission equipment	3336	106	2.0	1.8	-0.2	-2.7	-0.1	2.7
Other general purpose machinery	3339	277	2.6	1.9	-0.7	-4.3	-3.9	0.4
Computer and electronic products	334	1 255	12.2	9.8	-2.2	6.7	6.9	0.3
Computer and peripheral equipment	3341	185	24.8	20.1	-3.8	32.8	35.8	2.2
Communications equipment	3342	130	7.4	4.5	-2.7	-4.7	-2.4	2.4
Audio and video equipment	3343	28	3.9	0.3	-3.5	-15.7	-20.2	-5.3
Semiconductors and electronic components	3344	434	16.8	15.2	-1.4	4.4	3.1	-1.3
Electronic instruments	3345	444	4.4	2.5	-1.8	2.3	4.3	2.0
Magnetic media manufacturing and reproduction	3346	35	3.5	2.0	-1.5	19.3	3.7	-13.1
Electrical equipment and appliances	335	429	2.7	0.5	-2.1	-2.8	-3.3	-0.5
Electric lighting equipment	3351	59	2.1	0.3	-1.8	2.0	-3.1	-5.0
Household appliances	3352	71	4.0	0.9	-3.0	-3.9	-10.9	-7.3
Electrical equipment	3353	161	2.8	0.6	-2.1	-4.2	-0.1	4.2
Other electrical equipment and components	3359	138	2.0	0.2	-1.8	-2.3	-2.6	-0.3
Transportation equipment	336	1 622	2.9	1.4	-1.4	-5.5	-12.7	-7.7
Motor vehicles	3361	192	3.4	1.2	-2.2	-9.3	-19.9	-11.7
Motor vehicle bodies and trailers	3362	142	1.3	1.2	0.0	-5.8	-21.9	-17.1
Motor vehicle parts	3363	550	2.9	2.0	-0.8	-4.7	-17.1	-13.0
Aerospace products and parts	3364	508	1.7	-0.5	-2.1	-9.1	-6.9	2.4
Railroad rolling stock	3365	29	5.2	5.9	0.7	16.7	18.0	1.1
Ship and boat building	3366	157	2.2	1.3	-0.9	12.9	2.9	-8.9
Other transportation equipment	3369	44	6.8	7.2	0.4	3.8	9.0	5.0
Furniture and related products	337	513	1.9	0.6	-1.2	3.8	-8.9	-12.2
Household and institutional furniture	3371	335	1.8	0.3	-1.5	4.8	-10.1	-14.2
Office furniture and fixtures	3372	133	1.8	0.9	-0.9	0.9	-5.1	-5.9
Other furniture-related products	3379	45	2.3	1.8	-0.5	2.5	-13.6	-15.7
Miscellaneous manufacturing	339	699	3.0	3.0	0.0	1.6	1.1	-0.4
Medical equipment and supplies	3391	324	3.6	5.0	1.3	2.7	6.2	3.4
Other miscellaneous manufacturing	3399	375	2.2	1.3	-0.9	-0.6	-4.3	-3.7

Table 5-3. Average Annual Percent Change in Output Per Hour and Related Series, Wholesale Trade, Retail Trade, Food Service, and Drinking Places, 1987–2009 and 2008–2009

(Number, percent.)

Industry	NAICS code	2009 employment (thousands)	Average annual percent change, 1987–2009			Annual percent change, 2008–2009		
			Output per hour	Output	Hours	Output per hour	Output	Hours
Wholesale Trade								
Wholesale trade	42	5 793	2.6	2.9	0.3	-3.3	-10.1	-7.1
Durable goods	423	2 919	4.4	4.4	0.0	-6.6	-15.1	-9.1
Motor vehicles and parts	4231	327	1.9	1.3	-0.6	-14.7	-21.6	-8.1
Furniture and furnishings	4232	103	1.8	1.3	-0.5	2.9	-16.6	-18.9
Lumber and construction supplies	4233	208	0.6	0.9	0.3	-8.4	-23.3	-16.2
Commercial equipment	4234	634	14.5	14.8	0.3	1.8	-1.3	-3.1
Metals and minerals	4235	117	-1.3	-1.5	-0.3	-11.0	-25.0	-15.7
Electric goods	4236	332	8.3	7.7	-0.5	2.3	-8.3	-10.4
Hardware and plumbing	4237	237	1.1	1.7	0.6	-8.9	-17.2	-9.1
Machinery and supplies	4238	653	1.6	1.4	-0.1	-13.8	-19.7	-6.8
Miscellaneous durable goods	4239	307	1.0	1.6	0.6	-3.7	-16.2	-13.0
Nondurable goods	424	2 048	1.0	1.1	0.1	0.8	-4.6	-5.3
Paper and paper products	4241	132	1.7	0.7	-1.0	-1.3	-9.0	-7.7
Druggists' goods	4242	205	2.3	4.1	1.7	8.8	-1.5	-9.5
Apparel and piece goods	4243	142	2.9	2.3	-0.5	4.4	-5.1	-9.2
Grocery and related products	4244	744	0.7	1.5	0.7	0.0	-4.7	-4.7
Farm product raw materials	4245	76	1.4	-1.0	-2.4	8.3	10.0	1.6
Chemicals	4246	126	-0.2	0.3	0.5	-10.6	-13.7	-3.4
Petroleum	4247	100	2.3	-0.1	-2.3	-5.6	-8.8	-3.4
Alcoholic beverages	4248	164	0.3	1.9	1.6	2.2	-1.2	-3.4
Miscellaneous nondurable goods	4249	359	0.0	-0.2	-0.2	5.5	0.2	-5.0
Electronic markets and agents and brokers	425	826	0.6	2.9	2.3	-6.7	-10.2	-3.7
Retail Trade								
Retail trade	44	15 446	2.9	3.3	0.3	1.5	-4.4	-5.8
Motor vehicle and parts dealers	441	1 707	1.8	2.1	0.2	-1.8	-12.1	-10.5
Automobile dealers	4411	1 066	1.8	1.9	0.1	-1.0	-13.3	-12.4
Other motor vehicle dealers	4412	142	3.2	4.1	0.8	14.1	-7.6	-19.0
Auto parts, accessories, and tire stores	4413	499	1.7	2.0	0.3	-2.6	-5.9	-3.4
Furniture and home furnishings stores	442	486	3.8	3.3	-0.5	6.2	-10.9	-16.1
Furniture stores	4421	238	3.2	2.8	-0.4	4.2	-10.4	-14.0
Home furnishings stores	4422	249	4.6	4.0	-0.6	8.6	-11.5	-18.5
Electronics and appliance stores	443	511	13.5	14.2	0.6	13.8	0.5	-11.6
Building material and garden supply stores	444	1 211	2.5	3.4	0.9	-4.2	-11.6	-7.8
Building material and supplies dealers	4441	1 064	2.2	3.3	1.1	-5.3	-13.1	-8.2
Lawn and garden equipment and supplies stores	4442	147	4.3	3.5	-0.7	2.8	-2.1	-4.8
Food and beverage stores	445	2 924	0.4	0.2	-0.2	1.9	-1.1	-2.9
Grocery stores	4451	2 527	0.2	0.1	-0.1	1.4	-1.3	-2.7
Specialty food stores	4452	240	0.5	-0.1	-0.5	13.9	8.8	-4.4
Beer, wine and liquor stores	4453	157	2.0	0.7	-1.3	0.2	-2.5	-2.7
Health and personal care stores	446	1 028	2.5	3.7	1.2	3.3	0.1	-3.1
Gasoline stations	447	842	1.9	1.0	-0.8	-0.4	-3.2	-2.9
Clothing and clothing accessories stores	448	1 467	4.7	4.1	-0.5	-0.2	-4.6	-4.3
Clothing stores	4481	1 103	5.0	4.7	-0.4	0.8	-4.2	-5.0
Shoe stores	4482	184	3.4	2.3	-1.1	-6.6	-5.4	1.2
Jewelry, luggage, and leather goods stores	4483	180	3.9	3.2	-0.7	0.7	-5.5	-6.2
Sporting goods, hobby, book, and music stores	451	681	4.1	4.2	0.1	10.6	-1.1	-10.6
Sporting goods and musical instrument store	4511	507	4.8	5.1	0.3	11.4	0.3	-10.0
Book, periodical, and music stores	4512	174	2.5	2.1	-0.4	8.1	-5.2	-12.4
General merchandise stores	452	2 971	3.5	5.1	1.6	2.6	-0.4	-2.9
Department stores	4521	1 471	0.7	1.7	1.0	-1.4	-5.6	-4.3
Other general merchandise stores	4529	1 500	6.7	9.0	2.2	4.0	2.3	-1.6
Miscellaneous store retailers	453	969	4.0	3.8	-0.2	-0.5	-6.4	-5.9
Florists	4531	94	3.7	0.4	-3.2	16.0	-3.5	-16.8
Office supplies, stationery and gift stores	4532	355	6.4	5.6	-0.8	10.7	-0.9	-10.5
Used merchandise stores	4533	183	4.8	5.9	1.0	-4.9	1.4	6.7
Other miscellaneous store retailers	4539	337	1.5	2.6	1.1	-8.4	-11.8	-3.7
Nonstore retailers	454	649	8.8	8.9	0.1	7.1	3.8	-3.1
Electronic shopping and mail-order houses	4541	300	11.4	15.2	3.4	5.2	4.6	-0.6
Vending machine operators	4542	55	0.8	-1.9	-2.6	-9.2	-11.3	-2.3
Direct selling establishments	4543	294	3.6	1.7	-1.8	10.5	3.2	-6.5
Food Services and Drinking Places								
Food services and drinking places	722	9 648	0.7	2.0	1.4	1.0	-2.5	-3.5
Full-service restaurants	7221	4 518	0.6	2.1	1.4	0.3	-3.4	-3.6
Limited-service eating places	7222	4 120	0.7	2.3	1.6	1.9	-1.3	-3.1
Special food services	7223	651	1.6	2.6	0.9	-0.2	-3.8	-3.6
Drinking places, alcoholic beverages	7224	360	-0.3	-0.7	-0.4	2.8	-3.2	-5.8

Table 5-4. Indexes of Multifactor Productivity and Related Measures, 1989–2009

(2000 = 100.)

Sector	1989	1990	1991	1992	1993	1994	1995	1996	1997	1998	1999	2000
PRIVATE BUSINESS												
Productivity												
Output per hour of all persons	67.0	68.4	69.5	72.5	72.9	73.6	73.7	75.8	77.1	79.5	82.3	85.2
Output per unit of capital services	111.5	109.7	106.0	107.8	108.0	109.4	107.8	107.8	107.6	106.4	105.2	103.1
Multifactor productivity	82.0	82.6	81.8	83.9	84.1	84.7	84.4	85.9	86.6	87.9	89.5	91.0
Real value-added output	58.6	59.5	59.0	61.4	63.4	66.5	68.5	71.6	75.3	79.2	83.6	87.4
Inputs												
Labor input	81.6	81.5	80.7	81.5	84.0	87.8	90.1	91.9	95.5	97.7	100.0	101.2
Capital services	52.5	54.2	55.6	56.9	58.7	60.8	63.5	66.4	70.0	74.4	79.5	84.8
Combined input quantity	71.4	72.0	72.1	73.1	75.4	78.6	81.1	83.4	87.0	90.1	93.4	96.0
Capital hours ratio	60.1	62.3	65.6	67.2	67.5	67.3	68.3	70.3	71.7	74.7	78.2	82.6
PRIVATE NONFARM BUSINESS												
Productivity												
Output per hour of all persons	67.7	69.0	70.2	73.0	73.4	74.2	74.6	76.5	77.6	80.0	82.6	85.4
Output per unit of capital services	114.2	112.1	108.1	109.5	109.9	110.9	109.6	109.1	108.7	107.3	105.9	103.5
Multifactor productivity	83.0	83.3	82.6	84.5	84.8	85.4	85.4	86.5	87.1	88.4	89.9	91.3
Real value-added output	58.7	59.5	59.0	61.3	63.5	66.5	68.6	71.7	75.3	79.3	83.7	87.5
Inputs												
Labor input	80.9	80.9	80.0	80.8	83.5	87.0	89.3	91.3	94.9	97.2	99.8	101.0
Capital services	51.4	53.1	54.6	56.0	57.8	59.9	62.6	65.7	69.3	73.9	79.1	84.5
Combined input quantity	70.7	71.4	71.4	72.5	74.9	77.9	80.4	82.8	86.5	89.7	93.2	95.8
Capital hours ratio	59.3	61.5	64.9	66.7	66.8	66.9	68.1	70.1	71.4	74.5	78.0	82.5
MANUFACTURING												
Productivity												
Output per unit of labor	66.0	67.5	69.2	71.8	73.7	76.3	79.8	82.7	87.2	91.9	96.1	100.0
Output per unit of capital	98.7	95.8	92.0	92.8	94.0	97.0	98.5	97.9	100.5	100.7	100.4	100.0
Sector output	68.5	68.2	67.1	69.3	72.0	76.3	80.3	83.0	89.2	93.8	97.3	100.0
Inputs												
Labor hours	103.8	101.2	96.9	96.4	97.7	100.0	100.7	100.4	102.3	102.0	101.3	100.0
Combined input quantity	85.9	85.3	85.0	84.5	86.7	89.1	90.7	91.2	93.8	95.9	96.6	100.0
Energy	65.2	66.1	65.7	71.4	72.0	74.8	78.8	85.9	92.8	97.7	102.6	100.0
Materials	75.2	76.6	76.0	81.4	81.6	84.6	88.8	88.4	92.0	95.0	100.0	100.0
Capital services	69.4	71.3	72.9	74.7	76.6	78.6	81.5	84.8	88.7	93.2	97.0	100.0
Purchased services	79.7	80.0	78.9	82.0	83.0	85.6	88.5	91.1	95.1	97.8	100.7	100.0

Table 5-4. Indexes of Multifactor Productivity and Related Measures, 1989–2009—*Continued*

(2000 = 100.)

Sector	2001	2002	2003	2004	2005	2006	2007	2008	2009
PRIVATE BUSINESS									
Productivity									
Output per hour of all persons	87.9	91.9	95.5	98.3	100.0	101.0	102.9	105.0	109.0
Output per unit of capital services	99.2	97.8	98.2	99.8	100.0	100.0	99.3	96.7	92.3
Multifactor productivity	91.7	93.9	96.4	99.0	100.0	100.5	101.0	101.1	101.9
Real value-added output	88.2	90.0	92.8	96.7	100.0	103.1	105.5	105.4	101.7
Inputs									
Labor input	99.5	97.5	97.1	98.1	100.0	102.3	103.5	102.0	95.0
Capital services	89.0	92.0	94.5	96.9	100.0	103.1	106.2	109.1	110.3
Combined input quantity	96.2	95.8	96.2	97.7	100.0	102.6	104.4	104.3	99.9
Capital hours ratio	88.6	94.0	97.3	98.5	100.0	101.0	103.6	108.7	118.2
PRIVATE NONFARM BUSINESS									
Productivity									
Output per hour of all persons	88.1	92.2	95.7	98.4	100.0	101.0	102.9	105.0	109.0
Output per unit of capital services	99.5	98.0	98.2	99.9	100.0	99.8	98.9	96.1	91.6
Multifactor productivity	91.9	94.2	96.5	99.0	100.0	100.4	100.9	101.0	101.7
Real value-added output	88.4	90.1	92.8	96.7	100.0	103.2	105.6	105.5	101.6
Inputs									
Labor input	99.4	97.4	97.0	98.1	100.0	102.5	103.7	101.9	94.9
Capital services	88.8	91.9	94.5	96.8	100.0	103.4	106.8	109.7	111.0
Combined input quantity	96.1	95.7	96.2	97.7	100.0	102.8	104.7	104.4	100.0
Capital hours ratio	88.6	94.1	97.4	98.5	100.0	101.2	104.0	109.3	119.1
MANUFACTURING									
Productivity									
Output per unit of labor	101.6	108.6	115.4	118.0	123.6	124.6	128.8	. . .	. . .
Output per unit of capital	93.5	92.4	93.3	95.5	98.9	100.0	101.1	. . .	. . .
Sector output	94.9	94.3	95.3	97.0	100.4	102.0	103.6	. . .	. . .
Inputs									
Labor hours	93.5	86.8	82.6	82.2	81.3	81.9	80.4	. . .	. . .
Combined input quantity	98.7	102.4	105.3	108.1	108.1	110.8	116.0	. . .	. . .
Energy	93.3	88.4	87.7	87.3	92.7	90.4	83.1	. . .	. . .
Materials	100.7	98.3	99.1	97.0	105.2	103.9	103.5	. . .	. . .
Capital services	101.5	102.1	102.1	101.6	101.5	102.0	102.5	. . .	. . .
Purchased services	96.2	92.1	90.5	89.7	92.9	92.0	89.3	. . .	. . .

. . . = Not available.

Chapter Six

COMPENSATION OF EMPLOYEES

COMPENSATION OF EMPLOYEES

HIGHLIGHTS

This chapter discusses the Employment Cost Index (ECI), which covers changes in wages and salaries and benefits; the Employer Costs for Employee Compensation (ECEC); employee participation in various benefit plans; and occupational and hourly wage percentiles wages from the National Compensation Survey.

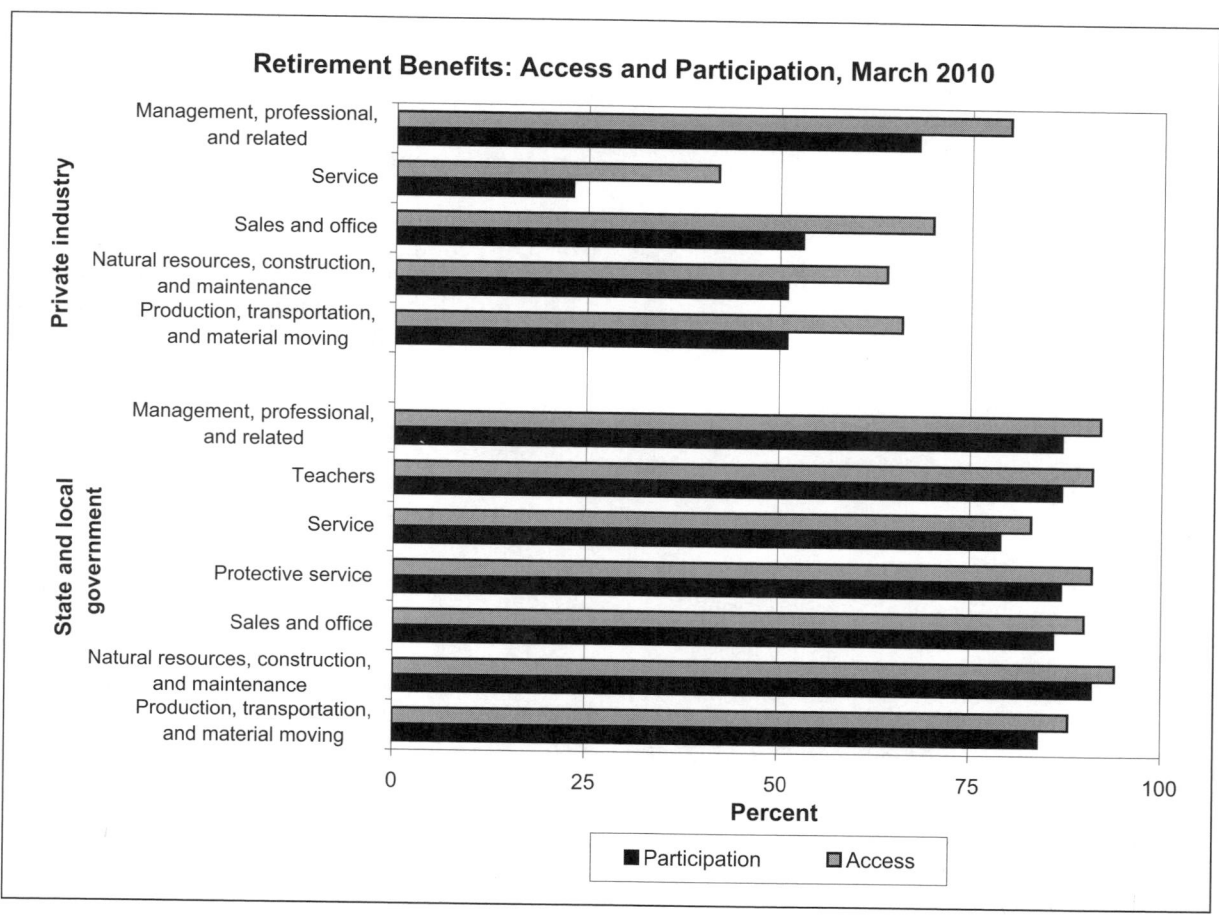

Ninety percent of state and local government employees had access to paid retirement benefits, compared with 65 percent in the private sector. Among those that had access to the plan, 85 percent of state and local government workers participated compared to 50 percent of private industry workers. (See Table 6-11.)

OTHER HIGHLIGHTS

- Total employer compensation costs per hour varied among the different Census divisions, ranging from $33.76 in the New England states (Connecticut, Maine, Massachusetts, New Hampshire, Rhode Island and Vermont) to $21.40 in the East South Central states (Alabama, Kentucky, Mississippi, and Tennessee). (See Table 6-7.)

- Wages and salaries accounted for 65.7 percent of employee compensation in June 2010 with benefits comprising the remaining 34.3 percent. Legally required benefits, such as social security, unemployment insurance and workers' compensation accounted for 6.0 percent. (See Table 6-8.)

- In March 2010, 91 percent of union workers had access to medical benefits compared to 68 percent of non-union workers in private industry. (See Tables 6-12)

NOTES AND DEFINITIONS

NATIONAL COMPENSATION SURVEY

The National Compensation Survey (NCS) is an establishment-based survey that provides data for the Employment Cost Index (ECI), the Employer Costs for Employee Compensation (ECEC), an experimental series, the occupational earnings series, and the employee benefits survey.

The NCS surveys workers in private industry establishments, and in state and local government, in each state and the District of Columbia. For the NCS, the term *civilian workers* denotes workers in private industry and workers in state and local government. Establishments with one or more workers are included in the survey. Major exclusions from the survey are workers in the federal government, military personnel, agricultural workers, workers in private households, the self-employed, volunteers, unpaid workers, individuals receiving long-term disability compensation, and U.S. citizens working overseas. Currently, the NCS also excludes individuals who set their own pay (for example, proprietors, owners, major stockholders, and partners in unincorporated firms) and family members being paid token wages; however, these exclusions are being reevaluated.

The NCS, which originally used the Standard Industrial Classification (SIC) system, began a transition from SIC to the 2002 version of North American Industry Classification System (NAICS) in 2004; the transition was completed in July 2007. NAICS revises its industry classifications every 5 years to stay current with industrial taxonomy in North America. In August 2007, the NCS began collecting and coding data under the 2007 NAICS. The 2007 NAICS includes revisions across several sectors. The most significant revisions are in the information sector, particularly within the telecommunications area; overall, the change from 2002 NAICS to 2007 NAICS had little effect on the resulting NCS estimates.

EMPLOYMENT COST INDEX

The Employment Cost Index (ECI) is a measure of the change in the cost of labor, free from the influence of employment shifts among occupations and industries. The compensation series includes changes in wages and salaries and employer costs for employee benefits. The wage and salary series and the benefit cost series are the two components of compensation.

The ECI provides data for the civilian economy, which includes the total private nonfarm economy excluding private households, and the public sector excluding the federal government. The private industry series and the state and local government series provide data for the two sectors separately.

To be included in the ECI, employees in occupations must receive cash payments from the establishment for services performed and the establishment must pay the employer's portion of Medicare taxes on that individual's wages. Major exclusions from the survey are the self-employed, individuals who set their own pay (for example, proprietors, owners, major stockholders, and partners in unincorporated firms), volunteers, unpaid workers, family members being paid token wages, individuals receiving long-term disability compensation, and U.S. citizens working overseas.

Data for the June 2010 reference period were collected from a probability sample of approximately 62,800 occupational observations selected from a sample of about 13,200 establishments in private industry and approximately 11,600 occupations from a sample of about 1,800 establishments in state and local governments. The state and local government sample, which is replaced less frequently than the private industry sample, was replaced in its entirety in September 2007. The private industry sample is rotated over approximately 5 years, which makes the sample more representative of the economy and reduces respondent burden. Data are collected for the pay period including the 12th day of the survey months of March, June, September, and December. The sample is replaced on a cross-area, cross-industry basis.

Beginning with the release of the March 2006 data, indexes were rebased to December 2005 = 100 from June 1989 = 100. The percentage changes shown in the current and constant-dollar historical tables were calculated from the rebased indexes. Thus, changes may differ from those published in previous edition of the handbook because of rounding.

Concepts and Definitions

Wages and salaries are defined as the hourly straight-time wage rate or, for workers not paid on an hourly basis, straight-time earnings divided by the corresponding hours. Straight-time wage and salary rates are total earnings before payroll deductions, excluding premium pay for overtime and for work on weekends and holidays, shift differentials, and nonproduction bonuses such as lump-sum payments provided in lieu of wage increases. Production bonuses, incentive earnings, commission payments, and cost-of-living adjustments are included in straight-time wage and salary rates.

Benefits covered by the ECI are: paid leave—vacations, holidays, sick leave, and personal leave; supplemental pay—premium pay for work in addition to the regular work schedule (such as overtime, weekends, and holidays), shift differentials, and nonproduction bonuses (such as referral bonuses and attendance bonuses); insurance benefits—life, health, short-term disability, and long-term disability; retirement and savings benefits—defined benefit and defined contribution plans; and legally required benefits—Social Security, Medicare, federal and state unemployment insurance, and workers' compensation.

Sources of Additional Information

Additional information on ECI methodology and more tables are available in Chapter 8 of the *BLS Handbook of Methods* and BLS new releases. The BLS publication *Compensation and Working Conditions* contains articles on all aspects of the NCS. All of these resources are on the BLS Web site at <http://www.bls.gov/ncs/ect/>.

Table 6-1. Employment Cost Index, Private Industry Workers, Total Compensation[1] and Wages and Salaries, by Industry and Occupation, 2001–2010

(December 2005 = 100.)

Characteristic and year	Total compensation					Wages and salaries				
	Indexes				Percent change for 12 months (ended December)	Indexes				Percent change for 12 months (ended December)
	March	June	September	December		March	June	September	December	
WORKERS BY INDUSTRY										
Total Private										
2001	85.0	85.8	86.7	87.3	4.1	87.6	88.4	89.2	89.9	3.8
2002	88.2	89.2	89.7	90.0	3.1	90.7	91.6	92.0	92.2	2.6
2003	91.4	92.3	93.2	93.6	4.0	93.3	94.0	94.8	95.1	3.1
2004	94.9	95.9	96.7	97.2	3.8	95.7	96.5	97.3	97.6	2.6
2005	98.2	98.9	99.5	100.0	2.9	98.3	98.9	99.5	100.0	2.5
2006	100.8	101.7	102.5	103.2	3.2	100.7	101.7	102.5	103.2	3.2
2007	104.0	104.9	105.7	106.3	3.0	104.3	105.1	106.0	106.6	3.3
2008	107.3	108.0	108.7	108.9	2.4	107.6	108.4	109.1	109.4	2.6
2009	109.3	109.6	110.0	110.2	1.2	109.8	110.1	110.6	110.9	1.4
2010	111.1	111.7	112.2	. . .	. . .	111.4	111.9	112.4	. . .	. . .
Goods-Producing[2]										
2001	83.9	84.7	85.3	86.0	3.6	87.9	88.8	89.3	90.0	3.6
2002	87.0	87.7	88.2	89.0	3.5	90.7	91.4	91.9	92.6	2.9
2003	90.5	91.5	92.1	92.6	4.0	93.3	94.1	94.6	94.9	2.5
2004	94.5	95.4	96.5	96.9	4.6	95.6	96.2	97.2	97.2	2.4
2005	98.0	99.0	99.8	100.0	3.2	97.9	98.7	99.5	100.0	2.9
2006	100.3	101.3	102.0	102.5	2.5	100.7	101.8	102.3	102.9	2.9
2007	102.9	103.9	104.4	105.0	2.4	103.9	104.7	105.4	106.0	3.0
2008	106.1	106.8	107.2	107.5	2.4	107.1	108.0	108.6	109.0	2.8
2009	107.9	108.2	108.4	108.6	1.0	109.2	109.5	109.8	110.0	0.9
2010	109.8	110.3	111.0	. . .	. . .	110.5	110.9	111.5	. . .	. . .
Service-Providing[3]										
2001	85.4	86.2	87.1	87.8	4.4	87.4	88.3	89.2	89.8	3.8
2002	88.7	89.7	90.2	90.4	3.0	90.7	91.7	92.0	92.1	2.6
2003	91.7	92.5	93.6	94.0	4.0	93.3	93.9	94.9	95.2	3.4
2004	95.1	96.1	96.8	97.3	3.5	95.8	96.6	97.3	97.7	2.6
2005	98.3	98.9	99.5	100.0	2.8	98.4	99.0	99.5	100.0	2.4
2006	101.0	101.8	102.7	103.4	3.4	100.8	101.7	102.6	103.3	3.3
2007	104.3	105.2	106.1	106.7	3.2	104.4	105.3	106.1	106.8	3.4
2008	107.7	108.5	109.1	109.4	2.5	107.7	108.6	109.3	109.6	2.6
2009	109.8	110.1	110.5	110.8	1.3	110.0	110.3	110.8	111.1	1.4
2010	111.6	112.2	112.6	. . .	. . .	111.7	112.3	112.7	. . .	. . .
WORKERS BY OCCUPATION										
Management, Professional, and Related[4]										
2001	85.0	86.0	86.8	87.4	4.5	87.0	88.0	88.9	89.5	4.1
2002	88.3	89.2	89.5	89.7	2.6	90.4	91.3	91.6	91.7	2.5
2003	91.6	92.3	93.3	93.8	4.6	93.3	94.0	94.8	95.3	3.9
2004	94.9	95.7	96.5	97.1	3.5	96.0	96.5	97.3	97.8	2.6
2005	98.5	99.1	99.6	100.0	3.0	98.6	99.2	99.6	100.0	2.2
2006	101.1	101.9	102.9	103.5	3.5	101.1	102.0	103.0	103.6	3.6
2007	104.6	105.5	106.4	106.8	3.2	104.9	105.8	106.7	107.2	3.5
2008	108.1	108.9	109.6	109.9	2.9	108.5	109.3	110.1	110.5	3.1
2009	110.4	110.5	110.6	110.7	0.7	111.1	111.1	111.3	111.5	0.9
2010	111.8	112.2	112.7	. . .	. . .	112.5	112.9	113.4	. . .	. . .
Management, Business, and Financial										
2001	86.1	87.1	87.8	88.5	4.4	87.3	88.3	89.1	89.8	4.1
2002	89.5	90.7	90.7	90.6	2.4	90.8	92.2	92.4	92.1	2.6
2003	93.3	93.9	94.9	95.4	5.3	94.8	95.5	96.4	96.7	5.0
2004	95.9	96.8	97.3	97.9	2.6	96.8	97.5	98.1	98.5	1.9
2005	99.1	99.6	99.7	100.0	2.1	99.2	99.7	99.5	100.0	1.5
2006	101.3	102.0	102.7	103.1	3.1	101.3	102.2	102.8	103.1	3.1
2007	104.3	105.1	106.0	106.3	3.1	104.7	105.5	106.3	106.6	3.4
2008	108.0	108.7	109.3	109.5	3.0	108.2	109.0	109.7	110.0	3.2
2009	109.6	109.7	109.7	109.9	0.4	110.3	110.3	110.4	110.8	0.7
2010	111.3	111.7	112.0	. . .	. . .	112.0	112.6	112.8	. . .	. . .

[1] Includes wages, salaries, and employer costs for employee benefits.
[2] Includes mining, construction, and manufacturing.
[3] Includes the following industries: wholesale trade; retail trade; transportation and warehousing; utilities; information; finance and insurance; real estate and rental and leasing; professional, scientific, and technical services; management of companies and enterprises; administrative and support and waste management and remediation services; education services; health care and social assistance; arts, entertainment, and recreation; accommodation and food services; and other services, except public administration.
[4] Includes the following occupational groups: management, business, and financial; professional and related; sales and related; and office and administrative support.
. . . = Not available.

Table 6-1. Employment Cost Index, Private Industry Workers, Total Compensation[1] and Wages and Salaries, by Industry and Occupation, 2001–2010—*Continued*

(December 2005 = 100.)

Characteristic and year	Total compensation					Wages and salaries				
	Indexes				Percent change for 12 months (ended December)	Indexes				Percent change for 12 months (ended December)
	March	June	September	December		March	June	September	December	
Professional and Related										
2001	84.1	85.0	86.0	86.5	4.7	86.9	87.8	88.7	89.3	4.1
2002	87.3	87.9	88.5	89.1	3.0	90.1	90.5	91.0	91.4	2.4
2003	90.3	91.0	92.0	92.6	3.9	92.1	92.7	93.6	94.2	3.1
2004	94.1	94.8	95.8	96.5	4.2	95.3	95.7	96.7	97.2	3.2
2005	98.0	98.8	99.5	100.0	3.6	98.2	98.8	99.6	100.0	2.9
2006	101.0	101.8	103.1	103.9	3.9	100.9	101.8	103.1	104.0	4.0
2007	104.9	105.9	106.7	107.3	3.3	105.1	106.0	107.0	107.6	3.5
2008	108.3	109.0	109.9	110.3	2.8	108.7	109.5	110.4	110.9	3.1
2009	111.0	111.1	111.4	111.4	1.0	111.6	111.8	112.1	112.1	1.1
2010	112.2	112.6	113.3	. . .	. . .	112.8	113.2	113.9	. . .	. . .
Sales and Office										
2001	84.5	85.4	86.1	86.9	4.1	86.9	87.8	88.4	89.1	3.5
2002	87.8	89.0	89.5	89.8	3.3	90.0	91.2	91.5	91.7	2.9
2003	90.8	91.9	93.0	93.1	3.7	92.4	93.3	94.4	94.3	2.8
2004	94.4	95.7	96.6	96.8	4.0	95.1	96.1	97.2	97.2	3.1
2005	97.8	98.5	99.3	100.0	3.3	97.8	98.5	99.3	100.0	2.9
2006	100.5	101.6	102.3	102.9	2.9	100.4	101.6	102.4	103.0	3.0
2007	103.7	104.7	105.3	106.1	3.1	103.8	104.8	105.3	106.2	3.1
2008	106.6	107.5	107.9	107.9	1.7	106.7	107.7	108.0	108.0	1.7
2009	107.9	108.3	108.8	109.2	1.2	107.9	108.3	109.0	109.4	1.3
2010	109.8	110.8	111.1	. . .	. . .	109.6	110.7	110.9	. . .	. . .
Sales and Related										
2001	84.9	86.0	86.3	87.2	3.3	86.8	88.0	87.9	88.6	2.4
2002	87.7	89.7	89.7	89.7	2.9	89.2	91.0	91.0	90.9	2.6
2003	90.6	91.7	93.2	92.9	3.6	91.5	92.5	94.3	93.8	3.2
2004	94.0	95.4	96.8	96.2	3.6	94.4	95.7	97.4	96.6	3.0
2005	97.2	97.9	99.2	100.0	4.0	97.3	97.8	99.2	100.0	3.5
2006	99.9	101.1	101.7	102.3	2.3	99.8	101.3	102.0	102.6	2.6
2007	102.4	103.6	104.2	105.2	2.8	102.8	104.0	104.4	105.5	2.8
2008	105.0	106.2	106.0	105.5	0.3	105.3	106.6	106.4	105.7	0.2
2009	104.3	104.5	105.3	105.8	0.3	104.3	104.7	105.7	106.2	0.5
2010	105.8	107.5	107.4	. . .	. . .	106.2	108.0	107.8	. . .	. . .
Office and Administrative Support										
2001	84.2	84.9	85.9	86.6	4.6	87.0	87.7	88.8	89.4	4.2
2002	87.9	88.6	89.3	89.9	3.8	90.7	91.3	91.8	92.4	3.4
2003	91.0	92.0	92.8	93.3	3.8	93.1	93.9	94.4	94.7	2.5
2004	94.7	95.8	96.5	97.2	4.2	95.6	96.4	97.1	97.6	3.1
2005	98.1	98.9	99.5	100.0	2.9	98.2	99.0	99.4	100.0	2.5
2006	100.9	101.9	102.7	103.4	3.4	100.9	101.9	102.6	103.3	3.3
2007	104.5	105.4	106.0	106.7	3.2	104.5	105.4	106.0	106.7	3.3
2008	107.8	108.5	109.2	109.6	2.7	107.7	108.5	109.2	109.7	2.8
2009	110.5	110.9	111.3	111.6	1.8	110.6	111.1	111.4	111.8	1.9
2010	112.6	113.1	113.7	. . .	. . .	112.2	112.6	113.3	. . .	. . .
Natural Resources, Construction, and Maintenance										
2001	84.3	85.0	86.4	86.6	4.0	87.6	88.4	89.9	90.0	3.8
2002	87.4	88.5	89.3	89.7	3.6	90.5	91.7	92.3	92.6	2.9
2003	90.8	92.0	92.8	93.3	4.0	93.2	94.1	94.8	95.2	2.8
2004	94.8	96.1	96.5	97.1	4.1	95.8	96.7	97.1	97.5	2.4
2005	97.9	98.9	99.5	100.0	3.0	97.8	98.7	99.4	100.0	2.6
2006	100.8	102.1	103.0	103.6	3.6	100.7	101.8	102.8	103.4	3.4
2007	104.0	105.0	105.9	106.7	3.0	104.2	105.1	106.2	107.1	3.6
2008	107.6	108.3	109.0	109.6	2.7	108.1	109.0	109.8	110.5	3.2
2009	109.9	110.3	110.9	111.2	1.5	110.6	111.0	111.6	112.0	1.4
2010	112.2	112.7	113.1	. . .	. . .	112.5	112.8	113.1	. . .	. . .
Construction, Extraction, Farming, Fishing, and Forestry										
2001	84.2	85.1	86.2	86.4	3.8	87.8	88.9	89.8	90.0	3.6
2002	87.3	88.1	88.8	89.5	3.6	90.6	91.3	91.9	92.4	2.7
2003	90.3	91.6	92.5	93.1	4.0	92.7	93.7	94.6	94.9	2.7
2004	94.7	95.8	96.4	97.2	4.4	95.8	96.6	96.9	97.5	2.7
2005	97.7	98.7	99.5	100.0	2.9	97.8	98.5	99.3	100.0	2.6
2006	100.7	102.2	103.1	103.7	3.7	100.7	102.0	103.0	103.7	3.7
2007	104.4	105.7	106.5	107.4	3.6	104.7	105.8	106.7	107.8	4.0
2008	108.6	109.7	110.3	110.8	3.2	109.2	110.1	110.8	111.5	3.4
2009	110.9	111.5	112.0	112.4	1.4	111.4	111.7	112.3	112.7	1.1
2010	113.1	113.6	114.3	. . .	. . .	112.9	113.3	113.9	. . .	. . .

[1]Includes wages, salaries, and employer costs for employee benefits.
. . . = Not available.

Table 6-1. Employment Cost Index, Private Industry Workers, Total Compensation[1] and Wages and Salaries, by Industry and Occupation, 2001–2010—*Continued*

(December 2005 = 100.)

Characteristic and year	Total compensation					Wages and salaries				
	Indexes				Percent change for 12 months (ended December)	Indexes				Percent change for 12 months (ended December)
	March	June	September	December		March	June	September	December	
Installation, Maintenance, and Repair										
2001	84.4	84.9	86.8	86.8	4.1	87.4	87.9	90.1	90.1	4.3
2002	87.4	89.1	90.0	90.1	3.8	90.4	92.2	92.9	92.9	3.1
2003	91.4	92.5	93.1	93.6	3.9	93.8	94.6	95.1	95.5	2.8
2004	95.0	96.3	96.7	97.0	3.6	95.9	96.8	97.3	97.4	2.0
2005	98.1	99.3	99.6	100.0	3.1	97.8	99.1	99.5	100.0	2.7
2006	100.9	102.1	103.0	103.4	3.4	100.7	101.6	102.6	103.0	3.0
2007	103.5	104.1	105.2	105.8	2.3	103.7	104.2	105.6	106.1	3.0
2008	106.3	106.6	107.4	108.1	2.2	106.8	107.6	108.5	109.3	3.0
2009	108.6	108.9	109.4	109.8	1.6	109.7	110.2	110.7	111.2	1.7
2010	111.1	111.5	111.5	. . .	. . .	112.1	112.1	112.1	. . .	. . .
Production, Transportation, and Material Moving										
2001	85.3	85.8	86.7	87.4	3.6	88.7	89.4	90.2	91.0	3.9
2002	88.4	89.1	89.7	90.3	3.3	91.9	92.4	92.8	93.3	2.5
2003	91.5	92.4	93.2	93.6	3.7	94.0	94.6	95.1	95.4	2.3
2004	95.5	96.5	97.4	97.8	4.5	96.0	96.7	97.6	97.8	2.5
2005	98.5	99.0	99.7	100.0	2.2	98.3	98.9	99.6	100.0	2.2
2006	100.4	101.1	101.7	102.3	2.3	100.6	101.2	101.8	102.4	2.4
2007	102.5	103.3	103.9	104.5	2.2	103.1	103.8	104.5	105.0	2.5
2008	105.5	106.0	106.6	106.9	2.3	106.0	106.8	107.5	107.8	2.7
2009	107.7	108.1	108.6	108.9	1.9	108.3	108.8	109.4	109.6	1.7
2010	109.9	110.5	111.3	. . .	. . .	109.8	110.3	111.1	. . .	. . .
Production										
2001	84.9	85.2	86.0	86.7	3.2	88.4	89.1	89.7	90.5	3.7
2002	87.7	88.3	88.8	89.4	3.1	91.3	91.8	92.3	92.8	2.5
2003	91.0	91.7	92.5	93.0	4.0	93.6	94.1	94.8	95.1	2.5
2004	95.3	96.4	97.4	97.7	5.1	95.6	96.5	97.4	97.5	2.5
2005	98.6	99.1	99.6	100.0	2.4	98.3	98.9	99.5	100.0	2.6
2006	100.4	101.0	101.6	102.0	2.0	100.7	101.2	101.7	102.2	2.2
2007	102.1	102.8	103.2	104.0	2.0	103.1	103.6	104.2	104.6	2.3
2008	104.8	105.2	105.8	106.1	2.0	105.6	106.4	107.2	107.4	2.7
2009	107.1	107.6	108.0	108.3	2.1	108.1	108.5	109.0	109.3	1.8
2010	109.5	110.0	110.7	. . .	. . .	109.6	110.0	110.5	. . .	. . .
Transportation and Material Moving										
2001	85.8	86.7	87.7	88.5	4.2	89.0	89.9	90.8	91.6	4.1
2002	89.5	90.2	90.9	91.4	3.3	92.6	93.1	93.6	94.0	2.6
2003	92.4	93.4	94.0	94.4	3.3	94.7	95.3	95.6	95.8	1.9
2004	95.7	96.7	97.5	97.9	3.7	96.4	97.1	97.9	98.2	2.5
2005	98.3	99.0	99.8	100.0	2.1	98.5	98.9	99.7	100.0	1.8
2006	100.4	101.2	102.0	102.6	2.6	100.4	101.2	102.0	102.6	2.6
2007	103.1	104.1	104.9	105.3	2.6	103.2	104.1	105.0	105.4	2.7
2008	106.4	107.2	107.7	107.9	2.5	106.5	107.4	108.0	108.3	2.8
2009	108.4	108.9	109.6	109.7	1.7	108.5	109.2	109.9	110.1	1.7
2010	110.5	111.2	112.2	. . .	. . .	110.2	110.8	111.8	. . .	. . .
Service										
2001	87.1	87.7	88.2	89.4	3.8	89.7	90.2	90.6	91.7	3.4
2002	90.2	90.6	91.5	92.0	2.9	92.5	92.8	93.4	93.9	2.4
2003	93.0	93.4	94.4	95.0	3.3	94.5	94.8	95.6	96.1	2.3
2004	95.9	96.7	97.2	97.7	2.8	96.4	96.9	97.4	97.9	1.9
2005	98.5	99.0	99.5	100.0	2.4	98.6	99.0	99.6	100.0	2.1
2006	100.8	101.5	102.3	103.1	3.1	100.6	101.3	102.0	102.9	2.9
2007	104.5	105.2	106.4	107.0	3.8	104.6	105.3	106.5	107.1	4.1
2008	107.8	108.7	109.4	109.8	2.6	107.9	108.8	109.7	110.1	2.8
2009	110.7	110.9	111.7	111.8	1.8	111.0	111.2	112.1	112.3	2.0
2010	112.4	112.7	113.3	. . .	. . .	112.6	112.7	113.3	. . .	. . .

[1]Includes wages, salaries, and employer costs for employee benefits.
. . . = Not available.

Table 6-2. Employment Cost Index, Private Industry Workers, Total Compensation[1] and Wages and Salaries, by Bargaining Status and Industry, 2001–2010

(December 2005 = 100.)

Characteristic and year	Total compensation					Wages and salaries				
	Indexes				Percent change for 12 months (ended December)	Indexes				Percent change for 12 months (ended December)
	March	June	September	December		March	June	September	December	
WORKERS BY BARGAINING STATUS AND INDUSTRY										
Union Workers										
2001	82.0	82.9	83.7	84.8	4.2	86.5	87.4	88.3	89.6	4.3
2002	85.7	86.5	87.5	88.2	4.0	90.2	91.1	91.9	92.6	3.3
2003	89.5	90.7	91.6	92.3	4.6	93.0	93.8	94.4	94.9	2.5
2004	94.5	95.9	96.7	97.3	5.4	95.6	96.4	97.1	97.6	2.8
2005	97.9	98.8	99.6	100.0	2.8	97.9	98.7	99.5	100.0	2.5
2006	100.5	101.8	102.4	103.0	3.0	100.3	101.2	101.7	102.3	2.3
2007	102.7	103.9	104.4	105.1	2.0	102.8	103.7	104.4	104.7	2.3
2008	105.9	106.7	107.4	108.0	2.8	105.5	106.7	107.4	108.1	3.2
2009	109.1	109.8	110.5	111.1	2.9	108.8	109.6	110.2	110.9	2.6
2010	112.8	113.7	114.6	...	...	111.5	112.1	112.7	...	...
Union Workers, Goods-Producing[2]										
2001	81.9	82.7	83.4	84.0	2.9	87.2	88.2	88.9	89.5	3.5
2002	84.8	85.5	86.4	87.1	3.7	90.0	90.9	91.7	92.4	3.2
2003	88.9	90.2	90.9	91.7	5.3	92.9	94.0	94.5	95.0	2.8
2004	94.6	95.9	96.7	97.2	6.0	95.4	96.3	96.9	97.1	2.2
2005	97.7	98.8	99.6	100.0	2.9	97.5	98.5	99.2	100.0	3.0
2006	99.9	101.2	101.8	102.2	2.2	100.5	101.6	101.9	102.3	2.3
2007	101.5	102.8	103.1	104.0	1.8	102.7	103.6	104.3	104.3	2.0
2008	104.6	105.6	106.2	106.9	2.8	105.2	106.4	107.1	107.7	3.3
2009	108.0	108.9	109.5	110.0	2.9	108.2	108.8	109.5	109.8	1.9
2010	112.0	112.7	113.8	...	...	110.2	110.7	111.1	...	...
Union Workers, Manufacturing										
2001	81.1	81.4	82.0	83.0	2.7	87.3	88.1	88.8	89.7	3.7
2002	84.1	84.7	85.4	86.5	4.2	90.3	90.8	91.6	92.5	3.1
2003	88.6	89.5	90.1	91.0	5.2	93.3	94.2	94.5	95.0	2.7
2004	95.6	96.7	97.5	97.8	7.5	95.5	96.2	97.0	97.1	2.2
2005	98.3	99.1	99.7	100.0	2.2	97.6	98.3	99.0	100.0	3.0
2006	99.3	100.1	100.5	100.8	0.8	100.6	101.2	101.4	101.7	1.7
2007	99.2	100.0	100.0	101.0	0.2	102.0	102.5	102.9	102.6	0.9
2008	101.4	101.7	102.1	102.8	1.8	103.4	104.4	104.9	105.5	2.8
2009	104.4	104.8	105.4	105.8	2.9	106.0	106.4	107.0	107.3	1.7
2010	108.6	109.1	110.5	...	...	107.8	108.2	108.6	...	...
Union Workers, Service-Providing[3]										
2001	82.0	83.0	84.0	85.5	5.2	85.9	86.8	87.8	89.6	4.9
2002	86.4	87.3	88.4	89.1	4.2	90.3	91.2	92.0	92.7	3.5
2003	90.1	91.1	92.3	92.8	4.2	93.1	93.6	94.4	94.8	2.3
2004	94.4	95.8	96.6	97.3	4.8	95.7	96.5	97.3	98.0	3.4
2005	98.1	98.8	99.6	100.0	2.8	98.2	99.0	99.7	100.0	2.0
2006	101.0	102.2	102.9	103.6	3.6	100.1	100.9	101.6	102.2	2.2
2007	103.7	104.7	105.4	106.0	2.3	102.9	103.8	104.6	104.9	2.6
2008	107.0	107.5	108.3	108.8	2.6	105.8	106.9	107.7	108.3	3.2
2009	109.9	110.6	111.3	111.9	2.8	109.2	110.1	110.8	111.6	3.0
2010	113.5	114.5	115.2	...	...	112.4	113.1	113.8	...	...
Nonunion Workers										
2001	85.5	86.3	87.2	87.8	4.2	87.7	88.6	89.3	89.9	3.7
2002	88.7	89.6	90.0	90.3	2.8	90.8	91.7	92.0	92.2	2.6
2003	91.8	92.5	93.5	93.9	4.0	93.3	94.0	94.9	95.1	3.1
2004	95.0	95.9	96.7	97.2	3.5	95.8	96.5	97.3	97.6	2.6
2005	98.3	98.9	99.5	100.0	2.9	98.3	98.9	99.5	100.0	2.5
2006	100.9	101.7	102.6	103.2	3.2	100.8	101.8	102.7	103.3	3.3
2007	104.2	105.1	105.9	106.5	3.2	104.5	105.3	106.2	106.9	3.5
2008	107.5	108.3	108.9	109.1	2.4	107.9	108.7	109.4	109.6	2.5
2009	109.4	109.6	109.9	110.1	0.9	110.0	110.2	110.6	110.9	1.2
2010	110.9	111.4	111.8	...	...	111.4	111.9	112.4	...	...

[1] Includes wages, salaries, and employer costs for employee benefits.
[2] Includes mining, construction, and manufacturing.
[3] Includes the following industries: wholesale trade; retail trade; transportation and warehousing; utilities; information; finance and insurance; real estate and rental and leasing; professional, scientific, and technical services; management of companies and enterprises; administrative and support and waste management and remediation services; education services; health care and social assistance; arts, entertainment, and recreation; accommodation and food services; and other services, except public administration.
. . . = Not available.

Table 6-2. Employment Cost Index, Private Industry Workers, Total Compensation[1] and Wages and Salaries, by Bargaining Status and Industry, 2001–2010—*Continued*

(December 2005 = 100.)

Characteristic and year	Total compensation					Wages and salaries				
	Indexes				Percent change for 12 months (ended December)	Indexes				Percent change for 12 months (ended December)
	March	June	September	December		March	June	September	December	
Nonunion, Goods-Producing[2]										
2001	84.7	85.5	86.0	86.7	3.8	88.1	89.0	89.5	90.1	3.6
2002	87.8	88.5	88.8	89.7	3.5	91.0	91.6	91.9	92.7	2.9
2003	91.1	91.9	92.6	92.9	3.6	93.4	94.1	94.6	94.9	2.4
2004	94.5	95.2	96.4	96.8	4.2	95.6	96.2	97.3	97.3	2.5
2005	98.1	99.0	99.9	100.0	3.3	98.0	98.7	99.6	100.0	2.8
2006	100.5	101.4	102.0	102.5	2.5	100.7	101.9	102.4	103.0	3.0
2007	103.3	104.2	104.8	105.4	2.8	104.2	105.0	105.8	106.4	3.3
2008	106.5	107.1	107.6	107.7	2.2	107.7	108.4	109.0	109.3	2.7
2009	107.9	108.0	108.0	108.2	0.5	109.5	109.7	109.9	110.1	0.7
2010	109.1	109.5	110.1	. . .	. . .	110.6	111.0	111.6	. . .	. . .
Nonunion Workers, Manufacturing										
2001	84.5	85.3	85.8	86.3	3.6	88.5	89.4	89.8	90.3	3.4
2002	87.6	88.4	88.7	89.4	3.6	91.4	92.0	92.4	92.9	2.9
2003	91.2	91.9	92.6	92.8	3.8	93.9	94.5	94.9	95.2	2.5
2004	94.4	95.3	96.4	96.6	4.1	95.8	96.5	97.5	97.5	2.4
2005	98.2	99.1	99.8	100.0	3.5	98.4	99.0	99.8	100.0	2.6
2006	100.3	101.3	101.7	102.1	2.1	100.7	101.8	102.0	102.5	2.5
2007	102.8	103.7	104.1	104.6	2.4	103.6	104.2	104.9	105.5	2.9
2008	105.6	106.2	106.6	106.8	2.1	106.6	107.3	108.0	108.2	2.6
2009	107.1	107.3	107.3	107.5	0.7	108.6	108.9	109.1	109.3	1.0
2010	108.5	109.2	109.9	. . .	. . .	109.8	110.5	111.1	. . .	. . .
Nonunion, Service-Providing[3]										
2001	85.7	86.5	87.5	88.0	4.1	87.6	88.5	89.3	89.9	3.8
2002	88.9	89.9	90.4	90.5	2.8	90.8	91.7	92.0	92.1	2.4
2003	91.9	92.7	93.7	94.1	4.0	93.3	94.0	94.9	95.2	3.4
2004	95.2	96.1	96.9	97.3	3.4	95.8	96.6	97.3	97.7	2.6
2005	98.3	98.9	99.4	100.0	2.8	98.4	99.0	99.5	100.0	2.4
2006	101.0	101.8	102.7	103.4	3.4	100.8	101.7	102.7	103.4	3.4
2007	104.4	105.3	106.2	106.8	3.3	104.6	105.4	106.3	107.0	3.5
2008	107.7	108.6	109.2	109.4	2.4	107.9	108.8	109.4	109.7	2.5
2009	109.8	110.0	110.4	110.6	1.1	110.1	110.3	110.8	111.0	1.2
2010	111.3	111.9	112.3	. . .	. . .	111.6	112.2	112.6	. . .	. . .

[1]Includes wages, salaries, and employer costs for employee benefits.
[2]Includes mining, construction, and manufacturing.
[3]Includes the following industries: wholesale trade; retail trade; transportation and warehousing; utilities; information; finance and insurance; real estate and rental and leasing; professional, scientific, and technical services; management of companies and enterprises; administrative and support and waste management and remediation services; education services; health care and social assistance; arts, entertainment, and recreation; accommodation and food services; and other services, except public administration.
. . . = Not available.

Table 6-3. Employment Cost Index, Private Industry Workers, Total Compensation[1] and Wages and Salaries, by·Region, and Metropolitan Area Status, 2001–2010

(December 2005 = 100.)

Geography type and year	Total compensation					Wages and salaries				
	Indexes				Percent change for 12 months (ended December)	Indexes				Percent change for 12 months (ended December)
	March	June	September	December		March	June	September	December	
CENSUS REGIONS AND DIVISIONS[1]										
Northeast										
2001	84.3	85.3	86.2	86.7	3.8	86.8	87.8	88.6	89.2	3.8
2002	87.7	88.6	88.9	89.3	3.0	90.2	91.0	91.1	91.5	2.6
2003	90.6	91.4	92.4	92.9	4.0	92.4	93.2	94.1	94.5	3.3
2004	94.2	95.5	96.3	96.6	4.0	95.3	96.3	97.1	97.2	2.9
2005	97.6	98.5	99.2	100.0	3.5	97.8	98.6	99.2	100.0	2.9
2006	100.9	101.8	102.5	103.3	3.3	100.8	101.7	102.5	103.1	3.1
2007	104.0	105.1	106.2	106.8	3.4	104.0	105.0	106.1	106.6	3.4
2008	107.4	108.1	108.7	109.5	2.5	107.5	108.2	108.7	109.6	2.8
2009	109.8	110.2	110.7	111.0	1.4	109.9	110.3	110.8	111.1	1.4
2010	111.8	112.7	113.1	. . .	. . .	111.7	112.6	112.9	. . .	. . .
New England										
2006	100.7	101.4	102.1	103.1	3.1	100.7	101.5	102.3	103.1	3.1
2007	103.6	104.8	105.4	106.1	2.9	103.6	104.8	105.7	106.3	3.1
2008	106.7	107.1	107.8	109.5	3.2	107.1	107.6	108.3	110.3	3.8
2009	109.9	110.2	111.2	111.5	1.8	110.5	110.6	111.7	112.1	1.6
2010	112.3	113.1	113.4	. . .	. . .	112.6	113.4	113.5	. . .	. . .
Middle Atlantic										
2006	100.9	101.9	102.6	103.3	3.3	100.8	101.7	102.5	103.1	3.1
2007	104.2	105.3	106.5	107.1	3.7	104.2	105.1	106.4	106.7	3.5
2008	107.8	108.6	109.1	109.5	2.2	107.6	108.4	109.0	109.4	2.5
2009	109.8	110.2	110.6	110.8	1.2	109.7	110.1	110.4	110.7	1.2
2010	111.6	112.5	113.0	. . .	. . .	111.3	112.3	112.7	. . .	. . .
South										
2001	86.4	87.2	88.1	88.7	4.2	88.9	89.7	90.5	91.0	3.6
2002	89.5	90.5	91.2	91.2	2.8	91.8	92.7	93.3	93.2	2.4
2003	92.0	92.7	93.6	93.9	3.0	93.5	94.1	94.9	95.0	1.9
2004	95.2	96.2	97.1	97.7	4.0	95.8	96.7	97.5	98.0	3.2
2005	98.9	99.3	99.7	100.0	2.4	98.9	99.3	99.7	100.0	2.0
2006	101.0	101.6	102.8	103.5	3.5	101.0	101.6	102.9	103.6	3.6
2007	104.3	105.3	106.1	106.7	3.1	104.6	105.6	106.5	107.0	3.3
2008	107.8	108.5	109.1	109.3	2.4	108.1	109.1	109.8	110.0	2.8
2009	109.8	110.1	110.6	110.7	1.3	110.4	110.7	111.3	111.5	1.4
2010	111.5	112.0	112.5	. . .	. . .	111.9	112.4	112.9	. . .	. . .
South Atlantic										
2006	101.2	101.9	103.1	103.8	3.8	101.3	101.9	103.2	103.9	3.9
2007	104.9	106.0	106.8	107.3	3.4	105.0	106.1	106.9	107.5	3.5
2008	108.5	109.1	109.7	109.8	2.3	108.6	109.5	110.2	110.3	2.6
2009	110.3	110.7	111.3	111.5	1.5	110.8	111.3	111.9	112.2	1.7
2010	112.2	112.6	113.0	. . .	. . .	112.5	112.9	113.3	. . .	. . .
East South Central										
2006	100.7	100.9	101.5	102.3	2.3	100.7	101.5	102.1	103.1	3.1
2007	103.3	103.8	104.8	105.4	3.0	104.2	104.5	105.6	106.3	3.1
2008	106.5	107.2	108.0	108.0	2.5	107.2	107.9	109.0	109.0	2.5
2009	108.5	108.7	109.2	109.3	1.2	109.2	109.5	110.1	110.2	1.1
2010	110.0	110.8	111.0	. . .	. . .	110.8	111.4	111.6	. . .	. . .
West South Central										
2006	100.7	101.4	102.7	103.4	3.4	100.6	101.2	102.7	103.4	3.4
2007	103.7	104.8	105.6	106.1	2.6	104.1	105.3	106.1	106.6	3.1
2008	107.3	108.2	108.7	109.0	2.7	107.8	108.8	109.4	109.8	3.0
2009	109.4	109.5	109.9	109.9	0.8	110.1	110.2	110.8	110.9	1.0
2010	110.8	111.4	112.2	. . .	. . .	111.3	111.9	112.8	. . .	. . .
Midwest										
2001	84.8	85.4	86.1	86.7	3.5	86.8	87.6	88.3	88.9	3.3
2002	88.0	88.7	89.0	89.5	3.2	90.3	91.0	91.3	91.7	3.1
2003	92.1	92.8	93.6	94.0	5.0	94.2	94.7	95.2	95.5	4.1
2004	95.0	95.9	96.6	96.9	3.1	95.6	96.1	96.9	97.1	1.7
2005	97.8	98.4	99.5	100.0	3.2	97.8	98.2	99.4	100.0	3.0
2006	100.7	101.7	102.3	102.8	2.8	100.4	101.4	102.0	102.6	2.6
2007	103.3	104.2	104.6	105.3	2.4	103.6	104.4	105.0	105.6	2.9
2008	106.0	107.0	107.4	107.6	2.2	106.3	107.5	107.9	108.0	2.3
2009	107.9	108.1	108.4	108.6	0.9	108.4	108.6	108.9	109.2	1.1
2010	109.9	110.4	111.0	. . .	. . .	109.9	110.4	110.9	. . .	. . .

[1]Includes wages, salaries, and employer costs for employee benefits.
. . . = Not available.

Table 6-3. Employment Cost Index, Private Industry Workers, Total Compensation[1] and Wages and Salaries, by Region, and Metropolitan Area Status, 2001–2010—*Continued*

(December 2005 = 100.)

Geography type and year	Total compensation					Wages and salaries				
	Indexes				Percent change for 12 months (ended December)	Indexes				Percent change for 12 months (ended December)
	March	June	September	December		March	June	September	December	
East North Central										
2006	100.7	101.7	102.3	102.8	2.8	100.3	101.4	101.9	102.5	2.5
2007	103.2	104.1	104.4	105.0	2.1	103.6	104.4	104.7	105.3	2.7
2008	105.5	106.5	106.9	107.0	1.9	105.8	107.0	107.3	107.4	2.0
2009	107.0	107.3	107.5	107.8	0.7	107.5	107.7	108.0	108.3	0.8
2010	109.2	109.8	110.3	. . .	. . .	109.1	109.7	110.0	. . .	. . .
West North Central										
2006	100.6	101.5	102.4	102.7	2.7	100.6	101.5	102.4	102.7	2.7
2007	103.5	104.3	105.3	105.9	3.1	103.8	104.5	105.6	106.3	3.5
2008	107.3	108.4	108.8	109.0	2.9	107.9	108.9	109.5	109.7	3.2
2009	109.9	110.2	110.6	110.7	1.6	110.7	110.8	111.2	111.4	1.5
2010	111.6	112.0	112.8	. . .	. . .	111.9	112.4	113.1	. . .	. . .
West										
2001	84.1	85.0	85.9	86.9	5.2	87.4	88.3	89.2	90.2	4.8
2002	87.4	88.5	89.1	89.8	3.3	90.4	91.5	92.0	92.4	2.4
2003	90.9	92.0	93.2	93.8	4.5	93.0	93.9	95.1	95.5	3.4
2004	95.3	96.2	96.9	97.4	3.8	96.4	97.0	97.7	98.0	2.6
2005	98.4	99.3	99.7	100.0	2.7	98.4	99.3	99.6	100.0	2.0
2006	100.6	101.8	102.5	103.0	3.0	100.7	102.1	102.7	103.2	3.2
2007	104.2	104.9	105.7	106.5	3.4	104.8	105.4	106.2	107.0	3.7
2008	107.8	108.4	109.3	109.4	2.7	108.3	108.9	109.9	110.1	2.9
2009	109.9	110.1	110.3	110.7	1.2	110.5	110.8	111.2	111.6	1.4
2010	111.4	111.8	112.2	. . .	. . .	112.1	112.4	112.9	. . .	. . .
Mountain										
2006	101.0	101.8	102.7	103.1	3.1	100.6	101.7	102.8	103.2	3.2
2007	105.2	105.2	106.6	107.5	4.3	105.3	105.5	106.7	107.8	4.5
2008	108.4	109.4	110.3	110.4	2.7	108.9	109.9	110.8	111.0	3.0
2009	110.5	110.6	110.9	111.0	0.5	111.1	111.4	111.9	111.9	0.8
2010	111.3	112.3	113.0	. . .	. . .	112.3	113.2	114.1	. . .	. . .
Pacific										
2006	100.5	101.8	102.5	103.0	3.0	100.8	102.2	102.7	103.3	3.3
2007	103.9	104.8	105.4	106.1	3.0	104.6	105.3	106.0	106.8	3.4
2008	107.6	108.1	108.9	109.1	2.8	108.1	108.6	109.6	109.8	2.8
2009	109.7	109.9	110.1	110.5	1.3	110.3	110.6	111.0	111.5	1.5
2010	111.4	111.6	112.0	. . .	. . .	112.0	112.1	112.4	. . .	. . .

[1]Includes wages, salaries, and employer costs for employee benefits.
. . . = Not available.

Table 6-4. Employment Cost Index, State and Local Government Workers, Total Compensation[1] and Wages and Salaries, by Industry and Occupation, 2001–2010

(December 2005 = 100.)

Characteristic and year	Total compensation					Wages and salaries				
	Indexes				Percent change for 12 months (ended December)	Indexes				Percent change for 12 months (ended December)
	March	June	September	December		March	June	September	December	
WORKERS BY INDUSTRY[1]										
Total State and Local Government										
2001	83.6	84.1	85.8	86.2	4.1	87.6	88.0	89.7	90.2	3.8
2002	86.7	87.0	89.0	89.7	4.1	90.5	90.8	92.4	93.0	3.1
2003	90.4	90.7	92.3	92.8	3.5	93.4	93.6	94.6	95.0	2.2
2004	93.5	93.9	95.4	96.1	3.6	95.4	95.6	96.6	97.0	2.1
2005	96.9	97.2	99.1	100.0	4.1	97.6	97.8	99.1	100.0	3.1
2006	100.5	100.9	103.2	104.1	4.1	100.3	100.8	102.8	103.5	3.5
2007	105.1	105.7	107.6	108.4	4.1	104.1	104.6	106.4	107.1	3.5
2008	108.9	109.4	111.3	111.6	3.0	107.7	108.2	110.1	110.4	3.1
2009	112.3	112.9	114.0	114.3	2.4	110.9	111.5	112.4	112.6	2.0
2010	114.6	114.9	115.9	. . .	. . .	112.9	113.1	113.6	. . .	. . .
Education and Health Services										
2001	84.3	84.7	86.9	87.1	3.9	87.8	88.1	90.2	90.4	3.6
2002	87.4	87.6	89.7	90.4	3.8	90.6	90.8	92.8	93.3	3.2
2003	90.8	91.1	92.7	93.2	3.1	93.5	93.6	94.7	95.0	1.8
2004	93.7	93.8	95.5	96.1	3.1	95.3	95.4	96.6	97.0	2.1
2005	96.7	97.0	99.0	100.0	4.1	97.4	97.6	99.0	100.0	3.1
2006	100.3	100.8	103.7	104.3	4.3	100.2	100.7	103.1	103.6	3.6
2007	104.8	105.3	107.5	108.2	3.7	104.0	104.2	106.3	107.1	3.4
2008	108.6	109.1	111.2	111.5	3.0	107.5	108.1	110.2	110.5	3.2
2009	111.9	112.4	113.7	114.0	2.2	110.7	111.1	112.1	112.3	1.6
2010	114.1	114.2	115.4	. . .	. . .	112.5	112.6	113.4	. . .	. . .
Education Services										
2001	84.4	84.7	86.9	87.2	3.9	87.9	88.2	90.3	90.5	3.4
2002	87.3	87.5	89.7	90.4	3.7	90.6	90.8	92.9	93.3	3.1
2003	90.8	91.1	92.7	93.1	3.0	93.4	93.6	94.7	95.0	1.8
2004	93.6	93.8	95.4	96.1	3.2	95.3	95.4	96.6	96.9	2.0
2005	96.6	96.9	98.9	100.0	4.1	97.3	97.5	98.9	100.0	3.2
2006	100.2	100.5	103.5	104.1	4.1	100.1	100.4	103.0	103.4	3.4
2007	104.6	105.0	107.4	108.0	3.7	103.7	103.9	106.1	106.8	3.3
2008	108.4	108.8	111.0	111.2	3.0	107.2	107.7	109.9	110.1	3.1
2009	111.8	112.1	113.5	113.7	2.2	110.4	110.7	111.7	111.9	1.6
2010	113.8	113.9	115.1	. . .	. . .	112.1	112.2	113.0	. . .	. . .
Schools[2]										
2001	84.4	84.7	87.0	87.2	3.9	87.9	88.2	90.3	90.5	3.4
2002	87.3	87.5	89.7	90.4	3.7	90.6	90.8	92.9	93.3	3.1
2003	90.8	91.1	92.7	93.1	3.0	93.4	93.6	94.7	95.0	1.8
2004	93.6	93.8	95.5	96.1	3.2	95.3	95.4	96.6	96.9	2.0
2005	96.6	96.9	98.9	100.0	4.1	97.3	97.5	98.9	100.0	3.2
2006	100.2	100.5	103.5	104.1	4.1	100.1	100.4	103.0	103.4	3.4
2007	104.6	104.9	107.4	108.0	3.7	103.6	103.9	106.1	106.8	3.3
2008	108.4	108.8	111.0	111.2	3.0	107.2	107.7	109.9	110.1	3.1
2009	111.8	112.1	113.5	113.7	2.2	110.4	110.7	111.7	111.9	1.6
2010	113.8	113.9	115.1	. . .	. . .	112.1	112.2	113.0	. . .	. . .
Elementary and Secondary Schools										
2001	84.1	84.3	86.5	86.7	3.5	87.8	88.2	90.0	90.3	3.1
2002	86.8	87.0	89.3	89.9	3.7	90.5	90.6	92.8	93.2	3.2
2003	90.3	90.6	92.4	92.7	3.1	93.2	93.4	94.6	94.8	1.7
2004	93.2	93.4	95.3	96.0	3.6	95.1	95.2	96.5	96.9	2.2
2005	96.4	96.6	98.8	100.0	4.2	97.1	97.2	98.9	100.0	3.2
2006	100.2	100.5	103.6	104.2	4.2	100.0	100.3	103.0	103.4	3.4
2007	104.7	105.0	107.4	108.0	3.6	103.6	103.8	106.0	106.6	3.1
2008	108.3	108.8	111.1	111.4	3.1	106.9	107.5	109.8	110.1	3.3
2009	112.0	112.2	114.0	114.1	2.4	110.3	110.5	112.0	112.1	1.8
2010	114.1	114.3	115.6	. . .	. . .	112.3	112.5	113.4	. . .	. . .
Health Care and Social Assistance[3]										
2001	83.4	84.5	86.0	86.8	5.0	86.1	87.1	88.6	89.5	4.8
2002	87.8	88.2	89.5	90.6	4.4	90.7	91.1	92.2	93.0	3.9
2003	91.2	91.4	92.9	93.5	3.2	93.5	93.9	94.7	95.3	2.5
2004	94.2	94.7	96.3	96.5	3.2	95.7	96.0	97.1	97.3	2.1
2005	97.6	98.0	99.5	100.0	3.6	98.1	98.5	99.4	100.0	2.8
2006	101.3	102.9	105.1	105.7	5.7	101.0	103.0	104.8	105.5	5.5
2007	107.1	107.6	108.6	109.3	3.4	106.6	107.2	108.2	109.2	3.5
2008	110.1	111.1	112.7	113.2	3.6	110.1	111.0	112.8	113.4	3.8
2009	113.3	114.8	115.3	115.8	2.3	113.1	114.8	115.2	115.6	1.9
2010	116.2	116.6	117.1	. . .	. . .	115.9	116.2	116.2	. . .	. . .

[1]Includes wages, salaries, and employer costs for employee benefits.
[2]Includes elementary and secondary schools, junior colleges, colleges, universities, and professional schools.
[3]Includes ambulatory health care services and social assistance, not shown separately.
. . . = Not available.

Table 6-4. Employment Cost Index, State and Local Government Workers, Total Compensation[1] and Wages and Salaries, by Industry and Occupation, 2001–2010—Continued

(December 2005 = 100.)

Characteristic and year	Total compensation					Wages and salaries				
	Indexes				Percent change for 12 months (ended December)	Indexes				Percent change for 12 months (ended December)
	March	June	September	December		March	June	September	December	
Hospitals										
2001	83.0	84.4	85.9	86.6	4.5	85.3	86.6	88.0	88.8	4.3
2002	87.6	88.1	89.3	90.6	4.6	90.0	90.6	91.7	92.8	4.5
2003	91.0	91.1	92.8	93.4	3.1	93.1	93.5	94.5	95.2	2.6
2004	93.9	94.4	96.1	96.7	3.5	95.6	95.9	97.1	97.7	2.6
2005	97.6	98.0	99.5	100.0	3.4	98.3	98.6	99.4	100.0	2.4
2006	100.9	101.3	103.3	104.3	4.3	100.9	101.4	103.1	104.4	4.4
2007	105.6	106.3	107.5	108.2	3.7	105.7	106.5	107.6	108.6	4.0
2008	109.2	109.7	110.8	111.3	2.9	109.8	110.3	111.4	112.1	3.2
2009	112.4	113.5	114.0	114.5	2.9	112.8	114.0	114.4	114.9	2.5
2010	115.2	115.8	116.1	. . .	. . .	115.4	115.7	115.7	. . .	. . .
WORKERS BY OCCUPATION										
Management, Professional, and Related[4]										
2001	84.1	84.6	86.5	86.8	4.1	87.5	88.0	89.8	90.2	3.8
2002	87.2	87.4	89.5	90.3	4.0	90.4	90.6	92.5	93.1	3.2
2003	90.8	91.1	92.6	93.1	3.1	93.4	93.6	94.6	95.0	2.0
2004	93.8	94.0	95.5	96.2	3.3	95.3	95.5	96.6	97.0	2.1
2005	97.0	97.3	99.0	100.0	4.0	97.5	97.8	99.0	100.0	3.1
2006	100.3	100.8	103.3	104.0	4.0	100.2	100.7	102.9	103.5	3.5
2007	104.9	105.4	107.5	108.3	4.1	104.0	104.3	106.3	107.0	3.4
2008	108.8	109.3	111.3	111.6	3.0	107.6	108.2	110.1	110.4	3.2
2009	112.0	112.6	113.7	113.9	2.1	110.7	111.2	112.1	112.3	1.7
2010	114.1	114.3	115.3	. . .	. . .	112.5	112.7	113.3	. . .	. . .
Professional and Related										
2001	84.0	84.4	86.4	86.7	4.0	87.5	87.9	89.8	90.1	3.7
2002	87.0	87.2	89.4	90.2	4.0	90.2	90.5	92.4	93.0	3.2
2003	90.7	91.0	92.5	93.0	3.1	93.3	93.4	94.5	94.9	2.0
2004	93.6	93.9	95.5	96.1	3.3	95.3	95.4	96.6	96.9	2.1
2005	96.8	97.1	98.9	100.0	4.1	97.4	97.7	98.9	100.0	3.2
2006	100.2	100.8	103.4	104.0	4.0	100.2	100.7	103.0	103.6	3.6
2007	104.8	105.3	107.5	108.2	4.0	103.9	104.2	106.3	107.0	3.3
2008	108.6	109.1	111.1	111.4	3.0	107.5	108.1	110.1	110.3	3.1
2009	111.9	112.4	113.7	114.0	2.3	110.6	111.1	112.1	112.3	1.8
2010	114.0	114.2	115.3	. . .	. . .	112.5	112.6	113.3	. . .	. . .
Sales and Office										
2001	82.8	83.1	84.5	85.2	3.9	87.4	87.8	89.1	89.6	3.1
2002	86.1	86.5	88.3	89.1	4.6	90.4	90.8	92.3	92.9	3.7
2003	89.8	90.3	92.4	92.8	4.2	93.5	93.8	95.1	95.4	2.7
2004	93.7	94.4	95.7	96.5	4.0	96.0	96.2	97.3	97.6	2.3
2005	97.5	97.6	99.3	100.0	3.6	98.1	98.0	99.4	100.0	2.5
2006	100.9	101.5	103.3	104.1	4.1	100.6	101.2	102.6	103.2	3.2
2007	105.6	106.2	107.9	108.6	4.3	104.5	104.8	106.3	107.0	3.7
2008	108.8	109.3	111.0	111.3	2.5	107.4	107.9	109.3	109.7	2.5
2009	112.4	113.0	114.3	114.7	3.1	110.5	111.2	112.1	112.4	2.5
2010	115.3	115.5	116.4	. . .	. . .	112.9	112.9	113.0	. . .	. . .
Office and Administrative Support										
2001	82.6	82.9	84.4	85.1	3.9	87.4	87.8	89.1	89.7	3.1
2002	86.0	86.5	88.2	88.9	4.5	90.5	91.0	92.4	92.8	3.5
2003	89.6	90.0	92.1	92.6	4.2	93.4	93.7	95.0	95.3	2.7
2004	93.5	94.2	95.6	96.4	4.1	95.9	96.1	97.1	97.5	2.3
2005	97.4	97.5	99.2	100.0	3.7	98.0	97.9	99.3	100.0	2.6
2006	101.0	101.6	103.5	104.2	4.2	100.7	101.4	102.7	103.4	3.4
2007	105.7	106.4	108.2	108.9	4.5	104.7	105.0	106.5	107.3	3.8
2008	109.3	109.8	111.4	111.8	2.7	107.8	108.3	109.7	110.1	2.6
2009	112.8	113.3	114.7	115.0	2.9	111.0	111.6	112.6	112.9	2.5
2010	115.6	115.9	116.8	. . .	. . .	113.3	113.4	113.5	. . .	. . .
Service										
2001	82.1	82.6	84.1	84.7	4.7	87.8	88.3	89.7	90.3	3.8
2002	85.2	85.8	87.4	88.0	3.9	90.8	91.2	92.1	92.4	2.3
2003	88.8	89.3	91.0	91.6	4.1	93.1	93.6	94.3	94.9	2.7
2004	92.3	92.7	94.9	95.5	4.3	95.3	95.4	96.4	96.8	2.0
2005	96.2	96.7	99.1	100.0	4.7	97.3	97.7	99.3	100.0	3.3
2006	100.6	101.2	103.1	104.5	4.5	100.3	100.8	102.4	103.9	3.9
2007	105.4	106.3	108.0	109.1	4.4	104.5	105.2	106.5	107.7	3.7
2008	109.7	110.0	111.9	112.4	3.0	108.3	108.6	110.4	110.9	3.0
2009	113.4	114.0	114.9	115.6	2.8	112.0	112.7	113.3	113.8	2.6
2010	116.1	116.4	117.6	. . .	. . .	114.3	114.5	114.9	. . .	. . .

[1]Includes wages, salaries, and employer costs for employee benefits.
[4]Includes the following occupational groups: management, business, and financial; professional and related; sales and related; and office and administrative support.
. . . = Not available.

Table 6-5. Employment Cost Index, Benefits, by Industry and Occupation, 2001–2010

(December 2005 = 100.)

Characteristic and year	Indexes				Percent change for 12 months (ended December)
	March	June	September	December	
Civilian Workers[1]					
2001	78.1	78.8	80.0	80.6	5.1
2002	81.6	82.5	83.6	84.3	4.6
2003	86.4	87.4	88.9	89.7	6.4
2004	92.2	93.6	94.8	95.7	6.7
2005	97.6	98.3	99.5	100.0	4.5
2006	100.9	101.6	102.8	103.6	3.6
2007	104.0	105.1	106.1	106.8	3.1
2008	107.6	108.1	108.9	109.1	2.2
2009	109.7	110.0	110.6	110.7	1.5
2010	112.1	112.7	113.6	. . .	. . .
Total Private					
2001	78.9	79.6	80.6	81.3	5.2
2002	82.4	83.4	84.1	84.7	4.2
2003	87.1	88.2	89.4	90.2	6.5
2004	93.0	94.6	95.4	96.2	6.7
2005	98.1	99.0	99.7	100.0	4.0
2006	101.0	101.7	102.5	103.1	3.1
2007	103.2	104.3	105.0	105.6	2.4
2008	106.5	107.0	107.5	107.7	2.0
2009	108.2	108.4	108.7	108.8	1.0
2010	110.4	111.1	111.7	. . .	. . .
State and Local Government Workers					
2001	75.3	75.8	77.7	78.1	5.1
2002	78.9	79.3	81.8	83.0	6.3
2003	84.1	84.7	87.3	88.2	6.3
2004	89.5	90.3	93.0	94.1	6.7
2005	95.5	96.0	99.0	100.0	6.3
2006	100.7	101.3	104.1	105.2	5.2
2007	107.0	108.0	110.3	111.0	5.5
2008	111.4	111.8	113.9	114.2	2.9
2009	115.2	115.8	117.5	117.9	3.2
2010	118.3	118.8	120.7	. . .	. . .
WORKERS BY OCCUPATION					
Management, Professional, and Related					
2001	79.8	80.7	81.5	82.0	5.8
2002	82.9	83.8	84.1	84.7	3.3
2003	87.4	88.1	89.4	90.1	6.4
2004	92.2	93.5	94.4	95.4	5.9
2005	98.2	99.0	99.8	100.0	4.8
2006	101.3	101.8	102.8	103.4	3.4
2007	103.8	104.9	105.6	106.0	2.5
2008	107.3	107.9	108.5	108.5	2.4
2009	108.8	108.8	108.9	108.8	0.3
2010	110.2	110.5	111.0	. . .	. . .
Sales and Office					
2001	78.1	78.9	80.1	81.1	6.0
2002	82.0	83.4	84.2	84.7	4.4
2003	86.8	88.2	89.3	90.0	6.3
2004	92.6	94.4	95.2	95.8	6.4
2005	97.6	98.5	99.3	100.0	4.4
2006	100.8	101.6	102.0	102.9	2.9
2007	103.4	104.3	105.2	106.0	3.0
2008	106.5	107.0	107.6	107.8	1.7
2009	108.0	108.1	108.5	108.7	0.8
2010	110.2	111.1	111.6	. . .	. . .
Natural Resources, Construction, and Maintenance					
2001	77.7	78.3	79.7	79.8	4.0
2002	81.2	82.3	83.5	84.1	5.4
2003	86.0	87.9	88.8	89.8	6.8
2004	92.9	94.9	95.4	96.4	7.3
2005	98.0	99.3	99.8	100.0	3.7
2006	101.1	102.7	103.5	104.0	4.0
2007	103.4	104.8	105.3	105.9	1.8
2008	106.5	107.0	107.5	107.7	1.7
2009	108.2	108.8	109.3	109.5	1.7
2010	111.6	112.4	113.0	. . .	. . .
Production, Transportation, and Material Moving					
2001	78.8	79.0	80.1	80.7	3.1
2002	82.0	82.9	83.7	84.5	4.7
2003	86.8	88.3	89.4	90.2	6.7
2004	94.5	96.1	97.1	97.7	8.3
2005	98.7	99.3	100.0	100.0	2.4
2006	100.1	101.0	101.6	102.0	2.0
2007	101.2	102.4	102.7	103.7	1.7
2008	104.4	104.5	104.8	105.1	1.4
2009	106.4	106.8	107.1	107.4	2.2
2010	110.0	110.8	111.8	. . .	. . .

[1]Includes workers in the private nonfarm economy, except those in private households, and workers in the public sector, except those in the federal government.
. . . = Not available.

Table 6-5. Employment Cost Index, Benefits, by Industry and Occupation, 2001–2010—*Continued*

(December 2005 = 100.)

Characteristic and year	Indexes				Percent change for 12 months (ended December)
	March	June	September	December	
Service					
2001	79.7	80.5	81.3	82.5	5.4
2002	83.7	84.4	85.9	86.5	4.8
2003	88.8	89.4	90.7	91.7	6.0
2004	94.6	95.9	96.7	97.0	5.8
2005	98.3	98.9	99.5	100.0	3.1
2006	101.5	102.2	103.0	103.6	3.6
2007	104.2	105.1	106.0	106.7	3.0
2008	107.6	108.5	108.7	108.8	2.0
2009	109.7	110.0	110.4	110.5	1.6
2010	111.7	112.5	113.2	...	...
WORKERS BY INDUSTRY					
Goods-Producing Industries[2]					
2001	76.5	77.1	77.9	78.5	3.7
2002	80.0	80.6	81.3	82.3	4.8
2003	85.3	86.5	87.5	88.2	7.2
2004	92.5	93.9	95.0	96.3	9.2
2005	98.3	99.6	100.4	100.0	3.8
2006	99.6	100.4	101.3	101.7	1.7
2007	100.9	102.2	102.4	103.2	1.5
2008	104.0	104.4	104.6	104.7	1.5
2009	105.4	105.7	105.7	105.8	1.1
2010	108.4	109.0	110.0	...	...
Manufacturing					
2001	75.5	75.8	76.4	77.2	3.5
2002	78.8	79.7	80.2	81.3	5.3
2003	84.7	85.8	86.7	87.3	7.4
2004	92.8	94.1	95.3	96.0	10.0
2005	98.3	99.4	100.0	100.0	4.2
2006	99.0	99.7	100.5	100.8	0.8
2007	99.6	101.0	100.7	101.7	0.9
2008	102.3	102.2	102.3	102.5	0.8
2009	103.5	103.6	103.4	103.6	1.1
2010	106.6	107.5	108.7	...	...
Aircraft Manufacturing					
2001	45.9	46.0	45.0	46.7	6.6
2002	48.4	48.9	48.9	51.8	10.9
2003	59.4	59.3	59.6	57.2	10.4
2004	70.0	70.7	71.1	71.1	24.3
2005	97.1	97.2	97.4	100.0	40.6
2006	79.1	79.2	84.3	83.2	-16.8
2007	72.6	73.4	68.5	68.6	-17.5
2008	71.1	71.3	73.1	73.3	6.9
2009	73.4	73.5	72.0	72.1	-1.6
2010	71.9	71.6	83.2	...	...
Service-Providing[3]					
2001	79.9	80.7	81.8	82.4	5.6
2002	83.4	84.5	85.3	85.8	4.1
2003	87.8	88.9	90.2	91.0	6.1
2004	93.2	94.9	95.5	96.1	5.6
2005	98.1	98.7	99.4	100.0	4.1
2006	101.5	102.3	103.0	103.7	3.7
2007	104.1	105.2	106.0	106.6	2.8
2008	107.6	108.1	108.7	108.9	2.2
2009	109.3	109.5	109.9	109.9	0.9
2010	111.3	111.9	112.3	...	...
WORKERS BY BARGAINING STATUS					
Union[2]					
2001	74.8	75.7	76.6	77.3	3.9
2002	78.6	79.3	80.5	81.2	5.0
2003	83.9	85.7	87.2	88.1	8.5
2004	92.8	95.0	96.0	96.8	9.9
2005	98.0	98.9	99.8	100.0	3.3
2006	100.8	102.7	103.4	104.2	4.2
2007	102.4	104.1	104.3	105.8	1.5
2008	106.6	106.6	107.2	107.8	1.9
2009	109.5	110.3	110.9	111.4	3.3
2010	114.9	116.2	117.7	...	...
Nonunion					
2001	79.9	80.5	81.6	82.2	5.4
2002	83.2	84.3	84.9	85.5	4.0
2003	87.8	88.8	89.9	90.6	6.0
2004	93.0	94.5	95.2	96.0	6.0
2005	98.2	99.0	99.6	100.0	4.2
2006	101.0	101.5	102.3	102.9	2.9
2007	103.4	104.3	105.1	105.6	2.6
2008	106.5	107.1	107.6	107.6	1.9
2009	107.9	108.0	108.2	108.2	0.6
2010	109.5	110.0	110.4	...	...

[2]Includes mining, construction, and manufacturing.
[3]Includes the following industries: wholesale trade; retail trade; transportation and warehousing; utilities; information; finance and insurance; real estate and rental and leasing; professional, scientific, and technical services; management of companies and enterprises; administrative and support and waste management and remediation services; education services; health care and social assistance; arts, entertainment, and recreation; accommodation and food services; and other services, except public administration.
. . . = Not available.

NOTES AND DEFINITIONS

EMPLOYER COSTS FOR EMPLOYEE COMPENSATION

The Employer Costs for Employee Compensation (ECEC) measures the average cost per employee hour worked that employers pay for wages and salaries and benefits.

Survey Scope

The ECEC consists of data for the civilian economy, obtained from both private industry and state and local government. Excluded from private industry are the self-employed and farm and private household workers. Federal government workers are excluded from the public sector. The private industry series and the state and local government series provide separate data for the two sectors.

The cost levels for June 2010 were collected from a probability sample of 62,800 occupations selected from a sample of about 13,200 establishments in private industry and approximately 11,600 occupations from a sample of about 1,800 establishments in state and local governments. The state and local government sample, which is replaced less frequently than the private industry sample, was replaced in its entirety in September 2007. The private industry sample is rotated over approximately 5 years, which makes the sample more representative of the economy and reduces respondent burden. Data are collected for the pay period including the 12th day of the survey months of March, June, September, and December. The sample is replaced on a cross-area, cross-industry basis.

To be included in the ECEC, employees in occupations must receive cash payments from the establishment for services performed and the establishment must pay the employer's portion of Medicare taxes on that individual's wages. Major exclusions from the survey are the self-employed, individuals who set their own pay (for example, proprietors, owners, major stockholders, and partners in unincorporated firms), volunteers, unpaid workers, family members being paid token wages, individuals receiving long-term disability compensation, and U.S. citizens working overseas.

Current employment weights are used to calculate cost levels. These weights are derived from two BLS programs: the Quarterly Census of Employment and Wages (QCEW) and the Current Employment Statistics (CES). Combined, these programs provide the appropriate industry coverage and currency of data needed to match the ECEC.

Sources of Additional Information

Additional information may be obtained from BLS news release 10-1241 "Employer Costs for Employee Compensation—June 2010," and in various articles in the BLS e-publication, *Compensation and Working Conditions*. These resources are available on the BLS Web site at <http://www.bls.gov/ncs/ect/>.

Table 6-6. Employer Compensation Costs Per Hour Worked for Employee Compensation and Costs as a Percent of Total Compensation: Private Industry Workers, by Major Industry Group, June 2010

(Dollars, percent of total cost.)

Compensation component	All workers		Goods-producing[1]						Service-providing[2]			
			All goods-producing[1]		Construction		Manufacturing		All service-providing[2]		Trade, transportation, and utilities	
	Cost	Percent	Cost	Percent	Cost	Percent	Cost	Percent	Cost	Percent	Cost	Percent
TOTAL COMPENSATION	27.64	100.0	32.56	100.0	31.44	100.0	32.36	100.0	26.60	100.0	23.75	100.0
Wages and Salaries	19.53	70.6	21.73	66.7	21.73	69.1	21.33	65.9	19.06	71.7	16.75	70.5
Total Benefits	8.11	29.4	10.84	33.3	9.72	30.9	11.03	34.1	7.53	28.3	7.00	29.5
Paid leave	1.86	6.7	2.09	6.4	1.14	3.6	2.46	7.6	1.81	6.8	1.43	6.0
Vacation	0.95	3.4	1.11	3.4	0.64	2.0	1.29	4.0	0.92	3.5	0.73	3.1
Holiday	0.59	2.1	0.74	2.3	0.39	1.2	0.88	2.7	0.56	2.1	0.44	1.9
Sick	0.23	0.8	0.17	0.5	0.08	0.2	0.21	0.7	0.24	0.9	0.19	0.8
Personal	0.08	0.3	0.06	0.2	0.03	0.1	0.07	0.2	0.09	0.3	0.06	0.3
Supplemental pay	0.78	2.8	1.20	3.7	1.05	3.3	1.21	3.8	0.69	2.6	0.54	2.3
Overtime and premium pay[3]	0.26	1.0	0.58	1.8	0.63	2.0	0.54	1.7	0.20	0.7	0.26	1.1
Shift differentials	0.07	0.2	0.09	0.3	(4)	(5)	0.12	0.4	0.06	0.2	0.02	0.1
Nonproduction bonuses	0.45	1.6	0.54	1.7	0.41	1.3	0.55	1.7	0.43	1.6	0.25	1.1
Insurance	2.22	8.0	3.09	9.5	2.33	7.4	3.37	10.4	2.03	7.6	2.07	8.7
Life insurance	0.04	0.2	0.07	0.2	0.06	0.2	0.07	0.2	0.04	0.1	0.04	0.1
Health insurance	2.08	7.5	2.89	8.9	2.20	7.0	3.15	9.7	1.91	7.2	1.96	8.3
Short-term disability	0.05	0.2	0.09	0.3	0.05	0.2	0.10	0.3	0.05	0.2	0.04	0.2
Long-term disability	0.04	0.1	0.04	0.1	(4)	(5)	0.05	0.2	0.04	0.2	0.03	0.1
Retirement and savings	0.96	3.5	1.50	4.6	1.68	5.3	1.30	4.0	0.85	3.2	0.88	3.7
Defined benefit plans	0.42	1.5	0.87	2.7	1.11	3.5	0.68	2.1	0.33	1.2	0.43	1.8
Defined contribution plans	0.54	2.0	0.62	1.9	0.57	1.8	0.62	1.9	0.52	2.0	0.45	1.9
Legally required benefits	2.29	8.3	2.95	9.1	3.53	11.2	2.68	8.3	2.15	8.1	2.08	8.8
Social Security and Medicare	1.64	5.9	1.85	5.7	1.80	5.7	1.85	5.7	1.59	6.0	1.39	5.9
Social Security[6]	1.31	4.8	1.49	4.6	1.46	4.6	1.49	4.6	1.28	4.8	1.12	4.7
Medicare	0.32	1.2	0.36	1.1	0.34	1.1	0.36	1.1	0.31	1.2	0.27	1.1
Federal unemployment insurance	0.03	0.1	0.03	0.1	0.03	0.1	0.03	0.1	0.03	0.1	0.04	0.2
State unemployment insurance	0.18	0.6	0.25	0.8	0.31	1.0	0.23	0.7	0.16	0.6	0.17	0.7
Workers' compensation	0.44	1.6	0.82	2.5	1.38	4.4	0.58	1.8	0.36	1.4	0.49	2.1

Compensation component	Service-providing[2]											
	Information		Financial activities		Professional and business services		Education and health services		Leisure and hospitality		Other services	
	Cost	Percent	Cost	Percent	Cost	Percent	Cost	Percent	Cost	Percent	Cost	Percent
TOTAL COMPENSATION	41.90	100.0	36.76	100.0	33.19	100.0	29.63	100.0	12.11	100.0	24.63	100.0
Wages and Salaries	28.67	68.4	25.00	68.0	24.10	72.6	21.27	71.8	9.56	79.0	18.15	73.7
Total Benefits	13.23	31.6	11.76	32.0	9.09	27.4	8.36	28.2	2.55	21.0	6.48	26.3
Paid leave	3.89	9.3	3.03	8.2	2.32	7.0	2.21	7.5	0.38	3.2	1.55	6.3
Vacation	2.01	4.8	1.54	4.2	1.20	3.6	1.09	3.7	0.21	1.8	0.72	2.9
Holiday	1.03	2.5	0.93	2.5	0.76	2.3	0.66	2.2	0.12	1.0	0.58	2.3
Sick	0.47	1.1	0.42	1.2	0.27	0.8	0.34	1.1	0.03	0.3	0.21	0.8
Personal	0.38	0.9	0.14	0.4	0.08	0.2	0.13	0.4	(4)	(5)	0.05	0.2
Supplemental pay	1.00	2.4	1.59	4.3	1.13	3.4	0.57	1.9	0.12	1.0	0.57	2.3
Overtime and premium pay[3]	0.37	0.9	0.15	0.4	0.20	0.6	0.21	0.7	0.07	0.5	0.16	0.6
Shift differentials	0.06	0.1	(4)	(5)	0.03	0.1	0.20	0.7	(4)	(5)	(4)	(5)
Nonproduction bonuses	0.57	1.4	1.43	3.9	0.90	2.7	0.16	0.5	0.05	0.4	0.41	1.7
Insurance	3.80	9.1	3.05	8.3	2.13	6.4	2.37	8.0	0.66	5.4	1.54	6.3
Life insurance	0.05	0.1	0.06	0.2	0.06	0.2	0.03	0.1	(4)	(5)	0.06	0.2
Health insurance	3.51	8.4	2.83	7.7	1.97	5.9	2.25	7.6	0.63	5.2	1.43	5.8
Short-term disability	0.17	0.4	0.09	0.3	0.06	0.2	0.04	0.1	(4)	(5)	0.03	0.1
Long-term disability	0.07	0.2	0.06	0.2	0.05	0.2	0.05	0.2	(4)	(5)	0.03	0.1
Retirement and savings	1.63	3.9	1.61	4.4	0.94	2.8	0.92	3.1	0.11	0.9	0.68	2.8
Defined benefit plans	0.70	1.7	0.63	1.7	0.31	0.9	0.28	0.9	0.02	0.2	0.28	1.1
Defined contribution plans	0.93	2.2	0.98	2.7	0.63	1.9	0.65	2.2	0.08	0.7	0.40	1.6
Legally required benefits	2.91	6.9	2.48	6.7	2.57	7.7	2.28	7.7	1.28	10.6	2.13	8.7
Social Security and Medicare	2.43	5.8	2.08	5.7	1.98	6.0	1.77	6.0	0.85	7.1	1.52	6.2
Social Security[6]	1.94	4.6	1.65	4.5	1.58	4.8	1.42	4.8	0.69	5.7	1.22	5.0
Medicare	0.49	1.2	0.43	1.2	0.40	1.2	0.35	1.2	0.16	1.3	0.29	1.2
Federal unemployment insurance	0.03	0.1	0.03	0.1	0.03	0.1	0.03	0.1	0.04	0.3	0.03	0.1
State unemployment insurance	0.18	0.4	0.17	0.5	0.20	0.6	0.14	0.5	0.14	1.2	0.16	0.6
Workers' compensation	0.26	0.6	0.20	0.5	0.36	1.1	0.34	1.2	0.25	2.0	0.43	1.7

Note: Individual items may not sum to totals due to rounding.

[1] Includes mining, construction, and manufacturing. The agriculture, forestry, farming, and hunting sector is excluded.
[2] Includes utilities; wholesale trade; retail trade; transportation and warehousing; information; finance and insurance; real estate and rental and leasing; professional and technical services; management of companies and enterprises; administrative and waste services; education services; health care and social assistance; arts, entertainment, and recreation; accommodation and food services; and other services, except public administration.
[3] Includes premium pay for work in addition to the regular work schedule (such as overtime, weekends, and holidays).
[4] Cost per hour worked is $0.01 or less.
[5] Less than 0.05 percent.
[6] Comprises the Old Age, Survivors, and Disability Insurance (OASDI) program.

Table 6-7. Employer Compensation Costs Per Hour Worked for Employee Compensation and Costs as a Percent of Total Compensation: Private Industry Workers, by Census Region and Area, June 2010

(Dollars, percent of total costs.)

Compensation component	Census region and division[1]					
	Northeast		Northeast divisions			
			New England		Middle Atlantic	
	Cost	Percent	Cost	Percent	Cost	Percent
TOTAL COMPENSATION	32.00	100.0	33.76	100.0	31.31	100.0
Wages and Salaries	22.09	69.0	23.26	68.9	21.63	69.1
Total Benefits	9.91	31.0	10.50	31.1	9.68	30.9
Paid leave	2.34	7.3	2.46	7.3	2.29	7.3
Vacation	1.17	3.6	1.25	3.7	1.13	3.6
Holiday	0.74	2.3	0.79	2.3	0.71	2.3
Sick	0.30	1.0	0.29	0.9	0.31	1.0
Personal	0.13	0.4	0.13	0.4	0.13	0.4
Supplemental pay	1.22	3.8	1.67	4.9	1.04	3.3
Overtime and premium pay[2]	0.27	0.8	0.26	0.8	0.27	0.9
Shift differentials	0.07	0.2	0.06	0.2	0.07	0.2
Nonproduction bonuses	0.88	2.8	1.35	4.0	0.70	2.2
Insurance	2.57	8.0	2.55	7.6	2.57	8.2
Life insurance	0.05	0.2	0.06	0.2	0.04	0.1
Health insurance	2.39	7.5	2.37	7.0	2.40	7.7
Short-term disability	0.08	0.3	0.07	0.2	0.08	0.3
Long-term disability	0.05	0.1	0.06	0.2	0.04	0.1
Retirement and savings	1.19	3.7	1.16	3.4	1.20	3.8
Defined benefit plans	0.51	1.6	0.46	1.4	0.53	1.7
Defined contribution plans	0.68	2.1	0.70	2.1	0.67	2.1
Legally required benefits	2.60	8.1	2.66	7.9	2.58	8.2
Social Security and Medicare	1.86	5.8	1.97	5.8	1.81	5.8
Social Security	1.48	4.6	1.57	4.6	1.45	4.6
Medicare	0.37	1.2	0.40	1.2	0.36	1.2
Federal unemployment insurance	0.03	0.1	0.03	0.1	0.03	0.1
State unemployment insurance	0.26	0.8	0.27	0.8	0.25	0.8
Workers' compensation	0.45	1.4	0.40	1.2	0.48	1.5

Compensation component	Census region and division[1]							
	South		South divisions					
			South Atlantic		East South Central		West South Central	
	Cost	Percent	Cost	Percent	Cost	Percent	Cost	Percent
TOTAL COMPENSATION	24.69	100.0	25.54	100.0	21.40	100.0	24.88	100.0
Wages and Salaries	17.76	71.9	18.40	72.1	15.20	71.0	17.93	72.1
Total Benefits	6.94	28.1	7.14	27.9	6.20	29.0	6.95	27.9
Paid leave	1.60	6.5	1.69	6.6	1.31	6.1	1.59	6.4
Vacation	0.81	3.3	0.85	3.3	0.69	3.2	0.81	3.3
Holiday	0.52	2.1	0.54	2.1	0.42	2.0	0.52	2.1
Sick	0.20	0.8	0.21	0.8	0.14	0.7	0.20	0.8
Personal	0.08	0.3	0.08	0.3	0.06	0.3	0.06	0.3
Supplemental pay	0.64	2.6	0.61	2.4	0.51	2.4	0.76	3.0
Overtime and premium pay[2]	0.25	1.0	0.24	1.0	0.24	1.1	0.28	1.1
Shift differentials	0.06	0.3	0.07	0.3	0.07	0.3	0.05	0.2
Nonproduction bonuses	0.32	1.3	0.30	1.2	0.20	0.9	0.43	1.7
Insurance	1.91	7.7	1.95	7.7	1.94	9.1	1.82	7.3
Life insurance	0.04	0.2	0.04	0.2	0.05	0.2	0.05	0.2
Health insurance	1.78	7.2	1.82	7.1	1.82	8.5	1.70	6.8
Short-term disability	0.04	0.2	0.05	0.2	0.04	0.2	0.04	0.2
Long-term disability	0.04	0.2	0.04	0.2	0.03	0.2	0.04	0.1
Retirement and savings	0.80	3.2	0.82	3.2	0.61	2.9	0.85	3.4
Defined benefit plans	0.31	1.3	0.29	1.2	0.28	1.3	0.36	1.4
Defined contribution plans	0.48	2.0	0.52	2.1	0.33	1.5	0.49	2.0
Legally required benefits	1.99	8.1	2.07	8.1	1.83	8.5	1.94	7.8
Social Security and Medicare	1.49	6.0	1.54	6.0	1.33	6.2	1.49	6.0
Social Security	1.20	4.9	1.24	4.9	1.08	5.0	1.19	4.8
Medicare	0.29	1.2	0.30	1.2	0.25	1.2	0.29	1.2
Federal unemployment insurance	0.03	0.1	0.03	0.1	0.03	0.2	0.03	0.1
State unemployment insurance	0.12	0.5	0.12	0.5	0.11	0.5	0.11	0.5
Workers' compensation	0.35	1.4	0.38	1.5	0.35	1.6	0.31	1.2

Note: Individual items may not sum to totals due to rounding.

[1] The states that comprise the Census divisions are: New England—Connecticut, Maine, Massachusetts, New Hampshire, Rhode Island, and Vermont; Middle Atlantic—New Jersey, New York, and Pennsylvania; South Atlantic—Delaware, District of Columbia, Florida, Georgia, Maryland, North Carolina, South Carolina, Virginia, and West Virginia; East South Central—Alabama, Kentucky, Mississippi, and Tennessee; West South Central—Arkansas, Louisiana, Oklahoma, and Texas; East North Central—Illinois, Indiana, Michigan, Ohio, and Wisconsin; West North Central—Iowa, Kansas, Minnesota, Missouri, Nebraska, North Dakota, and South Dakota; Mountain—Arizona, Colorado, Idaho, Montana, Nevada, New Mexico, Utah, and Wyoming; and Pacific—Alaska, California, Hawaii, Oregon, and Washington.
[2] Comprises the Old-Age, Survivors, and Disability Insurance (OASDI) program.

Table 6-7. Employer Compensation Costs Per Hour Worked for Employee Compensation and Costs as a Percent of Total Compensation: Private Industry Workers, by Census Region and Area, June 2010—*Continued*

(Dollars, percent of total costs.)

Compensation component	Census region and division[1]					
	Midwest		Midwest divisions			
			East North Central		West North Central	
	Cost	Percent	Cost	Percent	Cost	Percent
TOTAL COMPENSATION	26.64	100.0	27.02	100.0	25.86	100.0
Wages and Salaries	18.65	70.0	18.76	69.4	18.44	71.3
Total Benefits	7.99	30.0	8.27	30.6	7.42	28.7
Paid leave	1.74	6.5	1.80	6.7	1.63	6.3
Vacation	0.92	3.4	0.93	3.5	0.89	3.4
Holiday	0.56	2.1	0.59	2.2	0.50	1.9
Sick	0.19	0.7	0.19	0.7	0.19	0.7
Personal	0.08	0.3	0.09	0.3	0.05	0.2
Supplemental pay	0.69	2.6	0.72	2.7	0.61	2.4
Overtime and premium pay[2]	0.28	1.0	0.29	1.1	0.25	1.0
Shift differentials	0.08	0.3	0.08	0.3	0.06	0.2
Nonproduction bonuses	0.34	1.3	0.35	1.3	0.30	1.2
Insurance	2.36	8.9	2.47	9.1	2.13	8.2
Life insurance	0.05	0.2	0.05	0.2	0.04	0.2
Health insurance	2.22	8.3	2.32	8.6	2.00	7.7
Short-term disability	0.06	0.2	0.06	0.2	0.04	0.2
Long-term disability	0.04	0.2	0.04	0.1	0.05	0.2
Retirement and savings	1.00	3.8	1.02	3.8	0.95	3.7
Defined benefit plans	0.48	1.8	0.53	2.0	0.37	1.4
Defined contribution plans	0.52	2.0	0.49	1.8	0.58	2.2
Legally required benefits	2.20	8.3	2.25	8.3	2.10	8.1
Social Security and Medicare	1.56	5.9	1.59	5.9	1.51	5.8
Social Security	1.26	4.7	1.28	4.7	1.21	4.7
Medicare	0.31	1.2	0.31	1.1	0.30	1.2
Federal unemployment insurance	0.03	0.1	0.03	0.1	0.03	0.1
State unemployment insurance	0.19	0.7	0.19	0.7	0.17	0.6
Workers' compensation	0.42	1.6	0.43	1.6	0.39	1.5

Compensation component	Census region and division[1]					
	West		West divisions			
			Mountain		Pacific	
	Cost	Percent	Cost	Percent	Cost	Percent
TOTAL COMPENSATION	29.42	100.0	26.62	100.0	30.63	100.0
Wages and Salaries	20.96	71.2	19.32	72.6	21.67	70.7
Total Benefits	8.46	28.8	7.31	27.4	8.96	29.3
Paid leave	1.96	6.7	1.71	6.4	2.07	6.8
Vacation	1.01	3.4	0.88	3.3	1.08	3.5
Holiday	0.62	2.1	0.55	2.1	0.65	2.1
Sick	0.26	0.9	0.22	0.8	0.28	0.9
Personal	0.07	0.2	0.07	0.3	0.07	0.2
Supplemental pay	0.70	2.4	0.64	2.4	0.73	2.4
Overtime and premium pay[2]	0.26	0.9	0.22	0.8	0.28	0.9
Shift differentials	0.06	0.2	0.05	0.2	0.06	0.2
Nonproduction bonuses	0.38	1.3	0.38	1.4	0.39	1.3
Insurance	2.23	7.6	1.96	7.4	2.35	7.7
Life insurance	0.04	0.1	0.05	0.2	0.04	0.1
Health insurance	2.12	7.2	1.85	7.0	2.23	7.3
Short-term disability	0.04	0.1	0.03	0.1	0.04	0.1
Long-term disability	0.04	0.1	0.04	0.1	0.04	0.1
Retirement and savings	0.99	3.4	0.81	3.0	1.06	3.5
Defined benefit plans	0.46	1.5	0.30	1.1	0.52	1.7
Defined contribution plans	0.53	1.8	0.51	1.9	0.54	1.8
Legally required benefits	2.58	8.8	2.18	8.2	2.75	9.0
Social Security and Medicare	1.74	5.9	1.59	6.0	1.81	5.9
Social Security	1.40	4.8	1.27	4.8	1.46	4.8
Medicare	0.34	1.2	0.32	1.2	0.36	1.2
Federal unemployment insurance	0.03	0.1	0.03	0.1	0.03	0.1
State unemployment insurance	0.20	0.7	0.14	0.5	0.23	0.7
Workers' compensation	0.60	2.0	0.43	1.6	0.67	2.2

Note: Individual items may not sum to totals due to rounding.

[1]The states that comprise the Census divisions are: New England—Connecticut, Maine, Massachusetts, New Hampshire, Rhode Island, and Vermont; Middle Atlantic—New Jersey, New York, and Pennsylvania; South Atlantic—Delaware, District of Columbia, Florida, Georgia, Maryland, North Carolina, South Carolina, Virginia, and West Virginia; East South Central—Alabama, Kentucky, Mississippi, and Tennessee; West South Central—Arkansas, Louisiana, Oklahoma, and Texas; East North Central—Illinois, Indiana, Michigan, Ohio, and Wisconsin; West North Central—Iowa, Kansas, Minnesota, Missouri, Nebraska, North Dakota, and South Dakota; Mountain—Arizona, Colorado, Idaho, Montana, Nevada, New Mexico, Utah, and Wyoming; and Pacific—Alaska, California, Hawaii, Oregon, and Washington.
[2]Comprises the Old-Age, Survivors, and Disability Insurance (OASDI) program.

Table 6-8. Employer Compensation Costs Per Hour Worked for Employee Compensation and Costs as a Percent of Total Compensation: State and Local Government, by Major Occupational and Industry Group, June 2010

(Dollars, percent of total cost.)

Compensation component	All workers		Occupational group[1]						Industry group	
			Management, professional, and related		Sales and office		Service		Service-providing[2]	
	Cost	Percent	Cost	Percent	Cost	Percent	Cost	Percent	Cost	Percent
TOTAL COMPENSATION	39.74	100.0	48.28	100.0	27.66	100.0	29.97	100.0	39.79	100.0
Wages and Salaries	26.13	65.7	33.00	68.3	16.95	61.3	18.05	60.2	26.17	65.8
Total Benefits	13.62	34.3	15.29	31.7	10.72	38.7	11.92	39.8	13.61	34.2
Paid leave	3.01	7.6	3.35	6.9	2.48	9.0	2.67	8.9	3.01	7.6
Vacation	1.14	2.9	1.13	2.3	1.11	4.0	1.16	3.9	1.13	2.9
Holiday	0.89	2.2	0.94	1.9	0.78	2.8	0.86	2.9	0.89	2.2
Sick	0.77	1.9	0.98	2.0	0.48	1.7	0.53	1.8	0.77	1.9
Personal	0.21	0.5	0.30	0.6	0.11	0.4	0.12	0.4	0.21	0.5
Supplemental pay	0.34	0.9	0.25	0.5	0.20	0.7	0.56	1.9	0.34	0.8
Overtime and premium pay[3]	0.18	0.5	0.08	0.2	0.11	0.4	0.37	1.2	0.18	0.4
Shift differentials	0.05	0.1	0.03	0.1	0.02	0.1	0.09	0.3	0.05	0.1
Nonproduction bonuses	0.11	0.3	0.14	0.3	0.07	0.2	0.11	0.4	0.11	0.3
Insurance	4.70	11.8	5.23	10.8	4.26	15.4	3.82	12.7	4.70	11.8
Life insurance	0.09	0.2	0.12	0.3	0.04	0.2	0.04	0.1	0.09	0.2
Health insurance	4.55	11.4	5.02	10.4	4.16	15.0	3.73	12.4	4.55	11.4
Short-term disability	0.03	0.1	0.03	0.1	0.02	0.1	0.02	0.1	0.02	0.1
Long-term disability	0.05	0.1	0.06	0.1	0.03	0.1	0.03	0.1	0.04	0.1
Retirement and savings	3.17	8.0	3.72	7.7	2.03	7.3	2.86	9.6	3.17	8.0
Defined benefit plans	2.86	7.2	3.34	6.9	1.80	6.5	2.65	8.9	2.86	7.2
Defined contribution plans	0.31	0.8	0.39	0.8	0.23	0.8	0.21	0.7	0.31	0.8
Legally required benefits	2.39	6.0	2.74	5.7	1.75	6.3	2.01	6.7	2.39	6.0
Social Security and Medicare	1.85	4.7	2.26	4.7	1.34	4.8	1.32	4.4	1.85	4.7
Social Security[4]	1.44	3.6	1.74	3.6	1.06	3.8	1.02	3.4	1.44	3.6
Medicare	0.42	1.0	0.52	1.1	0.28	1.0	0.30	1.0	0.42	1.0
Federal unemployment insurance	([5])	([6])	([5])	([6])	([5])	([6])	([5])	([6])	([5])	([6])
State unemployment insurance	0.07	0.2	0.07	0.2	0.07	0.2	0.08	0.3	0.07	0.2
Workers' compensation	0.46	1.2	0.40	0.8	0.34	1.2	0.60	2.0	0.46	1.2

Note: Individual items may not sum to totals due to rounding.

[1]This table presents data for the three major occupational groups in state and local government: management, professional, and related occupations, including teachers; sales and office occupations, including clerical workers; and service occupations, including police and firefighters.
[2]Service-providing industries, which include health and education services, employ a large proportion of the state and local government workforce.
[3]Includes premium pay for work in addition to the regular work schedule (such as overtime, weekends, and holidays).
[4]Comprises the Old Age, Survivors, and Disability Insurance (OASDI) program.
[5]Cost per hour worked is $0.01 or less.
[6]Less than 0.05 percent.

Table 6-9. Employer Compensation Costs Per Hour Worked for Employee Compensation and Costs as a Percent of Total Compensation: State and Local Government, by Major Occupational and Industry Group, June 2010

(Dollars, percent of total compensation.)

Characteristic	Total compensation	Wages and salaries	Cost per hour worked					
			Total	Paid leave	Supplemental pay	Insurance	Retirement and savings	Legally required benefits
COSTS PER HOUR WORKED								
State and Local Government Workers	39.74	26.13	13.62	3.01	0.34	4.70	3.17	2.39
Occupational Group								
Management, professional, and related	48.28	33.00	15.29	3.35	0.25	5.23	3.72	2.74
Professional and related	47.36	32.51	14.85	3.03	0.24	5.24	3.69	2.66
Teachers[1]	54.71	38.76	15.95	2.79	0.14	5.75	4.32	2.96
Primary, secondary, and special education school teachers	53.69	38.08	15.61	2.52	0.15	6.06	4.10	2.79
Sales and office	27.66	16.95	10.72	2.48	0.20	4.26	2.03	1.75
Office and administrative support	27.88	17.03	10.85	2.52	0.20	4.33	2.06	1.75
Service	29.97	18.05	11.92	2.67	0.56	3.82	2.86	2.01
Industry Group								
Education and health services	41.80	28.45	13.36	2.70	0.21	4.95	3.15	2.36
Education services	42.87	29.40	13.46	2.61	0.15	5.04	3.30	2.37
Elementary and secondary schools	42.51	29.24	13.26	2.29	0.15	5.18	3.34	2.31
Junior colleges, colleges, and universities	44.50	30.21	14.29	3.81	0.12	4.57	3.18	2.61
Health care and social assistance	34.99	22.32	12.67	3.25	0.60	4.34	2.19	2.28
Hospitals	37.20	23.75	13.45	3.49	0.74	4.60	2.25	2.38
Public administration	37.82	23.30	14.52	3.62	0.55	4.47	3.43	2.45
PERCENT OF TOTAL COMPENSATION								
State and Local Government Workers	100.0	65.7	34.3	7.6	0.9	11.8	8.0	6.0
Occupational Group								
Management, professional, and related	100.0	68.3	31.7	6.9	0.5	10.8	7.7	5.7
Professional and related	100.0	68.6	31.4	6.4	0.5	11.1	7.8	5.6
Teachers[1]	100.0	70.9	29.1	5.1	0.2	10.5	7.9	5.4
Primary, secondary, and special education school teachers	100.0	70.9	29.1	4.7	0.3	11.3	7.6	5.2
Sales and office	100.0	61.3	38.7	9.0	0.7	15.4	7.3	6.3
Office and administrative support	100.0	61.1	38.9	9.0	0.7	15.5	7.4	6.3
Service	100.0	60.2	39.8	8.9	1.9	12.7	9.6	6.7
Industry Group								
Education and health services	100.0	68.1	31.9	6.5	0.5	11.8	7.5	5.6
Education services	100.0	68.6	31.4	6.1	0.3	11.8	7.7	5.5
Elementary and secondary schools	100.0	68.8	31.2	5.4	0.4	12.2	7.9	5.4
Junior colleges, colleges, and universities	100.0	67.9	32.1	8.6	0.3	10.3	7.2	5.9
Health care and social assistance	100.0	63.8	36.2	9.3	1.7	12.4	6.3	6.5
Hospitals	100.0	63.8	36.2	9.4	2.0	12.4	6.1	6.4
Public administration	100.0	61.6	38.4	9.6	1.4	11.8	9.1	6.5

Note: Individual items may not sum to totals due to rounding.

[1]Includes postsecondary teachers; primary, secondary, and special education teachers; and other teachers and instructors.

Table 6-10. Employer Costs Per Hour Worked for Employee Compensation and Costs as a Percent of Total Compensation: Private Industry Workers, by Establishment Employment Size, June 2010

(Dollars, percent.)

| Compensation component | 1–99 workers | | | | | |
| | 1–99 workers | | 1–49 workers | | 50–99 workers | |
	Cost	Percent	Cost	Percent	Cost	Percent
TOTAL COMPENSATION	22.77	100.0	22.08	100.0	24.88	100.0
Wages and Salaries	16.77	73.7	16.39	74.3	17.93	72.1
Total Benefits	6.00	26.3	5.68	25.7	6.95	27.9
Paid leave	1.24	5.5	1.18	5.3	1.45	5.8
Vacation	0.62	2.7	0.59	2.7	0.71	2.9
Holiday	0.42	1.9	0.40	1.8	0.49	2.0
Sick	0.15	0.6	0.14	0.6	0.18	0.7
Personal	0.05	0.2	0.05	0.2	0.07	0.3
Supplemental pay	0.60	2.6	0.57	2.6	0.67	2.7
Overtime and premium pay	0.19	0.8	0.17	0.8	0.26	1.0
Shift differentials	-2.00	-3.0	-2.00	-3.0	0.03	0.1
Nonproduction bonuses	0.39	1.7	0.39	1.8	0.39	1.5
Insurance	1.53	6.7	1.41	6.4	1.90	7.6
Life insurance	0.03	0.1	0.03	0.1	0.04	0.1
Health insurance	1.45	6.4	1.33	6.0	1.79	7.2
Short-term disability	0.03	0.1	0.03	0.1	0.04	0.2
Long-term disability	0.02	0.1	0.02	0.1	0.03	0.1
Retirement and savings	0.57	2.5	0.52	2.4	0.72	2.9
Defined benefit plans	0.22	1.0	0.19	0.9	0.29	1.2
Defined contribution plans	0.35	1.5	0.33	1.5	0.42	1.7
Legally required benefits	2.05	9.0	2.00	9.1	2.21	8.9
Social Security and Medicare	1.39	6.1	1.36	6.2	1.50	6.0
Social Security	1.12	4.9	1.10	5.0	1.21	4.8
Medicare	0.27	1.2	0.26	1.2	0.29	1.2
Federal unemployment insurance	0.04	0.2	0.04	0.2	0.03	0.1
State unemployment insurance	0.18	0.8	0.18	0.8	0.19	0.7
Workers' compensation	0.44	1.9	0.43	1.9	0.49	2.0

Table 6-10. Employer Costs Per Hour Worked for Employee Compensation and Costs as a Percent of Total Compensation: Private Industry Workers, by Establishment Employment Size, June 2010—*Continued*

(Dollars, percent.)

Compensation component	100 workers or more					
	100 workers or more		100–499 workers		500 workers or more	
	Cost	Percent	Cost	Percent	Cost	Percent
TOTAL COMPENSATION	33.25	100.0	28.58	100.0	39.61	100.0
Wages and Salaries	22.70	68.3	20.02	70.1	26.35	66.5
Total Benefits	10.55	31.7	8.56	29.9	13.26	33.5
Paid leave	2.57	7.7	1.95	6.8	3.41	8.6
Vacation	1.34	4.0	1.00	3.5	1.80	4.5
Holiday	0.78	2.4	0.63	2.2	1.00	2.5
Sick	0.33	1.0	0.24	0.8	0.45	1.1
Personal	0.12	0.4	0.09	0.3	0.16	0.4
Supplemental pay	0.99	3.0	0.73	2.6	1.34	3.4
Overtime and premium pay	0.35	1.0	0.32	1.1	0.39	1.0
Shift differentials	0.12	0.4	0.07	0.2	0.20	0.5
Nonproduction bonuses	0.52	1.6	0.34	1.2	0.76	1.9
Insurance	3.01	9.1	2.52	8.8	3.68	9.3
Life insurance	0.06	0.2	0.05	0.2	0.07	0.2
Health insurance	2.81	8.5	2.37	8.3	3.42	8.6
Short-term disability	0.08	0.2	0.06	0.2	0.10	0.3
Long-term disability	0.06	0.2	0.04	0.1	0.09	0.2
Retirement and savings	1.42	4.3	1.02	3.6	1.97	5.0
Defined benefit plans	0.66	2.0	0.44	1.5	0.96	2.4
Defined contribution plans	0.76	2.3	0.58	2.0	1.01	2.5
Legally required benefits	2.56	7.7	2.34	8.2	2.86	7.2
Social Security and Medicare	1.92	5.8	1.66	5.8	2.26	5.7
Social Security	1.53	4.6	1.33	4.7	1.81	4.6
Medicare	0.38	1.1	0.33	1.1	0.45	1.1
Federal unemployment insurance ...	0.03	0.1	0.03	0.1	0.03	0.1
State unemployment insurance	0.18	0.5	0.19	0.7	0.17	0.4
Workers' compensation	0.44	1.3	0.47	1.6	0.40	1.0

NOTES AND DEFINITIONS

EMPLOYEE BENEFITS SURVEY

The Employee Benefits Survey provides data on the incidence and provisions of selected employee benefit plans.

Collection and Coverage

The March 2010 National Compensation Survey (NCS) benefits survey represented approximately 118 million civilian workers; of this number, about 99 million were private industry workers, and 19 million were state and local government workers. This survey included a sample of 18,174 establishments.

Definitions

Access to a benefit is determined on an occupational basis within an establishment. An employee is considered to have access to a benefit if it is available for his or her use.

Participation refers to the proportion of employees covered by a benefit. There will be cases where employees with access to a plan will not participate. For example, some employees may decline to participate in a health insurance plan if there is an employee cost involved.

A *private establishment* is an economic unit that produces goods or services, a central administrative office, or an auxiliary unit providing support services to a company. For private industries, the establishment is usually at a single physical location. For state and local governments, an establishment is defined as an agency or entity such as a school district, college, university, hospital, nursing home, administrative body, court, police department, fire department, health or social service operation, highway maintenance operation, urban transit operation, or other governmental unit. It provides services under the authority of a specific state or local government organization within a defined geographic area or jurisdiction.

Take-up rates are the percentage of workers with access to a plan who participate in the plan. They are computed by using the number of workers participating in a plan divided by the number of workers with access to the plan, times 100 and rounded to the nearest one percent. Since the computation of take-up rates is based on the number of workers collected, rather the rounded percentage estimates, the take-up rates in the tables may not equal the ratio of participation to access estimates.

An employee is considered to be a *union worker* when all the following conditions are met: 1.) a labor organization is recognized as the bargaining agent for all workers in the occupation. 2.) Wage and salary rates are determined through collective bargaining or negotiations. 3.) Settlement terms, which must include earnings provisions and may include benefit provisions, are embodied in a signed, mutually binding collective bargaining agreement.

Sources of Additional Information

For more information, see Bureau of Labor Statistics (BLS) news release 10-1044 "Employee Benefits in the United States in the United States–March 2010". For a listing of selected benefit definitions, see the *Glossary of Compensation Terms*. These resources are available on the BLS Web site at <http://www.bls.gov/ncs/ebs/>.

Table 6-11. Retirement Benefits:[1] Access, Participation, and Take-Up Rates,[2] March 2010

(Percent.)

Characteristic	Civilian[3]			Private industry			State and local government		
	Access	Participation	Take-up rate	Access	Participation	Take-up rate	Access	Participation	Take-up rate
ALL WORKERS	69	55	80	65	50	76	90	85	95
Worker Characteristics									
Management, professional, and related	83	74	89	80	68	86	92	87	95
Management, business, and financial	86	78	90	85	76	89	...	...	...
Professional and related	82	73	88	77	65	84	91	87	95
Teachers	86	81	95	...	...	...	91	87	96
Primary, secondary, and special education school teachers	92	89	96	...	...	...	97	94	97
Registered nurses	82	69	85	...	...	...	...	...	...
Service	49	32	66	42	23	55	83	79	95
Protective service	75	63	84	50	26	51	91	87	96
Sales and office	71	56	78	70	53	76	90	86	96
Sales and related	66	43	66	66	43	65	...	...	...
Office and administrative support	74	63	84	72	59	82	91	88	96
Natural resources, construction, and maintenance	67	55	81	64	51	79	94	91	96
Construction, extraction, farming, fishing, and forestry	65	50	78	61	45	74	...	...	...
Installation, maintenance, and repair	70	59	84	68	56	83	...	...	...
Production, transportation, and material moving	67	52	78	66	51	77	88	84	96
Production	66	52	80	65	52	79	...	...	...
Transportation and material moving	68	53	77	67	50	75	...	...	...
Full-time workers	78	65	84	74	59	80	99	94	96
Part-time workers	39	23	58	39	21	54	40	36	89
Union workers	92	87	94	88	82	93	97	93	96
Nonunion workers	65	49	77	62	46	74	83	79	95
Average Wage Within the Following Percentiles[4]									
Less than 10	43	24	56	40	20	50	74	69	94
10 to under 25	31	12	39	30	10	34	60	56	94
25 to under 50	70	54	78	67	48	73	94	89	95
50 to under 75	80	68	86	75	62	82	95	91	96
75 to under 90	88	81	92	84	75	89	98	94	96
90 or greater	90	83	92	87	78	90	97	94	96
Establishment Characteristics									
Goods-producing industries	73	60	83	72	60	83	...	...	...
Service-providing industries	68	55	80	63	47	75	90	85	95
Education and health services	78	67	85	70	55	78	91	87	95
Educational services	87	82	94	74	63	86	91	87	96
Elementary and secondary schools	90	87	96	...	...	...	92	89	97
Junior colleges, colleges, and universities	87	79	91	88	78	89	86	79	92
Health care and social assistance	72	56	78	70	53	76	92	84	91
Hospitals	89	78	87	...	...	...	94	84	90
Public administration	90	86	96	...	...	...	90	86	96
1 to 99 workers	52	37	70	51	35	69	77	74	96
1 to 49 workers	48	34	71	47	32	69	71	68	95
50 to 99 workers	65	46	70	64	43	68	87	84	97
100 workers or more	84	72	86	81	66	82	91	87	95
100 to 499 workers	79	63	80	78	60	77	88	84	96
500 workers or more	88	80	91	85	75	88	93	88	95
Geographic Areas[5]									
New England	67	55	83	63	50	80	86	82	96
Middle Atlantic	72	60	84	68	56	82	92	87	94
East North Central	69	56	81	67	52	78	85	82	96
West North Central	72	58	81	69	54	78	89	82	92
South Atlantic	70	54	76	66	47	71	91	85	94
East South Central	68	54	79	62	45	73	90	86	96
West South Central	66	52	78	61	44	72	90	88	98
Mountain	70	55	79	66	49	75	89	87	97
Pacific	66	54	82	60	47	77	92	89	97

[1]Includes defined benefit pension plans and defined contribution retirement plans. Workers are considered as having access or as participating if they have access to or participate in at least one of these plan types.
[2]The take-up rate is an estimate of the percentage of workers with access to a plan who participate in the plan, rounded for presentation.
[3]Includes workers in the private nonfarm economy except those in private households, and workers in the public sector, except the federal government.
[4]The percentile groupings are based on the average wage for each occupation surveyed, which may include workers both above and below the threshold.
[5]The states that comprise the Census divisions are: New England—Connecticut, Maine, Massachusetts, New Hampshire, Rhode Island, and Vermont; Middle Atlantic—New Jersey, New York, and Pennsylvania; South Atlantic—Delaware, District of Columbia, Florida, Georgia, Maryland, North Carolina, South Carolina, Virginia, and West Virginia; East South Central—Alabama, Kentucky, Mississippi, and Tennessee; West South Central—Arkansas, Louisiana, Oklahoma, and Texas; East North Central—Illinois, Indiana, Michigan, Ohio, and Wisconsin; West North Central—Iowa, Kansas, Minnesota, Missouri, Nebraska, North Dakota, and South Dakota; Mountain—Arizona, Colorado, Idaho, Montana, Nevada, New Mexico, Utah, and Wyoming; and Pacific—Alaska, California, Hawaii, Oregon, and Washington.
... = Not available or not applicable.

Table 6-12. Medical Care Benefits: Access, Participation, and Take-Up Rates,[1] March 2010

(Percent.)

Characteristic	Civilian[2]			Private industry			State and local government		
	Access	Participation	Take-up rate	Access	Participation	Take-up rate	Access	Participation	Take-up rate
ALL WORKERS	73	55	75	71	51	73	88	73	83
Worker Characteristics									
Management, professional, and related	88	68	78	87	66	76	90	73	81
Management, business, and financial	94	74	79	94	74	78	...	...	...
Professional and related	85	66	78	83	63	76	89	73	82
Teachers	84	67	80	...	...	...	89	73	82
Primary, secondary, and special education school teachers	92	73	80	...	...	...	95	78	82
Registered nurses	81	62	76	...	...	...	...	...	...
Service	50	34	67	44	27	61	81	68	85
Protective service	73	59	81	48	31	64	89	77	87
Sales and office	73	52	71	72	50	70	88	75	84
Sales and related	64	41	65	64	41	64	...	...	...
Office and administrative support	79	59	74	78	56	72	89	75	84
Natural resources, construction, and maintenance	78	62	79	76	60	78	95	81	86
Construction, extraction, farming, fishing, and forestry	72	58	80	70	56	80	...	...	...
Installation, maintenance, and repair	84	66	78	83	64	77	...	...	...
Production, transportation, and material moving	76	59	77	76	59	77	82	69	84
Production	81	65	80	81	65	80	...	...	...
Transportation and material moving	72	53	74	71	52	73	...	...	...
Full-time workers	88	67	76	86	64	74	99	82	84
Part-time workers	24	14	59	24	14	57	28	19	68
Union workers	93	78	84	91	77	84	95	79	83
Nonunion workers	70	50	72	68	48	71	81	67	82
Average Wage Within the Following Percentiles[3]									
Less than 10	41	25	60	38	22	58	69	56	81
10 to under 25	25	13	54	23	12	52	53	41	79
25 to under 50	78	56	72	76	52	69	91	78	85
50 to under 75	88	70	79	86	66	77	95	79	83
75 to under 90	92	74	80	90	72	79	97	79	82
90 or greater	94	75	80	92	72	79	97	80	82
Establishment Characteristics									
Goods-producing industries	85	69	81	85	69	81	...	...	...
Service-providing industries	71	52	73	68	48	70	88	72	83
Education and health services	80	60	75	75	53	70	89	72	81
Educational services	86	68	80	76	54	72	88	72	81
Elementary and secondary schools	88	69	79	...	...	...	89	71	80
Junior colleges, colleges, and universities	87	72	83	90	69	76	86	75	87
Health care and social assistance	76	54	71	75	52	70	91	76	83
Hospitals	88	69	78	...	...	...	94	77	82
Public administration	88	75	84	...	...	...	88	75	84
1 to 99 workers	60	43	71	59	42	71	75	64	85
1 to 49 workers	56	39	71	55	39	70	68	58	86
50 to 99 workers	71	52	73	70	50	72	86	73	84
100 workers or more	86	66	77	84	63	74	89	74	82
100 to 499 workers	82	60	74	82	59	72	85	72	85
500 workers or more	89	71	79	88	68	78	91	74	82
Geographic Areas[4]									
New England	71	52	73	69	49	71	85	71	84
Middle Atlantic	74	57	78	71	53	75	87	78	91
East North Central	73	54	75	71	53	74	81	63	78
West North Central	72	54	76	70	52	74	84	67	80
South Atlantic	75	53	71	72	49	69	91	74	81
East South Central	78	60	77	74	55	74	94	80	85
West South Central	71	51	72	67	47	69	90	74	82
Mountain	73	52	71	71	49	69	86	68	79
Pacific	74	58	79	71	55	77	90	75	83

[1]The take-up rate is an estimate of the percentage of workers with access to a plan who participate in the plan, rounded for presentation.
[2]Includes workers in the private nonfarm economy except those in private households, and workers in the public sector, except the federal government.
[3]The percentile groupings are based on the average wage for each occupation surveyed, which may include workers both above and below the threshold.
[4]The states that comprise the Census divisions are: New England—Connecticut, Maine, Massachusetts, New Hampshire, Rhode Island, and Vermont; Middle Atlantic—New Jersey, New York, and Pennsylvania; South Atlantic—Delaware, District of Columbia, Florida, Georgia, Maryland, North Carolina, South Carolina, Virginia, and West Virginia; East South Central—Alabama, Kentucky, Mississippi, and Tennessee; West South Central—Arkansas, Louisiana, Oklahoma, and Texas; East North Central—Illinois, Indiana, Michigan, Ohio, and Wisconsin; West North Central—Iowa, Kansas, Minnesota, Missouri, Nebraska, North Dakota, and South Dakota; Mountain—Arizona, Colorado, Idaho, Montana, Nevada, New Mexico, Utah, and Wyoming; and Pacific—Alaska, California, Hawaii, Oregon, and Washington.
... = Not available or not applicable.

Table 6-13. Medical Plans: Share of Premiums Paid by Employer and Employee for Single Coverage, March 2010

(Percent.)

Characteristic	Civilian[1]		Private industry		State and local government	
	Employer share of premium	Employee share of premium	Employer share of premium	Employee share of premium	Employer share of premium	Employee share of premium
ALL WORKERS	82	18	80	20	89	11
Worker Characteristics						
Management, professional, and related	84	16	81	19	89	11
Management, business, and financial	82	18	81	19	...	...
Professional and related	84	16	82	18	88	12
Teachers	88	12	...	...	89	11
Primary, secondary, and special education school teachers	89	11	...	...	89	11
Registered nurses	81	19	...	...	...	...
Service	82	18	78	22	89	11
Protective service	86	14	74	26	89	11
Sales and office	80	20	79	21	89	11
Sales and related	76	24	76	24	...	...
Office and administrative support	82	18	80	20	89	11
Natural resources, construction, and maintenance	83	17	82	18	90	10
Construction, extraction, farming, fishing, and forestry	85	15	84	16	...	...
Installation, maintenance, and repair	82	18	81	19	...	...
Production, transportation, and material moving	82	18	81	19	89	11
Production	81	19	81	19	...	...
Transportation and material moving	82	18	81	19	...	...
Full-time workers	82	18	80	20	89	11
Part-time workers	80	20	79	21	86	14
Union workers	89	11	89	11	90	10
Nonunion workers	80	20	79	21	89	11
Average Wage Within the Following Percentiles[2]						
Less than 10	78	22	77	23	89	11
10 to under 25	76	24	75	25	89	11
25 to under 50	80	20	79	21	89	11
50 to under 75	83	17	81	19	90	10
75 to under 90	84	16	82	18	88	12
90 or greater	84	16	82	18	89	11
Establishment Characteristics						
Goods-producing industries	82	18	82	18	...	...
Service-providing industries	82	18	80	20	89	11
Education and health services	85	15	82	18	89	11
Educational services	88	12	80	20	89	11
Elementary and secondary schools	89	11	...	...	89	11
Junior colleges, colleges, and universities	86	14	79	21	89	11
Health care and social assistance	82	18	82	18	86	14
Hospitals	82	18	...	...	86	14
Public administration	89	11	...	...	89	11
1 to 99 workers	80	20	80	20	91	9
1 to 49 workers	81	19	80	20	92	8
50 to 99 workers	80	20	79	21	90	10
100 workers or more	83	17	81	19	89	11
100 to 499 workers	81	19	79	21	90	10
500 workers or more	84	16	82	18	88	12
Geographic Areas[3]						
New England	79	21	78	22	85	15
Middle Atlantic	84	16	82	18	92	8
East North Central	82	18	80	20	90	10
West North Central	82	18	80	20	90	10
South Atlantic	80	20	78	22	88	12
East South Central	81	19	77	23	91	9
West South Central	83	17	81	19	87	13
Mountain	83	17	81	19	90	10
Pacific	83	17	82	18	87	13

[1]Includes workers in the private nonfarm economy except those in private households, and workers in the public sector, except the federal government.
[2]The percentile groupings are based on the average wage for each occupation surveyed, which may include workers both above and below the threshold.
[3]The states that comprise the Census divisions are: New England—Connecticut, Maine, Massachusetts, New Hampshire, Rhode Island, and Vermont; Middle Atlantic—New Jersey, New York, and Pennsylvania; South Atlantic—Delaware, District of Columbia, Florida, Georgia, Maryland, North Carolina, South Carolina, Virginia, and West Virginia; East South Central—Alabama, Kentucky, Mississippi, and Tennessee; West South Central—Arkansas, Louisiana, Oklahoma, and Texas; East North Central—Illinois, Indiana, Michigan, Ohio, and Wisconsin; West North Central—Iowa, Kansas, Minnesota, Missouri, Nebraska, North Dakota, and South Dakota; Mountain—Arizona, Colorado, Idaho, Montana, Nevada, New Mexico, Utah, and Wyoming; and Pacific—Alaska, California, Hawaii, Oregon, and Washington.
... = Not available or not applicable.

Table 6-14. Medical Plans: Share of Premiums Paid by Employer and Employee for Family Coverage, March 2010

(Percent.)

Characteristic	Civilian[1]		Private industry		State and local government	
	Employer share of premium	Employee share of premium	Employer share of premium	Employee share of premium	Employer share of premium	Employee share of premium
ALL WORKERS	70	30	70	30	73	27
Worker Characteristics						
Management, professional, and related	72	28	71	29	72	28
Management, business, and financial	72	28	71	29	. . .	. . .
Professional and related	71	29	72	28	71	29
Teachers	69	31	. . .	. . .	70	30
Primary, secondary, and special education school teachers	67	33	. . .	. . .	69	31
Registered nurses	72	28	. . .	. . .	. . .	. . .
Service	68	32	65	35	74	26
Protective service	75	25	63	37	78	22
Sales and office	68	32	67	33	74	26
Sales and related	65	35	64	36	. . .	. . .
Office and administrative support	69	31	68	32	74	26
Natural resources, construction, and maintenance	70	30	69	31	76	24
Construction, extraction, farming, fishing, and forestry	70	30	68	32	. . .	. . .
Installation, maintenance, and repair	71	29	70	30	. . .	. . .
Production, transportation, and material moving	73	27	73	27	74	26
Production	74	26	74	26	. . .	. . .
Transportation and material moving	72	28	72	28	. . .	. . .
Full-time workers	70	30	70	30	73	27
Part-time workers	70	30	69	31	74	26
Union workers	82	18	83	17	81	19
Nonunion workers	67	33	67	33	65	35
Average Wage Within the Following Percentiles[2]						
Less than 10	63	37	63	37	66	34
10 to under 25	62	38	62	38	60	40
25 to under 50	67	33	66	34	75	25
50 to under 75	72	28	70	30	73	27
75 to under 90	75	25	74	26	76	24
90 or greater	76	24	75	25	81	19
Establishment Characteristics						
Goods-producing industries	74	26	74	26	. . .	. . .
Service-providing industries	69	31	68	32	73	27
Education and health services	69	31	68	32	70	30
Educational services	69	31	66	34	69	31
Elementary and secondary schools	68	32	. . .	. . .	68	32
Junior colleges, colleges, and universities	71	29	69	31	72	28
Health care and social assistance	69	31	68	32	74	26
Hospitals	75	25	. . .	. . .	74	26
Public administration	79	21	. . .	. . .	79	21
1 to 99 workers	65	35	65	35	71	29
1 to 49 workers	64	36	64	36	71	29
50 to 99 workers	66	34	66	34	71	29
100 workers or more	73	27	73	27	73	27
100 to 499 workers	71	29	70	30	73	27
500 workers or more	75	25	77	23	73	27
Geographic Areas[3]						
New England	74	26	72	28	82	18
Middle Atlantic	77	23	73	27	90	10
East North Central	76	24	74	26	85	15
West North Central	71	29	71	29	70	30
South Atlantic	65	35	65	35	66	34
East South Central	63	37	65	35	59	41
West South Central	63	37	66	34	54	46
Mountain	69	31	69	31	69	31
Pacific	71	29	69	31	79	21

[1]Includes workers in the private nonfarm economy except those in private households, and workers in the public sector, except the federal government.
[2]The percentile groupings are based on the average wage for each occupation surveyed, which may include workers both above and below the threshold.
[3]The states that comprise the Census divisions are: New England—Connecticut, Maine, Massachusetts, New Hampshire, Rhode Island, and Vermont; Middle Atlantic—New Jersey, New York, and Pennsylvania; South Atlantic—Delaware, District of Columbia, Florida, Georgia, Maryland, North Carolina, South Carolina, Virginia, and West Virginia; East South Central—Alabama, Kentucky, Mississippi, and Tennessee; West South Central—Arkansas, Louisiana, Oklahoma, and Texas; East North Central—Illinois, Indiana, Michigan, Ohio, and Wisconsin; West North Central—Iowa, Kansas, Minnesota, Missouri, Nebraska, North Dakota, and South Dakota; Mountain—Arizona, Colorado, Idaho, Montana, Nevada, New Mexico, Utah, and Wyoming; and Pacific—Alaska, California, Hawaii, Oregon, and Washington.
. . . = Not available or not applicable.

Table 6-15. Access to Paid Sick Leave, Vacation, and Holidays, March 2010

(Percent.)

Characteristic	Civilian[1]			Private industry			State and local government		
	Paid sick leave	Paid vacation	Paid holidays	Paid sick leave	Paid vacation	Paid holidays	Paid sick leave	Paid vacation	Paid holidays
ALL WORKERS	67	74	41	62	77	37	89	60	60
Worker Characteristics									
Management, professional, and related	87	74	58	86	87	54	90	44	65
Management, business, and financial	91	94	57	91	96	56	. . .	. . .	. . .
Professional and related	86	67	58	84	83	54	90	36	66
Teachers	84	17	64	. . .	. . .	. . .	88	12	70
Primary, secondary, and special education school teachers	92	12	76	. . .	. . .	. . .	93	9	79
Registered nurses	81	82	62	. . .	. . .	. . .	. . .	. . .	. . .
Service	48	61	28	42	59	24	85	75	51
Protective service	69	79	42	37	66	24	89	87	54
Sales and office	69	80	41	67	80	40	91	86	55
Sales and related	56	70	32	55	70	32	. . .	. . .	. . .
Office and administrative support	77	86	47	74	86	45	92	86	56
Natural resources, construction, and maintenance	56	80	28	51	78	26	94	94	46
Construction, extraction, farming, fishing, and forestry	42	69	20	36	66	17	. . .	. . .	. . .
Installation, maintenance, and repair	69	90	37	66	90	35	. . .	. . .	. . .
Production, transportation, and material moving	55	82	33	54	83	31	87	63	59
Production	53	90	30	53	90	30	. . .	. . .	. . .
Transportation and material moving	57	74	35	55	75	33	. . .	. . .	. . .
Full-time workers	79	86	47	74	91	43	98	67	65
Part-time workers	28	36	21	26	37	19	41	20	30
Union workers	83	73	58	71	87	48	97	57	71
Nonunion workers	64	75	38	61	76	36	83	62	50
Average Wage Within the Following Percentiles[2]									
Less than 10	35	54	21	32	53	19	75	56	45
10 to under 25	22	40	14	19	39	12	62	40	37
25 to under 50	70	83	41	66	84	39	93	83	58
50 to under 75	80	88	46	75	89	43	94	71	65
75 to under 90	87	77	59	84	89	53	96	37	70
90 or greater	90	73	59	86	89	54	98	34	65
Establishment Characteristics									
Goods-producing industries	55	88	30	54	88	30	. . .	. . .	. . .
Service-providing industries	69	72	43	64	75	39	89	59	60
Education and health services	83	65	58	78	79	53	90	43	65
Educational services	87	40	62	75	53	46	90	36	66
Elementary and secondary schools	90	27	70	. . .	. . .	. . .	90	27	72
Junior colleges, colleges, and universities	86	68	49	82	72	56	88	66	45
Health care and social assistance	79	84	55	78	83	54	91	90	58
Hospitals	89	89	67	. . .	. . .	. . .	93	94	53
Public administration	89	88	53	. . .	. . .	. . .	89	88	53
1 to 99 workers	54	70	27	53	70	26	78	67	45
1 to 49 workers	53	69	25	52	69	25	72	67	36
50 to 99 workers	58	75	34	56	75	32	89	66	58
100 workers or more	78	78	53	73	85	50	91	59	62
100 to 499 workers	70	79	47	67	82	44	88	59	62
500 workers or more	85	77	59	81	89	57	92	59	62
Geographic Areas[3]									
New England	72	71	51	69	75	46	86	48	80
Middle Atlantic	71	74	50	67	77	46	90	58	69
East North Central	62	74	44	58	78	40	85	52	64
West North Central	67	73	35	62	76	32	89	56	51
South Atlantic	65	77	40	60	79	36	93	68	57
East South Central	63	75	36	55	77	35	91	67	39
West South Central	67	74	37	63	78	32	86	52	61
Mountain	65	73	37	62	77	34	85	55	55
Pacific	70	75	37	65	76	33	93	68	58

[1] Includes workers in the private nonfarm economy except those in private households, and workers in the public sector, except the federal government.

[2] The percentile groupings are based on the average wage for each occupation surveyed, which may include workers both above and below the threshold.

[3] The states that comprise the Census divisions are: New England—Connecticut, Maine, Massachusetts, New Hampshire, Rhode Island, and Vermont; Middle Atlantic—New Jersey, New York, and Pennsylvania; South Atlantic—Delaware, District of Columbia, Florida, Georgia, Maryland, North Carolina, South Carolina, Virginia, and West Virginia; East South Central—Alabama, Kentucky, Mississippi, and Tennessee; West South Central—Arkansas, Louisiana, Oklahoma, and Texas; East North Central—Illinois, Indiana, Michigan, Ohio, and Wisconsin; West North Central—Iowa, Kansas, Minnesota, Missouri, Nebraska, North Dakota, and South Dakota; Mountain—Arizona, Colorado, Idaho, Montana, Nevada, New Mexico, Utah, and Wyoming; and Pacific—Alaska, California, Hawaii, Oregon, and Washington.

. . . = Not available or not applicable.

NOTES AND DEFINITIONS

OCCUPATIONAL EARNINGS

Collection and Coverage

Tables 6-16 through 6-20 present occupational pay estimates for the nation. The data were compiled from locality data collected between December 2008 and January 2010. The average reference period is July 2009.

Concepts and Definitions

Earnings. Regular payments from the employer to the employee as compensation for straight-time hourly work, or for any salaried work performed. The following components were included as part of earnings:

- Incentive pay, including commissions, production bonuses, and piece rates
- Cost-of-living allowances
- Hazard pay
- Payments of income deferred due to participation in a salary reduction plan
- Deadhead pay, defined as pay given to transportation workers returning in a vehicle without freight or passengers

Work levels are standardized measures of duties and responsibilities that apply to all occupations.

Percentiles designate position in the earnings distribution and are calculated from individual worker earnings and the hours those workers are scheduled to work. Table 6-20 provide estimates on the mean hourly wage for the 10th percentile, the 25th percentile, the 50th percentile (the median), the 75th percentile, and the 90th percentile of occupational wages, by ownership sector and for full- and part-time workers within the sectors.

An *incentive worker* is any employee whose earnings are at least partly tied to commissions, piece rates, production bonuses, or other incentives based on production or sales.

A *time-based worker* is any employee whose earnings are tied to an hourly rate or salary, and not to a specific level of production.

Sources of Additional Information

An extensive description of the sampling, weighting, and estimation steps and many additional detailed tables are available in BLS Bulletin 2738, "National Compensation Survey: Occupational Earnings in the United States, 2009," which is available on the BLS Web site at <http://www.bls.gov>.

Table 6-16. Mean Hourly Earnings[1] and Weekly Hours, by Selected Worker and Establishment Characteristics, National Compensation Survey, 2009

(Dollars, number of hours.)

Characteristic	Civilian workers		Private workers		State and local government workers	
	Mean hourly earnings	Mean weekly hours[2]	Mean hourly earnings	Mean weekly hours[2]	Mean hourly earnings	Mean weekly hours[2]
TOTAL	20.99	35.3	20.18	35.1	25.74	36.2
Worker Characteristics[3]						
Management, professional, and related occupations	33.90	36.8	34.35	37.1	32.61	35.9
Management, business, and financial occupations	37.77	39.4	38.30	39.8	34.86	37.5
Professional and related occupations	32.14	35.7	32.16	35.7	32.08	35.6
Service occupations	12.01	30.9	10.50	30.0	19.05	36.4
Sales and office occupations	16.40	34.8	16.33	34.7	17.19	36.4
Sales and related occupations	17.13	32.5	17.14	32.5	16.42	34.0
Office and administrative support occupations	16.01	36.2	15.84	36.2	17.21	36.5
Natural resources, construction, and maintenance occupations	21.03	39.1	21.06	39.1	20.67	38.8
Construction and extraction occupations	20.98	39.1	21.10	39.2	19.92	38.6
Installation, maintenance, and repair occupations	21.20	39.2	21.16	39.2	21.59	39.2
Production, transportation, and material moving occupations	15.85	37.1	15.73	37.2	19.14	34.4
Production occupations	16.16	38.8	16.07	38.8	21.33	39.6
Transportation and material moving occupations	15.54	35.6	15.37	35.7	18.46	33.1
Full-time workers	22.36	39.5	21.61	39.6	26.40	38.9
Part-time workers	12.03	20.7	11.70	20.9	16.27	18.3
Union workers	25.47	36.6	22.71	36.4	29.13	37.0
Nonunion workers	20.19	35.0	19.90	35.0	23.01	35.6
Time workers	20.76	35.1	19.87	34.9	25.74	36.2
Incentive workers	25.29	38.3	25.27	38.3		
Establishment Characteristics						
Goods-producing	(4)	(4)	21.86	39.4	(4)	(4)
Service-providing	(4)	(4)	19.75	34.1	(4)	(4)
1–49 workers	17.57	33.8	17.51	33.8	19.57	33.0
50–99 workers	19.18	34.7	19.07	34.6	20.90	35.8
100–499 workers	20.61	35.9	20.17	35.9	23.90	36.0
500 workers or more	26.51	36.9	26.04	37.0	27.35	36.7

[1]Earnings are the straight-time hourly wages or salaries paid to employees. They include incentive pay, cost-of-living adjustments, and hazard pay. Excluded are premium pay for overtime, vacations, and holidays; nonproduction bonuses; and tips. The mean is computed by totaling the pay of all workers and dividing by the number of workers, weighted by hours.
[2]Mean weekly hours are the hours an employee is scheduled to work in a week, not including overtime.
[3]Employees are classified as working either a full-time or part-time schedule based on the definition used by each establishment. Union workers are those whose wages are determined through collective bargaining. Wages of time workers are based solely on hourly rate or salary; incentive workers are those whose wages are at least partly based on productivity payments such as piece rates, commissions, and production bonuses.
[4]Classification of establishments into goods-producing and service-producing industries applies to private industry only.

Table 6-17. Mean Hourly Earnings[1] for Civilian Industry Workers by Size of Establishment, National Compensation Survey, 2009

(Dollars.)

Characteristic	Civilian workers	1–49 workers	50–99 workers	100–499 workers	500 workers or more
TOTAL	20.99	17.57	19.18	20.61	26.51
Worker Characteristics					
Management, professional, and related occupations	33.90	29.75	32.82	33.83	36.43
Management, business, and financial occupations	37.77	32.55	37.65	39.22	40.97
Professional and related occupations	32.14	28.03	29.78	31.21	34.89
Service occupations	12.01	10.07	9.98	12.29	15.54
Sales and office occupations	16.40	15.80	17.10	15.94	17.93
Sales and related occupations	17.13	16.53	18.86	16.12	22.45
Office and administrative support occupations	16.01	15.25	16.07	15.83	17.24
Natural resources, construction, and maintenance occupations	21.03	19.26	21.44	22.65	23.97
Construction and extraction occupations	20.98	. . .	. . .	. . .	. . .
Installation, maintenance, and repair occupations	21.20	19.32	21.84	22.08	24.29
Production, transportation, and material moving occupations	15.85	14.15	14.54	15.41	20.21
Production occupations	16.16	14.59	14.89	15.78	19.54
Transportation and material moving occupations	15.54	13.79	14.19	14.98	21.06

[1]Earnings are the straight-time hourly wages or salaries paid to employees. They include incentive pay, cost-of-living adjustments, and hazard pay. Excluded are premium pay for overtime, vacations, and holidays; nonproduction bonuses; and tips. The mean is computed by totaling the pay of all workers and dividing by the number of workers, weighed by hours.
. . . = Not available.

Table 6-18. Mean Hourly Earnings[1] by Major Occupational Groups for Full and Part-Time Workers,[2] National Compensation Survey, 2009

(Dollars.)

Characteristic	Full-time			Part-time		
	Civilian workers	Private industry workers	State and local government workers	Civilian workers	Private industry workers	State and local government workers
TOTAL	22.36	21.61	26.40	12.03	11.70	16.27
Worker Characteristics						
Management, professional, and related occupations	34.41	34.83	33.18	26.37	27.50	22.16
Management, business, and financial occupations	37.89	38.43	34.92	30.01	29.92	30.52
Professional and related occupations	32.70	32.67	32.76	26.06	27.28	21.69
Service occupations	13.40	11.51	19.83	8.68	8.52	11.48
Sales and office occupations	17.49	17.49	17.53	10.60	10.52	12.50
Sales and related occupations	19.87	19.90	17.66	9.35	9.35	10.29
Office and administrative support occupations	16.45	16.28	17.53	12.26	12.22	12.72
Natural resources, construction, and maintenance occupations	21.16	21.19	20.85	14.94	15.12	13.38
Construction and extraction occupations	21.02	21.13	20.05	18.03	18.73	13.43
Installation, maintenance, and repair occupations	21.40	21.36	21.80	13.72	13.89	11.61
Production, transportation, and material moving occupations	16.37	16.25	19.78	10.70	10.49	14.76
Production occupations	16.37	16.29	21.32	10.67	10.64	22.27
Transportation and material moving occupations	16.36	16.20	19.21	10.70	10.45	14.65

[1]Earnings are the straight-time hourly wages or salaries paid to employees. They include incentive pay, cost-of-living adjustments, and hazard pay. Excluded are premium pay for overtime, vacations, and holidays; nonproduction bonuses; and tips. The mean is computed by totaling the pay of all workers and dividing by the number of workers, weighted by hours.
[2]Employees are classified as working either a full-time or part-time schedule based on the definition used by each establishment. Union workers are those whose wages are determined through collective bargaining. Wages of time workers are based solely on hourly rate or salary; incentive workers are those whose wages are at least partly based on productivity payments such as piece rates, commissions, and production bonuses.

Table 6-19. Mean Hourly Earnings[1] for Civilian and Private Industry Workers Paid on Time or Incentive Basis,[2] National Compensation Survey, 2009

(Dollars.)

Characteristic	Time		Incentive	
	Civilian workers	Private industry workers	Civilian workers	Private industry workers
TOTAL	20.76	19.87	25.29	25.27
Worker Characteristics				
Management, professional, and related occupations	33.67	34.05	44.48	44.40
Management, business, and financial occupations	37.58	38.10	41.31	41.31
Professional and related occupations	31.97	31.92	53.71	53.46
Service occupations	11.96	10.41	15.15	15.15
Sales and office occupations	15.44	15.25	24.71	24.71
Sales and related occupations	14.07	14.04	27.19	27.19
Office and administrative support occupations	16.02	15.84	15.83	15.83
Natural resources, construction, and maintenance occupations	20.94	20.97	22.46	22.46
Construction and extraction occupations	. . .	21.09	. . .	21.60
Installation, maintenance, and repair occupations	21.03	20.97	22.76	22.76
Production, transportation, and material moving occupations	15.74	15.61	17.99	17.99
Production occupations	16.12	16.03	17.26	17.26
Transportation and material moving occupations	15.33	15.13	18.33	18.33

[1]Earnings are the straight-time hourly wages or salaries paid to employees. They include incentive pay, cost-of-living adjustments, and hazard pay. Excluded are premium pay for overtime, vacations, and holidays; nonproduction bonuses; and tips. The mean is computed by totaling the pay of all workers and dividing by the number of workers, weighed by hours.
[2]Earnings of time workers are based solely on hourly rate or salary. Incentive workers are those whose earnings are at least partially based on productivity payments such as piece rates, commissions, and production bonuses.
. . . = Not available.

Table 6-20. Private Industry Workers: Hourly Wage Percentiles,[1] 2009

(Dollars.)

Occupation	Wages fall at or below the following percentiles:				
	10	25	50	75	90
ALL OCCUPATIONS	8.10	10.63	15.70	24.53	37.02
Management	21.26	28.79	39.66	54.71	70.83
Chief executives	26.22	48.97	75.48	116.12	158.65
General and operations managers	20.98	28.97	40.00	60.63	87.50
Advertising and promotions managers	18.27	24.61	32.74	41.83	58.89
Marketing and sales managers	24.28	32.78	45.39	58.89	77.56
Marketing managers	27.32	36.00	48.08	61.26	73.87
Sales managers	22.36	31.59	43.31	57.69	86.54
Public relations managers	18.67	23.07	29.71	48.60	77.27
Administrative services managers	19.56	24.76	31.25	39.79	48.92
Computer and information systems managers	34.24	41.68	53.74	63.51	75.29
Financial managers	23.00	28.90	39.71	55.26	72.76
Human resources managers	23.10	29.28	40.33	52.85	66.48
Compensation and benefits managers	21.00	26.83	33.48	45.72	62.01
Training and development managers	27.05	33.70	41.70	54.76	67.83
Industrial production managers	26.44	33.75	40.83	48.52	59.84
Purchasing managers	23.17	29.97	40.81	54.70	67.56
Transportation, storage, and distribution managers	20.75	24.95	33.66	49.23	62.50
Agricultural managers	15.00	16.25	16.25	45.67	56.73
Farm, ranch, and other agricultural managers	15.00	16.25	16.25	45.67	56.73
Construction managers	22.50	28.85	37.01	47.12	53.58
Education administrators	17.19	21.11	29.72	35.54	51.20
Education administrators, preschool and child care center/program	14.68	17.49	24.04	30.85	30.85
Education administrators, elementary and secondary school	19.00	29.24	33.67	48.08	48.35
Education administrators, postsecondary	21.64	24.94	31.67	47.84	65.24
Engineering managers	36.06	46.15	56.82	68.56	74.71
Food service managers	15.30	18.25	24.14	29.57	36.91
Funeral directors	17.75	19.23	24.50	31.00	34.75
Lodging managers	12.33	17.48	19.50	31.46	40.98
Medical and health services managers	22.28	29.76	37.50	48.64	59.25
Natural sciences managers	22.36	40.96	42.80	47.31	59.11
Property, real estate, and community association managers	13.85	21.63	26.44	33.85	49.65
Social and community service managers	15.87	20.67	26.44	32.15	40.32
Business and Financial Operations	18.21	22.31	28.50	36.06	47.67
Buyers and purchasing agents	19.00	22.12	26.52	32.99	41.54
Purchasing agents and buyers, farm products	20.43	21.20	27.19	36.06	44.23
Wholesale and retail buyers, except farm products	18.81	21.39	25.51	32.00	41.38
Purchasing agents, except wholesale, retail, and farm products	19.12	22.40	27.05	32.90	41.97
Claims adjusters, appraisers, examiners, and investigators	18.47	20.98	26.83	32.96	39.73
Claims adjusters, examiners, and investigators	18.47	21.21	26.92	32.96	39.92
Insurance appraisers, auto damage	20.23	20.23	23.27	31.62	35.84
Compliance officers, except agriculture, construction, health and safety, and transportation	20.63	22.57	26.91	35.44	43.27
Cost estimators	18.50	21.34	28.88	38.26	47.10
Human resources, training, and labor relations specialists	18.04	21.62	26.97	34.46	43.71
Employment, recruitment, and placement specialists	16.63	19.16	22.72	29.84	38.70
Compensation, benefits, and job analysis specialists	20.19	21.68	27.24	33.70	39.23
Training and development specialists	17.46	23.52	30.37	35.58	42.70
Logisticians	19.62	23.28	30.63	38.65	49.52
Management analysts	21.84	28.05	34.52	47.84	59.44
Meeting and convention planners	16.45	18.51	21.72	25.73	29.23
Accountants and auditors	18.13	22.50	27.69	34.85	44.77
Appraisers and assessors of real estate	15.07	17.02	24.28	36.06	45.68
Budget analysts	23.33	28.08	28.16	36.97	46.93
Credit analysts	18.25	20.90	25.91	35.99	47.92
Financial analysts and advisors	19.63	24.04	31.25	42.07	55.64
Financial analysts	22.62	26.01	33.44	43.17	57.69
Personal financial advisors	15.28	18.78	23.40	36.54	56.89
Insurance underwriters	19.54	22.07	29.15	39.74	48.85
Financial examiners	19.42	21.95	28.55	32.18	35.99
Loan counselors and officers	15.56	18.50	25.94	34.36	46.88
Loan counselors	12.86	14.77	21.26	38.16	45.00
Loan officers	15.66	18.56	26.00	34.36	47.21
Tax examiners, collectors, preparers, and revenue agents	9.51	10.25	14.00	28.37	30.85
Tax preparers	9.35	10.25	14.00	17.57	30.85
Computer and Mathematical Science	20.09	26.02	35.91	45.33	54.09
Computer and information scientists, research	35.15	42.31	53.33	63.70	76.98
Computer programmers	19.61	25.00	34.83	41.84	52.40
Computer software engineers	28.10	35.48	43.03	51.18	60.10
Computer software engineers, applications	27.40	33.69	41.44	50.17	57.69
Computer software engineers, systems software	30.29	37.09	44.31	52.11	61.94
Computer support specialists	15.50	18.77	23.80	30.26	40.14
Computer systems analysts	26.53	31.25	39.44	46.84	54.09
Database administrators	22.30	25.77	35.30	44.39	50.58
Network and computer systems administrators	19.39	24.04	31.25	40.09	46.81
Network systems and data communications analysts	20.83	26.22	32.97	40.71	48.28
Actuaries	27.25	33.67	41.28	53.22	63.49
Operations research analysts	20.13	22.97	33.70	44.71	49.28
Statisticians	22.19	31.20	40.42	48.10	54.63

[1]Percentiles designate position in the earnings distribution and are calculated from individual worker earnings and the hours they are scheduled to work.

Table 6-20. Private Industry Workers: Hourly Wage Percentiles,[1] 2009—*Continued*

(Dollars.)

Occupation	Wages fall at or below the following percentiles:				
	10	25	50	75	90
Architecture and Engineering	19.38	25.67	33.64	43.95	55.29
Architects, except naval	19.38	23.46	29.72	34.17	47.17
Architects, except landscape and naval	19.23	22.90	29.77	37.02	48.08
Landscape architects	22.67	23.46	27.53	32.79	34.17
Surveyors, cartographers, and photogrammetrists	19.95	22.50	28.85	38.94	53.00
Surveyors	19.88	22.50	30.28	38.94	56.00
Engineers	26.83	32.00	39.49	49.22	60.17
Aerospace engineers	33.47	38.48	48.15	58.63	69.80
Chemical engineers	28.21	34.57	42.92	54.76	72.00
Civil engineers	23.46	28.37	36.20	44.03	50.66
Computer hardware engineers	30.54	36.89	45.14	55.12	68.28
Electrical and electronics engineers	26.83	32.17	39.58	46.80	57.21
Electrical engineers	25.70	30.56	38.91	46.05	55.18
Electronics engineers, except computer	28.40	32.76	40.43	47.49	59.42
Environmental engineers	25.77	30.57	39.44	50.45	54.98
Industrial engineers, including health and safety	25.26	29.23	35.41	43.03	52.46
Health and safety engineers, except mining safety engineers and inspectors	26.83	31.01	35.41	51.96	59.39
Industrial engineers	25.21	28.44	35.35	42.53	50.29
Materials engineers	27.33	29.81	36.91	51.14	60.01
Mechanical engineers	25.48	30.43	36.33	44.71	55.28
Mining and geological engineers, including mining safety	28.85	31.25	38.81	57.07	101.92
Nuclear engineers	34.09	38.45	44.16	46.21	56.39
Petroleum engineers	30.77	36.33	41.11	77.89	85.24
Drafters	14.45	18.00	22.12	29.28	36.54
Architectural and civil drafters	14.90	18.07	21.84	31.00	36.54
Electrical and electronics drafters	13.20	15.75	23.08	26.45	32.40
Mechanical drafters	16.71	19.23	22.74	26.44	30.53
Engineering technicians, except drafters	15.93	20.00	25.63	30.28	36.00
Aerospace engineering and operations technicians	22.62	25.02	27.92	33.27	38.04
Civil engineering technicians	12.00	14.00	16.00	19.15	26.84
Electrical and electronic engineering technicians	17.31	21.17	26.00	30.00	34.91
Electro-mechanical technicians	18.65	20.29	26.83	30.06	30.59
Environmental engineering technicians	14.00	18.00	18.03	29.58	29.59
Industrial engineering technicians	18.41	21.50	26.24	31.73	35.53
Mechanical engineering technicians	18.03	20.62	25.65	28.96	35.33
Surveying and mapping technicians	10.83	14.00	18.65	28.27	35.71
Life, Physical, and Social Science	17.05	21.43	27.78	38.80	52.59
Life scientists	19.89	23.72	33.91	42.91	53.32
Agricultural and food scientists	32.41	36.30	43.27	45.11	52.40
Food scientists and technologists	36.30	37.33	43.27	45.13	52.40
Biological scientists	19.80	21.75	34.55	42.32	47.82
Biochemists and biophysicists	19.80	23.01	39.57	44.50	52.40
Microbiologists	23.97	28.84	36.01	42.77	44.87
Medical scientists	19.83	24.17	31.21	45.70	58.27
Physical scientists	20.43	24.69	32.27	44.97	56.25
Astronomers and physicists	27.49	48.70	49.90	79.74	87.92
Physicists	27.20	48.22	49.18	79.74	87.92
Chemists and materials scientists	21.64	25.25	31.65	44.97	59.65
Chemists	21.64	24.52	30.65	39.73	59.62
Materials scientists	28.24	35.44	51.49	56.68	65.68
Environmental scientists and geoscientists	18.58	22.52	31.50	38.06	48.98
Environmental scientists and specialists, including health	18.58	21.02	29.33	34.65	48.98
Geoscientists, except hydrologists and geographers	22.31	25.30	35.39	38.94	46.38
Market and survey researchers	18.50	23.61	30.24	46.19	60.10
Market research analysts	17.85	23.37	28.85	45.34	58.94
Psychologists	17.95	18.27	27.00	40.63	57.79
Clinical, counseling, and school psychologists	18.11	19.08	29.73	44.56	61.62
Miscellaneous social scientists and related workers	13.35	20.38	27.14	36.03	66.54
Agricultural and food science technicians	14.91	15.27	17.80	22.60	28.25
Biological technicians	13.50	15.62	20.00	24.76	31.55
Chemical technicians	14.00	17.05	22.10	26.48	30.89
Geological and petroleum technicians	17.83	17.83	26.32	36.64	47.89
Nuclear technicians	28.75	31.16	35.23	45.27	46.50
Social science research assistants	15.63	21.63	24.65	25.00	25.82
Miscellaneous life, physical, and social science technicians	15.00	17.02	21.09	26.58	34.28
Environmental science and protection technicians, including health	15.65	18.56	23.21	34.28	34.28
Community and Social Services	11.08	13.74	16.99	21.02	27.55
Counselors	11.25	13.70	17.32	20.70	25.50
Substance abuse and behavioral disorder counselors	12.95	14.46	17.50	20.21	22.34
Educational, vocational, and school counselors	13.99	16.08	19.23	24.79	39.75
Mental health counselors	12.84	15.84	20.00	23.87	30.00
Rehabilitation counselors	10.50	12.00	15.02	19.18	21.11
Social workers	13.79	15.87	18.97	24.52	29.31
Child, family, and school social workers	12.05	13.98	16.41	20.56	23.89
Medical and public health social workers	17.12	19.39	24.71	29.28	32.63
Mental health and substance abuse social workers	14.00	16.00	18.54	22.59	28.84
Miscellaneous community and social service specialists	9.50	11.26	14.18	17.00	20.11
Health educators	10.00	15.39	19.00	36.02	42.23
Social and human service assistants	9.19	10.20	12.98	15.20	18.75
Clergy	14.10	14.10	17.05	21.22	24.76
Directors, religious activities and education	16.76	17.31	23.25	25.49	43.12
Legal	16.15	20.19	30.00	51.69	81.74
Lawyers	25.95	35.92	53.38	78.13	99.80
Paralegals and legal assistants	15.38	17.50	21.98	29.14	34.62
Miscellaneous legal support workers	13.59	16.75	20.87	25.98	33.77
Title examiners, abstractors, and searchers	14.90	17.13	20.87	25.98	29.44

[1]Percentiles designate position in the earnings distribution and are calculated from individual worker earnings and the hours they are scheduled to work.

Table 6-20. Private Industry Workers: Hourly Wage Percentiles,[1] 2009—*Continued*

(Dollars.)

Occupation	Wages fall at or below the following percentiles:				
	10	25	50	75	90
Education, Training, and Library	10.00	12.46	22.48	35.26	52.16
Postsecondary teachers	22.70	28.72	39.07	56.31	85.32
Business teachers, postsecondary	23.78	26.50	35.70	64.57	92.55
Math and computer teachers, postsecondary	31.60	32.75	42.52	55.74	79.68
Computer science teachers, postsecondary	24.37	38.74	52.93	63.18	85.32
Mathematical science teachers, postsecondary	32.75	32.75	36.27	51.28	74.23
Engineering and architecture teachers, postsecondary	39.07	48.90	78.33	91.37	105.11
Engineering teachers, postsecondary	39.07	48.90	80.73	92.63	105.87
Life sciences teachers, postsecondary	30.90	39.79	51.18	56.53	135.54
Biological science teachers, postsecondary	30.90	39.79	51.18	56.53	135.54
Physical sciences teachers, postsecondary	31.97	45.65	53.61	67.53	88.53
Chemistry teachers, postsecondary	31.97	39.60	46.03	58.78	78.11
Physics teachers, postsecondary	48.89	53.61	56.92	88.53	88.53
Social sciences teachers, postsecondary	31.67	35.51	45.85	55.75	73.76
Economics teachers, postsecondary	34.80	38.03	57.10	69.33	78.10
Political science teachers, postsecondary	48.08	48.08	49.77	49.77	62.73
Psychology teachers, postsecondary	27.69	31.67	43.32	57.20	76.84
Sociology teachers, postsecondary	35.16	36.70	42.62	58.60	96.63
Health teachers, postsecondary	26.28	35.00	49.60	81.33	104.00
Health specialties teachers, postsecondary	23.39	40.40	64.21	89.94	118.32
Nursing instructors and teachers, postsecondary	28.35	34.73	38.62	40.80	44.56
Education and library science teachers, postsecondary	25.25	28.23	38.13	38.13	49.88
Education teachers, postsecondary	25.25	28.23	38.13	38.13	49.88
Law, criminal justice, and social work teachers, postsecondary	34.68	49.82	72.66	88.72	108.06
Law teachers, postsecondary	52.90	68.41	75.68	95.21	108.06
Arts, communications, and humanities teachers, postsecondary	25.65	31.47	37.51	49.52	60.30
Art, drama, and music teachers, postsecondary	25.65	30.77	33.78	41.18	44.60
Communications teachers, postsecondary	20.96	24.19	33.43	58.60	75.28
English language and literature teachers, postsecondary	23.93	34.65	42.59	52.74	69.60
Foreign language and literature teachers, postsecondary	28.75	37.11	49.99	57.47	70.10
History teachers, postsecondary	33.83	33.83	44.21	54.29	63.06
Philosophy and religion teachers, postsecondary	25.75	30.94	35.14	47.46	60.01
Miscellaneous postsecondary teachers	19.23	22.70	28.85	39.25	54.42
Vocational education teachers, postsecondary	16.12	21.07	24.09	33.44	37.90
Primary, secondary, and special education school teachers	10.75	13.66	21.53	32.41	39.71
Preschool and kindergarten teachers	9.73	11.00	13.50	16.27	23.00
Preschool teachers, except special education	9.50	11.00	13.37	16.00	23.00
Kindergarten teachers, except special education	13.89	13.89	20.69	25.54	32.43
Elementary and middle school teachers	16.62	21.16	26.71	34.29	38.35
Elementary school teachers, except special education	16.51	20.95	26.88	34.17	38.35
Middle school teachers, except special and vocational	16.85	21.55	26.58	34.36	42.54
Secondary school teachers	21.17	26.91	34.09	42.29	53.21
Secondary school teachers, except special and vocational	21.74	27.49	34.34	42.46	53.60
Special education teachers	18.60	25.53	30.90	35.46	65.00
Special education teachers, preschool, kindergarten, and elementary school	18.88	25.53	28.85	33.87	39.05
Special education teachers, secondary school	25.00	32.15	53.72	66.98	66.98
Other teachers and instructors	10.00	14.00	20.00	28.70	35.00
Self-enrichment education teachers	17.00	19.23	21.58	25.00	33.67
Archivists, curators, and museum technicians	15.87	18.90	25.91	30.63	36.25
Archivists	13.34	14.84	18.46	23.87	27.16
Curators	23.85	25.91	27.60	36.25	36.25
Librarians	20.49	22.80	29.79	42.66	55.70
Library technicians	13.46	15.37	18.10	23.62	27.04
Instructional coordinators	20.77	22.94	24.46	34.75	38.99
Teacher assistants	8.50	9.60	10.30	11.83	13.86
Arts, Design, Entertainment, Sports, and Media	12.00	16.71	22.77	31.97	45.34
Artists and related workers	16.00	17.70	24.53	38.24	49.45
Art directors	16.00	17.70	28.23	49.45	49.93
Multi-media artists and animators	16.83	23.60	31.25	34.62	46.58
Designers	12.00	16.00	21.64	31.01	40.43
Commercial and industrial designers	21.50	28.85	31.88	41.74	45.34
Fashion designers	20.00	24.04	33.65	48.08	48.08
Floral designers	7.50	8.50	11.00	12.00	15.05
Graphic designers	14.00	16.83	20.43	27.24	35.10
Interior designers	17.12	21.64	28.48	32.78	47.14
Merchandise displayers and window trimmers	10.00	12.23	15.83	20.73	24.04
Set and exhibit designers	13.00	14.08	18.41	32.81	34.81
Actors, producers, and directors	13.13	17.83	25.46	43.27	61.64
Producers and directors	13.13	17.83	25.46	43.27	61.64
Athletes, coaches, umpires, and related workers	10.00	12.00	22.12	32.13	38.46
Coaches and scouts	10.00	12.00	22.12	33.52	40.06
Dancers and choreographers	15.96	18.34	20.33	25.37	34.17
Choreographers	15.96	18.00	18.34	20.33	25.00
Musicians, singers, and related workers	13.60	20.83	25.00	34.66	43.53
Music directors and composers	15.63	17.86	21.33	22.62	40.00
Musicians and singers	13.26	24.15	34.66	34.66	43.53
Announcers	8.17	11.77	20.45	34.58	98.56
Radio and television announcers	8.17	11.77	20.45	36.30	98.78
News analysts, reporters and correspondents	12.33	15.81	25.72	37.93	73.70
Reporters and correspondents	12.25	16.15	25.14	35.91	65.01

[1]Percentiles designate position in the earnings distribution and are calculated from individual worker earnings and the hours they are scheduled to work.

Table 6-20. Private Industry Workers: Hourly Wage Percentiles,[1] 2009—Continued

(Dollars.)

Occupation	Wages fall at or below the following percentiles:				
	10	25	50	75	90
Arts, Design, Entertainment, Sports, and Media—*Continued*					
Public relations specialists	16.83	21.51	25.55	32.65	50.89
Writers and editors	15.67	19.23	26.09	33.57	44.23
Editors	14.92	19.23	24.67	33.34	44.23
Technical writers	17.29	21.40	29.36	33.81	44.58
Writers and authors	15.00	18.54	19.19	29.38	48.72
Miscellaneous media and communication workers	15.38	17.61	21.92	24.57	27.47
Interpreters and translators	11.84	17.61	19.34	21.73	34.80
Broadcast and sound engineering technicians and radio operators	11.59	16.57	21.85	34.94	41.25
Audio and video equipment technicians	12.84	15.45	21.14	29.00	40.18
Broadcast technicians	8.83	14.24	19.23	27.61	37.76
Sound engineering technicians	18.50	26.92	35.00	49.13	52.89
Photographers	8.16	11.00	12.98	15.43	19.23
Television, video, and motion picture camera operators and editors	16.56	18.00	24.04	28.96	32.56
Camera operators, television, video, and motion picture	14.72	18.00	24.02	26.45	32.56
Film and video editors	17.50	24.04	28.96	28.96	29.09
Healthcare Practitioner and Technical	15.18	20.00	27.00	35.45	49.98
Dentists	52.89	55.29	73.82	73.82	114.64
Dentists, general	52.89	55.29	73.82	73.82	114.64
Dietitians and nutritionists	19.51	22.02	23.81	25.87	30.98
Optometrists	36.76	40.63	45.67	54.76	56.49
Pharmacists	44.00	50.00	53.50	56.00	58.89
Physicians and surgeons	24.80	31.82	83.86	116.63	181.73
Anesthesiologists	32.92	111.11	157.86	187.50	258.99
Family and general practitioners	30.50	57.70	76.46	104.00	151.66
Internists, general	24.24	51.94	88.35	105.77	169.23
Obstetricians and gynecologists	65.63	88.48	108.32	114.17	134.72
Pediatricians, general	23.85	24.59	67.70	80.53	96.88
Psychiatrists	62.50	71.81	79.56	86.65	92.29
Surgeons	65.14	100.00	155.71	181.73	181.73
Physician assistants	28.76	35.65	44.00	50.00	60.10
Registered nurses	22.27	26.00	30.84	37.25	44.99
Therapists	20.50	25.00	30.89	37.09	44.83
Audiologists	20.89	24.51	26.44	30.00	31.25
Occupational therapists	25.85	28.50	34.34	38.46	45.70
Physical therapists	25.00	28.84	34.06	39.03	45.67
Radiation therapists	26.37	29.78	37.54	45.67	49.99
Recreational therapists	13.04	15.14	16.51	20.44	23.32
Respiratory therapists	20.00	22.66	24.87	28.79	32.77
Speech-language pathologists	24.57	27.33	32.74	39.90	55.00
Veterinarians	32.72	41.16	44.22	52.89	58.65
Clinical laboratory technologists and technicians	13.25	16.25	20.90	25.96	30.52
Medical and clinical laboratory technologists	16.96	21.92	25.49	29.73	33.05
Medical and clinical laboratory technicians	12.22	14.75	17.51	21.18	25.78
Dental hygienists	22.34	28.75	33.00	38.00	46.88
Diagnostic related technologists and technicians	15.29	21.62	27.04	32.21	37.37
Cardiovascular technologists and technicians	11.85	14.62	23.50	30.96	37.85
Diagnostic medical sonographers	25.84	28.05	33.08	37.75	42.54
Nuclear medicine technologists	29.81	31.73	33.28	36.62	39.46
Radiologic technologists and technicians	16.34	20.50	25.55	30.14	34.09
Emergency medical technicians and paramedics	9.79	11.25	13.18	16.15	21.57
Health diagnosing and treating practitioner support technicians	10.20	12.79	16.00	19.25	23.00
Dietetic technicians	7.50	8.01	11.94	17.00	27.30
Pharmacy technicians	10.00	11.73	14.15	16.50	18.56
Psychiatric technicians	9.27	11.07	13.42	18.00	20.58
Respiratory therapy technicians	16.83	18.91	21.96	26.76	29.37
Surgical technologists	14.34	16.93	19.55	22.17	23.75
Veterinary technologists and technicians	11.00	12.50	15.00	16.70	19.00
Licensed practical and licensed vocational nurses	15.00	17.00	19.18	22.12	25.83
Medical records and health information technicians	10.25	12.85	15.91	18.80	23.12
Opticians, dispensing	11.31	14.00	19.50	26.25	26.50
Miscellaneous health technologists and technicians	11.75	14.00	17.25	21.32	27.93
Occupational health and safety specialists and technicians	15.91	24.94	30.00	30.71	40.78
Occupational health and safety specialists	15.42	22.67	30.05	35.02	46.41
Occupational health and safety technicians	21.97	28.31	30.00	30.00	30.64
Miscellaneous healthcare practitioner and technical workers	18.99	21.35	26.17	29.19	30.85
Athletic trainers	18.99	19.50	23.11	27.57	39.92
Healthcare Support	8.65	10.00	11.79	14.53	18.00
Nursing, psychiatric, and home health aides	8.25	9.40	10.60	12.62	14.94
Home health aides	7.25	8.35	9.87	10.81	12.62
Nursing aides, orderlies, and attendants	8.95	9.93	11.25	13.28	15.53
Psychiatric aides	8.41	9.25	10.20	12.00	13.26
Occupational therapist assistants and aides	15.13	17.66	24.69	30.70	30.70
Occupational therapist assistants	15.78	21.25	26.00	30.70	30.70
Occupational therapist aides	10.41	10.76	16.63	17.66	26.12
Physical therapist assistants and aides	10.00	11.47	16.23	24.72	32.00
Physical therapist assistants	12.00	17.25	23.50	29.14	34.00
Physical therapist aides	9.00	10.00	11.88	13.27	16.23
Massage therapists	8.63	14.58	20.49	21.68	24.24
Miscellaneous healthcare support occupations	9.84	11.44	13.74	16.91	19.76
Dental assistants	10.00	12.80	16.50	19.25	21.80
Medical assistants	10.00	11.00	13.18	16.00	18.52
Medical equipment preparers	11.41	12.14	14.22	17.40	20.00
Medical transcriptionists	11.33	13.09	15.27	17.47	20.28
Pharmacy aides	8.50	9.42	11.22	13.26	17.40
Veterinary assistants and laboratory animal caretakers	8.00	10.00	12.36	13.00	15.22

[1]Percentiles designate position in the earnings distribution and are calculated from individual worker earnings and the hours they are scheduled to work.

Table 6-20. Private Industry Workers: Hourly Wage Percentiles,[1] 2009—*Continued*

(Dollars.)

Occupation	Wages fall at or below the following percentiles:				
	10	25	50	75	90
Protective Service Occupations	8.00	9.33	10.95	13.81	17.50
First-line supervisors/managers, law enforcement workers	10.96	11.04	12.88	14.16	16.95
Bailiffs, correctional officers, and jailers	8.58	9.20	10.20	12.05	20.06
Correctional officers and jailers	8.52	9.07	10.20	12.01	20.06
Police officers	16.33	19.00	21.92	23.56	25.00
Police and sheriff's patrol officers	16.33	19.00	21.92	23.56	25.00
Private detectives and investigators	10.92	14.04	14.57	14.62	23.59
Security guards and gaming surveillance officers	8.00	9.36	10.75	12.84	15.91
Security guards	8.00	9.31	10.65	12.75	15.88
Miscellaneous protective service workers	7.25	7.50	8.34	10.63	13.48
Lifeguards, ski patrol, and other recreational protective	7.25	7.50	8.15	9.50	12.18
Food Preparation and Serving Related	3.82	7.00	8.00	10.00	13.00
First-line supervisors/managers, food preparation and serving	9.63	11.75	14.56	18.75	22.60
Chefs and head cooks	10.50	11.85	16.00	20.69	29.51
First-line supervisors/managers of food preparation and serving	9.50	11.72	14.42	18.30	21.98
Cooks	7.25	8.25	10.00	12.00	14.17
Cooks, fast food	7.15	7.25	8.00	9.00	10.00
Cooks, institution and cafeteria	8.28	9.56	11.49	13.83	17.50
Cooks, restaurant	8.00	9.00	10.50	12.49	14.33
Cooks, short order	7.40	8.00	9.08	11.00	13.25
Food preparation workers	7.25	7.72	8.55	10.38	12.40
Food service, tipped	2.15	3.26	5.00	8.00	8.87
Bartenders	4.00	5.00	7.30	8.55	10.00
Waiters and waitresses	2.13	2.75	4.23	6.85	8.08
Dining room and cafeteria attendants and bartender helpers	4.10	6.55	7.89	8.60	10.35
Fast food and counter workers	6.80	7.25	8.00	9.00	10.35
Combined food preparation and serving workers, including fast	6.75	7.25	7.85	8.80	10.13
Counter attendants, cafeteria, food concession, and coffee shop	7.08	7.33	8.20	9.36	11.75
Food servers, nonrestaurant	4.25	7.25	8.51	10.33	13.86
Dishwashers	7.15	7.55	8.40	9.37	10.81
Hosts and hostesses, restaurant, lounge, and coffee shop	5.11	7.25	8.00	9.35	11.00
Building and Grounds Cleaning and Maintenance	7.62	8.50	10.30	13.50	17.67
First-line supervisors/managers, building and grounds cleaning and	11.38	13.50	16.66	21.74	25.21
First-line supervisors/managers of housekeeping and janitorial	10.62	12.95	15.00	21.09	23.08
First-line supervisors/managers of landscaping, lawn service, and groundskeeing workers	13.00	15.50	17.57	22.83	27.00
Building cleaning workers	7.50	8.30	10.00	12.55	16.43
Janitors and cleaners, except maids and housekeeping cleaners	7.50	8.50	10.43	13.00	16.83
Maids and housekeeping cleaners	7.45	8.00	9.00	10.91	14.00
Pest control workers	12.00	13.27	15.18	17.16	18.68
Grounds maintenance workers	8.00	9.00	10.36	13.50	16.65
Landscaping and groundskeeping workers	8.00	9.00	10.20	13.06	16.00
Tree trimmers and pruners	13.25	15.00	16.00	20.00	22.50
Personal care and service	6.67	7.62	9.21	12.36	17.70
First-line supervisors/managers of gaming workers	10.32	11.60	14.74	18.51	21.64
Gaming supervisors	11.37	14.54	16.87	21.12	24.35
Slot key persons	9.77	10.61	11.89	13.32	15.20
First-line supervisors/managers of personal service workers	10.00	12.96	15.00	16.96	20.47
Nonfarm animal caretakers	7.25	8.39	9.67	11.25	15.10
Gaming services workers	5.50	5.89	6.81	7.86	8.61
Gaming dealers	5.46	5.84	6.64	7.65	8.15
Gaming and sports book writers and runners	7.50	8.06	8.60	12.21	17.17
Ushers, lobby attendants, and ticket takers	7.15	7.72	9.00	14.22	14.32
Miscellaneous entertainment attendants and related workers	7.00	7.30	8.04	10.00	13.19
Amusement and recreation attendants	6.85	7.25	8.00	9.34	12.75
Locker room, coatroom, and dressing room attendants	7.50	8.07	10.00	11.32	18.67
Funeral attendants	8.50	8.50	12.00	13.15	14.00
Barbers and cosmetologists	7.53	8.61	12.50	18.55	27.55
Hairdressers, hairstylists, and cosmetologists	7.50	8.55	12.50	19.60	27.55
Miscellaneous personal appearance workers	7.25	8.00	10.86	15.27	20.97
Manicurists and pedicurists	7.18	8.33	9.09	11.87	13.68
Shampooers	7.28	7.28	8.00	8.00	8.00
Skin care specialists	8.28	12.55	17.17	20.97	20.97
Baggage porters, bellhops, and concierges	7.03	8.00	10.00	13.50	16.49
Baggage porters and bellhops	6.55	7.53	8.00	10.50	14.15
Concierges	10.00	11.17	13.10	17.03	19.49
Tour and travel guides	7.36	8.84	12.77	16.73	16.73
Tour guides and escorts	7.36	8.84	12.77	16.62	16.73
Transportation attendants	6.55	17.71	32.30	43.04	48.46
Flight attendants	18.71	31.13	38.39	44.31	50.47
Transportation attendants, except flight attendants and baggage	6.55	6.55	7.99	12.56	15.53
Child care workers	7.25	7.97	8.93	10.16	12.09
Personal and home care aides	7.25	7.75	9.00	10.50	11.62
Recreation and fitness workers	7.50	8.84	11.00	15.38	22.14
Fitness trainers and aerobics instructors	8.25	9.70	15.00	19.93	25.00
Recreation workers	7.15	8.50	10.45	13.26	18.45
Residential advisors	10.40	12.55	14.07	16.33	19.85
Sales and Related	7.69	8.95	12.05	19.17	31.37
First-line supervisors/managers, sales workers	10.80	13.80	17.58	23.30	33.17
First-line supervisors/managers of retail sales workers	10.75	13.43	17.00	21.01	28.84
First-line supervisors/managers of non-retail sales workers	11.36	16.89	24.52	34.25	51.68
Retail sales workers	7.40	8.16	9.77	12.60	17.15
Cashiers, all workers	7.25	7.96	8.85	10.50	12.98
Cashiers	7.25	7.90	8.77	10.35	12.75
Gaming change persons and booth cashiers	9.68	11.66	13.66	14.64	15.47
Counter and rental clerks and parts salespersons	7.74	9.00	11.50	16.28	21.73
Counter and rental clerks	7.25	8.00	9.17	12.00	15.58
Parts salespersons	9.00	10.71	14.40	18.76	23.03
Retail salespersons	7.50	8.70	10.66	14.16	19.50
Advertising sales agents	10.99	14.32	19.20	27.39	38.89
Insurance sales agents	13.15	16.89	23.14	32.69	49.45

[1]Percentiles designate position in the earnings distribution and are calculated from individual worker earnings and the hours they are scheduled to work.

Table 6-20. Private Industry Workers: Hourly Wage Percentiles,[1] 2009—*Continued*

(Dollars.)

Occupation	Wages fall at or below the following percentiles:				
	10	25	50	75	90
Sales and Related—*Continued*					
Securities, commodities, and financial services sales agents	16.22	21.87	38.46	67.62	105.24
Travel agents	7.16	10.88	14.00	19.04	22.84
Sales representatives, wholesale and manufacturing	14.42	18.95	26.44	38.33	55.29
Sales representatives, wholesale and manufacturing, technical	17.60	23.63	35.28	52.85	60.10
Sales representatives, wholesale and manufacturing, except technical and scientific products	13.69	17.88	23.75	32.59	46.59
Models, demonstrators, and product promoters	8.62	11.03	13.30	17.29	22.76
Demonstrators and product promoters	8.62	11.01	13.30	17.29	22.76
Real estate brokers and sales agents	9.81	11.50	14.54	21.98	32.00
Real estate brokers	0.00	7.34	17.22	29.08	38.83
Real estate sales agents	10.50	11.50	14.53	21.10	31.34
Sales engineers	19.06	27.40	33.21	45.81	57.45
Telemarketers	8.00	9.00	11.25	14.71	20.92
Miscellaneous sales and related workers	8.06	9.64	14.72	20.25	29.27
Office and Administrative Support	9.77	11.74	14.78	18.73	23.24
First-line supervisors/managers of office and administrative	15.24	18.07	21.76	27.37	31.04
Switchboard operators, including answering service	8.15	9.36	10.97	13.11	16.24
Telephone operators	9.00	9.57	12.29	18.98	22.55
Financial clerks	10.15	12.00	14.79	18.00	21.66
Bill and account collectors	8.32	11.74	14.24	17.83	22.40
Billing and posting clerks and machine operators	11.00	13.00	15.28	17.95	21.09
Bookkeeping, accounting, and auditing clerks	11.02	13.19	15.89	19.11	22.87
Gaming cage workers	9.14	9.46	10.20	12.52	13.50
Payroll and timekeeping clerks	13.26	16.00	17.95	20.75	24.83
Procurement clerks	11.15	13.59	16.27	19.23	21.87
Tellers	9.50	10.32	11.68	13.49	15.65
Brokerage clerks	13.00	15.88	18.16	21.15	25.68
Correspondence clerks	13.10	14.98	16.54	18.73	21.74
Credit authorizers, checkers, and clerks	11.37	13.37	16.97	19.38	23.28
Customer service representatives	10.05	12.02	14.67	18.35	23.27
Eligibility interviewers, government programs	10.68	12.20	16.75	17.33	21.40
File clerks	8.73	10.25	11.65	14.72	16.63
Hotel, motel, and resort desk clerks	7.50	8.50	10.00	11.35	13.50
Interviewers, except eligibility and loan	8.69	10.50	12.89	15.15	18.34
Library assistants, clerical	9.55	11.59	13.82	16.29	18.74
Loan interviewers and clerks	11.32	13.10	15.92	18.75	22.73
New accounts clerks	10.50	12.36	14.38	16.76	20.55
Order clerks	10.00	11.75	14.50	17.95	21.81
Human resources assistants, except payroll and timekeeping	12.50	14.99	18.00	20.43	24.58
Receptionists and information clerks	9.00	10.40	12.26	14.93	17.50
Reservation and transportation ticket agents and travel clerks	9.45	10.86	15.20	20.54	21.72
Cargo and freight agents	12.75	14.75	18.63	22.94	39.00
Couriers and messengers	8.00	8.50	10.27	12.80	14.50
Dispatchers	10.75	13.00	16.83	20.50	25.00
Police, fire, and ambulance dispatchers	10.50	11.50	12.50	14.90	18.90
Dispatchers, except police, fire, and ambulance	10.85	13.62	17.00	20.70	25.16
Meter readers, utilities	12.00	15.09	18.95	22.65	26.84
Production, planning, and expediting clerks	13.10	15.00	18.81	23.20	27.00
Shipping, receiving, and traffic clerks	8.90	10.30	12.62	15.60	19.23
Stock clerks and order fillers	7.71	8.70	10.86	13.74	16.65
Weighers, measurers, checkers, and samplers, recordkeeping	9.10	11.00	13.60	15.69	19.75
Secretaries and administrative assistants	12.00	14.42	18.10	22.74	28.33
Executive secretaries and administrative assistants	15.00	17.62	21.40	25.64	30.26
Legal secretaries	13.00	16.13	21.00	28.77	33.85
Medical secretaries	10.50	12.48	15.00	18.25	21.13
Secretaries, except legal, medical, and executive	10.85	13.20	15.47	19.23	22.76
Computer operators	11.00	13.81	16.45	19.83	23.00
Data entry and information processing workers	10.00	11.50	13.00	15.69	18.26
Data entry keyers	9.79	11.09	12.85	14.93	16.83
Word processors and typists	10.80	12.10	17.00	19.44	25.25
Desktop publishers	11.98	15.16	19.71	23.57	26.83
Insurance claims and policy processing clerks	11.50	13.23	16.07	19.36	23.08
Mail clerks and mail machine operators, except postal service	8.50	10.25	11.59	14.01	16.54
Office clerks, general	9.90	11.50	14.00	17.17	20.88
Office machine operators, except computer	9.09	10.96	13.00	15.51	17.61
Proofreaders and copy markers	8.88	10.00	12.53	18.00	21.80
Statistical assistants	13.93	16.39	19.10	19.71	23.56
Farming, Fishing, and Forestry	7.25	8.75	11.61	16.08	20.60
First-line supervisors/managers of farming, fishing, and forestry	12.85	18.35	20.60	25.00	25.73
Graders and sorters, agricultural products	6.92	7.25	9.70	10.30	15.30
Miscellaneous agricultural workers	7.30	8.15	10.12	14.00	15.25
Farmworkers and laborers, crop, nursery, and greenhouse	8.25	9.10	10.54	14.64	15.87
Farmworkers, farm and ranch animals	7.00	7.15	7.44	8.50	10.35
Logging workers	11.19	13.34	17.41	18.28	24.85
Construction and Extraction	11.00	14.00	19.00	26.33	34.85
First-line supervisors/managers of construction trades and	18.67	22.00	28.00	35.63	43.46
Boilermakers	15.69	16.07	21.19	29.00	29.44
Brickmasons, blockmasons, and stonemasons	15.81	20.00	26.00	28.73	34.48
Brickmasons and blockmasons	16.86	21.00	26.70	28.73	34.48
Carpenters	13.79	16.00	20.10	26.98	36.95
Carpet, floor, and tile installers and finishers	14.24	16.50	18.00	20.00	25.00
Carpet installers	18.14	20.00	20.00	24.40	27.20
Tile and marble setters	15.00	16.50	17.00	20.00	24.49
Cement masons, concrete finishers, and terrazzo workers	13.05	16.00	20.00	25.00	30.00
Cement masons and concrete finishers	13.05	16.00	20.00	25.00	30.00
Construction laborers	9.00	10.00	14.00	19.87	27.55
Construction equipment operators	11.50	14.42	17.70	24.00	31.60
Paving, surfacing, and tamping equipment operators	10.74	13.00	16.00	20.50	23.40
Operating engineers and other construction equipment operators	11.60	14.63	18.50	27.54	32.16

[1]Percentiles designate position in the earnings distribution and are calculated from individual worker earnings and the hours they are scheduled to work.

Table 6-20. Private Industry Workers: Hourly Wage Percentiles,[1] 2009—Continued

(Dollars.)

Occupation	Wages fall at or below the following percentiles:				
	10	25	50	75	90
Construction and Extraction—*Continued*					
Drywall installers, ceiling tile installers, and tapers	13.29	15.00	18.75	26.03	34.85
Drywall and ceiling tile installers	13.25	15.00	18.18	25.33	34.85
Tapers	13.95	15.00	19.00	31.58	33.33
Electricians	13.00	16.50	21.95	31.43	37.56
Glaziers	8.68	14.00	20.00	31.25	33.73
Insulation workers	10.00	13.50	16.05	20.11	26.50
Insulation workers, floor, ceiling, and wall	9.50	11.00	14.00	19.00	26.50
Insulation workers, mechanical	14.00	15.12	16.05	21.05	24.28
Painters and paperhangers	12.00	13.20	15.81	20.83	24.38
Painters, construction and maintenance	12.00	13.54	15.81	20.00	23.73
Pipelayers, plumbers, pipefitters, and steamfitters	14.00	17.87	23.50	31.30	38.10
Pipelayers	11.00	12.50	14.00	23.77	30.15
Plumbers, pipefitters, and steamfitters	14.08	18.33	23.75	31.35	39.70
Plasterers and stucco masons	12.48	14.51	17.11	25.00	32.52
Reinforcing iron and rebar workers	12.50	18.00	31.83	32.75	35.25
Roofers	10.50	12.00	16.00	20.00	27.00
Sheet metal workers	12.58	15.82	19.50	28.50	38.20
Structural iron and steel workers	15.00	17.50	23.40	31.83	56.78
Helpers, construction trades	9.50	10.75	13.00	15.00	21.00
Helpers—brickmasons, blockmasons, stonemasons, and tile and marble setters	9.00	10.00	16.00	25.18	26.33
Helpers—carpenters	10.00	11.50	13.61	15.00	18.75
Helpers—electricians	10.00	10.90	12.48	13.35	15.50
Helpers—painters, paperhangers, plasterers, and stucco masons	8.50	9.54	10.90	11.72	13.16
Helpers—pipelayers, plumbers, pipefitters, and steamfitters	10.00	11.00	12.00	13.27	16.54
Helpers—roofers	10.00	11.00	13.00	14.00	15.42
Construction and building inspectors	18.36	21.28	27.29	33.88	40.21
Hazardous materials removal workers	11.00	14.00	18.00	22.00	39.95
Highway maintenance workers	9.75	18.50	22.66	24.20	25.38
Miscellaneous construction and related workers	10.63	11.73	15.15	19.48	27.00
Derrick, rotary drill, and service unit operators, oil, gas, and mining	12.47	12.47	20.70	32.65	34.75
Mining machine operators	16.00	19.76	23.25	24.50	29.74
Continuous mining machine operators	23.25	23.25	24.50	29.00	32.17
Roustabouts, oil and gas	11.11	11.11	16.44	17.50	30.84
Helpers—extraction workers	12.00	15.75	15.75	22.35	22.61
Installation, Maintenance, and Repair	11.25	15.00	19.85	26.48	31.80
First-line supervisors/managers of mechanics, installers, and repairers	17.67	20.81	26.19	34.14	42.35
Computer, automated teller, and office machine repairers	13.13	14.95	17.77	22.18	26.75
Radio and telecommunications equipment installers and repairers	19.00	25.43	30.03	32.30	34.86
Telecommunications equipment installers and repairers, except	19.00	25.43	30.03	32.30	34.86
Miscellaneous electrical and electronic equipment mechanics, installers, and repairers	13.02	14.27	19.23	26.46	33.12
Avionics technicians	15.65	18.08	24.22	29.70	36.75
Electric motor, power tool, and related repairers	10.00	12.50	14.50	18.07	22.91
Electrical and electronics repairers, commercial and industrial equipment	14.60	18.04	23.51	29.34	31.78
Electrical and electronics repairers, powerhouse, substation, and relay	25.80	31.08	36.12	38.21	39.04
Electronic equipment installers and repairers, motor vehicles	12.50	15.46	17.00	17.00	24.31
Electronic home entertainment equipment installers and repairers	10.50	13.83	13.89	14.27	17.48
Security and fire alarm systems installers	14.22	17.02	20.00	23.89	26.44
Aircraft mechanics and service technicians	18.50	22.75	27.44	31.81	41.16
Automotive technicians and repairers	10.00	13.00	17.57	22.69	28.88
Automotive body and related repairers	12.32	13.50	17.00	24.00	30.00
Automotive glass installers and repairers	12.00	14.50	18.00	20.34	28.88
Automotive service technicians and mechanics	9.75	12.50	17.75	22.65	28.48
Bus and truck mechanics and diesel engine specialists	13.93	16.22	20.00	23.89	28.11
Heavy vehicle and mobile equipment service technicians and mechanics	14.34	17.35	20.29	24.03	27.25
Farm equipment mechanics	11.75	13.00	17.30	21.06	25.00
Mobile heavy equipment mechanics, except engines	15.65	18.15	21.56	24.50	27.96
Rail car repairers	16.06	16.30	19.04	23.36	28.24
Small engine mechanics	10.88	12.50	14.90	19.23	23.11
Motorboat mechanics	10.88	11.47	13.00	16.00	20.18
Motorcycle mechanics	10.00	12.00	14.78	19.65	27.50
Outdoor power equipment and other small engine mechanics	12.50	13.00	16.75	19.23	21.25
Miscellaneous vehicle and mobile equipment mechanic, installers, and repairers	8.10	9.00	10.58	13.00	15.26
Recreational vehicle service technicians	10.58	11.06	18.00	20.19	21.00
Tire repairers and changers	8.00	9.00	10.50	12.75	14.30
Control and valve installers and repairers	12.36	16.28	23.13	26.09	31.50
Control and valve installers and repairers, except mechanical	17.57	21.06	24.20	29.07	34.02
Heating, air conditioning, and refrigeration mechanics and installers	13.00	16.00	20.90	28.61	36.43
Home appliance repairers	14.40	17.00	20.46	21.54	25.02
Industrial machinery installation, repair, and maintenance workers	12.48	15.20	19.15	23.78	29.51
Industrial machinery mechanics	17.06	19.60	22.50	27.04	32.19
Maintenance and repair workers, general	10.50	13.33	16.75	20.79	27.13
Maintenance workers, machinery	12.98	14.50	16.98	20.48	25.43
Millwrights	18.00	20.50	24.75	28.81	40.22
Line installers and repairers	16.60	22.80	28.13	30.91	33.67
Electrical power-line installers and repairers	20.07	26.40	30.43	34.85	38.65
Telecommunications line installers and repairers	15.00	20.95	27.02	30.03	31.46
Precision instrument and equipment repairers	13.95	17.00	21.86	28.88	39.12
Medical equipment repairers	13.81	15.34	21.27	26.01	28.88
Musical instrument repairers and tuners	14.00	20.00	20.00	20.50	25.20
Miscellaneous installation, maintenance, and repair workers	8.50	11.00	14.50	19.10	26.00
Coin, vending, and amusement machine servicers and repairers	11.00	11.00	14.35	17.69	19.27
Manufactured building and mobile home installers	9.00	10.75	12.65	12.65	15.00
Riggers	11.69	17.00	19.13	23.61	24.00
Helpers—installation, maintenance, and repair workers	7.87	9.00	11.32	14.00	16.97

[1]Percentiles designate position in the earnings distribution and are calculated from individual worker earnings and the hours they are scheduled to work.

Table 6-20. Private Industry Workers: Hourly Wage Percentiles,[1] 2009—*Continued*

(Dollars.)

Occupation	Wages fall at or below the following percentiles:				
	10	25	50	75	90
Production	8.91	11.00	14.50	19.30	25.97
First-line supervisors/managers of production and operating	15.29	19.45	24.06	30.92	36.14
Aircraft structure, surfaces, rigging, and systems assemblers	15.00	18.24	23.44	29.91	32.47
Electrical, electronics, and electromechanical assemblers	9.00	10.50	12.52	15.79	19.54
Coil winders, tapers, and finishers	9.37	10.47	12.00	14.25	18.33
Electrical and electronic equipment assemblers	8.65	10.16	12.48	15.25	19.50
Electromechanical equipment assemblers	9.64	11.15	13.92	17.85	19.54
Engine and other machine assemblers	12.16	14.65	17.60	21.71	28.49
Structural metal fabricators and fitters	8.75	13.24	15.41	19.00	27.00
Miscellaneous assemblers and fabricators	8.50	10.67	13.63	18.29	28.05
Fiberglass laminators and fabricators	10.75	11.96	12.95	15.66	16.00
Team assemblers	9.78	12.00	13.95	20.19	28.59
Bakers	8.00	9.27	12.00	14.50	19.15
Butchers and other meat, poultry, and fish processing workers	8.25	10.05	12.45	14.10	18.89
Butchers and meat cutters	9.75	12.75	15.63	19.23	21.50
Meat, poultry, and fish cutters and trimmers	7.20	8.35	10.10	11.71	13.05
Slaughterers and meat packers	10.00	11.05	12.57	13.48	15.54
Miscellaneous food processing workers	8.50	9.60	12.80	16.77	19.53
Food and tobacco roasting, baking, and drying machine operators	8.50	8.91	13.50	16.77	19.60
Food batchmakers	8.85	10.75	13.41	17.82	20.83
Food cooking machine operators and tenders	8.00	9.35	10.00	12.77	17.99
Computer control programmers and operators	12.50	14.36	18.30	21.75	26.29
Computer-controlled machine tool operators, metal and plastic	12.00	14.00	17.55	21.00	25.52
Numerical tool and process control programmers	18.60	19.90	22.50	25.33	32.35
Forming machine setters, operators, and tenders, metal and plastic	11.00	12.99	16.49	19.66	22.23
Extruding and drawing machine setters, operators, and tenders, metal and plastic	11.33	13.60	16.32	18.93	20.25
Forging machine setters, operators, and tenders, metal and plastic	12.05	12.50	18.15	20.24	23.25
Rolling machine setters, operators, and tenders, metal and plastic	8.70	11.45	15.18	19.77	22.23
Machine tool cutting setters, operators, and tenders, metal and plastic	9.54	12.28	14.50	18.50	21.26
Cutting, punching, and press machine setters, operators, and tenders, metal and plastic	9.27	11.97	13.77	17.14	20.30
Drilling and boring machine tool setters, operators, and tenders, metal and plastic	12.00	13.65	15.60	19.81	27.66
Grinding, lapping, polishing, and buffing machine tool setters, operators, and tenders, metal and plastic	9.54	12.00	14.21	17.40	19.77
Lathe and turning machine tool setters, operators, and tenders, metal and plastic	9.25	12.58	17.85	20.70	23.19
Milling and planing machine setters, operators, and tenders, metal and plastic	11.20	13.25	19.01	21.79	22.22
Machinists	14.20	17.50	20.57	25.36	30.57
Metal furnace and kiln operators and tenders	9.29	12.50	17.80	20.38	23.54
Metal-refining furnace operators and tenders	9.29	11.25	18.31	21.75	24.08
Pourers and casters, metal	9.12	14.05	17.80	19.38	20.38
Model makers and patternmakers, metal and plastic	11.00	15.68	22.25	32.78	34.52
Model makers, metal and plastic	14.25	16.25	23.77	32.69	36.05
Patternmakers, metal and plastic	9.00	12.01	15.50	32.78	34.52
Molders and molding machine setters, operators, and tenders, metal and plastic	8.50	10.00	12.90	16.12	19.44
Foundry mold and coremakers	9.98	10.50	15.27	17.85	19.44
Molding, coremaking, and casting machine setters, operators, and casting machine setters operators, and tenders, metal and plastic	8.26	10.00	12.84	15.98	19.50
Multiple machine tool setters, operators, and tenders, metal and plastic	10.00	11.73	14.50	18.76	24.75
Tool and die makers	18.00	20.23	24.42	27.50	32.83
Welding, soldering, and brazing workers	11.25	13.85	16.88	19.78	23.75
Welders, cutters, solderers, and brazers	11.44	14.00	17.00	20.10	23.57
Welding, soldering, and brazing machine setters, operators, and tenders	11.13	13.60	16.43	18.90	25.29
Miscellaneous metalworkers and plastic workers	9.00	11.43	14.80	17.92	23.00
Heat treating equipment setters, operators, and tenders, metal	9.50	11.65	16.53	18.97	20.77
Lay-out workers, metal and plastic	14.00	15.00	16.00	19.00	26.40
Plating and coating machine setters, operators, and tenders, metal and plastic	9.28	10.90	13.50	19.00	26.83
Tool grinders, filers, and sharpeners	8.34	8.34	14.80	18.12	23.19
Bookbinders and bindery workers	8.00	9.90	12.67	17.70	22.68
Bindery workers	8.00	9.90	12.67	17.70	22.68
Printers	9.57	12.78	16.86	21.75	26.33
Job printers	11.00	13.25	19.00	20.00	23.10
Prepress technicians and workers	10.00	13.35	19.82	24.09	27.62
Printing machine operators	9.50	12.62	16.00	20.81	26.00
Laundry and dry-cleaning workers	7.45	8.36	9.34	11.05	13.00
Pressers, textile, garment, and related materials	7.50	8.12	9.46	10.50	12.11
Sewing machine operators	8.00	8.25	10.50	14.07	16.61
Tailors, dressmakers, and sewers	9.00	10.75	12.14	18.50	24.31
Tailors, dressmakers, and custom sewers	9.00	10.75	12.14	16.20	24.31
Textile machine setters, operators, and tenders	8.65	9.87	11.75	13.71	15.81
Textile bleaching and dyeing machine operators and tenders	8.00	8.05	9.00	10.00	12.50
Textile cutting machine setters, operators, and tenders	9.00	9.30	9.94	12.81	13.55
Textile knitting and weaving machine setters, operators, and tenders	10.00	11.75	14.50	15.45	19.40
Textile winding, twisting, and drawing out machine setters, operators, and tenders	10.35	10.66	12.21	13.38	16.85
Miscellaneous textile, apparel, and furnishings workers	8.50	10.25	12.49	17.42	20.57
Extruding and forming machine setters, operators, and tenders, synthetic and glass fibers	9.47	11.20	17.42	19.55	19.85
Fabric and apparel patternmakers	13.13	13.13	17.57	20.37	22.00
Upholsterers	9.00	10.50	15.76	20.00	23.12
Cabinetmakers and bench carpenters	10.76	13.00	15.00	18.00	23.00
Furniture finishers	9.00	10.50	12.45	15.00	17.71
Model makers and patternmakers, wood	7.98	17.92	25.00	25.00	25.00
Woodworking machine setters, operators, and tenders	8.50	10.53	12.50	15.05	17.15
Sawing machine setters, operators, and tenders, wood	8.00	10.00	12.10	14.50	17.00
Woodworking machine setters, operators, and tenders, except sawing	9.00	11.47	13.82	15.55	17.24
Power plant operators, distributors, and dispatchers	25.58	28.43	34.32	35.33	40.78
Nuclear power reactor operators	28.77	35.08	35.08	38.75	42.03
Power distributors and dispatchers	31.37	33.59	38.08	44.36	45.31
Power plant operators	20.59	27.86	28.43	34.32	38.57
Stationary engineers and boiler operators	17.34	24.84	28.19	33.60	34.31
Water and liquid waste treatment plant and system operators	17.00	17.85	19.75	25.00	33.15
Miscellaneous plant and system operators	16.83	22.22	27.98	32.00	34.57
Chemical plant and system operators	17.16	20.43	24.52	29.57	31.30
Gas plant operators	26.06	28.43	34.57	34.57	37.08
Petroleum pump system operators, refinery operators, and gaugers	15.00	27.06	30.13	32.56	33.96

[1]Percentiles designate position in the earnings distribution and are calculated from individual worker earnings and the hours they are scheduled to work.

Table 6-20. Private Industry Workers: Hourly Wage Percentiles,[1] 2009—*Continued*

(Dollars.)

Occupation	Wages fall at or below the following percentiles:				
	10	25	50	75	90
Production—*Continued*					
Chemical processing machine setters, operators, and tenders	12.86	17.00	21.49	29.40	33.00
Chemical equipment operators and tenders	12.00	15.00	21.49	25.97	28.98
Separating, filtering, clarifying, precipitating, and still machine setters, operators, and tenders	13.78	17.50	22.17	30.51	35.37
Crushing, grinding, polishing, mixing, and blending workers	9.00	11.32	14.50	18.53	22.27
Crushing, grinding, and polishing machine setters, operators, and tenders	10.50	11.32	16.49	18.85	20.74
Grinding and polishing workers, hand	9.00	11.10	13.10	16.25	18.53
Mixing and blending machine setters, operators, and tenders	10.00	11.50	15.00	19.69	22.79
Cutting workers	9.25	11.00	14.00	16.95	19.50
Cutters and trimmers, hand	8.50	10.46	12.29	15.00	18.30
Cutting and slicing machine setters, operators, and tenders	9.50	11.45	14.00	17.15	19.80
Extruding, forming, pressing, and compacting machine setters, operators, and tenders	8.95	10.00	13.25	17.19	19.50
Furnace, kiln, oven, drier, and kettle operators and tenders	8.00	11.91	14.52	17.50	26.37
Inspectors, testers, sorters, samplers, and weighers	9.70	12.24	15.50	19.81	25.46
Jewelers and precious stone and metal workers	11.00	13.13	18.00	22.50	31.00
Medical, dental, and ophthalmic laboratory technicians	10.00	12.00	15.40	18.75	23.71
Dental laboratory technicians	9.04	13.25	16.00	20.20	24.25
Ophthalmic laboratory technicians	10.00	10.06	14.55	17.15	17.15
Packaging and filling machine operators and tenders	8.65	10.50	14.14	17.99	21.84
Painting workers	9.38	11.85	14.66	17.75	21.32
Coating, painting, and spraying machine setters, operators, and tenders	9.86	11.65	14.00	16.50	18.85
Painters, transportation equipment	13.22	15.56	18.64	24.00	29.39
Painting, coating, and decorating workers	7.50	8.00	11.50	15.25	18.13
Photographic process workers and processing machine operators	8.11	8.50	11.00	14.48	17.86
Photographic process workers	10.00	11.50	12.00	18.00	19.16
Photographic processing machine operators	8.08	8.16	10.00	14.48	17.63
Semiconductor processors	12.81	15.02	18.16	20.24	23.65
Miscellaneous production workers	8.16	9.84	12.15	16.74	21.13
Cementing and gluing machine operators and tenders	9.45	10.80	14.70	17.77	23.33
Cleaning, washing, and metal pickling equipment operators and tenders	11.40	12.23	14.20	22.81	29.28
Cooling and freezing equipment operators and tenders	8.95	8.95	12.45	19.56	24.67
Etchers and engravers	12.50	13.96	14.00	17.00	23.50
Molders, shapers, and casters, except metal and plastic	8.59	12.65	14.00	19.00	25.00
Paper goods machine setters, operators, and tenders	9.65	13.17	17.71	21.18	26.30
Tire builders	10.50	11.54	15.48	20.00	22.66
Helpers–production workers	8.00	9.27	11.00	13.41	17.92
Transportation and Material Moving	8.00	10.00	13.48	18.00	23.14
First-line supervisors/managers of helpers, laborers, and material	13.90	15.54	19.51	23.64	27.84
First-line supervisors/managers of transportation and material-moving machine and vehicle operators	16.48	19.95	24.05	30.38	37.48
Aircraft pilots and flight engineers	23.00	27.34	85.29	141.85	165.74
Airline pilots, copilots, and flight engineers	25.09	74.03	117.01	155.90	167.96
Commercial pilots	19.76	25.63	27.00	27.72	54.00
Ambulance drivers and attendants, except emergency medical	9.32	10.25	11.00	13.09	16.70
Bus drivers	10.00	11.00	14.47	17.00	19.86
Bus drivers, transit and intercity	10.00	11.90	15.00	17.12	23.35
Bus drivers, school	10.00	10.91	14.00	15.97	18.89
Driver/sales workers and truck drivers	9.47	12.30	16.17	20.60	25.40
Driver/sales workers	6.55	7.50	11.00	16.43	21.27
Truck drivers, heavy and tractor-trailer	12.11	14.50	17.63	21.05	24.85
Truck drivers, light or delivery services	9.00	10.53	14.00	19.70	28.88
Taxi drivers and chauffeurs	7.25	8.00	9.45	11.84	16.25
Locomotive engineers and operators	15.54	15.54	22.50	39.56	49.72
Locomotive engineers	15.54	15.54	22.50	41.41	49.72
Railroad conductors and yardmasters	14.43	14.43	20.75	36.45	38.11
Sailors and marine oilers	9.00	10.00	11.43	11.67	18.67
Ship and boat captains and operators	6.84	15.42	19.58	26.25	38.50
Captains, mates, and pilots of water vessels	6.84	15.42	19.58	26.25	38.50
Parking lot attendants	6.57	7.50	8.50	10.00	11.50
Service station attendants	7.50	8.15	9.25	12.00	15.63
Transportation inspectors	10.70	23.96	31.37	33.52	34.30
Conveyor operators and tenders	10.50	12.75	14.74	18.14	18.51
Crane and tower operators	13.35	16.40	20.00	25.50	31.31
Dredge, excavating, and loading machine operators	13.25	14.64	18.09	22.50	26.15
Excavating and loading machine and dragline operators	13.00	14.00	17.60	19.50	26.30
Hoist and winch operators	9.04	15.83	21.03	21.20	21.36
Industrial truck and tractor operators	9.65	11.50	14.07	17.00	21.74
Laborers and material movers, hand	7.69	8.50	10.50	13.35	16.84
Cleaners of vehicles and equipment	7.30	8.50	10.12	12.85	16.49
Laborers and freight, stock, and material movers, hand	7.95	9.00	11.00	13.95	17.86
Machine feeders and offbearers	8.00	8.71	10.50	13.52	16.04
Packers and packagers, hand	7.36	8.00	9.40	11.87	14.45
Pumping station operators	21.75	22.05	23.61	28.06	29.56
Refuse and recyclable material collectors	9.09	10.32	14.05	19.90	25.12
Tank car, truck, and ship loaders	14.00	15.00	19.99	20.83	25.16

[1]Percentiles designate position in the earnings distribution and are calculated from individual worker earnings and the hours they are scheduled to work.

Chapter Seven

RECENT TRENDS IN THE LABOR MARKET

RECENT TRENDS IN THE LABOR MARKET

HIGHLIGHTS

This chapter contains information on mass layoff events, initial claimants for unemployment insurance, movement of work, job openings, hires, and separations.

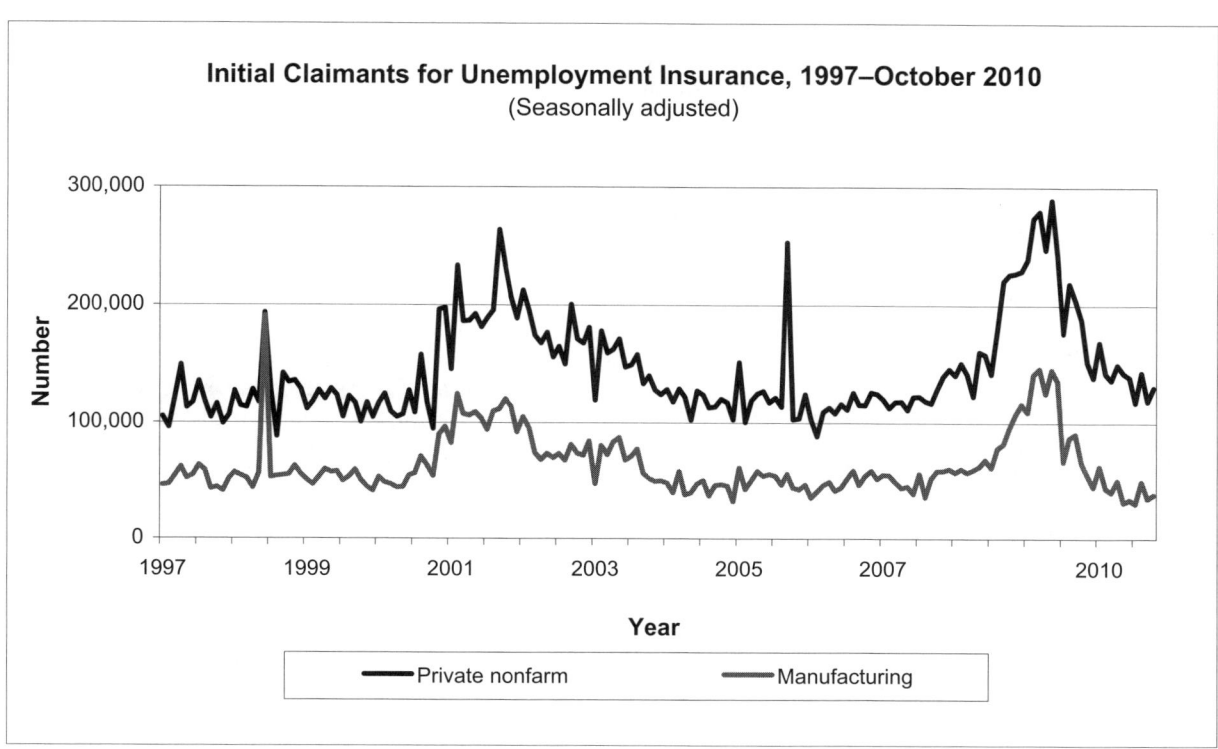

From December 2007 through October 2010, the total number of mass layoff events (seasonally adjusted) was 68,372, and the number of initial claims filed (seasonally adjusted) in those events was 6,805,798. December 2007 was the start of a recession as designated by the National Bureau of Economic Research. (See Table 7-1.)

OTHER HIGHLIGHTS

- In 2010, from January through October, the number of mass layoff events (seasonally adjusted), reached 16,394 while the number of initial claims rose to 1,562,958. During the same time period in 2009 there 24,884 mass layoff events and 2,530,115 initial claims. (See Table 7-1.)

- The manufacturing sector accounted for 34.3 percent of all mass layoff events and 40.7 percent of initial claims filed in 2009. In contrast, government only made up 5.7 percent of mass layoff events and 5.2 percent of initial claimants. (See Table 7-3.)

- Of the four census regions, the West had the highest number of mass layoff events in October 2010 (712), followed by the South (368), the Midwest (316), and the Northeast (246). (See Table 7-4.)

- In October 2010, the number of job openings reached 3,362,000 which is the highest level since August 2008. The number of job openings were the highest in professional and business services (744,000), educational and heath services (632,000) and trade, transportation, and utilities (488,000). (See Table 7-7.)

NOTES AND DEFINITIONS

MASS LAYOFFS

Collection and Coverage

The Mass Layoff Statistics (MLS) program is a federal-state program that identifies, describes, and tracks the effects of major job cutbacks, using data from each state's unemployment insurance database. Employers that have at least 50 initial claims filed against them during a consecutive 5-week period are contacted by the state agency to determine whether these separations are of at least 31 days duration, and, if so, information is obtained on the total number of persons separated, the reasons for these separations, and recall expectations. Employers are identified according to industry classification and location, and unemployment insurance claimants are identified by such demographic factors as age, race, gender, ethnic group, and place of residence. The program yields information on an individual's entire spell of unemployment, to the point when regular unemployment insurance benefits are exhausted.

A given month contains an aggregation of the weekly unemployment insurance claims filings for the Sunday through Saturday weeks in that month. All weeks are included for the particular month, except if the first day of the month falls on Saturday. In this case, the week is included in the prior month's tabulations. This means that some months will contain 4 weeks and others, 5 weeks, the number of weeks in a given month may be different from year to year, and the number of weeks in a year may vary. Therefore, analysis of over-the-month and over-the-year change in not seasonally adjusted series should take this calendar effect into consideration.

The latest quarterly data in these tables are considered preliminary. After the initial publication of quarterly information, more data are collected as remaining employer interviews for the quarter are completed and additional initial claimant information associated with extended layoff events is received.

The MLS program discontinued the collection of "domestic relocation" and "overseas relocation" as standard reasons for layoff beginning with data for the first quarter 2004. It was felt these reasons do not reflect an economic reason, and instead relate to the effect of the actual reason.

Concepts and Definitions

Employers in the MLS program include those covered by state unemployment insurance laws. Information on employers is obtained from the Quarterly Census of Employment and Wages (QCEW) program.

Extended layoff event is when there are fifty or more initial claims for unemployment insurance benefits from an employer during a 5-week period, with at least 50 workers separated for more than 30 days.

Initial claimant is a person who files any notice of unemployment to initiate a request either for a determination of entitlement to and eligibility for compensation, or for a subsequent period of unemployment within a benefit year or period of eligibility.

Layoff is the separation of persons from an employer as part of a mass layoff event. Such layoffs involve both persons subject to recall and those who are terminated by the establishment.

Mass layoff event is when there are fifty or more initial claims for unemployment insurance benefits from an employer during a five-week period, regardless of duration.

Movement-of-work action is relocation of work within the same company or to other companies, domestically or outside the United States. Because employers may cite more than one location to which work is moving, a layoff event may have more than one action associated with it.

Movement-of-work separations is the number of separations specifically associated with movement-of-work actions.

Outsourcing is the movement of work that was formerly conducted in-house by employees paid directly by a company to a different company under a contractual arrangement.

Seasonal adjustment is the process of estimating and removing the effect on time series data of regularly recurring seasonal events such as changes in the weather, holidays, and the beginning and ending of the school year. The use of seasonal adjustment makes it easier to observe fundamental changes in time series, particularly those associated with general economic expansions and contractions.

Separations is the total number of people laid-off in an extended mass layoff event for more than 30 days, according to the employer.

Worksite closure is the complete closure of either multi-unit or single-unit employers or the partial closure of a multi-unit employer where entire worksites affected by layoffs are closed or planned to be closed.

Sources of Additional Information

For more extensive information see BLS news release USDL 10-1627 "Mass Layoffs (Monthly)" and USDL 10-1548 "Extended Mass Layoffs (Quarterly)" on the BLS Web site at <http://www.bls.gov/mls/>.

Table 7-1. Mass Layoff Events and Initial Claimants for Unemployment Insurance, 1997–October 2010, Seasonally Adjusted

(Number.)

Year and month	Total		Private nonfarm		Manufacturing	
	Events	Initial claimants	Events	Initial claimants	Events	Initial claimants
1997						
January	1 154	117 136	985	105 049	355	45 970
February	985	104 805	868	95 846	383	46 614
March	1 233	134 334	1 051	121 521	399	54 344
April	1 353	162 965	1 165	149 073	504	62 166
May	1 229	123 446	1 102	112 769	452	52 241
June	1 383	137 275	1 106	117 005	467	54 828
July	1 436	153 734	1 220	135 080	484	63 442
August	1 197	129 375	1 040	117 754	485	58 941
September	1 132	118 918	933	104 136	337	42 572
October	1 235	130 351	1 050	116 063	377	43 911
November	1 157	109 533	1 018	99 067	378	40 752
December	1 238	118 146	1 072	106 346	430	51 879
1998						
January	1 316	143 061	1 089	126 988	406	57 309
February	1 234	129 602	1 046	114 166	438	54 440
March	1 181	124 912	1 030	112 851	436	52 061
April	1 362	145 440	1 142	128 241	428	43 403
May	1 248	129 030	1 089	117 332	466	56 728
June	1 332	205 228	1 162	193 631	684	190 810
July	1 422	147 574	1 187	128 085	444	53 057
August	1 076	100 917	887	88 347	433	54 085
September	1 268	150 904	1 139	141 911	450	54 589
October	1 389	153 632	1 174	134 417	468	55 517
November	1 331	151 957	1 138	135 741	467	63 022
December	1 400	150 760	1 115	128 451	415	55 676
1999						
January	1 399	129 104	1 122	111 713	429	50 593
February	1 321	136 296	1 074	117 827	404	46 526
March	1 354	148 022	1 112	127 562	460	53 087
April	1 251	134 118	1 058	120 142	457	60 125
May	1 278	146 682	1 063	128 874	438	57 589
June	1 217	138 397	1 053	123 191	446	58 202
July	1 136	117 941	951	104 930	358	49 567
August	1 188	140 981	1 000	122 361	408	53 579
September	1 355	134 430	1 152	116 756	374	59 783
October	995	115 894	797	100 478	344	50 194
November	1 258	138 992	1 025	117 116	337	44 140
December	1 174	119 033	973	104 519	298	40 825
2000						
January	1 100	126 440	968	116 846	371	53 270
February	1 280	151 107	1 018	124 497	379	48 372
March	1 159	126 309	965	109 445	393	46 564
April	1 030	115 068	913	104 865	407	43 829
May	1 196	126 525	976	106 893	376	44 019
June	1 220	145 766	1 020	127 239	406	54 672
July	1 065	118 649	922	108 499	417	56 465
August	1 282	178 789	1 060	157 762	423	71 141
September	1 260	134 153	1 045	117 266	407	63 394
October	938	107 676	798	94 783	385	54 006
November	1 643	215 381	1 447	196 166	599	89 869
December	1 691	214 601	1 514	197 944	575	96 295
2001						
January	1 288	158 580	1 144	145 584	529	82 504
February	1 912	253 943	1 684	233 524	828	124 430
March	1 761	202 344	1 569	186 565	800	107 481
April	1 622	200 683	1 484	186 898	776	106 255
May	1 676	206 062	1 523	192 500	750	108 773
June	1 608	195 802	1 432	181 264	740	103 468
July	1 710	201 363	1 574	189 030	721	93 949
August	1 732	207 416	1 568	195 777	791	109 611
September	2 407	277 955	2 236	263 773	841	111 520
October	2 177	242 507	2 051	232 371	923	119 873
November	2 104	218 378	1 940	206 999	948	113 776
December	1 824	200 677	1 673	188 836	746	92 019
2002						
January	1 841	224 765	1 711	212 461	764	104 909
February	1 823	207 788	1 663	194 840	701	95 406
March	1 697	187 212	1 525	174 281	604	74 492
April	1 666	183 005	1 494	167 848	584	68 282
May	1 730	190 129	1 561	176 744	613	73 612
June	1 632	171 213	1 436	155 960	547	70 137
July	1 632	179 407	1 461	164 741	557	73 479
August	1 468	161 431	1 324	149 847	563	67 831
September	1 918	217 299	1 737	200 635	615	81 292
October	1 749	187 851	1 573	171 346	611	73 940
November	1 651	178 739	1 507	167 723	590	72 329
December	1 834	194 852	1 646	180 976	676	84 247
2003						
January	1 336	132 819	1 160	119 199	382	46 839
February	1 831	191 434	1 650	178 003	650	80 285
March	1 784	175 384	1 589	159 467	609	72 679
April	1 702	172 252	1 555	162 323	637	83 268
May	1 744	185 159	1 556	171 221	646	87 077
June	1 726	164 597	1 518	147 553	640	68 197
July	1 661	165 130	1 450	149 233	567	71 319
August	1 546	171 996	1 383	157 968	563	77 405
September	1 571	149 250	1 370	133 276	479	56 454
October	1 525	157 759	1 319	140 086	422	51 872
November	1 370	139 572	1 225	127 963	379	49 219
December	1 395	136 166	1 226	124 009	428	49 789

Table 7-1. Mass Layoff Events and Initial Claimants for Unemployment Insurance, 1997–October 2010, Seasonally Adjusted—*Continued*

(Number.)

Year and month	Total		Private nonfarm		Manufacturing	
	Events	Initial claimants	Events	Initial claimants	Events	Initial claimants
2004						
January	1 414	145 593	1 221	128 305	396	47 882
February	1 257	130 205	1 111	117 788	365	39 214
March	1 362	138 397	1 222	129 094	396	58 213
April	1 349	136 837	1 175	121 841	347	37 115
May	1 240	116 392	1 077	102 443	340	39 208
June	1 397	139 975	1 231	127 229	370	46 998
July	1 315	135 186	1 165	123 768	371	49 945
August	1 417	127 814	1 226	112 867	344	36 298
September	1 275	124 279	1 149	113 689	337	45 732
October	1 265	129 312	1 153	120 337	366	46 319
November	1 306	129 014	1 161	117 300	374	44 939
December	1 163	114 258	1 009	102 732	285	31 445
2005						
January	1 509	161 805	1 367	151 530	413	61 483
February	1 075	111 437	948	100 564	344	42 035
March	1 193	129 288	1 045	118 827	361	50 086
April	1 238	135 353	1 107	124 881	384	58 255
May	1 266	139 915	1 124	127 071	395	54 052
June	1 185	125 919	1 072	117 229	359	55 621
July	1 257	133 036	1 116	121 311	392	53 945
August	1 118	124 738	996	113 784	340	46 067
September	2 241	299 151	2 028	253 431	423	55 855
October	1 113	111 868	994	102 840	323	43 326
November	1 176	115 215	1 040	103 701	328	41 868
December	1 272	135 737	1 142	124 459	356	46 211
2006						
January	1 110	112 550	979	102 802	289	34 737
February	938	96 542	846	88 629	304	40 029
March	1 069	117 725	965	109 241	312	45 687
April	1 189	123 056	1 055	112 922	352	48 731
May	1 121	117 834	1 003	107 929	302	40 703
June	1 150	125 318	1 039	115 883	349	43 476
July	1 182	121 056	1 056	111 432	373	51 691
August	1 238	135 707	1 104	125 704	372	58 962
September	1 154	124 200	1 043	115 261	393	45 972
October	1 208	123 691	1 094	115 102	409	53 957
November	1 244	135 465	1 128	125 976	413	58 509
December	1 227	134 176	1 123	124 570	376	51 403
2007						
January	1 264	130 834	1 113	119 874	404	55 217
February	1 191	121 289	1 075	112 607	374	54 581
March	1 225	126 391	1 113	117 760	386	48 298
April	1 268	129 098	1 135	118 175	362	43 205
May	1 172	118 648	1 070	111 103	345	44 391
June	1 241	131 394	1 125	122 123	338	37 931
July	1 274	130 331	1 169	122 381	403	55 973
August	1 247	126 108	1 158	118 575	323	34 902
September	1 255	123 632	1 160	116 744	436	51 814
October	1 370	137 108	1 248	128 387	449	58 360
November	1 415	148 952	1 289	139 665	424	58 543
December	1 569	155 095	1 448	145 666	483	60 368
2008						
January	1 481	151 269	1 348	140 570	436	57 147
February	1 578	162 152	1 432	150 712	470	60 276
March	1 487	151 539	1 372	141 574	436	56 919
April	1 327	133 318	1 201	122 651	460	59 377
May	1 604	170 619	1 465	160 529	468	62 345
June	1 674	170 329	1 523	158 084	501	68 403
July	1 531	152 447	1 389	141 707	461	61 417
August	1 845	189 798	1 711	179 737	607	78 172
September	2 222	235 755	2 049	220 832	634	81 989
October	2 287	239 768	2 125	226 098	721	95 301
November	2 489	240 181	2 334	227 368	929	107 072
December	2 461	243 505	2 277	229 171	962	115 961
2009						
January	2 279	251 807	2 115	238 990	764	109 124
February	2 737	289 162	2 592	274 040	1 186	141 264
March	2 913	295 970	2 715	279 671	1 202	146 381
April	2 663	263 162	2 461	247 329	1 033	125 093
May	2 794	306 788	2 589	289 012	1 183	145 166
June	2 598	260 596	2 371	241 864	1 072	135 844
July	2 039	196 578	1 818	176 542	565	66 918
August	2 480	238 911	2 244	218 425	798	87 201
September	2 326	221 639	2 109	204 462	783	90 440
October	2 055	205 502	1 856	187 880	594	65 801
November	1 813	163 823	1 650	151 810	485	54 858
December	1 726	153 127	1 542	138 747	433	44 072
2010						
January	1 761	182 261	1 585	168 466	486	62 556
February	1 570	155 718	1 406	142 240	376	43 100
March	1 628	150 864	1 432	136 446	356	39 290
April	1 646	164 325	1 478	149 621	388	50 083
May	1 676	164 115	1 416	142 594	320	30 729
June	1 757	158 479	1 529	139 029	332	33 012
July	1 520	135 389	1 301	117 546	286	29 826
August	1 655	165 528	1 448	143 056	400	48 858
September	1 530	138 220	1 317	118 741	334	34 096
October	1 651	148 059	1 445	130 448	356	37 438

Table 7-2. Mass Layoff Events and Initial Claimants for Unemployment Insurance, 1997–October 2010, Not Seasonally Adjusted

(Number.)

Year and month	Total		Private nonfarm		Manufacturing	
	Events	Initial claimants	Events	Initial claimants	Events	Initial claimants
1997						
January	2 139	212 860	1 950	197 137	727	82 978
February	755	63 352	632	55 848	277	26 507
March	783	84 069	678	76 804	265	33 141
April	1 269	152 168	1 111	139 164	402	55 181
May	1 152	101 476	1 037	91 900	352	35 472
June	1 238	121 256	952	99 210	277	28 786
July	1 899	237 410	1 623	211 580	794	124 062
August	973	99 513	878	92 768	363	42 472
September	548	59 062	447	52 310	181	18 881
October	1 414	139 297	1 108	116 157	408	47 579
November	1 156	100 051	953	86 994	386	39 757
December	1 634	172 029	1 500	161 797	639	78 387
1998						
January	2 360	255 203	2 117	235 263	823	104 790
February	970	81 455	773	68 345	315	31 692
March	762	78 210	673	71 258	289	31 369
April	1 253	132 476	1 076	117 601	342	37 312
May	1 180	107 952	1 038	97 493	365	38 553
June	1 208	183 590	1 012	169 411	409	103 501
July	2 220	286 055	1 903	255 245	1 014	152 044
August	617	53 665	558	50 149	259	26 593
September	637	79 629	564	74 941	248	25 134
October	1 553	160 830	1 220	132 258	507	60 529
November	1 368	144 343	1 076	123 066	478	62 829
December	1 776	207 661	1 552	188 787	618	82 871
1999						
January	2 421	226 995	2 142	206 615	861	94 887
February	1 067	89 800	810	73 846	289	28 322
March	880	91 890	737	80 063	302	31 317
April	1 270	136 885	1 100	123 987	450	56 668
May	1 032	102 738	895	93 006	303	32 958
June	1 140	130 951	925	109 848	268	32 610
July	1 741	221 334	1 496	201 412	808	137 688
August	698	75 691	638	70 285	246	26 606
September	717	75 288	592	64 942	212	28 968
October	1 098	118 938	814	97 984	373	55 222
November	1 336	139 508	977	110 200	347	45 431
December	1 509	162 381	1 353	150 171	446	60 349
2000						
January	1 934	223 322	1 807	212 805	741	100 397
February	1 045	103 898	780	81 103	268	30 358
March	986	106 748	827	92 565	329	38 434
April	924	101 359	838	93 631	323	34 061
May	984	92 193	841	81 125	262	25 838
June	1 597	192 025	1 269	160 685	404	60 258
July	1 333	164 978	1 159	152 243	664	100 874
August	751	97 215	679	90 877	256	35 687
September	936	106 842	767	93 327	319	46 865
October	874	103 755	684	84 922	321	48 877
November	1 697	216 514	1 397	190 626	617	93 966
December	2 677	326 743	2 477	311 623	1 074	166 928
2001						
January	1 522	200 343	1 405	188 504	632	107 028
February	1 501	172 908	1 285	156 183	576	79 784
March	1 527	171 466	1 371	158 108	659	86 874
April	1 450	176 265	1 353	166 167	608	78 845
May	1 434	159 365	1 331	151 186	528	64 887
June	2 107	253 826	1 784	226 022	737	116 005
July	2 117	273 807	1 952	259 128	1 144	168 877
August	1 490	166 148	1 386	158 307	603	79 515
September	1 327	160 402	1 214	151 161	485	58 544
October	1 831	215 483	1 676	202 053	742	107 030
November	2 721	295 956	2 373	270 268	1 122	151 969
December	2 440	268 893	2 319	259 497	1 103	136 820
2002						
January	2 146	263 777	2 028	252 245	892	128 825
February	1 382	138 808	1 253	129 849	481	58 784
March	1 460	161 316	1 335	151 305	500	59 613
April	1 506	165 814	1 378	153 216	461	50 897
May	1 723	179 799	1 571	166 801	488	52 720
June	1 584	162 189	1 266	136 424	336	42 130
July	2 042	245 294	1 819	226 892	907	135 271
August	1 248	128 103	1 151	119 874	427	48 668
September	1 062	124 522	957	114 736	352	43 755
October	1 497	171 100	1 270	149 327	493	64 655
November	2 153	240 171	1 860	216 237	719	92 712
December	2 474	264 158	2 324	252 807	984	126 826
2003						
January	2 315	225 430	2 130	210 918	822	90 244
February	1 363	124 965	1 222	116 264	435	48 161
March	1 207	113 026	1 099	104 468	390	41 063
April	1 581	161 412	1 470	152 937	499	62 349
May	1 703	174 204	1 538	160 729	499	61 278
June	1 691	157 552	1 336	127 743	389	40 845
July	2 087	226 435	1 815	206 901	946	136 410
August	1 258	133 839	1 163	124 131	405	52 620
September	868	82 647	756	73 914	271	31 428
October	1 523	158 240	1 265	137 706	438	53 741
November	1 438	138 543	1 234	123 524	408	48 419
December	1 929	192 633	1 793	182 750	648	77 915

Table 7-2. Mass Layoff Events and Initial Claimants for Unemployment Insurance, 1997–October 2010, Not Seasonally Adjusted—*Continued*

(Number.)

Year and month	Total		Private nonfarm		Manufacturing	
	Events	Initial claimants	Events	Initial claimants	Events	Initial claimants
2004						
January	2 428	239 454	2 226	220 687	848	89 551
February	941	84 201	832	76 577	240	23 043
March	920	92 554	847	87 782	258	34 686
April	1 458	157 314	1 316	142 657	343	36 172
May	988	87 501	878	78 786	219	22 141
June	1 379	134 588	1 077	110 804	222	27 307
July	2 094	253 929	1 860	234 877	885	145 895
August	809	69 033	745	63 876	194	17 698
September	708	68 972	637	63 102	189	25 808
October	1 242	127 918	1 101	117 375	372	48 265
November	1 399	130 423	1 201	115 549	412	44 243
December	1 614	161 271	1 487	152 092	436	50 726
2005						
January	2 564	263 952	2 421	253 409	823	108 985
February	810	74 644	722	68 372	230	24 931
March	806	88 937	733	83 793	246	33 030
April	1 373	158 582	1 263	148 133	395	59 129
May	986	101 358	891	93 332	249	30 424
June	1 157	120 463	941	103 307	216	32 783
July	1 981	244 216	1 745	222 377	856	136 210
August	645	67 582	598	63 484	188	22 531
September	1 662	213 281	1 505	179 042	318	47 497
October	905	91 941	757	80 694	249	37 276
November	1 254	116 127	1 079	102 182	363	41 442
December	2 323	254 258	2 168	242 753	706	96 382
2006						
January	1 245	117 946	1 123	108 701	331	35 097
February	719	66 555	658	62 208	210	24 892
March	921	111 838	856	106 177	285	44 688
April	1 140	121 589	1 038	112 964	296	39 538
May	872	84 809	794	78 663	192	23 570
June	1 489	164 761	1 224	140 687	319	41 095
July	1 511	166 857	1 335	154 342	648	96 152
August	708	72 844	656	69 054	203	28 494
September	865	87 699	785	81 274	296	39 076
October	964	98 804	820	88 133	311	46 737
November	1 315	136 186	1 172	125 009	455	58 473
December	2 249	254 503	2 126	244 783	735	105 462
2007						
January	1 407	134 984	1 263	124 475	456	53 615
February	935	86 696	861	82 097	273	36 170
March	1 082	123 974	1 015	118 431	367	49 886
April	1 219	127 444	1 115	118 040	309	35 229
May	923	85 816	856	81 153	224	26 527
June	1 599	172 810	1 318	148 669	313	36 571
July	1 599	175 419	1 450	164 939	684	101 390
August	963	93 458	908	88 345	220	23 361
September	717	67 385	667	64 026	246	29 381
October	1 083	108 455	929	97 716	338	50 918
November	1 799	198 220	1 593	181 184	514	75 413
December	2 167	224 214	2 071	216 898	699	91 754
2008						
January	1 647	154 503	1 520	144 191	488	54 418
February	1 269	119 508	1 178	113 587	361	42 527
March	1 089	114 541	1 039	110 147	333	43 740
April	1 272	130 810	1 172	121 625	394	48 188
May	1 552	159 471	1 438	150 462	388	51 698
June	1 622	166 742	1 315	140 916	309	42 097
July	1 891	200 382	1 687	186 018	760	108 733
August	1 427	139 999	1 343	133 146	414	51 912
September	1 292	129 586	1 202	122 505	361	46 391
October	2 125	221 784	1 917	205 553	689	100 457
November	2 574	241 589	2 389	226 657	997	107 620
December	3 377	351 305	3 232	340 220	1 378	172 529
2009						
January	3 806	388 813	3 633	375 293	1 461	172 757
February	2 262	218 438	2 173	210 755	945	103 588
March	2 191	228 387	2 107	221 397	940	114 747
April	2 547	256 930	2 385	243 321	887	100 872
May	2 738	289 628	2 572	274 047	1 005	123 683
June	2 519	256 357	2 051	216 063	674	85 726
July	3 054	336 654	2 659	296 589	1 133	154 208
August	1 428	125 024	1 334	117 193	436	41 151
September	1 371	123 177	1 258	115 141	448	51 126
October	1 934	193 904	1 678	172 883	566	69 655
November	1 870	164 496	1 679	150 751	517	55 053
December	2 310	214 648	2 166	203 655	615	64 540
2010						
January	2 860	278 679	2 682	265 074	962	104 846
February	1 183	102 818	1 091	96 022	282	30 728
March	1 197	111 727	1 111	105 514	273	29 745
April	1 840	199 690	1 697	184 654	424	55 178
May	1 354	123 333	1 170	109 203	216	19 334
June	1 861	171 190	1 355	125 872	212	21 083
July	2 124	206 254	1 732	172 248	532	64 200
August	976	92 435	897	83 021	230	23 088
September	920	77 654	806	67 987	187	19 403
October	1 642	148 638	1 373	127 865	351	40 861

Table 7-3. Industry Distribution: Mass Layoff Events and Initial Claimants for Unemployment Insurance, 1997–October 2010

(Number, not seasonally adjusted.)

Industry	1997	1998	1999	2000	2001	2002	2003	2004	2005	2006	2007	2008
						Mass layoff events						
ALL INDUSTRIES	14 960	15 904	14 909	15 738	21 467	20 277	18 963	15 980	16 466	13 998	15 493	21 137
Total, Private	14 164	15 098	14 197	15 028	20 763	19 376	17 846	15 018	15 534	13 238	14 714	20 130
Agriculture, forestry, fishing and hunting	1 295	1 536	1 718	1 503	1 314	1 164	1 025	811	711	651	668	698
Total, private nonfarm	12 869	13 562	12 479	13 525	19 449	18 212	16 821	14 207	14 823	12 587	14 046	19 432
Mining, quarrying, and oil and gas extraction	81	152	176	102	115	176	101	69	75	58	66	103
Utilities	31	40	31	37	33	44	40	25	25	20	20	28
Construction	1 512	1 477	1 509	1 638	1 688	1 939	2 013	1 821	1 975	1 546	1 952	2 393
Manufacturing	5 071	5 667	4 905	5 578	8 939	7 040	6 150	4 618	4 839	4 281	4 643	6 872
Food	924	909	830	826	879	826	850	797	751	648	595	678
Beverage and tobacco products	74	79	68	61	74	79	82	75	66	56	58	78
Textile mills	153	245	218	209	352	272	245	169	160	143	146	179
Textile product mills	82	84	70	83	91	113	111	93	86	66	63	69
Apparel	625	605	463	424	433	346	295	220	179	128	131	149
Leather and allied products	104	94	83	76	79	48	48	42	41	26	27	22
Wood products	296	271	240	377	355	377	345	225	273	339	418	557
Paper	121	142	91	148	212	167	156	82	98	86	78	146
Printing and related support activities	104	103	93	95	156	156	125	118	98	74	90	132
Petroleum and coal products	44	30	32	39	25	39	30	27	24	34	28	37
Chemicals	74	82	92	84	156	122	105	101	77	69	75	122
Plastics and rubber products	229	268	200	278	482	331	328	282	300	250	265	501
Nonmetallic mineral products	175	159	150	186	239	219	233	167	204	172	215	316
Primary metals	187	256	214	274	568	399	366	194	222	184	225	352
Fabricated metal products	233	284	268	327	675	482	397	322	311	288	293	574
Machinery	238	321	349	324	781	555	425	235	272	255	287	402
Computer and electronic products	253	489	344	231	1 050	817	481	230	217	173	190	285
Electrical equipment and appliance manufacturing	193	202	152	195	391	313	231	137	167	136	135	220
Transportation equipment	672	756	678	1 004	1 410	961	927	821	1 034	925	1 068	1 647
Furniture and related products	148	125	130	187	329	255	223	169	164	150	184	288
Miscellaneous manufacturing	142	163	140	150	202	163	147	112	95	79	72	118
Wholesale trade	245	234	228	236	334	336	318	222	251	184	220	363
Retail trade	1 023	935	830	906	1 249	1 351	1 327	1 165	1 196	991	1 048	1 457
Transportation and warehousing	712	661	595	717	908	947	965	853	1 011	934	982	1 267
Information	397	412	336	358	736	719	598	454	383	350	383	545
Finance and insurance	199	187	229	218	325	432	384	322	272	310	510	552
Real estate and rental and leasing	49	49	42	64	99	91	91	79	92	54	71	118
Professional and technical services	300	332	324	348	591	634	522	420	427	352	420	564
Management of companies and enterprises	31	26	43	40	47	40	35	38	27	28	42	61
Administrative and waste services	1 468	1 649	1 536	1 644	2 333	2 428	2 266	2 035	1 989	1 741	1 862	2 699
Educational services	32	36	35	34	51	69	82	60	70	63	67	100
Health care and social assistance	422	472	434	405	374	480	499	522	585	415	450	580
Arts, entertainment, and recreation	230	213	205	162	229	277	285	287	293	245	240	311
Accommodation and food services	811	790	738	729	1 032	916	886	980	1 083	844	905	1 238
Other services, except public administration	161	146	148	148	171	221	217	198	201	148	155	174
Unclassified	94	84	135	161	195	72	42	39	29	23	10	7
Government	796	806	712	710	704	901	1 117	962	932	760	779	1 007
Local	450	466	393	386	396	605	778	643	582	511	509	705

Table 7-3. Industry Distribution: Mass Layoff Events and Initial Claimants for Unemployment Insurance, 1997–October 2010—*Continued*

(Number, not seasonally adjusted.)

Industry	2009	January 2010	February 2010	March 2010	April 2010	May 2010	June 2010	July 2010	August 2010	September 2010	October 2010
					Mass layoff events						
ALL INDUSTRIES	28 030	2 860	1 183	1 197	1 840	1 354	1 861	2 124	976	920	1 642
Total, Private	26 437	2 739	1 128	1 149	1 761	1 197	1 398	1 832	923	823	1 493
Agriculture, forestry, fishing and hunting	742	57	37	38	64	27	43	100	26	17	120
Total, private nonfarm	25 695	2 682	1 091	1 111	1 697	1 170	1 355	1 732	897	806	1 373
Mining, quarrying, and oil and gas extraction	314	20	5	5	7	(1)	4	5	(1)	4	6
Utilities	39	(1)	...	3	(1)	5	5	6	...	3	(1)
Construction	2 833	328	166	117	163	159	121	135	105	89	175
Manufacturing	9 627	962	282	273	424	216	212	532	230	187	351
Food	771	93	45	53	100	47	46	75	54	31	80
Beverage and tobacco products	78	13	6	4	(1)	5	5	4	(1)	(1)	15
Textile mills	195	28	5	4	7	3	4	8	4	3	7
Textile product mills	76	18	5	3	5	3	...	3	3	...	4
Apparel	201	23	4	10	16	8	7	18	9	(1)	10
Leather and allied products	28	3	(1)	...	...	...	(1)	3	3	...	(1)
Wood products	552	62	27	16	17	11	20	24	17	22	26
Paper	241	16	10	5	14	3	4	4	7	4	4
Printing and related support activities	235	23	12	14	9	12	12	10	3	3	6
Petroleum and coal products	49	7	(1)	3	(1)	3	...	4	...	3	3
Chemicals	193	23	9	13	7	8	3	18	8	...	8
Plastics and rubber products	559	62	10	9	10	6	5	31	10	...	9
Nonmetallic mineral products	400	44	12	11	22	5	9	22	8	7	15
Primary metals	686	56	9	8	18	12	9	24	7	13	16
Fabricated metal products	949	99	12	18	21	12	8	27	12	13	20
Machinery	1 046	89	20	22	41	20	16	26	18	11	26
Computer and electronic products	626	37	18	16	27	13	8	18	15	8	13
Electrical equipment and appliance manufacturing	397	33	12	6	12	11	5	17	8	10	15
Transportation equipment	1 827	175	45	43	73	20	34	171	32	30	50
Furniture and related products	324	48	16	10	12	5	11	19	6	11	17
Miscellaneous manufacturing	194	10	(1)	5	10	9	3	6	4	8	6
Wholesale trade	653	67	27	29	25	18	14	33	18	16	30
Retail trade	1 965	259	128	124	156	121	107	142	108	99	126
Transportation and warehousing	1 491	212	51	62	178	47	159	148	45	31	45
Information	752	84	40	52	50	41	41	55	36	24	52
Finance and insurance	677	47	32	43	64	23	39	47	24	29	31
Real estate and rental and leasing	165	8	9	8	22	9	8	15	7	4	9
Professional and technical services	800	71	33	45	90	61	30	59	43	23	43
Management of companies and enterprises	104	15	6	(1)	6	4	(1)	5	6	(1)	3
Administrative and waste services	3 205	326	191	163	241	175	175	292	158	133	275
Educational services	149	18	4	10	7	10	40	30	6	13	11
Health care and social assistance	675	46	31	33	58	84	174	90	36	26	54
Arts, entertainment, and recreation	389	35	16	20	57	32	29	31	17	39	31
Accommodation and food services	1 606	163	61	112	131	129	141	89	50	72	118
Other services, except public administration	242	20	8	10	16	34	54	18	6	12	10
Unclassified	9	...	1	...	...	...	...	...	...	1	1
Government	1 593	121	55	48	79	157	463	292	53	97	149
Local	1 122	76	35	25	45	99	404	238	23	56	76

[1] Data do not meet BLS or state agency disclosure standards.
. . . = Not available.

Table 7-3. Industry Distribution: Mass Layoff Events and Initial Claimants for Unemployment Insurance, 1997–October 2010—*Continued*

(Number, not seasonally adjusted.)

Industry	1997	1998	1999	2000	2001	2002	2003	2004	2005	2006	2007	2008
	Initial claimants											
ALL INDUSTRIES	1542543	1 771 069	1 572 399	1 835 592	2 514 862	2 245 051	1 888 926	1 607 158	1 795 341	1 484 391	1598875	2130220
Total, Private	1470612	1 695 163	1 509 503	1 768 743	2 447 154	2 158 413	1 790 713	1 520 157	1 691 217	1 418 452	1533920	2046011
Agriculture, forestry, fishing and hunting	88 943	111 346	127 144	123 211	100 570	88 700	68 728	55 993	50 339	46 457	47 947	50 984
Total, private nonfarm	1381669	1 583 817	1 382 359	1 645 532	2 346 584	2 069 713	1 721 985	1 464 164	1 640 878	1 371 995	1485973	1995027
Mining, quarrying, and oil and gas extraction	6 680	12 206	19 537	9 271	14 887	16 672	9 852	5 985	6 483	5 582	5 327	9 273
Utilities	2 211	3 257	2 224	3 361	3 898	4 275	2 963	2 827	3 173	1 336	1 462	2 299
Construction	109 238	110 128	119 706	136 328	139 958	158 366	146 602	134 486	149 893	116 283	142 618	173 627
Manufacturing	613 203	757 217	631 026	782 543	1 236 178	904 856	744 473	565 535	670 620	583 274	610 215	870 310
Food	91 643	93 292	87 309	90 972	98 013	98 251	87 353	82 114	76 926	62 852	62 141	72 081
Beverage and tobacco products	5 995	6 421	7 229	5 955	6 242	6 564	6 775	6 594	4 714	4 404	4 679	6 466
Textile mills	18 001	32 403	33 744	33 064	57 009	43 511	37 734	19 669	22 213	19 070	19 527	21 620
Textile product mills	7 827	8 264	6 977	8 542	10 233	16 234	11 611	11 101	9 801	6 044	6 681	6 810
Apparel	61 019	65 714	47 715	40 474	50 423	41 320	29 887	24 729	21 889	14 170	11 508	13 970
Leather and allied products	11 507	12 343	8 492	8 204	7 867	3 903	5 170	4 733	4 960	2 757	3 077	2 862
Wood products	32 024	28 639	22 964	42 774	37 390	42 177	34 820	26 220	32 590	34 728	41 604	56 278
Paper	10 272	13 789	9 191	14 592	25 345	17 165	14 031	6 686	8 430	7 468	6 439	14 707
Printing and related support activities	8 002	8 624	8 981	9 030	13 799	15 019	9 976	10 534	8 005	6 131	7 414	12 000
Petroleum and coal products	3 713	2 500	2 761	3 609	2 518	3 611	2 292	2 343	2 262	2 874	2 333	3 114
Chemicals	6 557	8 980	9 338	8 960	15 659	11 161	10 811	8 707	7 713	6 164	6 665	10 227
Plastics and rubber products	25 645	27 693	26 551	35 828	59 024	38 596	35 054	28 409	30 714	26 098	24 611	49 196
Nonmetallic mineral products	16 103	16 125	16 035	19 272	25 246	21 712	22 031	15 389	18 956	15 980	19 204	27 834
Primary metals	19 810	29 975	26 928	38 835	81 601	48 671	40 641	23 193	27 469	21 866	27 016	37 765
Fabricated metal products	21 956	27 657	28 437	34 543	66 862	49 228	35 884	30 672	28 137	26 090	26 674	49 757
Machinery	38 032	43 662	72 480	57 793	121 724	87 710	60 370	28 407	33 713	40 069	45 831	53 673
Computer and electronic products	23 102	51 875	33 422	24 638	133 552	85 958	46 888	21 230	20 249	15 326	16 439	26 270
Electrical equipment and appliance manufacturing	30 270	30 547	31 223	39 205	60 387	48 413	36 496	24 443	30 804	24 503	23 274	37 732
Transportation equipment	151 398	214 826	123 741	228 380	303 139	176 505	178 282	163 026	253 681	221 257	228 213	323 622
Furniture and related products	17 393	15 887	14 799	23 821	40 267	34 743	25 225	16 379	18 168	17 499	19 510	33 617
Miscellaneous manufacturing	12 934	18 001	12 709	14 052	19 878	14 404	13 142	10 957	9 226	7 924	7 375	10 709
Wholesale trade	20 105	22 232	19 091	20 576	27 973	31 224	25 422	19 861	20 780	13 856	17 922	28 849
Retail trade	98 984	98 261	83 419	95 451	131 316	149 363	138 457	114 588	113 748	96 999	96 787	136 209
Transportation and warehousing	92 783	97 816	70 147	79 430	106 358	124 699	103 499	94 588	113 279	106 708	109 104	136 178
Information	91 162	99 124	55 890	80 618	103 122	100 982	80 715	72 820	72 100	64 365	64 404	70 066
Finance and insurance	15 787	14 619	17 804	17 532	27 881	36 099	27 870	24 954	20 884	22 213	40 917	42 152
Real estate and rental and leasing	3 710	2 816	2 991	4 564	7 611	7 324	6 412	6 329	7 615	4 082	5 139	8 754
Professional and technical services	29 105	33 922	47 941	57 135	77 862	82 223	52 700	49 547	49 719	40 739	49 223	57 144
Management of companies and enterprises	2 765	2 653	3 845	4 601	5 540	5 668	3 777	4 729	2 864	2 310	3 258	5 818
Administrative and waste services	142 440	175 144	154 902	191 073	258 542	257 530	206 765	184 369	187 156	153 655	168 460	246 670
Educational services	1 847	2 251	2 611	2 486	3 571	4 855	5 862	4 315	5 641	5 081	5 667	9 025
Health care and social assistance	33 920	36 658	36 229	36 759	32 255	40 364	38 108	40 118	51 371	33 972	38 848	44 139
Arts, entertainment, and recreation	16 501	17 040	16 629	14 399	20 542	23 517	21 387	21 191	27 564	16 531	16 874	21 550
Accommodation and food services	76 876	76 129	68 550	71 713	110 234	92 575	83 856	96 509	117 107	89 947	94 928	118 247
Other services, except public administration	12 093	11 802	12 806	13 287	15 742	20 049	18 617	18 226	18 753	13 478	13 936	14 310
Unclassified	12 259	10 542	17 011	24 405	23 114	9 072	4 648	3 187	2 128	1 584	884	407
Government	71 931	75 906	62 896	66 849	67 708	86 638	98 213	87 001	104 124	65 939	64 955	84 209
Local	37 458	38 545	30 264	32 271	35 003	53 323	66 279	57 331	69 351	41 689	40 690	58 272

Table 7-3. Industry Distribution: Mass Layoff Events and Initial Claimants for Unemployment Insurance, 1997–October 2010—Continued

(Number, not seasonally adjusted.)

Industry	2009	January 2010	February 2010	March 2010	April 2010	May 2010	June 2010	July 2010	August 2010	September 2010	October 2010
						Initial claimants					
ALL INDUSTRIES	2 796 456	278 679	102 818	111 727	199 690	123 333	171 190	206 254	92 435	77 654	148 638
Total, Private	2 650 289	268 595	98 241	107 880	191 664	110 968	128 691	179 524	84 610	68 913	136 178
Agriculture, forestry, fishing and hunting	53 201	3 521	2 219	2 366	7 010	1 765	2 819	7 276	1 589	926	8 313
Total, private nonfarm	2 597 088	265 074	96 022	105 514	184 654	109 203	125 872	172 248	83 021	67 987	127 865
Mining, quarrying, and oil and gas extraction	27 872	1 561	761	374	399	(1)	246	394	(1)	447	390
Utilities	3 355	(1)	(1)	207	(1)	449	343	689	(1)	186	...
Construction	205 765	24 148	12 200	8 206	11 947	12 129	8 405	9 570	6 910	6 137	13 500
Manufacturing	1 137 106	104 846	30 728	29 745	55 178	19 334	21 083	64 200	23 088	19 403	40 861
Food	78 345	9 134	4 031	6 122	10 200	4 015	3 315	9 535	4 312	3 216	8 639
Beverage and tobacco products	7 205	839	407	716	(1)	386	259	290	(1)	(1)	1 166
Textile mills	23 439	3 807	431	350	1 296	391	584	959	888	277	1 019
Textile product mills	8 306	2 503	557	172	414	407	(1)	347	272	(1)	(1)
Apparel	18 545	2 128	265	578	1 428	498	737	1 576	573	194	1 399
Leather and allied products	2 280	499	(1)	(1)	...	...	(1)	332	164	...	...
Wood products	49 686	6 657	1 850	1 445	1 591	913	2 012	2 051	1 355	1 726	2 570
Paper	23 238	1 421	721	313	1 134	277	382	311	559	239	334
Printing and related support activities	22 793	2 415	960	1 224	860	1 065	878	790	246	277	435
Petroleum and coal products	3 689	469	(1)	185	(1)	205	...	294	...	180	253
Chemicals	15 692	2 058	872	1 064	400	530	375	1 808	562	...	723
Plastics and rubber products	58 926	5 466	1 014	686	719	329	353	3 027	691	...	656
Nonmetallic mineral products	32 179	3 131	794	785	1 882	342	492	1 846	621	609	1 460
Primary metals	76 288	5 734	981	773	1 473	1 147	762	2 752	835	1 381	1 358
Fabricated metal products	84 702	9 256	681	1 361	1 581	910	621	2 497	925	1 006	1 667
Machinery	164 176	12 322	2 466	2 373	4 456	1 971	2 329	4 463	2 077	1 787	4 968
Computer and electronic products	58 693	4 239	1 538	1 278	1 964	1 015	654	1 492	999	562	851
Electrical equipment and appliance manufacturing	48 250	3 360	1 386	1 195	1 756	865	734	1 692	1 303	1 793	1 935
Transportation equipment	304 693	23 150	10 104	7 128	22 071	2 860	4 474	25 863	4 869	4 166	8 581
Furniture and related products	39 591	5 088	1 346	1 625	919	409	1 560	1 916	1 417	792	1 929
Miscellaneous manufacturing	16 390	1 170	(1)	372	833	799	232	359	319	573	596
Wholesale trade	54 003	5 310	1 754	2 016	2 224	1 183	955	2 691	1 324	1 011	2 079
Retail trade	193 492	28 109	10 802	13 337	16 188	9 982	10 102	14 907	10 430	9 764	13 260
Transportation and warehousing	157 661	23 788	5 372	6 444	23 013	4 781	19 790	17 270	4 356	2 268	3 948
Information	96 127	12 581	3 753	5 715	8 383	6 310	4 321	7 341	6 155	2 365	5 640
Finance and insurance	55 876	3 681	2 671	3 636	4 579	1 761	2 621	3 391	1 945	2 602	2 342
Real estate and rental and leasing	11 567	493	622	409	1 388	698	437	883	514	267	455
Professional and technical services	72 962	6 390	2 292	4 610	11 110	5 534	2 970	4 366	4 657	1 504	3 447
Management of companies and enterprises	11 064	1 462	1 990	(1)	425	395	(1)	419	490	(1)	265
Administrative and waste services	294 709	30 020	13 594	13 281	21 073	17 363	14 283	25 234	14 605	10 059	23 531
Educational services	13 670	2 460	242	824	958	766	2 588	2 912	902	786	657
Health care and social assistance	52 058	3 019	2 118	2 066	4 991	7 337	14 283	6 716	2 532	1 660	4 056
Arts, entertainment, and recreation	29 853	2 860	1 419	1 558	4 838	2 063	1 764	2 559	1 286	2 799	2 674
Accommodation and food services	160 464	12 838	5 044	12 269	16 214	16 045	18 121	7 184	3 424	5 735	10 024
Other services, except public administration	18 889	1 458	552	670	1 434	2 933	3 284	1 522	305	864	506
Unclassified	595	...	108	...	...	...	...	...	...	78	73
Government	146 167	10 084	4 577	3 847	8 026	12 365	42 499	26 730	7 825	8 741	12 460
Local	103 273	6 108	2 999	1 887	4 445	7 597	37 610	20 898	4 998	5 268	5 157

[1]Data do not meet BLS or state agency disclosure standards.
. . . = Not available.

Table 7-4. Mass Layoff Events and Initial Claimants for Unemployment Insurance, by Region and State, 1997–October 2010

(Number.)

Region and state	1997	1998	1999	2000	2001	2002	2003	2004	2005	2006	2007	2008
						Mass layoff events						
UNITED STATES[1]	14 960	15 904	14 909	15 738	21 467	20 277	18 963	15 980	16 466	13 998	15 493	21 137
Northeast	2 719	2 550	2 058	2 226	3 157	3 073	3 139	2 630	2 806	2 514	2 775	3 257
New England	376	395	383	427	691	615	493	359	426	352	358	427
Middle Atlantic	2 343	2 155	1 675	1 799	2 466	2 458	2 646	2 271	2 380	2 162	2 417	2 830
South	2 811	3 107	2 930	3 166	4 601	4 829	4 198	3 587	4 035	2 789	3 260	5 153
South Atlantic	1 536	1 608	1 423	1 538	2 249	2 275	2 068	1 802	1 585	1 475	1 727	2 561
East South Central	299	436	413	626	902	1 060	858	798	893	699	857	1 392
West South Central	976	1 063	1 094	1 002	1 450	1 494	1 272	987	1 557	615	676	1 200
Midwest	3 425	3 336	3 520	4 223	5 945	4 828	4 644	4 135	4 512	4 026	4 258	5 751
East North Central	2 594	2 591	2 710	3 309	4 682	3 679	3 622	3 292	3 585	3 183	3 381	4 551
West North Central	831	745	810	914	1 263	1 149	1 022	843	927	843	877	1 200
West	6 005	6 911	6 401	6 123	7 764	7 547	6 982	5 628	5 113	4 669	5 200	6 976
Mountain	478	481	508	596	836	726	638	512	537	443	558	831
Pacific	5 527	6 430	5 893	5 527	6 928	6 821	6 344	5 116	4 576	4 226	4 642	6 145
Alabama	45	90	105	119	169	428	332	274	244	138	276	444
Alaska	35	41	37	30	31	36	36	35	24	30	19	27
Arizona	120	105	103	107	161	170	146	110	109	72	99	146
Arkansas	115	105	103	85	95	76	60	54	52	40	69	116
California	5 049	5 881	5 342	5 008	6 145	6 045	5 651	4 547	4 104	3 702	4 130	5 403
Colorado	78	72	69	62	143	126	104	74	72	65	80	93
Connecticut	51	35	41	45	73	73	80	49	55	60	51	65
Delaware	17	13	13	13	33	19	23	13	9	9	17	38
District of Columbia	12	16	20	14	24	14	14	8	7	5	6	11
Florida	580	579	503	525	870	936	866	876	700	593	795	1 333
Georgia	143	155	165	164	215	310	403	323	323	317	350	476
Hawaii	57	53	62	38	77	74	55	37	33	48	46	88
Idaho	86	106	101	117	144	126	122	90	82	65	92	145
Illinois	571	532	549	647	870	824	775	663	647	600	641	871
Indiana	280	235	236	333	497	460	506	434	443	403	375	680
Iowa	142	153	196	230	319	251	249	169	212	188	192	303
Kansas	74	56	71	92	110	129	119	102	103	88	92	136
Kentucky	77	130	124	261	409	363	277	289	328	330	346	540
Louisiana	145	155	129	185	225	241	204	206	956	134	107	311
Maine	63	91	58	48	50	45	44	48	43	33	40	33
Maryland	162	67	57	68	73	85	94	80	55	120	128	85
Massachusetts	171	186	188	188	356	325	262	152	178	123	128	162
Michigan	467	489	791	969	1 359	612	604	866	1 032	922	949	1 156
Minnesota	194	172	162	198	304	279	260	213	237	205	199	245
Mississippi	42	95	53	102	121	82	81	61	155	71	80	167
Missouri	392	336	344	352	432	374	292	256	276	289	329	433
Montana	31	30	16	25	35	32	46	36	48	40	49	54
Nebraska	8	15	14	24	50	80	65	71	72	48	32	47
Nevada	97	92	148	214	246	178	148	121	138	117	135	251
New Hampshire	29	32	27	37	79	61	31	29	40	29	31	42
New Jersey	414	402	317	405	427	509	481	449	485	452	503	518
New Mexico	39	47	39	31	37	40	44	42	44	49	55	73
New York	621	446	311	244	441	765	932	836	806	717	733	897
North Carolina	114	124	123	172	288	245	246	167	166	129	93	196
North Dakota	16	6	12	10	30	24	22	22	14	18	22	26
Ohio	583	635	527	653	963	901	913	699	761	608	716	1 027
Oklahoma	61	74	74	61	122	122	121	86	58	55	69	79
Oregon	224	255	244	277	410	368	342	282	202	246	258	367
Pennsylvania	1 308	1 307	1 047	1 150	1 598	1 184	1 233	986	1 089	993	1 181	1 415
Rhode Island	59	47	58	71	82	72	41	51	65	52	54	64
South Carolina	225	369	334	288	452	364	170	159	142	140	177	284
South Dakota	5	7	11	8	18	12	15	10	13	7	11	10
Tennessee	135	121	131	144	203	187	168	174	166	160	155	241
Texas	655	729	788	671	1 008	1 055	887	641	491	386	431	694
Utah	26	29	30	39	66	50	24	33	37	30	43	61
Vermont	3	4	11	38	51	39	35	30	45	55	54	61
Virginia	266	258	200	271	275	263	229	156	170	143	142	116
Washington	162	200	208	174	265	298	260	215	213	200	189	260
West Virginia	17	27	8	23	19	39	23	20	13	19	19	22
Wisconsin	693	700	607	707	993	882	824	630	702	650	700	817
Wyoming	(²)	(²)	. . .	(²)	(²)	4	4	6	7	5	5	8

[1]Data for all states and the District of Columbia.
[2]Data do not meet BLS or state agency disclosure standards.
. . . = Not available.

Table 7-4. Mass Layoff Events and Initial Claimants for Unemployment Insurance, by Region and State, 1997–October 2010—*Continued*

(Number.)

Region and state	2009	January 2010	February 2010	March 2010	April 2010	May 2010	June 2010	July 2010	August 2010	September 2010	October 2010
	Mass layoff events										
UNITED STATES[1]	28 030	2 860	1 183	1 197	1 840	1 354	1 861	2 124	976	920	1 642
Northeast	4 864	593	215	195	397	203	288	434	183	160	246
New England	745	70	39	26	81	29	54	40	34	15	25
Middle Atlantic	4 119	523	176	169	316	174	234	394	149	145	221
South	7 089	753	319	262	412	428	442	512	274	259	368
South Atlantic	3 782	404	178	136	214	216	267	280	160	153	213
East South Central	1 694	220	69	54	80	94	73	142	55	41	70
West South Central	1 613	129	72	72	118	118	102	90	59	65	85
Midwest	7 434	807	221	252	364	261	390	490	157	155	316
East North Central	5 734	604	169	184	290	175	290	397	124	115	227
West North Central	1 700	203	52	68	74	86	100	93	33	40	89
West	8 643	707	428	488	667	462	741	688	362	346	712
Mountain	1 291	94	58	77	101	73	105	71	31	47	99
Pacific	7 352	613	370	411	566	389	636	617	331	299	613
Alabama	493	93	17	18	17	24	32	57	14	13	20
Alaska	72	9	3	(2)	11	11	(2)	(2)	10	4	5
Arizona	255	17	8	17	33	24	28	16	5	6	24
Arkansas	117	9	(2)	3	8	6	7	8	3	3	7
California	6 377	533	335	373	477	345	590	558	287	264	559
Colorado	188	13	10	7	20	10	14	16	5	10	17
Connecticut	125	6	10	9	9	10	11	13	8	(2)	7
Delaware	57	4	5	...	8	3	7	3	(2)	(2)	5
District of Columbia	17	(2)	(2)	...	...	4	(2)	(2)	(2)	...	(2)
Florida	1 748	141	87	68	118	104	123	137	93	91	105
Georgia	618	83	34	13	31	39	46	27	30	24	32
Hawaii	106	9	(2)	7	7	4	7	5	5	3	5
Idaho	137	11	11	9	8	6	8	5	7	7	5
Illinois	1 309	112	40	60	60	56	88	92	32	35	60
Indiana	730	59	22	22	32	21	30	38	14	10	26
Iowa	423	54	13	13	20	16	13	25	9	3	14
Kansas	211	27	...	4	5	15	14	5	4	8	6
Kentucky	719	76	32	25	40	28	15	50	18	10	20
Louisiana	282	18	12	16	32	29	26	23	16	11	19
Maine	68	8	(2)	3	8	3	5	3	(2)	(2)	...
Maryland	141	29	7	6	6	12	11	20	6	6	9
Massachusetts	275	27	8	7	20	9	13	16	16	7	11
Michigan	1 305	144	32	29	44	24	54	107	14	11	34
Minnesota	377	36	13	13	8	11	18	14	4	5	26
Mississippi	135	11	5	5	5	11	13	12	14	12	15
Missouri	551	74	24	31	28	30	48	34	12	19	37
Montana	93	9	4	3	7	4	10	4	(2)	4	9
Nebraska	66	7	(2)	6	10	6	6	10	(2)	5	6
Nevada	369	26	16	26	15	13	24	20	7	13	26
New Hampshire	90	12	7	5	14	3	8	(2)	6	(2)	3
New Jersey	690	87	(2)	28	69	34	56	113	31	22	31
New Mexico	123	31	37	40	44	42	44	49	(2)	73	123
New York	1 367	236	52	60	114	67	50	201	59	52	61
North Carolina	325	27	5	16	13	13	21	19	9	13	21
North Dakota	47	4	(2)	...	3	7	...	4	...	...	...
Ohio	1 205	145	35	34	61	47	58	87	27	22	45
Oklahoma	150	17	3	4	5	6	6	8	...	...	7
Oregon	472	35	19	18	42	18	27	32	18	17	22
Pennsylvania	2 062	200	108	81	133	73	128	80	59	71	129
Rhode Island	90	13	7	(2)	16	4	9	6	(2)	(2)	(2)
South Carolina	493	67	11	14	19	10	31	36	11	7	21
South Dakota	25	(2)	...	(2)	...	...	...	(2)	...	...	...
Tennessee	347	40	15	6	18	31	13	23	9	6	15
Texas	1 064	85	56	49	73	77	63	51	38	49	52
Utah	113	10	(2)	5	8	8	6	6	(2)	4	7
Vermont	97	4	(2)	(2)	14	...	(2)	(2)	(2)	(2)	3
Virginia	330	49	22	18	15	26	24	36	8	11	19
Washington	325	27	11	12	29	11	10	21	11	11	22
West Virginia	53	(2)	5	(2)	4	5	(2)	(2)	...	...	...
Wisconsin	1 185	144	40	39	93	27	60	73	37	37	62
Wyoming	13	(2)	(2)	(2)	(2)	...	(2)	...	(2)	...	4

[1]Data for all states and the District of Columbia.
[2]Data do not meet BLS or state agency disclosure standards.
. . . = Not available.

Table 7-4. Mass Layoff Events and Initial Claimants for Unemployment Insurance, by Region and State, 1997–October 2010—*Continued*

(Number.)

Region and state	1997	1998	1999	2000	2001	2002	2003	2004	2005	2006	2007	2008
	Initial claimants											
UNITED STATES[1]	1 542 543	1 771 069	1 572 399	1 835 592	2 514 862	2 245 051	1 888 926	1 607 158	1 795 341	1 484 391	1 598 875	2 130 220
Northeast	268 831	264 063	207 057	235 083	340 246	338 965	306 462	270 788	280 628	254 684	273 079	316 191
New England	36 796	40 074	40 473	56 909	75 283	67 846	50 708	35 020	45 064	37 359	34 860	40 915
Middle Atlantic	232 035	223 989	166 584	178 174	264 963	271 119	255 754	235 768	235 564	217 325	238 219	275 276
South	296 850	347 332	314 556	360 330	546 222	545 907	435 387	355 561	485 505	312 892	356 812	533 687
South Atlantic	154 809	173 436	155 192	185 615	257 113	247 353	206 290	165 280	159 131	152 443	163 761	225 596
East South Central	29 120	48 496	41 403	69 619	107 661	127 477	98 450	91 565	131 138	95 861	115 114	180 702
West South Central	112 921	125 400	117 961	105 096	181 448	171 077	130 647	98 716	195 236	64 588	77 937	127 389
Midwest	425 657	504 413	474 132	583 290	841 597	614 121	552 140	485 255	571 950	508 798	509 431	676 591
East North Central	326 665	390 667	359 364	465 917	663 997	457 002	414 489	387 065	457 592	406 432	414 919	538 429
West North Central	98 992	113 746	114 768	117 373	177 600	157 119	137 651	98 190	114 358	102 366	94 512	138 162
West	551 205	655 261	576 654	656 889	786 797	746 058	594 937	495 554	457 258	408 017	459 553	603 751
Mountain	47 055	45 541	51 863	61 090	94 490	76 484	58 247	47 929	50 830	41 696	49 308	75 567
Pacific	504 150	609 720	524 791	595 799	692 307	669 574	536 690	447 625	406 428	366 321	410 245	528 184
Alabama	4 480	10 721	10 175	13 491	18 228	59 821	44 523	34 012	29 603	14 530	30 543	57 324
Alaska	2 961	3 246	3 565	2 706	2 814	2 846	2 973	2 930	2 326	2 770	1 798	2 888
Arizona	11 915	11 350	11 710	10 782	16 148	17 775	12 566	11 020	11 831	7 950	10 839	14 274
Arkansas	13 557	11 819	13 896	9 050	11 328	6 868	6 131	5 926	7 611	5 056	8 647	11 914
California	460 613	556 078	469 814	536 673	600 501	576 110	467 573	394 114	360 138	317 907	357 994	446 480
Colorado	7 136	7 181	7 024	5 967	14 127	12 601	9 422	6 856	6 759	5 905	6 567	8 200
Connecticut	4 098	3 084	3 847	4 393	6 122	7 360	7 054	4 203	4 972	6 595	4 975	5 505
Delaware	1 307	5 764	3 477	8 271	8 200	4 927	8 084	3 764	5 034	4 185	4 522	6 335
District of Columbia	1 279	1 514	2 052	1 572	2 301	1 688	1 160	807	565	346	418	1 195
Florida	38 237	43 184	36 724	39 407	70 889	71 635	61 863	63 087	51 535	42 593	55 696	94 656
Georgia	13 319	16 992	15 903	16 967	22 141	41 888	49 009	33 406	40 854	35 947	39 624	48 603
Hawaii	4 714	5 148	5 107	3 042	7 803	7 467	5 151	2 938	2 692	3 706	3 988	9 590
Idaho	9 959	9 845	11 264	13 121	17 144	15 579	13 690	8 148	7 233	5 665	8 245	13 591
Illinois	72 749	74 206	86 768	108 726	135 126	116 592	90 181	75 763	71 399	75 118	80 477	103 685
Indiana	35 260	35 329	38 252	50 892	71 521	67 134	70 393	58 853	62 574	56 395	47 923	80 027
Iowa	16 912	19 467	30 779	32 479	44 997	35 460	32 744	18 126	30 291	27 804	23 637	43 574
Kansas	6 834	8 198	8 189	13 145	21 657	18 186	16 102	10 782	9 740	9 785	10 654	17 243
Kentucky	9 615	14 988	14 485	33 975	60 327	42 094	34 709	37 809	55 078	61 246	59 399	89 953
Louisiana	13 803	15 544	9 869	14 799	28 373	22 113	17 329	16 519	120 600	12 915	13 042	31 664
Maine	4 738	7 471	5 875	7 407	4 713	4 377	3 828	4 293	3 445	2 622	3 035	2 536
Maryland	24 521	10 295	4 527	5 868	6 259	9 386	7 911	7 951	4 998	11 771	12 172	7 116
Massachusetts	18 942	20 599	19 879	27 907	36 693	33 705	25 352	13 960	18 114	11 188	10 785	14 911
Michigan	60 558	101 297	99 284	129 640	196 459	63 350	66 866	99 124	131 411	127 964	125 942	132 468
Minnesota	21 462	29 806	19 936	24 169	38 739	33 348	27 725	24 607	26 689	25 729	19 231	23 370
Mississippi	3 541	9 651	4 576	8 684	10 501	7 162	5 239	4 384	29 971	5 524	9 647	13 818
Missouri	50 781	52 631	51 518	43 765	60 026	57 373	50 379	35 034	37 005	29 324	33 557	43 451
Montana	2 782	2 744	1 501	3 489	4 048	3 570	4 379	3 600	4 567	3 726	3 873	4 731
Nebraska	522	2 045	1 325	2 102	6 363	8 371	6 761	6 764	8 332	5 907	3 440	5 204
Nevada	9 121	7 652	14 611	21 976	32 414	19 115	12 897	11 795	13 224	11 130	11 344	22 389
New Hampshire	2 344	2 790	3 279	4 615	10 903	8 080	3 030	2 726	4 666	2 996	3 053	3 873
New Jersey	48 294	48 119	34 439	45 173	52 530	63 369	49 815	51 252	48 732	51 128	52 738	51 623
New Mexico	3 364	3 536	3 036	2 243	3 045	2 894	3 129	3 071	3 469	4 226	4 619	6 253
New York	63 296	50 700	30 753	22 318	46 404	85 578	93 583	95 228	87 649	76 638	77 353	95 612
North Carolina	11 947	11 723	18 592	23 902	33 021	27 324	28 977	14 435	16 670	13 316	10 694	21 037
North Dakota	1 684	961	2 022	912	4 303	3 140	2 577	1 980	1 184	3 065	2 992	4 354
Ohio	86 040	92 045	65 449	94 419	139 218	103 577	102 864	86 850	113 165	80 291	83 429	131 813
Oklahoma	7 287	9 646	9 889	7 531	21 086	16 203	17 502	14 124	10 090	7 234	9 627	10 187
Oregon	21 410	25 005	24 260	32 159	55 449	44 944	35 508	28 401	22 231	24 386	29 391	42 780
Pennsylvania	120 445	125 170	101 392	110 683	166 029	122 172	112 356	89 288	99 183	89 559	108 128	128 041
Rhode Island	6 341	5 675	6 788	8 441	10 851	9 567	5 251	6 907	9 151	8 211	7 362	7 040
South Carolina	26 108	49 051	46 724	45 084	74 891	51 006	21 001	22 241	17 450	16 909	21 787	32 063
South Dakota	797	638	999	801	1 515	1 241	1 363	897	1 117	752	1 001	966
Tennessee	11 484	13 136	12 167	13 469	18 605	18 400	13 979	15 360	16 486	14 561	15 525	19 607
Texas	78 274	88 391	84 307	73 716	120 661	125 893	89 685	62 147	56 935	39 383	46 621	73 624
Utah	78 274	88 391	84 307	73 716	120 661	125 893	89 685	62 147	56 935	39 383	46 621	73 624
Vermont	333	455	805	4 146	6 001	4 757	6 193	2 931	4 716	5 747	5 650	7 050
Virginia	36 645	32 636	26 515	42 651	37 911	36 059	26 377	17 802	20 927	25 642	17 496	12 738
Washington	14 452	20 243	22 045	21 219	25 740	38 207	25 485	19 242	19 041	17 552	17 074	26 446
West Virginia	1 446	2 277	678	1 893	1 500	3 440	1 908	1 787	1 098	1 734	1 352	1 853
Wisconsin	72 058	87 790	69 611	82 240	121 673	106 349	84 185	66 475	79 043	66 664	77 148	90 436
Wyoming	(²)	(²)	. . .	(²)	(²)	308	272	480	481	329	357	525

[1] Data for all states and the District of Columbia.
[2] Data do not meet BLS or state agency disclosure standards.
. . . = Not available.

Table 7-4. Mass Layoff Events and Initial Claimants for Unemployment Insurance, by Region and State, 1997–October 2010—*Continued*

(Number.)

Region and state	2009	January 2010	February 2010	March 2010	April 2010	May 2010	June 2010	July 2010	August 2010	September 2010	October 2010
					Initial claimants						
UNITED STATES[1]	2 796 456	278 679	102 818	111 727	199 690	123 333	171 190	206 254	92 435	77 654	148 638
Northeast	465 208	58 748	21 705	19 419	48 396	17 575	32 587	44 132	16 706	14 411	20 922
New England	70 288	6 503	4 682	2 168	9 523	2 421	6 003	3 136	3 743	1 357	1 940
Middle Atlantic	394 920	52 245	17 023	17 251	38 873	15 154	26 584	40 996	12 963	13 054	18 982
South	691 460	74 105	29 681	26 591	43 503	38 299	39 969	48 848	21 631	21 507	35 853
South Atlantic	344 284	37 846	13 052	10 762	20 768	19 282	23 150	26 937	12 404	11 811	21 191
East South Central	183 287	23 085	9 917	5 470	11 005	8 431	7 108	13 640	4 584	3 633	7 095
West South Central	163 889	13 174	6 712	10 359	11 730	10 586	9 711	8 271	4 643	6 063	7 567
Midwest	892 202	83 185	21 128	27 591	44 740	26 176	39 201	56 377	17 140	14 964	34 290
East North Central	706 233	63 706	16 776	21 613	37 448	17 981	29 931	46 473	13 603	11 280	25 674
West North Central	185 969	19 479	4 352	5 978	7 292	8 195	9 270	9 904	3 537	3 684	8 616
West	747 586	62 641	30 304	38 126	63 051	41 283	59 433	56 897	36 958	26 772	57 573
Mountain	117 890	8 992	4 276	6 324	11 433	6 357	9 136	6 593	2 197	4 461	9 563
Pacific	629 696	53 649	26 028	31 802	51 618	34 926	50 297	50 304	34 761	22 311	48 010
Alabama	56 284	11 204	1 758	1 517	2 148	2 171	3 783	5 642	1 407	1 021	2 244
Alaska	7 056	713	267	(²)	1 252	1 259	(²)	(²)	884	492	430
Arizona	24 316	1 502	700	1 417	4 943	2 369	2 197	1 710	268	477	2 392
Arkansas	12 353	1 433	(²)	214	1 039	553	521	765	275	301	790
California	532 028	46 474	23 191	28 180	42 426	31 197	44 939	44 343	31 007	19 288	42 458
Colorado	16 424	1 301	706	626	2 269	1 024	1 237	1 552	355	827	1 675
Connecticut	10 559	406	847	746	891	823	968	977	880	(²)	523
Delaware	5 513	287	378	...	611	162	477	212	(²)	(²)	403
District of Columbia	1 504	(²)	(²)	...	...	301	(²)	(²)	(²)	...	(²)
Florida	131 190	9 909	5 523	4 311	9 139	7 027	9 037	10 581	6 506	6 001	9 277
Georgia	64 642	8 861	2 708	1 202	3 375	4 227	4 398	4 020	2 996	2 438	2 969
Hawaii	9 173	735	(²)	534	672	264	562	471	381	182	401
Idaho	12 405	1 068	709	661	533	367	481	480	504	1 011	362
Illinois	193 495	11 615	4 311	7 479	7 059	6 699	8 046	10 969	3 707	5 053	7 281
Indiana	84 555	6 470	1 907	3 057	4 786	1 931	2 977	5 905	1 554	846	4 349
Iowa	54 587	6 647	1 122	2 135	2 876	1 984	1 686	3 463	1 743	362	1 397
Kansas	27 741	2 432	...	313	296	1 464	1 815	416	366	1 245	737
Kentucky	87 321	8 044	6 844	3 276	6 573	2 758	1 417	5 491	1 422	1 454	2 828
Louisiana	26 098	1 566	1 442	1 615	2 967	2 646	1 985	2 174	1 010	688	1 554
Maine	5 922	789	(²)	233	754	204	320	249	(²)	(²)	...
Maryland	11 932	2 586	724	557	496	816	1 172	1 844	363	528	796
Massachusetts	25 608	2 341	646	725	2 202	865	948	1 403	1 464	476	858
Michigan	153 361	16 035	3 694	4 729	7 624	2 924	5 047	12 383	2 385	758	3 010
Minnesota	34 255	3 614	1 456	921	576	965	1 526	1 462	307	412	3 056
Mississippi	10 116	735	282	241	461	922	768	1 094	1 057	741	1 017
Missouri	54 046	5 567	1 667	2 112	2 393	2 396	3 679	3 005	864	1 115	2 866
Montana	8 260	1 012	258	189	528	267	659	322	(²)	332	831
Nebraska	7 371	548	(²)	409	948	593	504	835	(²)	550	560
Nevada	34 364	2 463	1 331	2 131	1 432	994	2 956	1 644	484	1 238	2 396
New Hampshire	8 548	962	1 095	297	1 663	264	1 277	(²)	657	(²)	302
New Jersey	68 149	7 506	1 408	3 024	9 700	2 685	9 675	10 486	2 449	1 665	2 517
New Mexico	9 680	560	391	847	594	673	997	247	(²)	238	545
New York	144 247	28 309	6 833	6 046	15 919	6 338	5 201	23 920	5 547	5 499	5 443
North Carolina	37 488	2 072	451	1 610	1 438	2 462	2 378	1 264	698	1 372	1 697
North Dakota	5 870	595	(²)	...	203	681	...	666	...	...	...
Ohio	147 712	14 121	3 790	2 927	8 014	3 909	6 056	9 564	2 569	1 638	4 734
Oklahoma	16 986	1 666	306	1 287	608	350	494	665	...	...	484
Oregon	52 900	3 730	1 571	2 080	4 603	1 324	3 758	3 582	1 671	1 635	2 540
Pennsylvania	182 524	16 430	8 782	8 181	13 254	6 131	11 708	6 590	4 967	5 890	11 022
Rhode Island	10 159	1 696	1 545	(²)	2 525	265	1 723	396	(²)	(²)	(²)
South Carolina	53 172	7 274	886	1 513	3 832	839	3 414	5 430	792	724	3 479
South Dakota	2 099	(²)	...	(²)	...	(²)	(²)	(²)	...	...	1 006
Tennessee	29 566	3 102	1 033	436	1 823	2 580	1 140	1 413	698	417	1 006
Texas	108 452	8 509	4 894	7 243	7 116	7 037	6 711	4 667	3 058	4 814	4 739
Utah	108 452	1 086	(²)	393	889	663	461	638	(²)	338	758
Vermont	9 492	309	483	(²)	1 488	...	767	(²)	(²)	(²)	196
Virginia	33 637	6 570	1 704	1 416	1 489	3 151	1 999	3 427	747	689	2 444
Washington	28 539	1 997	769	949	2 665	882	839	1 848	818	714	2 181
West Virginia	5 206	(²)	509	(²)	388	297	(²)	(²)	...	...	...
Wisconsin	127 110	15 465	3 074	3 421	9 965	2 518	7 805	7 652	3 388	2 985	6 300
Wyoming	1 186	(²)	(²)	(²)	(²)	...	(²)	...	(²)	...	604

[1]Data for all states and the District of Columbia.
[2]Data do not meet BLS or state agency disclosure standards.
. . . = Not available.

Table 7-5. Extended Mass Layoff Events and Separations, Selected Measures, 2005–2010

(Number.)

Year and quarter	Layoff events					
	Total, private nonfarm	Total, excluding seasonal and vacation events[1]	Total, movement of work[2]	Movement of work actions		
				Total	With separations reported	With separations unknown
2005						
Quarter 1	1 142	769	71	90	66	24
Quarter 2	1 203	635	73	98	74	24
Quarter 3	1 136	953	68	83	62	21
Quarter 4	1 400	619	65	92	57	35
2006						
Quarter 1	963	715	53	80	51	29
Quarter 2	1 353	750	72	103	66	37
Quarter 3	929	752	58	72	49	23
Quarter 4	1 640	943	69	94	66	28
2007						
Quarter 1	1 110	849	70	86	61	25
Quarter 2	1 421	772	65	89	66	23
Quarter 3	1 018	800	63	87	60	27
Quarter 4	1 814	1 062	69	90	66	24
2008						
Quarter 1	1 340	1 094	59	76	41	35
Quarter 2	1 756	1 105	71	100	78	22
Quarter 3	1 581	1 365	84	106	78	28
Quarter 4	3 582	2 713	118	161	122	39
2009						
Quarter 1	3 979	3 639	92	124	87	37
Quarter 2	3 395	2 638	116	158	102	56
Quarter 3	2 034	1 748	77	109	73	36
Quarter 4	2 416	1 588	66	100	55	45
2010						
Quarter 1	1 870	1 452	72	101	67	34
Quarter 2[3]	2 011	1 210	57	75	48	27
Quarter 3[3]	1 297	933	47	71	38	33

Year and quarter	Separations					
	Total, private nonfarm	Total, excluding seasonal and vacation events[1]	Total, movement of work[2]	Movement of work actions		
				Total	With separations reported	With separations unknown
2005						
Quarter 1	186 506	129 261	13 980	. . .	9 422	. . .
Quarter 2	246 099	108 372	12 040	. . .	9 527	. . .
Quarter 3	201 878	164 224	15 578	. . .	8 035	. . .
Quarter 4	250 178	111 818	12 051	. . .	7 210	. . .
2006						
Quarter 1	183 089	141 448	10 519	. . .	7 080	. . .
Quarter 2	295 964	139 737	16 610	. . .	9 674	. . .
Quarter 3	160 254	132 563	12 840	. . .	6 820	. . .
Quarter 4	296 662	167 130	15 782	. . .	10 462	. . .
2007						
Quarter 1	225 600	186 345	11 438	. . .	8 467	. . .
Quarter 2	278 719	123 843	11 352	. . .	7 401	. . .
Quarter 3	160 024	119 663	12 367	. . .	7 159	. . .
Quarter 4	301 592	171 808	11 302	. . .	7 152	. . .
2008						
Quarter 1	230 098	186 991	13 314	. . .	6 180	. . .
Quarter 2	354 713	198 389	12 317	. . .	7 346	. . .
Quarter 3	290 453	246 532	14 943	. . .	9 631	. . .
Quarter 4	641 714	491 941	20 382	. . .	11 919	. . .
2009						
Quarter 1	705 141	648 916	15 501	. . .	9 089	. . .
Quarter 2	651 318	491 273	21 365	. . .	11 478	. . .
Quarter 3	345 531	289 220	12 854	. . .	7 088	. . .
Quarter 4	406 212	269 005	11 974	. . .	4 573	. . .
2010						
Quarter 1	314 296	245 671	11 275	. . .	5 949	. . .
Quarter 2[3]	382 007	210 879	11 080	. . .	4 797	. . .
Quarter 3[3]	187 091	138 013	6 840	. . .	3 074	. . .

[1]The questions on movement of work were not asked of employers when the reason for layoff was either seasonal work or vacation period.
[2]Movement of work can involve more than one action.
[3]Preliminary.
. . . = Not available.

Table 7-6. Movement of Work Actions by Type of Separation Where Number of Separations Is Known by Employers, 2005–2010

(Number.)

Actions[1]

Year and quarter	With separations reported	Location: Out-of-country relocations — Total	Within company	Different company	Domestic relocations — Total	Within company	Different company	Unable to assign place of relocation	Company: Within company — Total	Domestic	Out of country	Unable to assign	Different company — Total	Domestic	Out of country	Unable to assign
2005																
Quarter 1	66	21	17	4	45	37	8	. . .	54	37	17	. . .	12	8	4	. . .
Quarter 2	74	28	19	9	42	35	7	4	58	35	19	4	16	7	9	. . .
Quarter 3	62	20	15	5	42	32	10	. . .	47	32	15	. . .	15	10	5	. . .
Quarter 4	57	22	17	5	35	28	7	. . .	45	28	17	. . .	12	7	5	. . .
2006																
Quarter 1	51	22	17	5	29	24	5	. . .	41	24	17	. . .	10	5	5	. . .
Quarter 2	66	23	21	2	43	35	8	. . .	56	35	21	. . .	10	8	2	. . .
Quarter 3	49	12	9	3	37	31	6	. . .	40	31	9	. . .	9	6	3	. . .
Quarter 4	66	27	24	3	39	35	4	. . .	59	35	24	. . .	7	4	3	. . .
2007																
Quarter 1	61	14	13	1	46	41	5	1	55	41	13	1	6	5	1	. . .
Quarter 2	66	23	22	1	43	34	9	. . .	56	34	22	. . .	10	9	1	. . .
Quarter 3	60	21	11	10	38	34	4	1	46	34	11	1	14	4	10	. . .
Quarter 4	66	27	26	1	39	38	1	. . .	64	38	26	. . .	2	1	1	. . .
2008																
Quarter 1	41	15	12	3	26	24	2	. . .	36	24	12	. . .	5	2	3	. . .
Quarter 2	78	25	23	2	52	47	5	1	70	47	23	. . .	8	5	2	1
Quarter 3	78	19	17	2	59	50	9	. . .	67	50	17	. . .	11	9	2	. . .
Quarter 4	122	36	31	5	86	79	7	. . .	110	79	31	. . .	12	7	5	. . .
2009																
Quarter 1	87	25	23	2	62	57	5	. . .	80	57	23	. . .	7	5	2	. . .
Quarter 2	102	22	21	1	80	73	7	. . .	94	73	21	. . .	8	7	1	. . .
Quarter 3	73	19	16	3	54	42	12	. . .	58	42	16	. . .	15	12	3	. . .
Quarter 4	55	15	12	3	38	34	4	2	48	34	12	2	7	4	3	. . .
2010																
Quarter 1	67	14	11	3	53	47	6	. . .	58	47	11	. . .	9	6	3	. . .
Quarter 2[2]	48	11	10	1	37	35	2	. . .	45	35	10	. . .	3	2	1	. . .
Quarter 3[3]	38	6	3	3	32	27	5	. . .	30	27	3	. . .	8	5	3	. . .

Separations

Year and quarter	With separations reported	Location: Out-of-country relocations — Total	Within company	Different company	Domestic relocations — Total	Within company	Different company	Unable to assign place of relocation	Company: Within company — Total	Domestic	Out of country	Unable to assign	Different company — Total	Domestic	Out of country	Unable to assign
2005																
Quarter 1	9 422	3 811	3 353	458	5 611	4 626	985	. . .	7 979	4 626	3 353	. . .	1 443	985	458	. . .
Quarter 2	9 527	2 815	1 938	877	6 018	5 330	688	694	7 962	5 330	1 938	694	1 565	688	877	. . .
Quarter 3	8 035	2 702	2 137	565	5 333	3 075	2 258	. . .	5 212	3 075	2 137	. . .	2 823	2 258	565	. . .
Quarter 4	7 210	2 702	2 010	692	4 508	4 104	404	. . .	6 114	4 104	2 010	. . .	1 096	404	692	. . .
2006																
Quarter 1	7 080	2 682	2 408	274	4 398	3 873	525	. . .	6 281	3 873	2 408	. . .	799	525	274	. . .
Quarter 2	9 674	3 033	2 912	121	6 641	5 823	818	. . .	8 735	5 823	2 912	. . .	939	818	121	. . .
Quarter 3	6 820	2 071	1 030	1 041	4 749	4 020	729	. . .	5 050	4 020	1 030	. . .	1 770	729	1 041	. . .
Quarter 4	10 462	5 581	5 426	155	4 881	4 494	387	. . .	9 920	4 494	5 426	. . .	542	387	155	. . .
2007																
Quarter 1	8 467	2 135	2 086	49	6 261	5 221	1 040	71	7 378	5 221	2 086	71	1 089	1 040	49	. . .
Quarter 2	7 401	3 537	3 387	150	3 864	3 254	610	. . .	6 641	3 254	3 387	. . .	760	610	150	. . .
Quarter 3	7 159	3 187	1 504	1 683	3 793	3 396	397	179	5 079	3 396	1 504	179	2 080	397	1 683	. . .
Quarter 4	7 152	2 997	2 910	87	4 155	3 975	180	. . .	6 885	3 975	2 910	. . .	267	180	87	. . .
2008																
Quarter 1	6 180	1 901	1 602	299	4 279	3 364	915	. . .	4 966	3 364	1 602	. . .	1 214	915	299	. . .
Quarter 2	7 346	3 159	2 935	224	3 912	3 694	218	275	6 629	3 694	2 935	. . .	717	218	224	275
Quarter 3	9 631	2 312	2 135	177	7 319	6 522	797	. . .	8 657	6 522	2 135	. . .	974	797	177	. . .
Quarter 4	11 919	4 059	3 720	339	7 860	7 363	497	. . .	11 083	7 363	3 720	. . .	836	497	339	. . .
2009																
Quarter 1	9 089	3 967	3 794	173	5 122	4 776	346	. . .	8 570	4 776	3 794	. . .	519	346	173	. . .
Quarter 2	11 478	2 849	2 759	90	8 629	7 406	1 223	. . .	10 165	7 406	2 759	. . .	1 313	1 223	90	. . .
Quarter 3	7 088	2 006	1 786	220	5 082	3 642	1 440	. . .	5 428	3 642	1 786	. . .	1 660	1 440	220	. . .
Quarter 4	4 573	1 556	1 291	265	2 722	2 360	362	295	3 946	2 360	1 291	295	627	362	265	. . .
2010																
Quarter 1	5 949	1 023	933	90	4 926	3 992	934	. . .	4 925	3 992	933	. . .	1 024	934	90	. . .
Quarter 2[2]	4 797	1 200	1 160	40	3 597	3 138	459	. . .	4 298	3 138	1 160	. . .	499	459	40	. . .
Quarter 3[3]	3 074	737	279	458	2 337	1 785	552	. . .	2 064	1 785	279	. . .	1 010	552	458	. . .

[1]Only actions for which separations associated with the movement of work were reported are shown.
[2]Revised.
[3]Preliminary.
. . . = Not available.

NOTES AND DEFINITIONS

JOB OPENINGS AND LABOR TURNOVER SURVEY

The data for the Job Openings and Labor Turnover Survey (JOLTS) are collected and compiled monthly from a sample of business establishments by the Bureau of Labor Statistics (BLS). Each month, data are collected in a survey of business establishments for total employment, job openings, hires, quits, layoffs and discharges, and other separations. Data collection methods include computer-assisted telephone interviewing, touchtone data entry, fax, and mail.

Concepts and Definitions

The JOLTS program covers all private nonfarm establishments such as factories, offices, and stores, as well as federal, state, and local government entities in the 50 states and the District of Columbia.

Industry classification is in accordance with the 2007 version of the North American Industry Classification System (NAICS). In order to ensure the highest possible quality of data, state workforce agencies verify with employers and update, if necessary, the industry code, location, and ownership classification of all establishments on a 3-year cycle. Changes in establishment characteristics resulting from the verification process are always introduced into the JOLTS sampling frame with the data reported for the first month of the year.

Employment includes persons on the payroll who worked or received pay for the pay period that includes the 12th day of the reference month. Full-time, part-time, permanent, short-term, seasonal, salaried, and hourly employees are included, as are employees on paid vacations or other paid leave. Proprietors or partners of unincorporated businesses, unpaid family workers, or persons on leave without pay or on strike for the entire pay period, are not counted as employed. Employees of temporary help agencies, employee leasing companies, outside contractors, and consultants are counted by their employer of record, not by the establishment where they are working.

Job openings information is submitted by establishments for the last business day of the reference month. A job opening requires that: 1) a specific position exists and there is work available for that position, 2) work could start within 30 days regardless of whether a suitable candidate is found, and 3) the employer is actively recruiting from outside the establishment to fill the position. Included are full-time, part-time, permanent, short-term, and seasonal openings. Active recruiting means that the establishment is taking steps to fill a position by advertising in newspapers or on the Internet, posting help-wanted signs, accepting applications, or using other similar methods.

Jobs to be filled only by internal transfers, promotions, demotions, or recall from layoffs are excluded. Also excluded are jobs with start dates more than 30 days in the future, jobs for which employees have been hired but have not yet reported for work, and jobs to be filled by employees of temporary help agencies, employee leasing companies, outside contractors, or consultants. The job openings rate is computed by dividing the number of job openings by the sum of employment and job openings and multiplying that quotient by 100.

Hires are the total number of additions to the payroll occurring at any time during the reference month, including both new and rehired employees, full-time and part-time, permanent, short-term and seasonal employees, employees recalled to the location after a layoff lasting more than 7 days, on-call or intermittent employees who returned to work after having been formally separated, and transfers from other locations. The hires count does not include transfers or promotions within the reporting site, employees returning from strike, employees of temporary help agencies or employee leasing companies, outside contractors, or consultants. The hires rate is computed by dividing the number of hires by employment and multiplying that quotient by 100.

Separations are the total number of terminations of employment occurring at any time during the reference month, and are reported by type of separation—quits, layoffs and discharges, and other separations. Quits are voluntary separations by employees (except for retirements, which are reported as other separations). Layoffs and discharges are involuntary separations initiated by the employer and include layoffs with no intent to rehire, formal layoffs lasting or expected to last more than 7 days, discharges resulting from mergers, downsizing, or closings, firings or other discharges for cause, terminations of permanent or short-term employees, and terminations of seasonal employees. Other separations include retirements, transfers to other locations, deaths, and separations due to disability. Separations do not include transfers within the same location or employees on strike.

The separations rate is computed by dividing the number of separations by employment and multiplying that quotient by 100. The quits, layoffs and discharges, and other separations rates are computed similarly, dividing the number by employment and multiplying by 100.

The JOLTS annual level estimates for hires, quits, layoffs and discharges, other separations, and total separations are the sum of the 12 published monthly levels. The annual rate estimates are computed by dividing the annual level by the Current Employment Statistics (CES) annual average employment level, and multiplying that quotient by 100.

This figure will be approximately equal to the sum of the 12 monthly rates.

Annual estimates are not calculated for job openings because job openings are a stock, or point-in-time, measurement for the last business day of each month. Only jobs still open on the last day of the month are counted. For the same reason job openings cannot be cumulated throughout each month, annual figures for job openings cannot be created by summing the monthly estimates. Hires and separations are flow measures and are cumulated over the month with a total reported for the month. Therefore, the annual figures can be created by summing the monthly estimates.

Sources of Additional Information

For more extensive information see BLS news release USDL 10-1685 "Job Openings and Labor Turnover (Monthly)" on the BLS Web site at <http://www.bls.gov/jlt/>.

Table 7-7. Job Openings Levels and Rates, by Industry, December 2000–October 2010

(Seasonally adjusted, levels in thousands, rates per 100.)

Year and month	Level											
	Total[1]	Total private[1]	Construction	Manufacturing	Trade, transportation, and utilities[2]	Retail trade	Professional and business services	Education and health services	Leisure and hospitality[3]	Accommodation and food services	Government[4]	State and local government
2000												
December	5 111	4 716	226	467	879	543	830	842	591	555	396	322
2001												
January	5 082	4 601	189	422	929	496	689	782	658	597	481	401
February	4 885	4 394	228	417	877	519	796	808	617	567	491	421
March	4 992	4 511	200	405	699	430	1 044	787	678	569	481	422
April	4 803	4 307	232	322	894	550	836	709	600	547	496	433
May	4 560	4 063	221	313	699	464	813	791	585	521	498	430
June	4 491	3 953	188	347	694	436	746	770	526	467	538	475
July	4 392	3 859	191	304	665	408	623	795	599	511	534	482
August	4 293	3 792	112	277	626	404	594	921	595	533	501	450
September	4 165	3 724	146	313	587	362	647	757	638	560	441	385
October	3 726	3 264	128	262	615	362	511	771	440	381	461	408
November	3 670	3 216	140	231	566	353	563	709	491	421	455	408
December	3 621	3 163	121	220	567	369	520	728	466	411	458	405
2002												
January	3 702	3 299	110	260	570	374	564	759	429	370	403	367
February	3 505	3 040	109	259	542	350	495	750	424	359	464	418
March	3 687	3 243	128	242	598	354	597	740	428	355	444	393
April	3 485	3 058	98	244	567	352	537	709	412	353	427	384
May	3 614	3 161	111	249	556	340	655	673	429	364	453	397
June	3 429	3 030	130	257	544	339	525	742	391	342	400	369
July	3 466	3 045	103	259	516	345	599	698	402	362	421	374
August	3 506	3 048	112	249	535	322	597	702	405	351	457	405
September	3 371	2 954	132	241	497	319	588	720	380	346	417	364
October	3 698	3 289	134	230	593	395	724	680	407	354	409	355
November	3 646	3 181	120	238	503	298	677	736	427	382	465	397
December	3 127	2 752	86	218	436	246	556	659	383	321	375	334
2003												
January	3 622	3 203	109	216	518	313	853	642	395	360	420	359
February	3 444	3 035	101	202	555	358	774	609	342	286	409	355
March	3 180	2 784	87	199	481	301	660	590	362	332	396	328
April	3 260	2 883	137	206	455	293	523	626	440	353	377	341
May	3 190	2 854	92	203	497	308	624	669	378	344	335	282
June	3 339	2 932	114	195	510	333	618	609	482	411	407	341
July	3 249	2 895	155	189	522	322	706	574	345	289	354	283
August	3 223	2 901	109	225	539	336	729	559	365	316	322	260
September	3 140	2 819	66	209	553	361	651	551	393	342	321	270
October	3 305	2 958	85	225	558	360	597	626	416	372	347	300
November	3 338	3 011	90	267	584	382	613	586	408	365	327	275
December	3 293	2 964	100	217	607	345	619	524	459	404	329	279
2004												
January	3 524	3 111	141	235	556	349	592	639	425	360	413	347
February	3 502	3 135	122	224	561	390	657	604	445	386	368	307
March	3 514	3 148	127	251	620	388	589	611	436	393	366	317
April	3 574	3 207	136	265	607	386	669	617	416	377	367	305
May	3 728	3 337	138	288	639	427	661	617	439	375	391	348
June	3 500	3 148	102	269	637	402	729	528	463	420	352	297
July	3 894	3 510	117	277	681	428	759	608	474	430	385	339
August	3 734	3 371	129	283	649	431	674	608	506	426	362	315
September	3 817	3 447	124	274	702	479	708	610	466	398	371	316
October	3 961	3 539	156	290	656	450	746	675	451	403	422	361
November	3 464	3 076	144	255	553	320	593	624	420	365	389	336
December	3 916	3 490	153	274	669	412	709	636	465	393	426	351
2005												
January	3 895	3 515	154	292	657	447	689	637	522	459	381	352
February	3 864	3 482	153	283	711	443	695	618	502	443	382	336
March	3 943	3 568	150	286	697	462	734	672	496	436	375	322
April	4 191	3 797	135	294	731	472	801	651	600	525	393	340
May	3 912	3 531	138	281	696	411	776	693	495	436	381	324
June	4 161	3 779	144	294	690	415	888	653	529	450	382	334
July	4 175	3 769	158	320	686	417	801	693	523	421	407	354
August	4 112	3 711	154	302	680	424	825	669	482	415	402	350
September	4 290	3 862	171	330	678	396	824	694	499	453	428	364
October	4 276	3 889	182	286	759	453	813	660	497	429	387	338
November	4 465	4 067	199	395	826	542	847	661	532	466	398	348
December	4 433	3 977	174	362	736	467	872	669	547	489	456	396

[1]Includes natural resources and mining, information, financial activities, and other services, not shown separately.
[2]Includes wholesale trade and transportation, warehousing, and utilities, not shown separately.
[3]Includes arts, entertainment, and recreation, not shown separately.
[4]Includes federal government, not shown separately.

Table 7-7. Job Openings Levels and Rates, by Industry, December 2000–October 2010—*Continued*

(Seasonally adjusted, levels in thousands, rates per 100.)

Year and month	Rate											
	Total[1]	Total private[1]	Construction	Manufacturing	Trade, transportation, and utilities[2]	Retail trade	Professional and business services	Education and health services	Leisure and hospitality[3]	Accommodation and food services	Government[4]	State and local government
2000												
December	3.7	4.1	3.2	2.6	3.2	3.4	4.7	5.2	4.7	5.2	1.9	1.8
2001												
January	3.7	4.0	2.7	2.4	3.4	3.1	3.9	4.8	5.2	5.5	2.3	2.2
February	3.6	3.8	3.2	2.4	3.2	3.3	4.5	5.0	4.9	5.3	2.3	2.3
March	3.6	3.9	2.8	2.3	2.6	2.7	5.9	4.8	5.3	5.3	2.2	2.3
April	3.5	3.7	3.3	1.9	3.3	3.5	4.8	4.4	4.7	5.1	2.3	2.3
May	3.3	3.5	3.1	1.8	2.6	3.0	4.7	4.8	4.6	4.8	2.3	2.3
June	3.3	3.4	2.7	2.1	2.6	2.8	4.3	4.7	4.2	4.4	2.5	2.5
July	3.2	3.4	2.7	1.8	2.5	2.6	3.6	4.8	4.7	4.7	2.5	2.6
August	3.2	3.3	1.6	1.7	2.4	2.6	3.5	5.5	4.7	4.9	2.3	2.4
September	3.1	3.3	2.1	1.9	2.2	2.3	3.8	4.6	5.0	5.2	2.0	2.0
October	2.8	2.9	1.8	1.6	2.3	2.3	3.1	4.6	3.5	3.6	2.1	2.2
November	2.7	2.9	2.0	1.4	2.2	2.3	3.4	4.3	3.9	4.0	2.1	2.1
December	2.7	2.8	1.7	1.4	2.2	2.4	3.1	4.4	3.8	3.9	2.1	2.1
2002												
January	2.8	2.9	1.6	1.6	2.2	2.4	3.4	4.5	3.5	3.5	1.9	1.9
February	2.6	2.7	1.6	1.6	2.1	2.3	3.0	4.5	3.4	3.4	2.1	2.2
March	2.7	2.9	1.9	1.5	2.3	2.3	3.6	4.4	3.5	3.4	2.0	2.1
April	2.6	2.7	1.4	1.6	2.2	2.3	3.2	4.2	3.3	3.4	2.0	2.0
May	2.7	2.8	1.6	1.6	2.1	2.2	3.9	4.0	3.5	3.5	2.1	2.1
June	2.6	2.7	1.9	1.7	2.1	2.2	3.2	4.4	3.2	3.3	1.8	1.9
July	2.6	2.7	1.5	1.7	2.0	2.2	3.6	4.1	3.3	3.4	1.9	2.0
August	2.6	2.7	1.6	1.6	2.1	2.1	3.6	4.1	3.3	3.3	2.1	2.1
September	2.5	2.6	1.9	1.6	1.9	2.1	3.6	4.2	3.1	3.3	1.9	1.9
October	2.8	2.9	2.0	1.5	2.3	2.6	4.3	4.0	3.3	3.3	1.9	1.9
November	2.7	2.8	1.8	1.6	1.9	2.0	4.1	4.3	3.4	3.6	2.1	2.1
December	2.3	2.5	1.3	1.4	1.7	1.6	3.4	3.9	3.1	3.0	1.7	1.7
2003												
January	2.7	2.9	1.6	1.4	2.0	2.0	5.1	3.8	3.1	3.4	1.9	1.9
February	2.6	2.7	1.5	1.3	2.1	2.3	4.6	3.6	2.7	2.7	1.9	1.9
March	2.4	2.5	1.3	1.3	1.9	2.0	4.0	3.5	2.9	3.1	1.8	1.7
April	2.4	2.6	2.0	1.4	1.8	1.9	3.2	3.6	3.5	3.3	1.7	1.8
May	2.4	2.6	1.4	1.4	1.9	2.0	3.8	3.9	3.0	3.2	1.5	1.5
June	2.5	2.6	1.7	1.3	2.0	2.2	3.7	3.5	3.8	3.8	1.8	1.8
July	2.4	2.6	2.3	1.3	2.0	2.1	4.2	3.3	2.8	2.7	1.6	1.5
August	2.4	2.6	1.6	1.5	2.1	2.2	4.4	3.3	2.9	3.0	1.5	1.4
September	2.4	2.5	1.0	1.4	2.1	2.4	3.9	3.2	3.1	3.2	1.5	1.4
October	2.5	2.7	1.2	1.5	2.2	2.3	3.6	3.6	3.3	3.4	1.6	1.6
November	2.5	2.7	1.3	1.8	2.3	2.5	3.7	3.4	3.2	3.4	1.5	1.4
December	2.5	2.7	1.4	1.5	2.3	2.3	3.7	3.0	3.6	3.7	1.5	1.5
2004												
January	2.6	2.8	2.0	1.6	2.1	2.3	3.5	3.7	3.3	3.3	1.9	1.8
February	2.6	2.8	1.7	1.5	2.2	2.5	3.9	3.5	3.5	3.5	1.7	1.6
March	2.6	2.8	1.8	1.7	2.4	2.5	3.5	3.5	3.4	3.6	1.7	1.7
April	2.7	2.8	1.9	1.8	2.3	2.5	3.9	3.5	3.2	3.4	1.7	1.6
May	2.8	3.0	1.9	2.0	2.4	2.8	3.9	3.5	3.4	3.4	1.8	1.8
June	2.6	2.8	1.4	1.8	2.4	2.6	4.3	3.0	3.6	3.8	1.6	1.5
July	2.9	3.1	1.6	1.9	2.6	2.8	4.4	3.5	3.7	3.9	1.7	1.8
August	2.8	3.0	1.8	1.9	2.5	2.8	3.9	3.5	3.9	3.8	1.6	1.6
September	2.8	3.0	1.7	1.9	2.7	3.1	4.1	3.5	3.6	3.6	1.7	1.6
October	2.9	3.1	2.2	2.0	2.5	2.9	4.3	3.8	3.5	3.6	1.9	1.9
November	2.6	2.7	2.0	1.8	2.1	2.1	3.5	3.5	3.2	3.3	1.8	1.7
December	2.9	3.1	2.1	1.9	2.5	2.7	4.1	3.6	3.6	3.5	1.9	1.8
2005												
January	2.9	3.1	2.1	2.0	2.5	2.9	4.0	3.6	4.0	4.1	1.7	1.8
February	2.8	3.0	2.1	1.9	2.7	2.8	4.0	3.5	3.8	3.9	1.7	1.7
March	2.9	3.1	2.0	2.0	2.6	3.0	4.2	3.8	3.8	3.9	1.7	1.7
April	3.1	3.3	1.8	2.0	2.7	3.0	4.5	3.6	4.5	4.6	1.8	1.8
May	2.8	3.1	1.9	1.9	2.6	2.6	4.4	3.8	3.7	3.8	1.7	1.7
June	3.0	3.3	1.9	2.0	2.6	2.6	5.0	3.6	4.0	4.0	1.7	1.7
July	3.0	3.3	2.1	2.2	2.6	2.6	4.5	3.8	3.9	3.7	1.8	1.8
August	3.0	3.2	2.0	2.1	2.5	2.7	4.6	3.7	3.6	3.6	1.8	1.8
September	3.1	3.3	2.3	2.3	2.5	2.5	4.6	3.8	3.7	4.0	1.9	1.9
October	3.1	3.3	2.4	2.0	2.8	2.9	4.5	3.6	3.7	3.8	1.7	1.7
November	3.2	3.5	2.6	2.7	3.1	3.4	4.7	3.6	4.0	4.1	1.8	1.8
December	3.2	3.4	2.3	2.5	2.7	3.0	4.8	3.7	4.1	4.3	2.0	2.0

[1]Includes natural resources and mining, information, financial activities, and other services, not shown separately.
[2]Includes wholesale trade and transportation, warehousing, and utilities, not shown separately.
[3]Includes arts, entertainment, and recreation, not shown separately.
[4]Includes federal government, not shown separately.

Table 7-7. Job Openings Levels and Rates, by Industry, December 2000–October 2010—*Continued*

(Seasonally adjusted, levels in thousands, rates per 100.)

Year and month	Level											
	Total[1]	Total private[1]	Construc-tion	Manufac-turing	Trade, transpor-tation, and utilities[2]	Retail trade	Profes-sional and business services	Education and health services	Leisure and hospitality[3]	Accommo-dation and food services	Govern-ment[4]	State and local govern-ment
2006												
January	4 244	3 888	147	321	703	447	827	690	552	486	356	318
February	4 392	3 959	146	377	691	422	836	743	564	521	433	372
March	4 654	4 202	193	389	750	436	797	750	572	504	452	400
April	4 624	4 170	187	373	809	464	737	741	575	509	454	407
May	4 634	4 189	175	319	810	475	923	697	565	507	445	392
June	4 442	3 981	195	361	729	430	706	726	529	470	462	406
July	4 160	3 667	194	319	702	392	614	648	562	490	492	430
August	4 571	4 105	208	343	756	435	740	776	583	530	466	417
September	4 638	4 169	188	351	876	452	729	779	565	441	468	425
October	4 650	4 195	179	371	793	429	762	834	596	512	455	404
November	4 666	4 211	132	341	759	414	792	782	708	626	454	410
December	4 656	4 200	115	372	916	543	718	762	612	546	456	412
2007												
January	4 538	4 102	273	359	836	452	764	735	536	462	436	402
February	4 534	4 069	283	373	751	435	653	698	549	478	465	407
March	4 808	4 332	211	385	858	428	850	731	591	523	476	426
April	4 622	4 161	192	363	842	409	818	761	564	481	461	405
May	4 624	4 159	194	379	741	382	811	771	584	522	465	409
June	4 804	4 341	167	371	820	465	819	796	619	546	463	415
July	4 496	4 034	169	376	812	451	709	734	612	550	462	414
August	4 644	4 174	154	329	813	416	805	792	638	573	469	413
September	4 565	4 105	131	325	756	403	761	844	657	584	460	410
October	4 369	3 923	143	292	725	358	753	746	625	558	446	397
November	4 510	4 039	124	333	766	413	784	738	683	581	471	410
December	4 378	3 920	127	300	814	416	766	773	598	552	458	392
2008												
January	4 182	3 774	124	300	689	351	755	737	565	511	408	378
February	4 121	3 687	132	280	693	369	747	792	561	493	434	386
March	4 121	3 680	101	251	672	408	773	775	562	498	441	381
April	3 974	3 570	104	288	630	383	751	717	534	478	403	368
May	4 094	3 641	155	291	655	375	684	732	557	487	454	390
June	3 843	3 410	111	274	597	337	729	724	497	445	433	373
July	3 929	3 505	107	257	652	408	668	775	456	397	424	358
August	3 688	3 245	88	259	583	378	655	682	432	376	442	356
September	3 288	2 826	118	219	493	278	598	597	397	358	462	391
October	3 333	2 935	70	224	561	369	588	655	389	343	398	335
November	3 241	2 866	74	175	577	395	556	667	311	277	375	345
December	3 078	2 752	78	161	466	305	562	651	332	295	326	284
2009												
January	2 792	2 396	33	114	482	349	508	620	235	203	396	313
February	2 830	2 483	65	136	447	325	490	561	313	293	347	305
March	2 671	2 227	55	120	425	266	413	513	291	266	444	269
April	2 475	2 108	27	108	345	211	433	506	337	313	367	311
May	2 488	2 183	37	104	479	334	407	523	278	255	304	256
June	2 519	2 197	59	110	472	322	396	517	276	258	322	271
July	2 338	2 046	45	109	337	210	431	550	262	245	292	233
August	2 411	2 098	66	134	425	248	404	531	241	221	313	287
September	2 624	2 333	73	139	415	282	446	573	305	278	292	232
October	2 546	2 164	65	141	363	228	436	529	268	249	382	292
November	2 456	2 113	71	155	334	207	425	537	236	214	343	249
December	2 531	2 130	67	171	378	237	404	545	227	207	401	294
2010												
January	2 854	2 471	62	154	395	255	424	624	268	250	383	256
February	2 647	2 266	65	167	453	297	409	502	285	266	381	246
March	2 785	2 363	83	180	470	305	423	536	257	232	421	262
April	3 302	2 675	88	195	456	292	550	561	274	250	627	260
May	2 939	2 597	79	205	452	274	601	512	288	247	342	237
June	2 864	2 537	53	226	449	284	514	487	317	263	327	238
July	3 141	2 821	101	238	485	295	564	515	365	323	320	246
August	3 092	2 752	65	190	449	263	590	487	381	340	341	257
September	3 011	2 658	71	203	472	265	559	529	307	266	354	250
October[5]	3 362	3 027	56	205	488	280	744	632	339	303	335	265

[1]Includes natural resources and mining, information, financial activities, and other services, not shown separately.
[2]Includes wholesale trade and transportation, warehousing, and utilities, not shown separately.
[3]Includes arts, entertainment, and recreation, not shown separately.
[4]Includes federal government, not shown separately.
[5]Preliminary.

Table 7-7. Job Openings Levels and Rates, by Industry, December 2000–October 2010—*Continued*

(Seasonally adjusted, levels in thousands, rates per 100.)

Year and month	Rate											
	Total[1]	Total private[1]	Construction	Manufacturing	Trade, transportation, and utilities[2]	Retail trade	Professional and business services	Education and health services	Leisure and hospitality[3]	Accommodation and food services	Government[4]	State and local government
2006												
January	3.0	3.3	1.9	2.2	2.6	2.8	4.6	3.8	4.1	4.2	1.6	1.6
February	3.1	3.4	1.9	2.6	2.6	2.7	4.6	4.0	4.2	4.5	1.9	1.9
March	3.3	3.6	2.4	2.7	2.8	2.8	4.4	4.1	4.2	4.3	2.0	2.0
April	3.3	3.5	2.4	2.6	3.0	2.9	4.0	4.0	4.2	4.4	2.0	2.1
May	3.3	3.5	2.2	2.2	3.0	3.0	5.0	3.8	4.1	4.4	2.0	2.0
June	3.2	3.4	2.5	2.5	2.7	2.7	3.9	3.9	3.9	4.1	2.1	2.1
July	3.0	3.1	2.4	2.2	2.6	2.5	3.4	3.5	4.1	4.2	2.2	2.2
August	3.2	3.5	2.6	2.4	2.8	2.8	4.0	4.2	4.2	4.5	2.1	2.1
September	3.3	3.5	2.4	2.4	3.2	2.9	4.0	4.2	4.1	3.8	2.1	2.2
October	3.3	3.5	2.3	2.6	2.9	2.7	4.1	4.4	4.3	4.4	2.0	2.0
November	3.3	3.5	1.7	2.4	2.8	2.6	4.3	4.2	5.1	5.3	2.0	2.1
December	3.3	3.5	1.5	2.6	3.3	3.4	3.9	4.1	4.4	4.6	2.0	2.1
2007												
January	3.2	3.4	3.4	2.5	3.1	2.8	4.1	3.9	3.9	3.9	1.9	2.0
February	3.2	3.4	3.6	2.6	2.8	2.7	3.5	3.7	4.0	4.0	2.1	2.1
March	3.4	3.6	2.7	2.7	3.1	2.7	4.5	3.9	4.2	4.4	2.1	2.1
April	3.3	3.5	2.4	2.5	3.1	2.6	4.4	4.0	4.0	4.0	2.0	2.0
May	3.3	3.5	2.5	2.6	2.7	2.4	4.3	4.1	4.2	4.4	2.1	2.1
June	3.4	3.6	2.1	2.6	3.0	2.9	4.4	4.2	4.4	4.5	2.0	2.1
July	3.2	3.4	2.2	2.6	3.0	2.8	3.8	3.9	4.4	4.6	2.0	2.1
August	3.3	3.5	2.0	2.3	3.0	2.6	4.3	4.1	4.5	4.8	2.1	2.1
September	3.2	3.4	1.7	2.3	2.8	2.5	4.1	4.4	4.7	4.8	2.0	2.1
October	3.1	3.3	1.9	2.1	2.6	2.3	4.0	3.9	4.4	4.6	2.0	2.0
November	3.2	3.4	1.6	2.4	2.8	2.6	4.2	3.8	4.8	4.8	2.1	2.1
December	3.1	3.3	1.7	2.1	3.0	2.6	4.1	4.0	4.2	4.6	2.0	2.0
2008												
January	2.9	3.2	1.6	2.1	2.5	2.2	4.0	3.8	4.0	4.2	1.8	1.9
February	2.9	3.1	1.7	2.0	2.5	2.3	4.0	4.1	4.0	4.1	1.9	1.9
March	2.9	3.1	1.3	1.8	2.5	2.6	4.1	4.0	4.0	4.1	1.9	1.9
April	2.8	3.0	1.4	2.1	2.3	2.4	4.0	3.7	3.8	4.0	1.8	1.8
May	2.9	3.1	2.1	2.1	2.4	2.4	3.7	3.7	4.0	4.1	2.0	1.9
June	2.7	2.9	1.5	2.0	2.2	2.1	3.9	3.7	3.6	3.7	1.9	1.9
July	2.8	3.0	1.5	1.9	2.4	2.6	3.6	3.9	3.3	3.3	1.8	1.8
August	2.6	2.8	1.2	1.9	2.2	2.4	3.6	3.5	3.1	3.2	1.9	1.8
September	2.4	2.4	1.6	1.6	1.9	1.8	3.3	3.1	2.9	3.0	2.0	1.9
October	2.4	2.5	1.0	1.7	2.1	2.4	3.2	3.3	2.8	2.9	1.7	1.7
November	2.3	2.5	1.1	1.3	2.2	2.6	3.1	3.4	2.3	2.4	1.6	1.7
December	2.2	2.4	1.2	1.2	1.8	2.0	3.2	3.3	2.4	2.5	1.4	1.4
2009												
January	2.0	2.1	0.5	0.9	1.9	2.3	2.9	3.2	1.7	1.8	1.7	1.6
February	2.1	2.2	1.0	1.1	1.7	2.2	2.8	2.9	2.3	2.5	1.5	1.5
March	2.0	2.0	0.9	1.0	1.7	1.8	2.4	2.6	2.2	2.3	1.9	1.3
April	1.8	1.9	0.4	0.9	1.4	1.4	2.5	2.6	2.5	2.7	1.6	1.5
May	1.9	2.0	0.6	0.9	1.9	2.2	2.4	2.7	2.1	2.2	1.3	1.3
June	1.9	2.0	1.0	0.9	1.9	2.2	2.4	2.6	2.1	2.2	1.4	1.4
July	1.8	1.9	0.7	0.9	1.3	1.4	2.6	2.8	2.0	2.1	1.3	1.2
August	1.8	1.9	1.1	1.1	1.7	1.7	2.4	2.7	1.8	1.9	1.4	1.4
September	2.0	2.1	1.2	1.2	1.7	1.9	2.7	2.9	2.3	2.4	1.3	1.2
October	1.9	2.0	1.1	1.2	1.4	1.6	2.6	2.7	2.0	2.2	1.7	1.5
November	1.9	1.9	1.2	1.3	1.3	1.4	2.5	2.7	1.8	1.9	1.5	1.3
December	1.9	2.0	1.2	1.5	1.5	1.6	2.4	2.7	1.7	1.8	1.8	1.5
2010												
January	2.2	2.3	1.1	1.3	1.6	1.7	2.5	3.1	2.0	2.2	1.7	1.3
February	2.0	2.1	1.2	1.4	1.8	2.0	2.4	2.5	2.1	2.3	1.7	1.2
March	2.1	2.2	1.5	1.5	1.9	2.1	2.5	2.7	1.9	2.0	1.8	1.3
April	2.5	2.4	1.5	1.7	1.8	2.0	3.2	2.8	2.1	2.2	2.7	1.3
May	2.2	2.4	1.4	1.7	1.8	1.9	3.5	2.6	2.2	2.2	1.5	1.2
June	2.1	2.3	0.9	1.9	1.8	1.9	3.0	2.4	2.4	2.3	1.4	1.2
July	2.4	2.5	1.8	2.0	1.9	2.0	3.3	2.6	2.7	2.8	1.4	1.2
August	2.3	2.5	1.1	1.6	1.8	1.8	3.4	2.4	2.8	2.9	1.5	1.3
September	2.3	2.4	1.2	1.7	1.9	1.8	3.2	2.6	2.3	2.3	1.6	1.3
October[5]	2.5	2.7	1.0	1.7	1.9	1.9	4.2	3.1	2.5	2.6	1.5	1.3

[1]Includes natural resources and mining, information, financial activities, and other services, not shown separately.
[2]Includes wholesale trade and transportation, warehousing, and utilities, not shown separately.
[3]Includes arts, entertainment, and recreation, not shown separately.
[4]Includes federal government, not shown separately.
[5]Preliminary.

Table 7-8. Hires Levels[1] and Rates,[2] by Industry, December 2000–October 2010

(Seasonally adjusted, levels in thousands, rates per 100.)

Year and month	Level[3]											
	Total[4]	Total private[4]	Construc-tion	Manufac-turing	Trade, transpor-tation, and utilities[5]	Retail trade	Profes-sional and business services	Education and health services	Leisure and hospitality[6]	Accommo-dation and food services	Govern-ment[7]	State and local govern-ment
2000												
December	5 484	5 078	424	536	1 152	861	953	514	944	803	406	360
2001												
January	5 622	5 257	473	499	1 166	841	1 064	467	943	815	365	309
February	5 552	5 153	468	450	1 115	763	978	530	953	803	399	366
March	5 893	5 526	539	469	1 151	832	1 183	564	976	839	368	327
April	5 407	5 044	448	436	1 143	800	810	507	1 082	921	363	327
May	5 454	5 072	442	408	1 236	888	1 027	492	948	797	382	339
June	5 193	4 819	444	397	1 092	810	931	513	925	768	375	329
July	5 223	4 873	456	360	1 113	792	902	530	935	771	350	302
August	5 154	4 750	402	362	1 057	764	933	530	881	738	405	365
September	5 119	4 802	413	356	1 085	794	910	531	955	804	317	287
October	5 097	4 729	425	388	1 078	776	913	514	840	704	368	333
November	5 069	4 718	497	365	1 014	719	878	501	850	727	351	317
December	4 877	4 525	443	373	948	665	897	471	844	714	352	301
2002												
January	4 991	4 645	405	371	1 022	726	890	503	858	746	346	309
February	4 982	4 633	426	398	1 051	701	911	483	848	725	348	300
March	4 799	4 452	402	364	958	653	957	472	812	674	346	299
April	5 055	4 699	420	408	1 060	729	929	500	835	711	356	309
May	5 054	4 678	403	416	1 025	726	998	478	823	698	376	321
June	4 919	4 576	432	397	1 025	719	858	501	811	680	343	301
July	5 190	4 868	475	410	1 052	739	1 005	493	883	716	322	281
August	4 950	4 577	399	379	997	700	950	464	836	705	373	319
September	4 991	4 672	449	401	1 023	720	946	466	837	703	319	256
October	4 881	4 537	432	368	990	702	953	467	796	691	344	286
November	5 018	4 618	424	384	1 012	715	995	453	813	675	401	343
December	4 997	4 680	440	370	1 035	734	972	488	834	687	317	272
2003												
January	5 078	4 718	447	409	953	674	952	512	891	738	360	307
February	4 806	4 495	359	362	1 002	737	946	459	811	682	311	266
March	4 528	4 202	405	343	935	642	748	454	781	644	326	266
April	4 739	4 433	446	330	921	653	930	450	824	684	306	275
May	4 684	4 391	443	324	929	656	820	480	856	699	293	254
June	4 771	4 443	431	341	960	681	880	478	831	709	328	281
July	4 659	4 340	427	338	946	639	894	459	744	635	319	280
August	4 741	4 482	494	357	1 003	686	857	461	837	704	259	220
September	4 894	4 602	470	344	1 022	688	883	510	821	702	292	252
October	5 058	4 715	413	363	1 126	786	920	499	853	720	343	301
November	4 796	4 493	445	378	972	674	875	482	827	695	303	255
December	5 098	4 767	449	374	1 070	739	901	470	910	782	332	282
2004												
January	5 033	4 644	441	369	1 117	761	886	483	842	707	389	332
February	4 823	4 493	432	374	1 049	727	742	482	882	723	330	282
March	5 340	4 982	516	409	1 142	760	945	486	904	771	358	318
April	5 180	4 866	428	413	1 141	798	979	478	870	742	314	263
May	5 072	4 766	451	395	1 072	740	920	463	891	753	305	277
June	5 031	4 719	470	374	1 051	692	924	451	860	731	313	274
July	4 972	4 632	419	386	1 084	760	891	471	859	723	340	300
August	5 181	4 859	451	409	1 100	742	950	497	880	745	321	288
September	5 146	4 791	438	394	1 083	740	911	475	926	743	355	322
October	5 248	4 895	486	388	1 114	775	922	504	909	765	352	308
November	5 283	4 919	452	384	1 159	815	941	501	872	764	365	322
December	5 321	4 982	461	372	1 164	815	1 011	509	874	751	339	286
2005												
January	5 552	5 165	482	371	1 164	790	1 036	511	969	818	387	355
February	5 342	5 008	508	366	1 155	794	1 045	498	852	730	334	294
March	5 355	5 026	459	378	1 164	831	1 023	529	883	760	329	286
April	5 353	5 002	511	365	1 156	799	990	532	878	738	351	303
May	5 356	5 022	498	373	1 160	799	1 001	514	863	737	335	293
June	5 419	5 100	471	355	1 159	804	1 080	522	964	798	319	276
July	5 337	4 993	427	382	1 155	828	1 045	505	908	775	344	306
August	5 538	5 203	534	381	1 158	828	1 091	519	914	780	336	295
September	5 511	5 186	523	390	1 127	785	1 066	541	973	801	325	275
October	5 150	4 829	519	409	1 091	756	886	493	874	764	321	283
November	5 382	5 026	488	394	1 093	705	920	521	954	829	356	310
December	5 238	4 886	461	364	1 143	747	932	512	917	794	353	302

[1]Hires are the number of hires during the entire month.
[2]The hires rate is the number of hires during the entire month as a percent of total employment.
[3]Detail will not necessarily add to totals because of the independent seasonal adjustment of the various series.
[4]Includes natural resources and mining, information, financial activities, and other services, not shown separately.
[5]Includes wholesale trade and transportation, warehousing, and utilities, not shown separately.
[6]Includes arts, entertainment, and recreation, not shown separately.
[7]Includes federal government, not shown separately.

Table 7-8. Hires Levels[1] and Rates,[2] by Industry, December 2000–October 2010—*Continued*

(Seasonally adjusted, levels in thousands, rates per 100.)

Year and month	Rate											
	Total[4]	Total private[4]	Construction	Manufacturing	Trade, transportation, and utilities[5]	Retail trade	Professional and business services	Education and health services	Leisure and hospitality[6]	Accommodation and food services	Government[7]	State and local government
2000												
December	4.1	4.5	6.2	3.1	4.4	5.6	5.7	3.4	7.9	7.9	2.0	2.0
2001												
January	4.2	4.7	6.9	2.9	4.4	5.5	6.3	3.0	7.9	8.0	1.7	1.7
February	4.2	4.6	6.8	2.6	4.2	5.0	5.8	3.4	7.9	7.9	1.9	2.0
March	4.4	5.0	7.9	2.8	4.4	5.4	7.1	3.6	8.1	8.2	1.8	1.8
April	4.1	4.5	6.5	2.6	4.4	5.2	4.9	3.3	9.0	9.0	1.7	1.8
May	4.1	4.6	6.4	2.4	4.7	5.8	6.2	3.2	7.9	7.8	1.8	1.9
June	3.9	4.3	6.5	2.4	4.2	5.3	5.6	3.3	7.7	7.5	1.8	1.8
July	4.0	4.4	6.7	2.2	4.3	5.2	5.5	3.4	7.7	7.5	1.7	1.6
August	3.9	4.3	5.9	2.2	4.1	5.0	5.7	3.4	7.3	7.2	1.9	2.0
September	3.9	4.4	6.1	2.2	4.2	5.2	5.6	3.4	7.9	7.9	1.5	1.6
October	3.9	4.3	6.2	2.4	4.2	5.1	5.6	3.2	7.0	6.9	1.7	1.8
November	3.9	4.3	7.3	2.3	3.9	4.7	5.4	3.2	7.1	7.2	1.6	1.7
December	3.7	4.1	6.5	2.4	3.7	4.4	5.6	3.0	7.1	7.0	1.7	1.6
2002												
January	3.8	4.3	6.0	2.4	4.0	4.8	5.6	3.2	7.1	7.3	1.6	1.7
February	3.8	4.2	6.3	2.6	4.1	4.7	5.7	3.0	7.1	7.1	1.6	1.6
March	3.7	4.1	6.0	2.4	3.8	4.3	6.0	2.9	6.8	6.6	1.6	1.6
April	3.9	4.3	6.3	2.7	4.1	4.8	5.8	3.1	7.0	7.0	1.7	1.7
May	3.9	4.3	6.0	2.7	4.0	4.8	6.2	3.0	6.9	6.9	1.7	1.7
June	3.8	4.2	6.5	2.6	4.0	4.8	5.4	3.1	6.8	6.7	1.6	1.6
July	4.0	4.5	7.1	2.7	4.1	4.9	6.3	3.0	7.4	7.0	1.5	1.5
August	3.8	4.2	5.9	2.5	3.9	4.7	6.0	2.8	7.0	6.9	1.7	1.7
September	3.8	4.3	6.7	2.7	4.0	4.8	5.9	2.9	7.0	6.9	1.5	1.4
October	3.7	4.2	6.5	2.4	3.9	4.7	6.0	2.9	6.6	6.7	1.6	1.5
November	3.9	4.2	6.3	2.6	4.0	4.8	6.2	2.8	6.7	6.6	1.9	1.8
December	3.8	4.3	6.6	2.5	4.1	4.9	6.1	3.0	6.9	6.7	1.5	1.4
2003												
January	3.9	4.3	6.7	2.8	3.8	4.5	6.0	3.1	7.3	7.1	1.7	1.6
February	3.7	4.1	5.4	2.4	4.0	4.9	5.9	2.8	6.7	6.6	1.4	1.4
March	3.5	3.9	6.1	2.3	3.7	4.3	4.7	2.8	6.5	6.3	1.5	1.4
April	3.6	4.1	6.7	2.3	3.6	4.4	5.9	2.7	6.8	6.6	1.4	1.5
May	3.6	4.1	6.6	2.2	3.7	4.4	5.2	2.9	7.1	6.8	1.4	1.4
June	3.7	4.1	6.4	2.4	3.8	4.6	5.5	2.9	6.9	6.9	1.5	1.5
July	3.6	4.0	6.3	2.4	3.8	4.3	5.6	2.8	6.1	6.1	1.5	1.5
August	3.7	4.1	7.3	2.5	4.0	4.6	5.4	2.8	6.9	6.8	1.2	1.2
September	3.8	4.2	6.9	2.4	4.0	4.6	5.5	3.1	6.7	6.7	1.4	1.3
October	3.9	4.3	6.1	2.5	4.4	5.3	5.7	3.0	7.0	6.9	1.6	1.6
November	3.7	4.1	6.5	2.6	3.8	4.5	5.4	2.9	6.7	6.6	1.4	1.4
December	3.9	4.4	6.6	2.6	4.2	5.0	5.6	2.8	7.4	7.5	1.5	1.5
2004												
January	3.9	4.3	6.4	2.6	4.4	5.1	5.5	2.9	6.8	6.7	1.8	1.8
February	3.7	4.1	6.3	2.6	4.1	4.9	4.6	2.9	7.1	6.9	1.5	1.5
March	4.1	4.6	7.5	2.9	4.5	5.1	5.8	2.9	7.3	7.3	1.7	1.7
April	4.0	4.4	6.2	2.9	4.5	5.3	6.0	2.8	7.0	7.0	1.5	1.4
May	3.9	4.3	6.5	2.8	4.2	4.9	5.6	2.7	7.1	7.1	1.4	1.5
June	3.8	4.3	6.7	2.6	4.1	4.6	5.6	2.7	6.9	6.9	1.4	1.5
July	3.8	4.2	6.0	2.7	4.2	5.0	5.4	2.8	6.9	6.8	1.6	1.6
August	3.9	4.4	6.4	2.9	4.3	4.9	5.8	2.9	7.0	7.0	1.5	1.5
September	3.9	4.4	6.2	2.8	4.2	4.9	5.5	2.8	7.4	6.9	1.6	1.7
October	4.0	4.4	6.9	2.7	4.3	5.1	5.6	2.9	7.2	7.1	1.6	1.6
November	4.0	4.5	6.4	2.7	4.5	5.4	5.7	2.9	6.9	7.1	1.7	1.7
December	4.0	4.5	6.5	2.6	4.5	5.4	6.1	3.0	6.9	7.0	1.6	1.5
2005												
January	4.2	4.7	6.8	2.6	4.5	5.2	6.2	3.0	7.6	7.6	1.8	1.9
February	4.0	4.5	7.1	2.6	4.5	5.2	6.3	2.9	6.7	6.7	1.5	1.5
March	4.0	4.5	6.4	2.7	4.5	5.5	6.1	3.1	6.9	7.0	1.5	1.5
April	4.0	4.5	7.0	2.6	4.5	5.2	5.9	3.1	6.9	6.8	1.6	1.6
May	4.0	4.5	6.8	2.6	4.5	5.2	5.9	3.0	6.7	6.8	1.5	1.5
June	4.1	4.6	6.4	2.5	4.5	5.3	6.4	3.0	7.5	7.3	1.5	1.5
July	4.0	4.5	5.8	2.7	4.4	5.4	6.1	2.9	7.1	7.1	1.6	1.6
August	4.1	4.6	7.2	2.7	4.4	5.4	6.4	3.0	7.1	7.1	1.5	1.5
September	4.1	4.6	7.1	2.7	4.3	5.1	6.2	3.1	7.6	7.3	1.5	1.4
October	3.8	4.3	7.0	2.9	4.2	4.9	5.2	2.8	6.8	7.0	1.5	1.5
November	4.0	4.5	6.5	2.8	4.2	4.6	5.3	3.0	7.4	7.6	1.6	1.6
December	3.9	4.3	6.1	2.6	4.4	4.9	5.4	2.9	7.1	7.2	1.6	1.6

[1]Hires are the number of hires during the entire month.
[2]The hires rate is the number of hires during the entire month as a percent of total employment.
[4]Includes natural resources and mining, information, financial activities, and other services, not shown separately.
[5]Includes wholesale trade and transportation, warehousing, and utilities, not shown separately.
[6]Includes arts, entertainment, and recreation, not shown separately.
[7]Includes federal government, not shown separately.

Table 7-8. Hires Levels[1] and Rates,[2] by Industry, December 2000–October 2010—*Continued*

(Seasonally adjusted, levels in thousands, rates per 100.)

Year and month	Level[3]											
	Total[4]	Total private[4]	Construction	Manufacturing	Trade, transportation, and utilities[5]	Retail trade	Professional and business services	Education and health services	Leisure and hospitality[6]	Accommodation and food services	Government[7]	State and local government
2006												
January	5 125	4 834	483	378	1 107	777	920	483	928	818	291	246
February	5 506	5 142	474	377	1 206	835	976	502	989	872	364	309
March	5 412	5 020	470	421	1 132	799	932	492	967	834	392	333
April	5 215	4 845	457	377	1 157	816	865	519	880	757	370	311
May	5 586	5 215	486	394	1 166	810	1 154	583	882	750	371	305
June	5 448	5 062	402	413	1 205	851	1 032	509	922	783	385	319
July	5 563	5 193	463	394	1 173	798	1 015	576	955	806	370	305
August	5 344	4 969	432	388	1 166	778	967	530	913	784	375	306
September	5 388	4 980	407	351	1 133	789	1 025	544	896	780	409	327
October	5 362	5 011	411	344	1 142	795	990	553	938	805	351	313
November	5 586	5 224	466	370	1 127	798	1 094	531	1 036	897	361	310
December	5 375	5 035	451	383	1 088	757	1 000	533	1 001	855	340	294
2007												
January	5 288	4 929	419	390	1 129	792	986	529	927	787	359	304
February	5 262	4 878	330	399	1 138	791	986	524	941	799	384	319
March	5 461	5 068	457	378	1 164	794	980	539	921	781	392	314
April	5 277	4 897	394	375	1 090	728	930	534	976	830	380	309
May	5 398	4 992	403	389	1 112	787	986	547	927	803	406	317
June	5 337	4 948	422	395	1 106	716	894	559	953	807	389	313
July	5 214	4 858	414	380	1 059	719	959	527	916	796	356	263
August	5 228	4 832	398	377	1 063	749	941	546	919	793	396	310
September	5 228	4 843	395	375	1 079	757	953	531	940	792	386	297
October	5 297	4 956	392	385	1 113	772	983	537	945	807	341	306
November	5 221	4 871	388	410	1 113	791	957	546	917	770	349	304
December	5 023	4 650	364	350	1 041	730	906	503	920	787	374	322
2008												
January	4 943	4 612	374	350	1 036	707	882	566	865	730	332	300
February	4 962	4 630	371	322	1 037	714	847	573	931	785	332	294
March	4 914	4 578	400	320	1 004	693	888	568	863	726	337	302
April	4 973	4 652	402	352	1 020	682	897	567	863	746	322	289
May	4 785	4 465	374	331	924	616	846	541	898	760	319	292
June	4 907	4 572	404	325	1 025	701	937	528	822	711	334	308
July	4 653	4 352	382	271	1 014	701	823	545	819	706	301	278
August	4 666	4 362	404	279	982	674	815	535	829	682	305	280
September	4 460	4 167	356	285	926	640	756	506	834	730	293	270
October	4 452	4 159	366	288	934	637	756	533	786	665	293	266
November	4 046	3 766	339	258	800	567	736	508	706	623	280	253
December	4 321	4 044	351	268	940	611	772	527	730	618	277	250
2009												
January	4 330	4 005	358	213	928	572	726	552	725	616	325	286
February	4 095	3 837	344	250	806	546	722	520	702	607	257	248
March	3 935	3 670	314	248	863	564	640	469	697	607	265	241
April	4 182	3 795	339	248	891	646	720	470	691	598	387	244
May	3 962	3 690	328	204	843	562	739	460	683	602	272	251
June	3 856	3 580	268	217	758	519	640	528	689	586	276	251
July	4 065	3 805	338	263	788	526	687	530	717	577	260	227
August	3 975	3 696	278	254	798	545	680	531	711	596	279	252
September	4 091	3 833	349	271	854	566	698	532	693	572	258	236
October	4 001	3 689	325	243	772	518	709	522	663	563	312	271
November	4 160	3 878	329	259	847	554	808	512	693	582	282	247
December	3 997	3 715	335	244	849	547	652	496	657	562	282	254
2010												
January	4 087	3 790	312	289	822	584	729	487	715	613	297	254
February	4 011	3 710	306	267	821	572	767	470	652	564	301	258
March	4 331	3 970	400	279	897	646	744	503	712	598	360	268
April	4 292	3 935	349	305	856	593	780	496	711	584	357	248
May	4 581	3 846	321	266	819	567	805	479	678	573	735	246
June	4 250	3 946	289	267	876	589	825	523	691	564	304	247
July	4 275	3 985	361	297	864	608	810	515	712	593	289	247
August	4 156	3 891	357	274	798	571	831	492	688	579	264	228
September	4 208	3 953	336	260	863	606	818	514	714	595	254	222
October[8]	4 196	3 929	370	269	849	603	778	482	688	588	267	234

[1] Hires are the number of hires during the entire month.
[2] The hires rate is the number of hires during the entire month as a percent of total employment.
[3] Detail will not necessarily add to totals because of the independent seasonal adjustment of the various series.
[4] Includes natural resources and mining, information, financial activities, and other services, not shown separately.
[5] Includes wholesale trade and transportation, warehousing, and utilities, not shown separately.
[6] Includes arts, entertainment, and recreation, not shown separately.
[7] Includes federal government, not shown separately.
[8] Preliminary.

Table 7-8. Hires Levels[1] and Rates,[2] by Industry, December 2000–October 2010—*Continued*

(Seasonally adjusted, levels in thousands, rates per 100.)

Year and month	Rate											
	Total[4]	Total private[4]	Construction	Manufacturing	Trade, transportation, and utilities[5]	Retail trade	Professional and business services	Education and health services	Leisure and hospitality[6]	Accommodation and food services	Government[7]	State and local government
2006												
January	3.8	4.3	6.4	2.7	4.2	5.1	5.3	2.7	7.2	7.4	1.3	1.3
February	4.1	4.5	6.2	2.7	4.6	5.4	5.6	2.8	7.6	7.9	1.7	1.6
March	4.0	4.4	6.1	3.0	4.3	5.2	5.3	2.8	7.4	7.5	1.8	1.7
April	3.8	4.3	5.9	2.6	4.4	5.3	5.0	2.9	6.7	6.8	1.7	1.6
May	4.1	4.6	6.3	2.8	4.4	5.3	6.6	3.3	6.8	6.7	1.7	1.6
June	4.0	4.4	5.2	2.9	4.6	5.6	5.9	2.9	7.1	7.0	1.8	1.7
July	4.1	4.5	6.0	2.8	4.5	5.2	5.8	3.2	7.3	7.2	1.7	1.6
August	3.9	4.3	5.6	2.7	4.4	5.1	5.5	3.0	6.9	7.0	1.7	1.6
September	3.9	4.4	5.3	2.5	4.3	5.1	5.8	3.0	6.8	7.0	1.9	1.7
October	3.9	4.4	5.3	2.4	4.3	5.2	5.6	3.1	7.1	7.2	1.6	1.6
November	4.1	4.6	6.1	2.6	4.3	5.2	6.2	2.9	7.8	7.9	1.6	1.6
December	3.9	4.4	5.9	2.7	4.1	4.9	5.6	3.0	7.5	7.5	1.5	1.5
2007												
January	3.9	4.3	5.4	2.8	4.3	5.1	5.5	2.9	7.0	6.9	1.6	1.6
February	3.8	4.2	4.3	2.8	4.3	5.1	5.5	2.9	7.1	7.0	1.7	1.6
March	4.0	4.4	5.9	2.7	4.4	5.1	5.5	3.0	6.9	6.9	1.8	1.6
April	3.8	4.2	5.1	2.7	4.1	4.7	5.2	2.9	7.3	7.3	1.7	1.6
May	3.9	4.3	5.3	2.8	4.2	5.1	5.5	3.0	6.9	7.0	1.8	1.6
June	3.9	4.3	5.5	2.8	4.2	4.6	5.0	3.1	7.1	7.0	1.8	1.6
July	3.8	4.2	5.4	2.7	4.0	4.6	5.3	2.9	6.8	6.9	1.6	1.4
August	3.8	4.2	5.2	2.7	4.0	4.8	5.2	3.0	6.8	6.9	1.8	1.6
September	3.8	4.2	5.2	2.7	4.0	4.9	5.3	2.9	7.0	6.9	1.7	1.5
October	3.8	4.3	5.2	2.8	4.2	5.0	5.5	2.9	7.0	7.0	1.5	1.6
November	3.8	4.2	5.1	3.0	4.2	5.1	5.3	3.0	6.8	6.7	1.6	1.6
December	3.6	4.0	4.9	2.6	3.9	4.7	5.0	2.7	6.8	6.8	1.7	1.6
2008												
January	3.6	4.0	5.0	2.5	3.9	4.5	4.9	3.0	6.4	6.3	1.5	1.5
February	3.6	4.0	5.0	2.4	3.9	4.6	4.7	3.1	6.9	6.8	1.5	1.5
March	3.6	4.0	5.4	2.3	3.8	4.5	4.9	3.0	6.4	6.3	1.5	1.5
April	3.6	4.0	5.5	2.6	3.8	4.4	5.0	3.0	6.4	6.5	1.4	1.5
May	3.5	3.9	5.1	2.4	3.5	4.0	4.7	2.9	6.7	6.6	1.4	1.5
June	3.6	4.0	5.6	2.4	3.9	4.6	5.3	2.8	6.1	6.2	1.5	1.6
July	3.4	3.8	5.3	2.0	3.8	4.6	4.6	2.9	6.1	6.2	1.3	1.4
August	3.4	3.8	5.7	2.1	3.7	4.4	4.6	2.8	6.2	6.0	1.4	1.4
September	3.3	3.7	5.1	2.2	3.5	4.2	4.3	2.7	6.2	6.4	1.3	1.4
October	3.3	3.7	5.3	2.2	3.6	4.2	4.3	2.8	5.9	5.8	1.3	1.3
November	3.0	3.3	5.0	2.0	3.1	3.8	4.2	2.7	5.3	5.5	1.2	1.3
December	3.2	3.6	5.2	2.1	3.7	4.1	4.5	2.8	5.5	5.5	1.2	1.3
2009												
January	3.2	3.6	5.5	1.7	3.6	3.9	4.2	2.9	5.5	5.5	1.4	1.4
February	3.1	3.5	5.4	2.0	3.2	3.7	4.3	2.7	5.3	5.4	1.1	1.3
March	3.0	3.4	5.0	2.0	3.4	3.9	3.8	2.5	5.3	5.4	1.2	1.2
April	3.2	3.5	5.5	2.1	3.6	4.4	4.3	2.5	5.3	5.3	1.7	1.2
May	3.0	3.4	5.4	1.7	3.4	3.9	4.5	2.4	5.2	5.4	1.2	1.3
June	3.0	3.3	4.4	1.8	3.0	3.6	3.9	2.8	5.3	5.2	1.2	1.3
July	3.1	3.5	5.7	2.2	3.2	3.6	4.2	2.8	5.5	5.2	1.2	1.2
August	3.1	3.4	4.7	2.2	3.2	3.8	4.2	2.8	5.4	5.3	1.2	1.3
September	3.2	3.6	6.0	2.3	3.4	3.9	4.3	2.8	5.3	5.1	1.1	1.2
October	3.1	3.4	5.7	2.1	3.1	3.6	4.3	2.7	5.1	5.1	1.4	1.4
November	3.2	3.6	5.7	2.2	3.4	3.9	4.9	2.7	5.3	5.2	1.3	1.3
December	3.1	3.5	5.9	2.1	3.4	3.8	4.0	2.6	5.1	5.1	1.3	1.3
2010												
January	3.2	3.5	5.6	2.5	3.3	4.1	4.4	2.5	5.5	5.5	1.3	1.3
February	3.1	3.5	5.5	2.3	3.3	4.0	4.6	2.4	5.0	5.1	1.3	1.3
March	3.3	3.7	7.1	2.4	3.6	4.5	4.5	2.6	5.5	5.4	1.6	1.4
April	3.3	3.7	6.2	2.6	3.5	4.1	4.7	2.5	5.4	5.2	1.6	1.3
May	3.5	3.6	5.7	2.3	3.3	3.9	4.8	2.5	5.2	5.1	3.2	1.3
June	3.3	3.7	5.2	2.3	3.5	4.1	4.9	2.7	5.3	5.0	1.3	1.3
July	3.3	3.7	6.4	2.5	3.5	4.2	4.8	2.6	5.4	5.3	1.3	1.3
August	3.2	3.6	6.4	2.3	3.2	4.0	5.0	2.5	5.2	5.2	1.2	1.2
September	3.2	3.7	6.0	2.2	3.5	4.2	4.9	2.6	5.4	5.3	1.1	1.1
October[8]	3.2	3.6	6.6	2.3	3.4	4.2	4.6	2.4	5.2	5.2	1.2	1.2

[1] Hires are the number of hires during the entire month.
[2] The hires rate is the number of hires during the entire month as a percent of total employment.
[4] Includes natural resources and mining, information, financial activities, and other services, not shown separately.
[5] Includes wholesale trade and transportation, warehousing, and utilities, not shown separately.
[6] Includes arts, entertainment, and recreation, not shown separately.
[7] Includes federal government, not shown separately.
[8] Preliminary.

Table 7-9. Separations Levels[1] and Rates,[2] by Industry, December 2000–October 2010

(Seasonally adjusted, levels in thousands, rates per 100.)

Year and month	Level[3]											
	Total[4]	Total private[4]	Construc-tion	Manufac-turing	Trade, transpor-tation, and utilities[5]	Retail trade	Profes-sional and business services	Education and health services	Leisure and hospitality[6]	Accommo-dation and food services	Govern-ment[7]	State and local govern-ment
2000												
December	5 441	5 044	432	540	1 127	837	946	521	928	793	397	359
2001												
January	5 683	5 330	441	547	1 256	868	1 076	427	960	821	353	290
February	5 455	5 126	465	533	1 146	774	994	491	876	733	329	293
March	5 912	5 588	493	562	1 245	904	1 229	498	980	852	324	288
April	5 598	5 284	459	559	1 241	873	909	464	1 020	895	314	277
May	5 559	5 214	443	554	1 231	866	1 123	438	910	774	345	307
June	5 378	5 092	460	559	1 155	818	1 027	480	885	733	286	257
July	5 455	5 142	453	508	1 179	834	978	473	945	787	313	272
August	5 240	4 875	408	502	1 056	755	979	461	894	744	364	325
September	5 309	5 046	427	465	1 149	805	994	466	996	835	262	226
October	5 496	5 160	429	560	1 169	813	1 004	485	909	768	336	293
November	5 317	5 023	522	494	1 084	723	946	462	906	753	294	259
December	5 002	4 692	443	487	1 014	707	923	425	847	712	310	258
2002												
January	5 170	4 829	420	472	1 082	753	952	461	834	709	341	299
February	5 095	4 758	443	473	1 083	726	933	443	847	720	337	289
March	4 818	4 518	399	436	1 021	687	940	427	815	679	300	254
April	5 078	4 732	462	450	1 043	712	899	462	853	710	346	297
May	5 116	4 810	432	478	1 032	733	1 050	450	806	680	305	267
June	4 926	4 604	424	451	1 040	727	887	409	817	685	322	275
July	5 391	5 050	491	468	1 040	730	1 098	459	909	726	341	293
August	4 912	4 592	374	458	1 048	750	912	437	808	673	320	274
September	4 989	4 663	444	445	1 048	736	962	434	789	686	325	274
October	4 792	4 464	439	445	980	698	922	441	733	643	329	280
November	4 956	4 585	403	437	1 031	716	967	415	797	666	371	318
December	5 099	4 797	447	452	1 004	707	1 031	479	823	684	303	261
2003												
January	5 038	4 697	453	444	1 008	708	903	469	846	699	342	286
February	4 941	4 628	401	443	1 054	791	917	436	822	685	313	268
March	4 747	4 411	409	403	1 019	697	819	436	805	655	337	281
April	4 756	4 431	410	437	907	622	930	392	827	679	326	271
May	4 735	4 414	428	381	963	663	805	462	843	694	321	270
June	4 806	4 515	423	412	996	685	883	471	787	669	292	251
July	4 713	4 398	416	442	966	640	858	455	741	642	314	275
August	4 736	4 406	453	377	976	662	858	451	801	666	330	283
September	4 734	4 420	443	371	977	661	824	465	792	672	314	276
October	4 874	4 588	406	387	1 095	767	870	452	817	687	286	236
November	4 734	4 412	435	384	988	690	816	450	815	675	323	263
December	4 912	4 598	411	385	1 059	731	845	441	866	742	315	280
2004												
January	4 919	4 505	434	375	1 033	728	878	451	826	699	414	340
February	4 757	4 440	447	383	1 048	731	732	473	835	688	317	267
March	5 028	4 713	456	402	1 104	740	920	442	852	728	315	277
April	4 930	4 635	413	384	1 101	770	893	445	844	706	295	262
May	4 803	4 501	406	374	1 033	708	847	447	844	719	301	255
June	4 975	4 651	463	387	1 015	667	924	429	840	710	324	282
July	4 990	4 623	404	396	1 092	775	873	438	873	736	367	329
August	5 024	4 731	411	395	1 075	736	925	456	884	747	293	261
September	4 924	4 604	409	406	1 022	708	871	484	847	692	320	289
October	4 897	4 571	432	389	1 070	748	806	403	889	748	326	276
November	5 171	4 844	440	398	1 146	801	920	485	849	730	327	289
December	5 134	4 795	429	387	1 128	820	976	467	846	714	339	286
2005												
January	5 432	5 079	521	395	1 126	757	984	476	943	804	354	318
February	5 087	4 767	457	354	1 083	755	972	492	821	700	320	282
March	5 263	4 932	423	388	1 178	857	1 003	514	858	740	331	293
April	5 016	4 670	424	379	1 069	739	964	495	783	669	346	285
May	5 253	4 947	473	378	1 127	778	983	480	875	741	306	276
June	5 154	4 829	436	383	1 107	765	996	464	928	764	325	279
July	5 029	4 743	408	400	1 093	791	976	446	885	764	286	245
August	5 313	4 991	480	396	1 125	806	1 034	487	885	767	322	285
September	5 374	5 048	497	417	1 142	806	966	501	978	813	327	280
October	5 043	4 712	466	392	1 074	755	869	469	901	778	331	294
November	5 013	4 687	427	388	1 050	686	819	484	902	783	326	287
December	5 040	4 706	450	348	1 121	747	889	484	892	763	334	274

[1] Total separations are the number of separations during the entire month.
[2] The total separations rate is the number of total separations during the entire month as a percent of total employment.
[3] Detail will not necessarily add to totals because of the independent seasonal adjustment of the various series.
[4] Includes natural resources and mining, information, financial activities, and other services, not shown separately.
[5] Includes wholesale trade and transportation, warehousing, and utilities, not shown separately.
[6] Includes arts, entertainment, and recreation, not shown separately.
[7] Includes federal government, not shown separately.

Table 7-9. Separations Levels[1] and Rates,[2] by Industry, December 2000–October 2010—*Continued*

(Seasonally adjusted, levels in thousands, rates per 100.)

Year and month	Rate											
	Total[4]	Total private[4]	Construc-tion	Manufac-turing	Trade, transpor-tation, and utilities[5]	Retail trade	Profes-sional and business services	Education and health services	Leisure and hospitality[6]	Accommo-dation and food services	Govern-ment[7]	State and local govern-ment
2000												
December	4.1	4.5	6.4	3.1	4.3	5.4	5.6	3.4	7.7	7.8	1.9	2.0
2001												
January	4.3	4.8	6.5	3.2	4.8	5.6	6.4	2.8	8.0	8.1	1.7	1.6
February	4.1	4.6	6.8	3.1	4.4	5.0	5.9	3.2	7.3	7.2	1.6	1.6
March	4.5	5.0	7.2	3.3	4.8	5.9	7.3	3.2	8.2	8.4	1.5	1.6
April	4.2	4.8	6.7	3.3	4.8	5.7	5.5	3.0	8.5	8.8	1.5	1.5
May	4.2	4.7	6.5	3.3	4.7	5.7	6.8	2.8	7.5	7.6	1.6	1.7
June	4.1	4.6	6.7	3.4	4.4	5.4	6.2	3.1	7.3	7.2	1.4	1.4
July	4.1	4.6	6.6	3.1	4.5	5.5	5.9	3.0	7.8	7.7	1.5	1.5
August	4.0	4.4	6.0	3.1	4.1	5.0	6.0	2.9	7.4	7.3	1.7	1.8
September	4.0	4.6	6.3	2.9	4.4	5.3	6.1	3.0	8.3	8.2	1.2	1.2
October	4.2	4.7	6.3	3.5	4.5	5.4	6.2	3.1	7.6	7.5	1.6	1.6
November	4.1	4.6	7.7	3.1	4.2	4.8	5.9	2.9	7.6	7.4	1.4	1.4
December	3.8	4.3	6.5	3.1	4.0	4.7	5.7	2.7	7.1	7.0	1.5	1.4
2002												
January	4.0	4.4	6.2	3.0	4.2	5.0	5.9	2.9	6.9	7.0	1.6	1.6
February	3.9	4.4	6.6	3.1	4.2	4.8	5.8	2.8	7.1	7.1	1.6	1.5
March	3.7	4.1	5.9	2.8	4.0	4.6	5.9	2.7	6.8	6.7	1.4	1.4
April	3.9	4.3	6.9	2.9	4.1	4.7	5.6	2.9	7.2	7.0	1.6	1.6
May	3.9	4.4	6.5	3.1	4.0	4.9	6.6	2.8	6.8	6.7	1.4	1.4
June	3.8	4.2	6.3	2.9	4.1	4.8	5.5	2.5	6.9	6.8	1.5	1.5
July	4.1	4.6	7.3	3.1	4.1	4.9	6.9	2.8	7.6	7.1	1.6	1.6
August	3.8	4.2	5.6	3.0	4.1	5.0	5.7	2.7	6.8	6.6	1.5	1.5
September	3.8	4.3	6.6	2.9	4.1	4.9	6.0	2.7	6.6	6.7	1.5	1.5
October	3.7	4.1	6.6	3.0	3.9	4.7	5.8	2.7	6.1	6.3	1.5	1.5
November	3.8	4.2	6.0	2.9	4.1	4.8	6.1	2.5	6.6	6.5	1.7	1.7
December	3.9	4.4	6.7	3.0	3.9	4.7	6.5	2.9	6.8	6.6	1.4	1.4
2003												
January	3.9	4.3	6.8	3.0	4.0	4.7	5.7	2.9	6.9	6.8	1.6	1.5
February	3.8	4.3	6.0	3.0	4.2	5.3	5.7	2.6	6.8	6.6	1.4	1.4
March	3.7	4.1	6.2	2.7	4.0	4.7	5.2	2.6	6.6	6.4	1.6	1.5
April	3.7	4.1	6.1	3.0	3.6	4.2	5.9	2.4	6.8	6.6	1.5	1.4
May	3.6	4.1	6.4	2.6	3.8	4.5	5.1	2.8	7.0	6.7	1.5	1.4
June	3.7	4.2	6.3	2.8	3.9	4.6	5.5	2.8	6.5	6.5	1.4	1.3
July	3.6	4.1	6.2	3.1	3.8	4.3	5.4	2.7	6.1	6.2	1.5	1.5
August	3.6	4.1	6.7	2.6	3.9	4.4	5.4	2.7	6.6	6.4	1.5	1.5
September	3.6	4.1	6.5	2.6	3.9	4.4	5.1	2.8	6.5	6.5	1.5	1.5
October	3.7	4.2	6.0	2.7	4.3	5.1	5.4	2.7	6.7	6.6	1.3	1.3
November	3.6	4.1	6.4	2.7	3.9	4.6	5.1	2.7	6.6	6.5	1.5	1.4
December	3.8	4.2	6.0	2.7	4.2	4.9	5.2	2.6	7.0	7.1	1.5	1.5
2004												
January	3.8	4.1	6.3	2.6	4.1	4.9	5.4	2.7	6.7	6.7	1.9	1.8
February	3.6	4.1	6.5	2.7	4.1	4.9	4.5	2.8	6.7	6.5	1.5	1.4
March	3.8	4.3	6.6	2.8	4.3	4.9	5.7	2.6	6.9	6.9	1.5	1.5
April	3.8	4.2	6.0	2.7	4.3	5.1	5.5	2.6	6.8	6.7	1.4	1.4
May	3.7	4.1	5.8	2.6	4.1	4.7	5.2	2.6	6.8	6.8	1.4	1.3
June	3.8	4.2	6.6	2.7	4.0	4.4	5.6	2.5	6.7	6.7	1.5	1.5
July	3.8	4.2	5.8	2.8	4.3	5.1	5.3	2.6	7.0	6.9	1.7	1.7
August	3.8	4.3	5.9	2.8	4.2	4.9	5.6	2.7	7.1	7.0	1.4	1.4
September	3.7	4.2	5.8	2.8	4.0	4.7	5.3	2.9	6.8	6.5	1.5	1.5
October	3.7	4.1	6.1	2.7	4.2	4.9	4.9	2.4	7.1	7.0	1.5	1.5
November	3.9	4.4	6.2	2.8	4.5	5.3	5.5	2.8	6.7	6.8	1.5	1.5
December	3.9	4.3	6.0	2.7	4.4	5.4	5.9	2.7	6.7	6.6	1.6	1.5
2005												
January	4.1	4.6	7.3	2.8	4.4	5.0	5.9	2.8	7.4	7.4	1.6	1.7
February	3.8	4.3	6.4	2.5	4.2	5.0	5.8	2.9	6.5	6.5	1.5	1.5
March	4.0	4.4	5.9	2.7	4.6	5.6	6.0	3.0	6.7	6.8	1.5	1.5
April	3.8	4.2	5.8	2.7	4.1	4.8	5.7	2.9	6.1	6.1	1.6	1.5
May	3.9	4.4	6.5	2.6	4.3	5.1	5.8	2.8	6.8	6.8	1.4	1.4
June	3.9	4.3	5.9	2.7	4.3	5.0	5.9	2.7	7.2	7.0	1.5	1.5
July	3.8	4.2	5.5	2.8	4.2	5.2	5.7	2.6	6.9	7.0	1.3	1.3
August	4.0	4.4	6.5	2.8	4.3	5.2	6.1	2.8	6.9	7.0	1.5	1.5
September	4.0	4.5	6.7	2.9	4.4	5.3	5.6	2.9	7.6	7.4	1.5	1.5
October	3.8	4.2	6.3	2.8	4.1	4.9	5.1	2.7	7.0	7.1	1.5	1.5
November	3.7	4.2	5.7	2.7	4.0	4.5	4.8	2.8	7.0	7.1	1.5	1.5
December	3.7	4.2	6.0	2.5	4.3	4.9	5.2	2.8	6.9	6.9	1.5	1.4

[1]Total separations are the number of separations during the entire month.
[2]The total separations rate is the number of total separations during the entire month as a percent of total employment.
[4]Includes natural resources and mining, information, financial activities, and other services, not shown separately.
[5]Includes wholesale trade and transportation, warehousing, and utilities, not shown separately.
[6]Includes arts, entertainment, and recreation, not shown separately.
[7]Includes federal government, not shown separately.

Table 7-9. Separations Levels[1] and Rates,[2] by Industry, December 2000–October 2010—*Continued*

(Seasonally adjusted, levels in thousands, rates per 100.)

Year and month	Level[3]											
	Total[4]	Total private[4]	Construction	Manufacturing	Trade, transportation, and utilities[5]	Retail trade	Professional and business services	Education and health services	Leisure and hospitality[6]	Accommodation and food services	Government[7]	State and local government
2006												
January	4 873	4 544	422	364	1 061	769	881	423	896	783	329	277
February	5 179	4 844	409	379	1 150	813	913	450	956	843	335	285
March	5 161	4 805	449	425	1 120	794	860	461	920	789	356	296
April	5 061	4 708	424	357	1 141	830	878	495	838	734	353	293
May	5 628	5 258	495	429	1 196	861	1 087	581	917	768	370	306
June	5 324	4 949	417	403	1 172	835	952	500	917	781	374	312
July	5 377	5 042	452	434	1 150	800	967	539	886	757	335	274
August	5 185	4 836	412	409	1 156	772	924	488	885	761	349	276
September	5 224	4 871	412	386	1 107	776	1 010	473	885	765	354	278
October	5 265	4 939	439	391	1 095	757	995	505	893	773	325	282
November	5 364	5 017	480	397	1 093	778	1 005	490	965	832	347	296
December	5 190	4 856	432	406	1 040	751	980	500	952	813	335	289
2007												
January	5 086	4 739	399	392	1 064	740	925	485	909	770	347	291
February	5 178	4 819	422	424	1 065	740	956	487	920	782	359	293
March	5 278	4 916	374	410	1 121	753	962	499	916	772	362	283
April	5 188	4 835	409	385	1 066	727	944	484	948	801	353	280
May	5 330	4 946	419	411	1 112	799	939	526	920	791	384	296
June	5 208	4 849	408	419	1 104	734	865	511	935	798	359	278
July	5 267	4 842	443	407	1 040	713	954	481	922	795	424	335
August	5 281	4 926	446	427	1 067	748	942	498	913	792	355	282
September	5 113	4 802	421	420	1 063	752	936	473	884	755	311	227
October	5 149	4 840	405	410	1 096	760	950	484	897	765	309	271
November	5 110	4 792	410	407	1 078	743	943	528	878	737	318	284
December	4 966	4 639	413	366	1 048	728	878	467	910	779	327	291
2008												
January	4 956	4 632	408	365	1 046	715	886	509	872	736	324	268
February	5 040	4 740	404	367	1 058	729	902	527	930	782	300	267
March	4 994	4 689	432	360	1 022	708	940	530	867	732	305	275
April	5 093	4 791	460	384	1 082	736	918	516	875	756	302	275
May	5 087	4 789	439	368	1 032	704	908	512	964	802	298	274
June	5 021	4 731	468	378	1 086	738	934	485	831	724	290	266
July	4 883	4 604	433	348	1 072	739	888	495	846	724	279	259
August	4 980	4 683	449	357	1 088	740	904	491	843	699	298	279
September	4 872	4 586	422	376	1 052	708	822	494	872	753	286	269
October	4 948	4 656	449	420	1 053	701	889	508	809	688	292	267
November	4 798	4 530	489	381	1 002	686	891	471	765	675	268	247
December	5 040	4 755	455	455	1 119	709	912	503	763	652	285	262
2009												
January	5 121	4 833	523	502	1 085	662	855	499	757	644	288	267
February	4 869	4 588	465	433	936	602	918	508	732	632	281	260
March	4 710	4 444	458	413	1 011	649	782	470	756	655	266	248
April	4 651	4 396	449	378	986	674	862	474	723	611	256	235
May	4 401	4 076	393	364	905	597	790	427	684	596	325	250
June	4 310	3 968	352	351	823	547	722	496	706	594	343	264
July	4 424	4 102	417	309	880	577	744	507	715	585	322	297
August	4 166	3 883	335	297	826	558	711	501	718	602	283	259
September	4 274	3 990	415	313	916	605	705	503	677	591	284	267
October	4 171	3 901	381	293	844	567	717	473	707	579	269	242
November	4 130	3 846	347	285	853	544	706	486	716	600	284	249
December	4 195	3 884	382	273	901	567	649	486	688	578	311	283
2010												
January	4 155	3 858	405	276	856	577	698	457	709	598	296	269
February	3 969	3 663	362	260	806	551	716	440	621	543	306	273
March	4 048	3 743	365	245	866	620	699	455	677	558	305	268
April	4 013	3 726	345	249	803	551	733	475	684	570	287	248
May	4 146	3 816	340	238	800	574	806	446	707	585	331	263
June	4 436	3 884	314	260	874	604	777	493	668	555	552	275
July	4 390	3 940	361	271	855	613	830	491	701	580	450	268
August	4 210	3 796	321	279	814	583	808	454	663	557	414	267
September	4 139	3 761	334	261	813	569	774	487	675	570	378	269
October[8]	4 047	3 768	346	271	806	560	770	434	693	586	279	239

[1]Total separations are the number of separations during the entire month.
[2]The total separations rate is the number of total separations during the entire month as a percent of total employment.
[3]Detail will not necessarily add to totals because of the independent seasonal adjustment of the various series.
[4]Includes natural resources and mining, information, financial activities, and other services, not shown separately.
[5]Includes wholesale trade and transportation, warehousing, and utilities, not shown separately.
[6]Includes arts, entertainment, and recreation, not shown separately.
[7]Includes federal government, not shown separately.
[8]Preliminary.

Table 7-9. Separations Levels[1] and Rates,[2] by Industry, December 2000–October 2010—Continued

(Seasonally adjusted, levels in thousands, rates per 100.)

Year and month	Total[4]	Total private[4]	Construc-tion	Manufac-turing	Trade, transpor-tation, and utilities[5]	Retail trade	Profes-sional and business services	Education and health services	Leisure and hospitality[6]	Accommo-dation and food services	Govern-ment[7]	State and local govern-ment
2006												
January	3.6	4.0	5.6	2.6	4.1	5.0	5.1	2.4	6.9	7.1	1.5	1.4
February	3.8	4.3	5.3	2.7	4.4	5.3	5.3	2.5	7.4	7.6	1.5	1.5
March	3.8	4.2	5.8	3.0	4.3	5.2	4.9	2.6	7.1	7.1	1.6	1.5
April	3.7	4.1	5.5	2.5	4.4	5.4	5.0	2.8	6.4	6.6	1.6	1.5
May	4.1	4.6	6.4	3.0	4.6	5.6	6.2	3.3	7.0	6.9	1.7	1.6
June	3.9	4.3	5.4	2.8	4.5	5.4	5.4	2.8	7.0	7.0	1.7	1.6
July	3.9	4.4	5.9	3.1	4.4	5.2	5.5	3.0	6.7	6.8	1.5	1.4
August	3.8	4.2	5.3	2.9	4.4	5.0	5.2	2.7	6.7	6.8	1.6	1.4
September	3.8	4.3	5.3	2.7	4.2	5.1	5.7	2.6	6.7	6.8	1.6	1.4
October	3.9	4.3	5.7	2.8	4.2	4.9	5.6	2.8	6.8	6.9	1.5	1.5
November	3.9	4.4	6.3	2.8	4.1	5.1	5.7	2.7	7.3	7.4	1.6	1.5
December	3.8	4.2	5.6	2.9	3.9	4.9	5.5	2.8	7.2	7.2	1.5	1.5
2007												
January	3.7	4.1	5.2	2.8	4.0	4.8	5.2	2.7	6.8	6.8	1.6	1.5
February	3.8	4.2	5.5	3.0	4.0	4.8	5.3	2.7	6.9	6.9	1.6	1.5
March	3.8	4.3	4.8	2.9	4.2	4.8	5.4	2.7	6.9	6.8	1.6	1.5
April	3.8	4.2	5.3	2.8	4.0	4.7	5.3	2.7	7.1	7.0	1.6	1.4
May	3.9	4.3	5.5	3.0	4.2	5.1	5.2	2.9	6.9	6.9	1.7	1.5
June	3.8	4.2	5.3	3.0	4.1	4.7	4.8	2.8	7.0	7.0	1.6	1.4
July	3.8	4.2	5.8	2.9	3.9	4.6	5.3	2.6	6.9	6.9	1.9	1.7
August	3.8	4.3	5.9	3.1	4.0	4.8	5.2	2.7	6.8	6.9	1.6	1.4
September	3.7	4.2	5.6	3.0	4.0	4.8	5.2	2.6	6.6	6.6	1.4	1.2
October	3.7	4.2	5.4	3.0	4.1	4.9	5.3	2.6	6.6	6.6	1.4	1.4
November	3.7	4.1	5.4	3.0	4.0	4.8	5.2	2.9	6.5	6.4	1.4	1.5
December	3.6	4.0	5.5	2.7	3.9	4.7	4.9	2.5	6.7	6.7	1.5	1.5
2008												
January	3.6	4.0	5.5	2.7	3.9	4.6	4.9	2.7	6.4	6.4	1.4	1.4
February	3.7	4.1	5.4	2.7	4.0	4.7	5.0	2.8	6.9	6.8	1.3	1.4
March	3.6	4.1	5.8	2.6	3.8	4.6	5.2	2.8	6.4	6.3	1.4	1.4
April	3.7	4.2	6.3	2.8	4.1	4.8	5.1	2.7	6.5	6.6	1.3	1.4
May	3.7	4.2	6.0	2.7	3.9	4.6	5.1	2.7	7.1	7.0	1.3	1.4
June	3.7	4.1	6.5	2.8	4.1	4.8	5.2	2.6	6.2	6.3	1.3	1.3
July	3.6	4.0	6.0	2.6	4.1	4.8	5.0	2.6	6.3	6.3	1.2	1.3
August	3.6	4.1	6.3	2.7	4.1	4.9	5.1	2.6	6.3	6.1	1.3	1.4
September	3.6	4.0	6.0	2.8	4.0	4.7	4.7	2.6	6.5	6.6	1.3	1.4
October	3.6	4.1	6.5	3.2	4.1	4.6	5.1	2.7	6.1	6.0	1.3	1.3
November	3.6	4.0	7.2	2.9	3.9	4.6	5.1	2.5	5.8	6.0	1.2	1.2
December	3.8	4.3	6.8	3.5	4.4	4.8	5.3	2.6	5.8	5.8	1.3	1.3
2009												
January	3.8	4.4	8.0	4.0	4.3	4.5	5.0	2.6	5.7	5.7	1.3	1.3
February	3.7	4.2	7.2	3.5	3.7	4.1	5.4	2.7	5.6	5.6	1.2	1.3
March	3.6	4.1	7.3	3.4	4.0	4.4	4.7	2.5	5.8	5.8	1.2	1.3
April	3.5	4.0	7.3	3.1	3.9	4.6	5.2	2.5	5.5	5.5	1.1	1.2
May	3.4	3.8	6.4	3.1	3.6	4.1	4.8	2.2	5.2	5.3	1.4	1.3
June	3.3	3.7	5.8	3.0	3.3	3.8	4.4	2.6	5.4	5.3	1.5	1.3
July	3.4	3.8	7.0	2.6	3.5	4.0	4.5	2.6	5.5	5.2	1.4	1.5
August	3.2	3.6	5.7	2.5	3.3	3.9	4.3	2.6	5.5	5.4	1.3	1.3
September	3.3	3.7	7.1	2.7	3.7	4.2	4.3	2.6	5.2	5.3	1.3	1.4
October	3.2	3.6	6.6	2.5	3.4	3.9	4.4	2.5	5.4	5.2	1.2	1.2
November	3.2	3.6	6.1	2.5	3.5	3.8	4.3	2.5	5.5	5.4	1.3	1.3
December	3.2	3.6	6.7	2.4	3.7	3.9	3.9	2.5	5.3	5.2	1.4	1.4
2010												
January	3.2	3.6	7.2	2.4	3.5	4.0	4.2	2.4	5.5	5.4	1.3	1.4
February	3.1	3.4	6.5	2.3	3.3	3.8	4.3	2.3	4.8	4.9	1.4	1.4
March	3.1	3.5	6.5	2.1	3.5	4.3	4.2	2.3	5.2	5.0	1.4	1.4
April	3.1	3.5	6.1	2.1	3.2	3.8	4.4	2.4	5.2	5.1	1.3	1.3
May	3.2	3.5	6.1	2.0	3.2	4.0	4.8	2.3	5.4	5.2	1.4	1.3
June	3.4	3.6	5.6	2.2	3.5	4.2	4.7	2.5	5.1	5.0	2.4	1.4
July	3.4	3.7	6.5	2.3	3.5	4.2	5.0	2.5	5.3	5.2	2.0	1.4
August	3.2	3.5	5.7	2.4	3.3	4.0	4.8	2.3	5.0	5.0	1.8	1.4
September	3.2	3.5	5.9	2.2	3.3	3.9	4.6	2.5	5.1	5.1	1.7	1.4
October[8]	3.1	3.5	6.2	2.3	3.2	3.9	4.6	2.2	5.3	5.2	1.3	1.2

[1]Total separations are the number of separations during the entire month.
[2]The total separations rate is the number of total separations during the entire month as a percent of total employment.
[4]Includes natural resources and mining, information, financial activities, and other services, not shown separately.
[5]Includes wholesale trade and transportation, warehousing, and utilities, not shown separately.
[6]Includes arts, entertainment, and recreation, not shown separately.
[7]Includes federal government, not shown separately.
[8]Preliminary.

Table 7-10. Quits Levels[1] and Rates,[2] by Industry, December 2000–October 2010

(Seasonally adjusted, levels in thousands, rates per 100.)

Year and month	Level[3]											
	Total[4]	Total private[4]	Construction	Manufacturing	Trade, transportation, and utilities[5]	Retail trade	Professional and business services	Education and health services	Leisure and hospitality[6]	Accommodation and food services	Government[7]	State and local government
2000												
December	3 145	2 915	89	339	697	569	408	324	674	637	231	211
2001												
January	3 353	3 151	159	286	693	483	708	273	668	631	203	172
February	3 320	3 136	165	245	825	583	551	335	608	554	183	166
March	3 144	2 965	177	244	728	514	539	339	609	560	179	162
April	3 224	3 060	214	230	794	585	537	326	623	551	164	147
May	3 136	2 948	158	206	777	549	552	315	625	559	188	169
June	2 988	2 849	174	200	754	553	481	330	596	536	139	124
July	3 008	2 849	176	177	721	539	528	283	592	535	160	140
August	2 930	2 751	147	194	656	480	497	274	598	533	179	162
September	2 858	2 704	141	176	670	489	461	304	632	575	153	138
October	2 904	2 747	142	192	685	522	520	283	578	514	157	137
November	2 704	2 542	166	176	613	463	485	280	491	434	163	144
December	2 671	2 496	131	170	654	490	443	282	508	445	175	147
2002												
January	2 999	2 832	170	180	697	512	556	274	612	538	166	147
February	2 686	2 509	159	189	552	408	480	272	539	472	177	156
March	2 617	2 469	137	188	586	441	481	236	568	499	148	127
April	2 751	2 561	180	197	593	403	471	278	560	496	190	169
May	2 723	2 574	143	209	546	393	560	285	520	453	149	130
June	2 697	2 531	137	196	651	499	457	256	527	465	165	133
July	2 722	2 581	161	206	581	419	494	295	532	477	141	120
August	2 671	2 515	148	205	573	423	483	279	506	455	157	135
September	2 651	2 496	176	195	550	412	491	249	512	459	155	132
October	2 556	2 401	155	168	555	388	475	281	491	445	154	130
November	2 577	2 383	127	178	570	449	490	275	460	427	194	169
December	2 635	2 492	137	165	545	421	513	303	500	446	143	119
2003												
January	2 504	2 348	147	183	504	373	445	286	485	438	157	131
February	2 567	2 419	152	169	565	438	431	276	524	474	148	125
March	2 453	2 307	131	156	559	398	423	254	473	428	146	122
April	2 402	2 258	100	161	517	383	423	245	495	454	145	120
May	2 366	2 220	158	182	530	400	336	263	455	426	147	125
June	2 410	2 273	158	166	502	377	415	270	506	459	137	117
July	2 351	2 206	140	182	509	371	366	249	506	459	145	125
August	2 378	2 232	162	172	522	388	352	267	485	433	147	125
September	2 463	2 313	147	170	549	415	377	305	476	425	151	132
October	2 529	2 385	137	172	579	425	375	282	544	490	144	127
November	2 484	2 347	169	193	544	369	351	263	493	438	138	121
December	2 498	2 350	193	212	534	368	376	277	463	421	148	130
2004												
January	2 465	2 284	149	184	552	429	353	280	472	434	181	153
February	2 505	2 345	170	189	537	401	362	273	507	479	160	133
March	2 689	2 538	174	204	574	426	444	280	550	509	152	133
April	2 670	2 520	173	207	628	490	377	289	510	452	149	137
May	2 534	2 386	167	180	559	404	343	280	547	503	148	127
June	2 709	2 555	197	201	577	420	441	271	511	472	154	141
July	2 682	2 520	118	194	615	456	433	309	503	456	162	148
August	2 635	2 496	150	170	602	467	452	275	535	490	139	126
September	2 647	2 509	177	202	608	452	440	267	513	465	138	127
October	2 672	2 531	164	187	608	450	435	263	519	476	141	125
November	2 879	2 738	186	218	665	495	477	292	577	521	141	127
December	2 806	2 650	159	212	581	420	489	278	572	519	156	143
2005												
January	3 013	2 849	204	193	684	483	518	295	600	544	165	152
February	2 733	2 589	171	188	585	435	482	302	518	468	145	132
March	2 887	2 728	205	190	664	494	484	327	522	465	160	147
April	2 835	2 672	158	185	625	474	509	321	536	478	163	139
May	2 869	2 720	181	186	662	519	479	292	577	521	150	137
June	2 874	2 717	167	204	675	501	460	311	555	498	157	141
July	2 804	2 679	171	195	638	486	439	299	595	538	125	109
August	3 002	2 849	198	196	680	499	483	312	615	567	153	138
September	3 112	2 953	242	217	648	474	517	326	649	598	159	142
October	2 964	2 786	231	216	644	480	395	305	677	610	178	160
November	2 963	2 798	202	206	644	481	398	316	638	590	166	147
December	2 859	2 708	250	177	687	515	408	298	580	530	151	130

[1]Quits are the number of quits during the entire month.
[2]The quits rate is the number of quits during the entire month as a percent of total employment.
[3]Detail will not necessarily add to totals because of the independent seasonal adjustment of the various series.
[4]Includes natural resources and mining, information, financial activities, and other services, not shown separately.
[5]Includes wholesale trade and transportation, warehousing, and utilities, not shown separately.
[6]Includes arts, entertainment, and recreation, not shown separately.
[7]Includes federal government, not shown separately.

Table 7-10. Quits Levels[1] and Rates,[2] by Industry, December 2000–October 2010—*Continued*

(Seasonally adjusted, levels in thousands, rates per 100.)

Year and month	Rate											
	Total[4]	Total private[4]	Construction	Manufacturing	Trade, transportation, and utilities[5]	Retail trade	Professional and business services	Education and health services	Leisure and hospitality[6]	Accommodation and food services	Government[7]	State and local government
2000												
December	2.4	2.6	1.3	2.0	2.6	3.7	2.4	2.1	5.6	6.3	1.1	1.2
2001												
January	2.5	2.8	2.3	1.7	2.6	3.1	4.2	1.8	5.6	6.2	1.0	0.9
February	2.5	2.8	2.4	1.4	3.1	3.8	3.3	2.2	5.1	5.4	0.9	0.9
March	2.4	2.7	2.6	1.4	2.8	3.3	3.2	2.2	5.1	5.5	0.9	0.9
April	2.4	2.8	3.1	1.4	3.0	3.8	3.2	2.1	5.2	5.4	0.8	0.8
May	2.4	2.7	2.3	1.2	3.0	3.6	3.3	2.0	5.2	5.5	0.9	0.9
June	2.3	2.6	2.5	1.2	2.9	3.6	2.9	2.1	4.9	5.2	0.7	0.7
July	2.3	2.6	2.6	1.1	2.8	3.5	3.2	1.8	4.9	5.2	0.8	0.8
August	2.2	2.5	2.1	1.2	2.5	3.2	3.0	1.7	4.9	5.2	0.8	0.9
September	2.2	2.5	2.1	1.1	2.6	3.2	2.8	1.9	5.2	5.6	0.7	0.7
October	2.2	2.5	2.1	1.2	2.7	3.4	3.2	1.8	4.8	5.0	0.7	0.7
November	2.1	2.3	2.5	1.1	2.4	3.1	3.0	1.8	4.1	4.3	0.8	0.8
December	2.0	2.3	1.9	1.1	2.6	3.2	2.8	1.8	4.2	4.4	0.8	0.8
2002												
January	2.3	2.6	2.5	1.2	2.7	3.4	3.5	1.7	5.1	5.3	0.8	0.8
February	2.1	2.3	2.3	1.2	2.2	2.7	3.0	1.7	4.5	4.6	0.8	0.8
March	2.0	2.3	2.0	1.2	2.3	2.9	3.0	1.5	4.7	4.9	0.7	0.7
April	2.1	2.4	2.7	1.3	2.3	2.7	2.9	1.7	4.7	4.9	0.9	0.9
May	2.1	2.4	2.1	1.4	2.1	2.6	3.5	1.8	4.4	4.5	0.7	0.7
June	2.1	2.3	2.0	1.3	2.6	3.3	2.9	1.6	4.4	4.6	0.8	0.7
July	2.1	2.4	2.4	1.3	2.3	2.8	3.1	1.8	4.5	4.7	0.7	0.6
August	2.1	2.3	2.2	1.4	2.2	2.8	3.0	1.7	4.2	4.5	0.7	0.7
September	2.0	2.3	2.6	1.3	2.2	2.8	3.1	1.5	4.3	4.5	0.7	0.7
October	2.0	2.2	2.3	1.1	2.2	2.6	3.0	1.7	4.1	4.3	0.7	0.7
November	2.0	2.2	1.9	1.2	2.2	3.0	3.1	1.7	3.8	4.1	0.9	0.9
December	2.0	2.3	2.0	1.1	2.1	2.8	3.2	1.8	4.1	4.3	0.7	0.6
2003												
January	1.9	2.2	2.2	1.2	2.0	2.5	2.8	1.7	4.0	4.2	0.7	0.7
February	2.0	2.2	2.3	1.1	2.2	2.9	2.7	1.7	4.3	4.6	0.7	0.7
March	1.9	2.1	2.0	1.1	2.2	2.7	2.7	1.5	3.9	4.2	0.7	0.6
April	1.8	2.1	1.5	1.1	2.0	2.6	2.7	1.5	4.1	4.4	0.7	0.6
May	1.8	2.1	2.4	1.3	2.1	2.7	2.1	1.6	3.8	4.1	0.7	0.7
June	1.9	2.1	2.3	1.1	2.0	2.5	2.6	1.6	4.2	4.4	0.6	0.6
July	1.8	2.0	2.1	1.3	2.0	2.5	2.3	1.5	4.2	4.4	0.7	0.7
August	1.8	2.1	2.4	1.2	2.1	2.6	2.2	1.6	4.0	4.2	0.7	0.7
September	1.9	2.1	2.2	1.2	2.2	2.8	2.4	1.8	3.9	4.1	0.7	0.7
October	1.9	2.2	2.0	1.2	2.3	2.8	2.3	1.7	4.4	4.7	0.7	0.7
November	1.9	2.2	2.5	1.3	2.2	2.5	2.2	1.6	4.0	4.2	0.6	0.6
December	1.9	2.2	2.8	1.5	2.1	2.5	2.3	1.7	3.8	4.0	0.7	0.7
2004												
January	1.9	2.1	2.2	1.3	2.2	2.9	2.2	1.7	3.8	4.1	0.8	0.8
February	1.9	2.2	2.5	1.3	2.1	2.7	2.2	1.6	4.1	4.5	0.7	0.7
March	2.1	2.3	2.5	1.4	2.3	2.8	2.7	1.7	4.4	4.8	0.7	0.7
April	2.0	2.3	2.5	1.4	2.5	3.3	2.3	1.7	4.1	4.3	0.7	0.7
May	1.9	2.2	2.4	1.3	2.2	2.7	2.1	1.7	4.4	4.7	0.7	0.7
June	2.1	2.3	2.8	1.4	2.3	2.8	2.7	1.6	4.1	4.4	0.7	0.7
July	2.0	2.3	1.7	1.4	2.4	3.0	2.6	1.8	4.0	4.3	0.8	0.8
August	2.0	2.3	2.1	1.2	2.4	3.1	2.7	1.6	4.3	4.6	0.6	0.7
September	2.0	2.3	2.5	1.4	2.4	3.0	2.7	1.6	4.1	4.3	0.6	0.7
October	2.0	2.3	2.3	1.3	2.4	3.0	2.6	1.5	4.1	4.4	0.7	0.7
November	2.2	2.5	2.6	1.5	2.6	3.3	2.9	1.7	4.6	4.8	0.7	0.7
December	2.1	2.4	2.2	1.5	2.3	2.8	2.9	1.6	4.5	4.8	0.7	0.8
2005												
January	2.3	2.6	2.9	1.4	2.7	3.2	3.1	1.7	4.7	5.0	0.8	0.8
February	2.1	2.3	2.4	1.3	2.3	2.9	2.9	1.8	4.1	4.3	0.7	0.7
March	2.2	2.5	2.8	1.3	2.6	3.3	2.9	1.9	4.1	4.3	0.7	0.8
April	2.1	2.4	2.2	1.3	2.4	3.1	3.0	1.9	4.2	4.4	0.7	0.7
May	2.2	2.4	2.5	1.3	2.6	3.4	2.8	1.7	4.5	4.8	0.7	0.7
June	2.2	2.4	2.3	1.4	2.6	3.3	2.7	1.8	4.3	4.5	0.7	0.7
July	2.1	2.4	2.3	1.4	2.5	3.2	2.6	1.7	4.6	4.9	0.6	0.6
August	2.2	2.5	2.7	1.4	2.6	3.2	2.8	1.8	4.8	5.2	0.7	0.7
September	2.3	2.6	3.3	1.5	2.5	3.1	3.0	1.9	5.0	5.5	0.7	0.7
October	2.2	2.5	3.1	1.5	2.5	3.1	2.3	1.7	5.3	5.6	0.8	0.8
November	2.2	2.5	2.7	1.4	2.5	3.1	2.3	1.8	5.0	5.4	0.8	0.8
December	2.1	2.4	3.3	1.2	2.6	3.4	2.4	1.7	4.5	4.8	0.7	0.7

[1]Quits are the number of quits during the entire month.
[2]The quits rate is the number of quits during the entire month as a percent of total employment.
[4]Includes natural resources and mining, information, financial activities, and other services, not shown separately.
[5]Includes wholesale trade and transportation, warehousing, and utilities, not shown separately.
[6]Includes arts, entertainment, and recreation, not shown separately.
[7]Includes federal government, not shown separately.

Table 7-10. Quits Levels[1] and Rates,[2] by Industry, December 2000–October 2010—*Continued*

(Seasonally adjusted, levels in thousands, rates per 100.)

Year and month	Level[3]											
	Total[4]	Total private[4]	Construction	Manufacturing	Trade, transportation, and utilities[5]	Retail trade	Professional and business services	Education and health services	Leisure and hospitality[6]	Accommodation and food services	Government[7]	State and local government
2006												
January	2 866	2 714	208	194	646	481	427	261	651	581	152	131
February	3 054	2 882	197	204	709	528	458	307	654	605	173	150
March	3 098	2 927	211	205	703	526	489	292	648	590	171	145
April	2 836	2 663	202	186	707	518	469	301	535	481	173	145
May	3 101	2 913	205	236	707	518	486	339	623	578	188	160
June	3 116	2 931	204	196	656	481	508	336	685	629	185	153
July	3 034	2 871	177	225	673	517	484	335	594	552	163	137
August	3 062	2 876	175	207	707	480	492	337	615	566	186	155
September	3 014	2 844	159	181	670	498	551	309	619	572	170	138
October	2 999	2 833	178	208	640	471	530	330	598	548	166	142
November	3 151	2 980	161	237	717	527	552	314	639	574	171	145
December	3 140	2 968	172	257	653	470	559	348	674	622	172	150
2007												
January	2 956	2 788	162	220	647	465	533	288	605	568	169	148
February	3 041	2 874	136	221	690	495	527	327	632	579	167	143
March	3 098	2 913	155	229	666	470	509	315	634	581	186	153
April	2 958	2 788	149	209	662	478	490	319	640	592	170	146
May	3 087	2 903	160	230	711	514	472	345	609	567	184	154
June	2 873	2 704	131	211	665	478	438	302	634	586	169	143
July	2 928	2 752	182	194	578	427	513	321	644	590	176	147
August	3 000	2 838	187	214	602	442	489	331	645	582	162	139
September	2 656	2 502	140	185	611	446	463	277	484	433	154	128
October	2 883	2 724	164	204	626	460	471	292	637	579	159	142
November	2 773	2 613	151	183	562	408	482	326	634	578	160	147
December	2 858	2 712	164	217	649	477	401	300	653	588	145	134
2008												
January	2 790	2 641	144	194	646	475	426	309	577	516	149	133
February	2 870	2 715	167	198	621	429	486	310	605	551	154	141
March	2 741	2 607	129	196	579	410	464	320	595	550	135	124
April	2 914	2 762	160	187	620	436	523	334	612	561	152	142
May	2 743	2 598	139	173	603	411	464	277	650	593	145	137
June	2 712	2 571	150	164	579	409	490	294	589	543	141	133
July	2 529	2 392	149	147	556	404	433	302	567	514	137	129
August	2 469	2 321	160	145	553	399	366	291	518	475	148	140
September	2 521	2 374	110	142	586	429	397	290	555	509	147	142
October	2 417	2 282	116	147	517	358	427	289	528	488	135	127
November	2 136	2 017	91	124	474	353	361	251	474	440	119	114
December	2 084	1 954	79	101	499	370	351	241	454	430	130	125
2009												
January	1 980	1 872	80	105	454	351	329	245	439	409	108	103
February	2 003	1 889	88	100	410	309	311	266	437	403	114	110
March	1 942	1 836	99	90	470	335	294	248	424	393	106	102
April	1 821	1 723	64	85	384	277	285	240	432	395	99	95
May	1 807	1 706	77	91	394	291	309	251	381	339	100	97
June	1 830	1 727	72	98	408	308	268	266	419	376	103	99
July	1 822	1 709	70	86	411	294	282	242	407	367	113	110
August	1 779	1 669	68	82	408	307	263	247	410	368	110	100
September	1 716	1 616	77	90	387	285	265	270	345	331	100	96
October	1 723	1 620	62	80	382	287	277	267	356	317	102	98
November	1 837	1 731	92	75	413	276	264	262	397	355	106	101
December	1 753	1 639	76	75	392	291	248	271	375	344	114	106
2010												
January	1 772	1 661	99	85	368	266	259	248	401	353	112	106
February	1 851	1 719	84	97	432	333	300	237	393	358	132	121
March	1 918	1 802	83	89	424	316	315	253	406	371	117	105
April	1 972	1 871	67	99	442	330	323	299	419	379	101	93
May	1 929	1 828	64	96	438	338	330	254	428	390	101	88
June	1 951	1 819	67	105	443	331	325	268	373	347	131	105
July	1 974	1 855	72	97	451	347	357	258	401	370	119	100
August	1 998	1 881	81	107	425	322	385	249	407	370	117	101
September	1 983	1 860	85	95	452	351	350	245	394	355	124	112
October[8]	1 997	1 887	82	106	430	331	385	249	416	362	110	99

[1]Quits are the number of quits during the entire month.
[2]The quits rate is the number of quits during the entire month as a percent of total employment.
[3]Detail will not necessarily add to totals because of the independent seasonal adjustment of the various series.
[4]Includes natural resources and mining, information, financial activities, and other services, not shown separately.
[5]Includes wholesale trade and transportation, warehousing, and utilities, not shown separately.
[6]Includes arts, entertainment, and recreation, not shown separately.
[7]Includes federal government, not shown separately.
[8]Preliminary.

Table 7-10. Quits Levels[1] and Rates,[2] by Industry, December 2000–October 2010—*Continued*

(Seasonally adjusted, levels in thousands, rates per 100.)

Year and month	Rate											
	Total[4]	Total private[4]	Construc-tion	Manufac-turing	Trade, transpor-tation, and utilities[5]	Retail trade	Profes-sional and business services	Education and health services	Leisure and hospitality[6]	Accommo-dation and food services	Govern-ment[7]	State and local govern-ment
2006												
January	2.1	2.4	2.7	1.4	2.5	3.1	2.5	1.5	5.0	5.3	0.7	0.7
February	2.3	2.5	2.6	1.4	2.7	3.4	2.6	1.7	5.0	5.5	0.8	0.8
March	2.3	2.6	2.7	1.4	2.7	3.4	2.8	1.6	5.0	5.3	0.8	0.8
April	2.1	2.3	2.6	1.3	2.7	3.4	2.7	1.7	4.1	4.3	0.8	0.8
May	2.3	2.6	2.7	1.7	2.7	3.4	2.8	1.9	4.8	5.2	0.9	0.8
June	2.3	2.6	2.7	1.4	2.5	3.1	2.9	1.9	5.2	5.6	0.8	0.8
July	2.2	2.5	2.3	1.6	2.6	3.4	2.7	1.9	4.5	4.9	0.7	0.7
August	2.2	2.5	2.3	1.5	2.7	3.1	2.8	1.9	4.7	5.1	0.8	0.8
September	2.2	2.5	2.1	1.3	2.5	3.2	3.1	1.7	4.7	5.1	0.8	0.7
October	2.2	2.5	2.3	1.5	2.4	3.1	3.0	1.8	4.5	4.9	0.8	0.7
November	2.3	2.6	2.1	1.7	2.7	3.4	3.1	1.7	4.8	5.1	0.8	0.7
December	2.3	2.6	2.2	1.8	2.5	3.1	3.1	1.9	5.1	5.5	0.8	0.8
2007												
January	2.2	2.4	2.1	1.6	2.4	3.0	3.0	1.6	4.5	5.0	0.8	0.8
February	2.2	2.5	1.8	1.6	2.6	3.2	2.9	1.8	4.7	5.1	0.8	0.7
March	2.3	2.5	2.0	1.6	2.5	3.0	2.8	1.7	4.7	5.1	0.8	0.8
April	2.2	2.4	1.9	1.5	2.5	3.1	2.7	1.8	4.8	5.2	0.8	0.7
May	2.2	2.5	2.1	1.6	2.7	3.3	2.6	1.9	4.5	5.0	0.8	0.8
June	2.1	2.3	1.7	1.5	2.5	3.1	2.4	1.7	4.7	5.1	0.8	0.7
July	2.1	2.4	2.4	1.4	2.2	2.8	2.9	1.8	4.8	5.1	0.8	0.8
August	2.2	2.5	2.5	1.5	2.3	2.9	2.7	1.8	4.8	5.1	0.7	0.7
September	1.9	2.2	1.9	1.3	2.3	2.9	2.6	1.5	3.6	3.8	0.7	0.7
October	2.1	2.4	2.2	1.5	2.3	3.0	2.6	1.6	4.7	5.0	0.7	0.7
November	2.0	2.3	2.0	1.3	2.1	2.6	2.7	1.8	4.7	5.0	0.7	0.8
December	2.1	2.3	2.2	1.6	2.4	3.1	2.2	1.6	4.8	5.1	0.6	0.7
2008												
January	2.0	2.3	1.9	1.4	2.4	3.1	2.4	1.7	4.3	4.5	0.7	0.7
February	2.1	2.4	2.2	1.4	2.3	2.8	2.7	1.7	4.5	4.8	0.7	0.7
March	2.0	2.3	1.7	1.4	2.2	2.6	2.6	1.7	4.4	4.8	0.6	0.6
April	2.1	2.4	2.2	1.4	2.3	2.8	2.9	1.8	4.5	4.9	0.7	0.7
May	2.0	2.3	1.9	1.3	2.3	2.7	2.6	1.5	4.8	5.1	0.6	0.7
June	2.0	2.2	2.1	1.2	2.2	2.7	2.7	1.6	4.4	4.7	0.6	0.7
July	1.8	2.1	2.1	1.1	2.1	2.6	2.4	1.6	4.2	4.5	0.6	0.7
August	1.8	2.0	2.3	1.1	2.1	2.6	2.1	1.5	3.9	4.1	0.7	0.7
September	1.8	2.1	1.6	1.1	2.2	2.8	2.3	1.5	4.1	4.5	0.7	0.7
October	1.8	2.0	1.7	1.1	2.0	2.4	2.4	1.5	4.0	4.3	0.6	0.6
November	1.6	1.8	1.3	1.0	1.8	2.4	2.1	1.3	3.6	3.9	0.5	0.6
December	1.6	1.7	1.2	0.8	1.9	2.5	2.0	1.3	3.4	3.8	0.6	0.6
2009												
January	1.5	1.7	1.2	0.8	1.8	2.4	1.9	1.3	3.3	3.6	0.5	0.5
February	1.5	1.7	1.4	0.8	1.6	2.1	1.8	1.4	3.3	3.6	0.5	0.6
March	1.5	1.7	1.6	0.7	1.9	2.3	1.8	1.3	3.2	3.5	0.5	0.5
April	1.4	1.6	1.0	0.7	1.5	1.9	1.7	1.3	3.3	3.5	0.4	0.5
May	1.4	1.6	1.3	0.8	1.6	2.0	1.9	1.3	2.9	3.0	0.4	0.5
June	1.4	1.6	1.2	0.8	1.6	2.1	1.6	1.4	3.2	3.4	0.5	0.5
July	1.4	1.6	1.2	0.7	1.7	2.0	1.7	1.3	3.1	3.3	0.5	0.6
August	1.4	1.6	1.2	0.7	1.6	2.1	1.6	1.3	3.1	3.3	0.5	0.5
September	1.3	1.5	1.3	0.8	1.6	2.0	1.6	1.4	2.6	3.0	0.4	0.5
October	1.3	1.5	1.1	0.7	1.6	2.0	1.7	1.4	2.7	2.8	0.5	0.5
November	1.4	1.6	1.6	0.6	1.7	1.9	1.6	1.4	3.0	3.2	0.5	0.5
December	1.4	1.5	1.3	0.7	1.6	2.0	1.5	1.4	2.9	3.1	0.5	0.5
2010												
January	1.4	1.6	1.8	0.7	1.5	1.8	1.6	1.3	3.1	3.2	0.5	0.5
February	1.4	1.6	1.5	0.8	1.8	2.3	1.8	1.2	3.0	3.2	0.6	0.6
March	1.5	1.7	1.5	0.8	1.7	2.2	1.9	1.3	3.1	3.3	0.5	0.5
April	1.5	1.7	1.2	0.8	1.8	2.3	1.9	1.5	3.2	3.4	0.4	0.5
May	1.5	1.7	1.1	0.8	1.8	2.3	2.0	1.3	3.3	3.5	0.4	0.4
June	1.5	1.7	1.2	0.9	1.8	2.3	1.9	1.4	2.8	3.1	0.6	0.5
July	1.5	1.7	1.3	0.8	1.8	2.4	2.1	1.3	3.1	3.3	0.5	0.5
August	1.5	1.7	1.4	0.9	1.7	2.2	2.3	1.3	3.1	3.3	0.5	0.5
September	1.5	1.7	1.5	0.8	1.8	2.4	2.1	1.3	3.0	3.2	0.6	0.6
October[8]	1.5	1.7	1.5	0.9	1.7	2.3	2.3	1.3	3.2	3.2	0.5	0.5

[1]Quits are the number of quits during the entire month.
[2]The quits rate is the number of quits during the entire month as a percent of total employment.
[4]Includes natural resources and mining, information, financial activities, and other services, not shown separately.
[5]Includes wholesale trade and transportation, warehousing, and utilities, not shown separately.
[6]Includes arts, entertainment, and recreation, not shown separately.
[7]Includes federal government, not shown separately.
[8]Preliminary.

Table 7-11. Layoffs and Discharges Levels[1] and Rates,[2] by Industry, December 2000–October 2010

(Not seasonally adjusted, levels in thousands, rates per 100.)

Year and month	Level												
	Total	Total private	Mining and logging	Construc-tion	Manufac-turing	Durable goods	Non-durable goods	Trade, transpor-tation, and utilities	Whole-sale trade	Retail trade	Transpor-tation, ware-housing, and utilities	Infor-mation	Financial activities
2001	24 351	23 209	106	3 192	3 311	1 992	1 320	4 557	854	2 986	717	572	838
2002	23 325	22 124	106	3 118	2 690	1 653	1 038	4 536	810	2 990	735	534	950
2003	23 959	22 666	107	3 145	2 326	1 414	914	4 783	836	3 141	805	426	771
2004	23 389	22 011	83	2 945	1 998	1 219	782	4 809	790	3 070	946	390	785
2005	22 774	21 476	78	2 928	1 847	1 154	693	4 641	761	2 922	957	272	863
2006	21 460	20 094	74	2 634	1 819	1 022	797	4 174	645	2 848	681	259	869
2007	22 557	21 197	90	2 850	1 969	1 208	761	4 283	821	2 754	706	316	1 107
2008	24 549	23 368	119	3 448	2 259	1 445	814	4 890	1 035	3 061	796	316	1 105
2009	27 790	26 154	193	3 891	2 929	1 892	1 035	5 185	1 171	2 960	1 055	378	1 389
2000													
December	2 140	2 058	23	364	210	110	99	444	91	317	37	23	30
2001													
January	3 184	3 083	11	372	378	253	125	927	135	685	107	86	192
February	1 411	1 362	4	271	202	120	81	232	64	149	19	37	45
March	1 887	1 844	7	248	234	131	103	330	36	264	30	21	51
April	1 872	1 813	5	164	323	211	112	301	73	174	54	61	64
May	1 585	1 493	5	202	254	147	107	312	46	211	54	38	38
June	1 780	1 621	9	206	287	153	135	301	43	206	53	45	38
July	1 949	1 857	9	192	298	166	132	371	100	222	49	43	54
August	1 857	1 656	8	229	224	140	84	267	51	173	43	41	41
September	2 173	2 065	7	261	224	128	96	349	63	227	59	39	82
October	2 480	2 354	11	329	349	230	120	391	108	222	61	63	99
November	2 097	2 048	13	359	259	158	101	365	71	195	99	62	70
December	2 076	2 013	17	359	279	155	124	411	64	258	89	36	64
2002													
January	2 920	2 805	11	347	399	247	153	687	85	505	97	131	195
February	1 596	1 548	6	254	195	107	88	396	69	261	66	23	53
March	1 429	1 387	11	201	189	132	57	276	59	162	55	32	41
April	1 860	1 796	13	212	243	151	92	338	57	224	57	59	63
May	1 592	1 501	8	214	182	107	75	366	81	248	36	32	70
June	1 722	1 569	5	224	196	116	80	257	47	153	57	38	83
July	2 210	2 062	15	289	216	128	88	334	90	199	45	38	77
August	1 870	1 721	8	207	189	133	56	319	51	210	58	36	78
September	1 978	1 810	6	244	188	120	69	353	63	229	61	25	70
October	2 097	2 010	7	326	249	159	89	369	50	271	48	41	92
November	1 837	1 764	6	276	194	116	78	335	86	196	53	49	65
December	2 214	2 151	10	324	250	137	113	506	72	332	102	30	63
2003													
January	3 132	3 014	18	403	352	218	135	758	102	575	81	94	156
February	1 571	1 518	9	220	179	109	70	350	44	273	33	32	41
March	1 476	1 418	8	217	183	111	73	283	45	192	46	37	61
April	1 931	1 854	8	264	261	143	117	296	65	181	49	25	45
May	1 594	1 496	5	198	135	78	57	313	95	171	47	25	47
June	1 906	1 756	8	185	196	122	74	362	48	233	80	41	46
July	2 022	1 887	8	228	223	123	100	372	95	199	78	32	106
August	2 072	1 894	12	287	149	105	44	359	62	202	95	24	44
September	1 981	1 822	3	285	148	93	56	290	91	155	44	16	68
October	2 213	2 126	7	309	186	103	83	447	92	285	71	32	60
November	1 798	1 703	5	275	152	108	44	353	41	258	54	33	41
December	2 263	2 178	16	274	162	101	61	600	56	417	127	35	56
2004													
January	3 028	2 879	12	362	267	153	114	771	99	543	129	63	110
February	1 510	1 465	10	244	136	80	57	397	65	281	51	29	33
March	1 567	1 516	5	221	151	95	56	303	55	179	69	40	56
April	1 857	1 800	6	190	167	90	77	348	95	201	52	29	51
May	1 495	1 412	6	171	130	65	65	353	61	202	90	35	35
June	1 732	1 574	4	190	133	89	44	290	55	166	69	40	54
July	1 940	1 758	6	247	167	102	65	368	69	230	69	24	55
August	2 080	1 933	7	248	191	131	60	325	73	170	82	19	98
September	2 017	1 815	4	195	152	99	53	302	50	188	64	38	68
October	2 056	1 948	7	276	193	115	78	350	67	214	68	35	90
November	1 847	1 757	8	281	156	104	53	377	60	237	79	17	66
December	2 260	2 154	8	320	155	96	60	625	41	459	124	21	69
2005													
January	3 035	2 923	12	457	273	178	94	717	96	505	116	57	174
February	1 558	1 506	6	250	112	73	39	373	50	264	59	12	66
March	1 633	1 584	5	174	151	87	63	307	40	216	51	23	60
April	1 788	1 719	7	218	183	128	55	341	80	196	65	20	93
May	1 581	1 477	4	209	131	89	43	359	84	176	99	20	58
June	1 810	1 653	4	188	128	80	48	321	46	198	77	16	28
July	1 864	1 731	6	187	153	99	54	358	62	229	67	25	59
August	1 976	1 798	6	250	146	96	50	323	48	221	53	17	51
September	2 013	1 842	8	226	141	81	60	370	33	259	78	19	66
October	1 908	1 816	8	257	149	94	55	349	74	205	71	19	94
November	1 624	1 551	4	239	143	72	72	321	73	169	79	24	53
December	1 984	1 876	8	273	137	77	60	502	75	284	142	20	61

[1]Layoffs and discharges are the number of layoffs and discharges during the entire month.
[2]The layoffs and discharges rate is the number of layoffs and discharges during the entire month as a percent of total employment.

Table 7-11. Layoffs and Discharges Levels[1] and Rates,[2] by Industry, December 2000–October 2010
—Continued

(Not seasonally adjusted, levels in thousands, rates per 100.)

Year and month	Finance and insurance	Real estate and rental and leasing	Professional and business services	Education and health services	Educational services	Health care and social assistance	Leisure and hospitality	Arts, entertainment, and recreation	Accommodation and food services	Other services	Government	Federal	State and local government
2001	538	300	4 848	1 537	264	1 274	3 554	963	2 590	686	1 147	112	1 031
2002	577	374	4 637	1 626	247	1 380	3 090	804	2 286	841	1 202	143	1 058
2003	421	349	4 924	1 732	359	1 372	3 408	966	2 442	1 042	1 292	160	1 134
2004	427	358	4 907	1 655	287	1 370	3 584	1 061	2 522	853	1 380	162	1 217
2005	474	389	5 080	1 680	301	1 381	3 232	907	2 328	855	1 298	166	1 134
2006	465	406	4 585	1 686	339	1 348	3 053	836	2 218	937	1 365	190	1 174
2007	607	501	4 749	1 737	388	1 351	3 175	911	2 263	915	1 360	224	1 135
2008	661	448	4 997	2 042	396	1 644	3 161	899	2 262	968	1 179	111	1 070
2009	784	603	5 115	2 255	469	1 785	3 467	859	2 607	1 291	1 634	217	1 419
2000													
December	26	5	635	119	43	76	174	53	121	36	81	7	75
2001													
January	172	20	542	184	29	156	288	79	209	103	102	28	73
February	23	22	323	84	9	75	138	44	94	25	49	5	44
March	22	29	546	92	11	81	243	37	205	73	43	6	37
April	48	16	324	96	24	72	397	62	335	76	59	7	53
May	28	10	360	98	18	80	159	25	133	26	93	7	86
June	20	18	336	138	23	115	212	41	172	48	159	5	154
July	45	9	314	220	35	185	293	73	220	61	93	7	85
August	27	14	320	172	59	113	257	97	161	95	201	8	193
September	30	52	434	113	13	100	500	248	251	57	107	12	95
October	60	38	461	168	24	144	435	101	334	48	127	12	114
November	34	37	378	95	10	85	401	115	286	46	50	6	43
December	29	35	510	77	9	68	231	41	190	28	64	9	54
2002													
January	152	43	471	227	33	193	253	43	209	85	116	26	90
February	39	14	287	103	9	94	188	26	162	42	47	8	39
March	23	19	344	116	19	98	146	30	116	31	42	9	32
April	44	19	368	135	20	115	275	91	184	90	64	12	53
May	51	19	283	135	24	110	171	21	150	42	91	7	84
June	57	26	329	148	24	124	210	23	187	79	153	9	144
July	45	33	468	177	27	150	335	103	232	113	149	12	136
August	41	37	312	148	29	119	292	114	179	131	150	8	141
September	26	44	370	136	31	105	346	129	217	73	168	16	152
October	30	61	424	125	10	116	326	62	264	51	86	14	72
November	33	32	399	71	3	69	320	111	209	49	73	14	60
December	36	27	582	105	18	87	228	51	177	55	63	8	55
2003													
January	89	67	548	199	25	173	362	83	279	123	118	26	92
February	32	9	345	98	13	86	177	46	131	66	53	7	46
March	33	28	283	103	9	94	202	54	148	42	57	9	49
April	27	18	457	113	20	93	312	115	196	74	77	10	68
May	28	19	301	166	41	124	265	78	187	41	98	9	88
June	23	23	383	201	61	140	224	33	191	111	150	11	139
July	50	56	389	229	63	166	196	33	163	106	134	11	124
August	21	23	404	190	56	134	297	97	201	126	178	11	167
September	36	32	377	112	17	96	405	169	236	117	159	13	146
October	36	24	485	135	22	112	367	103	264	99	87	20	67
November	23	17	392	102	15	87	294	101	193	54	95	27	68
December	23	33	560	84	17	67	307	54	253	83	86	6	80
2004													
January	62	48	673	187	26	161	357	74	282	78	149	27	122
February	23	10	260	110	13	97	196	66	131	49	45	9	36
March	27	29	385	111	19	92	206	42	164	38	51	6	45
April	28	23	487	135	14	121	308	89	219	79	57	7	50
May	22	13	314	134	28	106	181	49	132	52	84	9	75
June	26	28	373	163	48	115	279	49	230	47	158	21	137
July	34	21	368	134	24	110	322	62	260	68	182	12	170
August	61	37	374	170	34	137	336	125	211	164	148	10	138
September	32	36	360	171	35	136	440	234	206	86	202	12	190
October	46	44	353	107	9	98	498	136	361	40	108	14	94
November	38	28	387	109	17	93	249	80	169	106	90	7	82
December	28	41	573	124	20	104	212	55	157	46	106	28	78
2005													
January	115	60	581	199	22	177	344	69	275	109	112	14	98
February	24	42	324	117	10	107	187	39	149	59	51	8	43
March	35	24	436	137	14	123	233	29	205	59	49	7	42
April	63	30	432	155	23	132	221	59	162	49	69	13	56
May	35	23	266	156	45	112	191	48	143	84	104	9	95
June	19	8	451	148	30	119	320	59	261	49	157	18	140
July	35	24	507	142	31	110	236	31	206	57	133	13	120
August	40	11	436	165	24	141	252	89	163	153	178	15	163
September	24	42	362	127	34	93	442	243	199	80	171	18	153
October	41	53	428	122	19	103	325	92	234	66	92	9	83
November	18	36	367	93	12	81	268	92	175	38	73	10	64
December	25	36	490	119	37	83	213	57	156	52	109	32	77

[1]Layoffs and discharges are the number of layoffs and discharges during the entire month.
[2]The layoffs and discharges rate is the number of layoffs and discharges during the entire month as a percent of total employment.

Table 7-11. Layoffs and Discharges Levels[1] and Rates,[2] by Industry, December 2000–October 2010
—Continued

(Not seasonally adjusted, levels in thousands, rates per 100.)

Year and month	Total	Total private	Mining and logging	Construction	Manufacturing	Durable goods	Non-durable goods	Trade, transportation, and utilities	Wholesale trade	Retail trade	Transportation, warehousing, and utilities	Information	Financial activities
2001	18.5	21.0	17.5	46.8	20.1	19.3	21.6	17.5	14.8	19.6	14.4	15.8	10.7
2002	17.9	20.3	18.2	46.4	17.6	17.4	18.0	17.8	14.3	19.9	15.2	15.7	12.1
2003	18.4	20.9	18.7	46.7	16.0	15.8	16.5	18.9	14.9	21.1	16.9	13.4	9.7
2004	17.8	20.0	14.0	42.2	14.0	13.7	14.5	18.8	14.0	20.4	19.7	12.5	9.8
2005	17.0	19.2	12.4	39.9	13.0	12.9	13.1	17.9	13.2	19.1	19.5	8.9	10.6
2006	15.8	17.6	10.8	34.2	12.9	11.4	15.4	15.9	10.9	18.6	13.6	8.5	10.4
2007	16.4	18.4	12.4	37.4	14.2	13.7	15.0	16.1	13.6	17.7	13.9	10.4	13.3
2008	17.9	20.4	15.5	48.1	16.9	17.1	16.5	18.6	17.4	20.0	15.7	12.7	13.6
2009	21.2	24.1	27.6	64.5	24.6	25.9	22.6	20.8	20.8	20.4	22.0	15.6	17.9
2000													
December	1.6	1.8	3.9	5.4	1.2	1.0	1.6	1.6	1.5	2.0	0.7	0.6	0.4
2001													
January	2.4	2.8	1.9	5.8	2.2	2.4	2.0	3.6	2.3	4.5	2.1	2.3	2.5
February	1.1	1.2	0.7	4.2	1.2	1.1	1.3	0.9	1.1	1.0	0.4	1.0	0.6
March	1.4	1.7	1.2	3.8	1.4	1.2	1.7	1.3	0.6	1.8	0.6	0.6	0.7
April	1.4	1.6	0.9	2.5	1.9	2.0	1.8	1.2	1.3	1.2	1.1	1.7	0.8
May	1.2	1.3	0.9	2.9	1.5	1.4	1.7	1.2	0.8	1.4	1.1	1.0	0.5
June	1.3	1.4	1.5	2.9	1.7	1.5	2.2	1.2	0.7	1.3	1.1	1.2	0.5
July	1.5	1.7	1.4	2.7	1.8	1.6	2.2	1.4	1.7	1.5	1.0	1.2	0.7
August	1.4	1.5	1.3	3.2	1.4	1.4	1.4	1.0	0.9	1.1	0.9	1.1	0.5
September	1.6	1.9	1.2	3.7	1.4	1.3	1.6	1.4	1.1	1.5	1.2	1.1	1.0
October	1.9	2.1	1.8	4.7	2.2	2.3	2.0	1.5	1.9	1.5	1.2	1.8	1.3
November	1.6	1.9	2.1	5.2	1.6	1.6	1.7	1.4	1.2	1.3	2.0	1.7	0.9
December	1.6	1.8	2.8	5.4	1.8	1.6	2.1	1.6	1.1	1.6	1.8	1.0	0.8
2002													
January	2.3	2.6	2.0	5.5	2.6	2.6	2.6	2.7	1.5	3.4	2.0	3.8	2.5
February	1.2	1.4	1.1	4.0	1.3	1.1	1.5	1.6	1.2	1.8	1.4	0.7	0.7
March	1.1	1.3	1.9	3.1	1.2	1.4	1.0	1.1	1.0	1.1	1.2	0.9	0.5
April	1.4	1.7	2.3	3.2	1.6	1.6	1.6	1.3	1.0	1.5	1.2	1.7	0.8
May	1.2	1.4	1.3	3.2	1.2	1.1	1.3	1.4	1.4	1.7	0.8	0.9	0.9
June	1.3	1.4	0.9	3.2	1.3	1.2	1.4	1.0	0.8	1.0	1.2	1.1	1.1
July	1.7	1.9	2.5	4.1	1.4	1.4	1.5	1.3	1.6	1.3	0.9	1.1	1.1
August	1.4	1.6	1.4	3.0	1.2	1.4	1.0	1.3	0.9	1.4	1.2	1.1	1.0
September	1.5	1.7	1.0	3.5	1.2	1.3	1.2	1.4	1.1	1.5	1.3	0.7	0.9
October	1.6	1.8	1.3	4.7	1.6	1.7	1.6	1.4	0.9	1.8	1.0	1.2	1.2
November	1.4	1.6	1.0	4.1	1.3	1.2	1.4	1.3	1.5	1.3	1.1	1.5	0.8
December	1.7	2.0	1.7	4.9	1.7	1.5	2.0	1.9	1.3	2.1	2.1	0.9	0.8
2003													
January	2.4	2.8	3.3	6.4	2.4	2.4	2.4	3.0	1.8	3.9	1.7	2.9	2.0
February	1.2	1.4	1.5	3.5	1.2	1.2	1.3	1.4	0.8	1.9	0.7	1.0	0.5
March	1.1	1.3	1.4	3.4	1.3	1.2	1.3	1.1	0.8	1.3	1.0	1.1	0.8
April	1.5	1.7	1.4	4.0	1.8	1.6	2.1	1.2	1.2	1.2	1.0	0.8	0.6
May	1.2	1.4	0.9	2.9	0.9	0.9	1.0	1.2	1.7	1.2	1.0	0.8	0.6
June	1.5	1.6	1.3	2.7	1.3	1.4	1.3	1.4	0.9	1.6	1.7	1.3	0.6
July	1.6	1.7	1.3	3.2	1.5	1.4	1.8	1.5	1.7	1.3	1.7	1.0	1.3
August	1.6	1.7	2.1	4.1	1.0	1.2	0.8	1.4	1.1	1.4	2.0	0.8	0.5
September	1.5	1.7	0.6	4.1	1.0	1.0	1.0	1.1	1.6	1.0	0.9	0.5	0.8
October	1.7	1.9	1.2	4.4	1.3	1.2	1.5	1.8	1.6	1.9	1.5	1.0	0.7
November	1.4	1.6	0.9	4.0	1.1	1.2	0.8	1.4	0.7	1.7	1.1	1.1	0.5
December	1.7	2.0	2.8	4.1	1.1	1.1	1.1	2.3	1.0	2.7	2.6	1.1	0.7
2004													
January	2.4	2.7	2.1	5.6	1.9	1.7	2.1	3.1	1.8	3.7	2.7	2.0	1.4
February	1.2	1.4	1.8	3.8	1.0	0.9	1.1	1.6	1.2	1.9	1.1	0.9	0.4
March	1.2	1.4	0.8	3.4	1.1	1.1	1.0	1.2	1.0	1.2	1.5	1.3	0.7
April	1.4	1.6	1.1	2.8	1.2	1.0	1.4	1.4	1.7	1.4	1.1	0.9	0.6
May	1.1	1.3	0.9	2.4	0.9	0.7	1.2	1.4	1.1	1.3	1.9	1.1	0.4
June	1.3	1.4	0.7	2.6	0.9	1.0	0.8	1.1	1.0	1.1	1.4	1.3	0.7
July	1.5	1.6	0.9	3.4	1.2	1.1	1.2	1.4	1.2	1.1	1.4	0.8	0.7
August	1.6	1.7	1.1	3.4	1.3	1.5	1.1	1.3	1.3	1.1	1.7	0.6	1.2
September	1.5	1.6	0.7	2.7	1.1	1.1	1.0	1.2	0.9	1.3	1.3	1.2	0.8
October	1.5	1.8	1.2	3.8	1.3	1.3	1.4	1.4	1.2	1.4	1.4	1.1	1.1
November	1.4	1.6	1.4	3.9	1.1	1.2	1.0	1.4	1.1	1.5	1.6	0.6	0.8
December	1.7	1.9	1.4	4.6	1.1	1.1	1.1	2.4	0.7	2.9	2.5	0.7	0.9
2005													
January	2.3	2.7	2.1	6.8	1.9	2.0	1.8	2.8	1.7	3.4	2.4	1.9	2.2
February	1.2	1.4	1.0	3.7	0.8	0.8	0.7	1.5	0.9	1.8	1.2	0.4	0.8
March	1.2	1.4	0.8	2.5	1.1	1.0	1.2	1.2	0.7	1.4	1.1	0.8	0.7
April	1.3	1.5	1.2	3.1	1.3	1.4	1.0	1.3	1.4	1.3	1.3	0.6	1.2
May	1.2	1.3	0.6	2.8	0.9	1.0	0.8	1.4	1.5	1.2	2.0	0.6	0.7
June	1.3	1.5	0.7	2.5	0.9	0.9	0.9	1.2	0.8	1.3	1.6	0.5	0.3
July	1.4	1.5	0.9	2.4	1.1	1.1	1.1	1.4	1.1	1.5	1.4	0.8	0.7
August	1.5	1.6	1.0	3.2	1.0	1.1	0.9	1.2	0.8	1.4	1.1	0.6	0.6
September	1.5	1.6	1.3	2.9	1.0	0.9	1.1	1.4	0.6	1.7	1.6	0.6	0.8
October	1.4	1.6	1.2	3.3	1.0	1.1	1.0	1.3	1.3	1.3	1.4	0.6	1.1
November	1.2	1.4	0.6	3.1	1.0	0.8	1.4	1.2	1.3	1.1	1.6	0.8	0.6
December	1.5	1.7	1.2	3.7	1.0	0.9	1.2	1.9	1.3	1.8	2.9	0.6	0.7

[1] Layoffs and discharges are the number of layoffs and discharges during the entire month.
[2] The layoffs and discharges rate is the number of layoffs and discharges during the entire month as a percent of total employment.

Table 7-11. Layoffs and Discharges Levels[1] and Rates,[2] by Industry, December 2000–October 2010 —*Continued*

(Not seasonally adjusted, levels in thousands, rates per 100.)

Year and month	Rate												
	Finance and insurance	Real estate and rental and leasing	Professional and business services	Education and health services	Educational services	Health care and social assistance	Leisure and hospitality	Arts, entertainment, and recreation	Accommodation and food services	Other services	Government	Federal	State and local government
2001	9.3	14.7	29.4	9.8	10.5	9.7	29.5	52.8	25.4	13.0	5.4	4.1	5.6
2002	9.9	18.4	29.0	10.0	9.3	10.2	25.8	45.1	22.4	15.7	5.6	5.2	5.6
2003	7.1	17.0	30.8	10.4	13.3	9.9	28.0	53.3	23.6	19.3	6.0	5.8	6.0
2004	7.2	17.2	29.9	9.8	10.4	9.7	28.7	57.4	23.7	15.8	6.4	5.9	6.4
2005	7.9	18.2	30.0	9.7	10.6	9.5	25.2	47.9	21.3	15.8	6.0	6.1	5.9
2006	7.6	18.7	26.1	9.5	11.7	9.0	23.3	43.4	19.8	17.2	6.2	7.0	6.1
2007	9.9	23.1	26.5	9.5	13.2	8.8	23.6	46.3	19.8	16.7	6.1	8.2	5.8
2008	11.0	21.0	28.2	10.8	13.0	10.4	23.5	45.6	19.7	17.6	5.2	4.0	5.4
2009	13.6	30.2	30.9	11.8	15.2	11.1	26.5	44.9	23.3	24.1	7.2	7.7	7.2
2000													
December	0.5	0.2	3.8	0.8	1.7	0.6	1.5	3.3	1.2	36.0	0.4	0.2	0.4
2001													
January	3.0	1.0	3.3	1.2	1.2	1.2	2.5	5.0	2.1	103.0	0.5	1.0	0.4
February	0.4	1.1	2.0	0.5	0.3	0.6	1.2	2.8	1.0	25.0	0.2	0.2	0.2
March	0.4	1.4	3.3	0.6	0.4	0.6	2.1	2.3	2.1	73.0	0.2	0.2	0.2
April	0.8	0.8	2.0	0.6	0.9	0.6	3.3	3.5	3.3	76.0	0.3	0.2	0.3
May	0.5	0.5	2.2	0.6	0.7	0.6	1.3	1.3	1.3	26.0	0.4	0.2	0.5
June	0.4	0.9	2.0	0.9	1.0	0.9	1.7	1.9	1.6	48.0	0.8	0.2	0.8
July	0.8	0.4	1.9	1.4	1.6	1.4	2.3	3.4	2.1	61.0	0.5	0.3	0.5
August	0.5	0.7	1.9	1.1	2.7	0.9	2.0	4.6	1.5	95.0	1.0	0.3	1.1
September	0.5	2.5	2.6	0.7	0.5	0.8	4.1	13.1	2.4	57.0	0.5	0.4	0.5
October	1.0	1.9	2.8	1.1	0.9	1.1	3.6	5.6	3.3	48.0	0.6	0.4	0.6
November	0.6	1.8	2.3	0.6	0.4	0.6	3.4	6.9	2.8	46.0	0.2	0.2	0.2
December	0.5	1.7	3.2	0.5	0.3	0.5	2.0	2.5	1.9	28.0	0.3	0.3	0.3
2002													
January	2.6	2.1	3.0	1.4	1.3	1.4	2.2	2.7	2.1	85.0	0.5	1.0	0.5
February	0.7	0.7	1.8	0.6	0.3	0.7	1.6	1.6	1.6	42.0	0.2	0.3	0.2
March	0.4	0.9	2.2	0.7	0.7	0.7	1.3	1.8	1.2	31.0	0.2	0.3	0.2
April	0.8	0.9	2.3	0.8	0.7	0.9	2.3	5.3	1.8	90.0	0.3	0.4	0.3
May	0.9	0.9	1.8	0.8	0.9	0.8	1.4	1.2	1.5	42.0	0.4	0.2	0.4
June	1.0	1.3	2.0	0.9	1.0	0.9	1.7	1.2	1.8	79.0	0.7	0.3	0.8
July	0.8	1.6	2.9	1.1	1.1	1.1	2.7	5.1	2.2	113.0	0.7	0.4	0.8
August	0.7	1.8	1.9	0.9	1.2	0.9	2.3	5.7	1.7	131.0	0.7	0.3	0.8
September	0.5	2.1	2.3	0.8	1.2	0.8	2.8	7.0	2.1	73.0	0.8	0.6	0.8
October	0.5	3.0	2.6	0.8	0.3	0.8	2.7	3.5	2.6	51.0	0.4	0.5	0.4
November	0.6	1.6	2.5	0.4	0.1	0.5	2.7	6.7	2.1	49.0	0.3	0.5	0.3
December	0.6	1.3	3.7	0.6	0.6	0.6	1.9	3.1	1.7	55.0	0.3	0.3	0.3
2003													
January	1.5	3.4	3.5	1.2	1.0	1.3	3.1	5.1	2.8	123.0	0.5	0.9	0.5
February	0.5	0.5	2.2	0.6	0.4	0.6	1.5	2.8	1.3	66.0	0.2	0.3	0.2
March	0.6	1.4	1.8	0.6	0.3	0.7	1.7	3.2	1.5	42.0	0.3	0.3	0.3
April	0.5	0.9	2.9	0.7	0.7	0.7	2.6	6.6	1.9	74.0	0.4	0.3	0.4
May	0.5	0.9	1.9	1.0	1.5	0.9	2.2	4.2	1.8	41.0	0.4	0.3	0.5
June	0.4	1.1	2.4	1.2	2.4	1.0	1.8	1.6	1.8	111.0	0.7	0.4	0.7
July	0.8	2.6	2.4	1.4	2.6	1.2	1.5	1.6	1.5	106.0	0.7	0.4	0.7
August	0.4	1.1	2.5	1.2	2.4	1.0	2.3	4.7	1.9	126.0	0.9	0.4	0.9
September	0.6	1.5	2.3	0.7	0.6	0.7	3.3	9.0	2.2	117.0	0.7	0.5	0.8
October	0.6	1.1	3.0	0.8	0.8	0.8	3.0	5.9	2.5	99.0	0.4	0.7	0.4
November	0.4	0.8	2.4	0.6	0.5	0.6	2.4	6.0	1.9	54.0	0.4	1.0	0.4
December	0.4	1.6	3.5	0.5	0.6	0.5	2.5	3.2	2.4	83.0	0.4	0.2	0.4
2004													
January	1.0	2.4	4.3	1.1	1.0	1.2	3.0	4.6	2.8	78.0	0.7	0.9	0.6
February	0.4	0.5	1.6	0.7	0.4	0.7	1.7	4.0	1.3	49.0	0.2	0.3	0.2
March	0.5	1.4	2.4	0.7	0.7	0.6	1.7	2.5	1.6	38.0	0.2	0.3	0.2
April	0.5	1.1	3.0	0.8	0.5	0.9	2.5	4.9	2.1	79.0	0.3	0.3	0.3
May	0.4	0.6	1.9	0.8	1.0	0.7	1.4	2.6	1.2	52.0	0.4	0.3	0.4
June	0.4	1.3	2.3	1.0	1.9	0.8	2.1	2.4	2.1	47.0	0.7	0.4	0.7
July	0.6	1.0	2.2	0.8	1.0	0.8	2.5	2.9	2.4	68.0	0.9	0.4	1.0
August	1.0	1.7	2.2	1.0	1.4	1.0	2.6	5.9	1.9	164.0	0.7	0.4	0.8
September	0.5	1.7	2.2	1.0	1.3	1.0	3.5	12.1	1.9	86.0	0.9	0.5	1.0
October	0.8	2.1	2.1	0.6	0.3	0.7	4.0	7.5	3.4	40.0	0.5	0.7	0.5
November	0.6	1.3	2.3	0.6	0.6	0.6	2.0	4.6	1.6	106.0	0.4	1.0	0.4
December	0.5	2.0	3.5	0.7	0.7	0.7	1.7	3.2	1.5	46.0	0.5	0.2	0.4
2005													
January	1.9	2.9	3.6	1.2	0.8	1.2	2.8	4.2	2.6	109.0	0.5	0.5	0.5
February	0.4	2.0	2.0	0.7	0.4	0.7	1.5	2.3	1.4	59.0	0.2	0.3	0.2
March	0.6	1.2	2.6	0.8	0.5	0.9	1.9	1.7	1.9	59.0	0.2	0.3	0.2
April	1.1	1.4	2.6	0.9	0.8	0.9	1.7	3.2	1.5	49.0	0.3	0.5	0.3
May	0.6	1.1	1.6	0.9	1.6	0.8	1.5	2.4	1.3	84.0	0.5	0.3	0.5
June	0.3	0.4	2.6	0.9	1.1	0.8	2.4	2.7	2.3	49.0	0.7	0.6	0.7
July	0.6	1.1	3.0	0.8	1.2	0.8	1.7	1.4	1.8	57.0	0.6	0.5	0.7
August	0.7	0.5	2.5	1.0	1.0	1.0	1.9	4.1	1.4	153.0	0.9	0.5	0.9
September	0.4	2.0	2.1	0.7	1.2	0.6	3.4	12.3	1.8	80.0	0.8	0.7	0.8
October	0.7	2.5	2.5	0.7	0.6	0.7	2.5	4.9	2.1	66.0	0.4	0.3	0.4
November	0.3	1.7	2.1	0.5	0.4	0.6	2.1	5.2	1.6	38.0	0.3	0.3	0.3
December	0.4	1.7	2.8	0.7	1.2	0.6	1.7	3.3	1.4	52.0	0.5	1.2	0.4

[1]Layoffs and discharges are the number of layoffs and discharges during the entire month.
[2]The layoffs and discharges rate is the number of layoffs and discharges during the entire month as a percent of total employment.

Table 7-11. Layoffs and Discharges Levels[1] and Rates,[2] by Industry, December 2000–October 2010
—Continued

(Not seasonally adjusted, levels in thousands, rates per 100.)

Year and month	Level												
	Total	Total private	Mining and logging	Construction	Manufacturing	Durable goods	Non-durable goods	Trade, transportation, and utilities	Wholesale trade	Retail trade	Transportation, warehousing, and utilities	Information	Financial activities
2006													
January	2 386	2 272	8	321	203	100	104	649	55	497	97	22	113
February	1 392	1 341	6	178	114	61	53	309	46	230	32	17	63
March	1 318	1 258	8	176	164	79	85	221	36	149	36	15	71
April	1 765	1 695	10	147	161	69	92	314	50	236	28	33	81
May	1 629	1 510	3	169	138	82	56	315	47	209	59	12	51
June	1 608	1 404	2	126	133	71	62	340	48	240	53	13	53
July	1 869	1 716	4	212	150	94	56	350	101	191	58	25	82
August	1 746	1 608	5	209	151	90	60	305	50	197	58	19	78
September	1 883	1 694	10	208	155	98	58	303	55	186	62	16	61
October	2 036	1 939	6	263	161	97	64	346	68	201	77	31	74
November	1 826	1 746	5	322	139	90	49	287	45	188	54	23	62
December	2 002	1 911	7	303	150	91	58	435	44	324	67	33	80
2007													
January	2 509	2 397	14	333	223	136	87	606	68	423	114	78	131
February	1 405	1 356	6	230	147	93	54	278	37	204	37	25	64
March	1 474	1 423	4	156	141	92	49	255	50	151	54	18	101
April	1 840	1 777	6	223	153	94	59	307	67	180	60	20	101
May	1 500	1 378	5	170	128	76	52	296	53	197	45	21	70
June	1 778	1 614	4	214	135	87	48	286	77	163	47	21	58
July	1 916	1 684	7	201	179	110	69	359	91	207	61	33	107
August	1 940	1 760	9	236	159	94	65	336	64	218	54	27	100
September	2 160	2 020	7	259	172	108	64	343	68	231	43	19	98
October	2 101	2 014	9	265	199	122	77	389	91	235	64	21	113
November	1 919	1 856	9	272	184	114	70	389	65	247	77	14	76
December	2 015	1 918	10	291	149	82	67	439	90	298	50	19	88
2008													
January	2 681	2 566	16	377	221	148	73	637	125	423	89	54	178
February	1 485	1 449	9	198	135	77	58	312	56	215	41	16	58
March	1 534	1 481	6	225	122	78	44	265	58	163	44	30	69
April	1 790	1 738	9	236	196	123	73	326	85	184	56	18	98
May	1 618	1 513	4	212	144	89	55	317	74	197	46	15	64
June	1 816	1 666	6	232	157	94	63	370	75	244	52	32	70
July	2 026	1 893	11	246	162	113	49	410	65	254	91	22	125
August	2 269	2 104	5	263	167	120	47	395	72	253	70	17	115
September	2 017	1 878	6	293	178	112	65	354	72	220	63	33	79
October	2 368	2 285	11	363	257	162	96	455	102	279	75	55	87
November	2 192	2 130	17	401	215	132	82	392	72	244	76	38	75
December	2 753	2 665	19	402	305	197	109	657	179	385	93	48	87
2009													
January	3 859	3 733	21	587	533	368	164	877	270	483	124	98	296
February	2 071	2 015	17	318	278	191	88	406	98	234	74	32	117
March	2 041	1 984	23	281	283	210	73	360	79	194	87	33	123
April	2 546	2 477	20	343	308	225	83	493	112	308	73	45	116
May	1 924	1 738	16	246	219	147	72	376	107	206	64	25	78
June	2 025	1 756	11	226	187	122	65	310	68	170	72	29	94
July	2 406	2 204	17	342	195	108	86	382	85	209	88	34	140
August	2 239	2 036	10	266	185	97	88	300	85	157	59	22	112
September	2 281	2 092	12	321	176	100	75	432	68	267	97	17	70
October	2 283	2 193	18	362	220	128	92	343	59	216	68	29	119
November	1 896	1 815	11	273	177	101	76	343	56	202	85	29	45
December	2 219	2 111	17	326	168	95	73	563	84	314	164	45	79
2010													
January	2 836	2 698	18	414	271	190	81	674	103	474	97	56	122
February	1 424	1 373	8	220	135	79	56	251	58	152	42	23	58
March	1 428	1 362	7	204	123	72	51	305	54	221	30	19	57
April	1 650	1 572	9	242	142	75	67	277	69	161	46	21	69
May	1 543	1 373	8	212	98	65	33	229	58	129	42	25	66
June	1 977	1 556	5	191	111	56	56	306	45	200	62	27	44
July	2 170	1 857	7	280	146	77	69	306	65	198	43	28	83
August	1 946	1 643	7	220	137	72	65	244	55	157	32	27	52
September	1 817	1 583	7	225	136	74	61	257	69	145	43	17	44
October	1 884	1 788	8	280	167	99	68	309	65	171	72	24	95

[1]Layoffs and discharges are the number of layoffs and discharges during the entire month.
[2]The layoffs and discharges rate is the number of layoffs and discharges during the entire month as a percent of total employment.

Table 7-11. Layoffs and Discharges Levels[1] and Rates,[2] by Industry, December 2000–October 2010
—Continued

(Not seasonally adjusted, levels in thousands, rates per 100.)

Year and month	Level												
	Finance and insurance	Real estate and rental and leasing	Profes- sional and business services	Education and health services	Educa- tional services	Health care and social assistance	Leisure and hospitality	Arts, enter- tainment, and recreation	Accommo- dation and food services	Other services	Govern- ment	Federal	State and local govern- ment
2006													
January	71	43	415	179	28	152	269	37	232	91	114	18	97
February	43	21	339	86	8	79	178	32	146	51	50	9	41
March	31	40	285	111	20	91	180	37	143	29	60	11	48
April	43	37	381	151	25	126	261	48	214	157	69	12	57
May	29	23	360	227	50	177	185	66	119	48	118	13	106
June	29	24	311	171	53	118	190	43	147	64	205	18	186
July	36	46	404	183	40	143	228	54	173	79	153	22	131
August	43	35	327	147	28	119	266	94	173	101	139	25	113
September	35	26	399	120	26	93	329	155	173	92	189	26	163
October	34	40	434	122	22	100	397	111	286	103	97	10	87
November	22	40	418	87	13	74	339	96	244	62	80	9	71
December	49	31	512	102	26	76	231	63	168	60	91	17	74
2007													
January	75	56	446	184	43	141	312	88	223	71	112	21	91
February	34	31	300	96	20	76	184	47	137	25	49	12	37
March	48	53	384	128	19	110	186	47	139	48	51	14	37
April	51	50	447	143	32	111	263	88	175	113	63	14	49
May	27	43	282	160	41	119	217	54	163	30	122	17	104
June	40	18	323	212	68	144	261	51	210	99	164	25	139
July	62	45	365	141	22	119	186	29	157	106	232	28	204
August	72	28	335	183	61	122	248	58	190	127	180	24	156
September	54	44	392	149	19	130	480	160	320	100	140	30	110
October	71	42	471	132	15	117	354	124	231	59	87	10	77
November	21	55	462	103	21	82	266	116	150	81	63	9	54
December	52	36	542	106	27	80	218	49	168	56	97	20	77
2008													
January	122	56	510	217	36	181	274	68	206	82	115	28	87
February	34	25	318	127	14	112	222	51	172	53	36	6	30
March	47	22	380	144	15	128	188	52	136	52	53	6	47
April	68	30	431	145	34	111	220	60	160	58	52	8	45
May	31	33	259	207	39	168	204	63	141	88	105	5	100
June	51	20	346	204	56	148	200	31	169	49	150	10	140
July	74	51	394	206	48	158	192	31	161	125	133	7	126
August	72	43	417	208	51	157	372	141	231	144	164	6	158
September	40	38	348	145	21	124	363	129	233	80	139	7	132
October	43	45	440	149	28	121	375	134	241	93	82	9	73
November	33	43	531	107	22	85	291	74	217	63	63	5	58
December	46	42	623	183	32	151	260	65	195	81	87	14	74
2009													
January	195	101	588	244	31	213	331	71	260	159	125	10	115
February	68	48	455	141	17	124	196	36	160	55	56	6	50
March	68	55	420	138	14	124	236	39	197	87	56	5	52
April	75	40	586	203	30	173	270	67	203	93	69	6	63
May	54	24	323	153	56	97	221	24	198	80	185	62	124
June	53	41	351	215	59	156	232	37	195	99	269	66	204
July	84	56	396	295	92	202	247	56	192	155	202	8	194
August	48	64	364	269	77	193	342	103	238	165	203	9	194
September	27	43	370	168	29	138	369	127	242	158	190	8	181
October	54	65	407	153	25	128	448	144	303	94	90	7	83
November	19	26	414	132	13	119	325	96	228	66	81	18	63
December	39	40	441	144	26	118	250	59	191	80	108	12	96
2010													
January	74	48	490	213	27	186	326	56	270	114	137	12	126
February	30	29	324	126	11	116	145	18	127	81	51	8	42
March	32	25	298	127	14	113	171	52	120	51	66	12	54
April	44	25	378	151	21	131	226	66	160	57	78	17	61
May	39	27	313	161	37	124	203	54	150	57	170	42	128
June	27	17	332	230	65	164	242	54	187	68	421	242	179
July	43	40	422	253	67	187	242	66	176	89	314	153	161
August	36	16	318	223	65	158	256	89	167	160	303	127	176
September	35	9	323	204	37	166	311	115	196	61	234	92	142
October	63	32	333	122	14	110	367	100	267	85	96	22	74

[1]Layoffs and discharges are the number of layoffs and discharges during the entire month.
[2]The layoffs and discharges rate is the number of layoffs and discharges during the entire month as a percent of total employment.

Table 7-11. Layoffs and Discharges Levels[1] and Rates,[2] by Industry, December 2000–October 2010
—Continued

(Not seasonally adjusted, levels in thousands, rates per 100.)

Year and month	Rate												
	Total	Total private	Mining and logging	Construction	Manufacturing	Durable goods	Non-durable goods	Trade, transportation, and utilities	Whole-sale trade	Retail trade	Transportation, ware-housing, and utilities	Infor-mation	Financial activities
2006													
January	1.8	2.0	1.3	4.5	1.4	1.1	2.0	2.5	0.9	3.3	2.0	0.7	1.4
February	1.0	1.2	1.0	2.5	0.8	0.7	1.0	1.2	0.8	1.5	0.7	0.6	0.8
March	1.0	1.1	1.2	2.4	1.2	0.9	1.6	0.9	0.6	1.0	0.7	0.5	0.9
April	1.3	1.5	1.5	1.9	1.1	0.8	1.8	1.2	0.6	1.6	0.6	1.1	1.0
May	1.2	1.3	0.4	2.2	1.0	0.9	1.1	1.2	0.8	1.4	1.2	0.4	0.6
June	1.2	1.2	0.3	1.6	0.9	0.8	1.2	1.3	0.8	1.6	1.1	0.4	0.6
July	1.4	1.5	0.6	2.6	1.1	1.0	1.1	1.3	1.7	1.2	1.2	0.8	1.0
August	1.3	1.4	0.8	2.6	1.1	1.0	1.2	1.2	0.8	1.3	1.2	0.6	0.9
September	1.4	1.5	1.5	2.6	1.1	1.1	1.1	1.2	0.9	1.2	1.2	0.5	0.7
October	1.5	1.7	0.8	3.3	1.1	1.1	1.2	1.3	1.1	1.3	1.5	1.0	0.9
November	1.3	1.5	0.8	4.1	1.0	1.0	1.0	1.1	0.8	1.2	1.1	0.8	0.7
December	1.5	1.7	1.0	4.0	1.1	1.0	1.1	1.6	0.7	2.0	1.3	1.1	1.0
2007													
January	1.9	2.1	2.0	4.6	1.6	1.5	1.7	2.3	1.2	2.8	2.3	2.6	1.6
February	1.0	1.2	0.8	3.2	1.1	1.1	1.1	1.1	0.6	1.3	0.7	0.8	0.8
March	1.1	1.2	0.6	2.1	1.0	1.0	1.0	1.0	0.8	1.0	1.1	0.6	1.2
April	1.3	1.5	0.8	3.0	1.1	1.1	1.2	1.2	1.1	1.2	1.2	0.7	1.2
May	1.1	1.2	0.8	2.2	0.9	0.9	1.0	1.1	1.1	1.2	1.2	0.7	0.8
June	1.3	1.4	0.6	2.7	1.0	1.0	0.9	1.1	0.9	1.3	0.9	0.7	0.7
July	1.4	1.4	1.0	2.5	1.3	1.3	1.3	1.3	1.5	1.3	1.2	1.1	1.3
August	1.4	1.5	1.2	3.0	1.1	1.1	1.3	1.3	1.1	1.4	1.1	0.9	1.2
September	1.6	1.7	1.0	3.3	1.2	1.2	1.3	1.3	1.1	1.5	0.8	0.6	1.2
October	1.5	1.7	1.3	3.4	1.4	1.4	1.5	1.5	1.1	1.5	1.2	0.7	1.4
November	1.4	1.6	1.3	3.6	1.3	1.3	1.4	1.4	1.1	1.5	1.5	0.5	0.9
December	1.5	1.7	1.3	3.9	1.1	0.9	1.3	1.6	1.5	1.8	1.0	0.6	1.1
2008													
January	2.0	2.3	2.1	5.3	1.6	1.7	1.5	2.4	2.1	2.7	1.8	1.8	2.2
February	1.1	1.3	1.3	2.8	1.0	0.9	1.2	1.2	0.9	1.4	0.8	0.5	0.7
March	1.1	1.3	0.8	3.2	0.9	0.9	0.9	1.0	1.0	1.1	0.9	1.0	0.8
April	1.3	1.5	1.2	3.3	1.5	1.4	1.5	1.2	1.4	1.2	1.1	0.6	1.2
May	1.2	1.3	0.5	2.9	1.1	1.0	1.1	1.2	1.2	1.3	0.9	0.5	0.8
June	1.3	1.4	0.7	3.1	1.2	1.1	1.3	1.4	1.2	1.6	1.0	1.0	0.9
July	1.5	1.6	1.4	3.3	1.2	1.2	1.0	1.6	1.1	1.7	1.8	0.7	1.5
August	1.7	1.8	0.6	3.5	1.2	1.4	0.9	1.5	1.2	1.7	1.4	0.6	1.4
September	1.5	1.6	0.7	4.0	1.3	1.3	1.3	1.4	1.2	1.5	1.2	1.1	1.0
October	1.7	2.0	1.5	5.0	1.9	1.9	1.9	1.7	1.7	1.8	1.5	1.1	1.1
November	1.6	1.9	2.1	5.8	1.6	1.6	1.7	1.5	1.2	1.6	1.5	1.9	1.1
December	2.0	2.4	2.5	6.1	2.4	2.4	2.3	2.5	3.1	2.5	1.9	1.6	1.1
2009													
January	2.9	3.4	2.8	9.5	4.3	4.7	3.5	3.5	4.7	3.3	2.5	3.4	3.7
February	1.6	1.9	2.3	5.3	2.3	2.5	1.9	1.6	1.7	1.6	1.5	1.1	1.5
March	1.6	1.8	3.2	4.7	2.3	2.8	1.6	1.4	1.4	1.3	1.8	1.2	1.6
April	1.9	2.3	2.9	5.7	2.6	3.0	1.8	2.0	2.0	2.1	1.5	1.6	1.5
May	1.5	1.6	2.2	4.0	1.8	2.0	1.6	1.5	1.9	1.4	1.3	0.9	1.0
June	1.5	1.6	1.6	3.6	1.6	1.7	1.4	1.2	1.2	1.2	1.5	1.0	1.2
July	1.9	2.0	2.5	5.5	1.7	1.5	1.9	1.5	1.5	1.4	1.9	1.2	1.8
August	1.7	1.9	1.5	4.3	1.6	1.3	1.9	1.2	1.5	1.1	1.2	0.8	1.5
September	1.8	1.9	1.7	5.3	1.5	1.4	1.6	1.7	1.2	1.9	2.0	0.6	0.9
October	1.7	2.0	2.7	6.0	1.9	1.8	2.0	1.4	1.1	1.5	1.4	1.1	1.6
November	1.4	1.7	1.6	4.6	1.5	1.4	1.7	1.4	1.0	1.4	1.8	1.1	0.6
December	1.7	2.0	2.5	5.8	1.4	1.3	1.6	2.2	1.5	2.1	3.4	1.6	1.0
2010													
January	2.2	2.6	2.7	7.9	2.4	2.7	1.8	2.8	1.9	3.3	2.1	2.1	1.6
February	1.1	1.3	1.2	4.3	1.2	1.1	1.3	1.0	1.0	1.1	0.9	0.9	0.8
March	1.1	1.3	1.1	3.9	1.1	1.0	1.1	1.2	1.0	1.6	0.6	0.7	0.8
April	1.3	1.5	1.3	4.4	1.2	1.1	1.5	1.1	1.2	1.1	1.0	0.8	0.9
May	1.2	1.3	1.1	3.8	0.8	0.9	0.7	0.9	1.0	0.9	0.9	0.9	0.9
June	1.5	1.4	0.7	3.3	0.9	0.8	1.2	1.2	0.8	1.4	1.3	1.0	0.6
July	1.7	1.7	1.0	4.8	1.2	1.1	1.5	1.2	1.2	1.4	0.9	1.0	1.1
August	1.5	1.5	1.0	3.7	1.2	1.0	1.4	1.0	1.0	1.1	0.7	1.0	0.7
September	1.4	1.5	1.0	3.8	1.2	1.0	1.4	1.0	1.2	1.0	0.9	0.6	0.6
October	1.4	1.6	1.0	4.8	1.4	1.4	1.5	1.2	1.2	1.2	1.5	0.9	1.3

[1] Layoffs and discharges are the number of layoffs and discharges during the entire month.
[2] The layoffs and discharges rate is the number of layoffs and discharges during the entire month as a percent of total employment.

Table 7-11. Layoffs and Discharges Levels[1] and Rates,[2] by Industry, December 2000–October 2010 —Continued

(Not seasonally adjusted, levels in thousands, rates per 100.)

Year and month	Rate												
	Finance and insurance	Real estate and rental and leasing	Profes-sional and business services	Education and health services	Educa-tional services	Health care and social assistance	Leisure and hospitality	Arts, enter-tainment, and recreation	Accommo-dation and food services	Other services	Govern-ment	Federal	State and local govern-ment
2006													
January	1.2	2.0	2.5	1.0	1.0	1.0	2.2	2.2	2.2	91.0	0.5	0.7	0.5
February	0.7	1.0	2.0	0.5	0.3	0.5	1.4	1.9	1.4	51.0	0.2	0.3	0.2
March	0.5	1.9	1.7	0.6	0.7	0.6	1.4	2.1	1.3	29.0	0.3	0.4	0.2
April	0.7	1.7	2.2	0.8	0.8	0.9	2.0	2.5	1.9	157.0	0.3	0.5	0.3
May	0.5	1.0	2.1	1.3	1.7	1.2	1.4	3.3	1.1	48.0	0.5	0.5	0.5
June	0.5	1.1	1.7	1.0	2.0	0.8	1.4	2.0	1.3	64.0	0.9	0.7	1.0
July	0.6	2.1	2.3	1.0	1.6	1.0	1.7	2.4	1.5	79.0	0.7	0.8	0.7
August	0.7	1.6	1.8	0.8	1.1	0.8	1.9	4.3	1.5	101.0	0.7	0.9	0.6
September	0.6	1.2	2.2	0.7	0.9	0.6	2.5	7.8	1.5	92.0	0.9	0.9	0.9
October	0.6	1.9	2.4	0.7	0.7	0.7	3.0	5.9	2.5	103.0	0.4	0.4	0.4
November	0.4	1.8	2.3	0.5	0.4	0.5	2.6	5.3	2.2	62.0	0.4	0.3	0.4
December	0.8	1.4	2.9	0.6	0.9	0.5	1.8	3.5	1.5	60.0	0.4	0.6	0.4
2007													
January	1.2	2.6	2.6	1.0	1.5	0.9	2.5	5.1	2.0	71.0	0.5	0.8	0.5
February	0.5	1.4	1.7	0.5	0.7	0.5	1.4	2.6	1.2	25.0	0.2	0.4	0.2
March	0.8	2.5	2.2	0.7	0.6	0.7	1.4	2.6	1.2	48.0	0.2	0.5	0.2
April	0.8	2.3	2.5	0.8	1.0	0.7	2.0	4.6	1.5	113.0	0.3	0.5	0.2
May	0.4	2.0	1.6	0.9	1.4	0.8	1.6	2.6	1.4	30.0	0.5	0.6	0.5
June	0.6	0.8	1.8	1.2	2.5	0.9	1.9	2.3	1.8	99.0	0.7	0.9	0.7
July	1.0	2.0	2.0	0.8	0.8	0.8	1.3	1.3	1.3	106.0	1.1	1.0	1.1
August	1.2	1.3	1.8	1.0	2.3	0.8	1.8	2.6	1.6	127.0	0.9	0.9	0.9
September	0.9	2.0	2.2	0.8	0.7	0.8	3.5	7.9	2.8	100.0	0.6	1.1	0.6
October	1.2	2.0	2.6	0.7	0.5	0.8	2.6	6.4	2.0	59.0	0.4	0.4	0.4
November	0.3	2.6	2.5	0.5	0.7	0.5	2.0	6.3	1.3	81.0	0.3	0.3	0.3
December	0.9	1.7	3.0	0.6	0.9	0.5	1.6	2.7	1.5	56.0	0.4	0.7	0.4
2008													
January	2.0	2.6	2.9	1.2	1.2	1.2	2.1	3.9	1.9	82.0	0.5	1.0	0.4
February	0.6	1.2	1.8	0.7	0.5	0.7	1.7	2.8	1.5	53.0	0.2	0.2	0.1
March	0.8	1.0	2.1	0.8	0.5	0.8	1.4	2.8	1.2	52.0	0.2	0.2	0.2
April	1.1	1.4	2.4	0.8	1.1	0.7	1.6	3.1	1.4	58.0	0.2	0.3	0.2
May	0.5	1.6	1.5	1.1	1.3	1.1	1.5	3.1	1.2	88.0	0.5	0.2	0.5
June	0.8	0.9	1.9	1.1	2.0	0.9	1.4	1.4	1.4	49.0	0.7	0.3	0.7
July	1.2	2.3	2.2	1.1	1.7	1.0	1.4	1.3	1.4	125.0	0.6	0.2	0.7
August	1.2	2.0	2.3	1.1	1.8	1.0	2.6	6.3	2.0	144.0	0.8	0.2	0.8
September	0.7	1.8	2.0	0.8	0.7	0.8	2.7	6.4	2.0	80.0	0.6	0.3	0.7
October	0.7	2.1	2.5	0.8	0.9	0.8	2.8	7.0	2.1	93.0	0.4	0.3	0.4
November	0.6	2.0	3.0	0.6	0.7	0.5	2.2	4.1	1.9	63.0	0.3	0.2	0.3
December	0.8	2.0	3.6	1.0	1.0	0.9	2.0	3.6	1.7	81.0	0.4	0.5	0.4
2009													
January	3.3	5.0	3.5	1.3	1.0	1.3	2.6	4.1	2.4	159.0	0.6	0.4	0.6
February	1.2	2.4	2.7	0.7	0.5	0.8	1.6	2.1	1.5	55.0	0.2	0.2	0.2
March	1.2	2.8	2.5	0.7	0.4	0.8	1.9	2.2	1.8	87.0	0.2	0.2	0.3
April	1.3	2.0	3.5	1.1	0.9	1.1	2.1	3.6	1.8	93.0	0.3	0.2	0.3
May	0.9	1.2	2.0	0.8	1.8	0.6	1.7	1.2	1.7	80.0	0.8	2.2	0.6
June	0.9	2.0	2.1	1.1	2.0	1.0	1.7	1.7	1.7	99.0	1.2	2.3	1.0
July	1.5	2.8	2.4	1.6	3.3	1.3	1.8	2.5	1.7	155.0	1.0	0.3	1.1
August	0.8	3.2	2.2	1.4	2.8	1.2	2.5	4.8	2.1	165.0	1.0	0.3	1.0
September	0.5	2.2	2.2	0.9	1.0	0.9	2.8	6.4	2.1	158.0	0.9	0.3	0.9
October	0.9	3.3	2.4	0.8	0.8	0.8	3.4	7.7	2.7	94.0	0.4	0.3	0.4
November	0.3	1.3	2.5	0.7	0.4	0.7	2.5	5.5	2.1	66.0	0.4	0.6	0.3
December	0.7	2.0	2.7	0.7	0.8	0.7	2.0	3.4	1.7	80.0	0.5	0.4	0.5
2010													
January	1.3	2.5	3.0	1.1	0.9	1.1	2.6	3.4	2.5	114.0	0.6	0.4	0.6
February	0.5	1.5	2.0	0.6	0.3	0.7	1.2	1.0	1.2	81.0	0.2	0.3	0.2
March	0.6	1.3	1.8	0.6	0.4	0.7	1.4	3.0	1.1	51.0	0.3	0.4	0.3
April	0.8	1.3	2.3	0.8	0.6	0.8	1.7	3.6	1.4	57.0	0.3	0.6	0.3
May	0.7	1.4	1.9	0.8	1.2	0.8	1.5	2.7	1.3	57.0	0.7	1.2	0.6
June	0.5	0.9	2.0	1.2	2.2	1.0	1.8	2.5	1.6	68.0	1.9	7.6	0.9
July	0.8	2.0	2.5	1.3	2.3	1.1	1.8	3.0	1.5	89.0	1.5	5.0	0.9
August	0.6	0.8	1.9	1.2	2.3	1.0	1.9	4.1	1.4	160.0	1.4	4.3	1.0
September	0.6	0.4	1.9	1.0	1.2	1.0	2.3	5.7	1.7	61.0	1.1	3.2	0.7
October	1.1	1.6	2.0	0.6	0.4	0.7	2.8	5.4	2.4	95.0	0.4	0.8	0.4

[1]Layoffs and discharges are the number of layoffs and discharges during the entire month.
[2]The layoffs and discharges rate is the number of layoffs and discharges during the entire month as a percent of total employment.

Table 7-12. Other Separations Levels[1] and Rates,[2] by Industry, December 2000–October 2010

(Not seasonally adjusted, levels in thousands, rates per 100.)

Year and month	Level											
	Total[3]	Total private[3]	Construc-tion	Manufac-turing	Trade, transpor-tation, and utilities[4]	Retail trade	Profes-sional and business services	Education and health services	Leisure and hospitality[5]	Accommo-dation and food services	Govern-ment[6]	State and local govern-ment
2001	4 851	4 145	270	515	850	549	990	407	452	382	707	547
2002	4 711	3 901	215	495	897	543	964	407	369	333	807	661
2003	4 537	3 766	181	462	871	492	768	435	410	364	772	610
2004	4 425	3 634	231	349	952	551	669	385	406	369	791	610
2005	4 369	3 646	199	429	797	469	796	389	365	340	723	576
2006	4 871	4 125	353	431	1 104	668	849	424	326	280	749	546
2007	4 464	3 592	220	391	958	623	646	443	323	265	871	562
2008	4 018	3 370	231	345	960	650	603	455	315	278	648	535
2009	3 921	3 273	131	288	931	597	632	538	295	254	650	541
2000												
December	348	297	24	47	86	35	46	28	30	20	51	41
2001												
January	642	540	33	67	155	120	66	46	67	61	102	54
February	270	234	8	33	69	50	17	28	37	35	36	27
March	343	307	16	51	53	33	88	31	30	27	36	28
April	462	402	29	47	89	60	82	36	30	23	60	49
May	318	263	17	36	62	36	75	21	27	22	55	47
June	479	400	17	46	35	18	172	49	30	30	79	71
July	492	401	41	44	61	32	88	29	56	48	92	79
August	442	386	40	60	53	31	104	44	42	23	56	44
September	368	306	21	29	67	45	72	35	36	30	62	53
October	384	338	22	44	95	53	67	33	40	32	46	35
November	271	235	17	22	49	32	49	27	22	18	36	27
December	380	333	9	36	62	39	110	28	35	33	47	33
2002												
January	636	530	20	72	118	74	146	51	35	31	106	79
February	300	253	10	37	65	33	62	27	19	18	47	35
March	324	280	16	34	38	21	79	33	30	29	44	35
April	421	368	24	40	67	43	91	47	38	36	52	40
May	316	256	11	39	54	30	75	26	26	23	60	50
June	381	284	7	37	66	38	69	28	42	38	96	88
July	499	402	7	47	113	83	100	37	37	34	97	83
August	367	299	23	39	94	62	60	30	25	24	68	57
September	401	340	18	30	92	56	76	39	35	26	60	47
October	366	297	19	46	62	30	63	37	29	26	69	60
November	303	263	17	40	68	40	46	25	25	23	41	29
December	397	329	43	34	60	33	97	27	28	25	67	58
2003												
January	746	624	29	71	164	88	121	72	64	61	121	82
February	292	249	11	44	83	54	36	19	20	19	43	33
March	331	278	11	36	53	31	82	41	38	37	53	40
April	381	324	14	49	58	22	79	34	33	30	58	43
May	333	265	10	28	61	37	54	35	29	28	68	53
June	367	283	22	27	66	36	53	42	27	26	84	74
July	428	345	19	40	81	47	90	35	26	25	83	75
August	357	291	9	42	45	27	71	25	45	26	67	57
September	364	301	8	29	89	54	48	35	31	28	63	54
October	355	310	16	42	66	37	46	32	33	27	45	34
November	268	232	19	25	53	31	43	24	41	37	36	26
December	315	264	13	29	52	28	45	41	23	20	51	39
2004												
January	649	501	46	47	110	61	48	57	60	58	147	84
February	258	213	12	25	46	25	38	37	19	18	46	37
March	300	256	11	29	89	56	55	18	17	15	44	36
April	346	304	13	31	86	38	57	27	34	33	42	34
May	344	280	9	31	66	48	57	39	39	35	63	50
June	400	296	11	31	87	48	75	31	21	18	104	95
July	428	332	18	31	85	57	68	28	38	34	96	82
August	378	313	15	26	94	47	52	40	49	48	65	56
September	359	309	30	29	61	33	50	33	39	31	50	39
October	379	329	46	20	99	56	57	30	20	16	50	35
November	265	232	8	16	62	45	48	22	44	39	34	23
December	319	269	12	33	67	37	64	23	26	24	50	39
2005												
January	584	481	12	52	101	53	59	53	60	55	103	75
February	311	262	10	29	63	39	77	25	20	19	48	36
March	283	233	7	28	72	55	46	15	19	19	50	39
April	342	289	16	35	72	37	54	27	22	20	53	37
May	339	287	12	32	48	26	79	41	34	32	51	45
June	342	230	21	25	56	32	41	35	21	20	113	99
July	357	285	10	47	64	40	41	38	20	18	72	58
August	370	312	26	42	58	35	66	39	38	35	59	50
September	320	263	18	33	67	35	65	31	16	13	57	40
October	351	313	27	34	60	37	88	32	26	24	38	31
November	303	273	28	33	49	27	57	19	23	22	30	25
December	467	418	12	39	87	53	123	34	66	63	49	41

[1]Other separations are the number of other separations during the entire month.
[2]The other separations rate is the number of other separations during the entire month as a percent of total employment.
[3]Includes natural resources and mining, information, financial activities, and other services, not shown separately.
[4]Includes wholesale trade and transportation, warehousing, and utilities, not shown separately.
[5]Includes arts, entertainment, and recreation, not shown separately.
[6]Includes federal government, not shown separately.

Table 7-12. Other Separations Levels[1] and Rates,[2] by Industry, December 2000–October 2010—*Continued*

(Not seasonally adjusted, levels in thousands, rates per 100.)

Year and month	Rate											
	Total[3]	Total private[3]	Construction	Manufacturing	Trade, transportation, and utilities[4]	Retail trade	Professional and business services	Education and health services	Leisure and hospitality[5]	Accommodation and food services	Government[6]	State and local government
2001	3.7	3.7	4.0	3.1	3.3	3.6	6.0	2.6	3.8	3.7	3.3	3.0
2002	3.6	3.6	3.2	3.2	3.5	3.6	6.0	2.5	3.1	3.3	3.8	3.5
2003	3.5	3.5	2.7	3.2	3.4	3.3	4.8	2.6	3.4	3.5	3.6	3.2
2004	3.4	3.3	3.3	2.4	3.7	3.7	4.1	2.3	3.2	3.5	3.7	3.2
2005	3.3	3.3	2.7	3.0	3.1	3.1	4.7	2.2	2.8	3.1	3.3	3.0
2006	3.6	3.6	4.6	3.0	4.2	4.4	4.8	2.4	2.5	2.5	3.4	2.8
2007	3.2	3.1	2.9	2.8	3.6	4.0	3.6	2.4	2.4	2.3	3.9	2.9
2008	2.9	2.9	3.2	2.6	3.7	4.3	3.4	2.4	2.3	2.4	2.9	2.7
2009	3.0	3.0	2.2	2.4	3.7	4.1	3.8	2.8	2.3	2.3	2.9	2.7
2000												
December	0.3	0.3	0.4	0.3	0.3	0.2	0.3	0.2	0.3	0.2	0.2	0.2
2001												
January	0.5	0.5	0.5	0.4	0.6	0.8	0.4	0.3	0.6	0.6	0.5	0.3
February	0.2	0.2	0.1	0.2	0.3	0.3	0.1	0.2	0.3	0.4	0.2	0.1
March	0.3	0.3	0.2	0.3	0.2	0.2	0.5	0.2	0.3	0.3	0.2	0.1
April	0.3	0.3	0.4	0.3	0.3	0.4	0.5	0.2	0.3	0.2	0.3	0.3
May	0.2	0.2	0.2	0.2	0.2	0.2	0.5	0.1	0.2	0.2	0.3	0.3
June	0.4	0.4	0.2	0.3	0.1	0.1	1.0	0.3	0.2	0.3	0.4	0.4
July	0.4	0.4	0.6	0.3	0.2	0.2	0.5	0.2	0.4	0.5	0.5	0.5
August	0.3	0.3	0.6	0.4	0.2	0.2	0.6	0.3	0.3	0.2	0.3	0.3
September	0.3	0.3	0.3	0.2	0.3	0.3	0.4	0.2	0.3	0.3	0.3	0.3
October	0.3	0.3	0.3	0.3	0.4	0.3	0.4	0.2	0.3	0.3	0.2	0.2
November	0.2	0.2	0.3	0.1	0.2	0.2	0.3	0.2	0.2	0.2	0.2	0.1
December	0.3	0.3	0.1	0.2	0.2	0.2	0.7	0.2	0.3	0.3	0.2	0.2
2002												
January	0.5	0.5	0.3	0.5	0.5	0.5	0.9	0.3	0.3	0.3	0.5	0.4
February	0.2	0.2	0.2	0.2	0.3	0.2	0.4	0.2	0.2	0.2	0.2	0.2
March	0.2	0.2	0.2	0.2	0.2	0.1	0.5	0.2	0.3	0.3	0.2	0.2
April	0.3	0.3	0.4	0.3	0.3	0.3	0.6	0.3	0.3	0.4	0.2	0.2
May	0.2	0.2	0.2	0.3	0.2	0.2	0.5	0.2	0.2	0.2	0.3	0.3
June	0.3	0.3	0.1	0.2	0.3	0.3	0.4	0.2	0.3	0.4	0.4	0.5
July	0.4	0.4	0.1	0.3	0.4	0.6	0.6	0.2	0.3	0.3	0.5	0.5
August	0.3	0.3	0.3	0.3	0.4	0.4	0.4	0.2	0.2	0.2	0.3	0.3
September	0.3	0.3	0.3	0.2	0.4	0.4	0.5	0.2	0.3	0.3	0.3	0.3
October	0.3	0.3	0.3	0.3	0.2	0.2	0.4	0.2	0.2	0.3	0.3	0.3
November	0.2	0.2	0.2	0.3	0.3	0.3	0.3	0.1	0.2	0.2	0.2	0.2
December	0.3	0.3	0.7	0.2	0.2	0.2	0.6	0.2	0.2	0.2	0.3	0.3
2003												
January	0.6	0.6	0.5	0.5	0.6	0.6	0.8	0.4	0.6	0.6	0.6	0.4
February	0.2	0.2	0.2	0.3	0.3	0.4	0.2	0.1	0.2	0.2	0.2	0.2
March	0.3	0.3	0.2	0.2	0.2	0.2	0.5	0.2	0.3	0.4	0.2	0.2
April	0.3	0.3	0.2	0.3	0.2	0.2	0.5	0.2	0.3	0.3	0.3	0.2
May	0.3	0.3	0.1	0.2	0.2	0.2	0.3	0.2	0.2	0.3	0.3	0.3
June	0.3	0.3	0.3	0.2	0.3	0.2	0.3	0.3	0.2	0.2	0.4	0.4
July	0.3	0.3	0.3	0.3	0.3	0.3	0.6	0.2	0.2	0.2	0.4	0.4
August	0.3	0.3	0.1	0.3	0.2	0.2	0.4	0.2	0.4	0.2	0.3	0.3
September	0.3	0.3	0.1	0.2	0.4	0.4	0.3	0.2	0.3	0.3	0.3	0.3
October	0.3	0.3	0.2	0.3	0.3	0.2	0.3	0.2	0.3	0.3	0.2	0.2
November	0.2	0.2	0.3	0.2	0.2	0.2	0.3	0.1	0.3	0.4	0.2	0.1
December	0.2	0.2	0.2	0.2	0.2	0.2	0.3	0.2	0.2	0.2	0.2	0.2
2004												
January	0.5	0.5	0.7	0.3	0.4	0.4	0.3	0.3	0.5	0.6	0.7	0.4
February	0.2	0.2	0.2	0.2	0.2	0.2	0.2	0.2	0.2	0.2	0.2	0.2
March	0.2	0.2	0.2	0.2	0.4	0.4	0.3	0.1	0.1	0.1	0.2	0.2
April	0.3	0.3	0.2	0.2	0.3	0.3	0.3	0.2	0.3	0.3	0.2	0.2
May	0.3	0.3	0.1	0.2	0.3	0.3	0.3	0.2	0.3	0.3	0.3	0.3
June	0.3	0.3	0.2	0.2	0.3	0.3	0.5	0.2	0.2	0.2	0.5	0.5
July	0.3	0.3	0.2	0.2	0.3	0.4	0.4	0.2	0.3	0.3	0.5	0.5
August	0.3	0.3	0.4	0.2	0.4	0.3	0.3	0.2	0.4	0.4	0.3	0.3
September	0.3	0.3	0.6	0.1	0.4	0.4	0.3	0.2	0.3	0.3	0.2	0.2
October	0.3	0.3	0.6	0.1	0.4	0.4	0.3	0.2	0.2	0.1	0.2	0.2
November	0.2	0.2	0.1	0.1	0.2	0.3	0.3	0.1	0.4	0.4	0.2	0.1
December	0.2	0.2	0.2	0.2	0.3	0.2	0.4	0.1	0.2	0.2	0.2	0.2
2005												
January	0.4	0.4	0.2	0.4	0.4	0.4	0.4	0.3	0.5	0.5	0.5	0.4
February	0.2	0.2	0.2	0.2	0.2	0.3	0.5	0.1	0.2	0.2	0.2	0.2
March	0.2	0.2	0.1	0.2	0.3	0.4	0.3	0.1	0.2	0.2	0.2	0.2
April	0.3	0.3	0.2	0.2	0.3	0.2	0.3	0.2	0.2	0.2	0.2	0.2
May	0.3	0.3	0.2	0.2	0.2	0.2	0.5	0.2	0.3	0.3	0.2	0.2
June	0.3	0.3	0.3	0.2	0.2	0.2	0.2	0.2	0.2	0.2	0.5	0.5
July	0.3	0.3	0.1	0.3	0.2	0.3	0.2	0.2	0.1	0.2	0.4	0.3
August	0.3	0.3	0.3	0.3	0.2	0.2	0.4	0.2	0.3	0.3	0.3	0.3
September	0.2	0.2	0.2	0.2	0.3	0.2	0.4	0.2	0.1	0.1	0.3	0.2
October	0.3	0.3	0.4	0.2	0.2	0.2	0.5	0.2	0.2	0.2	0.2	0.2
November	0.2	0.2	0.4	0.2	0.2	0.2	0.3	0.1	0.2	0.2	0.1	0.1
December	0.3	0.3	0.2	0.3	0.3	0.3	0.7	0.2	0.5	0.6	0.2	0.2

[1]Other separations are the number of other separations during the entire month.
[2]The other separations rate is the number of other separations during the entire month as a percent of total employment.
[3]Includes natural resources and mining, information, financial activities, and other services, not shown separately.
[4]Includes wholesale trade and transportation, warehousing, and utilities, not shown separately.
[5]Includes arts, entertainment, and recreation, not shown separately.
[6]Includes federal government, not shown separately.

Table 7-12. Other Separations Levels[1] and Rates,[2] by Industry, December 2000–October 2010—*Continued*

(Not seasonally adjusted, levels in thousands, rates per 100.)

Year and month	Level											
	Total[3]	Total private[3]	Construction	Manufacturing	Trade, transportation, and utilities[4]	Retail trade	Professional and business services	Education and health services	Leisure and hospitality[5]	Accommodation and food services	Government[6]	State and local government
2006												
January	612	520	25	68	110	60	177	40	27	20	92	57
February	318	280	20	40	86	49	37	21	32	28	38	25
March	341	293	20	36	85	47	61	27	23	21	48	33
April	425	376	41	33	91	49	63	52	38	34	49	35
May	430	362	44	28	118	74	61	28	32	28	69	49
June	478	371	24	42	113	74	83	37	25	24	107	94
July	484	410	27	47	96	53	84	62	24	22	75	58
August	363	280	18	32	72	46	43	35	33	27	83	63
September	368	302	36	27	84	59	43	26	18	15	65	37
October	420	383	45	31	91	53	79	36	30	27	38	31
November	297	264	31	23	66	48	67	30	16	12	34	25
December	335	284	22	24	92	56	51	30	28	22	51	39
2007												
January	595	506	30	52	141	102	67	78	28	23	89	56
February	325	265	25	37	67	40	59	21	20	19	59	38
March	315	264	22	29	86	59	45	26	22	18	51	28
April	381	322	9	49	81	53	54	30	32	26	59	32
May	311	231	22	33	51	31	38	31	18	14	80	48
June	421	289	8	37	91	58	49	43	23	20	132	99
July	466	358	23	22	75	44	73	52	43	35	108	69
August	358	267	10	26	69	43	54	28	45	31	91	56
September	338	258	11	34	70	49	64	25	17	14	79	35
October	341	307	19	23	66	37	51	42	30	26	34	26
November	278	246	23	27	75	58	37	28	22	20	32	26
December	335	279	18	22	86	49	55	39	23	19	57	49
2008												
January	445	363	18	45	84	56	66	47	60	57	83	52
February	292	252	17	25	83	70	36	40	16	15	39	31
March	329	288	21	35	80	65	74	35	15	14	41	31
April	401	357	36	30	125	103	27	44	34	31	44	37
May	289	237	18	28	61	44	46	35	27	24	53	43
June	306	215	20	23	66	41	29	29	27	25	91	84
July	368	299	13	26	77	44	55	29	41	38	69	62
August	346	289	16	24	85	50	75	44	17	14	58	51
September	345	286	9	29	83	41	55	33	25	13	59	51
October	350	308	24	43	77	47	56	42	20	19	41	35
November	265	236	21	19	75	53	32	41	21	18	28	22
December	282	240	18	18	64	36	52	36	12	10	42	36
2009												
January	531	461	23	46	131	75	60	99	25	18	70	58
February	264	234	8	18	51	35	62	47	29	28	30	24
March	294	262	9	24	80	52	50	49	18	15	32	26
April	357	318	22	24	112	87	69	39	14	13	39	31
May	271	224	6	22	80	56	32	32	24	23	47	39
June	335	244	8	34	43	31	43	58	30	28	91	82
July	370	273	11	22	73	46	64	36	29	25	98	82
August	338	282	5	21	75	63	52	52	29	24	56	48
September	305	254	6	27	77	39	42	42	33	30	52	44
October	357	308	6	18	118	52	62	25	25	17	49	36
November	220	188	7	12	47	34	56	21	18	14	32	28
December	279	225	20	20	44	27	40	38	21	19	54	43
2010												
January	532	457	27	36	122	63	57	66	31	24	75	55
February	277	236	17	14	67	44	43	28	20	17	40	32
March	300	259	18	21	52	26	77	38	24	23	41	33
April	359	311	25	26	63	43	80	29	28	27	48	37
May	304	233	10	19	69	54	49	27	25	22	70	60
June	389	261	10	19	62	42	49	45	20	17	127	119
July	431	323	16	24	77	48	63	48	50	42	108	98
August	359	280	7	21	102	79	39	37	40	36	79	72
September	354	285	15	14	80	49	74	31	36	34	69	58
October	302	257	25	20	66	44	45	30	29	25	44	37

[1]Other separations are the number of other separations during the entire month.
[2]The other separations rate is the number of other separations during the entire month as a percent of total employment.
[3]Includes natural resources and mining, information, financial activities, and other services, not shown separately.
[4]Includes wholesale trade and transportation, warehousing, and utilities, not shown separately.
[5]Includes arts, entertainment, and recreation, not shown separately.
[6]Includes federal government, not shown separately.

Table 7-12. Other Separations Levels[1] and Rates,[2] by Industry, December 2000–October 2010—*Continued*

(Not seasonally adjusted, levels in thousands, rates per 100.)

Year and month	Rate											
	Total[3]	Total private[3]	Construction	Manufacturing	Trade, transportation, and utilities[4]	Retail trade	Professional and business services	Education and health services	Leisure and hospitality[5]	Accommodation and food services	Government[6]	State and local government
2006												
January	0.5	0.5	0.3	0.5	0.4	0.4	1.0	0.2	0.2	0.2	0.4	0.3
February	0.2	0.2	0.3	0.3	0.3	0.3	0.2	0.1	0.3	0.3	0.2	0.1
March	0.3	0.3	0.3	0.3	0.3	0.3	0.4	0.2	0.2	0.2	0.2	0.2
April	0.3	0.3	0.5	0.2	0.4	0.3	0.4	0.3	0.3	0.3	0.2	0.2
May	0.3	0.3	0.6	0.2	0.5	0.5	0.3	0.2	0.2	0.2	0.3	0.2
June	0.3	0.3	0.3	0.3	0.4	0.5	0.5	0.2	0.2	0.2	0.5	0.5
July	0.4	0.4	0.3	0.3	0.4	0.3	0.5	0.4	0.2	0.2	0.4	0.3
August	0.3	0.3	0.2	0.2	0.3	0.3	0.2	0.2	0.2	0.2	0.4	0.3
September	0.3	0.3	0.4	0.2	0.3	0.4	0.2	0.1	0.1	0.1	0.3	0.2
October	0.3	0.3	0.6	0.2	0.3	0.3	0.4	0.2	0.2	0.2	0.2	0.2
November	0.2	0.2	0.4	0.2	0.2	0.3	0.4	0.2	0.1	0.1	0.1	0.1
December	0.2	0.2	0.3	0.2	0.3	0.3	0.3	0.2	0.2	0.2	0.2	0.2
2007												
January	0.4	0.4	0.4	0.4	0.5	0.7	0.4	0.4	0.2	0.2	0.4	0.3
February	0.2	0.2	0.3	0.3	0.3	0.3	0.3	0.1	0.2	0.2	0.3	0.2
March	0.2	0.2	0.3	0.2	0.3	0.4	0.3	0.1	0.2	0.2	0.2	0.1
April	0.3	0.3	0.1	0.4	0.3	0.3	0.3	0.2	0.2	0.2	0.3	0.2
May	0.2	0.2	0.3	0.2	0.2	0.2	0.2	0.2	0.1	0.1	0.4	0.2
June	0.3	0.3	0.1	0.3	0.3	0.4	0.3	0.2	0.2	0.2	0.6	0.5
July	0.3	0.3	0.3	0.2	0.3	0.3	0.4	0.3	0.3	0.3	0.5	0.4
August	0.3	0.3	0.1	0.2	0.3	0.3	0.3	0.2	0.3	0.3	0.4	0.3
September	0.2	0.2	0.1	0.2	0.3	0.3	0.4	0.1	0.1	0.1	0.4	0.2
October	0.2	0.2	0.2	0.2	0.2	0.2	0.3	0.2	0.2	0.2	0.2	0.1
November	0.2	0.2	0.3	0.2	0.3	0.4	0.2	0.2	0.2	0.2	0.1	0.1
December	0.2	0.2	0.2	0.2	0.3	0.3	0.3	0.2	0.2	0.2	0.3	0.2
2008												
January	0.3	0.3	0.3	0.3	0.3	0.4	0.4	0.3	0.5	0.5	0.4	0.3
February	0.2	0.2	0.2	0.2	0.3	0.5	0.2	0.2	0.1	0.1	0.2	0.2
March	0.2	0.2	0.3	0.3	0.3	0.4	0.4	0.2	0.1	0.1	0.2	0.2
April	0.3	0.3	0.5	0.2	0.5	0.7	0.1	0.2	0.3	0.3	0.2	0.2
May	0.2	0.2	0.2	0.2	0.2	0.3	0.3	0.2	0.2	0.2	0.2	0.2
June	0.2	0.2	0.3	0.2	0.3	0.3	0.2	0.2	0.2	0.2	0.4	0.4
July	0.3	0.3	0.2	0.2	0.3	0.3	0.3	0.2	0.3	0.3	0.3	0.3
August	0.3	0.3	0.2	0.2	0.3	0.3	0.4	0.2	0.1	0.1	0.3	0.3
September	0.3	0.3	0.1	0.2	0.3	0.3	0.3	0.2	0.2	0.2	0.3	0.3
October	0.3	0.3	0.3	0.3	0.3	0.3	0.3	0.2	0.2	0.2	0.2	0.2
November	0.2	0.2	0.3	0.1	0.3	0.3	0.2	0.2	0.2	0.2	0.1	0.1
December	0.2	0.2	0.3	0.1	0.2	0.2	0.3	0.2	0.1	0.1	0.2	0.2
2009												
January	0.4	0.4	0.4	0.4	0.5	0.5	0.4	0.5	0.2	0.2	0.3	0.3
February	0.2	0.2	0.1	0.1	0.2	0.2	0.4	0.2	0.2	0.3	0.1	0.1
March	0.2	0.2	0.2	0.2	0.3	0.4	0.3	0.3	0.1	0.1	0.1	0.1
April	0.3	0.3	0.4	0.2	0.5	0.6	0.4	0.2	0.1	0.1	0.2	0.2
May	0.2	0.2	0.1	0.2	0.3	0.4	0.2	0.2	0.2	0.2	0.2	0.2
June	0.3	0.3	0.1	0.3	0.2	0.2	0.3	0.3	0.2	0.2	0.4	0.4
July	0.3	0.3	0.2	0.2	0.3	0.3	0.4	0.2	0.2	0.2	0.5	0.4
August	0.3	0.3	0.1	0.2	0.3	0.4	0.3	0.3	0.2	0.2	0.3	0.3
September	0.2	0.2	0.1	0.2	0.3	0.3	0.3	0.2	0.2	0.3	0.2	0.2
October	0.3	0.3	0.1	0.2	0.5	0.4	0.4	0.1	0.2	0.2	0.2	0.2
November	0.2	0.2	0.1	0.1	0.2	0.2	0.3	0.1	0.1	0.1	0.1	0.1
December	0.2	0.2	0.4	0.2	0.2	0.2	0.2	0.2	0.2	0.2	0.2	0.2
2010												
January	0.4	0.4	0.5	0.3	0.5	0.4	0.4	0.3	0.3	0.2	0.3	0.3
February	0.2	0.2	0.3	0.1	0.3	0.3	0.3	0.1	0.2	0.2	0.2	0.2
March	0.2	0.2	0.3	0.2	0.2	0.2	0.5	0.2	0.2	0.2	0.2	0.2
April	0.3	0.3	0.4	0.2	0.3	0.3	0.5	0.1	0.2	0.2	0.2	0.2
May	0.2	0.2	0.2	0.2	0.3	0.4	0.3	0.1	0.2	0.2	0.3	0.3
June	0.3	0.3	0.2	0.2	0.3	0.3	0.3	0.2	0.1	0.1	0.6	0.6
July	0.3	0.3	0.3	0.2	0.3	0.3	0.4	0.2	0.4	0.4	0.5	0.5
August	0.3	0.3	0.1	0.2	0.4	0.5	0.2	0.2	0.3	0.3	0.4	0.4
September	0.3	0.3	0.2	0.1	0.3	0.3	0.4	0.2	0.3	0.3	0.3	0.3
October	0.2	0.2	0.4	0.2	0.3	0.3	0.3	0.2	0.2	0.2	0.2	0.2

[1]Other separations are the number of other separations during the entire month.
[2]The other separations rate is the number of other separations during the entire month as a percent of total employment.
[3]Includes natural resources and mining, information, financial activities, and other services, not shown separately.
[4]Includes wholesale trade and transportation, warehousing, and utilities, not shown separately.
[5]Includes arts, entertainment, and recreation, not shown separately.
[6]Includes federal government, not shown separately.

Chapter Eight

LABOR-MANAGEMENT RELATIONS

LABOR-MANAGEMENT RELATIONS

HIGHLIGHTS

This chapter contains information on historical trends in union membership, earnings, and work stoppages.

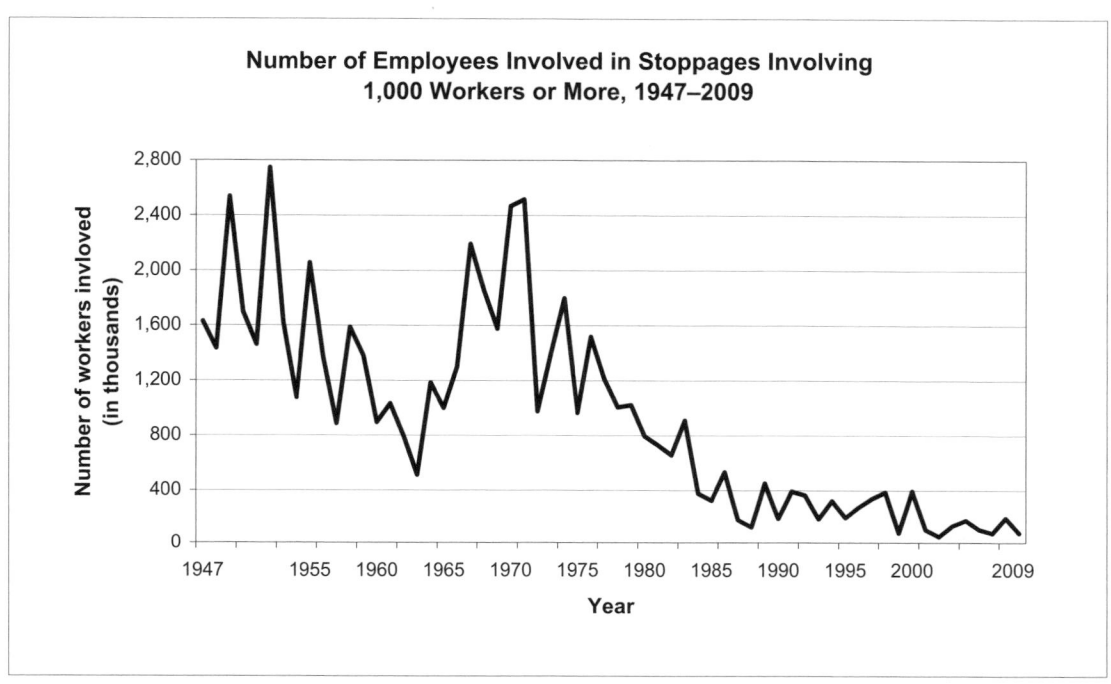

The number of work stoppages and the number of employees involved in work stoppages has declined dramatically since 1947 and has been gradually declining since the early 1980s. In 2009, there were only 5 work stoppages that involved 1,000 workers or more, which, is the lowest amount ever recorded since the Bureau of Labor Statistics (BLS) first began recording data in 1947. There was a record-high 470 work stoppages involving 1,000 workers or more in 1952. (See Table 8-1.)

OTHER HIGHLIGHTS

- In 2009, the number of workers belonging to a union declined to 15,327,000 after increasing in 2007 and 2008. Union members accounted for 12.3 percent of employed wage and salary workers in 2009, down slightly from 12.4 percent in 2008. In 1983, the first year for which comparable union data are available, the union membership rate was 20.1 percent. (See Tables 8-2 and 8-5.)

- Education, training, and library occupations had the highest unionization rate among all occupations at 38.1 percent, followed by protective service occupations at 35.6 percent, and construction and extraction workers at 21.0 percent. Sales and related occupations had the lowest rate of unionization at 3.1 percent followed by management occupations at 4.1 percent. (See Table 8-3.)

- The median weekly earnings of union members were significantly higher than that of non-union members in both the private and public sector. In the private sector, the median weekly earnings of union members were $856 compared to $697 of non-union members. In the public sector, union members had a median weekly earning of $947 compared to $782 for non-union members. (See Table 8-4.)

- Four states had union membership rates over 20 percent in 2009—New York (25.2 percent), Hawaii (23.5 percent), and Alaska (22.3 percent), and Washington (20.2 percent). North Carolina reported the lowest union membership again in 2009 at 3.1 percent. (See Table 8-6.)

NOTES AND DEFINITIONS

WORK STOPPAGES

Collection and Coverage

Data on work stoppages measure the number and duration of major strikes or lockouts (involving 1,000 workers or more) during the year, the number of workers involved in these stoppages, and the amount of time lost due to these stoppages.

Information on work stoppages is obtained from reports issued by the Federal Mediation and Conciliation Service, state labor market information offices, Bureau of Labor Statistics (BLS) Strike Reports from the Office of Employment and Unemployment Statistics, and media sources such as the *Daily Labor Report* and the *Wall Street Journal*. One or both parties involved in the work stoppage (employer and/or union) is contacted to verify the duration of the stoppage and number of workers idled by the stoppage.

Concepts and Definitions

Major work stoppage includes both worker-initiated strikes and employer-initiated lockouts involving 1,000 workers or more. BLS does not distinguish between lockouts and strikes in its statistics.

Workers involved consists of workers directly involved in the stoppage. This category does not measure the indirect or secondary effect of stoppages on other establishments whose employees are idle from material shortages or lack of service.

Days of idleness is calculated by taking the number of workers involved in the strike or lockout and multiplying it by the number of days workers are off the job. The number of working days lost for every major work stoppage is based on a 5-day workweek (Monday through Friday), excluding federal holidays.

Sources of Additional Information

Additional information is available in BLS news release USDL 10-0170, "Major Work Stoppages in 2009" on the BLS Web site at <http://www.bls.gov/wsp/home.htm>.

UNION MEMBERSHIP

Collection and Coverage

The estimates of union membership are obtained from the Current Population Survey (CPS), which provides basic information on the labor force, employment, and unem-ployment. The survey is conducted monthly for the Bureau of Labor Statistics by the U.S. Census Bureau from a scien-tifically selected national sample of about 60,000 house-holds. The union membership and earnings data are tabulated from one-quarter of the CPS monthly sample and are limited to wage and salary workers. All self-employed workers are excluded. The data in these tables are annual averages.

Union membership data for 2009 are not strictly compara-ble with data for 2008 and earlier years because of the introduction of updated population controls with the release of January data. The effect of the revised popula-tion controls on the union membership estimates is unknown. However, the effect of the new controls on the monthly CPS estimates was to decrease the December 2008 employment level by 407,000. The updated controls had lit-tle or no effect on unemployment rates and other ratios.

Concepts and Definitions

Union members are members of a labor union or an employee association similar to a union.

Represented by unions refers to union members, as well as to workers who have no union affiliation but whose jobs are covered by a union contract.

Usual weekly earnings represent earnings before taxes and other deductions and include any overtime pay, commis-sions, or tips usually received (at the main job in the case of multiple jobholders). Prior to 1994, respondents were asked how much they usually earned per week. Since January 1994, respondents have been asked to identify the easiest way for them to report earnings (hourly, weekly, biweekly, twice monthly, monthly, annually, other) and how much they usually earn in the reported time period. Earnings reported on a basis other than weekly are converted to a weekly equivalent. The term "usual" is as perceived by the respon-dent. If the respondent asks for a definition of "usual," inter-viewers are instructed to define the term as more than half of the weeks worked during the past 4 or 5 months.

Median earnings is the amount which divides a given earn-ings distribution into two equal groups, one having earnings above the median and the other having earnings below the median. The estimating procedure places each reported or calculated weekly earnings value into $50-wide intervals which are centered around multiples of $50. The actual value is estimated through the linear interpolation of the interval in which the median lies.

Wage and salary workers are workers who receive wages, salaries, commissions, tips, payment in kind, or piece rates. The group includes employees in both the private and public sectors, but, for the purposes of the union membership and earnings series, excludes all self-employed persons, regardless of whether or not their businesses are incorporated.

Full-time workers are workers who usually work 35 hours or more per week at their sole or principal job.

Part-time workers are workers who usually work fewer than 35 hours per week at their sole or principal job.

Hispanic or Latino ethnicity refers to persons who identified themselves in the enumeration process as being Spanish, Hispanic, or Latino. Persons whose ethnicity is identified as Hispanic or Latino may be of any race.

Sources of Additional Information

For additional information see BLS news release USDL 10-0069, "Union Members in 2009."

Table 8-1. Work Stoppages Involving 1,000 Workers or More, 1947–2009

(Number, percent.)

Year	Stoppages beginning during the year		Days idle during the year[1]	
	Number	Workers involved (thousands)[2]	Number (thousands)	Percent of estimated total working time[3]
1947	270	1 629	25 720	. . .
1948	245	1 435	26 127	0.22
1949	262	2 537	43 420	0.38
1950	424	1 698	30 390	0.26
1951	415	1 462	15 070	0.12
1952	470	2 746	48 820	0.38
1953	437	1 623	18 130	0.14
1954	265	1 075	16 630	0.13
1955	363	2 055	21 180	0.16
1956	287	1 370	26 840	0.20
1957	279	887	10 340	0.07
1958	332	1 587	17 900	0.13
1959	245	1 381	60 850	0.43
1960	222	896	13 260	0.09
1961	195	1 031	10 140	0.07
1962	211	793	11 760	0.08
1963	181	512	10 020	0.07
1964	246	1 183	16 220	0.11
1965	268	999	15 140	0.10
1966	321	1 300	16 000	0.10
1967	381	2 192	31 320	0.18
1968	392	1 855	35 367	0.20
1969	412	1 576	29 397	0.16
1970	381	2 468	52 761	0.29
1971	298	2 516	35 538	0.19
1972	250	975	16 764	0.09
1973	317	1 400	16 260	0.08
1974	424	1 796	31 809	0.16
1975	235	965	17 563	0.09
1976	231	1 519	23 962	0.12
1977	298	1 212	21 258	0.10
1978	219	1 006	23 774	0.11
1979	235	1 021	20 409	0.09
1980	187	795	20 844	0.09
1981	145	729	16 908	0.07
1982	96	656	9 061	0.04
1983	81	909	17 461	0.08
1984	62	376	8 499	0.04
1985	54	324	7 079	0.03
1986	69	533	11 861	0.05
1987	46	174	4 481	0.02
1988	40	118	4 381	0.02
1989	51	452	16 996	0.07
1990	44	185	5 926	0.02
1991	40	392	4 584	0.02
1992	35	364	3 989	0.01
1993	35	182	3 981	0.01
1994	45	322	5 021	0.02
1995	31	192	5 771	0.02
1996	37	273	4 889	0.02
1997	29	339	4 497	0.01
1998	34	387	5 116	0.02
1999	17	73	1 996	0.01
2000	39	394	20 419	0.06
2001	29	99	1 151	([4])
2002	19	46	660	([4])
2003	14	129	4 091	0.01
2004	17	171	3 344	0.01
2005	22	100	1 736	0.01
2006	20	70	2 688	0.01
2007	21	189	1 265	([4])
2008	15	72	1 954	0.01
2009	5	13	124	([4])

[1]Days idle include all stoppages in effect during the reference period. For work stoppages that are still ongoing at the end of the calendar year, only those days of idleness during the calendar year are counted.
[2]Workers are counted more than once if involved in more than one stoppage during the reference period.
[3]Agricultural and government workers are included in the calculation of estimated working time; private household, forestry, and fishery workers are excluded.
[4]Less than 0.005 percent.
. . . = Not available.

Table 8-2. Union Affiliation of Employed Wage and Salary Workers, by Selected Characteristics, 2004–2009

(Numbers in thousands, percent.)

Characteristic	2004					2005					2006				
	Total employed	Member of union[1]		Represented by union[2]		Total employed	Member of union[1]		Represented by union[2]		Total employed	Member of union[1]		Represented by union[2]	
		Total	Percent of employed	Total	Percent of employed		Total	Percent of employed	Total	Percent of employed		Total	Percent of employed	Total	Percent of employed
SEX AND AGE															
Both Sexes, 16 Years and Over	123 554	15 472	12.5	17 087	13.8	125 889	15 685	12.5	17 223	13.7	128 237	15 359	12.0	16 860	13.1
16 to 24 years	19 109	890	4.7	1 019	5.3	19 283	878	4.6	1 019	5.3	19 538	857	4.4	978	5.0
25 years and over	104 444	14 581	14.0	16 069	15.4	106 606	14 808	13.9	16 204	15.2	108 699	14 502	13.3	15 883	14.6
25 to 34 years	28 202	2 982	10.6	3 316	11.8	28 450	3 044	10.7	3 368	11.8	28 805	2 899	10.1	3 195	11.1
35 to 44 years	30 470	4 173	13.7	4 590	15.1	30 654	4 211	13.7	4 579	14.9	30 526	3 997	13.1	4 356	14.3
45 to 54 years	28 039	4 771	17.0	5 233	18.7	28 714	4 731	16.5	5 158	18.0	29 401	4 710	16.0	5 131	17.5
55 to 64 years	14 239	2 390	16.8	2 617	18.4	15 158	2 496	16.5	2 732	18.0	16 095	2 568	16.0	2 832	17.6
65 years and over	3 495	264	7.5	314	9.0	3 631	325	8.9	366	10.1	3 872	328	8.5	370	9.5
Men, 16 Years and Over	64 145	8 878	13.8	9 638	15.0	65 466	8 870	13.5	9 597	14.7	66 811	8 657	13.0	9 360	14.0
16 to 24 years	9 835	557	5.7	627	6.4	9 860	523	5.3	603	6.1	10 130	543	5.4	608	6.0
25 years and over	54 310	8 321	15.3	9 010	16.6	55 606	8 347	15.0	8 994	16.2	56 682	8 114	14.3	8 752	15.4
25 to 34 years	15 391	1 722	11.2	1 873	12.2	15 559	1 754	11.3	1 915	12.3	15 677	1 650	10.5	1 793	11.4
35 to 44 years	16 035	2 449	15.3	2 658	16.6	16 196	2 422	15.0	2 582	15.9	16 159	2 309	14.3	2 488	15.4
45 to 54 years	14 026	2 699	19.2	2 903	20.7	14 421	2 658	18.4	2 849	19.8	14 867	2 617	17.6	2 807	18.9
55 to 64 years	7 117	1 309	18.4	1 414	19.9	7 606	1 346	17.7	1 458	19.2	7 990	1 370	17.1	1 474	18.4
65 years and over	1 741	142	8.2	163	9.4	1 824	167	9.1	190	10.4	1 989	167	8.4	190	9.6
Women, 16 Years and Over	59 408	6 593	11.1	7 450	12.5	60 423	6 815	11.3	7 626	12.6	61 426	6 702	10.9	7 501	12.2
16 to 24 years	9 274	333	3.6	391	4.2	9 423	354	3.8	417	4.4	9 408	315	3.3	370	3.9
25 years and over	50 134	6 260	12.5	7 058	14.1	51 000	6 461	12.7	7 210	14.1	52 018	6 388	12.3	7 131	13.7
25 to 34 years	12 811	1 261	9.8	1 443	11.3	12 891	1 290	10.0	1 454	11.3	13 127	1 249	9.5	1 401	10.7
35 to 44 years	14 435	1 725	11.9	1 931	13.4	14 457	1 790	12.4	1 997	13.8	14 368	1 687	11.7	1 867	13.0
45 to 54 years	14 014	2 072	14.8	2 330	16.6	14 293	2 073	14.5	2 309	16.2	14 534	2 093	14.4	2 325	16.0
55 to 64 years	7 122	1 081	15.2	1 203	16.9	7 552	1 150	15.2	1 274	16.9	8 106	1 198	14.8	1 358	16.8
65 years and over	1 753	121	6.9	151	8.6	1 806	158	8.8	176	9.8	1 883	160	8.5	180	9.5
RACE, HISPANIC ORIGIN, AND SEX															
White, 16 Years and Over[3]	101 340	12 381	12.2	13 657	13.5	102 967	12 520	12.2	13 755	13.4	104 668	12 259	11.7	13 424	12.8
Men	53 432	7 260	13.6	7 854	14.7	54 462	7 275	13.4	7 858	14.4	55 459	7 115	12.8	7 668	13.8
Women	47 908	5 121	10.7	5 803	12.1	48 505	5 245	10.8	5 897	12.2	49 209	5 144	10.5	5 756	11.7
Black, 16 Years and Over[3]	14 090	2 130	15.1	2 355	16.7	14 459	2 178	15.1	2 391	16.5	14 878	2 163	14.5	2 391	16.1
Men	6 409	1 085	16.9	1 185	18.5	6 603	1 062	16.1	1 166	17.7	6 788	1 056	15.6	1 158	17.1
Women	7 681	1 045	13.6	1 170	15.2	7 857	1 115	14.2	1 225	15.6	8 090	1 107	13.7	1 233	15.2
Asian, 16 Years and Over[3]	5 280	603	11.4	670	12.7	5 479	614	11.2	666	12.2	5 703	592	10.4	657	11.5
Men	2 815	328	11.7	371	13.2	2 881	314	10.9	337	11.7	3 015	286	9.5	316	10.5
Women	2 465	275	11.1	299	12.1	2 598	299	11.5	329	12.7	2 688	306	11.4	340	12.7
Hispanic, 16 Years and Over[4]	16 533	1 676	10.1	1 888	11.4	17 191	1 793	10.4	1 981	11.5	18 121	1 770	9.8	1 935	10.7
Men	9 857	1 016	10.3	1 130	11.5	10 324	1 093	10.6	1 185	11.5	10 842	1 064	9.8	1 144	10.6
Women	6 676	661	9.9	758	11.4	6 866	700	10.2	796	11.6	7 279	706	9.7	791	10.9
FULL- OR PART-TIME STATUS[5]															
Full-time workers	101 224	14 029	13.9	15 463	15.3	103 560	14 207	13.7	15 551	15.0	106 106	13 938	13.1	15 244	14.4
Part-time workers	22 047	1 406	6.4	1 587	7.2	22 052	1 441	6.5	1 630	7.4	21 863	1 382	6.3	1 573	7.2

Note: Beginning in January 2006, data reflect revised population controls used in the household survey.

[1]Data refer to members of a labor union or to an employee association similar to a union.

[2]Data refer to members of a labor union or to an employee association similar to a union, as well as to workers who report no union affiliation but whose jobs are covered by a union or an employee association contract.

[3]Beginning in 2003, persons who selected this race group only; persons who selected more than one race group are not included. Prior to 2003, persons who reported more than one race group were included in the group they identified as their main race. Additionally, estimates for the above race groups (White, Black, and Asian) do not sum to totals because data are not presented for all races.

[4]May be of any race.

[5]The distinction between full- and part-time workers is based on hours usually worked. Data will not sum to totals because full- or part-time status on the principal job is not identifiable for a small number of multiple job holders.

Table 8-2. Union Affiliation of Employed Wage and Salary Workers, by Selected Characteristics, 2004–2009
—Continued

(Numbers in thousands, percent.)

Characteristic	2007					2008					2009				
	Total employed	Member of union[1]		Represented by union[2]		Total employed	Member of union[1]		Represented by union[2]		Total employed	Member of union[1]		Represented by union[2]	
		Total	Percent of employed	Total	Percent of employed		Total	Percent of employed	Total	Percent of employed		Total	Percent of employed	Total	Percent of employed
SEX AND AGE															
Both Sexes, 16 Years and Over	129 767	15 670	12.1	17 243	13.3	129 377	16 098	12.4	17 761	13.7	124 490	15 327	12.3	16 904	13.6
16 to 24 years	19 395	939	4.8	1 068	5.5	18 705	930	5.0	1 062	5.7	17 173	813	4.7	941	5.5
25 years and over	110 372	14 731	13.3	16 176	14.7	110 672	15 168	13.7	16 699	15.1	107 317	14 514	13.5	15 962	14.9
25 to 34 years	29 409	3 050	10.4	3 358	11.4	29 276	3 120	10.7	3 443	11.8	28 067	2 942	10.5	3 262	11.6
35 to 44 years	30 296	3 972	13.1	4 362	14.4	29 708	3 993	13.4	4 365	14.7	28 066	3 669	13.1	4 035	14.4
45 to 54 years	29 731	4 664	15.7	5 087	17.1	29 787	4 767	16.0	5 228	17.6	29 054	4 551	15.7	4 994	17.2
55 to 64 years	16 752	2 691	16.1	2 967	17.7	17 430	2 887	16.6	3 209	18.4	17 599	2 926	16.6	3 186	18.1
65 years and over	4 183	355	8.5	402	9.6	4 471	401	9.0	454	10.2	4 530	425	9.4	485	10.7
Men, 16 Years and Over	67 468	8 767	13.0	9 494	14.1	66 846	8 938	13.4	9 724	14.5	63 539	8 441	13.3	9 176	14.4
16 to 24 years	9 959	551	5.5	627	6.3	9 537	555	5.8	617	6.5	8 555	493	5.8	560	6.5
25 years and over	57 509	8 217	14.3	8 867	15.4	57 309	8 383	14.6	9 107	15.9	54 984	7 947	14.5	8 616	15.7
25 to 34 years	15 994	1 736	10.9	1 884	11.8	15 780	1 750	11.1	1 909	12.1	14 952	1 633	10.9	1 786	11.9
35 to 44 years	16 070	2 318	14.4	2 501	15.6	15 653	2 307	14.7	2 491	15.9	14 679	2 077	14.1	2 250	15.3
45 to 54 years	15 040	2 578	17.1	2 745	18.3	14 988	2 608	17.4	2 812	18.8	14 421	2 492	17.3	2 693	18.7
55 to 64 years	8 286	1 403	16.9	1 532	18.5	8 657	1 525	17.6	1 682	19.4	8 647	1 536	17.8	1 654	19.1
65 years and over	2 119	181	8.5	205	9.7	2 230	193	8.7	213	9.6	2 285	211	9.2	233	10.2
Women, 16 Years and Over	62 299	6 903	11.1	7 749	12.4	62 532	7 160	11.4	8 036	12.9	60 951	6 887	11.3	7 727	12.7
16 to 24 years	9 436	388	4.1	441	4.7	9 168	374	4.1	445	4.8	8 619	320	3.7	381	4.4
25 years and over	52 863	6 514	12.3	7 308	13.8	53 364	6 785	12.7	7 592	14.2	52 333	6 567	12.5	7 346	14.0
25 to 34 years	13 416	1 313	9.8	1 474	11.0	13 496	1 370	10.1	1 534	11.4	13 116	1 309	10.0	1 476	11.3
35 to 44 years	14 226	1 653	11.6	1 861	13.1	14 055	1 685	12.0	1 874	13.3	13 387	1 593	11.9	1 785	13.3
45 to 54 years	14 691	2 086	14.2	2 341	15.9	14 799	2 159	14.6	2 416	16.3	14 633	2 060	14.1	2 302	15.7
55 to 64 years	8 466	1 288	15.2	1 435	17.0	8 773	1 363	15.5	1 527	17.4	8 952	1 390	15.5	1 532	17.1
65 years and over	2 065	174	8.4	197	9.5	2 241	208	9.3	241	10.7	2 245	215	9.6	252	11.2
RACE, HISPANIC ORIGIN, AND SEX															
White, 16 Years and Over[3]	105 515	12 487	11.8	13 715	13.0	105 052	12 863	12.2	14 222	13.5	101 581	12 330	12.1	13 595	13.4
Men	55 771	7 134	12.8	7 708	13.8	55 197	7 309	13.2	7 961	14.4	52 691	6 918	13.1	7 512	14.3
Women	49 743	5 352	10.8	6 007	12.1	49 855	5 555	11.1	6 261	12.6	48 889	5 412	11.1	6 083	12.4
Black, 16 Years and Over[3]	15 177	2 165	14.3	2 403	15.8	15 030	2 178	14.5	2 370	15.8	14 127	1 966	13.9	2 172	15.4
Men	6 945	1 097	15.8	1 205	17.3	6 809	1 081	15.9	1 159	17.0	6 257	964	15.4	1 046	16.7
Women	8 232	1 067	13.0	1 198	14.6	8 221	1 097	13.3	1 211	14.7	7 870	1 002	12.7	1 126	14.3
Asian, 16 Years and Over[3]	6 016	654	10.9	720	12.0	6 157	653	10.6	714	11.6	5 847	664	11.4	730	12.5
Men	3 168	324	10.2	348	11.0	3 216	310	9.6	339	10.6	3 075	332	10.8	370	12.0
Women	2 849	330	11.6	372	13.1	2 941	344	11.7	374	12.7	2 772	333	12.0	361	13.0
Hispanic, 16 Years and Over[4]	18 778	1 837	9.8	2 026	10.8	18 572	1 960	10.6	2 168	11.7	18 034	1 841	10.2	2 036	11.3
Men	11 163	1 108	9.9	1 208	10.8	10 998	1 204	11.0	1 317	12.0	10 518	1 108	10.5	1 199	11.4
Women	7 615	728	9.6	818	10.7	7 574	756	10.0	852	11.2	7 515	733	9.7	836	11.1
FULL- OR PART-TIME STATUS[5]															
Full-time workers	107 339	14 201	13.2	15 570	14.5	106 648	14 561	13.7	16 029	15.0	99 820	13 602	13.6	14 960	15.0
Part-time workers	22 172	1 437	6.5	1 635	7.4	22 497	1 505	6.7	1 697	7.5	24 431	1 698	7.0	1 913	7.8

Note: Beginning in January 2006, data reflect revised population controls used in the household survey.

[1]Data refer to members of a labor union or to an employee association similar to a union.
[2]Data refer to members of a labor union or to an employee association similar to a union, as well as to workers who report no union affiliation but whose jobs are covered by a union or an employee association contract.
[3]Beginning in 2003, persons who selected this race group only; persons who selected more than one race group are not included. Prior to 2003, persons who reported more than one race group were included in the group they identified as their main race. Additionally, estimates for the above race groups (White, Black, and Asian) do not sum to totals because data are not presented for all races.
[4]May be of any race.
[5]The distinction between full- and part-time workers is based on hours usually worked. Data will not sum to totals because full- or part-time status on the principal job is not identifiable for a small number of multiple job holders.

Table 8-3. Union Affiliation of Wage and Salary Workers, by Occupation and Industry, 2008–2009

(Thousands of people, percent.)

Occupation and industry	2008					2009				
	Total employed	Member of union[1]		Represented by union[2]		Total employed	Member of union[1]		Represented by union[2]	
		Total	Percent of employed	Total	Percent of employed		Total	Percent of employed	Total	Percent of employed
OCCUPATION										
Management, professional, and related	45 538	6 110	13.4	6 948	15.3	44 845	6 027	13.4	6 821	15.2
Management, business, and financial operations	17 326	866	5.0	1 039	6.0	16 978	822	4.8	997	5.9
Management	11 843	564	4.8	679	5.7	11 548	473	4.1	585	5.1
Business and financial operations	5 483	302	5.5	360	6.6	5 430	348	6.4	412	7.6
Professional and related	28 212	5 244	18.6	5 909	20.9	27 867	5 206	18.7	5 824	20.9
Computer and mathematical	3 488	170	4.9	210	6.0	3 306	175	5.3	207	6.3
Architecture and engineering	2 746	203	7.4	233	8.5	2 512	194	7.7	228	9.1
Life, physical, and social science	1 209	106	8.8	132	10.9	1 220	122	10.0	141	11.6
Community and social service	2 222	363	16.3	406	18.3	2 269	366	16.1	396	17.5
Legal	1 318	74	5.6	87	6.6	1 335	79	5.9	97	7.3
Education, training, and library	8 424	3 259	38.7	3 630	43.1	8 318	3 172	38.1	3 503	42.1
Arts, design, entertainment, sports, and media	1 994	141	7.1	167	8.4	1 840	136	7.4	157	8.5
Health care practitioner and technical	6 813	928	13.6	1 045	15.3	7 067	962	13.6	1 096	15.5
Services	22 114	2 624	11.9	2 831	12.8	22 364	2 588	11.6	2 830	12.7
Health care support	3 028	296	9.8	317	10.5	3 159	317	10.0	353	11.2
Protective service	3 023	1 069	35.4	1 122	37.1	3 120	1 111	35.6	1 180	37.8
Food preparation and serving related	7 694	401	5.2	444	5.8	7 621	334	4.4	389	5.1
Building and grounds cleaning and maintenance	4 648	534	11.5	592	12.7	4 592	521	11.3	570	12.4
Personal care and service	3 721	324	8.7	357	9.6	3 873	306	7.9	338	8.7
Sales and office	32 479	2 395	7.4	2 710	8.3	30 998	2 231	7.2	2 499	8.1
Sales and related	13 708	447	3.3	531	3.9	13 331	411	3.1	480	3.6
Office and administrative support	18 770	1 949	10.4	2 179	11.6	17 667	1 820	10.3	2 019	11.4
Natural resources, construction, and maintenance	12 444	2 208	17.7	2 303	18.5	11 231	1 989	17.7	2 088	18.6
Farming, fishing, and forestry	901	39	4.3	46	5.1	880	24	2.8	26	2.9
Construction and extraction	6 876	1 391	20.2	1 445	21.0	5 820	1 220	21.0	1 269	21.8
Installation, maintenance, and repair	4 668	778	16.7	812	17.4	4 531	744	16.4	793	17.5
Production, transportation, and material moving	16 802	2 760	16.4	2 968	17.7	15 052	2 492	16.6	2 666	17.7
Production	8 601	1 269	14.8	1 370	15.9	7 309	1 082	14.8	1 164	15.9
Transportation and material moving	8 202	1 491	18.2	1 599	19.5	7 742	1 410	18.2	1 502	19.4
INDUSTRY										
Private sector	108 073	8 265	7.6	9 084	8.4	103 357	7 431	7.2	8 226	8.0
Agriculture and related industries	1 057	30	2.8	35	3.4	1 045	12	1.1	14	1.4
Nonagricultural industries	107 016	8 236	7.7	9 049	8.5	102 312	7 419	7.3	8 212	8.0
Mining	776	54	6.9	61	7.9	662	57	8.6	63	9.5
Construction	7 652	1 195	15.6	1 241	16.2	6 613	958	14.5	993	15.0
Manufacturing	15 131	1 723	11.4	1 862	12.3	13 454	1 470	10.9	1 595	11.9
Durable goods	9 728	1 139	11.7	1 223	12.6	8 438	907	10.8	985	11.7
Nondurable goods	5 403	584	10.8	639	11.8	5 016	562	11.2	610	12.2
Wholesale and retail trade	18 622	976	5.2	1 096	5.9	17 851	937	5.3	1 032	5.8
Wholesale trade	3 635	194	5.3	214	5.9	3 386	167	4.9	185	5.5
Retail trade	14 987	782	5.2	881	5.9	14 465	770	5.3	847	5.9
Transportation and utilities	5 544	1 231	22.2	1 298	23.4	5 162	1 144	22.2	1 210	23.4
Transportation and warehousing	4 639	988	21.3	1 041	22.4	4 256	908	21.3	960	22.6
Utilities	906	243	26.9	257	28.3	906	237	26.1	249	27.5
Information[3]	3 056	388	12.7	420	13.7	2 790	280	10.0	312	11.2
Publishing, except Internet	717	52	7.2	62	8.7	633	34	5.3	41	6.5
Motion pictures and sound recording	337	38	11.4	39	11.7	331	42	12.8	43	13.0
Broadcasting, except Internet	561	53	9.5	59	10.6	534	25	4.7	30	5.5
Telecommunications	1 184	228	19.3	242	20.4	1 088	174	16.0	192	17.7
Financial activities	8 654	157	1.8	199	2.3	8 236	150	1.8	193	2.3
Finance and insurance	6 536	86	1.3	115	1.8	6 199	88	1.4	120	1.9
Finance	4 312	45	1.0	62	1.4	4 043	56	1.4	73	1.8
Insurance	2 224	41	1.9	53	2.4	2 155	32	1.5	48	2.2
Real estate and rental and leasing	2 118	71	3.3	84	4.0	2 037	61	3.0	73	3.6
Professional and business services	11 967	253	2.1	324	2.7	11 325	256	2.3	314	2.8
Professional and technical services	7 234	93	1.3	128	1.8	6 915	78	1.1	107	1.5
Management, administrative, and waste services	4 733	159	3.4	196	4.1	4 410	178	4.0	207	4.7
Education and health services	18 841	1 723	9.1	1 940	10.3	19 269	1 655	8.6	1 912	9.9
Education services	3 657	504	13.8	584	16.0	3 816	494	12.9	580	15.2
Health care and social assistance	15 184	1 219	8.0	1 356	8.9	15 454	1 161	7.5	1 332	8.6
Leisure and hospitality	11 187	361	3.2	408	3.6	11 352	349	3.1	407	3.6
Arts, entertainment, and recreation	2 044	131	6.4	150	7.3	2 143	138	6.4	152	7.1
Accommodation and food services	9 144	231	2.5	258	2.8	9 209	211	2.3	255	2.8
Accommodation	1 447	115	7.9	120	8.3	1 390	108	7.8	115	8.3
Food services and drinking places	7 696	116	1.5	138	1.8	7 819	103	1.3	140	1.8
Other services[3]	5 585	175	3.1	200	3.6	5 598	164	2.9	182	3.2
Other services, except private households	4 785	164	3.4	185	3.9	4 775	147	3.1	163	3.4
Public sector	21 305	7 832	36.8	8 676	40.7	21 133	7 896	37.4	8 677	41.1
Federal government	3 542	994	28.1	1 167	33.0	3 594	1 005	28.0	1 192	33.2
State government	6 176	1 955	31.6	2 167	35.1	6 294	2 025	32.2	2 222	35.3
Local government	11 586	4 884	42.2	5 342	46.1	11 244	4 867	43.3	5 263	46.8

Note: Updated population controls are introduced annually with the release of January data. Data refer to the sole or principal job of full- and part-time workers. Excluded are all self-employed workers, regardless of whether or not their businesses are incorporated.

[1]Data refer to members of a labor union or an employee association similar to a union.
[2]Data refer to members of a labor union or an employee association similar to a union, as well as to workers who report no union affiliation but whose jobs are covered by a union or an employee association contract.
[3]Includes other industries, not shown separately.

Table 8-4. Median Weekly Earnings of Full-Time Wage and Salary Workers, by Union Affiliation, Occupation, and Industry, 2008–2009

(Dollars.)

Occupation and industry	2008				2009			
	Total	Member of union[1]	Represented by union[2]	Non-union	Total	Member of union[1]	Represented by union[2]	Non-union
OCCUPATION								
Management, professional, and related	1 025	1 028	1 017	1 028	1 044	1 047	1 040	1 045
Management, business, and financial operations	1 128	1 113	1 120	1 129	1 138	1 116	1 123	1 139
Management	1 204	1 235	1 236	1 199	1 208	1 192	1 208	1 208
Business and financial operations	974	925	943	978	996	1 002	1 009	995
Professional and related	980	1 018	1 004	973	994	1 036	1 026	983
Computer and mathematical	1 242	1 149	1 139	1 248	1 253	1 078	1 107	1 263
Architecture and engineering	1 244	1 223	1 243	1 244	1 266	1 230	1 210	1 271
Life, physical, and social science	1 035	1 169	1 144	1 018	1 059	1 099	1 135	1 040
Community and social service	788	983	978	743	783	957	948	746
Legal	1 174	1 186	1 265	1 169	1 200	1 266	1 258	1 191
Education, training, and library	866	974	957	765	887	1 010	996	782
Arts, design, entertainment, sports, and media	882	1 110	1 098	858	888	1 105	1 059	877
Health care practitioner and technical	962	1 070	1 061	943	970	1 089	1 070	952
Services	475	691	679	440	470	702	682	435
Health care support	465	526	526	457	472	518	518	464
Protective service	748	990	983	620	747	992	980	611
Food preparation and serving related	402	502	496	398	398	463	456	395
Building and grounds cleaning and maintenance	431	596	593	412	444	597	588	418
Personal care and service	475	580	570	463	440	576	567	429
Sales and office	614	741	736	603	624	768	761	613
Sales and related	656	679	683	655	665	678	673	665
Office and administrative support	601	749	744	585	612	782	773	595
Natural resources, construction, and maintenance	702	990	984	647	719	1 009	1 003	657
Farming, fishing, and forestry	420	(3)	(3)	418	416	(3)	(3)	411
Construction and extraction	688	992	989	621	718	1 023	1 011	643
Installation, maintenance, and repair	774	1 002	994	729	781	999	999	733
Production, transportation, and material moving	594	777	770	560	605	786	780	578
Production	595	765	759	567	610	783	778	587
Transportation and material moving	593	789	779	550	599	789	782	563
INDUSTRY								
Private sector	694	838	829	680	711	856	845	697
Agriculture and related industries	444	(3)	(3)	446	462	(3)	(3)	457
Nonagricultural industries	698	840	831	683	715	857	846	701
Mining	1 007	1 024	1 032	1 003	1 050	1 013	1 015	1 058
Construction	712	1 014	1 012	668	744	1 072	1 052	698
Manufacturing	741	796	795	733	767	800	799	762
Durable goods	772	829	827	763	806	836	832	801
Nondurable goods	685	729	729	675	706	735	741	698
Wholesale and retail trade	603	643	638	601	611	648	641	609
Wholesale trade	741	775	763	739	760	761	767	760
Retail trade	564	598	596	561	577	612	607	575
Transportation and utilities	787	958	950	747	798	975	964	748
Transportation and warehousing	744	897	895	710	749	923	911	707
Utilities	1 061	1 161	1 142	1 010	1 043	1 120	1 104	1 008
Information[4]	898	1 011	1 001	871	905	1 105	1 083	883
Publishing, except Internet	856	(3)	979	846	847	(3)	(3)	843
Motion pictures and sound recording	883	(3)	(3)	800	1 047	(3)	(3)	924
Broadcasting, except Internet	806	(3)	944	794	827	(3)	(3)	828
Telecommunications	969	1 006	1 000	953	964	1 095	1 079	924
Financial activities	814	782	782	816	839	843	831	839
Finance and insurance	857	762	774	859	881	845	837	882
Finance	864	(3)	829	865	889	842	817	892
Insurance	846	(3)	(3)	849	868	(3)	(3)	868
Real estate and rental and leasing	703	789	783	696	726	842	822	718
Professional and business services	835	814	817	836	864	761	748	868
Professional and technical services	1 065	1 129	1 140	1 064	1 094	1 081	1 096	1 094
Management, administrative, and waste services	544	682	695	538	560	658	640	553
Education and health services	685	795	798	671	715	839	838	698
Education services	773	892	868	762	819	886	879	795
Health care and social assistance	661	756	768	652	685	801	802	673
Leisure and hospitality	470	584	575	462	464	583	576	458
Arts, entertainment, and recreation	590	651	638	586	601	673	671	593
Accommodation and food services	435	563	552	427	423	526	505	421
Accommodation	508	605	602	494	505	582	582	496
Food services and drinking places	417	497	491	416	412	424	423	412
Other services[4]	610	878	810	606	605	886	862	599
Other services, except private households	629	893	849	622	627	893	868	620
Public sector	842	923	918	766	865	947	943	782
Federal government	972	949	959	989	1 002	981	989	1 019
State government	812	900	889	753	829	906	899	767
Local government	814	925	917	719	834	956	948	720

Note: Updated population controls are introduced annually with the release of January data. Data refer to the sole or principal job of full- and part-time workers. Excluded are all self-employed workers, regardless of whether or not their businesses are incorporated.

[1]Data refer to members of a labor union or an employee association similar to a union.
[2]Data refer to members of a labor union or an employee association similar to a union, as well as to workers who report no union affiliation but whose jobs are covered by a union or an employee association contract.
[3]Data not shown where base is less than 50,000.
[4]Includes other industries, not shown separately.

Table 8-5. Union or Employee Association Members Among Wage and Salary Employees, 1977–2009

(Numbers in thousands, percent.)

Year	Total wage and salary employment	Union or employee association member	Union or association members as a percent of total wage and salary employment
1977	81 334	19 335	23.8
1978	84 968	19 548	23.0
1979	87 117	20 986	24.1
1980	87 480	20 095	23.0
1981	. . .	. . .	. . .
1982	. . .	. . .	. . .
1983[1]	88 290	17 717	20.1
1984	92 194	17 340	18.8
1985	94 521	16 996	18.0
1986	96 903	16 975	17.5
1987	99 303	16 913	17.0
1988	101 407	17 002	16.8
1989	103 480	16 980	16.4
1990	103 905	16 740	16.1
1991	102 786	16 568	16.1
1992	103 688	16 390	15.8
1993	105 087	16 598	15.8
1994[2]	107 989	16 748	15.5
1995	110 038	16 360	14.9
1996	111 960	16 269	14.5
1997	114 533	16 110	14.1
1998	116 730	16 211	13.9
1999	118 963	16 477	13.9
2000	120 786	16 258	13.5
2001	122 482	16 387	13.4
2002	121 826	16 145	13.3
2003	122 358	15 776	12.9
2004	123 554	15 472	12.5
2005	125 889	15 685	12.5
2006	128 237	15 359	12.0
2007	129 767	15 670	12.1
2008	129 377	16 098	12.4
2009	124 490	15 327	12.3

Note: Beginning in January 2006, updated population controls are introduced annually with the release of January data.

[1]Annual average data beginning in 1983 are not directly comparable with the data for 1977–1980.
[2]Data beginning in 1994 are not strictly comparable with data for 1993 and earlier years because of the introduction of a major redesign of the Current Population Survey questionnaire and collection methodology and the introduction of 1990 census–based population controls.
. . . = Not available.

Table 8-6. Union Affiliation of Employed Wage and Salary Workers, by State, 2008–2009

(Numbers in thousands, percent.)

State	2008					2009				
	Total employed	Member of union[1]		Represented by union[2]		Total employed	Member of union[1]		Represented by union[2]	
		Total	Percent of employed	Total	Percent of employed		Total	Percent of employed	Total	Percent of employed
UNITED STATES	129 377	16 098	12.4	17 761	13.7	124 490	15 327	12.3	16 904	13.6
Alabama	1 858	181	9.8	199	10.7	1 763	191	10.9	212	12.0
Alaska	289	68	23.5	71	24.7	293	65	22.3	69	23.6
Arizona	2 579	227	8.8	254	9.8	2 471	162	6.5	194	7.9
Arkansas	1 158	68	5.9	85	7.3	1 103	47	4.2	55	5.0
California	14 889	2 740	18.4	2 909	19.5	14 297	2 453	17.2	2 622	18.3
Colorado	2 254	181	8.0	208	9.2	2 175	153	7.0	181	8.3
Connecticut	1 625	275	16.9	291	17.9	1 538	265	17.3	282	18.4
Delaware	391	52	13.4	57	14.7	367	44	11.9	47	12.8
District of Columbia	288	35	12.2	41	14.3	276	29	10.4	35	12.5
Florida	7 573	482	6.4	601	7.9	7 097	411	5.8	489	6.9
Georgia	4 084	151	3.7	189	4.6	3 869	177	4.6	226	5.9
Hawaii	562	136	24.3	143	25.5	526	123	23.5	128	24.3
Idaho	602	42	7.1	48	8.0	577	36	6.3	46	7.9
Illinois	5 662	939	16.6	993	17.5	5 435	951	17.5	997	18.3
Indiana	2 811	349	12.4	386	13.7	2 612	277	10.6	319	12.2
Iowa	1 437	153	10.6	187	13.0	1 398	156	11.1	185	13.3
Kansas	1 273	89	7.0	111	8.7	1 249	77	6.2	104	8.4
Kentucky	1 703	146	8.6	163	9.6	1 657	142	8.6	173	10.5
Louisiana	1 724	80	4.6	97	5.6	1 704	99	5.8	110	6.5
Maine	574	71	12.3	84	14.7	543	63	11.7	74	13.7
Maryland	2 610	329	12.6	380	14.5	2 555	323	12.6	366	14.3
Massachusetts	2 909	458	15.7	491	16.9	2 864	476	16.6	516	18.0
Michigan	4 089	771	18.8	801	19.6	3 785	710	18.8	752	19.9
Minnesota	2 430	392	16.1	412	17.0	2 400	362	15.1	377	15.7
Mississippi	1 089	57	5.3	79	7.3	1 029	49	4.8	66	6.4
Missouri	2 543	285	11.2	327	12.8	2 481	234	9.4	264	10.6
Montana	389	47	12.2	61	15.7	374	52	13.9	68	18.1
Nebraska	840	70	8.3	90	10.7	823	76	9.2	94	11.4
Nevada	1 192	199	16.7	217	18.2	1 097	173	15.7	188	17.2
New Hampshire	635	67	10.6	79	12.4	616	67	10.8	76	12.3
New Jersey	3 843	703	18.3	731	19.0	3 734	721	19.3	742	19.9
New Mexico	807	58	7.2	94	11.6	759	51	6.7	77	10.2
New York	8 165	2 029	24.9	2 170	26.6	8 021	2 019	25.2	2 182	27.2
North Carolina	3 799	132	3.5	189	5.0	3 707	115	3.1	162	4.4
North Dakota	308	19	6.1	25	8.2	301	21	6.8	30	9.8
Ohio	5 046	716	14.2	783	15.5	4 827	685	14.2	742	15.4
Oklahoma	1 529	102	6.6	127	8.3	1 456	83	5.7	107	7.3
Oregon	1 566	259	16.6	272	17.4	1 471	250	17.0	272	18.5
Pennsylvania	5 504	847	15.4	899	16.3	5 220	782	15.0	844	16.2
Rhode Island	471	78	16.5	82	17.4	444	80	17.9	83	18.7
South Carolina	1 792	70	3.9	105	5.8	1 672	75	4.5	91	5.4
South Dakota	369	18	5.0	24	6.4	357	20	5.5	24	6.6
Tennessee	2 534	139	5.5	166	6.6	2 387	121	5.1	156	6.6
Texas	9 991	449	4.5	559	5.6	9 920	508	5.1	615	6.2
Utah	1 178	68	5.8	84	7.1	1 136	79	6.9	90	8.0
Vermont	284	29	10.4	36	12.8	285	35	12.3	40	14.1
Virginia	3 597	146	4.1	178	5.0	3 503	166	4.7	191	5.4
Washington	2 912	578	19.8	626	21.5	2 847	574	20.2	612	21.5
West Virginia	736	101	13.8	112	15.3	699	97	13.9	108	15.4
Wisconsin	2 642	396	15.0	422	16.0	2 528	385	15.2	400	15.8
Wyoming	241	19	7.7	21	8.9	239	18	7.7	20	8.3

Note: Updated population controls are introduced annually with the release of January data. Data refer to the sole or principal job of full- and part-time workers. Excluded are all self-employed workers, regardless of whether or not their businesses are incorporated.

[1]Data refer to members of a labor union or an employee association similar to a union.
[2]Data refer to members of a labor union or an employee association similar to a union, as well as to workers who report no union affiliation but whose jobs are covered by a union or an employee association contract.

Chapter Nine

PRICES

PRICES

HIGHLIGHTS

This chapter examines the movement of prices, which is one of the most important indicators of the state of the economy. Several indexes are covered: the Producer Price Index (PPI), which gives information about prices received by producers; the Consumer Price Index (CPI), which gives information about prices paid by consumers; and the Import Price Index (MPI) and the Export Price Index (XPI), which give information about prices involved in various foreign trade, export, and import price indexes.

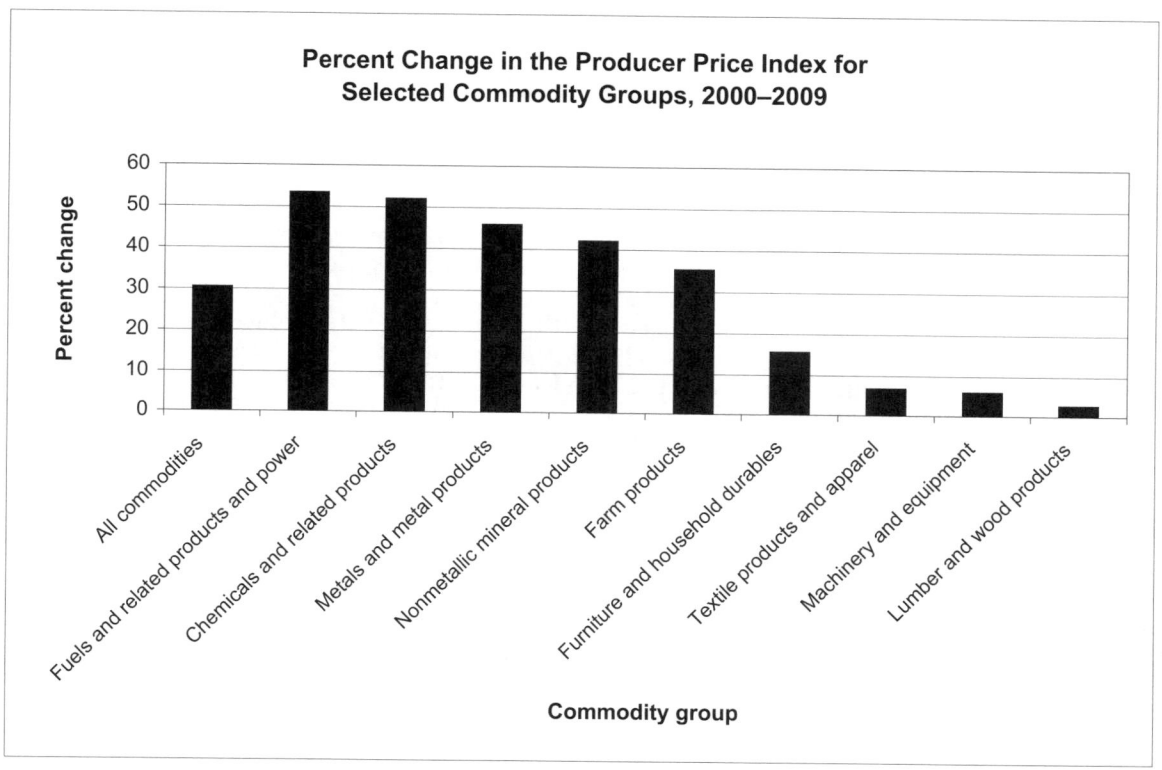

From 2000 through 2009, the producer price index for all commodities grew 30.3 percent. Fuels and related products and power (53.3 percent), chemicals and related products (51.9 percent), and metals and metal products (45.8 percent) experienced the fastest growth while lumber and wood products (2.6 percent), machinery and equipment (5.9 percent), and textile products and apparel (6.7 percent) grew at a far slower pace. (See Table 9-2.)

OTHER HIGHLIGHTS

- Although the PPI for all commodities increased 30.3 percent from 2000 and 2009, it actually declined 8.8 percent between 2008 and 2009 marking the greatest decline in one year since 1938 when it dropped 9.4 percent. (See Table 9-2)

- While the PPI for most commodities declined in 2009, it increased for furniture and household durables (2.8 percent), nonmetallic mineral products (2.7 percent), transportation equipment (2.3 percent), and textile products and apparel (0.5 percent). (See Table 9-2.)

- In 2008, the PPI for consumer goods declined 3.9 percent while the PPI for finished goods declined 2.6 percent. However, the PPI for capital equipment grew 1.9 percent. (See Table 9-1.)

NOTES AND DEFINITIONS

PRODUCER PRICE INDEX

Coverage

The *Producer Price Index (PPI)* measures average changes in prices received by domestic producers of goods and services. PPIs measure price change from the perspective of the seller. This contrasts with other measures, such as the Consumer Price Index (CPI). CPIs measure price change from the purchaser's perspective. Sellers' and purchasers' prices can differ due to government subsidies, sales and excise taxes, and distribution costs.

Over 25,000 establishments provide approximately 100,000 price quotations per month. Establishments report selling prices on the Tuesday that includes the 13th of each month and they usually respond by mail.

PPIs are typically organized into one of three groups: (1) stage-of-processing indexes, (2) commodity indexes, and (3) indexes for the net output of industries and their products. The stage-of-processing structure organizes products by class of buyer and degree of fabrication. The commodity structure organizes products by similarity of end use or material composition. The entire output of various industries is sampled to derive price indexes for the net output of industries and their products.

Within the stage-of-processing system, finished goods are commodities that will not undergo further processing and that are ready for sale to the final demand user— either an individual consumer or a business firm. Consumer foods include unprocessed foods, such as eggs and fresh vegetables, and processed foods, such as bakery products and meats. Other finished consumer goods include durable goods, such as automobiles, household furniture, and appliances; and

nondurable goods, such as apparel and home heating oil. Capital equipment includes producer durable goods, such as heavy motor trucks, tractors, and machine tools.

The stage-of-processing category for intermediate materials, supplies, and components includes commodities that have been processed but require further processing, such as flour, cotton, yarn, steel mill products, and lumber. The intermediate goods category also encompasses physically complete nondurable goods purchased by business firms as inputs for their operations, such as diesel fuel, belts and belting, paper boxes, and fertilizers.

Crude materials for further processing are products entering the market for the first time that have not been manufactured or fabricated; these products will not be sold directly to consumers. Crude foodstuffs and feedstuffs includes items such as grains and livestock; examples of crude nonfood materials include raw cotton, crude petroleum, coal, hides and skins, and iron and steel scrap.

PPIs for the net output of industries and their products are grouped according to the North American Industry Classification System (NAICS). Prior to the release of January 2004, industry-based PPIs were published according to the Standard Industrial Classification (SIC) system. Industry price indexes are compatible with other economic time series organized by industry, such as data on employment, wages, and productivity.

Sources of Additional Information

For more information on the underlying concepts and methodology of the Producer Price Index, see Chapter 14 in the *BLS Handbook of Methods*, which is available on the BLS Web site at <http://www.bls.gov/opub/hom/>.

Table 9-1. Producer Price Indexes, by Stage of Processing, 1947–2009

(1982 = 100.)

Year	Crude materials for further processing				Intermediate materials, supplies, and components						Finished goods		
	Total	Foodstuffs and feedstuffs	Nonfood materials, except fuel	Fuel	Total	Materials and components for construction	Components for manufacturing	Processed fuels and lubricants	Containers	Supplies	Total	Consumer goods	Capital equipment
1947	31.7	45.1	24.0	7.5	23.3	22.5	21.3	14.4	23.4	28.5	26.4	28.6	19.8
1948	34.7	48.8	26.7	8.9	25.2	24.9	23.0	16.4	24.4	29.8	28.5	30.8	21.6
1949	30.1	40.5	24.3	8.8	24.2	24.9	23.4	14.9	24.5	28.0	27.7	29.4	22.7
1950	32.7	43.4	27.8	8.8	25.3	26.2	24.3	15.2	25.2	29.0	28.2	29.9	23.2
1951	37.6	50.2	32.0	9.0	28.4	28.7	27.6	15.9	29.6	32.6	30.8	32.7	25.5
1952	34.5	47.3	27.8	9.0	27.5	28.5	27.6	15.7	28.0	32.6	30.6	32.3	25.9
1953	31.9	42.3	26.6	9.3	27.7	29.0	28.1	15.8	28.0	31.0	30.3	31.7	26.3
1954	31.6	42.3	26.1	8.9	27.9	29.1	28.3	15.8	28.5	31.7	30.4	31.7	26.7
1955	30.4	38.4	27.5	8.9	28.4	30.3	29.5	15.8	28.9	31.2	30.5	31.5	27.4
1956	30.6	37.6	28.6	9.5	29.6	31.8	32.2	16.3	31.0	32.0	31.3	32.0	29.5
1957	31.2	39.2	28.2	10.1	30.3	32.0	33.5	17.2	32.4	32.3	32.5	32.9	31.3
1958	31.9	41.6	27.1	10.2	30.4	32.0	33.8	16.2	33.2	33.1	33.2	33.6	32.1
1959	31.1	38.8	28.1	10.4	30.8	32.9	34.2	16.2	33.0	33.5	33.1	33.3	32.7
1960	30.4	38.4	26.9	10.5	30.8	32.7	34.0	16.6	33.4	33.3	33.4	33.6	32.8
1961	30.2	37.9	27.2	10.5	30.6	32.2	33.7	16.8	33.2	33.7	33.4	33.6	32.9
1962	30.5	38.6	27.1	10.4	30.6	32.1	33.4	16.7	33.6	34.5	33.5	33.7	33.0
1963	29.9	37.5	26.7	10.5	30.7	32.2	33.4	16.6	33.2	35.0	33.4	33.5	33.1
1964	29.6	36.6	27.2	10.5	30.8	32.5	33.7	16.2	32.9	34.7	33.5	33.6	33.4
1965	31.1	39.2	27.7	10.6	31.2	32.8	34.2	16.5	33.5	35.0	34.1	34.2	33.8
1966	33.1	42.7	28.3	10.9	32.0	33.6	35.4	16.8	34.5	36.5	35.2	35.4	34.6
1967	31.3	40.3	26.5	11.3	32.2	34.0	36.5	16.9	35.0	36.8	35.6	35.6	35.8
1968	31.8	40.9	27.1	11.5	33.0	35.7	37.3	16.5	35.9	37.1	36.6	36.5	37.0
1969	33.9	44.1	28.4	12.0	34.1	37.7	38.5	16.6	37.2	37.8	38.0	37.9	38.3
1970	35.2	45.2	29.1	13.8	35.4	38.3	40.6	17.7	39.0	39.7	39.3	39.1	40.1
1971	36.0	46.1	29.4	15.7	36.8	40.8	41.9	19.5	40.8	40.8	40.5	40.2	41.7
1972	39.9	51.5	32.3	16.8	38.2	43.0	42.9	20.1	42.7	42.5	41.8	41.5	42.8
1973	54.5	72.6	42.9	18.6	42.4	46.5	44.3	22.2	45.2	51.7	45.6	46.0	44.2
1974	61.4	76.4	54.5	24.8	52.5	55.0	51.1	33.6	53.3	56.8	52.6	53.1	50.5
1975	61.6	77.4	50.0	30.6	58.0	60.1	57.8	39.4	60.0	61.8	58.2	58.2	58.2
1976	63.4	76.8	54.9	34.5	60.9	64.1	60.8	42.3	63.1	65.8	60.8	60.4	62.1
1977	65.5	77.5	56.3	42.0	64.9	69.3	64.5	47.7	65.9	69.3	64.7	64.3	66.1
1978	73.4	87.3	61.9	48.2	69.5	76.5	69.2	49.9	71.0	72.9	69.8	69.4	71.3
1979	85.9	100.0	75.5	57.3	78.4	84.2	75.8	61.6	79.4	80.2	77.6	77.5	77.5
1980	95.3	104.6	91.8	69.4	90.3	91.3	84.6	85.0	89.1	89.9	88.0	88.6	85.8
1981	103.0	103.9	109.8	84.8	98.6	97.9	94.7	100.6	96.7	96.9	96.1	96.6	94.6
1982	100.0	100.0	100.0	100.0	100.0	100.0	100.0	100.0	100.0	100.0	100.0	100.0	100.0
1983	101.3	101.8	98.8	105.1	100.6	102.8	102.4	95.4	100.4	101.8	101.6	101.3	102.8
1984	103.5	104.7	101.0	105.1	103.1	105.6	105.0	95.7	105.9	104.1	103.7	103.3	105.2
1985	95.8	94.8	94.3	102.7	102.7	107.3	106.4	92.8	109.0	104.4	104.7	103.8	107.5
1986	87.7	93.2	76.0	92.2	99.1	108.1	107.5	72.7	110.3	105.6	103.2	101.4	109.7
1987	93.7	96.2	88.5	84.1	101.5	109.8	108.8	73.3	114.5	107.7	105.4	103.6	111.7
1988	96.0	106.1	85.9	82.1	107.1	116.1	112.3	71.2	120.1	113.7	108.0	106.2	114.3
1989	103.1	111.2	95.8	85.3	112.0	121.3	116.4	76.4	125.4	118.1	113.6	112.1	118.8
1990	108.9	113.1	107.3	84.8	114.5	122.9	119.0	85.9	127.7	119.4	119.2	118.2	122.9
1991	101.2	105.5	97.5	82.9	114.4	124.5	121.0	85.3	128.1	121.4	121.7	120.5	126.7
1992	100.4	105.1	94.2	84.0	114.7	126.5	122.0	84.5	127.7	122.7	123.2	121.7	129.1
1993	102.4	108.4	94.1	87.1	116.2	132.0	123.0	84.7	126.4	125.0	124.7	123.0	131.4
1994	101.8	106.5	97.0	82.4	118.5	136.6	124.3	83.1	129.7	127.0	125.5	123.3	134.1
1995	102.7	105.8	105.8	72.1	124.9	142.1	126.5	84.2	148.8	132.1	127.9	125.6	136.7
1996	113.8	121.5	105.7	92.6	125.7	143.6	126.9	90.0	141.1	135.9	131.3	129.5	138.3
1997	111.1	112.2	103.5	101.3	125.6	146.5	126.4	89.3	136.0	135.9	131.8	130.2	138.2
1998	96.8	103.9	84.5	86.7	123.0	146.8	125.9	81.1	140.8	134.8	130.7	128.9	137.6
1999	98.2	98.7	91.1	91.2	123.2	148.9	125.7	84.6	142.5	134.2	133.0	132.0	137.6
2000	120.6	100.2	118.0	136.9	129.2	150.7	126.2	102.0	151.6	136.9	138.0	138.2	138.8
2001	121.0	106.1	101.5	151.4	129.7	150.6	126.4	104.5	153.1	138.7	140.7	141.5	139.7
2002	108.1	99.5	101.0	117.3	127.8	151.3	126.1	96.3	152.1	138.9	138.9	139.4	139.1
2003	135.3	113.5	116.9	185.7	133.7	153.6	125.9	112.6	153.7	141.5	143.3	145.3	139.5
2004	159.0	127.0	149.2	211.4	142.6	166.4	127.4	124.3	159.3	146.7	148.5	151.7	141.4
2005	182.2	122.7	176.7	279.7	154.0	176.6	129.9	150.0	167.1	151.9	155.7	160.4	144.6
2006	184.8	119.3	210.0	241.5	164.0	188.4	134.5	162.8	175.0	157.0	160.4	166.0	146.9
2007	207.1	146.7	238.7	236.8	170.7	192.5	136.3	173.9	180.3	161.7	166.6	173.5	149.5
2008	251.8	163.4	308.5	298.3	188.3	205.4	140.3	206.2	191.8	173.8	177.1	186.3	153.8
2009	175.2	134.5	211.1	166.3	172.5	202.9	141.0	161.9	195.8	172.2	172.5	179.1	156.7

Table 9-2. Producer Price Indexes, by Commodity Group, 1913–2009

(1982 = 100.)

Year	All commodities	Farm products	Processed foods and feeds	Industrial commodities													
				Total	Textile products and apparel	Hides, leather, and related products	Fuels and related products and power	Chemicals and related products	Rubber and plastics products	Lumber and wood products	Pulp, paper, and allied products	Metals and metal products	Machinery and equipment	Furniture and household durables	Non-metallic mineral products	Transportation equipment	Miscellaneous products
1913	12.0	18.0	. . .	11.9	. . .	. . .	. . .	. . .	. . .	. . .	. . .	. . .	. . .	. . .	. . .	. . .	. . .
1914	11.8	17.9	. . .	11.3	. . .	. . .	. . .	. . .	. . .	. . .	. . .	. . .	. . .	. . .	. . .	. . .	. . .
1915	12.0	18.0	. . .	11.6	. . .	. . .	. . .	. . .	. . .	. . .	. . .	. . .	. . .	. . .	. . .	. . .	. . .
1916	14.7	21.3	. . .	15.0	. . .	. . .	. . .	. . .	. . .	. . .	. . .	. . .	. . .	. . .	. . .	. . .	. . .
1917	20.2	32.6	. . .	19.5	. . .	. . .	. . .	. . .	. . .	. . .	. . .	. . .	. . .	. . .	. . .	. . .	. . .
1918	22.6	37.4	. . .	21.1	. . .	. . .	. . .	. . .	. . .	. . .	. . .	. . .	. . .	. . .	. . .	. . .	. . .
1919	23.9	39.8	. . .	22.0	. . .	. . .	. . .	. . .	. . .	. . .	. . .	. . .	. . .	. . .	. . .	. . .	. . .
1920	26.6	38.0	. . .	27.4	. . .	. . .	. . .	. . .	. . .	. . .	. . .	. . .	. . .	. . .	. . .	. . .	. . .
1921	16.8	22.3	. . .	17.8	. . .	. . .	. . .	. . .	. . .	. . .	. . .	. . .	. . .	. . .	. . .	. . .	. . .
1922	16.7	23.7	. . .	17.4	. . .	. . .	. . .	. . .	. . .	. . .	. . .	. . .	. . .	. . .	. . .	. . .	. . .
1923	17.3	24.9	. . .	17.8	. . .	. . .	. . .	. . .	. . .	. . .	. . .	. . .	. . .	. . .	. . .	. . .	. . .
1924	16.9	25.2	. . .	17.0	. . .	. . .	. . .	. . .	. . .	. . .	. . .	. . .	. . .	. . .	. . .	. . .	. . .
1925	17.8	27.7	. . .	17.5	. . .	. . .	. . .	. . .	. . .	. . .	. . .	. . .	. . .	. . .	. . .	. . .	. . .
1926	17.2	25.3	. . .	17.0	. . .	17.1	10.3	. . .	47.1	9.3	. . .	13.7	. . .	28.6	16.4	. . .	. . .
1927	16.5	25.1	. . .	16.0	. . .	18.4	9.1	. . .	35.7	8.8	. . .	12.9	. . .	27.9	15.7	. . .	. . .
1928	16.7	26.7	. . .	15.8	. . .	20.7	8.7	. . .	28.3	8.5	. . .	12.9	. . .	27.2	16.2	. . .	. . .
1929	16.4	26.4	. . .	15.6	. . .	18.6	8.6	. . .	24.6	8.8	. . .	13.3	. . .	27.0	16.0	. . .	. . .
1930	14.9	22.4	. . .	14.5	. . .	17.1	8.1	. . .	21.5	8.0	. . .	12.0	. . .	26.5	15.9	. . .	. . .
1931	12.6	16.4	. . .	12.8	. . .	14.7	7.0	. . .	18.3	6.5	. . .	10.8	. . .	24.4	14.9	. . .	. . .
1932	11.2	12.2	. . .	11.9	. . .	12.5	7.3	. . .	15.9	5.6	. . .	9.9	. . .	21.5	13.9	. . .	. . .
1933	11.4	13.0	. . .	12.1	. . .	13.8	6.9	16.2	16.7	6.7	. . .	10.2	. . .	21.6	14.7	. . .	. . .
1934	12.9	16.5	. . .	13.3	. . .	14.8	7.6	17.0	19.5	7.8	. . .	11.2	. . .	23.4	15.7	. . .	. . .
1935	13.8	19.8	. . .	13.3	. . .	15.3	7.6	17.7	19.6	7.5	. . .	11.2	. . .	23.2	15.7	. . .	. . .
1936	13.9	20.4	. . .	13.5	. . .	16.3	7.9	17.8	21.1	7.9	. . .	11.4	. . .	23.6	15.8	. . .	. . .
1937	14.9	21.8	. . .	14.5	. . .	17.9	8.0	18.6	24.9	9.3	. . .	13.1	. . .	26.1	16.1	. . .	. . .
1938	13.5	17.3	. . .	13.9	. . .	15.8	7.9	17.7	24.4	8.5	. . .	12.6	. . .	25.5	15.6	. . .	. . .
1939	13.3	16.5	. . .	13.9	. . .	16.3	7.5	17.6	25.4	8.7	. . .	12.5	14.8	25.4	15.3	. . .	. . .
1940	13.5	17.1	. . .	14.1	. . .	17.2	7.4	17.9	23.7	9.6	. . .	12.5	14.9	26.0	15.3	. . .	. . .
1941	15.1	20.8	. . .	15.1	. . .	18.4	7.9	19.5	25.5	11.5	. . .	12.8	15.1	27.6	15.7	. . .	. . .
1942	17.0	26.7	. . .	16.2	. . .	20.1	8.1	21.7	29.7	12.5	. . .	13.0	15.4	29.9	16.3	. . .	. . .
1943	17.8	30.9	. . .	16.5	. . .	20.1	8.3	21.9	30.5	13.2	. . .	12.9	15.2	29.7	16.4	. . .	. . .
1944	17.9	31.2	. . .	16.7	. . .	19.9	8.6	22.2	30.1	14.3	. . .	12.9	15.1	30.5	16.7	. . .	. . .
1945	18.2	32.4	. . .	17.0	. . .	20.1	8.7	22.3	29.2	14.5	. . .	13.1	15.1	30.5	17.4	. . .	. . .
1946	20.8	37.5	. . .	18.6	. . .	23.3	9.3	24.1	29.3	16.6	. . .	14.7	16.6	32.4	18.5	. . .	. . .
1947	25.6	45.1	33.0	22.7	50.6	31.7	11.1	32.1	29.2	25.8	25.1	18.2	19.3	37.2	20.7	. . .	26.6
1948	27.7	48.5	35.3	24.6	52.8	32.1	13.1	32.8	30.2	29.5	26.2	20.7	20.9	39.4	22.4	. . .	27.7
1949	26.3	41.9	32.1	24.1	48.3	30.4	12.4	30.0	29.2	27.3	25.1	20.9	21.9	40.1	23.0	. . .	28.2
1950	27.3	44.0	33.2	25.0	50.2	32.9	12.6	30.4	35.6	31.4	25.7	22.0	22.6	40.9	23.5	. . .	28.6
1951	30.4	51.2	36.9	27.6	56.0	37.7	13.0	34.8	43.7	34.1	30.5	24.5	25.3	44.4	25.0	. . .	30.3
1952	29.6	48.4	36.4	26.9	50.5	30.5	13.0	33.0	39.6	33.2	29.7	24.5	25.3	43.5	25.0	. . .	30.2
1953	29.2	43.8	34.8	27.2	49.3	31.0	13.4	33.4	36.9	33.1	29.6	25.3	25.9	44.4	26.0	. . .	31.0
1954	29.3	43.2	35.4	27.2	48.2	29.5	13.2	33.8	37.5	32.5	29.6	25.5	26.3	44.9	26.6	. . .	31.3
1955	29.3	40.5	33.8	27.8	48.2	29.4	13.2	33.7	42.4	34.1	30.4	27.2	27.2	45.1	27.3	. . .	31.3
1956	30.3	40.0	33.8	29.1	48.2	31.2	13.6	33.9	43.0	34.6	32.4	29.6	29.3	46.3	28.5	. . .	31.7
1957	31.2	41.1	34.8	29.9	48.3	31.2	14.3	34.6	42.8	32.8	33.0	30.2	31.4	47.5	29.6	. . .	32.6
1958	31.6	42.9	36.5	30.0	47.4	31.6	13.7	34.9	42.8	32.5	33.4	30.0	32.1	47.9	29.9	. . .	33.3
1959	31.7	40.2	35.6	30.5	48.1	35.9	13.7	34.8	42.6	34.7	33.7	30.6	32.8	48.0	30.3	. . .	33.4
1960	31.7	40.1	35.6	30.5	48.6	34.6	13.9	34.8	42.7	33.5	34.0	30.6	33.0	47.8	30.4	. . .	33.6
1961	31.6	39.7	36.2	30.4	47.8	34.9	14.0	34.5	41.1	32.0	33.0	30.5	33.0	47.5	30.5	. . .	33.7
1962	31.7	40.4	36.5	30.4	48.2	35.3	14.0	33.9	39.9	32.2	33.4	30.2	33.0	47.2	30.5	. . .	33.9
1963	31.6	39.6	36.8	30.3	48.2	34.3	13.9	33.5	40.1	32.8	33.1	30.3	33.1	46.9	30.3	. . .	34.2
1964	31.6	39.0	36.7	30.5	48.5	34.4	13.5	33.6	39.6	33.5	33.0	31.1	33.3	47.1	30.4	. . .	34.4

. . . = Not available.

Table 9-2. Producer Price Indexes, by Commodity Group, 1913–2009—*Continued*

(1982 = 100.)

Year	All commodities	Farm products	Processed foods and feeds	Industrial commodities													
				Total	Textile products and apparel	Hides, leather, and related products	Fuels and related products and power	Chemicals and related products	Rubber and plastics products	Lumber and wood products	Pulp, paper, and allied products	Metals and metal products	Machinery and equipment	Furniture and household durables	Nonmetallic mineral products	Transportation equipment	Miscellaneous products
1965	32.3	40.7	38.0	30.9	48.8	35.9	13.8	33.9	39.7	33.7	33.3	32.0	33.7	46.8	30.4	. . .	34.7
1966	33.3	43.7	40.2	31.5	48.9	39.4	14.1	34.0	40.5	35.2	34.2	32.8	34.7	47.4	30.7	. . .	35.3
1967	33.4	41.3	39.8	32.0	48.9	38.1	14.4	34.2	41.4	35.1	34.6	33.2	35.9	48.3	31.2	. . .	36.2
1968	34.2	42.3	40.6	32.8	50.7	39.3	14.3	34.1	42.8	39.8	35.0	34.0	37.0	49.7	32.4	. . .	37.0
1969	35.6	45.0	42.7	33.9	51.8	41.5	14.6	34.2	43.6	44.0	36.0	36.0	38.2	50.7	33.6	40.4	38.1
1970	36.9	45.8	44.6	35.2	52.4	42.0	15.3	35.0	44.9	39.9	37.5	38.7	40.0	51.9	35.3	41.9	39.8
1971	38.1	46.6	45.5	36.5	53.3	43.4	16.6	35.6	45.2	44.7	38.1	39.4	41.4	53.1	38.2	44.2	40.8
1972	39.8	51.6	48.0	37.8	55.5	50.0	17.1	35.6	45.3	50.7	39.3	40.9	42.3	53.8	39.4	45.5	41.5
1973	45.0	72.7	58.9	40.3	60.5	54.5	19.4	37.6	46.6	62.2	42.3	44.0	43.7	55.7	40.7	46.1	43.3
1974	53.5	77.4	68.0	49.2	68.0	55.2	30.1	50.2	56.4	64.5	52.5	57.0	50.0	61.8	47.8	50.3	48.1
1975	58.4	77.0	72.6	54.9	67.4	56.5	35.4	62.0	62.2	62.1	59.0	61.5	57.9	67.5	54.4	56.7	53.4
1976	61.1	78.8	70.8	58.4	72.4	63.9	38.3	64.0	66.0	72.2	62.1	65.0	61.3	70.3	58.2	60.5	55.6
1977	64.9	79.4	74.0	62.5	75.3	68.3	43.6	65.9	69.4	83.0	64.6	69.3	65.2	73.2	62.6	64.6	59.4
1978	69.9	87.7	80.6	67.0	78.1	76.1	46.5	68.0	72.4	96.9	67.7	75.3	70.3	77.5	69.6	69.5	66.7
1979	78.7	99.6	88.5	75.7	82.5	96.1	58.9	76.0	80.5	105.5	75.9	86.0	76.7	82.8	77.6	75.3	75.5
1980	89.8	102.9	95.9	88.0	89.7	94.7	82.8	89.0	90.1	101.5	86.3	95.0	86.0	90.7	88.4	82.9	93.6
1981	98.0	105.2	98.9	97.4	97.6	99.3	100.2	98.4	96.4	102.8	94.8	99.6	94.4	95.9	96.7	94.3	96.1
1982	100.0	100.0	100.0	100.0	100.0	100.0	100.0	100.0	100.0	100.0	100.0	100.0	100.0	100.0	100.0	100.0	100.0
1983	101.3	102.4	101.8	101.1	100.3	103.2	95.9	100.3	100.8	107.9	103.3	101.8	102.7	103.4	101.6	102.8	104.8
1984	103.7	105.5	105.4	103.3	102.7	109.0	94.8	102.9	102.3	108.0	110.3	104.8	105.1	105.7	105.4	105.2	107.0
1985	103.2	95.1	103.5	103.7	102.9	108.9	91.4	103.7	101.9	106.6	113.3	104.4	107.2	107.1	108.6	107.9	109.4
1986	100.2	92.9	105.4	100.0	103.2	113.0	69.8	102.6	101.9	107.2	116.1	103.2	108.8	108.2	110.0	110.5	111.6
1987	102.8	95.5	107.9	102.6	105.1	120.4	70.2	106.4	103.0	112.8	121.8	107.1	110.4	109.9	110.0	112.5	114.9
1988	106.9	104.9	112.7	106.3	109.2	131.4	66.7	116.3	109.3	118.9	130.4	118.7	113.2	113.1	111.2	114.3	120.2
1989	112.2	110.9	117.8	111.6	112.3	136.3	72.9	123.0	112.6	126.7	137.8	124.1	117.4	116.9	112.6	117.7	126.5
1990	116.3	112.2	121.9	115.8	115.0	141.7	82.3	123.6	113.6	129.7	141.2	122.9	120.7	119.2	114.7	121.5	134.2
1991	116.5	105.7	121.9	116.5	116.3	138.9	81.2	125.6	115.1	132.1	142.9	120.2	123.0	121.2	117.2	126.4	140.8
1992	117.2	103.6	122.1	117.4	117.8	140.4	80.4	125.9	115.1	146.6	145.2	119.2	123.4	122.2	117.3	130.4	145.3
1993	118.9	107.1	124.0	119.0	118.0	143.7	80.0	128.2	116.0	174.0	147.3	119.2	124.0	123.7	120.0	133.7	145.4
1994	120.4	106.3	125.5	120.7	118.3	148.5	77.8	132.1	117.6	180.0	152.5	124.8	125.1	126.1	124.2	137.2	141.9
1995	124.7	107.4	127.0	125.5	120.8	153.7	78.0	142.5	124.3	178.1	172.2	134.5	126.6	128.2	129.0	139.7	145.4
1996	127.7	122.4	133.3	127.3	122.4	150.5	85.8	142.1	123.8	176.1	168.7	131.0	126.5	130.4	131.0	141.7	147.7
1997	127.6	112.9	134.0	127.7	122.6	154.2	86.1	143.6	123.2	183.8	167.9	131.8	125.9	130.8	133.2	141.6	150.9
1998	124.4	104.6	131.6	124.8	122.9	148.0	75.3	143.9	122.6	179.1	171.7	127.8	124.9	131.3	135.4	141.2	156.0
1999	125.5	98.4	131.1	125.5	121.1	146.0	80.5	144.2	122.5	183.6	174.1	124.6	124.3	131.7	138.9	141.8	166.6
2000	132.7	99.5	133.1	134.8	121.4	151.5	103.5	151.0	125.5	178.2	183.7	128.1	124.0	132.6	142.5	143.8	170.8
2001	134.2	103.8	137.3	135.7	121.3	158.4	105.3	151.8	127.2	174.4	184.8	125.4	123.7	133.2	144.3	145.2	181.3
2002	131.1	99.0	136.2	132.4	119.9	157.6	93.2	151.9	126.8	173.3	185.9	125.9	122.9	133.5	146.2	144.6	182.4
2003	138.1	111.5	143.4	139.1	119.8	162.3	112.9	161.8	130.1	177.4	190.0	129.2	121.9	133.9	148.2	145.7	179.6
2004	146.7	123.3	151.2	147.6	121.0	164.5	126.9	174.4	133.8	195.6	195.7	149.6	122.1	135.1	153.2	148.6	183.2
2005	157.4	118.5	153.1	160.2	122.8	165.4	156.4	192.0	143.8	196.5	202.6	160.8	123.7	139.4	164.2	151.0	195.1
2006	164.7	117.0	153.8	168.8	124.5	168.4	166.7	205.8	153.8	194.4	209.8	181.6	126.2	142.6	179.9	152.6	205.6
2007	172.6	143.4	165.1	175.1	125.8	173.6	177.6	214.8	155.0	192.4	216.9	193.5	127.3	144.7	186.2	155.0	210.3
2008	189.6	161.3	180.5	192.3	128.9	173.1	214.6	245.5	165.9	191.3	226.8	213.0	129.7	148.9	197.1	158.6	216.6
2009	172.9	134.6	176.2	174.8	129.5	157.0	158.7	229.4	165.2	182.8	225.6	186.8	131.3	153.1	202.4	162.2	217.5

. . . = Not available.

Table 9-3. Producer Price Indexes for the Net Output of Selected Industries, 1999–2009

(December 2003 = 100, unless otherwise specified.)

Industry	1999	2000	2001	2002	2003	2004	2005	2006	2007	2008	2009
Agriculture, Forestry, Fishing, and Hunting											
Logging[1]	182.7	177.5	167.5	165.0	168.7	175.2	179.0	176.6	175.0	171.5	160.3
Mining											
Oil and gas extraction[2]	78.5	126.8	127.5	107.0	160.1	192.7	262.0	252.5	267.1	347.5	187.3
Mining (except oil and gas)	...	...	...	...	...	109.5	126.6	147.9	158.4	180.8	187.3
Coal mining [2]	87.3	84.8	91.3	93.9	94.4	104.1	118.2	126.9	130.6	162.2	185.7
Metal ore mining[3]	70.3	73.8	70.8	73.6	81.6	111.8	146.0	204.6	226.4	232.6	203.4
Iron ore mining[3]	94.0	93.9	95.2	94.2	95.0	97.2	115.7	131.2	127.5	141.0	143.5
Gold ore and silver ore mining[3]	58.2	57.0	55.2	62.6	72.6	82.6	89.5	121.3	138.8	143.9	161.9
Copper, nickel, lead, and zinc mining[4]	71.3	88.7	81.7	80.1	90.1	147.7	195.2	350.2	386.5	390.3	288.6
Other metal ore mining[2]	25.9	26.4	24.7	28.9	34.9	80.0	159.1	128.7	145.5	147.8	110.9
Nonmetallic mineral mining and quarrying[3]	134.0	137.0	141.0	143.5	146.4	151.2	161.3	176.0	191.1	217.6	228.9
Stone mining and quarrying[3]	142.1	147.3	152.2	156.1	160.2	166.1	176.7	192.7	210.2	224.7	236.8
Sand, gravel, clay, and refractory minerals mining	...	...	...	...	...	102.4	108.8	117.6	126.1	135.1	142.2
Other nonmetallic mineral mining and quarrying[3]	108.0	106.8	107.1	107.7	108.4	111.4	120.8	133.8	148.3	222.5	233.3
Mining support activities	...	...	...	...	68.0	86.8	111.5	110.8	112.8	103.2	102.0
Utilities	...	...	...	...	...	104.9	117.6	123.1	127.0	136.5	130.2
Electric power generation, transmission, and distribution	...	...	...	...	...	103.3	111.3	118.8	122.7	130.7	129.3
Electric power generation	...	...	...	...	...	105.2	121.6	128.0	132.0	145.5	132.3
Electric power transmission, control, and distribution	...	...	...	...	...	102.5	107.1	115.1	118.9	124.8	127.7
Natural gas distribution	...	...	...	...	...	107.3	126.6	129.3	129.0	142.9	117.9
Manufacturing											
Food[3]	126.3	128.5	132.8	132.0	137.4	144.3	146.1	146.8	158.6	173.8	169.5
Animal food	...	...	...	...	...	103.3	98.2	101.8	118.6	147.8	142.1
Grain and oilseed milling	...	...	...	...	...	103.1	99.8	104.7	121.2	157.4	136.3
Flour milling and malt	...	...	...	...	...	102.6	100.5	109.1	128.5	178.8	145.3
Starch and vegetable fats and oils	...	...	...	...	...	103.6	97.9	102.4	122.2	163.1	138.9
Breakfast cereal manufacturing	...	...	...	...	...	101.7	105.0	106.9	108.9	112.1	115.7
Sugar and confectionery product[3]	129.4	127.5	129.3	133.7	139.5	141.4	147.3	154.7	155.4	166.7	180.2
Sugar	...	...	...	...	...	99.7	105.6	123.4	111.1	114.4	129.1
Chocolate and confectionery from cacao beans	...	...	...	...	...	100.1	101.7	103.9	107.2	116.9	125.2
Confectionery from purchased chocolate	...	...	...	...	...	100.1	102.2	103.8	109.1	120.0	127.6
Non-chocolate confectionery	...	...	...	...	...	104.0	111.0	113.0	114.9	121.1	131.1
Fruit and vegetable preserving and specialty food[3]	131.7	132.1	133.3	135.2	136.6	139.2	141.7	144.5	147.6	156.5	165.2
Frozen food	...	...	...	...	...	101.6	103.9	107.7	108.9	113.5	118.7
Fruit and vegetable canning, pickling, and drying	...	...	...	...	...	100.5	104.0	107.3	112.5	120.5	128.0
Dairy product[3]	133.8	129.9	141.2	133.3	135.8	151.0	151.3	147.4	174.5	179.1	157.9
Dairy product (except frozen)	...	...	...	...	...	108.4	108.5	105.0	126.9	130.0	112.1
Ice cream and frozen dessert	...	...	...	...	...	103.3	104.7	106.9	110.6	114.8	115.8
Animal slaughtering and processing[3]	108.9	115.0	120.3	114.0	125.8	134.2	135.8	130.8	139.1	145.8	140.3
Seafood product preparation and packaging	...	...	...	...	...	102.4	106.2	107.0	112.8	123.6	124.8
Bakery and tortilla	...	...	...	...	...	100.8	102.6	105.3	109.8	123.5	127.7
Bread and bakery product	...	...	...	...	...	101.1	103.4	106.6	111.1	125.0	129.6
Cookie, cracker, and pasta	...	...	...	...	...	100.5	101.3	103.2	107.3	120.3	124.8
Tortilla	...	...	...	...	...	100.4	102.5	103.9	113.3	129.6	126.0
Other food	...	...	...	...	...	101.1	105.4	107.0	110.6	119.9	122.3
Snack food	...	...	...	...	...	101.4	108.4	108.5	109.5	119.2	127.1
Coffee and tea	...	...	...	...	...	101.7	115.1	117.3	124.3	135.4	137.1
Flavoring syrup and concentrate	...	...	...	...	...	101.0	103.1	106.5	109.1	113.4	117.1
Seasoning and dressing	...	...	...	...	...	101.1	101.3	102.7	106.7	116.2	121.8
All other food	...	...	...	...	...	100.4	100.8	103.1	108.2	118.5	112.8
Beverage and tobacco product	...	...	...	...	...	101.0	104.8	106.3	109.6	114.4	119.8
Beverage[3]	129.8	134.4	138.6	140.8	142.7	146.4	150.4	153.3	155.2	162.2	168.4
Soft drink and ice	...	...	...	...	...	102.1	104.1	106.8	109.3	114.5	119.1
Breweries	...	...	...	...	...	101.3	105.6	105.6	104.0	108.7	114.4
Wineries	...	...	...	...	...	100.7	104.2	109.8	112.0	114.6	116.8
Distilleries	...	...	...	...	...	100.1	100.6	101.9	106.5	113.7	114.5
Tobacco[3]	325.7	345.8	386.1	401.9	377.9	379.7	401.0	403.8	429.5	446.9	474.8
Tobacco stemming and redrying[5]	104.7	109.0	112.3	114.7	117.5	119.4	119.9	109.4	112.6	113.4	115.2
Tobacco product[6]	356.7	379.3	425.8	442.8	411.7	412.5	436.3	440.2	468.4	487.6	518.2
Textile mills	...	...	...	...	...	101.1	103.6	106.6	108.2	112.4	112.3
Fiber, yarn, and thread mills[3]	106.9	105.5	103.0	99.8	100.9	105.6	108.8	111.1	114.0	121.1	117.6
Fabric mills	...	...	...	...	...	101.0	103.0	105.8	106.2	109.7	109.2
Broadwoven fabric mills	...	...	...	...	...	101.1	103.2	106.7	108.1	111.7	108.0
Narrow fabric mills and schiffli mach embroidery[5]	124.3	125.3	126.2	126.0	125.1	126.2	129.3	131.1	132.5	134.6	136.9
Nonwoven fabric mills	...	...	...	...	...	101.5	105.6	108.1	108.2	112.8	113.7
Knit fabric mills	...	...	...	...	...	100.4	100.5	101.3	99.4	101.2	107.4
Textile and fabric finishing mills	...	...	...	...	...	99.9	102.8	106.5	109.5	113.4	116.3
Fabric coating mills	...	...	...	...	...	100.2	104.9	113.4	116.5	123.9	126.2
Textile product mills	...	...	...	...	...	101.4	105.3	108.4	109.6	112.4	115.4
Textile furnishings mills	...	...	...	...	...	101.1	105.1	108.6	110.0	112.2	116.3
Carpet and rug mills[3]	115.4	117.8	118.9	119.0	121.8	124.6	132.9	140.2	141.6	144.6	151.0
Curtain and linen mills	...	...	...	...	...	100.2	100.3	100.5	102.1	103.5	106.3
Other textile product mills	...	...	...	...	...	102.0	105.4	107.9	108.8	113.3	113.4
Textile bag and canvas mills	...	...	...	...	...	102.7	104.9	107.5	111.5	115.1	116.3
All other textile product mills	...	...	...	...	...	101.7	105.6	108.0	107.8	112.7	112.4

[1]December 1981 = 100.
[2]December 1985 = 100.
[3]December 1984 = 100.
[4]June 1988 = 100.
[5]June 1984 = 100.
[6]December 1982 = 100.
... = Not available.

Table 9-3. Producer Price Indexes for the Net Output of Selected Industries, 1999–2009—*Continued*

(December 2003 = 100, unless otherwise specified.)

Industry	1999	2000	2001	2002	2003	2004	2005	2006	2007	2008	2009
Manufacturing—*Continued*											
Apparel	...	...	...	...	...	100.0	100.0	100.5	101.5	102.4	103.5
Apparel knitting mills[3]	114.0	113.9	113.7	112.7	111.6	110.3	109.6	110.5	110.9	112.9	113.9
Cut and sew apparel	...	...	...	...	...	100.2	100.2	100.6	101.7	102.4	103.5
Cut and sew apparel contractors	...	...	...	...	...	100.2	103.0	105.3	105.9	106.3	106.3
Men's and boys' cut and sew apparel	...	...	...	...	...	100.4	104.8	108.8	110.6	111.6	113.2
Women's and girls' cut and sew apparel	...	...	...	...	...	100.1	102.4	103.9	104.1	104.3	103.8
Other cut and sew apparel	...	...	...	...	...	100.2	102.3	107.1	111.8	114.7	116.5
Accessories and other apparel	...	...	...	...	...	100.5	101.6	102.2	103.5	106.5	106.9
Leather and allied product[3]	136.5	137.9	141.3	141.1	142.8	143.6	144.5	146.6	149.7	153.5	153.8
Leather and hide tanning and finishing[7]	168.8	174.6	191.7	191.4	200.5	205.7	204.8	208.4	215.9	221.3	212.1
Footwear	...	...	...	...	...	100.1	101.1	102.2	103.3	106.3	107.7
Other leather and allied product	...	...	...	...	...	99.8	100.7	102.6	104.7	106.6	109.8
Wood product	...	...	...	...	...	106.7	108.6	108.5	107.0	107.4	103.2
Sawmills and wood preservation	...	...	...	...	...	110.5	110.7	107.9	103.8	99.3	88.7
Plywood, and engineered wood product	...	...	...	...	...	107.0	105.2	99.6	94.6	95.8	90.6
Other wood product	...	...	...	...	...	105.0	111.3	115.9	118.0	122.3	122.1
Millwork	...	...	...	...	...	104.8	105.4	106.7	107.3	107.5	106.3
Wood container and pallet	...	...	...	...	...	102.8	107.1	110.9	109.9	111.7	110.8
All other wood product	...	...	...	...	...	105.0	111.3	115.9	118.0	122.3	122.1
Paper	...	...	...	...	...	102.6	106.9	112.3	115.7	122.8	123.3
Pulp, paper, and paperboard mills	...	...	...	...	...	103.8	109.4	115.7	119.3	129.0	126.6
Pulp mills[6]	122.7	143.4	122.9	116.5	120.9	131.3	137.4	144.8	163.2	175.5	162.1
Paper mills[7]	139.7	148.8	150.5	144.1	145.7	151.1	161.0	168.1	170.8	184.6	183.9
Paperboard mills[6]	166.9	192.2	187.3	179.5	180.2	189.9	196.0	212.7	224.1	242.4	230.9
Converted paper product	...	...	...	...	...	101.9	105.5	110.5	113.9	119.4	121.8
Paper container[3]	144.1	157.1	158.9	157.0	157.3	161.5	167.1	177.1	182.9	192.3	195.0
Paper bag and coated and treated paper	...	...	...	...	...	101.7	105.8	110.4	113.3	117.8	120.3
Stationery product	...	...	...	...	...	101.7	106.8	110.5	114.7	120.2	122.9
Other converted paper product	...	...	...	...	...	97.0	98.7	100.0	102.8	107.9	112.0
Printing and related support activities	...	...	...	...	...	101.1	103.1	105.6	106.7	109.4	109.3
Printing	...	...	...	...	...	101.2	103.3	105.9	107.1	109.9	109.8
Printing support activities	...	...	...	...	...	100.4	100.0	100.4	100.9	101.2	101.2
Petroleum and coal product[3]	76.8	112.8	105.3	98.8	122.0	149.9	200.4	235.5	260.3	329.2	218.8
Petroleum refineries[8]	73.6	111.6	103.1	96.3	121.2	151.5	205.3	241.0	266.9	338.3	217.0
Asphalt paving, roofing, and saturated materials[3]	102.8	113.5	116.9	119.7	125.1	127.1	138.6	164.8	174.2	213.5	229.9
Other petroleum and coal product[3]	142.1	150.3	159.3	160.5	165.3	172.0	197.8	238.3	253.5	320.2	313.4
Chemical[3]	149.7	156.7	158.4	157.3	164.6	172.8	187.3	196.8	203.3	228.2	224.7
Basic chemical[3]	161.4	177.3	173.5	170.6	183.0	197.7	225.9	244.3	254.4	309.0	290.3
Petrochemical	...	...	...	...	...	120.7	151.0	164.7	168.5	212.6	141.2
Industrial gas	...	...	...	...	...	108.3	118.3	123.0	123.2	140.9	129.0
Synthetic dye and pigment	...	...	...	...	...	104.2	108.7	112.0	118.1	125.5	118.4
Other basic inorganic chemical	...	...	...	...	...	103.1	120.4	149.4	159.5	206.6	219.7
Other basic organic chemical	...	...	...	...	...	...	...	...	...	...	...
Resin, synthetic rubber, and artificial and synthetic fiber and filament[3]	115.4	128.0	126.2	119.7	131.0	145.5	169.4	175.2	174.6	193.0	174.3
Resin and synthetic rubber	...	...	...	...	...	115.1	136.5	141.2	140.4	156.3	140.6
Artificial and synthetic fiber and filament	...	...	...	...	...	101.2	107.8	111.1	110.6	113.7	107.2
Pesticide, fertilizer, and other agricultural chemical[3]	123.2	124.9	132.0	127.0	135.3	142.7	151.3	156.6	179.4	278.7	198.8
Fertilizer	...	...	...	...	...	107.3	118.1	123.5	151.8	277.5	162.1
Pesticide and other agricultural chemical	...	...	...	...	...	100.6	102.2	104.4	106.9	115.5	125.9
Pharmaceutical and medicine[3]	210.1	215.7	220.5	226.3	235.4	244.2	255.2	266.3	276.0	293.3	311.7
Paint, coating, and adhesive	...	...	...	...	...	101.9	108.8	116.9	121.5	129.8	137.4
Adhesive	...	...	...	...	...	100.5	106.4	114.8	119.0	127.4	133.6
Soap, cleaners, and toilet preparation[3]	130.3	132.5	134.2	134.2	134.9	136.9	140.5	144.6	147.2	153.0	157.0
Soap and cleaning compound	...	...	...	...	...	102.0	105.8	110.5	112.5	120.8	126.1
Toilet preparation	...	...	...	...	...	100.0	101.2	102.1	103.9	104.3	104.7
Other chemical product and preparation	...	...	...	...	...	101.6	108.6	114.2	118.0	126.5	128.0
Printing ink	...	...	...	...	...	100.0	103.0	107.2	114.2	123.5	131.8
Explosives[9]	...	...	...	...	...	...	...	...	103.1	113.1	108.5
All other chemical product and preparation	...	...	...	...	...	101.8	109.4	115.3	118.7	127.0	127.8
Plastics and rubber product[3]	...	...	...	...	...	102.8	106.3	109.4	111.4	115.2	118.7
Plastics product[10]	107.1	109.8	111.0	110.2	113.0	116.2	125.8	134.1	133.9	143.4	142.4
Unsupported plastics film, sheet, and bag	...	...	...	...	...	104.2	116.9	124.4	123.8	137.9	132.2
Plastics pipe, fitting, and unsupported shape	...	...	...	...	...	108.5	122.6	142.8	136.2	147.6	142.7
Laminated plastics plate, sheet, and shape	...	...	...	...	...	101.7	105.0	108.4	107.7	112.5	113.2
Polystyrene foam product	...	...	...	...	...	104.6	117.0	120.8	125.7	136.1	135.4
Foam product (except polystyrene)	...	...	...	...	...	100.2	110.0	136.6	132.5	140.0	142.4
Plastics bottle	...	...	...	...	...	103.1	114.8	119.5	118.3	126.8	114.3
Other plastics product	...	...	...	...	...	101.3	107.1	111.7	112.5	118.6	120.6
Rubber product	...	...	...	...	...	102.1	106.7	111.8	115.2	123.6	127.1
Tire[7]	100.4	100.4	101.5	102.7	105.6	110.5	116.9	123.8	128.6	140.2	143.5
Rubber and plastics hose and belting	...	...	...	...	...	102.3	107.4	111.0	113.6	120.1	127.1
Other rubber product	119.9	120.5	121.3	121.4	121.8	121.9	125.1	130.2	133.0	140.4	143.9
Nonmetallic mineral product[3]	132.6	134.7	136.0	137.1	138.0	142.7	152.0	163.4	166.8	170.9	174.0
Clay product and refractory	...	...	...	...	...	101.5	105.1	110.4	113.1	116.0	119.4
Pottery, ceramics, and plumbing fixture[3]	138.1	139.7	150.2	150.1	150.6	152.1	154.3	159.8	163.3	164.1	168.5
Clay building material and refractories	...	...	...	...	...	102.2	107.8	114.5	117.5	122.1	125.8
Glass and glass product	...	...	...	...	...	100.1	101.6	103.7	105.8	108.6	110.2

[3]December 1984 = 100.
[6]December 1982 = 100.
[7]June 1981 = 100.
[8]June 1985 = 100.
[9]December 2006 = 100.
[10]June 1993 = 100.
. . . = Not available.

Table 9-3. Producer Price Indexes for the Net Output of Selected Industries, 1999–2009—*Continued*

(December 2003 = 100, unless otherwise specified.)

Industry	1999	2000	2001	2002	2003	2004	2005	2006	2007	2008	2009
Manufacturing—*Continued*											
Cement and concrete product	...	...	...	...	...	104.2	114.8	126.6	131.9	136.4	138.0
Cement[11]	149.1	148.6	148.7	151.1	150.5	155.4	175.2	197.7	208.4	207.8	204.3
Ready-mix concrete	...	...	...	...	...	104.5	117.3	130.6	135.6	139.7	143.3
Concrete pipe, brick, and block ...	...	...	...	...	...	102.5	109.2	116.7	121.0	127.9	128.5
Other concrete products	...	...	...	...	...	104.7	111.3	121.0	126.6	132.2	131.3
Lime and gypsum product	...	...	...	...	...	110.0	124.5	145.1	128.1	119.4	123.6
Lime	...	...	...	...	...	110.0	124.5	145.1	128.1	119.4	123.6
Gypsum product	...	...	...	...	...	111.9	127.9	151.6	128.6	116.0	115.3
Other nonmetallic mineral product[3]	131.3	130.9	132.0	132.6	133.4	137.2	142.5	150.2	152.0	154.9	160.6
Abrasive product	...	...	...	...	...	100.2	103.1	107.2	110.4	118.1	124.6
All other nonmetallic mineral product ...	...	...	...	...	...	103.5	108.0	114.5	115.2	115.7	119.3
Primary metal[3]	115.8	119.8	116.1	116.2	118.4	142.8	156.3	179.3	190.5	211.9	172.5
Iron and steel mills and ferroalloy	...	...	...	...	...	127.7	136.7	150.9	160.8	189.7	138.1
Steel product from purchased steel	...	...	...	...	...	133.1	146.2	148.2	151.1	189.8	156.8
Iron/steel pipe and tube from purchased steel ...	...	...	...	...	...	147.9	160.1	164.1	168.1	206.6	164.7
Rolling and drawing of purchased steel ...	...	...	...	...	...	123.7	137.5	138.1	140.8	180.6	154.0
Alumina and aluminum production and processing ...	...	...	...	...	...	...	114.0	131.2	136.3	139.0	111.3
Nonferrous (except aluminum) production and processing ...	...	...	...	...	...	113.6	137.6	202.8	223.0	218.6	186.0
Copper rolling, drawing, extruding, and alloying ...	...	...	...	...	...	118.2	138.9	222.0	232.8	232.9	196.9
Other nonferrous rolling, drawing, extruding, and alloying ...	...	...	...	...	...	110.3	136.2	181.2	206.0	195.8	168.3
Foundries	...	...	...	...	...	103.9	110.9	118.7	126.3	138.6	133.5
Ferrous metal foundries[3]	130.4	132.1	132.7	133.0	133.5	140.4	152.5	160.1	168.5	188.7	183.5
Nonferrous metal foundries[3]	131.6	133.5	134.1	134.4	135.6	140.0	145.0	160.4	173.2	185.6	176.4
Fabricated metal product[3]	129.1	130.3	131.0	131.7	132.9	141.3	149.5	155.7	162.3	174.4	175.2
Forging and stamping	...	...	...	...	...	107.0	113.3	116.8	120.9	130.8	128.0
Cutlery and handtool	...	...	...	...	...	...	105.5	108.9	111.8	115.8	119.7
Architectural and structural metals	...	...	...	...	...	111.2	118.0	122.6	127.4	140.9	135.6
Plate work and fabricated structural product ...	...	...	...	...	...	115.2	124.2	128.9	135.2	155.4	143.2
Ornamental and architectural metal product ...	...	...	...	...	...	108.3	113.5	118.1	121.7	129.9	130.1
Boiler, tank, and shipping container	...	...	...	...	...	106.8	115.7	120.3	126.2	136.5	143.0
Power boiler and heat exchanger	...	...	...	...	...	...	124.2	132.4	136.9	147.3	143.3
Metal tank (heavy gauge)	...	...	...	...	...	...	120.8	125.6	132.3	143.2	142.3
Light gauge metal container[3]	100.7	101.0	100.8	102.7	105.4	110.4	117.5	121.0	127.1	137.8	149.9
Hardware	...	...	...	...	...	103.4	107.2	110.7	115.3	122.4	125.1
Spring and wire product	...	...	...	...	...	108.9	114.4	117.9	120.7	138.4	140.8
Machine shops; turned product; and screw, nut, and bolt	...	...	...	...	...	102.8	108.4	113.0	118.8	125.2	126.4
Machine shops	...	...	...	...	...	102.4	107.4	109.8	112.4	119.4	122.7
Turned product and screw, nut, and bolt[3] ...	121.8	122.9	122.8	123.4	123.6	128.4	136.6	147.1	161.2	167.9	165.3
Coating, engraving, heat treating, and other activity ...	...	...	...	...	...	102.0	104.2	110.6	115.5	119.5	118.9
Other fabricated metal product	...	...	...	...	...	103.8	109.8	115.7	121.5	128.4	133.0
Metal valve	...	...	...	...	...	103.0	109.8	118.1	126.6	132.8	136.5
All other fabricated metal product	...	...	...	...	...	104.5	109.9	113.7	117.1	124.7	129.9
Machinery	...	...	...	...	...	101.9	105.6	108.8	112.1	117.0	120.3
Agricultural, construction, and mining machinery	...	...	...	...	...	102.4	107.4	111.7	115.4	120.3	124.2
Agricultural implement	...	...	...	...	...	101.8	105.8	107.8	110.5	114.5	117.8
Construction machinery	...	...	...	...	...	102.9	107.7	112.5	115.8	119.4	123.7
Mining and oil and gas field machinery ...	...	...	...	...	...	102.7	110.6	119.5	127.3	137.9	142.1
Industrial machinery[3]	147.2	148.7	149.9	149.6	150.1	153.0	155.9	158.9	162.8	166.4	166.2
Sawmill and woodworking machinery	...	...	...	...	...	110.5	110.7	107.9	103.8	99.3	88.7
Plastics and rubber industry machinery ...	122.2	124.6	125.9	125.5	128.4	131.7	141.2	149.7	150.6	161.3	161.3
Other industrial machinery[3]	147.2	148.7	149.9	149.6	150.1	152.7	155.3	158.0	162.0	165.2	164.2
Commercial and service industry machinery ...	...	...	...	...	...	101.3	102.9	103.9	106.0	109.3	111.8
HVAC and commercial refrigeration equipment ...	...	...	...	...	...	101.9	108.0	112.1	117.8	123.0	124.1
Metalworking machinery	...	...	...	...	...	100.8	103.3	105.8	106.8	108.8	109.2
Turbine, and power transmission equipment[3] ...	135.7	136.6	137.7	138.9	139.1	140.8	143.2	148.0	152.6	162.9	174.6
Other general purpose machinery	...	...	...	...	...	103.0	107.6	111.2	115.0	121.4	125.4
Pump and compressor	...	...	...	...	...	102.2	108.4	112.6	117.9	123.6	127.5
Material handling equipment	...	...	...	...	...	104.6	110.6	114.4	118.2	125.3	129.5
All other general purpose machinery ...	...	...	...	...	...	102.5	105.7	108.7	112.0	118.1	122.2
Computer and electronic product	...	...	...	...	...	99.0	97.5	96.5	94.2	92.7	92.1
Computer and peripheral equipment[9]	172.8	162.2	153.1	139.5	123.9	115.4	107.8	102.1	94.5	86.4	81.1
Communications equipment[2]	113.0	110.4	108.6	105.0	101.7	98.4	97.0	95.9	95.8	97.1	97.2
Telephone apparatus	...	...	...	...	...	95.3	93.2	91.1	90.5	91.3	90.7
Radio/TV broadcast and wireless communication equipment ...	...	...	...	...	...	99.4	98.7	98.2	98.6	100.3	100.8
Other communications equipment	...	...	...	...	...	99.8	99.7	101.2	101.6	103.5	104.9
Audio and video equipment	...	...	...	...	...	98.1	95.6	93.7	90.9	89.3	85.5
Semiconductor and other electronic component[3] ...	90.1	88.8	86.4	84.9	81.1	78.3	76.5	75.1	70.2	66.3	65.4
Navigation, measuring, medical, and control instruments ...	...	...	...	...	...	100.6	101.9	103.5	104.9	106.5	108.2
Manufacturing and reproducing magnetic and optical media ...	...	...	...	...	...	98.0	97.0	95.5	92.2	93.8	92.4
Electrical equipment, appliance and component ...	...	...	...	...	...	103.2	108.0	116.6	122.2	127.8	128.6
Electric lighting equipment	...	...	...	...	...	100.8	103.5	105.9	108.2	110.9	112.7
Electric lamp bulb and part	...	...	...	...	...	98.1	100.2	98.6	98.8	99.6	110.0
Lighting fixture	...	...	...	...	...	101.7	104.6	108.2	111.2	114.3	116.3
Household appliance[3]	107.2	106.2	104.6	104.2	103.1	103.1	106.3	107.7	109.3	112.6	117.7
Small electrical appliance	...	...	...	...	...	99.9	101.8	103.0	105.3	106.0	109.2
Major appliance	...	...	...	...	...	100.6	104.2	105.6	106.8	110.8	116.1
Electrical equipment	...	...	...	...	...	101.9	107.2	113.7	120.6	127.3	129.5
Other electrical equipment and component ...	...	...	...	...	...	106.6	112.5	129.1	136.7	144.0	140.5
Battery	...	...	...	...	...	102.2	105.7	112.6	126.2	138.9	138.2
Communications and energy wire and cable ...	...	...	...	...	...	106.8	115.8	150.3	161.3	167.9	154.8
Wiring device	...	...	...	...	...	113.6	118.9	128.6	133.9	140.9	139.9
All other electrical equipment and component ...	...	...	...	...	...	101.7	105.4	109.3	110.3	114.0	119.5

[2]December 1985 = 100.
[3]December 1984 = 100.
[9]December 2006 = 100.
[11]June 1982 = 100.
. . . = Not available.

Table 9-3. Producer Price Indexes for the Net Output of Selected Industries, 1999–2009—*Continued*

(December 2003 = 100, unless otherwise specified.)

Industry	1999	2000	2001	2002	2003	2004	2005	2006	2007	2008	2009
Manufacturing—*Continued*											
Transportation equipment	. . .	. . .	. . .	. . .	. . .	100.9	102.5	103.2	104.9	107.3	109.5
Motor vehicle	. . .	. . .	. . .	. . .	. . .	99.4	98.7	96.1	96.6	98.0	100.9
Automobile and light truck motor vehicle	. . .	. . .	. . .	. . .	. . .	99.2	98.2	95.1	95.3	96.6	99.4
Motor vehicle body and trailer	. . .	. . .	. . .	. . .	. . .	104.0	109.7	113.7	117.2	121.5	122.4
Motor vehicle parts	. . .	. . .	. . .	. . .	. . .	101.4	102.7	104.8	106.8	108.8	108.5
Motor vehicle steering and suspension parts	. . .	. . .	. . .	. . .	. . .	101.8	105.1	106.3	105.0	106.5	105.3
Aerospace product and parts[8]	144.8	149.9	154.7	157.3	162.2	168.0	176.0	182.8	188.6	196.2	200.6
Railroad rolling stock[5]	128.2	128.6	128.3	127.7	129.0	135.8	150.5	158.4	165.6	169.3	171.5
Ship and boat building[3]	145.6	149.0	152.6	156.8	163.0	169.6	175.0	181.4	188.3	193.8	199.2
Other transportation equipment	. . .	. . .	. . .	. . .	. . .	101.1	103.6	104.8	106.3	106.4	107.2
Furniture and related product[3]	141.3	143.3	145.1	146.3	147.4	151.5	157.8	162.5	165.7	171.7	176.6
Household and institutional furniture and kitchen cabinet[3]	140.3	142.5	144.4	146.2	147.0	148.6	152.6	157.4	160.8	166.5	171.1
Wood kitchen cabinet and countertop	. . .	. . .	. . .	. . .	. . .	101.1	103.2	106.3	108.4	111.2	113.4
Household and institutional furniture	. . .	. . .	. . .	. . .	. . .	101.1	104.0	107.4	109.7	114.0	117.6
Office furniture (including fixtures)	. . .	. . .	. . .	. . .	. . .	105.1	111.5	113.8	116.7	121.2	124.6
Other furniture-related product	. . .	. . .	. . .	. . .	. . .	104.0	110.6	115.2	114.9	118.5	122.9
Mattress	. . .	. . .	. . .	. . .	. . .	105.6	115.0	120.6	119.2	123.9	127.7
Blind and shade	. . .	. . .	. . .	. . .	. . .	101.3	103.9	106.9	108.3	109.9	115.5
Miscellaneous	. . .	. . .	. . .	. . .	. . .	101.2	102.9	104.7	107.0	109.9	111.5
Medical equipment and supplies	. . .	. . .	. . .	. . .	. . .	101.3	102.5	103.8	105.1	107.4	108.9
Other miscellaneous[2]	130.3	130.9	132.4	133.3	133.9	135.2	138.4	142.0	146.5	151.1	153.5
Jewelry and silverware[2]	126.4	127.1	128.0	129.1	131.0	134.6	138.7	146.5	152.6	161.7	165.6
Sporting and athletic goods	. . .	. . .	. . .	. . .	. . .	101.3	102.0	103.6	107.6	106.2	108.2
Doll, toy, and game	. . .	. . .	. . .	. . .	. . .	100.3	101.7	102.7	104.9	107.9	113.9
Office supplies (except paper)[2]	132.0	132.0	131.4	132.8	132.9	133.1	135.8	136.2	139.0	141.1	144.1
Sign	. . .	. . .	. . .	. . .	. . .	100.9	104.6	106.9	109.1	111.2	111.5
All other miscellaneous	. . .	. . .	. . .	. . .	. . .	101.0	103.7	106.7	110.2	115.4	116.4
Wholesale Trade											
Merchant wholesalers, durable goods[12]	. . .	. . .	. . .	. . .	. . .	. . .	102.0	106.3	110.4	116.4	119.8
Merchant wholesalers, nondurable goods[13]	. . .	. . .	. . .	. . .	. . .	. . .	. . .	106.2	112.2	120.5	133.4
Wholesale trade agents and brokers[13]	. . .	. . .	. . .	. . .	. . .	. . .	. . .	102.4	105.5	110.4	110.9
Retail Trade											
Motor vehicle and parts dealers	. . .	. . .	. . .	. . .	. . .	103.5	106.9	112.8	115.5	118.0	120.0
Automobile dealers	. . .	. . .	. . .	. . .	. . .	102.9	105.4	110.8	113.2	115.8	116.2
New car dealers[14]	. . .	99.7	103.1	108.7	111.5	113.5	116.3	122.3	125.0	125.7	128.2
Recreational vehicle dealers[15]	. . .	. . .	98.8	112.2	109.7	121.4	133.6	133.8	142.4	143.5	119.1
Automotive parts, accessories, and tire stores[16]	. . .	. . .	. . .	100.9	104.2	109.4	115.1	124.3	128.2	142.0	148.2
Automotive parts and accessories stores	. . .	. . .	. . .	. . .	. . .	106.8	110.9	119.7	125.6	140.3	148.1
Tire dealers	. . .	. . .	. . .	. . .	. . .	102.0	110.7	119.3	117.5	128.1	130.5
Furniture and home furnishings stores	. . .	. . .	. . .	. . .	. . .	102.4	110.7	116.6	117.4	120.3	121.5
Furniture stores	. . .	. . .	. . .	. . .	. . .	100.8	108.0	111.0	110.6	113.7	117.2
Floor covering stores	. . .	. . .	. . .	. . .	. . .	104.6	114.4	124.3	127.0	129.8	128.2
Electronics and appliance stores	. . .	. . .	. . .	. . .	. . .	99.0	98.9	99.4	106.1	110.8	104.5
Appliance, TV, and other electronics stores	. . .	. . .	. . .	. . .	. . .	101.8	103.5	103.8	104.9	112.8	109.6
Computer and software stores	. . .	. . .	. . .	. . .	. . .	95.2	92.4	91.7	91.7	84.6	61.9
Camera and photographic supplies stores	. . .	. . .	. . .	. . .	. . .	88.6	82.0	95.5	91.3	86.7	89.2
Building material and garden equipment and supplies dealers	. . .	. . .	. . .	. . .	. . .	108.3	109.9	118.4	120.1	119.2	119.5
Building material and supplies dealers	. . .	. . .	. . .	. . .	. . .	108.7	109.9	119.8	122.4	121.0	120.8
Home centers	. . .	. . .	. . .	. . .	. . .	107.0	109.6	122.5	121.8	115.7	118.4
Paint and wallpaper stores	. . .	. . .	. . .	. . .	. . .	99.5	104.4	106.2	110.3	121.8	129.7
Hardware stores	. . .	. . .	. . .	. . .	. . .	103.1	108.2	112.3	114.3	114.3	118.2
Other building material dealers	. . .	. . .	. . .	. . .	. . .	111.4	110.8	121.3	128.9	130.6	125.7
Lawn and garden equipment and supplies stores	. . .	. . .	. . .	. . .	. . .	105.8	110.3	111.5	106.8	110.1	114.5
Nursery, garden, and farm supply stores	. . .	. . .	. . .	. . .	. . .	105.8	110.3	111.5	106.8	110.1	114.5
Food and beverage stores[14]	. . .	103.8	109.6	113.4	117.6	123.2	131.0	134.7	139.6	149.3	151.2
Grocery stores	. . .	. . .	. . .	. . .	. . .	103.5	110.7	114.0	117.9	126.1	127.4
Grocery (except convenience) stores	. . .	. . .	. . .	. . .	. . .	103.5	110.7	114.0	117.9	126.1	127.4
Specialty food stores	. . .	. . .	. . .	. . .	. . .	107.1	110.2	114.1	122.9	132.4	141.0
Beer, wine, and liquor stores[17]	. . .	. . .	102.9	103.5	106.9	110.7	111.0	111.3	113.2	120.6	119.8
Health and personal care stores	. . .	. . .	. . .	. . .	. . .	101.7	107.6	118.7	123.1	130.5	137.9
Pharmacies and drug stores[17]	. . .	. . .	102.4	112.4	116.6	119.8	127.9	142.0	148.5	158.7	169.4
Optical goods stores	. . .	. . .	. . .	. . .	. . .	99.8	100.1	101.5	103.0	104.8	107.0
Gasoline stations[15]	. . .	. . .	105.6	66.8	54.1	51.3	51.0	50.9	74.0	70.3	68.5
Gasoline stations with convenience stores	. . .	. . .	. . .	. . .	. . .	102.5	104.3	110.0	123.0	135.0	129.7
Other gasoline stations	. . .	. . .	. . .	. . .	. . .	132.8	118.1	84.2	216.2	151.4	152.7
Clothing and clothing accessories stores	. . .	. . .	. . .	. . .	. . .	100.5	103.3	105.4	107.0	110.7	111.9
Clothing stores	. . .	. . .	. . .	. . .	. . .	99.3	102.4	104.4	105.3	107.5	108.3
Men's clothing stores	. . .	. . .	. . .	. . .	. . .	100.2	102.1	98.9	99.8	98.3	91.1
Women's clothing stores	. . .	. . .	. . .	. . .	. . .	102.9	103.3	108.6	110.7	114.6	122.7
Family clothing stores	. . .	. . .	. . .	. . .	. . .	97.8	102.2	104.3	104.0	105.9	103.8
Shoe stores	. . .	. . .	. . .	. . .	. . .	103.9	105.0	105.7	109.7	114.0	114.7
Jewelry, luggage, and leather goods stores	. . .	. . .	. . .	. . .	. . .	101.8	104.9	108.7	110.9	120.4	123.7
Jewelry stores	. . .	. . .	. . .	. . .	. . .	101.8	104.8	108.6	110.8	120.7	124.1
Luggage and leather goods stores	. . .	. . .	. . .	. . .	. . .	101.4	106.5	111.0	113.5	116.8	118.9

[2]December 1985 = 100.
[3]December 1984 = 100.
[5]June 1984 = 100.
[8]June 1985 = 100.
[12]June 2004 = 100.
[13]June 2005 = 100.
[14]December 1999 = 100.
[15]June 2001 = 100.
[16]December 2001 = 100.
[17]June 2000 = 100.
. . . = Not available.

Table 9-3. Producer Price Indexes for the Net Output of Selected Industries, 1999–2009—*Continued*

(December 2003 = 100, unless otherwise specified.)

Industry	1999	2000	2001	2002	2003	2004	2005	2006	2007	2008	2009
Retail Trade—*Continued*											
Sporting goods, hobby, book, and music stores	...	...	...	...	...	96.6	96.6	98.4	103.4	111.6	113.9
Sporting goods, hobby, and musical instrument stores	...	...	...	...	...	97.8	99.0	102.5	107.7	119.5	123.2
Sporting goods stores	...	...	...	...	...	95.0	96.1	99.2	112.7	130.7	134.5
Hobby, toy, and game stores	...	...	...	...	...	100.5	101.7	105.7	101.9	108.5	112.2
Sewing, needlework, and piece goods stores	...	...	...	...	...	103.2	104.7	109.0	108.2	110.5	113.7
Book, periodical, and music stores	...	...	...	...	...	94.7	92.5	91.6	95.4	96.2	95.6
Bookstores and news dealers	...	...	...	...	...	95.0	92.0	94.2	97.1	98.0	101.3
Prerecorded tape, CD, and record stores	...	...	...	...	...	93.9	93.8	84.4	91.0	91.5	80.2
General merchandise stores	...	...	...	...	...	103.1	103.4	106.6	110.0	112.9	105.7
Department stores	...	...	...	...	...	105.4	105.1	105.6	111.4	117.8	111.3
Other general merchandise stores	...	...	...	...	...	97.7	99.5	108.9	110.0	107.9	99.5
Florists	...	...	...	...	...	100.2	100.2	102.8	107.3	108.6	107.5
Office supplies, stationery, and gift stores	...	...	...	...	...	99.7	101.7	104.3	107.8	112.0	116.5
Office supplies and stationery stores	...	...	...	...	...	100.4	102.9	107.1	113.6	119.4	130.7
Gift, novelty, and souvenir stores	...	...	...	...	...	98.7	100.0	100.1	101.2	104.0	102.8
Manufactured (mobile) home dealers	...	...	...	...	...	107.7	116.7	123.2	118.3	113.6	113.5
Nonstore retailers	...	...	...	...	...	107.5	119.8	118.9	129.2	144.1	147.7
Vending machine operators	...	...	...	...	...	101.5	104.4	105.7	106.4	110.6	111.9
Fuel dealers[17]	...	...	120.5	113.8	122.7	129.4	147.3	138.9	138.3	174.2	179.2
Transportation and Warehousing											
Air transportation[18]	130.8	147.7	157.2	157.8	162.1	162.3	171.0	180.4	183.7	203.8	188.5
Scheduled air transportation[19]	157.3	180.1	193.0	193.3	198.5	198.6	209.3	220.5	224.5	248.9	229.1
Nonscheduled air transportation[20]	102.2	107.3	112.7	114.7	117.8	119.9	126.7	136.8	148.5	165.8	160.4
Rail transportation[20]	101.3	102.6	104.5	106.6	108.8	113.4	125.2	135.9	140.9	157.3	148.5
Water transportation	...	...	...	...	...	101.3	106.4	111.1	113.5	127.0	116.1
Inland water transportation	...	...	...	...	...	103.2	119.3	144.1	146.7	172.0	166.7
Truck transportation	...	...	...	...	...	103.1	109.0	113.2	115.4	123.0	117.3
General freight trucking	...	...	...	...	...	103.5	110.0	114.1	116.5	123.6	117.5
General freight trucking, local	...	...	...	...	...	105.2	111.5	115.3	119.6	130.2	126.0
General freight trucking, long distance	...	...	...	...	...	103.2	109.7	113.8	115.9	122.2	115.5
Specialized freight trucking	...	...	...	...	...	102.3	107.0	111.4	113.1	122.1	117.4
Used household and office goods moving	...	...	...	...	...	102.6	106.0	107.8	108.8	112.2	112.8
Specialized freight (except used) trucking, local	...	...	...	...	...	102.7	107.1	112.3	114.2	126.7	123.9
Specialized freight (except used) trucking, long distance	...	...	...	...	...	101.7	107.5	112.8	114.8	123.6	113.2
Pipeline transportation of crude oil	...	...	...	...	...	103.9	113.3	122.0	125.4	137.1	141.0
Other pipeline transportation	...	...	...	...	...	101.4	105.2	108.2	115.0	121.6	128.7
Pipeline transportation of refined petroleum products	...	...	...	...	...	101.4	105.2	108.2	115.0	121.6	128.7
Transportation support activities	...	...	...	...	...	101.1	104.1	106.5	108.5	111.7	108.6
Air transportation support activities[20]	108.6	114.2	117.5	121.4	125.1	128.1	134.2	138.6	141.0	145.4	149.2
Airport operations	...	...	...	...	...	101.1	104.8	108.6	109.6	112.3	117.9
Other air transportation support activities	...	...	...	...	...	102.0	107.5	110.8	112.9	117.0	117.5
Water transportation support activities	...	...	...	...	...	101.0	103.5	107.7	112.7	117.3	116.8
Port and harbor operations	...	...	...	...	...	102.4	105.9	108.8	114.8	117.7	120.5
Marine cargo handling	...	...	...	...	...	100.5	102.2	105.1	109.0	110.7	113.3
Navigational services to shipping	...	...	...	...	...	101.5	105.7	113.8	120.6	133.8	122.9
Freight transportation arrangement[20]	97.3	98.3	98.2	97.5	97.9	98.9	99.1	98.8	100.2	102.5	94.8
Postal service[21]	135.3	135.2	143.4	150.2	155.0	155.0	155.0	164.7	171.9	178.9	185.0
Couriers and messengers	...	...	...	...	...	106.1	113.8	121.5	131.5	142.0	141.5
Couriers	...	...	...	...	...	106.6	115.0	123.2	133.5	144.4	143.8
Local messengers and local delivery	...	...	...	...	...	101.1	102.7	104.4	108.1	112.2	114.3
Warehousing and storage[9]	89.0	90.8	93.2	94.5	95.8	...	...	102.5	106.5	107.2	
General warehousing and storage	...	...	...	...	...	100.3	101.5	103.8	107.3	111.9	112.2
Refrigerated warehousing and storage	...	...	...	...	...	100.5	101.0	102.4	104.0	106.7	109.5
Farm product warehousing and storage	...	...	...	...	...	100.2	101.5	103.8	104.0	108.7	108.1
Information											
Publishing industries, except Internet	...	...	...	...	...	101.5	104.1	106.2	108.1	110.6	111.3
Newspaper, book, and directory publishers	...	...	...	...	...	102.1	105.5	108.3	111.8	115.1	117.6
Newspaper publishers[22]	339.3	351.3	367.9	381.9	395.7	409.7	426.2	439.0	450.3	459.2	466.3
Periodical publishers[22]	284.9	292.6	305.9	320.4	332.4	339.1	347.6	354.4	369.5	383.1	391.7
Book publishers[3]	184.7	190.2	195.6	201.5	208.2	215.7	224.3	232.8	240.2	250.9	260.7
Directory and mailing list publishers	...	...	...	...	...	101.3	103.3	105.4	108.4	111.1	113.0
Other publishers	...	...	...	...	...	100.7	103.9	104.9	107.9	108.8	109.2
Software publishers	...	...	...	...	...	99.8	99.8	100.1	99.6	100.7	98.9
Broadcasting, except Internet	...	...	...	...	...	101.2	102.1	102.8	101.4	106.7	105.3
Radio and television broadcasting[15]	...	...	98.2	97.1	99.8	102.8	101.9	101.1	101.3	101.7	92.5
Radio broadcasting	...	...	...	...	...	102.7	106.3	105.8	104.3	103.7	99.5
Television broadcasting	...	...	...	...	...	100.5	97.3	96.3	97.3	98.0	85.8
Cable networks	...	...	...	...	...	101.4	104.3	106.7	103.6	111.9	115.2
Telecommunications	...	...	...	...	...	99.8	98.1	98.3	100.8	101.1	101.1
Wired telecommunications carriers[23]	...	96.4	93.6	89.9	88.1	86.3	85.8	86.6	89.3	90.7	91.1
Wireless telecommunications carriers	...	...	...	...	...	98.4	86.4	80.9	80.4	76.1	73.6
Cable and other program distribution	...	...	...	...	...	102.2	106.5	109.6	113.7	116.2	118.7
ISPs and Web search portals[12]	...	...	...	...	...	...	95.9	87.6	72.8	73.4	71.1
Data processing and related services	...	...	...	...	...	98.8	98.8	99.7	100.3	100.9	100.9

[3]December 1984 = 100.
[9]December 2006 = 100.
[12]June 2004 = 100.
[15]June 2001 = 100.
[17]June 2000 = 100.
[18]December 1992 = 100.
[19]December 1989 = 100.
[20]December 1996 = 100.
[21]June 1989 = 100.
[22]December 1979 = 100.
[23]June 1999 = 100.
. . . = Not available.

Table 9-3. Producer Price Indexes for the Net Output of Selected Industries, 1999–2009—*Continued*

(December 2003 = 100, unless otherwise specified.)

Industry	1999	2000	2001	2002	2003	2004	2005	2006	2007	2008	2009
Other Services											
Depository credit intermediation	...	...	...	...	...	102.5	105.0	111.2	112.8	102.6	97.5
Security, commodity contracts, and like activity	...	...	...	...	...	103.4	109.4	113.8	119.9	119.5	112.2
Security and commodity contracts, intermediation, and brokerage[17]	...	...	88.1	81.8	82.5	84.2	88.1	90.1	92.8	94.2	90.1
Investment banking and securities dealing	...	...	...	...	...	102.6	109.1	111.0	113.6	125.4	119.0
Securities brokerage	...	...	...	...	...	100.0	102.2	105.2	109.7	103.4	99.6
Portfolio management	...	...	...	...	...	108.1	117.8	124.8	137.1	131.2	116.0
Investment advice	...	...	...	...	...	102.0	104.8	119.4	129.7	133.4	134.7
Insurance carriers and related activities	...	...	...	...	...	101.9	104.5	106.3	107.7	110.1	113.3
Insurance carriers	...	...	...	...	...	101.9	104.5	106.4	107.7	110.2	113.4
Direct life/health/medical insurance carriers	...	...	...	...	...	102.2	105.1	107.6	109.5	112.6	116.2
Other direct insurance carriers[24]	100.7	101.9	104.3	108.7	115.0	118.7	121.0	121.7	122.1	123.6	126.7
Insurance agencies and brokerages	...	...	...	...	...	100.8	101.8	102.2	102.9	103.4	103.7
Lessors of nonresidential building (except miniwarehouse)	...	...	...	...	...	102.3	105.1	107.7	107.2	110.6	109.4
Lessors of miniwarehouse and self-storage units	...	...	...	...	...	102.0	105.6	109.2	110.6	113.4	112.9
Offices of real estate agents and brokers	...	...	...	...	...	101.8	108.1	110.9	110.8	106.5	101.9
Real estate property managers	...	...	...	...	...	100.9	102.2	102.9	103.8	108.1	108.5
Automotive equipment rental and leasing[15]	...	...	...	103.9	106.6	107.8	109.0	115.2	118.0	126.4	135.2
Passenger car rental and leasing	...	...	...	...	...	98.2	99.9	108.0	108.2	116.5	131.0
Truck, utility trailer, and RV rental and leasing	...	...	...	...	...	99.9	99.9	101.2	107.7	114.7	111.8
Legal services[20]	108.7	112.5	117.9	121.7	125.6	131.8	138.5	145.2	153.6	161.6	166.2
Offices of lawyers[20]	108.7	112.5	117.9	121.7	125.6	131.8	138.5	145.2	153.6	161.6	166.2
Architectural, engineering, and related services[20]	108.5	111.8	115.9	121.1	124.3	126.8	129.2	134.4	140.0	141.0	142.9
Architectural services	...	...	...	...	...	99.7	102.0	106.0	109.3	110.5	110.2
Engineering services	...	...	...	...	...	101.5	103.4	107.6	112.2	113.0	114.9
Management and technical consulting services[25]	...	...	...	...	...	...	...	...	102.8	105.7	107.3
Advertising agencies	...	...	...	...	...	100.1	101.4	104.1	105.0	106.0	105.1
Employment services[20]	105.2	107.3	108.2	108.9	111.4	113.9	116.3	119.2	121.7	123.2	123.5
Employment placement agencies	...	...	...	...	...	102.2	104.4	104.4	105.8	106.4	106.9
Temporary help services	...	...	...	...	...	101.7	104.0	106.9	109.4	110.7	110.3
Employee leasing services	...	...	...	...	...	101.3	102.9	105.4	107.6	109.0	110.2
Travel agencies	...	...	...	...	...	96.9	95.9	99.5	101.0	99.7	99.6
Janitorial services	...	...	...	...	...	100.9	101.9	103.7	106.0	109.1	110.0
Waste collection	...	...	...	...	...	101.3	102.5	104.5	107.6	112.4	115.5
Amusement and theme parks[25]	...	...	...	...	...	...	...	...	105.2	109.8	112.5
Accommodations[20]	112.7	116.2	121.3	121.3	122.0	125.2	131.9	136.7	142.9	146.0	141.5
Hotels (except casino hotels) and motels	...	...	...	...	...	103.5	110.0	114.1	119.8	124.2	120.8
Casino hotels	...	...	...	...	...	105.0	107.5	110.8	113.0	110.9	106.3
Health Care and Social Assistance											
Offices of physicians[20]	105.5	107.3	110.4	110.3	112.1	114.3	116.4	117.5	122.3	123.6	126.6
Medical and diagnostic laboratories	...	...	...	...	...	100.0	104.1	104.4	107.0	107.3	108.4
Home health care services[20]	107.1	111.1	114.0	116.6	117.0	119.8	121.1	121.8	124.0	126.1	128.0
Hospitals[18]	116.4	119.4	123.0	127.5	134.9	141.5	146.9	153.3	158.6	163.4	168.3
General medical and surgical hospitals	...	...	...	...	...	102.9	106.7	111.2	115.1	118.6	122.3
Psychiatric and substance abuse hospitals	...	...	...	...	...	101.1	103.7	106.2	110.0	113.4	115.2
Other specialty hospitals	...	...	...	...	...	103.8	109.6	122.8	126.7	128.4	130.7
Nursing care facilities	...	...	...	...	...	102.6	106.4	109.6	114.7	119.2	123.2
Residential mental retardation facilities	...	...	...	...	...	101.2	104.5	108.5	112.7	118.3	123.0

[15]June 2001 = 100.
[17]June 2000 = 100.
[18]December 1992 = 100.
[20]December 1996 = 100.
[24]December 1998 = 100.
[25]June 2006 = 100.
. . . = Not available.

CONSUMER PRICE INDEX

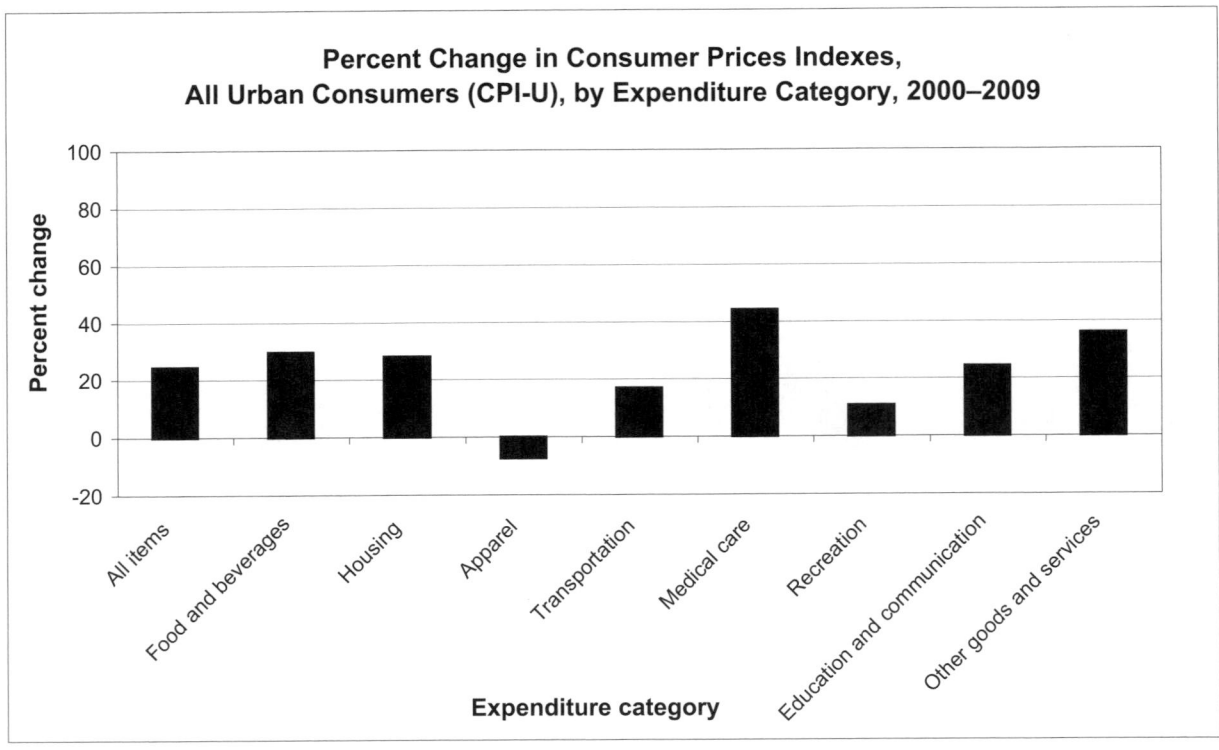

While the Consumer Price Index for all Urban Consumers (CPI-U) for all items increased by 24.6 percent from 2000 to 2009, the CPI-U for medical care increased by 44.0 percent. The CPI-U also increased rapidly for food and beverages (29.6 percent), housing (28.0 percent) and transportation (17.0 percent) from 2000 to 2009. The CPI-U for apparel declined by 7.3 percent from 2000 to 2009. (See Table 9-8.)

OTHER HIGHLIGHTS

- The CPI-U for energy commodities declined 27.8 percent in 2009 after increasing 18 percent from 2007 to 2008. (See Table 9-5.)

- Water, sewer, and trash collection services were the fastest growing component of housing in 2009, increasing by 5.9 percent, followed by rent of primary residence (2.3 percent), and tenant and household insurance (2.2 percent). (See Table 9-8.)

- In 2009, the CPI grew 1.2 percent in Anchorage, AK, making it the only metropolitan statistical area (MSA) listed on Table 9-10 in which the CPI grew by more than 1 percent. The CPI declined in 16 of the 27 MSAs listed. (See Table 9-10.)

NOTES AND DEFINITIONS

CONSUMER PRICE INDEX

The Consumer Price Index (CPI) is a measure of the average change over time in the prices of consumer items—goods and services that people buy for day-to-day living. The CPI is a complex construct that combines economic theory with sampling and other statistical techniques and uses data from several surveys to produce a timely and precise measure of average price change for the consumption sector of the American economy.

The Bureau of Labor Statistics (BLS) publishes CPIs for two population groups: (1) the CPI for Urban Wage Earners and Clerical Workers (CPI-W), which covers households of wage earners and clerical workers that comprise approximately 32 percent of the total population and (2) the CPI for All Urban Consumers (CPI-U) and the Chained CPI for All Urban Consumers (C-CPI-U), which cover approximately 87 percent of the total population and include in addition to wage earners and clerical worker households, groups such as professional, managerial, and technical workers, the self-employed, short-term workers, the unemployed, and retirees and others not in the labor force. BLS began publishing the CPI-U in January 1978, but did not begin publishing the C-CPI-U until August 2002 with data beginning in January 2000. The CPI-W is much older than either the CPI-U or C-CPI-U.

The CPIs are based on prices of food, clothing, shelter, fuels, transportation fares, charges for doctors' and dentists' services, drugs, and other goods and services that people buy for day-to-day living. Prices are collected each month in 87 urban areas across the country from about 4,000 housing units and approximately 25,000 retail establishments-department stores, supermarkets, hospitals, filling stations, and other types of stores and service establishments. All taxes directly associated with the purchase and use of items are included in the index. Prices of fuels and a few other items are obtained every month in all 87 locations. Prices of most other commodities and services are collected every month in the three largest geographic areas and every other month in other areas. Prices of most goods and services are obtained by personal visits or telephone calls from BLS trained representatives.

In calculating the index, price changes for the various items in each location are averaged together with weights, which represent their importance in the spending of the appropriate population group. Local data are then combined to obtain a U.S. city average. For the CPI-U and CPI-W separate indexes are also published by size of city, by region of the country, for cross-classifications of regions and population-size classes, and for 27 local areas. Area indexes do not measure differences in the level of prices among cities; they only measure the average change in prices for each area since the base period. For the C-CPI-U data are issued only at the national level. It is important to note that the CPI-U and CPI-W are considered final when released, but the C-CPI-U is issued in preliminary form and subject to two annual revisions. The prices used in the C-CPI-U are the same as those used to produce the CPI-U and the CPI-W, but the C-CPI-U uses a different formula and different weights to combine basic indexes.

The Consumer Price Index Research Series Using Current Methods (CPI-U-RS), shown in Table 9-11, provides estimates for the period since 1977 of what the CPI would have been had the most current methods been in effect. Each time there are new methods introduced into the CPI, the CPI-U-RS is revised from 1978 forward.

Sources of Additional Information

An extensive description of the methodology is available in the updated version of Chapter 17 in the *BLS Handbook of Methods*. Additional detailed data can be found in the *Consumer Price Index Detailed Report* and in special reports. These resources can be found on the BLS Web site at <http://www.bls.gov>.

Table 9-4. Consumer Price Indexes, All Urban Consumers (CPI-U): U.S. City Average, Major Groups, 1957–2009

(1982–1984 = 100, unless otherwise specified.)

Year	All items	Food and beverages	Housing	Apparel	Transportation	Medical care	Recreation[1]	Education and communication[1]	Other goods and services
1957	28.1	. . .	. . .	44.5	27.7	19.7	. . .	. . .	. . .
1958	28.9	. . .	. . .	44.6	28.6	20.6	. . .	. . .	. . .
1959	29.1	. . .	. . .	45.0	29.8	21.5	. . .	. . .	. . .
1960	29.6	. . .	. . .	45.7	29.8	22.3	. . .	. . .	. . .
1961	29.9	. . .	. . .	46.1	30.1	22.9	. . .	. . .	. . .
1962	30.2	. . .	. . .	46.3	30.8	23.5	. . .	. . .	. . .
1963	30.6	. . .	. . .	46.9	30.9	24.1	. . .	. . .	. . .
1964	31.0	. . .	. . .	47.3	31.4	24.6	. . .	. . .	. . .
1965	31.5	. . .	. . .	47.8	31.9	25.2	. . .	. . .	. . .
1966	32.4	. . .	. . .	49.0	32.3	26.3	. . .	. . .	. . .
1967	33.4	35.0	30.8	51.0	33.3	28.2	. . .	. . .	35.1
1968	34.8	36.2	32.0	53.7	34.3	29.9	. . .	. . .	36.9
1969	36.7	38.1	34.0	56.8	35.7	31.9	. . .	. . .	38.7
1970	38.8	40.1	36.4	59.2	37.5	34.0	. . .	. . .	40.9
1971	40.5	41.4	38.0	61.1	39.5	36.1	. . .	. . .	42.9
1972	41.8	43.1	39.4	62.3	39.9	37.3	. . .	. . .	44.7
1973	44.4	48.8	41.2	64.6	41.2	38.8	. . .	. . .	46.4
1974	49.3	55.5	45.8	69.4	45.8	42.4	. . .	. . .	49.8
1975	53.8	60.2	50.7	72.5	50.1	47.5	. . .	. . .	53.9
1976	56.9	62.1	53.8	75.2	55.1	52.0	. . .	. . .	57.0
1977	60.6	65.8	57.4	78.6	59.0	57.0	. . .	. . .	60.4
1978	65.2	72.2	62.4	81.4	61.7	61.8	. . .	. . .	64.3
1979	72.6	79.9	70.1	84.9	70.5	67.5	. . .	. . .	68.9
1980	82.4	86.7	81.1	90.9	83.1	74.9	. . .	. . .	75.2
1981	90.9	93.5	90.4	95.3	93.2	82.9	. . .	. . .	82.6
1982	96.5	97.3	96.9	97.8	97.0	92.5	. . .	. . .	91.1
1983	99.6	99.5	99.5	100.2	99.3	100.6	. . .	. . .	101.1
1984	103.9	103.2	103.6	102.1	103.7	106.8	. . .	. . .	107.9
1985	107.6	105.6	107.7	105.0	106.4	113.5	. . .	. . .	114.5
1986	109.6	109.1	110.9	105.9	102.3	122.0	. . .	. . .	121.4
1987	113.6	113.5	114.2	110.6	105.4	130.1	. . .	. . .	128.5
1988	118.3	118.2	118.5	115.4	108.7	138.6	. . .	. . .	137.0
1989	124.0	124.9	123.0	118.6	114.1	149.3	. . .	. . .	147.7
1990	130.7	132.1	128.5	124.1	120.5	162.8	. . .	. . .	159.0
1991	136.2	136.8	133.6	128.7	123.8	177.0	. . .	. . .	171.6
1992	140.3	138.7	137.5	131.9	126.5	190.1	. . .	. . .	183.3
1993	144.5	141.6	141.2	133.7	130.4	201.4	90.7	78.4	192.9
1994	148.2	144.9	144.8	133.4	134.3	211.0	92.7	83.3	198.5
1995	152.4	148.9	148.5	132.0	139.1	220.5	94.5	88.0	206.9
1996	156.9	153.7	152.8	131.7	143.0	228.2	97.4	92.7	215.4
1997	160.5	157.7	156.8	132.9	144.3	234.6	99.6	97.3	224.8
1998	163.0	161.1	160.4	133.0	141.6	242.1	101.1	102.1	237.7
1999	166.6	164.6	163.9	131.3	144.4	250.6	102.0	107.0	258.3
2000	172.2	168.4	169.6	129.6	153.3	260.8	103.3	112.5	271.1
2001	177.1	173.6	176.4	127.3	154.3	272.8	104.9	118.5	282.6
2002	179.9	176.8	180.3	124.0	152.9	285.6	106.2	126.0	293.2
2003	184.0	180.5	184.8	120.9	157.6	297.1	107.5	134.4	298.7
2004	188.9	186.6	189.5	120.4	163.1	310.1	108.6	143.7	304.7
2005	195.3	191.2	195.7	119.5	173.9	323.2	109.4	152.7	313.4
2006	201.6	195.7	203.2	119.5	180.9	336.2	110.9	162.1	321.7
2007	207.3	203.3	209.6	119.0	184.7	351.1	111.4	171.4	333.3
2008	215.3	214.2	216.3	118.9	195.5	364.1	113.3	181.3	345.4
2009	214.5	218.2	217.1	120.1	179.3	375.6	114.3	190.9	368.6

[1]December 1997 = 100.
. . . = Not available.

Table 9-5. Consumer Price Indexes, All Urban Consumers (CPI-U): U.S. City Average, Commodity, Service, and Special Groups, 1957–2009

(1982–1984 = 100, unless otherwise specified.)

Year	All items less food	All items less shelter	All items less medical care	All items less energy	All items less food and energy	Commodities	Commodities less food and beverages	Commodities less food and energy	Energy commodities	Nondurables	Nondurables less food	Nondurables less food and apparel
1957	28.0	29.7	28.7	28.9	28.9	32.6	. . .	37.4	21.6	30.9	32.9	28.5
1958	28.6	30.6	29.5	29.7	29.6	33.3	. . .	37.9	21.3	31.7	33.1	28.8
1959	29.2	30.8	29.8	29.9	30.2	33.3	. . .	38.4	21.5	31.5	33.5	29.2
1960	29.7	31.3	30.2	30.4	30.6	33.6	. . .	38.5	21.9	32.0	34.1	29.7
1961	30.0	31.7	30.5	30.7	31.0	33.8	. . .	38.6	21.9	32.2	34.3	29.8
1962	30.3	32.0	30.8	31.1	31.4	34.1	. . .	38.9	22.0	32.5	34.5	30.1
1963	30.7	32.4	31.1	31.5	31.8	34.4	. . .	39.2	22.1	32.9	34.8	30.4
1964	31.1	32.8	31.5	32.0	32.3	34.8	. . .	39.6	21.9	33.2	35.1	30.6
1965	31.6	33.3	32.0	32.5	32.7	35.2	. . .	39.8	22.6	33.8	35.6	31.2
1966	32.3	34.3	33.0	33.5	33.5	36.1	. . .	40.3	23.2	35.1	36.4	31.8
1967	33.4	35.2	33.7	34.4	34.7	36.8	38.3	41.3	23.9	35.7	37.6	32.6
1968	34.9	36.7	35.1	35.9	36.3	38.1	39.7	42.9	24.4	37.1	39.1	33.7
1969	36.8	38.4	37.0	38.0	38.4	39.9	41.4	44.7	25.2	38.9	40.9	34.9
1970	39.0	40.3	39.2	40.3	40.8	41.7	43.1	46.7	25.6	40.8	42.5	36.3
1971	40.8	42.0	40.8	42.0	42.7	43.2	44.7	48.5	26.1	42.1	44.0	37.6
1972	42.0	43.3	42.1	43.4	44.0	44.5	45.8	49.7	26.4	43.5	45.0	38.6
1973	43.7	46.2	44.8	46.1	45.6	47.8	47.3	51.1	29.1	47.5	46.9	40.3
1974	48.0	51.4	49.8	50.6	49.4	53.5	52.4	55.0	40.4	54.0	52.9	46.9
1975	52.5	56.0	54.3	55.1	53.9	58.2	57.3	60.1	43.4	58.3	57.0	51.5
1976	56.0	59.3	57.2	58.2	57.4	60.7	60.2	63.2	45.4	60.5	59.5	54.1
1977	59.6	63.1	60.8	61.9	61.0	64.2	63.6	66.5	48.7	64.0	62.5	57.2
1978	63.9	67.4	65.4	66.7	65.5	68.8	67.3	70.5	51.0	68.6	65.5	60.4
1979	71.2	74.2	72.9	73.4	71.9	76.6	75.2	76.4	68.7	77.2	74.6	71.2
1980	81.5	82.9	82.8	81.9	80.8	86.0	85.7	83.5	95.2	87.6	88.4	87.1
1981	90.4	91.0	91.4	90.1	89.2	93.2	93.1	90.0	107.6	95.2	96.7	96.8
1982	96.3	96.2	96.8	96.1	95.8	97.0	96.9	95.3	102.9	97.8	98.3	98.2
1983	99.7	99.8	99.6	99.6	99.6	99.8	100.0	100.2	99.0	99.7	100.0	100.0
1984	104.0	103.9	103.7	104.3	104.6	103.2	103.1	104.4	98.1	102.5	101.7	101.8
1985	108.0	107.0	107.2	108.4	109.1	105.4	105.2	107.1	98.2	104.8	104.1	104.1
1986	109.8	108.0	108.8	112.6	113.5	104.4	101.4	108.6	77.2	103.5	98.5	96.9
1987	113.6	111.6	112.6	117.2	118.2	107.7	104.0	111.8	80.2	107.5	101.8	100.3
1988	118.3	115.9	117.0	122.3	123.4	111.5	107.3	115.8	80.8	111.8	105.8	104.0
1989	123.7	121.6	122.4	128.1	129.0	116.7	111.6	119.6	87.9	118.2	111.7	111.3
1990	130.3	128.2	128.8	134.7	135.5	122.8	117.0	123.6	101.2	126.0	119.9	120.9
1991	136.1	133.5	133.8	140.9	142.1	126.6	120.4	128.8	99.1	130.3	124.5	125.7
1992	140.8	137.3	137.5	145.4	147.3	129.1	123.2	132.5	98.3	132.8	127.6	128.9
1993	145.1	141.4	141.2	150.0	152.2	131.5	125.3	135.2	97.3	135.1	129.3	130.7
1994	149.0	144.8	144.7	154.1	156.5	133.8	126.9	137.1	97.6	136.8	129.7	131.6
1995	153.1	148.6	148.6	158.7	161.2	136.4	128.9	139.3	98.8	139.3	130.9	134.1
1996	157.5	152.8	152.8	163.1	165.6	139.9	131.5	141.1	105.7	143.5	134.5	139.5
1997	161.1	155.9	156.3	167.1	169.5	141.8	132.2	142.3	105.7	146.4	136.3	141.8
1998	163.4	157.2	158.6	170.9	173.4	141.9	130.5	143.2	92.1	146.9	134.6	139.2
1999	167.0	160.2	162.0	174.4	177.0	144.4	132.5	144.1	100.0	151.2	139.4	147.5
2000	173.0	165.7	167.3	178.6	181.3	149.2	137.7	144.9	129.5	158.2	149.1	162.9
2001	177.8	169.7	171.9	183.5	186.1	150.7	137.2	145.3	125.2	160.6	149.1	164.1
2002	180.5	170.8	174.3	187.7	190.5	149.7	134.2	143.7	117.1	161.1	147.4	163.3
2003	184.7	174.6	178.1	190.6	193.2	151.2	134.5	140.9	136.7	165.3	151.9	172.1
2004	189.4	179.3	182.7	194.4	196.6	154.7	136.7	139.6	161.2	172.2	159.3	183.8
2005	196.0	186.1	188.7	198.7	200.9	160.2	142.5	140.3	197.4	180.2	170.1	201.2
2006	202.7	191.9	194.7	203.7	205.9	164.0	145.9	140.6	223.0	186.7	178.2	213.9
2007	208.1	196.6	200.1	208.9	210.7	167.5	147.5	140.1	241.0	193.5	184.0	223.4
2008	215.5	205.5	207.8	214.8	215.6	174.8	153.0	140.2	284.4	205.9	197.3	244.4
2009	214.0	203.3	206.6	218.4	219.2	169.7	144.4	142.0	205.3	198.5	181.5	218.7

. . . = Not available.

Table 9-5. Consumer Price Indexes, All Urban Consumers (CPI-U): U.S. City Average, Commodity, Service, and Special Groups, 1957–2009—*Continued*

(1982–1984 = 100, unless otherwise specified.)

Year	Total services[1]	Rent of shelter[2]	Gas (piped) and electricity	Transportation services	Medical care services	Other services	Services less medical care	Energy	Services less energy
1957	21.8	...	21.1	24.1	17.0	...	...	21.5	21.9
1958	22.6	...	21.9	25.6	17.9	...	...	21.5	22.7
1959	23.3	...	22.4	26.5	18.7	...	...	21.9	23.4
1960	24.1	...	23.3	27.2	19.5	...	...	22.4	24.2
1961	24.5	...	23.5	27.8	20.2	...	...	22.5	24.7
1962	25.0	...	23.5	28.3	20.9	...	...	22.6	25.2
1963	25.5	...	23.5	28.6	21.5	...	...	22.6	25.7
1964	26.0	...	23.5	29.2	22.0	...	...	22.5	26.2
1965	26.6	...	23.5	30.3	22.7	...	...	22.9	26.9
1966	27.6	...	23.6	31.6	23.9	...	...	23.3	28.0
1967	28.8	...	23.7	32.6	26.0	36.0	29.3	23.8	29.3
1968	30.3	...	23.9	33.9	27.9	38.1	30.8	24.2	30.9
1969	32.4	...	24.3	36.3	30.2	40.0	32.9	24.8	33.2
1970	35.0	...	25.4	40.2	32.3	42.2	35.6	25.5	36.0
1971	37.0	...	27.1	43.4	34.7	44.4	37.5	26.5	38.0
1972	38.4	...	28.5	44.4	35.9	45.6	38.9	27.2	39.4
1973	40.1	...	29.9	44.7	37.5	47.7	40.6	29.4	41.1
1974	43.8	...	34.5	46.3	41.4	51.3	44.3	38.1	44.8
1975	48.0	...	40.1	49.8	46.6	55.1	48.3	42.1	48.8
1976	52.0	...	44.7	56.9	51.3	58.4	52.2	45.1	52.7
1977	56.0	...	50.5	61.5	56.4	62.1	55.9	49.4	56.5
1978	60.8	...	55.0	64.4	61.2	66.4	60.7	52.5	61.3
1979	67.5	...	61.0	69.5	67.2	71.9	67.5	65.7	68.2
1980	77.9	...	71.4	79.2	74.8	78.7	78.2	86.0	78.5
1981	88.1	...	81.9	88.6	82.8	86.1	88.7	97.7	88.7
1982	96.0	...	93.2	96.1	92.6	93.5	96.4	99.2	96.3
1983	99.4	102.7	101.5	99.1	100.7	100.0	99.2	99.9	99.2
1984	104.6	107.7	105.4	104.8	106.7	106.5	104.4	100.9	104.5
1985	109.9	113.9	107.1	110.0	113.2	113.0	109.6	101.6	110.2
1986	115.4	120.2	105.7	116.3	121.9	119.4	114.6	88.2	116.5
1987	120.2	125.9	103.8	121.9	130.0	125.7	119.1	88.6	122.0
1988	125.7	132.0	104.6	128.0	138.3	132.6	124.3	89.3	127.9
1989	131.9	138.0	107.5	135.6	148.9	140.9	130.1	94.3	134.4
1990	139.2	145.5	109.3	144.2	162.7	150.2	136.8	102.1	142.3
1991	146.3	152.1	112.6	151.2	177.1	159.8	143.3	102.5	149.8
1992	152.0	157.3	114.8	155.7	190.5	168.5	148.4	103.0	155.9
1993	157.9	162.0	118.5	162.9	202.9	177.0	153.6	104.2	161.9
1994	163.1	167.0	119.2	168.6	213.4	185.4	158.4	104.6	167.6
1995	168.7	172.4	119.2	175.9	224.2	193.3	163.5	105.2	173.7
1996	174.1	178.0	122.1	180.5	232.4	201.4	168.7	110.1	179.4
1997	179.4	183.4	125.1	185.0	239.1	209.6	173.9	111.5	185.0
1998	184.2	189.6	121.2	187.9	246.8	216.9	178.4	102.9	190.6
1999	188.8	195.0	120.9	190.7	255.1	223.1	182.7	106.6	195.7
2000	195.3	201.3	128.0	196.1	266.0	229.9	188.9	124.6	202.1
2001	203.4	208.9	142.4	201.9	278.8	238.0	196.6	129.3	209.6
2002	209.8	216.7	134.4	209.1	292.9	246.4	202.5	121.7	217.5
2003	216.5	221.9	145.0	216.3	306.0	254.4	208.7	136.5	223.8
2004	222.8	227.9	150.6	220.6	321.3	261.3	214.5	151.4	230.2
2005	230.1	233.7	166.5	225.7	336.7	268.4	221.2	177.1	236.6
2006	238.9	241.9	182.1	230.8	350.6	277.5	229.6	196.9	244.7
2007	246.8	250.8	186.3	233.7	369.3	285.6	236.8	207.7	253.1
2008	255.5	257.2	202.2	244.1	384.9	295.8	245.0	236.7	261.0
2009	259.2	259.9	193.6	251.0	397.3	304.0	248.1	193.1	265.9

[1]Includes tenants, household insurance, water, sewer, trash, and household operations services, not shown separately.
[2]December 1982 = 100.
. . . = Not available.

Table 9-6. Consumer Price Indexes, All Urban Consumers (CPI-U): U.S. City Average, Selected Groups and Purchasing Power of the Consumer Dollar, 1913–2009

(1982–1984 = 100, unless otherwise specified.)

Year	All items	Food	Rent of primary residence	Owners' equivalent of primary residence[1]	Apparel	Purchasing power of the consumer dollar[2]
1913	9.9	10.0	21.0	. . .	14.9	10.08
1914	10.0	10.2	21.0	. . .	15.0	9.94
1915	10.1	10.0	21.1	. . .	15.3	9.84
1916	10.9	11.3	21.3	. . .	16.8	9.15
1917	12.8	14.5	21.2	. . .	20.2	7.79
1918	15.1	16.7	21.5	. . .	27.3	6.64
1919	17.3	18.6	23.3	. . .	36.2	5.78
1920	20.0	21.0	27.4	. . .	43.1	4.99
1921	17.9	15.9	31.5	. . .	33.2	5.59
1922	16.8	14.9	32.4	. . .	27.0	5.96
1923	17.1	15.4	33.2	. . .	27.1	5.86
1924	17.1	15.2	34.4	. . .	26.8	5.85
1925	17.5	16.5	34.6	. . .	26.3	5.70
1926	17.7	17.0	34.2	. . .	25.9	5.65
1927	17.4	16.4	33.7	. . .	25.3	5.76
1928	17.1	16.3	32.9	. . .	25.0	5.83
1929	17.1	16.5	32.1	. . .	24.7	5.83
1930	16.7	15.6	31.2	. . .	24.2	5.99
1931	15.2	12.9	29.6	. . .	22.0	6.56
1932	13.7	10.7	26.5	. . .	19.5	7.32
1933	13.0	10.4	22.9	. . .	18.8	7.71
1934	13.4	11.6	21.4	. . .	20.6	7.46
1935	13.7	12.4	21.4	. . .	20.8	7.28
1936	13.9	12.6	21.9	. . .	21.0	7.21
1937	14.4	13.1	22.9	. . .	22.0	6.96
1938	14.1	12.1	23.7	. . .	21.9	7.09
1939	13.9	11.8	23.7	. . .	21.6	7.20
1940	14.0	12.0	23.7	. . .	21.8	7.13
1941	14.7	13.1	24.2	. . .	22.8	6.79
1942	16.3	15.4	24.7	. . .	26.7	6.13
1943	17.3	17.1	24.7	. . .	27.8	5.78
1944	17.6	16.9	24.8	. . .	29.8	5.68
1945	18.0	17.3	24.8	. . .	31.4	5.55
1946	19.5	19.8	25.0	. . .	34.4	5.12
1947	22.3	24.1	25.8	. . .	39.9	4.47
1948	24.1	26.1	27.5	. . .	42.5	4.15
1949	23.8	25.0	28.7	. . .	40.8	4.19
1950	24.1	25.4	29.7	. . .	40.3	4.15
1951	26.0	28.2	30.9	. . .	43.9	3.85
1952	26.5	28.7	32.2	. . .	43.5	3.77
1953	26.7	28.3	33.9	. . .	43.1	3.74
1954	26.9	28.2	35.1	. . .	43.1	3.72
1955	26.8	27.8	35.6	. . .	42.9	3.73
1956	27.2	28.0	36.3	. . .	43.7	3.68
1957	28.1	28.9	37.0	. . .	44.5	3.55
1958	28.9	30.2	37.6	. . .	44.6	3.46
1959	29.1	29.7	38.2	. . .	45.0	3.43
1960	29.6	30.0	38.7	. . .	45.7	3.37
1961	29.9	30.4	39.2	. . .	46.1	3.34
1962	30.2	30.6	39.7	. . .	46.3	3.30
1963	30.6	31.1	40.1	. . .	46.9	3.27
1964	31.0	31.5	40.5	. . .	47.3	3.22
1965	31.5	32.2	40.9	. . .	47.8	3.17
1966	32.4	33.8	41.5	. . .	49.0	3.08
1967	33.4	34.1	42.2	. . .	51.0	2.99
1968	34.8	35.3	43.3	. . .	53.7	2.87
1969	36.7	37.1	44.7	. . .	56.8	2.73
1970	38.8	39.2	46.5	. . .	59.2	2.57
1971	40.5	40.4	48.7	. . .	61.1	2.47
1972	41.8	42.1	50.4	. . .	62.3	2.39
1973	44.4	48.2	52.5	. . .	64.6	2.25
1974	49.3	55.1	55.2	. . .	69.4	2.03
1975	53.8	59.8	58.0	. . .	72.5	1.86
1976	56.9	61.6	61.1	. . .	75.2	1.76
1977	60.6	65.5	64.8	. . .	78.6	1.65
1978	65.2	72.0	69.3	. . .	81.4	1.53
1979	72.6	79.9	74.3	. . .	84.9	1.38

[1]December 1982 = 100.
[2]Purchasing power in 1982–1984 = $1.00.
. . . = Not available.

Table 9-6. Consumer Price Indexes, All Urban Consumers (CPI-U): U.S. City Average, Selected Groups and Purchasing Power of the Consumer Dollar, 1913–2009—*Continued*

(1982–1984 = 100, unless otherwise specified.)

Year	All items	Food	Rent of primary residence	Owners' equivalent of primary residence[1]	Apparel	Purchasing power of the consumer dollar[2]
1980	82.4	86.8	80.9	. . .	90.9	1.22
1981	90.9	93.6	87.9	. . .	95.3	1.10
1982	96.5	97.4	94.6	. . .	97.8	1.04
1983	99.6	99.4	100.1	102.5	100.2	1.00
1984	103.9	103.2	105.3	107.3	102.1	0.96
1985	107.6	105.6	111.8	113.2	105.0	0.93
1986	109.6	109.0	118.3	119.4	105.9	0.91
1987	113.6	113.5	123.1	124.8	110.6	0.88
1988	118.3	118.2	127.8	131.1	115.4	0.85
1989	124.0	125.1	132.8	137.4	118.6	0.81
1990	130.7	132.4	138.4	144.8	124.1	0.77
1991	136.2	136.3	143.3	150.4	128.7	0.73
1992	140.3	137.9	146.9	155.5	131.9	0.71
1993	144.5	140.9	150.3	160.5	133.7	0.69
1994	148.2	144.3	154.0	165.8	133.4	0.68
1995	152.4	148.4	157.8	171.3	132.0	0.66
1996	156.9	153.3	162.0	176.8	131.7	0.64
1997	160.5	157.3	166.7	181.9	132.9	0.62
1998	163.0	160.7	172.1	187.8	133.0	0.61
1999	166.6	164.1	177.5	192.9	131.3	0.60
2000	172.2	167.8	183.9	198.7	129.6	0.58
2001	177.1	173.1	192.1	206.3	127.3	0.57
2002	179.9	176.2	199.7	214.7	124.0	0.56
2003	184.0	180.0	205.5	219.9	120.9	0.54
2004	188.9	186.2	211.0	224.9	120.4	0.53
2005	195.3	190.7	217.3	230.2	119.5	0.51
2006	201.6	195.2	225.1	238.2	119.5	0.50
2007	207.3	202.9	234.7	246.2	119.0	0.48
2008	215.3	214.1	243.3	252.4	118.9	0.47
2009	214.5	218.0	248.8	256.6	120.1	0.47

[1]December 1982 = 100.
[2]Purchasing power in 1982–1984 = $1.00.
. . . = Not available.

Table 9-7. Consumer Price Indexes, Urban Wage Earners and Clerical Workers (CPI-W): U.S. City Average, Major Groups, 1913–2009

(1982–1984 = 100, unless otherwise specified.)

Year	All items	Food and beverages	Housing	Apparel	Transportation	Medical care	Recreation[1]	Education and communication[1]	Other goods and services
1913	10.0	. . .	. . .	15.0	. . .	. . .	. . .	. . .	. . .
1914	10.1	. . .	. . .	15.1	. . .	. . .	. . .	. . .	. . .
1915	10.2	. . .	. . .	15.4	. . .	. . .	. . .	. . .	. . .
1916	11.0	. . .	. . .	16.9	. . .	. . .	. . .	. . .	. . .
1917	12.9	. . .	. . .	20.3	. . .	. . .	. . .	. . .	. . .
1918	15.1	. . .	. . .	27.5	. . .	. . .	. . .	. . .	. . .
1919	17.4	. . .	. . .	36.4	. . .	. . .	. . .	. . .	. . .
1920	20.1	. . .	. . .	43.3	. . .	. . .	. . .	. . .	. . .
1921	18.0	. . .	. . .	33.4	. . .	. . .	. . .	. . .	. . .
1922	16.9	. . .	. . .	27.2	. . .	. . .	. . .	. . .	. . .
1923	17.2	. . .	. . .	27.2	. . .	. . .	. . .	. . .	. . .
1924	17.2	. . .	. . .	26.9	. . .	. . .	. . .	. . .	. . .
1925	17.6	. . .	. . .	26.4	. . .	. . .	. . .	. . .	. . .
1926	17.8	. . .	. . .	26.0	. . .	. . .	. . .	. . .	. . .
1927	17.5	. . .	. . .	25.5	. . .	. . .	. . .	. . .	. . .
1928	17.2	. . .	. . .	25.1	. . .	. . .	. . .	. . .	. . .
1929	17.2	. . .	. . .	24.8	. . .	. . .	. . .	. . .	. . .
1930	16.8	. . .	. . .	24.3	. . .	. . .	. . .	. . .	. . .
1931	15.3	. . .	. . .	22.1	. . .	. . .	. . .	. . .	. . .
1932	13.7	. . .	. . .	19.6	. . .	. . .	. . .	. . .	. . .
1933	13.0	. . .	. . .	18.9	. . .	. . .	. . .	. . .	. . .
1934	13.5	. . .	. . .	20.7	. . .	. . .	. . .	. . .	. . .
1935	13.8	. . .	. . .	20.9	14.1	10.2	. . .	. . .	. . .
1936	13.9	. . .	. . .	21.1	14.2	10.3	. . .	. . .	. . .
1937	14.4	. . .	. . .	22.1	14.5	10.4	. . .	. . .	. . .
1938	14.2	. . .	. . .	22.0	14.6	10.4	. . .	. . .	. . .
1939	14.0	. . .	. . .	21.7	14.2	10.4	. . .	. . .	. . .
1940	14.1	. . .	. . .	21.9	14.1	10.4	. . .	. . .	. . .
1941	14.8	. . .	. . .	23.0	14.6	10.5	. . .	. . .	. . .
1942	16.4	. . .	. . .	26.8	15.9	10.8	. . .	. . .	. . .
1943	17.4	. . .	. . .	28.0	15.8	11.3	. . .	. . .	. . .
1944	17.7	. . .	. . .	30.0	15.8	11.6	. . .	. . .	. . .
1945	18.1	. . .	. . .	31.5	15.8	11.9	. . .	. . .	. . .
1946	19.6	. . .	. . .	34.6	16.6	12.6	. . .	. . .	. . .
1947	22.5	. . .	. . .	40.1	18.4	13.6	. . .	. . .	. . .
1948	24.2	. . .	. . .	42.7	20.4	14.5	. . .	. . .	. . .
1949	24.0	. . .	. . .	41.0	22.0	14.9	. . .	. . .	. . .
1950	24.2	. . .	. . .	40.5	22.6	15.2	. . .	. . .	. . .
1951	26.1	. . .	. . .	44.1	24.0	15.9	. . .	. . .	. . .
1952	26.7	. . .	. . .	43.7	25.6	16.8	. . .	. . .	. . .
1953	26.9	. . .	. . .	43.3	26.3	17.4	. . .	. . .	. . .
1954	27.0	. . .	. . .	43.3	25.9	17.9	. . .	. . .	. . .
1955	26.9	. . .	. . .	43.1	25.6	18.3	. . .	. . .	. . .
1956	27.3	. . .	. . .	44.0	26.1	19.0	. . .	. . .	. . .
1957	28.3	. . .	. . .	44.7	27.6	19.8	. . .	. . .	. . .
1958	29.1	. . .	. . .	44.8	28.4	20.7	. . .	. . .	. . .
1959	29.3	. . .	. . .	45.2	29.6	21.6	. . .	. . .	. . .
1960	29.8	. . .	. . .	45.9	29.6	22.4	. . .	. . .	. . .
1961	30.1	. . .	. . .	46.3	30.0	23.0	. . .	. . .	. . .
1962	30.4	. . .	. . .	46.6	30.6	23.6	. . .	. . .	. . .
1963	30.8	. . .	. . .	47.1	30.8	24.2	. . .	. . .	. . .
1964	31.2	. . .	. . .	47.5	31.2	24.7	. . .	. . .	. . .
1965	31.7	. . .	. . .	48.0	31.7	25.3	. . .	. . .	. . .
1966	32.6	. . .	. . .	49.2	32.2	26.4	. . .	. . .	. . .
1967	33.6	35.0	31.1	51.2	33.1	28.3	. . .	. . .	35.4
1968	35.0	36.2	32.3	54.0	34.1	30.0	. . .	. . .	37.2
1969	36.9	38.0	34.3	57.1	35.5	32.1	. . .	. . .	39.1
1970	39.0	40.1	36.7	59.5	37.3	34.1	. . .	. . .	41.3
1971	40.7	41.3	38.3	61.4	39.2	36.3	. . .	. . .	43.3
1972	42.1	43.1	39.8	62.7	39.7	37.5	. . .	. . .	45.1
1973	44.7	48.8	41.5	65.0	41.0	39.0	. . .	. . .	46.9
1974	49.6	55.5	46.2	69.8	45.5	42.6	. . .	. . .	50.2
1975	54.1	60.2	51.1	72.9	49.8	47.7	. . .	. . .	54.4
1976	57.2	62.0	54.2	75.6	54.7	52.3	. . .	. . .	57.6
1977	60.9	65.7	57.9	79.0	58.6	57.3	. . .	. . .	60.9
1978	65.6	72.1	62.9	81.7	61.5	62.1	. . .	. . .	64.8
1979	73.1	79.9	70.7	85.2	70.4	68.0	. . .	. . .	69.4

[1]December 1997 = 100.
. . . = Not available.

Table 9-7. Consumer Price Indexes, Urban Wage Earners and Clerical Workers (CPI-W): U.S. City Average, Major Groups, 1913–2009—*Continued*

(1982–1984 = 100, unless otherwise specified.)

Year	All items	Food and beverages	Housing	Apparel	Transportation	Medical care	Recreation[1]	Education and communication[1]	Other goods and services
1980	82.9	86.9	81.7	90.9	82.9	75.6	. . .	. . .	75.6
1981	91.4	93.6	91.1	95.6	93.0	83.5	. . .	. . .	82.5
1982	96.9	97.3	97.7	97.8	97.0	92.5	. . .	. . .	90.9
1983	99.8	99.5	100.0	100.2	99.2	100.5	. . .	. . .	101.3
1984	103.3	103.2	102.2	102.0	103.8	106.9	. . .	. . .	107.9
1985	106.9	105.5	106.6	105.0	106.4	113.6	. . .	. . .	114.2
1986	108.6	108.9	109.7	105.8	101.7	122.0	. . .	. . .	120.9
1987	112.5	113.3	112.8	110.4	105.1	130.2	. . .	. . .	127.8
1988	117.0	117.9	116.8	114.9	108.3	139.0	. . .	. . .	136.5
1989	122.6	124.6	121.2	117.9	113.9	149.6	. . .	. . .	147.4
1990	129.0	131.8	126.4	123.1	120.1	162.7	. . .	. . .	158.9
1991	134.3	136.5	131.2	127.4	123.1	176.5	. . .	. . .	171.7
1992	138.2	138.3	135.0	130.7	125.8	189.6	. . .	. . .	183.3
1993	142.1	141.2	138.5	132.4	129.4	200.9	91.2	86.0	192.2
1994	145.6	144.4	142.0	132.2	133.4	210.4	93.0	89.1	196.4
1995	149.8	148.3	145.4	130.9	138.8	219.8	94.7	92.3	204.2
1996	154.1	153.2	149.6	130.9	142.8	227.6	97.5	95.4	212.2
1997	157.6	157.2	153.4	132.1	143.6	234.0	99.7	98.5	221.6
1998	159.7	160.4	156.7	131.6	140.5	241.4	100.9	100.4	236.1
1999	163.2	163.8	160.0	130.1	143.4	249.7	101.3	101.5	261.9
2000	168.9	167.7	165.4	128.3	152.8	259.9	102.4	102.7	276.5
2001	173.5	173.0	172.1	126.1	153.6	271.8	103.6	105.3	289.5
2002	175.9	176.1	175.7	123.1	151.8	284.6	104.6	107.6	302.0
2003	179.8	179.9	180.4	120.0	156.3	296.3	105.5	109.0	307.0
2004	184.5	186.2	185.0	120.0	161.5	309.5	106.3	110.0	312.6
2005	191.0	190.5	191.2	119.1	173.0	322.8	106.8	111.4	322.2
2006	197.1	194.9	198.5	119.1	180.3	335.7	108.2	113.9	330.9
2007	202.8	202.5	204.8	118.5	184.3	350.9	108.6	116.3	344.0
2008	211.1	213.5	211.8	118.7	195.7	364.2	110.1	119.8	357.9
2009	209.6	217.5	213.1	119.8	176.7	376.1	111.0	123.0	391.6

[1]December 1997 = 100.
. . . = Not available.

Table 9-8. Consumer Price Indexes, All Urban Consumers (CPI-U): U.S. City Average, by Expenditure Category, 1990–2009

(1982–1984 = 100, unless otherwise specified.)

Expenditure category	1990	1991	1992	1993	1994	1995	1996	1997	1998	1999
ALL ITEMS	130.7	136.2	140.3	144.5	148.2	152.4	156.9	160.5	163.0	166.6
Food and Beverages	132.1	136.8	138.7	141.6	144.9	148.9	153.7	157.7	161.1	164.6
Food	132.4	136.3	137.9	140.9	144.3	148.4	153.3	157.3	160.7	164.1
Food at home	132.3	135.8	136.8	140.1	144.1	148.8	154.3	158.1	161.1	164.2
Cereals and bakery product	140.0	145.8	151.5	156.6	163.0	167.5	174.0	177.6	181.1	185.0
Meats, poultry, fish, and eggs	130.0	132.6	130.9	135.5	137.2	138.8	144.8	148.5	147.3	147.9
Dairy and related product	126.5	125.1	128.5	129.4	131.7	132.8	142.1	145.5	150.8	159.6
Fruits and vegetables	149.0	155.8	155.4	159.0	165.0	177.7	183.9	187.5	198.2	203.1
Nonalcoholic beverages and beverage materials	113.5	114.1	114.3	114.6	123.2	131.7	128.6	133.4	133.0	134.3
Other food at home	123.4	127.3	128.8	130.5	135.6	140.8	142.9	147.3	150.8	153.5
Sugar and sweets	124.7	129.3	133.1	133.4	135.2	137.5	143.7	147.8	150.2	152.3
Fats and oils	126.3	131.7	129.8	130.0	133.5	137.3	140.5	141.7	146.9	148.3
Other food	131.2	137.1	140.1	143.7	147.5	151.1	156.2	161.2	165.5	168.9
Other miscellaneous food[1]	. . .	. . .	. . .	. . .	. . .	. . .	. . .	. . .	102.6	104.9
Food away from home	133.4	137.9	140.7	143.2	145.7	149.0	152.7	157.0	161.1	165.1
Other food away from home[1]	. . .	. . .	. . .	. . .	. . .	. . .	. . .	. . .	101.6	105.2
Alcoholic beverages	129.3	142.8	147.3	149.6	151.5	153.9	158.5	162.8	165.7	169.7
Housing	128.5	133.6	137.5	141.2	144.8	148.5	152.8	156.8	160.4	163.9
Shelter	140.0	146.3	151.2	155.7	160.5	165.7	171.0	176.3	182.1	187.3
Rent of primary residence	138.4	143.3	146.9	150.3	154.0	157.8	162.0	166.7	172.1	177.5
Lodging away from home[1]	. . .	. . .	. . .	. . .	. . .	. . .	. . .	. . .	109.0	112.3
Owners' equivalent rent of primary residence[2]	144.8	150.4	155.5	160.5	165.8	171.3	176.8	181.9	187.8	192.9
Tenants' and household insurance[1]	. . .	. . .	. . .	. . .	. . .	. . .	. . .	. . .	99.8	101.3
Fuels and utilities	111.6	115.3	117.8	121.3	122.8	123.7	127.5	130.8	128.5	128.8
Household energy	104.5	106.7	108.1	111.2	111.7	111.5	115.2	117.9	113.7	113.5
Fuel oil and other fuels	99.3	94.6	90.7	90.3	88.8	88.1	99.2	99.8	90.0	91.4
Gas (piped) and electricity	109.3	112.6	114.8	118.5	119.2	119.2	122.1	125.1	121.2	120.9
Water, sewer, and trash collection services[1]	. . .	. . .	. . .	. . .	. . .	. . .	. . .	. . .	101.6	104.0
Household furnishings and operations	113.3	116.0	118.0	119.3	121.0	123.0	124.7	125.4	126.6	126.7
Household operations[1]	. . .	. . .	. . .	. . .	. . .	. . .	. . .	. . .	101.5	104.5
Apparel	124.1	128.7	131.9	133.7	133.4	132.0	131.7	132.9	133.0	131.3
Men's and boys' apparel	120.4	124.2	126.5	127.5	126.4	126.2	127.7	130.1	131.8	131.1
Women's and girls' apparel	122.6	127.6	130.4	132.6	130.9	126.9	124.7	126.1	126.0	123.3
Infants' and toddlers' apparel	125.8	128.9	129.3	127.1	128.1	127.2	129.7	129.0	126.1	129.0
Footwear	117.4	120.9	125.0	125.9	126.0	125.4	126.6	127.6	128.0	125.7
Transportation	120.5	123.8	126.5	130.4	134.3	139.1	143.0	144.3	141.6	144.4
Private transportation	118.8	121.9	124.6	127.5	131.4	136.3	140.0	141.0	137.9	140.5
New and used motor vehicles[1]	. . .	. . .	. . .	91.8	95.5	99.4	101.0	100.5	100.1	100.1
New vehicles	121.4	126.0	129.2	132.7	137.6	141.0	143.7	144.3	143.4	142.9
Used cars and trucks	117.6	118.1	123.2	133.9	141.7	156.5	157.0	151.1	150.6	152.0
Motor fuel	101.2	99.4	99.0	98.0	98.5	100.0	106.3	106.2	92.2	100.7
Gasoline (all types)	101.0	99.2	99.0	97.7	98.2	99.8	105.9	105.8	91.6	100.1
Motor vehicle parts and equipment	100.9	102.2	103.1	101.6	101.4	102.1	102.2	101.9	101.1	100.5
Motor vehicle maintenance and repair	130.1	136.0	141.3	145.9	150.2	154.0	158.4	162.7	167.1	171.9
Public transportation	142.6	148.9	151.4	167.0	172.0	175.9	181.9	186.7	190.3	197.7
Medical Care	162.8	177.0	190.1	201.4	211.0	220.5	228.2	234.6	242.1	250.6
Medical care commodities	163.4	176.8	188.1	195.0	200.7	204.5	210.4	215.3	221.8	230.7
Medical care services	162.7	177.1	190.5	202.9	213.4	224.2	232.4	239.1	246.8	255.1
Professional services	156.1	165.7	175.8	184.7	192.5	201.0	208.3	215.4	222.2	229.2
Hospital and related services	178.0	196.1	214.0	231.9	245.6	257.8	269.5	278.4	287.5	299.5
Recreation[1]	. . .	. . .	. . .	90.7	92.7	94.5	97.4	99.6	101.1	102.0
Video and audio[1]	. . .	. . .	. . .	96.5	95.4	95.1	96.6	99.4	101.1	100.7
Education and Communication[1]	. . .	. . .	. . .	85.5	88.8	92.2	95.3	98.4	100.3	101.2
Education[1]	. . .	. . .	. . .	78.4	83.3	88.0	92.7	97.3	102.1	107.0
Educational books and supplies	171.3	180.3	190.3	197.6	205.5	214.4	226.9	238.4	250.8	261.7
Tuition, other school fees, and childcare	175.7	191.4	208.5	225.3	239.8	253.8	267.1	280.4	294.2	308.4
Communication[1]	. . .	. . .	. . .	96.7	97.6	98.8	99.6	100.3	98.7	96.0
Information and information processing[1]	. . .	. . .	. . .	97.7	98.6	98.7	99.5	100.4	98.5	95.5
Telephone services[1]	. . .	. . .	. . .	. . .	. . .	. . .	. . .	. . .	100.7	100.1
Information technology, hardware, and services[3]	93.5	88.6	83.7	78.8	72.0	63.8	57.2	50.1	39.9	30.5
Personal computers and peripheral equipment[1]	. . .	. . .	. . .	. . .	. . .	. . .	. . .	. . .	875.1	598.7
Other Goods and Services	159.0	171.6	183.3	192.9	198.5	206.9	215.4	224.8	237.7	258.3
Tobacco and smoking product	181.5	202.7	219.8	228.4	220.0	225.7	232.8	243.7	274.8	355.8
Personal care	130.4	134.9	138.3	141.5	144.6	147.1	150.1	152.7	156.7	161.1
Personal care product	128.2	132.8	136.5	139.0	141.5	143.1	144.3	144.2	148.3	151.8
Personal care services	132.8	137.0	140.0	144.0	147.9	151.5	156.6	162.4	166.0	171.4
Miscellaneous personal services	158.4	168.8	177.5	186.1	195.9	205.9	215.6	226.1	234.7	243.0

[1]December 1997 = 100.
[2]December 1982 = 100.
[3]December 1988 = 100.
. . . = Not available.

Table 9-8. Consumer Price Indexes, All Urban Consumers (CPI-U): U.S. City Average, by Expenditure Category, 1990–2009—*Continued*

(1982–1984 = 100, unless otherwise specified.)

Expenditure category	2000	2001	2002	2003	2004	2005	2006	2007	2008	2009
ALL ITEMS	172.2	177.1	179.9	184.0	188.9	195.3	201.6	207.3	215.3	214.5
Food and Beverages	168.4	173.6	176.8	180.5	186.6	191.2	195.7	203.3	214.2	218.2
Food	167.8	173.1	176.2	180.0	186.2	190.7	195.2	202.9	214.1	218.0
Food at home	167.9	173.4	175.6	179.4	186.2	189.8	193.1	201.2	214.1	215.1
Cereals and bakery product	188.3	193.8	198.0	202.8	206.0	209.0	212.8	222.1	244.9	252.6
Meats, poultry, fish, and eggs	154.5	161.3	162.1	169.3	181.7	184.7	186.6	195.6	204.7	203.8
Dairy and related product	160.7	167.1	168.1	167.9	180.2	182.4	181.4	194.8	210.4	197.0
Fruits and vegetables	204.6	212.2	220.9	225.9	232.7	241.4	252.9	262.6	278.9	272.9
Nonalcoholic beverages and beverage materials	137.8	139.2	139.2	139.8	140.4	144.4	147.4	153.4	160.0	163.0
Other food at home	155.6	159.6	160.8	162.6	164.9	167.0	169.6	173.3	184.2	191.2
Sugar and sweets	154.0	155.7	159.0	162.0	163.2	165.2	171.5	176.8	186.6	196.9
Fats and oils	147.4	155.7	155.4	157.4	167.8	167.7	168.0	172.9	196.8	201.2
Other food	172.2	176.0	177.1	178.8	179.7	182.5	185.0	188.2	198.1	205.5
Other miscellaneous food[1]	107.5	108.9	109.2	110.3	110.4	111.3	113.9	115.1	119.9	122.4
Food away from home	169.0	173.9	178.3	182.1	187.5	193.4	199.4	206.7	215.8	223.3
Other food away from home[1]	109.0	113.4	117.7	121.3	125.3	131.3	136.6	144.1	150.6	155.9
Alcoholic beverages	174.7	179.3	183.6	187.2	192.1	195.9	200.7	207.0	214.5	220.8
Housing	169.6	176.4	180.3	184.8	189.5	195.7	203.2	209.6	216.3	217.1
Shelter	193.4	200.6	208.1	213.1	218.8	224.4	232.1	240.6	246.7	249.4
Rent of primary residence	183.9	192.1	199.7	205.5	211.0	217.3	225.1	234.7	243.3	248.8
Lodging away from home[1]	117.5	118.6	118.3	119.3	125.9	130.3	136.0	142.8	143.7	134.2
Owners' equivalent rent of primary residence[2]	198.7	206.3	214.7	219.9	224.9	230.2	238.2	246.2	252.4	256.6
Tenants' and household insurance[1]	103.7	106.2	108.7	114.8	116.2	117.6	116.5	117.0	118.8	121.5
Fuels and utilities	137.9	150.2	143.6	154.5	161.9	179.0	194.7	200.6	220.0	210.7
Household energy	122.8	135.4	127.2	138.2	144.4	161.6	177.1	181.7	200.8	188.1
Fuel oil and other fuels	129.7	129.3	115.5	139.5	160.5	208.6	234.9	251.5	334.4	239.8
Gas (piped) and electricity	128.0	142.4	134.4	145.0	150.6	166.5	182.1	186.3	202.2	193.6
Water, sewer, and trash collection services[1]	106.5	109.6	113.0	117.2	124.0	130.3	136.8	143.7	152.1	161.1
Household furnishings and operations	128.2	129.1	128.3	126.1	125.5	126.1	127.0	126.9	127.8	128.7
Household operations[1]	110.5	115.6	119.0	121.8	125.0	130.3	136.6	140.6	147.5	150.3
Apparel	129.6	127.3	124.0	120.9	120.4	119.5	119.5	119.0	118.9	120.1
Men's and boys' apparel	129.7	125.7	121.7	118.0	117.5	116.1	114.1	112.4	113.0	113.6
Women's and girls' apparel	121.5	119.3	115.8	113.1	113.0	110.8	110.7	110.3	107.5	108.1
Infants' and toddlers' apparel	130.6	129.2	126.4	122.1	118.5	116.7	116.5	113.9	113.8	114.5
Footwear	123.8	123.0	121.4	119.6	119.3	122.6	123.5	122.4	124.2	126.9
Transportation	153.3	154.3	152.9	157.6	163.1	173.9	180.9	184.7	195.5	179.3
Private transportation	149.1	150.0	148.8	153.6	159.4	170.2	177.0	180.8	191.0	174.8
New and used motor vehicles[1]	100.8	101.3	99.2	96.5	94.2	95.6	95.6	94.3	93.3	93.5
New vehicles	142.8	142.1	140.0	137.9	137.1	137.9	137.6	136.3	134.2	135.6
Used cars and trucks	155.8	158.7	152.0	142.9	133.3	139.4	140.0	135.7	134.0	127.0
Motor fuel	129.3	124.7	116.6	135.8	160.4	195.7	221.0	239.1	279.7	202.0
Gasoline (all types)	128.6	124.0	116.0	135.1	159.7	194.7	219.9	238.0	277.5	201.6
Motor vehicle parts and equipment	101.5	104.8	106.9	107.8	108.7	111.9	117.3	121.6	128.7	134.1
Motor vehicle maintenance and repair	177.3	183.5	190.2	195.6	200.2	206.9	215.6	223.0	233.9	243.3
Public transportation	209.6	210.6	207.4	209.3	209.1	217.3	226.6	230.0	250.5	236.3
Medical Care	260.8	272.8	285.6	297.1	310.1	323.2	336.2	351.1	364.1	375.6
Medical care commodities	238.1	247.6	256.4	262.8	269.3	276.0	285.9	290.0	296.0	305.1
Medical care services	266.0	278.8	292.9	306.0	321.3	336.7	350.6	369.3	384.9	397.3
Professional services	237.7	246.5	253.9	261.2	271.5	281.7	289.3	300.8	311.0	319.4
Hospital and related services	317.3	338.3	367.8	394.8	417.9	439.9	468.1	498.9	534.0	567.9
Recreation[1]	103.3	104.9	106.2	107.5	108.6	109.4	110.9	111.4	113.3	114.3
Video and audio[1]	101.0	101.5	102.8	103.6	104.2	104.2	104.6	102.9	102.6	101.3
Education and Communication[1]	102.5	105.2	107.9	109.8	111.6	113.7	116.8	119.6	123.6	127.4
Education[1]	112.5	118.5	126.0	134.4	143.7	152.7	162.1	171.4	181.3	190.9
Educational books and supplies	279.9	295.9	317.6	335.4	351.0	365.6	388.9	420.4	450.2	482.1
Tuition, other school fees, and childcare	324.0	341.1	362.1	386.7	414.3	440.9	468.1	494.1	522.1	549.0
Communication[1]	93.6	93.3	92.3	89.7	86.7	84.7	84.1	83.4	84.2	85.0
Information and information processing[1]	92.8	92.3	90.8	87.8	84.6	82.6	81.7	80.7	81.4	81.9
Telephone services[1]	98.5	99.3	99.7	98.3	95.8	94.9	95.8	98.2	100.5	102.4
Information technology, hardware, and services[3]	25.9	21.3	18.3	16.1	14.8	13.6	12.5	10.6	10.1	9.7
Personal computers and peripheral equipment[1]	459.9	330.1	248.4	196.9	171.2	143.2	120.9	108.4	94.9	82.3
Other Goods and Services	271.1	282.6	293.2	298.7	304.7	313.4	321.7	333.3	345.4	368.6
Tobacco and smoking product	394.9	425.2	461.5	469.0	478.0	502.8	519.9	554.2	588.7	730.3
Personal care	165.6	170.5	174.7	178.0	181.7	185.6	190.2	195.6	201.3	204.6
Personal care product	153.7	155.1	154.7	153.5	153.9	154.4	155.8	158.3	159.3	162.6
Personal care services	178.1	184.3	188.4	193.2	197.6	203.9	209.7	216.6	223.7	227.6
Miscellaneous personal services	252.3	263.1	274.4	283.5	293.9	303.0	313.6	325.0	338.9	344.5

[1]December 1997 = 100.
[2]December 1982 = 100.
[3]December 1988 = 100.

Table 9-9. Relative Importance of Components in the Consumer Price Index: U.S. City Average, Selected Groups, December 1997–December 2009

(Percent distribution.)

Index and year	All items	Food and beverages	Housing	Apparel	Transportation	Medical care	Recreation	Education and communication	Other goods and services
ALL URBAN CONSUMERS (CPI-U)									
December 1997	100.0	16.3	39.6	4.9	17.6	5.6	6.1	5.5	4.3
December 1998	100.0	16.4	39.8	4.8	17.0	5.7	6.1	5.5	4.6
December 1999	100.0	16.3	39.6	4.7	17.5	5.8	6.0	5.4	4.7
December 2000	100.0	16.2	40.0	4.4	17.6	5.8	5.9	5.3	4.8
December 2001[1]	100.0	16.4	40.5	4.2	16.6	6.0	5.9	5.4	4.9
December 2001[2]	100.0	15.7	40.9	4.4	17.1	5.8	6.0	5.8	4.3
December 2002	100.0	15.6	40.9	4.2	17.3	6.0	5.9	5.8	4.4
December 2003	100.0	15.4	42.1	4.0	16.9	6.1	5.9	5.9	3.8
December 2004	100.0	15.3	42.0	3.8	17.4	6.1	5.7	5.8	3.8
December 2005	100.0	15.1	42.2	3.7	17.7	6.2	5.6	5.8	3.7
December 2006	100.0	15.0	42.7	3.7	17.2	6.3	5.6	6.0	3.5
December 2007	100.0	14.9	42.4	3.7	17.7	6.2	5.6	6.1	3.3
December 2008	100.0	15.8	43.4	3.7	15.3	6.4	5.7	6.3	3.4
December 2009	100.0	14.8	42.0	3.7	16.7	6.5	6.4	6.4	3.5
URBAN WAGE EARNERS AND WORKERS (CPI-W)									
December 1997	100.0	17.9	36.5	5.3	19.8	4.6	6.0	5.4	4.5
December 1998	100.0	18.0	36.7	5.2	19.2	4.7	5.9	5.4	5.0
December 1999	100.0	17.9	36.5	5.0	19.7	4.7	5.8	5.3	5.1
December 2000	100.0	17.8	36.8	4.8	19.9	4.7	5.7	5.2	5.2
December 2001[1]	100.0	18.0	37.3	4.6	18.8	4.9	5.7	5.3	5.4
December 2001[2]	100.0	17.2	38.1	4.8	19.4	4.6	5.6	5.6	4.5
December 2002	100.0	17.1	38.1	4.6	19.7	4.7	5.6	5.6	4.6
December 2003	100.0	17.2	39.1	4.4	19.1	5.0	5.7	5.6	3.9
December 2004	100.0	17.0	39.0	4.2	19.8	5.0	5.5	5.5	3.9
December 2005	100.0	16.8	39.2	4.0	20.1	5.1	5.4	5.4	3.9
December 2006	100.0	16.5	40.5	4.0	19.5	5.2	5.0	5.6	3.7
December 2007	100.0	15.9	40.0	4.0	20.1	5.2	5.3	6.0	3.5
December 2008	100.0	16.9	41.3	4.0	17.1	5.4	5.5	6.2	3.7
December 2009	100.0	16.4	39.8	3.8	18.6	5.3	6.0	6.2	3.9

[1]1993–1995 weights.
[2]1999–2000 weights.

Table 9-10. Consumer Price Indexes, All Urban Consumers (CPI-U), All Items: Selected Metropolitan Statistical Areas, Selected Years, 1970–2009

(1982–1984 = 100, unless otherwise specified.)

Area	1970	1975	1980	1985	1986	1987	1988	1989	1990	1991	1992	1993	1994	1995
NORTHEAST														
Boston-Brockton-Nashua, MA-NH-ME-CT	40.2	55.8	82.6	109.4	112.2	117.1	124.2	131.3	138.9	145.0	148.6	152.9	154.9	158.6
New York-Northern New Jersey-Long Island, NY-NJ-CT-PA	41.2	57.6	82.1	108.7	112.3	118.0	123.7	130.6	138.5	144.8	150.0	154.5	158.2	162.2
Philadelphia-Wilmington-Atlantic City, PA-NJ-DE-MD	40.8	56.8	83.6	108.8	111.5	116.8	122.4	128.3	135.8	142.2	146.6	150.2	154.6	158.7
Pittsburgh, PA	38.1	52.4	81.0	106.9	108.2	111.4	114.9	120.1	126.2	131.3	136.0	139.9	144.6	149.2
NORTH CENTRAL														
Chicago-Gary-Kenosha, IL-IN-WI	38.9	52.8	82.2	107.7	110.0	114.5	119.0	125.0	131.7	137.0	141.1	145.4	148.6	153.3
Cincinnati-Hamilton, OH-KY-IN	37.4	51.8	82.1	106.6	107.6	111.9	116.1	120.9	126.5	131.4	134.1	137.8	142.4	146.2
Cleveland-Akron, OH	37.2	50.2	78.9	107.8	109.4	112.7	116.7	122.7	129.0	134.2	136.8	140.3	144.4	147.9
Detroit-Ann Arbor-Flint, MI	39.5	53.9	85.3	106.8	108.3	111.7	116.1	122.3	128.6	133.1	135.9	139.6	144.0	148.6
Kansas City, MO-KS	39.0	53.2	83.6	107.7	108.7	113.1	117.4	121.6	126.0	131.2	134.3	138.1	141.3	145.3
Milwaukee-Racine, WI	37.5	50.8	81.4	107.0	107.4	111.5	115.9	120.8	126.2	132.2	137.1	142.1	147.0	151.0
Minneapolis-St. Paul, MN-WI	37.4	51.2	78.9	107.0	108.4	111.6	117.2	122.0	127.0	130.4	135.0	139.2	143.6	147.0
St. Louis, MO-IL	38.8	52.6	82.5	107.1	108.6	112.2	115.7	121.8	128.1	132.1	134.7	137.5	141.3	145.2
SOUTH														
Atlanta, GA	38.6	53.6	80.3	108.9	112.2	116.5	120.4	126.1	131.7	135.9	138.5	143.4	146.7	150.9
Dallas-Fort Worth, TX	37.6	50.4	81.5	108.2	109.9	112.9	116.1	119.1	125.1	130.8	133.9	137.3	141.2	144.9
Houston-Galveston-Brazoria, TX	36.4	51.4	82.7	104.9	103.9	106.5	109.5	114.1	120.6	125.1	129.1	133.4	137.9	139.8
Miami-Fort Lauderdale, FL	...	...	81.1	106.5	107.9	111.8	116.8	121.5	128.0	132.3	134.5	139.1	143.6	148.9
Tampa-St. Petersburg-Clearwater, FL[1]	...	...	...	...	...	100.0	103.7	107.2	111.7	116.4	119.2	124.0	126.5	129.7
Washington-Baltimore, DC-MD-VA-WV[2]	...	...	...	...	...	...	...	...	...	...	...	...	...	...
WEST														
Anchorage, AK	41.1	57.1	85.5	105.8	107.8	108.2	108.6	111.7	118.6	124.0	128.2	132.2	135.0	138.9
Denver-Boulder-Greeley, CO	34.5	48.4	78.4	107.1	107.9	110.8	113.7	115.8	120.9	125.6	130.3	135.8	141.8	147.9
Honolulu, HI	41.5	56.3	83.0	106.8	109.4	114.9	121.7	128.7	138.1	148.0	155.1	160.1	164.5	168.1
Los Angeles-Riverside-Orange County, CA	38.7	53.3	83.7	108.4	111.9	116.7	122.1	128.3	135.9	141.4	146.5	150.3	152.3	154.6
Phoenix-Mesa, AZ	...	...	...	...	...	...	...	...	...	...	...	...	...	...
Portland-Salem, OR-WA	38.7	53.5	87.2	106.7	108.2	110.9	114.7	120.4	127.4	133.9	139.8	144.7	148.9	153.2
San Diego, CA	34.1	47.6	79.4	110.4	113.5	117.5	123.4	130.6	138.4	143.4	147.4	150.6	154.5	156.8
San Francisco-Oakland-San Jose, CA	37.7	51.8	80.4	108.4	111.6	115.4	120.5	126.4	132.1	137.9	142.5	146.3	148.7	151.6
Seattle-Tacoma-Bremerton, WA	37.4	51.1	82.7	105.6	106.7	109.2	112.8	118.1	126.8	134.1	139.0	142.9	147.8	152.3

Area	1996	1997	1998	1999	2000	2001	2002	2003	2004	2005	2006	2007	2008	2009
NORTHEAST														
Boston-Brockton-Nashua, MA-NH-ME-CT	163.3	167.9	171.7	176.0	183.6	191.5	196.5	203.9	209.5	216.4	223.1	227.4	235.4	233.8
New York-Northern New Jersey-Long Island, NY-NJ-CT-PA	166.9	170.8	173.6	177.0	182.5	187.1	191.9	197.8	204.8	212.7	220.7	226.9	235.8	236.8
Philadelphia-Wilmington-Atlantic City, PA-NJ-DE-MD	162.8	166.5	168.2	171.9	176.5	181.3	184.9	188.8	196.5	204.2	212.1	216.7	224.1	223.3
Pittsburgh, PA	153.2	157.0	159.2	162.5	168.0	172.5	174.0	177.5	183.0	189.8	195.7	201.5	211.3	212.1
NORTH CENTRAL														
Chicago-Gary-Kenosha, IL-IN-WI	157.4	161.7	165.0	168.4	173.8	178.3	181.2	184.5	188.6	194.3	198.3	204.8	212.5	210.0
Cincinnati-Hamilton, OH-KY-IN	149.6	152.1	155.1	159.2	164.8	167.9	170.0	173.4	176.5	181.6	188.6	193.9	201.5	200.6
Cleveland-Akron, OH	152.0	156.1	159.8	162.5	168.0	172.9	173.3	176.2	181.6	187.9	191.1	196.0	203.0	200.5
Detroit-Ann Arbor-Flint, MI	152.5	156.3	159.8	163.9	169.8	174.4	178.9	182.5	185.4	190.8	196.6	200.1	204.7	203.5
Kansas City, MO-KS	151.6	155.8	157.8	160.1	166.6	172.2	174.0	177.0	180.7	185.3	190.1	194.5	201.2	201.0
Milwaukee-Racine, WI	154.7	157.7	160.3	163.7	168.6	171.7	174.0	177.7	180.2	185.2	189.9	194.1	203.0	203.0
Minneapolis-St. Paul, MN-WI	151.9	155.4	158.3	163.3	170.1	176.5	179.6	182.7	187.9	193.1	196.2	201.2	209.0	207.9
St. Louis, MO-IL	149.6	152.9	154.5	157.6	163.1	167.3	169.1	173.4	180.3	186.2	189.5	193.2	198.7	198.5
SOUTH														
Atlanta, GA	156.0	158.9	161.2	164.8	170.6	176.2	178.2	180.8	183.2	188.9	193.8	200.0	206.5	201.0
Dallas-Fort Worth, TX	148.8	151.4	153.6	158.0	164.7	170.4	172.7	176.2	178.7	184.7	190.1	193.2	201.8	200.5
Houston-Galveston-Brazoria, TX	142.7	145.4	146.8	148.7	154.2	158.8	159.2	163.7	169.5	175.6	180.6	183.8	190.0	190.5
Miami-Fort Lauderdale, FL	153.7	158.4	160.5	162.4	167.8	173.0	175.5	180.6	185.6	194.3	203.9	212.4	222.1	221.4
Tampa-St. Petersburg-Clearwater, FL[1]	131.6	134.0	137.5	140.6	145.7	148.8	153.9	158.1	162.0	168.5	175.2	184.3	190.1	189.9
Washington-Baltimore, DC-MD-VA-WV[2]	...	100.8	102.1	104.2	107.6	110.4	113.0	116.2	119.5	124.3	128.8	133.5	139.5	139.8
WEST														
Anchorage, AK	142.7	144.8	146.9	148.4	150.9	155.2	158.2	162.5	166.7	171.8	177.3	181.2	189.5	191.7
Denver-Boulder-Greeley, CO	153.1	158.1	161.9	166.6	173.2	181.3	184.8	186.8	187.0	190.9	197.7	202.0	209.9	208.5
Honolulu, HI	170.7	171.9	171.5	173.3	176.3	178.4	180.3	184.5	190.6	197.8	209.4	219.5	228.9	230.0
Los Angeles-Riverside-Orange County, CA	157.5	160.0	162.3	166.1	171.6	177.3	182.2	187.0	193.2	201.8	210.4	217.3	225.0	223.2
Phoenix-Mesa, AZ	...	...	...	...	...	101.2	103.3	105.2	108.3	111.5	115.3	119.3	117.6	
Portland-Salem, OR-WA	158.6	164.0	167.1	172.6	178.0	182.4	183.8	186.3	191.1	196.0	201.1	208.6	215.4	215.6
San Diego, CA	160.9	163.7	166.9	172.8	182.8	191.2	197.9	205.3	212.8	220.6	228.1	233.3	242.3	242.3
San Francisco-Oakland-San Jose, CA	155.1	160.4	165.5	172.5	180.2	189.9	193.0	196.4	198.8	202.7	209.2	216.0	222.8	224.4
Seattle-Tacoma-Bremerton, WA	157.5	163.0	167.7	172.8	179.2	185.7	189.3	192.3	194.7	200.2	207.6	215.7	224.7	226.0

[1] 1987 = 100.
[2] November 1996 = 100.
. . . = Not available.

Table 9-11. Consumer Price Index Research Series, Using Current Methods (CPI-U-RS), by Month and Annual Average, 1977–2009

(December 1977 = 100.)

Year	January	February	March	April	May	June	July	August	September	October	November	December	Annual average
1977	. . .	. . .	. . .	. . .	. . .	. . .	. . .	. . .	. . .	. . .	. . .	100.0	. . .
1978	100.5	101.1	101.8	102.7	103.6	104.6	105.0	105.5	106.1	106.7	107.3	107.9	104.4
1979	108.7	109.7	110.7	111.8	113.0	114.1	115.2	116.0	117.1	117.9	118.5	119.5	114.4
1980	120.9	122.4	123.8	124.8	125.8	126.7	127.6	128.6	130.0	130.8	131.5	132.4	127.1
1981	133.6	135.3	136.4	137.1	137.9	138.7	139.7	140.7	141.8	142.4	142.9	143.4	139.2
1982	144.2	144.7	144.9	145.1	146.1	147.5	148.5	148.8	149.5	150.2	150.5	150.7	147.6
1983	151.1	151.2	151.3	152.4	153.2	153.8	154.4	154.8	155.6	156.0	156.2	156.4	153.9
1984	157.3	158.0	158.4	159.1	159.5	160.0	160.5	161.1	161.9	162.3	162.3	162.4	160.2
1985	162.6	163.3	164.0	164.7	165.3	165.8	166.1	166.4	167.0	167.4	167.9	168.3	165.7
1986	168.8	168.3	167.5	167.1	167.7	168.5	168.5	168.7	169.7	169.7	169.8	169.9	168.7
1987	170.9	171.6	172.3	173.2	173.7	174.3	174.6	175.6	176.4	176.8	176.9	176.8	174.4
1988	177.3	177.6	178.3	179.2	179.8	180.5	181.1	181.9	183.0	183.5	183.6	183.7	180.8
1989	184.6	185.2	186.2	187.5	188.4	188.8	189.3	189.5	190.2	190.9	191.2	191.5	188.6
1990	193.3	194.2	195.2	195.5	195.8	196.9	197.6	199.3	200.9	202.1	202.3	202.4	198.0
1991	203.3	203.5	203.6	203.9	204.4	204.9	205.0	205.6	206.4	206.6	207.1	207.2	205.1
1992	207.5	208.1	209.0	209.3	209.6	210.1	210.4	211.0	211.6	212.2	212.5	212.3	210.3
1993	212.9	213.7	214.3	214.9	215.3	215.5	215.6	216.1	216.4	217.1	217.3	217.1	215.5
1994	217.4	218.0	218.8	219.0	219.2	219.9	220.4	221.1	221.5	221.6	221.9	221.8	220.1
1995	222.6	223.3	224.0	224.7	225.1	225.6	225.7	226.1	226.5	227.1	226.9	226.8	225.4
1996	227.9	228.7	229.8	230.6	231.2	231.3	231.7	232.0	232.7	233.4	233.8	233.8	231.4
1997	234.5	235.2	235.6	235.9	235.8	236.2	236.3	236.7	237.5	237.9	237.8	237.4	236.4
1998	237.8	238.2	238.6	239.1	239.4	239.6	239.8	240.2	240.5	241.0	241.0	240.7	239.7
1999	241.4	241.7	242.4	244.1	244.1	244.2	244.9	245.6	246.7	247.2	247.3	247.3	244.7
2000	248.0	249.4	251.4	251.6	251.8	253.2	253.7	253.8	255.1	255.5	255.7	255.5	252.9
2001	257.1	258.2	258.8	259.8	260.9	261.4	260.6	260.7	261.8	260.9	260.4	259.4	260.0
2002	260.1	261.1	262.5	264.0	264.0	264.2	264.5	265.3	265.8	266.3	266.3	265.7	264.2
2003	266.8	268.9	270.5	269.9	269.5	269.8	270.1	271.1	271.9	271.7	270.9	270.6	270.1
2004	272.0	273.5	275.2	276.1	277.6	278.5	278.2	278.3	278.8	280.4	280.5	279.5	277.4
2005	280.0	281.6	283.8	285.7	285.5	285.6	286.9	288.3	291.9	292.5	290.2	288.9	286.7
2006	291.2	291.8	293.5	295.9	297.3	297.9	298.8	299.5	298.0	296.4	295.9	296.4	296.1
2007	297.2	298.8	301.6	303.5	305.4	306.0	305.9	305.3	306.2	306.8	308.6	308.4	304.5
2008	310.0	310.9	313.6	315.5	318.1	321.3	323.0	321.7	321.3	318.0	311.9	308.7	316.2
2009	310.1	311.6	312.4	313.1	314.0	316.7	316.2	316.9	317.1	317.5	317.7	317.1	315.0

. . . = Not available.

NOTES AND DEFINITIONS

IMPORT AND EXPORT PRICE INDEXES

Collection and Coverage

The International Price Program (IPP) at the Bureau of Labor Statistics (BLS) produces Import/Export Price Indexes (MXP) which contain data on changes in the prices of nonmilitary goods and services traded between the U.S. and the rest of the world.

The MXP are primarily used to deflate foreign trade statistics produced by the U.S. government. The MXP are also a valuable input into the processes of measuring inflation, formulating fiscal and monetary policy, forecasting future prices, conducting elasticity studies, measuring U.S. industrial competitiveness, analyzing exchange rates, negotiating trade contracts, and analyzing import prices by locality of origin. The IPP collects prices as close as possible to the first day of each reference month.

The formula used to calculate the MXP is a modified form of the Laspeyres index. A Laspeyres index uses fixed base period quantities to aggregate prices. This means that the quality of goods and services is fixed; new goods do not appear, and the prices of goods that disappear must be observable. Because these implications are not consistent with the actually workings of the economy, adjustments must be made to the index.

The merchandise item price indexes are classified by end use for the Bureau of Economic Analysis System, by industry according to the North American Industry Classification System (NAICS), and product category according to the Harmonized System (HS). While classification by end use and product category are self-explanatory, a couple of notes are in order for classifying items by industry. In the NAICS tables, for both imports and exports, items are classified by output industry, not input industry. As an example, NAICS import index 326 (plastics and rubber products) includes outputs such as manufactured plastic rather than inputs such as petroleum. The NAICS classification structure also matches the classification system used by the PPI to produce the NAICS primary products indexes.

The Import Price Indexes (MPI) are based on U.S. dollar prices paid by the U.S. importer. The prices are generally either "free on board" (f.o.b.) foreign port or "cost, insur-ance, and freight" (c.i.f.) U.S. port transaction prices, depending on the practices of the individual industry. The index for crude petroleum is calculated from data collected by the Department of Energy.

Prices used in the import indexes by locality of origin are a subset of the data collected for the Import Price Indexes. Beginning with January 2002, the indexes are defined by locality of origin using a nomenclature based upon the North American Industry Classification System (NAICS). Nonmanufactured goods are defined as NAICS 11 and 21, and manufactured goods are defined as NAICS 31–33.

The Export Price Indexes (XPI) are classified by end use, determined by BEA. The prices used are generally either "free alongside ship" (f.a.s.) factory or "free on board" (f.o.b.) transaction prices, depending on the practices of the individual industry. Prices used in the grain index, excluding rice, are obtained from the Department of Agriculture.

Starting in September 2008 the Import Air Passenger Fares Indexes represent changes in the average revenue per passenger received by foreign carriers from U.S. residents and are calculated from data obtained from an airline consulting service. These data include tickets sold by travel agencies and travel websites. Tickets sold directly by the airlines are excluded, as are frequent flyer tickets generally. Starting in January 2008 the Export Air Passenger Fares Indexes represent changes in the average revenue per passenger received by U.S. carriers from foreign residents and are calculated from data collected directly from airlines. These data include frequent flyer tickets and those sold by consolidators. Taxes and fees are included in the Import Air Passenger Fares Index and excluded from the Export Air Passenger Fares Index. The Air Freight Indexes are calculated from data collected directly from airlines. These data exclude mail and passenger baggage. The scope of the service being priced is the movement of freight from airport to airport only, and does not include any ground transportation or port service.

Sources of Additional Information

Concepts and methodology are described in Chapter 15 of the *BLS Handbook of Methods* and in monthly BLS press releases. These resources are available on the BLS Web site at <http://www.bls.gov>.

Table 9-12. U.S. Export Price Indexes for Selected Categories of Goods, by End Use, 1999–2009

(2000 = 100, unless otherwise indicated.)

Commodity	1999				2000				2001			
	March	June	September	December	March	June	September	December	March	June	September	December
ALL COMMODITIES	97.9	98.2	98.5	99.0	100.0	100.1	100.4	100.1	100.0	99.4	99.0	97.6
Foods, Feeds, and Beverages	101.1	102.9	101.4	99.5	100.8	100.8	98.7	101.2	101.0	100.4	102.6	100.7
Agricultural foods, feeds, and beverages excluding distilled beverages	100.6	101.6	101.5	99.3	100.9	100.9	98.6	101.5	101.2	101.2	103.6	101.6
Nonagricultural foods (fish, distilled beverages)	105.4	115.2	100.0	101.4	99.6	99.9	99.7	98.2	99.4	92.6	92.9	92.1
Industrial Supplies and Materials	91.1	92.1	94.2	96.5	100.1	100.2	101.7	100.0	98.9	97.2	95.2	91.4
Industrial supplies and materials, durable	96.2	96.1	96.2	98.6	100.7	99.9	100.4	99.5	98.6	97.6	95.9	93.8
Industrial supplies and materials, nondurable	88.1	89.7	93.0	95.3	99.8	100.4	102.4	100.2	99.0	96.9	94.8	90.0
Agricultural industrial supplies and materials	100.7	98.8	96.5	96.7	98.0	98.6	103.2	104.6	101.7	99.3	96.8	93.3
Nonagricultural industrial supplies and materials	90.5	91.6	94.1	96.5	100.3	100.3	101.6	99.7	98.7	97.0	95.1	91.3
Fuels and lubricants	66.3	71.6	80.3	86.4	103.1	97.3	111.3	104.9	100.3	102.8	103.2	83.5
Nonagricultural supplies and materials excluding fuels and building materials	93.8	94.3	96.0	97.9	99.8	100.8	100.2	98.8	98.5	96.1	93.8	92.3
Selected building materials	97.4	97.9	97.4	98.8	100.5	100.2	99.7	99.2	97.5	97.0	95.5	94.2
Capital Goods	100.8	100.4	100.0	99.9	99.9	99.9	100.0	100.2	100.6	100.3	100.0	99.4
Electrical generating equipment	99.9	99.8	99.1	99.3	99.6	100.0	100.7	100.5	100.9	101.7	101.6	101.5
Nonelectrical machinery	101.8	101.3	100.8	100.4	100.2	100.0	99.8	99.7	99.7	99.1	98.6	97.7
Transportation equipment excluding motor vehicles[1]	. . .	. . .	. . .	. . .	. . .	. . .	. . .	. . .	. . .	. . .	. . .	. . .
Automotive Vehicles, Parts, and Engines	98.8	99.0	99.1	99.6	99.9	99.9	100.3	100.1	100.3	100.4	100.4	100.5
Consumer Goods, Excluding Automotives	99.5	99.6	99.6	100.1	100.0	99.9	99.9	99.7	99.6	99.4	99.7	99.9
Nondurables, manufactured	99.8	99.8	99.8	100.6	100.1	99.8	99.8	99.6	99.0	99.0	99.1	99.1
Durables, manufactured	99.1	99.3	99.4	99.5	99.8	100.1	100.1	99.9	100.2	100.0	100.4	100.5
Agricultural Commodities	100.6	101.1	100.7	98.9	100.4	100.5	99.4	102.0	101.3	100.9	102.5	100.2
Nonagricultural Commodities	97.7	97.9	98.3	99.0	100.0	100.0	100.5	99.9	99.9	99.3	98.6	97.4

Commodity	2002				2003				2004			
	March	June	September	December	March	June	September	December	March	June	September	December
ALL COMMODITIES	97.6	98.0	98.8	98.6	99.7	99.5	99.8	100.8	103.0	103.4	103.8	104.8
Foods, Feeds, and Beverages	99.7	101.5	109.8	108.7	108.2	111.3	115.3	122.4	130.5	129.1	118.7	116.9
Agricultural foods, feeds, and beverages excluding distilled beverages	100.0	101.7	110.7	109.5	108.1	111.2	116.3	123.8	132.4	131.1	119.3	116.6
Nonagricultural foods (fish, distilled beverages)	98.3	100.7	101.3	102.3	110.0	113.1	106.5	108.5	112.1	110.7	113.0	118.4
Industrial Supplies and Materials	91.9	94.6	95.9	96.0	100.6	100.1	100.2	102.5	108.1	109.9	114.0	118.0
Industrial supplies and materials, durable	94.4	96.0	96.4	96.6	99.2	99.7	100.4	103.3	110.3	111.8	116.0	120.2
Industrial supplies and materials, nondurable	90.4	93.9	95.8	95.8	101.7	100.6	100.4	102.2	107.0	108.9	112.9	116.9
Agricultural industrial supplies and materials	93.6	95.8	98.4	101.9	104.8	104.4	107.3	117.5	117.2	110.7	109.4	109.5
Nonagricultural industrial supplies and materials	91.8	94.5	95.8	95.7	100.3	99.8	99.8	101.7	107.7	109.9	114.3	118.6
Fuels and lubricants	85.6	86.7	92.9	91.3	108.0	97.0	97.6	99.0	108.9	114.9	121.5	125.4
Nonagricultural supplies and materials excluding fuels and building materials	92.6	95.7	96.4	96.4	99.9	100.7	100.5	102.5	108.1	110.0	114.4	118.9
Selected building materials	94.2	94.2	96.2	96.2	96.4	96.3	98.4	99.5	102.3	103.4	104.0	104.4
Capital Goods	99.4	98.7	98.4	98.1	98.3	97.6	97.5	97.5	98.0	97.8	97.8	98.2
Electrical generating equipment	102.1	102.0	102.0	101.9	101.6	101.6	101.7	101.7	102.0	102.0	102.4	103.6
Nonelectrical machinery	97.5	96.6	96.0	95.4	95.6	94.5	94.3	94.1	94.5	94.1	93.9	93.9
Transportation equipment excluding motor vehicles[1]	100.9	100.8	101.7	102.5	103.5	104.0	105.1	105.7	106.6	107.2	108.3	109.5
Automotive Vehicles, Parts, and Engines	100.9	100.9	101.1	101.3	101.5	101.6	101.8	101.8	101.9	102.3	102.5	102.9
Consumer Goods, Excluding Automotives	99.1	99.1	99.3	99.3	99.4	99.6	99.4	99.9	100.2	100.4	101.0	101.2
Nondurables, manufactured	98.1	98.5	98.7	98.7	98.7	98.8	98.5	99.2	99.9	100.0	101.0	101.0
Durables, manufactured	99.7	99.4	99.6	99.6	99.7	100.1	100.1	100.3	100.1	100.7	100.9	101.1
Agricultural Commodities	98.9	100.7	108.6	108.2	107.5	110.0	114.7	122.7	129.7	127.4	117.6	115.4
Nonagricultural Commodities	97.5	97.8	98.0	97.8	99.1	98.7	98.6	99.1	100.9	101.5	102.8	104.1

[1]December 2001 = 100.
. . . = Not available.

Table 9-12. U.S. Export Price Indexes for Selected Categories of Goods, by End Use, 1999–2009—Continued

(2000 = 100, unless otherwise indicated.)

Commodity	2005				2006				2007			
	March	June	September	December	March	June	September	December	March	June	September	December
ALL COMMODITIES	106.4	106.7	107.5	107.7	108.8	111.2	111.7	112.5	114.7	116.0	116.7	119.3
Foods, Feeds, and Beverages	120.9	125.2	122.8	121.9	121.7	125.6	128.8	138.7	146.9	148.6	157.8	171.1
Agricultural foods, feeds, and beverages excluding distilled beverages	120.7	125.6	122.6	121.7	121.5	125.7	129.1	140.5	149.2	151.0	160.8	175.2
Nonagricultural foods (fish, distilled beverages)	121.8	120.1	123.6	123.6	123.2	125.0	126.0	123.5	128.0	128.5	133.0	136.1
Industrial Supplies and Materials	122.3	122.3	127.4	127.9	131.3	138.8	139.5	139.4	145.5	149.0	148.8	154.1
Industrial supplies and materials, durable	122.6	122.7	123.4	129.1	135.7	146.2	146.9	150.1	160.2	160.9	155.5	159.2
Industrial supplies and materials, nondurable	122.2	122.1	129.8	127.4	129.0	134.9	135.7	133.9	137.6	142.8	145.5	151.9
Agricultural industrial supplies and materials	115.6	115.8	116.4	117.4	116.8	117.3	118.1	123.9	127.3	128.7	140.0	144.7
Nonagricultural industrial supplies and materials	122.8	122.8	128.2	128.7	132.3	140.2	140.9	140.5	146.7	150.4	149.5	154.9
Fuels and lubricants	143.8	148.8	184.8	163.4	173.5	196.3	191.1	183.5	188.8	201.1	200.9	222.8
Nonagricultural supplies and materials excluding fuels and building materials	121.4	120.6	122.2	125.7	128.5	134.7	136.3	136.8	143.5	146.1	145.0	148.5
Selected building materials	105.3	106.2	105.7	106.5	108.5	109.8	110.0	111.5	112.7	113.9	114.4	113.7
Capital Goods	98.4	98.4	97.6	97.7	98.2	98.4	98.5	98.8	99.2	99.6	99.9	100.6
Electrical generating equipment	103.9	103.4	102.6	103.6	104.4	104.8	105.1	106.2	106.0	106.5	106.7	107.5
Nonelectrical machinery	93.9	93.7	92.7	92.5	92.7	92.7	92.6	92.6	92.8	92.9	93.1	93.6
Transportation equipment excluding motor vehicles[1]	111.1	111.8	112.6	113.8	116.0	117.1	117.7	119.1	121.1	122.3	123.4	125.0
Automotive Vehicles, Parts, and Engines	103.3	103.4	103.7	103.9	104.4	104.9	105.2	105.5	105.9	106.1	106.3	106.7
Consumer Goods, Excluding Automotives	101.6	101.5	101.9	101.9	102.3	103.5	104.0	104.0	104.8	105.8	106.2	107.3
Nondurables, manufactured	101.5	101.2	101.5	101.6	102.4	103.3	103.8	104.0	105.0	106.7	107.0	108.2
Durables, manufactured	101.5	101.5	101.8	101.5	101.3	102.4	103.1	102.8	103.4	103.7	104.2	105.2
Agricultural Commodities	119.9	123.9	121.5	121.0	120.7	124.1	127.1	137.3	145.0	146.7	156.8	169.3
Nonagricultural Commodities	105.4	105.4	106.5	106.8	108.0	110.3	110.6	110.7	112.6	113.8	113.8	115.7

Commodity	2008				2009			
	March	June	September	December	March	June	September	December
ALL COMMODITIES	123.8	126.1	124.9	115.8	115.5	117.8	117.9	119.7
Foods, Feeds, and Beverages	196.9	198.0	190.4	155.1	156.7	174.8	158.2	165.1
Agricultural foods, feeds, and beverages excluding distilled beverages	202.6	204.0	195.6	156.6	158.3	178.6	160.7	167.9
Nonagricultural foods (fish, distilled beverages)	148.3	146.1	145.5	143.5	144.4	141.5	137.3	140.9
Industrial Supplies and Materials	165.5	173.2	169.4	139.6	136.5	140.4	143.9	150.1
Industrial supplies and materials, durable	172.7	172.9	167.1	141.5	143.4	144.0	150.7	157.7
Industrial supplies and materials, nondurable	162.0	174.2	171.6	139.1	133.1	139.0	140.5	146.2
Agricultural industrial supplies and materials	159.3	158.0	157.4	126.1	122.9	131.0	142.2	152.5
Nonagricultural industrial supplies and materials	166.1	174.3	170.3	140.5	137.5	141.2	144.3	150.2
Fuels and lubricants	249.5	297.2	267.2	166.8	146.9	175.2	171.9	189.6
Nonagricultural supplies and materials excluding fuels and building materials	158.2	161.6	160.8	138.8	138.2	138.5	142.7	147.3
Selected building materials	114.2	113.8	115.4	115.1	114.0	113.0	114.0	113.5
Capital Goods	101.2	102.0	101.8	101.5	102.3	103.1	103.5	103.3
Electrical generating equipment	108.6	108.9	109.5	109.0	106.8	107.2	107.4	109.3
Nonelectrical machinery	93.7	94.2	93.9	93.3	93.8	94.4	94.9	94.5
Transportation equipment excluding motor vehicles[1]	128.1	130.3	130.7	131.5	135.1	137.3	137.2	136.5
Automotive Vehicles, Parts, and Engines	107.1	107.4	107.9	108.0	108.2	108.0	108.0	108.2
Consumer Goods, Excluding Automotives	108.0	108.2	109.3	109.0	108.5	108.4	109.2	109.4
Nondurables, manufactured	109.3	110.1	109.0	107.2	107.1	108.5	109.4	110.0
Durables, manufactured	105.4	105.2	108.7	109.7	109.9	108.1	109.5	109.2
Agricultural Commodities	194.3	195.2	188.3	150.8	151.6	169.7	156.9	164.7
Nonagricultural Commodities	118.8	121.2	120.4	113.2	112.9	114.1	115.1	116.5

[1]December 2001 = 100.

Table 9-13. U.S. Import Price Indexes for Selected Categories of Goods, by End Use, 1999–2009

(2000 = 100, unless otherwise indicated.)

Commodity	1999				2000				2001			
	March	June	September	December	March	June	September	December	March	June	September	December
ALL COMMODITIES	91.5	92.9	95.8	97.4	99.9	100.2	101.6	100.5	98.3	97.6	95.9	91.4
Foods, Feeds, and Beverages	101.5	102.2	100.7	103.4	101.0	99.4	98.9	99.3	98.9	95.4	95.0	94.6
Agricultural foods, feeds, and beverages, excluding distilled beverages	104.6	105.4	103.3	106.0	102.1	99.2	97.3	99.3	101.0	97.0	97.8	98.3
Nonagricultural foods (fish and distilled beverages)	95.0	95.7	95.4	97.9	98.5	99.7	102.3	99.2	94.5	92.2	89.2	86.8
Industrial Supplies and Materials	70.1	75.9	85.3	90.4	99.0	100.7	105.5	102.9	96.0	95.5	91.0	77.6
Fuels and lubricants	43.9	55.3	74.8	83.5	97.2	101.3	111.3	106.1	91.1	90.9	86.1	61.6
Paper and paper base stocks	90.1	88.4	90.1	93.4	95.5	100.0	103.2	104.5	104.4	100.0	93.9	90.7
Materials associated with nondurable supplies and materials	95.3	95.2	95.5	97.0	98.5	99.9	101.1	101.5	102.8	100.3	97.9	96.2
Selected building materials	103.0	109.0	108.3	106.1	107.1	100.3	94.3	94.7	91.9	111.1	103.7	92.9
Unfinished metals related to durable goods	83.3	84.6	86.0	90.9	102.7	100.7	101.5	99.5	99.5	93.6	87.1	82.1
Finished metals related to durable goods	99.8	99.7	99.2	100.0	100.6	100.5	100.3	99.4	98.3	99.4	98.2	97.9
Nonmetals related to durable goods	100.9	99.5	99.9	99.9	100.2	99.5	99.7	99.7	101.6	100.6	100.4	99.0
Industrial Supplies and Materials, Durable	92.4	94.1	94.6	96.7	102.9	100.4	99.6	98.5	98.1	99.1	94.1	89.1
Industrial Supplies and Materials, Excluding Fuels[1]	. . .	. . .	. . .	. . .	. . .	. . .	. . .	. . .	. . .	. . .	. . .	100.0
Industrial Supplies and Materials, Excluding Petroleum	89.9	90.9	92.6	94.8	98.9	99.9	101.0	105.4	102.1	99.8	94.2	90.0
Industrial Supplies and Materials, Nondurable, Excluding Petroleum	87.2	87.4	90.4	92.7	94.6	99.3	102.6	112.9	106.4	100.7	94.2	90.9
Capital Goods	103.5	102.1	101.4	101.0	100.5	100.0	99.7	98.9	98.7	97.7	96.8	96.2
Electric generating equipment	99.5	98.1	98.2	97.7	98.7	101.1	100.3	99.8	102.1	101.8	101.4	100.6
Nonelectrical machinery	104.5	103.0	102.1	101.6	100.9	99.9	99.5	98.6	98.0	96.7	95.6	94.9
Transportation equipment, excluding motor vehicles[1]	. . .	. . .	. . .	. . .	. . .	. . .	. . .	. . .	. . .	. . .	. . .	100.0
Automotive Parts and Accessories	97.8	98.2	98.5	99.1	99.4	100.9	100.3	100.0	99.3	98.7	98.0	97.4
Consumer Goods, Excluding Automotive	101.2	100.6	100.9	100.7	100.3	99.6	99.8	99.5	99.8	99.3	99.1	98.7
Nondurables, manufactured	101.0	100.4	100.8	100.6	100.3	99.6	99.8	99.6	100.2	99.8	99.6	99.7
Nonmanufactured consumer goods	99.2	98.2	100.1	100.0	100.3	98.2	99.8	99.0	99.3	99.2	97.9	96.4
All Imports, Excluding Fuels	. . .	. . .	. . .	. . .	. . .	. . .	. . .	. . .	. . .	. . .	. . .	100.0
All Imports, Excluding Petroleum	99.0	98.8	98.9	99.4	100.0	99.9	100.0	100.7	100.0	98.9	97.3	96.2

Commodity	2002				2003				2004			
	March	June	September	December	March	June	September	December	March	June	September	December
ALL COMMODITIES	92.8	94.1	95.5	95.2	99.1	96.2	96.2	97.5	100.2	101.7	104.1	104.0
Foods, Feeds, and Beverages	95.0	96.2	99.7	100.2	102.6	100.7	101.8	103.2	105.9	106.9	108.7	111.5
Agricultural foods, feeds, and beverages, excluding distilled beverages	99.5	101.3	105.4	106.0	109.6	107.1	108.3	110.9	113.0	114.3	116.4	120.7
Nonagricultural foods (fish and distilled beverages)	85.5	85.1	87.3	87.5	86.9	86.6	87.6	86.0	90.1	90.3	91.4	91.0
Industrial Supplies and Materials	84.9	89.8	95.2	94.6	109.7	98.2	98.9	103.6	112.7	119.3	128.5	126.4
Fuels and lubricants	76.4	85.8	96.2	94.7	125.2	100.3	99.4	107.2	120.2	130.9	146.2	141.0
Paper and paper base stocks	88.0	87.1	90.5	89.1	91.0	94.1	94.0	93.9	95.6	99.0	101.1	101.3
Materials associated with nondurable supplies and materials	95.9	97.1	99.4	100.1	104.2	103.0	102.5	104.4	105.4	106.0	108.0	109.8
Selected building materials	100.7	99.1	97.6	95.0	96.3	96.7	110.3	108.0	118.4	120.5	125.6	115.6
Unfinished metals related to durable goods	83.8	88.5	89.7	91.5	92.8	92.2	93.4	99.2	114.9	124.4	133.1	138.5
Finished metals related to durable goods	97.1	96.5	97.1	96.8	96.1	97.4	99.0	101.0	104.8	108.1	112.4	114.7
Nonmetals related to durable goods	97.2	96.7	96.9	97.1	97.9	98.2	97.5	98.2	99.3	98.7	98.8	99.7
Industrial Supplies and Materials, Durable	91.1	92.3	92.7	92.7	93.6	93.7	97.3	99.5	108.5	112.8	117.8	118.0
Industrial Supplies and Materials, Excluding Fuels[1]	101.0	102.1	103.4	103.6	105.8	105.7	107.9	110.1	116.5	119.8	124.1	124.8
Industrial Supplies and Materials, Excluding Petroleum	90.3	92.9	93.9	95.2	104.3	99.9	100.3	102.1	107.9	112.5	114.4	118.8
Industrial Supplies and Materials, Nondurable, Excluding Petroleum	89.3	93.4	95.2	98.1	117.1	107.2	103.8	105.0	107.1	112.0	110.2	119.7
Capital Goods	95.2	95.1	94.7	93.9	93.7	93.8	93.5	92.9	93.1	92.2	92.0	92.2
Electric generating equipment	95.5	95.1	95.7	94.9	95.5	96.6	95.8	96.8	97.8	97.0	97.4	98.0
Nonelectrical machinery	94.4	94.4	93.7	92.8	92.5	92.3	92.1	91.1	91.2	90.1	89.8	89.9
Transportation equipment, excluding motor vehicles[1]	100.5	100.4	101.0	101.0	101.6	102.0	102.2	102.8	103.5	104.0	103.9	104.5
Automotive Parts and Accessories	97.1	98.0	98.3	98.0	98.0	98.3	97.8	98.8	99.6	100.1	100.2	101.5
Consumer Goods, Excluding Automotive	98.2	98.1	98.1	98.0	97.9	98.1	97.9	98.1	98.7	98.5	98.4	99.0
Nondurables, manufactured	99.2	99.1	99.5	99.7	99.7	99.8	99.7	100.1	101.3	100.9	100.8	101.4
Nonmanufactured consumer goods	96.1	95.6	95.4	95.4	95.7	96.2	95.7	96.2	96.4	96.8	97.9	98.2
All Imports, Excluding Fuels	99.7	99.9	100.1	100.0	100.3	100.3	100.6	101.0	102.4	102.7	103.4	104.0
All Imports, Excluding Petroleum	95.8	96.2	96.4	96.5	98.1	97.3	97.3	97.7	99.1	99.7	100.1	101.3

[1]December 2001 = 100.
. . . = Not available.

Table 9-13. U.S. Import Price Indexes for Selected Categories of Goods, by End Use, 1999–2009—*Continued*

(2000 = 100, unless otherwise indicated.)

Commodity	2005				2006				2007			
	March	June	September	December	March	June	September	December	March	June	September	December
ALL COMMODITIES	107.8	109.2	114.4	112.3	112.7	117.3	116.2	115.1	115.9	120.0	121.8	127.3
Foods, Feeds, and Beverages	115.9	114.1	114.2	117.5	117.0	118.0	120.9	122.6	124.6	127.8	131.8	134.4
Agricultural foods, feeds, and beverages, excluding distilled beverages	125.7	123.5	122.6	127.2	125.4	126.8	130.4	133.7	135.1	139.5	144.4	148.3
Nonagricultural foods (fish and distilled beverages)	94.0	93.1	95.6	95.9	98.3	98.5	99.8	97.9	101.3	101.5	103.5	103.0
Industrial Supplies and Materials	139.8	145.5	167.2	158.6	160.4	178.1	172.2	166.6	169.8	185.6	190.7	211.3
Fuels and lubricants	165.6	178.0	222.1	202.4	201.5	230.2	216.3	204.3	209.6	238.2	250.0	290.3
Paper and paper base stocks	103.8	103.8	104.3	106.1	107.7	111.3	113.1	112.8	111.5	110.8	111.2	109.2
Materials associated with nondurable supplies and materials	113.0	113.5	117.3	117.8	119.3	120.6	121.8	123.0	124.0	125.4	128.2	135.3
Selected building materials	122.7	118.1	117.6	116.9	118.0	117.2	115.8	110.6	111.4	113.1	116.9	116.0
Unfinished metals related to durable goods	140.4	139.9	138.2	145.8	161.1	193.2	194.4	195.9	202.9	219.7	209.6	217.2
Finished metals related to durable goods	115.9	116.6	117.3	117.6	119.2	125.3	128.4	128.9	125.4	133.7	134.8	135.0
Nonmetals related to durable goods	100.8	100.9	100.7	100.5	100.8	101.1	101.3	101.7	101.8	101.6	102.5	103.8
Industrial Supplies and Materials, Durable	120.8	119.7	119.1	121.4	127.2	139.1	139.8	139.2	141.0	148.4	146.3	149.1
Industrial Supplies and Materials, Excluding Fuels[1]	128.0	127.5	128.5	130.3	134.9	143.7	144.7	144.7	146.2	151.6	151.2	155.4
Industrial Supplies and Materials, Excluding Petroleum	119.9	120.2	126.8	132.2	128.1	133.9	135.1	138.3	139.3	144.6	141.0	147.5
Industrial Supplies and Materials, Nondurable, Excluding Petroleum	118.7	120.7	135.4	144.3	128.3	126.7	128.5	136.3	136.3	139.1	133.6	144.5
Capital Goods	91.1	91.2	91.3	91.5	91.1	91.2	91.3	91.5	91.1	91.3	91.9	92.2
Electric generating equipment	98.8	98.8	99.0	99.3	100.1	102.1	102.7	103.0	104.3	105.7	106.5	107.9
Nonelectrical machinery	89.8	89.8	88.7	88.1	88.0	87.8	87.8	87.9	87.2	87.2	87.7	87.7
Transportation equipment, excluding motor vehicles[1]	105.6	106.0	106.4	106.1	107.0	107.9	108.3	109.1	110.1	111.0	113.4	114.7
Automotive Parts and Accessories	101.8	102.0	102.1	101.8	101.6	102.7	103.2	103.0	103.5	103.3	103.6	104.8
Consumer Goods, Excluding Automotive	99.9	99.9	99.7	99.6	99.6	99.8	100.5	101.0	101.3	101.4	102.1	102.6
Nondurables, manufactured	102.8	102.8	103.1	102.7	102.8	102.6	103.0	103.4	104.1	104.3	105.0	105.5
Nonmanufactured consumer goods	100.3	101.8	100.6	101.2	98.2	98.6	100.5	101.8	102.2	102.6	103.4	103.8
All Imports, Excluding Fuels	105.0	104.9	104.8	105.1	105.7	107.2	107.8	108.1	108.4	109.5	110.1	111.4
All Imports, Excluding Petroleum	102.0	102.0	102.8	103.7	103.0	104.2	104.8	105.7	105.9	107.1	107.1	108.9

Commodity	2008				2009			
	March	June	September	December	March	June	September	December
ALL COMMODITIES	133.5	145.5	137.8	114.5	113.6	120.0	121.3	124.4
Foods, Feeds, and Beverages	141.8	147.7	147.9	142.3	137.0	139.8	140.6	143.7
Agricultural foods, feeds, and beverages, excluding distilled beverages	157.3	165.1	165.1	159.4	151.3	155.5	156.8	160.8
Nonagricultural foods (fish and distilled beverages)	106.8	108.4	109.1	103.8	104.8	104.4	104.1	104.9
Industrial Supplies and Materials	234.5	283.0	248.9	150.4	149.3	177.3	183.0	196.2
Fuels and lubricants	329.0	423.7	346.3	153.9	162.3	222.1	228.5	249.7
Paper and paper base stocks	114.1	117.3	119.9	113.2	106.6	101.8	99.1	103.1
Materials associated with nondurable supplies and materials	147.8	152.9	162.4	148.5	136.7	137.5	134.8	140.6
Selected building materials	114.1	119.2	122.7	118.1	116.2	116.0	118.9	120.9
Unfinished metals related to durable goods	241.5	273.2	255.4	185.7	171.6	178.3	204.0	221.5
Finished metals related to durable goods	145.8	158.7	159.9	140.8	132.7	133.2	137.1	140.4
Nonmetals related to durable goods	105.2	107.6	111.4	109.0	105.2	103.0	104.3	105.4
Industrial Supplies and Materials, Durable	158.9	173.5	169.7	141.8	134.7	136.0	145.7	152.5
Industrial Supplies and Materials, Excluding Fuels[1]	166.8	178.8	179.5	155.1	145.5	146.5	151.7	158.6
Industrial Supplies and Materials, Excluding Petroleum	159.4	173.7	167.4	146.0	133.1	132.1	134.4	145.2
Industrial Supplies and Materials, Nondurable, Excluding Petroleum	159.3	173.0	163.5	150.8	131.0	127.4	121.0	136.3
Capital Goods	92.2	93.2	93.3	92.7	91.8	91.9	91.9	91.9
Electric generating equipment	109.3	112.0	112.9	111.4	109.4	110.0	110.3	111.3
Nonelectrical machinery	87.5	88.2	88.2	87.5	86.6	86.5	86.5	86.4
Transportation equipment, excluding motor vehicles[1]	115.3	117.7	118.2	120.2	120.6	122.4	123.2	122.6
Automotive Parts and Accessories	106.2	106.7	107.4	108.8	108.9	108.5	109.2	110.0
Consumer Goods, Excluding Automotive	104.0	104.9	105.1	104.4	103.9	104.3	104.1	104.3
Nondurables, manufactured	107.5	107.9	108.2	108.2	108.4	108.1	107.8	107.9
Nonmanufactured consumer goods	104.3	106.6	106.6	103.6	101.2	101.4	101.2	102.1
All Imports, Excluding Fuels	113.9	116.5	116.8	112.7	110.7	111.2	111.9	113.0
All Imports, Excluding Petroleum	111.6	114.9	114.0	109.9	107.3	107.4	107.9	109.7

[1]December 2001 = 100.

Table 9-14. U.S. Import Price Indexes for Selected Categories of Goods, by Locality of Origin, 1995–2009

(2000 = 100, unless otherwise indicated.)

Category and year	Percent of U.S. imports[1]	Month			
		March	June	September	December
INDUSTRIALIZED COUNTRIES[2]					
Total Goods	41.1				
1995		97.4	99.8	100.0	100.0
1996		99.7	98.8	99.3	99.4
1997		97.4	96.5	96.4	96.1
1998		94.6	94.0	93.3	93.8
1999		94.1	94.8	96.4	97.5
2000		99.5	100.1	100.9	101.4
2001		100.2	99.0	96.5	93.7
2002		94.3	95.7	96.9	96.7
2003		100.0	98.4	98.6	100.0
2004		103.4	104.7	106.3	107.5
2005		109.7	110.0	113.5	114.1
2006		113.5	117.4	117.0	116.4
2007		117.9	119.7	120.4	124.2
2008		130.9	139.6	135.1	119.1
2009		117.5	119.3	120.4	123.9
Manufactured Goods	34.9				
1995		100.0	102.6	102.9	102.9
1996		102.1	101.1	101.4	100.7
1997		99.5	98.9	98.8	98.6
1998		97.8	97.5	96.7	97.3
1999		97.6	97.7	98.1	98.9
2000		100.2	99.9	100.2	99.8
2001		99.9	99.2	97.6	96.0
2002		95.6	96.3	96.9	96.7
2003		97.8	97.7	98.2	99.4
2004		102.1	102.8	104.0	104.6
2005		106.3	106.6	106.7	107.7
2006		109.0	111.8	111.8	111.1
2007		112.5	113.5	114.5	116.3
2008		120.1	124.3	124.2	115.7
2009		114.9	114.9	116.1	117.9
Nonmanufactured Goods	5.7				
1995		66.3	67.6	65.2	66.0
1996		71.6	72.3	76.0	84.3
1997		73.3	68.9	69.4	68.5
1998		59.3	56.8	57.2	55.7
1999		56.9	65.1	78.7	83.2
2000		92.7	102.2	107.5	118.2
2001		103.9	97.2	85.2	69.9
2002		82.9	93.8	102.4	102.7
2003		134.3	113.7	108.9	112.4
2004		122.9	133.1	138.7	147.1
2005		156.7	158.0	203.0	199.2
2006		170.9	190.0	183.7	184.9
2007		185.6	197.9	195.4	228.2
2008		275.6	346.8	279.0	154.5
2009		143.9	170.6	169.1	198.8
OTHER COUNTRIES					
Total Goods	58.9				
1995		97.5	98.7	97.4	97.6
1996		99.8	99.0	101.3	102.7
1997		100.6	99.4	98.7	96.6
1998		92.4	90.7	89.5	86.8
1999		87.7	90.3	94.5	96.9
2000		99.8	100.4	102.5	99.5
2001		97.0	96.6	95.0	88.6
2002		90.9	92.2	94.3	93.4
2003		96.7	93.1	93.3	94.1
2004		96.3	97.9	101.5	99.7
2005		105.0	107.0	112.1	109.5
2006		110.8	115.5	114.0	111.8
2007		113.1	118.0	121.1	127.5
2008		133.3	147.3	139.0	111.2
2009		110.3	118.7	120.0	122.1

[1]Based on 2008 trade values.
[2]Includes Western Europe, Canada, Japan, Australia, New Zealand and South Africa.

Table 9-14. U.S. Import Price Indexes for Selected Categories of Goods, by Locality of Origin, 1995–2009
—Continued

(2000 = 100, unless otherwise indicated.)

Category and year	Percent of U.S. imports[1]	Month			
		March	June	September	December
Manufactured Goods	43.0				
1995		107.3	108.8	108.6	108.4
1996		108.9	108.4	107.9	108.6
1997		108.4	107.8	107.0	105.3
1998		103.5	102.2	100.6	99.6
1999		98.8	98.9	99.0	99.3
2000		99.8	99.7	100.3	100.2
2001		99.6	98.8	97.9	96.0
2002		95.6	95.9	96.2	95.8
2003		96.5	95.1	95.1	94.5
2004		95.2	96.2	97.2	97.1
2005		98.4	98.7	99.3	99.6
2006		99.4	101.2	101.2	100.7
2007		102.0	103.6	104.1	106.0
2008		107.8	111.8	111.3	103.4
2009		101.7	103.5	104.3	104.5
Nonmanufactured Goods	15.7				
1995		69.5	70.3	66.1	67.3
1996		73.7	72.1	80.9	84.5
1997		75.8	72.6	72.2	68.8
1998		57.1	54.9	54.5	46.8
1999		53.0	63.6	80.3	89.2
2000		99.9	102.4	109.2	97.4
2001		88.9	89.7	86.1	65.3
2002		81.3	88.2	99.6	96.4
2003		113.3	98.0	98.8	106.5
2004		118.1	123.2	141.5	130.3
2005		158.0	169.5	199.8	181.3
2006		191.7	215.4	204.6	191.1
2007		192.4	220.6	241.6	279.0
2008		314.6	402.3	336.0	160.2
2009		166.8	225.6	231.3	247.8
CANADA					
Total Goods	15.9				
1995		92.1	93.8	94.8	94.7
1996		94.3	93.5	93.8	95.1
1997		93.2	92.6	93.2	92.0
1998		90.1	89.7	89.3	88.7
1999		88.8	90.6	93.5	94.7
2000		97.2	99.8	102.4	105.6
2001		102.6	101.8	97.0	93.2
2002		96.1	97.8	99.6	99.2
2003		106.6	103.1	103.9	104.4
2004		110.0	112.3	114.4	116.6
2005		120.1	119.6	128.2	129.6
2006		125.4	130.6	129.7	129.2
2007		130.2	135.0	135.0	142.3
2008		152.0	171.2	160.1	129.8
2009		124.4	129.0	131.1	137.7
Manufactured Goods	10.3				
1995		98.0	99.4	100.7	100.5
1996		99.0	98.0	97.7	97.4
1997		98.0	98.0	98.3	97.3
1998		96.7	96.6	96.3	95.5
1999		95.5	96.1	96.9	97.7
2000		98.8	98.9	101.3	101.8
2001		101.6	102.8	99.9	98.1
2002		99.1	98.7	99.5	98.9
2003		100.9	101.1	103.2	103.3
2004		107.4	108.2	110.3	110.7
2005		113.7	112.9	113.1	115.6
2006		117.2	120.0	119.9	118.7
2007		119.5	123.7	125.3	127.6
2008		128.8	137.5	138.7	126.8
2009		122.7	123.0	125.8	127.3

[1]Based on 2008 trade values.

Table 9-14. U.S. Import Price Indexes for Selected Categories of Goods, by Locality of Origin, 1995–2009
—*Continued*

(2000 = 100, unless otherwise indicated.)

Category and year	Percent of U.S. imports[1]	Month			
		March	June	September	December
Nonmanufactured Goods	5.3				
1995		61.7	64.4	63.9	64.8
1996		70.3	70.7	74.4	84.3
1997		69.9	66.6	68.1	66.4
1998		58.4	56.6	56.5	56.3
1999		56.5	64.2	76.8	79.9
2000		89.3	103.6	107.6	124.4
2001		108.1	97.9	83.1	69.8
2002		83.8	96.8	104.1	104.9
2003		143.1	119.0	111.5	114.0
2004		126.1	138.0	138.9	150.5
2005		157.9	159.8	210.8	207.4
2006		171.3	189.2	183.1	187.1
2007		187.8	195.9	187.7	222.3
2008		273.7	345.1	273.0	150.8
2009		139.7	163.4	161.6	192.5
EUROPEAN UNION					
Total Goods	16.8				
1995		97.7	99.5	99.7	100.4
1996		101.3	101.0	101.7	101.9
1997		100.5	100.0	99.1	100.1
1998		98.9	98.8	98.7	99.4
1999		98.8	99.1	99.9	100.3
2000		100.8	100.1	100.0	98.9
2001		99.0	98.8	98.2	97.4
2002		97.4	99.2	101.0	100.9
2003		103.2	102.8	102.8	104.3
2004		107.4	108.5	110.0	111.6
2005		113.8	114.1	115.7	114.5
2006		117.7	120.4	120.5	119.6
2007		121.3	121.6	122.3	124.1
2008		129.7	133.9	131.5	124.3
2009		123.6	124.4	125.4	127.4
Manufactured Goods	16.5				
1995		98.6	100.4	100.9	101.5
1996		102.3	101.8	102.4	102.3
1997		101.0	100.8	100.1	101.0
1998		100.4	100.6	100.5	101.5
1999		100.9	100.6	100.8	100.8
2000		100.8	99.9	99.6	98.6
2001		99.2	98.8	98.7	98.4
2002		98.1	99.9	101.5	101.4
2003		103.3	103.2	103.2	104.5
2004		107.4	108.4	109.3	110.9
2005		112.8	113.0	113.8	112.9
2006		116.0	118.0	118.4	118.0
2007		119.5	119.2	119.7	121.1
2008		126.5	130.1	128.2	121.8
2009		121.5	122.1	123.0	124.9
Nonmanufactured Goods	0.2				
1995		72.8	74.5	71.2	73.0
1996		78.8	80.6	85.7	91.7
1997		89.3	82.2	76.5	78.4
1998		65.6	58.7	58.8	53.4
1999		53.6	66.6	81.3	88.7
2000		100.4	102.9	107.9	106.2
2001		96.0	99.5	89.1	75.7
2002		86.6	88.7	99.6	104.1
2003		118.8	106.7	111.5	118.8
2004		128.4	135.1	157.9	163.1
2005		177.1	177.5	209.7	191.1
2006		211.4	231.9	219.9	198.7
2007		205.2	234.6	274.9	304.8
2008		323.4	400.2	332.3	230.8
2009		188.3	230.0	235.3	250.2

[1]Based on 2008 trade values.

Table 9-14. U.S. Import Price Indexes for Selected Categories of Goods, by Locality of Origin, 1995–2009
    —Continued

(2000 = 100, unless otherwise indicated.)

Category and year	Percent of U.S. imports[1]	Month			
		March	June	September	December
LATIN AMERICA					
Total Goods	18.0				
1998		84.3	83.9	83.0	80.4
1999		81.7	85.3	90.7	94.2
2000		98.9	100.9	103.5	99.5
2001		99.5	98.9	97.2	90.6
2002		94.0	96.2	100.0	98.9
2003		104.8	99.6	99.8	102.6
2004		106.3	108.6	114.7	113.1
2005		122.1	126.3	133.8	131.0
2006		134.0	142.8	140.2	136.4
2007		138.1	146.3	152.3	161.5
2008		171.6	193.9	181.7	135.4
2009		132.1	146.7	148.5	154.0
Manufactured Goods	11.7				
1998		94.8	95.0	93.8	93.5
1999		92.0	93.6	94.6	96.0
2000		98.3	99.6	101.6	102.3
2001		104.2	103.5	102.5	101.4
2002		101.5	102.4	104.2	103.8
2003		108.2	103.6	104.4	105.8
2004		107.5	109.1	112.0	113.9
2005		117.1	118.6	120.1	122.2
2006		123.2	128.9	128.4	125.8
2007		127.4	131.4	132.5	134.3
2008		139.3	146.0	145.4	127.7
2009		121.7	125.0	126.5	129.3
Nonmanufactured Goods	6.2				
1998		60.8	59.7	59.4	51.9
1999		59.3	67.2	82.1	90.2
2000		100.2	103.5	107.8	93.6
2001		89.3	89.0	86.0	67.3
2002		83.5	90.7	103.0	99.3
2003		111.7	103.5	100.9	109.8
2004		121.1	125.9	144.6	130.1
2005		161.0	175.1	205.1	184.6
2006		195.5	217.2	205.7	197.1
2007		199.3	225.0	250.7	289.5
2008		320.9	409.2	348.3	181.5
2009		188.9	254.3	257.1	273.9
CHINA					
Total Goods	16.4				
2004		99.5	99.7	99.6	99.0
2005		98.8	98.8	98.4	98.5
2006		97.9	97.4	97.4	97.3
2007		97.4	98.1	99.1	99.6
2008		101.1	102.8	103.7	102.4
2009		100.9	100.4	100.5	100.6

[1]Based on 2008 trade values.

Table 9-14. U.S. Import Price Indexes for Selected Categories of Goods, by Locality of Origin, 1995–2009
—Continued

(2000 = 100, unless otherwise indicated.)

Category and year	Percent of U.S. imports[1]	Month			
		March	June	September	December
JAPAN					
Total Goods	6.7				
1995		108.6	112.5	112.0	111.0
1996		110.1	108.4	107.8	106.5
1997		104.6	103.2	102.7	101.0
1998		99.8	98.2	96.8	98.0
1999		98.2	98.2	98.6	99.6
2000		99.6	100.0	99.9	99.9
2001		99.4	98.6	97.8	97.0
2002		95.6	95.4	95.0	94.6
2003		94.4	94.2	93.8	94.7
2004		95.2	95.1	95.3	95.9
2005		95.9	95.8	95.8	95.2
2006		94.6	94.7	94.4	94.1
2007		93.9	94.0	93.9	94.2
2008		94.6	95.1	94.9	96.0
2009		96.3	96.9	97.2	97.8
ASIAN NEWLY INDUSTRIALIZED COUNTRIES[2]					
Total Goods	5.0				
1995		120.9	121.3	121.5	120.8
1996		120.6	119.6	118.1	117.3
1997		116.6	115.3	113.8	111.3
1998		108.7	105.2	103.0	102.0
1999		101.3	100.8	100.7	100.8
2000		100.6	99.9	100.0	99.3
2001		97.3	96.4	95.2	93.8
2002		93.3	92.6	92.5	91.3
2003		91.2	91.5	91.7	90.9
2004		90.3	90.6	91.0	90.6
2005		90.9	90.0	89.7	88.5
2006		88.8	89.2	89.3	89.1
2007		88.7	88.5	88.8	88.9
2008		89.2	91.1	93.2	89.2
2009		85.4	85.7	86.1	86.5

[1]Based on 2008 trade values.
[2]Includes Western Europe, Canada, Japan, Australia, New Zealand and South Africa.

Table 9-15. U.S. International Price Indexes for Selected Transportation Services, 1995–2009

(2000 = 100.)

Category and year	March	June	September	December
AIR FREIGHT				
Import Air Freight				
1995	115.8	118.7	112.9	115.1
1996	113.7	112.2	112.0	110.6
1997	104.1	104.5	102.5	100.1
1998	93.0	94.2	92.8	100.2
1999	101.5	98.7	100.6	102.8
2000	100.7	100.1	100.2	99.0
2001	98.9	96.0	95.9	95.6
2002	96.7	99.7	101.2	106.9
2003	110.2	111.5	116.8	114.9
2004	117.1	117.5	120.0	126.8
2005	128.6	128.4	129.7	128.9
2006	129.7	135.2	133.1	131.2
2007	130.7	132.3	134.2	141.8
2008	144.4	158.7	157.1	138.5
2009	132.9	132.8	134.8	163.9
Export Air Freight				
1996	. . .	. . .	. . .	112.9
1997	111.1	110.4	109.0	105.4
1998	107.1	106.6	108.0	109.2
1999	102.1	102.5	100.8	99.1
2000	99.1	100.8	100.8	99.4
2001	99.7	98.4	98.6	97.9
2002	95.5	97.9	98.3	95.2
2003	96.3	95.2	95.1	95.4
2004	97.1	99.1	100.3	106.1
2005	106.4	110.1	110.9	112.0
2006	113.6	115.9	117.9	116.7
2007	117.0	117.0	119.8	127.1
2008	132.0	140.8	144.3	135.0
2009	124.1	117.4	121.6	122.9
Inbound Air Freight				
1995	113.6	116.5	111.0	111.7
1996	108.6	107.7	108.2	107.6
1997	101.3	101.8	100.3	97.9
1998	93.9	94.4	92.7	99.0
1999	99.6	97.6	99.5	102.8
2000	100.7	100.1	100.2	99.0
2001	97.9	95.1	94.9	95.1
2002	93.9	98.3	100.3	105.9
2003	108.8	109.4	112.5	112.9
2004	116.2	116.6	118.7	125.1
2005	126.3	125.6	127.5	124.6
2006	124.6	129.2	128.9	127.1
2007	126.6	127.3	129.6	138.1
2008	140.7	152.1	151.6	136.8
2009	127.5	125.1	127.4	147.3
Outbound Air Freight				
1995	108.2	108.1	108.6	107.8
1996	107.3	107.6	107.0	107.3
1997	108.0	107.3	107.7	105.7
1998	105.2	103.8	103.7	103.0
1999	100.3	100.4	100.3	99.2
2000	99.2	100.3	100.2	100.2
2001	100.1	98.0	97.6	97.8
2002	95.9	98.4	97.3	95.4
2003	97.2	95.4	95.5	94.9
2004	96.1	99.0	100.7	104.7
2005	103.8	107.2	112.4	112.0
2006	113.5	117.2	116.9	113.8
2007	112.3	114.3	117.0	124.3
2008	128.9	143.7	147.0	130.4
2009	119.7	112.1	111.9	114.6

. . . = Not available.

Table 9-15. U.S. International Price Indexes for Selected Transportation Services, 1995–2009—*Continued*

(2000 = 100.)

Category and year	March	June	September	December
AIR PASSENGER FARES				
Import Air Passenger Fares				
1995	80.2	88.1	86.4	82.6
1996	82.0	88.1	86.8	84.3
1997	84.7	95.5	94.0	88.0
1998	87.1	94.9	95.1	88.6
1999	87.5	98.9	99.5	89.7
2000	92.5	103.5	105.1	98.9
2001	101.1	112.8	116.4	105.7
2002	103.1	119.1	125.2	107.2
2003	108.6	122.3	125.9	107.0
2004	103.6	123.1	121.0	111.7
2005	110.0	128.1	124.0	116.3
2006	114.9	136.7	130.9	125.4
2007	122.9	144.6	140.2	135.3
2008	131.3	171.6	161.3	157.3
2009	134.9	147.3	137.9	152.3
Export Air Passenger Fares				
1995	92.4	99.4	96.4	91.6
1996	93.0	94.4	97.7	94.7
1997	85.3	97.7	95.0	87.4
1998	89.5	90.2	90.6	93.1
1999	95.5	96.8	100.6	98.6
2000	98.1	101.5	102.6	97.7
2001	99.6	100.4	102.5	98.4
2002	97.5	103.2	108.1	103.2
2003	108.4	117.0	118.0	118.4
2004	123.2	123.8	130.1	134.0
2005	136.3	136.2	139.5	128.3
2006	130.8	139.3	142.4	137.3
2007	140.2	147.3	154.6	155.7
2008	156.4	171.4	171.9	164.6
2009	141.7	138.2	141.3	156.1

Chapter Ten

INTERNATIONAL LABOR COMPARISONS

INTERNATIONAL LABOR COMPARISONS

HIGHLIGHTS

This chapter compares several summary statistics of labor force status, manufacturing productivity, and consumer prices for the United States with similar statistics for other countries. Different concepts and methodologies can make comparisons between countries difficult, but the Bureau of Labor Statistics (BLS) makes adjustments to reconcile as much of the data as possible.

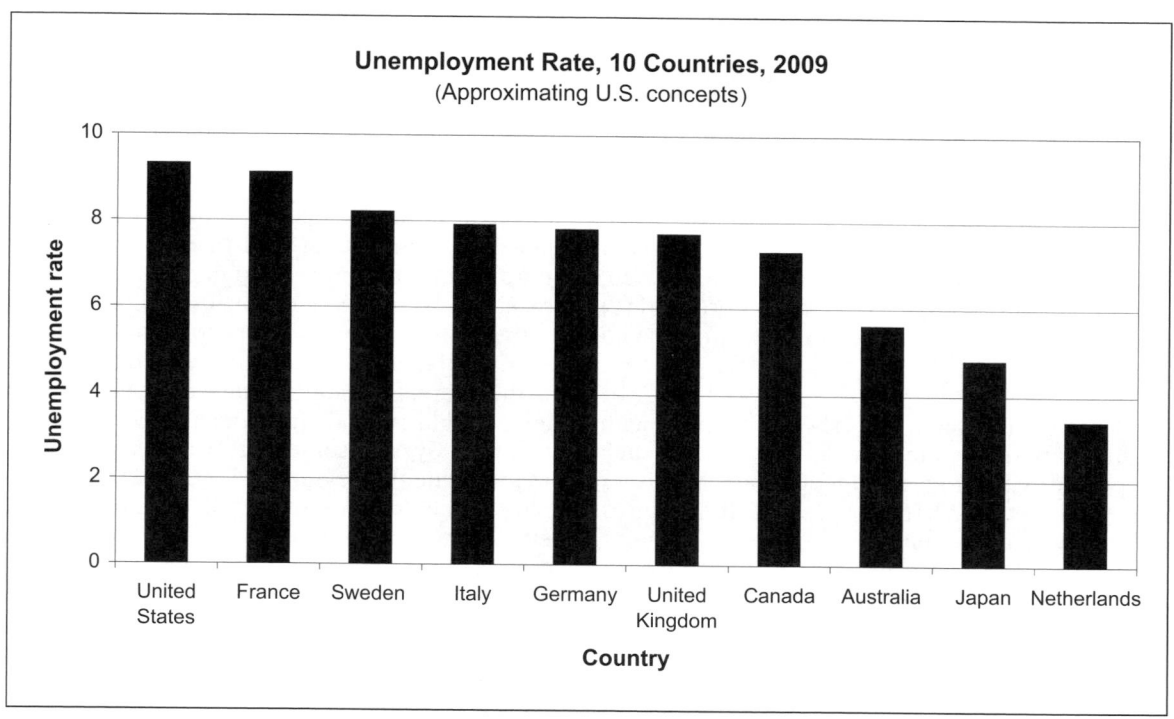

Unemployment Rate, 10 Countries, 2009
(Approximating U.S. concepts)

Unemployment rates have typically been higher in Western European countries than in the United States, however, in 2009, the U.S. had the highest unemployment rate of all countries compared. The unemployment rate in the United States increased significantly in 2009 from 5.8 to 9.3—the highest the unemployment rate has been since 1983. (See Table 10-1.)

OTHER HIGHLIGHTS

- The unemployment rate grew in 2009 for each of the 10 countries compared. The United States experienced the highest increase in its unemployment rate (3.5 percent) followed by Sweden (2.2 percent), Canada, and the United Kingdom (both at 2.0 percent) (See Table 10-1.)

- In 2009, the unemployment rates for men ranged from 3.4 percent in the Netherlands to 10.3 percent in the United States while the unemployment rates for women ranged from 3.5 in the Netherlands to 9.3 percent in Italy and France. (See Table 10-2.) The unemployment rates among youth also varied by country, ranging from 6.7 percent in the Netherlands to 25.7 percent in Italy. Youth are defined as 16- to 24-year-olds in the United States, Canada, France, Sweden, and the United Kingdom; otherwise, they are defined as 15- to 24-year-olds. (See Table 10-3.)

- The percent of women in the labor force continued to increase in each county compared except for Sweden where the share of women in the labor force declined slightly from 47.5 to 47.4 percent in 2009 (See Table 10-5.)

- Real gross domestic product (GDP) per capita, stated in U.S. dollars, declined in all of the 16 countries compared in Table 10-12. The United States, which experienced a decrease of 3.5 percent, had the second highest real gross domestic product (GDP) per capita in 2009 ($45,918), exceeded only by Norway ($55,653). (See Table 10-12.)

NOTES AND DEFINITIONS

Collection and Coverage

From its inception, the Bureau of Labor Statistics (BLS) has conducted a program of research and statistical analysis that compares labor conditions in the United States with those in selected foreign countries. The principal comparative measures of the International Labor Comparisons (ILC) program (formerly called the Foreign Labor Statistics program) cover the labor force, employment, and unemployment; trends in labor productivity and unit labor costs in manufacturing; hourly compensation costs for manufacturing production workers, and consumer prices. All of the measures are based upon statistical data and other source materials from (a) the statistical agencies of the foreign countries studied; (b) international and supranational bodies such as the United Nations, the International Labour Office (ILO), the Organisation for Economic Co-operation and Development (OECD), and the Statistical Office of the European Communities (EUROSTAT), which attempt to obtain comparable country data; and (c) private agencies such as banks, industry associations, and research institutions.

International statistical comparisons should be made with caution, as the statistical concepts and methods in each country are primarily fashioned to meet domestic (rather than international) needs. Whenever possible, BLS adjusts the data to improve comparability.

Labor Force, Employment, and Unemployment

To compare unemployment across countries, BLS publishes monthly, quarterly, and annual unemployment rates for 10 countries that have been adjusted as closely as possible to U.S. concepts. The 10 countries are the United States, Canada, Australia, Japan, France, Germany, Italy, the Netherlands, Sweden, and the United Kingdom. BLS publishes additional annual labor force statistics on a civilian basis for the same 10 countries: working-age population, labor force, employment by major economic sector (agriculture, industry, manufacturing, and services), unemployment, employment-population ratios by sex, unemployment rates by age and sex, and women's share of the labor force.

Foreign country data are adjusted as closely as possible to the U.S. definitions. Primary areas of adjustment address conceptual differences in upper age limits and definitions of employment and unemployment, provided that reliable data are available to make these adjustments. Adjustments are made where applicable to include employed and unemployed persons above upper age limits; some European countries do not include persons older than age 64 in their labor force measures, because a large portion of this population has retired. Adjustments are made to exclude active duty military from employment figures, although a small number of career military may be included in some

European countries. Adjustments are made to exclude unpaid family workers who worked fewer than 15 hours per week from employment figures; U.S. concepts do not include them in employment; most foreign countries include all unpaid family workers regardless of the number of hours worked. Adjustments are made to include full-time students seeking work and available for work as unemployed when they are classified as not in the labor force.

Where possible, lower age limits are based on the age at which compulsory schooling ends in each country, rather than based on the U.S. standard of 16 years of age and over. Lower age limits have ranged between 13 and 16 over the years covered; currently, the lower age limits are either 15 or 16 in all 10 countries.

Some adjustments for comparability are not made because data are unavailable for adjustment purposes. For example, no adjustments to unemployment are usually made for deviations from U.S. concepts in the treatment of persons waiting to start a new job or passive job seekers. These conceptual differences have little impact on the measures. Furthermore, BLS studies have concluded that no adjustments should be made for persons on layoff who are counted as employed in some countries because of their strong job attachment as evidenced by, for example, payment of salary or the existence of a recall date. In the United States, persons on layoff have weaker job attachment and are classified as unemployed. Finally, employment data by economic sector are not fully comparable with U.S. definitions for some countries because all data required to make adjustments at the sector level are not available. Therefore, the sum of employment by sector may not equal total adjusted employment

Hourly Compensation Costs

Measures of hourly compensation costs are prepared by BLS to assess international differences in manufacturing employer labor costs. For several reasons, comparisons based on the more readily available average earnings statistics published by many countries can be misleading. National definitions of average earnings differ considerably; average earnings do not include all items of labor compensation, and the omitted items of compensation frequently represent a large proportion of total compensation. For many years, data on hourly compensation costs covered production workers only; recently, the series has been extended to cover all employees as well.

Hourly compensation costs include (1) hourly direct pay and (2) employer social insurance expenditures and other labor taxes. Hourly direct pay includes all payments made directly to the worker, before payroll deductions of any kind, consisting of pay for time worked and other direct pay. Social insurance expenditures and other labor taxes include employer expenditures for legally required insurance programs, contractual and private benefit plans, and other labor taxes. Other labor taxes refer to taxes on payrolls or employment (or reductions to reflect subsidies), even if they do not finance programs that directly benefit workers, because such taxes are regarded as labor costs.

Productivity and Unit Labor Costs

Time series indexes of manufacturing labor productivity (output per hour) and unit labor costs are constructed from three basic aggregate measures: Total real output, hours worked, and nominal compensation. Indexes for unit labor costs are prepared on a national currency basis and, using currency exchange rates, a U.S. dollar basis. With the additional collection of annual employment in manufacturing and the use of consumer price indexes, a total of 15 time series indexes are constructed.

The employment, hours, and compensation measures refer to employees (wage and salary workers) in Belgium and Taiwan and to all employed persons (employees plus the self-employed and unpaid family workers) in all other economies.

In general, the measures relate to total manufacturing as defined by the International Standard Industrial Classification (ISIC). However, the measures for France include parts of mining. Data for the United States are in accordance with the North American Industry Classification System (NAICS), except compensation data before 1987, which are based on SIC 1987. Canadian data are in accordance with NAICS 97 starting in 1961.

The data for the most recent years are based on the United Nations System of National Accounts 1993 (SNA 93). For earlier years, data were compiled according to previously used systems.

To obtain historical time series, BLS sometimes links together data series that were compiled according to different accounting systems by national statistical offices.

Consumer Price Index

The indexes and percent changes in this chapter are based upon national consumer price indexes as published by each country. They have not been adjusted for comparability. National differences exist, for example, in population coverage, frequency of market basket weight changes, and treatment of homeowner costs. The data in these tables are not available in this form from the foreign statistical agencies.

The indexes in Table 10-10 are calculated by rebasing the official indexes of each country to the official U.S. base year. Because of the change in base year, the indexes may differ from the official indexes published by national statistical agencies.

Percent change in Table 10-11 is computed using the compound rate method. The figures may differ from official percent changes published by national statistical agencies because of rounding. In Sweden and Switzerland, the national statistical agencies calculate the official percent changes from more precise index values than those that they publish.

Real Gross Domestic Product per Capita and per Employed Person

Measures of gross domestic product (GDP), population, and employment are obtained from national statistical sources. While these data are generally comparable to one another, some differences remain in the countries' statistical methodologies, which may affect comparability. The GDP measures used for all countries come from their national accounts sources. For all countries, the most recent series use the 1993 United Nations System of National Accounts (SNA 93). However, some earlier series have been prepared using 1968 United Nations System of National Accounts (SNA 68). The U.S. GDP series is based on the system of national income and product accounts (NIPAs) estimated by the Bureau of Economic Analysis (BEA).

Sources of Additional Information

An extensive description of the methodology can be found in Chapter 12 in the *BLS Handbook of Methods*. For more information on international comparisons see the BLS report titled, "International Comparisons of Annual Labor Force Statistics, Adjusted to U.S. Concepts, 10 Countries, 1970–2009" on the BLS Web site at <http://www.bls.gov/fls/>.

Table 10-1. Employment Status of the Working-Age Population, Adjusted to U.S. Concepts, 10 Countries, 1970–2009

(Numbers in thousands, percent.)

Category and year	United States	Canada	Australia	Japan	France	Germany[1]	Italy	Netherlands	Sweden	United Kingdom
Employed										
1970	78 678	7 919	5 388	50 150	20 270	26 107	19 083	. . .	3 850	. . .
1971	79 367	8 104	5 517	50 470	20 420	26 222	19 016	. . .	3 854	24 315
1972	82 153	8 344	5 601	50 590	20 540	26 289	18 710	. . .	3 856	24 385
1973	85 064	8 761	5 765	51 920	20 840	26 593	18 874	5 050	3 873	24 777
1974	86 794	9 125	5 891	51 710	21 030	26 247	19 284	5 100	3 956	24 849
1975	85 846	9 284	5 866	51 530	20 869	25 536	19 395	5 070	4 056	24 758
1976	88 752	9 652	5 946	52 030	21 041	25 396	19 504	5 100	4 082	24 611
1977	92 017	9 825	6 000	52 720	21 235	25 428	19 668	5 210	4 093	24 638
1978	96 048	10 124	6 038	53 370	21 326	25 647	19 725	5 260	4 109	24 774
1979	98 824	10 561	6 111	54 040	21 392	26 074	19 932	5 350	4 174	25 031
1980	99 303	10 872	6 284	54 600	21 443	26 486	20 195	5 520	4 226	24 917
1981	100 397	11 192	6 416	55 060	21 345	26 453	20 279	5 550	4 219	24 256
1982	99 526	10 847	6 415	55 620	21 390	26 149	20 246	5 520	4 213	23 782
1983	100 834	10 936	6 300	56 550	21 378	25 765	20 320	5 420	4 218	23 607
1984	105 005	11 211	6 494	56 870	21 199	25 826	20 392	5 490	4 249	24 115
1985	107 150	11 557	6 697	57 250	21 128	26 018	20 492	5 650	4 293	24 422
1986	109 597	11 895	6 984	57 740	21 244	26 383	20 614	5 740	4 326	24 578
1987	112 440	12 221	7 142	58 310	21 321	26 584	20 591	5 756	4 340	25 073
1988	114 968	12 591	7 413	59 300	21 521	26 799	20 868	5 917	4 410	25 905
1989	117 342	12 876	7 734	60 490	21 842	27 201	20 773	6 048	4 480	26 588
1990	118 793	12 964	7 877	61 710	22 075	27 952	21 080	6 251	4 513	26 713
1991	117 718	12 754	7 698	62 920	22 113	36 871	21 364	6 427	4 447	26 007
1992	118 492	12 643	7 660	63 630	22 000	36 390	21 233	6 559	4 265	25 388
1993	120 259	12 705	7 699	63 830	21 715	35 989	20 549	6 554	4 027	25 162
1994	123 060	12 975	7 942	63 860	22 350	35 756	20 176	6 614	3 990	25 374
1995	124 900	13 210	8 256	63 900	22 547	35 780	20 034	6 821	4 053	25 694
1996	126 708	13 338	8 364	64 200	22 640	35 637	20 124	6 966	4 014	25 941
1997	129 558	13 637	8 444	64 900	22 791	35 508	20 169	7 189	3 974	26 413
1998	131 463	13 973	8 618	64 450	23 224	36 059	20 370	7 408	4 036	26 684
1999	133 488	14 331	8 762	63 920	23 712	36 042	20 617	7 605	4 116	27 058
2000	136 891	14 681	8 989	63 790	24 326	36 236	20 973	7 813	4 230	27 375
2001	136 933	14 866	9 088	63 460	24 792	36 350	21 359	8 014	4 303	27 604
2002	136 485	15 223	9 271	62 650	24 976	36 018	21 666	8 114	4 311	27 815
2003	137 736	15 586	9 485	62 510	24 990	35 615	21 972	8 069	4 301	28 077
2004	139 252	15 861	9 662	62 640	25 016	35 604	22 124	8 052	4 279	28 380
2005	141 730	16 080	9 998	62 910	25 187	36 185	22 290	8 056	4 334	28 674
2006	144 427	16 393	10 255	63 210	25 446	36 978	22 721	8 205	4 416	28 929
2007	146 047	16 767	10 539	63 509	25 806	37 815	22 953	8 408	4 530	29 129
2008	145 362	17 025	10 777	63 250	25 951	38 406	23 144	8 537	4 581	29 346
2009	139 877	16 769	10 809	62 242	25 755	38 324	22 765	8 542	4 486	28 880
Unemployed										
1970	4 093	476	91	590	530	140	640	. . .	59	. . .
1971	5 016	535	107	640	580	160	640	. . .	101	1 058
1972	4 882	553	150	730	610	190	740	. . .	107	1 116
1973	4 365	515	136	680	590	190	720	160	98	946
1974	5 156	514	162	730	630	420	620	190	80	948
1975	7 929	690	303	1 000	793	890	690	270	67	1 174
1976	7 406	716	298	1 080	893	890	790	290	66	1 414
1977	6 991	836	358	1 100	1 015	900	840	270	75	1 470
1978	6 202	898	405	1 240	1 063	870	850	280	94	1 453
1979	6 137	831	408	1 170	1 212	780	920	290	88	1 432
1980	7 637	854	409	1 140	1 306	770	920	350	86	1 833
1981	8 273	887	394	1 260	1 547	1 090	1 040	540	108	2 609
1982	10 678	1 298	495	1 360	1 692	1 560	1 160	630	137	2 875
1983	10 717	1 437	697	1 560	1 766	1 900	1 270	700	151	3 081
1984	8 539	1 377	641	1 610	2 074	1 970	1 280	710	136	3 241
1985	8 312	1 293	603	1 470	2 210	2 010	1 310	600	124	3 151
1986	8 237	1 205	601	1 630	2 234	1 860	1 680	640	117	3 160
1987	7 425	1 123	612	1 570	2 272	1 800	1 760	622	100	2 940
1988	6 701	999	558	1 440	2 194	1 810	1 790	609	86	2 445
1989	6 528	982	490	1 340	2 052	1 640	1 760	558	74	2 082
1990	7 047	1 083	563	1 280	1 995	1 460	1 590	516	84	2 053
1991	8 628	1 386	788	1 270	2 047	2 204	1 580	490	147	2 530
1992	9 613	1 507	897	1 350	2 283	2 615	1 680	478	261	2 821
1993	8 940	1 533	914	1 600	2 559	3 113	2 227	437	416	2 928
1994	7 996	1 372	829	1 720	2 726	3 318	2 421	492	426	2 674
1995	7 404	1 246	739	1 920	2 584	3 200	2 544	523	404	2 441
1996	7 236	1 285	751	2 040	2 743	3 505	2 555	489	441	2 301
1997	6 739	1 248	759	2 110	2 785	3 907	2 584	423	445	1 991
1998	6 210	1 162	721	2 540	2 685	3 693	2 634	337	368	1 791
1999	5 880	1 072	652	2 810	2 630	3 333	2 559	277	313	1 728
2000	5 692	956	602	2 920	2 265	3 065	2 388	239	260	1 587
2001	6 801	1 026	658	3 020	2 075	3 110	2 164	186	227	1 489
2002	8 378	1 143	630	3 216	2 137	3 396	2 062	231	234	1 528
2003	8 774	1 147	599	2 985	2 295	3 661	2 048	310	264	1 488
2004	8 149	1 093	551	2 726	2 408	4 107	1 960	387	300	1 423
2005	7 591	1 028	531	2 476	2 429	4 575	1 889	402	360	1 463
2006	7 001	958	516	2 346	2 435	4 272	1 673	336	330	1 670
2007	7 078	929	482	2 400	2 222	3 601	1 506	278	292	1 652
2008	8 924	962	477	2 410	2 070	3 136	1 692	243	294	1 780
2009	14 265	1 329	638	3 120	2 576	3 222	1 945	304	401	2 395

[1]Unified Germany from 1991 onward; data for previous years relate to the former West Germany.
. . . = Not available.

Table 10-1. Employment Status of the Working-Age Population, Adjusted to U.S. Concepts, 10 Countries, 1970–2009—*Continued*

(Numbers in thousands, percent.)

Category and year	United States	Canada	Australia	Japan	France	Germany¹	Italy	Netherlands	Sweden	United Kingdom
Civilian Labor Force Participation Rate										
1970	60.4	57.8	62.1	64.5	57.5	56.9	49.0	. . .	64.0	. . .
1971	60.2	58.1	62.2	64.3	57.4	56.5	48.7	. . .	64.2	. . .
1972	60.4	58.6	62.3	63.8	57.2	56.2	47.7	. . .	64.1	62.8
1973	60.8	59.7	62.6	64.0	57.4	56.3	47.6	53.4	64.1	62.9
1974	61.3	60.5	63.0	63.1	57.4	55.7	47.7	53.5	64.8	63.1
1975	61.2	61.1	63.2	62.4	57.0	55.0	47.7	54.5	65.9	63.1
1976	61.6	62.5	62.7	62.4	57.2	54.6	48.0	54.1	66.0	63.0
1977	62.3	62.8	62.7	62.5	57.5	54.4	48.2	54.2	65.9	62.7
1978	63.2	63.7	61.9	62.8	57.4	54.4	47.8	54.0	66.1	62.6
1979	63.7	64.5	61.6	62.7	57.4	54.5	48.0	54.2	66.6	62.7
1980	63.8	65.0	62.1	62.6	57.2	54.7	48.1	55.4	66.9	62.8
1981	63.9	65.6	61.9	62.6	57.1	54.7	48.3	56.7	66.8	62.7
1982	64.0	64.9	61.7	62.7	57.0	54.6	47.7	56.6	66.8	61.9
1983	64.0	65.2	61.4	63.1	56.7	54.3	47.5	55.7	66.7	61.6
1984	64.4	65.5	61.5	62.7	56.5	54.4	47.3	55.7	66.6	62.7
1985	64.8	66.0	61.7	62.2	56.2	54.7	47.2	55.5	66.9	62.9
1986	65.3	66.4	62.8	62.1	56.1	54.9	47.8	56.0	67.0	62.9
1987	65.6	66.8	62.9	61.8	55.9	55.0	47.6	55.2	66.5	63.2
1988	65.9	67.1	63.3	61.8	55.7	55.1	47.4	55.9	67.0	63.8
1989	66.5	67.5	64.1	62.1	55.6	55.2	47.3	56.1	67.3	64.3
1990	66.5	67.4	64.7	62.6	55.5	55.0	47.2	57.0	67.4	64.3
1991	66.2	66.8	64.2	63.1	55.4	58.8	47.8	57.7	67.0	63.7
1992	66.4	65.9	63.9	63.3	55.3	58.1	47.5	58.3	65.8	62.9
1993	66.3	65.5	63.5	63.2	55.0	57.8	48.3	57.5	64.5	62.6
1994	66.6	65.2	63.9	62.9	56.2	57.4	47.6	58.0	63.7	62.4
1995	66.6	64.9	64.5	62.8	56.1	57.1	47.3	59.6	64.0	62.4
1996	66.8	64.8	64.6	62.8	56.3	57.1	47.3	60.2	63.9	62.4
1997	67.1	65.1	64.3	63.0	56.4	57.3	47.3	61.1	63.2	62.5
1998	67.1	65.4	64.3	62.6	56.9	57.7	47.7	61.8	62.8	62.4
1999	67.1	65.9	64.0	62.0	57.4	56.9	47.9	62.5	62.7	62.8
2000	67.1	66.0	64.4	61.7	57.6	56.7	48.1	63.4	63.7	62.8
2001	66.8	66.1	64.4	61.2	57.7	56.7	48.3	64.0	63.7	62.7
2002	66.6	67.1	64.3	60.4	57.8	56.4	48.5	64.7	63.9	62.9
2003	66.2	67.7	64.6	59.9	57.7	56.0	49.1	64.6	63.9	62.9
2004	66.0	67.7	64.6	59.6	57.5	56.4	49.1	64.8	63.6	63.0
2005	66.0	67.4	65.4	59.5	57.4	57.6	48.7	64.7	64.8	63.1
2006	66.2	67.4	65.8	59.6	57.5	58.2	48.9	65.1	64.9	63.5
2007	66.0	67.7	66.2	59.8	57.4	58.4	48.6	65.9	65.3	63.3
2008	66.0	67.9	66.6	59.5	57.1	58.5	49.0	66.2	65.3	63.3
2009	65.4	67.3	66.5	59.3	57.3	58.6	48.4	66.4	64.6	63.3
Unemployment Rate										
1970	4.9	5.7	1.7	1.2	2.5	0.5	3.2	. . .	1.5	. . .
1971	5.9	6.2	1.9	1.3	2.8	0.6	3.3	. . .	2.6	4.2
1972	5.6	6.2	2.6	1.4	2.9	0.7	3.8	. . .	2.7	4.4
1973	4.9	5.6	2.3	1.3	2.8	0.7	3.7	3.1	2.5	3.7
1974	5.6	5.3	2.7	1.4	2.9	1.6	3.1	3.6	2.0	3.7
1975	8.5	6.9	4.9	1.9	3.7	3.4	3.4	5.1	1.6	4.5
1976	7.7	6.9	4.8	2.0	4.1	3.4	3.9	5.4	1.6	5.4
1977	7.1	7.8	5.6	2.0	4.6	3.4	4.1	4.9	1.8	5.6
1978	6.1	8.1	6.3	2.3	4.7	3.3	4.1	5.1	2.2	5.5
1979	5.8	7.3	6.3	2.1	5.4	2.9	4.4	5.1	2.1	5.4
1980	7.1	7.3	6.1	2.0	5.7	2.8	4.4	6.0	2.0	6.9
1981	7.6	7.3	5.8	2.2	6.8	4.0	4.9	8.9	2.5	9.7
1982	9.7	10.7	7.2	2.4	7.3	5.6	5.4	10.2	3.1	10.8
1983	9.6	11.6	10.0	2.7	7.6	6.9	5.9	11.4	3.5	11.5
1984	7.5	10.9	9.0	2.8	8.9	7.1	5.9	11.5	3.1	11.8
1985	7.2	10.1	8.3	2.5	9.5	7.2	6.0	9.6	2.8	11.4
1986	7.0	9.2	7.9	2.7	9.5	6.6	7.5	10.0	2.6	11.4
1987	6.2	8.4	7.9	2.6	9.6	6.3	7.9	9.8	2.3	10.5
1988	5.5	7.4	7.0	2.4	9.3	6.3	7.9	9.3	1.9	8.6
1989	5.3	7.1	6.0	2.2	8.6	5.7	7.8	8.4	1.6	7.3
1990	5.6	7.7	6.7	2.0	8.3	5.0	7.0	7.6	1.8	7.1
1991	6.8	9.8	9.3	2.0	8.5	5.6	6.9	7.1	3.2	8.9
1992	7.5	10.6	10.5	2.1	9.4	6.7	7.3	6.8	5.8	10.0
1993	6.9	10.8	10.6	2.4	10.5	8.0	9.8	6.3	9.4	10.4
1994	6.1	9.6	9.4	2.6	10.9	8.5	10.7	6.9	9.6	9.5
1995	5.6	8.6	8.2	2.9	10.3	8.2	11.3	7.1	9.1	8.7
1996	5.4	8.8	8.2	3.1	10.8	9.0	11.3	6.6	9.9	8.1
1997	4.9	8.4	8.3	3.1	10.9	9.9	11.4	5.6	10.1	7.0
1998	4.5	7.7	7.7	3.8	10.4	9.3	11.5	4.4	8.4	6.3
1999	4.2	7.0	6.9	4.2	10.0	8.5	11.0	3.5	7.1	6.0
2000	4.0	6.1	6.3	4.4	8.5	7.8	10.2	3.0	5.8	5.5
2001	4.7	6.5	6.8	4.5	7.7	7.9	9.2	2.3	5.0	5.1
2002	5.8	7.0	6.4	4.9	7.9	8.6	8.7	2.8	5.1	5.2
2003	6.0	6.9	5.9	4.6	8.4	9.3	8.5	3.7	5.8	5.0
2004	5.5	6.4	5.4	4.2	8.8	10.3	8.1	4.6	6.6	4.8
2005	5.1	6.0	5.0	3.8	8.8	11.2	7.8	4.8	7.7	4.9
2006	4.6	5.5	4.8	3.6	8.7	10.4	6.9	3.9	7.0	5.5
2007	4.6	5.3	4.4	3.6	8.0	8.7	6.2	3.2	6.1	5.4
2008	5.8	5.3	4.2	3.7	7.4	7.5	6.8	2.8	6.1	5.7
2009	9.3	7.3	5.6	4.8	9.1	7.8	7.9	3.4	8.2	7.7

¹Unified Germany from 1991 onward; data for previous years relate to the former West Germany.
. . . = Not available.

Table 10-2. Unemployment Rates by Sex and Country, Adjusted to U.S. Concepts, 10 Countries, 1970–2009

(Percent.)

Sex and year	United States	Canada	Australia	Japan	France	Germany[1]	Italy	Netherlands	Sweden	United Kingdom
Men										
1970	4.4	5.6	1.1	1.2	1.5	0.5	2.5	. . .	1.4	. . .
1971	5.3	6.0	1.3	1.2	1.7	0.5	2.5	. . .	2.4	3.6
1972	5.0	5.8	1.9	1.5	1.8	0.7	2.9	. . .	2.5	3.9
1973	4.2	4.9	1.6	1.3	1.6	0.6	2.7	2.6	2.2	3.0
1974	4.9	4.8	1.9	1.4	1.8	1.5	2.3	2.8	1.7	3.0
1975	7.9	6.2	3.8	1.8	2.7	3.3	2.5	3.9	1.4	4.1
1976	7.1	6.3	3.9	2.2	2.9	3.0	2.7	4.1	1.3	5.2
1977	6.3	7.3	4.6	2.0	3.3	2.9	2.8	3.8	1.5	5.3
1978	5.3	7.5	5.4	2.2	3.6	2.7	2.8	3.6	2.1	5.1
1979	5.1	6.7	5.2	1.9	4.0	2.3	3.0	3.6	1.9	4.9
1980	6.9	6.9	5.1	1.7	4.0	2.3	2.9	4.2	1.7	6.7
1981	7.4	7.0	4.8	2.0	5.0	3.4	3.3	6.9	2.4	10.3
1982	9.9	11.1	6.4	2.1	5.7	5.0	3.8	8.6	3.0	11.6
1983	9.9	12.2	9.7	2.5	6.1	6.2	4.1	10.4	3.4	12.3
1984	7.4	11.1	8.7	2.5	7.4	6.2	4.2	10.4	3.0	12.0
1985	7.0	10.2	7.9	2.2	8.1	6.2	4.2	8.4	2.8	11.8
1986	6.9	9.3	7.6	2.4	8.1	5.6	5.2	7.9	2.6	11.8
1987	6.2	8.3	7.6	2.2	7.9	5.4	5.5	7.3	2.3	10.9
1988	5.5	7.2	6.6	2.0	7.5	5.3	5.5	7.3	1.9	8.8
1989	5.2	7.0	5.6	1.8	6.7	4.6	5.4	6.4	1.6	7.4
1990	5.7	7.9	6.6	1.7	6.5	4.2	4.8	5.6	1.9	7.4
1991	7.2	10.5	9.7	1.7	6.7	4.6	4.9	5.4	3.5	9.9
1992	7.9	11.6	11.2	1.8	7.7	5.5	5.3	5.4	6.8	11.8
1993	7.2	11.5	11.3	2.1	9.2	6.7	7.4	5.3	11.0	12.4
1994	6.2	10.2	9.8	2.3	9.6	7.3	8.4	6.1	11.0	11.3
1995	5.6	9.1	8.6	2.6	8.9	7.3	8.7	5.9	9.9	10.1
1996	5.4	9.2	8.5	2.8	9.6	8.4	8.8	5.3	10.4	9.5
1997	4.9	8.7	8.5	2.8	9.8	9.4	8.8	4.5	10.4	7.9
1998	4.4	8.1	8.0	3.5	9.2	8.9	8.9	3.5	8.7	7.0
1999	4.1	7.3	7.1	4.0	8.8	8.1	8.6	2.8	7.4	6.6
2000	3.9	6.3	6.5	4.1	7.3	7.6	7.9	2.3	6.2	6.0
2001	4.8	6.9	7.0	4.4	6.5	7.8	7.2	1.8	5.3	5.7
2002	5.9	7.5	6.5	4.7	7.1	8.8	6.8	2.5	5.6	5.8
2003	6.3	7.3	5.9	4.3	7.6	9.7	6.6	3.5	6.3	5.6
2004	5.6	6.8	5.3	3.9	8.0	10.6	6.5	4.4	6.9	5.2
2005	5.1	6.3	4.9	3.5	8.0	11.5	6.3	4.5	7.8	5.3
2006	4.6	5.8	4.7	3.3	8.0	10.5	5.5	3.6	6.9	5.8
2007	4.7	5.6	4.0	3.2	7.4	8.6	5.0	2.8	5.8	5.7
2008	6.1	5.8	4.0	3.2	6.9	7.5	5.6	2.6	5.8	6.2
2009	10.3	8.5	5.7	4.4	8.9	8.1	6.9	3.4	8.6	8.7
Women										
1970	5.9	5.8	2.8	2.2	4.2	0.6	5.2	. . .	1.7	. . .
1971	6.9	6.6	3.1	3.0	4.6	0.8	5.2	. . .	2.8	5.1
1972	6.6	7.0	3.9	3.4	4.7	0.8	5.9	. . .	3.0	5.1
1973	6.0	6.7	3.6	2.6	4.6	0.9	6.2	4.3	2.8	4.8
1974	6.7	6.4	4.1	3.2	4.7	1.8	5.2	5.6	2.4	4.7
1975	9.3	8.1	7.0	3.9	5.1	3.5	5.8	8.2	2.0	5.2
1976	8.6	7.9	6.4	3.9	5.9	3.9	6.5	8.6	2.0	5.8
1977	8.2	8.8	7.5	4.3	6.5	4.3	6.8	7.6	2.2	6.2
1978	7.2	9.1	7.9	4.3	6.6	4.2	6.8	8.6	2.4	6.2
1979	6.8	8.3	8.2	4.1	7.4	3.9	7.3	8.8	2.3	6.2
1980	7.4	7.9	7.9	3.3	8.3	3.6	7.4	9.7	2.3	7.1
1981	7.9	7.8	7.4	3.5	9.2	4.8	8.1	12.9	2.7	8.8
1982	9.4	10.1	8.5	3.5	9.7	6.5	8.6	13.3	3.4	9.5
1983	9.2	10.8	10.4	3.7	9.8	7.9	9.4	13.9	3.5	10.5
1984	7.6	10.7	9.5	3.3	11.0	8.5	9.4	13.9	3.2	11.6
1985	7.4	9.9	8.8	3.0	11.3	8.6	9.4	11.9	2.9	11.0
1986	7.1	9.1	8.5	3.2	11.4	8.1	11.8	13.7	2.7	10.9
1987	6.2	8.6	8.3	3.2	11.8	7.8	12.0	13.7	2.3	10.0
1988	5.6	7.6	7.5	2.9	11.5	7.8	12.3	12.6	1.9	8.3
1989	5.4	7.1	6.5	2.7	11.0	7.2	12.1	11.6	1.7	7.1
1990	5.5	7.5	6.8	2.5	10.6	6.1	10.8	10.8	1.8	6.8
1991	6.4	9.0	8.7	2.5	10.7	7.0	10.4	9.6	2.9	7.5
1992	7.0	9.4	9.5	2.5	11.5	8.4	10.8	8.9	4.6	7.7
1993	6.6	9.9	9.7	3.0	12.2	9.6	13.8	7.7	7.6	7.9
1994	6.0	8.8	9.0	3.1	12.3	10.1	14.6	8.1	8.2	7.4
1995	5.6	8.0	7.7	3.4	11.9	9.4	15.4	8.8	8.1	6.9
1996	5.4	8.2	7.8	3.5	12.2	9.6	15.3	8.4	9.3	6.4
1997	5.0	8.0	7.9	3.7	12.1	10.6	15.4	7.0	9.7	5.9
1998	4.6	7.2	7.4	4.2	11.7	9.8	15.4	5.5	8.0	5.4
1999	4.3	6.6	6.7	4.5	11.3	8.9	14.8	4.5	6.7	5.2
2000	4.1	5.8	6.1	4.8	9.9	8.1	13.7	3.8	5.4	4.9
2001	4.7	6.0	6.4	4.8	9.1	7.9	12.2	2.8	4.7	4.5
2002	5.6	6.4	6.2	5.2	8.8	8.3	11.5	3.1	4.7	4.5
2003	5.7	6.4	6.0	4.9	9.3	8.8	11.4	3.9	5.2	4.4
2004	5.4	6.0	5.5	4.6	9.7	10.0	10.6	4.9	6.1	4.3
2005	5.1	5.6	5.2	4.1	9.7	10.9	10.1	5.1	7.5	4.4
2006	4.6	5.2	4.9	4.0	9.5	10.2	8.8	4.4	7.1	5.0
2007	4.5	4.8	4.8	4.2	8.5	8.8	7.9	3.7	6.4	5.0
2008	5.4	4.8	4.6	4.3	7.9	7.7	8.5	3.0	6.3	5.1
2009	8.1	6.1	5.4	5.2	9.3	7.3	9.3	3.5	7.9	6.5

[1]Unified Germany from 1991 onward; data for previous years relate to the former West Germany.
. . . = Not available.

Table 10-3. Unemployment Rates Among Youth, Adjusted to U.S. Concepts, 10 Countries, 1970–2009

(Percent.)

Year	United States	Canada	Australia	Japan	France	Germany[1]	Italy	Netherlands	Sweden	United Kingdom
1970	11.0	. . .	. . .	2.0	4.9	0.4	10.4	. . .	2.9	. . .
1971	12.7	. . .	. . .	2.1	5.5	0.6	10.3	. . .	5.1	. . .
1972	12.1	. . .	. . .	2.5	5.9	0.7	13.6	. . .	5.8	. . .
1973	10.5	. . .	. . .	2.3	5.8	0.8	13.2	3.8	5.3	. . .
1974	11.9	. . .	. . .	2.4	6.3	2.2	12.0	5.1	4.5	. . .
1975	16.1	. . .	. . .	3.1	7.9	4.7	13.2	8.2	3.8	
1976	14.7	12.4	. . .	3.2	9.1	4.8	15.2	9.3	3.8	. . .
1977	13.6	13.8	. . .	3.6	10.7	5.0	14.9	8.9	4.5	. . .
1978	12.3	13.9	12.6	3.8	11.2	4.5	15.4	9.6	5.6	. . .
1979	11.8	12.6	13.0	3.7	12.9	3.6	16.0	10.2	5.1	. . .
1980	13.9	12.7	12.5	3.5	14.3	3.7	15.8	11.9	5.1	
1981	14.9	12.6	11.4	4.0	16.9	5.7	17.3	16.8	6.4	. . .
1982	17.8	18.1	13.8	4.3	18.4	8.2	19.4	19.8	7.7	. . .
1983	17.2	19.1	18.3	4.6	19.4	9.6	20.9	20.9	8.1	. . .
1984	13.9	17.2	16.8	4.9	23.6	10.7	21.6	20.8	6.1	19.8
1985	13.6	15.6	15.2	4.7	24.1	10.0	22.2	17.4	5.9	18.0
1986	13.3	14.5	14.8	5.2	22.3	8.0	25.5	16.8	5.7	18.2
1987	12.2	13.0	14.6	5.0	21.3	7.4	25.8	15.2	5.3	15.4
1988	11.0	11.2	13.1	4.7	20.1	6.9	24.8	14.1	4.3	12.6
1989	10.9	10.5	10.8	4.4	17.7	5.5	23.9	12.5	4.0	10.1
1990	11.2	12.0	12.6	4.3	17.9	4.6	21.3	11.5	4.6	10.6
1991	13.4	15.4	17.0	4.2	19.0	5.5	21.2	10.7	8.0	14.3
1992	14.2	16.8	18.8	4.4	20.6	6.4	22.8	9.7	13.9	16.8
1993	13.4	16.7	18.2	5.1	24.4	7.8	27.8	9.9	23.5	18.0
1994	12.5	14.9	16.5	5.2	25.9	8.5	29.4	10.4	23.8	16.8
1995	12.1	13.9	14.8	5.9	24.2	8.4	30.6	12.9	20.2	15.8
1996	12.0	14.5	15.1	6.4	25.6	9.7	30.6	12.1	21.5	15.4
1997	11.3	15.5	15.7	6.4	26.4	10.6	30.4	9.5	21.1	14.2
1998	10.4	14.6	14.6	7.4	24.2	9.4	30.1	8.2	17.1	13.6
1999	9.9	13.4	13.3	8.7	24.0	8.8	29.0	7.1	14.6	13.0
2000	9.3	11.7	12.1	8.9	19.1	8.6	27.3	5.8	12.0	12.5
2001	10.6	11.9	13.5	9.1	17.8	8.4	24.4	4.6	12.0	12.0
2002	12.0	12.8	12.8	9.5	19.0	10.0	23.4	5.1	13.1	12.2
2003	12.4	12.8	12.0	9.6	16.9	10.8	24.0	6.4	14.0	12.4
2004	11.8	12.4	11.4	9.0	18.5	12.9	23.8	8.0	17.2	12.3
2005	11.3	11.3	10.6	8.1	19.0	15.5	24.2	8.3	22.2	13.0
2006	10.5	10.6	10.0	7.5	20.2	13.8	22.0	6.6	21.1	14.2
2007	10.5	10.1	9.4	7.6	17.9	11.9	20.6	6.0	18.7	14.4
2008	12.8	10.6	8.9	7.0	17.5	10.5	21.5	5.3	19.1	15.1
2009	17.6	14.0	11.6	8.8	21.6	11.2	25.7	6.7	24.6	19.2

Note: Youth are defined as 16- to 24-year-olds in the United States, Canada, France, Sweden, and the United Kingdom; otherwise, they are defined as 15- to 24-year-olds.

[1] Unified Germany from 1991 onward; data for previous years relate to the former West Germany.
. . . = Not available.

Table 10-4. Employment-Population Ratios by Sex, Adjusted to U.S. Concepts, 10 Countries, 1970–2009

(Ratio.)

Sex and year	United States	Canada	Australia	Japan	France	Germany[1]	Italy	Netherlands	Sweden	United Kingdom
Men										
1970	76.2	73.4	83.2	80.5	76.3	78.4	71.9	. . .	77.4	. . .
1971	74.9	72.7	82.7	80.9	75.3	77.1	71.6	. . .	76.2	80.1
1972	75.0	73.0	82.0	80.6	74.4	75.9	69.9	. . .	75.4	79.5
1973	75.5	74.3	81.8	80.8	74.3	75.4	69.3	77.3	75.1	79.9
1974	74.9	74.9	81.1	80.5	74.0	73.5	69.4	77.1	75.6	79.0
1975	71.7	73.5	79.1	79.5	72.3	70.9	68.8	76.9	76.0	77.9
1976	72.0	74.2	78.3	79.2	71.9	70.3	68.5	75.9	75.6	76.7
1977	72.8	73.3	77.3	78.7	71.4	69.9	67.5	75.7	74.5	75.9
1978	73.8	73.4	75.5	78.2	70.6	69.7	66.8	75.0	73.5	75.3
1979	73.8	74.3	75.3	78.2	69.8	69.8	66.3	74.3	73.7	75.0
1980	72.0	74.0	75.1	77.9	69.1	69.6	66.0	74.1	73.6	73.3
1981	71.3	73.9	75.1	77.8	67.6	68.5	65.6	72.2	72.0	70.1
1982	69.0	69.3	73.4	77.4	66.5	67.0	64.4	69.5	71.3	68.0
1983	68.8	68.3	70.1	77.1	65.3	65.8	63.5	67.4	70.4	66.7
1984	70.7	68.9	70.5	76.4	63.7	65.7	62.9	66.6	70.2	67.2
1985	70.9	69.6	70.6	75.9	62.5	65.8	62.5	67.6	70.5	67.1
1986	71.0	70.4	70.8	75.4	62.0	66.3	61.8	66.7	70.6	66.6
1987	71.5	71.0	70.3	74.9	61.4	66.2	60.9	64.8	69.7	67.2
1988	72.0	71.6	71.0	75.0	61.2	65.9	60.4	65.0	70.3	69.0
1989	72.5	71.8	72.1	75.0	61.4	65.9	59.9	65.7	70.9	70.2
1990	72.0	70.6	71.4	75.4	61.4	65.6	60.0	66.5	70.6	70.0
1991	70.4	67.6	68.2	75.8	60.7	67.9	60.6	66.8	69.2	67.3
1992	69.8	65.7	66.6	76.1	59.5	66.3	59.8	67.2	65.7	64.8
1993	70.0	65.3	66.0	75.9	57.8	64.7	58.8	65.5	61.6	63.7
1994	70.4	65.9	67.2	75.4	57.7	63.8	57.2	65.2	60.9	64.2
1995	70.8	66.1	68.2	75.0	57.9	63.1	56.2	66.7	62.0	64.7
1996	70.9	65.8	68.1	74.9	57.5	62.1	55.8	67.5	61.5	64.9
1997	71.3	66.4	67.7	74.9	57.4	61.3	55.5	68.5	61.0	65.9
1998	71.6	66.8	67.9	73.9	58.1	61.9	55.4	69.8	62.1	66.2
1999	71.6	67.6	68.2	73.0	59.0	60.7	55.5	70.4	62.5	66.6
2000	71.9	68.2	68.4	72.5	60.1	60.6	55.8	71.4	64.2	66.9
2001	70.9	67.7	67.6	71.5	60.8	60.2	56.0	72.0	64.4	66.9
2002	69.7	67.9	67.8	70.4	60.6	58.9	56.3	71.9	64.3	66.7
2003	68.9	68.3	68.1	69.9	59.7	57.5	56.9	70.6	63.7	66.9
2004	69.2	68.5	68.8	69.6	59.1	57.3	56.9	70.0	63.0	66.9
2005	69.6	68.6	69.4	69.7	58.8	57.9	56.8	69.2	63.8	66.8
2006	70.1	68.6	69.8	69.8	58.8	58.8	57.3	70.0	64.5	66.7
2007	69.8	68.8	70.3	70.1	59.0	59.9	57.3	70.9	65.5	66.7
2008	68.5	68.8	70.6	69.6	58.8	60.8	56.9	71.2	65.5	66.4
2009	64.5	66.0	69.0	68.0	57.6	60.2	55.4	70.5	62.8	64.2
Women										
1970	40.8	36.1	39.3	48.2	38.1	38.1	25.0	. . .	49.1	. . .
1971	40.4	36.8	39.7	47.2	38.4	38.2	24.9	. . .	49.5	42.3
1972	41.0	37.4	39.6	46.2	38.7	38.6	24.1	. . .	50.0	42.6
1973	42.0	39.1	40.9	46.8	39.2	39.1	24.5	27.3	50.3	43.6
1974	42.6	40.2	41.7	45.1	39.4	38.7	25.1	27.1	52.0	44.2
1975	42.0	40.8	41.4	44.0	39.2	37.9	25.3	27.1	54.1	44.2
1976	43.2	42.6	41.5	44.1	39.7	37.8	25.8	27.3	54.7	44.0
1977	44.5	42.9	41.5	44.9	40.1	37.7	26.9	28.2	55.5	44.0
1978	46.4	44.0	41.0	45.5	40.4	37.9	26.9	28.4	56.1	44.4
1979	47.5	45.7	40.7	45.7	40.5	38.4	27.3	29.2	57.2	45.0
1980	47.7	46.9	41.9	45.7	40.4	38.9	27.9	31.0	58.0	45.1
1981	48.0	48.2	42.1	45.7	40.3	38.7	28.0	31.9	58.5	44.3
1982	47.7	47.0	41.5	45.9	40.6	38.1	27.7	32.8	58.4	43.5
1983	48.0	47.3	40.8	46.7	40.7	37.3	27.6	31.9	58.6	43.3
1984	49.5	48.2	41.8	46.5	40.6	37.3	27.6	32.7	59.1	44.4
1985	50.4	49.5	43.0	46.3	40.5	37.6	27.8	33.4	59.7	45.2
1986	51.4	50.7	45.1	46.2	40.7	38.1	28.1	34.7	60.1	45.8
1987	52.5	51.6	45.8	46.2	40.8	38.5	28.3	35.4	60.5	46.9
1988	53.4	53.0	47.0	46.6	40.9	39.0	28.3	37.0	61.2	48.4
1989	54.3	53.9	48.8	47.4	41.3	39.7	28.6	37.7	61.7	49.9
1990	54.3	54.1	49.5	48.0	41.5	40.5	29.2	39.4	61.8	50.3
1991	53.7	53.2	48.4	48.6	41.7	44.3	29.7	40.9	60.6	49.6
1992	53.8	52.4	48.0	48.7	41.7	43.4	29.7	41.9	58.4	49.1
1993	54.1	51.9	47.7	48.3	41.5	42.7	29.7	42.8	55.5	49.0
1994	55.3	52.4	48.8	48.0	43.2	42.3	29.2	43.3	54.3	49.3
1995	55.6	52.7	50.5	47.7	43.4	42.7	29.1	44.4	54.7	49.8
1996	56.0	52.6	50.6	47.7	43.6	42.8	29.4	45.3	53.9	50.3
1997	56.8	53.2	50.5	47.9	43.8	42.7	29.6	47.3	53.0	51.0
1998	57.1	54.3	51.0	47.4	44.5	43.5	30.1	48.7	53.3	51.4
1999	57.4	55.2	51.3	46.6	45.1	44.1	30.8	50.5	54.2	52.0
2000	57.5	56.0	52.5	46.4	45.9	44.4	31.6	52.0	56.1	52.5
2001	57.0	56.2	52.6	46.2	46.5	44.8	32.7	53.4	56.7	52.7
2002	56.3	57.1	52.9	45.4	46.7	44.7	33.3	54.3	57.1	53.0
2003	56.1	58.0	53.6	45.3	46.7	44.5	34.0	54.1	56.8	53.1
2004	56.0	58.3	53.7	45.5	46.5	44.3	34.2	54.0	56.1	53.4
2005	56.2	58.3	55.0	45.7	46.5	44.9	34.1	54.3	56.0	53.7
2006	56.6	58.9	55.7	46.0	46.8	46.0	34.7	55.2	56.4	53.8
2007	56.6	59.7	56.4	46.1	47.4	47.1	34.9	56.8	57.4	53.6
2008	56.2	59.8	57.1	45.9	47.5	47.8	35.3	57.7	57.4	53.7
2009	54.4	58.8	56.8	45.7	47.2	48.3	34.7	57.9	55.8	53.1

[1]Unified Germany from 1991 onward; data for previous years relate to the former West Germany.
. . . = Not available.

Table 10-5. Women's Share of the Labor Force, Adjusted to U.S. Concepts, 10 Countries, 1970–2009

(Percent.)

Year	United States	Canada	Australia	Japan	France	Germany[1]	Italy	Netherlands	Sweden	United Kingdom
1970	38.1	33.6	32.8	38.9	36.6	36.5	28.2	. . .	39.6	. . .
1971	38.2	34.4	33.2	38.4	37.0	36.8	28.3	. . .	40.3	37.4
1972	38.5	34.9	33.4	37.9	37.4	37.3	28.1	. . .	40.8	37.6
1973	38.9	35.6	34.1	38.2	37.7	37.7	28.7	27.1	41.1	38.2
1974	39.4	36.1	34.8	37.4	38.0	38.0	29.1	27.2	41.9	38.7
1975	40.0	36.9	35.5	37.0	38.2	38.5	29.4	27.5	42.7	38.8
1976	40.5	37.4	35.6	37.1	38.8	38.8	30.2	28.0	43.1	38.9
1977	41.0	37.9	36.1	37.7	39.3	39.0	31.4	28.6	43.8	39.2
1978	41.7	38.6	36.3	38.1	39.8	39.2	31.5	29.2	44.4	39.7
1979	42.1	39.2	36.4	38.3	40.2	39.3	32.2	30.1	44.8	40.1
1980	42.5	39.8	37.1	38.4	40.6	39.5	32.7	31.5	45.3	40.4
1981	43.0	40.5	37.2	38.4	41.0	39.7	33.0	33.0	46.1	40.6
1982	43.3	40.9	37.3	38.7	41.6	39.8	33.2	34.1	46.4	40.7
1983	43.5	41.4	37.5	39.2	42.0	39.8	33.5	34.0	46.7	41.1
1984	43.8	41.9	38.0	39.3	42.6	39.9	33.7	34.8	47.0	41.8
1985	44.2	42.4	38.6	39.6	42.9	40.1	34.0	34.9	47.2	42.2
1986	44.5	42.7	39.6	39.6	43.2	40.2	34.9	36.7	47.3	42.7
1987	44.8	43.1	40.0	39.8	43.7	40.3	35.3	37.9	47.7	43.0
1988	45.0	43.6	40.5	40.0	43.9	40.7	35.6	38.7	47.8	43.2
1989	45.2	43.9	41.1	40.3	44.0	41.0	35.9	38.7	47.8	43.5
1990	45.2	44.2	41.6	40.5	44.1	41.5	36.2	39.5	47.8	43.7
1991	45.3	44.6	41.8	40.6	44.4	42.8	36.3	40.0	47.7	43.8
1992	45.4	44.7	41.9	40.6	44.9	42.8	36.7	40.2	47.7	44.0
1993	45.5	44.9	42.0	40.5	45.3	42.8	37.4	41.1	47.7	44.4
1994	46.0	44.9	42.4	40.5	46.0	42.9	37.6	41.3	47.6	44.5
1995	46.1	45.1	42.9	40.5	46.2	43.1	38.0	41.5	47.6	44.7
1996	46.2	45.1	43.0	40.5	46.3	43.3	38.4	41.8	47.7	44.9
1997	46.2	45.3	43.1	40.7	46.4	43.4	38.6	42.3	47.5	45.1
1998	46.3	45.5	43.3	40.7	46.5	43.5	39.1	42.4	47.2	45.3
1999	46.5	45.7	43.5	40.6	46.5	44.0	39.5	43.0	47.4	45.4
2000	46.5	45.9	44.0	40.8	46.6	44.3	39.8	43.3	47.5	45.6
2001	46.5	46.0	44.3	40.9	46.6	44.4	40.3	43.6	47.7	45.6
2002	46.5	46.2	44.4	40.9	46.6	44.7	40.5	44.0	47.8	45.7
2003	46.6	46.5	44.8	41.1	47.0	45.0	40.7	44.3	47.8	45.7
2004	46.4	46.6	44.6	41.3	47.2	45.1	40.7	44.5	47.8	45.8
2005	46.4	46.6	45.0	41.4	47.3	45.1	40.5	45.0	47.5	45.9
2006	46.3	46.9	45.2	41.6	47.4	45.4	40.6	45.2	47.5	46.0
2007	46.4	47.0	45.3	41.6	47.5	45.6	40.6	45.6	47.6	45.8
2008	46.5	47.0	45.4	41.7	47.6	45.6	41.0	45.8	47.5	45.8
2009	46.7	47.3	45.5	42.1	47.7	45.8	41.1	46.0	47.4	46.1

[1]Unified Germany from 1991 onward; data for previous years relate to the former West Germany.
. . . = Not available.

Table 10-6. Percent of Employment in Agriculture, Adjusted to U.S. Concepts, 10 Countries, 1970–2009

(Percent.)

Year	United States	Canada	Australia	Japan	France	Germany[1]	Italy	Netherlands	Sweden	United Kingdom[2]
1970	4.5	7.6	8.1	16.9	13.5	8.5	20.1	. . .	8.2	. . .
1971	4.4	7.5	7.7	15.5	12.9	8.0	20.1	. . .	7.8	3.2
1972	4.4	6.9	7.9	14.4	12.1	7.6	19.0	. . .	7.5	3.0
1973	4.2	6.5	7.4	13.1	11.3	7.2	18.2	6.1	7.2	3.0
1974	4.2	6.3	7.0	12.6	10.8	6.9	17.4	6.0	6.7	2.8
1975	4.1	6.1	6.9	12.4	10.4	6.7	16.7	5.9	6.5	2.8
1976	3.9	5.7	6.6	11.9	9.9	6.2	16.4	5.7	6.2	2.8
1977	3.7	5.5	6.7	11.6	9.5	5.9	15.8	5.6	6.1	2.8
1978	3.7	5.2	6.4	11.4	9.2	5.7	15.4	5.6	6.1	2.8
1979	3.5	5.2	6.5	10.8	8.9	5.3	14.9	5.4	5.8	2.7
1980	3.6	5.0	6.5	10.1	8.6	5.2	14.2	5.2	5.6	2.6
1981	3.5	4.9	6.5	9.7	8.3	5.0	13.3	5.2	5.6	2.7
1982	3.6	5.0	6.5	9.4	8.0	4.9	12.4	5.3	5.6	2.7
1983	3.5	5.1	6.6	8.9	7.7	4.8	12.3	5.3	5.5	2.7
1984	3.3	4.9	6.2	8.5	7.5	4.7	11.7	5.2	5.2	2.6
1985	3.1	4.7	6.1	8.4	7.3	4.5	11.0	5.1	4.9	2.3
1986	3.1	4.7	6.1	8.1	7.0	4.3	10.7	5.0	4.7	2.2
1987	3.0	4.5	5.8	8.0	6.7	4.1	10.4	4.9	4.5	2.3
1988	2.9	4.4	5.8	7.6	6.4	3.9	9.8	4.7	4.4	2.3
1989	2.9	4.2	5.5	7.3	6.0	3.7	9.3	4.7	4.3	2.2
1990	2.9	4.2	5.6	6.9	5.7	3.5	8.9	4.6	3.9	2.1
1991	2.9	4.3	5.5	6.4	5.4	4.1	8.5	4.5	3.8	2.3
1992	2.9	4.2	5.3	6.1	5.2	3.8	8.2	4.0	3.8	2.2
1993	2.7	4.3	5.3	5.7	5.0	3.5	7.1	3.9	3.9	2.0
1994	2.9	4.2	5.1	5.6	4.7	3.3	6.9	4.0	3.9	2.1
1995	2.9	4.0	4.9	5.5	4.5	3.1	6.6	3.8	3.5	2.1
1996	2.8	4.0	5.0	5.3	4.3	3.0	6.2	3.9	3.3	1.9
1997	2.7	3.8	5.1	5.1	4.2	2.9	6.2	3.8	3.1	1.8
1998	2.7	3.8	4.9	5.0	4.1	2.8	5.9	3.3	2.9	1.7
1999	2.6	3.5	4.9	4.9	3.9	2.8	5.5	3.2	3.1	1.6
2000	1.8	3.3	4.9	4.8	3.7	2.6	5.3	3.2	2.9	1.5
2001	1.7	2.8	4.8	4.7	3.6	2.6	5.3	3.0	2.6	1.4
2002	1.7	2.8	4.4	4.5	3.5	2.5	5.0	3.0	2.5	1.3
2003	1.7	2.8	3.9	4.4	3.4	2.5	4.9	3.0	2.5	1.3
2004	1.6	2.6	3.7	4.3	3.4	2.4	4.5	3.1	2.5	1.3
2005	1.6	2.7	3.6	4.2	3.3	2.4	4.2	3.3	2.3	1.4
2006	1.5	2.6	3.4	4.1	3.2	2.3	4.3	3.3	2.2	1.4
2007	1.4	2.5	3.3	4.1	3.0	2.3	4.0	3.0	2.2	1.4
2008	1.5	2.3	3.3	4.0	2.9	2.3	3.7	2.7	2.2	1.5
2009	1.5	2.3	3.3	4.0	. . .	2.1	3.7	2.7	2.2	1.6

Note: Agriculture includes agriculture, forestry, hunting, and fishing.

[1]Unified Germany from 1991 onward; data for previous years relate to the former West Germany.
[2]Sectoral employment is only partially adjusted to U.S. concepts prior to 1984.
. . . = Not available.

Table 10-7. Percent of Employment in Industry, Adjusted to U.S. Concepts, 10 Countries, 1970–2009

(Percent.)

Year	United States	Canada	Australia	Japan	France	Germany[1]	Italy	Netherlands	Sweden	United Kingdom[2]
1970	33.1	29.8	34.6	35.7	38.4	48.7	38.8	. . .	37.9	. . .
1971	31.7	29.4	34.3	35.9	38.5	47.7	39.0	. . .	37.1	. . .
1972	31.4	29.2	33.5	36.2	38.5	47.0	38.8	. . .	36.3	42.0
1973	32.0	29.5	33.4	37.0	38.7	46.8	38.4	35.1	36.3	41.2
1974	31.4	29.5	33.0	36.8	38.6	45.9	38.4	34.3	36.3	40.9
1975	29.5	28.1	31.5	35.6	37.8	44.5	38.3	33.2	35.8	40.6
1976	29.6	27.8	31.0	35.6	37.1	44.1	37.5	32.3	34.8	39.0
1977	29.7	27.4	30.4	35.1	36.6	43.8	37.6	32.1	33.7	38.1
1978	30.0	27.3	29.3	34.8	35.9	43.5	37.4	31.8	32.4	38.0
1979	30.2	27.5	29.0	34.7	35.2	43.3	37.0	31.0	31.9	37.7
1980	29.3	27.1	28.6	35.1	34.9	42.9	37.0	29.7	31.5	37.3
1981	28.9	26.8	28.3	35.1	34.0	42.2	36.5	28.4	30.6	36.2
1982	27.2	24.8	27.4	34.5	33.6	41.3	36.1	27.5	29.5	34.3
1983	26.8	24.1	25.9	34.4	32.8	40.6	35.1	27.3	29.1	33.1
1984	27.3	24.2	25.5	34.5	31.9	40.3	33.4	27.3	29.0	32.0
1985	26.9	24.3	24.8	34.6	31.0	40.1	32.6	26.6	29.0	34.2
1986	26.6	24.2	24.1	34.2	30.4	39.9	32.0	26.1	29.1	33.8
1987	26.0	24.1	23.9	33.5	29.8	39.5	31.5	26.3	28.7	33.1
1988	25.8	24.3	23.8	33.9	29.4	39.0	31.5	25.7	28.3	31.9
1989	25.6	24.3	24.2	34.1	29.2	38.9	31.5	25.9	28.4	31.9
1990	25.1	23.6	23.2	33.9	28.7	38.9	31.4	25.9	28.2	31.8
1991	24.2	22.0	22.0	34.2	28.3	39.8	31.4	25.1	27.2	31.2
1992	23.5	21.3	21.7	34.3	27.5	38.9	31.3	24.3	25.6	31.4
1993	23.0	20.7	21.8	33.9	23.4	37.8	33.3	24.0	24.5	29.1
1994	23.0	20.9	21.8	33.7	23.2	36.6	33.2	22.9	24.0	28.4
1995	23.0	21.2	21.4	33.1	22.9	35.3	33.0	22.8	25.0	26.8
1996	22.9	21.1	21.1	32.9	22.5	34.4	32.7	22.3	25.2	26.6
1997	23.0	21.4	20.8	32.8	22.1	33.9	32.4	22.3	25.0	26.5
1998	22.7	21.5	20.6	31.7	21.8	33.6	32.3	21.7	24.9	26.2
1999	22.2	21.7	20.2	31.3	21.5	33.2	32.1	21.6	24.2	25.8
2000	22.0	21.9	20.6	30.9	21.5	32.8	31.6	21.2	23.6	25.1
2001	21.3	21.7	19.8	30.1	21.3	32.3	31.4	21.1	23.1	24.3
2002	20.3	21.8	20.0	29.0	21.0	31.7	31.3	20.2	22.5	23.9
2003	20.0	21.5	19.9	28.5	20.8	31.0	31.4	19.6	21.9	23.3
2004	20.0	21.6	20.3	27.6	20.5	30.7	30.3	20.0	21.9	22.5
2005	19.8	21.3	20.1	27.1	20.3	29.1	30.4	20.0	21.4	21.9
2006	19.9	20.9	20.2	27.1	20.2	29.0	29.8	19.7	21.4	21.6
2007	19.8	20.5	20.2	27.0	20.1	29.1	29.9	18.8	21.1	21.5
2008	19.1	20.3	20.5	26.5	20.0	29.0	28.9	17.8	21.2	21.5
2009	17.6	19.1	19.9	25.5	. . .	28.5	28.3	17.1	19.7	20.7

Note: Industry includes manufacturing, mining, and construction.

[1]Unified Germany from 1991 onward; data for previous years relate to the former West Germany.
[2]Sectoral employment is only partially adjusted to U.S. concepts prior to 1984.
. . . = Not available.

Table 10-8. Percent of Employment in Manufacturing, Adjusted to U.S. Concepts, 10 Countries, 1970–2009

(Percent.)

Year	United States	Canada	Australia	Japan	France	Germany[1]	Italy	Netherlands	Sweden	United Kingdom[2]
1970	26.4	22.3	24.4	27.4	27.5	39.5	27.7	. . .	27.7	. . .
1971	24.7	21.8	24.1	27.4	27.8	37.4	28.0	. . .	27.4	33.9
1972	24.3	21.8	23.5	27.3	28.0	36.9	27.9	. . .	27.2	32.9
1973	24.8	22.0	23.3	27.8	28.2	36.7	27.9	25.3	27.6	32.3
1974	24.2	21.7	22.9	27.6	28.3	36.5	28.1	25.1	28.4	32.4
1975	22.7	20.2	21.3	26.1	27.8	35.7	28.0	24.5	28.1	31.0
1976	22.8	19.2	21.2	25.8	27.3	35.2	27.7	23.6	27.0	30.2
1977	22.7	18.8	20.9	25.3	26.9	35.1	27.6	23.2	26.0	30.4
1978	22.7	18.9	19.9	24.8	26.4	34.8	27.3	22.7	25.0	30.1
1979	22.7	19.2	19.6	24.6	26.0	34.5	26.9	22.0	24.7	29.5
1980	22.1	19.1	19.4	25.0	25.6	34.0	26.9	21.3	24.3	28.3
1981	21.7	18.5	19.2	25.1	24.9	33.4	26.3	20.8	23.4	26.5
1982	20.4	17.2	18.6	24.7	24.7	32.8	25.8	20.1	22.5	25.5
1983	19.8	16.8	17.8	24.8	24.3	32.2	25.0	19.6	22.4	24.3
1984	20.0	17.1	17.3	25.2	23.8	32.1	23.9	19.6	22.5	25.1
1985	19.5	17.0	16.1	25.3	23.2	32.3	23.2	19.5	22.6	25.0
1986	19.1	17.1	15.5	24.9	22.7	32.3	22.9	19.4	22.8	24.8
1987	18.6	16.7	15.4	24.4	22.1	32.0	22.5	19.5	22.0	23.4
1988	18.5	16.6	15.3	24.5	21.6	31.6	22.6	18.8	21.7	23.6
1989	18.5	16.5	15.1	24.5	21.4	31.6	22.8	19.1	21.7	22.8
1990	18.0	15.8	14.4	24.3	21.0	31.6	22.6	19.1	21.0	22.4
1991	17.5	14.8	13.7	24.6	20.7	30.7	22.1	18.3	19.9	22.9
1992	17.0	14.3	13.7	24.6	20.1	29.5	22.0	18.1	18.9	21.4
1993	16.4	14.0	13.5	23.9	19.5	28.1	24.6	17.7	18.3	21.2
1994	16.4	14.0	13.5	23.4	18.4	26.6	24.7	16.7	18.2	19.1
1995	16.4	14.4	13.0	22.7	18.2	25.2	24.9	16.4	19.0	19.1
1996	16.2	14.4	12.8	22.5	18.0	24.3	24.6	15.9	19.3	19.2
1997	16.1	14.7	12.9	22.2	17.7	24.0	24.2	15.7	19.3	18.8
1998	15.8	15.0	12.3	21.4	17.4	24.1	24.3	15.2	19.1	18.4
1999	15.0	15.3	11.8	21.0	17.0	23.8	24.1	15.1	18.5	17.7
2000	14.4	15.3	12.0	20.7	16.8	23.9	23.6	14.8	18.0	16.9
2001	13.5	15.0	11.6	20.2	16.6	23.7	23.1	14.5	17.5	16.2
2002	12.6	15.0	11.5	19.1	16.3	23.6	23.0	13.8	16.7	15.7
2003	12.3	14.6	11.0	18.8	15.9	23.3	22.9	13.5	16.2	14.5
2004	11.8	14.4	10.9	18.3	15.5	23.1	21.9	13.7	16.0	13.7
2005	11.5	13.7	10.4	18.1	15.0	22.2	21.6	13.7	15.3	13.2
2006	11.3	12.9	10.0	18.3	14.5	22.0	21.2	13.3	15.0	12.9
2007	11.2	12.2	9.9	18.3	14.6	22.2	21.2	12.5	14.6	12.8
2008	10.9	11.6	9.8	18.0	14.1	22.2	20.1	11.4	14.3	12.0
2009	10.2	10.7	9.3	17.2	. . .	21.8	19.5	10.7	13.0	10.6

[1]Unified Germany from 1991 onward; data for previous years relate to the former West Germany.
[2]Sectoral employment is only partially adjusted to U.S. concepts prior to 1984.
. . . = Not available.

Table 10-9. Percent of Employment in Services, Adjusted to U.S. Concepts, 10 Countries, 1970–2009

(Percent.)

Category and year	United States	Canada	Australia	Japan	France	Germany[1]	Italy	Netherlands	Sweden	United Kingdom
1970	62.3	62.6	57.3	47.4	48.0	42.8	41.1	. . .	53.9	. . .
1971	63.8	63.1	57.9	48.5	48.6	44.4	40.9	. . .	55.1	54.8
1972	64.2	63.9	58.6	49.4	49.4	45.4	42.2	. . .	56.2	55.8
1973	63.8	63.9	59.3	49.9	50.0	46.0	43.4	58.9	56.6	56.1
1974	64.5	64.2	60.1	50.6	50.6	47.2	44.2	59.7	57.0	56.5
1975	66.4	65.8	61.5	52.0	51.8	48.8	45.1	60.8	57.7	58.2
1976	66.5	66.5	62.4	52.5	52.9	49.6	46.1	61.9	59.0	59.1
1977	66.6	67.2	62.9	53.3	53.9	50.3	46.6	62.3	60.2	59.2
1978	66.3	67.5	64.3	53.8	55.0	50.8	47.2	62.6	61.5	59.5
1979	66.3	67.4	64.5	54.5	55.9	51.4	48.2	63.6	62.3	60.1
1980	67.1	67.8	64.9	54.8	56.5	51.9	48.8	65.1	62.9	61.2
1981	67.6	68.3	65.2	55.3	57.6	52.8	50.2	66.4	63.8	63.0
1982	69.2	70.1	66.1	56.0	58.4	53.7	51.6	67.3	64.9	64.2
1983	69.7	70.8	67.4	56.6	59.5	54.5	52.6	67.5	65.5	65.3
1984	69.4	70.9	68.2	56.9	60.6	55.1	54.8	67.5	65.9	63.2
1985	70.0	71.0	69.1	57.0	61.7	55.4	56.4	68.3	66.1	63.9
1986	70.4	71.1	69.8	57.6	62.6	55.8	57.3	68.9	66.1	64.6
1987	71.0	71.3	70.3	58.5	63.5	56.4	58.1	68.8	66.8	65.8
1988	71.3	71.4	70.3	58.5	64.3	57.0	58.8	69.5	67.3	65.8
1989	71.5	71.5	70.3	58.7	64.8	57.4	59.3	69.4	67.3	66.0
1990	72.0	72.3	71.2	59.2	65.6	57.6	59.6	69.5	67.9	66.7
1991	72.9	73.6	72.6	59.4	66.3	56.2	60.2	70.4	69.0	66.2
1992	73.6	74.4	73.0	59.5	67.3	57.3	60.6	71.7	70.6	68.7
1993	74.3	75.0	72.9	60.3	71.5	58.7	59.5	72.0	71.6	69.5
1994	74.1	74.9	73.1	60.8	72.1	60.1	59.9	73.0	72.1	71.1
1995	74.1	74.8	73.7	61.4	72.6	61.5	60.4	73.4	71.5	71.3
1996	74.3	75.0	73.9	61.8	73.2	62.6	61.2	73.7	71.6	71.5
1997	74.3	74.8	74.1	62.1	73.6	63.2	61.4	73.9	71.9	72.0
1998	74.6	74.7	74.5	63.3	74.1	63.6	61.8	75.0	72.2	72.5
1999	75.3	74.8	74.9	63.8	74.6	64.0	62.4	75.3	72.7	73.3
2000	76.2	74.8	74.4	64.3	74.8	64.5	63.0	75.6	73.5	74.1
2001	77.1	75.5	75.4	65.2	75.1	65.1	63.4	75.9	74.3	74.7
2002	78.0	75.5	75.6	66.5	75.5	65.7	63.6	76.8	75.0	75.3
2003	78.3	75.7	76.2	67.1	75.8	66.4	63.7	77.4	75.6	76.2
2004	78.4	75.8	76.0	68.0	76.1	66.9	65.2	76.9	75.6	76.8
2005	78.6	76.0	76.3	68.7	76.4	68.5	65.4	76.7	76.3	77.0
2006	78.5	76.5	76.3	68.8	76.7	68.8	65.9	77.1	76.4	77.1
2007	78.8	77.1	76.5	68.9	76.9	68.6	66.1	78.2	76.7	77.1
2008	79.5	77.3	76.2	69.5	77.1	68.7	67.4	79.4	76.7	77.8
2009	80.9	78.6	76.8	70.5	. . .	69.4	68.0	80.2	78.1	79.4

[1]Unified Germany from 1991 onward; data for previous years relate to the former West Germany.
. . . = Not available.

Table 10-10. Consumer Price Indexes, 16 Countries, 1950–2009

(1982–1984 = 100.)

Year	Consumer Price Index[1]															
	United States[2]	Canada[3]	Japan[4]	Australia[5]	Austria[6]	Bel- gium[7]	Den- mark[8]	France[9]	Ger- many[10]	Italy	Nether- lands[11]	Norway[12]	Spain[13]	Sweden	Switzer- land[14]	United Kingdom
1950	24.1	21.6	...	12.6	...	24.0	12.2	11.2	34.0	...	21.0	13.5	5.5	13.4	33.2	9.8
1951	26.0	23.8	...	15.1	...	26.3	13.6	13.1	36.6	...	23.1	15.7	6.0	15.7	34.8	10.7
1952	26.5	24.5	...	17.7	...	26.5	13.9	14.7	37.3	...	23.1	17.1	5.9	16.8	35.7	11.7
1953	26.7	24.2	...	18.4	...	26.4	13.8	14.4	36.7	10.3	23.1	17.5	6.0	16.9	35.5	12.1
1954	26.9	24.4	...	18.6	...	26.9	14.1	14.4	36.8	10.6	24.0	18.2	6.1	17.0	35.7	12.3
1955	26.8	24.4	...	19.0	...	26.7	15.0	14.6	37.3	10.9	24.5	18.4	6.3	17.5	36.0	12.8
1956	27.2	24.7	...	20.1	...	27.4	15.8	14.9	38.4	11.2	24.9	19.1	6.7	18.4	36.6	13.5
1957	28.1	25.6	...	20.6	...	28.2	16.0	15.3	39.1	11.4	26.5	19.7	7.4	19.2	37.3	14.0
1958	28.9	26.3	...	20.9	31.6	28.6	16.2	17.6	40.0	11.7	27.0	20.6	8.4	20.0	38.0	14.4
1959	29.1	26.4	...	21.3	32.0	29.0	16.5	18.7	40.3	11.7	27.2	21.2	9.0	20.2	37.7	14.5
1960	29.6	26.8	...	22.1	32.6	29.0	16.9	19.4	40.9	11.9	27.9	21.2	9.1	21.0	38.3	14.6
1961	29.9	27.1	...	22.6	33.8	29.3	17.6	20.0	42.0	12.2	28.4	21.7	9.2	21.5	39.0	15.1
1962	30.2	27.5	...	22.6	35.3	29.8	18.8	21.0	43.1	12.7	28.9	22.8	9.7	22.5	40.7	15.8
1963	30.6	27.8	...	22.7	36.2	30.4	19.7	22.0	44.4	13.7	30.0	23.3	10.6	23.2	42.1	16.1
1964	31.0	28.3	...	23.2	37.6	31.7	20.5	22.7	45.5	14.5	31.7	24.6	11.3	23.9	43.4	16.6
1965	31.5	29.0	...	24.1	39.5	32.9	21.8	23.3	46.9	15.2	33.3	25.7	12.8	25.2	44.8	17.4
1966	32.4	30.2	...	24.9	40.3	34.3	23.3	23.9	48.5	15.5	35.3	26.6	13.6	26.8	47.0	18.1
1967	33.4	31.3	...	25.7	41.9	35.3	25.0	24.6	49.4	16.1	36.4	27.7	14.5	27.9	48.9	18.6
1968	34.8	32.5	...	26.4	43.1	36.3	27.0	25.7	50.2	16.3	37.7	28.8	15.2	28.5	50.1	19.4
1969	36.7	34.0	...	27.2	44.4	37.6	27.9	27.3	51.1	16.7	40.5	29.5	15.5	29.2	51.3	20.5
1970	38.8	35.1	38.4	28.2	46.4	39.1	29.7	28.8	52.9	17.5	42.3	32.6	16.4	31.3	53.2	21.8
1971	40.5	36.1	40.9	29.8	48.5	40.8	31.5	30.3	55.7	18.4	45.5	34.8	17.7	33.6	56.6	23.8
1972	41.8	37.8	42.9	31.7	51.6	43.0	33.6	32.2	58.7	19.4	49.1	37.2	19.2	35.6	60.4	25.5
1973	44.4	40.8	47.9	34.6	55.5	46.0	36.7	34.6	62.8	21.6	53.0	40.1	21.4	38.0	65.7	27.8
1974	49.3	45.3	59.0	39.9	60.8	51.8	42.3	39.3	67.2	25.7	58.1	43.8	24.8	41.7	72.1	32.3
1975	53.8	50.1	65.9	45.9	65.9	58.5	46.4	43.9	71.2	30.0	64.0	48.9	29.0	45.8	77.0	40.1
1976	56.9	53.7	72.2	52.0	70.8	63.8	50.5	48.2	74.2	35.1	69.6	53.4	34.1	50.6	78.3	46.8
1977	60.6	58.1	78.1	58.5	74.6	68.4	56.2	52.7	77.0	41.0	74.3	58.4	42.4	56.3	79.3	54.2
1978	65.2	63.2	81.4	63.1	77.3	71.4	61.8	57.3	79.1	46.0	77.3	63.1	50.8	62.0	80.1	58.7
1979	72.6	69.1	84.3	68.8	80.2	74.6	67.7	63.6	82.3	52.8	80.6	66.0	58.8	66.4	83.0	66.6
1980	82.4	76.0	91.0	75.8	85.2	79.6	76.1	72.3	86.8	64.0	85.8	73.3	67.9	75.5	86.4	78.5
1981	90.9	85.5	95.3	83.1	91.0	85.6	85.0	82.0	92.2	75.4	91.6	83.2	77.8	84.6	92.0	87.9
1982	96.5	94.9	98.1	92.5	96.0	93.1	93.6	91.6	97.1	87.8	97.1	92.6	89.0	91.8	97.1	95.4
1983	99.6	100.4	99.8	101.8	99.2	100.3	100.1	100.5	100.2	100.0	100.7	99.8	100.5	99.9	100.1	100.0	99.8
1984	103.9	104.7	102.1	105.8	104.8	106.6	106.3	107.9	102.7	111.5	103.1	106.9	111.1	108.1	102.9	104.8
1985	107.6	108.9	104.2	112.9	108.2	111.8	111.3	114.2	104.8	121.8	105.4	112.9	120.9	116.1	106.4	111.1
1986	109.6	113.4	104.8	123.2	110.0	113.3	115.4	117.7	104.7	129.0	105.6	120.9	131.6	121.0	107.2	114.9
1987	113.6	118.4	104.9	133.6	111.6	115.0	120.1	120.9	104.9	135.1	105.1	131.5	138.5	126.0	108.7	119.7
1988	118.3	123.0	105.6	143.3	113.7	116.4	125.5	124.2	106.2	141.9	105.8	140.2	145.2	133.4	110.7	125.6
1989	124.0	129.3	108.0	154.1	116.6	120.0	131.5	128.6	109.2	150.8	107.0	146.6	155.0	142.0	114.2	135.4
1990	130.7	135.5	111.3	165.3	120.4	124.1	135.0	133.0	112.1	160.5	109.6	152.6	165.4	156.8	120.5	148.2
1991	136.2	143.1	115.1	170.7	124.4	128.1	138.2	137.3	116.3	170.6	113.8	157.9	175.2	171.5	127.6	156.9
1992	140.3	145.2	117.0	172.4	129.4	131.2	141.1	140.5	122.3	179.6	118.1	161.6	185.6	175.4	132.6	162.7
1993	144.5	147.9	118.5	175.5	134.1	134.8	142.9	142.5	127.6	187.8	120.5	165.2	194.1	183.5	137.1	165.3
1994	148.2	148.1	119.2	178.8	138.1	138.0	145.7	145.8	131.2	195.5	123.8	167.6	203.3	187.5	138.3	169.3
1995	152.4	151.4	119.1	187.1	141.2	140.1	148.8	148.4	133.4	205.8	126.0	171.8	212.8	192.3	140.7	175.2
1996	156.9	153.6	119.2	192.0	143.8	142.9	151.9	151.3	135.3	214.0	128.7	173.8	220.3	193.2	141.8	179.4
1997	160.5	156.2	121.5	192.5	145.7	145.3	155.2	153.2	137.9	218.3	131.5	178.4	224.7	194.2	142.6	185.1
1998	163.0	157.8	122.2	194.1	147.0	146.6	158.1	154.3	139.3	222.6	134.1	182.4	228.8	194.0	142.6	191.4
1999	166.6	160.5	121.8	197.0	147.9	148.3	162.0	155.0	140.0	226.3	137.0	186.6	234.1	194.8	143.8	194.3
2000	172.2	164.9	120.9	205.8	151.4	152.1	166.8	157.7	142.0	232.1	140.2	192.4	242.1	196.8	145.9	200.1
2001	177.1	169.0	120.1	214.8	155.4	155.8	170.7	160.3	144.8	238.5	146.1	198.2	250.8	201.6	147.5	203.6
2002	179.9	172.8	119.0	221.2	158.2	158.4	174.8	163.4	146.9	244.5	150.9	200.8	259.7	205.9	148.4	207.0
2003	184.0	177.6	118.7	227.4	160.3	160.9	178.5	166.8	148.5	251.0	154.0	205.7	267.7	209.9	149.3	213.0
2004	188.9	180.9	118.7	232.7	163.6	164.3	180.5	170.3	150.9	256.6	156.0	206.6	275.9	210.7	150.5	219.4
2005	195.3	184.9	118.3	238.9	167.4	168.8	183.8	173.4	153.2	261.5	158.6	209.9	285.1	211.6	152.2	225.6
2006	201.6	188.5	118.7	247.4	169.9	171.9	187.3	176.2	155.7	267.1	160.4	214.7	295.1	214.5	153.9	232.8
2007	207.3	192.7	118.7	253.1	173.6	175.0	190.5	178.9	159.2	272.0	163.0	216.3	303.4	219.3	155.0	242.7
2008	215.3	197.2	120.3	264.1	179.1	182.9	197.0	183.9	163.3	281.1	167.1	224.5	315.8	226.9	158.8	252.4
2009	214.5	197.7	118.7	269.0	180.0	182.8	199.6	184.1	163.9	283.3	169.0	229.2	314.9	226.2	158.0	251.1

[1] The figures may differ from official indexes published by national statistical agencies because of rounding.
[2] Urban wage earners and clerical workers prior to 1978 and all urban consumers from 1978 onward.
[3] All households from January 1995, all urban households from September 1978 to December 1994, and middle-income urban households prior to September 1978.
[4] Excluding imputed rent for owner-occupied households prior to 1970.
[5] Urban worker households prior to September 1998.
[6] Worker households prior to 1966.
[7] Excluding rent and several other services prior to 1976.
[8] Excluding rent prior to 1964.
[9] All households from 1991, urban worker households prior to 1991; worker households in Paris only prior to 1962.
[10] Unified Germany from 1991 onward; data for previous years relate to the former West Germany.
[11] Employee households from 2001, low-income employee households prior to 2001.
[12] Urban worker households prior to 1960.
[13] All family households from 1993, middle-income family households prior to 1993.
[14] Urban worker households prior to May 1993.
. . . = Not available.

Table 10-11. Consumer Price Indexes, Average Annual Percent Change, 16 Countries, 1950–2009

(Percent.)

Year	Average annual percent change in Consumer Price Index[1]															
	United States[2]	Canada[3]	Japan[4]	Australia[5]	Austria[6]	Bel-gium[7]	Den-mark[8]	France[9]	Ger-many[10]	Italy	Nether-lands[11]	Norway[12]	Spain[13]	Sweden	Switzer-land[14]	United Kingdom
1950–2009	3.8	3.8	...	5.3	...	3.5	4.9	4.9	2.7	...	3.6	4.9	7.1	4.9	2.7	5.6
1960–2009	4.1	4.2	...	5.2	3.5	3.8	5.2	4.7	2.9	6.7	3.7	5.0	7.5	5.0	2.9	6.0
1970–2009	4.5	4.5	2.9	6.0	3.5	4.0	5.0	4.9	2.9	7.4	3.6	5.1	7.9	5.2	2.8	6.5
1980–2009	3.4	3.3	0.9	4.5	2.6	2.9	3.4	3.3	2.2	5.3	2.4	4.0	5.4	3.9	2.1	4.1
1990–2009	2.6	2.0	0.3	2.6	2.1	2.1	2.1	1.7	2.0	3.0	2.3	2.2	3.4	1.9	1.4	2.8
2000–2009	2.5	2.0	-0.2	3.0	1.9	2.1	2.0	1.7	1.6	2.2	2.1	2.0	3.0	1.6	0.9	2.6
1950–1955	2.1	2.4	...	8.6	...	2.2	4.3	5.4	1.9	...	3.0	6.4	2.8	5.4	1.6	5.5
1955–1960	2.0	1.9	...	3.1	...	1.7	2.3	5.8	1.9	1.9	2.7	2.8	7.6	3.7	1.2	2.6
1960–1965	1.3	1.6	...	1.8	3.9	2.5	5.3	3.7	2.8	4.9	3.6	4.0	7.0	3.7	3.2	3.5
1965–1970	4.3	3.9	...	3.2	3.3	3.5	6.4	4.3	2.4	3.0	4.9	4.9	5.1	4.4	3.5	4.6
1970–1975	6.8	7.4	11.4	10.3	7.3	8.4	9.3	8.8	6.1	11.3	8.6	8.4	12.1	8.0	7.7	13.0
1975–1980	8.9	8.7	6.7	10.6	5.3	6.4	10.4	10.5	4.0	16.3	6.0	8.4	18.6	10.5	2.3	14.4
1980–1985	5.5	7.4	2.8	8.3	4.9	7.0	7.9	9.6	3.8	13.7	4.2	9.0	12.2	9.0	4.3	7.2
1985–1990	4.0	4.5	1.3	7.9	2.2	2.1	3.9	3.1	1.4	5.7	0.8	6.2	6.5	6.2	2.5	5.9
1990–1995	3.1	2.2	1.4	2.5	3.2	2.4	2.0	2.2	3.5	5.1	2.8	2.4	5.2	4.2	3.1	3.4
1995–2000	2.5	1.7	0.3	1.9	1.4	1.7	2.3	1.2	1.3	2.4	2.2	2.3	2.6	0.5	0.7	2.7
2000–2005	2.5	2.3	-0.4	3.0	2.0	2.1	2.0	1.9	1.5	2.4	2.5	1.8	3.3	1.5	0.8	2.4
1950–1951	7.9	10.4	...	19.7	...	9.4	11.7	16.9	7.6	...	9.6	16.2	9.4	16.9	4.8	9.1
1951–1952	1.9	2.9	...	17.3	...	0.9	2.3	11.8	2.1	...	0.0	9.3	-2.0	7.2	2.6	9.2
1952–1953	0.8	-1.4	...	4.3	...	-0.3	-0.7	-1.2	-1.7	...	0.0	2.1	1.6	0.6	-0.7	3.1
1953–1954	0.7	0.7	...	0.9	...	1.8	1.8	-0.4	0.4	2.8	4.0	4.2	1.2	0.6	0.7	2.0
1954–1955	-0.4	0.0	...	2.2	...	-0.5	6.8	1.2	1.4	2.3	1.9	1.0	4.0	2.7	0.9	4.4
1955–1956	1.5	1.4	...	5.9	...	2.4	5.1	2.0	2.8	3.4	1.9	4.0	5.9	5.0	1.5	5.1
1956–1957	3.3	3.5	...	2.6	...	3.2	1.2	2.7	2.0	1.3	6.5	2.9	10.8	4.5	1.9	3.5
1957–1958	2.8	2.7	...	1.2	...	1.3	1.0	15.0	2.3	2.8	1.7	4.6	13.4	4.3	1.8	3.2
1958–1959	0.7	0.7	...	1.9	1.1	1.2	2.0	6.2	0.6	-0.4	0.8	2.7	7.3	0.8	-0.7	0.4
1959–1960	1.7	1.3	...	3.8	1.9	0.3	2.3	3.7	1.6	2.3	2.5	0.0	1.2	4.1	1.4	1.0
1960–1961	1.0	1.3	...	2.5	3.6	1.0	4.5	3.3	2.5	2.1	1.7	2.6	0.8	2.2	1.9	3.5
1961–1962	1.0	1.3	...	-0.2	4.4	1.4	6.5	4.7	2.8	4.7	1.9	5.0	5.7	4.8	4.3	4.3
1962–1963	1.3	1.3	...	0.4	2.7	2.1	5.2	4.8	3.0	7.5	3.8	2.4	8.7	3.0	3.4	1.9
1963–1964	1.3	1.9	...	2.5	3.8	4.2	3.7	3.4	2.4	5.9	5.5	5.5	7.0	3.1	3.1	3.3
1964–1965	1.6	2.4	...	3.8	5.0	4.1	6.4	2.5	3.2	4.6	5.2	4.4	13.2	5.2	3.4	4.7
1965–1966	2.9	4.2	...	3.2	2.2	4.2	6.9	2.7	3.3	2.3	5.8	3.5	6.2	6.6	4.7	3.9
1966–1967	3.1	3.4	...	3.2	4.0	2.9	7.4	2.6	1.9	3.7	3.1	4.1	6.4	4.0	4.0	2.6
1967–1968	4.2	3.9	...	2.7	2.8	2.8	8.0	4.6	1.6	1.4	3.7	3.9	5.0	2.0	2.4	4.7
1968–1969	5.5	4.8	...	3.0	3.1	3.7	3.5	6.5	1.8	2.7	7.4	2.5	2.2	2.7	2.5	5.4
1969–1970	5.7	3.0	...	3.7	4.4	3.9	6.5	5.2	3.6	4.9	4.4	10.5	5.7	6.9	3.6	6.4
1970–1971	4.4	3.0	6.5	6.0	4.7	4.3	5.9	5.5	5.2	4.8	7.5	6.7	8.2	7.4	6.6	9.4
1971–1972	3.2	4.8	4.9	6.0	6.3	5.4	6.7	6.2	5.4	5.7	7.8	6.8	8.3	6.0	6.7	7.1
1972–1973	6.2	7.8	11.6	9.2	7.6	7.0	9.3	7.3	7.1	10.8	8.0	7.8	11.4	6.7	8.7	9.1
1973–1974	11.0	11.0	23.2	15.3	9.5	12.7	15.3	13.7	6.9	19.1	9.6	9.1	11.7	9.9	9.8	16.0
1974–1975	9.1	10.7	11.6	15.2	8.4	12.8	9.6	11.8	6.0	17.0	10.2	11.7	17.0	9.8	6.7	24.2
1975–1976	5.8	7.2	9.5	13.4	7.3	9.2	9.0	9.6	4.2	16.8	8.8	9.3	17.6	10.4	1.7	16.5
1976–1977	6.5	8.0	8.2	12.3	5.5	7.1	11.1	9.4	3.7	17.0	6.7	9.2	24.5	11.3	1.3	15.8
1977–1978	7.6	8.9	4.2	8.0	3.6	4.5	10.0	9.1	2.7	12.1	4.1	8.1	19.8	10.1	1.1	8.3
1978–1979	11.3	9.3	3.6	9.1	3.7	4.5	9.6	10.8	4.1	14.8	4.2	4.6	15.7	7.2	3.6	13.4
1979–1980	13.5	10.0	7.9	10.2	6.3	6.6	12.3	13.6	5.4	21.2	6.5	11.0	15.6	13.6	4.0	18.0
1980–1981	10.3	12.5	4.8	9.6	6.8	7.6	11.7	13.4	6.3	17.8	6.7	13.4	14.5	12.1	6.6	11.9
1981–1982	6.2	10.9	2.9	11.2	5.4	8.7	10.1	11.8	5.2	16.5	6.0	11.4	14.4	8.6	5.5	8.6
1982–1983	3.2	5.8	1.8	10.1	3.3	7.7	6.9	9.6	3.2	14.7	2.8	8.5	12.2	9.0	3.0	4.6
1983–1984	4.3	4.3	2.3	3.9	5.7	6.4	6.3	7.4	2.5	10.8	3.3	6.4	11.3	8.0	2.9	5.0
1984–1985	3.6	4.0	2.1	6.7	3.2	4.9	4.7	5.8	2.0	9.2	2.2	5.6	8.8	7.4	3.4	6.1

[1]The figures may differ from official indexes published by national statistical agencies because of rounding.
[2]Urban wage earners and clerical workers prior to 1978 and all urban consumers from 1978 onward.
[3]All households from January 1995, all urban households from September 1978 to December 1994, and middle-income urban households prior to September 1978.
[4]Excluding imputed rent for owner-occupied households prior to 1970.
[5]Urban worker households prior to September 1998.
[6]Excluding rent and several other services prior to 1976.
[7]Excluding rent prior to 1964.
[8]All households from 1991, urban worker households prior to 1991; worker households in Paris only prior to 1962.
[9]Unified Germany from 1991 onward; data for previous years relate to the former West Germany.
[10]Employee households from 2001, low-income employee households prior to 2001.
[11]Urban worker households prior to 1960.
[12]All family households from 1993, middle-income family households prior to 1993.
[13]Urban worker households prior to May 1993.
. . . = Not available.

Table 10-11. Consumer Price Indexes, Average Annual Percent Change, 16 Countries, 1950–2009
—Continued

(Percent.)

Year	United States[2]	Canada[3]	Japan[4]	Australia[5]	Austria[6]	Belgium[7]	Denmark[8]	France[9]	Germany[10]	Italy	Netherlands[11]	Norway[12]	Spain[13]	Sweden	Switzerland[14]	United Kingdom
1985–1986	1.9	4.1	0.6	9.1	1.7	1.3	3.7	2.7	-0.1	5.9	0.2	7.1	8.8	4.2	0.7	3.4
1986–1987	3.6	4.4	0.1	8.5	1.4	1.6	4.0	3.1	0.2	4.7	-0.5	8.7	5.2	4.2	1.4	4.2
1987–1988	4.1	3.9	0.7	7.3	1.9	1.2	4.5	2.7	1.2	5.0	0.7	6.7	4.8	5.8	1.8	4.9
1988–1989	4.8	5.1	2.2	7.5	2.6	3.1	4.8	3.6	2.8	6.3	1.1	4.6	6.8	6.5	3.2	7.8
1989–1990	5.4	4.8	3.1	7.3	3.3	3.4	2.6	3.4	2.6	6.5	2.5	4.1	6.7	10.5	5.5	9.5
1990–1991	4.2	5.6	3.4	3.2	3.3	3.2	2.4	3.2	3.7	6.3	3.9	3.5	5.9	9.3	5.8	5.9
1991–1992	3.0	1.4	1.6	1.0	4.0	2.4	2.1	2.4	5.1	5.3	3.7	2.3	5.9	2.3	4.0	3.7
1992–1993	3.0	1.9	1.3	1.8	3.6	2.8	1.2	2.1	4.4	4.6	2.1	2.3	4.6	4.6	3.3	1.6
1993–1994	2.6	0.1	0.6	1.9	2.9	2.4	2.0	1.6	2.8	4.1	2.8	1.4	4.7	2.2	0.9	2.4
1994–1995	2.8	2.2	-0.1	4.6	2.2	1.5	2.1	1.8	1.8	5.3	1.8	2.5	4.7	2.5	1.8	3.5
1995–1996	3.0	1.5	0.1	2.6	1.9	2.1	2.1	2.0	1.4	4.0	2.1	1.2	3.6	0.5	0.8	2.4
1996–1997	2.3	1.7	1.9	0.3	1.3	1.6	2.2	1.2	1.9	2.0	2.2	2.6	2.0	0.5	0.5	3.1
1997–1998	1.6	1.0	0.6	0.9	0.9	0.9	1.8	0.7	1.0	2.0	2.0	2.2	1.8	-0.1	0.0	3.4
1998–1999	2.2	1.8	-0.3	1.5	0.6	1.1	2.5	0.5	0.6	1.7	2.2	2.3	2.3	0.4	0.9	1.5
1999–2000	3.4	2.7	-0.8	4.5	2.3	2.5	2.9	1.7	1.4	2.5	2.3	3.1	3.4	1.0	1.5	3.0
2000–2001	2.8	2.5	-0.7	4.4	2.7	2.5	2.4	1.7	1.9	2.7	4.2	3.0	3.6	2.5	1.0	1.8
2001–2002	1.6	2.2	-0.9	3.0	1.8	1.6	2.4	1.9	1.5	2.5	3.3	1.3	3.5	2.1	0.6	1.7
2002–2003	2.3	2.8	-0.3	2.8	1.4	1.6	2.1	2.1	1.0	2.7	2.1	2.5	3.1	1.9	0.6	2.9
2003–2004	2.7	1.8	0.0	2.3	2.1	2.1	1.2	2.1	1.7	2.2	1.2	0.4	3.1	0.4	0.8	3.0
2004–2005	3.4	2.2	-0.3	2.7	2.3	2.8	1.8	1.8	1.5	1.9	1.7	1.6	3.3	0.4	1.1	2.8
2005–2006	3.2	2.0	0.3	3.5	1.5	1.8	1.9	1.6	1.6	2.1	1.2	2.3	3.5	1.4	1.1	3.2
2006–2007	2.8	2.2	0.0	2.3	2.2	1.8	1.7	1.5	2.3	1.8	1.6	0.8	2.8	2.2	0.7	4.3
2007–2008	3.8	2.3	1.4	4.4	3.2	4.5	3.4	2.8	2.6	3.3	2.5	3.8	4.1	3.5	2.5	4.0
2008–2009	-0.4	0.3	-1.4	1.8	0.5	-0.1	1.3	0.1	0.4	0.8	1.2	2.1	-0.3	-0.3	-0.5	-0.5

[1]The figures may differ from official indexes published by national statistical agencies because of rounding.
[2]Urban wage earners and clerical workers prior to 1978 and all urban consumers from 1978 onward.
[3]All households from January 1995, all urban households from September 1978 to December 1994, and middle-income urban households prior to September 1978.
[4]Excluding imputed rent for owner-occupied households prior to 1970.
[5]Urban worker households prior to September 1998.
[7]Excluding rent and several other services prior to 1976.
[8]Excluding rent prior to 1964.
[9]All households from 1991, urban worker households prior to 1991; worker households in Paris only prior to 1962.
[10]Unified Germany from 1991 onward; data for previous years relate to the former West Germany.
[11]Employee households from 2001, low-income employee households prior to 2001.
[12]Urban worker households prior to 1960.
[13]All family households from 1993, middle-income family households prior to 1993.
[14]Urban worker households prior to May 1993.

Table 10-12. Real Gross Domestic Product (GDP) Per Capita, 16 Countries, 1960–2009

(2009 U.S. dollars.)

Year	United States	Canada	Australia	Japan	Korea, Republic of	Austria	Belgium	Denmark	France	Germany[1]	Italy	Netherlands	Norway	Spain	Sweden	United Kingdom
1960	17 167	14 281	15 132	5 879	1 491	11 215	11 212	13 449	10 845	12 982	10 048	13 830	14 583	. . .	13 872	14 031
1961	17 282	14 437	14 645	6 516	1 532	11 746	11 731	14 144	11 264	13 404	10 800	14 043	15 355	. . .	14 592	14 240
1962	18 049	15 162	15 204	7 011	1 520	11 954	12 294	14 811	11 821	13 865	11 393	14 443	15 642	. . .	15 129	14 263
1963	18 568	15 672	15 799	7 551	1 614	12 362	12 733	14 762	12 352	14 118	11 945	14 716	16 112	. . .	15 847	14 784
1964	19 374	16 375	16 512	8 307	1 724	13 021	13 491	15 958	13 016	14 907	12 178	15 770	16 792	10 757	16 802	15 489
1965	20 361	17 105	16 972	8 682	1 777	13 307	13 845	16 594	13 524	15 532	12 471	16 379	17 543	11 308	17 279	15 729
1966	21 440	17 905	17 166	9 491	1 944	13 959	14 187	16 843	14 116	15 823	13 115	16 618	18 059	11 998	17 473	15 946
1967	21 743	18 099	18 023	10 432	2 011	14 272	14 654	17 643	14 696	15 737	13 955	17 302	19 025	12 370	17 923	16 245
1968	22 570	18 692	18 687	11 543	2 188	14 833	15 210	18 508	15 232	16 536	14 775	18 274	19 286	13 054	18 468	16 848
1969	23 043	19 353	19 580	12 774	2 435	15 710	16 174	19 611	16 194	17 602	15 587	19 294	19 988	14 051	19 256	17 121
1970	22 821	19 663	20 445	13 925	2 591	16 770	17 186	19 668	17 031	18 310	16 328	20 229	20 248	14 471	20 317	17 452
1971	23 292	19 878	20 291	14 347	2 806	17 549	17 785	20 154	17 752	18 683	16 548	20 843	21 245	14 944	20 370	17 723
1972	24 269	20 719	20 395	15 340	2 933	18 530	18 651	20 876	18 413	19 370	17 061	21 359	22 193	15 969	20 774	18 315
1973	25 431	21 892	21 020	16 343	3 308	19 329	19 690	21 530	19 464	20 195	18 154	22 341	23 025	17 023	21 559	19 589
1974	25 059	22 385	21 009	15 926	3 557	20 057	20 431	21 255	20 203	20 350	19 027	22 930	23 756	17 820	22 183	19 328
1975	24 764	22 463	21 210	16 213	3 754	20 037	20 070	20 935	19 914	20 247	18 519	22 734	24 813	17 754	22 660	19 211
1976	25 841	23 322	21 778	16 677	4 192	20 991	21 151	22 155	20 710	21 352	19 739	23 552	26 127	18 128	22 819	19 721
1977	26 759	23 848	21 897	17 243	4 615	22 034	21 225	22 520	21 349	22 113	20 159	24 001	27 094	18 386	22 373	20 198
1978	27 954	24 545	22 141	17 988	5 013	22 020	21 785	22 961	22 097	22 806	20 738	24 502	28 031	18 411	22 699	20 855
1979	28 511	25 228	22 747	18 814	5 352	23 261	22 230	23 808	22 779	23 740	21 910	24 826	29 153	18 283	23 520	21 390
1980	28 106	25 443	23 148	19 192	5 170	23 676	23 164	23 691	23 045	23 993	22 615	24 956	30 369	18 423	23 873	20 911
1981	28 533	26 012	23 739	19 848	5 467	23 581	23 099	23 493	23 127	24 075	22 779	24 589	30 733	18 294	23 796	20 625
1982	27 713	24 969	23 348	20 374	5 829	24 023	23 242	24 381	23 549	23 997	22 856	24 173	30 658	18 423	24 066	21 081
1983	28 703	25 395	22 938	20 855	6 443	24 773	23 317	25 048	23 703	24 460	23 115	24 578	31 738	18 661	24 490	21 836
1984	30 498	26 619	24 062	21 644	6 992	24 789	23 892	26 106	23 939	25 252	23 855	25 234	33 514	18 916	25 511	22 382
1985	31 479	27 638	25 098	22 872	7 441	25 386	24 279	27 148	24 228	25 904	24 516	25 768	35 203	19 284	26 029	23 128
1986	32 274	28 027	25 254	23 395	8 269	25 958	24 713	28 455	24 697	26 478	25 216	26 343	36 494	19 851	26 710	24 001
1987	33 011	28 835	25 961	24 239	9 192	26 291	25 262	28 494	25 176	26 845	26 018	26 674	36 970	20 901	27 541	25 043
1988	34 057	29 878	26 744	25 860	10 164	27 007	26 371	28 440	26 184	27 671	27 090	27 413	36 708	21 917	28 148	26 251
1989	34 942	30 114	27 409	27 145	10 743	27 891	27 187	28 591	27 114	28 465	27 993	28 458	36 922	22 931	28 736	26 775
1990	35 200	29 718	27 345	28 560	11 627	28 834	27 957	29 003	27 681	29 397	28 544	29 449	37 504	23 763	28 803	26 908
1991	34 654	28 751	26 782	29 398	12 631	29 500	28 364	29 345	27 825	30 386	28 953	29 925	38 485	24 311	28 288	26 440
1992	35 356	28 659	27 173	29 526	13 221	29 728	28 682	29 783	28 067	30 827	29 165	30 207	39 611	24 456	27 783	26 411
1993	35 895	29 007	27 948	29 483	13 915	29 595	28 295	29 651	27 693	30 359	28 889	30 370	40 474	24 130	27 054	26 938
1994	36 908	30 069	28 942	29 657	14 985	30 133	29 117	31 192	28 204	31 073	29 504	31 085	42 277	24 638	27 967	28 019
1995	37 391	30 593	29 609	30 141	16 159	30 851	29 719	31 996	28 700	31 568	30 338	31 890	43 819	25 258	28 919	28 793
1996	38 340	30 764	30 415	30 864	17 156	31 497	30 079	32 702	28 918	31 790	30 662	32 836	45 820	25 809	29 304	29 553
1997	39 573	31 747	31 347	31 273	17 976	32 130	31 130	33 604	29 464	32 302	31 219	34 063	48 030	26 737	30 109	30 452
1998	40 819	32 774	32 561	30 557	16 827	33 248	31 662	34 212	30 386	32 967	31 648	35 183	49 026	27 834	31 345	31 463
1999	42 302	34 306	33 589	30 459	18 501	34 292	32 709	34 974	31 249	33 607	32 106	36 584	49 678	29 005	32 767	32 440
2000	43 571	35 766	34 270	31 270	19 961	35 458	33 832	36 086	32 252	34 643	33 276	37 756	50 962	30 215	34 198	33 595
2001	43 591	36 014	34 647	31 240	20 601	35 507	33 980	36 213	32 615	35 007	33 860	38 193	51 714	30 966	34 535	34 289
2002	43 951	36 651	35 569	31 267	21 951	35 914	34 291	36 258	32 714	34 947	33 907	37 976	52 208	31 346	35 276	34 884
2003	44 626	36 984	36 308	31 659	22 455	36 041	34 418	36 303	32 838	34 855	33 638	37 925	52 429	31 786	35 957	35 723
2004	45 802	37 764	37 178	32 497	23 404	36 726	35 376	37 044	33 406	35 284	33 818	38 646	54 134	32 296	37 318	36 600
2005	46 766	38 537	37 840	33 123	24 280	37 374	35 803	37 841	33 786	35 566	33 789	39 338	55 240	32 918	38 358	37 152
2006	47 563	39 223	38 289	33 800	25 453	38 468	36 552	38 994	34 298	36 735	34 282	40 601	56 046	33 721	39 783	37 991
2007	48 012	39 652	39 374	34 598	26 665	39 673	37 373	39 485	34 900	37 688	34 536	42 100	56 984	34 295	40 814	38 716
2008	47 570	39 385	39 497	34 198	27 194	40 314	37 504	38 913	34 779	38 229	33 820	42 726	57 300	34 044	40 310	38 669
2009	45 918	37 946	39 178	32 445	27 169	38 701	36 161	36 813	33 679	36 452	31 887	40 839	55 653	32 565	37 919	36 528

[1]Unified Germany from 1991 onward; data for previous years relate to the former West Germany.

. . . = Not available.

Table 10-13. Real Gross Domestic Product (GDP) Per Employed Person, 16 Countries, 1960–2009

(2009 U.S. dollars.)

Year	United States	Canada	Australia	Japan	Korea, Republic of	Austria	Belgium	Denmark	France	Germany[1]	Italy	Netherlands	Norway	Spain	Sweden	United Kingdom
1960	45 438	40 949	37 411	11 669	. . .	22 976	29 361	28 885	25 315	27 581	24 106	37 583	34 145	. . .	28 407	30 785
1961	46 480	41 603	37 063	12 873	. . .	24 064	30 593	30 143	26 579	28 461	25 919	38 117	35 748	. . .	29 780	31 142
1962	48 437	43 287	38 267	13 801	. . .	24 757	31 698	31 325	28 411	29 686	27 608	38 975	36 510	. . .	30 880	31 306
1963	49 859	44 551	39 409	14 887	5 817	25 945	32 846	31 087	29 972	30 448	29 649	39 720	37 738	. . .	32 364	32 568
1964	51 614	45 812	40 614	16 338	6 268	27 557	34 637	33 183	31 576	32 448	30 584	42 392	39 518	. . .	34 082	33 896
1965	53 613	47 007	41 244	16 991	6 289	28 537	35 733	34 150	33 024	33 993	32 373	44 262	41 238	. . .	35 142	34 304
1966	55 448	48 166	40 693	18 356	6 875	30 399	36 731	34 368	34 517	35 049	34 880	45 150	42 627	. . .	35 826	34 884
1967	55 534	48 066	42 437	20 006	7 028	31 832	38 323	36 306	36 141	36 117	36 924	47 690	45 026	. . .	37 431	36 164
1968	57 024	49 406	43 676	22 021	7 447	33 698	39 977	38 075	37 865	38 055	39 361	50 417	45 999	. . .	38 386	37 849
1969	57 384	50 310	45 588	24 467	8 274	35 880	41 916	39 773	39 995	40 267	42 063	52 964	47 652	. . .	39 564	38 619
1970	57 172	51 222	46 662	26 697	8 688	38 358	44 547	39 837	41 896	41 766	44 092	55 558	47 831	. . .	41 317	39 589
1971	58 864	52 049	47 349	27 674	9 278	39 881	45 860	41 093	43 907	42 880	44 479	57 613	50 099	35 414	41 788	40 445
1972	60 218	53 277	47 669	29 847	9 469	42 047	48 384	41 966	45 695	44 479	46 656	60 171	52 137	37 833	42 605	41 801
1973	61 675	54 227	48 475	31 532	10 310	43 494	50 793	43 007	48 041	46 048	49 283	63 420	54 086	39 763	44 130	44 116
1974	60 210	53 928	48 682	31 277	10 805	44 629	52 092	43 006	49 764	46 902	51 199	64 971	55 419	41 844	44 656	43 426
1975	60 762	53 916	49 860	32 324	11 330	44 798	52 070	43 047	49 717	47 692	50 090	65 475	57 250	42 921	44 910	43 322
1976	62 001	55 607	51 217	33 336	12 107	46 691	55 267	44 908	51 521	50 262	53 122	68 220	58 606	44 830	45 229	44 727
1977	62 610	56 553	51 241	34 387	13 116	48 440	55 754	45 911	52 925	51 827	54 315	69 269	59 385	46 403	44 417	45 747
1978	63 398	57 052	52 333	35 850	13 819	48 129	57 233	46 620	54 753	52 864	55 889	70 288	60 626	48 276	45 027	46 976
1979	63 599	56 756	53 424	37 431	14 769	50 539	57 924	48 003	56 398	54 014	58 569	70 714	62 397	49 414	46 085	47 747
1980	63 117	56 335	53 516	38 224	14 404	50 976	60 503	48 193	57 201	53 872	59 714	69 546	63 665	51 266	46 353	46 956
1981	64 003	56 658	54 607	39 519	15 096	51 104	61 466	48 561	57 950	54 092	60 267	67 629	63 832	52 455	46 185	47 579
1982	63 275	56 838	54 660	40 522	15 942	52 820	62 644	50 204	59 287	54 298	60 393	67 586	63 892	53 568	46 825	49 546
1983	65 282	57 966	55 420	41 140	17 729	54 744	63 675	51 530	60 182	55 659	60 903	69 858	66 498	54 707	47 563	51 722
1984	67 237	59 833	57 111	42 831	19 580	54 826	65 263	52 892	61 459	56 740	62 871	71 586	69 892	56 956	49 185	51 988
1985	68 637	60 939	58 562	45 298	20 282	56 010	66 030	53 749	62 742	57 258	64 024	72 100	71 647	58 883	49 750	53 187
1986	69 454	60 555	57 358	46 343	21 979	57 138	66 810	55 090	64 041	57 464	65 405	72 982	72 174	59 422	50 859	54 977
1987	69 892	61 358	58 563	48 056	23 394	57 941	67 849	55 003	65 137	57 467	67 339	66 703	71 994	59 851	52 200	56 362
1988	71 216	62 518	59 096	50 900	25 324	59 091	69 707	55 363	67 515	58 761	69 418	67 077	72 270	60 770	52 866	57 311
1989	72 305	62 745	59 060	52 854	25 970	60 567	71 025	55 927	69 163	59 927	71 284	68 642	75 128	61 477	53 554	57 131
1990	72 804	62 435	58 736	54 884	27 561	61 905	72 472	57 145	70 431	61 149	71 606	69 252	77 264	61 467	53 601	57 315
1991	73 314	62 216	59 605	55 578	29 324	63 180	73 552	58 230	71 069	62 929	71 369	69 136	80 460	62 283	53 806	58 048
1992	75 411	63 390	61 521	55 408	30 427	64 007	74 775	60 092	72 461	65 279	72 446	68 910	83 469	63 750	55 634	59 549
1993	76 533	64 566	64 579	55 293	31 974	64 559	74 539	60 990	72 736	65 625	73 784	69 861	85 192	64 934	57 497	61 440
1994	77 928	66 307	64 579	55 708	33 703	65 954	77 268	64 595	74 239	67 439	76 634	71 446	88 289	66 796	60 439	63 565
1995	78 786	66 977	64 367	56 576	35 695	67 753	77 906	65 557	75 144	68 558	78 958	71 586	90 112	67 357	61 824	64 709
1996	80 623	67 455	66 131	58 024	37 454	68 988	78 778	66 596	75 693	69 430	79 370	72 550	92 833	68 008	63 254	65 960
1997	82 412	68 867	68 274	58 524	38 940	69 946	81 183	67 584	77 049	70 749	80 604	73 327	95 051	68 637	65 876	66 944
1998	84 784	69 965	70 240	58 008	39 065	71 735	81 311	68 001	78 553	71 332	80 933	74 049	95 066	69 012	67 479	68 665
1999	87 563	71 995	72 111	58 735	42 504	73 027	83 043	69 079	79 539	71 795	81 237	75 484	96 105	69 759	69 145	70 074
2000	88 961	73 938	72 613	60 792	44 353	74 987	84 403	71 021	80 491	72 737	82 635	76 383	98 671	70 812	70 549	71 981
2001	89 868	74 339	73 609	61 369	45 226	74 837	83 923	70 740	80 551	73 316	82 472	75 938	100 282	71 132	69 963	73 148
2002	91 740	74 688	74 986	62 509	47 155	76 141	85 193	70 980	80 875	73 729	81 454	75 073	101 399	71 483	71 664	74 118
2003	93 099	74 341	75 757	63 600	48 542	76 805	85 841	72 103	81 652	74 272	80 238	75 756	103 494	71 451	73 746	75 483
2004	95 384	75 347	77 035	65 205	49 843	77 679	87 795	74 194	83 579	74 871	81 109	77 600	106 993	71 313	77 378	76 897
2005	96 626	76 554	76 800	66 214	51 138	78 432	88 109	75 192	84 693	75 522	81 173	79 138	108 598	71 022	79 643	77 776
2006	97 414	77 211	76 899	67 270	53 101	80 023	89 475	76 165	85 729	77 434	81 233	80 338	107 187	70 978	81 685	79 290
2007	98 229	77 125	78 340	68 604	55 140	81 392	90 636	75 223	86 512	78 047	81 410	81 490	105 807	71 300	82 375	80 773
2008	98 671	76 349	78 401	68 017	56 063	81 623	89 894	73 652	86 185	77 940	80 107	81 776	104 489	72 247	81 228	80 620
2009	99 763	75 676	79 188	65 507	56 342	79 381	87 515	72 551	84 978	74 120	77 363	78 542	103 156	74 616	78 646	77 878

[1]Unified Germany from 1991 onward; data for previous years relate to the former West Germany.
. . . = Not available.

Table 10-14. Real Gross Domestic Product (GDP) Per Hour Worked, 16 Countries, 1970–2009

(2009 U.S. dollars.)

Year	United States	Canada	Australia	Japan	Korea, Republic of	Austria	Belgium	Denmark	France	Germany[1]	Italy	Netherlands	Norway	Spain	Sweden	United Kingdom
1970	29.90	26.68	...	12.12	...	...	23.74	21.14	20.45	21.24	...	...	26.07	...	...	...
1971	31.05	27.37	...	12.71	...	...	24.57	22.16	21.46	22.17	...	...	27.63	...	...	22.04
1972	31.82	28.17	...	13.72	...	...	26.29	23.34	22.95	23.27	...	...	29.28	...	...	22.52
1973	32.62	28.74	...	14.64	...	...	28.01	24.52	24.32	24.46	...	...	30.62	...	...	23.65
1974	32.32	28.80	...	14.81	...	...	29.18	24.67	25.63	25.45	...	...	31.76	...	...	23.47
1975	33.20	29.04	...	15.53	...	...	29.32	25.71	25.97	26.40	...	...	33.13	...	...	23.82
1976	34.00	30.42	...	15.88	...	...	31.07	26.66	26.54	27.63	...	...	35.00	...	...	24.68
1977	34.35	31.05	...	16.26	...	...	31.80	27.64	27.83	28.77	...	...	36.25	25.26	...	25.11
1978	34.64	31.22	28.44	16.85	...	...	32.96	28.38	29.28	29.66	...	...	37.85	26.60	...	25.77
1979	34.78	31.11	28.73	17.56	...	...	33.68	29.35	30.20	30.51	...	...	39.49	27.98	...	26.23
1980	34.78	31.32	29.18	17.92	5.14	...	35.58	29.05	30.75	30.77	32.12	...	40.30	29.24	30.28	26.23
1981	35.59	31.50	29.62	18.61	5.42	...	36.65	29.76	31.47	31.28	32.31	...	40.65	30.38	30.34	27.13
1982	35.43	31.97	30.46	19.13	5.48	...	37.67	30.58	33.56	31.60	32.18	...	40.98	31.03	30.47	28.31
1983	36.38	32.65	31.07	19.45	6.15	...	38.15	31.46	34.41	32.64	32.47	...	42.81	32.26	30.77	29.65
1984	37.12	33.62	31.61	20.13	6.83	...	38.55	32.40	35.29	33.50	33.70	...	45.14	34.31	31.77	29.70
1985	37.79	33.98	32.54	21.47	7.08	...	38.89	33.21	36.76	34.27	34.39	...	46.46	35.85	32.05	30.34
1986	38.64	33.82	31.76	21.98	7.84	...	39.79	33.97	37.63	34.79	34.97	...	46.92	36.17	32.81	31.46
1987	38.83	34.06	32.14	22.74	8.12	...	40.78	34.65	37.99	35.27	35.64	...	47.66	37.52	33.45	32.16
1988	39.25	34.35	32.61	24.06	8.73	...	42.20	35.28	39.16	36.18	36.67	...	47.75	37.99	33.45	32.57
1989	39.56	34.58	32.63	25.30	9.16	...	43.21	36.04	40.49	37.44	37.97	...	49.74	38.23	33.91	32.40
1990	40.24	34.75	32.77	26.62	9.85	...	43.77	37.14	41.32	38.76	38.36	...	51.42	38.22	34.02	32.74
1991	40.72	35.09	33.20	27.58	10.56	...	45.43	37.97	41.94	40.65	38.38	...	53.63	38.94	34.45	33.64
1992	42.07	35.78	34.01	28.09	11.15	...	46.79	38.66	42.76	41.68	38.89	...	55.27	39.94	35.22	34.65
1993	42.28	35.91	35.42	28.83	11.67	...	47.96	39.22	43.25	42.34	39.61	...	56.53	40.91	36.00	35.82
1994	42.66	36.55	35.74	29.19	12.37	...	49.73	41.73	44.32	43.59	41.28	...	58.67	42.16	36.96	36.84
1995	42.68	37.12	35.66	29.61	13.08	39.88	49.31	42.56	45.53	44.70	42.48	47.33	60.57	42.31	37.69	37.46
1996	43.73	37.05	37.26	30.34	13.77	40.35	50.70	43.51	45.74	45.74	42.37	47.73	62.62	42.73	38.26	38.19
1997	44.38	38.18	37.90	31.08	14.57	40.71	51.81	43.77	46.73	46.89	43.26	48.59	64.33	42.84	39.73	38.80
1998	45.34	38.96	38.98	31.17	14.99	41.69	51.53	43.61	47.97	47.45	43.06	49.58	64.42	42.76	40.74	39.88
1999	46.62	40.00	40.13	31.87	16.22	42.66	52.53	44.03	48.78	48.13	43.31	50.71	65.21	42.81	41.53	40.90
2000	47.91	41.19	40.36	32.73	16.86	43.58	54.63	44.91	50.58	49.38	44.40	51.62	67.81	42.84	42.96	42.40
2001	49.02	41.63	42.08	33.38	17.26	43.53	53.22	44.58	51.03	50.27	44.75	51.97	70.17	43.14	43.24	43.02
2002	50.57	42.23	42.73	34.29	18.21	44.37	53.92	44.96	52.62	51.01	44.49	52.31	71.71	43.41	44.93	44.05
2003	52.10	42.38	42.97	34.88	19.01	44.45	54.50	45.73	53.28	51.62	43.95	53.02	74.00	43.78	46.63	45.11
2004	53.36	42.52	44.18	35.69	19.68	45.25	56.68	46.98	53.53	51.94	44.42	54.75	75.49	44.09	48.20	46.05
2005	54.16	43.44	43.79	36.51	20.45	46.17	56.30	47.63	54.40	52.66	44.63	55.84	76.47	44.46	49.62	46.46
2006	54.61	43.88	44.52	36.92	21.32	47.35	57.14	48.04	55.82	54.17	44.76	56.83	75.81	44.83	51.08	47.54
2007	55.29	43.97	46.10	37.78	22.51	48.41	58.10	47.87	55.60	54.54	44.82	57.71	74.56	45.59	51.01	48.36
2008	55.90	43.75	44.81	37.90	23.44	48.56	57.33	46.93	55.25	54.52	44.27	58.38	73.45	45.96	49.99	48.42
2009	57.54	44.14	46.27	37.10	23.61	47.45	56.84	46.32	54.50	53.32	43.62	56.75	73.26	47.27	48.83	47.39

[1]Unified Germany from 1991 onward; data for previous years relate to the former West Germany.
. . . = Not available.

Table 10-15. Real Gross Domestic Product (GDP) Per Capita and Per Employed Person, Average Annual Percent Change, 16 Countries, Selected Years, 1979–2009

(Percent.)

Category and country	1979–2009	1979–1990	1990–1995	1995–2000	2000–2009	2007–2008	2008–2009
Real GDP Per Capita							
United States	1.6	1.9	1.2	3.1	0.6	-0.9	-3.5
Canada	1.4	1.5	0.6	3.2	0.7	-0.7	-3.7
Australia	1.8	1.7	1.6	3.0	1.5	0.3	-0.8
Japan	1.8	3.9	1.1	0.7	0.4	-1.2	-5.1
Korea, Republic of	5.6	7.3	6.8	4.3	3.5	2.0	-0.1
Austria	1.7	2.0	1.4	2.8	1.0	1.6	-4.0
Belgium	1.6	2.1	1.2	2.6	0.7	0.4	-3.6
Denmark	1.5	1.8	2.0	2.4	0.2	-1.4	-5.4
France	1.3	1.8	0.7	2.4	0.5	-0.3	-3.2
Germany[1]	. . .	2.0	. . .	1.9	0.6	1.4	-4.6
Italy	1.3	2.4	1.2	1.9	-0.5	-2.1	-5.7
Netherlands	1.7	1.6	1.6	3.4	0.9	1.5	-4.4
Norway	2.2	2.3	3.2	3.1	1.0	0.6	-2.9
Spain	1.9	2.4	1.2	3.6	0.8	-0.7	-4.3
Sweden	1.6	1.9	0.1	3.4	1.2	-1.2	-5.9
United Kingdom	1.8	2.1	1.4	3.1	0.9	-0.1	-5.5
Real GDP Per Employed Person							
United States	1.5	1.2	1.6	2.5	1.3	0.4	1.1
Canada	1.0	0.9	1.4	2.0	0.3	-1.0	-0.9
Australia	1.3	0.9	1.8	2.4	1.0	0.1	1.0
Japan	1.9	3.5	0.6	1.4	0.8	-0.9	-3.7
Korea, Republic of	4.6	5.8	5.3	4.4	2.7	1.7	0.5
Austria	1.5	1.9	1.8	2.0	0.6	0.3	-2.7
Belgium	1.4	2.1	1.5	1.6	0.4	-0.8	-2.6
Denmark	1.4	1.6	2.8	1.6	0.2	-2.1	-1.5
France	1.4	2.0	1.3	1.4	0.6	-0.4	-1.4
Germany[1]	. . .	1.1	. . .	1.2	0.2	-0.1	-4.9
Italy	0.9	1.8	2.0	0.9	-0.7	-1.6	-3.4
Netherlands	0.4	-0.2	0.7	1.3	0.3	0.4	-4.0
Norway	1.7	2.0	3.1	1.8	0.5	-1.2	-1.3
Spain	1.4	2.0	1.8	1.0	0.6	1.3	3.3
Sweden	1.8	1.4	2.9	2.7	1.2	-1.4	-3.2
United Kingdom	1.6	1.7	2.5	2.2	0.9	-0.2	-3.4

[1]Data for Germany for years before 1991 pertain to the former West Germany.
. . . = Not available.

Table 10-16. Real Gross Domestic Product (GDP) Per Hour Worked, Average Annual Percent Change, 16 Countries, Selected Years, 1979–2009

(Percent.)

Country	1979–2009	1979–1990	1990–1995	1995–2000	2000–2009	2007–2008	2008–2009
Real GDP Per Capita							
United States	1.8	1.3	1.2	2.3	2.1	1.1	2.9
Canada	1.2	1.0	1.3	2.1	0.8	-0.5	0.9
Australia	1.7	1.2	1.7	2.5	1.5	-2.8	3.3
Japan	2.6	3.9	2.1	2.0	1.4	0.3	-2.1
Korea, Republic of	. . .	. . .	5.8	5.2	3.8	4.1	0.7
Austria	1.8	2.4	2.4	2.1	0.4	-1.3	-0.8
Belgium	1.6	2.2	2.8	1.1	0.3	-2.0	-1.3
Denmark	2.1	2.9	2.0	2.1	0.8	-0.6	-1.4
France	. . .	2.2	. . .	2.0	0.9	0.0	-2.2
Germany[1]	. . .	. . .	2.1	0.9	-0.2	-1.2	-1.5
Italy	. . .	. . .	. . .	1.8	1.1	1.1	-2.8
Netherlands	2.2	2.4	3.3	2.3	0.9	-1.5	-0.3
Norway	1.8	2.9	2.1	0.2	1.1	0.8	2.8
Spain	. . .	. . .	2.1	2.7	1.4	-2.0	-2.3
Sweden	2.1	2.0	2.7	2.5	1.2	0.1	-2.1

[1]Data for Germany for years before 1991 pertain to the former West Germany.
. . . = Not available.

Chapter Eleven

CONSUMER EXPENDITURES

CONSUMER EXPENDITURES

HIGHLIGHTS

The principal objective of the Consumer Expenditure (CE) Survey is to collect information about the buying habits of American households. The survey breaks down expenditures for different demographic categories, such as income, age, family size, and geographic location. These data are used in a variety of government, business, and academic research projects and provide important weights for the periodic revisions of the Consumer Price Index (CPI).

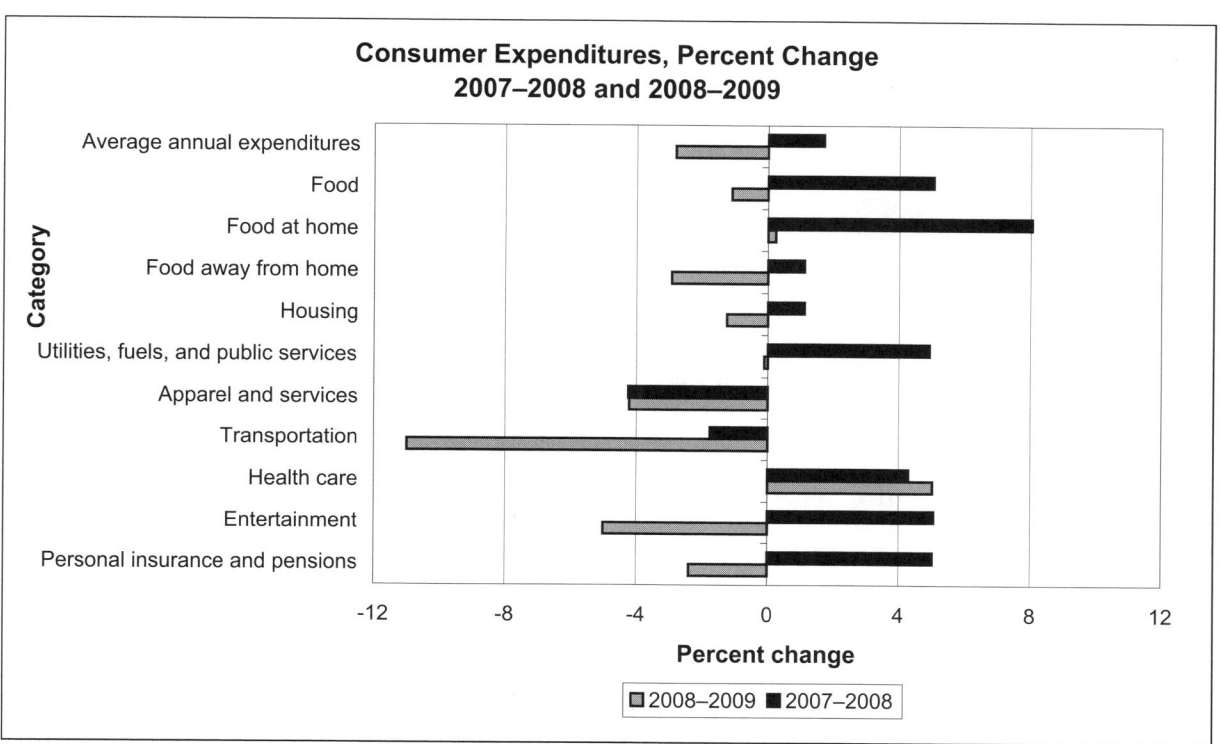

Average annual expenditures declined 2.8 percent in 2009 after increasing each year from 2000 to 2008. While spending declined in most categories, it increased for heath care (5.0 percent) and education (2.1 percent). (See Table 11-1.)

OTHER HIGHLIGHTS

- In 2009, average annual expenditures for transportation dropped significantly—11.0 percent—after only declining by 1.8 percent the year before. (See Table 11-1.)

- Average annual expenditures ranged from $35,707 for retired persons to $70,143 for managers and professional workers. Self-employee workers had the second highest average annual expenditures at $57,073. (See Table 11-6.)

- As educational attainment increased, so did average annual expenditures. Those with less than a high school diploma had average annual expenditures of $30,323 while those with a master's, professional, or doctoral degree had average annual expenditures of $76,072. (See Table 11-13.)

- In 2009, average annual expenditures were highest for those in the Northeast ($53,868), followed by those in the West ($53,005), the South ($46,551), and the Midwest ($45,749). (See Table 11-16.)

NOTES AND DEFINITIONS

Purpose, Collection, and Coverage

The buying habits of American consumers change over time because of changes in relative prices, real income, family size and composition, and other determinants of tastes and preferences. The introduction of new products into the marketplace and the emergence of new concepts in retailing also influence consumer buying habits. Data from the Consumer Expenditure Survey (CE), the only national survey that relates family expenditures to demographic characteristics, are of great importance to researchers. The survey data are also used to revise the Consumer Price Index market baskets and item samples.

Until the 1970s, the Bureau of Labor Statistics (BLS) conducted surveys of consumer expenditures approximately once every 10 years. The last such survey was conducted in 1972–1973. In late 1979, in a significant departure from previous methodology, BLS initiated a survey to be conducted on a continuous basis with rotating panels of respondents.

The current CE is similar to its 1972–1973 predecessor in that it consists of two separate components. Each component has its own questionnaire and sample: (1) the Interview Survey, in which an interviewer visits each consumer unit every three months for a twelve-month period; and (2) the Diary Survey, a record-keeping survey completed by other consumer units for two consecutive one-week periods. The Census Bureau, under contract to BLS, collects the data for both components of the survey. Beginning in 1999, the sample was increased from 5,000 to 7,500 households.

In 2003, the survey modified the questions on race and Hispanic origin to comply with the new standards for maintaining, collecting, and presenting federal data on race and ethnicity for federal statistical agencies. Beginning with the data collected in 2003, the CE tables use data collected from the new race and ethnicity questions. A number of new classifications were made with publication of the 2003 data.

Beginning with the publication of the 2004 tables, the CE has been implementing multiple imputations of income data. Prior to 2004, the CE only published income data collected from complete income reporters. The introduction of multiply imputed income data affects the published CE tables in several ways, because income data are now published for all consumer units (instead of for complete reporters only). The most obvious result of this change is seen on the tables showing expenditures categorized by income before taxes, including income by quintile. Starting with the 2004 data, columns describing income, expenditures, and characteristics for "total complete reporting" and "incomplete reporting of income" no longer appear in these tables, and the column entitled "all consumer units" appears on all income tables. Due to the implementation of income imputation, data for 2004 are not strictly comparable to those of prior years, especially for the income tables. Averages for demographic characteristics and annual expenditures will change due to differences between the incomplete and complete income reporters in these categories. Furthermore, certain expenditures (such as personal insurance and pensions) are computed using income data. As a result of imputation, average annual values for these expenditures may be substantially different in the 2004 CE tables than in tables for previous years. The regular flow of data resulting from this design substantially enhances the usefulness of the survey by providing more timely information on consumption patterns within different kinds of consumer units.

The *Interview Survey* is designed to collect data on the types of expenditures that respondents can be expected to recall after a period of three months or longer. These include relatively large expenditures (such as those for property, travel, automobiles, and major appliances) and expenditures that occur on a regular basis (such as those for rent, utilities, insurance premiums, and clothing). The interview also obtains "global estimates" for food and other selected items. The survey collects data for approximately 95 percent of total expenditures. Each sample household is interviewed once per quarter, for five consecutive quarters.

The *Diary Survey* is designed to collect data on expenditures for frequently purchased items that are more difficult to recall over longer periods of time. Respondents complete a diary of expenses for two consecutive 1-week periods. Expenditures for tobacco, drugs (including nonprescription drugs), and personal care supplies and services are also collected in the Diary Survey.

Participants in both surveys record dollar amounts for goods and services purchased during the reporting period, regardless of whether payment was made at the time of purchase. Excluded from both surveys are business-related expenditures and expenditures for which the family is reimbursed. Information is collected on demographic and family characteristics at the initial interview for each survey.

The tables in this chapter present integrated data from the Diary Survey and the Interview Survey and provide a complete accounting of consumer expenditures and income, which neither survey component is designed to do alone. Data for some expenditure items are only collected in one of the surveys. For example, the Diary Survey does not collect data for expenditures on overnight travel or information on reimbursements, while the Interview Survey records these purchases. Examples of expenditures for which reimbursements are netted out include those for medical care, auto repair, and construction, repairs, alterations, and maintenance of property.

For items unique to one survey or the other, the choice of which survey to use as the source of data is obvious. However, there is considerable overlap in coverage between the two surveys. Integrating the data thus presents the problem of determining the appropriate survey component. When data are available from both survey sources, the more reliable of the two (as determined by statistical methods) is selected. As a result, some items are selected from the Interview Survey and others are selected from the Diary Survey.

Data Included in This Book

Data for single characteristics are for calendar year 2009, and data for two cross-classified characteristics are for an average of calendar years 2008 and 2009. Income values from the survey are derived from "complete income reporters" only. Complete income reporters are defined as consumer units that provide values for at least one of the major sources of their income: wages and salaries, self-employment income, retirement income, dividends and interest, and welfare benefits. Some consumer units are defined as complete income reporters, even though they may not have provided a full accounting of all income from all sources.

Consumer units are classified by quintiles of income before taxes, age of reference person, size of consumer unit, region, composition of consumer unit, number of earners in consumer unit, housing tenure, race, type of area (urban or rural), and occupation.

Concepts and Definitions

A *consumer unit* comprises either (1) all members of a particular household related by blood, marriage, adoption, or other legal arrangements; (2) a person living alone, sharing a household with others, living as a roomer in a private home or lodging house or in permanent living quarters in a hotel or motel, but who is financially independent; or (3) two or more persons living together who pool their income to make joint expenditure decisions. Financial independence is determined by the three major expense categories: housing, food, and other living expenses. To be considered financially independent, at least two of the three major expense categories have to be provided by the respondent.

The terms "family," "household," and "consumer unit" are used interchangeably in descriptions of the CE.

An *earner* is a consumer unit member, 14 years of age or older, who reported having worked at least 1 week during the 12 months prior to the interview date.

The *education of reference person* refers to the number of years of formal education of the reference person, on the basis of the highest grade completed. If enrolled at time of the interview, the interviewer records the grade currently attended. Persons not reporting the extent of their education are classified under no school or not reported.

Housing tenure refers to the family's principal place of residence during the survey. "Owner" includes families living in their own homes, cooperatives or condominium apartments, or townhouses. "Renter" includes families paying rent, as well as families living rent-free in lieu of wages.

The *householder* or *reference person* is the first member of the consumer unit mentioned by the respondent as owner or renter of the premises at the time of the initial interview.

Quintiles of income before taxes refers to the ranking of complete income reporters in ascending order, according to the level of total before-tax income reported by the consumer unit. The ranking is then divided into five equal groups. Incomplete income reporters are not ranked and are shown separately.

Total expenditures include the transaction costs, including excise and sales taxes of goods and services acquired during the interview period. Estimates include expenditures for gifts and contributions and payments for pensions and personal insurance.

Sources of Additional Information

More extensive descriptions and tables can be found in an updated version of Chapter 16 in the *BLS Handbook of Methods* and in an anthology of articles relating to consumer expenditures. These resources can be found on the BLS Web site at <http://www.bls.gov>.

Table 11-1. Consumer Expenditures, Annual Average of All Consumer Units, 1999–2009

(Number, dollar, percent.)

Item	1999	2000	2001	2002	2003	2004	2005	2006	2007	2008	2009
NUMBER OF CONSUMER UNITS (THOUSANDS)	108 465	109 367	110 339	112 108	115 356	116 282	117 356	118 843	120 171	120 770	120 847
CONSUMER UNIT CHARACTERISTICS											
Income Before Taxes	43 951	44 649	47 507	49 430	51 128	54 453	58 712	60 533	63 091	63 563	62 857
Age of Reference Person	47.9	48.2	48.1	48.1	48.0	48.5	48.6	48.7	48.8	49.1	49.4
Average Number in Consumer Unit											
All persons	2.5	2.5	2.5	2.5	2.5	2.5	2.5	2.5	2.5	2.5	2.5
Children under 18 years	0.7	0.7	0.7	0.7	0.6	0.6	0.6	0.6	0.6	0.6	0.6
Persons 65 years and over	0.3	0.3	0.3	0.3	0.3	0.3	0.3	0.3	0.3	0.3	0.3
Earners	1.3	1.4	1.4	1.4	1.3	1.3	1.3	1.3	1.3	1.3	1.3
Vehicles	1.9	1.9	1.9	2.0	1.9	1.9	2.0	1.9	1.9	2.0	2.0
Percent Homeowner	65	66	66	66	67	68	67	67	67	66	66
With mortgage	38	39	40	41	41	42	43	43	43	42	41
Without mortgage	27	27	26	26	26	25	25	24	23	24	25
AVERAGE ANNUAL EXPENDITURES	36 995	38 045	39 518	40 677	40 817	43 395	46 409	48 398	49 638	50 486	49 067
Food	5 031	5 158	5 321	5 375	5 340	5 781	5 931	6 111	6 133	6 443	6 372
Food at home	2 915	3 021	3 086	3 099	3 129	3 347	3 297	3 417	3 465	3 744	3 753
Cereals and bakery products	448	453	452	450	442	461	445	446	460	507	506
Meats, poultry, fish, and eggs	448	453	452	798	825	880	764	797	777	846	841
Dairy products	322	325	332	328	328	371	378	368	387	430	406
Fruits and vegetables	500	521	522	552	535	561	552	592	600	657	656
Other food at home	896	927	952	970	999	1 075	1 158	1 212	1 241	1 305	1 343
Food away from home	2 116	2 137	2 235	2 276	2 211	2 434	2 634	2 694	2 668	2 698	2 619
Alcoholic Beverages	318	372	349	376	391	459	426	497	457	444	435
Housing	12 057	12 319	13 011	13 283	13 432	13 918	15 167	16 366	16 920	17 109	16 895
Shelter	7 016	7 114	7 602	7 829	7 887	7 998	8 805	9 673	10 023	10 183	10 075
Owned dwellings	4 525	4 602	4 979	5 165	5 263	5 324	5 958	6 516	6 730	6 760	6 543
Rented dwellings	2 027	2 034	2 134	2 160	2 179	2 201	2 345	2 590	2 602	2 724	2 860
Other lodging	465	478	489	505	445	473	502	567	691	698	672
Utilities, fuels, and public services	2 377	2 489	2 767	2 684	2 811	2 927	3 183	3 397	3 477	3 649	3 645
Household operations	666	684	676	706	707	753	801	948	984	998	1 011
Housekeeping supplies	498	482	509	545	529	594	611	640	639	654	659
Household furnishings and equipment	1 499	1 549	1 458	1 518	1 497	1 646	1 767	1 708	1 797	1 624	1 506
Apparel and Services	1 743	1 856	1 743	1 749	1 640	1 816	1 886	1 874	1 881	1 801	1 725
Transportation	7 011	7 417	7 633	7 759	7 781	7 801	8 344	8 508	8 758	8 604	7 658
Vehicle purchases (net outlay)	3 305	3 418	3 579	3 665	3 732	3 397	3 544	3 421	3 244	2 755	2 657
Gasoline and motor oil	1 055	1 291	1 279	1 235	1 333	1 598	2 013	2 227	2 384	2 715	1 986
Other vehicle expenses	2 254	2 281	2 375	2 471	2 331	2 365	2 339	2 355	2 592	2 621	2 536
Public transportation	397	427	400	389	385	441	448	505	538	513	479
Health Care	1 959	2 066	2 182	2 350	2 416	2 574	2 664	2 766	2 853	2 976	3 126
Health insurance	923	983	1 061	1 168	1 252	1 332	1 361	1 465	1 545	1 653	1 785
Medical services	558	568	573	590	591	648	677	670	709	727	736
Drugs	370	416	449	487	467	480	521	514	481	482	486
Medical supplies	109	99	100	105	107	114	105	117	118	114	119
Entertainment	1 891	1 863	1 953	2 079	2 060	2 218	2 388	2 376	2 698	2 835	2 693
Personal Care Products and Services	408	564	465	526	527	581	541	585	588	616	596
Reading	159	146	141	139	127	130	126	117	118	116	110
Education	635	632	648	752	783	905	940	888	945	1 046	1 068
Tobacco Products and Smoking Supplies	300	319	308	320	290	288	319	327	323	317	380
Miscellaneous	867	776	750	792	606	690	808	846	808	840	816
Cash Contributions	1 181	1 192	1 258	1 277	1 370	1 408	1 663	1 869	1 821	1 737	1 723
Personal Insurance and Pensions	3 436	3 365	3 737	3 899	4 055	4 823	5 204	5 270	5 336	5 605	5 471
Life and other personal insurance	394	399	410	406	397	390	381	322	309	317	309
Pensions and Social Security	3 042	2 966	3 326	3 493	3 658	4 433	4 823	4 948	5 027	5 288	5 162

Table 11-2. Shares of Annual Average Consumer Expenditures and Characteristics of All Consumer Units, 1999–2009

(Number, dollar, percent.)

Item	1999	2000	2001	2002	2003	2004	2005	2006	2007	2008	2009
NUMBER OF CONSUMER UNITS (THOUSANDS)	108 465	109 367	110 339	112 108	115 356	116 282	117 356	118 843	120 171	120 770	120 847
CONSUMER UNIT CHARACTERISTICS											
Income Before Taxes	43 951	44 649	47 507	49 430	51 128	54 453	58 712	60 533	63 091	63 563	62 857
Age of Reference Person	47.9	48.2	48.1	48.1	48.4	48.5	48.6	48.7	48.8	49.1	49.4
Average Number in Consumer Unit											
All persons	2.5	2.5	2.5	2.5	2.5	2.5	2.5	2.5	2.5	2.5	2.5
Children under 18 years	0.7	0.7	0.7	0.7	0.6	0.6	0.6	0.6	0.6	0.6	0.6
Persons 65 years and over	0.3	0.3	0.3	0.3	0.3	0.3	0.3	0.3	0.3	0.3	0.3
Earners	1.3	1.4	1.4	1.4	1.3	1.3	1.3	1.3	1.3	1.3	1.3
Vehicles	1.9	1.9	1.9	2.0	1.9	1.9	2.0	1.9	1.9	2.0	2.0
Percent Homeowner	65	66	66	66	67	68	67	67	67	66	66
With mortgage	38	39	40	41	41	42	43	43	43	42	41
Without mortgage	27	27	26	26	26	25	25	24	23	24	25
AVERAGE ANNUAL EXPENDITURES	36 995	38 045	39 518	40 677	40 817	43 395	46 409	48 398	49 638	50 486	49 067
Food	13.6	13.6	13.5	13.2	13.1	13.3	12.8	12.6	12.4	12.8	13.0
Food at home	7.9	7.9	7.8	7.6	7.7	7.7	7.1	7.1	7.0	7.4	7.6
Cereals and bakery products	1.2	1.2	1.1	1.1	1.1	1.1	1.0	0.9	0.9	1.0	1.0
Meats, poultry, fish, and eggs	2.0	2.1	2.1	2.0	2.0	2.0	1.6	1.6	1.6	1.7	1.7
Dairy products	0.9	0.9	0.8	0.8	0.8	0.9	0.8	0.8	0.8	0.9	0.8
Fruits and vegetables	1.4	1.4	1.3	1.4	1.3	1.3	1.2	1.2	1.2	1.3	1.3
Other food at home	2.4	2.4	2.4	2.4	2.4	2.5	2.5	2.5	2.5	2.6	2.7
Food away from home	5.7	5.6	5.7	5.6	5.4	5.6	5.7	5.6	5.4	5.3	5.3
Alcoholic Beverages	0.9	1.0	0.9	0.9	1.0	1.1	0.9	1.0	0.9	0.9	0.9
Housing	32.6	32.4	32.9	32.7	32.9	32.1	32.7	33.8	34.1	33.9	34.4
Shelter	19.0	18.7	19.2	19.2	19.3	18.4	19.0	20.0	20.2	20.2	20.5
Owned dwellings	12.2	12.1	12.6	12.7	12.9	12.3	12.8	13.5	13.6	13.4	13.3
Rented dwellings	5.5	5.3	5.4	5.3	5.3	5.1	5.1	5.4	5.2	5.4	5.8
Other lodging	1.3	1.3	1.2	1.2	1.1	1.1	1.1	1.2	1.4	1.4	1.4
Utilities, fuels, and public services	6.4	6.5	7.0	6.6	6.9	6.7	6.9	7.0	7.0	7.2	7.4
Household operations	1.8	1.8	1.7	1.7	1.7	1.7	1.7	2.0	2.0	2.0	2.1
Housekeeping supplies	1.3	1.3	1.3	1.3	1.3	1.4	1.3	1.3	1.3	1.3	1.3
Household furnishings and equipment	4.1	4.1	3.7	3.7	3.7	3.8	3.8	3.5	3.6	3.2	3.1
Apparel and Services	4.7	4.9	4.4	4.3	4.0	4.2	4.1	3.9	3.8	3.6	3.5
Transportation	19.0	19.5	19.3	19.1	19.1	18.0	18.0	17.6	17.6	17.0	15.6
Vehicle purchases (net outlay)	8.9	9.0	9.1	9.0	9.1	7.8	7.6	7.1	6.5	5.5	5.4
Gasoline and motor oil	2.9	3.4	3.2	3.0	3.3	3.7	4.3	4.6	4.8	5.4	4.0
Other vehicle expenses	6.1	6.0	6.0	6.1	5.7	5.5	5.0	4.9	5.2	5.2	5.2
Public transportation	1.1	1.1	1.0	1.0	0.9	1.0	1.0	1.0	1.1	1.0	1.0
Health Care	5.3	5.4	5.5	5.8	5.9	5.9	5.7	5.7	5.7	5.9	6.4
Health insurance	2.5	2.6	2.7	2.9	3.1	3.1	2.9	3.0	3.1	3.3	3.6
Medical services	1.5	1.5	1.4	1.5	1.4	1.5	1.5	1.4	1.4	1.4	1.5
Drugs	1.0	1.1	1.1	1.2	1.1	1.1	1.1	1.1	1.0	1.0	1.0
Medical supplies	0.3	0.3	0.3	0.3	0.3	0.3	0.2	0.2	0.2	0.2	0.2
Entertainment	5.1	4.9	4.9	5.1	5.0	5.1	5.1	4.9	5.4	5.6	5.5
Personal Care Products and Services	1.1	1.5	1.2	1.3	1.3	1.3	1.2	1.2	1.2	1.2	1.2
Reading	0.4	0.4	0.4	0.3	0.3	0.3	0.3	0.2	0.2	0.2	0.2
Education	1.7	1.7	1.6	1.8	1.9	2.1	2.0	1.8	1.9	2.1	2.2
Tobacco Products and Smoking Supplies	0.8	0.8	0.8	0.8	0.7	0.7	0.7	0.7	0.7	0.6	0.8
Miscellaneous	2.3	2.0	1.9	1.9	1.5	1.6	1.7	1.7	1.6	1.7	1.7
Cash Contributions	3.2	3.1	3.2	3.1	3.4	3.2	3.6	3.9	3.7	3.4	3.5
Personal Insurance and Pensions	9.3	8.8	9.5	9.6	9.9	11.1	11.2	10.9	10.8	11.1	11.2
Life and other personal insurance	1.1	1.0	1.0	1.0	1.0	0.9	0.8	0.7	0.6	0.6	0.6
Pensions and Social Security	8.2	7.8	8.4	8.6	9.0	10.2	10.4	10.2	10.1	10.5	10.5

Table 11-3. Consumer Expenditures, Averages by Income Before Taxes, 2009

(Number, dollar, percent.)

Item	All consumer units	Less than $5,000	$5,000 to $9,999	$10,000 to $14,999	$15,000 to $19,999	$20,000 to $29,999	$30,000 to $39,999	$40,000 to $49,999	$50,000 to $69,999	$70,000 and over
NUMBER OF CONSUMER UNITS (THOUSANDS)	120 847	4 749	5 203	7 726	7 669	15 022	13 053	11 444	17 799	38 181
CONSUMER UNIT CHARACTERISTICS										
Income Before Taxes	62 857	-2 587	8 015	12 598	17 527	24 888	34 721	44 733	59 009	129 528
Income After Taxes	60 753	-2 676	8 163	12 749	17 699	25 089	34 432	43 940	57 610	123 705
Age of Reference Person	49.4	42.5	48.8	56.2	53.9	52.4	50.0	48.6	48.6	47.3
Average Number in Consumer Unit										
All persons	2.5	1.7	1.6	1.7	2.0	2.2	2.4	2.5	2.7	3.1
Children under 18 years	0.6	0.4	0.4	0.4	0.5	0.5	0.6	0.6	0.6	0.8
Persons 65 years and over	0.3	0.2	0.3	0.5	0.5	0.5	0.4	0.3	0.3	0.2
Earners	1.3	0.5	0.5	0.4	0.6	0.9	1.1	1.3	1.5	1.9
Vehicles	2.0	0.9	0.8	1.0	1.2	1.5	1.7	1.9	2.3	2.7
Percent Distribution										
Male	47	46	36	35	40	41	43	48	51	54
Female	53	54	64	65	60	59	57	52	49	46
Percent Homeowner	66	31	31	43	49	55	62	65	74	86
With mortgage	41	13	12	12	16	23	32	39	49	68
Without mortgage	25	17	19	32	33	32	30	26	25	18
AVERAGE ANNUAL EXPENDITURES	49 067	22 731	18 032	21 741	23 706	29 397	35 929	39 553	48 900	82 060
Food	6 372	3 833	3 026	3 710	3 348	4 415	4 737	5 384	6 420	9 761
Food at home	3 753	2 429	2 187	2 695	2 385	2 996	2 959	3 362	3 755	5 236
Cereals and bakery products	506	354	292	334	320	422	394	457	512	701
Meats, poultry, fish, and eggs	841	553	500	636	566	675	717	780	851	1 125
Dairy products	406	269	262	273	259	313	308	363	402	577
Fruits and vegetables	656	431	379	439	416	525	505	576	659	928
Other food at home	1 343	821	754	1 013	823	1 061	1 035	1 185	1 329	1 904
Food away from home	2 619	1 404	839	1 015	963	1 419	1 778	2 022	2 666	4 525
Alcoholic Beverages	435	246	190	168	103	233	296	324	431	765
Housing	16 895	8 933	7 751	8 994	10 015	11 440	12 986	14 309	16 788	26 386
Shelter	10 075	5 652	4 720	5 458	5 706	6 575	7 579	8 477	9 989	15 916
Owned dwellings	6 543	2 363	1 398	1 942	2 225	3 117	4 038	4 847	6 473	12 306
Rented dwellings	2 860	3 096	3 248	3 408	3 311	3 228	3 296	3 295	2 977	2 098
Other lodging	672	193	74	108	170	229	245	336	539	1 511
Utilities, fuels, and public services	3 645	1 935	2 000	2 251	2 648	3 028	3 289	3 513	3 899	4 849
Household operations	1 011	456	280	361	566	587	613	706	845	1 873
Housekeeping supplies	659	316	276	366	388	499	494	540	632	1 018
Household furnishings and equipment	1 506	573	475	558	707	751	1 011	1 072	1 424	2 730
Apparel and Services	1 725	802	797	1 086	768	1 080	1 225	1 336	1 608	2 850
Transportation	7 658	2 851	2 299	2 666	3 493	4 355	6 311	6 393	8 352	12 603
Vehicle purchases (net outlay)	2 657	934	649	673	953	1 201	2 112	2 099	2 742	4 775
Gasoline and motor oil	1 986	932	761	894	1 110	1 450	1 689	1 955	2 250	2 881
Other vehicle expenses	2 536	805	773	949	1 217	1 508	2 264	2 064	2 951	3 976
Public transportation	479	180	115	151	213	196	246	275	409	971
Health Care	3 126	1 345	1 099	1 785	2 050	2 536	2 684	2 937	3 454	4 393
Health insurance	1 785	725	705	1 089	1 236	1 519	1 684	1 705	1 995	2 380
Medical services	736	340	189	362	361	468	476	607	806	1 212
Drugs	486	207	174	292	372	469	443	528	507	621
Medical supplies	119	72	32	42	81	81	80	97	147	180
Entertainment	2 693	1 248	835	971	1 080	1 504	1 970	2 008	2 611	4 733
Personal Care Products and Services	596	273	225	273	291	372	438	476	578	991
Reading	110	41	34	49	62	71	81	86	108	182
Education	1 068	1 466	507	373	249	303	557	441	654	2 257
Tobacco Products and Smoking Supplies	380	289	252	304	353	439	405	381	436	371
Miscellaneous	816	308	234	389	297	438	668	738	853	1 351
Cash Contributions	1 723	600	450	493	767	744	1 208	1 256	1 728	3 176
Personal Insurance and Pensions	5 471	496	333	481	829	1 466	2 362	3 485	4 881	12 241
Life and other personal insurance	309	113	87	108	110	123	177	212	275	607
Pensions and Social Security	5 162	383	246	373	719	1 343	2 185	3 273	4 605	11 634

Table 11-4. Consumer Expenditures, Averages by Higher Income Before Taxes, 2009

(Number, dollar, percent.)

Item	All consumer units	Less than $70,000	$70,000 to $79,000	$80,000 to $99,999	$100,000 and over	$100,000 to $119,000	$120,000 to $149,999	$150,000 and over
NUMBER OF CONSUMER UNITS (THOUSANDS)	120 847	82 665	6 640	9 951	21 589	7 260	5 882	8 447
CONSUMER UNIT CHARACTERISTICS								
Income Before Taxes	62 857	32 063	74 594	89 096	165 062	108 564	132 565	236 246
Income After Taxes	60 753	31 677	72 124	86 130	156 890	104 701	127 030	222 535
Age of Reference Person	49.4	50.4	46.3	46.7	47.9	46.9	47.3	49.2
Average Number in Consumer Unit								
All persons	2.5	2.2	2.9	3.0	3.1	3.0	3.2	3.2
Children under 18 years	0.6	0.5	0.7	0.8	0.8	0.8	0.8	0.8
Persons 65 years and over	0.3	0.4	0.2	0.2	0.2	0.2	0.2	0.2
Earners	1.3	1.0	1.7	1.9	2.0	1.9	2.1	2.1
Vehicles	2.0	1.6	2.5	2.6	2.9	2.8	2.8	3.0
Percent Distribution								
Male	47	44	51	54	56	51	55	60
Female	53	56	49	46	44	49	45	40
Percent Homeowner	66	57	81	83	90	87	89	93
With mortgage	41	29	60	65	72	68	73	74
Without mortgage	25	28	21	18	18	19	16	18
AVERAGE ANNUAL EXPENDITURES	49 067	33 810	57 833	65 027	97 576	76 140	85 806	124 306
Food	6 372	4 798	7 818	8 359	11 088	9 622	9 886	13 234
Food at home	3 753	3 064	4 471	4 713	5 752	5 319	5 201	6 529
Cereals and bakery products	506	416	607	636	765	700	714	860
Meats, poultry, fish, and eggs	841	709	963	1 040	1 221	1 134	1 080	1 401
Dairy products	406	327	492	525	632	594	568	712
Fruits and vegetables	656	530	772	808	1 041	934	954	1 197
Other food at home	1 343	1 082	1 637	1 704	2 092	1 957	1 885	2 359
Food away from home	2 619	1 734	3 347	3 646	5 336	4 303	4 685	6 704
Alcoholic Beverages	435	282	534	569	936	735	832	1 188
Housing	16 895	12 509	19 127	21 666	30 831	23 907	27 923	38 824
Shelter	10 075	7 377	11 393	12 815	18 736	14 190	16 872	23 941
Owned dwellings	6 543	3 880	8 296	9 663	14 759	11 090	13 496	18 790
Rented dwellings	2 860	3 212	2 404	2 325	1 900	2 069	1 832	1 802
Other lodging	672	284	694	828	2 078	1 031	1 544	3 349
Utilities, fuels, and public services	3 645	3 089	4 188	4 470	5 226	4 618	5 100	5 837
Household operations	1 011	613	1 054	1 309	2 385	1 587	2 010	3 330
Housekeeping supplies	659	492	776	824	1 195	944	1 044	1 526
Household furnishings and equipment	1 506	938	1 716	2 247	3 289	2 567	2 896	4 190
Apparel and Services	1 725	1 203	1 795	2 388	3 428	2 595	2 934	4 508
Transportation	7 658	5 373	9 880	9 929	14 674	12 378	13 028	17 799
Vehicle purchases (net outlay)	2 657	1 679	3 410	3 386	5 835	4 800	4 713	7 506
Gasoline and motor oil	1 986	1 573	2 470	2 669	3 105	2 942	3 090	3 257
Other vehicle expenses	2 536	1 869	3 452	3 313	4 442	3 806	4 245	5 129
Public transportation	479	252	547	560	1 292	830	980	1 907
Health Care	3 126	2 541	3 679	4 158	4 723	4 385	4 399	5 242
Health insurance	1 785	1 510	2 019	2 264	2 544	2 408	2 442	2 732
Medical services	736	516	974	1 168	1 306	1 152	1 145	1 552
Drugs	486	424	555	573	665	632	636	715
Medical supplies	119	90	132	153	208	192	177	243
Entertainment	2 693	1 749	3 364	3 625	5 690	4 616	4 824	7 228
Personal Care Products and Services	596	412	653	782	1 200	960	1 082	1 492
Reading	110	76	118	130	226	174	198	292
Education	1 068	519	783	1 259	3 170	1 828	2 442	4 831
Tobacco Products and Smoking Supplies	380	384	449	377	344	408	307	314
Miscellaneous	816	569	979	1 005	1 630	1 327	1 396	2 054
Cash Contributions	1 723	1 052	1 685	2 414	3 986	2 443	2 996	6 002
Personal Insurance and Pensions	5 471	2 344	6 968	8 368	15 649	10 764	13 559	21 302
Life and other personal insurance	309	171	432	391	761	472	639	1 095
Pensions and Social Security	5 162	2 173	6 536	7 977	14 887	10 292	12 919	20 207

Table 11-5. Consumer Expenditures, Averages by Quintiles of Income Before Taxes, 2009

(Number, dollar, percent.)

Item	All consumer units	Lowest 20 percent	Second 20 percent	Third 20 percent	Fourth 20 percent	Highest 20 percent
NUMBER OF CONSUMER UNITS (THOUSANDS)	120 847	24 165	24 120	24 212	24 154	24 196
CONSUMER UNIT CHARACTERISTICS						
Income Before Taxes	62 857	9 846	27 227	46 012	73 417	157 631
Income After Taxes	60 753	9 956	27 275	45 199	71 241	149 951
Age of Reference Person	49.4	51.4	51.4	49.3	47.1	47.8
Average Number in Consumer Unit						
All persons	2.5	1.7	2.3	2.5	2.9	3.1
Children under 18 years	0.6	0.4	0.6	0.6	0.7	0.8
Persons 65 years and over	0.3	0.4	0.5	0.3	0.2	0.2
Earners	1.3	0.5	0.9	1.3	1.7	2.0
Vehicles	2.0	1.0	1.5	2.0	2.5	2.8
Percent Distribution						
Male	47	38	42	49	51	56
Female	53	62	58	51	49	44
Percent Homeowner	66	40	56	67	79	89
With mortgage	41	13	25	40	57	72
Without mortgage	25	26	31	27	22	18
AVERAGE ANNUAL EXPENDITURES	49 067	21 611	31 382	41 150	56 879	94 244
Food	6 372	3 501	4 569	5 483	7 522	10 780
Food at home	3 753	2 463	2 999	3 355	4 316	5 629
Cereals and bakery products	506	327	414	451	587	753
Meats, poultry, fish, and eggs	841	575	709	784	933	1 203
Dairy products	406	266	311	354	475	624
Fruits and vegetables	656	421	521	570	758	1 013
Other food at home	1 343	874	1 045	1 197	1 563	2 037
Food away from home	2 619	1 038	1 569	2 127	3 206	5 151
Alcoholic Beverages	435	170	250	330	541	883
Housing	16 895	8 961	11 829	14 805	18 862	29 998
Shelter	10 075	5 392	6 807	8 804	11 173	18 185
Owned dwellings	6 543	1 964	3 287	5 168	7 944	14 337
Rented dwellings	2 860	3 291	3 308	3 210	2 582	1 911
Other lodging	672	137	211	426	647	1 936
Utilities, fuels, and public services	3 645	2 238	3 069	3 574	4 172	5 167
Household operations	1 011	417	583	721	1 039	2 295
Housekeeping supplies	659	349	501	550	741	1 153
Household furnishings and equipment	1 506	565	869	1 157	1 738	3 197
Apparel and Services	1 725	873	1 161	1 402	1 848	3 339
Transportation	7 658	2 855	5 078	6 717	9 525	14 105
Vehicle purchases (net outlay)	2 657	778	1 488	2 232	3 280	5 501
Gasoline and motor oil	1 986	926	1 498	1 982	2 457	3 067
Other vehicle expenses	2 536	984	1 872	2 199	3 294	4 327
Public transportation	479	167	220	303	494	1 211
Health Care	3 126	1 628	2 491	3 069	3 762	4 677
Health insurance	1 785	978	1 524	1 825	2 080	2 516
Medical services	736	323	437	642	995	1 283
Drugs	486	274	448	503	536	669
Medical supplies	119	53	82	99	151	208
Entertainment	2 693	1 015	1 668	2 106	3 197	5 474
Personal Care Products and Services	596	268	397	496	650	1 167
Reading	110	48	72	91	119	217
Education	1 068	573	369	548	881	2 966
Tobacco Products and Smoking Supplies	380	303	413	400	439	342
Miscellaneous	816	323	522	756	921	1 558
Cash Contributions	1 723	559	868	1 435	1 949	3 801
Personal Insurance and Pensions	5 471	534	1 694	3 512	6 664	14 937
Life and other personal insurance	309	104	140	217	355	728
Pensions and Social Security	5 162	429	1 554	3 295	6 308	14 209

Table 11-6. Consumer Expenditures, Averages by Occupation of Reference Person, 2009

(Number, dollar, percent.)

| Item | Self-employed workers | Wage and salary earners | | | | | | Retired | All others, including those not reporting |
		Total wage and salary earners	Managers and professional workers	Technical sales and clerical workers	Service workers	Construction workers and mechanics	Operators, fabricators, and laborers		
NUMBER OF CONSUMER UNITS (THOUSANDS)	5 824	77 087	29 707	21 239	12 844	4 163	9 133	21 163	16 772
CONSUMER UNIT CHARACTERISTICS									
Income Before Taxes	81 240	74 168	103 040	62 755	49 816	56 949	48 895	35 336	39 211
Income After Taxes	78 537	71 304	97 900	60 728	49 066	55 537	47 849	34 838	38 784
Age of Reference Person	48.3	43.6	44.8	42.5	42.7	43.4	43.8	73.8	45.5
Average Number in Consumer Unit									
All persons	2.7	2.6	2.6	2.5	2.6	2.9	2.7	1.7	2.9
Children under 18 years	0.7	0.7	0.7	0.7	0.8	0.8	0.7	0.1	0.9
Persons 65 years and over	0.2	0.1	0.1	0.1	0.1	0.1	0.1	1.2	0.2
Earners	1.7	1.7	1.7	1.7	1.6	1.7	1.7	0.2	0.7
Vehicles	2.3	2.1	2.2	2.0	1.8	2.4	2.1	1.6	1.6
Percent Distribution									
Male	58	52	50	42	44	92	73	42	28
Female	42	48	50	58	56	8	27	58	72
Percent Homeowner	74	65	75	60	53	62	58	79	53
With mortgage	49	49	61	44	38	43	39	20	33
Without mortgage	25	16	15	17	15	19	19	60	21
AVERAGE ANNUAL EXPENDITURES	57 073	54 465	70 143	48 516	41 759	44 034	39 904	35 707	38 382
Food	7 198	6 857	8 212	6 298	5 683	5 935	5 801	4 816	5 839
Food at home	4 219	3 827	4 302	3 495	3 554	3 585	3 533	3 185	3 973
Cereals and bakery products	576	518	579	486	465	478	480	433	525
Meats, poultry, fish, and eggs	912	856	896	804	865	812	849	696	931
Dairy products	457	413	472	368	372	396	385	340	441
Fruits and vegetables	750	658	777	582	589	568	585	598	691
Other food at home	1 525	1 383	1 578	1 254	1 263	1 331	1 233	1 118	1 385
Food away from home	2 979	3 031	3 910	2 804	2 129	2 350	2 268	1 630	1 866
Alcoholic Beverages	546	502	664	411	308	486	451	275	294
Housing	18 173	18 525	23 699	16 552	14 951	14 813	13 016	12 863	14 053
Shelter	10 882	11 302	14 740	9 914	9 108	8 662	7 633	6 842	8 235
Owned dwellings	7 303	7 431	10 574	6 051	5 290	5 213	4 441	4 527	4 738
Rented dwellings	2 590	3 129	2 908	3 320	3 519	3 108	2 869	1 741	3 129
Other lodging	988	741	1 258	543	299	342	323	575	368
Utilities, fuels, and public services	3 966	3 790	4 247	3 587	3 476	3 636	3 290	3 260	3 348
Household operations	1 001	1 143	1 737	907	733	738	525	834	632
Housekeeping supplies	648	644	777	616	571	478	468	759	604
Household furnishings and equipment	1 675	1 646	2 199	1 527	1 063	1 299	1 101	1 168	1 234
Apparel and Services	1 638	2 017	2 505	1 802	1 620	1 249	1 830	913	1 440
Transportation	7 585	8 709	10 722	8 100	6 776	7 449	6 869	5 291	5 844
Vehicle purchases (net outlay)	1 979	3 097	3 897	2 985	2 164	2 550	2 319	1 926	1 791
Gasoline and motor oil	2 263	2 230	2 419	2 081	2 022	2 357	2 192	1 239	1 716
Other vehicle expenses	2 761	2 822	3 491	2 622	2 271	2 267	2 141	1 799	2 073
Public transportation	583	560	915	413	318	276	218	327	265
Health Care	3 723	2 798	3 496	2 616	2 096	2 396	2 119	4 800	2 316
Health insurance	1 997	1 580	1 954	1 488	1 221	1 257	1 233	2 936	1 199
Medical services	1 159	698	927	638	443	670	463	892	569
Drugs	461	400	470	376	342	339	339	822	467
Medical supplies	106	119	146	114	90	130	84	150	80
Entertainment	3 183	2 962	3 958	2 537	2 183	2 600	1 970	2 061	2 087
Personal Care Products and Services	595	651	855	617	490	404	414	517	441
Reading	134	109	163	91	66	62	63	142	61
Education	962	1 328	1 922	1 071	988	875	684	185	1 023
Tobacco Products and Smoking Supplies	331	400	275	441	433	710	521	210	518
Miscellaneous	1 542	889	1 124	877	621	663	634	555	563
Cash Contributions	2 176	1 737	2 442	1 362	1 196	1 375	1 243	2 039	1 102
Personal Insurance and Pensions	9 287	6 980	10 107	5 740	4 348	5 017	4 290	1 041	2 800
Life and other personal insurance	400	335	481	292	202	207	200	275	203
Pensions and Social Security	8 887	6 646	9 626	5 448	4 146	4 809	4 089	766	2 597

Table 11-7. Consumer Expenditures, Averages by Number of Earners, 2009

(Number, dollar, percent.)

Item	All consumer units	Single consumer — No earner	Single consumer — One earner	Consumer units of two or more persons — No earner	Consumer units of two or more persons — One earner	Consumer units of two or more persons — Two earners	Consumer units of two or more persons — Three or more earners
NUMBER OF CONSUMER UNITS (THOUSANDS)	120 847	13 715	21 056	11 110	26 304	39 535	9 127
CONSUMER UNIT CHARACTERISTICS							
Income Before Taxes	62 857	17 514	42 723	31 182	56 147	92 660	106 232
Income After Taxes	60 753	17 383	40 504	31 059	54 817	88 948	103 753
Age of Reference Person	49.4	68.2	43.5	64.3	47.5	43.8	46.2
Average Number in Consumer Unit							
All persons	2.5	1.0	1.0	2.3	3.1	3.0	4.4
Children under 18 years	0.6	X	X	0.4	1.1	0.8	1.0
Persons 65 years and over	0.3	0.7	0.1	1.2	0.3	0.1	0.1
Earners	1.3	X	1.0	X	1.0	2.0	3.3
Vehicles	2.0	0.9	1.2	1.7	1.9	2.5	3.2
Percent Distribution							
Male	47	34	54	46	42	51	48
Female	53	66	46	54	58	49	52
Percent Homeowner	66	56	46	75	66	76	79
With mortgage	41	12	30	22	41	59	61
Without mortgage	25	44	16	54	25	16	18
AVERAGE ANNUAL EXPENDITURES	49 067	21 768	34 314	36 882	49 285	64 241	72 854
Food	6 372	2 937	3 782	5 609	6 742	8 137	9 879
Food at home	3 753	2 057	1 892	3 795	4 339	4 495	5 715
Cereals and bakery products	506	283	238	529	579	609	793
Meats, poultry, fish, and eggs	841	416	403	879	988	1 000	1 347
Dairy products	406	224	208	395	466	494	605
Fruits and vegetables	656	366	344	712	768	761	978
Other food at home	1 343	768	699	1 281	1 538	1 630	1 992
Food away from home	2 619	880	1 890	1 814	2 403	3 641	4 165
Alcoholic Beverages	435	141	484	276	381	566	539
Housing	16 895	9 455	12 643	12 854	17 861	21 267	21 073
Shelter	10 075	5 616	8 522	6 678	10 455	12 636	12 299
Owned dwellings	6 543	2 535	4 119	4 426	6 702	9 158	8 942
Rented dwellings	2 860	2 873	3 930	1 669	3 070	2 572	2 465
Other lodging	672	207	473	583	683	906	892
Utilities, fuels, and public services	3 645	2 256	2 325	3 512	3 915	4 322	5 227
Household operations	1 011	666	471	723	1 031	1 493	985
Housekeeping supplies	659	364	334	733	796	790	795
Household furnishings and equipment	1 506	553	991	1 208	1 665	2 026	1 768
Apparel and Services	1 725	568	1 224	1 018	1 906	2 286	2 545
Transportation	7 658	2 360	5 362	5 780	7 416	10 052	13 594
Vehicle purchases (net outlay)	2 657	662	1 949	1 976	2 427	3 572	4 819
Gasoline and motor oil	1 986	624	1 280	1 431	2 053	2 618	3 410
Other vehicle expenses	2 536	926	1 729	2 018	2 514	3 205	4 672
Public transportation	479	147	405	355	423	658	693
Health Care	3 126	2 687	1 566	4 891	3 301	3 350	3 768
Health insurance	1 785	1 622	873	3 028	1 812	1 901	2 039
Medical services	736	504	408	822	824	845	1 018
Drugs	486	477	228	867	549	461	562
Medical supplies	119	83	57	174	116	144	150
Entertainment	2 693	1 052	1 801	2 243	2 724	3 560	3 928
Personal Care Products and Services	596	294	376	513	610	769	872
Reading	110	83	90	121	103	126	126
Education	1 068	183	693	422	974	1 498	2 463
Tobacco Products and Smoking Supplies	380	199	288	345	398	445	570
Miscellaneous	816	398	672	557	739	1 052	1 300
Cash Contributions	1 723	1 211	1 306	1 829	1 641	2 007	2 336
Personal Insurance and Pensions	5 471	202	4 027	424	4 489	9 126	9 863
Life and other personal insurance	309	118	119	305	318	429	494
Pensions and Social Security	5 162	84	3 907	[1]120	4 170	8 697	9 369

[1]Data are likely to have large sampling errors.
X = Not applicable.

Table 11-8. Consumer Expenditures, Averages by Size of Consumer Unit, 2009

(Number, dollar, percent.)

Item	All consumer units	One person	Two or more persons	Two persons	Three persons	Four persons	Five or more persons
NUMBER OF CONSUMER UNITS (THOUSANDS)	120 847	34 770	86 076	39 531	17 990	16 474	12 081
CONSUMER UNIT CHARACTERISTICS							
Income Before Taxes	62 857	32 780	75 006	68 393	76 545	85 436	80 132
Income After Taxes	60 753	31 384	72 616	65 435	74 521	82 990	79 132
Age of Reference Person	49.4	53.2	47.8	54.0	44.5	41.4	41.5
Average Number in Consumer Unit							
All persons	2.5	1.0	3.1	2.0	3.0	4.0	5.6
Children under 18 years	0.6	X	0.9	0.1	0.7	1.6	2.7
Persons 65 years and over	0.3	0.3	0.3	0.5	0.2	0.1	0.1
Earners	1.3	0.6	1.6	1.2	1.7	1.9	2.1
Vehicles	2.0	1.1	2.3	2.2	2.2	2.5	2.5
Percent Distribution							
Male	47	46	48	50	43	48	44
Female	53	54	52	50	57	52	56
Percent Homeowner	66	50	73	76	69	74	69
With mortgage	41	23	49	42	49	61	57
Without mortgage	25	27	24	34	20	13	12
AVERAGE ANNUAL EXPENDITURES	49 067	29 405	57 002	51 650	56 645	65 503	63 439
Food	6 372	3 460	7 544	6 308	7 506	8 730	10 034
Food at home	3 753	1 953	4 477	3 631	4 454	5 187	6 324
Cereals and bakery products	506	255	607	470	588	719	937
Meats, poultry, fish, and eggs	841	408	1 015	813	1 024	1 170	1 457
Dairy products	406	214	483	391	472	568	689
Fruits and vegetables	656	352	779	664	778	860	1 048
Other food at home	1 343	724	1 592	1 293	1 592	1 871	2 194
Food away from home	2 619	1 507	3 067	2 677	3 052	3 543	3 710
Alcoholic Beverages	435	355	467	537	381	486	336
Housing	16 895	11 388	19 119	17 145	19 353	22 193	21 035
Shelter	10 075	7 376	11 165	10 078	11 114	13 038	12 243
Owned dwellings	6 543	3 495	7 774	6 906	7 526	9 530	8 589
Rented dwellings	2 860	3 513	2 596	2 257	2 874	2 711	3 138
Other lodging	672	368	795	916	714	797	516
Utilities, fuels, and public services	3 645	2 298	4 189	3 740	4 233	4 658	4 951
Household operations	1 011	548	1 198	845	1 345	1 811	1 303
Housekeeping supplies	659	345	785	779	771	803	798
Household furnishings and equipment	1 506	821	1 782	1 702	1 891	1 884	1 741
Apparel and Services	1 725	975	2 027	1 566	2 046	2 571	2 767
Transportation	7 658	4 182	9 061	8 306	8 775	10 707	9 716
Vehicle purchases (net outlay)	2 657	1 441	3 148	3 039	2 659	4 004	3 065
Gasoline and motor oil	1 986	1 022	2 376	1 993	2 470	2 761	2 964
Other vehicle expenses	2 536	1 417	2 987	2 714	3 086	3 374	3 203
Public transportation	479	303	550	559	560	568	484
Health Care	3 126	2 007	3 578	4 021	3 273	3 300	2 960
Health insurance	1 785	1 169	2 034	2 332	1 890	1 772	1 628
Medical services	736	446	854	855	783	981	781
Drugs	486	326	551	673	466	441	425
Medical supplies	119	67	140	161	134	105	126
Entertainment	2 693	1 510	3 170	2 913	2 860	3 775	3 635
Personal Care Products and Services	596	345	697	646	719	779	717
Reading	110	87	119	136	113	100	95
Education	1 068	492	1 301	793	1 563	1 906	1 746
Tobacco Products and Smoking Supplies	380	253	431	403	463	443	458
Miscellaneous	816	565	918	838	942	1 115	872
Cash Contributions	1 723	1 268	1 907	2 028	1 776	1 718	1 964
Personal Insurance and Pensions	5 471	2 518	6 664	6 011	6 875	7 680	7 101
Life and other personal insurance	309	118	386	393	409	371	350
Pensions and Social Security	5 162	2 399	6 278	5 618	6 466	7 309	6 751

X = Not applicable.

Table 11-9. Consumer Expenditures, Averages by Composition of Consumer Unit, 2009

(Number, dollar, percent.)

Item		Husband and wife consumer units						One parent, at least one child under 18 years	Single person and other consumer units
	Total	Husband and wife only	Husband and wife with children				Other husband and wife consumer units		
			Total	Oldest child under 6 years	Oldest child 6 to 17 years	Oldest child 18 years or over			
NUMBER OF CONSUMER UNITS (THOUSANDS)	61 271	26 852	29 480	5 154	14 983	9 342	4 939	6 810	52 766
CONSUMER UNIT CHARACTERISTICS									
Income Before Taxes	84 785	75 876	92 616	81 821	94 302	95 867	86 478	35 845	40 880
Income After Taxes	81 782	72 316	89 803	80 113	91 218	92 878	85 375	35 993	39 530
Age of Reference Person	49.7	57.7	42.6	32.6	40.4	51.6	48.6	38.0	50.5
Average Number in Consumer Unit									
All persons	3.2	2.0	4.0	3.5	4.1	3.9	4.9	2.9	1.7
Children under 18 years	0.9	X	1.5	1.5	2.1	0.6	1.4	1.7	0.2
Persons 65 years and over	0.4	0.7	0.1	(^{1})	(^{1})	0.2	0.5	(^{1})	0.3
Earners	1.6	1.2	1.9	1.6	1.7	2.4	2.2	1.0	0.9
Vehicles	2.6	2.5	2.6	2.0	2.5	3.1	2.7	1.2	1.3
Percent Distribution									
Male	53	56	52	50	51	54	45	16	44
Female	47	44	48	50	49	46	55	84	56
Percent Homeowner	82	87	79	67	77	89	77	37	51
With mortgage	56	46	65	59	67	63	57	29	26
Without mortgage	27	41	15	8	10	26	20	8	25
AVERAGE ANNUAL EXPENDITURES	63 104	56 777	68 481	62 138	70 329	69 089	65 654	36 763	34 450
Food	8 264	6 906	9 369	7 813	9 827	9 525	9 182	5 348	4 352
Food at home	4 827	3 975	5 451	4 833	5 606	5 567	5 868	3 480	2 568
Cereals and bakery products	657	508	770	622	826	765	811	485	338
Meats, poultry, fish, and eggs	1 069	887	1 167	930	1 198	1 262	1 522	837	583
Dairy products	530	427	615	599	637	587	588	350	273
Fruits and vegetables	853	748	921	859	951	908	1 040	542	448
Other food at home	1 718	1 404	1 977	1 824	1 993	2 045	1 908	1 266	926
Food away from home	3 436	2 930	3 917	2 980	4 221	3 958	3 314	1 868	1 785
Alcoholic Beverages	511	582	470	507	485	422	345	177	382
Housing	20 654	18 140	22 858	24 503	23 906	20 258	21 203	14 836	12 810
Shelter	11 960	10 414	13 412	14 005	14 410	11 485	11 706	8 610	8 074
Owned dwellings	9 049	7 835	10 226	10 279	10 796	9 284	8 626	3 711	3 997
Rented dwellings	1 936	1 413	2 308	3 273	2 602	1 305	2 563	4 626	3 705
Other lodging	975	1 166	878	454	1 012	896	517	272	372
Utilities, fuels, and public services	4 403	3 937	4 708	3 853	4 731	5 144	5 115	3 438	2 791
Household operations	1 336	873	1 784	3 537	1 716	928	1 176	1 215	608
Housekeeping supplies	886	916	851	796	867	858	943	583	410
Household furnishings and equipment	2 069	2 001	2 101	2 312	2 182	1 842	2 263	991	926
Apparel and Services	2 170	1 630	2 600	2 281	2 844	2 387	2 597	1 708	1 220
Transportation	10 021	9 202	10 487	9 889	9 988	11 673	11 750	5 337	5 224
Vehicle purchases (net outlay)	3 504	3 460	3 406	3 650	3 190	3 618	4 323	1 679	1 800
Gasoline and motor oil	2 572	2 139	2 868	2 417	2 838	3 166	3 159	1 573	1 360
Other vehicle expenses	3 315	2 962	3 557	3 191	3 293	4 241	3 838	1 801	1 736
Public transportation	631	641	656	631	668	649	430	283	328
Health Care	4 182	4 852	3 556	2 884	3 460	4 082	4 282	1 381	2 127
Health insurance	2 365	2 802	1 975	1 669	1 941	2 200	2 315	743	1 246
Medical services	1 011	1 034	984	819	981	1 080	1 054	382	463
Drugs	642	820	465	302	408	647	746	194	344
Medical supplies	163	196	132	94	131	155	166	62	75
Entertainment	3 606	3 259	4 030	2 894	4 532	3 852	2 935	1 907	1 743
Personal Care Products and Services	758	708	798	779	800	802	799	552	415
Reading	135	160	118	78	122	133	106	62	86
Education	1 478	840	2 105	378	2 096	3 071	1 207	874	617
Tobacco Products and Smoking Supplies	375	335	357	258	326	461	706	345	389
Miscellaneous	1 016	923	1 014	860	1 091	971	1 540	613	611
Cash Contributions	2 245	2 456	2 130	1 435	1 979	2 756	1 781	792	1 237
Personal Insurance and Pensions	7 689	6 785	8 590	7 580	8 873	8 695	7 220	2 830	3 237
Life and other personal insurance	481	512	464	292	488	521	410	123	134
Pensions and Social Security	7 208	6 273	8 126	7 288	8 384	8 174	6 810	2 707	3 103

^{1}Value less than or equal to 0.05.
X = Not applicable.

Table 11-10. Consumer Expenditures, Averages by Age of Reference Person, 2009

(Number, dollar, percent.)

Item	All consumer units	Under 25 years	25 to 34 years	35 to 44 years	45 to 54 years	55 to 64 years	65 years and over	65 to 74 years	75 years and over
NUMBER OF CONSUMER UNITS (THOUSANDS)	120 847	7 875	20 044	22 199	25 440	20 731	24 557	12 848	11 709
CONSUMER UNIT CHARACTERISTICS									
Income Before Taxes	62 857	25 695	58 946	77 005	80 976	70 609	39 862	47 286	31 715
Income After Taxes	60 753	25 522	57 239	74 900	77 460	67 586	39 054	46 147	31 272
Age of Reference Person	49.4	21.4	29.7	39.7	49.5	59.1	75.0	68.9	81.6
Average Number in Consumer Unit									
All persons	2.5	2.0	2.8	3.3	2.8	2.1	1.7	1.9	1.6
Children under 18 years	0.6	0.4	1.1	1.3	0.6	0.2	0.1	0.1	1.6
Persons 65 years and over	0.3	([1])	([1])	([1])	([1])	0.1	1.4	1.4	1.4
Earners	1.3	1.3	1.5	1.6	1.7	1.3	0.5	0.6	1.4
Vehicles	2.0	1.2	1.7	2.1	2.4	2.2	1.6	1.9	0.2 1.3
Percent Distribution									
Male	47	47	48	49	49	48	43	46	39
Female	53	53	52	51	51	52	57	54	61
Percent Homeowner	66	14	46	65	74	81	79	81	77
With mortgage	41	10	39	56	55	47	22	31	12
Without mortgage	25	4	7	9	20	34	58	51	65
AVERAGE ANNUAL EXPENDITURES	49 067	28 119	46 494	57 301	58 708	52 463	37 562	42 957	31 676
Food	6 372	4 179	6 169	7 760	7 445	6 303	4 901	5 561	4 189
Food at home	3 753	2 449	3 478	4 446	4 343	3 678	3 222	3 567	2 851
Cereals and bakery products	506	307	473	629	586	465	439	463	414
Meats, poultry, fish, and eggs	841	571	757	983	978	849	720	849	581
Dairy products	406	281	376	495	465	386	346	381	308
Fruits and vegetables	656	398	593	739	750	663	618	684	546
Other food at home	1 343	891	1 280	1 600	1 564	1 314	1 100	1 190	1 002
Food away from home	2 619	1 731	2 691	3 314	3 102	2 626	1 679	1 994	1 338
Alcoholic Beverages	435	344	481	498	502	440	292	389	188
Housing	16 895	9 735	17 258	20 705	19 004	16 991	13 196	14 462	11 811
Shelter	10 075	6 306	10 856	12 753	11 356	9 749	7 173	7 828	6 454
Owned dwellings	6 543	1 245	5 581	8 832	8 093	7 149	4 838	5 802	3 781
Rented dwellings	2 860	4 885	4 877	3 328	2 369	1 570	1 741	1 320	2 202
Other lodging	672	176	398	593	894	1 031	594	706	471
Utilities, fuels, and public services	3 645	1 821	3 249	4 093	4 275	3 896	3 282	3 568	2 967
Household operations	1 011	370	1 231	1 377	964	871	876	801	957
Housekeeping supplies	659	309	506	698	703	825	682	773	584
Household furnishings and equipment	1 506	929	1 416	1 786	1 705	1 651	1 184	1 491	850
Apparel and Services	237	134	243	227	295	284	177	204	147
Transportation	7 658	5 334	7 671	8 364	9 409	8 323	5 409	7 033	3 631
Vehicle purchases (net outlay)	2 657	2 319	2 820	2 761	3 233	2 752	1 862	2 597	1 055
Gasoline and motor oil	1 986	1 483	2 071	2 359	2 398	2 074	1 241	1 573	877
Other vehicle expenses	2 536	1 298	2 293	2 694	3 199	2 962	1 968	2 488	1 402
Public transportation	479	234	487	549	579	535	338	376	297
Health Care	3 126	676	1 805	2 520	3 173	3 895	4 846	4 906	4 779
Health insurance	1 785	381	1 083	1 436	1 688	2 017	3 027	3 042	3 011
Medical services	736	167	466	650	862	1 054	821	818	824
Drugs	486	97	195	335	485	679	828	865	787
Medical supplies	119	30	61	100	139	144	170	181	158
Entertainment	2 693	1 233	2 504	3 317	3 176	2 906	2 062	2 498	1 587
Personal Care Products and Services	596	360	555	685	666	617	531	600	456
Reading	110	42	69	85	119	147	145	154	134
Education	1 068	1 910	808	935	2 055	1 003	162	181	141
Tobacco Products and Smoking Supplies	380	330	368	417	513	410	207	275	133
Miscellaneous	816	243	631	967	1 051	952	663	820	491
Cash Contributions	1 723	349	1 001	1 581	2 056	2 092	2 226	2 087	2 378
Personal Insurance and Pensions	5 471	1 988	5 303	7 122	7 654	6 793	1 856	2 669	964
Life and other personal insurance	309	31	156	270	427	446	320	397	234
Pensions and Social Security	5 162	1 957	5 147	6 851	7 226	6 347	1 537	2 272	730

[1]Value less than or equal to 0.05.

Table 11-11. Consumer Expenditures, Averages by Race of Reference Person, 2009

(Number, dollar, percent.)

Item	All consumer units	White, Asian, and other races			Black
		Total	White and other races	Asian	
NUMBER OF CONSUMER UNITS (THOUSANDS)	120 847	106 187	101 604	4 584	14 659
CONSUMER UNIT CHARACTERISTICS					
Income Before Taxes	62 857	65 405	64 898	76 633	44 397
Income After Taxes	60 753	63 113	62 663	73 107	43 654
Age of Reference Person	49.4	49.7	49.9	45.1	47.1
Average Number in Consumer Unit					
All persons	2.5	2.5	2.5	2.7	2.6
Children under 18 years	0.6	0.6	0.6	0.6	0.8
Persons 65 years and over	0.3	0.3	0.3	0.3	0.2
Earners	1.3	1.3	1.3	1.4	1.2
Vehicles	2.0	2.0	2.1	1.5	1.3
Percent Distribution					
Male	47	49	48	59	36
Female	53	51	52	41	64
Percent Homeowner	66	69	70	57	46
With mortgage	41	43	43	45	29
Without mortgage	25	26	27	12	16
AVERAGE ANNUAL EXPENDITURES	49 067	50 957	50 723	56 308	35 311
Food	6 372	6 622	6 585	7 565	4 524
Food at home	3 753	3 871	3 870	3 905	2 880
Cereals and bakery products	506	522	522	520	390
Meats, poultry, fish, and eggs	841	840	835	966	845
Dairy products	406	426	429	346	258
Fruits and vegetables	656	680	671	903	484
Other food at home	1 343	1 403	1 412	1 169	903
Food away from home	2 619	2 751	2 715	3 660	1 645
Alcoholic Beverages	435	466	471	350	201
Housing	16 895	17 362	17 224	20 395	13 503
Shelter	10 075	10 372	10 228	13 571	7 919
Owned dwellings	6 543	6 944	6 872	8 543	3 632
Rented dwellings	2 860	2 697	2 619	4 411	4 046
Other lodging	672	731	737	616	241
Utilities, fuels, and public services	3 645	3 641	3 658	3 270	3 668
Household operations	1 011	1 064	1 051	1 347	633
Housekeeping supplies	659	690	696	536	429
Household furnishings and equipment	1 506	1 594	1 591	1 671	854
Apparel and Services	1 725	1 721	1 704	2 150	1 755
Transportation	7 658	7 983	7 950	8 784	5 302
Vehicle purchases (net outlay)	2 657	2 818	2 829	2 582	1 489
Gasoline and motor oil	1 986	2 037	2 045	1 871	1 618
Other vehicle expenses	2 536	2 626	2 605	3 153	1 876
Public transportation	479	501	471	1 178	319
Health Care	3 126	3 314	3 351	2 498	1 763
Health insurance	1 785	1 875	1 891	1 509	1 133
Medical services	736	797	807	575	294
Drugs	486	515	524	307	279
Medical supplies	119	127	128	107	57
Entertainment	2 693	2 869	2 894	2 270	1 404
Personal Care Products and Services	596	603	606	557	536
Reading	110	118	119	111	46
Education	1 068	1 134	1 080	2 327	591
Tobacco Products and Smoking Supplies	380	400	413	122	230
Miscellaneous	816	843	853	611	626
Cash Contributions	1 723	1 784	1 799	1 452	1 280
Personal Insurance and Pensions	5 471	5 736	5 674	7 117	3 550
Life and other personal insurance	309	319	321	283	235
Pensions and Social Security	5 162	5 417	5 353	6 834	3 315

Table 11-12. Consumer Expenditures, Averages by Hispanic Origin of Reference Person, 2009

(Number, dollar, percent.)

Item	All consumer units	Hispanic[1]	Not Hispanic		
			Total	White, Asian, and other races	Black
NUMBER OF CONSUMER UNITS (THOUSANDS)	120 847	14 295	106 552	92 119	14 432
CONSUMER UNIT CHARACTERISTICS					
Income Before Taxes	62 857	49 930	64 591	67 784	44 211
Income After Taxes	60 753	49 185	62 305	65 259	43 449
Age of Reference Person	49.4	43.1	50.2	50.7	47.1
Average Number in Consumer Unit					
All persons	2.5	3.3	2.4	2.4	2.6
Children under 18 years	0.6	1.1	0.6	0.5	0.8
Persons 65 years and over	0.3	0.2	0.3	0.4	0.2
Earners	1.3	1.5	1.3	1.3	1.2
Vehicles	2.0	1.6	2.0	2.1	1.3
Percent Distribution					
Male	47	49	47	48	36
Female	53	51	53	52	64
Percent Homeowner	66	51	68	72	46
With mortgage	41	36	42	44	29
Without mortgage	25	15	26	28	16
AVERAGE ANNUAL EXPENDITURES	49 067	41 981	50 015	52 320	35 198
Food	6 372	6 094	6 409	6 696	4 524
Food at home	3 753	3 784	3 749	3 882	2 875
Cereals and bakery products	506	479	510	529	388
Meats, poultry, fish, and eggs	841	955	826	823	846
Dairy products	406	403	406	429	258
Fruits and vegetables	656	734	646	671	483
Other food at home	1 343	1 213	1 360	1 430	900
Food away from home	2 619	2 310	2 660	2 814	1 649
Alcoholic Beverages	435	267	457	496	201
Housing	16 895	15 983	17 016	17 579	13 409
Shelter	10 075	10 043	10 079	10 429	7 847
Owned dwellings	6 543	5 298	6 710	7 198	3 594
Rented dwellings	2 860	4 415	2 652	2 437	4 020
Other lodging	672	330	718	794	233
Utilities, fuels, and public services	3 645	3 532	3 660	3 660	3 660
Household operations	1 011	714	1 051	1 119	618
Housekeeping supplies	659	517	677	714	434
Household furnishings and equipment	1 506	1 177	1 549	1 657	850
Apparel and Services	1 725	2 002	1 689	1 678	1 761
Transportation	7 658	7 156	7 725	8 109	5 269
Vehicle purchases (net outlay)	2 657	2 333	2 700	2 897	1 446
Gasoline and motor oil	1 986	2 104	1 971	2 026	1 614
Other vehicle expenses	2 536	2 309	2 566	2 670	1 896
Public transportation	479	410	489	516	313
Health Care	3 126	1 568	3 335	3 581	1 762
Health insurance	1 785	848	1 910	2 033	1 128
Medical services	736	418	779	855	296
Drugs	486	241	519	556	280
Medical supplies	119	61	126	137	58
Entertainment	2 693	1 664	2 829	3 050	1 406
Personal Care Products and Services	596	532	604	614	536
Reading	110	36	119	131	47
Education	1 068	707	1 116	1 197	599
Tobacco Products and Smoking Supplies	380	182	406	434	232
Miscellaneous	816	544	853	887	633
Cash Contributions	1 723	1 015	1 818	1 903	1 277
Personal Insurance and Pensions	5 471	4 230	5 638	5 966	3 542
Life and other personal insurance	309	119	335	350	236
Pensions and Social Security	5 162	4 111	5 303	5 616	3 306

[1]May be of any race.

Table 11-13. Consumer Expenditures, Averages by Education of Reference Person, 2009

(Number, dollar, percent.)

Item	All consumer units	Less than a college graduate					College graduate or more		
		Total	Less than a high school graduate	High school graduate	High school graduate with some college	Associate's degree	Total	Bachelor's degree	Master's, professional, or doctoral degree
NUMBER OF CONSUMER UNITS (THOUSANDS)	120 847	85 270	16 692	31 015	25 512	12 051	35 576	23 410	12 166
CONSUMER UNIT CHARACTERISTICS									
Income Before Taxes	62 857	48 449	33 262	47 338	53 065	62 570	97 390	90 318	110 998
Income After Taxes	60 753	47 446	33 032	46 531	51 686	60 788	92 648	86 107	105 234
Age of Reference Person	49.4	50.0	53.8	51.8	46.1	48.0	48.0	46.5	51.0
Average Number in Consumer Unit									
All persons	2.5	2.5	2.8	2.5	2.4	2.5	2.5	2.5	2.4
Children under 18 years	0.6	0.6	0.8	0.6	0.6	0.7	0.6	0.6	0.6
Persons 65 years and over	0.3	0.3	0.5	0.4	0.3	0.2	0.2	0.2	0.3
Earners	1.3	1.2	1.0	1.2	1.3	1.4	1.4	1.5	1.4
Vehicles	2.0	1.9	1.5	1.9	2.0	2.2	2.1	2.1	2.1
Percent Distribution									
Male	47	45	45	45	45	44	52	52	53
Female	53	55	55	55	55	56	48	48	47
Percent Homeowner	66	62	54	65	59	69	77	75	80
With mortgage	41	36	26	35	37	47	56	55	57
Without mortgage	25	26	29	30	22	23	21	20	23
AVERAGE ANNUAL EXPENDITURES	49 067	40 520	30 323	38 693	44 697	50 446	69 389	65 908	76 072
Food	6 372	5 622	4 735	5 426	5 977	6 588	8 097	7 775	8 704
Food at home	3 753	3 476	3 343	3 439	3 547	3 598	4 386	4 275	4 595
Cereals and bakery products	506	469	454	468	470	493	590	588	595
Meats, poultry, fish, and eggs	841	810	856	826	797	728	912	931	876
Dairy products	406	370	333	363	387	400	488	472	519
Fruits and vegetables	656	580	570	568	596	590	831	773	939
Other food at home	1 343	1 247	1 129	1 213	1 297	1 387	1 565	1 511	1 667
Food away from home	2 619	2 146	1 392	1 987	2 430	2 991	3 711	3 500	4 110
Alcoholic Beverages	435	325	213	298	384	424	686	676	705
Housing	16 895	14 047	11 181	13 261	15 142	17 702	23 695	22 456	26 074
Shelter	10 075	8 111	6 556	7 547	8 737	10 391	14 782	14 106	16 084
Owned dwellings	6 543	4 841	3 263	4 556	5 259	6 876	10 621	10 187	11 456
Rented dwellings	2 860	2 885	3 126	2 652	2 997	2 911	2 802	2 767	2 869
Other lodging	672	385	167	339	481	603	1 359	1 152	1 759
Utilities, fuels, and public services	3 645	3 462	3 101	3 491	3 479	3 848	4 083	3 989	4 264
Household operations	1 011	705	346	598	889	1 090	1 745	1 510	2 198
Housekeeping supplies	659	573	414	568	607	723	854	741	1 067
Household furnishings and equipment	1 506	1 197	764	1 057	1 431	1 650	2 230	2 110	2 460
Apparel and Services	1 725	1 452	1 454	1 369	1 432	1 742	2 358	2 385	2 308
Transportation	7 658	6 547	4 762	6 295	7 329	7 970	10 312	10 007	10 897
Vehicle purchases (net outlay)	2 657	2 138	1 430	2 017	2 477	2 714	3 901	3 844	4 010
Gasoline and motor oil	1 986	1 893	1 529	1 865	1 972	2 305	2 209	2 205	2 218
Other vehicle expenses	2 536	2 242	1 611	2 149	2 581	2 595	3 229	3 146	3 390
Public transportation	479	273	193	264	299	356	972	812	1 279
Health Care	3 126	2 749	2 010	2 913	2 917	3 000	4 026	3 778	4 503
Health insurance	1 785	1 584	1 215	1 712	1 635	1 660	2 266	2 121	2 544
Medical services	736	608	364	624	691	729	1 044	974	1 177
Drugs	486	460	356	487	487	476	548	525	591
Medical supplies	119	98	76	90	105	135	169	157	191
Entertainment	2 693	2 261	1 406	2 184	2 626	2 848	3 716	3 458	4 212
Personal Care Products and Services	596	489	361	459	555	602	845	799	933
Reading	110	78	40	70	98	107	186	157	241
Education	1 068	648	236	447	1 039	907	2 074	1 833	2 538
Tobacco Products and Smoking Supplies ...	380	462	430	531	419	418	183	219	113
Miscellaneous	816	689	437	596	843	957	1 122	1 167	1 037
Cash Contributions	1 723	1 193	784	1 123	1 354	1 600	2 993	2 734	3 491
Personal Insurance and Pensions	5 471	3 958	2 275	3 721	4 580	5 580	9 098	8 465	10 318
Life and other personal insurance	309	233	151	239	248	298	492	451	571
Pensions and Social Security	5 162	3 725	2 124	3 482	4 332	5 282	8 607	8 014	9 746

Table 11-14. Consumer Expenditures, Averages by Housing Tenure and Type of Area, 2009

(Number, dollar, percent.)

Item	All consumer units	Housing tenure				Type of area			
		Homeowner			Renter	Urban			Rural
		Total	Homeowner with mortgage	Homeowner without mortgage		Total	Central city	Other urban	
NUMBER OF CONSUMER UNITS (THOUSANDS)	120 847	80 068	50 080	29 988	40 778	110 241	35 043	75 198	10 605
CONSUMER UNIT CHARACTERISTICS									
Income Before Taxes	62 857	75 858	88 237	55 185	37 329	64 316	55 385	68 477	47 692
Income After Taxes	60 753	73 035	85 062	52 949	36 637	62 164	53 636	66 138	46 080
Age of Reference Person	49.4	53.3	47.8	62.5	41.7	49.0	46.6	50.1	53.7
Average Number in Consumer Unit									
All persons	2.5	2.6	2.9	2.1	2.3	2.5	2.4	2.6	2.4
Children under 18 years	0.6	0.6	0.8	0.3	0.6	0.6	0.6	0.6	0.5
Persons 65 years and over	0.3	0.4	0.2	0.7	0.2	0.3	0.3	0.3	0.4
Earners	1.3	1.4	1.6	0.9	1.1	1.3	1.2	1.3	1.2
Vehicles	2.0	2.4	2.5	2.2	1.2	1.9	1.5	2.1	2.6
Percent Distribution									
Male	47	48	49	45	46	48	46	48	42
Female	53	52	51	55	54	52	54	52	58
Percent Homeowner	66	100	100	100	X	65	50	72	82
With mortgage	41	63	100	X	X	42	32	46	40
Without mortgage	25	37	X	100	X	23	17	26	42
AVERAGE ANNUAL EXPENDITURES	49 067	57 047	64 493	44 130	33 404	49 807	43 962	52 501	41 325
Food	6 372	7 198	7 682	6 125	4 753	6 435	5 922	6 662	5 675
Food at home	3 753	4 214	4 377	3 837	2 849	3 757	3 407	3 911	3 707
Cereals and bakery products	506	566	594	501	390	508	456	530	494
Meats, poultry, fish, and eggs	841	932	966	852	663	844	797	865	803
Dairy products	406	459	478	415	302	404	360	423	429
Fruits and vegetables	656	744	760	704	486	658	614	677	638
Other food at home	1 343	1 514	1 580	1 366	1 008	1 343	1 181	1 414	1 344
Food away from home	2 619	2 984	3 306	2 288	1 904	2 678	2 515	2 752	1 968
Alcoholic Beverages	435	477	525	370	352	448	458	444	289
Housing	16 895	18 901	22 846	12 287	12 958	17 356	16 058	17 953	12 110
Shelter	10 075	10 733	14 050	5 193	8 783	10 483	10 060	10 681	5 828
Owned dwellings	6 543	9 761	13 059	4 254	223	6 731	5 095	7 493	4 589
Rented dwellings	2 860	60	48	80	8 359	3 063	4 374	2 452	753
Other lodging	672	912	943	859	202	690	591	736	486
Utilities, fuels, and public services	3 645	4 276	4 554	3 811	2 406	3 650	3 245	3 838	3 592
Household operations	1 011	1 217	1 424	873	607	1 056	929	1 116	542
Housekeeping supplies	659	804	804	803	374	652	533	704	738
Household furnishings and equipment	1 506	1 872	2 015	1 607	788	1 515	1 292	1 615	1 409
Apparel and Services	1 725	1 857	2 085	1 371	1 466	1 762	1 777	1 755	1 328
Transportation	7 658	9 089	10 005	7 568	4 849	7 623	6 273	8 249	8 028
Vehicle purchases (net outlay)	2 657	3 247	3 554	2 734	1 499	2 611	1 950	2 920	3 130
Gasoline and motor oil	1 986	2 276	2 555	1 809	1 419	1 964	1 563	2 151	2 218
Other vehicle expenses	2 536	3 023	3 288	2 589	1 579	2 545	2 180	2 711	2 446
Public transportation	479	544	608	436	353	503	580	467	234
Health Care	3 126	3 944	3 627	4 478	1 520	3 105	2 423	3 422	3 352
Health insurance	1 785	2 253	2 003	2 671	865	1 775	1 364	1 967	1 884
Medical services	736	932	936	928	351	737	590	806	726
Drugs	486	609	544	722	245	474	384	516	612
Medical supplies	119	149	143	157	60	118	84	133	129
Entertainment	2 693	3 256	3 578	2 655	1 588	2 716	2 269	2 920	2 453
Personal Care Products and Services	596	693	744	599	404	613	555	639	413
Reading	110	136	135	137	58	111	99	117	91
Education	1 068	1 234	1 503	778	743	1 127	951	1 209	456
Tobacco Products and Smoking Supplies	380	359	375	332	421	362	314	384	566
Miscellaneous	816	965	1 028	863	525	795	720	830	1 030
Cash Contributions	1 723	2 164	2 079	2 306	858	1 749	1 404	1 910	1 451
Personal Insurance and Pensions	5 471	6 776	8 282	4 260	2 910	5 605	4 739	6 008	4 084
Life and other personal insurance	309	417	466	336	97	306	240	337	336
Pensions and Social Security	5 162	6 359	7 816	3 924	2 813	5 298	4 499	5 670	3 748

X = Not applicable.

Table 11-15. Consumer Expenditures, Averages by Population Size of Area of Residence, 2009

(Number, dollar, percent.)

Item	All consumer units	Outside urban area	Urban consumer units						
			Total	Less than 100,000	100,000 to 249,999	250,000 to 999,999	1,000,000 to 2,499,999	2,500,000 to 4,999,999	5,000,000 and over
NUMBER OF CONSUMER UNITS (THOUSANDS)	120 847	24 704	96 142	18 615	9 486	19 817	15 575	16 791	15 858
CONSUMER UNIT CHARACTERISTICS									
Income Before Taxes	62 857	59 715	63 664	51 157	56 252	59 060	65 415	75 629	74 144
Income After Taxes	60 753	57 609	61 561	49 556	55 052	57 201	63 190	72 206	72 122
Age of Reference Person	49.4	53.0	48.5	48.8	48.2	47.9	48.7	47.4	50.0
Average Number in Consumer Unit									
All persons	2.5	2.5	2.5	2.4	2.5	2.5	2.5	2.5	2.6
Children under 18 years	0.6	0.6	0.6	0.6	0.7	0.6	0.6	0.6	0.6
Persons 65 years and over	0.3	0.4	0.3	0.3	0.3	0.3	0.3	0.2	0.3
Earners	1.3	1.3	1.3	1.2	1.3	1.3	1.3	1.4	1.3
Vehicles	2.0	2.6	1.8	1.9	1.9	1.8	1.8	1.7	1.5
Percent Distribution									
Male	47	47	47	46	45	46	49	49	48
Female	53	53	53	54	55	54	51	51	52
Percent Homeowner	66	83	62	61	64	64	64	62	57
With mortgage	41	45	41	34	42	42	45	44	38
Without mortgage	25	38	21	27	22	22	19	18	19
AVERAGE ANNUAL EXPENDITURES	49 067	46 890	49 627	40 605	43 895	48 083	50 416	57 380	56 351
Food	6 372	6 147	6 429	5 275	5 948	6 560	6 600	6 952	7 072
Food at home	3 753	3 865	3 724	3 099	3 461	3 899	3 913	3 885	3 990
Cereals and bakery products	506	521	503	414	472	533	525	533	526
Meats, poultry, fish, and eggs	841	877	832	684	742	857	897	853	926
Dairy products	406	432	400	339	389	437	402	412	411
Fruits and vegetables	656	624	665	519	578	668	654	740	793
Other food at home	1 343	1 411	1 326	1 142	1 280	1 404	1 435	1 347	1 334
Food away from home	2 619	2 282	2 705	2 176	2 487	2 660	2 687	3 067	3 081
Alcoholic Beverages	435	356	455	340	390	468	510	554	442
Housing	16 895	14 329	17 555	13 233	15 132	16 125	17 915	20 898	21 967
Shelter	10 075	7 547	10 724	7 230	8 892	9 415	10 974	13 149	14 746
Owned dwellings	6 543	5 941	6 697	4 559	5 955	6 203	7 118	7 969	8 511
Rented dwellings	2 860	1 025	3 332	2 163	2 362	2 670	3 213	4 245	5 260
Other lodging	672	581	695	508	575	542	644	935	975
Utilities, fuels, and public services	3 645	3 737	3 621	3 341	3 467	3 491	3 702	3 878	3 852
Household operations	1 011	712	1 088	745	841	1 002	1 060	1 448	1 394
Housekeeping supplies	659	749	636	575	617	739	653	630	581
Household furnishings and equipment	1 506	1 583	1 486	1 342	1 315	1 479	1 526	1 792	1 394
Apparel and Services	1 725	1 412	1 805	1 406	1 425	1 724	1 852	2 344	1 933
Transportation	7 658	8 510	7 440	6 794	6 531	7 198	7 363	8 534	7 925
Vehicle purchases (net outlay)	2 657	3 038	2 559	2 730	2 068	2 655	2 326	2 929	2 369
Gasoline and motor oil	1 986	2 440	1 870	1 796	1 775	1 847	1 939	2 031	1 803
Other vehicle expenses	2 536	2 767	2 476	1 972	2 285	2 334	2 529	2 898	2 832
Public transportation	479	264	534	295	403	362	569	677	921
Health Care	3 126	3 587	3 008	2 939	2 899	3 199	3 051	3 017	2 864
Health insurance	1 785	2 067	1 712	1 623	1 719	1 805	1 782	1 698	1 644
Medical services	736	765	729	774	588	729	721	794	699
Drugs	486	609	455	442	473	535	435	416	420
Medical supplies	119	145	112	99	118	130	113	109	102
Entertainment	2 693	2 859	2 650	2 434	2 429	2 627	2 759	2 964	2 622
Personal Care Products and Services	596	504	619	470	548	629	611	795	639
Reading	110	104	111	98	106	124	108	121	106
Education	1 068	712	1 159	862	899	1 105	1 021	1 254	1 766
Tobacco Products and Smoking Supplies	380	547	337	404	403	355	312	301	257
Miscellaneous	816	894	796	608	785	796	925	909	774
Cash Contributions	1 723	1 832	1 695	1 424	1 418	1 856	1 656	1 806	1 898
Personal Insurance and Pensions	5 471	5 097	5 567	4 319	4 983	5 318	5 733	6 931	6 087
Life and other personal insurance	309	365	295	251	271	331	302	286	317
Pensions and Social Security	5 162	4 732	5 272	4 067	4 712	4 987	5 431	6 645	5 770

Table 11-16. Consumer Expenditures, Averages by Region of Residence, 2009

(Number, dollar, percent.)

Item	All consumer units	Region[1]			
		Northeast	South	Midwest	West
NUMBER OF CONSUMER UNITS (THOUSANDS)	120 847	22 411	27 536	43 819	27 080
CONSUMER UNIT CHARACTERISTICS					
Income Before Taxes	62 857	71 731	59 908	58 641	65 332
Income After Taxes	60 753	68 986	57 866	56 795	63 279
Age of Reference Person	49.4	51.2	48.9	49.6	48.1
Average Number in Consumer Unit					
All persons	2.5	2.4	2.4	2.5	2.6
Children under 18 years	0.6	0.5	0.6	0.6	0.7
Persons 65 years and over	0.3	0.3	0.3	0.3	0.3
Earners	1.3	1.3	1.3	1.3	1.3
Vehicles	2.0	1.7	2.1	1.9	2.0
Percent Distribution					
Male	47	44	48	45	52
Female	53	56	52	55	48
Percent Homeowner	66	65	68	68	62
With mortgage	41	40	42	40	44
Without mortgage	25	25	26	28	18
AVERAGE ANNUAL EXPENDITURES	49 067	53 868	46 551	45 749	53 005
Food	6 372	6 975	6 031	5 944	6 903
Food at home	3 753	4 043	3 682	3 481	4 023
Cereals and bakery products	506	563	510	469	516
Meats, poultry, fish, and eggs	841	919	762	829	875
Dairy products	406	435	419	367	432
Fruits and vegetables	656	751	616	581	740
Other food at home	1 343	1 374	1 375	1 235	1 461
Food away from home	2 619	2 932	2 349	2 463	2 880
Alcoholic Beverages	435	468	418	368	530
Housing	16 895	19 343	15 109	15 387	19 127
Shelter	10 075	11 944	8 756	8 524	12 378
Owned dwellings	6 543	7 513	6 126	5 613	7 667
Rented dwellings	2 860	3 507	1 986	2 361	4 021
Other lodging	672	924	643	550	690
Utilities, fuels, and public services	3 645	4 095	3 421	3 741	3 343
Household operations	1 011	1 196	780	969	1 164
Housekeeping supplies	659	640	682	667	638
Household furnishings and equipment	1 506	1 467	1 471	1 485	1 605
Apparel and Services	1 725	1 782	1 461	1 786	1 844
Transportation	7 658	8 108	7 649	7 400	7 711
Vehicle purchases (net outlay)	2 657	2 754	2 921	2 612	2 380
Gasoline and motor oil	1 986	1 787	1 933	2 103	2 018
Other vehicle expenses	2 536	2 885	2 375	2 371	2 673
Public transportation	479	682	420	314	640
Health Care	3 126	3 132	3 272	3 030	3 128
Health insurance	1 785	1 916	1 845	1 730	1 703
Medical services	736	625	780	672	889
Drugs	486	481	508	521	414
Medical supplies	119	111	139	108	122
Entertainment	2 693	2 767	2 627	2 467	3 062
Personal Care Products and Services	596	601	538	593	653
Reading	110	141	112	85	121
Education	1 068	1 710	1 103	820	902
Tobacco Products and Smoking Supplies	380	439	409	394	278
Miscellaneous	816	821	798	768	910
Cash Contributions	1 723	1 568	1 684	1 692	1 941
Personal Insurance and Pensions	5 471	6 013	5 340	5 015	5 894
Life and other personal insurance	309	350	340	298	262
Pensions and Social Security	5 162	5 662	5 000	4 717	5 633

[1]The states that comprise the Census regions are: Northeast—Connecticut, Maine, Massachusetts, New Hampshire, New Jersey, New York, Pennsylvania, Rhode Island, and Vermont; South—Alabama, Arkansas, Delaware, District of Columbia, Florida, Georgia, Kentucky, Louisiana, Maryland, Mississippi, North Carolina, Oklahoma, South Carolina, Tennessee, Texas, Virginia, and West Virginia; Midwest—Illinois, Indiana, Iowa, Kansas, Michigan, Minnesota, Missouri, Nebraska, North Dakota, Ohio, South Dakota, and Wisconsin; and West—Alaska, Arizona, California, Colorado, Hawaii, Idaho, Montana, Nevada, New Mexico, Oregon, Utah, Washington, and Wyoming.

Table 11-17. Consumer Expenditures, Averages for Single Men by Income Before Taxes, 2008–2009

(Number, dollar, percent.)

Item	All single men	Complete reporting of income						
		Less than $5,000	$5,000 to $9,999	$10,000 to $14,999	$15,000 to $19,999	$20,000 to $29,999	$30,000 to $39,999	$40,000 and over
NUMBER OF CONSUMER UNITS (THOUSANDS)	16 180	1 494	1 484	1 719	1 632	2 398	1 916	5 538
CONSUMER UNIT CHARACTERISTICS								
Income Before Taxes	37 058	1 319	7 825	12 540	17 515	24 523	34 375	74 260
Income After Taxes	35 381	1 417	7 780	12 580	17 374	24 294	33 704	69 704
Age of Reference Person	47.1	36.4	43.2	52.7	53.9	49.3	46.6	46.4
Average Number in Consumer Unit								
All persons	1.0	1.0	1.0	1.0	1.0	1.0	1.0	1.0
Persons 65 years and over	0.2	0.1	0.2	0.4	0.4	0.3	0.2	0.1
Earners	0.7	0.5	0.5	0.4	0.5	0.7	0.9	0.9
Vehicles	1.3	0.7	0.8	1.0	1.2	1.3	1.4	1.6
Percent Homeowner	43	19	18	31	40	43	45	60
With mortgage	23	5	6	7	9	16	25	43
Without mortgage	20	14	12	24	31	27	20	17
AVERAGE ANNUAL EXPENDITURES	30 673	16 704	15 350	19 489	20 656	24 845	30 291	46 878
Food	3 779	2 927	2 468	2 844	2 605	3 119	3 597	4 998
Food at home	1 841	1 612	1 423	1 795	1 599	1 685	1 851	2 075
Cereals and bakery products	236	226	175	233	229	219	224	261
Meats, poultry, fish, and eggs	421	405	353	440	347	370	426	465
Dairy products	203	175	144	189	190	195	202	227
Fruits and vegetables	314	254	229	309	255	277	337	357
Other food at home	667	551	522	624	577	623	663	764
Food away from home	1 939	1 315	1 046	1 048	1 006	1 433	1 745	2 923
Alcoholic Beverages	521	344	339	322	232	421	505	747
Housing	11 218	6 243	5 991	7 772	8 154	9 249	10 770	16 833
Shelter	7 550	4 357	4 165	4 857	5 154	5 874	7 153	11 723
Owned dwellings	3 450	1 069	743	1 190	1 465	2 008	2 763	6 967
Rented dwellings	3 761	3 116	3 321	3 536	3 585	3 656	4 172	4 078
Other lodging	339	172	[1]101	131	104	211	218	678
Utilities, fuels, and public services	2 131	1 126	1 192	1 593	1 949	2 190	2 345	2 773
Household operations	428	152	147	167	474	444	329	673
Housekeeping supplies	275	205	155	351	194	188	174	375
Household furnishings and equipment	834	403	332	804	383	552	769	1 288
Apparel and Services	877	595	418	1 604	325	680	851	1 048
Transportation	4 861	2 070	2 160	2 275	3 666	4 711	5 705	7 170
Vehicle purchases (net outlay)	1 603	538	646	[1]236	1 197	1 749	2 324	2 378
Gasoline and motor oil	1 432	876	822	884	1 067	1 408	1 588	1 981
Other vehicle expenses	1 531	562	597	973	1 281	1 334	1 619	2 253
Public transportation	294	94	96	182	121	220	174	559
Health Care	1 450	634	674	1 271	1 597	1 537	1 527	1 817
Health insurance	847	323	350	817	977	910	849	1 064
Medical services	323	154	201	177	262	329	370	446
Drugs	231	116	101	240	299	257	255	245
Medical supplies	49	[1]40	[1]22	37	58	40	53	61
Entertainment	1 630	1 010	899	870	1 130	1 376	1 549	2 480
Personal Care Products and Services	201	151	111	143	126	197	184	275
Reading	75	31	38	42	74	67	66	115
Education	653	1 504	1 194	558	388	329	680	514
Tobacco Products and Smoking Supplies	318	247	246	341	339	349	379	308
Miscellaneous	590	344	146	354	276	353	602	1 024
Cash Contributions	1 413	311	342	649	967	856	1 272	2 657
Personal Insurance and Pensions	3 087	292	324	444	776	1 601	2 606	6 893
Life and other personal insurance	109	[1]60	32	80	68	80	79	187
Pensions and Social Security	2 978	232	292	365	708	1 521	2 526	6 706

[1]Data are likely to have large sampling errors.

Table 11-18. Consumer Expenditures, Averages for Single Women by Income Before Taxes, 2008–2009

(Number, dollar, percent.)

Item	All single women	Complete reporting of income						
		Less than $5,000	$5,000 to $9,999	$10,000 to $14,999	$15,000 to $19,999	$20,000 to $29,999	$30,000 to $39,999	$40,000 and over
NUMBER OF CONSUMER UNITS (THOUSANDS)	19 049	1 554	2 250	3 214	2 436	3 132	2 207	4 256
CONSUMER UNIT CHARACTERISTICS								
Income Before Taxes	28 620	1 286	8 110	12 610	17 072	24 576	34 236	68 204
Income After Taxes	27 692	1 359	8 176	12 714	17 083	24 233	33 309	64 637
Age of Reference Person	57.5	45.4	56.5	67.3	65.6	60.4	52.2	50.9
Average Number in Consumer Unit								
All persons	1.0	1.0	1.0	1.0	1.0	1.0	1.0	1.0
Persons 65 years and over	0.4	0.3	0.4	0.7	0.6	0.5	0.3	0.2
Earners	0.5	0.4	0.3	0.2	0.4	0.6	0.8	0.9
Vehicles	0.9	0.5	0.5	0.7	0.9	1.1	1.1	1.2
Percent Homeowner	55	25	33	54	59	58	57	71
With mortgage	24	11	7	10	16	20	33	51
Without mortgage	31	14	26	44	43	38	24	20
AVERAGE ANNUAL EXPENDITURES	28 598	15 809	14 675	18 224	23 335	26 902	32 553	50 199
Food	3 226	2 344	2 057	2 485	2 602	2 986	3 578	4 908
Food at home	1 960	1 434	1 465	1 686	1 744	1 887	2 178	2 600
Cereals and bakery products	263	192	199	235	268	259	270	329
Meats, poultry, fish, and eggs	401	309	316	400	301	407	449	492
Dairy products	229	164	170	196	224	208	258	305
Fruits and vegetables	372	280	295	310	313	355	430	496
Other food at home	694	488	485	544	638	658	772	978
Food away from home	1 267	910	592	799	859	1 099	1 400	2 308
Alcoholic Beverages	231	184	83	107	104	143	261	522
Housing	11 528	6 791	6 464	7 859	10 309	11 021	12 865	19 011
Shelter	7 225	4 484	3 829	4 531	6 101	6 818	8 261	12 459
Owned dwellings	3 684	1 401	1 039	1 856	2 816	3 140	3 961	8 049
Rented dwellings	3 160	2 910	2 719	2 590	3 097	3 456	3 811	3 395
Other lodging	381	173	71	85	189	222	489	1 015
Utilities, fuels, and public services	2 336	1 343	1 657	2 149	2 390	2 396	2 585	2 993
Household operations	590	169	214	371	616	553	530	1 149
Housekeeping supplies	397	225	240	303	369	384	438	590
Household furnishings and equipment	981	570	523	504	832	869	1 049	1 820
Apparel and Services	1 053	762	514	687	755	782	1 158	1 974
Transportation	3 929	1 770	1 955	2 256	3 351	4 085	5 130	6 562
Vehicle purchases (net outlay)	1 104	¹319	¹675	741	¹892	1 252	¹1 282	1 812
Gasoline and motor oil	1 090	621	609	668	883	1 201	1 435	1 692
Other vehicle expenses	1 415	535	527	705	1 411	1 419	2 093	2 326
Public transportation	320	295	145	142	165	214	320	732
Health Care	2 200	920	1 101	1 975	2 620	2 575	2 416	2 785
Health insurance	1 246	556	609	1 384	1 658	1 512	1 241	1 300
Medical services	489	128	198	287	388	492	675	887
Drugs	385	204	255	237	505	475	423	472
Medical supplies	81	32	39	67	70	96	78	126
Entertainment	1 451	711	675	823	974	1 377	1 458	2 866
Personal Care Products and Services	531	331	253	305	433	485	590	964
Reading	102	50	41	70	94	106	96	182
Education	500	1 199	703	272	236	309	516	589
Tobacco Products and Smoking Supplies	148	126	168	139	103	196	172	128
Miscellaneous	518	161	190	236	288	464	540	1 192
Cash Contributions	1 100	271	249	702	897	997	1 323	2 228
Personal Insurance and Pensions	2 082	188	223	309	568	1 377	2 451	6 288
Life and other personal insurance	116	35	59	105	142	113	144	155
Pensions and Social Security	1 966	153	164	204	426	1 265	2 307	6 132

¹Data are likely to have large sampling errors.

Table 11-19. Consumer Expenditures, Averages for Age Groups by Income Before Taxes: Reference Person Under 25 Years of Age, 2008–2009

(Number, dollar, percent.)

Item	Total	Complete reporting of income						
		Less than $5,000	$5,000 to $9,999	$10,000 to $14,999	$15,000 to $19,999	$20,000 to $29,999	$30,000 to $39,999	$40,000 and over
NUMBER OF CONSUMER UNITS (THOUSANDS)	8 051	1 431	1 141	912	856	1 070	809	1 834
CONSUMER UNIT CHARACTERISTICS								
Income Before Taxes	26 938	2 467	7 495	12 226	17 481	24 498	34 409	67 971
Income After Taxes	26 741	2 601	7 586	12 510	17 724	24 892	34 490	66 425
Age of Reference Person	21.5	20.4	20.9	21.4	21.7	21.8	21.9	22.3
Average Number in Consumer Unit								
All persons	2.0	1.2	1.4	1.7	2.1	2.2	2.4	2.8
Children under 18 years	0.4	0.1	0.2	0.4	0.5	0.5	0.5	0.5
Persons 65 years and over	(1)	(1)	(1)	(1)	(1)	(1)	(1)	(1)
Earners	1.3	0.7	0.9	0.9	1.2	1.4	1.5	2.1
Vehicles	1.2	0.5	0.7	0.8	1.1	1.3	1.7	2.0
Percent Distribution								
Male	47	52	49	45	49	44	43	45
Female	53	48	51	55	51	56	57	55
Percent Homeowner	15	1	2	5	11	13	24	36
With mortgage	10	1	1	3	5	9	17	28
Without mortgage	4	1	1	2	6	4	7	9
AVERAGE ANNUAL EXPENDITURES	28 728	13 469	17 675	19 785	23 042	26 745	36 001	49 999
Food	4 315	2 568	3 123	3 131	2 919	3 869	4 486	6 664
Food at home	2 389	1 280	1 730	1 931	1 810	2 230	2 498	3 537
Cereals and bakery products	294	171	210	278	228	266	310	417
Meats, poultry, fish, and eggs	572	310	392	448	395	570	547	873
Dairy products	269	142	190	164	252	263	306	385
Fruits and vegetables	384	187	264	255	324	367	382	594
Other food at home	871	469	674	785	610	764	953	1 268
Food away from home	1 926	1 288	1 394	1 201	1 109	1 639	1 987	3 127
Alcoholic Beverages	396	143	151	291	152	382	363	750
Housing	9 857	4 393	5 951	7 298	8 936	9 747	12 050	17 091
Shelter	6 420	3 167	4 111	4 840	5 907	6 363	7 823	10 833
Owned dwellings	1 316	[2]153	[2]136	252	501	955	1 684	3 912
Rented dwellings	4 913	2 793	3 780	4 401	5 325	5 351	5 900	6 644
Other lodging	191	220	195	[2]187	[2]81	[2]57	[2]239	277
Utilities, fuels, and public services	1 849	600	974	1 425	1 774	2 100	2 466	3 194
Household operations	347	79	142	263	298	268	404	770
Housekeeping supplies	306	144	150	222	153	277	354	516
Household furnishings and equipment	935	403	575	547	804	739	1 004	1 778
Apparel and Services	1 373	712	1 010	1 133	867	1 585	1 222	2 088
Transportation	5 398	1 571	2 731	3 533	4 840	4 782	9 411	9 488
Vehicle purchases (net outlay)	2 149	[2]492	1 199	1 450	2 089	1 178	5 309	3 583
Gasoline and motor oil	1 734	720	962	1 203	1 531	1 861	2 405	2 993
Other vehicle expenses	1 283	253	411	730	1 046	1 475	1 552	2 461
Public transportation	231	105	159	150	174	268	145	451
Health Care	679	142	228	311	492	581	1 107	1 500
Health insurance	386	63	88	116	253	329	663	928
Medical services	155	23	75	97	104	113	297	321
Drugs	107	41	43	73	90	105	134	198
Medical supplies	32	[2]15	[2]21	[2]25	[2]45	34	[2]13	53
Entertainment	1 423	572	752	956	1 344	1 343	1 669	2 538
Personal Care Products and Services	365	182	225	253	251	237	511	636
Reading	45	24	35	34	54	48	48	67
Education	1 798	2 802	2 570	1 476	1 336	1 326	1 011	1 537
Tobacco Products and Smoking Supplies	290	103	159	289	284	435	428	372
Miscellaneous	262	52	122	146	125	251	672	444
Cash Contributions	389	64	216	232	229	337	407	926
Personal Insurance and Pensions	2 139	141	401	702	1 213	1 822	2 616	5 898
Life and other personal insurance	34	[2]1	[2]1	[2]6	[2]18	[2]28	70	89
Pensions and Social Security	2 105	140	400	696	1 195	1 795	2 546	5 809

[1]Value less than or equal to 0.5.
[2]Data are likely to have large sampling errors.

Table 11-20. Consumer Expenditures, Averages for Age Groups by Income Before Taxes: Reference Person 25 to 34 Years of Age, 2008–2009

(Number, dollar, percent.)

Item	Total	Complete reporting of income								
		Less than $5,000	$5,000 to $9,999	$10,000 to $14,999	$15,000 to $19,999	$20,000 to $29,999	$30,000 to $39,999	$40,000 to $49,999	$50,000 to $69,999	$70,000 and over
NUMBER OF CONSUMER UNITS (THOUSANDS)	20 126	613	613	945	1 047	2 535	2 349	2 344	3 549	6 131
CONSUMER UNIT CHARACTERISTICS										
Income Before Taxes	59 414	-1 110	7 776	12 865	17 586	25 001	34 610	44 614	59 007	114 567
Income After Taxes	58 027	-489	8 558	13 803	18 441	25 770	34 903	44 521	58 226	109 642
Age of Reference Person	29.6	29.3	29.1	29.3	29.4	29.2	29.2	29.4	29.6	30.2
Average Number in Consumer Unit										
All persons	2.8	2.3	2.5	2.6	2.7	2.6	2.7	2.8	2.9	3.0
Children under 18 years	1.1	1.0	1.2	1.2	1.2	1.1	1.1	1.1	1.0	1.0
Persons 65 years and over	([1])	([1])	([1])	([1])	([1])	([1])	([1])	([1])	([1])	([1])
Earners	1.5	0.5	0.7	0.9	1.1	1.2	1.3	1.5	1.7	1.9
Vehicles	1.7	0.9	0.9	1.0	1.0	1.3	1.5	1.7	1.9	2.2
Percent Distribution										
Male	49	45	36	32	45	45	48	48	54	52
Female	51	55	64	68	55	55	52	52	46	48
Percent Homeowner	46	19	12	18	18	23	34	42	54	72
With mortgage	40	14	10	11	11	15	25	35	47	69
Without mortgage	6	5	3	7	8	8	9	7	8	3
AVERAGE ANNUAL EXPENDITURES	47 334	25 727	22 125	24 739	24 345	29 832	36 231	39 045	48 958	73 263
Food	6 199	5 108	3 738	4 210	4 193	4 507	4 926	5 254	6 337	8 742
Food at home	3 436	3 573	2 344	2 916	2 868	2 816	2 975	2 904	3 423	4 399
Cereals and bakery products	464	507	309	415	351	383	412	399	442	599
Meats, poultry, fish, and eggs	749	876	610	667	735	681	678	629	729	892
Dairy products	385	347	246	315	337	319	334	322	382	499
Fruits and vegetables	588	562	449	525	405	486	493	475	596	769
Other food at home	1 250	1 282	730	994	1 040	947	1 058	1 078	1 274	1 641
Food away from home	2 763	1 534	1 394	1 294	1 325	1 691	1 951	2 351	2 915	4 343
Alcoholic Beverages	486	203	266	131	121	263	381	441	544	770
Housing	17 288	9 785	9 416	10 884	10 271	11 482	13 007	14 833	17 176	26 069
Shelter	10 896	6 434	5 913	6 731	6 407	7 137	8 148	9 584	10 794	16 415
Owned dwellings	5 728	1 656	1 166	1 604	914	1 541	2 550	4 206	5 762	11 559
Rented dwellings	4 805	4 751	4 596	5 060	5 450	5 477	5 479	5 165	4 713	4 061
Other lodging	363	[2]28	[2]151	[2]67	[2]42	119	119	213	319	795
Utilities, fuels, and public services	3 201	2 092	2 170	2 319	2 352	2 555	2 943	3 137	3 390	3 975
Household operations	1 184	412	534	513	431	609	702	780	1 089	2 189
Housekeeping supplies	550	315	277	454	415	432	420	353	531	829
Household furnishings and equipment	1 458	531	521	868	665	749	793	979	1 373	2 660
Apparel and Services	1 918	1 772	1 412	1 408	1 161	1 558	1 549	1 356	1 902	2 732
Transportation	8 191	4 042	3 254	3 822	3 925	5 413	7 162	6 679	8 948	12 188
Vehicle purchases (net outlay)	2 985	[2]1 484	[2]1 021	[2]1 094	[2]1 051	1 849	2 662	1 872	3 350	4 760
Gasoline and motor oil	2 414	1 076	1 216	1 432	1 522	1 780	2 184	2 495	2 662	3 147
Other vehicle expenses	2 341	1 323	870	1 045	1 166	1 549	2 116	2 006	2 540	3 420
Public transportation	451	159	147	251	187	235	200	307	396	860
Health Care	1 771	730	650	596	573	994	1 317	1 641	2 069	2 747
Health insurance	1 033	[2]237	385	323	285	501	836	1 018	1 264	1 581
Medical services	469	236	114	159	168	281	254	396	525	782
Drugs	205	92	140	88	90	171	176	177	220	288
Medical supplies	64	[2]165	[2]11	[2]25	[2]30	41	51	50	60	95
Entertainment	2 636	1 155	956	1 230	1 059	1 576	1 942	2 081	3 077	4 092
Personal Care Products and Services	551	432	289	362	268	343	403	440	495	895
Reading	74	28	30	36	31	46	52	68	81	114
Education	784	1 497	583	632	314	606	920	439	645	1 071
Tobacco Products and Smoking Supplies	333	276	355	297	336	355	362	360	427	256
Miscellaneous	679	183	237	161	247	299	580	626	704	1 123
Cash Contributions	1 019	345	473	226	619	537	756	881	1 121	1 624
Personal Insurance and Pensions	5 407	172	467	742	1 226	1 854	2 873	3 945	5 431	10 841
Life and other personal insurance	155	[2]24	[2]11	[2]31	29	52	79	147	130	313
Pensions and Social Security	5 251	148	456	711	1 197	1 802	2 794	3 797	5 300	10 528

[1]Value less than or equal to 0.05.
[2]Data are likely to have large sampling errors.

Table 11-21. Consumer Expenditures, Averages for Age Groups by Income Before Taxes: Reference Person 35 to 44 Years of Age, 2008–2009

(Number, dollar, percent.)

Item	Total	Less than $5,000	$5,000 to $9,999	$10,000 to $14,999	$15,000 to $19,999	$20,000 to $29,999	$30,000 to $39,999	$40,000 to $49,999	$50,000 to $69,999	$70,000 and over
					Complete reporting of income					
NUMBER OF CONSUMER UNITS (THOUSANDS)	22 516	509	543	734	855	2 186	2 162	2 035	3 787	9 706
CONSUMER UNIT CHARACTERISTICS										
Income Before Taxes	77 297	-2 606	8 022	12 813	17 597	24 916	34 759	44 530	59 430	130 613
Income After Taxes	75 294	-1 821	8 169	13 386	18 344	25 729	35 376	44 707	59 175	125 548
Age of Reference Person	39.7	39.6	39.5	39.5	39.3	39.5	39.5	39.7	39.6	39.9
Average Number in Consumer Unit										
All persons	3.3	2.7	2.3	2.5	2.7	2.9	3.1	3.1	3.3	3.6
Children under 18 years	1.3	1.1	0.9	1.1	1.2	1.2	1.4	1.2	1.3	1.5
Persons 65 years and over	([1])	([1])	([1])	([1])	([1])	([1])	([1])	([1])	([1])	([1])
Earners	1.6	0.6	0.5	0.8	1.0	1.3	1.4	1.6	1.8	2.0
Vehicles	2.1	1.2	0.9	1.1	1.2	1.4	1.6	1.8	2.2	2.7
Percent Distribution										
Male	48	40	45	39	33	39	45	44	49	52
Female	52	60	55	61	67	61	55	56	51	48
Percent Homeowner	66	43	28	26	29	41	49	55	70	86
With mortgage	57	28	16	16	16	28	38	46	60	79
Without mortgage	9	15	12	10	12	13	11	8	10	7
AVERAGE ANNUAL EXPENDITURES	58 070	30 495	21 482	24 018	25 399	29 753	36 847	41 601	50 136	84 679
Food	7 805	4 994	3 579	4 019	4 126	4 905	5 723	5 970	6 973	10 646
Food at home	4 477	3 053	2 334	2 971	2 875	3 260	3 615	3 765	4 068	5 710
Cereals and bakery products	624	414	278	368	420	440	483	497	590	808
Meats, poultry, fish, and eggs	998	707	502	786	691	760	925	946	917	1 196
Dairy products	506	394	357	329	296	325	406	393	449	661
Fruits and vegetables	746	508	417	512	431	537	565	634	692	956
Other food at home	1 602	1 031	780	976	1 037	1 197	1 236	1 295	1 420	2 088
Food away from home	3 328	1 941	1 245	1 048	1 251	1 645	2 108	2 205	2 905	4 936
Alcoholic Beverages	480	501	248	188	200	167	305	323	363	724
Housing	20 678	13 288	9 280	9 991	10 745	12 007	14 027	15 583	17 917	28 965
Shelter	12 720	8 289	5 212	5 894	6 431	7 406	8 697	9 573	11 036	17 853
Owned dwellings	8 945	5 028	1 658	1 631	1 669	2 888	4 068	5 038	7 562	14 563
Rented dwellings	3 168	3 116	3 440	4 201	4 669	4 398	4 390	4 308	3 170	2 156
Other lodging	607	[2]145	[2]115	[2]61	[2]93	120	239	227	305	1 135
Utilities, fuels, and public services	4 112	2 913	2 447	2 512	2 743	3 131	3 381	3 768	4 072	4 981
Household operations	1 376	592	360	342	506	422	595	633	878	2 368
Housekeeping supplies	681	461	307	421	392	398	467	525	588	939
Household furnishings and equipment	1 789	1 033	953	822	673	649	888	1 084	1 344	2 823
Apparel and Services	2 291	1 230	1 113	2 482	959	1 338	1 507	1 823	1 721	3 205
Transportation	9 095	4 250	3 171	2 764	4 311	4 788	5 957	6 875	8 752	12 861
Vehicle purchases (net outlay)	2 944	[2]966	[2]563	[2]392	[2]1 104	1 238	1 806	2 289	2 601	4 446
Gasoline and motor oil	2 860	1 734	1 269	1 363	1 580	2 046	2 162	2 423	2 993	3 613
Other vehicle expenses	2 751	1 393	1 231	871	1 275	1 348	1 775	1 897	2 824	3 875
Public transportation	540	158	107	138	352	156	216	267	334	927
Health Care	2 510	1 407	852	795	1 075	1 086	1 824	1 836	2 400	3 574
Health insurance	1 388	837	410	422	615	553	1 000	1 069	1 385	1 955
Medical services	681	417	280	182	217	282	492	409	625	1 006
Drugs	342	131	129	169	193	191	278	288	303	467
Medical supplies	99	[2]21	[2]33	[2]23	[2]50	59	55	70	86	147
Entertainment	3 460	1 965	984	951	1 149	1 283	1 857	2 022	2 612	5 550
Personal Care Products and Services	706	387	404	254	310	430	436	553	574	1 017
Reading	94	32	18	32	27	48	38	55	72	151
Education	944	376	[2]229	464	198	198	470	335	642	1 635
Tobacco Products and Smoking Supplies	385	372	345	521	472	476	420	434	409	322
Miscellaneous	914	349	270	355	314	534	519	702	997	1 260
Cash Contributions	1 565	931	689	505	411	536	900	1 230	1 351	2 364
Personal Insurance and Pensions	7 143	412	300	696	1 101	1 958	2 862	3 860	5 354	12 407
Life and other personal insurance	277	[2]86	[2]23	[2]52	[2]47	79	129	161	196	473
Pensions and Social Security	6 866	326	277	644	1 055	1 879	2 734	3 699	5 159	11 934

[1]Value less than or equal to 0.05.
[2]Data are likely to have large sampling errors.

Table 11-22. Consumer Expenditures, Averages for Age Groups by Income Before Taxes: Reference Person 45 to 54 Years of Age, 2008–2009

(Number, dollar, percent.)

Item	Total	Complete reporting of income								
		Less than $5,000	$5,000 to $9,999	$10,000 to $14,999	$15,000 to $19,999	$20,000 to $29,999	$30,000 to $39,999	$40,000 to $49,999	$50,000 to $69,999	$70,000 and over
NUMBER OF CONSUMER UNITS (THOUSANDS)	25 527	630	705	810	865	2 081	2 308	2 371	4 209	11 549
CONSUMER UNIT CHARACTERISTICS										
Income Before Taxes	81 411	-4 592	8 105	12 598	17 488	25 057	34 740	45 017	59 460	135 143
Income After Taxes	78 001	-5 239	8 323	12 975	17 785	25 187	34 336	44 318	57 914	128 342
Age of Reference Person	49.4	49.8	49.6	49.8	49.3	49.3	49.3	49.2	49.5	49.5
Average Number in Consumer Unit										
All persons	2.7	2.0	1.7	2.1	2.2	2.4	2.5	2.5	2.7	3.1
Children under 18 years	0.6	0.5	0.4	0.4	0.5	0.5	0.5	0.6	0.6	0.7
Persons 65 years and over	(1)	(1)	(1)	(1)	(1)	(1)	(1)	(1)	(1)	(1)
Earners	1.7	0.5	0.4	0.7	0.9	1.2	1.3	1.5	1.7	2.2
Vehicles	2.4	1.0	0.7	1.1	1.2	1.6	1.7	2.0	2.4	3.1
Percent Distribution										
Male	48	50	34	33	40	40	40	50	44	54
Female	52	50	66	67	60	60	60	50	56	46
Percent Homeowner	75	40	30	37	48	53	61	71	76	91
With mortgage	56	21	16	19	21	33	42	52	56	73
Without mortgage	19	19	14	18	27	19	19	19	21	19
AVERAGE ANNUAL EXPENDITURES	59 953	26 947	18 645	24 078	24 907	30 419	35 605	39 160	48 941	88 155
Food	7 573	4 509	3 060	4 317	3 945	4 741	4 809	5 241	6 245	10 662
Food at home	4 399	3 106	2 310	2 952	2 977	3 296	3 063	3 342	3 764	5 784
Cereals and bakery products	593	469	345	417	372	421	377	455	522	781
Meats, poultry, fish, and eggs	998	677	528	678	811	753	813	802	848	1 272
Dairy products	486	349	277	324	327	359	329	368	402	647
Fruits and vegetables	765	576	394	481	460	566	528	546	656	1 020
Other food at home	1 557	1 034	766	1 051	1 007	1 197	1 017	1 171	1 335	2 065
Food away from home	3 174	1 403	750	1 366	968	1 445	1 746	1 899	2 481	4 877
Alcoholic Beverages	503	402	403	227	156	259	302	332	368	742
Housing	19 285	11 471	8 382	9 699	10 129	11 735	13 177	14 249	16 314	26 469
Shelter	11 493	7 576	4 827	5 557	5 654	6 775	7 813	8 512	9 587	15 860
Owned dwellings	8 350	4 373	1 707	1 994	2 354	3 340	4 593	5 612	6 615	12 716
Rented dwellings	2 203	2 886	3 095	3 471	3 262	3 294	3 014	2 633	2 522	1 379
Other lodging	940	[2]317	[2]25	[2]92	[2]38	141	206	267	450	1 765
Utilities, fuels, and public services	4 261	2 683	2 440	2 769	2 848	3 290	3 497	3 689	4 094	5 175
Household operations	964	397	233	307	387	431	429	503	637	1 546
Housekeeping supplies	735	317	346	515	498	477	411	408	561	1 071
Household furnishings and equipment	1 832	498	536	551	742	763	1 028	1 137	1 434	2 817
Apparel and Services	2 059	845	1 061	1 275	958	1 032	1 248	1 165	1 545	3 076
Transportation	10 052	3 202	2 400	3 518	3 945	4 813	6 225	6 610	8 963	14 641
Vehicle purchases (net outlay)	3 292	[2]735	[2]595	[2]1 018	[2]865	1 175	1 761	1 793	2 614	5 180
Gasoline and motor oil	2 850	1 162	840	1 301	1 413	1 916	2 151	2 324	2 777	3 723
Other vehicle expenses	3 307	978	793	1 097	1 528	1 558	2 046	2 307	3 172	4 717
Public transportation	603	327	173	103	140	164	269	186	401	1 020
Health Care	3 051	1 523	803	1 296	1 351	1 762	2 033	2 262	2 924	4 168
Health insurance	1 605	705	316	825	605	883	1 157	1 209	1 593	2 168
Medical services	850	463	149	804	290	479	429	558	748	1 205
Drugs	458	291	212	-399	426	356	359	419	440	601
Medical supplies	138	[2]64	[2]127	65	[2]30	44	88	75	144	195
Entertainment	3 237	1 642	1 056	1 050	1 261	1 685	1 561	1 739	2 409	5 012
Personal Care Products and Services	702	286	183	246	270	413	406	457	593	1 029
Reading	122	57	28	28	49	44	60	75	92	190
Education	2 033	[2]565	[2]144	326	115	273	624	780	890	3 768
Tobacco Products and Smoking Supplies	475	626	428	672	434	594	478	501	544	407
Miscellaneous	1 003	292	293	358	351	390	790	764	876	1 433
Cash Contributions	2 104	752	169	480	803	775	912	1 006	1 474	3 439
Personal Insurance and Pensions	7 753	775	235	586	1 140	1 903	2 979	3 981	5 705	13 120
Life and other personal insurance	411	[2]181	69	83	140	139	173	208	281	673
Pensions and Social Security	7 343	595	166	503	1 000	1 764	2 806	3 773	5 423	12 448

[1]Value less than or equal to 0.05.
[2]Data are likely to have large sampling errors.

Table 11-23. Consumer Expenditures, Averages for Age Groups by Income Before Taxes: Reference Person 55 to 64 Years of Age, 2008–2009

(Number, dollar, percent.)

Item	Total	Complete reporting of income								
		Less than $5,000	$5,000 to $9,999	$10,000 to $14,999	$15,000 to $19,999	$20,000 to $29,999	$30,000 to $39,999	$40,000 to $49,999	$50,000 to $69,999	$70,000 and over
NUMBER OF CONSUMER UNITS (THOUSANDS)	20 279	683	799	1 103	1 015	2 179	1 994	1 913	3 205	7 387
CONSUMER UNIT CHARACTERISTICS										
Income Before Taxes	71 120	-2 431	8 043	12 718	17 394	25 147	34 645	44 648	59 191	136 282
Income After Taxes	68 282	-2 107	8 087	12 667	17 184	25 171	34 150	43 409	57 129	129 836
Age of Reference Person	59.2	59.1	59.3	59.5	59.6	59.6	59.7	59.3	59.1	58.9
Average Number in Consumer Unit										
All persons	2.1	1.4	1.4	1.5	1.7	1.8	1.9	2.1	2.2	2.5
Children under 18 years	0.2	[1]0.1	[1]0.1	[1]0.1	0.2	0.1	0.1	0.2	0.2	0.2
Persons 65 years and over	0.1	([2])	[1]0.1	0.1	0.1	0.1	0.1	0.1	0.1	0.1
Earners	1.3	0.3	0.3	0.4	0.6	0.9	1.1	1.3	1.5	1.9
Vehicles	2.2	1.4	1.0	1.3	1.5	1.7	1.9	2.1	2.6	2.8
Percent Distribution										
Male	49	47	35	41	41	40	42	47	51	56
Female	51	53	65	59	59	60	58	53	49	44
Percent Homeowner	81	58	47	54	62	74	77	84	86	94
With mortgage	47	26	19	16	24	32	39	44	55	63
Without mortgage	34	32	29	38	38	42	39	41	31	31
AVERAGE ANNUAL EXPENDITURES	53 602	28 606	18 495	20 968	26 699	29 625	34 267	41 871	51 409	84 566
Food	6 330	3 646	3 213	3 535	3 404	3 813	4 625	5 262	6 259	9 250
Food at home	3 694	2 544	2 586	2 507	2 345	2 543	2 869	3 335	3 753	4 920
Cereals and bakery products	478	399	304	308	320	333	349	434	484	640
Meats, poultry, fish, and eggs	847	553	693	679	464	566	735	844	860	1 082
Dairy products	402	289	279	291	286	256	293	343	385	557
Fruits and vegetables	673	480	450	402	422	480	519	613	670	905
Other food at home	1 293	822	861	827	854	909	972	1 100	1 354	1 736
Food away from home	2 636	1 102	627	1 028	1 058	1 270	1 756	1 927	2 505	4 330
Alcoholic Beverages	482	202	201	182	127	216	270	281	495	815
Housing	17 295	11 284	7 715	8 470	10 113	10 918	12 136	13 823	16 965	25 521
Shelter	9 932	6 955	4 310	4 851	5 785	6 102	6 613	7 628	9 687	14 871
Owned dwellings	7 265	3 987	1 806	2 000	2 848	3 846	4 337	5 797	7 306	11 714
Rented dwellings	1 588	2 436	2 446	2 629	2 508	1 913	1 968	1 425	1 475	1 028
Other lodging	1 078	532	[1]59	222	429	343	308	406	906	2 129
Utilities, fuels, and public services	3 934	2 391	2 441	2 415	2 886	3 183	3 341	3 584	4 087	5 015
Household operations	875	427	209	235	297	451	512	623	760	1 501
Housekeeping supplies	785	430	352	396	390	457	508	663	757	1 194
Household furnishings and equipment	1 770	1 080	402	573	754	726	1 161	1 325	1 675	2 940
Apparel and Services	1 606	627	566	389	615	838	1 394	1 047	1 479	2 610
Transportation	8 842	3 844	2 774	2 964	5 261	5 329	5 887	7 971	9 223	13 214
Vehicle purchases (net outlay)	2 873	[1]837	[1]420	[1]588	1 638	1 735	1 432	2 817	3 240	4 417
Gasoline and motor oil	2 438	1 441	1 127	1 185	1 552	1 716	1 884	2 272	2 563	3 331
Other vehicle expenses	2 946	1 302	1 146	1 035	1 930	1 682	2 356	2 603	2 952	4 326
Public transportation	586	264	81	156	142	196	214	279	469	1 141
Health Care	3 860	2 531	1 427	1 891	2 396	2 570	2 737	3 551	4 073	5 413
Health insurance	1 982	1 447	769	1 044	1 300	1 420	1 583	1 863	1 953	2 713
Medical services	1 038	601	321	306	504	472	513	802	1 186	1 646
Drugs	696	411	316	478	497	601	587	753	740	848
Medical supplies	144	72	22	63	95	77	55	133	193	207
Entertainment	2 970	2 358	1 082	1 020	1 117	1 620	1 979	2 309	3 387	4 429
Personal Care Products and Services	623	478	209	170	260	366	434	444	569	998
Reading	152	81	40	52	63	72	82	104	159	250
Education	936	[1]469	[1]14	[1]145	[1]227	85	206	555	449	2 053
Tobacco Products and Smoking Supplies	383	296	337	441	497	377	408	341	417	362
Miscellaneous	1 130	980	178	678	714	641	540	836	1 101	1 759
Cash Contributions	2 127	624	359	484	936	797	1 004	1 551	1 541	3 964
Personal Insurance and Pensions	6 867	1 185	381	545	970	1 983	2 566	3 795	5 291	13 928
Life and other personal insurance	482	176	105	149	129	217	244	310	445	852
Pensions and Social Security	6 385	1 009	277	396	841	1 765	2 323	3 485	4 847	13 075

[1]Data are likely to have large sampling errors.
[2]Value less than or equal to 0.05.

Table 11-24. Consumer Expenditures, Averages for Age Groups by Income Before Taxes: Reference Person 65 Years of Age and Over, 2008–2009

(Number, dollar, percent.)

Item		Complete reporting of income								
	Total	Less than $5,000	$5,000 to $9,999	$10,000 to $14,999	$15,000 to $19,999	$20,000 to $29,999	$30,000 to $39,999	$40,000 to $49,999	$50,000 to $69,999	$70,000 and over
NUMBER OF CONSUMER UNITS (THOUSANDS)	24 310	742	1 470	3 300	3 010	4 810	3 004	2 099	2 693	3 181
CONSUMER UNIT CHARACTERISTICS										
Income Before Taxes	39 604	-7 481	8 435	12 613	17 471	24 724	34 875	44 960	58 726	121 184
Income After Taxes	38 949	-7 990	8 500	12 786	17 579	24 809	34 838	44 444	58 106	116 756
Age of Reference Person	75.0	74.7	76.2	77.7	77.3	75.5	74.3	73.9	73.0	71.9
Average Number in Consumer Unit										
All persons	1.7	1.3	1.2	1.2	1.3	1.7	1.8	2.0	2.1	2.3
Children under 18 years	0.1	([1])	([1])	([1])	([1])	([1])	([1])	0.1	0.1	0.1
Persons 65 years and over	1.4	1.2	1.1	1.1	1.2	1.4	1.5	1.5	1.5	1.5
Earners	0.4	0.2	0.1	0.1	0.1	0.2	0.4	0.6	0.8	1.2
Vehicles	1.6	0.9	0.8	0.9	1.2	1.5	1.8	1.9	2.2	2.5
Percent Distribution										
Male	43	36	27	26	37	42	42	49	56	62
Female	57	64	73	74	63	58	58	51	44	38
Percent Homeowner	79	51	51	62	73	82	89	87	91	95
With mortgage	21	11	10	10	15	17	21	25	31	43
Without mortgage	58	39	41	52	58	64	67	62	60	52
AVERAGE ANNUAL EXPENDITURES	37 204	23 097	16 640	19 457	24 022	30 562	36 128	39 072	50 304	77 079
Food	4 797	3 335	2 577	2 933	2 955	4 117	4 819	5 177	6 199	8 322
Food at home	3 149	2 262	2 074	2 186	2 153	2 893	3 205	3 421	3 931	4 686
Cereals and bakery products	437	331	299	286	317	425	450	460	549	613
Meats, poultry, fish, and eggs	704	431	474	463	442	675	731	735	916	1 039
Dairy products	354	259	253	234	252	304	359	410	453	522
Fruits and vegetables	597	513	395	375	433	537	619	594	735	938
Other food at home	1 058	728	654	828	708	952	1 046	1 222	1 278	1 574
Food away from home	1 648	1 073	504	747	802	1 224	1 614	1 756	2 267	3 635
Alcoholic Beverages	272	[2]86	[2]21	139	68	196	260	216	408	702
Housing	13 095	9 655	7 390	8 264	10 048	11 365	11 992	13 848	16 189	24 520
Shelter	7 054	5 929	4 456	4 656	5 400	5 964	6 089	7 132	8 617	13 758
Owned dwellings	4 763	2 365	1 872	2 126	3 135	3 904	4 447	5 098	6 464	10 868
Rented dwellings	1 700	3 408	2 527	2 404	2 074	1 652	1 192	1 454	1 289	895
Other lodging	592	[2]156	[2]57	125	190	408	450	580	864	1 995
Utilities, fuels, and public services	3 297	2 428	2 050	2 349	2 767	3 167	3 429	3 612	3 894	4 924
Household operations	880	609	229	420	746	727	676	798	1 227	2 032
Housekeeping supplies	655	306	290	371	409	585	702	792	803	1 081
Household furnishings and equipment	1 209	385	365	470	727	923	1 096	1 514	1 648	2 725
Apparel and Services	1 080	553	325	555	745	736	988	951	1 554	2 413
Transportation	5 512	2 993	2 053	2 160	3 186	4 754	5 663	6 050	8 508	11 307
Vehicle purchases (net outlay)	1 684	[2]50	[2]541	[2]264	845	1 487	1 676	1 907	2 932	3 960
Gasoline and motor oil	1 433	890	588	694	925	1 313	1 546	1 805	1 963	2 580
Other vehicle expenses	2 002	1 425	568	1 010	1 252	1 741	2 090	2 035	3 172	3 611
Public transportation	394	628	355	193	164	214	351	303	440	1 156
Health Care	4 726	3 004	2 213	2 688	3 441	4 567	5 288	5 627	6 567	7 125
Health insurance	2 937	1 808	1 410	1 833	2 294	2 932	3 335	3 534	3 845	4 126
Medical services	807	525	371	342	454	693	863	895	1 365	1 481
Drugs	825	551	355	438	590	805	930	1 033	1 141	1 207
Medical supplies	158	[2]121	77	74	103	138	159	165	216	311
Entertainment	1 988	927	693	843	1 048	1 659	2 244	2 027	2 575	4 415
Personal Care Products and Services	521	325	212	296	379	393	533	524	741	1 013
Reading	143	72	52	66	102	115	153	160	208	290
Education	216	[2]16	[2]25	[2]198	23	96	90	129	344	792
Tobacco Products and Smoking Supplies	184	122	97	127	161	236	184	172	209	231
Miscellaneous	626	408	229	255	363	444	746	805	765	1 359
Cash Contributions	2 191	1 265	559	707	1 090	1 185	2 154	1 748	3 239	6 705
Personal Insurance and Pensions	1 851	336	195	226	414	699	1 015	1 639	2 800	7 885
Life and other personal insurance	325	249	135	151	134	180	284	293	437	976
Pensions and Social Security	1 526	[2]87	60	75	280	519	732	1 345	2 363	6 909

[1]Value less than or equal to 0.05.
[2]Data are likely to have large sampling errors.

Chapter Twelve

AMERICAN TIME USE SURVEY

AMERICAN TIME USE SURVEY

HIGHLIGHTS

This chapter presents data from the American Time Use Survey (ATUS). The survey was introduced in the sixth edition of the *Handbook of U.S. Labor Statistics*. Its purpose is to collect data on the activities people do during the day and the amount of time they spend on each activity.

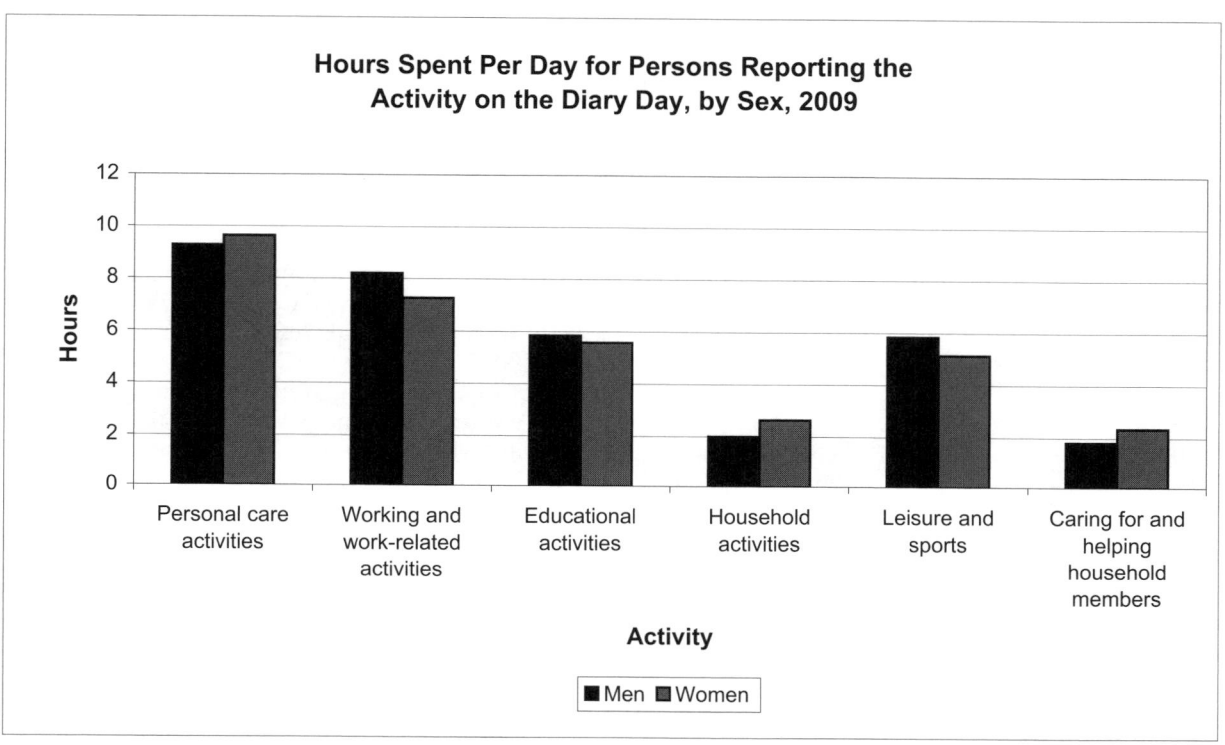

Hours Spent Per Day for Persons Reporting the Activity on the Diary Day, by Sex, 2009

In 2009, on days that they worked, men worked nearly one hour more than women. This difference partly reflects women's greater likelihood of working part-time. Men also spent more time more on educational activities and leisure and sports than women when reporting that activity on the diary day. (See Table 12-1.)

OTHER HIGHLIGHTS

- On an average day in 2009, 20.2 percent of men cared for household members compared to 29.9 percent of women. In addition, 20.2 percent of men did housework—such as cleaning or doing laundry—while 51.3 percent of women did. (See Table 12-1.)

- The number of hours spent on work and work-related activities increased for each age group from 15 to 34 years. However, for each age group from 35 to 75 years, the number of hours spent working declined. (See Table 12-2.)

- Production workers had the longest average workday (8.37 hours), followed by installation, maintenance, and repair workers (8.26 hours) and transportation and material moving occupations (7.9 hours). (See Table 12-4.)

- The more education a person attained, the greater the likelihood they worked at home in 2009. Over 40 percent of employed people age 25 and over with a Bachelor's degree reported working at home on an average day compared to 13.0 percent of those with a high school diploma and 10.2 percent of those with less than a high school diploma. (See Table 12-5.)

NOTES AND DEFINITIONS

Survey Methodology

While the Bureau of Labor Statistics (BLS) has long produced statistics about the labor market, including information about employment, hours, and earnings, the American Time Use Survey (ATUS) marks the first time that a federal statistical agency has produced estimates on how Americans spend another critical resource—their time. Data collection for the ATUS began in January 2003. Sample cases for the survey are selected monthly, and interviews are conducted continuously throughout the year. In 2009, approximately 13,100 individuals were interviewed.

ATUS sample households are chosen from the households that have completed their eighth (final) interview for the Current Population Survey (CPS), the nation's monthly household labor force survey. (See Chapter 1 of this *Handbook* for a description of the CPS.) ATUS sample households are selected to ensure that estimates will be representative of the nation.

An individual age 15 years or older is randomly chosen from each sample household. This "designated person" takes part in a one-time telephone interview about his or her activities on the previous day (the "diary day").

All ATUS interviews are conducted using Computer Assisted Telephone Interviewing. Procedures are in place to collect information from the small number of households that did not provide a telephone number during the CPS interview.

Concepts and Definitions

Average day. The average day measure reflects an average distribution across all persons in the reference population and all days of the week. Average day measures for the entire population provide a mechanism for seeing the overall distribution of time allocation for society as a whole. The ATUS collects data about daily activities from all segments of the population age 15 and over, including persons who are employed and not employed. Many activities are not typically done on a daily basis, and some activities are only done by a subset of the population.

Average hours per day. The average number of hours spent in a 24-hour day (between 4 a.m. on the diary day and 4 a.m. on the interview day) doing a specified activity.

Average hours per day, population. The average number of hours per day spent on a particular activity is computed using all responses from the sample population, including those from respondents who did not do the particular activity on their diary day. These estimates reflect the total number of respondents engaged in an activity and the total amount of time they spent on the activity.

Average hours per day, persons reporting the activity on the diary day. The average number of hours per day spent on a particular activity is computed using responses only from those engaged in the particular activity on the diary day.

Diary day. The diary day is the day about which the designated person reports. For example, the diary day of a designated person interviewed on Tuesday would be Monday.

Earnings

Usual weekly earnings. Data represent the earnings of full-time wage and salary workers before taxes and other deductions and include any overtime pay, commissions, or tips usually received (at the main job in the case of multiple jobholders). Usual weekly earnings are only updated in ATUS for about a third of employed respondents—if the respondent changed jobs or employment status or if the CPS weekly earnings value was imputed. This means that the earnings information could be out of date because the CPS interview was done 2 to 5 months prior to the ATUS interview. Respondents are asked to identify the easiest way for them to report earnings (hourly, weekly, biweekly, twice monthly, annually, or other) and how much they usually earn in the reported time period. Earnings reported on a basis other than weekly are converted to a weekly equivalent. The term "usual" is as perceived by the respondent. If the respondent asks for a definition of usual, interviewers are instructed to define the term as more than half the weeks worked during the past 4 or 5 months.

Weekly earnings ranges. The ranges used represent approximately 25 percent of full-time wage and salary workers. For example, 25 percent of full-time wage and salary workers with one job only had weekly earnings of $500 or less. These dollar values vary from year to year.

Employment Status

Employed. All persons who, at any time during the seven days prior to the interview: 1) did any work at all as paid employees, worked in their own business professions, or on their own farms, or usually worked 15 hours or more an unpaid workers in family-operated enterprises; and 2) all those who were not working but had jobs or businesses from which they were temporarily absent due to illness, bad weather, vacation, childcare problems, labor-management disputes, maternity or paternity leave, job training, or other family or personal reasons, whether or not they were paid for the time off or were seeking other jobs.

Employed full time. Full-time workers are those who usually work 35 hours or more per week at all jobs combined.

Employed part time. Part-time workers are those who usually work fewer than 35 hours per week at all jobs combined.

Not employed. Persons are not employed if they do not meet the conditions for employment. Not employed workers include those classified as unemployed as well as those classified as not in the labor force (using CPS definitions).

The numbers of employed and not employed persons in this report do not correspond to published totals from the CPS. While the information on employment from the ATUS is useful for assessing work in the context of other daily activities, the employment data are not intended for analysis of current employment trends. Compared to the CPS and other estimates of employment, the ATUS estimates are based on a much smaller sample and are only available with a substantial lag.

Household children. Household children are children under 18 years of age who reside in the household of the ATUS respondent. The children may be related to the respondent (such as their own children, grandchildren, nieces, nephews, brothers, or sisters) or not related (such as foster children or children of roommates). For secondary childcare calculations, respondents are asked about care of household children under 13 years of age.

Primary activity. A primary activity is the main activity of a respondent at a specified time.

Secondary activities. A secondary (or simultaneous) activity is an activity done at the same time as a primary activity. With the exception of the care of children under age 13, information on secondary activities is not systematically collected in the ATUS.

Major Activity Category Definitions

Personal care activities. Personal care activities include sleeping, bathing, dressing, health-related self-care, and personal or private activities. Receiving unpaid personal care from others (for example, "my sister put polish on my nails") is also captured in this category.

Eating and drinking. All time spent eating or drinking (except when identified by the respondent as part of a work or volunteer activity), whether alone, with others, at home, at a place of purchase, in transit, or somewhere else, is classified in this category.

Household activities. Household activities are those done by respondents to maintain their households. These include housework, cooking, yard care, pet care, vehicle maintenance and repair, and home maintenance, repair, decoration, and renovation. Food preparation is always classified as a household activity. Household management and organizational activities—such as filling out paperwork, balancing a checkbook, or planning a party—are also included in this category.

Purchasing goods and services. This category includes the purchase of consumer goods as well as the purchase or use of professional and personal care services, household services, and government services. Most purchases and rentals of consumer goods, regardless of mode or place of purchase or rental (in person, via telephone, over the Internet, at home, or in a store), are classified in this category. Time spent obtaining, receiving, and purchasing professional and personal care services provided by someone else is also classified in this category, which also includes time spent arranging for and purchasing household services provided by someone else.

Caring for and helping household members. Time spent doing activities to care for or help any child (under age 18) or adult in the household, regardless of relationship to the respondent or the physical or mental health status of the person being helped, is classified here. Caring for and helping activities for household children and adults are coded separately in subcategories.

Caring for and helping non-household members. Time spent caring for and helping any child or adult who is not part of the respondent's household, regardless of the relationship to the respondent or the physical or mental health status of the person being helped, is classified in this category.

Working and work-related activities. This category includes time spent working, doing activities as part of one's job, engaging in income-generating activities (not as part of one's job), and job search activities. "Working" includes hours spent doing the specific tasks required of one's main or other job, regardless of location or time of day. Travel time related to working and work-related activities includes time spent commuting to and from one's job, as well as time spent traveling for work-related activities, generating income, and job searching.

Educational activities. Educational activities include taking classes (including Internet and other distance-learning courses), doing research and homework, and taking care of administrative tasks, such as registering for classes or obtaining a school ID. For high school students, before- and after-school extracurricular activities (except sports) also are classified as educational activities.

Organizational, civic, and religious activities. This category captures time spent volunteering for or through an organization, performing civic obligations, and participating in religious and spiritual activities.

Leisure and sports. The leisure and sports category includes sports, exercise, and recreation; socializing and communicating; and other leisure activities, such as watching television, reading or attending entertainment events.

Telephone calls, mail, and e-mail. This category captures telephone communication and handling household or personal mail and e-mail. Telephone and Internet purchases are classified in purchasing goods and services.

Other activities, not elsewhere classified. This residual category includes security procedures related to traveling, traveling not associated with a specific activity category, ambiguous activities that could not be coded, or missing activities that were considered too private to report.

Sources of Additional Information

Additional information, including expanded definitions and estimation methodology, is available from BLS news release USDL 10-0855, "American Time Use Survey—2008 Results"; the June 2005 edition of the *Monthly Labor Review;* and the *ATUS User's Guide,* June 2008. All of these resources are available on the BLS Web site at <http://www.bls.gov/tus/>.

Table 12-1. Average Hours Per Day Spent in Primary Activities[1] for the Total Population and for Persons Reporting the Activity on the Diary Day, by Activity Category and Sex, 2008 and 2009 Annual Averages

(Hours, percent.)

Activity	Hours per day, total population			Percent of population reporting the activity on the diary day			Hours per day for persons reporting the activity on the diary day		
	Both sexes	Men	Women	Both sexes	Men	Women	Both sexes	Men	Women
2008									
All Activities[2]	24.00	24.00	24.00	X	X	X	X	X	X
Personal care activities	9.39	9.22	9.55	100.0	100.0	100.0	9.39	9.23	9.55
Sleeping	8.60	8.56	8.64	99.9	99.9	99.9	8.61	8.57	8.64
Eating and drinking	1.23	1.28	1.18	96.0	96.5	95.6	1.28	1.33	1.23
Household activities	1.73	1.30	2.13	73.7	64.2	82.6	2.34	2.02	2.58
Housework	0.58	0.24	0.90	35.5	19.7	50.3	1.64	1.23	1.79
Food preparation and cleanup	0.52	0.30	0.73	52.3	38.4	65.3	1.00	0.78	1.12
Lawn and garden care	0.19	0.26	0.12	9.4	11.0	7.9	2.00	2.35	1.56
Household management	0.13	0.10	0.15	18.1	14.5	21.5	0.70	0.68	0.71
Purchasing goods and services	0.77	0.60	0.92	44.8	39.2	50.0	1.71	1.53	1.85
Consumer goods purchases	0.38	0.28	0.48	40.7	35.6	45.4	0.94	0.79	1.05
Professional and personal care services	0.08	0.06	0.11	8.9	6.7	11.0	0.92	0.84	0.97
Caring for and helping household members	0.53	0.36	0.70	26.1	20.7	31.2	2.04	1.72	2.24
Caring for and helping household children	0.42	0.27	0.55	22.4	17.2	27.2	1.86	1.59	2.01
Caring for and helping non-household members	0.23	0.18	0.27	13.3	11.0	15.6	1.69	1.66	1.72
Caring for and helping non-household adults	0.07	0.08	0.07	8.5	7.8	9.1	0.87	0.98	0.78
Working and work-related activities	3.73	4.52	2.99	46.7	53.5	40.3	7.99	8.44	7.42
Working	3.38	4.06	2.73	44.7	51.1	38.7	7.56	7.95	7.06
Educational activities	0.47	0.42	0.52	7.9	6.9	9.0	5.94	6.15	5.79
Attending class	0.27	0.27	0.27	5.2	5.0	5.3	5.22	5.37	5.09
Homework and research	0.16	0.12	0.20	5.8	4.6	7.0	2.72	2.49	2.87
Organizational, civic, and religious activities	0.33	0.30	0.37	14.6	12.4	16.7	2.29	2.42	2.20
Religious and spiritual activities	0.14	0.12	0.17	9.2	7.7	10.7	1.55	1.54	1.55
Volunteering (organizational and civic activities)	0.15	0.14	0.16	7.0	6.0	7.9	2.15	2.38	1.99
Leisure and sports	5.18	5.52	4.86	96.2	96.4	96.0	5.39	5.73	5.06
Socializing and communicating	0.71	0.66	0.76	38.9	36.1	41.6	1.83	1.83	1.82
Watching television	2.77	3.01	2.55	80.9	82.3	79.6	3.43	3.66	3.20
Participating in sports, exercise, and recreation	0.30	0.40	0.20	17.9	21.0	15.0	1.64	1.91	1.30
Telephone calls, mail, and e-mail	0.21	0.14	0.28	26.3	20.3	31.9	0.80	0.67	0.89
Other activities n.e.c.	0.20	0.17	0.24	14.6	12.6	16.5	1.39	1.32	1.44
2009									
All Activities[2]	24.00	24.00	24.00	X	X	X	X	X	X
Personal care activities	9.45	9.25	9.63	100.0	100.0	100.0	9.45	9.26	9.63
Sleeping	8.67	8.62	8.73	99.9	99.8	100.0	8.68	8.63	8.73
Eating and drinking	1.22	1.26	1.19	96.4	96.1	96.8	1.27	1.31	1.23
Household activities	1.80	1.33	2.24	76.1	66.6	85.0	2.36	2.00	2.63
Housework	0.60	0.26	0.92	36.3	20.2	51.3	1.65	1.27	1.79
Food preparation and cleanup	0.54	0.29	0.77	54.6	39.9	68.3	0.99	0.73	1.13
Lawn and garden care	0.20	0.28	0.12	9.4	11.5	7.4	2.11	2.42	1.67
Household management	0.13	0.11	0.16	19.1	16.4	21.6	0.70	0.67	0.72
Purchasing goods and services	0.76	0.64	0.88	44.4	39.2	49.2	1.71	1.62	1.78
Consumer goods purchases	0.38	0.30	0.46	40.2	35.8	44.4	0.94	0.83	1.03
Professional and personal care services	0.09	0.06	0.11	8.6	6.4	10.7	0.99	0.98	1.00
Caring for and helping household members	0.54	0.37	0.70	25.2	20.2	29.9	2.13	1.81	2.34
Caring for and helping household children	0.43	0.28	0.57	21.6	16.4	26.5	1.98	1.71	2.14
Caring for and helping non-household members	0.21	0.19	0.22	13.4	11.4	15.2	1.55	1.69	1.46
Caring for and helping non-household adults	0.07	0.08	0.06	8.7	7.8	9.6	0.82	1.02	0.67
Working and work-related activities	3.53	4.26	2.85	45.4	51.9	39.2	7.78	8.20	7.26
Working	3.18	3.81	2.58	42.7	48.4	37.3	7.44	7.86	6.93
Educational activities	0.46	0.43	0.50	8.2	7.4	8.9	5.68	5.84	5.56
Attending class	0.26	0.26	0.27	5.2	5.1	5.3	5.03	5.01	5.05
Homework and research	0.16	0.14	0.18	5.6	4.9	6.3	2.82	2.84	2.81
Organizational, civic, and religious activities	0.34	0.32	0.36	14.5	12.6	16.4	2.32	2.53	2.17
Religious and spiritual activities	0.15	0.12	0.17	9.0	7.0	10.8	1.62	1.78	1.53
Volunteering (organizational and civic activities)	0.15	0.15	0.15	7.2	7.1	7.2	2.11	2.17	2.07
Leisure and sports	5.25	5.59	4.93	96.1	95.9	96.2	5.46	5.83	5.13
Socializing and communicating	0.70	0.63	0.76	39.2	34.6	43.4	1.78	1.81	1.76
Watching television	2.82	3.10	2.56	81.8	82.7	81.0	3.45	3.75	3.17
Participating in sports, exercise, and recreation	0.31	0.41	0.21	18.2	20.9	15.7	1.69	1.96	1.36
Telephone calls, mail, and e-mail	0.20	0.14	0.25	25.7	19.6	31.4	0.77	0.71	0.80
Other activities n.e.c.	0.24	0.23	0.26	15.7	13.6	17.8	1.55	1.69	1.44

Note: Data refer to respondents age 15 years and over, unless otherwise specified.

n.e.c. = Not elsewhere classified.

[1]A primary activity is designated by a respondent as his or her main activity. Other activities done simultaneously are not included.
[2]All major activity categories include related travel time.
X = Not applicable.

Table 12-2. Average Hours Per Day Spent in Primary Activities[1] for the Total Population, by Age, Sex, Race, Hispanic Origin, and Educational Attainment, 2009 Annual Averages

(Hours.)

Characteristic	Hours per day spent in primary activities[2]											
	Personal care activities	Eating and drinking	Household activities	Purchasing goods and services	Caring for and helping household members	Caring for and helping non-household members	Working and work-related activities	Edu-cational activities	Organiza-tional, civic, and religious activities	Leisure activities	Telephone calls, mail, and e-mail	Other activities n.e.c.
Both Sexes, 15 Years and Over	9.45	1.22	1.80	0.76	0.54	0.21	3.53	0.46	0.34	5.25	0.20	0.24
15 to 19 years	10.29	1.06	0.70	0.54	0.19	0.26	1.04	3.27	0.31	5.75	0.32	0.27
20 to 24 years	10.25	1.04	1.13	0.68	0.41	0.17	3.83	1.01	0.15	4.94	0.15	0.24
25 to 34 years	9.20	1.18	1.46	0.70	1.16	0.16	4.70	0.30	0.21	4.57	0.13	0.23
35 to 44 years	9.12	1.18	1.84	0.78	1.12	0.18	4.67	0.12	0.33	4.27	0.15	0.23
45 to 54 years	9.09	1.20	2.01	0.81	0.39	0.22	4.65	0.06	0.37	4.83	0.18	0.19
55 to 64 years	9.25	1.29	2.16	0.88	0.12	0.28	3.72	0.03	0.38	5.44	0.21	0.23
65 to 74 years	9.55	1.45	2.58	0.86	0.07	0.30	1.26	0.03	0.55	6.77	0.25	0.34
75 years and over	10.01	1.49	2.42	0.72	0.06	0.11	0.30	0.01	0.48	7.76	0.32	0.33
Men, 15 Years and Over	9.25	1.26	1.33	0.64	0.37	0.19	4.26	0.43	0.32	5.59	0.14	0.23
15 to 19 years	10.38	1.00	0.55	0.38	0.18	0.26	1.10	3.06	0.37	6.24	0.27	0.21
20 to 24 years	10.07	1.04	0.83	0.58	0.18	0.19	4.50	0.84	0.15	5.21	0.11	0.29
25 to 34 years	9.01	1.17	1.04	0.61	0.65	0.16	5.55	0.25	0.19	5.06	0.11	0.21
35 to 44 years	8.91	1.24	1.27	0.65	0.77	0.19	5.60	0.11	0.31	4.65	0.12	0.19
45 to 54 years	8.85	1.26	1.52	0.66	0.34	0.18	5.44	0.03	0.35	5.07	0.09	0.21
55 to 64 years	9.02	1.36	1.67	0.74	0.09	0.20	4.49	0.02	0.33	5.74	0.12	0.21
65 to 74 years	9.30	1.54	2.07	0.72	0.07	0.28	1.57	0.03	0.52	7.35	0.20	0.35
75 years and over	9.82	1.61	1.84	0.71	0.08	0.11	0.48	0.00	0.48	8.34	0.24	0.29
Women, 15 Years and Over	9.63	1.19	2.24	0.88	0.70	0.22	2.85	0.50	0.36	4.93	0.25	0.26
15 to 19 years	10.21	1.12	0.86	0.71	0.19	0.26	0.98	3.49	0.25	5.25	0.37	0.33
20 to 24 years	10.43	1.03	1.43	0.79	0.64	0.14	3.15	1.17	0.16	4.67	0.19	0.19
25 to 34 years	9.40	1.19	1.88	0.78	1.68	0.16	3.85	0.35	0.24	4.08	0.16	0.24
35 to 44 years	9.33	1.12	2.39	0.91	1.46	0.17	3.75	0.14	0.36	3.91	0.18	0.28
45 to 54 years	9.32	1.15	2.47	0.96	0.43	0.25	3.90	0.10	0.39	4.60	0.26	0.17
55 to 64 years	9.46	1.23	2.62	1.01	0.15	0.35	2.99	0.04	0.42	5.17	0.29	0.25
65 to 74 years	9.76	1.38	3.01	0.97	0.08	0.31	0.99	0.02	0.57	6.28	0.29	0.33
75 years and over	10.14	1.41	2.79	0.73	0.05	0.12	0.19	0.01	0.48	7.38	0.37	0.35
White, 15 Years and Over	9.38	1.26	1.88	0.77	0.53	0.21	3.58	0.44	0.32	5.17	0.19	0.25
Men	9.17	1.29	1.39	0.64	0.37	0.20	4.39	0.42	0.30	5.46	0.13	0.24
Women	9.59	1.23	2.36	0.89	0.69	0.23	2.80	0.47	0.33	4.89	0.25	0.27
Black, 15 Years and Over	9.91	0.92	1.25	0.71	0.47	0.19	3.19	0.46	0.47	5.99	0.24	0.19
Men	9.87	0.91	1.03	0.61	0.30	0.19	3.28	0.38	0.44	6.58	0.20	0.20
Women	9.95	0.94	1.44	0.79	0.61	0.19	3.12	0.53	0.49	5.50	0.27	0.18
Hispanic,[3] 15 Years and Over	9.72	1.16	1.80	0.74	0.73	0.21	3.58	0.63	0.29	4.70	0.12	0.32
Men	9.58	1.15	1.20	0.64	0.48	0.21	4.33	0.61	0.24	5.16	0.09	0.30
Women	9.87	1.18	2.43	0.84	0.99	0.21	2.79	0.65	0.34	4.21	0.16	0.34
Marital Status and Sex												
Married, spouse present	9.15	1.32	2.15	0.80	0.76	0.20	3.89	0.09	0.39	4.83	0.16	0.25
Men	8.95	1.36	1.55	0.66	0.53	0.18	4.75	0.08	0.39	5.20	0.11	0.25
Women	9.36	1.27	2.75	0.95	0.99	0.22	3.03	0.11	0.39	4.46	0.21	0.26
Other marital statuses	9.78	1.12	1.39	0.71	0.28	0.22	3.12	0.89	0.28	5.73	0.24	0.24
Men	9.62	1.13	1.05	0.61	0.17	0.21	3.65	0.86	0.23	6.06	0.18	0.21
Women	9.92	1.11	1.69	0.80	0.38	0.22	2.66	0.91	0.32	5.43	0.29	0.26
Educational Attainment, 25 Years and Over												
Less than a high school diploma	9.82	1.05	2.10	0.66	0.55	0.17	2.38	0.04	0.37	6.53	0.11	0.22
High school graduate, no college[4]	9.35	1.21	2.09	0.74	0.46	0.25	3.37	0.04	0.33	5.79	0.16	0.21
Some college or associate degree	9.22	1.22	2.00	0.81	0.59	0.20	4.04	0.19	0.32	4.95	0.20	0.25
Bachelor's degree and higher[5]	9.04	1.42	1.82	0.88	0.73	0.18	4.46	0.15	0.41	4.41	0.24	0.27

Note: Data refer to persons age 15 years and over, unless otherwise specified

n.e.c. = Not elsewhere classified.

[1] A primary activity is designated by a respondent as his or her main activity. Other activities done simultaneously are not included.
[2] All major activity categories include related travel time.
[3] May be of any race.
[4] Includes persons with a high school diploma or equivalent.
[5] Includes persons with bachelor's, master's, professional, and doctoral degrees.

Table 12-3. Average Hours Worked Per Day by Employed Persons on Weekdays and Weekends, by Selected Characteristics, 2009 Annual Averages

(Number, percent.)

Characteristic	Total employed (thousands)	Worked on an average day			Worked on an average weekday			Worked on an average Saturday, Sunday, or holiday[1]		
		Number (thousands)	Percent	Hours per day[2]	Number[3] (thousands)	Percent	Hours per day[2]	Number[4] (thousands)	Percent	Hours per day[2]
Both Sexes[5]	148 720	101 379	68.2	7.48	122 636	82.5	7.92	51 652	34.7	5.03
Full-time worker	114 618	82 511	72.0	7.97	100 923	88.1	8.44	39 044	34.1	5.13
Part-time worker	34 102	18 868	55.3	5.34	21 636	63.4	5.50	12 587	36.9	4.72
Men[5]	78 264	55 676	71.1	7.90	67 121	85.8	8.34	28 417	36.3	5.46
Full-time worker	65 641	48 043	73.2	8.29	58 529	89.2	8.75	23 473	35.8	5.59
Part-time worker	12 623	7 633	60.5	5.47	8 657	68.6	5.63	4 971	39.4	4.77
Women[5]	70 456	45 703	64.9	6.97	55 485	78.8	7.42	23 267	33.0	4.52
Full-time worker	48 977	34 468	70.4	7.53	42 398	86.6	8.01	15 557	31.8	4.42
Part-time worker	21 479	11 235	52.3	5.25	12 936	60.2	5.40	7 659	35.7	4.69
Multiple Job Holding Status										
Single job holder	132 834	88 563	66.7	7.48	108 470	81.7	7.90	42 513	32.0	4.97
Multiple job holder	15 886	12 816	80.7	7.51	14 134	89.0	8.08	9 424	59.3	5.31
Educational Attainment, 25 Years and Over										
Less than a high school diploma	9 087	5 968	65.7	7.75	7 348	80.9	7.92	2 886	31.8	6.80
High school graduate, no college[6]	36 852	24 251	65.8	8.03	30 571	83.0	8.22	9 625	26.1	6.60
Some college or associate degree	33 136	23 045	69.5	7.76	28 092	84.8	8.19	11 139	33.6	5.22
Bachelor's degree or higher[7]	47 722	34 855	73.0	7.20	41 919	87.8	7.90	18 251	38.2	3.44

Note: Data refer to persons age 15 years and over, unless otherwise specified.

[1]Holidays are New Year's Day, Easter, Memorial Day, the Fourth of July, Labor Day, Thanksgiving Day, and Christmas Day.
[2]Includes work at main and other job(s) and excludes travel related to work.
[3]Number was derived by multiplying the "total employed" by the percentage of employed persons who worked on an average weekday.
[4]Number was derived by multiplying the "total employed" by the percentage of employed persons who worked on an average Saturday, Sunday, or holiday.
[5]Includes workers whose hours vary.
[6]Includes persons with a high school diploma or equivalent.
[7]Includes persons with bachelor's, master's, professional, and doctoral degrees.

Table 12-4. Average Hours Worked Per Day at Main Job Only by Employed Persons on Weekdays and Weekend Days, by Selected Characteristics, 2009 Annual Averages

(Number, percent.)

Characteristic	Total employed (thousands)	Worked on an average day			Worked on an average weekday			Worked on an average Saturday, Sunday, or holiday[1]		
		Number (thousands)	Percent	Hours per day[2]	Number[3] (thousands)	Percent	Hours per day[2]	Number[4] (thousands)	Percent	Hours per day[2]
Class of Worker										
Wage and salary workers	137 890	92 192	66.9	7.48	113 051	82.0	7.89	43 575	31.6	4.98
Self-employed workers	10 753	7 198	66.9	6.46	8 081	75.1	7.02	5 035	46.8	4.24
Occupation										
Management, business, and financial operations	22 801	16 656	73.1	7.69	20 614	90.4	8.25	7 502	32.9	4.13
Professional and related	34 308	23 634	68.9	7.14	28 866	84.1	7.82	11 908	34.7	3.47
Services	25 460	15 240	59.9	6.94	17 832	70.0	7.10	9 249	36.3	6.20
Sales and related	15 716	11 245	71.6	7.18	12 144	77.3	7.68	8 863	56.4	5.38
Office and administrative support	19 196	12 117	63.1	7.18	15 514	80.8	7.44	3 971	20.7	4.75
Farming, fishing, and forestry	1 346	763	56.7	(5)	993	73.7	(5)	411	30.5	(5)
Construction and extraction	6 863	4 526	65.9	7.80	5 791	84.4	8.25	1 707	24.9	(5)
Installation, maintenance, and repair	5 454	3 552	65.1	8.26	4 669	85.6	8.59	1 214	22.2	(5)
Production	8 981	5 864	65.3	8.37	7 594	84.6	8.48	1 370	15.3	(5)
Transportation and material moving	8 595	5 827	67.8	7.90	7 146	83.1	8.11	2 623	30.5	(5)
Earnings of Full-Time Wage and Salary Earners[6]										
$0 to $480	23 168	14 934	64.5	7.83	18 708	80.7	8.08	6 694	28.9	6.33
$481 to $730	23 207	16 848	72.6	8.16	21 153	91.1	8.40	5 736	24.7	5.83
$731 to $1,150	22 954	15 562	67.8	7.96	19 625	85.5	8.36	6 323	27.5	5.17
$1,151 and higher	23 039	17 101	74.2	8.05	21 217	92.1	8.70	7 360	31.9	3.60

Note: Data refer to persons age 15 years and over, unless otherwise specified.

[1]Holidays are New Year's Day, Easter, Memorial Day, the Fourth of July, Labor Day, Thanksgiving Day, and Christmas Day.
[2]Includes work at main job only and excludes travel related to work.
[3]Number was derived by multiplying the "total employed" by the percentage of employed persons who worked on an average weekday.
[4]Number was derived by multiplying the "total employed" by the percentage of employed persons who worked on an average Saturday, Sunday, or holiday.
[5]Data not shown where base is less than 1.2 million.
[6]These values are based on usual weekly earnings. Each earnings range represents approximately 25 percent of full-time wage and salary workers.

Table 12-5. Average Hours Worked Per Day at All Jobs by Employed Persons at Workplaces or at Home, by Selected Characteristics, 2009 Annual Averages

(Number, percent.)

Characteristic	Total employed (thousands)	Employed persons who reported working on an average day[1]							
		Number (thousands)	Percent	Hours of work	Location of work[2]				
					Persons who reported working at their workplaces on an average day			Persons who reported working at home on an average day[3]		
					Number (thousands)	Percent	Hours of work at workplace	Number (thousands)	Percent	Hours of work at home
Full- and Part-Time Status and Sex										
Both sexes[4]	148 720	101 379	68.2	7.48	85 267	84.1	7.82	23 925	23.6	2.98
Full-time worker	114 618	82 511	72.0	7.97	70 365	85.3	8.24	19 353	23.5	3.13
Part-time worker	34 102	18 868	55.3	5.34	14 902	79.0	5.81	4 572	24.2	2.35
Men[4]	78 264	55 676	71.1	7.90	47 411	85.2	8.17	13 033	23.4	3.12
Full-time worker	65 641	48 043	73.2	8.29	41 289	85.9	8.51	11 081	23.1	3.24
Part-time worker	12 623	7 633	60.5	5.47	6 121	80.2	5.93	1 952	25.6	2.49
Women[4]	70 456	45 703	64.9	6.97	37 856	82.8	7.38	10 892	23.8	2.81
Full-time worker	48 977	34 468	70.4	7.53	29 076	84.4	7.87	8 272	24.0	2.99
Part-time worker	21 479	11 235	52.3	5.25	8 780	78.2	5.74	2 620	23.3	2.24
Multiple Job Holding Status										
Single job holder	132 834	88 563	66.7	7.48	74 876	84.5	7.81	19 828	22.4	3.13
Multiple job holder	15 886	12 816	80.7	7.51	10 391	81.1	7.88	4 097	32.0	2.24
Educational Attainment, 25 Years and Over										
Less than a high school diploma	9 087	5 968	65.7	7.75	5 538	92.8	7.92	609	10.2	(5)
High school graduate, no college[6]	36 852	24 251	65.8	8.03	21 559	88.9	8.14	3 154	13.0	4.97
Some college or associate degree	33 136	23 045	69.5	7.76	19 748	85.7	8.07	4 759	20.7	3.02
Bachelor's degree or higher[7]	47 722	34 855	73.0	7.20	26 371	75.7	7.82	14 049	40.3	2.64

Note: Data refer to persons age 15 years and over, unless otherwise specified.

[1]Includes work at main and other job(s) and excludes travel related to work.
[2]Respondents may have worked at more than one location.
[3]"Working at home" includes any time the respondent reported doing activities that were identified as "part of one's job"; this category is not restricted to persons whose usual workplace is their home.
[4]Includes workers whose hours vary.
[5]Data not shown where base is less than 1.2 million.
[6]Includes persons with a high school diploma or equivalent.
[7]Includes persons with bachelor's, master's, professional, and doctoral degrees.

Table 12-6. Average Hours Worked Per Day at Main Job Only by Employed Persons at Workplaces or at Home, by Selected Characteristics, 2009 Annual Averages

(Number, percent.)

Characteristic	Total employed (thousands)	Employed persons who reported working on an average day[1]								
		Number (thousands)	Percent	Hours of work	Location of work[2]					
					Persons who reported working at their workplaces on an average day			Persons who reported working at home on an average day[3]		
					Number (thousands)	Percent	Hours of work at workplace	Number (thousands)	Percent	Hours of work at home
Class of Worker										
Wage and salary worker	137 890	92 192	66.9	7.48	80 442	87.3	7.79	18 022	19.5	2.62
Self-employed worker	10 753	7 198	66.9	6.46	3 533	49.1	6.72	4 324	60.1	4.66
Occupation										
Management, business, and financial operations	22 801	16 656	73.1	7.69	12 925	77.6	8.23	5 918	35.5	3.14
Professional and related	34 308	23 634	68.9	7.14	18 214	77.1	7.63	9 054	38.3	2.80
Services	25 460	15 240	59.9	6.94	13 293	87.2	7.11	2 082	13.7	3.96
Sales and related	15 716	11 245	71.6	7.18	9 389	83.5	7.42	2 436	21.7	3.12
Office and administrative support	19 196	12 117	63.1	7.18	11 057	91.2	7.47	1 091	9.0	2.83
Farming, fishing, and forestry	1 346	763	56.7	([4])	600	78.7	([4])	153	20.0	([4])
Construction and extraction	6 863	4 526	65.9	7.80	4 078	90.1	8.35	518	11.4	([4])
Installation, maintenance, and repair	5 454	3 552	65.1	8.26	3 252	91.5	8.42	425	12.0	([4])
Production	8 981	5 864	65.3	8.37	5 611	95.7	8.49	302	5.2	([4])
Transportation and material moving	8 595	5 827	67.8	7.90	5 575	95.7	7.91	382	6.6	([4])
Earnings of Full-Time Wage and Salary Earners[5]										
$0 to $480	23 168	14 934	64.5	7.83	14 241	95.4	7.86	1 209	8.1	([4])
$481 to $730	23 207	16 848	72.6	8.16	15 605	92.6	8.36	1 658	9.8	2.54
$731 to $1,150	22 954	15 562	67.8	7.96	13 850	89.0	8.38	2 925	18.8	2.27
$1,151 and higher	23 039	17 101	74.2	8.05	13 654	79.8	8.51	6 095	35.6	3.00

Note: Data refer to persons age 15 years and over, unless otherwise specified.

[1]Includes work at main job only and excludes travel related to work.
[2]Respondents may have worked at more than one location.
[3]"Working at home" includes any time the respondent reported doing activities that were identified as "part of one's job"; this category is not restricted to persons whose usual workplace is their home.
[4]Data not shown where base is less than 1.2 million.
[5]These values are based on usual weekly earnings. Each earnings range covers approximately 25 percent of full-time wage and salary workers.

Table 12-7. Average Hours Per Day Spent by Persons Age 18 Years and Over Caring for Household Children Under 18 Years, by Sex of Respondent, Age of Youngest Household Child, and Day, 2005–2009 Combined Annual Averages

(Number.)

Activity	Hours per day caring for household children								
	Total			Weekdays			Weekends and holidays[1]		
	Both sexes	Men	Women	Both sexes	Men	Women	Both sexes	Men	Women
Persons in Households with Children Under 18 Years									
Caring for household children as a primary activity	1.33	0.86	1.73	1.42	0.84	1.91	1.13	0.90	1.31
Physical care	0.45	0.24	0.63	0.48	0.25	0.67	0.39	0.24	0.52
Education-related activities	0.10	0.06	0.13	0.13	0.07	0.17	0.03	0.02	0.04
Reading to/with children	0.04	0.02	0.05	0.04	0.02	0.05	0.03	0.02	0.04
Talking to/with children	0.05	0.03	0.07	0.06	0.03	0.08	0.04	0.02	0.05
Playing/doing hobbies with children	0.27	0.25	0.30	0.26	0.22	0.29	0.31	0.31	0.31
Looking after children	0.08	0.06	0.09	0.07	0.05	0.09	0.09	0.08	0.10
Attending children's events	0.06	0.05	0.07	0.05	0.04	0.06	0.08	0.07	0.08
Travel related to care of household children	0.17	0.11	0.23	0.21	0.12	0.28	0.09	0.08	0.10
Other childcare activities	0.11	0.05	0.17	0.14	0.06	0.20	0.06	0.05	0.08
Persons in Households with Youngest Child 6 to 17 Years									
Caring for household children as a primary activity	0.79	0.51	1.03	0.87	0.52	1.18	0.58	0.48	0.67
Physical care	0.15	0.08	0.21	0.17	0.09	0.25	0.09	0.06	0.13
Education-related activities	0.12	0.07	0.16	0.15	0.09	0.20	0.04	0.03	0.05
Reading to/with children	0.02	0.01	0.02	0.02	0.01	0.03	0.01	0.01	0.02
Talking to/with children	0.07	0.03	0.09	0.07	0.04	0.11	0.05	0.03	0.06
Playing/doing hobbies with children	0.06	0.08	0.05	0.06	0.07	0.04	0.08	0.08	0.08
Looking after children	0.04	0.03	0.06	0.04	0.02	0.05	0.06	0.05	0.06
Attending children's events	0.08	0.06	0.09	0.06	0.04	0.08	0.11	0.10	0.12
Travel related to care of household children	0.16	0.10	0.21	0.19	0.11	0.26	0.09	0.08	0.10
Other childcare activities	0.09	0.05	0.13	0.11	0.05	0.16	0.05	0.04	0.06
Persons in Households with Youngest Child Under 6 Years									
Caring for household children as a primary activity	1.98	1.30	2.54	2.08	1.25	2.75	1.76	1.42	2.03
Physical care	0.81	0.45	1.10	0.84	0.44	1.16	0.74	0.47	0.96
Education-related activities	0.08	0.05	0.10	0.10	0.06	0.13	0.02	0.01	0.03
Reading to/with children	0.06	0.04	0.08	0.07	0.04	0.08	0.05	0.04	0.07
Talking to/with children	0.03	0.02	0.05	0.04	0.02	0.05	0.02	0.01	0.03
Playing/doing hobbies with children	0.52	0.45	0.58	0.50	0.39	0.58	0.58	0.59	0.57
Looking after children	0.11	0.09	0.13	0.11	0.07	0.13	0.13	0.13	0.14
Attending children's events	0.04	0.03	0.05	0.04	0.02	0.05	0.05	0.05	0.04
Travel related to care of household children	0.19	0.11	0.25	0.23	0.13	0.31	0.09	0.07	0.10
Other childcare activities	0.14	0.06	0.20	0.17	0.07	0.25	0.08	0.05	0.10

Note: Universe includes respondents age 18 years and over living in households with children under 18 years of age, whether or not they provided childcare.

[1]Holidays are New Year's Day, Easter, Memorial Day, the Fourth of July, Labor Day, Thanksgiving Day, and Christmas Day. Data were not collected for Christmas Day in 2003, Thanksgiving Day from 2003 to 2005, and New Year's Day in 2007.

Table 12-8. Average Hours Per Day Spent in Primary Activities[1] by the Total Population Age 18 Years and Over, by Activity Category, Employment Status, Presence and Age of Household Children, and Sex, 2009 Annual Averages

(Number.)

Activity	Hours spent per day in primary activities								
	Household with children under 6 years			Household with children 6 to 17 years			Household with no children under 18 years		
	Both sexes	Men	Women	Both sexes	Men	Women	Both sexes	Men	Women
TOTAL									
All Activities[2]	24.00	24.00	24.00	24.00	24.00	24.00	24.00	24.00	24.00
Personal care activities	9.19	9.02	9.33	9.30	9.09	9.48	9.48	9.25	9.71
Sleeping	8.51	8.41	8.59	8.56	8.45	8.66	8.68	8.61	8.74
Eating and drinking	1.16	1.21	1.12	1.15	1.20	1.11	1.28	1.31	1.26
Household activities	1.80	1.18	2.28	1.83	1.23	2.39	1.91	1.49	2.33
Housework	0.65	0.28	0.94	0.69	0.26	1.09	0.60	0.26	0.92
Food preparation and cleanup	0.70	0.33	0.99	0.61	0.32	0.88	0.52	0.29	0.73
Lawn and garden care	0.12	0.17	0.09	0.16	0.23	0.09	0.24	0.34	0.16
Household management	0.12	0.11	0.14	0.10	0.08	0.12	0.16	0.13	0.18
Purchasing goods and services	0.73	0.62	0.81	0.73	0.57	0.88	0.80	0.69	0.92
Consumer goods purchases	0.36	0.31	0.41	0.38	0.28	0.47	0.39	0.31	0.47
Professional and personal care services	0.10	0.06	0.13	0.05	0.04	0.06	0.10	0.07	0.12
Caring for and helping household members	2.13	1.50	2.63	0.85	0.59	1.09	0.05	0.05	0.05
Caring for and helping household children	1.92	1.36	2.35	0.63	0.41	0.83	X	X	X
Caring for and helping non-household members	0.12	0.13	0.12	0.17	0.16	0.19	0.24	0.22	0.26
Caring for and helping non-household adults	0.06	0.07	0.06	0.07	0.08	0.07	0.08	0.09	0.06
Working and work-related activities	4.03	5.42	2.94	4.33	5.14	3.59	3.43	4.06	2.81
Working	3.64	4.90	2.66	3.92	4.61	3.27	3.08	3.63	2.54
Educational activities	0.17	0.14	0.20	0.38	0.35	0.40	0.24	0.21	0.27
Attending class	0.05	0.04	0.06	0.18	0.16	0.20	0.09	0.08	0.10
Homework and research	0.10	0.08	0.12	0.16	0.17	0.15	0.12	0.11	0.13
Organizational, civic, and religious activities	0.25	0.23	0.27	0.38	0.41	0.35	0.35	0.30	0.39
Religious and spiritual activities	0.12	0.11	0.14	0.16	0.16	0.16	0.15	0.11	0.18
Volunteering (organizational and civic activities)	0.09	0.09	0.10	0.17	0.20	0.14	0.16	0.15	0.17
Leisure and sports	4.02	4.23	3.86	4.48	4.89	4.10	5.77	6.06	5.48
Socializing and communicating	0.70	0.59	0.78	0.70	0.64	0.75	0.68	0.61	0.75
Watching television	2.26	2.47	2.09	2.36	2.65	2.09	3.18	3.48	2.88
Participating in sports, exercise, and recreation	0.21	0.28	0.15	0.30	0.42	0.19	0.29	0.38	0.21
Telephone calls, mail, and e-mail	0.13	0.09	0.16	0.15	0.11	0.19	0.22	0.15	0.28
Other activities n.e.c.	0.27	0.23	0.29	0.25	0.26	0.24	0.23	0.22	0.24
EMPLOYED									
All Activities[2]	24.00	24.00	24.00	24.00	24.00	24.00	24.00	24.00	24.00
Personal care activities	8.95	8.80	9.11	9.09	8.89	9.30	9.19	8.94	9.48
Sleeping	8.27	8.20	8.35	8.34	8.22	8.46	8.38	8.30	8.48
Eating and drinking	1.17	1.22	1.11	1.17	1.22	1.11	1.25	1.28	1.22
Household activities	1.43	1.09	1.82	1.63	1.18	2.10	1.51	1.22	1.84
Housework	0.45	0.23	0.70	0.57	0.26	0.92	0.46	0.22	0.75
Food preparation and cleanup	0.55	0.30	0.82	0.54	0.31	0.79	0.38	0.24	0.54
Lawn and garden care	0.13	0.16	0.08	0.16	0.22	0.09	0.18	0.26	0.10
Household management	0.11	0.11	0.11	0.10	0.08	0.12	0.13	0.10	0.16
Purchasing goods and services	0.69	0.64	0.75	0.70	0.56	0.84	0.73	0.63	0.84
Consumer goods purchases	0.33	0.30	0.36	0.36	0.27	0.45	0.36	0.29	0.44
Professional and personal care services	0.09	0.07	0.11	0.05	0.04	0.06	0.07	0.05	0.09
Caring for and helping household members	1.86	1.44	2.33	0.75	0.56	0.96	0.03	0.04	0.03
Caring for and helping household children	1.66	1.31	2.07	0.56	0.41	0.71	X	X	X
Caring for and helping non-household members	0.11	0.12	0.11	0.16	0.14	0.17	0.22	0.20	0.24
Caring for and helping non-household adults	0.06	0.06	0.05	0.07	0.07	0.07	0.07	0.07	0.06
Working and work-related activities	5.58	6.23	4.84	5.66	6.26	5.02	5.67	6.25	5.02
Working	5.11	5.66	4.48	5.17	5.66	4.64	5.19	5.70	4.61
Educational activities	0.11	0.08	0.14	0.24	0.21	0.27	0.26	0.19	0.33
Attending class	0.03	0.02	0.03	0.10	0.07	0.13	0.10	0.07	0.13
Homework and research	0.07	0.05	0.09	0.12	0.13	0.11	0.13	0.10	0.15
Organizational, civic, and religious activities	0.23	0.24	0.23	0.33	0.36	0.29	0.27	0.26	0.28
Religious and spiritual activities	0.11	0.11	0.11	0.13	0.12	0.15	0.11	0.09	0.13
Volunteering (organizational and civic activities)	0.09	0.10	0.08	0.15	0.19	0.11	0.12	0.13	0.11
Leisure and sports	3.54	3.84	3.19	3.97	4.31	3.60	4.54	4.73	4.32
Socializing and communicating	0.59	0.56	0.62	0.58	0.52	0.65	0.62	0.56	0.69
Watching television	1.96	2.17	1.72	2.08	2.34	1.80	2.38	2.56	2.18
Participating in sports, exercise, and recreation	0.19	0.25	0.12	0.30	0.40	0.20	0.29	0.35	0.21
Telephone calls, mail, and e-mail	0.10	0.08	0.12	0.12	0.10	0.14	0.16	0.11	0.22
Other activities n.e.c.	0.23	0.22	0.24	0.20	0.20	0.20	0.17	0.16	0.17

n.e.c. = Not elsewhere classified.

[1]A primary activity is designated by a respondent as his or her main activity. Other activities done simultaneously are not included.
[2]All major activity categories include related travel time.
X = Not applicable.

Table 12-8. Average Hours Per Day Spent in Primary Activities[1] by the Total Population Age 18 Years and Over, by Activity Category, Employment Status, Presence and Age of Household Children, and Sex, 2009 Annual Averages—*Continued*

(Number.)

Activity	Hours spent per day in primary activities								
	Household with children under 6 years			Household with children 6 to 17 years			Household with no children under 18 years		
	Both sexes	Men	Women	Both sexes	Men	Women	Both sexes	Men	Women
NOT EMPLOYED									
All Activities[2]	24.00	24.00	24.00	24.00	24.00	24.00	24.00	24.00	24.00
Personal care activities	9.81	10.43	9.65	9.93	9.96	9.91	9.90	9.79	9.99
Sleeping	9.11	9.74	8.94	9.24	9.43	9.13	9.10	9.16	9.05
Eating and drinking	1.13	1.17	1.13	1.11	1.09	1.11	1.33	1.37	1.30
Household activities	2.69	1.71	2.94	2.46	1.42	3.07	2.49	1.95	2.93
Housework	1.15	0.61	1.29	1.06	0.30	1.51	0.79	0.34	1.14
Food preparation and cleanup	1.07	0.49	1.22	0.83	0.40	1.09	0.71	0.38	0.97
Lawn and garden care	0.12	0.21	0.09	0.16	0.28	0.09	0.33	0.47	0.22
Household management	0.16	0.07	0.18	0.11	0.11	0.12	0.19	0.18	0.21
Purchasing goods and services	0.82	0.55	0.90	0.83	0.62	0.96	0.91	0.78	1.02
Consumer goods purchases	0.44	0.34	0.47	0.45	0.34	0.52	0.43	0.33	0.51
Professional and personal care services	0.13	0.01	0.16	0.07	0.05	0.08	0.14	0.12	0.16
Caring for and helping household members	2.82	1.88	3.06	1.14	0.71	1.39	0.07	0.07	0.07
Caring for and helping household children	2.54	1.71	2.76	0.86	0.44	1.10	X	X	X
Caring for and helping non-household members	0.14	0.18	0.13	0.23	0.23	0.23	0.26	0.24	0.28
Caring for and helping non-household adults	0.08	0.12	0.07	0.08	0.10	0.08	0.09	0.11	0.07
Working and work-related activities	0.20	0.22	0.19	0.26	0.33	0.22	0.20	0.31	0.10
Working	0.03	0.01	0.03	0.07	0.09	0.06	0.04	0.07	0.02
Educational activities	0.33	0.52	0.28	0.80	0.95	0.71	0.21	0.23	0.20
Attending class	0.11	0.21	0.09	0.41	0.52	0.35	0.08	0.10	0.06
Homework and research	0.19	0.26	0.17	0.30	0.38	0.25	0.11	0.12	0.10
Organizational, civic, and religious activities	0.29	0.16	0.32	0.54	0.64	0.47	0.46	0.38	0.53
Religious and spiritual activities	0.15	0.08	0.17	0.25	0.34	0.20	0.20	0.15	0.24
Volunteering (organizational and civic activities)	0.10	0.07	0.11	0.24	0.25	0.23	0.21	0.18	0.24
Leisure and sports	5.22	6.75	4.82	6.04	7.36	5.27	7.54	8.34	6.90
Socializing and communicating	0.98	0.80	1.02	1.05	1.18	0.98	0.77	0.70	0.83
Watching television	2.99	4.34	2.63	3.22	3.97	2.78	4.32	5.06	3.74
Participating in sports, exercise, and recreation	0.25	0.51	0.18	0.30	0.49	0.19	0.30	0.42	0.21
Telephone calls, mail, and e-mail	0.19	0.11	0.20	0.26	0.16	0.32	0.30	0.22	0.37
Other activities n.e.c.	0.36	0.31	0.37	0.41	0.51	0.34	0.33	0.33	0.32

n.e.c. = Not elsewhere classified.

[1]A primary activity is designated by a respondent as his or her main activity. Other activities done simultaneously are not included.
[2]All major activity categories include related travel time.
X = Not applicable.

Table 12-9. Average Hours Per Day Spent in Leisure and Sports Activities for the Total Population, by Selected Characteristics, 2009 Annual Averages

(Number.)

Characteristic	Total, all leisure and sports activities			Participating in sports, exercise, and recreation		Socializing and communicating		Watching TV	
	Total, all days	Weekdays	Weekends and holidays[1]	Weekdays	Weekends and holidays[1]	Weekdays	Weekends and holidays[1]	Weekdays	Weekends and holidays[1]
Sex									
Men	5.59	4.95	7.09	0.39	0.45	0.47	0.98	2.80	3.81
Women	4.93	4.48	5.99	0.20	0.24	0.57	1.22	2.43	2.87
Age									
Total, 15 years and over	5.25	4.71	6.53	0.29	0.34	0.52	1.10	2.61	3.32
15 to 19 years	5.75	5.36	6.67	0.68	0.64	0.73	1.26	2.19	2.62
20 to 24 years	4.94	4.32	6.43	0.32	0.48	0.57	1.29	2.28	2.86
25 to 34 years	4.57	3.83	6.37	0.25	0.40	0.50	1.27	2.06	3.16
35 to 44 years	4.27	3.64	5.77	0.24	0.30	0.46	1.03	2.13	2.91
45 to 54 years	4.83	4.21	6.21	0.24	0.35	0.50	1.10	2.43	3.24
55 to 64 years	5.44	4.91	6.71	0.23	0.23	0.45	0.99	3.03	3.69
65 to 74 years	6.77	6.53	7.35	0.35	0.21	0.59	1.01	3.58	4.17
75 years and over	7.76	7.62	8.08	0.24	0.17	0.56	0.81	4.38	4.52
Race and Hispanic Origin									
White	5.17	4.61	6.52	0.29	0.36	0.52	1.13	2.51	3.23
Black[2]	5.99	5.61	6.92	0.29	0.18	0.62	1.04	3.48	4.13
Hispanic[2]	4.70	4.14	6.03	0.24	0.28	0.53	1.38	2.52	3.18
Employment Status									
Employed	4.24	3.50	5.98	0.25	0.37	0.41	1.08	1.92	2.93
Full-time workers	4.08	3.26	6.00	0.22	0.37	0.37	1.08	1.85	2.98
Part-time workers	4.80	4.31	5.91	0.34	0.37	0.54	1.08	2.18	2.77
Not employed	6.89	6.67	7.43	0.37	0.29	0.71	1.14	3.73	3.97
Earnings of Full-Time Wage and Salary Earners[3]									
$0 to $480	4.47	3.75	6.04	0.16	0.32	0.35	1.14	2.28	3.31
$481 to $730	4.22	3.38	6.39	0.18	0.26	0.38	1.06	1.94	3.44
$731 to $1,150	4.21	3.34	6.19	0.25	0.34	0.42	1.12	1.97	2.99
$1,151 and higher	3.93	3.02	6.09	0.27	0.47	0.35	0.99	1.54	2.76
Presence and Age of Children									
No household children under 18 years	5.78	5.26	7.01	0.31	0.32	0.54	1.04	2.91	3.69
Household children under 18 years	4.40	3.82	5.77	0.27	0.37	0.50	1.20	2.13	2.74
Children 13 to 17 years, none younger ...	4.92	4.26	6.31	0.35	0.41	0.57	1.26	2.23	2.89
Children 6 to 12 years, none younger	4.41	3.84	5.77	0.34	0.43	0.47	1.11	2.10	2.67
Youngest child under 6 years	4.11	3.56	5.44	0.18	0.30	0.50	1.24	2.10	2.71
Marital Status and Sex									
Married, spouse present	4.83	4.24	6.20	0.26	0.30	0.47	1.08	2.41	3.18
Men	5.20	4.49	6.81	0.33	0.39	0.41	0.95	2.68	3.77
Women	4.46	4.00	5.56	0.20	0.21	0.54	1.21	2.14	2.58
Other marital status	5.73	5.23	6.91	0.33	0.39	0.58	1.13	2.84	3.48
Men	6.06	5.50	7.45	0.47	0.54	0.55	1.03	2.94	3.85
Women	5.43	5.00	6.45	0.21	0.27	0.61	1.23	2.75	3.16
Educational Attainment, 25 Years and Over									
Less than a high school diploma	6.53	6.20	7.23	0.21	0.16	0.58	1.19	4.16	4.40
High school graduate, no college[4]	5.79	5.32	6.91	0.24	0.24	0.49	1.10	3.25	3.94
Some college or associate degree	4.95	4.33	6.38	0.23	0.30	0.51	0.99	2.37	3.32
Bachelor's degree or higher[5]	4.41	3.76	5.95	0.30	0.41	0.47	1.05	1.85	2.67

Note: Data refer to respondents age 15 years and over, unless otherwise specified.

[1]Holidays are New Year's Day, Easter, Memorial Day, the Fourth of July, Labor Day, Thanksgiving Day, and Christmas Day.
[2]May be of any race.
[3]These values are based on usual weekly earnings. Each earnings range covers approximately 25 percent of full-time wage and salary workers.
[4]Includes persons with a high school diploma or equivalent.
[5]Includes persons with bachelor's, master's, professional, and doctoral degrees.

Table 12-9. Average Hours Per Day Spent in Leisure and Sports Activities for the Total Population, by Selected Characteristics, 2009 Annual Averages—*Continued*

(Number.)

Characteristic	Reading		Relaxing/thinking		Playing games and computer use for leisure		Other leisure and sports activities, including travel[6]	
	Weekdays	Weekends and holidays[1]	Weekdays	Weekends and holidays[1]	Weekdays	Weekends and holidays[1]	Weekdays	Weekends and holidays[1]
Sex								
Men	0.26	0.28	0.24	0.28	0.41	0.58	0.39	0.71
Women	0.41	0.45	0.24	0.27	0.32	0.33	0.31	0.62
Age								
Total, 15 years and over	0.33	0.37	0.24	0.28	0.36	0.45	0.35	0.66
15 to 19 years	0.17	0.09	0.13	0.11	0.84	1.02	0.63	0.91
20 to 24 years	0.19	0.15	0.19	0.22	0.40	0.52	0.38	0.92
25 to 34 years	0.17	0.15	0.18	0.17	0.35	0.51	0.32	0.70
35 to 44 years	0.16	0.24	0.14	0.22	0.23	0.45	0.28	0.62
45 to 54 years	0.26	0.35	0.21	0.26	0.25	0.28	0.32	0.63
55 to 64 years	0.43	0.57	0.24	0.35	0.29	0.31	0.24	0.58
65 to 74 years	0.71	0.68	0.44	0.45	0.41	0.31	0.45	0.54
75 years and over	1.03	1.03	0.64	0.63	0.42	0.44	0.35	0.48
Race and Hispanic Origin								
White	0.37	0.41	0.22	0.26	0.34	0.45	0.35	0.68
Black	0.14	0.14	0.38	0.43	0.39	0.39	0.31	0.62
Hispanic[2]	0.13	0.10	0.22	0.24	0.19	0.25	0.32	0.61
Employment Status								
Employed	0.22	0.30	0.19	0.22	0.22	0.40	0.30	0.68
Full-time workers	0.20	0.28	0.18	0.21	0.18	0.40	0.26	0.67
Part-time workers	0.28	0.34	0.20	0.24	0.35	0.41	0.42	0.70
Not employed	0.52	0.49	0.33	0.37	0.59	0.53	0.43	0.64
Earnings of Full-Time Wage and Salary Earners[3]								
$0 to $480	0.14	0.18	0.28	0.22	0.19	0.39	0.34	0.48
$481 to $730	0.22	0.22	0.21	0.23	0.21	0.45	0.24	0.72
$731 to $1,150	0.20	0.28	0.12	0.26	0.18	0.41	0.20	0.79
$1,151 and higher	0.25	0.46	0.16	0.14	0.15	0.52	0.30	0.75
Presence and Age of Children								
No household children under 18 years	0.42	0.48	0.29	0.33	0.42	0.49	0.38	0.66
Household children under 18 years	0.19	0.19	0.16	0.20	0.26	0.39	0.29	0.67
Children 13 to 17 years, none younger	0.26	0.30	0.18	0.24	0.31	0.48	0.37	0.74
Children 6 to 12 years, none younger	0.19	0.20	0.14	0.19	0.30	0.45	0.31	0.72
Youngest child under 6 years	0.15	0.13	0.18	0.19	0.21	0.29	0.24	0.58
Marital Status and Sex								
Married, spouse present	0.35	0.41	0.23	0.27	0.25	0.37	0.28	0.59
Men	0.30	0.34	0.25	0.31	0.25	0.41	0.28	0.65
Women	0.39	0.48	0.20	0.23	0.25	0.32	0.27	0.53
Other marital status	0.32	0.32	0.25	0.28	0.49	0.55	0.42	0.74
Men	0.21	0.22	0.23	0.24	0.60	0.80	0.51	0.77
Women	0.42	0.41	0.28	0.32	0.39	0.34	0.35	0.72
Educational Attainment, 25 Years and Over								
Less than a high school diploma	0.23	0.21	0.54	0.66	0.23	0.21	0.25	0.41
High school graduate, no college[4]	0.39	0.32	0.31	0.37	0.32	0.34	0.31	0.60
Some college or associate degree	0.34	0.47	0.22	0.20	0.35	0.49	0.31	0.61
Bachelor's degree or higher[5]	0.41	0.56	0.12	0.17	0.28	0.41	0.34	0.69

Note: Data refer to respondents age 15 years and over, unless otherwise specified.

[1]Holidays are New Year's Day, Easter, Memorial Day, the Fourth of July, Labor Day, Thanksgiving Day, and Christmas Day.
[2]May be of any race.
[3]These values are based on usual weekly earnings. Each earnings range covers approximately 25 percent of full-time wage and salary workers.
[4]Includes persons with a high school diploma or equivalent.
[5]Includes persons with bachelor's, master's, professional, and doctoral degrees.
[6]Includes other leisure and sports activities, not elsewhere classified, and travel related to leisure and sports activities.

Chapter Thirteen

INCOME IN THE UNITED STATES
(CENSUS BUREAU)

INCOME IN THE UNITED STATES (CENSUS BUREAU)

This chapter presents data on income and earnings in the United States collected by the Census Bureau. Income, as distinguished from earnings, includes income from pensions, investments, and other sources and is measured as real income in 2009 dollars.

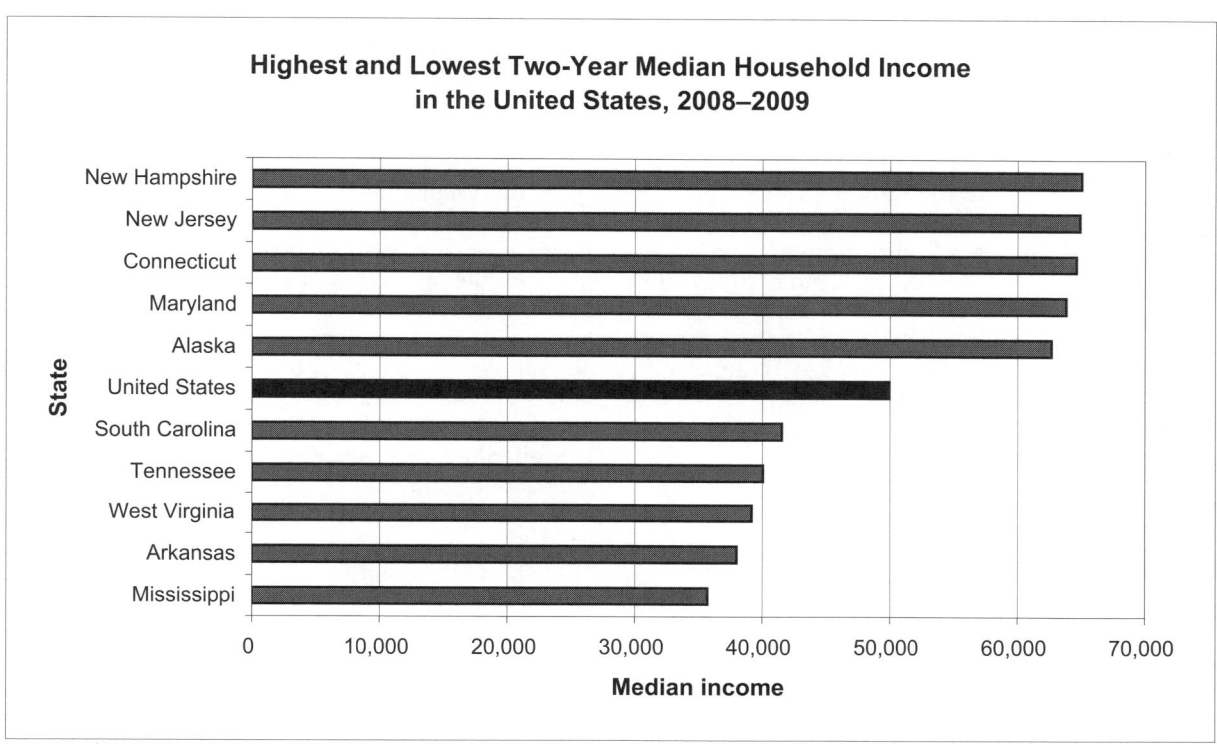

The two-year average median household income in the United States for 2008–2009 was $49,945, a 3.2 percent decline from the two-year median income of $51,622 in 2006–2007. New Hampshire again had the highest two-year median income at $65,028, followed by Connecticut ($64,644) and Maryland ($63,828). (See Table 13-5.)

OTHER HIGHLIGHTS

- Real median household income fell between 2008 and 2009 in every region except the South which experienced a slight increase of 0.4 percent. The Midwest experienced the greatest decline in real median income (-2.1) followed by the Northeast (-2.0) and the West (-1.9). (See Table 13-1.)

- In 2009, real median income declined 4.4 percent for Blacks, and 1.6 percent for non-Hispanic Whites while it increased 0.7 percent for Hispanics and 0.1 for Asians. (See Table 13-1.)

- Asians continued to have the highest median income in 2009 at $65,469—more than double the median income of Blacks. (See Table 13-1.)

- Median family income ranged from $45,601 in Mississippi to $84,254 in Maryland in 2009. The median for the United States was $61,082 (See Table 13-6.)

NOTES AND DEFINITIONS

Collection and Coverage

The data in tables 13-1 through 13-5 are from the Annual Social and Economic Supplement (ASEC) to the 2010 Current Population Survey (CPS). The CPS ASEC provides timely estimates of household income and individual earnings, as well as the distribution of that income. The population represented (the population universe) is the civilian noninstitutionalized population living in the United States. Members of the Armed Forces living off post or with their families on post are included if at least one civilian adult lives in the household. Most of the data from the CPS ASEC were collected in March (with some data collected in February and April), and the data were controlled to independent population estimates for March 2010. The estimates in these tables are based on responses from a sample of the population and may differ from actual values because of sampling variability or other factors. As a result, apparent differences between the estimates for two or more groups may not be statistically significant. All comparative statements have undergone statistical testing and are significant at the 90 percent confidence level unless otherwise noted.

For tables 13-6 and 13-7, the data are from the American Community Survey (ACS). The ACS is an annual survey that covers the same type of information that had been collected every 10 years from the decennial census long form questionnaire. The ACS eliminated the need for a separate long form in the 2010 Census. The CPS ASEC and ACS surveys differ in the length and detail of its questionnaire, the number of households interviewed, the methodology used to collect and process the data, and, consequently, in the income and poverty estimates produced.

The sample size of the ACS is much larger (approximately 3 million) compared to the sample size of the CPS ASEC (100,000). Although it is smaller, the CPS ASEC is a high quality source of information due to its detailed questionnaire and experienced interviewing staff. Another notable difference between the two surveys is that the ACS is a mandatory whereas the CPS ASEC is voluntary. More information on the differences between the two surveys is available on the Census Bureau Web site at <http://www.census.gov/hhes/www/income/definitions.html>.

Concepts and Definitions

The *Gini index of income inequality* (also known as the Gini ratio, Gini coefficient, or index of income concentration) is a statistical measure that summarizes the dispersion of income across an entire income distribution. Values range from 0 to 1. A Gini value of 1 indicates "perfect" inequality; that is, one household has all the income and the rest have none. A value of zero indicates "perfect" equality, a situation in which all households have equal income.

Equivalence-adjusted income inequality is another way to measure income inequality. Equivalence adjusted income takes into consideration the number of people living in the household and how these people share resources and take advantage of economies of scale. For example, the household-income-based distribution treats income of $30,000 for a single-person household and a family household similarly, while the equivalence-adjusted income of $30,000 for a single-person household would be more than twice the equivalence-adjusted income of $30,000 for a family household with two adults and two children. The equivalence adjustment used here is based on a three-parameter scale that reflects:

1. On average, children consume less than adults.
2. As family size increases, expenses do not increase at the same rate
3. The increase in expenses is larger for a first child of a single-parent family than the first child of a two-adult family.

Additional Information

Additional information is available in the Census publication "Income, Poverty, and Health Insurance Coverage in the United States: 2009," on the Census Bureau Web site at <http://www.census.gov/hhes/www/income/income.html>.

Table 13-1. Income and Earnings Summary Measures, by Selected Characteristics, 2008 and 2009

(Numbers in thousands, dollars, percent; income in 2009 dollars.)

Characteristic	2008			2009			Percent change in real median income (2008–2009)	
		Median income (dollars)			Median income (dollars)			
	Number	Estimate	90 percent confidence interval[1] (+/-)	Number	Estimate	90 percent confidence interval[1] (+/-)	Estimate	90 percent confidence interval[1] (+/-)
Households								
All households	117 181	50 112	225	117 538	49 777	350	-0.7	0.68
Type of Household								
Family households	78 850	62 383	421	78 833	61 265	311	-1.8	0.68
Married-couple	59 118	72 733	538	58 410	71 830	410	-1.2	0.75
Female householder, no husband present	14 480	32 947	618	14 843	32 597	541	-1.1	2.00
Male householder, no wife present	5 252	48 999	1 088	5 580	48 084	1 156	-1.9	2.59
Nonfamily households	38 331	29 964	305	38 705	30 444	281	1.6	1.13
Female householder	20 637	24 919	382	20 442	25 269	345	1.4	1.68
Male householder	17 694	35 869	434	18 263	36 611	456	2.1	1.43
Race[2] and Hispanic Origin of Householder								
White	95 297	52 113	249	95 489	51 861	253	-0.5	0.55
White, not Hispanic	82 884	55 319	369	83 158	54 461	459	-1.6	0.86
Black	14 595	34 088	723	14 730	32 584	648	-4.4	2.24
Asian	4 573	65 388	2 271	4 687	65 469	2 084	0.1	3.81
Hispanic[3]	13 425	37 769	796	13 298	38 039	826	0.7	2.04
Age of Householder								
Under 65 years	92 346	56 575	339	92 268	55 821	321	-1.3	0.66
15 to 24 years	6 357	32 148	615	6 233	30 733	693	-4.4	2.29
25 to 34 years	19 302	51 205	534	19 257	50 199	551	-2.0	1.20
35 to 44 years	22 171	62 715	941	21 519	61 083	536	-2.6	1.41
45 to 54 years	24 633	64 105	929	24 871	64 235	929	0.2	1.65
55 to 64 years	19 883	57 048	872	20 387	56 973	714	-0.1	1.60
65 years and over	24 834	29 631	369	25 270	31 354	372	5.8	1.47
Nativity of Householder								
Native	101 585	50 862	244	102 039	50 503	252	-0.7	0.55
Foreign-born	15 596	43 328	1 018	15 499	43 923	1 234	1.4	3.01
Naturalized citizen	7 668	51 328	946	7 834	51 975	859	1.3	2.02
Not a citizen	7 928	37 807	1 052	7 666	36 089	865	-4.5	2.84
Region								
Northeast	21 309	54 140	1 101	21 479	53 073	924	-2.0	2.12
Midwest	26 282	49 922	533	26 390	48 877	711	-2.1	1.44
South	43 423	45 417	444	43 611	45 615	464	0.4	1.14
West	26 166	54 876	864	26 058	53 833	895	-1.9	1.81
Metropolitan Status								
Inside metropolitan statistical areas	97 865	51 656	244	98 379	51 522	255	-0.3	0.55
Inside principal cities	39 065	44 029	562	38 850	44 852	569	1.9	1.48
Outside principal cities	58 800	57 684	577	59 529	56 582	428	-1.9	1.00
Outside metropolitan statistical areas[4]	19 315	40 630	660	19 159	40 135	642	-1.2	1.82
Earnings of Full-Time Year-Round Workers								
Men with earnings	59 861	46 191	238	56 053	47 127	242	2.0	0.62
Women with earnings	44 156	35 609	174	43 217	36 278	173	1.9	0.58
Per Capita Income[5]								
All races[2]	301 483	26 862	161	304 280	26 530	160	-1.2	0.70
White	240 852	28 394	185	242 403	28 034	183	-1.3	0.76
White, not Hispanic	197 159	31 194	216	197 436	30 941	214	-0.8	0.81
Black	38 076	18 336	326	38 624	18 135	327	-1.1	2.10
Asian	13 315	30 177	916	14 011	30 653	1 053	1.6	3.90
Hispanic[3]	47 485	15 615	292	48 901	15 063	276	-3.5	1.87

[1]A 90-percent confidence interval is a measure of an estimate's variability. The larger the confidence interval in relation to the size of the estimate, the less reliable the estimate.
[2]Federal surveys now give respondents the option of reporting more than one race. Therefore, there are two basic ways of defining a race group. A group such as Asian may be defined as those who reported Asian and no other race (the race-alone or single-race concept) or as those who reported Asian regardless of whether they also reported another race (the race-alone-or-in-combination concept). This table shows data using the race-alone concept. The use of the single-race population does not imply that it is the preferred method of presenting or analyzing data; the Census Bureau uses a variety of approaches. Information on people who reported more than one race, such as White and American Indian and Alaska Native or Asian and Black or African American, is available from Census 2000 through American FactFinder. About 2.6 percent of respondents reported more than one race in Census 2000.
[3]May be of any race.
[4]The "outside metropolitan statistical areas" category includes both micropolitan statistical areas and territory outside of metropolitan and micropolitan statistical areas.
[5]The data shown in this section are per capita incomes and their respective confidence intervals. Per capita income is the mean income computed for every man, woman, and child in a particular group. It is derived by dividing the total income of a particular group by the total population in that group (excluding patients or inmates in institutional quarters).

Table 13-2. Households, by Total Money Income, Race, and Hispanic Origin of Householder, 1967–2009

(Numbers in thousands, percent, dollars; income in 2009 CPI-U-RS adjusted dollars.)

Race and Hispanic origin of householder and year	Number	Percent distribution										Median income (dollars)		Mean income (dollars)	
		Total	Under $15,000	$15,000 to $24,999	$25,000 to $34,999	$35,000 to $49,999	$50,000 to $74,999	$75,000 to $99,999	$100,000 to $149,999	$150,000 to $199,000	$200,000 and over	Value	Standard error	Value	Standard error
All Races															
1967[1]	60 813	100.0	17.8	12.1	13.7	20.0	22.1	8.3	4.4	0.9	0.8	40 108	146	44 858	146
1968	62 214	100.0	16.2	12.2	12.6	20.4	22.8	9.6	4.7	0.9	0.6	41 836	151	47 331	151
1969	63 401	100.0	15.9	11.7	11.9	19.1	23.4	10.5	5.7	1.1	0.8	43 391	160	49 366	155
1970	64 778	100.0	16.3	11.8	12.0	19.2	22.7	10.4	5.6	1.2	0.8	43 055	158	49 301	158
1971[2]	66 676	100.0	16.5	12.3	12.1	18.7	22.5	10.3	5.7	1.1	0.8	42 636	165	49 035	156
1972[3]	68 251	100.0	15.6	12.1	11.6	17.5	22.8	11.1	6.8	1.5	1.0	44 462	170	51 748	160
1973	69 859	100.0	14.9	12.2	11.4	16.9	22.7	11.8	7.4	1.5	1.2	45 360	173	52 458	160
1974[4,5]	71 163	100.0	14.9	12.5	11.9	18.2	22.0	11.3	6.8	1.4	1.0	43 923	169	51 365	161
1975[5]	72 867	100.0	15.8	13.0	12.3	17.3	22.1	11.0	6.2	1.4	0.8	42 773	174	49 947	156
1976[6]	74 142	100.0	15.3	13.0	12.3	16.4	22.4	11.4	6.8	1.5	0.9	43 483	161	51 147	158
1977	76 030	100.0	15.2	13.1	11.9	16.8	21.7	11.8	7.0	1.6	1.0	43 758	164	51 909	158
1978	77 330	100.0	14.6	12.9	11.6	16.2	21.8	12.2	7.8	1.9	1.1	45 452	184	53 496	205
1979[7]	80 776	100.0	14.8	12.3	12.1	15.8	21.9	12.1	7.9	1.9	1.2	45 325	215	53 842	204
1980	82 368	100.0	15.5	12.7	12.1	16.4	21.4	11.5	7.8	1.6	1.0	43 892	226	52 202	191
1981	83 527	100.0	15.8	13.2	12.4	16.2	20.8	11.2	7.8	1.6	1.0	43 163	226	51 565	188
1982	83 918	100.0	16.2	12.7	12.3	16.7	20.5	10.9	7.7	1.9	1.2	43 048	194	51 879	192
1983[8]	85 407	100.0	15.9	13.1	12.2	16.3	20.2	11.1	7.9	2.0	1.2	42 747	194	51 990	194
1984	86 789	100.0	15.4	12.7	11.9	16.3	19.9	11.7	8.5	2.2	1.3	44 074	201	54 002	199
1985[9]	88 458	100.0	15.3	12.4	11.7	16.0	20.1	11.9	8.8	2.3	1.4	44 898	243	55 255	219
1986	89 479	100.0	15.1	11.7	11.5	15.3	20.4	12.2	9.5	2.6	1.7	46 488	241	57 434	233
1987[10]	91 124	100.0	14.8	11.7	11.2	15.3	20.1	12.3	10.0	2.7	1.9	47 071	222	58 539	240
1988	92 830	100.0	14.5	11.6	11.4	15.0	20.1	12.3	10.1	3.0	1.9	47 433	232	59 266	265
1989	93 347	100.0	13.7	11.6	11.3	15.0	20.1	12.4	10.6	3.1	2.2	48 279	266	60 996	266
1990	94 312	100.0	14.0	11.8	11.2	15.7	20.0	12.2	9.9	3.0	2.1	47 637	243	59 505	251
1991	95 669	100.0	14.5	12.3	11.3	15.9	19.3	12.0	9.9	2.9	1.9	46 269	223	58 242	240
1992[11]	96 426	100.0	15.0	12.5	11.1	15.5	19.3	12.1	9.7	2.7	2.1	45 888	217	58 177	244
1993[12]	97 107	100.0	15.1	12.6	11.0	15.8	18.5	11.7	10.0	3.0	2.3	45 665	213	60 556	327
1994[13]	98 990	100.0	14.6	12.6	11.5	14.8	19.0	11.6	10.3	3.2	2.6	46 175	210	61 731	332
1995[14]	99 627	100.0	13.7	12.2	11.4	15.0	19.2	12.1	10.6	3.1	2.6	47 622	275	62 802	344
1996	101 018	100.0	13.7	12.3	11.2	14.7	18.8	12.3	10.7	3.5	2.8	48 315	244	64 148	359
1997	102 528	100.0	13.2	11.8	11.3	14.4	18.8	12.2	11.4	3.7	3.1	49 309	228	66 214	370
1998	103 874	100.0	12.7	11.4	10.7	14.5	18.7	12.6	12.0	4.0	3.4	51 100	302	68 145	368
1999[15]	106 434	100.0	11.8	11.3	10.9	14.0	18.4	12.8	12.5	4.3	4.0	52 388	245	70 462	366
2000[16]	108 209	100.0	12.1	11.1	10.5	14.5	18.4	12.7	12.3	4.5	3.8	52 301	164	71 165	280
2001	109 297	100.0	12.4	11.4	10.5	14.8	17.9	12.6	12.2	4.3	3.9	51 161	156	70 521	281
2002	111 278	100.0	12.9	11.4	10.6	14.5	18.0	12.5	12.3	4.2	3.7	50 563	166	68 976	259
2003	112 000	100.0	13.2	11.6	10.9	14.0	17.7	12.2	12.3	4.4	3.7	50 519	219	68 886	252
2004[17]	113 343	100.0	13.3	11.6	11.0	14.1	18.1	12.0	11.9	4.4	3.6	50 343	223	68 662	259
2005	114 384	100.0	13.0	11.5	10.8	14.2	18.1	12.1	12.0	4.3	4.0	50 899	170	69 597	263
2006	116 011	100.0	12.6	11.2	11.1	14.1	18.2	11.6	12.5	4.7	4.0	51 278	220	70 819	273
2007	116 783	100.0	12.9	11.3	10.5	14.0	18.0	12.0	12.7	4.7	4.0	51 965	145	69 940	244
2008	117 181	100.0	13.4	12.0	11.0	14.1	17.6	11.9	11.9	4.3	3.7	50 112	136	68 164	241
2009	117 538	100.0	13.0	11.9	11.1	14.1	18.1	11.5	11.9	4.4	3.8	49 777	213	67 976	243
White[18]															
1967[1]	54 188	100.0	16.2	11.4	13.4	20.6	23.2	8.8	4.6	0.9	0.8	41 826	152	46 498	157
1968	55 394	100.0	14.8	11.4	12.3	20.9	23.8	10.1	5.0	1.0	0.7	43 560	162	49 033	162
1969	56 248	100.0	14.5	10.9	11.5	19.3	24.5	11.2	6.1	1.2	0.9	45 284	166	51 197	171
1970	57 575	100.0	14.9	11.2	11.6	19.5	23.7	11.0	6.0	1.3	0.9	44 844	173	51 026	168
1971[2]	59 463	100.0	15.0	11.7	11.8	19.0	23.4	10.9	6.2	1.2	0.9	44 596	170	50 811	165
1972[3]	60 618	100.0	14.1	11.4	11.2	17.8	23.7	11.8	7.3	1.6	1.1	46 645	179	53 761	174
1973	61 965	100.0	13.5	11.6	11.0	17.0	23.6	12.5	7.9	1.7	1.3	47 539	181	54 486	173
1974[4,5]	62 984	100.0	13.4	11.9	11.6	18.4	23.0	11.8	7.4	1.5	1.1	45 936	173	53 268	173
1975[5]	64 392	100.0	14.1	12.5	12.1	17.5	23.1	11.7	6.6	1.5	0.9	44 731	163	51 792	170
1976[6]	65 353	100.0	13.7	12.4	12.1	16.6	23.3	12.1	7.3	1.6	1.0	45 550	189	53 115	171
1977	66 934	100.0	13.6	12.3	11.7	16.9	22.6	12.5	7.5	1.7	1.1	46 015	193	53 937	174
1978	68 028	100.0	13.0	12.3	11.4	16.3	22.7	12.8	8.2	2.1	1.2	47 250	208	55 478	223
1979[7]	70 766	100.0	13.1	11.7	11.9	16.0	22.8	12.7	8.5	2.0	1.3	47 523	226	55 965	223

[1]Implementation of a new Curent Population Survey (CPS) Annual Social and Economic Supplements (ASEC) processing system.
[2]Introduction of 1970 census sample design and population controls.
[3]Full implementation of 1970 census–based sample design.
[4]Implementation of a new CPS ASEC processing system. Questionnaire expanded to ask 11 income questions.
[5]Some of these estimates were derived using Pareto interpolation and may differ from published data that were derived using linear interpolation.
[6]First-year medians were derived using both Pareto and linear interpolation. Before this year, all medians were derived using linear interpolation.
[7]Implementation of 1980 census population controls. Questionnaire expanded to show 27 possible values from a list of 51 possible sources of income.
[8]Implementation of Hispanic population weighting controls and introduction of 1980 census–based sample design.
[9]Recording of amounts for earnings from longest job increased to $299,999. Full implementation of 1980 census–based sample design.
[10]Implementation of a new CPS ASEC processing system.
[11]Implementation of 1990 census population controls.
[12]Data collection method changed from paper and pencil to computer-assisted interviewing. In addition, the 1994 ASEC was revised to allow for the coding of different income amounts on selected questionnaire items. Limits either increased or decreased in the following categories: earnings limits increased to $999,999, Social Security limits increased to $49,999, Supplemental Security Income and public assistance limits increased to $24,999, veterans' benefits limits increased to $99,999, and child support and alimony limits decreased to $49,999.
[13]Introduction of 1990 census sample design.
[14]Full implementation of 1990 census–based sample design and metropolitan definitions, 7,000 household sample reduction, and revised editing of responses on race.
[15]Implementation of the 2000 census–based population controls.
[16]Implementation of a 28,000 household sample expansion.
[17]Data revised to reflect a correction to the weights in the 2005 ASEC.
[18]For 2001 and earlier years, the CPS allowed respondents to report only one race group.

Table 13-2. Households, by Total Money Income, Race, and Hispanic Origin of Householder, 1967–2009
—Continued

(Numbers in thousands, percent, dollars; income in 2009 CPI-U-RS adjusted dollars.)

Race and Hispanic origin of householder and year	Number	Percent distribution											Median income (dollars)		Mean income (dollars)	
		Total	Under $15,000	$15,000 to $24,999	$25,000 to $34,999	$35,000 to $49,999	$50,000 to $74,999	$75,000 to $99,999	$100,000 to $149,999	$150,000 to $199,000	$200,000 and over	Value	Standard error	Value	Standard error
White[18]—Continued															
1980	71 872	100.0	13.6	12.1	12.0	16.6	22.3	12.1	8.4	1.8	1.1	46 306	238	54 308	208
1981	72 845	100.0	13.9	12.6	12.3	16.5	21.6	11.8	8.4	1.7	1.1	45 605	210	53 727	204
1982	73 182	100.0	14.4	12.1	12.2	16.9	21.3	11.6	8.2	2.0	1.3	45 067	205	54 017	211
1983[8]	74 376	100.0	13.8	12.6	12.1	16.7	21.1	11.7	8.5	2.1	1.4	44 829	203	54 148	211
1984	75 328	100.0	13.5	12.1	11.8	16.6	20.8	12.3	9.1	2.4	1.4	46 497	234	56 230	218
1985[9]	76 576	100.0	13.5	11.9	11.5	16.2	20.8	12.4	9.5	2.5	1.6	47 351	253	57 523	241
1986	77 284	100.0	13.2	11.2	11.3	15.4	21.1	12.8	10.1	2.9	1.9	48 874	237	59 826	256
1987[10]	78 519	100.0	12.7	11.2	11.1	15.4	21.0	13.1	10.7	2.9	2.0	49 594	249	61 040	264
1988	79 734	100.0	12.4	11.1	11.4	15.2	20.9	12.9	10.8	3.2	2.1	50 144	296	61 794	291
1989	80 163	100.0	11.8	11.2	11.1	15.2	20.8	13.0	11.2	3.3	2.4	50 784	247	63 536	294
1990	80 968	100.0	12.0	11.5	11.1	16.0	20.6	12.9	10.5	3.2	2.3	49 686	228	61 905	277
1991	81 675	100.0	12.4	12.0	11.2	16.0	19.9	12.6	10.6	3.2	2.0	48 485	235	60 701	264
1992[11]	81 795	100.0	12.9	12.1	11.0	15.8	19.9	12.8	10.4	2.9	2.3	48 245	234	60 804	271
1993[12]	82 387	100.0	13.0	12.2	10.8	15.9	19.4	12.4	10.6	3.3	2.5	48 178	281	63 270	365
1994[13]	83 737	100.0	12.7	12.1	11.4	15.0	19.5	12.1	11.0	3.4	2.8	48 700	273	64 451	375
1995[14]	84 511	100.0	11.9	11.8	11.3	15.2	19.7	12.7	11.2	3.4	2.8	49 984	261	65 305	379
1996	85 059	100.0	11.9	11.9	11.0	14.8	19.4	12.9	11.3	3.8	3.0	50 586	261	66 695	395
1997	86 106	100.0	11.6	11.5	11.0	14.4	19.2	12.7	12.1	4.0	3.5	51 930	329	69 159	421
1998	87 212	100.0	11.0	10.9	10.5	14.5	19.2	13.2	12.6	4.3	3.8	53 764	269	71 236	419
1999[15]	88 893	100.0	10.3	11.0	10.8	14.1	18.8	13.3	13.2	4.4	4.3	54 485	275	73 023	413
2000[16]	90 030	100.0	10.8	10.8	10.3	14.4	18.6	13.2	13.0	4.8	4.1	54 700	242	73 804	316
2001	90 682	100.0	11.0	11.1	10.1	14.8	18.2	13.1	12.8	4.6	4.2	53 934	253	73 313	315
White Alone[18]															
2002	91 645	100.0	11.4	11.0	10.4	14.3	18.4	13.1	13.0	4.4	4.0	53 755	218	71 735	292
2003	91 962	100.0	11.6	11.1	10.8	14.0	18.1	12.7	13.0	4.6	4.1	53 216	209	71 825	288
2004[17]	92 880	100.0	11.7	11.2	10.9	14.0	18.4	12.5	12.6	4.6	3.9	52 982	208	71 436	294
2005	93 588	100.0	11.3	11.1	10.7	14.3	18.4	12.7	12.6	4.6	4.3	53 347	233	72 473	300
2006	94 705	100.0	10.9	10.8	10.9	14.1	18.7	12.1	13.3	4.9	4.3	53 907	156	73 518	306
2007	95 112	100.0	11.2	11.1	10.3	14.0	18.3	12.5	13.3	5.0	4.3	53 912	159	72 756	277
2008	95 297	100.0	11.8	11.7	10.7	14.0	18.1	12.5	12.5	4.6	4.0	52 113	151	70 921	273
2009	95 489	100.0	11.4	11.6	10.8	14.2	18.7	12.0	12.6	4.7	4.1	51 861	154	70 544	272
White, Not Hispanic[19]															
1972[3]	58 005	100.0	13.9	11.1	11.0	17.6	24.0	12.0	7.6	1.7	1.1	47 310	225	54 384	243
1973	59 236	100.0	13.4	11.4	10.7	16.9	23.7	12.8	8.1	1.7	1.3	47 958	224	55 095	233
1974[4,5]	60 164	100.0	13.2	11.6	11.4	18.3	23.1	12.1	7.6	1.5	1.1	46 328	228	53 868	235
1975[5]	61 533	100.0	13.8	12.2	12.0	17.4	23.3	11.9	6.8	1.5	0.9	45 068	239	52 426	254
1976[6]	62 365	100.0	13.4	12.1	12.0	16.5	23.5	12.4	7.5	1.7	1.0	46 479	271	53 797	240
1977	63 721	100.0	13.4	12.1	11.5	16.8	22.8	12.8	7.7	1.8	1.2	46 928	264	54 604	258
1978	64 836	100.0	12.8	12.2	11.2	16.2	22.9	13.0	8.4	2.2	1.2	48 140	253	56 133	241
1979[7]	67 203	100.0	12.9	11.6	11.7	15.9	23.0	12.9	8.7	2.1	1.3	48 192	267	56 612	248
1980	68 106	100.0	13.3	11.9	11.8	16.6	22.6	12.4	8.6	1.8	1.1	47 126	108	55 022	248
1981	68 996	100.0	13.6	12.4	12.2	16.4	21.9	12.0	8.7	1.8	1.2	46 263	235	54 403	226
1982	69 214	100.0	13.9	11.8	12.1	16.9	21.6	11.8	8.5	2.1	1.3	45 822	230	54 811	235
1983[8]	69 648	100.0	13.2	12.4	12.0	16.6	21.4	12.0	8.7	2.2	1.4	45 981	...	55 570	...
1984	70 586	100.0	13.0	11.8	11.7	16.6	21.0	12.6	9.4	2.5	1.5	47 462	263	57 207	256
1985[9]	71 540	100.0	13.0	11.4	11.4	16.2	21.1	12.8	9.8	2.7	1.7	48 415	247	58 643	266
1986	72 067	100.0	12.7	10.8	11.2	15.4	21.4	13.2	10.4	3.0	2.0	49 985	258	61 013	280
1987[10]	73 120	100.0	12.1	10.8	10.9	15.3	21.3	13.4	11.1	3.0	2.1	50 958	284	62 234	289
1988	74 067	100.0	11.8	10.7	11.2	15.2	21.2	13.2	11.2	3.3	2.2	51 525	303	63 056	296
1989	74 495	100.0	11.2	11.0	10.9	15.1	21.0	13.3	11.7	3.5	2.5	51 876	254	64 809	317
1990	75 035	100.0	11.4	11.1	11.0	15.9	20.8	13.3	10.9	3.3	2.4	50 822	237	63 277	286
1991	75 625	100.0	11.8	11.6	11.1	16.0	20.1	13.0	11.0	3.3	2.2	49 643	244	62 003	276
1992[11]	75 107	100.0	12.1	11.7	10.7	15.7	20.1	13.3	10.8	3.1	2.4	49 864	309	62 348	288
1993[12]	75 697	100.0	12.2	11.8	10.6	15.7	19.8	12.7	11.1	3.5	2.7	49 951	292	64 938	387
1994[13]	77 004	100.0	11.9	11.7	11.2	14.9	19.8	12.5	11.4	3.6	3.0	50 271	266	66 093	392

[3]Full implementation of 1970 census–based sample design.
[4]Implementation of a new CPS ASEC processing system. Questionnaire expanded to ask 11 income questions.
[5]Some of these estimates were derived using Pareto interpolation and may differ from published data that were derived using linear interpolation.
[6]First-year medians were derived using both Pareto and linear interpolation. Before this year, all medians were derived using linear interpolation.
[7]Implementation of 1980 census population controls. Questionnaire expanded to show 27 possible values from a list of 51 possible sources of income.
[8]Implementation of Hispanic population weighting controls and introduction of 1980 census–based sample design.
[9]Recording of amounts for earnings from longest job increased to $299,999. Full implementation of 1980 census–based sample design.
[10]Implementation of a new CPS ASEC processing system.
[11]Implementation of 1990 census population controls.
[12]Data collection method changed from paper and pencil to computer-assisted interviewing. In addition, the 1994 ASEC was revised to allow for the coding of different income amounts on selected questionnaire items. Limits either increased or decreased in the following categories: earnings limits increased to $999,999, Social Security limits increased to $49,999, Supplemental Security Income and public assistance limits increased to $24,999, veterans' benefits limits increased to $99,999, and child support and alimony limits decreased to $49,999.
[13]Introduction of 1990 census sample design.
[14]Full implementation of 1990 census–based sample design and metropolitan definitions, 7,000 household sample reduction, and revised editing of responses on race.
[15]Implementation of the 2000 census–based population controls.
[16]Implementation of a 28,000 household sample expansion.
[17]Data revised to reflect a correction to the weights in the 2005 ASEC.
[18]For 2001 and earlier years, the CPS allowed respondents to report only one race group.
[19]Beginning with the 2003 CPS, respondents were allowed to choose one or more races. White alone refers to people who reported White and did not report any other race category. The use of this single-race population does not imply that it is the preferred method of presenting or analyzing the data; the Census Bureau uses a variety of approaches. Information on people who reported more than one race, such as White and American Indian and Alaska Native or Asian and Black or African American, is available from Census 2000 through American FactFinder. About 2.6 percent of respondents reported more than one race in Census 2000.
. . . = Not available.

Table 13-2. Households, by Total Money Income, Race, and Hispanic Origin of Householder, 1967–2009
—Continued

(Numbers in thousands, percent, dollars; income in 2009 CPI-U-RS adjusted dollars.)

Race and Hispanic origin of householder and year	Number	Percent distribution										Median income (dollars)		Mean income (dollars)	
		Total	Under $15,000	$15,000 to $24,999	$25,000 to $34,999	$35,000 to $49,999	$50,000 to $74,999	$75,000 to $99,999	$100,000 to $149,999	$150,000 to $199,000	$200,000 and over	Value	Standard error	Value	Standard error
White, Not Hispanic[19]—Continued															
1995[14]	76 932	100.0	10.9	11.3	10.9	15.1	20.2	13.1	11.8	3.6	3.0	51 957	271	67 434	404
2000[16]	77 240	100.0	11.1	11.3	10.7	14.7	19.7	13.4	11.9	4.0	3.2	52 800	362	68 712	...
1997	77 936	100.0	10.7	11.1	10.6	14.3	19.4	13.2	12.8	4.2	3.7	54 068	282	71 375	...
1998	78 577	100.0	10.2	10.4	10.2	14.2	19.4	13.7	13.3	4.5	4.0	55 771	321	73 517	449
1999[15]	79 819	100.0	9.8	10.5	10.4	13.7	18.9	13.7	13.8	4.7	4.6	56 843	359	75 417	447
2000[16]	80 527	100.0	10.4	10.2	10.0	14.1	18.6	13.6	13.6	5.1	4.4	56 826	228	76 050	341
2001	80 818	100.0	10.6	10.6	9.8	14.3	18.3	13.4	13.5	4.9	4.5	56 100	233	75 653	343
White Alone, Not Hispanic[19]															
2002	81 166	100.0	10.9	10.5	10.0	13.9	18.5	13.5	13.7	4.7	4.3	55 918	219	74 058	315
2003	81 148	100.0	11.1	10.5	10.3	13.7	18.2	13.1	13.7	5.0	4.4	55 719	269	74 507	316
2004[17]	81 628	100.0	11.1	10.7	10.4	13.6	18.5	13.0	13.3	5.0	4.3	55 539	254	74 103	322
2005	82 003	100.0	10.8	10.5	10.2	13.9	18.5	13.2	13.3	4.9	4.7	55 797	189	75 375	333
2006	82 675	100.0	10.4	10.2	10.5	13.7	18.7	12.5	14.0	5.3	4.7	55 769	200	76 324	337
2007	82 765	100.0	10.6	10.5	9.8	13.6	18.3	12.9	14.2	5.4	4.7	56 814	256	75 706	305
2008	82 884	100.0	10.9	11.2	10.2	13.6	18.4	13.0	13.3	4.9	4.4	55 319	224	73 821	302
2009	83 158	100.0	10.6	11.0	10.3	14.0	18.8	12.4	13.4	5.1	4.4	54 461	279	73 240	299
Black[18]															
1967[1]	5 728	100.0	32.5	19.1	16.9	14.5	11.8	3.1	1.5	0.3	0.2	24 285	404	29 181	326
1968	5 870	100.0	29.1	20.1	15.5	16.5	12.9	4.0	1.7	0.2	-	25 686	373	31 284	330
1969	6 053	100.0	27.9	18.9	15.7	17.4	13.6	4.4	1.8	0.1	0.1	27 372	403	32 586	347
1970	6 180	100.0	28.9	17.6	15.4	16.5	14.2	5.1	2.0	0.2	0.2	27 295	375	33 329	360
1971[2]	6 578	100.0	29.9	18.3	14.7	16.2	13.7	5.0	1.7	0.2	0.1	26 343	392	32 643	335
1972[3]	6 809	100.0	29.1	17.9	14.5	15.6	14.7	5.7	2.0	0.3	0.3	27 227	408	34 393	367
1973	7 040	100.0	27.5	17.9	15.0	15.5	15.7	5.1	2.6	0.5	0.2	27 983	436	34 749	345
1974[4,5]	7 263	100.0	28.2	18.1	14.6	16.6	14.1	6.2	1.9	0.3	0.1	27 318	330	33 975	302
1975[5]	7 489	100.0	30.1	17.3	13.6	16.0	15.2	5.2	2.2	0.3	-	26 853	395	33 519	297
1976[6]	7 776	100.0	28.6	18.4	13.9	15.1	15.5	5.7	2.4	0.3	0.1	27 085	336	34 605	308
1977	7 977	100.0	27.8	19.4	14.1	15.4	14.4	5.7	2.8	0.3	0.2	27 154	364	34 792	310
1978	8 066	100.0	28.6	17.1	12.9	15.6	14.7	7.2	3.4	0.5	0.1	28 395	600	36 288	474
1979[7]	8 586	100.0	28.9	17.5	13.8	14.2	15.2	6.9	3.1	0.3	0.1	27 901	509	35 801	441
1980	8 847	100.0	30.6	17.8	13.6	14.2	14.2	6.2	2.9	0.4	0.1	26 677	503	34 623	426
1981	8 961	100.0	31.6	18.0	13.2	14.2	13.8	5.9	3.1	0.2	0.1	25 591	430	33 618	407
1982	8 916	100.0	31.7	17.4	13.2	14.6	14.7	5.6	2.3	0.4	0.1	25 541	410	33 606	420
1983[8]	9 236	100.0	32.2	17.0	13.4	13.8	13.8	6.2	3.2	0.4	0.1	25 439	477	33 835	418
1984	9 480	100.0	30.7	17.5	13.2	14.5	13.2	6.5	3.7	0.6	0.1	26 488	509	35 326	435
1985[9]	9 797	100.0	29.7	16.5	13.3	14.3	14.7	6.8	3.7	0.7	0.2	28 171	547	36 756	477
1986	9 922	100.0	30.1	15.8	12.6	14.4	14.8	6.7	4.4	0.7	0.4	28 158	553	37 778	513
1987[10]	10 192	100.0	30.5	15.4	12.6	15.0	14.0	6.7	4.4	1.0	0.5	28 307	542	38 221	526
1988	10 561	100.0	30.1	15.7	12.4	13.7	14.0	7.5	4.9	1.3	0.4	28 585	596	39 161	571
1989	10 486	100.0	28.2	14.9	13.1	13.9	15.7	7.1	5.6	1.1	0.4	30 202	615	40 076	544
1990	10 671	100.0	29.1	15.1	12.2	14.4	15.4	7.3	5.0	0.9	0.5	29 712	678	39 477	533
1991	11 083	100.0	30.4	15.3	11.5	14.6	15.2	7.1	4.6	1.0	0.3	28 884	607	38 462	502
1992[11]	11 269	100.0	30.7	15.8	12.1	14.1	14.6	7.0	4.3	0.9	0.5	28 092	574	38 121	517
1993[12]	11 281	100.0	30.0	15.6	12.5	15.1	13.4	6.9	4.7	1.2	0.6	28 552	564	39 801	661
1994[13]	11 655	100.0	27.7	16.1	12.2	13.6	15.0	7.9	5.5	1.3	0.8	30 093	560	41 875	601
1995[14]	11 577	100.0	26.0	15.6	13.2	14.4	16.0	7.8	5.5	0.9	0.7	31 295	534	42 484	727
1996	12 109	100.0	25.8	15.8	12.4	14.5	15.4	8.4	5.7	1.2	0.8	31 966	629	44 187	863
1997	12 474	100.0	24.4	14.8	13.6	14.7	16.1	8.7	5.7	1.3	0.8	33 379	574	43 923	630
1998	12 579	100.0	24.4	15.3	12.7	14.4	15.5	8.4	6.7	1.8	0.9	33 315	522	44 864	599
1999[15]	12 838	100.0	22.0	14.5	12.7	14.1	16.3	9.0	7.6	2.7	1.1	35 928	669	49 512	711
2000[16]	13 174	100.0	21.0	14.4	12.9	15.4	17.2	8.8	7.2	1.9	1.2	36 952	490	48 798	494
2001	13 315	100.0	22.1	14.5	12.8	15.5	16.1	9.1	7.1	1.7	1.1	35 704	420	47 550	502

[1]Implementation of a new Curent Population Survey (CPS) Annual Social and Economic Supplements (ASEC) processing system.
[2]Introduction of 1970 census sample design and population controls.
[3]Full implementation of 1970 census–based sample design.
[4]Implementation of a new CPS ASEC processing system. Questionnaire expanded to ask 11 income questions.
[5]Some of these estimates were derived using Pareto interpolation and may differ from published data that were derived using linear interpolation.
[6]First-year medians were derived using both Pareto and linear interpolation. Before this year, all medians were derived using linear interpolation.
[7]Implementation of 1980 census population controls. Questionnaire expanded to show 27 possible values from a list of 51 possible sources of income.
[8]Implementation of Hispanic population weighting controls and introduction of 1980 census–based sample design.
[9]Recording of amounts for earnings from longest job increased to $299,999. Full implementation of 1980 census–based sample design.
[10]Implementation of a new CPS ASEC processing system.
[11]Implementation of 1990 census population controls.
[12]Data collection method changed from paper and pencil to computer-assisted interviewing. In addition, the 1994 ASEC was revised to allow for the coding of different income amounts on selected questionnaire items. Limits either increased or decreased in the following categories: earnings limits increased to $999,999, Social Security limits increased to $49,999, Supplemental Security Income and public assistance limits increased to $24,999, veterans' benefits limits increased to $99,999, and child support and alimony limits decreased to $49,999.
[13]Introduction of 1990 census sample design.
[14]Full implementation of 1990 census–based sample design and metropolitan definitions, 7,000 household sample reduction, and revised editing of responses on race.
[15]Implementation of the 2000 census–based population controls.
[16]Implementation of a 28,000 household sample expansion.
[17]Data revised to reflect a correction to the weights in the 2005 ASEC.
[18]For 2001 and earlier years, the CPS allowed respondents to report only one race group.
[19]Beginning with the 2003 CPS, respondents were allowed to choose one or more races. White alone refers to people who reported White and did not report any other race category. The use of this single-race population does not imply that it is the preferred method of presenting or analyzing the data; the Census Bureau uses a variety of approaches. Information on people who reported more than one race, such as White and American Indian and Alaska Native or Asian and Black or African American, is available from Census 2000 through American FactFinder. About 2.6 percent of respondents reported more than one race in Census 2000.
. . . = Not available.
- = Quantity zero.

Table 13-2. Households, by Total Money Income, Race, and Hispanic Origin of Householder, 1967–2009
—Continued

(Numbers in thousands, percent, dollars; income in 2009 CPI-U-RS adjusted dollars.)

Race and Hispanic origin of householder and year	Number	Percent distribution										Median income (dollars)		Mean income (dollars)	
		Total	Under $15,000	$15,000 to $24,999	$25,000 to $34,999	$35,000 to $49,999	$50,000 to $74,999	$75,000 to $99,999	$100,000 to $149,999	$150,000 to $199,000	$200,000 and over	Value	Standard error	Value	Standard error
Black Alone[20]															
2002	13 465	100.0	23.3	14.9	12.4	15.9	14.9	8.7	6.8	1.9	1.3	34 607	466	47 704	551
2003	13 629	100.0	23.6	14.8	13.0	14.5	15.7	8.5	7.0	1.8	1.1	34 573	450	46 802	501
2004[17]	13 809	100.0	24.3	14.6	12.8	15.1	15.7	8.2	6.4	1.7	1.2	34 174	355	46 141	500
2005	14 002	100.0	23.9	15.5	12.3	14.6	15.9	8.3	6.6	1.9	1.1	33 904	331	46 645	507
2006	14 354	100.0	23.4	14.6	13.3	14.3	16.0	8.1	7.0	1.9	1.4	34 010	256	48 007	594
2007	14 551	100.0	23.6	14.1	12.4	14.5	16.3	8.6	7.4	1.9	1.2	35 086	491	48 239	538
2008	14 595	100.0	23.6	15.0	13.7	15.0	14.9	8.1	6.6	2.0	1.0	34 088	439	46 356	496
2009	14 730	100.0	23.5	15.4	13.4	14.6	15.1	8.7	6.3	1.8	1.2	32 584	394	46 046	525
Black Alone or in Combination															
2002	13 778	100.0	23.1	14.9	12.4	15.9	14.9	8.7	6.8	1.9	1.3	34 787	458	48 089	560
2003	13 969	100.0	23.5	14.8	13.0	14.4	15.7	8.5	7.0	1.8	1.2	34 624	435	47 018	498
2004[17]	14 151	100.0	24.2	14.6	12.7	15.1	15.8	8.3	6.5	1.7	1.2	34 333	315	46 284	492
2005	14 399	100.0	23.8	15.5	12.3	14.5	15.9	8.3	6.7	2.0	1.1	34 009	324	46 945	511
2006	14 709	100.0	23.2	14.5	13.3	14.4	16.0	8.2	7.0	2.0	1.4	34 183	253	48 397	594
2007	14 976	100.0	23.6	14.0	12.3	14.6	16.2	8.6	7.4	2.0	1.3	35 267	481	48 446	530
2008	15 056	100.0	23.5	14.9	13.7	15.1	14.9	8.1	6.6	2.0	1.1	34 215	437	46 502	486
2009	15 212	100.0	23.4	15.4	13.4	14.5	15.2	8.7	6.3	1.8	1.2	32 750	418	46 280	516
Asian and Pacific Islander[18]															
1987[10]	. . .	100.0	12.1	12.3	8.7	11.3	18.9	12.9	15.8	5.0	2.8	58 206	2 164	. . .	. . .
1988	1 913	100.0	10.5	11.5	8.2	13.6	20.5	12.1	15.3	5.4	2.9	56 217	2 310	70 284	2 099
1989	1 988	100.0	10.4	8.2	9.0	13.1	19.8	15.8	14.5	4.7	4.5	60 298	1 630	74 959	2 181
1990	1 958	100.0	10.6	9.5	8.2	12.5	20.9	14.0	15.4	5.4	3.6	61 170	1 812	73 837	2 090
1991	2 094	100.0	11.6	8.7	10.5	14.7	18.2	13.9	13.9	5.0	3.6	55 980	1 806	71 075	2 095
1992[11]	2 262	100.0	12.0	10.2	8.9	12.9	21.4	11.9	14.7	4.6	3.4	56 621	1 634	70 175	1 929
1993[12]	2 233	100.0	14.6	9.4	9.8	13.4	15.2	14.5	15.1	4.6	3.4	56 052	2 757	73 443	2 957
1994[13]	2 040	100.0	11.9	10.2	8.3	13.4	19.3	13.2	13.9	5.2	4.5	57 937	2 195	75 225	2 681
1995[14]	2 777	100.0	12.5	9.8	7.7	13.9	19.6	13.7	13.6	4.7	4.4	56 759	1 424	77 182	3 114
1996	2 998	100.0	12.3	9.1	8.4	12.2	19.1	12.8	16.7	5.6	3.7	58 911	2 111	76 976	2 761
1997	3 125	100.0	11.4	8.5	8.5	12.5	19.1	13.7	16.2	6.0	4.0	60 294	1 676	78 470	2 432
1998	3 308	100.0	10.7	8.7	9.0	13.1	17.8	13.7	16.7	5.8	4.5	61 288	1 706	79 122	2 285
1999[15]	3 742	100.0	11.0	7.2	7.9	13.0	17.1	13.7	14.6	7.7	7.8	65 600	2 312	86 747	2 199
2000[16]	3 963	100.0	9.3	7.7	7.4	12.4	16.9	14.8	16.4	8.7	6.4	69 448	1 185	90 672	1 882
2001	4 071	100.0	10.3	8.0	8.6	12.8	17.5	12.7	16.3	7.5	6.3	64 981	1 551	88 635	2 092
Asian Alone[21]															
2002	3 917	100.0	10.2	8.8	8.1	13.2	18.1	12.7	16.0	6.7	6.1	62 745	1 098	83 516	1 629
2003	4 040	100.0	13.1	9.3	6.0	11.5	16.8	13.9	16.1	7.8	5.4	64 958	1 276	81 605	1 445
2004[17]	4 123	100.0	10.2	8.3	8.1	11.4	19.0	12.6	16.7	7.7	6.1	65 298	1 388	86 888	1 681
2005	4 273	100.0	11.2	7.9	7.2	10.5	18.6	13.0	16.9	6.9	7.8	67 125	782	88 002	1 552
2006	4 454	100.0	10.1	7.1	8.5	11.4	17.1	13.1	17.0	8.8	6.9	68 338	1 781	93 929	2 021
2007	4 494	100.0	10.3	8.1	7.5	11.4	17.0	13.1	17.9	7.9	6.8	68 382	1 433	87 950	1 552
2008	4 573	100.0	12.1	8.7	8.2	12.1	15.1	12.6	17.1	7.5	6.6	65 388	1 381	85 858	1 497
2009	4 687	100.0	11.7	7.9	8.2	11.1	16.9	11.8	16.9	7.8	7.7	65 469	1 267	90 811	1 845
Asian Alone or in Combination															
2002	4 079	100.0	10.4	8.7	8.1	13.3	18.3	12.8	16.0	6.5	5.9	62 338	943	82 835	1 575
2003	4 235	100.0	13.1	9.3	6.2	11.5	16.9	14.0	16.0	7.7	5.3	64 448	1 437	80 951	1 392
2004[17]	4 346	100.0	10.2	8.3	8.1	11.5	19.0	12.8	16.6	7.6	5.8	65 236	1 315	86 450	1 632
2005	4 500	100.0	11.1	7.8	7.2	10.7	18.4	13.1	17.0	6.9	7.7	67 074	801	87 893	1 534
2006	4 664	100.0	10.0	7.0	8.4	11.6	17.3	13.2	17.1	8.6	6.7	67 979	1 720	93 115	1 949
2007	4 715	100.0	10.3	8.0	7.4	11.6	17.1	13.1	17.7	8.0	6.8	68 148	1 434	87 477	1 496
2008	4 805	100.0	11.9	8.7	8.3	12.1	15.2	12.7	17.0	7.4	6.6	65 318	1 408	85 995	1 481
2009	4 940	100.0	11.7	8.0	8.2	11.4	16.6	11.9	16.7	7.8	7.7	65 073	1 435	90 110	1 770

[10]Implementation of a new CPS ASEC processing system.
[11]Implementation of 1990 census population controls.
[12]Data collection method changed from paper and pencil to computer-assisted interviewing. In addition, the 1994 ASEC was revised to allow for the coding of different income amounts on selected questionnaire items. Limits either increased or decreased in the following categories: earnings limits increased to $999,999, Social Security limits increased to $49,999, Supplemental Security Income and public assistance limits increased to $24,999, veterans' benefits limits increased to $99,999, and child support and alimony limits decreased to $49,999.
[13]Introduction of 1990 census sample design.
[14]Full implementation of 1990 census–based sample design and metropolitan definitions, 7,000 household sample reduction, and revised editing of responses on race.
[15]Implementation of the 2000 census–based population controls.
[16]Implementation of a 28,000 household sample expansion.
[17]Data revised to reflect a correction to the weights in the 2005 ASEC.
[18]For 2001 and earlier years, the CPS allowed respondents to report only one race group.
[20]Black alone refers to persons who reported Black and did not report any other race category.
[21]Asian alone refers to persons who reported Asian and did not report any other race category.
. . . = Not available.

Table 13-2. Households, by Total Money Income, Race, and Hispanic Origin of Householder, 1967–2009
—Continued

(Numbers in thousands, percent, dollars; income in 2009 CPI-U-RS adjusted dollars.)

Race and Hispanic origin of householder and year	Number	Percent distribution										Median income (dollars)		Mean income (dollars)	
		Total	Under $15,000	$15,000 to $24,999	$25,000 to $34,999	$35,000 to $49,999	$50,000 to $74,999	$75,000 to $99,999	$100,000 to $149,999	$150,000 to $199,000	$200,000 and over	Value	Standard error	Value	Standard error
Hispanic[22]															
1972	2 655	100.0	16.9	18.1	16.2	21.6	17.8	5.9	2.8	0.3	0.5	35 200	688	40 459	688
1973	2 722	100.0	15.9	17.1	17.4	18.8	20.6	6.7	3.1	0.4	0.2	35 142	798	40 829	665
1974	2 897	100.0	17.2	18.4	14.7	20.1	19.2	6.5	3.0	0.5	0.3	34 936	765	40 471	659
1975	2 948	100.0	20.4	18.2	15.6	18.8	18.3	5.6	2.3	0.5	0.3	32 134	710	38 148	678
1976	3 081	100.0	20.9	17.6	15.6	17.5	18.3	6.8	2.7	0.4	0.2	32 799	699	38 760	631
1977	3 304	100.0	18.5	16.8	16.0	19.3	18.5	6.6	3.5	0.5	0.3	34 328	603	40 512	625
1978	3 291	100.0	17.9	16.4	15.2	18.7	19.4	7.7	3.8	0.8	0.2	35 613	863	42 066	851
1979	3 684	100.0	17.8	15.5	15.6	18.1	19.0	8.1	4.5	0.8	0.5	35 911	1 035	43 450	873
1980	3 906	100.0	19.9	17.0	15.2	17.9	17.3	7.8	4.0	0.6	0.5	33 832	917	41 324	823
1981	3 980	100.0	19.5	17.0	14.5	18.0	17.6	8.3	4.1	0.7	0.3	34 623	948	41 577	794
1982	4 085	100.0	22.6	16.8	14.5	17.3	16.6	7.5	3.4	0.8	0.5	32 392	856	39 977	811
1983	4 326	100.0	23.1	16.3	14.6	17.8	16.2	6.9	4.1	0.7	0.2	32 556	825	39 644	761
1984	4 883	100.0	22.1	16.0	13.8	17.0	17.3	8.2	4.2	1.0	0.3	33 411	838	41 546	810
1985	5 213	100.0	21.6	17.6	13.3	16.7	16.8	7.7	5.1	0.8	0.3	33 201	776	41 486	675
1986	5 418	100.0	21.1	16.3	14.0	16.0	17.5	8.0	5.7	1.1	0.4	34 267	893	43 269	711
1987	5 642	100.0	21.4	15.6	13.5	16.6	17.1	8.6	5.2	1.1	1.0	34 925	759	44 768	829
1988	5 910	100.0	20.8	15.5	13.9	16.2	17.7	8.6	4.9	1.6	0.8	35 471	899	45 286	960
1989	5 933	100.0	19.3	14.5	14.4	16.2	17.9	9.5	5.9	1.5	0.9	36 612	710	46 752	803
1990	6 220	100.0	19.7	16.5	12.9	17.6	18.2	7.8	5.3	1.3	0.8	35 525	729	44 501	733
1991	6 379	100.0	20.2	16.6	13.5	16.9	17.2	8.1	5.3	1.6	0.6	34 850	725	44 343	710
1992	7 153	100.0	21.3	16.6	13.5	16.9	16.8	8.0	5.1	1.1	0.6	33 847	700	43 171	679
1993	7 362	100.0	21.6	16.7	13.5	17.9	14.9	8.1	5.3	1.0	1.0	33 453	672	44 277	931
1994	7 735	100.0	22.2	16.3	13.8	15.7	16.5	7.6	5.7	1.4	0.9	33 519	623	45 199	1 128
1995	7 939	100.0	22.3	17.1	15.1	15.8	14.9	8.0	4.9	1.2	0.8	31 947	696	43 604	978
1996	8 225	100.0	20.1	17.5	14.5	15.5	16.3	8.1	5.4	1.5	1.1	33 904	657	46 290	1 071
1997	8 590	100.0	20.1	15.3	14.4	15.9	17.4	7.9	6.0	1.6	1.3	35 481	633	47 814	965
1998	9 060	100.0	18.3	15.3	13.7	17.3	16.8	8.9	6.6	1.8	1.3	37 230	718	50 305	1 070
1999	9 579	100.0	15.1	15.3	14.2	16.8	17.9	10.1	7.4	2.0	1.4	39 579	575	51 994	923
2000	10 034	100.0	14.5	15.1	12.6	17.6	18.9	10.4	7.3	2.0	1.7	41 312	595	54 777	788
2001	10 499	100.0	14.9	15.0	12.9	17.9	17.4	10.6	7.6	2.2	1.4	40 665	516	53 772	680
2002	11 339	100.0	15.2	14.9	14.0	17.1	18.1	9.6	7.6	2.1	1.5	39 468	575	53 518	715
2003	11 693	100.0	15.6	15.5	14.9	16.5	17.1	9.5	7.3	2.1	1.6	38 482	535	51 860	574
2004	12 178	100.0	16.1	15.1	14.5	16.6	17.8	9.0	7.4	2.0	1.5	38 916	545	52 095	637
2005	12 519	100.0	15.6	15.2	14.0	17.2	17.8	9.3	7.2	2.2	1.6	39 517	392	51 791	521
2006	12 973	100.0	15.5	14.5	13.5	17.1	18.1	9.3	8.0	2.6	1.5	40 193	537	53 803	617
2007	13 339	100.0	15.6	14.7	13.8	16.5	18.3	10.0	7.5	2.2	1.5	40 013	538	52 581	553
2008	13 425	100.0	17.8	14.8	14.5	16.4	16.2	9.0	7.5	2.4	1.4	37 769	484	51 376	532
2009	13 298	100.0	16.5	15.2	14.3	15.4	17.6	9.1	7.8	2.2	1.7	38 039	502	52 229	573

[22]Because Hispanics may be of any race, data in this report for Hispanics overlap with data for racial groups. Hispanic origin was reported by 12.7 percent of White householders who reported only one race, 3.1 percent of Black householders who reported only one race, and 1.4 percent of Asian householders who reported only one race. Data users should exercise caution when interpreting aggregate results for the Hispanic population and for race groups, because these populations consist of many distinct groups that differ in socioeconomic characteristics, culture, and recentness of immigration. Data were first collected for Hispanics in 1972.

Table 13-3. Change in Real Median Household Income, Number of Workers, and Median Earnings During Recessions, 1969 to 2009

(Percent.)

Recessions[1]	Income years	Percent change in real median household income	Change in number of workers with earnings		Percentage change in median earnings of all workers	
			Male	Female	Male	Female
December 1969 to November 1970	1969 to 1971	-1.7	1 613	748	-2.2	6.3
November 1973 to March 1975	1973 to 1975	-5.7	-170	1 343	-6.4	1.6
January 1980 to July 1980 and July 1981 to November 1982	1978 to 1983	-6.0	2 235	4 710	-10.1	6.4
July 1990 to March 1991	1989 to 1991	-4.2	-5	458	-6.0	1.0
March 2001 to November 2001	1999 to 2002	-3.5	1 178	358	-2.6	7.6
December 2007, trough not yet defined	2007 to 2008	-4.2	-2 548	-1 323	-4.1	-2.8

[1]Recessions are determined by the National Bureau of Economic Research, a private research organization.

Table 13-4. Income Distribution Measures Using Money Income and Equivalence-Adjusted Income 2008 and 2009

(Percent distribution.)

Measure	2008				2009				Percent change (2008–2009)			
	Money income		Equivalence-adjusted income		Money income		Equivalence-adjusted income		Money income		Equivalence-adjusted income	
	Estimate	90 percent confidence interval[1] (+/-)	Estimate	90 percent confidence interval[1] (+/-)	Estimate	90 percent confidence interval[1] (+/-)	Estimate	90 percent confidence interval[1] (+/-)	Estimate	90 percent confidence interval[1] (+/-)	Estimate	90 percent confidence interval[1] (+/-)
Shares of Aggregate Income by Percentile												
Lowest quintile	3.4	0.04	3.6	0.03	3.4	0.04	3.4	0.03	0.0	1.27	0.0	0.96
Second quintile	8.6	0.09	9.4	0.07	8.6	0.09	9.2	0.07	0.0	1.24	0.0	0.87
Middle quintile	14.7	0.16	15.1	0.11	14.6	0.16	15.0	0.11	0.0	1.23	0.0	0.85
Fourth quintile	23.3	0.25	22.9	0.17	23.2	0.25	22.9	0.17	0.0	1.24	0.0	0.84
Highest quintile	50.0	0.54	49.0	0.36	50.3	0.55	49.4	0.36	0.6	1.25	0.8	0.83
Top 5 percent	21.5	0.49	21.4	0.31	21.7	0.49	21.7	0.33	0.9	2.61	1.4	1.76
Summary Measures												
Gini index of income inequality	0.466	0.005	0.451	0.003	0.468	0.005	0.458	0.003	0.40	1.11	1.60	0.72

[1]A 90-percent confidence interval is a measure of an estimate's variability. The larger the confidence interval in relation to the size of the estimate, the less reliable the estimate.

Table 13-5. Two-Year-Average[1] Median Household Income by State, 2006 to 2009

(Income in 2009 dollars, percent.)

| State | 2-year-average | | | | Change in median income (2008–2009 average less 2006–2007 average) | |
| | 2006–2007 | | 2008–2009 | | | |
	Median money income	90 percent confidence interval[2]	Median money income	90 percent confidence interval[2]	Dollars	Percent change
UNITED STATES	51 622	249	49 945	239	-1 677	-3.2
Alabama	42 021	1 731	42 144	1 763	123	0.3
Alaska	62 592	2 181	62 675	2 745	83	0.1
Arizona	49 239	1 987	46 238	1 597	-3 002	-6.1
Arkansas	40 812	1 518	37 987	1 424	-2 825	-6.9
California	58 253	933	56 466	981	-1 787	-3.1
Colorado	61 251	1 824	58 321	2 360	-2 930	-4.8
Connecticut	66 370	2 988	64 644	3 383	-1 726	-2.6
Delaware	56 128	2 759	51 312	2 146	-4 816	-8.6
District of Columbia	52 053	1 997	54 260	2 602	2 208	4.2
Florida	47 983	851	45 159	1 057	-2 824	-5.9
Georgia	51 406	1 625	44 696	1 633	-6 710	-13.1
Hawaii	65 280	2 627	58 469	2 378	-6 811	-10.4
Idaho	50 022	1 846	47 009	1 995	-3 013	-6.0
Illinois	53 047	1 508	52 961	1 538	-86	-0.2
Indiana	48 698	1 766	45 324	1 532	-3 374	-6.9
Iowa	50 896	2 087	50 337	1 911	-560	-1.1
Kansas	49 315	2 176	46 206	2 165	-3 109	-6.3
Kentucky	41 409	1 603	41 828	1 453	419	1.0
Louisiana	40 778	1 699	42 423	2 231	1 646	4.0
Maine	49 051	2 280	47 276	2 147	-1 775	-3.6
Maryland	67 813	2 312	63 828	2 322	-3 985	-5.9
Massachusetts	59 671	3 054	59 732	2 309	62	0.1
Michigan	51 413	1 256	47 797	1 456	-3 616	-7.0
Minnesota	59 930	2 217	55 404	1 799	-4 526	-7.6
Mississippi	37 757	1 832	35 693	1 457	-2 064	-5.5
Missouri	47 508	1 787	47 316	1 861	-192	-0.4
Montana	44 445	1 755	41 587	1 898	-2 858	-6.4
Nebraska	51 044	2 036	50 065	1 973	-979	-1.9
Nevada	55 771	1 805	52 985	2 633	-2 786	-5.0
New Hampshire	67 916	2 359	65 028	3 468	-2 888	-4.3
New Jersey	67 499	2 458	64 918	2 848	-2 582	-3.8
New Mexico	44 234	1 936	42 742	1 940	-1 492	-3.4
New York	50 966	1 354	50 243	865	-724	-1.4
North Carolina	43 676	1 340	42 337	967	-1 339	-3.1
North Dakota	46 250	1 907	49 759	1 991	3 509	7.6
Ohio	49 811	1 232	46 318	999	-3 494	-7.0
Oklahoma	43 012	2 166	45 907	1 400	2 896	6.7
Oregon	51 033	1 953	50 315	2 040	-718	-1.4
Pennsylvania	50 840	1 276	49 690	1 043	-1 150	-2.3
Rhode Island	56 623	2 603	52 337	2 630	-4 286	-7.6
South Carolina	43 942	2 056	41 548	1 507	-2 394	-5.4
South Dakota	48 173	1 849	48 615	1 547	443	0.9
Tennessee	42 953	1 333	40 034	1 486	-2 919	-6.8
Texas	46 856	1 087	46 895	956	39	0.1
Utah	56 745	2 067	60 396	2 101	3 651	6.4
Vermont	52 162	1 888	51 416	1 647	-746	-1.4
Virginia	60 983	2 103	61 126	1 784	143	0.2
Washington	59 150	2 119	58 404	2 204	-746	-1.3
West Virginia	42 207	1 569	39 170	1 579	-3 037	-7.2
Wisconsin	54 019	1 552	51 122	1 118	-2 897	-5.4
Wyoming	50 234	2 035	52 803	2 515	2 569	5.1

[1]The 2-year-average median is the sum of two inflation-adjusted single-year medians divided by 2.
[2]A 90-percent confidence interval is a measure of an estimate's variability. The larger the confidence interval in relation to the size of the estimate, the less reliable the estimate.

Table 13-6. Median Family Income in the Past Twelve Months, by the Number of Earners and State, 2009

(Income in 2009 inflation-adjusted dollars.)

State	Total	No earners	1 earner	2 earners	3 or more earners
UNITED STATES	61 082	29 575	42 149	78 296	95 943
Alabama	50 779	25 183	38 018	70 015	85 621
Alaska	79 934	40 215	51 112	89 785	118 346
Arizona	57 855	33 960	41 915	74 461	92 045
Arkansas	46 868	25 409	32 304	63 508	79 668
California	67 038	29 514	47 234	86 906	97 571
Colorado	68 943	35 712	47 814	83 137	98 864
Connecticut	83 069	34 392	56 929	100 833	117 818
Delaware	67 582	37 176	47 634	85 535	107 920
District of Columbia	71 208	14 161	48 034	116 274	126 012
Florida	53 509	34 124	39 383	69 898	85 308
Georgia	56 176	24 615	38 748	75 790	88 413
Hawaii	75 066	36 763	49 846	86 149	116 809
Idaho	51 851	33 460	38 420	62 729	78 704
Illinois	66 806	30 254	45 607	83 149	99 615
Indiana	56 432	29 770	39 487	71 299	90 391
Iowa	61 156	32 392	39 803	72 320	88 700
Kansas	60 994	32 576	40 982	72 680	92 214
Kentucky	49 801	22 637	36 999	68 960	89 397
Louisiana	53 427	22 528	37 493	74 933	94 866
Maine	56 566	28 814	38 860	69 347	88 243
Maryland	84 254	35 822	54 874	102 736	122 598
Massachusetts	81 033	29 034	54 161	98 513	119 700
Michigan	56 681	32 291	41 875	74 517	90 974
Minnesota	69 374	35 853	45 022	81 592	98 019
Mississippi	45 601	20 508	32 131	64 262	83 046
Missouri	56 318	29 400	38 697	71 181	91 311
Montana	55 010	30 889	37 954	68 000	88 037
Nebraska	60 102	31 735	38 287	70 309	88 339
Nevada	60 829	32 810	42 346	76 027	96 008
New Hampshire	73 856	35 553	50 630	86 462	106 235
New Jersey	83 381	32 767	58 107	102 955	119 698
New Mexico	51 994	29 276	36 672	69 503	84 915
New York	66 891	26 645	45 548	88 327	109 333
North Carolina	54 288	28 103	37 171	72 194	85 472
North Dakota	63 507	30 333	40 774	72 786	90 289
Ohio	57 360	28 903	40 091	74 488	91 812
Oklahoma	52 403	27 438	36 289	68 361	86 278
Oregon	59 174	34 253	43 986	72 113	87 238
Pennsylvania	62 185	29 619	44 172	78 250	98 043
Rhode Island	69 350	26 317	45 391	86 886	102 328
South Carolina	52 406	27 585	36 457	69 729	87 343
South Dakota	57 764	31 847	35 008	66 399	80 345
Tennessee	51 344	24 235	37 528	68 357	85 101
Texas	56 607	25 106	37 676	74 750	86 196
Utah	62 935	35 831	49 818	67 893	95 781
Vermont	63 483	32 551	42 347	76 056	92 223
Virginia	71 270	33 647	49 484	88 825	108 017
Washington	68 360	37 725	49 124	84 439	100 832
West Virginia	47 659	25 316	39 109	67 419	87 527
Wisconsin	62 638	33 713	40 486	75 608	92 303
Wyoming	65 532	40 896	45 427	76 314	94 714

Table 13-7. Median Family Income in the Past Twelve Months, by Size of Family and State, 2009

(Income in 2009 inflation-adjusted dollars.)

State	Total	2-person families	3-person families	4-person families	5-person families	6-person families	7-or-more-person families
UNITED STATES	61 082	54 500	62 064	73 714	68 544	64 079	64 511
Alabama	50 779	46 143	51 613	62 983	57 904	51 011	44 169
Alaska	79 934	74 242	80 133	84 577	83 941	90 151	75 571
Arizona	57 855	54 510	58 696	66 030	57 193	59 921	55 893
Arkansas	46 868	43 370	48 799	53 523	50 470	49 553	43 538
California	67 038	61 954	67 562	77 596	66 106	63 109	70 741
Colorado	68 943	63 635	69 717	82 621	72 673	66 580	63 827
Connecticut	83 069	70 800	82 305	101 647	100 989	103 804	105 588
Delaware	67 582	61 424	67 412	83 928	73 851	70 269	78 579
District of Columbia	71 208	78 878	56 599	70 862	51 400	74 088	53 733
Florida	53 509	49 321	53 713	64 084	60 656	56 679	59 498
Georgia	56 176	51 184	55 767	68 122	60 785	55 834	52 666
Hawaii	75 066	63 143	74 449	85 190	80 552	94 304	112 585
Idaho	51 851	47 863	54 558	60 488	57 737	51 953	57 629
Illinois	66 806	59 104	68 782	79 788	72 240	68 061	66 662
Indiana	56 432	50 279	58 075	68 109	64 746	61 668	65 998
Iowa	61 156	55 132	62 485	74 349	71 627	61 746	61 726
Kansas	60 994	56 251	63 816	68 154	69 210	58 082	55 196
Kentucky	49 801	44 353	51 046	62 739	59 928	52 502	51 315
Louisiana	53 427	45 950	54 800	66 154	66 029	56 745	56 870
Maine	56 566	50 767	58 097	67 361	68 365	74 776	55 433
Maryland	84 254	73 291	85 746	101 693	98 508	95 648	89 529
Massachusetts	81 033	67 142	82 385	100 462	103 475	99 351	85 558
Michigan	56 681	49 919	59 190	70 600	67 658	58 968	52 657
Minnesota	69 374	60 694	72 886	83 772	81 598	74 597	59 021
Mississippi	45 601	40 908	46 299	54 812	50 335	43 202	42 982
Missouri	56 318	50 295	57 664	68 705	67 260	66 013	59 043
Montana	55 010	51 566	55 357	66 825	58 198	55 539	75 761
Nebraska	60 102	53 251	64 429	69 950	70 363	62 928	66 384
Nevada	60 829	56 612	59 802	69 371	61 443	61 962	77 129
New Hampshire	73 856	62 509	81 134	88 538	83 081	94 246	74 257
New Jersey	83 381	69 539	84 192	99 474	102 931	95 995	89 623
New Mexico	51 994	51 018	51 459	52 842	54 788	53 387	58 222
New York	66 891	56 845	67 292	82 587	80 441	77 582	79 704
North Carolina	54 288	49 813	54 573	66 487	59 925	52 913	49 349
North Dakota	63 507	55 501	68 209	78 352	81 369	61 814	61 413
Ohio	57 360	50 491	59 275	71 453	66 204	63 512	54 910
Oklahoma	52 403	48 909	53 261	63 004	54 994	48 107	51 810
Oregon	59 174	54 656	59 546	71 593	63 550	60 536	60 959
Pennsylvania	62 185	52 839	66 030	78 626	76 895	71 035	66 099
Rhode Island	69 350	57 567	71 019	87 163	83 848	59 839	103 575
South Carolina	52 406	49 685	51 887	62 056	54 010	57 259	53 655
South Dakota	57 764	52 581	57 845	66 918	69 880	63 830	56 326
Tennessee	51 344	46 432	52 368	62 197	60 602	57 289	49 448
Texas	56 607	54 288	55 534	64 420	57 130	53 786	53 299
Utah	62 935	55 220	60 944	68 707	68 386	74 140	80 272
Vermont	63 483	57 013	64 767	77 127	70 777	72 307	65 422
Virginia	71 270	62 586	72 078	85 586	81 234	81 611	96 185
Washington	68 360	62 204	71 354	81 269	71 181	73 241	61 582
West Virginia	47 659	41 919	50 521	59 307	58 004	52 450	52 307
Wisconsin	62 638	55 175	65 187	76 188	73 813	68 159	59 348
Wyoming	65 532	59 847	68 553	75 129	73 284	75 307	62 473

Chapter Fourteen

OCCUPATIONAL SAFETY AND HEALTH

OCCUPATIONAL SAFETY AND HEALTH

HIGHLIGHTS

This chapter includes data on work-related illnesses and injuries and fatal work injuries from the Injuries, Illnesses, and Fatalities (IIF) program. Data are classified by industry and selected worker characteristics.

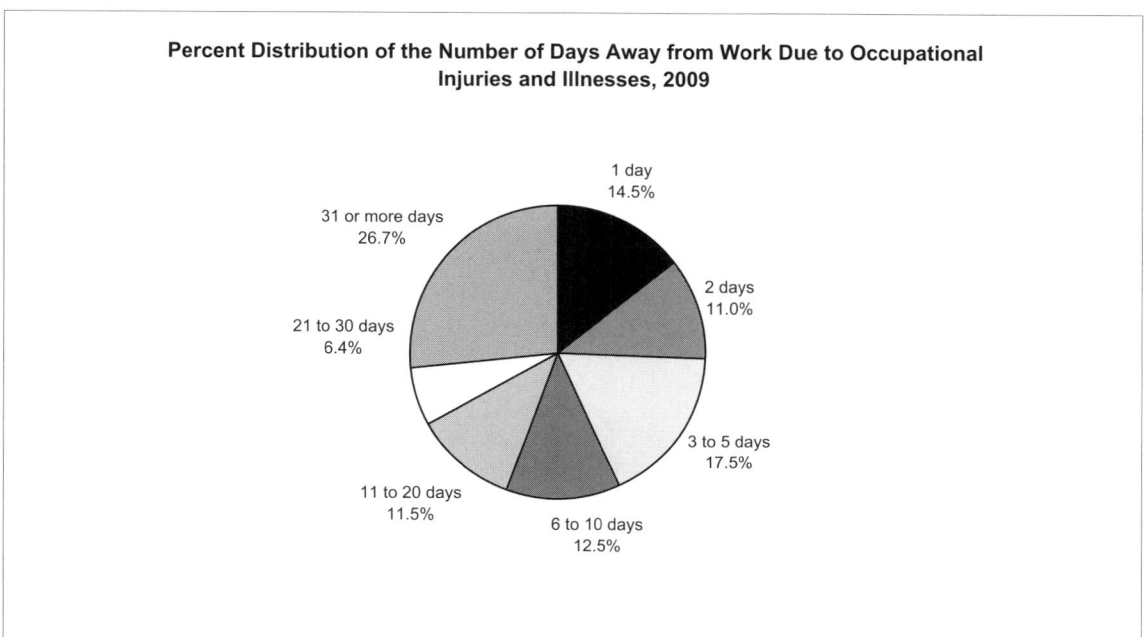

Percent Distribution of the Number of Days Away from Work Due to Occupational Injuries and Illnesses, 2009

There were 964,990 nonfatal occupational injuries and illnesses requiring days away from work in the private sector 2009, a decrease of 11 percent from 2008 and the first time it has been below 1 million since data has been collected by the Bureau of Labor Statistics (BLS). Nearly 27 percent of these injuries and illnesses required an employee to be away from work for 31 or more days while another 6.4 percent caused a worker to be away for 21 to 30 days. The median number of days away from work due to occupational injury and illness remained at 8. (See Tables 14-2 and 14-3.)

OTHER HIGHLIGHTS

- The rate of nonfatal occupational injuries and illnesses declined in 2009 to 3.6 cases per 100 equivalent full-time workers in 2009, down from 3.9 cases in 2008 and 4.2 cases in 2007. Workers in transportation and warehousing and health care and social assistance continued to have the highest rates. (See Table 14-1.)

- Although the total nonfatal occupational injuries and illnesses incidence rate declined, it increased for light or delivery service truck drivers, landscapers and groundskeepers, restaurant cooks, and registered nurses. (See Table 14-1)

- The preliminary number of fatalities declined 16.8 percent in 2009 to 4,340—the lowest number ever recorded since BLS began the Census of Fatal Occupational Injuries. (See Table 14-5.)

- Men accounted for 92.6 percent of fatal occupational injuries but only 61.9 percent of nonfatal occupational injuries and illness involving days away from work in the private sector. (See Tables 14-2 and 14-4.)

NOTES AND DEFINITIONS

Collection and Coverage

The Injuries, Illnesses, and Fatalities (IIF) program at the Bureau of Labor Statistics (BLS) provides annual reports on the number of workplace injuries, illnesses, and fatalities. BLS has reported annually on the number of work-related injuries, illnesses, and fatalities since the early 1970s after the Occupational Safety and Health Act of 1970 was passed.

Nonfatal Occupational Injuries and Illnesses

The Survey of Occupational Injuries and Illnesses is a federal-state program in which employer's reports are collected annually from about 230,000 private industry establishments and processed by state agencies cooperating with the BLS. Summary information on the number of injuries and illnesses is copied by these employers directly from their recordkeeping logs to the survey questionnaire. The questionnaire also asks for the number of employee hours worked (needed in the calculation of incidence rates) as well as its average employment (needed to verify the unit's employment-size class).

Occupational injury and illness data for coal, metal, and nonmetal mining and for railroad activities were provided by the Department of Labor's Mine Safety and Health Administration and the Department of Transportation's Federal Railroad Administration. The survey excludes all work-related fatalities as well as nonfatal work injuries and illnesses to the self employed; to workers on farms with 10 or fewer employees; to private household workers; and, nationally, to federal, state, and local government workers.

Injuries and illnesses logged by employers conform with definitions and recordkeeping guidelines set by the Occupational Safety and Health Administration, U.S. Department of Labor. Under those guidelines, nonfatal cases are recordable if they are occupational illnesses or if they are occupational injuries which involve lost worktime, medical treatment other than first aid, restriction of work or motion, loss of consciousness, or transfer to another job. Employers keep counts of injuries separate from illnesses and also identify for each whether a case involved any days away from work or days of restricted work activity, or both, beyond the day of injury or onset of illness.

Occupational injuries, such as sprains, cuts, and fractures, account for the vast majority of all cases that employers log and report to the BLS survey. Occupational illnesses are new cases recognized, diagnosed, and reported during the year. Overwhelmingly, those reported are easier to directly relate to workplace activity (e.g., contact dermatitis or carpal tunnel syndrome) than are long-term latent illnesses, such as cancers. The latter illnesses are believed to be under recorded and, thus, understated in the BLS survey.

Concepts and Definitions

Days away from work are cases that involve days away from work, days of restricted work activity, or both.

The data are presented in the form of *incidence rates*, defined as the number of injuries and illnesses or cases of days away from work per 100 full-time employees. The formula is (N/EH) x 200,000, where N = number of injuries and illnesses or days away from work, EH = total hours worked by all employees during the calendar year, and 200,000 represents the base for 100 full-time equivalent workers (working 40 hours per week, 50 weeks per year).

Median days away from work is a measure used to summarize the varying lengths of absences from work among the cases with days away from work. The median is the point at which half of the cases involved more days away from work and half involved less days away from work.

Occupational illness is an abnormal condition or disorder (other than one resulting from an occupational injury) caused by exposure to environmental factors associated with employment. It includes acute and chronic illnesses and diseases that may have been caused by inhalation, absorption, ingestion, or direct contact. Long-term latent illnesses can be difficult to relate to the workplace and are believed to be understated in this survey.

Occupational injury is any injury—such as a cut, fracture, sprain, or amputation—that results from a work accident or from exposure to an incident in the work environment

Fatal Occupational Injuries

The Bureau of Labor Statistics (BLS) Census of Fatal Occupational Injuries (CFOI) produces comprehensive, accurate, and timely counts of fatal work injuries. CFOI is a federal-state cooperative program that has been implemented in all 50 states and the District of Columbia since 1992. To compile counts that are as complete as possible, the census uses multiple sources to identify, verify, and profile fatal worker injuries. Information about each workplace fatality—occupation and other worker characteristics, equipment involved, and circumstances of the event—is obtained by cross referencing the source records, such as death certificates, workers' compensation reports, and federal and state agency administrative reports. To ensure that fatalities are work-related, cases are substantiated with two or more independent source documents, or a source document and a follow-up questionnaire.

Data compiled by the CFOI program are issued annually for the preceding calendar year. These data are used by safety and health policy analysts and researchers to help prevent fatal work injuries by:

- Informing workers of life threatening hazards associated with various jobs;
- Promoting safer work practices through enhanced job safety training;
- Assessing and improving workplace safety standards; and
- Identifying new areas of safety research.

The National Safety Council has adopted the Census of Fatal Occupational Injuries figure, beginning with the 1992 data year, as the authoritative count for work related deaths in the United States.

Sources of Additional Information

For more extensive definitions and descriptions of collection methods see Chapter 9 in the *BLS Handbook of Methods* and BLS news release USDL 10-1451, "Workplace Injuries and Illnesses in 2009," for injuries and illnesses; USDL 10-1142, "National Census of Fatal Occupational Injuries in 2009," available on the BLS Web site at <http://www.bls.gov/iif/>.

Table 14-1. Incidence Rates[1] of Nonfatal Occupational Injuries and Illnesses, by Selected Industries and Case Types, 2009

(Number, rate per 100 full-time workers.)

Industry[2]	NAICS code[3]	2009 average annual employment (thousands)[4]	Total recordable cases	Cases with days away from work, job transfer, or restriction			Other recordable cases
				Total	Cases with days away from work[5]	Cases with job transfer or restriction	
PRIVATE INDUSTRY[6]		111 469	3.6	1.8	1.1	0.8	1.8
Goods-Producing[6]		21 064	4.3	2.3	1.2	1.1	2.0
Natural resources and mining[6,7]		1 667	4.0	2.2	1.4	0.8	1.7
Agriculture, forestry, fishing, and hunting[6]	11	978	5.3	2.9	1.6	1.2	2.4
Crop production[6]	111	414	4.9	2.7	1.5	1.3	2.2
Animal production	112	164	6.9	3.6	2.0	1.6	3.3
Forestry and logging	113	60	4.3	1.8	1.6	0.1	2.5
Fishing, hunting and trapping	114	9	0.9	0.6	0.4	. . .	0.3
Support activities for agriculture and forestry	115	331	5.0	2.8	1.6	1.2	2.2
Mining[7]	21	689	2.4	1.5	1.1	0.4	1.0
Oil and gas extraction	211	158	1.6	0.9	0.7	0.2	0.7
Mining (except oil and gas)[8]	212	221	3.2	2.2	1.7	0.5	1.1
Support activities for mining	213	310	2.3	1.3	0.8	0.4	1.0
Construction	23	6 701	4.3	2.3	1.6	0.7	2.0
Construction of buildings	236	1 552	3.7	1.9	1.2	0.6	1.8
Heavy and civil engineering construction	237	926	3.8	2.2	1.4	0.7	1.6
Specialty trade contractors	238	4 222	4.6	2.5	1.7	0.8	2.1
Manufacturing	31-33	12 697	4.3	2.3	1.0	1.3	2.0
Food	311	1 470	5.7	3.6	1.3	2.3	2.1
Beverage and tobacco product	312	194	6.4	4.6	1.7	2.8	1.8
Textile mills	313	137	2.9	1.6	0.7	0.9	1.2
Textile product mills	314	138	3.7	1.9	0.8	1.1	1.8
Apparel	315	193	2.6	1.3	0.4	0.9	1.2
Leather and allied product	316	32	6.2	3.4	0.9	2.5	2.8
Wood product	321	402	6.5	3.3	1.8	1.5	3.2
Paper	322	422	3.2	1.8	0.9	0.9	1.4
Printing and related support activities	323	562	2.7	1.6	0.7	0.9	1.2
Petroleum and coal products	324	116	1.5	0.9	0.5	0.4	0.6
Chemical manufacturing	325	848	2.3	1.4	0.6	0.7	1.0
Plastics and rubber products	326	674	4.8	2.7	1.2	1.5	2.1
Nonmetallic mineral product	327	429	5.2	3.0	1.6	1.5	2.2
Primary metal	331	405	6.2	3.2	1.5	1.8	2.9
Fabricated metal product	332	1 441	5.5	2.6	1.3	1.3	2.8
Machinery	333	1 118	4.3	2.0	0.9	1.1	2.3
Computer and electronic product	334	1 199	1.6	0.8	0.4	0.4	0.8
Electrical equipment, appliance, and component	335	406	3.5	1.8	0.7	1.1	1.7
Transportation equipment	336	1 461	5.2	2.7	1.1	1.5	2.5
Furniture and related product	337	430	5.2	2.7	1.3	1.4	2.5
Miscellaneous	339	619	3.1	1.6	0.7	0.8	1.5
Service-Providing		90 405	3.4	1.7	1.0	0.7	1.7
Trade, transportation, and utilities[9]		25 648	4.1	2.4	1.4	1.0	1.8
Wholesale trade	42	5 851	3.3	2.0	1.1	0.9	1.3
Merchant wholesalers, durable goods	423	2 965	3.1	1.7	1.0	0.7	1.4
Merchant wholesalers, nondurable goods	424	2 036	4.3	2.9	1.5	1.4	1.4
Retail trade	44-45	15 059	4.2	2.2	1.2	1.0	2.0
Motor vehicle and parts dealers	441	1 724	3.8	1.7	1.2	0.5	2.1
Furniture and home furnishings stores	442	482	4.0	2.3	1.4	0.9	1.7
Electronics and appliance stores	443	505	1.8	0.8	0.5	0.3	0.9
Building material and garden equipment and supplies dealers	444	1 218	5.3	3.3	1.5	1.8	2.0
Food and beverage stores	445	2 889	5.2	2.8	1.5	1.4	2.3
Health and personal care stores	446	1 016	2.3	1.0	0.6	. . .	1.4
Gasoline stations	447	844	3.4	1.5	1.0	0.4	1.9
Clothing and clothing accessories stores	448	1 419	3.0	1.1	0.8	. . .	1.9
Sporting goods, hobby, book, and music stores	451	641	3.0	1.0	0.6	0.5	2.0
General merchandise stores	452	3 061	5.2	3.1	1.4	1.8	2.1
Miscellaneous store retailers	453	827	4.3	1.6	1.0	0.6	2.7
Nonstore retailers	454	433	3.6	1.9	1.4	0.6	1.7

Note: Components may not sum to totals because of rounding.

[1]The incidence rates represent the number of injuries and illnesses per 100 full-time workers and were calculated as: (N/EH) x 200,000 (where N = number of injuries and illnesses; EH = total hours worked by all employees during the calendar year; 200,000 = base for 100 equivalent full-time workers working 40 hours per week, 50 weeks per year).
[2]Totals include data for industries not shown separately.
[3]North American Industry Classification System—United States, 2002.
[4]Employment is expressed as an average annual value and is derived primarily from the Bureau of Labor Statistics's (BLS) Quarterly Census of Employment and Wages (QCEW) program.
[5]Days away from work cases include those that result in days away from work with or without job transfer or restriction.
[6]Excludes farms with fewer than 11 employees.
[7]Data for mining include establishments not governed by the Department of Labor's Mine Safety and Health Administration (MSHA) rules and reporting, such as those in oil and gas extraction and related support activities. Data for mining operators in coal, metal, and nonmetal mining are provided to BLS by MSHA. Independent mining contractors are excluded from the coal, metal, and nonmetal mining industries. These data do not reflect the changes the Occupational Safety and Health Administration (OSHA) made to its record-keeping requirements effective January 1, 2002; thus, estimates for these industries are not comparable to estimates in other industries.
[8]Data for mining operators in this industry are provided to BLS by MSHA. Independent mining contractors are excluded. These data do not reflect the changes OSHA made to its record-keeping requirements effective January 1, 2002; thus, estimates for these industries are not comparable to estimates in other industries.
[9]Data for employers in rail transportation are provided to BLS by the Department of Transportation's Federal Railroad Administration (FRA).
. . . = Not available.

Table 14-1.   Incidence Rates[1] of Nonfatal Occupational Injuries and Illnesses, by Selected Industries and Case Types, 2009—*Continued*

(Number, rate per 100 full-time workers.)

Industry[2]	NAICS code[3]	2009 average annual employment (thousands)[4]	Total recordable cases	Cases with days away from work, job transfer, or restriction			Other recordable cases
				Total	Cases with days away from work[5]	Cases with job transfer or restriction	
Service-Providing—*Continued*							
Transportation and warehousing	48-49	4 171	5.2	3.5	2.3	1.3	1.6
Air transportation	481	478	8.5	6.5	4.6	1.8	2.1
Rail transportation[9]	482	. . .	2.2	1.6	1.4	0.2	0.6
Water transportation	483	66	2.5	1.7	1.2	0.5	0.8
Truck transportation	484	1 334	4.6	3.0	2.3	0.7	1.6
Transit and ground passenger transportation	485	417	5.0	3.1	2.2	0.9	1.9
Pipeline transportation	486	41	1.9	0.7	0.5	0.2	1.2
Scenic and sightseeing transportation	487	29	3.6	2.0	1.8	0.2	1.5
Support activities for transportation	488	580	4.0	2.7	1.8	0.9	1.3
Couriers and messengers	492	560	7.2	4.7	2.6	2.0	2.5
Warehousing and storage	493	662	5.9	4.3	1.7	2.6	1.6
Utilities	221	568	3.3	1.8	1.0	0.8	1.5
Information	51	2 932	1.9	1.0	0.7	0.3	0.9
Publishing industries (except Internet)	511	844	1.5	0.7	0.4	. . .	0.7
Motion picture and sound recording industries	512	370	3.6	0.6	0.4	0.2	3.0
Broadcasting (except Internet)	515	315	2.0	1.1	0.7	0.4	1.0
Telecommunications	517	1 010	2.4	1.5	1.1	0.4	0.9
Data processing, hosting, and related services	518	257	0.6	0.2	0.1	0.1	0.4
Other information services	519	137	0.6	0.2	0.2	([10])	0.4
Financial activities		7 905	1.5	0.6	0.4	0.2	0.8
Finance and insurance		5 814	0.8	0.2	0.2	0.1	0.6
Monetary authorities—central bank	521	22	1.0	0.5	0.3	0.2	0.6
Credit intermediation and related activities	522	2 681	1.0	0.2	0.2	0.1	0.8
Securities, commodity contracts, and other financial investments and related activities	523	857	0.2	0.1	0.1	([10])	0.1
Insurance carriers and related activities	524	2 164	0.9	0.3	0.2	0.1	0.6
Funds, trusts, and other financial vehicles	525	89	0.7	0.3	0.2	0.1	0.4
Real estate and rental and leasing	53	2 091	3.3	1.9	1.2	0.7	1.5
Real estate	531	1 477	3.1	1.7	1.2	0.6	1.4
Rental and leasing services	532	587	3.8	2.3	1.4	0.9	1.5
Lessors of nonfinancial intangible assets (except copyrighted works)	533	27	0.6	0.2	0.2	. . .	0.4
Professional and business services		17 367	1.8	0.9	0.6	0.3	0.9
Professional, scientific, and technical services		7 832	1.2	0.5	0.3	0.1	0.7
Management of companies and enterprises	55	1 933	1.7	0.8	0.4	0.4	0.9
Administrative and support and waste management and remediation services	56	7 601	2.9	1.6	1.1	0.5	1.3
Administrative and support services	561	7 241	2.7	1.5	1.0	0.5	1.2
Waste management and remediation services		360	5.2	3.3	1.8	1.4	2.0
Education and health services		18 360	5.0	2.2	1.3	1.0	2.7
Education services		2 455	2.4	0.8	0.6	0.2	1.5
Health care and social assistance	62	15 905	5.4	2.4	1.4	1.1	2.9
Ambulatory health care services	621	5 787	2.7	0.9	0.6	0.3	1.8
Hospitals	622	4 637	7.3	2.9	1.6	1.2	4.4
Nursing and residential care facilities	623	3 060	8.4	5.0	2.4	2.6	3.4
Social assistance		2 420	4.0	2.0	1.4	0.6	1.9
Leisure and hospitality		13 586	3.9	1.6	1.0	0.6	2.3
Arts, entertainment, and recreation		2 106	4.9	2.3	1.3	1.0	2.6
Performing arts, spectator sports, and related industries	711	415	6.4	3.0	1.6	. . .	3.4
Museums, historical sites, and similar institutions	712	130	4.5	2.4	1.4	0.9	2.2
Amusement, gambling, and recreation industries	713	1 561	4.5	2.1	1.2	0.9	2.4
Accommodation and food services	72	11 480	3.7	1.5	1.0	0.5	2.3
Accommodation	721	1 884	5.0	2.6	1.4	1.1	2.5
Food services and drinking places	722	9 596	3.4	1.2	0.9	0.4	2.2
Other services, except public administration	81	4 607	2.9	1.4	1.0	0.5	1.5
Repair and maintenance		1 200	3.8	1.8	1.3	0.5	2.0
Personal and laundry services	812	1 325	2.5	1.4	0.8	0.6	1.1
Religious, grantmaking, civic, professional, and similar organizations	813	1 361	2.4	1.0	0.7	0.3	1.4

Note: Components may not sum to totals because of rounding.

[1]The incidence rates represent the number of injuries and illnesses per 100 full-time workers and were calculated as: (N/EH) x 200,000 (where N = number of injuries and illnesses; EH = total hours worked by all employees during the calendar year; 200,000 = base for 100 equivalent full-time workers working 40 hours per week, 50 weeks per year).
[2]Totals include data for industries not shown separately.
[3]North American Industry Classification System—United States, 2002.
[4]Employment is expressed as an average annual value and is derived primarily from the Bureau of Labor Statistics's (BLS) Quarterly Census of Employment and Wages (QCEW) program.
[5]Days away from work cases include those that result in days away from work with or without job transfer or restriction.
[9]Data for employers in rail transportation are provided to BLS by the Department of Transportation's Federal Railroad Administration (FRA).
[10]Data too small to be displayed.
. . . = Not available.

Table 14-2. Number of Nonfatal Occupational Injuries and Illnesses Involving Days Away from Work,[1] by Selected Worker Characteristics and Private Industry, 2009

(Number.)

Characteristic	Total private[2]	Goods-producing[2]			
		All goods-producing	Natural resources and mining[3]	Construction	Manufacturing
TOTAL CASES	964 990	241 310	21 640	92 540	127 130
Sex					
Men	596 930	208 360	18 720	89 990	99 650
Women	363 930	32 840	2 920	2 530	27 390
Age[4]					
14 to 15 years	160	. . .	. . .	. . .	. . .
16 to 19 years	22 330	3 210	400	1 430	1 380
20 to 24 years	91 780	19 590	2 350	8 290	8 940
25 to 34 years	209 670	56 320	5 530	25 850	24 940
35 to 44 years	231 750	66 070	5 490	28 660	31 930
45 to 54 years	236 030	58 070	4 500	18 720	34 850
55 to 64 years	132 110	30 660	2 450	7 960	20 250
65 years and over	27 620	4 220	380	1 060	2 780
Length of Service with Employer					
Less than 3 months	78 750	21 890	3 460	10 810	7 610
3 to 11 months	169 300	38 220	4 040	16 450	17 730
1 to 5 years	379 030	90 260	7 820	37 760	44 680
More than 5 years	324 950	89 100	6 030	27 150	55 920
Race and Hispanic Origin					
White only	412 730	124 870	5 450	53 910	65 510
Black only	78 840	14 780	850	3 640	10 300
Hispanic only[5]	125 790	44 940	7 330	17 560	20 060
Asian only	12 630	3 030	60	970	1 990
Native Hawaiian or Pacific Islander only	3 110	450	40	160	250
American Indian or Alaskan Native only	3 950	1 000	40	430	520
Hispanic[5] and other race	520	150	20	40	90
Multiple races	1 360	110	. . .	50	50
Not reported	326 080	51 990	7 850	15 770	28 370

Characteristic	Service-providing							
	All service-providing	Trade, transportation, and utilities[6]	Information	Financial activities	Professional and business services	Education and health services	Leisure and hospitality	Other services
TOTAL CASES	723 680	295 700	17 040	30 270	80 650	183 260	87 740	29 020
Sex								
Men	388 570	206 820	12 590	18 790	50 990	38 560	42 260	18 560
Women	331 090	85 200	4 440	11 480	29 650	144 530	45 340	10 450
Age[4]								
14 to 15 years	150	. . .	. . .	. . .	. . .	. . .	90	. . .
16 to 19 years	19 110	7 110	80	310	2 170	3 140	5 660	630
20 to 24 years	72 190	28 720	860	3 000	8 190	14 840	13 690	2 880
25 to 34 years	153 360	56 940	3 800	5 080	20 980	39 250	20 490	6 810
35 to 44 years	165 680	70 120	4 410	6 750	19 580	39 630	17 380	7 820
45 to 54 years	177 960	75 170	5 020	7 550	16 920	48 810	17 630	6 850
55 to 64 years	101 450	42 710	2 510	5 180	9 350	29 960	8 890	2 860
65 years and over	23 400	10 110	260	1 810	2 520	5 460	2 620	610
Length of Service with Employer								
Less than 3 months	56 870	19 210	490	1 470	8 930	12 500	10 490	3 780
3 to 11 months	131 080	46 780	1 220	5 510	18 520	32 650	21 150	5 230
1 to 5 years	288 770	118 260	5 370	12 450	33 260	73 500	34 470	11 470
More than 5 years	235 850	104 360	9 850	10 310	19 190	63 060	20 620	8 460
Race and Hispanic Origin								
White only	287 860	113 080	4 420	12 860	33 380	78 540	31 260	14 320
Black only	64 060	18 560	1 110	2 030	6 460	28 410	6 020	1 460
Hispanic only[5]	80 850	27 640	810	4 320	13 970	14 290	15 570	4 250
Asian only	9 600	2 650	120	330	820	3 030	2 260	390
Native Hawaiian or Pacific Islander only	2 660	810	30	90	230	700	350	460
American Indian or Alaskan Native only	2 950	1 010	30	170	260	820	590	80
Hispanic[5] and other race	370	140	. . .	30	20	60	120	. . .
Multiple races	1 250	200	. . .	. . .	750	130	140	. . .
Not reported	274 100	131 610	10 510	10 440	24 760	57 280	31 440	8 060

Note: Components may not sum to totals because of rounding.

[1]Days away from work cases include those that result in days away from work with or without restricted work activity.
[2]Excludes farms with fewer than 11 employees.
[3]Data for mining include establishments not governed by the Department of Labor's Mine Safety and Health Administration (MSHA) rules and reporting, such as those in oil and gas extraction and related support activities. Data for mining operators in coal, metal, and nonmetal mining are provided to the Bureau of Labor Statistics (BLS) by MSHA. Independent mining contractors are excluded from the coal, metal, and nonmetal mining industries. These data do not reflect the changes the Occupational Safety and Health Administration (OSHA) made to its record-keeping requirements effective January 1, 2002; thus, estimates for these industries are not comparable to estimates in other industries.
[4]Data are not shown separately for injured workers under 14 years of age; these workers accounted for fewer than 50 cases.
[5]May be of any race.
[6]Data for employers in rail transportation are provided to BLS by the Department of Transportation's Federal Railroad Administration (FRA).
. . . = Not available.

Table 14-3. Percent Distribution of Nonfatal Occupational Injuries and Illnesses Involving Days Away from Work¹ by Selected Occupation and Number of Days Away from Work, Private Industry, 2009

(Number, percent.)

Occupation	Percent of days away from work cases involving:								Median days away from work
	Total	1 day	2 days	3 to 5 days	6 to 10 days	11 to 20 days	21 to 30 days	31 days or more	
TOTAL CASES	100.0	14.5	11.0	17.5	12.5	11.5	6.4	26.7	8
Sex									
Men	100.0	14.0	10.0	16.8	12.3	11.9	6.6	28.4	9
Women	100.0	15.4	12.6	18.7	12.9	10.7	6.0	23.7	6
Age									
14 to 15 years	100.0	18.8	. . .	31.2	. . .	. . .	43.8	. . .	18
16 to 19 years	100.0	25.0	14.6	20.3	14.0	8.9	7.5	9.8	4
20 to 24 years	100.0	20.5	14.4	20.5	12.8	10.7	4.6	16.4	5
25 to 34 years	100.0	16.9	13.3	18.3	12.7	11.6	6.2	20.9	6
35 to 44 years	100.0	14.1	10.4	17.5	12.6	11.8	6.0	27.7	9
45 to 54 years	100.0	11.5	9.0	16.4	12.6	11.6	6.7	32.2	11
55 to 64 years	100.0	11.3	9.6	15.6	11.4	11.4	7.8	32.9	12
65 years and over	100.0	10.7	7.3	17.6	11.3	11.7	7.2	34.1	13
Length of Service with Employer									
Less than 3 months	100.0	17.3	14.1	17.1	13.3	9.8	5.3	23.0	6
3 to 11 months	100.0	16.3	13.0	19.3	12.1	11.2	5.7	22.5	6
1 to 5 years	100.0	14.7	11.1	17.8	12.9	11.1	6.5	25.9	7
More than 5 years	100.0	12.7	9.1	16.4	11.9	12.5	6.8	30.6	10
Race and Hispanic Origin									
White only	100.0	16.6	11.0	17.9	12.1	11.4	6.3	24.7	7
Black only	100.0	13.5	11.3	19.4	13.4	10.9	5.5	26.0	7
Hispanic only	100.0	13.0	11.8	18.5	12.9	10.6	6.2	27.0	8
Asian only	100.0	11.2	13.2	19.7	13.5	11.6	5.0	25.8	7
Native Hawaiian or Pacific Islander only	100.0	11.9	13.8	15.8	10.3	10.3	6.4	31.8	10
American Indian or Alaskan Native only	100.0	16.2	11.9	15.9	13.7	9.9	5.1	27.6	7
Hispanic and other race	100.0	15.4	9.6	23.1	5.8	11.5	15.4	17.3	8
Multiple races	100.0	8.8	35.3	27.9	9.6	3.7	4.4	10.3	3
Not reported	100.0	13.0	10.3	15.9	12.6	12.0	6.8	29.4	10

Note: Percentages may not sum to 100 because of rounding.

¹Days away from work cases include those that result in days away from work with or without restricted work activity.
. . . = Not available.

Table 14-4. Fatal Occupational Injuries, by Selected Worker Characteristics and Selected Event or Exposure, 2009

(Number, percent.)

Characteristic	Fatalities		Selected event or exposure[1] (percent of total for characteristic category)			
	Number	Percent	Highway[2]	Homicides	Falls	Struck by object
TOTAL	4 340	100	20	12	14	10
Employee Status						
Wage and salary workers[3]	3 335	77	23	11	14	9
Self-employed[4]	1 005	23	11	15	14	13
Sex						
Men	4 021	93	20	11	14	10
Women	319	7	25	26	13	3
Age[5]						
Under 16 years	13	(6)	. . .	. . .	. . .	. . .
16 to 17 years	14	(6)	36	. . .	. . .	. . .
18 to 19 years	55	1	20	16	7	9
20 to 24 years	261	6	18	13	13	7
25 to 34 years	681	16	19	15	11	9
35 to 44 years	872	20	21	15	11	9
45 to 54 years	1 113	26	21	11	14	10
55 to 64 years	806	19	21	11	18	9
65 years and over	521	12	19	5	20	11
Race and Hispanic Origin						
White	3 059	70	22	8	14	10
Black	407	9	25	28	7	7
Hispanic[7]	668	15	14	13	20	11
American Indian or Alaskan Native	32	1	19	22	12	9
Asian	122	3	12	43	7	6
Native Hawaiian or Pacific Islander	7	(6)	. . .	. . .	. . .	. . .
Multiple races	7	(6)	. . .	. . .	. . .	. . .
Other or not reported	38	1	8	21	8	. . .

Note: Totals for 2009 are preliminary. Totals for major categories may include subcategories not shown separately. Components may not sum to totals because of rounding.

[1]The figure shown is the percentage of the total fatalities for that demographic group.
[2]"Highway" includes deaths to vehicle occupants resulting from traffic incidents that occur on the public roadway, shoulder, or surrounding area. It excludes incidents occurring entirely off the roadway, such as in parking lots or on farms; incidents involving trains; and deaths of pedestrians or other non-passengers.
[3]May include volunteers and other workers receiving compensation.
[4]Includes self-employed workers, owners of unincorporated businesses and farms, paid and unpaid family workers, and members of partnerships; may also include owners of incorporated businesses.
[5]There were eight fatalities for which there was insufficient information to determine the age of the decedent.
[6]Less than or equal to 0.5 percent.
[7]May be of any race.
. . . = Not available.

Table 14-5. Fatal Occupational Injuries, by Occupation and Selected Event or Exposure, Preliminary 2009

(Number, percent.)

Occupation[1]	Fatalities		Selected event or exposure (percent of total for characteristic category)[2]			
	Number	Percent	Highway[3]	Homicide	Falls	Struck by object
TOTAL	4 340	100	20	12	14	10
Management	514	12	14	11	9	13
Top executives	37	1	19	22	8	. . .
Operations specialties managers	27	1	19	11	11	11
Other management	433	10	12	10	9	15
Business and financial operations	24	1	17	. . .	. . .	. . .
Computer and mathematical	6	(4)	. . .	. . .	. . .	. . .
Architecture and engineering	41	1	15	7	20	. . .
Engineers	18	(4)	. . .	. . .	33	. . .
Life, physical, and social science	16	(4)	19	. . .	. . .	. . .
Community and social services	29	1	34	31	17	. . .
Legal	12	(4)	42	. . .	. . .	. . .
Education, training, and library	21	(4)	. . .	19	43	. . .
Arts, design, entertainment, sports, and media	41	1	12	15	15	12
Entertainers and performers, sports and related workers	31	1	13	10	13	13
Health care practitioners and technical	54	1	24	19	6	. . .
Health diagnosing and treating practitioners	30	1	27	17	. . .	. . .
Health technologists and technicians	23	1	22	22	. . .	. . .
Health care support	24	1	29	33	12	. . .
Protective service	243	6	26	37	6	2
Fire fighting and prevention workers	29	1	24	. . .	21	. . .
Law enforcement workers	108	2	36	45	. . .	. . .
Other protective service workers	81	2	10	46	7	4
Food preparation and serving related	55	1	7	56	11	7
Supervisors, food preparation and serving workers	13	(4)	. . .	62	. . .	. . .
Building and grounds cleaning and maintenance	248	6	7	5	27	17
Building cleaning and pest control workers	55	1	. . .	16	36	7
Grounds maintenance workers	147	3	9	. . .	27	17
Personal care and service	42	1	12	38	7	. . .
Sales and related	269	6	16	50	7	4
Supervisors, sales workers	150	3	10	53	6	5
Retail sales workers	72	2	6	65	8	. . .
Sales representatives, services	11	(4)	45	. . .	. . .	. . .
Sales representatives, wholesale and manufacturing	25	(4)	68	. . .	. . .	. . .
Office and administrative support	86	2	33	23	15	. . .
Material recording, scheduling, dispatching, and distributing workers	38	1	50	11	13	. . .
Farming, fishing, and forestry	229	5	10	2	4	18
Agricultural workers	120	3	15	. . .	7	8
Fishing and hunting workers	57	1	. . .	. . .	. . .	. . .
Forest, conservation, and logging workers	37	1	11	. . .	. . .	65
Construction and extraction	818	19	10	2	32	12
Supervisors, construction and extraction workers	111	3	14	3	21	10
Construction trades workers	607	14	8	1	38	10
Extraction workers	58	1	19	. . .	7	29
Installation, maintenance, and repair	317	7	11	6	16	16
Vehicle and mobile equipment mechanics, installers, and repairers	120	3	8	4	6	28
Other installation, maintenance, and repair	164	4	12	6	22	9
Production	191	4	5	4	10	17
Supervisors, production workers	22	1	. . .	. . .	14	. . .
Metal workers and plastic workers	72	2	6	. . .	11	24
Transportation and material moving	988	23	45	6	7	6
Air transportation workers	66	2	. . .	. . .	. . .	. . .
Motor vehicle operators	660	15	64	7	5	4
Water transportation workers	27	1	. . .	. . .	. . .	. . .
Material moving workers	187	4	10	3	14	15
Military	69	2	4	22	. . .	. . .

Note: Totals for 2009 are preliminary. Totals for major categories may include subcategories not shown separately. Components may not sum to totals because of rounding. There were three fatalities for which there was insufficient information to determine a specific occupation classification.

[1]Based on the 2000 Standard Occupational Classification (SOC) system.
[2]The figure shown is the percentage of total fatalities for that occupation group.
[3]"Highway" includes deaths to vehicle occupants resulting from traffic incidents that occur on the public roadway, shoulder, or surrounding area. It excludes incidents occurring entirely off the roadway, such as in parking lots or on farms; incidents involving trains; and deaths of pedestrians or other non-passengers.
[4]Less than or equal to 0.5 percent.
. . . = Not available.

INDEX